CEDU쎄듀는 A **C**omprehensive **E**nglish e**DU**cation(**종합적 영어교육**)**의 약자입니다.**

펴낸이 김기훈 I 김진희
펴낸곳 (주)쎄듀 I 서울특별시 강남구 논현로 305 (역삼동)
발행일 2022년 4월 15일 제1개정판 1쇄
내용문의 www.cedubook.com
구입문의 콘텐츠 마케팅 사업본부
Tel. 02-6241-2007
Fax. 02-2058-0209
등록번호 제 22-2472호
ISBN 978-89-6806-252-0

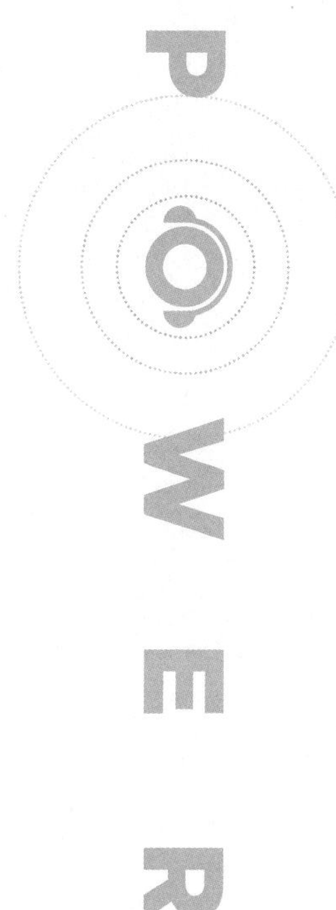

파워업

듣기 모의고사

40회

저자

김기훈 現 ㈜ 쎄듀 대표이사
現 메가스터디 영어영역 대표강사
前 서울특별시 교육청 외국어 교육정책자문위원회 위원
저서 천일문 / 천일문 Training Book / 천일문 GRAMMAR / 어법끝 / 어휘끝
첫단추 / 쎈쓰업 / 파워업 / 빈칸백서 / 오답백서
쎄듀 본영어 / 문법의 골든룰 101 / Grammar Q
거침없이 Writing / ALL씀 서술형 / 수능실감 등

쎄듀 영어교육연구센터
쎄듀 영어교육센터는 영어 콘텐츠에 대한 전문지식과 경험을 바탕으로
최고의 교육 콘텐츠를 만들고자 최선의 노력을 다하는 전문가 집단입니다.

이혜진 선임연구원 · **이혜경** 전임연구원

마케팅 콘텐츠 마케팅 사업본부
영업 문병구
제작 정승호
인디자인 편집 올댓에디팅
디자인 문한나 · 이연수
영문교열 Stephen Daniel White

본 교재는 <쎄듀 파워업 듣기 모의고사>를 최신 수능에 맞게 새롭게 개정한 것으로서, 수능 영어 영역 듣기 말하기 파트인 1~17번으로 이루어진 총 40회, 680문항이 실려 있습니다.
최신 대학수학능력시험 및 평가원 모의평가의 출제 경향을 분석하고 이러한 사항을 철저히 반영하여 절대평가 수능에 완벽히 대비할 수 있도록 하였습니다.

수능의 듣기 말하기 파트는 실전 수능 수준보다 난이도가 약간 높게 구성된 교재로 충분한 양을 학습하는 것이 중요합니다. 듣기 말하기 파트의 난이도에 영향을 미칠 수 있는 요소는 1. 녹음 속도와 성우의 목소리 2. 어휘나 표현 3. 대화·담화의 길이 4. 오답의 매력도 및 함정의 난이도 5. 말하기 문제의 선택지 길이 6. 답안 체크에 주어진 시간 등 여러 가지가 있을 수 있습니다. 본 교재는 이런 모든 요소들을 감안하여 현재 출제되고 있는 수능보다 난이도를 한 단계 높여서 구성하여 수능 시험 이전에 청취 훈련을 충분히 할 수 있도록 했습니다.

이 책은 특히 다음과 같은 특징이 있습니다.

1. **꾸준한 연습을 통하여 청취 능력 자체가 향상될 수 있도록 만들었습니다. 실제 수능보다 약간 빠른 속도로 녹음하였고, 다양한 목소리와 억양에 익숙해지도록 총 4명의 성우를 녹음에 참여시켰습니다.**

2. **총 17문항으로 구성된 실전모의고사 40회와 받아쓰기 연습을 할 수 있는 Dictation이 매회 실려 있습니다.**

3. **학습자의 편의를 고려하여 듣기 파일을 문제풀이용(회별) 파일과 연습용(문항별) 파일의 두 종류로 제작하였으므로 학습자가 필요에 따라 원하는 파일을 활용할 수 있습니다.**

영어를 듣고 말하는 능력은 단기간에 형성되지 않습니다. 장기간에 걸쳐 꾸준히 반복 학습해야만 실력의 향상을 이룰 수 있습니다. 부디 이 책으로 공부하는 모든 분들이 인내심을 가지고 꾸준히 학습하여 수능 듣기 말하기 시험에서 강한 자신감을 가지게 되기를 바랍니다.

저자

HOW TO USE THIS BOOK

이 책의 구성과 특징

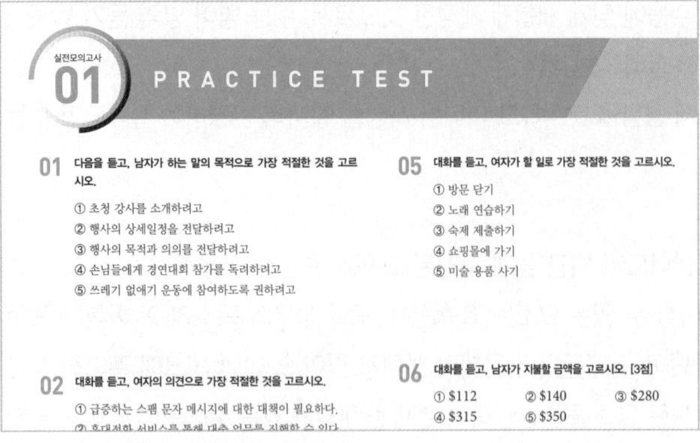

실전모의고사 01 PRACTICE TEST

01 다음을 듣고, 남자가 하는 말의 목적으로 가장 적절한 것을 고르시오.

① 초청 강사를 소개하려고
② 행사의 상세일정을 전달하려고
③ 행사의 목적과 의의를 전달하려고
④ 손님들에게 경연대회 참가를 독려하려고
⑤ 쓰레기 없애기 운동에 참여하도록 권하려고

02 대화를 듣고, 여자의 의견으로 가장 적절한 것을 고르시오.

① 급증하는 스팸 문자 메시지에 대한 대책이 필요하다.

05 대화를 듣고, 여자가 할 일로 가장 적절한 것을 고르시오.

① 방문 닫기
② 노래 연습하기
③ 숙제 제출하기
④ 쇼핑몰에 가기
⑤ 미술 용품 사기

06 대화를 듣고, 남자가 지불할 금액을 고르시오. [3점]

① $112 ② $140 ③ $280 ④ $315 ⑤ $350

1 실전모의고사

최신 수능 및 모의평가를 반영하여 수능 영어 듣기 시험을 완벽히 준비할 수 있도록 40회분의 모의고사가 제공됩니다. 실제 시험보다 문제의 난이도를 약간 높이고 말하는 속도도 빠르게 하여 난이도가 높은 듣기 문제까지도 실전처럼 대비할 수 있도록 했습니다.

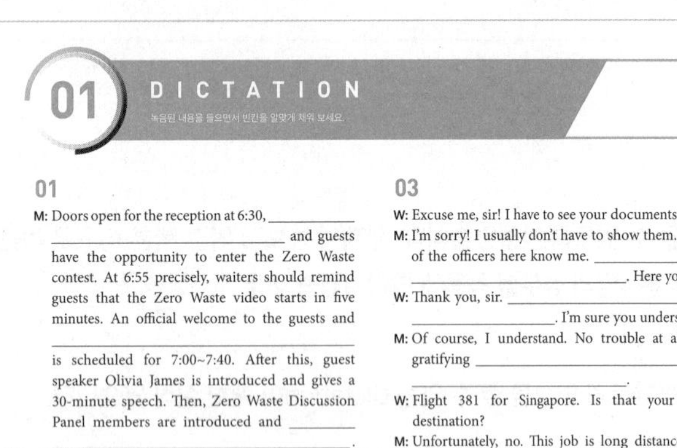

01 DICTATION

01

M: Doors open for the reception at 6:30, ____________ ____________ and guests have the opportunity to enter the Zero Waste contest. At 6:55 precisely, waiters should remind guests that the Zero Waste video starts in five minutes. An official welcome to the guests and ____________ is scheduled for 7:00~7:40. After this, guest speaker Olivia James is introduced and gives a 30-minute speech. Then, Zero Waste Discussion Panel members are introduced and ____________ ____________.

03

W: Excuse me, sir! I have to see your documents!

M: I'm sorry! I usually don't have to show them. M of the officers here know me. ____________ ____________. Here you

W: Thank you, sir. ____________ ____________. I'm sure you understa

M: Of course, I understand. No trouble at all. gratifying ____________ ____________.

W: Flight 381 for Singapore. Is that your fi destination?

M: Unfortunately, no. This job is long distance.

2 받아쓰기를 통해 기초를 탄탄히!

매회 모의고사가 끝나고 의미 단위로 받아쓰는 연습을 통해 듣기 실력의 기초를 다지도록 구성했습니다.

3 다양한 성우와 살아있는 회화체 표현!

다양한 원어민들의 목소리에 익숙해질 수 있도록 총 4명의 남/여 성우를 동원해서 녹음을 했습니다. 또한 원어민들의 사용빈도가 높은 회화체 표현과 실용 어휘를 문제에 적극 반영하여 이러한 표현과 어휘를 자연스럽게 익힐 수 있도록 만들었습니다.

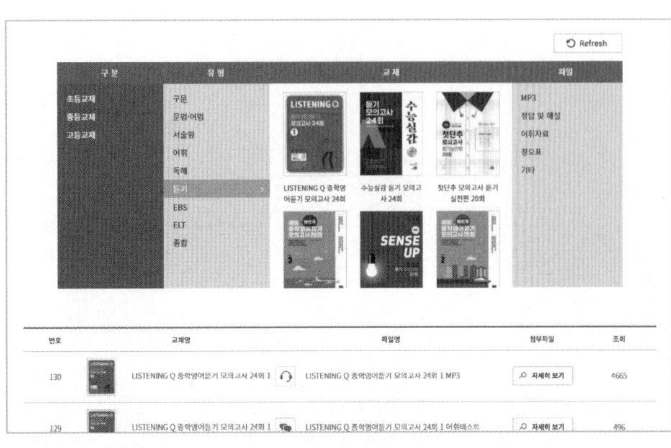

4 복습을 위한 다양한 부가서비스!

문제풀이용(회별) MP3 파일과 더불어 연습용(문항별) MP3 파일을 별도로 무료 제공합니다. 쎄듀북 홈페이지(www.cedubook.com)에서 다운받아 필요에 따라 원하시는 파일로 복습하십시오.

교재에 나온 어휘를 따로 학습할 수 있도록 어휘리스트와 어휘테스트를 제공합니다. 쎄듀북 홈페이지(www.cedubook.com)에서 무료로 다운받아 이용하실 수 있습니다.

CONTENTS

이 책의 목차

PRACTICE TEST

01 **다음을 듣고, 남자가 하는 말의 목적으로 가장 적절한 것을 고르시오.**

① 초청 강사를 소개하려고
② 행사의 상세일정을 전달하려고
③ 행사의 목적과 의의를 전달하려고
④ 손님들에게 경연대회 참가를 독려하려고
⑤ 쓰레기 없애기 운동에 참여하도록 권하려고

02 **대화를 듣고, 여자의 의견으로 가장 적절한 것을 고르시오.**

① 급증하는 스팸 문자 메시지에 대한 대책이 필요하다.
② 휴대전화 서비스를 통해 대출 업무를 진행할 수 있다.
③ 스팸 문자 메시지는 사용자의 관심사에 따라 다양하다.
④ 문자 메시지 무료 전송 응용프로그램이 많아지고 있다.
⑤ 응용프로그램을 통해 스팸 문자 메시지를 차단할 수 있다.

03 **대화를 듣고, 두 사람의 관계를 가장 잘 나타낸 것을 고르시오.**

① 여행사 직원 – 관광객
② 선장 – 출입국관리원
③ 항공정비사 – 항공관제사
④ 공항보안 요원 – 항공기 조종사
⑤ 경찰관 – 비행기 승객

04 **대화를 듣고, 그림에서 대화의 내용과 일치하지 않는 것을 고르시오.**

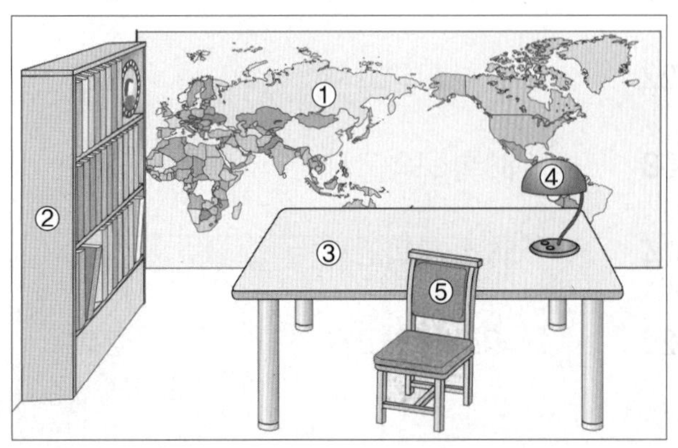

05 **대화를 듣고, 여자가 할 일로 가장 적절한 것을 고르시오.**

① 방문 닫기
② 노래 연습하기
③ 숙제 제출하기
④ 쇼핑몰에 가기
⑤ 미술 용품 사기

06 **대화를 듣고, 남자가 지불할 금액을 고르시오. [3점]**

① $112 ② $140 ③ $280
④ $315 ⑤ $350

07 **대화를 듣고, 남자가 창문을 닫으려는 이유를 고르시오.**

① 날씨가 추워서
② 모기가 들어와서
③ 바깥이 시끄러워서
④ 에어컨을 켜기 위해서
⑤ 비가 내리기 시작해서

08 **대화를 듣고, 모로코에 관해 언급되지 않은 것을 고르시오.**

① 위치 ② 수도 ③ 언어
④ 종교 ⑤ 정부 형태

09 **젬베(jembe)에 관한 다음 내용을 듣고, 일치하지 않는 것을 고르시오.**

① 맨손으로 연주하는 북이다.
② 서아프리카 속담에서 이름이 유래하였다.
③ 윗부분은 대개 염소 가죽으로 덮여 있다.
④ 소리가 매우 크고 다채롭다.
⑤ 전통적으로 여성만 연주할 수 있다.

10 다음 표를 보면서 대화를 듣고, 두 사람이 선택한 쇼를 고르시오.

Show	Starting Time	Duration	Price	Hands-on Activities
① Farm Animals	1:00 p.m.	1 hr.	$40	yes
② Tropical Birds (parrots)	11:00 a.m.	1 hr.	$35	yes
③ Monkey Play	2:00 p.m.	40 min.	$30	yes
④ Jungle King (lion cubs)	2:00 p.m.	40 min.	$40	no
⑤ Oceanside (dolphins)	1:30 p.m.	30 min.	$25	no

11 대화를 듣고, 여자의 마지막 말에 대한 남자의 응답으로 가장 적절한 것을 고르시오.

① I don't like any of them.
② The blue one doesn't fit.
③ I'll wait until it's on sale.
④ This is my favorite store.
⑤ I've already made up my mind.

12 대화를 듣고, 남자의 마지막 말에 대한 여자의 응답으로 가장 적절한 것을 고르시오.

① Only a few times a month.
② I made the plans yesterday.
③ I often take my car and park there.
④ I couldn't find what I wanted last time.
⑤ I take walks in the park every weekend.

13 대화를 듣고, 여자의 마지막 말에 대한 남자의 응답으로 가장 적절한 것을 고르시오.

▶ Man : ______

① That's too bad that you missed your stop.
② Call the subway company's lost property number.
③ I think you should move it to a more secure place.
④ They have lockers where you can store your sneakers.
⑤ There's no problem. Your luggage will be safe with me.

14 대화를 듣고, 남자의 마지막 말에 대한 여자의 응답으로 가장 적절한 것을 고르시오. [3점]

▶ Woman : ______

① I'll do it tomorrow. OK, Dad? Good night.
② Well, it's too bad that I won't get to ride a horse.
③ I wish I didn't have to do it. I want to travel overseas.
④ I just feel like I can't wait until all my exams are over.
⑤ You can't be serious. I'm way too busy to do any farm work!

15 다음 상황 설명을 듣고, Alex가 Polly에게 할 말로 가장 적절한 것을 고르시오. [3점]

▶ Alex : ______

① Art is long, life is short.
② Good idea. Fortune telling is very interesting.
③ I know a better, cheaper fortune teller. Let's go there now.
④ If it's just for fun, sure, but don't believe anything will come true!
⑤ I've already had my fortune told. But here's some money for you.

[16~17] 다음을 듣고, 물음에 답하시오.

16 남자가 하는 말의 주제로 가장 적절한 것은?

① various uses for herbs
② medical benefits of peppermint
③ different types of folk medicine
④ reasons to use herbs in moderation
⑤ the use of herbs as medicine in ancient times

17 valerian의 부작용으로 언급되지 않은 것은?

① 현기증
② 소화불량
③ 방향감각 상실
④ 피부 발진
⑤ 호흡 곤란

01 DICTATION

녹음된 내용을 들으면서 빈칸을 알맞게 채워 보세요.

01

M: Doors open for the reception at 6:30, ______________________________________ and guests have the opportunity to enter the Zero Waste contest. At 6:55 precisely, waiters should remind guests that the Zero Waste video starts in five minutes. An official welcome to the guests and ______________________ is scheduled for 7:00~7:40. After this, guest speaker Olivia James is introduced and gives a 30-minute speech. Then, Zero Waste Discussion Panel members are introduced and ______________________. Twenty minutes of audience question time follows. Finally, ______________________ and guests have their final opportunity to enter the Zero Waste contest.

02

W: Your phone is buzzing again. I think someone is texting you.

M: No, it's just a spam message. They are probably offering me a loan or some other thing that ______________________.

W: Do you get many messages like that?

M: I get several each day. It's really annoying.

W: You know, there are applications ______________________. They work just like the spam filter in your email.

M: Something like that might be helpful. Maybe ______________________.

W: I'd be happy to. I can also check if your phone-service provider has an option to block spam. Many do.

M: ______________________. Thanks for your help.

03

W: Excuse me, sir! I have to see your documents!

M: I'm sorry! I usually don't have to show them. Most of the officers here know me. ______________________. Here you are.

W: Thank you, sir. ______________________. I'm sure you understand.

M: Of course, I understand. No trouble at all. It's gratifying ______________________.

W: Flight 381 for Singapore. Is that your final destination?

M: Unfortunately, no. This job is long distance. We refuel in Singapore, ______________________, and continue to Auckland.

W: Here are your documents. ______________________. Fly safely!

M: Thank you.

04

M: Hello?

W: Hi, Grandpa!

M: Hi, Jessica. How do you like your new study room?

W: It's great! I especially love the world map that ______________________. It covers the entire wall.

M: I'm glad it fits. And how about the 5-shelf bookshelf that I bought for you?

W: I think I'll really appreciate the extra space. ______________________ I originally chose.

M: Good. Also, I heard your father gave you a rectangular desk as a present.

W: Yes, and I have a lamp, too. It's on top of my desk.

M: Great. Are you sure the seat and backrest of your chair are comfortable enough?

W: Of course. It's the same wooden chair ______________________.

M: Everything sounds great. ______________________.

정답 및 해설 p.2

05

M: Sounds good, honey. You've got a nice voice.

W: Thanks, Dad. I'm practicing for my singing test tomorrow.

M: I'm sure you'll do well. But I'm trying to read some reports for work, so ______________________________ ______________________________?

W: Actually, ______________________________, Dad.

M: You've got other homework to do?

W: I do. But before I can do it, I have to ______________ ______________________________ to make a poster.

M: Why don't you wait until after dinner?

W: I'm not going to the shopping mall. I'm going to the stationery store on the corner.

M: OK. ____________________. Your mom needs some help getting dinner ready and ____________________ ______________________________.

W: OK. I'll just be 10 minutes.

06

W: Good morning. How can I help you?

M: ______________________________ tickets for the park. How much are they?

W: A single-day ticket is 40 dollars for adults and 20 dollars for children.

M: Is it a one-day ticket?

W: Yes. If you're thinking about visiting our park more than once during the year, consider buying annual passes. You can get a 10% discount on food ______________________________.

M: That sounds great. ______________________________ ______________________________?

W: 100 dollars for adults and 50 dollars for children.

M: Then I want annual passes for three adults and one child. We're Michigan residents. ______________ ______________________________?

W: Yes, for Michigan residents, a 20% discount is available on the annual pass. Do you have a valid Michigan ID?

M: Sure. Here are my ID and card.

W: Okay. Here's your receipt. Have a nice day.

07

M: Honey, do you mind if I close the window?

W: I'm really enjoying the breeze. So maybe we can keep it open until ______________________________ ______________________________?

M: I agree that it's still hot in here, but I'm worried about mosquitoes.

W: Oh, are they ______________________________?

M: Yes, they're coming in through the window.

W: I guess they are getting worse now that it's the rainy season.

M: And ______________________________ once they are inside the house.

W: In that case, I'll ______________________________ ______________________________. It will be nice to block some of the street noise, too.

M: Good idea.

08

M: Have you talked to Cindy, the new girl in our class?

W: Not yet, but I heard she is from Morocco. That's a country in North Africa, right?

M: Yes, it's ____________________. Cindy said it's a beautiful country.

W: Can she speak English well?

M: She said that Arabic is her first language, but she ________________________________.

W: That's impressive. I hope she is enjoying her time here.

M: I think she is experiencing a bit of a culture shock. Almost 99% of Moroccans ________________ ________________________.

W: A lot of things here must be different to her. Morocco also has a different type of government, right?

M: Yeah, it's a constitutional monarchy. They have a king whose power ____________________ ________________________.

W: Wow, that's interesting. I look forward to meeting her.

09

W: A jembe is a West African drum played ________ ________________. The name of the jembe comes from a West African country's saying that means "everyone gather together in peace." The jembe has a body carved of hard wood and the upper part ________________________. This drum can be heard clearly when ________ ________________________ because its sounds are very loud and various. Another special feature of the jembe is that it is traditionally played only by men. Even today, ____________ ________________________ the jembe in West Africa, and many African women are startled when they do see a female jembe player.

10

W: There are so many great shows that Charlotte would love. Which should we choose?

M: Well, you know ________________________ ________________________. And parrots are her favorite.

W: I know. But look at the time. It's before lunchtime and she'll probably get hungry during the show, so maybe something after lunch ____________ ________________________.

M: You have a point. Then should we choose something after 1 p.m.?

W: Yeah, it'll give us enough time to eat. How about this show?

M: Well, a one-hour show might be too long for Charlotte. She starts to get distracted after about 40 minutes.

W: You're right. Then let's ____________________ ________________________. And I don't want to spend too much money on a show.

M: Yes, we should spend our money on other attractions, too.

W: ________________________________ $30 per person.

M: We have two choices left. Which do you prefer?

W: Oh, this one offers a hands-on activity for Charlotte.

M: That'll be good. Let me go get the tickets.

11

W: I think you should buy the yellow sweater.

M: I don't think so. ________________________ ________________________.

W: Oh, really? Then, which one do you have in mind?

12

M: I'm going to the park. Do you want to come?

W: Sorry, ________________________________ ________________________.

M: You just went shopping yesterday. ____________ ________________________?

13

M: Good morning, Lisa.
W: Hi, Mr. Park.
M: Lisa? What's the matter? ____________________ ________________________________? You look a little upset.
W: Yes! I feel so stupid!
M: Did you forget to bring your P.E. gear to school today?
W: Well, not exactly.
M: ____________________________, "not exactly"?
W: I had my sneakers and gym clothes in a shopping bag. ____ and when I woke up I was at my station already. So I jumped up and quickly ____________________ ________________________________.
M: Did you forget the shopping bag?
W: Yes. It's probably still ________________________ ________________________________.

14

W: Dad, I'm exhausted.
M: It's tough, isn't it, honey? But ________________ ____.
W: It's so stressful! I have to write two more essays tonight!
M: ______________________________. You'll do great. And think of all the things you can do when you've finished!
W: Yeah, ____ will be wonderful.
M: That's right.
W: Actually, you know what I'd really like to do after my exams? To go and work for Uncle Kevin and Aunt Maureen on their farm again.
M: Really, sweetheart?
W: Oh, yeah. It was so much fun that summer, and I ______________________________ every day!
M: Well, I'm sure they'd love to have you again. They'll have lots of work for you!

15

W: Alex studies physics at a university. He believes only science holds the answers to life's mysteries. He firmly rejects fortune tellers, star signs, and ____. On the other hand, Alex's girlfriend, Polly, __________ ________________________________. Alex never tells lies and never says no to Polly. He adores her and hopes to marry her after graduation. One day, ____ when Polly says "Look at the sign! It says, 'Your fortune told for $25.' What fun! ________________ ________________________________! Please!" Alex worries Polly will take the fortune too seriously. In this situation, what would Alex most likely say to Polly?

16-17

M: Herbal medicine, the oldest form of medicine known to humans, is the traditional medical practice of using plants to treat illnesses and disease. Depending on the plant and the illness ________________________________; leaves, seeds, flowers, stems, and roots may all be used. People ____ on every continent for thousands of years. For example, the records of King Hammurabi of Babylon included instructions for using medicinal plants in 1800 BC. Specifically, Hammurabi prescribed the use of mint for ________________ ______________________________. Modern research has confirmed that peppermint does indeed relieve nausea and vomiting __________________ ______________________. In ancient Greece, the great physician Hippocrates described valerian, a plant with heads of sweetly scented pink flowers, __________________________________. However, although valerian root is nontoxic, it sometimes ________________________________, such as dizziness and a loss of sense of direction. Also, in rare cases, it causes skin rashes and difficulty breathing. For this reason, small doses have always been recommended.

실전모의고사 02

PRACTICE TEST

01 **다음을 듣고, 여자가 하는 말의 목적으로 가장 적절한 것을 고르시오.**

① 영어 학원의 수업을 홍보하려고
② 이번 시험의 결과를 발표하려고
③ 내일 시험에 대해 안내해 주려고
④ 학교 동아리 활동 참여를 독려하려고
⑤ 학생들에게 선택과목에 대해 알려 주려고

02 **대화를 듣고, 남자의 의견으로 가장 적절한 것을 고르시오.**

① 대중교통 수단을 확대해야 한다.
② 카풀을 할 때는 배려심이 필요하다.
③ 카풀을 하면 환경 보호에 도움이 된다.
④ 카풀을 하기 위한 조건을 맞추기가 힘들다.
⑤ 환경을 위해 자동차의 운행 제한이 필요하다.

03 **대화를 듣고, 두 사람의 관계를 가장 잘 나타낸 것을 고르시오.**

① 부인 – 남편
② 팬 – 축구팀 코치
③ 고객 – 기념품 판매상
④ 사진 기자 – 잡지 편집자
⑤ 기념품 수집상 – 신문 기자

04 **대화를 듣고, 그림에서 대화의 내용과 일치하지 않는 것을 고르시오.**

05 **대화를 듣고, 여자가 남자를 위해 할 일로 가장 적절한 것을 고르시오.**

① 역사 자료 검색해주기 ② 컴퓨터 수리 맡기기
③ 콘서트 표 예매하기 ④ 약속을 다른 날로 미루기
⑤ 예매를 대신 부탁하기

06 **대화를 듣고, 두 사람이 지불할 금액을 고르시오.**

① $30 ② $33 ③ $35
④ $37 ⑤ $39

07 **대화를 듣고, 남자가 아침에 일찍 일어난 이유를 고르시오.**

① 누나가 깨워서
② 중요한 시험이 있어서
③ 개가 아침부터 짖어서
④ 축구 중계방송을 보고 싶어서
⑤ 아침마다 조깅하기로 결심해서

08 **다음을 듣고, 장미 축제에 관해 언급되지 않은 것을 고르시오.**

① 전시 기간 ② 전시되는 장미 종류
③ 전시장 규모 ④ 전시 장소
⑤ 관람 시간

09 **화재 대피 훈련에 관한 다음 내용을 듣고, 일치하지 않는 것을 고르시오.**

① 훈련은 테러의 위험이 높아져서 실시된다.
② 경보가 울리면 건물에서 대피해야 한다.
③ 각 층에 두 명의 화재 훈련대장이 배치된다.
④ 대피 시에는 엘리베이터의 사용이 제한된다.
⑤ 건강상 문제가 있는 사람은 훈련에서 제외된다.

10 다음 표를 보면서 대화를 듣고, 두 사람이 구매할 바비큐 그릴을 고르시오.

Barbecue Grills				
Model	Price	Fuel Type	Burner Material	Size (square inches)
① A	$429	Charcoal	Stainless Steel	350
② B	$315	Gas	Aluminum	320
③ C	$399	Gas	Stainless Steel	310
④ D	$325	Gas	Aluminum	280
⑤ E	$217	Charcoal	Aluminum	180

11 대화를 듣고, 여자의 마지막 말에 대한 남자의 응답으로 가장 적절한 것을 고르시오.

① That's a great idea.
② I've been working on it all week.
③ I like to take walks in old palaces.
④ Thanks, but we're supposed to work alone.
⑤ The project involves visiting a history museum.

12 대화를 듣고, 남자의 마지막 말에 대한 여자의 응답으로 가장 적절한 것을 고르시오.

① I wish I had a better laptop.
② Games just don't interest me.
③ I mainly use it to surf the Internet.
④ This laptop used to be my brother's.
⑤ I lost the instruction manual long ago.

13 대화를 듣고, 여자의 마지막 말에 대한 남자의 응답으로 가장 적절한 것을 고르시오. [3점]

▶ Man : ____________________

① Slow down. You're walking too fast.
② Watch out! Be careful where you step.
③ It's surprising. I never would've known.
④ OK. I can turn up the heat in the house.
⑤ Don't litter. Put your garbage in the wastebasket.

14 대화를 듣고, 남자의 마지막 말에 대한 여자의 응답으로 가장 적절한 것을 고르시오. [3점]

▶ Woman : ____________________

① That's OK. My father has a farm.
② Wow! That's great! I've won a car!
③ Oh, no! What can I do with a goat?
④ Phew! Great! I've still got a chance.
⑤ It's not good. Open another door quickly.

15 다음 상황 설명을 듣고, Jones 선생님이 Sally에게 할 말로 가장 적절한 것을 고르시오. [3점]

▶ Mr. Jones : ____________________

① I have also visited Britain once.
② That was great, Sally. Thank you.
③ Could you get on with the topic, please?
④ Where did you go after you left London?
⑤ Could you please slow down your speaking pace?

[16~17] 다음을 듣고, 물음에 답하시오.

16 여자가 하는 말의 주제로 가장 적절한 것은?

① the speed at which animals evolve
② ways to survive in a warmer world
③ benefits of global warming for animals
④ various species adapting to climate change
⑤ how to help animals adjust to climate change

17 언급된 동물이 아닌 것은?

① polar bears ② parrots
③ owls ④ mosquitos
⑤ jellyfish

02 DICTATION

녹음된 내용을 들으면서 빈칸을 알맞게 채워 보세요.

01

W: Class, I'd like to remind you about tomorrow's speaking test. The test is optional. ____________ ____________________ if you don't want to. But you will ____________________ if you do take it. I will give three extra points to ____________________; two extra points to those who do OK; and one point to those who take it. It also gives you a chance to evaluate how much your speaking skills have improved. The test results will show which part of your speaking skills ____________________ ____________________. The test will be based on one of the short passages that I've asked you to listen to and recite at home. Are there any questions?

02

W: Lucas! Do you have to work overtime today?

M: No, I'm waiting for Mia and Ethan. ____________ ____________________.

W: Good. Who drives?

M: We take turns driving each week.

W: That sounds nice. But I think it's a bit inconvenient on days like today when you three have different schedules. Why don't you take the subway?

M: There's no subway station near my home. And carpooling is very convenient ____________ ____________________.

W: Oh, yes. You can save money on your commute, too.

M: That's right. But most importantly, carpooling ____________________ on the road.

W: Oh, that's right.

M: That means there is ____________________ ____________________ getting into the air. It saves the environment by keeping the air cleaner.

W: I didn't think about that.

03

W: That autograph on the magazine, ____________ ____________?

M: That's Pablo Rossini's.

W: My husband would love to have that autograph. He's a big fan of soccer.

M: ____________________ to have one of his autographs. But it's very expensive.

W: How much?

M: $5,000.

W: Wow! ____________________?

M: Well, he never gave a lot of autographs. _______ ____________________ and therefore the price is high. He signed this magazine after the 1992 World Cup.

W: Can you show me anything else for my husband?

M: Sure, over here is a newspaper photograph of the 2002 Korean soccer team. All the players ____________________.

W: Oh, ____________________ of his office. How much is it?

M: It's $300.

04

W: Dad, this amusement park looks amazing!

M: It really looks like ____________________ ____________________. What do you want to do first?

W: I want to start by trying the merry-go-round.

M: All right. I'm sure you also want to visit that castle.

W: I do. Right after trying the merry-go-round.

M: Okay. Then ____________________ the roller coaster, afterward?

W: Sounds great. I also want to ____________ ____________________ with that princess character. She's standing right over there.

M: Oh, you mean the one with a polka-dotted dress?

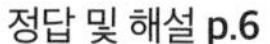

W: Right. Actually, I expected her to be wearing a star-patterned dress ________________________________ ________________________________, but I think her new dress is far more beautiful.

M: I agree. Would you like to have hot dogs at that stand on the right, afterward?

W: Yes, please.

05

W: Hello?

M: Mom, this is Kevin.

W: What's up? Don't you have class soon?

M: Yes, but I ________________________________.

W: Oh? What do you need?

M: Could you go on your computer and ____________ ________________ for DJ Dawnstar's concert for me? It's urgent.

W: I'm sorry, but I'm on my way to your grandmother's place. Can't you use the school's computer lab?

M: The computer lab ________________________ ________________________________, so I can't. And I'm not going to be home until 7, which will be too late.

W: I ________________________________ either. Why not ask your sister?

M: Okay, but I have to go to history class right now.

W: Then I'll call her instead. She'll text you if she can help.

M: Thanks, Mom. I'll wait for a text.

06

M: Mom, click on the title of the book.

W: Let's see. It says it is $8.

M: That's 20% cheaper than the bookstore. Is shipping included?

W: I'm not sure.

M: ________________________________ "Prices and Shipping Policy." On the left.

W: Oh, the two-day shipping cost is $8.

M: Then I'll go to the bookstore.

W: Hold on. ________________________________ over $30, shipping is free.

M: But the book is only $8.

W: Well, your big sister needs more study guides to prepare for the SAT.

M: She's not going to be happy if you give her more study books.

W: She has no choice. I'll get this one for $15 and this vocabulary book for $10.

M: Then we're over $30 ________________________ ________________________________.

07

W: You looked like ________________________ ____________________ in class today, Jim. Tired?

M: Yeah, really tired. I woke up at 5 a.m. today.

W: Oh, do you have ________________________ ________________________________?

M: No, our dog was barking and woke me up.

W: I didn't know your family had a dog.

M: It's my sister's. She usually wakes up early and goes jogging with it, but she's traveling right now.

W: Oh, poor thing. Why didn't you take it jogging instead?

M: Well, I wanted to get plenty of sleep so I could ________________________________.

W: Oh, ________________________________. Why don't you go home and take a nap before it starts?

M: That's a good idea. Talk to you later.

08

M: Want to fall in love? Come to Lincoln City during its 33rd annual Rose Festival and you'll __________ __________. From April 29th to May 15th, there will be three types of garden roses __________: miniatures, shrubs and climbers. Miniature roses are less than 40 centimeters tall, shrubs are __________ __________ and climbing roses can be 7 meters long. All the types of roses will be on display in both the outdoor and the indoor exhibition areas. The exhibition areas are open from 9 a.m. until 8 p.m. But these areas will close __________. Roses symbolize love. Come to Lincoln City this spring and feel the love.

09

W: To be ready for the upcoming winter season, __________ today. When you hear the alarm, please treat it __________. Each floor of the building has two fire captains. You will soon __________ __________. So please follow their instructions for the evacuation. During the drill you will not be able to use the elevators. But if you have a health problem and __________ __________, please see your fire captain immediately after this announcement. It is to confirm you don't have to participate in this drill. If you have any question about the drill, __________. Thank you.

10

W: Honey, we need to buy a new grill for barbecuing in the backyard. We can buy one from this online store.

M: Sure. The success of the barbecue often comes down to the quality of the grill. First, do you __________?

W: I don't want to spend over $400.

M: Then we have great options at that price range. And we need to choose between gas and charcoal.

W: My friend Lily says gas is __________ __________. So I'd like to buy a gas grill.

M: Okay. Next is the material the burners __________ __________. I think the best burner is the stainless steel burner.

W: But I've heard aluminum will outlast stainless steel. It's also less expensive than stainless steel.

M: Okay. __________. It looks like we'll have to choose the size. How big do you think the grill should be?

W: I think we need one with at least 300 square inches for our family.

M: Then we should go with this one. Let's order it now.

11

W: I don't have a partner for my history project.

M: __________. I'm not sure what to do.

W: Why don't we __________?

12

M: Is your laptop __________ __________?

W: No, but I don't play a lot of games anyway.

M: Then __________?

13

M: Sang-mi, thanks for bringing me to this beautiful park.

W: You're welcome, Eric.

M: It's relaxing __________ __________ and up the mountain.

W: I don't think you know, but this park used to be a garbage dump. For 50 years, __________ __________.

M: Really?

W: Yes. A few years ago they covered all the garbage with layers and layers of plastic. __________ __________ and planted trees.

M: A garbage mountain! Wow!

W: It is producing energy, too. ________________ ________________ breaks down, it produces gas.

M: They collect the gas coming out of the mountain?

W: That's right. ________________ ________________.

M: Everything looks so natural and clean.

W: But we're really walking on garbage.

14

M: You've defeated the others in the quiz round of our show. Now you're ready to enter ________________ ________________, a new car!

W: Oh, this is so exciting! I really want to win the new car.

M: Let me explain how to play. Sharon, there are three doors.

W: Yes, I know.

M: There is a new car behind one door. There are ________________.

W: I know. I don't want a goat!

M: Well, choose your door.

W: I'll take door no. 3.

M: Sharon, I'll open door no. 2 first instead of door no. 3. ________________? No, it's a goat!

15

M: Mr. Jones is a teacher at a high school. One of his students, Sally, is giving a presentation. Her presentation is on World War Ⅱ. She is talking about how the people in Britain ________________ ________________ by the Germans. She says that London was bombed particularly hard. Then she says that her family visited London last year. And she talks on and on about ________________ ________________, where they stayed and what they ate. Mr. Jones knows Sally ________________. He wants her to get back to her presentation. ________________. In this situation, what would Mr. Jones most likely say to Sally?

16-17

W: Good morning, class. As you know, we've been discussing climate change by talking about the animals ________________, such as the polar bear. Today, we'll continue by introducing a few animals that are ________________ ________________ to their changing environments. For example, some parrots living in Australia are growing larger wings to adapt to climate change. Larger wings allow the birds to release more heat from their bodies. This ________________ in warmer temperatures. A European owl is another adapting species. As less and less snow falls in Europe, more brown owls and fewer white owls are being seen. This is because white is no longer a useful color for hiding when there isn't snow. Unfortunately for us, the mosquitos of North America are also adapting. As the winters get shorter and shorter, their active season is ________________. This gives them more time to breed and grow. How might other animals adapt to the changing climate?

PRACTICE TEST

01 **다음을 듣고, 남자가 하는 말의 목적으로 가장 적절한 것을 고르시오.**

① 소방관들의 노고를 위로하려고
② 가정용 화재 감지 장치를 홍보하려고
③ 응급 상황에 대처하는 방법을 알리려고
④ 화재 대책 수립 시 유의사항을 설명하려고
⑤ 화재 발생 시 줄사다리의 중요성을 홍보하려고

02 **대화를 듣고, 여자의 의견으로 가장 적절한 것을 고르시오.**

① 반려동물을 기르는 결정은 심사숙고해야 한다.
② 반려동물과 함께 하면 정서 안정에 도움이 된다.
③ 반려동물을 기르는 데는 많은 비용과 노력이 든다.
④ 반려동물을 기르는 것은 아이들에게 좋은 교육이 된다.
⑤ 반려동물을 선택할 때는 경험자들의 조언이 도움이 된다.

03 **대화를 듣고, 두 사람의 관계를 가장 잘 나타낸 것을 고르시오.**

① 의사 – 의사
② 구급대원 – 환자
③ 의학 박사 – 조수
④ 배달원 – 손님
⑤ 물리치료사 – 간호사

04 **대화를 듣고, 그림에서 대화의 내용과 일치하지 않는 것을 고르시오.**

05 **대화를 듣고, 남자가 여자를 위해 할 일로 가장 적절한 것을 고르시오.**

① 정장 사주기
② 함께 쇼핑하기
③ 회의 시간 확인하기
④ 면접 결과를 알려주기
⑤ 면접장까지 운전해주기

06 **대화를 듣고, 남자가 지불할 금액을 고르시오. [3점]**

① $300
② $310
③ $340
④ $810
⑤ $880

07 **대화를 듣고, 여자가 헬스클럽에 등록한 이유를 고르시오.**

① 살을 빼고 싶어서
② 요가가 지겨워져서
③ 특별 할인 기간이어서
④ 친구가 함께 운동하자고 해서
⑤ 날씨에 상관없이 운동하고 싶어서

08 **대화를 듣고, 미어캣에 관해 언급되지 않은 것을 고르시오.**

① 별명
② 먹이 습성
③ 서식지
④ 몸 크기
⑤ 평균 수명

09 **Ecotours 여행사에 관한 다음 내용을 듣고, 일치하지 않는 것을 고르시오.**

① 환경을 해치지 않을 것을 약속한다.
② 영업에 지역민을 고용할 것이다.
③ 지역민이 소유하고 있는 숙소를 이용할 것이다.
④ 자연 보호 활동을 위한 기부를 약속한다.
⑤ 코스타리카에서의 모든 수익을 기부할 것이다.

10 다음 표를 보면서 대화를 듣고, 두 사람이 선택할 회의 장소를 고르시오.

Top Conference Venues in Redwood City

Name of Venue	Number of Seats	Rental fee (per session)	Indoor Catering	Parking Available
① Library Club	150	$960	○	Available
② Council Chamber	90	$620	×	Not Available
③ Durban Center	150	$1,180	○	Available
④ Niles Hall	180	$850	○	Available
⑤ Moorgate Place	120	$776	×	Not Available

11 대화를 듣고, 여자의 마지막 말에 대한 남자의 응답으로 가장 적절한 것을 고르시오.

① I like to listen to the radio.
② I prefer instrumental music.
③ I enjoyed his performance a lot.
④ DJ Antonie's music isn't hip hop.
⑤ I'm looking forward to the concert.

12 대화를 듣고, 남자의 마지막 말에 대한 여자의 응답으로 가장 적절한 것을 고르시오.

① I need to get him a gift as well.
② Kevin Smith's books are amazing.
③ I'm sorry, but her books are sold out.
④ You'd better purchase the book online.
⑤ He'll appreciate whatever you get for him.

13 대화를 듣고, 여자의 마지막 말에 대한 남자의 응답으로 가장 적절한 것을 고르시오.

▶ Man : ______________________

① I hope you feel better soon.
② Send a payment before you go.
③ We will begin delivery on that date.
④ I will inform them of your new address.
⑤ I will let your delivery boy know immediately.

14 대화를 듣고, 남자의 마지막 말에 대한 여자의 응답으로 가장 적절한 것을 고르시오. [3점]

▶ Woman : ______________________

① Do you know who broke this?
② Why do you need such a long break?
③ You have to repay your debt to the bank.
④ Do you want me to lend you some money?
⑤ How much money did your mom give you?

15 다음 상황 설명을 듣고, Robert가 Sandra에게 할 말로 가장 적절한 것을 고르시오. [3점]

▶ Robert: I'm sorry, but ______________________

① the group will be fine without me.
② can you write my presentation for me?
③ I can't be part of the study group anymore.
④ my parents are transferring me to a new school.
⑤ I had a family emergency and wasn't able to do the work.

[16~17] 다음을 듣고, 물음에 답하시오.

16 여자가 하는 말의 주제로 가장 적절한 것은?

① the list of ancient languages to be researched
② the reason why languages are worth preserving
③ essential effects of languages on culture and society
④ languages that might disappear by the end of the century
⑤ several different methods to protect endangered languages

17 만주어(manchu language)에 대해 언급되지 않은 것은?

① 사용되는 지역
② 구사하는 사람 수
③ 사용되는 상황
④ 처음 사용된 시기
⑤ 쇠퇴 이유

03 DICTATION

녹음된 내용을 들으면서 빈칸을 알맞게 채워 보세요.

01

M: In the event of a fire, many people are not prepared. Therefore, they easily panic. When they __________________________________, it becomes very hard for them to survive even in a small fire. This is why each and every person in the house must know __________________________________ at any time and from any place. For taller apartment buildings, each home should be equipped with a fire-proof rope. This is __________________________ to the ground. In homes closer to the ground, a rope ladder may be good enough. You should ______________________________________ for your individual situation. If you don't have a fire plan, call your local fire department for a consultation.

02

M: Stephanie, this article says that raising companion animals is great for one's mental and physical health.

W: I've heard that, too.

M: I want to raise a dog. Walking a dog would be great for my health.

W: Raising a dog ________________________________. Do you know it takes a great amount of effort and care?

M: I know I would be responsible for ____.

W: But you aren't home much because you go on so many business trips. Who's going to look after your dog then?

M: Oh, I heard there are places ____.

W: I don't think it's a good idea to leave him too often. You really have to treat them like your kids.

M: Oh, you have a point.

W: You have to ____________________________________ before you bring a dog into your life.

M: You're right. I didn't really think this through.

03

M: Linda, I'd like you to take a look at this X-ray.

W: Oh my, Bob. ____. Where is the patient?

M: He's lying on bed number five. He crashed his motorcycle while delivering food.

W: That's terrible. What have you decided to do?

M: That's the reason I asked you to look at it. What do you think is the best treatment?

W: I think surgery is not necessary, but it will ____.

M: I agree with your opinion. ____?

W: That will be fine. Let me tell my assistant that I will be busy for the next several hours.

M: Great. I'm glad ____.

W: You go tell the patient, and I'll meet you downstairs for the operation.

04

W: Next, I'll show you how to prepare the tables in the guest rooms.

M: Okay. I can see that the black coffeepot _____________________________________.

W: Yes, please try and remember that, as it is ____.

M: I think I can handle that. Also, the tea bags go on a square-shaped plate just next to the coffeepot.

W: Right. Then, next to that, we place two mugs that can ____.

M: Okay, so the mugs, and then a magazine next to them?

W: No, please put the notepad and pen in between the mugs and the magazine.

M: All right. ____.

W: Great. I think you are going to do well here.

05

M: Why are you in such a hurry, Nicole?

W: I need to go to the mall ______________________ ______________________, Dad.

M: I heard your mother was going to take you. Where is she?

W: She just called me and said her meeting ______________________.

M: Really? I hope it doesn't finish too late. It's already 7 p.m.

W: I'm so sad that she can't go shopping with me. ______________________.

M: Then, do you want me to accompany you instead? ______________________, but I can be helpful.

W: That would be great. Thanks, Dad.

M: I'll get the car keys. ______________________ ______________________.

W: OK. I'll wait for you.

06

W: Welcome to Susan's Calligraphy School. How may I help you?

M: Hello, I'd like to sign up for a calligraphy class. ______________________?

W: We have a beginner class and an advanced class.

M: How much are the class fees?

W: It costs $160 a month for beginners and $180 a month for advanced students.

M: I should take a beginner's class since I'm a beginner. What day is the beginner's class?

W: The class ______________________, on Fridays from 7 p.m. to 9 p.m.

M: That's perfect. I want to enroll with my friend. Is there a discount available?

W: Sure. If ______________________, both of you get a $10 discount each.

M: That sounds great. Then both my friend and I ______________________ the beginner's class. I'll pay for the two of us now.

W: All right. If you pay for 3 months in advance, you can receive an additional 10% discount.

M: Thank you, but we'll start with one month.

W: Okay.

07

W: I'm going to work out, Dad. I'll be back before dinner.

M: You aren't going to jog in this rain, are you?

W: Of course not! ______________________ ______________________ across the street. Didn't I tell you?

M: I don't remember hearing anything about it, but didn't you want to do yoga before?

W: Yes, but Hannah ______________________ ______________________ at the fitness center, so I decided to go to the fitness center instead.

M: Oh, it's great that you have a friend to exercise with.

W: I agree. It's really ______________________ ______________________.

M: Well, have fun. And please let me know if they ______________________. I also need to find a new gym.

W: Sure, Dad. I will.

08

M: Hello. I can answer any questions for you about the meerkat exhibit.

W: Great. It's fun to ______________________________ ______________________________. Also, that one standing on two feet is really cute.

M: Right now, the others are looking for food. The one that is standing ______________________________ ______________________________.

W: That's a really clever way for them to protect each other. Oh, look, that one just caught a small snake.

M: Yes, they eat many things including insects, reptiles, and even scorpions.

W: And all of these meerkats were brought from South Africa?

M: That's correct. South Africa is ______________________________ ______________________________.

W: I see. How large is a typical adult?

M: Meerkats grow to be 25 to 35 centimeters. And they typically ______________________________.

09

W: In Cambodia, temples are being damaged by tourists. And throughout the world, ______________________________ they came to see. Ecotours is a different kind of travel company. We pledge to preserve the environment. Our company also ______________________________ ______________________________. Too often, travel companies don't help the local people. So we promise to employ locals to run our trips. And our customers will stay in lodges and hotels owned by locals, too. Finally, we pledge to donate money to conservation activities in the countries ______________________________. For example, in Costa Rica, we will donate a percentage of profits ______________________________ ______________________________.

10

W: Noah, could you ______________________________ ______________________________ our annual conference next month?

M: Sure. I know a nice website that will help us find a conference venue. Look here.

W: Wow! Thanks. First, we have to think about the size of the venue.

M: ______________________________ the conference?

W: So far 96 people have applied and we're expecting about 120 people.

M: Okay. Then it should have more than 100 seats. Next, what is our budget range for the venue rental?

W: We ______________________________ more than $1,000.

M: All right. And we should think about dining.

W: Of course. I'd like a place where indoor catering is possible in case of rain.

M: We have these two options, then. Both of these places provide parking, so you can choose between them. ______________________________?

W: Of course we should choose the cheaper place.

M: Then this one is perfect for us.

11

W: ______________________________ to see DJ Antonie's performance?

M: Thanks, but I don't really like hip hop.

W: Then ______________________________ do you enjoy?

12

M: I'm thinking of getting this Mary Clark book for my brother. What do you think?

W: In my opinion, ______________________________ ______________________________.

M: Then could you recommend something better?

13

M: Hello. This is Daily News. How may I help you?
W: I'm going on vacation for a month, but I don't want to ________________________.
M: Well, we can stop delivery for you, if you would like.
W: ________________________?
M: No. We will also ________________________ when you are gone.
W: Great. What do I have to do?
M: Just give me your name and address.
W: My name is Lucinda Williams and I live at 722 Fremont Avenue.
M: And ________________________?
W: I am leaving next Friday, the 10th.

14

W: Hi, Sean. What's up?
M: Nothing really. ________________________ in the mall all afternoon.
W: By yourself?
M: No, with Cole and Claire. ____________. They're going to a movie at the theater in the mall.
W: That's where I am going. ________________________? I want to see *Save Oscar*.
M: I can't.
W: Are you busy? Homework?
M: No, I've done all my homework for this weekend.
W: Well then, come on. Let's go.
M: Mia, I can't. ________________________ on my new books yesterday.
W: Oh, that's the problem.
M: Yeah. ________________________.

15

M: Robert has agreed to join Sandra's study group. Each week, a different member of the study group presents a topic that they are currently studying in class and teaches the rest of the group. This week, ________________________ the rest of the group about photosynthesis in plants. However, during the weekend, his grandmother ________________________ and he had to leave town with his parents to visit her in the hospital. At the time, he was too worried about his grandmother to remember to take along his book, so ________________________. He has always thought that ________________________. In this situation, what would Robert most likely say to Sandra?

16-17

W: Experts estimate that only 50% of the languages that are alive today will be spoken by the year 2100. ________________________ means the loss of valuable scientific and cultural information. So, I'd like to discuss ________________________ today. The Ainu language is spoken by members of the Ainu ethnic group on the Japanese island of Hokkaido. However, most of the ethnic Ainu in Japan speak only Japanese now. There are ________________________, out of which only 15 use the language every day. Another endangered language is the Manchu language spoken in Northeast China. Out of nearly 10 million Manchu people, there are ________________________ of the Manchu language. And even those who speak Manchu only use it in specific circumstances, such as ceremonies, proverbs, or songs. Most Manchu ________________________ Mandarin Chinese in all situations. ________________________ most endangered languages, Manchu is being abandoned for languages spoken by wealthier people.

실전모의고사 04 PRACTICE TEST

01 다음을 듣고, 남자가 하는 말의 목적으로 가장 적절한 것을 고르시오.

① 흡연의 실태를 고발하려고
② 간접흡연 피해자를 도우려고
③ 건강 검진의 필요성을 알리려고
④ 간접흡연을 피하도록 조언하려고
⑤ 공공장소 흡연 금지 법안을 홍보하려고

02 대화를 듣고, 두 사람이 하는 말의 주제로 가장 적절한 것을 고르시오.

① 여행에 적합한 옷차림
② 배낭여행 시 챙겨야 할 물품들
③ 여행할 때 도난 및 분실 예방법
④ 배낭여행에 알맞은 배낭 고르는 법
⑤ 여행 가방을 가볍게 싸야 하는 이유

03 대화를 듣고, 두 사람의 관계를 가장 잘 나타낸 것을 고르시오.

① 영화감독 – 잡지 기자
② 배우 – 사진작가
③ 편집장 – 조수
④ 매니저 – 프로듀서
⑤ 연예인 – 팬

04 대화를 듣고, 그림에서 대화의 내용과 일치하지 않는 것을 고르시오.

05 대화를 듣고, 여자가 할 일로 가장 적절한 것을 고르시오.

① 차를 정비소로 가져가기
② 비행기 표 출력하기
③ 여권 찾아오기
④ Lisa 데려오기
⑤ 세탁물 찾아오기

06 대화를 듣고, 여자가 지불할 금액을 고르시오. [3점]

① $150　② $165　③ $180
④ $300　⑤ $330

07 대화를 듣고, 남자가 올여름에 아버지를 만나러 갈 수 없는 이유를 고르시오.

① 비행기 표가 매진되어서
② 아버지가 너무 바쁘셔서
③ 캠프에 참가하기 때문에
④ 연구실 인턴십 일정 때문에
⑤ 소프트웨어 결함이 발견되어서

08 대화를 듣고, 보고서 작성에 관해 언급되지 않은 것을 고르시오.

① 제출 방법　② 제출 기한　③ 작성 인원
④ 구성 자료　⑤ 작성 분량

09 Big Tree 천문대에 관한 다음 내용을 듣고, 일치하지 않는 것을 고르시오.

① 여름에는 화요일부터 일요일까지 운영한다.
② 전시와 소극장 상영은 오후 프로그램이다.
③ 오후 프로그램은 전문가의 안내를 받을 수 있다.
④ 저녁 8시부터 천문 관측을 할 수 있다.
⑤ 12세 미만 어린이는 입장료를 5% 할인해준다.

10 다음 표를 보면서 대화를 듣고, 두 사람이 수강할 강좌를 고르시오.

Fitness First Gym's Spring Schedule			
Course	**Level**	**Days**	**Age**
① **Tennis**	Basic	Mon & Wed	Junior(8-10)
② **Yoga**	Basic	Wed & Fri	All ages
③ **Yoga**	Advanced	Sat & Sun	All ages
④ **Swimming**	Basic	Tue & Thu	All ages
⑤ **Swimming**	Advanced	Sat & Sun	All ages

11 대화를 듣고, 여자의 마지막 말에 대한 남자의 응답으로 가장 적절한 것을 고르시오.

① I sent it one hour before the deadline.
② Thanks for giving me a second chance.
③ I'll get better grades on my book report.
④ The deadline for the report was delayed.
⑤ I'm sorry. I'll submit the report on time next time.

12 대화를 듣고, 남자의 마지막 말에 대한 여자의 응답으로 가장 적절한 것을 고르시오.

① Hurry up, or we will miss the subway.
② You can take a shuttle bus over there.
③ Let's get one now. There's a taxi stand.
④ The meeting ended almost an hour later.
⑤ I don't have enough money to take a bus.

13 대화를 듣고, 여자의 마지막 말에 대한 남자의 응답으로 가장 적절한 것을 고르시오. [3점]

▶ Man : ______

① I was happy to be able to help you.
② Your rehearsal was really impressive.
③ A little bit, but I can make a presentation.
④ Not really. Just call me after you've analyzed the data.
⑤ You should postpone the meeting until you're prepared.

14 대화를 듣고, 남자의 마지막 말에 대한 여자의 응답으로 가장 적절한 것을 고르시오.

▶ Woman : ______

① You shouldn't forget to take them on time.
② You don't have to eat health supplements.
③ Well, it's okay if you take them one at a time.
④ I believe this can even keep you from getting sick.
⑤ Yes. It's important not to exceed the stated dose.

15 다음 상황 설명을 듣고, Jacob의 엄마가 Jacob에게 할 말로 가장 적절한 것을 고르시오. [3점]

▶ Jacob's mother : ______

① Don't bite off more than you can chew.
② You'd better get in the habit of saving your money.
③ I forbid you to play until you finish your homework.
④ I'm so surprised that you earned the money by yourself.
⑤ Whatever you choose to do, give it your complete attention.

[16~17] 다음을 듣고, 물음에 답하시오.

16 남자가 하는 말의 주제로 가장 적절한 것은?

① the major contributor to climate change
② the dangers of extreme heat during summer
③ ways to lower the electricity bill in summer
④ tips to help you stay safe during hot weather
⑤ advantages and disadvantages of the air conditioner

17 올바른 에어컨 사용법으로 언급되지 않은 것은?

① 그늘진 곳에 설치하기
② 선풍기와 함께 사용하기
③ 2주마다 필터 청소하기
④ 에어컨 앞에 여유 공간 확보하기
⑤ 자주 켰다 껐다 하지 않기

04 DICTATION

녹음된 내용을 들으면서 빈칸을 알맞게 채워 보세요.

01

M: Every year, more than 10 million people die from illnesses related to smoking. Whether it is lung cancer, or ______________________________, they can be avoided simply by not smoking and avoiding being around those who do smoke. Second-hand smoke ______________________________. Until more laws are passed to protect the lungs of non-smokers, children and ______________________________, the best choice is to stay away. If enough people say no to second-hand smoke, smoking itself will become a thing of the past. ______________________________.

02

M: Hi, Gina. What are you doing?

W: I'm trying to pack for our backpacking trip.

M: It looks like you have a good start, but I wouldn't bring those cotton shirts ______________.

W: Oh, really? Why is that?

M: Cotton absorbs sweat and quickly ______________________. Man-made fabrics and wool are better.

W: Okay, I'll trust you about that. Also, I'm bringing ______________________.

M: That's a great idea. Footwear is the most important thing when hiking. Plus, ______________________ several pairs of socks.

W: Of course, and I've also purchased some money belts that we can use to safely hide our money.

M: Good thinking. ______________________________.

W: Right. We should always be careful while we're traveling.

03

M: Hello?

W: Hi. This is Tanya Paulson. How have you been?

M: Great, Ms. Paulson. It's been a while.

W: It has. By the way, ______________________________ on winning the Best Director award for your movie, *Trading Lives*. ______________________________!

M: Thank you. I wasn't expecting to win, but it felt great.

W: ______________________, my magazine, *Hollywood Weekly*, is planning a feature on your movie next month.

M: Yes, and I think ______________________________ I directed in the desert.

W: Sounds good. And I'd also like to interview you about the script and the actors.

M: That's not a problem. How about Wednesday afternoon?

W: That would be perfect. And we'd like to use still shots from the movie for the article, too.

M: I can ______________________________.

W: Thanks.

04

M: Hi, Nicole. Did you finish our election poster?

W: Yes. I just printed it, so ______________________________.

M: Okay. What did you change?

W: First, I moved our candidate number ______________________ like we talked about.

M: Good! What else?

W: Well, the title, "Nicole and Adam for Student Council," is now ______________________________.

M: Much better. Are the photos back from the studio?

W: Yes. I picked one ______________________________.

M: Okay. I like that you put our names and positions in round speech bubbles beside the photo.
W: It looks like we're talking, doesn't it?
M: Exactly. And you didn't forget to show our pledges.
W: Of course not. They are at the bottom in three lines.
M: I think ______________________________.

05

W: There are so many things I have to do before our trip this Friday.
M: I thought ______________________________ ______________________________. Don't worry. There's nothing to be anxious about. I can help you.
W: I appreciate it. I just got the smog check notice in the mail for our car.
M: ______________________________. I can take the car to the repair shop tomorrow after work.
W: That'd be great. Our printer broke down so could you print the flight tickets at your office?
M: Not a problem. By the way, where are you going? Are you going to pick up Lisa from her ballet lesson?
W: No, ______________________________ the passports. Lisa's lesson will finish at 4. Can you pick her up?
M: Sure. Anything else?
W: One last thing. Since I won't have the car tomorrow, ______________________________ the dry cleaners and pick up the shirts?
M: No worries. I can take care of that.
W: Thanks for helping me.

06

M: How can I help you?
W: ______________________________ inline skates for my daughters.
M: Do you know their exact sizes?
W: My younger daughter takes a size 2 and my older daughter takes a size 4.
M: The inline skates for kids are here. The size 2 pair costs \$150 and size 4 is \$180.
W: Wow, they're so expensive. My daughters are beginners and they're growing quickly. Do you have ______________________________?
M: Yes, we do. We have used skates ______________________________ ______________________________. They are good quality.
W: Can I see them?
M: Sure. Please wait a moment. Okay. Here you are.
W: Hmm, they look brand new. ______________________________ ______________________________?
M: The total is exactly 50% cheaper than the new ones.
W: Wow, that's a great deal! Okay, I'll take these used skates for my daughters.
M: You've made the right choice.

07

M: Hi, Anna. How was camping with your father?
W: Great! We ______________________________ and went fishing.
M: Sounds like an unforgettable experience.
W: It was. At night, we ______________________________ ______________________________. I feel much closer to my father now.
M: I bet you do. I really miss my father. He's been in England for almost a year.
W: No wonder you miss him. Then, ______________________________ ______________________________ now to visit him during the summer?
M: I'd love to, but ______________________________ ______________________________ at Dyson Lab during the vacation.
W: Oh, I forgot about that. Dyson is famous for its anti-virus software, right?
M: Yes. It's a great opportunity, so I think my father will understand.
W: I'm sure you're right.

08

W: Dan, what are you doing?

M: ______________________________ about the problems that cities have.

W: I see. When's the deadline?

M: There are only two days left, so I have to hurry.

W: Isn't it a team project? What about your team members?

M: We have five members in our team, so we each chose one topic to research.

W: ______________________________. Then what topic are you researching?

M: I'm researching about ______________________________.

W: Then you should present accurate numbers in the report.

M: You're right. I've put lots of graphs and tables about the topic.

W: It seems like you are working hard.

M: Of course. ______________________________ for this 50-page report.

W: Okay. I'm glad to hear that.

09

W: Do you like to look at the night sky? If so, the Big Tree Observatory is the perfect place for you. We are open from 2 to 10 p.m., Tuesday through Sunday, during the summer. Our afternoon program ______________________________, a small theater presentation, and hands-on instruction with telescopes. Additionally, our professional instructors ______________________________ and basic astronomy during these programs. Our evening program, starting at 8 p.m., is the highlight of what we offer and ______________________________ with a telescope. All of our programs are open to the public for $5, but children under 12 ______________________________. Due to the popularity, reservations are highly recommended. For more information, visit our website www.bigtreeobservatory.com.

10

W: Brad, have you seen this? It's a schedule of courses ______________________________.

M: A few of them look interesting.

W: What do you think about tennis? You've mentioned before that you want to learn.

M: Unfortunately, ______________________________. Besides, it's for young children.

W: Have you considered yoga?

M: I'm worried that ______________________________ because I'm not very flexible.

W: Well, that only leaves swimming classes.

M: I'm interested in that, especially if it's for beginners. Also, I think ______________________________.

W: I should sign up too, ______________________________.

M: Good idea. Let's take it together.

W: I'm looking forward to it.

11

W: Fred, you didn't send your book report to me.

M: Oops, ______________________________? Can I send it now?

W: It's too late. The due date was yesterday, and it would be unfair ______________________________.

12

M: ______________________________ will the shuttle bus to the conference come?

W: I don't know, but if we continue to wait, we'll be late for the meeting.

M: You're right. We ______________________________. What should we do?

13

M: Hi, Carolyn. Here's the USB you asked to borrow.
W: Oh. Thanks, Paul.
M: Is it for next Friday's economics presentation?
W: Yes. ______________________________ for the past few days.
M: Really? ______________________________. What do you have left to do?
W: Well, first ______________________________ that's on my friend's laptop.
M: Ah, that's why you need the USB.
W: Right. And then I have to rehearse the presentation.
M: You know, I'd ______________________________ and give you some feedback.
W: Really? That would be helpful, but I thought you were busy.

14

W: Hi, Luke. Is that medicine? Are you sick?
M: No, but I haven't been eating right. So, I bought these dietary supplements last week.
W: That's smart, but it's best ______________________________.
M: I agree, but people say supplements are helpful ______________________________.
W: I see. So, what else are you taking?
M: Well, these are iron supplements.
W: You're taking iron and calcium?
M: Don't sound so concerned. I ______________________________.
W: That's not what I mean. Iron and calcium ______________________________, because calcium blocks the absorption of iron.
M: Then what should I do? Would it be better to quit taking one of them?

15

W: During the winter vacation, Jacob decided to buy a new game console. To pay for it, he ______________________________ and started saving. Two months later, he purchased the console and began playing. These days, ______________________________ playing games. He rarely studies and sometimes doesn't ______________________________ because he is so focused on his games. Jacob's mother is concerned. She knows that Jacob even has an important exam next week but still continues to play his games. So, ______________________________ Jacob's behavior. In this situation, what would Jacob's mother most likely say to Jacob?

16-17

M: This summer has been particularly hot, hasn't it? In fact, the entire Earth ______________________________ because of global warming. As a result, many of us are suffering from skyrocketing electricity bills for air conditioning. To save yourself some money, there are a few things you can do. First, ______________________________ without spending money because light colors reflect heat and sunlight. Second, unplug electronic devices when you aren't using them. This is because electronics ______________________________. Third, use your air conditioner properly. Air conditioning is energy intensive and can quickly run up a huge bill. To use it properly, there are several things you must do. To begin with, ______________________________. Then, remember to clean its filter at least once every two weeks because blocked filters waste electricity. For the same reason, leave some space in front of the unit. Finally, ______________________________, since additional electricity is required to activate the unit. By following these tips, you can hopefully remain cool without breaking the bank.

PRACTICE TEST

01 다음을 듣고, 여자가 하는 말의 목적으로 가장 적절한 것을 고르시오.

① 새로운 제품을 홍보하려고
② 살충제의 유해성을 알리려고
③ 살충제의 사용을 줄이게 하려고
④ 세제의 올바른 사용법을 알리려고
⑤ 가족 건강의 중요성을 인식시키려고

02 대화를 듣고, 두 사람이 하는 말의 주제로 가장 적절한 것을 고르시오.

① 만리장성의 역사
② 거리에 따른 마라톤 종류
③ 마라톤 기록을 향상하는 방법
④ 전 세계의 다양한 마라톤 대회
⑤ 만리장성에서 열리는 마라톤 대회

03 대화를 듣고, 두 사람의 관계를 가장 잘 나타낸 것을 고르시오.

① 고용인 – 피고용인
② 배관공 – 집 소유주
③ 이웃주민 – 이웃주민
④ 경비 – 아파트 거주자
⑤ 직장 동료 – 직장 동료

04 대화를 듣고, 그림에서 대화의 내용과 일치하지 않는 것을 고르시오.

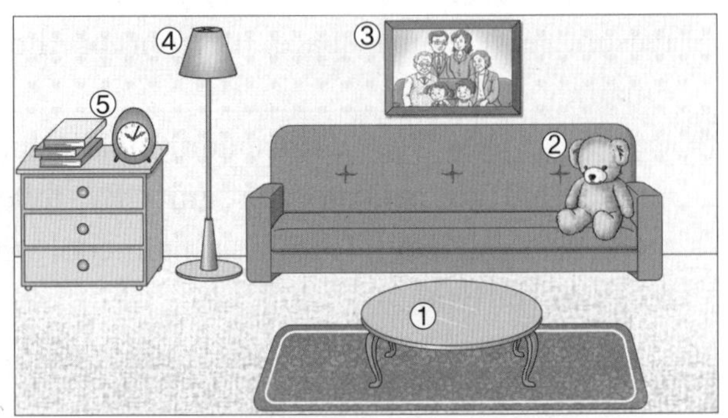

05 대화를 듣고, 남자가 할 일로 가장 적절한 것을 고르시오.

① 캠페인 전단 나눠주기
② 온라인으로 기부금 보내기
③ 시의회에 항의 편지 보내기
④ 건물 보존 단체에 가입하기
⑤ 건물 보존 시위에 참여하기

06 대화를 듣고, 여자가 지불할 금액을 고르시오.

① \$70 ② \$85 ③ \$90
④ \$100 ⑤ \$110

07 대화를 듣고, 남자가 여자에게 Lee 교수의 수업을 추천하는 이유를 고르시오.

① 과제가 많지 않아서
② 여자의 시간표와 맞아서
③ 좋은 성적을 받기 쉬워서
④ 재미있는 팀 과제가 있어서
⑤ 학계 최고인 교수의 수업이라서

08 대화를 듣고, 레인보우 브릿지(Rainbow Bridge)에 관해 언급되지 않은 것을 고르시오.

① 위치 ② 길이 ③ 설계자
④ 통행 수단 ⑤ 통행 허용 요건

09 quinoa에 관한 다음 내용을 듣고, 일치하지 않는 것을 고르시오.

① 안데스 산맥에서 재배된다.
② 빈민을 위한 음식으로 여겨져 왔다.
③ 단백질 함량이 풍부하다.
④ 볼리비아에는 재배에 적합한 땅이 많다.
⑤ 재배 지역에서의 소비량은 많지 않다.

10

다음 표를 보면서 대화를 듣고, 여자가 구매할 무선 진공청소기를 고르시오.

Cordless Vacuum Cleaners				
Model	Price	Weight	HEPA filter	Maximum Run Time
① Victory11	$782	3.2 kg	○	60 mins.
② Alpha08	$389	3.1 kg	○	40 mins.
③ Joy12	$448	2.6 kg	○	60 mins.
④ Green-9	$319	4.2 kg	×	60 mins.
⑤ CL5	$212	3.5 kg	×	40 mins.

11

대화를 듣고, 여자의 마지막 말에 대한 남자의 응답으로 가장 적절한 것을 고르시오.

① Math is my favorite subject.
② Art, because I love to draw.
③ I have a history class tomorrow.
④ I'll help you with your homework.
⑤ The science club is very popular at our school.

12

대화를 듣고, 남자의 마지막 말에 대한 여자의 응답으로 가장 적절한 것을 고르시오.

① Some drugs can be addictive.
② Ask for it at your local pharmacy.
③ I think it will help to get some rest.
④ I'm not sure. I wasn't paying attention.
⑤ Right, but you should bring the prescription.

13

대화를 듣고, 여자의 마지막 말에 대한 남자의 응답으로 가장 적절한 것을 고르시오. [3점]

▶ Man : ______________________

① OK. I will sell the book to you.
② Can I get you a cup of coffee while you wait?
③ Would you like a book about the Korean War?
④ I can order a copy for you, but it will take a week.
⑤ I can answer all of your questions about Gettysburg.

14

대화를 듣고, 남자의 마지막 말에 대한 여자의 응답으로 가장 적절한 것을 고르시오. [3점]

▶ Woman : ______________________

① Stop it! I'm too busy to talk with you now.
② Me too. I can't remember why we broke up.
③ I'm sorry. I didn't mean to tease you so much.
④ Really? But you never asked me out on a date.
⑤ That's right. You look really young with that haircut.

15

다음 상황 설명을 듣고, Andrew가 미용사에게 할 말로 가장 적절한 것을 고르시오. [3점]

▶ Andrew : ______________________

① No. Just trim it a little bit.
② No, I want to have long hair.
③ Please shampoo my hair first. OK?
④ I wish. But my mom won't allow it.
⑤ Please show me how to use hair wax properly.

[16~17] 다음을 듣고, 물음에 답하시오.

16

남자가 하는 말의 주제로 가장 적절한 것은?

① the threat of very dangerous allergies
② the best way to handle an allergic reaction
③ the connection between food and allergies
④ the reason why you should avoid bee stings
⑤ how to stay clear of food and insect allergies

17

벌에게 쏘이는 것을 피하기 위한 방법으로 언급되지 <u>않은</u> 것은?

① 벌이 다가오면 천천히 멀어지기
② 밝은 색 옷 입지 않기
③ 벌집 근처에 가지 않기
④ 향수 뿌리지 않기
⑤ 당도가 높은 음식 덮어놓기

05 DICTATION

녹음된 내용을 들으면서 빈칸을 알맞게 채워 보세요.

01

W: It doesn't matter how long you wash an apple under tap water. Water alone can't remove all those harmful pesticides ______________________ ______________________ because the pesticides are trapped under the wax coating ____________ ______________________ to make it look 'perfect.' But Veggie-Wash can do the job! It is a type of soap for your fruits and vegetables made from all natural ingredients. ______________________ ______________________ 98% of the pesticides on the fruits and vegetables you eat. It comes in an easy-to-use spray bottle ____________ ______________________. Start using it today for the health of your family.

02

M: I think our report on The Great Wall of China is almost finished.

W: It's good, but I'd like to include something about The Wall's modern role.

M: We could ______________________ that is held on The Wall in May.

W: Good idea. I remember reading that they have 5 km, 10 km, half marathon, and full marathon races.

M: And competitors in the full marathon must climb ______________________.

W: Yes, it's a very challenging race. It takes even well-prepared runners five to six hours to complete the run.

M: ______________________, but I heard the race is for everyone. There are no time limits and the course remains open with full support ______________________.

W: In that case, I'd like to try it.

03

M: Thanks for holding the elevator.

W: No problem, Sam. I haven't seen you for a while.

M: Well, I've gotten a promotion and ____________ ______________________ a lot of work in the evenings and on weekends.

W: Oh, that's too bad.

M: Yeah. But ______________________ so I can rest.

W: Good for you.

M: But I can't seem to get much rest in my apartment.

W: Oh! Sam. I'm sorry about the renovations. ________ ______________________, isn't it?

M: It really is! I was trying to read in my living room this morning and all I heard was 'Bang! Bang!'

W: We're putting in a new bathroom. The plumber was installing the pipes today.

M: ______________________?

W: Yes, by tomorrow.

04

W: I rearranged the living room this morning, honey. What do you think?

M: I like this round table on the carpet. Is it new?

W: Actually, one of our neighbors ______________ ______________. I took it home instead.

M: Good job. There's something different about the sofa, too. The teddy bear!

W: Right. I bought it at a small shop and put it on the sofa. I think it's cute.

M: It's nice. Our family picture looks good ________ ______________ the sofa, as well.

W: That's what I thought.

M: Now, you placed the floor lamp ______________ ______________.

W: I thought it would be good for reading, but I'm thinking about moving it again.

M: You can if you want. Do you have ______________ ______________________?

정답 및 해설 p.18

W: No, I'll think about it. Oh, I also threw out the books and other things that were on the chest of drawers.

M: That's good. The room looks more neat and tidy.

W: I agree.

05

W: Can I have everyone's attention?

M: Oh, Emma. What are you doing with a picket sign? Are you demonstrating against something?

W: Oh, Lucas. The city council ____________________ ____________________ the Bridgeport Library. Look at this flyer.

M: You mean that beautiful old library? It's a historically significant structure in our city.

W: Yes! They say there is a new city library, so they want to tear down the old one and build a 30-story hotel there.

M: That's a terrible idea! ____________________ ____________________.

W: That's why we're protesting here. We sent a letter of protest to the city council.

M: ____________________ this kind of campaign. How can I help you?

W: You can support us by making an online donation.

M: That sounds nice. I'll go home and sponsor you online right away.

W: Thanks a lot! ____________________.

06

W: I need shorts for this summer weather.

M: Summer shorts are over here. Pure cotton, soft and comfortable.

W: ____________________ they are $20 a pair.

M: That's right.

W: Well, they look nice, so I'll take the brown ones and the blue ones in a 24 waist.

M: Good. ____________________.
What about summer T-shirts? These ones here are 2 for $15 or 4 for $20.

W: Hmm... very cheap. ____________________ ____________________, too. I'll take 2 blue ones and 2 pink ones. I need a small size.

M: OK. $20 for the T-shirts.

W: Oh, and I need a long-sleeved white cardigan in a cool summer material.

M: How about ____________________ ____________________? I have it in your size. It's $30.

W: Fine. ____________________?

07

M: Hey, Karen. Have you chosen your classes for next semester?

W: Almost. ____________________ except for history.

M: Why don't you take history from Professor Lee? I'm taking it.

W: I heard that ____________________.
I don't have time for a lot of extra assignments and group projects.

M: I'm sure you can handle it. Besides, he is ____________________ ____________________. Studying under Lee is a great opportunity.

W: Hmm... I guess it does ____________________.
And are you sure I can pass his class?

M: Of course. You ____________________ ____________________ in the past.

W: Okay, I'll do it. Thanks for your advice.

M: Anytime.

08

M: These pictures from your trip are great. Where is this?

W: That's the Rainbow Bridge. It's ____________________ ____________________.

M: Really? It looks like a typical steel bridge. Why is it famous?

W: It's built across the Niagara river, and the famous Niagara Falls are located nearby.

M: Oh, I understand. Then ____________________ ____________________ of Canada and the U.S. Right?

W: Exactly. It's only 290 meters in length, so it can be crossed ______________________________.

M: Did you cross it on foot, too?

W: Well, I rode a bicycle. Cars can drive on it, too, but commercial trucks are not allowed.

M: I see. By the way, ________________________ to cross the bridge?

W: That's right. My nephew, Franklin, ____________ ____________________, so he couldn't cross.

M: That's too bad.

09

M: Quinoa is a grain-like crop grown in the Andes mountains of Peru and Bolivia. While usually ______________________________, what we call "quinoa grain" is actually the plant's seed. For centuries, quinoa ____________________ ____________________ for the poor, but in recent years, things have changed rapidly. Quinoa has become popular for its high protein and dietary fiber content. In the last few years, Peru has almost ________________________ from quinoa exports. Bolivia has also __________ ____________________ from quinoa, although it doesn't have much land suitable for growing quinoa. Ironically, the local consumption of quinoa still remains low because ____________ ____________________.

10

M: How can I help you?

W: I'm looking for a cordless vacuum cleaner.

M: Come this way. These five are the best-selling cordless vacuum cleaners these days. What is ______________________________?

W: No more than $500. And I want a lightweight vacuum cleaner that ________________________.

M: Okay. We need to eliminate this one. It weighs more than 4 kg.

W: All right. And my husband and I have allergies. I heard there's a vacuum cleaner that has a special filter.

M: You're talking about the HEPA filter. These ones have HEPA filters.

W: Great. Now I have these two options.

M: ________________________ between these two is around $60. Do you want the cheaper one?

W: It doesn't matter. I'd like a vacuum cleaner ________ ______________________________.

M: Then this one is for you. Good choice.

W: Okay. I'll take it.

11

W: You're really good at math. You must love it.

M: ________________________. I only study it ________________________.

W: Then what is your favorite subject?

12

M: How are you doing? ____________________?

W: I really don't feel well. Can we stop and get some medicine?

M: Of course. ____________________________ at the last intersection that we just passed?

13

W: I'm looking for a book about the U.S. Civil War.

M: We have a large selection on that war. ____________ ____?

W: There was a famous battle in Pennsylvania. I can't remember what it was called.

M: That was the battle of Gettysburg. Let me see ____.

W: If there isn't one about that battle, then maybe just ____________________________________ would be OK.

M: Well, I have good news and bad news.

W: Uh-oh! That doesn't sound promising.

M: We carry a book called *The Ghosts of Gettysburg*, but, unfortunately, ______________________ now.

W: I really need that book.

14

W: It's great ________________________________, Matt.

M: Yeah. It's been 10 years.

W: ________________________________! Your hairstyle is even the same.

M: Yes, I've still got the same hairstyle. Umm... I think ________________________ about your hairstyle.

W: Yes. My hair was short, so you said I had a boy's hairstyle.

M: Well, I'm sorry. By the way, in high school you wanted to be a teacher, right?

W: Yes. ______________________________. And yours?

M: Not yet. ______________________________. It's a small part in a new play at the Royal Playhouse.

W: That's great. I remember ______________________ in several school plays.

M: Yeah. Umm, you know, I used to tease you because I really liked you.

15

W: Andrew spends a lot of time on his hair. ________ ____________________ but a little below his ears. At home he styles his hair with lots of hair wax. At school, he frequently checks his hair. His mom is angry. Andrew's mom ______________________ ____________________________. It must be above his ears. If he doesn't, ______________________ ____________________________. Andrew walks unhappily into a hairdresser's near his house. The hairdresser says he looks good with long hair and suggests that ________________________________. In this situation, what would Andrew most likely say to the hairdresser?

16-17

M: There are millions of people who suffer from allergies worldwide, and many of these people can ____________________________________. Allergies occur when your immune system _____________ ____________________ that normally shouldn't cause a reaction. Although allergic reactions can be caused by many things, there are a few that are especially dangerous. Peanut allergies are ____ of life-threatening reactions. More than 3 million people in the United States report being allergic to peanuts, and about 150 of them ____________ ________________ allergic reactions. That's more than the number of people killed by lightning strikes. Bee stings are also very dangerous to anyone who is allergic. At least 40 Americans die each year from bee stings. To avoid getting stung, __________________________ whenever bees are nearby. Stay calm, and slowly move away. You can somewhat ________________________________ near you by not wearing bright clothing and not using perfume. Also, if you're picnicking outdoors, don't open the food _________________________ ________________, and cover up high-sugar foods and drinks like sodas that can attract bees.

PRACTICE TEST

01 다음을 듣고, 남자가 하는 말의 목적으로 가장 적절한 것을 고르시오.

① 학교 행사의 계획 변경을 알리려고
② 학교의 개교 기념행사를 소개하려고
③ 매년 열리는 학교 행사를 연기하려고
④ 태풍 피해에 대해서 학생들에게 알리려고
⑤ 자선 행사를 위한 행사 진행요원을 모집하려고

02 대화를 듣고, 여자의 의견으로 가장 적절한 것을 고르시오.

① 유기견 문제에 대한 의식 개선이 필요하다.
② 공공장소에서 반려견 배설물은 주인이 치워야 한다.
③ 반려견의 건강을 위해 정기적으로 산책시켜야 한다.
④ 깨끗한 공원 환경을 위해 관리 인력을 충원해야 한다.
⑤ 반려견을 공원에 데리고 나올 때는 목줄을 채워야 한다.

03 대화를 듣고, 두 사람의 관계를 가장 잘 나타낸 것을 고르시오.

① 의사 – 간호사
② 선생님 – 선생님
③ 아나운서 – 리포터
④ 방송 진행자 – 청취자
⑤ 생물학 교수 – 프로듀서

04 대화를 듣고, 그림에서 대화의 내용과 일치하지 않는 것을 고르시오.

05 대화를 듣고, 여자가 남자에게 부탁한 일로 가장 적절한 것을 고르시오.

① 새 자전거 사주기
② 자전거 타이어 고쳐주기
③ 자전거 타는 법 가르쳐주기
④ 공원으로 함께 자전거 타러 가기
⑤ 자전거 수리점 찾는 것 도와주기

06 대화를 듣고, 남자가 지불할 금액을 고르시오. [3점]

① $180 ② $190 ③ $209
④ $210 ⑤ $220

07 대화를 듣고, 여자가 영화 시사회에 갈 수 없는 이유를 고르시오.

① 영화를 좋아하지 않아서
② 친구 이사를 도와야 해서
③ 갑자기 출장을 가야 해서
④ 다른 친구와 가기로 해서
⑤ 배우의 사인회에 가야 해서

08 다음을 듣고, Josephine Baker에 관해 언급되지 않은 것을 고르시오.

① 성격 ② 별명 ③ 고국을 떠난 이유
④ 출연작 ⑤ 참여한 사회 운동

09 Tour de France에 관한 다음 내용을 듣고, 일치하지 않는 것을 고르시오.

① Tour de France는 매년 22일간 개최된다.
② 참가자는 3,000km가 넘는 거리를 자전거로 달려야 한다.
③ 경주에서 부정행위는 최근 들어 시작되었다.
④ 경기력 향상 약물을 복용한 부정행위자들이 있었다.
⑤ 경기력 향상 약물은 정당하지 않으므로 금지되었다.

10 다음 표를 보면서 대화를 듣고, 두 사람이 등록할 강좌를 고르시오.

Online Real Estate Courses (non-credit)

Class	Topics	Duration	Fees	Student Ratings
① A	Investment	7 weeks	$380	★★★★
② B	Apartments	6 weeks	$320	★★★
③ C	Commercial Properties	5 weeks	$275	★★★★
④ D	Apartments	5 weeks	$250	★★
⑤ E	Commercial Properties	8 weeks	$345	★★★

11 대화를 듣고, 여자의 마지막 말에 대한 남자의 응답으로 가장 적절한 것을 고르시오.

① That movie looks amazing.
② I turned 21 years old last Sunday.
③ I think you have to be over fifteen.
④ The original was made 10 years ago.
⑤ A horror movie would really scare him.

12 대화를 듣고, 남자의 마지막 말에 대한 여자의 응답으로 가장 적절한 것을 고르시오.

① I'm not sure, but it's a lot.
② It's much cheaper than calling.
③ I'll try to stop texting so much.
④ There are many errors in the text.
⑤ The maximum size is 80 characters.

13 대화를 듣고, 여자의 마지막 말에 대한 남자의 응답으로 가장 적절한 것을 고르시오.

▶ Man : ______________________

① But it's too far to walk.
② If you go just a bit further, you'll see it.
③ Thank you, but I'm going to pass this time.
④ I think we should go back. It's getting dark.
⑤ I'll drive. You can have a nap in the back seat.

14 대화를 듣고, 남자의 마지막 말에 대한 여자의 응답으로 가장 적절한 것을 고르시오. [3점]

▶ Woman : ______________________

① I shouldn't have hired her for the job.
② Yeah, I know. She called me half an hour ago.
③ She'll get in trouble for being so late to work.
④ I'd better hurry to have lunch with her at Mario's!
⑤ Well, I'm free for lunch. How about going together?

15 다음 상황 설명을 듣고, Grant 선생님이 Sylvia에게 할 말로 가장 적절한 것을 고르시오. [3점]

▶ Mr. Grant : ______________________

① If you think that will help, we'll try that.
② He doesn't want to discuss his problems with me.
③ I think we should try to pay him more attention.
④ I hope you can figure out what's going on with him.
⑤ I don't think his problem is related to schoolwork.

[16~17] 다음을 듣고, 물음에 답하시오.

16 여자가 하는 말의 주제로 가장 적절한 것은?

① sports world records
② the fastest objects in sports
③ the history of balls in sports
④ the reasons people love sports
⑤ sports that are popular worldwide

17 언급된 스포츠가 아닌 것은?

① badminton ② golf
③ tennis ④ baseball
⑤ soccer

06 DICTATION

녹음된 내용을 들으면서 빈칸을 알맞게 채워 보세요.

01

M: I'm terribly sorry to inform you that our school's anniversary event ______________________ ______________________. Since our neighborhood is still suffering from the terrible damage done by last summer's typhoon, we decided to cancel this event. Instead, ______________________ ______________________, we are planning a charity bazaar event. Soon your homeroom teacher will ______________________ of next week's event, which every student should attend. Of course, your family members are most welcome too. This is ______________________ ______________________ for those who lost everything overnight. Please bring anything that would ______________________ this difficult time.

02

M: It was a great idea to come to the park. The weather is perfect.

W: Yeah, but ______________________ with their dogs.

M: I guess I haven't even noticed any dogs since we got here.

W: I don't think there are any. But ______________________ ______________________. Look at that.

M: Ugh, is that dog waste?

W: How could the owner of that dog just walk off and leave that there? ______________________ ______________________?

M: I suppose some unfortunate park employee will have to.

W: That's simply unacceptable. Sometimes the careless behavior of others really______________________ ______________________.

M: You have a point.

03

M: ... and our next caller is Andrea from Sydney.

W: Hi, Dr. Karl. I love your show. I listen every week.

M: That's terrific, Andrea. ______________________ ______________________ today?

W: Yes. Dr. Karl, I'm always tired. Mom says ________ ______________________, but I can never sleep until 2 a.m.

M: How old are you, Andrea?

W: Sixteen.

M: Oh, that's a natural teenage sleep pattern. Teenagers have very special sleep needs.

W: You mean ______________________ ______________________?

M: Yes, so you don't have to worry about it too much. ______________________ on weekends.

W: OK, thank you.

M: Thanks for calling, Andrea.

04

M: Hello?

W: Hi, Chuck. It's me. Sorry I couldn't be there to ______________________.

M: That's okay. I think we can ______________________ ______________________.

W: Good. I really want Ms. Wilson's farewell party to be a success. Did you get balloons?

M: Yes, and I taped them on the board.

W: Okay, but the board still says "Thank You, Teacher," right?

M: Of course. And I ______________________ ______________________ and set it on the table.

W: Great. Do you need me to bring any flowers?

M: No, I already have some on the table. They're between the cake and the cards from the other students.

W: Then I'll just bring my card and add it to the pile.

M: Right. ______________________.

정답 및 해설 p.22

05

M: Are you busy on Saturday afternoon, Julie?

W: I don't have any plans. ______________________ ______________________?

M: I'd love to go bicycling in Lake Park with you. I remember that you once said you love bicycling in the park.

W: That was right after I had bought my new bike. But ______________________.

M: Why not?

W: My bicycle is broken. OK, it's not really broken. There's a hole in my tire and ______________. But there aren't any bicycle repair shops near my house.

M: I know how to fix a flat tire. I've patched a hole before.

W: Well, then ______________________ ______________________ on Saturday morning? Afterwards, I'd love to go to the park with you.

M: OK. No problem.

06

W: Glory Office Supplies. How can I help you?

M: Hi, this is Michael Whittier of Lloyd Trading Company. ______________________ ______________________ for some office supplies.

W: Okay, Mr. Whittier. ______________________ ______________________?

M: First, we'd like to purchase 10 boxes of A4 printer paper. How much is it?

W: It costs $15 a box.

M: I see. And we need 10 plastic binders. I want the one with 40 pockets.

W: It's $5 each, and you need 10 binders. Will there be anything else?

M: No, ______________________. You offer a bulk discount, right?

W: I can give you 5% discount as usual.

M: Okay. We need them today. ______________________ ______________________ for a rush order?

W: Yes, you'll have to pay $20 for delivery. We can get it to you today after 3 p.m.

M: Okay. We'll pay with our corporate credit card.

W: Thanks.

07

M: Today is truly my lucky day. My brother just called and told me the best news ever.

W: Well, what did he say?

M: ______________________ of the movie *Blue Moon*, but he can't make it. So he's giving them to me. Do you want to see it?

W: Are you kidding me? Of course I do. I heard it's a great movie.

M: We can get some autographs from the actors ______________________.

W: Really? I'm a big fan of Timothy Dalton! I can't believe it! By the way, why can't he go?

M: He had an unexpected business trip to Seattle so he'll be ______________________. Anyway, it begins at 6 p.m. tomorrow, so let's meet at 5.

W: Tomorrow? Oh, no! My best friend is moving tomorrow and ______________________ ______________________ her move. I already promised to go.

M: Oh, I understand.

W: I really want to go and get Timothy's autograph.

M: If you want, I'll get his autograph for you.

W: Great! That's very nice of you! I really appreciate it!

08

M: American dancer, singer, and actress Josephine Baker spent most of her career in France, captivating audiences with her wonderful performances and outgoing personality. Nicknamed "The Black Venus," she left the U.S. for France ______________________________. She made the decision because she wanted to experience the freedom of acting in Paris. After arriving, her style of dance quickly ______________________________. During the late 1920s, Baker was the highest-paid entertainer in Europe and the most photographed. She ______________________________ during World War Ⅱ, and remained a lifelong fighter against racism. She even ______________________________ from varying ethnic backgrounds and named them her "Rainbow Tribe."

09

W: The Tour de France is the world's most famous bicycle race. It is held in France every July. Cyclists ride for 22 days across a distance of more than 3,000 kilometers. Unfortunately, some cyclists ______________________________ that they cheat. The very first cheats on the Tour de France were caught in 1904. They ______________________________ in between towns. More recently, cheats have used performance-enhancing drugs. These drugs ______________________________, reduce pain, and give enormous energy. They are forbidden because they are not fair. American Floyd Landis won the 1997 Tour de France, but then a blood test showed he had used performance-enhancing drugs. ______________________________, and he returned to America in disgrace.

10

M: Miranda, you said you're interested in getting a real estate license.

W: Yes, I am. ______________________________ an online real estate course. I've already downloaded the course list.

M: Good. How about taking a course together?

W: Sure. Why don't we take a look at the course list? Do you have ______________________________?

M: I'm afraid we can't take the investment course because we are beginners.

W: You're right. And I need to finish this course within 6 weeks because I'll leave on my two-month vacation in December.

M: I also think a 5-6 week course would be perfect. By the way, fees are very expensive. ______________________________?

W: I don't want to spend more than $300 for just one course.

M: Me either. Well, it seems we have two choices. The difference is the course fee. Want to choose the cheaper one?

W: But the student ratings of that course are ______________________________.

M: You're right. Then I guess we need to take this course.

W: It looks like it.

11

W: Let's go watch that new horror movie with your brother.

M: Sounds great. But I don't think he's old enough.

W: ______________________________?

12

M: ______________________________ you are always texting these days.

W: I ______________________________ on the phone.

M: How many texts do you think you send in a day?

13

W: Look. ________________________________ — "Lake Victoria National Park, 320 kilometers."

M: Three hours to go.

W: I can't wait! I hope we get the same campsite we had last summer.

M: We need to get there before the school holiday crowds. ________________________________ and we'll get there in time.

W: We don't have any time to stop, do we?

M: No, we don't. Ha-bin, I just ________________ ________________________ and yawning!

W: Yeah, I'm feeling really sleepy.

M: Take a rest! You've been driving too long. ________ ________________________________ at the wheel?

W: But we can't stop. We have to keep going if we want to get our campsite!

14

W: Hi, Ben. What are you doing here?

M: Waiting for someone.

W: ____!

M: I know. ________________________________. I wonder where she is.

W: Why don't you call?

M: I can't. Stupidly, ________________________ ____________________ at home! And I can't remember her number.

W: Oh! Anyway, are you meeting for something important?

M: Oh, no. She's a friend. We have lunch together every Tuesday at Mario's.

W: Oh, I love Mario's! ______________________ ____________________! So, who's the friend?

M: Do you know Joanna?

W: Joanna! I saw her just before. She's working at Smokey's Burgers.

M: Oh, I completely forgot! She told me last week she got a new job! But ________________________ ____________________.

15

M: Sylvia is Anthony's mother. Today she comes to Anthony's school to meet his teacher, Mr. Grant, because he wants to talk with her about Anthony. Mr. Grant says Anthony ________________ ________________ in the class, but recently he rarely participates and he doesn't get along with his classmates. He says Anthony looks stressed. Sylvia is very surprised to hear this at first, but she says it's probably because ________________ ____________ last month. She thinks he is upset because everyone in the family __________ ____________________. Mr. Grant thinks it would ____________________________. In this situation, what would Mr. Grant most likely say to Sylvia?

16-17

W: Hello, everyone. At the end of last class, we spent some time talking about popular sports and why people love them. Certainly, one reason for their popularity is the fast-paced action that attracts a viewer's attention. Continuing with this idea, I'd like to introduce some facts about ________ ____. Surprisingly, the fastest object recorded in a major sport isn't a ball. It's the shuttlecock from badminton, ________________________ ______________ traveling at 493 km/h. In second place is the golf ball. In 2012, one was recorded traveling at 340 km/h. Now, you might have already guessed that tennis balls ________ ____________________________. In fact, tennis serves have been recorded traveling at over 260 km/h, making the tennis ball the fifth-fastest object in sports. The objects ______________ ________________________ have all been small. So, you might not expect that a soccer ball can travel at over 210 km/h. What other sports ________________________________ belong on this list?

실전모의고사 07 PRACTICE TEST

01 다음을 듣고, 남자가 하는 말의 목적으로 가장 적절한 것을 고르시오.

① 축가를 부를 사람을 모집하려고
② 음악 선생님의 결혼을 축하하려고
③ 합창 경연대회에 대해 알려주려고
④ 학생들의 실력 향상을 칭찬하려고
⑤ 합창단의 다음 공연에 대해 설명하려고

02 대화를 듣고, 여자의 의견으로 가장 적절한 것을 고르시오.

① 아이들에게 휴대 전화를 사주는 것은 좋지 않다.
② 어린이용 애플리케이션이 다양해질 필요가 있다.
③ 휴대 전화의 전자파 차단 기능을 강화해야 한다.
④ 휴대 전화의 가격을 좀 더 낮춰야 할 필요가 있다.
⑤ 부모가 올바른 휴대 전화 사용법을 가르쳐야 한다.

03 대화를 듣고, 두 사람의 관계를 가장 잘 나타낸 것을 고르시오.

① 식당 손님 – 요리사
② 주방 보조원 – 주방장
③ 식당 종업원 – 매니저
④ 요리학원 교습생 – 강사
⑤ 잡지 기자 – 요리 평론가

04 대화를 듣고, 그림에서 대화의 내용과 일치하지 <u>않는</u> 것을 고르시오.

05 대화를 듣고, 남자가 여자에게 부탁한 일로 가장 적절한 것을 고르시오.

① 피자 데우기
② 치킨 주문하기
③ 거실 청소하기
④ 휴대 전화 찾기
⑤ 부엌 식탁 치우기

06 대화를 듣고, 여자가 지불할 금액을 고르시오. [3점]

① $62　② $70　③ $72
④ $75　⑤ $80

07 대화를 듣고, 남자가 자원봉사 프로그램에 지원할 수 <u>없는</u> 이유를 고르시오.

① 클럽 회원이 아니라서
② 여행 일정이 한 달 미뤄져서
③ 최소 봉사 기간을 채울 수 없어서
④ 유소년 축구 지도자 자격증이 없어서
⑤ 자원봉사자 교육을 미리 받지 못해서

08 대화를 듣고, 해파리(jellyfish)에 관해 언급되지 <u>않은</u> 것을 고르시오.

① 모양　② 유독성　③ 먹이
④ 크기　⑤ 수명

09 the Shiny Pool에 관한 다음 내용을 듣고, 일치하지 <u>않는</u> 것을 고르시오.

① 이번 주 금요일에 개장한다.
② 최대 300명까지 수용할 수 있다.
③ 14세 미만 어린이는 입장료가 무료이다.
④ 백화점 회원은 입장료를 할인받을 수 있다.
⑤ 매일 자정까지 운영한다.

정답 및 해설 p.26

10 다음 표를 보면서 대화를 듣고, 남자가 빌릴 차를 고르시오.

Model	Rental Price (per day)	GPS Navigation System	Capacity (person)
① RC700	$60	×	5
② RC710	$70	○	5
③ RV720	$75	×	7
④ RV730	$80	○	7
⑤ RV740	$85	○	7

11 대화를 듣고, 여자의 마지막 말에 대한 남자의 응답으로 가장 적절한 것을 고르시오.

① I also like many genres of film.
② Alright. I'll let you choose this time.
③ I really enjoyed that romantic comedy.
④ Then we can come back another time.
⑤ This one has less action than the original.

12 대화를 듣고, 남자의 마지막 말에 대한 여자의 응답으로 가장 적절한 것을 고르시오.

① Sure, I love teaching the students.
② No, I'm on my way home right now.
③ I made it because it's getting colder.
④ If you'd like, I could make one for you.
⑤ Actually, my aunt has been teaching me.

13 대화를 듣고, 여자의 마지막 말에 대한 남자의 응답으로 가장 적절한 것을 고르시오. [3점]

▶ Man : ______________________

① Don't be sorry. What are friends for?
② Then, let's drop by my place tomorrow.
③ No thanks. I have to leave within an hour.
④ Well, I don't have a choice then. I owe you.
⑤ Are you sure you don't want to take the subway?

14 대화를 듣고, 남자의 마지막 말에 대한 여자의 응답으로 가장 적절한 것을 고르시오.

▶ Woman : ______________________

① I wish I had a larger yard.
② I hope you do well in the race.
③ I'm happy that they will come on Sunday.
④ How much do you want for your bicycle?
⑤ Then, I can keep it for you until the weekend.

15 다음 상황 설명을 듣고, Kyle의 엄마가 Kyle에게 할 말로 가장 적절한 것을 고르시오. [3점]

▶ Kyle's mom: Kyle, ______________________

① there's no rush, so just take it slow.
② your health must always come first.
③ that's okay. There's always next time.
④ you'd better review after class from now on.
⑤ you can get a good score since you studied hard.

[16~17] 다음을 듣고, 물음에 답하시오.

16 여자가 하는 말의 주제로 가장 적절한 것은?

① how weather affects travel
② good ways to enjoy a day off
③ the features of a new library
④ vacation strategies for families
⑤ tips for saving money while traveling

17 도서관에서 할 수 있는 일로 언급되지 않은 것은?

① DVD 관람
② 특별 강연 참석
③ 도서열람실 이용
④ 미니 콘서트 관람
⑤ 구내식당에서 식사

07 DICTATION

녹음된 내용을 들으면서 빈칸을 알맞게 채워 보세요.

01

M: Great job today, class. ______________________ ______________________, I'm very pleased to see that your singing is improving. You're sure to do well at this fall's competition. Now, before you leave for the day, ______________________ ______________________. Ms. Hathaway, the music teacher, is getting married next month. She has asked if someone from our choir ______ ______________________ at her wedding. I believe this is a great opportunity to show your appreciation for one of the nicest and most dedicated teachers at our school, ____________ ______________________. Those who are interested should speak to me after class. I will be happy to help with selecting a song and practicing for the performance. Let's show Ms. Hathaway ______________________________!

02

W: Hi, Tony. What are you reading?

M: It's an article in today's paper about a new cell phone.

W: Oh, I saw that phone on TV.

M: It has several amazing features and applications, but the price is high.

W: They say it's selling well ______________________ ______________________.

M: Right. It's especially popular with younger children. I think parents buy it ______________________ ______________________.

W: I'm not sure if that's right.

M: What do you mean?

W: It's dangerous because young kids can't control themselves. They focus entirely on their phones and ______________________________ around them.

M: True. Kids these days become ______________________ ______________________________.

W: In addition, there's evidence that suggests cell phone radiation is harmful to developing brains.

M: That is something to worry about.

03

W: Hello, I'm Jenny Harper.

M: It's nice to meet you, Jenny.

W: ______________________________. I saw your interview in a cooking magazine last month.

M: I'm glad to hear that. Now, let's go over ________ ______________________________.

W: Okay. I'm ready.

M: First, ______________________________. That's the first rule you should never forget while working here.

W: Got it. And then?

M: Peel the onions in this bowl and ______________ ______________________________.

W: No problem. By the way, I heard a group is coming to taste your special dish, salmon with salad.

M: Right. I should cook especially well for them.

W: ______________________________, as well. Please tell me if you need anything.

M: Great. Let's get started.

04

W: What ______________________________, Harry?

M: I went to the park with my friends. Do you want to see a picture?

W: Of course. Oh, the wooden hut beside the bench looks great.

M: Yes, we ate lunch inside of it.

W: Wonderful. Who are the people ______________ ______________________________?

M: They're Sandra and Nick. They hadn't met for a while, so they had a lot to talk about. And the man ______________________________ is my friend Jake.

W: Since he's holding a racket, he ____.

M: That's right. And the girl with a long-sleeved shirt is my younger sister Carol.

W: She looks excited, and the puppy running in front of her is so cute. Is it her dog?

M: Yeah. It loves to run with her.

05

M: It's almost 1:00 p.m. What should we have for lunch?

W: We have leftover pizza in the refrigerator. We ____.

M: That's not an option.

W: ____?

M: No, I ate it all last night. How about ordering some food?

W: That's fine with me. I'm ________________________________.

M: Sounds good. I have the number saved in my cell phone.

W: Could you order it while I clean the kitchen table? It's ____.

M: I think the living room is worse. Could you please take care of it first?

W: I'm too hungry to bother with the living room.

M: If Mom sees it, ________________________________.

W: Alright. I'll do that right now.

06

W: Excuse me. How much are your camera bags?

M: They ____ $15 to $150. What are you looking for?

W: I want something decent that's under $70.

M: Then ____. It's priced at $50, but it's very well-made.

W: Great! I'll take it. Can I also get two 16GB memory cards?

M: Of course. They're $15 each. ____?

W: Yes. I have two coupons I'd like to use: one is for 10% off and the other is for $5 off the total price.

M: I'm sorry, but you can't combine the two coupons. Our store policy is to accept only one at a time. ____ the coupons.

W: Oh, then I guess I'll use the 10% off coupon today. Here's my credit card.

M: OK. Thank you for shopping with us!

07

W: Jonathan, I've just signed up for a volunteer program.

M: What kind of volunteer program?

W: Have you heard of Evergreen Youth Club? They are looking for people ________________________________ their voluntary work project.

M: This is the first time I've heard of it. Can you tell me more?

W: ____, such as opening sports classes for underprivileged children, doing environmental clean-ups and so on.

M: It sounds quite rewarding. I'd like to sign up, too. ____ or skills that I need?

W: No, just sign up as a member of the club. I think you can volunteer in the soccer class.

M: That would be great. Thanks for the information.

W: Oh, most importantly, they require that ____ for the minimum period of three months from next month.

M: Oh, no. Then I can't. I'm planning a trip to Europe for a month next month.

W: Too bad. Okay, then you can apply next time.

08

M: Do you have any questions about the equipment?
W: No, I think I'm ready to dive.
M: Good. Then the only thing left before we enter the sea is ______________________________.
W: Jellyfish? You mean the fish that looks like an umbrella?
M: That's right. Most aren't deadly, but they __________ ______________________________. It's extremely painful.
W: How can I avoid them?
M: These jellyfish are about a meter in length and will be easy to see.
W: One meter? That's ______________________________ ______________________________. How many years do they usually live?
M: It ______________________________.
Most large coastal jellyfish live for 2 to 6 months.
W: I guess jellyfish are something ______________________________.
M: That's true, but don't worry too much. I'll be with you.
W: Okay. Let's go.

09

W: Attention shoppers. Thank you for visiting Shiny Department Store, ______________________________ ______________________________ in the city. This announcement is to invite you to the Shiny Pool, which opens this Friday. ______________________________, it offers an incredible view of the city for you to enjoy while you swim. ______________________________ up to 300 people and there are shower facilities available. The entrance fee is $10 per person and children under 14 can swim for free. And ______________________________ for those with department store membership cards. If you aren't already a Shiny Member, ______________________________. The pool is open every day from 10 a.m. until 10 p.m., and it's open until midnight on Fridays and Saturdays. So come to the Shiny Pool and enjoy your summer.

10

W: Hello, sir. How may I help you?
M: I need to rent a car for a trip.
W: You've come to the right place. As you can see, we have five options. ______________________________ ______________________________?
M: I think $80 is the most I'm willing to spend.
W: Okay. And would you like a GPS navigation system?
M: I definitely need one. ______________________________ ______________________________ where I'm going.
W: Then I recommend this model. It has a navigation system and ______________________________ ______________________________.
M: That sounds good, but I really don't need that much space. A car ______________________________ ______________________________ would be fine.
W: Then we have just the thing for you. And it will save you some money.
M: Great. I'll take it.

11

W: It looks like there are three movies we could see.
M: Oh, let's watch *Iron Man 3*! ______________________________ ______________________________!
W: Another sci-fi movie? I ______________________________ ______________________________.

12

M: Jenny, did you make this muffler? It's great!
W: Thank you. ______________________________ ______________________________ since last month.
M: Oh, ______________________________ ______________________________?

13

W: Do you think we'll finish by tonight, Matthew?
M: We have to. That's the deadline. Besides, we can finish in a few hours.
W: Okay, then I'll start on this next file. Did you hear something?
M: It sounds like rain. Look out the window! ________ ______________________________ outside!

W: It's quite a storm. Will you ________________ ____________________________ after work?

M: I'm not worried. The rain will probably stop later.

W: I don't think so. I heard the rain will last through the night.

M: Oh, I ______________________________________ ____________________________.

W: I could drive you home. It's no trouble.

M: Thanks, but my house is ________________ ________________________. I'll take the subway.

W: ____. Also, the subway might stop before we finish tonight.

14

W: Where are you going, Tony? Oh, nice bicycle!

M: Hi, Mina. Thanks, I just bought it at the mall and ____.

W: It looks great! By the way, don't you already have one?

M: Yes, but I had to buy this high-performance bicycle for next month's race.

W: I see. So, what are you going to do with your old one?

M: ________________________________, I guess.

W: Is there ____________________________________ ____________________________?

M: No, but I don't need it anymore.

W: Hey, my family __________________________ ____________________________ on Sunday. You could sell it there.

M: That's a great idea, but I don't have room in my yard to keep both bicycles until then.

W: Your yard isn't ____________________________ ____________________________?

M: Well, my brother and sister each have bicycles also.

15

M: It's late on a Thursday night, and Kyle is studying history for next week's final exam. Since Kyle did not prepare for the exam in advance, ________ ________________________________ to study. In fact, Kyle has gotten less than four hours of sleep each night this week. Kyle's mom has noticed that this behavior is ______________________________ __________________________ that is repeated each semester. She thinks it is a poor study habit and bad for Kyle's health, __________________ ______________________________ at school. Furthermore, she believes Kyle could ________ ______________________________ by spending a little time each day __________________ __________________. Since Kyle doesn't seem to realize this, she decides to tell him her opinion. In this situation, what would Kyle's mom most likely say to Kyle?

16-17

W: We all ____________________________________, but it can sometimes be difficult to find fun and interesting activities to do. But there are a few tips that can help you out. For example, a one-day trip outside the city can be fun. ________________ ____________________________ about the best local foods and places to explore. Then take ____________________________________ for a cheap and relaxing journey to your destination. While exploring, you can listen to music. And don't forget to take pictures. Now, if the weather isn't so nice, you can __________________________ ______________________________. You will be surprised how many things you can do there. Watching a DVD in a multimedia room will be a great start. Special lectures from authors or professors also make a nice change of pace. ______ ____________________________ such as mini concerts or plays. Watching one is a great way to spend an evening. And finally, don't forget the cafeteria. It may not be the best, but there will be ______________________________________.

PRACTICE TEST

01 **다음을 듣고, 남자가 하는 말의 목적으로 가장 적절한 것을 고르시오.**

① 학교의 다양한 과외 활동을 소개하려고
② 공정한 회장 선거가 되도록 협조를 구하려고
③ 적절한 교우관계를 유지하는 방법을 알리려고
④ 학급 회장을 뽑을 때 고려할 사항들을 알리려고
⑤ 대학 입학 지원서를 돋보이게 하는 법을 알리려고

02 **대화를 듣고, 여자의 의견으로 가장 적절한 것을 고르시오.**

① 학생들에게 스트레스 관리 방법을 가르쳐야 한다.
② 학생들의 학업 부담을 덜어줄 해결책을 찾아야 한다.
③ 학생들을 위한 상담 체계를 학교 내에 마련해야 한다.
④ 친구 사이의 갈등은 대화로 해결하는 것이 바람직하다.
⑤ 전공을 선택할 때 선생님에게 조언을 구하는 것이 좋다.

03 **대화를 듣고, 두 사람의 관계를 가장 잘 나타낸 것을 고르시오.**

① 수사관 - 검사　② 경찰 - 범인
③ 판사 - 피고인　④ 변호사 - 의뢰인
⑤ 강도 피해자 - 강도

04 **대화를 듣고, 그림에서 대화의 내용과 일치하지 않는 것을 고르시오.**

05 **대화를 듣고, 여자가 할 일로 가장 적절한 것을 고르시오.**

① 전화해서 구급차 부르기
② 약국에 가서 붕대를 사오기
③ 벤치에 앉는 것을 도와주기
④ 집에 가서 무릎 보호대 가져오기
⑤ 롤러블레이드 타는 법을 가르쳐주기

06 **대화를 듣고, 남자가 지불할 금액을 고르시오.**

① $60　② $75　③ $90
④ $105　⑤ $110

07 **대화를 듣고, 여자가 어제 산 구두를 환불한 이유를 고르시오.**

① 구두끈이 끊어져 있어서
② 온라인 상점보다 가격이 비싸서
③ 구두를 신으면 발이 너무 아파서
④ 구두 대신 워킹 슈즈가 필요해서
⑤ 온라인 상점의 제품이 더 다양해서

08 **다음을 듣고, 공연 취소에 관해 언급되지 않은 것을 고르시오.**

① 취소 기간　② 취소 이유
③ 환불 여부　④ 취소 극장 이름
⑤ 공연 여부 문의처

09 **Amity 해변 청소의 날에 관한 다음 내용을 듣고, 일치하지 않는 것을 고르시오.**

① 이 행사는 매년 행해진다.
② 오렌지색 봉지는 재활용품을 담기 위함이다.
③ 검은색 봉지는 음식물 쓰레기용이다.
④ 참가자들을 위한 음식이 마련된다.
⑤ 참가자들은 두 명이 한 팀으로 활동한다.

정답 및 해설 p.30

10 다음 표를 보면서 대화를 듣고, 두 사람이 구입하기로 한 미끄럼틀을 고르시오.

Slide Climbers for Playground

Model	Age Range	Type of Material	Number of Slides	Price
① A	6-8	metal	3	$850
② B	4-6	plastic	1	$410
③ C	4-6	plastic	2	$480
④ D	4-6	plastic	2	$570
⑤ E	4-6	metal	3	$660

11 대화를 듣고, 남자의 마지막 말에 대한 여자의 응답으로 가장 적절한 것을 고르시오.

① I think you should get a dog.
② Sometimes it can be difficult.
③ The black one is my favorite.
④ I can give you some dog food.
⑤ I'm working at an animal hospital.

12 대화를 듣고, 여자의 마지막 말에 대한 남자의 응답으로 가장 적절한 것을 고르시오.

① I'll do that right now.
② I like studying with Jennifer.
③ I don't mind. Let's go home.
④ The library closes too early.
⑤ I know where her house is located.

13 대화를 듣고, 남자의 마지막 말에 대한 여자의 응답으로 가장 적절한 것을 고르시오. [3점]

▶ Woman : ______________________

① We don't sell clothing here. Try next door.
② The complaint department is on the fourth floor.
③ If you have a coupon, we will gladly sell you wool.
④ I'm sorry, but we have a new selection of scarves.
⑤ My family doesn't like to be in pictures together.

14 대화를 듣고, 여자의 마지막 말에 대한 남자의 응답으로 가장 적절한 것을 고르시오. [3점]

▶ Man : ______________________

① I really want to see the rock concert.
② They are as comfortable as I have imagined.
③ I don't like standing on the train during rush hour.
④ That's expensive. What about the upper deck seats?
⑤ I would pay twice as much to get the orchestra seats.

15 다음 상황 설명을 듣고, Jess가 Carter에게 할 말로 가장 적절한 것을 고르시오. [3점]

▶ Jess : ______________________

① Don't worry. I don't mind seeing it a second time.
② We should see a movie that none of us has seen.
③ I'll be in the next theater watching an action movie.
④ That movie is fantastic. It has a surprise ending.
⑤ Have a great time! I'll wait for you at the coffee shop.

[16~17] 다음을 듣고, 물음에 답하시오.

16 여자가 하는 말의 주제로 가장 적절한 것은?

① the effectiveness of caffeine
② why caffeine is highly addictive
③ how to handle caffeine addiction
④ various effects of coffee on the body
⑤ differences between coffee and herbal tea

17 카페인 섭취 대신 할 수 있는 행동으로 언급되지 않은 것은?

① 허브티 마시기
② 아침 식사하기
③ 운동하기
④ 친구와 대화하기
⑤ 카페인을 줄인 커피 마시기

08 DICTATION

녹음된 내용을 들으면서 빈칸을 알맞게 채워 보세요.

01

M: Selecting a class president is a very important choice. Although someone may be popular among the students and teachers, it will not necessarily ________________________. Other things to consider are whether the candidate can handle ________________________. Will it interfere with doing school work and other activities? Will they ________________________ to represent your voice in school matters? Will they bring about positive changes, or will they simply use the position to ________________________? Ask the candidates these questions and choose the one who will best serve you, not just themselves.

02

W: Hi, Jim. You look really tired. Are you feeling alright?

M: ________________________. I'm failing two of my classes and I'm thinking about changing my major.

W: That's too bad. Actually, I'm also ________________________ on my school work. ________________________ about our problems.

M: I think you're right. I know that many of our classmates are feeling a lot of pressure right now.

W: There are also a lot of students that are ________________________ who are making them feel uncomfortable. A school counseling system might be able to help with those things.

M: That's a great idea. I would really appreciate having someone to talk to.

W: Don't forget that you can talk to me anytime.

03

M: Do you understand the charges against you?

W: I understand, your honor.

M: It is my job to see that there is justice and ________________________.

W: That's why I want it known that ________________________ the convenience store.

M: So you are saying you are not guilty?

W: ________________________. I am not guilty.

M: We will then have to ________________________. This means we will have to select a jury who will decide whether or not you are guilty.

W: I understand. Then how should I start to prepare for the trial?

M: You should start ________________________.

04

W: Honey, Sean is having his second birthday next month. I'd like to ________________________ for him like this photo.

M: Let me see. Wow! Its theme is the Baby Shark.

W: He really loves the Baby Shark song and dance. What do you think of the triangular flags ________________________?

M: I like them. They give it a festive mood. I also like the banner behind the table.

W: It has Papa, Mama, and Baby Shark. They put their son's name on the banner, too.

M: Good idea. They decorated the table with three balloons on the right.

W: That's another decoration detail.

M: They also ________________________ of the table. What a great idea!

W: That's my favorite part. They put a cake with three candles on the fish net.

M: Are you going to organize Sean's birthday party just like this picture?

W: Almost the same, ________________________. I'm going to put a number 2-shaped candle on the cake.

M: That would be great!

정답 및 해설 p.30

05

W: Johnny! Watch out! You're going to hit that other rollerblader.

M: Ahhh! Ouch!

W: Oh, no! Oh, no! Are you OK? ________________ ________________.

M: It hurts, but I think I'm OK. Let me try to get up.

W: No, ______________________________. I'll get some help. I'll call an ambulance.

M: Mom, it's not that bad. Ouch! I can sit down on that bench.

W: Hmm.... There's a pharmacy ________________ ____________________ of the park. I'll go and get some bandages.

M: OK. I'll wait here. I guess I should have worn my knee pads.

W: I told you to go back and get your knee pads and helmet, but you said it was alright.

M: Well, I ____ today.

W: I hope so.

06

M: I would like three tickets, please, for my mother, my son and myself. Do any of us qualify for a special ticket?

W: A regular ticket costs $30. If your child is under 12 years old, ________________________________.
And anyone 65 years old or older gets in for $20.

M: Oh, no! Today is my son's 13th birthday. ________ ____.

W: Actually, we also have a birthday special. If you ________________________________, then you can take $5 off the price of a regular ticket.

M: That would be $25? Here's his passport.

W: And how about the rest of your family?

M: ____.
That means she can get in for $20. And I guess I just get a regular ticket.

07

M: Honey, ____ for a while?

W: Can you wait just a little longer? I'm buying some shoes online.

M: Really? I thought you went shopping yesterday and bought a pair of high heels.

W: I did, but ____ when I got home.

M: Were you able to get your money back?

W: Sure. I paid in cash and I kept the receipt. I ____ this morning.

M: That's good. So what kind are you ordering today?

W: I've decided to get these walking shoes. I think I have too many high heels that are hurting my feet, anyway.

M: Good idea. And please ________________________ when you are finished with the computer.

08

W: Starting tonight, performances of some musicals, including *The Lion King*, are cancelled __________ ____________________. The workers who operate the theater ______________________________. The workers' union and theater owners tried very hard but ____. Tickets for any performance that is cancelled will be refunded. Some musicals performed in other parts of the city ______________________________. Those theater workers are represented by a different union. *Phantom of the Opera*, *Cats* and *West Side Story* are going on without a problem. Phone the theater if you have tickets to a show and ____ because of the strike.

09

M: Welcome to the annual Amity Beach Clean-Up Day. ____________________, the recent bad weather has made our once-beautiful beach quite ugly. To my left, you will see a table with trash bags and gloves. The orange bags ____________________, such as glass, plastic and aluminum. The black bags will be used for trash, such as cigarette butts and old shoes. The table to my right has food and drinks, so please, help yourselves. Now, if everyone will get a partner and ____________________, each team will get one orange bag, one black bag and two pairs of gloves. Let's make this beach ____________________ once again!

10

W: Bill, I think we need to replace the slide climber in the kindergarten playground.

M: I thought about that, too. ____________________?

W: I have a catalog here. Let's take a look.

M: Oh, very nice! We need to find something for kids between the ages of 4 and 6.

W: You're right. ____________________ plastic would be better for the kids? Metal can be dangerous.

M: Of course. They could ____________________, and it can also rust over time.

W: How many slides should it have?

M: There should at least be two slides so that the kids don't have to wait long.

W: You're right. The kids can start fighting if they wait too long. But three slides ____________________. It would be too big for our playground.

M: Then let's get one with two slides. How much should we spend?

W: We can't spend more than $500.

M: Well, we'll have to get this one. Let's hurry and order.

11

M: ____________________. You have one, right?

W: Actually, I have three. They are so much fun to play with.

M: ____________________?

12

W: The library is closing soon. We need to find ____________________.

M: Let's go to Jennifer's house.

W: Shouldn't we call her first ____________________?

13

M: I saw a red scarf in your catalogue. Do you have it here?

W: We might. Do you remember what it was called?

M: I thought it was called a red wool scarf. Sorry, I didn't notice the style name.

W: That's OK. I have the current catalogue right here.

M: That isn't the same catalogue I was looking at. ____________________ wearing ski clothes.

W: I'm sorry, but I think you were looking at last year's book!

M: How could that happen? ____________________.

W: Well, we ____________________ and complain that the old one was sent to them.

M: Does that mean you don't ____________________ in your store?

14

W: Thank you for calling Ticketron. What can I do for you?

M: I'd like to buy two tickets for the rock concert on Saturday at the concert hall.

W: OK. ________________________________ in the orchestra pit and seats in the upper deck.

M: Which ones ____________________________?

W: The orchestra seats have a better view, but you will find yourself standing for most of the show.

M: Hmm. I was hoping to enjoy the concert from ____________________________________.

W: Oh, there is another option, but they are very expensive.

M: What option is that?

W: We have stage-side seats. There are ____________ ______________________ and we have two left.

M: Great. How much are they?

W: They are $250 each.

15

M: Every Saturday, Jess and Lucinda go out with their friends, Carter and Patty. They usually go to dinner and then a movie and then for a late night cup of coffee. Every week, Carter ________________ ____________________________. Even if Jess doesn't want to see the movie Carter has chosen, he doesn't want to argue with his good friend, so ____________________________. This week, Carter says he wants to see a movie that Jess has already seen. Carter says that it isn't his or the girls' fault that Jess ____________________________. Although Jess does want to see a movie with her friends, she doesn't ____________________ __________________________. And she thinks Carter should respect his friends' opinion this time. In this situation, what would Jess most likely say to Carter?

16-17

W: You can't work before your morning coffee? Does your IQ jump a couple of points after a cup from your favorite coffee shop? If so, ______________ ______________________________. You might think this is a harmless addiction, but caffeine can hurt you if you have too much. In order to get rid of your caffeine addiction, you will first have to accept the fact that you are addicted to it. Then, write down your resolution to quit caffeine on a piece of paper and paste it in a place where you will see it every day. You can also try to find a caffeine alternative whenever ________________ ________________________________. Even decaffeinated coffee may contain caffeine, so ________________________________. A hot cup of tea can provide an uplifting sensation that is similar to coffee. And ____________________ ________________________. Having a healthy breakfast makes it much easier to get through the morning. Finally, try to stay active. ____________ ______________________________ to prevent fatigue. Even ______________________________ will help take your mind off caffeine.

실전모의고사 09 PRACTICE TEST

01 **다음을 듣고, 여자가 하는 말의 목적으로 가장 적절한 것을 고르시오.**

① 선로 보수에 따른 열차 지연을 통보하려고
② 열차 정보 서비스의 신규 개통을 알리려고
③ 철도 건널목에서의 차량 사고의 위험을 알리려고
④ 열차 운행 중지에 따른 대체 교통수단을 설명하려고
⑤ 역과 시내를 연결하는 셔틀버스의 운행 노선을 알리려고

02 **대화를 듣고, 남자의 의견으로 가장 적절한 것을 고르시오.**

① 공연 관람 예절을 지켜야 한다.
② 공연 관람은 혼자 하는 것이 좋다.
③ 공연은 같이 보는 사람이 중요하다.
④ 공연 관람은 훌륭한 사교 활동이다.
⑤ 공연은 좌석 위치에 따라 만족도가 다르다.

03 **대화를 듣고, 두 사람의 관계를 가장 잘 나타낸 것을 고르시오.**

① 마사지사 – 환자
② 내과 의사 – 간호사
③ 외과 의사 – 물리치료사
④ 병원 접수원 – 청소부
⑤ 치과 의사 – 병원 접수원

04 **대화를 듣고, 그림에서 대화의 내용과 일치하지 않는 것을 고르시오.**

05 **대화를 듣고, 여자가 할 일로 가장 적절한 것을 고르시오.**

① 친구 집을 방문하기
② 안경 배달을 신청하기
③ 콘택트렌즈를 새로 사기
④ 퇴근 후 안경을 찾아오기
⑤ 회사에서 메시지를 확인하기

06 **대화를 듣고, 여자가 지불할 금액을 고르시오.**

① 1,200원　② 1,800원　③ 2,000원
④ 2,400원　⑤ 3,000원

07 **대화를 듣고, 여자가 노래 대회에 참가할 수 없는 이유를 고르시오.**

① 참가비가 비싸서
② 참가 자격이 안 되어서
③ 시간제 근무 시간과 겹쳐서
④ 감기로 목 상태가 안 좋아서
⑤ 오디션 일자에 여행 계획이 있어서

08 **대화를 듣고, 이산화탄소에 관해 두 사람이 언급하지 않은 것을 고르시오.**

① 무게　② 대기 중 비율　③ 용도
④ 색깔　⑤ 냄새

09 **kabuki에 관한 다음 내용을 듣고, 일치하지 않는 것을 고르시오.**

① 1603년 일본에서 시작되었다.
② 중산층과 하류층의 취향을 만족시켰다.
③ 특수 효과를 사용했다.
④ 정치인을 풍자하는 내용도 다루었다.
⑤ 내용 검열이 심해 한때 쇠퇴하기도 했다.

10 다음 자료를 보면서 대화를 듣고, 남자가 구입할 자전거를 고르시오.

Last-minute sale!

barrysbicycles.com

Brand/Style	Retail/Sale Price	Wheel Size(inches)	Warranty (months)
① Huffy Comfort Bike	~~$269~~/$99	26	12
② Milo Road Bike	~~$319~~/$179	26	12
③ Ultimate Hybrid Bike	~~$499~~/$279	26	36
④ Giant Hybrid Bike	~~$469~~/$299	24	24
⑤ Apollo Folding Bike	~~$799~~/$499	26	lifetime

11 대화를 듣고, 남자의 마지막 말에 대한 여자의 응답으로 가장 적절한 것을 고르시오.

① Let's take turns driving.
② I'll go back and lock up the house.
③ I've already double-checked everything.
④ Traveling gives you unforgettable memories.
⑤ I think we should have taken a train instead.

12 대화를 듣고, 여자의 마지막 말에 대한 남자의 응답으로 가장 적절한 것을 고르시오.

① Try another Internet browser.
② I don't think we can finish our report.
③ Online information is not that reliable.
④ I'm going to post my report on the web.
⑤ Sure, I'll send you an email about it later.

13 대화를 듣고, 남자의 마지막 말에 대한 여자의 응답으로 가장 적절한 것을 고르시오. [3점]

▶ Woman : __________

① OK, enjoy the conference and have a great day.
② Well, you'd better hurry or you will miss the train.
③ I'd like to see the opera too. Can I come with you?
④ Don't worry. I'll go and tell them you are on the way.
⑤ Just call and get them to meet you at another place.

14 대화를 듣고, 여자의 마지막 말에 대한 남자의 응답으로 가장 적절한 것을 고르시오. [3점]

▶ Man : __________

① But I won't be ready by then.
② It shouldn't take more than 15 minutes.
③ I need you to help me prepare lunch then.
④ But I don't know how to make Greek salad.
⑤ Go ahead and have lunch. Don't wait for me.

15 다음 상황 설명을 듣고, Miriam이 여자아이의 어머니에게 할 말로 가장 적절한 것을 고르시오. [3점]

▶ Miriam : __________

① I have great news about your daughter.
② Your daughter is very concerned about you.
③ The pool is too crowded, Mom. Can I go home?
④ Your daughter missed her swimming lesson today.
⑤ I'm sorry but your daughter has had an accident.

[16~17] 다음을 듣고, 물음에 답하시오.

16 남자가 하는 말의 주제로 가장 적절한 것은?

① how copyright law affects the music industry
② reasons we shouldn't download music illegally
③ how intellectual property rights protect creativity
④ conflicts between file sharing sites and copyright law
⑤ building a system to prevent downloading files illegally

17 바이러스가 일으킬 수 있는 문제로 언급되지 <u>않은</u> 것은?

① 개인 정보 유출
② 자료 손실
③ 인터넷 연결 속도 저하
④ 백신 프로그램 오류
⑤ 과도한 팝업 광고

09 DICTATION

녹음된 내용을 들으면서 빈칸을 알맞게 채워 보세요.

01

W: Attention please, passengers. There has been a major accident involving an express train and several cars ______________________ at Church Street. Emergency services ______________________. All trains have been stopped until further notice. We sincerely apologize for the inconvenience. ______________________, we have several shuttle buses waiting at exit 4. Each of the buses will ______________________, so please check the destination before you get on a bus. ______________________, please call our information hotline at 111-333. That's 111-333. Thank you.

02

M: Hi, Yumi. Did you just come from the ballet performance?

W: Jason! You surprised me. Yes, I just watched it with my friends.

M: Oh? So did I. I was in row C.

W: Wow, ______________________. Who did you come with?

M: No one. I was able to get one good seat for myself.

W: That's too bad. ______________________ if I'd known.

M: Yeah, but don't worry about it. I really enjoyed the performance.

W: Do you mind doing things alone? I go with friends whenever I watch something.

M: Friends are great, but I can focus on the performance when I'm alone. It ______________________.

W: I see what you mean. Maybe I should try it someday.

M: Plus, it gives me a chance to meet new people.

W: That's true, too. But ______________________.

M: I'd love to. Talk to you later.

03

W: Sam, I've finished with Ms. Walsh. Here are her charts. Please ______________________ of oral X-rays.

M: As well as the regular clean-and-polish treatment?

W: Yes, and I need to see her again next week.

M: OK, ______________________?

W: Implants. So please make it a 60-minute appointment.

M: Yes, I'll ask her ______________________ when she comes through to reception.

W: Good. Now, who's next?

M: Ken Chang. Wisdom tooth removal. He's not here yet. Here are his records.

W: Thanks. ______________________ as soon as he arrives.

04

W: Welcome home, brother. How was your trip to Europe?

M: It was very exciting! I bought some gifts for the family. Can you guess which one is for you?

W: Is it the mug on the left?

M: No, that's for Mom. ______________________ next to Dad's gift.

W: Oh, that's great. Dad will love a checkered handkerchief.

M: I hope so, and the necklace with a flower-shaped pendant is for you. Do you like it?

W: I love it. ______________________ with a heart-shaped pendant that you gave me for my birthday.

M: ______________________. Next to it, I placed a teddy bear for our little sister.

W: That's so sweet, but what about the star-shaped box of chocolates?

M: That's for all of us to share.

05

M: Goodman Optical, Gary speaking.

W: Hi, Gary. This is Stephanie Lee. You called and left a message earlier. You said ________________ ____________________________?

M: Oh, I'm afraid ____________________________.

W: What's wrong?

M: Your glasses won't be ready until 8 p.m. tonight. I can have them delivered to you by 10 a.m. tomorrow.

W: That's OK. ______________________________ on my way home from work tonight.

M: Are you sure?

W: Definitely. I can't stand another day wearing contact lenses. ____________________________.

M: I know what you mean.

06

W: I'm full, but this is so tasty. What's it called again?

M: Eomuk Kkochi.

W: Eomuk Kkochi? Yum. ______________________ ______________?

M: It's just mashed fish ______________________ ______________.

W: What a great snack! But why are the sticks different colors?

M: They're different prices. Red sticks are 300 won each, blue are 400 won, and white sticks are 500 won.

W: That's cheap.

M: Isn't it? Here, ____________________________.

W: No! You can pay next time.

M: OK, ____________________________________. That's 1,200 won.

W: And I had two blue sticks at 400 won per stick, and two white sticks at 500, right?

M: Right.

07

M: Sophia, did you hear about the English Song Contest that's being held at Merriam College?

W: Yes, I did. I really want to enter but I ___________ ___________________________. I'm not a college student.

M: Of course you can. College and high school students are all accepted this time.

W: I'm so excited. I ____________________________ ______________. I'd like to know about the cost to participate.

M: It's $20.

W: That's not as expensive as I thought. When is the contest?

M: It's September 20th, but you _________________ _________________ an audition. The audition is on August 17th and 18th.

W: Really? Then I won't be able to participate.

M: Why? Is it because of your part-time job? You can switch shifts with someone.

W: My family ______________________________ to Alaska from August 11th to 19th. I'm afraid I'll have to wait for another chance.

M: I'm sorry to hear that.

08

W: I brought some snacks for you to eat while you work on your presentation.
M: Thanks, Mom. I was getting really hungry.
W: Are you researching about global warming?
M: Right now, I'm reading about carbon dioxide. It's ______________________________ of global warming.
W: Okay. You know it's ______________________ ________________, right?
M: Yes, but it's only around 0.03% of the atmosphere. However, it's ______________________________ ______________________________.
W: Oh, I know that it can be turned into dry ice and that it's used in fire extinguishers.
M: Right. I've also learned that __________________ ______________________________, which is why it can be added to soda pop.
W: You're really learning a lot from this presentation.

09

M: As you can see, we are now inside the Japanese kabuki theater. The history of kabuki __________ ________________________. As a new form of drama, kabuki satisfied the tastes of the new social classes, ______________________________ who began to increase in the urban centers. With beautiful costumes, exaggerated movements, and ______________________________, it is no wonder that this spectacular event has remained popular for centuries. The stories deal with a wide range of subjects from historical events to daily life. Sometimes the stories ______________________________. So, during the 1600s, government officials banned some performances that they felt were too controversial. However, these bans seem to have made kabuki ________________________ ________________.

10

M: This website has ______________________________.
W: You should buy one.
M: I know. Which one, though?
W: The Apollo folding bike is a bargain.
M: And ______________________________ on the subway.
W: ______________________________, though.
M: Um, I really can't afford more than $300.
W: Hybrid-style bikes are great for city riding.
M: True. OK, I'll get the Giant Hybrid!
W: That was easy!
M: Oh, no. It's only 24 inches. I need a 26-inch.
W: How about the Milo road bike?
M: No, ______________________________.
W: That leaves two. ______________________________ to get the one with the longer warranty.
M: Good thinking. I'll do that.

11

M: I put our luggage in the trunk and ____________ ______________________________ properly.
W: Then let's ______________________________.
M: Are you sure we aren't forgetting anything?

12

W: I'm ______________________________ for my report.
M: I found most of my ideas on the Internet.
W: Really? ______________________________ for me?

13

W: Hey Joe, what are you up to?

M: ________________________________ to meet up with Dan and Tim.

W: Oh, yeah? Where are you meeting them?

M: Museum Station. ____________________ the Opera House.

W: But you can't! The APEC conference is on. Leaders from all over the world are there. The Opera House area ____________________________.

M: That's all right. We'll do something else.

W: Joe, you won't find them. Museum Station is off-limits too, and the police are everywhere to stop people from going there.

M: Dan and Tim will ____________________. I have to go find them.

14

W: Matt, can you go to the grocery store for me?

M: Why?

W: I'm making a Greek salad for lunch. I need some Greek-style cheese and olives.

M: I love Greek salad. And I'm starving. I'll go right away.

W: Thanks. Black olives please, not green. Oh, and ________________________________.

M: OK, anything else? ____________________ ______________?

W: Oh, yeah. Some wholemeal bread would be nice. We've got some tomatoes and cucumbers. So don't worry about them. Do you want some money?

M: No, that's okay. I'll pay. ________________ ____________________?

W: That depends on when you get back with the cheese and other things.

15

W: Miriam is a lifeguard and swimming instructor at the local swimming pool. One day she ______ ______________________ in the crowded pool. Miriam ____________________ and checks if the girl is OK, but the girl is unconscious and not breathing. Shouting, "Call an ambulance!" she ____________________ ____________ and applies emergency rescue techniques. Miriam saves the girl's life, but the girl still has to go to a hospital. The ambulance arrives. Miriam asks the girl for her mother's phone number ____________________ what has happened. Miriam calls and the mother answers the phone. In this situation, what would Miriam most likely say to the girl's mother?

16-17

M: When a song is produced and marketed, it is protected by copyright law so that it cannot be copied, reproduced or resold without the copyright holder's permission. If you do not pay for a song that is under copyright, then downloading that song is a crime. Today, I'd like to talk about ________________________. I'll start by explaining intellectual property. Intellectual property is something that someone has created or invented and that no one is legally allowed to make, copy, or sell. It is basically ______________ __________________. Intellectual property rights were created to reward people for their efforts and stimulate investment. In the music industry, intellectual property rights ________ ____________________ by providing a guarantee that the company will end up making money. Violating these rights hurts these companies. Another reason not to download music illegally ________________________. Illegally downloaded files are typically passed through file sharing sites, some of which contain viruses designed to steal your identity. Other viruses might ____________________ ________________________. And at the very least, you will probably have to ______ ________________________.

실전모의고사
10 PRACTICE TEST

01 다음을 듣고, 여자가 하는 말의 목적으로 가장 적절한 것을 고르시오.

① 공연의 성공을 기원하려고
② 본인의 공연을 홍보하려고
③ 공연 취소에 대해 사과하려고
④ 팬들에게 감사의 말을 전하려고
⑤ 새로운 앨범의 출시를 알리려고

02 대화를 듣고, 남자의 의견으로 가장 적절한 것을 고르시오.

① 새로운 곳으로 여행 가는 것은 흥미롭다.
② 자유여행은 만족스러운 여행이 되기 어렵다.
③ 자유여행 계획은 되도록 세세하게 짜야 한다.
④ 편안한 여행을 위해서는 숙소 선택이 중요하다.
⑤ 패키지 단체 여행이 관광하는 데 더 효율적이다.

03 대화를 듣고, 두 사람의 관계를 가장 잘 나타낸 것을 고르시오.

① 팬 – 모델
② 매니저 – 프로듀서
③ 아나운서 – 리포터
④ 사진작가 – 배우
⑤ 영화감독 – 각본가

04 대화를 듣고, 그림에서 대화의 내용과 일치하지 않는 것을 고르시오.

05 대화를 듣고, 여자가 남자에게 부탁한 일로 가장 적절한 것을 고르시오.

① 컴퓨터에서 파일 지우기
② 여자에게 춤을 보여 주기
③ 사진기에서 파일을 내려받기
④ 친구에게 오지 말라고 전하기
⑤ 비디오 파일을 남에게 보여 주지 말기

06 대화를 듣고, 여자가 지불할 금액을 고르시오. [3점]

① $35 ② $45 ③ $50
④ $55 ⑤ $60

07 대화를 듣고, 남자가 딸의 발표회에 참석할 수 없는 이유를 고르시오.

① 출장을 가야 해서
② 치과 예약이 있어서
③ 꽃다발을 사느라 늦어서
④ 발표회 스케줄이 바뀌어서
⑤ 예정에 없던 회사 일이 생겨서

08 음악 축제에 관한 다음 내용을 듣고, 언급되지 않은 것을 고르시오.

① 축제 기간 ② 출연진 ③ 기념품 판매
④ 입장료 ⑤ 교통편

09 Brockton Point에 관한 다음 내용을 듣고, 일치하지 않는 것을 고르시오.

① 도심 한복판에 위치해 있다.
② 시장이 청혼 장소로 명명했다.
③ 대형 스크린 TV와 스피커가 설치되었다.
④ 현장에서 청혼 영상이 녹화된다.
⑤ 청혼 영상 서비스는 인터넷으로 신청 가능하다.

10 다음 표를 보면서 대화를 듣고, 여자가 주문할 블루투스 스피커를 고르시오.

The Best Outdoor Bluetooth Speakers

Brand	Price	Battery Life	Channel	Water-resistant
① Anker	$99	8 hours	mono	×
② Sonos	$148	12 hours	stereo	×
③ Bosa	$179	18 hours	mono	○
④ JBO	$189	15 hours	stereo	○
⑤ Ultimate	$249	20 hours	mono	○

11 대화를 듣고, 여자의 마지막 말에 대한 남자의 응답으로 가장 적절한 것을 고르시오.

① It's so hard to please her.
② Next time, let's go together.
③ She would barely speak to me.
④ I was upset because she was late.
⑤ We had dinner at a nice restaurant.

12 대화를 듣고, 남자의 마지막 말에 대한 여자의 응답으로 가장 적절한 것을 고르시오.

① Then, I guess we're both hungry.
② Yes, teachers eat in the cafeteria.
③ No, I'm happy to share it with you.
④ Yes, so I want to take a cooking class.
⑤ No, but we can eat it during the break.

13 대화를 듣고, 여자의 마지막 말에 대한 남자의 응답으로 가장 적절한 것을 고르시오.

▶ Man : ____________________

① Thank you for holding the door.
② Good idea. You might catch a cold.
③ Wait a minute. Those gloves fit well.
④ Don't worry. Brad will be fine by himself.
⑤ You didn't hear me! You don't need them.

14 대화를 듣고, 남자의 마지막 말에 대한 여자의 응답으로 가장 적절한 것을 고르시오. [3점]

▶ Woman : ____________________

① No way, you are my friend. Take one.
② How much would you pay for those books?
③ You are really kind to offer me such a good job.
④ No thanks, you don't have to draw anything for me.
⑤ They are very valuable paintings. They cost a fortune.

15 다음 상황 설명을 듣고, Harry가 Paula에게 할 말로 가장 적절한 것을 고르시오. [3점]

▶ Harry : ____________________

① I can't. I'm grounded.
② You're being so unfair to me.
③ Great. Let's meet at 8 o'clock.
④ It's not a problem for me at all.
⑤ Good. I've changed my behavior recently.

[16~17] 다음을 듣고, 물음에 답하시오.

16 남자가 하는 말의 주제로 가장 적절한 것은?

① effects of caffeine on the body
② disadvantages of drinking coffee
③ how to select a tea for good health
④ potential side effects of drinking tea
⑤ the properties of various herbal teas

17 언급된 차가 아닌 것은?

① black tea
② green tea
③ rosemary tea
④ jasmine tea
⑤ chamomile tea

10 DICTATION

녹음된 내용을 들으면서 빈칸을 알맞게 채워 보세요.

01

W: This is it! This is my last performance. I can't believe that after four years and 300 performances, it's over. It was really hard at the beginning. I ______________________________ and wanted to quit. But you, ____________________________. Some of you saw the show 50, 60, even more than 70 times. At the beginning I had my critics, but you stood by me. I also want to thank the supporting cast of dancers and musicians. Thank you! I'll miss you. I'm going to work on a new album; then ______________________. But I'll never forget all of you!

02

M: Honey, have you thought about our trip?

W: Well, it's our first trip to Europe. I want it to be special.

M: Right. __________________________________.

W: I know! Why don't you reserve the hotels? Then I'll plan the flights.

M: What do you think about a package tour? We don't have much time to plan.

W: I don't want ______________________________, though. I want to feel free.

M: I'm afraid we'll spend too much time on small details. A group tour would allow us to see all the famous sights.

W: What about the price? ______________________ ______________ our own holiday?

M: If we book a package tour soon, we can probably get a good deal. Then we can see everything without wasting money.

W: Okay. I agree. ______________________________.

M: Great. This is going to be so much fun.

03

M: Beth! Beth! Look over here.

W: Yes?

M: Is it all right if I take a few pictures?

W: Sure. ____________________________________?

M: No. I work for *Stars* magazine.

W: Well, take good pictures for the magazine. ______ ____________________________?

M: We're not in the studio. Just walk down the street holding your daughter and I want to ____________ __________________________ of the two of you.

W: OK. Finished?

M: Yes. Thanks for being understanding.

W: Well, ____________________________________. I am promoting my new movie, *The Good Girl*.

M: I hope it'll be a blockbuster.

04

M: Hi, Mom.

W: Jimmy, ____________________________________ at the store?

M: I think so. I got ____________________________.

W: That's good. And you got some broccoli, too?

M: Yes, of course. I ____________________________, just to be safe.

W: Okay. Hmm... I can't remember what else I sent you to buy.

M: You told me to get bacon and onions. I got _______ ____________________, and three onions.

W: Oh, that's right, and don't forget to get __________ ______________________. Parmesan cheese is the most important ingredient for the cream spaghetti that you love so much.

M: I didn't forget anything. Don't worry. And I didn't buy bread because we have leftovers at home.

W: Okay. I'll see you at home soon.

정답 및 해설 p.38

05

W: What are you doing?

M: Just downloading these pictures and video files from the camera.

W: Are those the pictures from when you visited my dance academy?

M: Yeah, you danced well.

W: Thanks.

M: I'm going to show the video files to William ______ ______________________ in a few minutes.

W: What? Please, don't show them to anyone!

M: Do you ______________________________?

W: No, I just don't want you to show them to anyone.

M: Tell me why.

W: ______________________________. That dance clothing was too tight.

M: Don't worry. Your dance was so great that ______ ______________________.

06

M: How can I help you, ma'am?

W: I'd like to have my car hand washed.

M: Welcome. You've come to the right place. Is this your car?

W: Yes, how much is it?

M: If you have a Basic Car Wash, it's $25. ________ ____________________ hand wash, vacuum, windows, and tire shine.

W: Does it include full interior cleaning?

M: No. The Super Clean service, which is 10 dollars more expensive, includes full interior cleaning and wheel shine.

W: Then I'd like a Super Clean service. And ______ ________________________ waxing?

M: Yes, if you pay an extra $20, we'll treat your car's surface with premium wax.

W: Okay. I want that. And I have this discount coupon ______________________________. Can I use it now?

M: Sure. We'll give you a $5 discount on the total.

W: Thank you. I'll be in the waiting room.

07

W: Honey, do you remember Cindy's violin recital next Tuesday?

M: Next Tuesday? Isn't it next Friday?

W: No, it's Tuesday. Actually, I ______________ ____________________ that afternoon, but I cancelled it.

M: Oh, I may be mixed up on the dates. I'm sorry, but I can't make it.

W: What are you talking about? It's our daughter's first violin recital!

M: I have to go to New York on business on Monday. I'll return on Thursday.

W: ______________________________? This is such an important event. Cindy will be disappointed if you don't come.

M: I'll tell Cindy about it. And I'll order a beautiful flower bouquet for her. Where will the recital be held?

W: It's the Riverside Youth Center, near City Hall.

M: I see. By the way, ______________________ ____________ a recital?

W: It seats 50 people, and it's okay because it's just for the students and their families.

08

W: Are you going camping this summer? Instead of listening to mosquitoes buzzing, ______________________________________? Come to the Vincent Island Music Camping Festival 2011. Running from July 3rd to the 4th, the festival ______________________________________ while listening to James Johnson, Bonnie Blue, the Lawrence Sisters and other pop stars. There are two sizes of tents for rent: a 2-to-3 person tent or a 4-to-6 person tent. Two-day festival passes ______________________________________. The pass doesn't include the tent rental. During the festival, you can take a ferryboat to get to Vincent Island. If you're interested, please ______________________________________ on the festival website at www.vincentmusic.com.

09

M: Where is the perfect place to ask your loved one to marry you? Of course it is the famous Brockton Point of Fraser Stream ______________________________. In a special ceremony last Monday, Mayor Moore came to this special place and named Brockton Point as "the marriage proposal spot." At Brockton Point, a big screen TV and a speaker system ______________________________. Citizens can prerecord their marriage proposal, and then ______________________________________ on a specific day and at a specific time. And ______________________________________ for them. Citizens can apply to use the service by logging onto the city government's website.

10

W: I'm looking for a portable Bluetooth speaker to ______________________________________ next weekend. Could you help me choose one from this website?

M: Sure. First, what's your budget?

W: I can't spend over $200.

M: Okay. Now you need to think about battery life. I recommend one that ______________________________________.

W: Okay. What is the difference between mono and stereo Bluetooth speakers?

M: Hmm, to put it simply, mono speakers come with a single speaker while stereo ones contain two.

W: Then stereo speakers ______________________________________ mono speakers. I'd like a stereo speaker.

M: Now you've narrowed the choice down to these two options. The more expensive one is waterproof and the other isn't.

W: I'll choose the one that's waterproof. There's a chance of rain and ______________________________________ when I'm camping, so that feature is important.

M: Good choice.

W: I'll order it now. Thanks for helping me.

11

W: How was your date with Jemma?

M: Not so good. I think ______________________________________.

W: How could you tell that she was upset?

12

M: Are you going to bring that sandwich to class?

W: Yeah, I didn't eat breakfast. I'll give you some ______________________________.

M: ______________________________________ in class, are we?

13

M: Lisa, you've got to get ready as soon as I ask you to.
W: I was playing with Brad.
M: Lisa, you're not a baby anymore. ______________________________. If I ask you to do something, you do it right away.
W: Yes, Dad. I'll try. ____. I've got my jacket, gloves....
M: You don't need gloves. It's not cold today.
W: Huh?
M: Hurry up! You'll be late for your piano lesson.
W: No problem, Dad. It only takes a few minutes to walk there.
M: OK. Let's go then.
W: Hold on. ______________________________.

14

M: You are really good at drawing, Betty.
W: Thanks, Peter. ____.
M: During a recess ____, aren't you?
W: Yeah. I like to play outside, but I love to draw.
M: Well, ______________________________ from cartoon books.
W: They are. These are my favorite characters.
M: They are some of my favorite characters, too.
W: Do you want one of the drawings? I've got so many.
M: Sure, but I don't want you ______________________________.
W: What do you mean?
M: Let me pay even just a little for your work.

15

W: Harry's mother, Mrs. Henderson, is really angry at him. He doesn't clean his room ____ when she tells him to. And he doesn't speak politely to her. ______________________________ his cell phone and not giving him money. But Harry ______________________________. So last night, Mrs. Henderson told him he couldn't go anywhere with his friends. He must stay in his room after school and on weekends. Today, Harry's friend, Paula, ______________________________, asks to speak to Harry and invites him to a movie tonight. In this situation, what would Harry most likely say to his friend, Paula?

16-17

M: What kind of tea do you drink? Everyone likes a good cup of tea. In the morning, black tea can provide the boost of energy you need to start your day. In the evening, herbal tea can ____ before bed. Depending on how much tea you drink and its specific type, however, tea ______________________________ some unpleasant side effects. Drinking green tea can cause problems with sleeplessness, as coffee can. ______________________________ to drink green tea only in the morning. Trouble with sleeping, however, isn't the only potential downside to drinking tea. Drinking herbal teas, like rosemary tea, can have a negative impact on the medicine you are currently using. So, be sure to speak with your doctor if you are currently taking any medications. It is also known that some herbal teas contain chemicals which ____ getting kidney stones. Although rare, allergic reactions to chamomile tea may occur. If you experience symptoms of a serious allergic reaction, including difficulty breathing, you should stop drinking chamomile tea. Despite these side effects, drinking herbal tea ______________________________ health. Side effects are related to people who drink more than 5-6 cups of tea a day, and most people don't.

실전모의고사

11 PRACTICE TEST

01 다음을 듣고, 남자가 하는 말의 목적으로 가장 적절한 것을 고르시오.

① 사이버 범죄의 여러 유형을 알리려고
② 스팸메일을 차단하는 방법을 알리려고
③ 개인정보 보호 법안 마련을 요구하려고
④ 개인정보 유출의 위험성을 인식시키려고
⑤ 불법 웹사이트 접속으로 인한 피해를 신고하려고

02 대화를 듣고, 두 사람이 하는 말의 주제로 가장 적절한 것을 고르시오.

① 포장 용기를 재활용하는 방법
② 과대 포장을 제한해야 하는 이유
③ 가정에서 만들 수 있는 천연 세제
④ 일회용품 사용이 환경에 미치는 영향
⑤ 일상생활에서 실천하는 환경 보호 방법

03 대화를 듣고, 두 사람의 관계를 가장 잘 나타낸 것을 고르시오.

① 신문 기자 – 방송 진행자
② 방송 출연자 – 분장사
③ 팬 – 영화배우
④ 조수 – 무대감독
⑤ 방청객 – 방송 프로듀서

04 대화를 듣고, 그림에서 대화의 내용과 일치하지 <u>않는</u> 것을 고르시오.

05 대화를 듣고, 여자가 남자에게 부탁한 일로 가장 적절한 것을 고르시오.

① 노트북 찾아오기
② 식료품 사러 가기
③ 도서관에 책 반납하기
④ 크리스마스카드 보내기
⑤ 세탁소에서 셔츠를 찾기

06 대화를 듣고, 남자가 지불할 금액을 고르시오. [3점]

① $300　② $320　③ $360
④ $380　⑤ $400

07 대화를 듣고, 여자가 수학여행을 가고 싶어 하지 <u>않는</u> 이유를 고르시오.

① 비행 공포증이 있어서
② 비용이 너무 많이 들어서
③ 엄마 생신 날짜와 겹쳐서
④ 장소가 마음에 들지 않아서
⑤ 친구들과 아직 친해지지 않아서

08 대화를 듣고, 가족 소풍에 관해 언급되지 <u>않은</u> 것을 고르시오.

① 장소　② 인원수　③ 교통수단
④ 점심 메뉴　⑤ 출발 시각

09 Monarch Band에 관한 다음 내용을 듣고, 일치하지 <u>않는</u> 것을 고르시오.

① 밴드의 이름은 나비에서 유래되었다.
② 창단한 지 25년이 되었다.
③ 매년 총 두 번의 콘서트를 연다.
④ 여름 콘서트에서는 외국의 전통 음악을 들려준다.
⑤ 신입 단원은 1년에 한 번만 모집한다.

10 다음 표를 보면서 대화를 듣고, 남자가 지원할 일자리를 고르시오.

Part-time Jobs at Sunshine Department Store

Job	Days	Pay (per hour)	Requirements
① Greeter	Mon. ~ Fri.	$5	—
② Information Desk	Sat. ~ Sun.	$6	English proficiency
③ Product Salesperson	Sat. ~ Sun.	$7	English proficiency
④ Valet Parking	Mon. ~ Fri.	$7	Driver's license
⑤ Cashier in Snack Bar	Sat. ~ Sun.	$6	Experience

11 대화를 듣고, 여자의 마지막 말에 대한 남자의 응답으로 가장 적절한 것을 고르시오.

① I'd like them to fit into this frame.
② Sorry, the medium size is sold out.
③ I hope they'll be ready by tomorrow.
④ I'll need at least three copies of each.
⑤ Sure, thirty dollars should be enough.

12 대화를 듣고, 남자의 마지막 말에 대한 여자의 응답으로 가장 적절한 것을 고르시오.

① He sure is growing up fast.
② Then we have two weeks to prepare.
③ Cheer up! You'll see your friends again.
④ Didn't you graduate from the same school?
⑤ How about throwing a party for him and his friends?

13 대화를 듣고, 여자의 마지막 말에 대한 남자의 응답으로 가장 적절한 것을 고르시오. [3점]

▶ Man : ______________________

① I'll keep my fingers crossed for you.
② It's okay. I'll write a note for your teacher.
③ Why don't you ask the teacher in the session?
④ I'm afraid you can't choose your classes freely.
⑤ The school's class schedule is the same as ours.

14 대화를 듣고, 남자의 마지막 말에 대한 여자의 응답으로 가장 적절한 것을 고르시오.

▶ Woman : ______________________

① I agree. We have to look out for cars.
② I'm sorry I couldn't visit you in the hospital.
③ Okay. I'll make an appointment with a doctor.
④ Why don't we eat something after the movie?
⑤ Great. Then let's meet in front of the hospital.

15 다음 상황 설명을 듣고, Roger가 Ms. Harrison에게 할 말로 가장 적절한 것을 고르시오. [3점]

▶ Roger: Ms. Harrison, ______________________

① Amy is going to be thrilled to get this job.
② if you give me a chance, I promise I'll do my best.
③ I think I know someone who would be perfect.
④ let me know the board's decision as soon as possible.
⑤ I hope you accept my suggestion as the new marketing manager.

[16~17] 다음을 듣고, 물음에 답하시오.

16 남자가 하는 말의 주제로 가장 적절한 것은?

① the importance of a balanced diet
② the possible causes of high cholesterol
③ reasons to worry about your cholesterol
④ introducing various kinds of healthy tea
⑤ good methods for reducing cholesterol levels

17 maté에 관해 언급되지 않은 것은?

① 원료의 주요 재배지 ② 음용 방법
③ 항암 효과 ④ 향미
⑤ 부작용

11 **DICTATION**

녹음된 내용을 들으면서 빈칸을 알맞게 채워 보세요.

01

M: Has your personal information ever been shared ______________________________? Unfortunately, many of us ______________________________. If you're lucky, it will only result in an increase in spam mail, but it can be much worse. Your resident registration number could ______________________________. Often, we are partly to blame when this happens. For example, we might use passwords that include our date of birth or phone number, or use identical passwords for several websites. Moreover, some free websites sell their data to other sites ______________________________. To protect ourselves, we need to change passwords frequently and investigate websites before we join them. Otherwise, ______________________________ our personal information, and it may be used for illegal purposes.

02

M: Thanks for bringing takeout for dinner, but next time, let's eat out instead.

W: Sure, honey, but I thought ______________________________.

M: I do, but recently ______________________________ how much waste there is after we eat takeout.

W: I know what you mean. We can recycle these plastic containers, but ______________________________.

M: Right. I've also begun to buy larger containers of juice and cola for the same reason.

W: Good idea. ______________________________.

M: Good thinking. I'm also doing some other things for the environment. For instance, I bought natural soaps and detergents the other day.

W: That's great. I'm glad we won't be pouring so many harsh chemicals down the drain anymore.

03

W: It's really exciting to be ______________________________!

M: My pleasure. But I only have an hour before the show will be aired live.

W: OK, ______________________________. Isn't it difficult because it's a live show?

M: It's not an easy job, but it's a lot of fun to host my own show and talk with different celebrities every week.

W: I see. So, ______________________________ is the most challenging? It must be stressful sometimes.

M: Exactly. I can't make any mistakes. It's also thrilling, though. Oh, ______________________________.

W: OK. Then, quickly, is there anything you'd like to say to our newspaper readers?

M: I truly appreciate all of my fans. ______________________________.

W: Alright. Thank you for answering my questions.

M: It was no trouble.

04

M: Hello?

W: Hi, Martin. Have you finished ______________________________?

M: Almost, Mom. I just finished putting the couch with two cushions on one side of the living room.

W: Wasn't it hard to move it?

M: Not really. ______________________________.

W: And I'm sure the table is in front of the couch, too.

M: Yes, ______________________________. I also put up some curtains. They have a nice striped pattern.

W: Sounds nice. And what about your 4-shelf bookshelf?

M: ______________________________ to the right of the window. It's more space efficient.

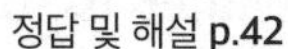

W: Also, don't forget to place the flower pot that I bought for you next to the couch.

M: I tried to, but there was very little room, so I put it beside the bookshelf.

W: Hmm.... Okay. ______________________________ ______________________________.

05

W: I have ______________________________ today.

M: Well, maybe I can help you.

W: That would be great. Here's my list.

M: Wow. It looks like you have to drive all over town.

W: Maybe ______________________________. Let's see.... If I go to the supermarket to buy bread and milk, I will have to go past the dry cleaners, ______________________________.

M: That's true. And you can also go to the computer repair shop to pick up your laptop.

W: OK, I will do those three things. But I won't be anywhere near the post office to mail my Christmas cards. ______________________________?

M: Sure. But you'll be closer to the library. These books are all late.

W: It looks like I have a lot more to do than you.

M: ______________________________?

W: Sure! See you then.

06

W: Can I help you find anything, sir?

M: Yes, thanks. ______________________________ buying a new hiking jacket, and I heard you have a good selection.

W: We certainly do. All of our hiking jackets are on this rack here.

M: Okay. Now ______________________________ these two jackets?

W: The blue one is a standard jacket that is $300. The yellow one costs $380 because it's waterproof.

M: I see. Well, I should be prepared for rain. I'll take the waterproof one.

W: Excellent choice. And how about some hiking socks? They ______________________________ and cost only $10 per pair.

M: Why not? I'll take two pairs.

W: Great. Now, ______________________________ a member of our store, you can get 10% off on everything you buy today.

M: Great! Then I'll sign up now.

07

M: Jenna, why didn't you mention next week's school trip?

W: I didn't tell you ______________________________. Is that okay, Dad?

M: I guess so, but it sounds like it would be fun.

W: Well, it would be fun to fly. I guess I'm just not excited to go back to Jeju Island __________ ______________________________ as a family.

M: We did see most of the island on your mom's birthday, but it would be ______________________________ ______________________________.

W: You're right, but several of my friends won't be going either. I don't think I'll miss anything interesting.

M: Okay. You don't have to go, but I still think it would be ______________________________ ______________________________.

08

M: Mom, the weather is so nice today. Let's go on a family picnic.

W: Why not? Do you ______________________________ ______________________?

M: How about Lake Park? I heard the Rose Festival ______________________________ right now.

W: Great idea! I'm sure your dad and Sally will love it.

M: Why don't we invite Grandma? She'd like some fresh air.

W: You're so sweet. Then, that makes five including your grandmother.

M: Right. So, ______________________________?

W: Hmm. I think restaurants in the park will be too crowded. I'll make sandwiches and bring some fruit.

M: Great. I love your homemade sandwiches. I'll call Grandmother ______________________________ ______________.

W: Alright. Tell her that we're going to leave home at eleven and get there at eleven thirty.

M: Got it.

09

W: Hi, I'm Jennifer Taylor, a junior in the Department of Music. If you are looking for ______________ ________________, why not join the Monarch Band? Named for the Monarch butterflies commonly found around the band practice room, the Monarch Band is the university's original club band. ______________________________ 25 years ago, hundreds of students have formed lasting friendships within the Monarch Band. But there is ______________________________. We play 2 regular concerts and a Christmas special each year. Our annual summer concert, where we choose one country and ____________________ ______________________, is especially popular. Anyone can join, but unlike other clubs that recruit twice a year, we do so annually. So _______ ______________________________ for fun and friendship.

10

M: Hi, Vanessa. ______________________________?

W: Sure, Derrick. What's up?

M: I'm trying to pick one of these five part-time jobs at a department store, and I'd like your opinion.

W: I see. Well, how about being a greeter? It seems easy.

M: Yeah, but ______________________________.

W: Then how about this job? I think you'd be great at it. Plus, it's on weekends and it pays more.

M: Ah, I see. But I don't have any experience.

W: Hmm.... ______________________________, then? You're an English major, so it'd be easy for you.

M: That's true, but I'd really ____________________ ______________________________.

W: Then there's only one left.

M: I guess so. I'll apply now.

11

W: Hello. How can I help you today?

M: I'd like to ______________________________, please.

W: Alright. Do you ______________________________ ____________________?

12

M: My little brother's graduation is two weeks from now.

W: Oh, he ______________________________ ____________________.

M: Yes. I'm afraid that he'll miss his friends. _______ ______________________________?

13

M: Great work today, Stacy.
W: Thank you, Mr. Cho. I really love studying Chinese.
M: It shows. ______________________________ ______________________ to visit Shanghai High School in China.
W: Really? You mean our sister school? I'm so excited! Please, tell me everything about the trip.
M: Actually, one of the teachers from Shanghai High School is coming to visit our school tomorrow.
W: Then, can I ______________________________ ____________________?
M: Of course. She will lead an information session about the trip in the auditorium at 3 p.m.
W: I really want to go, but ____________________ ______________________.
M: Why not?
W: I'm worried because ______________________ __________________________.

14

M: Hi, Rachel. It's Dan.
W: Oh, hi. What's up?
M: Are you free this afternoon?
W: No, I'm going to the cooking class that I have at 4 every Friday.
M: Oh, now I remember. ______________________ __________________________. How's the class?
W: So far, so good. The instructor said __________ __________________________.
M: Good for you! Then, what about after class? Actually, I got two free tickets to a newly released movie.
W: Sorry, but ______________________________ the West Lake Hospital to visit Janice.
M: What happened to Janice?
W: She had a minor car accident last night. ________ ____________________________? She'll be glad.
M: Sure. I want to see if she's okay. We can use the free tickets later.

15

W: Roger is an employee at a large company, and Ms. Harrison is his boss. Two weeks ago, Ms. Harrison recommended Roger ______________________ ______________________. Today, the board accepted her recommendation. So, Ms. Harrison gives the good news to Roger, and Roger thanks Ms. Harrison ____________________________. Then, Ms. Harrison tells Roger that a replacement is necessary for Roger's current position and ____ ______________________________. At the moment, Roger's friend Amy is looking to ______ ____________________________. Roger knows that Amy is well-qualified and ______________ ____________________________, so he wants to recommend her. In this situation, what would Roger most likely say to Ms. Harrison?

16-17

M: If you are worried about your cholesterol, there are a few things to keep in mind. First, fatty foods raise cholesterol levels, so ______________________ ________________________ with lots of fruits and vegetables. Exercise is also important. Studies have shown that even ____________________ ____________________ cholesterol levels. Now, if you are still worried, there are some specific foods that can actually lower cholesterol, such as oatmeal, fish, and nuts. And along with these, try a cup of maté since it also has the ability to fight cholesterol. It is a type of tea made from the maté tree, which is grown mainly in South America. ________________________________ of the tree, you add them to hot water and drink it. Traditionally, people serve it in a special container and drink it through a metal straw. The flavor is strongly herbal and grassy, similar to green tea. Though it's rich in vitamins and low in caffeine, large quantities of hot maté may ___________ ____________________________. So, drink less than one liter per day. By following these tips, you'll soon be ______________________ __________________.

실전모의고사

12 PRACTICE TEST

01 다음을 듣고, 남자가 하는 말의 목적으로 가장 적절한 것을 고르시오.

① 환경 보호의 중요성을 알리려고
② 재활용 센터의 문제점을 알리려고
③ 생활 쓰레기 처리 과정을 가르쳐주려고
④ 정부에 재활용 법안 마련을 요구하려고
⑤ 사람들에게 폐기물 안전 처리를 촉구하려고

02 대화를 듣고, 여자의 의견으로 가장 적절한 것을 고르시오.

① 졸업 전에 실무를 경험해보는 것이 좋다.
② 구직 시 면접 준비를 철저하게 해야 한다.
③ 학창시절에 진로를 미리 결정할 필요가 있다.
④ 채용 시 가산점 관련 내용을 명확히 밝혀야 한다.
⑤ 인턴십 지원 시 대학 전공과 연계하는 것이 좋다.

03 대화를 듣고, 두 사람의 관계를 가장 잘 나타낸 것을 고르시오.

① 교수 – 학생
② 조종사 – 승무원
③ 비행 강사 – 수강생
④ 항공기 전문가 – 기자
⑤ 응급 의료 요원 – 환자

04 대화를 듣고, 그림에서 대화의 내용과 일치하지 않는 것을 고르시오.

05 대화를 듣고, 남자가 할 일로 가장 적절한 것을 고르시오.

① 학원에서 수업받기
② 친구에게 도움 청하기
③ 스터디 모임에 가입하기
④ 개인 교사와 함께 공부하기
⑤ 아빠께 가르쳐 달라고 부탁하기

06 대화를 듣고, 여자가 지불할 금액을 고르시오.

① $150 ② $175 ③ $275
④ $300 ⑤ $350

07 대화를 듣고, 남자가 책을 사려는 이유를 고르시오.

① 수업에 필요해서
② 특별 한정판이라서
③ 작가의 사인이 있어서
④ 친구가 삽화를 그려서
⑤ 여동생에게 선물하기 위해서

08 대화를 듣고, Waris Dirie에 관해 언급되지 않은 것을 고르시오.

① 직업 ② 저서 ③ 출연작
④ 출신 국가 ⑤ 고향을 떠난 나이

09 Bauhaus에 관한 다음 내용을 듣고, 일치하지 않는 것을 고르시오.

① 1919년부터 1933년까지 운영되었다.
② 독일어로 '건축 학교'라는 뜻이다.
③ 설립 초기에는 건축학과가 없었다.
④ 재정적인 문제로 폐교했다.
⑤ 현대 건축물과 가구 양식에 영향을 주었다.

정답 및 해설 p.46

10 다음 자료를 보면서 대화를 듣고, 두 사람이 예약할 호텔을 고르시오.

Beachfront Hotels and Facilities

Hotels	Pool	Internet	Kitchen	Hotel Rate
① Lily Inn	no	yes	no	$90/night
② Desert Rose Hotel	yes	yes	yes	$120/night
③ Cactus Creek Spa	yes	no	no	$99/night
④ Ocean View Resort	yes	no	yes	$100/night
⑤ Sea Breeze Hotel	no	yes	yes	$95/night

11 대화를 듣고, 여자의 마지막 말에 대한 남자의 응답으로 가장 적절한 것을 고르시오.

① I do, but I'm just too busy.
② I'm sorry I missed the game.
③ I don't want to miss baseball.
④ No, but I think I'll sign up tomorrow.
⑤ Baseball is traditionally played in the summer.

12 대화를 듣고, 남자의 마지막 말에 대한 여자의 응답으로 가장 적절한 것을 고르시오.

① Sorry, I have to leave now.
② The next project will begin soon.
③ The due date is approaching fast.
④ This project is beyond our ability.
⑤ I thought you're not available tomorrow.

13 대화를 듣고, 여자의 마지막 말에 대한 남자의 응답으로 가장 적절한 것을 고르시오. [3점]

▶ Man : ______________________

① Your brother is really good at tennis.
② My family is going away for the weekend.
③ I'm too busy to play tennis with you anyway.
④ Your mother will be really upset if you don't win.
⑤ I'll tell the coach that you had a family emergency.

14 대화를 듣고, 남자의 마지막 말에 대한 여자의 응답으로 가장 적절한 것을 고르시오. [3점]

▶ Woman : ______________________

① All of our models are from France.
② The microwaves are on sale this month.
③ I'll send someone now with the right machine.
④ The combo meal comes with a deluxe burger.
⑤ We will add the cost of the dryer onto the bill.

15 다음 상황 설명을 듣고, Susan이 Jane에게 할 말로 가장 적절한 것을 고르시오. [3점]

▶ Susan : ______________________

① I don't like your boyfriend. He is very mean to me.
② You don't look so good. Is everything OK with you?
③ Now that I have a boyfriend, we can go on a double date.
④ I'm glad you have a boyfriend, but I don't want to lose you.
⑤ I don't want to complain, but would you be honest with me?

[16~17] 다음을 듣고, 물음에 답하시오.

16 여자가 하는 말의 주제로 가장 적절한 것은?

① the long history of eco-friendly fashion
② the pros and cons of reusing old clothing
③ natural fabrics popular in the fashion industry
④ recommending the best natural dyes for clothing
⑤ the fashion trend that aims to preserve the environment

17 천연 염색제의 재료로 언급되지 않은 것은?

① 사과　② 블랙베리　③ 대나무
④ 장미　⑤ 라벤더

12 DICTATION

녹음된 내용을 들으면서 빈칸을 알맞게 채워 보세요.

01

M: Do you know where your trash goes once you put it in the bag and set it outside? ____________ ____________________ on trash mountains called 'landfills.' Often, these landfills are filled with common household items such as batteries, motor oil and old computers. ______________________ ________________ causes a lot of problems. When it rains, toxic chemicals from these items ________________________________. From here, some harmful substances make their way into rivers and ______________________________. We used to think we could throw anything into landfills. But some things have to go to special recycling centers. To ask for a list of harmful household items and ______________________ __________, call your local government office now.

02

W: Well, the semester is over. Are you going to be around this summer?

M: No, I'll be traveling in South America. What about you?

W: I managed to get an internship. I'll be staying in the city and working.

M: You're going to work all summer? Don't you need a vacation?

W: This is the only chance ____________________ ______________________, and I think I'll need internship experience to get a job.

M: Hmm... I assumed I would start getting work experience after I graduated. I ________________ ________________________ now.

W: I'm afraid that those who gain work experience before graduation will ______________________ __________________________ those who don't. Employers like to hire people who have experience.

M: It certainly ________________________________ some internship experience.

03

M: OK. Now just gently pull the stick toward you and you will feel the airplane climb.

W: Wow. This is very exciting.

M: All right. ________________________________. If you push the pedals left and right, one at a time, you will feel ____________________ ____________________ swing gently behind us.

W: You mean like this?

M: Just like that. You'll notice it doesn't ____________ ____.

W: Yeah. It's very sensitive.

M: And now if you pull that knob right there out a bit, the plane will go faster.

W: Oh boy! It's getting louder too!

M: Do you think you are ready to ________________ ______________________?

W: I'm afraid to try that. Maybe next time.

04

W: Hello?

M: Amanda. It's me. __________________________ ______________ the table for Halloween?

W: I'm almost done, Dad.

M: Great! Did you have any trouble putting up the "Trick or Treat!" banner by yourself?

W: Not at all. ________________________________. I also put the tablecloth on our round table.

M: Good job. Also, __________________________ the witch's hat.

W: Right. I've already set it on the table, and it looks great.

M: You also have candy and chocolates, right? That's the most important thing.

W: Of course, they're on the rectangular plate.

M: Fantastic. Oh, I almost forgot about the pumpkins.

W: Don't worry, I placed two pumpkins on the table, just like every Halloween.

M: Okay. Then everything ______________________ ______________________.

05

M: My math grade is so terrible. My father is going to be so disappointed.
W: He'll understand.
M: Ji-won! My father is a mathematics professor. It should be "_______________________________."
W: Oh, that's not true. My mother is good at piano, but I hate it. Just ask him for help.
M: He wants to help me, but I don't want his help. _______________________________.
W: Then join a study group. Your friends can help you.
M: All my classmates have different schedules. _______________________________. I tried a month ago.
W: Lessons at an academy?
M: My mom won't agree since she knows my father said he'd teach me.
W: Then you _______________________________ your dad.
M: Hmm.... I know. I'll do it tonight.

06

W: I'd like to rent a car.
M: OK. We have different cars and different rates.
W: _______________________________?
M: For a compact car, it is $50 a day during the week and $75 a day on the weekends.
W: $50 and $75, hmm... how much is a convertible?
M: A convertible is $100 a day during the week and $150 a day on Saturdays and Sundays.
W: OK. I think I will just _______________________________. It only costs half as much as a convertible.
M: And _______________________________?
W: I would like it for Thursday through Saturday.
M: So _______________________________ two weekdays and one weekend day.
W: Right.

07

M: Mary, take a look at this book.
W: I really don't think that's a good gift for my sister. She's a bit old for picture books.
M: No, no, take a look inside, _______________________________.
W: Oh, wow! It was illustrated by Neil Jurgen, your old roommate.
M: Yeah! You know, _______________________________ since I've talked to him. I didn't know that he was illustrating books these days.
W: Well, you always said he was talented. And I remember being impressed by the pictures he drew for his art classes.
M: You're right. _______________________________. I'm glad he's doing well.
W: So, are you going to get the book?
M: I am, and _______________________________ when we get home.

08

W: Honey, let's stop for a minute. I want to get a copy of that magazine.
M: Okay. Who is that on the cover?
W: That's Waris Dirie. She was a model, and is now _______________________________.
M: Oh, right. I didn't recognize her. She's also an author, right?
W: Yeah. She wrote *Desert Flower* in 1998, which was turned into a movie, and *Letter to My Mother* in 2007. _______________________________ her experiences.
M: I remember watching the movie *Desert Flower*. Anyway, she was born to a poor tribe in Somalia, right?
W: Yes, and she had to _______________________________ at the age of 13 to avoid an arranged marriage.
M: She had a difficult life, but she _______________________________ and is now an inspiration to many.

09

W: Bauhaus was a design school in Germany that operated from 1919 to 1933. Bauhaus designers primarily tried to ______________________________ ______________________________ through a new design philosophy. Its name means "School of Building" in German; however, Bauhaus did not have an architecture department ______________________________. However, in pursuit of the establishment of a unified school of the arts, an architecture department was eventually added. Bauhaus ______________________________ ______________________________ art and design before being forever shut down by Adolf Hitler's Nazi party, which was opposed to it for political reasons. However, through the many modern buildings, offices, and pieces of furniture that ______________________________ in the style of Bauhaus, we can see that its influence still remains today.

10

W: I can't wait for our trip to Cancun!

M: Yeah, me too. Now all we need to do is choose a hotel.

W: Well, I want to go swimming every day!

M: All of these hotels in this brochure are right on the beach. You can swim in the sea. I don't think ______________________________.

W: Right, and since you have to check in with work every morning on the big project, we need to have access to the Web.

M: Well, that ______________________________.

W: What will we do about eating? With your special diet, it looks like a kitchen would be helpful.

M: Sure, and ______________________________?

W: The rate should be cheaper than $100 per night.

M: I guess that leaves only one choice.

11

W: Today is the last day to ______________________________ ______________________________.

M: I know, but I don't think ______________________________.

W: Don't you want to play this season?

12

M: I think we can complete this project ______________ ______________________________.

W: Great. Let's meet tomorrow and finish it up.

M: Wouldn't you rather stay and ______________________________ ______________________________?

13

M: Where are you going, Valerie?

W: I have to pick up my little brother from school.

M: But we have tennis practice ______________________________ ______________________________.

W: I know, but my mother is too busy to get Oscar, so ______________________________.

M: But the finals are coming up this weekend! Can't your little brother walk home by himself?

W: No. He's only in first grade and he has to ______________________________. It might be dangerous for him to go back home by himself. Family comes first.

M: I guess you're right, but the coach is really going to be mad.

W: Hopefully he'll understand. Anyway, ______________ ______________________________.

14

W: Sammy's Appliances, this is Gladys. How may I help you?

M: Hi. ______________________________ to be delivered from your store yesterday.

W: Have you received the machine yet?

M: A machine was delivered today, but ____________ ____________________.

W: OK. ____________________________________ on my computer. What is your name and address, sir?

M: My name is Bill Bixby. 115 Oak Street.

W: Yes sir. It looks like you ordered the deluxe washer-dryer combo.

M: Well, ________________________________, but I didn't order that. I asked for the deluxe washer, but no dryer.

W: It looks like we made a mistake at the store. Are you sure you don't want to keep the model we sent?

M: No. That one was more expensive. I just want the one I ordered.

15

M: Susan and Jane have been friends all their lives. Now Jane has a boyfriend and she doesn't ____________________________ to spend with Susan as before. In fact, Jane sees her boyfriend almost every evening and doesn't __________________________________. This hurts Susan's feelings, but she doesn't want to upset her best friend by complaining. If Jane ____________________________, Susan is afraid they will not be friends anymore. In this situation, what would Susan most likely say to Jane?

16-17

W: Many of the fabrics, materials, and dyes that are used to create today's clothing _____________ ___________________ the Earth's ecosystems. For example, nylon and polyester are both made from petroleum and harmful to the ozone layer. ____________________________________ on the environment, there is a new trend toward eco-fashion. Eco-fashion is simply the use of natural fabrics and dyes ______________________ _________________. Examples of this include using organic raw materials, such as cotton grown without pesticides, or reused materials such as recycled plastic from old soda bottles. Bamboo is especially useful to eco-fashion designers because it grows quickly and can be turned into a soft, breathable fabric that is biodegradable. This means that old clothing made from bamboo ____________________________________. Also, eco-fashion avoids the use of harmful chemicals and bleaches to color fabrics, and instead uses natural sources of dyes. For example, apples ______________________________ shades of green, while blackberries can make deep purples. Roses can be used for lighter shades of red, and lavender can produce darker shades.

실전모의고사

13 PRACTICE TEST

01 **다음을 듣고, 여자가 하는 말의 목적으로 가장 적절한 것을 고르시오.**

① 개인정보 유출 가능성을 알리려고
② 인터넷 회사에 불편함을 항의하려고
③ 웹사이트 점검에 대해 양해를 구하려고
④ 웹사이트 이용 불편에 대해 해명하려고
⑤ 새로 개설된 인터넷 서비스를 홍보하려고

02 **대화를 듣고, 남자의 의견으로 가장 적절한 것을 고르시오.**

① 소셜 미디어에서 맺는 인간관계는 진정성이 없다.
② 소셜 미디어 사용 시간을 줄여 중독을 예방해야 한다.
③ 가족과의 시간에는 휴대전화를 사용하지 않아야 한다.
④ 스마트폰 앱은 유익한 것을 선별해 다운로드해야 한다.
⑤ 소셜 미디어 중독의 원인을 찾는 것이 치료의 시작이다.

03 **대화를 듣고, 두 사람의 관계를 가장 잘 나타낸 것을 고르시오.**

① 학생 – 역사학자
② 형사 – 기자
③ 도서관 이용자 – 도서관 사서
④ 소설 작가 – 영화감독
⑤ 서점 고객 – 서점 직원

04 **대화를 듣고, 그림에서 대화의 내용과 일치하지 않는 것을 고르시오.**

05 **대화를 듣고, 여자가 남자에게 부탁한 일로 가장 적절한 것을 고르시오.**

① 하드 드라이브를 청소하기
② 컴퓨터를 수리할 사람 보내 주기
③ 교체용 컴퓨터를 집으로 보내주기
④ 집에서 인터넷 케이블 서비스를 설치하기
⑤ 컴퓨터에 바이러스 퇴치 프로그램을 설치하기

06 **대화를 듣고, 남자가 지불할 금액을 고르시오. [3점]**

① $28　② $31　③ $34
④ $40　⑤ $43

07 **대화를 듣고, 여자가 약속을 연기한 이유를 고르시오.**

① 눈보라가 심해서
② 교통사고가 나서
③ 심부름을 가야 해서
④ 병원 진료를 받아야 해서
⑤ 할아버지를 모셔 와야 해서

08 **다음을 듣고, 수소 연료 자동차에 관해 언급되지 않은 것을 고르시오.**

① 경제성　② 환경친화성　③ 출시일
④ 배출물질　⑤ 연비

09 **Korea International Toilet Expo and Conference에 관한 다음 내용을 듣고, 일치하지 않는 것을 고르시오.**

① 이 행사는 서울 코엑스에서 개최된다.
② 40개가 넘는 국가에서 관계자들이 참석한다.
③ 공중위생 문제에 대한 해결책을 찾기 위한 행사이다.
④ 이 행사는 일주일간 지속될 예정이다.
⑤ 행사의 일환으로 화장실 시찰의 일정도 있다.

10 다음 표를 보면서 대화를 듣고, 두 사람이 선택할 회사를 고르시오.

Bathroom Remodeling Company

Company	Price	Warranty	Years in Business	Customer Reviews
① Booher	$1,800	none	10	★★
② Ambath	$2,400	1 year	7	★★★
③ Mr. Handyman	$2,900	1 year	15	★★★
④ Re-Bath	$3,200	1 year	12	★★★★
⑤ Lowe's	$4,800	2 years	19	★★★★

11 대화를 듣고, 남자의 마지막 말에 대한 여자의 응답으로 가장 적절한 것을 고르시오.

① I'm bringing a gift.
② No, but I'll introduce you.
③ It's going to be a lot of fun.
④ More than 30 people will be there.
⑤ The party will be held in her house.

12 대화를 듣고, 여자의 마지막 말에 대한 남자의 응답으로 가장 적절한 것을 고르시오.

① I don't like their colors.
② I plan on using it every day.
③ The basic model is too simple.
④ Yes, please. That will help me decide.
⑤ They looked different in the advertisement.

13 대화를 듣고, 남자의 마지막 말에 대한 여자의 응답으로 가장 적절한 것을 고르시오.

▶ Woman : ____________________

① It's not that bad. Don't worry.
② Great. What's the brand name?
③ No ice-cream for me. I'm on a diet.
④ Sure, I'd like to meet your German friend.
⑤ That's OK. I have already taken some medicine.

14 대화를 듣고, 여자의 마지막 말에 대한 남자의 응답으로 가장 적절한 것을 고르시오. [3점]

▶ Man : ____________________

① I think about it all the time.
② Can't you give me a discount?
③ If it's as much fun as you say, sure.
④ Definitely. Thanks for letting me know.
⑤ No, thanks. I don't want to go to the beach.

15 다음 상황 설명을 듣고, Jeff가 Mandy에게 할 말로 가장 적절한 것을 고르시오. [3점]

▶ Jeff : ____________________

① Can you give me a ride to my place?
② Long time no see! How have you been?
③ Can you tell me how to get to the subway station?
④ What took you so long? I've been waiting for so long.
⑤ Why didn't you come to the baseball game with me?

[16~17] 다음을 듣고, 물음에 답하시오.

16 남자가 하는 말의 주제로 가장 적절한 것은?

① objects that can be seen in the night sky
② how telescopes have advanced astronomy
③ how to locate various planets in the night sky
④ differences between man-made satellites and stars
⑤ the closest objects to the planet Earth in the solar system

17 언급된 행성이 아닌 것은?

① Venus ② Mercury ③ Saturn
④ Mars ⑤ Jupiter

13 DICTATION

녹음된 내용을 들으면서 빈칸을 알맞게 채워 보세요.

01

W: Important message concerning last night's network happenings. Although all of our servers were fine, Domain Name Service — which was outside our direct control — ________________ many of our websites. We outsource DNS to a specialist company which has many redundant servers. These also didn't work. We resolved the problem early this morning ________________ ________________ our own DNS service. We intend to make this permanent so that we do not ________________ in the future. We appreciate your understanding in this matter, especially if you were affected. You can ________________ ________________, and what we're doing to ________________ again, on our website. Thank you.

02

M: Evelyn, you keep checking your smartphone every few minutes.

W: I am checking to see ________________ ________________ on Facebook and Instagram.

M: Have you heard about FOMO? It stands for "Fear of Missing Out."

W: What does it mean?

M: It's the uneasy feeling that ________________ ________________ that your peers are doing. It's among the biggest causes of social media addiction.

W: You're right. I'm depressed when I have no internet access.

M: I stopped using it. Now I have more free time to do other things. You should try it.

W: But it's very difficult to quit using social media.

M: The first step is ________________. I use a smartphone app that enables you to monitor your screen time and limit it.

W: That's a good idea.

M: Keep one thing in mind when you spend all your time staring at pictures on social media. ________________ ________________.

03

M: Hi, where can I find newspapers and magazines?

W: ________________. Are you looking for something in particular?

M: Actually, I am researching a local murder that happened in 1925.

W: Oh, in that case, you need to search our microfilm catalogue. All newspapers from 1970 or earlier ________________.

M: Is it possible to make copies?

W: Of course, you can buy a copier card downstairs.

M: I'm also looking for ________________ ________________. Do you keep those?

W: No, I suggest you try the National War Archives website. You can use the computers ________________ ________________ just over there.

M: Thanks for your help!

04

W: Josh, ________________?

M: It's a picture of my family's vacation to Hard Rock Resort. This is the kids' pool.

W: It's quite a big swimming pool. ________________ ________________? It looks like a mushroom.

M: It's a kind of waterfall. That's my daughter, Stephanie, who is standing under the mushroom and ________________.

W: That looks fun. They also have a big water slide in the pool.

M: Yeah. I especially like the waterfall bucket at the top of the slide.

W: That looks great. Where is your son? Is he the boy ________________?

M: No, he is my nephew. My son is sitting with his feet in the water.
W: He is so cute. Oh, you are sitting on a sun chair near your son. You look very comfortable.
M: Yeah. I was drinking tropical fruit juice __________ __________________________.
W: I want to go there with my family, too. Let me know some information about this place.
M: Sure. I'll send you a link to the resort's site.

05

M: Hello, Total Computer Solutions, Kevin speaking.
W: Hi, Kevin. This is Carolyn Jones. It's an emergency!
M: What's wrong?
W: I have a major assignment due tomorrow and _____ __________________________________!
M: Do you have virus protection?
W: Umm... no, I don't think so.
M: You really should __________________________. If you bring your computer in, we'll probably have it repaired for you by this afternoon. We can __________________________________ for you too.
W: But I can't bring it in! I'm too busy! _____________ ____?
M: Of course I can do that.
W: How much will that cost?
M: $30 per hour, ________________________________ ________________________.
W: OK. How quickly can someone come?
M: Right away. What's your address?

06

M: See you tonight, Aunt Heather. _________________ _________________________!
W: Make sure you buy a subway card.
M: Oh? Why is that?
W: ____. And you don't have to buy a new ticket each time you go somewhere.
M: Cool, how much is it?
W: The blank card costs $3, but _________________ ________________________ before you can use it.
M: How much do I need to add?
W: As much as you like. You're in town for seven days. The discounted fare is $1 per trip.
M: So, $1 for each trip. And I'll probably _________ ______________________________. Then the total amount for one week is....
W: Don't forget to add the $3 fee for the blank card.

07

M: Hello?
W: Hi, David. It's me, Gina. Listen, I'm sorry, but I don't think I'll be able to meet you today.
M: Oh, really? Did something happen?
W: Yeah, unfortunately. I need to _________________ ____________________ from the hospital.
M: Okay. It's nothing serious, is it?
W: No, not at all. Normally his nurse takes him and picks him up, but someone _________________ __________________ last night. It's a long story.
M: I heard there were several accidents last night. It was quite a snowstorm.
W: Right. So, anyway, I hope ____________________ __________________. Tomorrow, maybe?
M: Well, ____ _________________ tomorrow. How about Friday?
W: Sounds good. See you then.

08

W: Green Motors has finally done it! We've made a ______________________________ hydrogen-powered car costing as much as a gasoline-powered car. Now you don't have to spend a lot of money ______________________________________. Hydrogen-powered cars are environmentally friendly because they don't discharge harmful chemicals into the air. Hydrogen engines produce only water as they run. Green Motors' hydrogen cars can travel 200 kilometers on a tank of hydrogen. You can drive only ____________ ______________ that on one tank of gasoline, but when you drive this car, you can feel good that ______________________________________.

09

M: Welcome to the Korea International Toilet EXPO and Conference at the Seoul COEX convention center! Experts from more than 40 nations ______________________________________ of global sanitation issues and to find solutions to the problems. Over the five days of the conference, we will plan direct action __________ ______________________________ around the world. Today's keynote speaker is the distinguished German scientist, Lisa Kirchner. ______________ __________________ at the reception desk for her keynote address, and for the afternoon tour of the famous toilets in Suwon.

10

W: James, I've contacted five different bathroom remodeling companies, since ________________ ________________. I want to discuss it with you.

M: Okay. How should we do this?

W: ________________________________ the five companies. Take a look.

M: Let me see. The price is the most important factor for us.

W: Right. We can spend up to $4,000.

M: We'll have to go with the company that __________ ___________________________.

W: But that company doesn't offer any warranty.

M: Really? Then we must rule it out. A warranty is essential ______________________________.

W: I think experience is also important in ensuring that the remodeling is done correctly.

M: Sure. I think we have to choose a company with at least ten years of experience. Then, there are two options left.

W: We also need to check customer reviews. Let's ______________________________________.

M: Sounds good. I think we've found one.

11

M: Beth, what are you doing this weekend?

W: I'm going to my cousin Amy's birthday party. ___________________________________. You should come.

M: ______________________________________?

12

W: Here are two exercise machines ________________ ____________________.

M: I like both of them. Should I get the basic model or the more expensive one?

W: ____________________________. Would you like me to explain the differences?

13

M: What's the matter, Yun-hee? You've been scratching yourself all day.

W: I'm itchy! ________________________________!

M: Are you allergic to something?

W: I don't know. The itching started yesterday and ______________________________________.

M: Have you taken anything for it?

W: No, but ________________________________ at an allergy clinic on Saturday.

M: Then you could get some medicine that stops the itching ________________________.

W: Do you know any medicine for this?

M: Yes, sure, but it can make you very sleepy.

W: ______________________________, I'll try it. I can't stand this!

M: You should get some soothing cream, too. ______________________________.

W: I should do that.

M: A friend of mine told me about a really good German brand.

14

M: Sonia, hi. ______________________________?

W: Hi, Won-jun. I've been working. I got myself a part-time job for the summer.

M: Really? Where?

W: Charmaine's ice-cream parlor at Sandy Beach. It's lots of fun. I'm really enjoying it.

M: ______________________________? I'm looking for a summer job, too.

W: Sorry, no. But my dad needs summer workers at his construction company. ______________________________!

M: I don't know. Construction work is really hard....

W: It can be. But the pay is high. Think about it and let me know by the end of the week.

15

W: Jeff had a great time at a baseball game Friday night. After the game, his friends decided to go to a barbecue restaurant. But since he had to get up early the next day, Jeff said goodnight to his friends and ______________________________. Unfortunately, ______________________________ and got lost. When he found the subway at last, it was too late. ______________________________. Disappointed, he stood on the sidewalk, wondering what to do. ______________________________ and then suddenly stopped. It was his friend Mandy. She had been at the game with Jeff and their friends. She's on her way home, and her house is near Jeff's. In this situation, what would Jeff most likely say to Mandy?

16-17

M: Hello, class. I want to thank all of you for showing so much interest in astronomy. Of course, most professional astronomy research today is done with large telescopes. However, there are ______________________________ that can be seen with the eye. For instance, the planet Venus is often the second-brightest object in the night sky after the moon. It ______________________________ on any clear night. Mercury, being so close to the sun, is much harder to find, but ______________________________. For something a bit easier, try to find Mars. With a telescope, you can even see it in the late afternoon. Asteroids can also be seen at certain times of the year. They are easy to spot when they ______________________________. Though it is quite far from us, Jupiter is also visible on some nights. Incredibly, those with very good vision can sometimes even see three or four of its moons. Finally, there are hundreds of man-made satellites and thousands of stars ______________________________ each night.

실전모의고사

14 PRACTICE TEST

01 다음을 듣고, 남자가 하는 말의 목적으로 가장 적절한 것을 고르시오.

① 노숙자 문제를 쟁점화하려고
② 지적 장애의 원인을 설명하려고
③ 자선행위의 중요성을 강조하려고
④ 노숙자들에게 집을 마련해 주려고
⑤ 정치 문제에 대한 관심을 촉구하려고

02 대화를 듣고, 두 사람이 하는 말의 주제로 가장 적절한 것을 고르시오.

① 산사태 방지 대책
② 열대우림 기후의 특징
③ 자연과 공존하는 개발의 필요성
④ 열대우림 파괴가 미치는 악영향
⑤ 가축 사육 지역을 제한해야 하는 이유

03 대화를 듣고, 두 사람의 관계를 가장 잘 나타낸 것을 고르시오.

① 행사 주최자 – 자원봉사자
② 사장 – 비서
③ 리포터 – 사업가
④ 변호사 – 의뢰인
⑤ 고객 – 접수 담당자

04 대화를 듣고, 그림에서 대화의 내용과 일치하지 않는 것을 고르시오.

05 대화를 듣고, 남자가 여자를 위해 할 일로 가장 적절한 것을 고르시오.

① 봉사 활동 소개해주기
② 여자가 예산 세우는 것 도와주기
③ 여자에게 캠프 웹사이트를 알려주기
④ 여자를 자신의 전 직장에 추천해주기
⑤ 아르바이트에 관한 이메일 보내주기

06 대화를 듣고, 여자가 지불할 금액을 고르시오.

① $360 ② $400 ③ $450
④ $540 ⑤ $600

07 대화를 듣고, 여자가 햄버거를 먹지 않는 이유를 고르시오.

① 식욕이 없어서
② 다이어트 중이어서
③ 어제 햄버거를 먹어서
④ 식습관을 바꾸기로 해서
⑤ 저녁을 직접 만들고 싶어서

08 대화를 듣고, 새로 개봉한 영화관에 관해 언급되지 않은 것을 고르시오.

① 위치 ② 개관일 ③ 할인 혜택
④ 규모 ⑤ 상영 영화 수

09 Theodore Roosevelt National Park에 관한 다음 내용을 듣고, 일치하지 않는 것을 고르시오.

① 대통령이 사냥을 하기 위해 방문한 적이 있다.
② 야생 동물의 침입을 막는 울타리가 있다.
③ 서식하는 새들은 대부분 철새이다.
④ 곳곳에 빙하가 존재했음을 보여주는 흔적이 남아 있다.
⑤ 사전에 허가를 받아야 캠핑을 할 수 있다.

10 다음 표를 보면서 대화를 듣고, 두 사람이 주문할 포토북을 고르시오.

Custom Photo Books: Options and Pricing

Type	Size	Captions	Pages	Price
① A	Small	Not Available	24	$20
② B	Medium	Not Available	30	$25
③ C	Medium	Available	36	$30
④ D	Large	Available	28	$35
⑤ E	Large	Available	36	$40

11 대화를 듣고, 여자의 마지막 말에 대한 남자의 응답으로 가장 적절한 것을 고르시오.

① I had to call her that day.
② The password is my cat's name.
③ Let me look it up in my cell phone.
④ She said she would come a little late.
⑤ I can't understand why she behaved like that.

12 대화를 듣고, 남자의 마지막 말에 대한 여자의 응답으로 가장 적절한 것을 고르시오.

① This item is not on sale.
② Sure. I'll wait for you outside.
③ I'd love to, but it's too crowded.
④ I'm afraid the sale has already ended.
⑤ I hope we can sell everything by tonight.

13 대화를 듣고, 여자의 마지막 말에 대한 남자의 응답으로 가장 적절한 것을 고르시오. [3점]

▶ Man : ______

① Don't worry. Your final grade was great.
② I can explain what you don't understand.
③ You'd better stay in bed for one more day.
④ A doctor's note is required for long absences.
⑤ You always take careful notes during the lectures.

14 대화를 듣고, 남자의 마지막 말에 대한 여자의 응답으로 가장 적절한 것을 고르시오. [3점]

▶ Woman : ______

① I dropped it in the sink by mistake.
② I put my cell phone on vibration mode.
③ My brother spilt his milk on your book.
④ I should have charged the phone last night.
⑤ I didn't have an additional battery in my bag.

15 다음 상황 설명을 듣고, Nina가 Andy에게 할 말로 가장 적절한 것을 고르시오. [3점]

▶ Nina : ______

① You did a great job at the festival.
② You should have attended rehearsal.
③ Be confident and believe in your ability.
④ Don't be careless and stay on your guard.
⑤ I would be pleased if you wished me luck.

[16~17] 다음을 듣고, 물음에 답하시오.

16 여자가 하는 말의 주제로 가장 적절한 것은?

① information about in-flight events and services
② notification of changes in the rewards system
③ travel tips useful when flying with children
④ special offers available to all the passengers
⑤ recommendation of a family travel package

17 7세 미만 어린이에게 제공되는 서비스로 언급되지 않은 것은?

① 특별 기내식
② 만화영화 상영
③ 동화책 대여
④ 기념품 증정
⑤ 안전 의자 제공

14 DICTATION

녹음된 내용을 들으면서 빈칸을 알맞게 채워 보세요.

01

M: The homeless, or people living on the streets, are a serious problem in many cities around the world. These people ______________________________ an "unpleasant" problem. Thus, homelessness is not an issue that people will talk about because ______________________________ of dirty, poor and sometimes mentally-ill people. Sometimes homelessness is ______________________________. The good inside of every person is tested ______________________________. Can we make a difference by ourselves? I believe the answer is "yes," and the first step is to talk about it and ______________________________ that can no longer be ignored.

02

M: Hi, Pam. How was your trip to South America?

W: I'm glad I went, but to be honest, ______________________________ how much of the rainforest is being destroyed.

M: That's a shame. The rainforests are so important to the environment.

W: On the third day that I was there, it started raining heavily. There were terrible landslides in areas where ______________________________.

M: I saw a bit about that on the news.

W: The worst areas were places where forests are being cut down to ______________________________.

M: Raising cattle is an important business, but I'm worried about the effect on the native people.

W: Me, too. Many of them are losing their villages and their way of life. ______________________________ I could do to help.

03

M: Good morning, Christine.

W: Mr. Kruger, Suzzane Gorey from Bellcore Manufacturing called just a moment ago.

M: ______________________________?

W: Yes. She hopes tomorrow's conference call can be moved to Tuesday afternoon.

M: I see. Is my schedule free that afternoon?

W: Actually, ______________________________ Mr. Anderson, the CEO of DIA Lighting, in your office at that time.

M: ______________________________ Mr. Anderson would prefer to meet that evening.

W: Then I'll check your schedule for that day.

M: Please do. If I'm free, ______________________________ at the Lexington Hotel at 7 p.m.

W: I'll set that up right away, sir.

M: Thank you, Christine. I'll be in my office. ______________________________.

04

W: Dan, did you ______________________________?

M: Yes, Mom. What do you think?

W: You put a bookshelf to the right of the monitor. Where did you get it?

M: I bought it at Kelly's garage sale. The pencil vase in front of it is also from there.

W: I like the polka-dot pattern of the vase. Oh, you put a calendar next to it. That will ______________________________.

M: Right. Do you see anything else that is different?

W: ______________________________.... You put away the duck-shaped cell phone holder that was on the left side of your desk.

M: You're right. Instead, I placed a lamp there.

W: Why did you put it away? There is still room in front of the lamp.

M: If my cell phone is on my desk, ______________________________.

W: Okay. I understand.

정답 및 해설 p.54

05

M: Tina, do you have any plans for summer vacation?
W: Actually, my goal is to find a part-time job.
M: Oh? Are you ______________________________ ____________________?
W: Mainly, it's to pay next semester's tuition.
M: I see. Well, last year I helped out at an elementary school English camp. The work was meaningful, and I saved enough for school.
W: That sounds perfect. I want a rewarding job like that, but I can't find any.
M: If you are interested, you could ______________ ______________________________. The school recently sent out an email looking for helpers.
W: Really? Wow, I'd love to work there.
M: I'll ______________________________________ so you can decide.
W: Oh, what about the hours and pay?
M: I'm not sure ______________________________ _____________, but everything is in the email.
W: OK, that'll be very helpful. Thanks.

06

M: Good morning. What can I do for you?
W: I need to ________________________________ ____________, but I'm not sure how many I need.
M: Where are you going to decorate with them?
W: They are for the Pinebrook Primary School's auditorium.
M: School auditoriums usually need around 150 balloons.
W: Hmm.... I think our auditorium is ____________ ______________________________.
M: Well, then how about 50 more? I can give you a 10 percent discount if you buy 200 or more.
W: Okay, I'll get 200. ___________________________ ____________________________ for elementary school students?
M: I have round and heart-shaped balloons that are two dollars each. I also have rabbit and bear-shaped balloons that are three dollars each.
W: Then ___________________________________ of the hearts and the rabbits.
M: Yes, that would be great.

07

M: Liz, let's go out for hamburgers. _____________ __________________ Burger Queen's new menu.
W: I don't want a hamburger, Robert.
M: You aren't hungry?
W: I am.
M: Then why? Just the other day, ________________ ____________________________.
W: Yes, but that was a few days ago.
M: I don't understand why you don't want one all of a sudden. Are you on a diet again?
W: Actually, _________________________________ last night called *Grease: The Silent Killer*.
M: I think I've heard of that. It's on the dangers of greasy foods, right?
W: Right! So, I decided to ______________________ _________________________.
M: Then why don't we go shopping and cook dinner instead? We can make soup and some salad.
W: Great idea! Sounds delicious.

08

M: What did you do on the weekend, Sara?
W: I went with some friends to see a movie at the new theater.
M: You mean the one that is on 10th avenue?
W: Right. ______________________________, but it just opened on Saturday.
M: ___________________________________ while it's still new.
W: Then, you should ________________________ ________________________. Tickets are 50% off.
M: That's a good deal. How are the facilities?
W: Great. _________________________________ __________________ in the city.
M: In that case, I'll definitely go there.

09

W: Theodore Roosevelt National Park ______________ ____ of western North Dakota in the United States. The park was founded to pay respect to President Theodore Roosevelt on a location ____________ ________________________. To keep the native animals in, the entire park has been surrounded with a 7-foot tall wire fence. More than 185 different bird species live in the park, and most of them are migratory. Despite its current landscape, fossil evidence suggests that the park ____ today. Today, there are no glaciers in the park, but the evidence of their geologically recent presence is everywhere. For those who are looking for adventure, camping is permitted in the park, but ____ ____________________.

10

M: Kate, did you choose our honeymoon photo book?

W: Not yet, honey. I'm still ____________________ ________________________. Can you help me with the choice?

M: Sure, let me see. Let's start with the size.

W: ____________________________ would be okay.

M: I agree. Would you like to add some captions to the photos?

W: Sure. I'd like the captions to bring back memories ____ ________________________.

M: That'll be great. And how about the length? We need more than 30 pages, don't you think?

W: I think you're right. The remaining choices have the same number of pages, so ____________________ ____________________________.

M: Okay. So, you've decided?

W: Yes. Thanks for your help, honey.

11

W: Bella ____ ____________________ and nobody knows the reason.

M: Really? I thought she would definitely come. ______ ________________________________?

W: But I don't have her number now. Do you?

12

M: Unbelievable! Look over there! ______________ ______________________________!

W: That's because it's having a huge clearance sale.

M: Do you want to ______________________________ ____________________?

13

M: Jessica! ________________________________? I didn't see you in the lecture last week.

W: I've been sick. I spent last week in the hospital.

M: Why were you in the hospital? ______________ ____________________________?

W: I had a bad cold, but I'm fine now. Anyway, I'm worried because I've already missed a week of class.

M: Don't worry. You can copy my notes. But we are also having a quiz next week.

W: Oh, I didn't know about that. Is it part of the final grade?

M: Yes, Professor Han said that.

W: Really? I'm not ready for a quiz.

M: It'll be next Friday. So ______________________ ____________________.

W: You're right, but I'm a little worried about ________ ____.

14

M: Charlotte! ______________________________ __________________.

W: Really? Why?

M: I need ______________________________. I called you several times, but you didn't answer.

W: Oh, I didn't know that you called me.

M: Well, I did, but all I got was a message saying that your mobile phone is turned off.

W: I'm so sorry, but I couldn't turn on my phone. Here's your book.

M: Thanks. You were busy ____________________ __________________________, I guess.

W: No. My cell phone is broken.

M: Come on. ______________________________ __________________, didn't you?

W: You're right, but now the battery won't charge.

M: ____?

15

M: Andy is the MC for his high school's annual festival. He has a passion for presenting, and all of his friends think he is very talented. However, ____, Andy becomes nervous. He begins to focus on ____ during rehearsal. His friend Nina sees that he is worried and asks him about it. Andy explains that ____ and worried that other students will make fun of him. Nina listens to this and ___________ ____________________________________. In this situation, what would Nina most likely say to Andy?

16-17

W: Good morning, passengers. _______________ ____________________ Desert Fox Airlines. Throughout May, Desert Fox Airlines will be offering ______________________________ _______________ to celebrate Children's Day and Parents' Day. First, passengers will receive an additional 5% of their total bonus mileage when traveling during the month of May. Also, we'll be offering packages of tickets for families who are traveling together. ______________________ ____________________, we will provide free, specially-made in-flight meals. We also provide animated films for children as part of our VOD service. If your children prefer to read, our flight attendants have a selection of storybooks. And of course, we provide child safety seats ______ ______________________. If you have children under seven, ___________________________ _________________ by letting us know when you reserve your tickets. For further details, please check inside your copy of *Desert Fox Airlines Magazine*, ______________________ __________________ in front of you. We hope you have a pleasant flight today with Desert Fox Airlines.

실전모의고사

15 PRACTICE TEST

01 다음을 듣고, 여자가 하는 말의 목적으로 가장 적절한 것을 고르시오.

① 금융사기에 대해 경고하려고
② 신용카드 가입을 권유하려고
③ 스팸을 차단하는 방법을 알리려고
④ 인터넷 쇼핑의 편리성을 설명하려고
⑤ 은행계좌의 안전한 사용법을 조언하려고

02 대화를 듣고, 두 사람이 하는 말의 주제로 가장 적절한 것을 고르시오.

① 세계의 주요 산맥들
② 산맥이 만들어지는 과정
③ 산의 높이가 변하는 이유
④ 산의 높이를 측정하는 방법
⑤ 알프스 산맥과 히말라야 산맥의 차이

03 대화를 듣고, 두 사람의 관계를 가장 잘 나타낸 것을 고르시오.

① 팬 – 배우
② 작가 – 작가
③ 손님 – 여행사 직원
④ 출판사 직원 – 광고사 직원
⑤ 서점 관계자 – 서점 고객

04 대화를 듣고, 그림에서 대화의 내용과 일치하지 않는 것을 고르시오.

05 대화를 듣고, 여자가 할 일로 가장 적절한 것을 고르시오.

① 이젤 옮기기
② 기념사진 찍기
③ 이젤 설치하기
④ 홍보용 표지판 만들기
⑤ 음료수를 놓을 탁자 설치하기

06 대화를 듣고, 남자와 그 친구가 식사 후 지불할 금액을 고르시오. [3점]

① $8　② $16　③ $24
④ $40　⑤ $48

07 대화를 듣고, 여자가 당분간 식물을 돌볼 수 없는 이유를 고르시오.

① 집을 수리해야 해서
② 장기 휴가를 가야 해서
③ 엄마 병문안을 가야 해서
④ 엄마에게 꽃 알레르기가 있어서
⑤ 충분한 장소를 마련하지 못해서

08 대화를 듣고, 전주 한옥마을에 관해 언급되지 않은 것을 고르시오.

① 교통편　② 숙박 가능 여부
③ 보유 시설　④ 전통 가옥 수
⑤ 조성 시기

09 개복치(ocean sunfish)에 관한 다음 내용을 듣고, 일치하지 않는 것을 고르시오.

① 평균 무게가 약 1톤에 가깝다.
② 먹이를 구하기 위해 해수면 가까이에 떠 있는다.
③ 공격을 받으면 몸 색깔을 바꾼다.
④ 인간에게 공격적이지 않다.
⑤ 여러 아시아 국가에서 식용으로 쓰인다.

10 다음 표를 보면서 대화를 듣고, 여자가 주문할 샌드위치를 고르시오.

The Sandwich Shack			
Name	Ingredients	Fat	Calories
① Italian Meatball	beef meatballs (barbecue sauce)	35 grams	600
② Golden Delight	tofu (pea sauce)	12 grams	250
③ Super Club	roast chicken, turkey, bacon	30 grams	450
④ Asian Chicken	chicken (teriyaki sauce)	20 grams	300
⑤ Tuna	tuna, cheese	20 grams	390

11 대화를 듣고, 여자의 마지막 말에 대한 남자의 응답으로 가장 적절한 것을 고르시오.

① It's only been 15 stops.
② I took the line number 4 today.
③ Maybe I should try the bus instead.
④ Twice, but it's not too inconvenient.
⑤ It saves me at least fifteen minutes.

12 대화를 듣고, 남자의 마지막 말에 대한 여자의 응답으로 가장 적절한 것을 고르시오.

① I wish I were photogenic.
② Here are some souvenirs for you.
③ Sure, I'd be happy to show them to you.
④ It was as beautiful as the pictures I showed you.
⑤ I bought a collection of Claude Monet's paintings.

13 대화를 듣고, 여자의 마지막 말에 대한 남자의 응답으로 가장 적절한 것을 고르시오.

▶ Man : ____________________

① Great. I also thought about that.
② It's OK, Mom. Don't worry about it.
③ No, I want pizza and chicken this time.
④ I've already had them over to celebrate.
⑤ Thanks. I'd love some cake and a drink.

14 대화를 듣고, 남자의 마지막 말에 대한 여자의 응답으로 가장 적절한 것을 고르시오. [3점]

▶ Woman : ____________________

① What do I need my cup for?
② I'd like these refilled, please.
③ Oh, silly me. I have to take it.
④ That's OK. I will not eat fast food.
⑤ Wow! I've forgotten how good burgers are.

15 다음 상황 설명을 듣고, Sylvia가 David에게 할 말로 가장 적절한 것을 고르시오. [3점]

▶ Sylvia : ____________________

① You should check out a site before shopping on it.
② You need to pay the extra charge for faster shipping.
③ Although I do check reviews, I treat them with caution.
④ I try to be totally honest when I write customer reviews.
⑤ If I were you, I would not complain and just wait for a while.

[16~17] 다음을 듣고, 물음에 답하시오.

16 남자가 하는 말의 주제로 가장 적절한 것은?

① the four reasons why people become refugees
② the meaning and purpose of World Refugee Day
③ difficulties refugees are facing and how to help them
④ a fundraiser for refugees held by the United Nations
⑤ the accomplishments of volunteer groups for refugees

17 난민이 되는 이유로 언급되지 <u>않은</u> 것은?

① 인종 차별 ② 자연재해
③ 종교적 박해 ④ 정치적 견해
⑤ 전쟁

15 DICTATION

녹음된 내용을 들으면서 빈칸을 알맞게 채워 보세요.

01

W: The Internet is a sea of information. And some 21st century pirates ______________________________ ______________ by using the Internet. When you open an email, ______________________________ ______________________ they represent your bank or your credit card company. Then they ask you for your bank account numbers and account passwords, or credit card numbers. These pirates want this information so that they can ______________________________ or use your credit card. You need to be careful. Banks or credit card companies don't ask for this kind of information. You should never ______________ ______________________________.

02

W: I think our report about mountain ranges is almost finished. What about you?

M: It's almost finished, but we are still missing a few details.

W: Like what?

M: Well, I ______________________________ for Mount Whitney. Why is that?

W: Oh, that's the highest peak in the US. As measurement techniques have become more accurate, the official height has changed.

M: Okay. I thought maybe ______________________ ______________________.

W: It is growing slowly, about a millimeter a year.

M: We should mention that in our report, also. Is every mountain getting taller?

W: ______________________________________, like the Alps and the Himalayas, are still growing.

M: And the older ones are slowly shrinking, right?

W: That's right. ______________________________ ____________________, too.

03

M: Austin is sending me on a book tour to __________ ______________________.

W: Oh, I like going on book tours.

M: I don't really like going on them.

W: Really? I like meeting the people who read my stories.

M: Not me. I just like writing. ________________ ______________. I'll be visiting 10 cities in 10 days.

W: And you will visit two or three bookstores in every city, won't you?

M: That's right. It's exhausting. ________________ ______________________?

W: Good. When it's done, Austin will ____________ ______________________, too.

M: What's the new book called?

W: It's called *The Lover's Triangle*.

M: ______________________________________.

04

W: Hello?

M: Hi, Vanessa. How's the concert?

W: It's great. A huge banner that says "Beautiful Day" ______________________________________. I wish you could be here.

M: That's cool. Maybe we can go together next time. Do you ______________________________ of the stage?

W: I can see the drummer clearly. He's wearing his usual striped shirt.

M: Okay. I'm sure the guitarist still has long hair.

W: Right. ______________________________. And the lead singer is wearing sunglasses as always.

M: Can you see the second guitarist?

W: Yes. He's at ______________________________, wearing checkered pants.

M: It sounds like you have a great seat.

W: Yes, I booked the tickets early.

정답 및 해설 p.58

05

W: Sorry ______________________ the photography club meeting yesterday.

M: That's OK, Sally.

W: Did you discuss our exhibition for the school festival this Friday?

M: Yes. Everyone has a job.

W: What's mine?

M: Oh, no. We forgot about you. Hmm.... Eddie's setting up the easels ______________________.

W: I could help him.

M: Ted will help him. And Johnny and Fred are going to bring the easels down from the art room.

W: I can make promotional signs.

M: Carol's doing that. And ______________________ a drink's table.

W: I have nothing to do!

M: I know; we need ______________________ the club members and important guests.

W: Good idea. I'll do that. That's the best job for me!

06

W: Are you ready to order?

M: Umm... ______________________. If we order a main dish, like this steak for $20, then is the salad bar free?

W: No, it isn't. The salad bar is $4 extra with any main dish.

M: And ______________________?

W: Then the salad bar is $12 per person.

M: Umm... but it says right here that it's $8.

W: The lunch price is $8, but it's only available between 11 a.m. and 2 p.m.

M: ______________________?

W: Yes, it's a few minutes past two.

M: Could you check with the manager? ______________________.

W: OK. The manager has agreed to the lunchtime price.

M: We'd just like the salad bar then. ______________________.

W: OK.

07

W: Hi, Chris. I was hoping to meet you.

M: Why, Susan? Can I help you with something?

W: I hope so. I'd like you to ______________________ for a couple of weeks.

M: Does that mean you're taking a vacation?

W: Unfortunately not. My mom is quite sick.

M: I'm really sorry to hear that. Are you going to visit her?

W: No. I was going to, but I decided to ______________________.

M: I see. Then, why do you want me to care for your plants?

W: Well, she's allergic to some of my flowers. I want you to keep them at your house.

M: I understand. Are there any special instructions for ______________________?

W: No, they just need water and sunlight.

M: Okay. ______________________.

W: Thanks. You're the best.

08

W: Hi, Chris. Are you enjoying your time in Korea?

M: ______________________________, but I don't feel like I've seen enough Korean culture.

W: If you want to experience Korean culture, why don't you visit the Jeonju Hanok Village?

M: I've heard about that place. They have ______________________________.

W: They also have souvenir shops, traditional restaurants, museums, and temples.

M: It sounds like ______________________________.

W: You won't be disappointed. There are over 500 traditional houses that still have people living in them.

M: That's a lot. How was the village first formed?

W: The village was established by Koreans in the 1930's to ______________________ during the period when Korea was controlled by Japan.

09

M: The ocean sunfish is one of the heaviest fish on Earth, with an average weight of about a ton. It lives in temperate and tropical seas and oceans. It is flat and it often ______________________ so birds can remove tiny worms from its body. Besides its unique appearance and habits, the ocean sunfish ______________________. For example, its skin is usually gray or white, but it can become lighter or darker in color ______________________. They are not aggressive toward humans, so the largest danger they can pose is damage to boats ______________________. Meanwhile, the meat of ocean sunfish is eaten in many Asian countries. However, the meat ______________________ before consumption.

10

M: I'm having the Italian Meatball sandwich. I love that barbecue sauce.

W: Yikes! It's got 35 grams of fat!

M: But it tastes great! And I didn't have any breakfast. It's what I want.

W: My doctor told me to have only 50 grams of fat a day. Then ______________________.

M: Do you like tofu? ______________________.

W: No, I don't like it. Hmm... let's see, my doctor recommended I ______________________ to 20 grams at lunch.

M: Well, you still have two choices.

W: Actually ______________________.

M: Really? Should we go somewhere else?

W: No, I don't have much time. I will take the one which has fewer calories between the two.

M: Good. Let's order then.

11

W: Jeff, you ______________________, right?

M: Actually, I take the subway. ______________________.

W: Oh, really? How many times do you have to transfer?

12

M: Hi, Karen! ______________________ for a few weeks.

W: That's because I went to France with my sister. It was amazing.

M: Sounds like you had a great time. ______________________?

13

W: How are your plans for your birthday party going?
M: My birthday party?
W: Yes. ______________________________ in our apartment. You and your friends had pizza and chicken.
M: We did that when I was a child.
W: You're still a child.
M: No, I'm not. I'm in high school.
W: So you don't want a birthday party at home this year?
M: No. ______________________________ for two or three years.
W: I know, but I thought maybe this year you would have one. ______________________________ on your birthday then?
M: I just want to spend some time with my friends. Maybe they'll buy me some lunch and we'll have some cake.
W: But ______________________________ if we invite them to the apartment?

14

W: I'm becoming ______________________________.
M: You've just been working hard. You're tired.
W: I'm getting old!
M: ______________________________! Let's finish our shopping after we eat.
W: OK. How's your hamburger? Mine is great. I haven't had a hamburger in a long time.
M: Well, ______________________________ too frequently.
W: Simon, don't worry. I don't eat too much fast food. I rarely visit food courts like this.
M: Are you finished with your cola?
W: Yeah. All that walking and shopping has ______________________________.
M: Me, too. Can you ______________________________?
W: Good idea. Just a minute.
M: Gloria, Gloria, wait! You've forgotten my cup.

15

W: Sylvia happens to meet her friend David at school. ______________________________. David says he ordered sunglasses online 20 days ago and they still have not shipped them. When Sylvia asks him if he's contacted the seller, David says he sent them an e-mail but ______________________________. He also called them, but ______________________________. Sylvia asks David to show her what site he bought the item on. She's never heard of that site and ______________________________. Sylvia thinks it's ______________________________ whenever people buy something online. She wants to say that to David. In this situation, what would Sylvia most likely say to David?

16-17

M: As you may already know, June 20th is World Refugee Day. Each year the United Nations and other civic groups celebrate this day. But ______________________________? Refugees are people who have left their home country and ______________________________. This often happens because a refugee's race, religion, or political opinion isn't respected in his or her home country. Also, when countries go to war, people may choose to leave their home country or ______________________________. In 2020, there were 26.4 million refugees around the world. These people typically have few rights and limited access to food, shelter, and medical care. They need our help. Fortunately, ______________________________ them. You can start by participating in a volunteer program for refugees. You can help them to understand the culture and language of their new country. ______________________________ is difficult, but a little effort from you can help refugees to overcome the challenges.

실전모의고사

16 PRACTICE TEST

01 다음을 듣고, 남자가 하는 말의 목적으로 가장 적절한 것을 고르시오.

① 비타민의 중요성을 설명하려고
② 적절한 채식 방법을 알려주려고
③ 과일과 채소의 섭취를 권장하려고
④ 과일의 색깔에 숨겨진 비밀을 밝히려고
⑤ 천천히 먹는 습관의 중요성을 일깨우려고

02 대화를 듣고, 여자의 의견으로 가장 적절한 것을 고르시오.

① 관중을 위한 편의시설을 확대하는 것이 좋다.
② 큰 소음을 발생시키는 응원을 금지해야 한다.
③ 좌석에 따라 입장권 가격을 다르게 책정해야 한다.
④ 관중의 시야 확보를 보장하는 규정이 있어야 한다.
⑤ 경기 관람 시 좋은 좌석을 얻으려면 예매해야 한다.

03 대화를 듣고, 두 사람의 관계를 가장 잘 나타낸 것을 고르시오.

① 도서관 사서 – 학생
② 매니저 – 종업원
③ 경찰 – 용의자
④ 배달부 – 고객
⑤ 우체국 사무원 – 우체국장

04 대화를 듣고, 그림에서 대화의 내용과 일치하지 않는 것을 고르시오.

05 대화를 듣고, 여자가 남자를 위해 할 일로 가장 적절한 것을 고르시오.

① 진료 기록을 작성하기
② 썩은 치아를 치료해 주기
③ 다음 주 진료 예약을 해 주기
④ 통증을 참을 수 있도록 도와주기
⑤ 진료를 당장 받을 수 있는지 알아보기

06 대화를 듣고, 여자가 지불할 금액을 고르시오. [3점]

① $20 ② $20 ③ $35
④ $45 ⑤ $50

07 대화를 듣고, 남자가 영화에 출연하지 않는 이유를 고르시오.

① 뮤지컬이 아니라서
② 감독이 너무 상업적이라서
③ 영화 각본이 재미없어서
④ 다른 드라마에 출연하고 있어서
⑤ 주연 여배우가 마음에 안 들어서

08 다음을 듣고, floating island에 관해 언급되지 않은 것을 고르시오.

① 위치 ② 형성 물질
③ 최초 거주 이유 ④ 거주 형태
⑤ 날씨 형태

09 Spelling Championship에 관한 다음 내용을 듣고, 일치하지 않는 것을 고르시오.

① 1년에 한 번 열리는 행사이다.
② 오디션에서는 단어의 철자를 소리 내어 말해야 한다.
③ 진출을 위해 오디션에서 모든 문제를 맞춰야 한다.
④ 오디션은 모든 학생들에게 공개로 진행된다.
⑤ 오디션을 통과한 학생들에게 추가 정보가 주어질 것이다.

10 다음 자료를 보면서 대화를 듣고, 남자가 가입할 회원 자격 (membership)을 고르시오.

Save the Polar Bears Club Membership Form				
	Cost	T-shirt	Hat	Mug
① Lifetime Member	$199.99	yes	yes	yes
② 1 year Gold Member	$49.99	yes	yes	yes
③ 1 year Silver Member	$39.99	yes	yes	no
④ 1 year Bronze Member	$35	no	yes	yes
⑤ 6 month Basic Member	$25	yes	no	no

11 대화를 듣고, 여자의 마지막 말에 대한 남자의 응답으로 가장 적절한 것을 고르시오.

① I thought I would be alone.
② My hometown is quite far from here.
③ Please tell me the way to the cafeteria.
④ It's as good as it looked in the pictures.
⑤ My brother graduated from a school nearby.

12 대화를 듣고, 남자의 마지막 말에 대한 여자의 응답으로 가장 적절한 것을 고르시오.

① I always prefer gift cards.
② Ask the clerk to help you.
③ I shouldn't spend that much.
④ No, but I want something nicer.
⑤ You should check the price tag first.

13 대화를 듣고, 여자의 마지막 말에 대한 남자의 응답으로 가장 적절한 것을 고르시오. [3점]

▶ Man : ______________________

① Thank you! It's very kind of you.
② But these diamonds are also very good.
③ Most of my investments have lost money.
④ I'm sorry, but I have to buy a genuine diamond.
⑤ Yes, but I think I'd rather look around for something cheaper.

14 대화를 듣고, 남자의 마지막 말에 대한 여자의 응답으로 가장 적절한 것을 고르시오.

▶ Woman : ______________________

① I don't think anyone can play that character.
② You need permission to put up posters on the wall.
③ Great, we're having auditions Saturday at 11 a.m.
④ Can you tell me something about the character?
⑤ Yes, that's true; my mother was quite a famous singer.

15 다음 상황 설명을 듣고, Mary가 Sarah에게 할 말로 가장 적절한 것을 고르시오. [3점]

▶ Mary : ______________________

① I'll do anything to go to your party!
② Well, it is dangerous. We have to be careful.
③ I need to do my best to get good scores this time.
④ I'd like to help you, but not this. I won't help you to cheat.
⑤ I'm also having a party this weekend. I hope you can come.

[16~17] 다음을 듣고, 물음에 답하시오.

16 여자가 하는 말의 주제로 가장 적절한 것은?

① factors necessary for improving yoga skills
② a suitable type of yoga studio for the beginner
③ various styles of yoga developed in recent years
④ things to consider before choosing a yoga studio
⑤ an overview of the fundamentals of yoga philosophy

17 요가 수련 공간의 환경 요소로 언급되지 않은 것은?

① temperature
② classroom size
③ light
④ noise
⑤ cleanliness

16 DICTATION

녹음된 내용을 들으면서 빈칸을 알맞게 채워 보세요.

01

M: It is important to eat ________________ in order to stay healthy. This means eating a wide variety of foods every day. The most important foods are fruits and vegetables. ________________, they provide the nutrients you need to stay healthy, ________________. The best way ________________ is to make sure you eat fruits and vegetables of many colors, because the colors reflect what kinds of vitamins are in the food. ________________ is five fist-sized servings a day.

02

M: It sure is a great day to watch a baseball game.

W: Yeah, but I feel bad for Susan. She can't see very well.

M: You're right. Those people in front of her are ________________.

W: I know they just want to support their team, but it's rude to the people behind them.

M: I agree with you, but I think ________________.

W: Well, maybe there should be ________________ of another spectator. After all, we all paid the same amount to see the game.

M: I understand your point. In the meantime, I'll ask them to ________________.

W: That's a good idea.

03

M: Are you Mary Ellen Park?

W: Yes, I am. What can I do for you?

M: I just need you to ________________.

W: Right here, next to the X?

M: Yes, that's right. And this is for you.

W: Wow! It's from Korea. But ________________.

M: Do you have family there? How about an old high school friend?

W: Hmm... ________________, but I only know their Korean names.

M: Well, the family name is 'Kim.'

W: Maybe 'June' is the Western name of my cousin Ji-eun.

M: ________________. Have a nice day!

04

M: Wow, your house looks great. I guess the remodeling went well.

W: It did. My daughter and I especially love ________________.

M: That's lovely. By the way, you didn't have a fence before, correct?

W: That's right. ________________, but the remodeling company offered us a discount, so we decided to have it built.

M: I think you two made the right choice. It is ________________, especially when you have a kid.

W: I hadn't thought of that. Good point! The only disappointment was ________________.

M: I remember that you were really excited about that. What happened?

W: It was going to cost a lot of money, and my daughter really wanted the swimming pool. Therefore, it was either the door or the swimming pool.

M: And you decided ________________. Good choice!

W: Yeah, it's going to be a lot of fun in the summer. And I put a table and chairs next to it.

M: Awesome!

정답 및 해설 p.62

05

W: Welcome to Kim's Dental Clinic. What can we do for you today?

M: ________________________________ and would like to see a dentist.

W: Have you ever been here before?

M: No. ________________________________. My regular dentist is back in Denver.

W: Well, ________________________________ to see the dentist at 1 p.m., if you don't mind waiting an hour.

M: That's a long time. Ouch! ________________________________.

W: Here are a few forms to fill out for now.

M: OK. But I don't know ________________________________.

W: Well, if it's that bad, I'll see if I can get Dr. Kim to see you right now.

M: That would be great.

06

W: I need film for this instant camera.

M: Color or black and white?

W: Color, please.

M: Well, 10 exposures is $10.

W: It's very expensive. $1 a picture. I never knew because I just ________________________________ a few weeks ago.

M: Well, black and white film is $6 for 10 exposures.

W: ________________________________? Say packs of 20 or 30 exposures. Larger packs would be cheaper per exposure, wouldn't they?

M: Sorry, not right now.

W: Hey, what are these?

M: Films which print cartoon characters on ________________________________. There's Mickey, Winnie the Pooh....

W: Mickey's cute. I love Mickey. ________________________________.

M: They're $15 a pack.

W: One pack of Mickey, then, and two packs of color film.

M: OK. Thank you for shopping with us!

07

W: Michael. I heard you're going to appear in a movie directed by John Williams.

M: You heard that? I ________________________________ at how fast word travels.

W: Is it a musical? I know you'd like to appear in a musical.

M: No, it's a historical drama. I read the script last week but I ________________________________.

W: Oh, I'm sorry to hear that. You don't like the script?

M: Well, I do. Its ending is sad but ________________________________.

W: Then what's the problem? The director is John Williams!

M: Yeah, I know that he ________________________________.

W: Definitely. Who is the main actress in that movie?

M: Jennifer Anderson. I really wanted to work with her, but I'm busy making another drama show for TVB until next July.

W: I see. You have to ________________________________.

M: Yes, so I didn't really have a choice.

08

W: It's not often you come across a real "floating island," but they do exist in Lake Titicaca in Peru. These floating islands ______________________________, a type of grass that grows in the lake, and are large enough for people to live on. The islands ______ ________________, and more are being created as the need arises. The Uros, the people that live on the islands, originally moved onto the floating islands centuries ago to _____________ ________________. This strategy turned out to be effective, so they have lived like that ever since. Since the islands are slowly sinking, every 6 months or so they have to lift all the houses and other buildings to ______________________________. The residents must also wear layers of clothing, to protect themselves from the cold, the wind, and the intense sunshine.

09

M: The annual spelling championship for Rockville High School ______________________ ___________. In order to enter, interested students must attend an audition tomorrow. During the audition you will be asked ________________ ______________________ in front of the judges. If you miss any of the words in the audition, you will not make it to the championship round next Monday. The audition will not be open to non-participating students. ______________ ______________________ will be given further information about when and where to go, and the format of the contest. ______________________ ______________________!

10

W: What are you doing, Max?

M: I'm going to join the 'Save the Polar Bears Club.'

W: Oh, ___________________________________. Good for you.

M: Thanks. Look at this membership form. There are five memberships available.

W: Right.

M: ______________________________ Lifetime Membership. It costs almost two hundred dollars.

W: I see they give T-shirts, hats and coffee mugs to certain members.

M: Hmm... if I wear the Save the Polar Bears Club T-shirt, that will let people know.

W: Yes, ___________________________________!

M: True. And I would like a hat too.

W: If I ___________________________________ _______________, would you give me the hat?

M: Sure.

W: But I don't think we need the coffee mug.

M: No, we don't. Then, the membership will cost less than $40.

11

W: You're a new student, right?

M: Yes, today is ____________________________ at this school.

W: Well, I hope you like it here. _______________ ______________________ so far?

12

M: What do you think of this book as a present for Carol?

W: It's nice, but I think ______________________ ______________________.

M: Does the cost of the gift really matter?

13

W: Welcome to the Jewelry Barn. What can I do for you today?

M: I'm trying to find a gift for my wife's birthday.

W: Oh, how romantic! What do you have in mind?

M: I was thinking about diamond earrings, but _____ ____.

W: Well, we have a small pair for $300.

M: Wow. ____ ______________.

W: We do have small diamond pendants that start at $150. We also have synthetic diamonds that look like the real thing ________________________ ______________.

M: No, I couldn't get her a fake diamond. I would ____. But $300 is too expensive.

W: ______________________________ in your future!

14

W: Roundhouse Theater Company.

M: Hello, may I speak to Jenna Paine, please?

W: Speaking.

M: Oh, ____ outside the community center.

W: For the musical?

M: Yes, ____.

W: OK, do you have any acting experience?

M: Yes, ____.

W: And singing?

M: Oh yes, I love singing. Actually, I won some prizes for my singing.

W: Lovely. Can I get your name, please?

M: It's Blake Lee.

W: OK. Now, do you know the musical at all?

M: *Jesus Christ Superstar*? Yes, __________________ __________________.

15

M: Mary and Sarah sit next to each other in math class. Mary ____ and Sarah has always gotten average grades. Mary sometimes lets Sarah see her homework ____. On the day of the final exam, Sarah confronts Mary with an offer. She says that she is having a party on the weekend and will invite Mary if she will ______________________________. Although Mary would like to go to the party, she knows that cheating is not right and __________________ __________________. In this situation, what would Mary most likely say to Sarah?

16-17

W: As yoga has become popular over the years, you can now find yoga studios in most major cities. With a number of options available, it may be difficult to decide ________________________. There are a few things to consider. First of all, it's a good idea to check out __________________ ________________ the studio offers. There are classes that focus more on the physical aspect of yoga and others that focus more on the spiritual. The latter might include meditation and yoga philosophy. Once you identify what appeals to you, you can choose a studio that has classes of that style. ____________________________ is also important. Would you prefer __________ ____? Some studios ______________________________ for calm practices and others have bright rooms for an active atmosphere. If you want to focus on the spiritual practice, look for ones __________ ________________________. For some people, ________________________________ is the most important factor. You can check out all of the information by simply visiting them.

실전모의고사

17 PRACTICE TEST

01 **다음을 듣고, 여자가 하는 말의 목적으로 가장 적절한 것을 고르시오.**

① 새로운 은퇴 계획을 발표하려고
② 실의에 빠진 동료들을 격려하려고
③ 적십자의 자원봉사자를 모집하려고
④ 신입 사원 환영 행사를 준비하려고
⑤ 동료들에게 감사 인사를 전하려고

02 **대화를 듣고, 두 사람이 하는 말의 주제로 가장 적절한 것을 고르시오.**

① 취침 시 적정 실내 온도
② 낮잠이 건강에 좋은 이유
③ 운전할 때 졸음을 쫓는 방법
④ 장시간 운전에 좋은 스트레칭
⑤ 고속도로에서 운전 시 주의사항

03 **대화를 듣고, 두 사람의 관계를 가장 잘 나타낸 것을 고르시오.**

① 아내 – 남편
② 선생님 – 학생
③ 제빵사 – 고객
④ 아이들 엄마 – 베이비시터
⑤ 아들 – 아버지

04 **대화를 듣고, 그림에서 대화의 내용과 일치하지 않는 것을 고르시오.**

05 **대화를 듣고, 여자가 남자에게 부탁한 일로 가장 적절한 것을 고르시오.**

① 설거지를 도와주기
② 저녁 식사를 준비하기
③ 음식물 쓰레기를 버려 주기
④ 음식물 쓰레기를 봉투에 담기
⑤ 가게에서 저녁 찬거리를 사 오기

06 **대화를 듣고, 남자가 지불할 금액을 고르시오. [3점]**

① $60 ② $70 ③ $84
④ $107 ⑤ $120

07 **대화를 듣고, 남자가 여자에게 동물 보호소에 함께 가자고 부탁한 이유를 고르시오.**

① 봉사활동을 하고 싶어서
② 고양이를 입양하고 싶어서
③ 유기 고양이를 데려다 주고 싶어서
④ 잃어버린 고양이를 찾아보고 싶어서
⑤ 그곳에서 일하는 친구를 방문하고 싶어서

08 **대화를 듣고, 부르즈 칼리파(Burj Khalifa)에 관해 언급되지 않은 것을 고르시오.**

① 높이 ② 면적 ③ 건축비용
④ 건설한 이유 ⑤ 준공 시기

09 **Spruce Goose에 관한 다음 내용을 듣고, 일치하지 않는 것을 고르시오.**

① 8개의 엔진을 가지고 있다.
② 전투기 용도로 설계되었다.
③ 목재를 주재료로 하여 만들어졌다.
④ 비행은 단 한 번 이루어졌다.
⑤ 현재 실물을 관람할 수 있다.

10 다음 자료를 보면서 대화를 듣고, 두 사람이 관람할 영화를 고르시오.

THE ASTOR CINEMA Sunday Classics			
Title	Genre	Start	Running Time
① The Godfather	Gangster	11:00 a.m.	2 hrs 55 mins
② The Wizard of Oz	Fantasy	2:30 p.m.	1 hr 32 mins
③ Citizen Kane	Drama	4:10 p.m.	1 hr 59 mins
④ City Lights	Romantic Comedy	9:10 p.m.	1 hr 46 mins
⑤ 2001: A Space Odyssey	Science Fiction	10:00 p.m.	2 hrs 29 mins

11 대화를 듣고, 여자의 마지막 말에 대한 남자의 응답으로 가장 적절한 것을 고르시오.

① I applied for it online.
② You should apply soon.
③ I only did it for a month.
④ It was a great experience.
⑤ I worked as a part-time translator.

12 대화를 듣고, 남자의 마지막 말에 대한 여자의 응답으로 가장 적절한 것을 고르시오.

① I'd rather sit in a row.
② All the desks need to be cleaned.
③ I want new desks with a modern design.
④ She is thinking of new arrangements these days.
⑤ I think the circular arrangement is good for discussions.

13 대화를 듣고, 여자의 마지막 말에 대한 남자의 응답으로 가장 적절한 것을 고르시오.

▶ Man : ____________________

① I'll go get the doctor's note right away.
② The professors will be happy to see me.
③ I didn't want to drop out of this course anyway.
④ How about if I bring a doctor's note tomorrow?
⑤ OK, I'll be back after lunch. Thank you so much!

14 대화를 듣고, 남자의 마지막 말에 대한 여자의 응답으로 가장 적절한 것을 고르시오. [3점]

▶ Woman : ____________________

① Midlands is too far from here.
② Why are shuttle bus tickets so expensive?
③ I am sorry that you couldn't make it on time.
④ Soccer supporters tend to be too aggressive.
⑤ I would be happy to drive all of you there.

15 다음 상황 설명을 듣고, Angelina가 판매원에게 할 말로 가장 적절한 것을 고르시오. [3점]

▶ Angelina : ____________________

① I've been waiting 45 minutes already!
② May I exchange this? It doesn't fit me.
③ I'd like to have this dry-cleaned, please.
④ I'm just browsing at the moment, thank you.
⑤ This cream-colored coat looks great on you.

[16~17] 다음을 듣고, 물음에 답하시오.

16 남자가 하는 말의 주제로 가장 적절한 것은?

① how to find appropriate volunteer activities
② volunteering as a way of developing social skills
③ mental and physical health benefits of volunteering
④ volunteering as an opportunity for career development
⑤ a variety of volunteer activities for all personal interests

17 언급된 장소가 아닌 것은?

① animal shelter
② hospital
③ national park
④ daycare center
⑤ kindergarten

17 DICTATION

녹음된 내용을 들으면서 빈칸을 알맞게 채워 보세요.

01

W: Thank you all for coming! In a company as big as ours, we see many people come and go, so ______________________ that you all came to say farewell. You brought such wonderful gifts and food, thank you! Now, I understand that ______________________ we are expected to say something about our plans for retirement. But all of you know I'm joining the Red Cross ______________________. So, I'll just say this: I'll never forget these last six years. I may be closing one chapter of my life, but the next chapter will ______________________ ______________________. Thanks to all of you.

02

W: Chris, you're home! I didn't expect to see you until tomorrow.

M: Well, I wasn't tired, so I decided to ______________________ ______________________.

W: But you usually stay at a hotel. ______________________ ______________________?

M: If I had gotten tired, I would have stopped for a nap, but I was able to stay awake by eating nuts and chewing gum.

W: I guess ______________________ might be enough to keep you awake.

M: It worked well, and I also listened to the radio and tried not to turn the heat up very high.

W: Those are good tips, but I hope you aren't ______________________.

M: Don't worry. I know how dangerous it can be to drive while sleepy.

03

W: Now, John, you've got my cell phone number?

M: Yes, Ms. Bennett. And your husband's is on the kitchen counter?

W: Yes, ______________________ for the restaurant too?

M: Sure.

W: Um... ______________________, that won't be necessary.

M: Okay. Where are Tom and Nicky?

W: Their father is dressing them in their pajamas. Darling, hurry! We'll be late!

M: Are they going to bed already?

W: No! I told them they can watch a DVD, but they must go to bed ______________________.

M: Got it.

W: Help yourself to the cake and sandwiches ______________________ ______________________, won't you?

M: Thanks, Ms. Bennett. Have a good time!

04

W: Grimeville Police Department. How may I help you?

M: I think someone ______________________!

W: Okay, sir. Please describe the scene to me first.

M: The first thing I noticed is that the window was open. I think that's how they came in.

W: Okay. What else?

M: They broke my vase. Oh, why would they do that?

W: ______________________?

M: I had several trophies, and now my soccer trophy is gone and my star trophy is on the floor.

W: Okay. Did they take anything else?

M: I'm not sure. ______________________. Oh, they broke my guitar, too.

W: Alright. Any detail can be helpful.

M: I guess they also ______________________. It's on the floor now.

W: Alright, sir. Please tell me your address.

정답 및 해설 p.66

05

W: Honey! What are you doing at the moment?

M: ______________________________ ______________. Do you want to watch it with me?

W: I'd love to, but I've got things to do.

M: Anything I can help you with? ______________ ______________________?

W: Actually, the dishes are done. You know how much I ______________________________________?

M: Yeah, that big food waste bucket downstairs really stinks.

W: So, could you do that for me? ______________ ____________________ and buy some things for our dinner.

M: OK, see you soon. Anyway, where is the food waste?

W: In the yellow plastic bag near the back door.

06

M: Excuse me, ______________________________ to Wally's Land?

W: The next train leaves in 20 minutes. There's one ________________________________ until 2 in the afternoon during any national holiday.

M: Great. __________________________________?

W: It's $40 ____________________________.

M: And for children?

W: Children's tickets are 50% off the adult price.

M: Well, I need tickets for two adults and two children.

W: May I suggest buying our Wally's Land Family Ticket? The family ticket is good for a family of four to travel to and from Wally's Land.

M: ______________________________________?

W: Yes, it's 30% cheaper. It's our holiday gift to families.

M: Oh, that's great. I'll take one family pack, please.

07

M: Helen, you have a cat, right?

W: Yes, I have had one for years. Why?

M: I've been kind of lonely these days and I want to get a cat, but ______________________________.

W: There are several ways to get a cat. You could buy one in a shop or get one from someone who wants to ________________________. You could also adopt one from an animal shelter.

M: I think I'll ______________________________. It will feel good to take in an abandoned animal. Would you go there with me?

W: Of course. My friend works in a shelter and I'm sure he can help you.

M: Great. How about this Saturday?

W: Sounds good. Also, I can ____________________ ____.

M: Thanks a lot.

08

W: Hi, Ted. ________________________ to Dubai?

M: It was good. I had a great time with my uncle.

W: That's great. Did you see much of the city?

M: Sure. On the second day, we went to see the Burj Khalifa. It's ______________________________ in the world, at 829 meters.

W: I've heard about that. The project cost 1.5 billion dollars to complete.

M: It's truly an amazing structure. I heard the Dubai government decided to ____________________ ____.

W: In that case, I would say it's worth the money.

M: I agree. Having such a tall building definitely impresses visitors.

W: Right! And I think ________________________ ____________________________.

M: It sure did. Construction of the Burj Khalifa began in September of 2004, and __________________ ____________________ October of 2009.

W: I hope I get the chance to see it someday.

09

M: Welcome to the Springfield Aviation Museum. Did you know that the plane with ______________ ______________________ was nicknamed the Spruce Goose? It measured almost 100 meters from wing tip to wing tip, and weighed 200 tons. It needed ____________________________ to power it. This U.S. plane was designed _______________________ during the war. It was made of wood because wood is _________ ________________________ in wartime than metal. The plane was so difficult to build that it never really got used. It was flown one time only on November 2, 1947. Today, the Spruce Goose is ______________________________ in Long Beach, California.

10

W: Let's go see a movie at the Astor Cinema tomorrow. ______________________________ with the screening times. *Citizen Kane* is showing at 4:10.

M: Great! Some critics say it's _______________ _______________. Oh, no! I forgot. I'm having dinner at my grandmother's tomorrow. I have to be there by 6. Sorry.

W: Oh, well. How about one of the earlier movies?

M: Umm, I don't like gangster movies. What about a fantasy movie?

W: That's a good one, but ____________________ _________________.

M: Really? Wait! I can leave Grandma's place at 8:30. How about one of the late movies?

W: Sure, but _____________________________ before midnight. I have an early class the following day.

M: OK. Let's see this one. I'll have to hurry from Grandma's place to ______________________ _______________.

11

W: Nate, didn't you _________________________ last summer?

M: I did. I worked in the mayor's office.

W: ____________________________________?

12

M: I really love going to Ms. Carpenter's class. Don't you?

W: She's a great teacher. But I hate ______________ ________________________.

M: How would you prefer to _________________ ________________________?

13

W: What can I do for you today, Chris?

M: I'd like to drop out of my Calculus class and switch into Advanced Psychology.

W: Well, __________________________________ was yesterday.

M: I know, but I was very sick yesterday.

W: I'm sorry, but I don't think there is anything I can do for you.

M: __________________________ from a doctor?

W: That won't be good enough. Yesterday was _____ _______________________.

M: It's really important that __________________. I'm changing my major!

W: I'll tell you what, if _______________________ ____________________ today, then I'll change it for you.

14

M: Hi, Mom. I'm home.

W: Hi, Luke. How was soccer training this evening?

M: OK. We play Midlands High School on Saturday. It's the finals.

W: I know. ______________________________.

M: We're playing an away game though, and Midlands is ______________________________.

W: Don't worry. You'll have lots of supporters there. And I'm coming to watch you!

M: You know ______________________________ there with Dan and Chris and their mom?

W: Uh-huh.

M: Well, she can't go now. She has to work on Saturday. And ______________________________ on the coach's shuttle bus!

15

W: Angelina and her friends are going to see a movie together. She goes to the subway station to meet her friends. She is 45 minutes early, so she ______________________________ in the nearby department store. She only has enough money to pay for the movie and lunch. She goes up to the young fashion department. There's a 50% discount sale on winter coats, so she happily ______________________________. She loves one cream-colored coat in particular, though she ______________________________. When she tries it on and ______________________________, the sales assistant comes and asks, "How may I help you?" In this situation, what would Angelina most likely say to the sales assistant?

16-17

M: Volunteers make a big difference in the lives of others. Oftentimes, they work with the core ______________________________. But did you know that volunteering can do more than that? Research has shown that volunteering ______________________________. By enjoying time spent in service to others, you will feel a sense of meaning and appreciation, which can have a stress-reducing effect. Volunteer activities also get you moving and thinking at the same time. One study found that adults age 60 and over who volunteered received ______________________________. According to another research study, in general, volunteers are physically healthier than are non-volunteers. Older volunteers experience greater increases in life satisfaction and greater positive changes in their health. In addition, ______________________________. If you enjoy caring for animals, you can walk dogs for an animal shelter. ______________________________, you could volunteer at a hospital or a nursing home. If you like children, you can volunteer to help at a daycare center or kindergarten. Now, how about experiencing some of those yourself? Go volunteer today!

실전모의고사

18 PRACTICE TEST

01 다음을 듣고, 남자가 하는 말의 목적으로 가장 적절한 것을 고르시오.

① 작가의 강연 소식을 알리려고
② 초청 강사의 저서를 소개하려고
③ 강연회 일정 변경을 공지하려고
④ 작가에게 순회 강연을 제안하려고
⑤ 강연 관련 질문에 대해 응답하려고

02 대화를 듣고, 여자의 의견으로 가장 적절한 것을 고르시오.

① 적성에 맞는 직업을 찾기는 어렵지 않다.
② 직장 선택 시 회사 위치가 가장 중요하다.
③ 연봉이 높은 회사일수록 업무 강도가 높다.
④ 비슷한 성향의 룸메이트를 고르는 것이 좋다.
⑤ 주변 집세를 고려하여 직장을 선택해야 한다.

03 대화를 듣고, 두 사람의 관계를 가장 잘 나타낸 것을 고르시오.

① 기관사 – 정비사
② 기차 승무원 – 승객
③ 식당 종업원 – 손님
④ 비행기 승무원 – 기장
⑤ 여행 가이드 – 여행객

04 대화를 듣고, 그림에서 대화의 내용과 일치하지 않는 것을 고르시오.

05 대화를 듣고, 남자가 여자를 위해 할 일로 가장 적절한 것을 고르시오.

① 호텔 예약해주기
② 관광 명소 알려주기
③ 입장료 할인 쿠폰 제공하기
④ 호텔 웹사이트 주소를 메일로 보내주기
⑤ 유료 관광 안내 책자를 우편으로 발송하기

06 대화를 듣고, 여자가 지불할 금액을 고르시오. [3점]

① $100 ② $160 ③ $170
④ $180 ⑤ $200

07 대화를 듣고, 남자가 잠을 자지 못하는 이유를 고르시오.

① 배가 아파서
② 불면증이 있어서
③ 시험공부를 해야 해서
④ 연극 대사를 외워야 해서
⑤ 카페인을 너무 많이 섭취해서

08 대화를 듣고, 선풍기에 관해 언급되지 않은 것을 고르시오.

① 크기 ② 색상
③ 날개의 날 수 ④ 리모컨 기능
⑤ 절전 기능

09 Helping Hands에 관한 다음 내용을 듣고, 일치하지 않는 것을 고르시오.

① 주로 아프리카에서 활동한다.
② 참가자들의 주업무는 집 지어주기다.
③ 참가자들은 경비 대부분을 지원받는다.
④ 매년 참가자 중 절반 이상이 정규직에 지원한다.
⑤ 대학생도 참가할 수 있다.

10 다음 표를 보면서 대화를 듣고, 두 사람이 영화제를 관람할 날짜를 고르시오.

Independent Film Festival

Date	Film Genre	Place	Film Discussion
① September 4 (Wed)	Action	Big Culture Center	×
② September 5 (Thu)	Animation	Royal Theater	○
③ September 6 (Fri)	Romance	Royal Theater	×
④ September 7 (Sat)	Documentary	Royal Theater	○
⑤ September 8 (Sun)	Sci-fi	Big Culture Center	○

11 대화를 듣고, 여자의 마지막 말에 대한 남자의 응답으로 가장 적절한 것을 고르시오.

① It's only three blocks from here.
② The play will be performed there.
③ No, but my sister recommended it.
④ No, I don't care for Mongolian food.
⑤ I went to the theater twice last year.

12 대화를 듣고, 남자의 마지막 말에 대한 여자의 응답으로 가장 적절한 것을 고르시오.

① I'll let you know after I check.
② We will have to buy tickets in advance.
③ The exhibit will last for five more weeks.
④ Over twenty sculptures will be on display.
⑤ Her sculptures are worth thousands of dollars.

13 대화를 듣고, 여자의 마지막 말에 대한 남자의 응답으로 가장 적절한 것을 고르시오. [3점]

▶ Man : ____________________

① I'm so pleased to be able to help you.
② I believe you can do better next time.
③ Well, there's no use crying over spilled milk.
④ It takes practice to get used to live broadcasts.
⑤ I'll be standing beside the camera and I'll signal you.

14 대화를 듣고, 남자의 마지막 말에 대한 여자의 응답으로 가장 적절한 것을 고르시오. [3점]

▶ Woman : ____________________

① I recovered the data with your help.
② Then, could you come to my house?
③ Why don't you go to a computer lab?
④ Sorry, but I don't think I can help you.
⑤ It sounds difficult. I can't understand your instructions.

15 다음 상황 설명을 듣고, Amanda가 Billy에게 할 말로 가장 적절한 것을 고르시오.

▶ Amanda : ____________________

① Aren't you interested in your health?
② Running outdoors is better than in a gym.
③ Why don't you try running outside with me?
④ I'd be happy to join you on one of your runs.
⑤ Thanks for your offer, but I work overtime these days.

[16~17] 다음을 듣고, 물음에 답하시오.

16 여자가 하는 말의 주제로 가장 적절한 것은?

① reasons we need to exercise
② ways to improve our concentration
③ how light exercise affects our efficiency
④ various effects of meditation on the body
⑤ the most appropriate place for meditation

17 명상을 할 수 있는 장소로 언급되지 않은 것은?

① bedroom ② library ③ park
④ lounge ⑤ bus

18 DICTATION

녹음된 내용을 들으면서 빈칸을 알맞게 채워 보세요.

01

M: May I have your attention, please? I'm your principal, Mr. Baker. If you like reading, I'm sure you've heard of Nathan Jenkins. He is ________ ________________________________ of the year and has attracted attention with his first book, *The Sound of Your Mind*. Also, he is ______________ ____________________ to meet and communicate with his audience. Fortunately, he's chosen to speak at our school. He will lecture about his teenage years and ________________________ ________________, next Friday in our school auditorium. After the lecture, there will be a question-and-answer session, where you may ask anything you like. I hope many students ______________________________________.

02

W: Jason, I heard ____________________________ ______________. Is that true?

M: It is. One is Yescom, a software company, and the other is ComHealer, an anti-virus software company.

W: ____?

M: Yescom. The salaries are similar, but for me, the work is more interesting at Yescom.

W: Isn't Yescom ______________________________? You'll have to find a house, and rent is high these days.

M: I know. ________________________________ who's joining the company at the same time. We can help each other.

W: I guess we're different. I'd choose ComHealer.

M: How come?

W: They are similar companies, so I think location is the most important factor.

M: What if Yescom offered a higher salary?

W: ____ ____________________.

M: I understand.

03

M: Excuse me, ma'am. May I see your ticket, please?

W: Of course. I have it in my phone. Electronic tickets are ____ paper ones.

M: Aren't they? Alright. Thank you for your cooperation.

W: Oh, wait. ________________________________ to Busan?

M: We'll arrive in about two hours.

W: I see. Will the food cart be coming anytime soon? I'm a bit hungry.

M: No, but ________________________________. It is in the fourth car.

W: Oh, I didn't know that. I think I'll visit it now.

M: Is there ________________________________?

W: I think everything's fine. Thank you.

M: Great. Enjoy the rest of your trip and ____________ ____.

04

W: How long before class begins?

M: I'll check. Hey, where's the clock?

W: I put it above the left side of the blackboard so ____.

M: Oh, I see. We still have plenty of time.

W: Well, everything looks nice, ________________ ________________ on the blackboard.

M: Yes, that was a good idea.

W: ____ the heart-shaped frame with "Happy Teacher's Day!" written inside of it in the middle of the board?

M: You did a great job! And I'm sure the flowers we ordered will ____________________________ ________________________.

W: You reminded Min-ji ____________________ ______________________________, right?

M: Of course. I also put our teacher's rectangular desk in front of the blackboard for the party.

W: Great. I can't wait for the party.

05

M: Hello, Golden Travel Agency. How may I help you?

W: I'm planning a trip to Canada next month.

M: I see. ________________________________ that you wish to visit?

W: Yes. I want to visit Niagara Falls, and I'd like to stay nearby.

M: In that case, the Maple Leaf Hotel is the perfect place for you. It is offering 20 percent discounts ________________________________.

W: Oh, that sounds good. But I'd like to discuss it with my husband ________________________.

M: Then, I'd be happy to send a free brochure to you by mail or give you the website of the hotel.

W: The website of the hotel would be helpful.

M: Great. Then ________________________.

W: Thanks for your help.

06

M: Honey, look! These are exactly the same chairs we saw at the department store!

W: Oh, they are! You said they would ____________ ________________________.

M: Yes. They were 100 dollars each at the department store, but they're 20 percent cheaper here.

W: ____________________! How about buying them here?

M: That would be great. How many should we buy?

W: Well, I think four will be too many. How about two?

M: Two will be enough. Wait, the sign says _________ ________________________.

W: Really? How much is it?

M: It's 10 dollars within 20 kilometers from here and 20 dollars in other areas.

W: Our house is ________________________. It will be less than 5 kilometers.

M: Great. Let's buy them here.

W: Okay. I'll ________________________.

07

W: Justin, are you still awake?

M: Yes, Mom. Why?

W: I'm worried about you. It's 2 a.m. ____________ ________________________ for tomorrow's math test?

M: Yes. Actually, the test was delayed until next week.

W: Then are you still memorizing your lines for the school play?

M: No, I already did that. ________________ __________ and can't go to bed.

W: Hmm.... You aren't normally this energetic late at night.

M: Well, I guess I drank too much coffee and too many energy drinks.

W: Then ________________________________! What were you thinking?

M: Well, I had some important assignments for class. ________________________________.

W: I understand, but too much caffeine can cause ________________________________.

M: I promise I'll be more careful in the future.

08

W: Hello. Are you looking for something?

M: Yes. I'd like to buy an electric fan before summer starts.

W: Let's see. First, ________________________. We have 35-, 40-, and 50- centimeter fans.

M: Forty centimeters sounds appropriate.

W: Good. Do you have a specific color in mind?

M: ________________________________?

W: We have black, white, and blue right now.

M: Hmm.... ____________. Also, I wonder about the difference between 3- blade and 4-blade fans.

W: More blades offer more cooling power.

M: Oh, I didn't know that. And ______________ ________________________.

W: Okay. The ones with this mark will save on power.

M: Sounds good. Thanks for your help.

09

W: If you are ______________________________, consider volunteering for Helping Hands. Helping Hands is an NGO that does its work primarily in Africa. As a volunteer, you will have many jobs, but most of your time will be spent ______________ ______________________. There is no need to worry about money, because Helping Hands pays for most of its volunteers' expenses. And it's such a rewarding experience that each year around 25 percent of its volunteers ________________ ______________________. Unlike some NGOs, Helping Hands welcomes university students. So, if you are thinking of ________________ ______________________, Helping Hands is the ideal choice for you.

10

M: Mary, you remember we planned to visit an independent film festival this week, right?

W: Of course. I saved the schedule on my phone. Take a look.

M: Wow, there's a lot to see. ____________________ ____________________?

W: Actually, I've got an important meeting with a client on Wednesday.

M: No problem. We can choose another day. So, how about this one? I love science fiction.

W: I know you do, but the Big Culture Center is ____ ______________________________.

M: That's true. Hmm.

W: Let's go on Thursday. It's at the Royal Theater.

M: I think those films are for kids. How about going on Friday?

W: I do like romantic movies, but I think __________ ________________________ a conversation.

M: That would be fun. Okay, ____________________ ____________.

W: Great.

11

W: You know, ______________________________ ____________________ before the play.

M: Let's go to the Mongolian place beside the theater. It's the best in the city.

W: Wow, it sounds like ____________________________ ____________________.

12

M: Did you hear that the sculptures of Sarah Milburn are on display?

W: I didn't know __________________________. Why don't we go see it this weekend?

M: Sounds great! Do you know __________________ ______________________?

13

M: How are you feeling, Ms. Edwards?

W: A little nervous, but I'm ____________________ ______________________________.

M: I'm sure you'll do well, but I'll just check a few things before we begin, ____________________ ____________________.

W: Oh, alright. Can you hear me clearly?

M: Yes, it's working perfectly. Now, when we begin recording, please remember to face camera number two.

W: It's that one on the left, correct?

M: Right. When this red light comes on, __________ ____________________.

W: There's a lot to remember. I'm starting to ______ ______________________________.

M: There's no need to be nervous. We're going to do a rehearsal first, so you'll have time to get comfortable.

W: ______________________________________ when we're on air?

14

M: Hello?

W: Hi, Chris. It's Lindsey.

M: Oh. Hi, Lindsey. What's up?

W: Well, I know you're good with computers, so I'm hoping you can help me. ____________________ ____________________.

M: I'll try. What's the problem?

W: I was working on an assignment on my laptop when, all of a sudden, ______________________ ______________.

M: Sounds serious. Were you able to reboot?

W: Yes, but now it won't connect to the Internet. ____ ___________________. It's due tomorrow! Can anything be done?

M: Sure. I know a few tricks for recovering lost data.

W: I was hoping you'd say that! So, what do I do?

M: Oh.... Well, ______________________________. I think I'd have to see the laptop.

15

M: Amanda is on her way to a cafe to meet her friend Billy. When she arrives, Billy mentions that Amanda has seemed especially positive and energetic recently. Amanda tells him that _______ ____________________________ every day after work. Billy looks interested and asks whether ______________________________________. So, Amanda explains about __________________ ________________________ in the fresh air and seeing a variety of scenery. While Amanda talks, she notices Billy becoming _________________ ____________________________. Since Amanda has been wanting a workout partner for some time, she decides to find out if Billy ______________ __________________________. In this situation, what would Amanda most likely say to Billy?

16-17

W: How many times have you tried to focus on a task, ___________________________________ ________________? Just like muscles, the mind needs training ___________________________ _________________. So, I'd like to discuss some useful tips for when we're distracted. The next time you lose focus, ________________________ __________________. These are accomplished by closing your eyes and rolling your eyeballs clockwise and counterclockwise. Then try counting backwards from 100 by multiples of 2. And if that's not helping, take a short walk. Research has shown that walking helps ____.

Now, if you're truly serious about improving your mind, consider meditation. Start by meditating in your bedroom, or _________________________ _______________, for a few minutes every day. After that, you can try meditating in other quiet places, such as libraries. Meditating in a park can also be a wonderful experience. When you have truly mastered your technique, you will even be able to meditate in noisy places, like buses. It's an amazing way ___________________________ what is going on in the present.

실전모의고사

19 PRACTICE TEST

01 다음을 듣고, 여자가 하는 말의 목적으로 가장 적절한 것을 고르시오.

① 수업에 방해가 된 것을 사과하려고
② 학교 축제일의 날짜 변경을 알리려고
③ 수업 종이 울린 후 하교하도록 지도하려고
④ 축제 준비에 관한 새로운 방침을 알리려고
⑤ 학생들이 학교 축제에 참여하도록 독려하려고

02 대화를 듣고, 남자의 의견으로 가장 적절한 것을 고르시오.

① 에너지를 절약하는 건축 설계 방식을 고수해야 한다.
② 전통적인 건축 방식이 건축 비용을 아낄 수 있다.
③ 새집증후군 예방을 위해 환기가 중요하다.
④ 건축 시 친환경적인 재료 사용을 고려해야 한다.
⑤ 단열재를 고를 때에는 환경을 먼저 생각해야 한다.

03 대화를 듣고, 두 사람의 관계를 가장 잘 나타낸 것을 고르시오.

① 환자 – 의사
② 팬 – 운동선수
③ 고객 – 운동용품 영업사원
④ 옷 가게 주인 – 옷 가게 점원
⑤ 헬스클럽 회원 – 헬스클럽 트레이너

04 대화를 듣고, 그림에서 대화의 내용과 일치하지 않는 것을 고르시오.

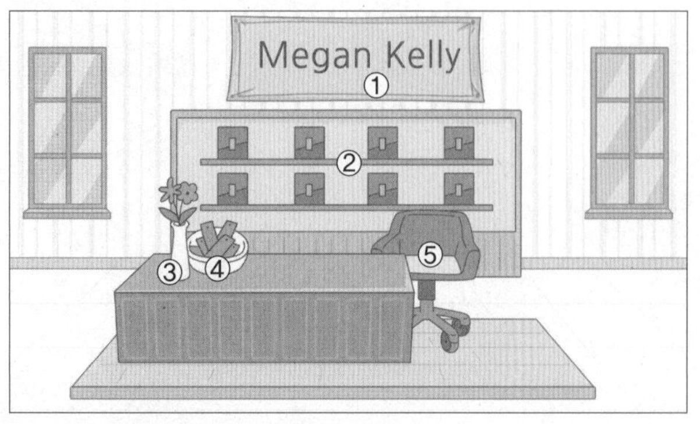

05 대화를 듣고, 남자가 여자에게 부탁한 일로 가장 적절한 것을 고르시오.

① 퇴원할 날짜를 알아봐 주기
② 남자가 사용할 목발을 구해 주기
③ 남자의 상태를 의사에게 확인하기
④ 휴대전화 배터리를 집에서 찾아보기
⑤ 휴대전화 배터리 충전기를 가져오기

06 대화를 듣고, 여자가 선글라스를 구입하며 지불한 금액을 고르시오. [3점]

① $120 ② $160 ③ $200
④ $240 ⑤ $400

07 대화를 듣고, 남자가 인도로 여행가는 이유를 고르시오.

① 여행 경비가 적게 들어서
② 동료가 인도 여행을 추천해서
③ 새로운 문화를 경험할 수 있어서
④ 인도에 사는 친구를 방문하기 위해서
⑤ 아름다운 풍경과 유적지가 많이 있어서

08 다음을 듣고, Pamukkale에 관해 언급되지 않은 것을 고르시오.

① 이름의 의미 ② 온천의 개수
③ 형성 과정 ④ 온천의 효능
⑤ 구역 내 금지 행위

09 부부간의 말다툼에 관한 다음 내용을 듣고, 일치하지 않는 것을 고르시오.

① 말다툼하는 부부는 더 오래 사는 경향이 있다.
② 말다툼하지 않는 부부는 5~10년 정도 수명이 더 짧다.
③ 분노를 억누르면 건강 문제를 야기할 수도 있다.
④ 최근 연구 결과는 이전의 연구 결과와 완전히 반대된다.
⑤ 감정 표현은 자신이 삶을 통제하고 있다는 느낌을 준다.

10 다음 표를 보면서 대화를 듣고, 두 사람이 주문할 실험실 가운을 고르시오.

Labwear.com: Lab Coats Online				
Model	Price	Length (inches)	Fabric	Free Logo Embroidery
① A	$19	31	Polycotton	×
② B	$22	40	Polycotton	×
③ C	$24	41	Polycotton	○
④ D	$24	37	100% Cotton	○
⑤ E	$27	32	100% Cotton	○

11 대화를 듣고, 남자의 마지막 말에 대한 여자의 응답으로 가장 적절한 것을 고르시오.

① No. I would move if I could.
② Yes, it's much too noisy here.
③ Of course. I'm moving nearby also.
④ No, our neighbors are nice and friendly.
⑤ Yes, I had to walk twenty minutes to the bus stop!

12 대화를 듣고, 여자의 마지막 말에 대한 남자의 응답으로 가장 적절한 것을 고르시오.

① I do, so never you mind.
② It's really no trouble at all.
③ We can finish it tomorrow.
④ We can do better next time.
⑤ Let's take a break for a while.

13 대화를 듣고, 남자의 마지막 말에 대한 여자의 응답으로 가장 적절한 것을 고르시오. [3점]

▶ Woman : ____________________

① We aren't very close at all.
② I'm close to finishing the game.
③ Thanks for closing the cupboards.
④ I think your clothes fit really well.
⑤ Harry, put your clothes in the closet first.

14 대화를 듣고, 여자의 마지막 말에 대한 남자의 응답으로 가장 적절한 것을 고르시오. [3점]

▶ Man : ____________________

① Yes, those names are too modern for you.
② Yes, we use Jacob's nickname, Jake, all the time.
③ I agree. It's a bad idea to follow changing trends.
④ Oh, I really like your choice of name for the baby.
⑤ They are getting popular again, so they sound modern.

15 다음 상황 설명을 듣고, Ben의 어머니가 Ben에게 할 말로 가장 적절한 것을 고르시오.

▶ Ben's Mom : ____________________

① Right. The root of all evil is money.
② You shouldn't run after money all the time.
③ Don't worry. Our family has money to burn.
④ You should know money doesn't grow on trees.
⑤ Never mind. A bad workman always blames his tools.

[16~17] 다음을 듣고, 물음에 답하시오.

16 남자가 하는 말의 주제로 가장 적절한 것은?

① educational benefits of family dinners
② the importance of healthy eating habits
③ ways of improving family relationships
④ family meals as a bonding time for the family
⑤ the importance of making family dinners enjoyable

17 언급된 과목이 아닌 것은?

① sociology ② science
③ history ④ math
⑤ literature

19 DICTATION

녹음된 내용을 들으면서 빈칸을 알맞게 채워 보세요.

01

W: Your attention, please. ______________________ ________________. Between classes and during lunchtime today, I noticed that different groups of students were practicing dances and songs. They were also practicing other material that ________ ______________________________ next week. Everywhere in the school it was too noisy. And the teachers told me that when classes began, the students were not focusing on their lessons. As a result, ______________________________ ______________ for the festival until the school day has finished at 3:30. ____________________ ________________________ will automatically be given an after-school detention for three days.

02

M: I think we should use stone for the walls of our new house.

W: That might look really nice. Where did you get the idea?

M: I was watching a show about construction and they said that ________________________________.

W: Is that because it's a natural material?

M: Yes, and it's very good at maintaining its temperature. Homes made of stone __________ ________________________________.

W: Okay, and how about using some bamboo for the floors?

M: I was going to suggest that, too. Bamboo grows more quickly than most trees, which means its use ______________________________________.

W: Great. What other materials could we include in our house?

M: We could consider using straw and earth as ______ ____________________________ to save energy.

W: I'm interested in all of those options.

03

M: In university my waist was 30 inches, and ________ ____________________________.

W: We all ______________________________________.

M: I really want to be slim again.

W: I'll help you ______________________________.

M: Great. My doctor warned me to lose 10 kilograms or I'd develop health problems.

W: 10 kilograms?

M: Yes.

W: Exercising will help, but I can also give you some advice on your eating habits.

M: Great. Where should we start?

W: ______________________________________. Let's go over to the stationary bikes.

M: Do you want to ____________________________?

W: That's right. I want to design a program that's appropriate for your current fitness level.

04

M: Sandra, have you finished the preparations for the Megan Kelly book signing event?

W: Yes, I'm all finished! ______________________ ______________________ and sent you a photo.

M: Hold on, let me check. Oh, you did a good job. You set a stage in front of a bookcase.

W: Yes, I hung up the banner that says the author's name, "Megan Kelly," above the bookcase.

M: Make sure you have the correct spelling of her name. It's ________________________________ ________________ on the bookshelves.

W: What do you think about the table decoration? I placed a flower vase on the left side of the table.

M: That's a great idea. Flowers __________________ ________________________. By the way, what is the basket next to the flower vase for?

W: Oh, I put some bookmarks there. They're gifts for the participants.

M: Good. Well, we normally provide a movable chair with wheels for the author. ______________________________ this time?

W: It's because the author asked. She said she wants a chair with no wheels.

M: You really thought of everything! Thanks for all your help.

05

M: Hello.

W: Hi, honey. How are you doing this afternoon?

M: ______________________________.

W: Well, the doctor did say it'd be a few days before you could go home.

M: ______________________________ this morning.

W: Won't you need crutches for a few weeks?

M: Yes, I will.

W: I'll look for some this afternoon.

M: You don't need to. Dylan is going to lend me the crutches ______________________________ last year.

W: OK. Do you want me to bring today's newspaper?

M: It's OK. ______________________________. I normally keep my phone charger in my bag, but now I can't find it.

W: You've lost it.

M: Maybe. Could you bring me another one?

W: Sure. I'll be right there.

06

W: Blake, look at my new Gangster Shades sunglasses.

M: Gangster Shades sunglasses! ______________________________.

W: Well, AM Department Store sells them for $400.

M: $400! Did you pay all that money?

W: I didn't buy them at AM Department Store. I bought them at a second-hand shop that ______________________________ brand-name luxury items.

M: Shopping in second-hand shops. Wow! You're really changing.

W: Well, ______________________________, but they still look brand new.

M: They do look good. And the price?

W: They were 60% less than the price the department store ______________________________.

M: That means you saved more than $200. Good for you.

07

W: Ted, are you going to take any vacations this summer?

M: ______________________________, I'm planning to spend two weeks in India in August.

W: You're going to have such a good time. I went two years ago and the scenery and culture were both amazing!

M: Really? I never knew you went to India.

W: I did, and I visited so many great places. If you want, ______________________________.

M: Thanks, but I'll be ______________________________ who lives there. I'm sure he'll be able to ______________________________.

W: That will be nice. You haven't seen each other for a long time?

M: Not since he got a job there three years ago. ______________________________.

W: Good for you. India is a wonderful place to visit, and very affordable, too.

08

W: Pamukkale is a natural wonder in southwestern Turkey. ________________________ "Cotton Castle," and when you see it, you will understand why. Pamukkale is a collection of seventeen hot springs on top of a small hill. Over time, the calcium from the surrounding rock ________________________ and hardened, forming small pools. These pools sit at various levels, each a few meters above or below its neighbor. When approached from below, Pamukkale does indeed ________________________. In the past, Pamukkale was not officially protected, but now the area ________________________. People are allowed to bathe in some of the pools but are not allowed to wear shoes as these may ________________________.

09

M: Do you think arguing is good for your health? Maybe your first reaction is "No!" Well, a recent study revealed that ________________________. The main finding is that partners who try not to argue die 5 to 10 years earlier than those who argue strongly. Not expressing your anger ________________________, which can cause health problems. The researchers say ________________________ with other research which shows that expressing your feelings is good for you. It makes people feel like they are ________________________. People who don't express themselves can ________________________.

10

M: Sophia, I'm looking at lab coats online. Could you help me choose?

W: Sure. First, what's the laboratory's budget for them?

M: We ________________________ $25 per coat.

W: I see. How about the length?

M: Long coats are ________________________ accidental spills and drops, so I think the length should be more than 36 inches.

W: Okay. What do you want them to be made of? 100% cotton or polycotton?

M: What do you think about that?

W: think polycotton coats are ________________________.

M: I agree. Now it looks like we have two choices left. It'd be better to ________________________.

W: It'd saved money, but this one includes free logo embroidery and I think that's ________________________ $2.

M: You're right. Let's go with this, then.

11

M: I think I'm going to move into an apartment near here.

W: Really? ________________________, and the rent is really high.

M: So you don't like ________________________, do you?

12

W: I'm so tired. It seems like we are never going to finish this report.

M: Actually, ________________________. Just go home and I can finish it myself.

W: Are you sure ________________________?

13

W: Harry, ________________________! I can't understand why your coat is on the floor.

M: I just don't like cleaning up my room. It's not fun.

W: Well, you're old enough ________________________.

M: I'm sorry, Mom. ________________________.

W: I want you to pick up all your clothes right now and put them in the closet.

M: OK. In a minute, ________________________.

W: Turn the computer off! Right now!

M: OK, OK.

W: And why do you always ________________________?

M: I don't know.

W: Well, put your clothes away, and then close the closet. You always leave the kitchen cupboards open, too.

M: I guess it's just a bad habit. Look, I'm closing the closet now.

14

W: I need a name for my new baby.

M: I think you should call your baby Abraham.

W: But Abraham is ______________________________ ______________.

M: Well, you won't have to use his full first name all the time. You could call him Abe.

W: Hmm... Abe. ______________________________ ______________.

M: But last year when your mother and I were choosing Jacob ______________________________, we looked at a list of popular baby names.

W: ____?

M: Well, for boys, names like Jacob, Matthew, Joshua and Abraham were high on the list. I like these names.

W: I'm really not sure. Those names seem too traditional.

15

W: Whenever Ben gets his allowance, ____________ ____________________________. His mom wants to teach him to save some money, but she finds it really difficult to do so. Last week, Ben saw ______________________________________. He asked his mom to buy it. Even though it was quite expensive, Ben's mom ____________________. She thought it might help him. Then a day later, Ben's bike was stolen. ______________________ ______________________ a new bike, but also he asked her to buy one of the most expensive models. She was not happy. What Ben wanted ____________________________________. In this situation, what would Ben's mom most likely say to Ben?

16-17

M: When's the last time you sat down with your children together for dinner? During the day your children are learning about the world from many sources, often without parental filters or input. Perhaps the only opportunity of the day to talk with each other is at the dinner table. Family meals allow conversations to take place. ____________________ ______________________ the body, they benefit the mind too. A national poll of high school seniors showed that students who ate more often with their families ______________________________ sociology and science than those that did less often. Another study reports that teens who have five to seven family dinners per week compared to ____________________________________ three received mostly As and Bs in school. In addition, researchers at the University of Illinois found that children ages 7 to 11 that spent a large amount of time eating meals with their families ___________ __________________ school achievement tests of history and literature. Preschoolers that ate more often with their family did better in language skills than those who didn't as often; it is believed that these meal times give preschoolers more opportunity to hear and have conversations with their parents. Giving your kids ______________ ____________________________________ is a great excuse for having more family meals together.

PRACTICE TEST

01 다음을 듣고, 남자가 하는 말의 목적으로 가장 적절한 것을 고르시오.

① 무료 동화 사이트를 소개하려고
② 동화 번역 봉사자를 모집하려고
③ 이민자 자녀 공부방을 안내하려고
④ 다국어 번역 프로그램을 판매하려고
⑤ 모국어 교육의 중요성을 강조하려고

02 대화를 듣고, 여자의 의견으로 가장 적절한 것을 고르시오.

① 목표가 같으면 그룹을 이루어 활동하는 것이 좋다.
② 성공한 사람들의 생활 습관을 본받을 필요가 있다.
③ 과학적으로 검증된 이론만 실생활에 적용해야 한다.
④ 성공하기 위해서는 일정을 효율적으로 관리해야 한다.
⑤ 능률을 높이려면 자신의 생체 리듬을 잘 파악해야 한다.

03 대화를 듣고, 두 사람의 관계를 가장 잘 나타낸 것을 고르시오.

① 감독 – 운동선수
② 정신과 의사 – 환자
③ 이민국 관리 – 이민자
④ 신문 기자 – 뉴스 앵커
⑤ 스포츠 기자 – 운동선수

04 대화를 듣고, 그림에서 대화의 내용과 일치하지 않는 것을 고르시오.

05 대화를 듣고, 남자가 할 일로 가장 적절한 것을 고르시오.

① 컴퓨터 챙기기
② 피자 주문하기
③ 이메일 확인하기
④ 옷 챙기는 것 도와주기
⑤ 인터넷 서비스 취소하기

06 대화를 듣고, 남자가 지불할 금액을 고르시오.

① $40 ② $60 ③ $70
④ $80 ⑤ $100

07 대화를 듣고, 여자가 주말에 영화를 보지 못한 이유를 고르시오.

① 표가 매진돼서
② 상영이 종료돼서
③ 영화관이 공사 중이어서
④ 친구가 상영 시간에 늦어서
⑤ 영화보다 미술 전시회를 보고 싶어서

08 대화를 듣고, 국립 박물관(National Museum)에 관해 언급되지 않은 것을 고르시오.

① 위치 ② 입장료
③ 예약 필요 여부 ④ 관람 가능 시간
⑤ 특별 전시 내용

09 다음 방송 내용을 듣고, 일치하지 않는 것을 고르시오.

① 학생 모두가 내일 조회에 참석하도록 요청되었다.
② 조회는 배치 고사에 대한 정보를 주기 위한 것이다.
③ 10월 배치 고사로 학생들이 들을 수업이 결정된다.
④ 출판사 관계자들이 조회에 참석할 예정이다.
⑤ 무료 공부 모임은 이번 주 금요일부터 시작된다.

10 다음 자료를 보면서 대화를 듣고, 남자가 구입할 컴퓨터를 고르시오.

Back to School Computer Sale
(All computers feature a CD-ROM drive)
*The bonus gift is an inkjet printer.

Name	RAM	EX2 Graphics Card	Price	Bonus Gift
① M-550	8 GB		$299	
② D-425	8 GB	✓	$499	
③ L-670	32 GB		$799	✓
④ Pi-1000	16 GB	✓	$899	✓
⑤ XL-2000	32 GB	✓	$1,199	✓

11 대화를 듣고, 남자의 마지막 말에 대한 여자의 응답으로 가장 적절한 것을 고르시오.

① I only have two meals a day.
② You can bring your own food.
③ Saturdays are not good for me.
④ Pasta and salad are my favorites.
⑤ I think it's better to be a vegetarian.

12 대화를 듣고, 여자의 마지막 말에 대한 남자의 응답으로 가장 적절한 것을 고르시오.

① No, traveling was too expensive.
② Job opportunities are quite scarce here.
③ I'll focus on studying during the semester.
④ I chose the job for its work environment.
⑤ Yes, but I spent it all on a new computer.

13 대화를 듣고, 남자의 마지막 말에 대한 여자의 응답으로 가장 적절한 것을 고르시오. [3점]

▶ Woman : ____________________

① You can check them out on your library card.
② Just put them in your backpack. You can pay later.
③ You should use the Internet to download the books.
④ Please don't photocopy the books you can't check out.
⑤ No, it's not possible. I cannot make an exception just for you.

14 대화를 듣고, 여자의 마지막 말에 대한 남자의 응답으로 가장 적절한 것을 고르시오. [3점]

▶ Man : ____________________

① When the weather is fair, the flying is easy.
② The planes are taking off in the scheduled order.
③ I will check on the status of your flight right now.
④ The pilot is doing his best to get the direction right.
⑤ I will schedule a new bus ticket for you, if you would like.

15 다음 상황 설명을 듣고, Michelle이 Jody에게 할 말로 가장 적절한 것을 고르시오. [3점]

▶ Michelle : ____________________

① As your best friend, I'll cover for you anytime.
② As your supervisor, I must insist you be on time.
③ You're lucky that we're friends. You should be thankful.
④ Customer service will suffer if you don't work this week.
⑤ I'm telling your supervisor the next time you're late.

[16~17] 다음을 듣고, 물음에 답하시오.

16 여자가 하는 말의 주제로 가장 적절한 것은?

① how to make healthy lifestyle decisions
② the most efficient way to clean your home
③ everyday activities that function as workouts
④ reasons to avoid going to the gym to exercise
⑤ ways to burn calories while doing your shopping

17 언급된 집안일이 아닌 것은?

① vacuuming ② doing dishes
③ cooking ④ mopping
⑤ ironing

20 **DICTATION**

녹음된 내용을 들으면서 빈칸을 알맞게 채워 보세요.

01

M: Many families ______________________________ ______________________________. And many children of immigrant families are growing up without knowledge of their family heritage and first language. They ______________________ ______________________ to the books of their culture, as well as the majority culture, regardless of where they live. That's why our organization translates children's stories into various languages. We depend upon a network of individuals who ______________________________________. If you want to help children, become a volunteer translator. You don't need to give up a great deal of your time to do it. Please sign up today! Fill out and ______________________________________.

02

M: Jenny! Since we both have interviews soon, ______ ______________________________?

W: Great idea! Can we start tomorrow, around 8 a.m.?

M: Eight in the morning is too early. I can't wake up. How about in the evening, after class?

W: Maybe you should find someone else. I'm energetic in the mornings, but I can't concentrate later in the day.

M: ______________________________________. I can't get anything done before noon.

W: ______________________________________ ________________, like Mr. Watson talked about in science class.

M: I remember. Our biological clocks determine when we are sleepy and alert.

W: Right. He said successful people ______________ ______________________________ and told us to think about this when planning our schedules.

M: You're right, and I see your point.

W: I think you can find someone else like you.

M: Okay, I will.

03

W: Can you tell our audience why you decided to play for the English team?

M: ______________________________________ in many different ways.

W: In what ways are you now being challenged?

M: For one thing, the size of the league is much larger, so ______________________________________.

W: What else is challenging?

M: There is also ______________________________. Living in England like an Englishman — it's not so easy for me as a Korean.

W: I imagine there are some differences. __________ ______________________________ about Korea?

M: Umm... I think the thing I miss most is the food. You know I love spicy food.

W: Thank you for your time. That's all the time we have. See you tomorrow!

04

M: Kent's Gym. How may I help you?

W: Hi. ______________________________________ that says "New Kent Gym Center" at the top, and I have a few questions.

M: Certainly. Right now, all new members are getting a 30% discount.

W: Yes, I can see that. What I'd really like to know about are your stationary bikes, ______________ ______________________ in your advertisement.

M: They are all brand new and available to use in our fitness center. A basic membership also includes screen golf as you can see.

W: I'm more interested in yoga classes, but they aren't shown in the flyer. ________________________ ________________?

M: Yoga classes were offered until last month, but they ______________________________________ screen golf. However, membership does include swimming classes, which are pictured on your flyer.

W: Okay. Thank you.

정답 및 해설 p.78

05

M: I'm glad the real estate agent was able to find a new place that was ______________________________ this place.

W: Yeah. I'm so excited to be moving, too. But ______ ______________________________ tonight.

M: Oh, relax. The movers are coming tomorrow morning, and it's their job to _______________ _______________. Everything, that is, except my computer. I'll do it myself. It's too valuable.

W: Yeah. I'd rather pack my clothes myself, too.

M: Well, I'm going to check my email.

W: You can't! I canceled the cable and Internet service today. We can't use the Internet until we have Internet service available in our new house.

M: OK. Then what are you cooking for dinner? ______ ____________.

W: Cooking? There is stuff everywhere. I cannot cook. We're having pizza tonight.

M: OK. ______________________________.

06

W: Welcome to Mt. Baekdu Sauna. Los Angeles' finest Korean-style sauna.

M: ______________________________?

W: It's $5 for adults, and to enter the family sauna area it's $2 extra.

M: We won't be going to the family sauna. Oh, I see you sell books of tickets.

W: Yes, for $40 you get a book of 10 tickets. You can get a 20% discount ______________________ _______________.

M: We've just moved here. Maybe I should _______ _______________________. We'll probably be coming here every weekend.

W: In that case, you can also buy 20 tickets. And the discount is 30%.

M: Sounds good. I'll take the book of 20 tickets. ______________________________.

W: Thank you. Just a second.

07

W: Good morning, Robert. Did you have a good weekend?

M: Yeah, I took my son to a baseball game. How about you? Did you see that movie you were talking about?

W: No. I planned to go with my friend, but ________ _________________________.

M: Why? Were the tickets sold out?

W: Well, my friend's house is on the other side of town, so she decided to meet me at the theater. But she ______________________________.

M: So you missed the opening?

W: Right. We didn't want to start in the middle, so we ______________________________ instead.

M: I guess there is always next weekend.

W: Actually, I'm going by myself tonight. _________ ______________________________.

08

W: National Museum. How may I help you?

M: Hi, I'd like to bring my class to visit your museum. ______________________________?

W: Admission is free, but there is an extra $5 charge for certain exhibits.

M: All right. I have 23 students. Should I __________ _________________________?

W: Reservations are only required for groups larger than 30.

M: Okay. And you're open from 9 a.m. to 6 p.m. every day, right?

W: Yes, except for Wednesdays and Saturdays, when we close at 9 p.m.

M: Oh, ______________________________ about your children's museum.

W: We have a special exhibit on traditional Korean instruments as well as musical performances _____ ______________________________.

M: Great. Thanks so much.

09

W: Attention everyone. Tomorrow at 8:15 a.m., all students ________________________ ________________ in the gymnasium. We will be presenting information about the upcoming placement tests in October. These tests will ____ ________________________ next year. There will also be representatives from several test prep companies and study guide publishers here. They are going to give you information regarding their services and products. We will also ________________ ________________ free study sessions at the school. ________________________ ________ will be required to attend a special session on Friday after school.

10

M: I can't wait to start college next year!

W: That's why we're getting you a computer today.

M: ________________________! I'm sure we'll find something here. Look at this leaflet.

W: Look, they have one for only $299.

M: But, Mom, the M-550 is a dinosaur! It ________ ________________________.

W: Well, you have to decide what is most important. We aren't going to spend more than $1,000 on a computer and printer.

M: ________________________________, I will need the top graphics card.

W: I don't know much about computers, but graphics cards use a lot of RAM, right?

M: Yeah, so I don't think the D-425 will have enough. Now ________________________ ____________.

W: It looks like you're getting a new computer after all.

M: And don't forget the free printer!

11

M: ________________________________ on Saturday. Want to come?

W: Well, I don't eat meat, so I think I'll pass.

M: I'll have other things too. ________________ ________________?

12

W: Kevin, it's good to see you again. Did you go anywhere during the summer?

M: No, ________________________ and worked during the vacation.

W: Good for you. Did you ________________ ________________?

13

M: I'd like to check out these four books, please.

W: I'll need your student ID, please.

M: Here you go.

W: Oh, I'm sorry. It looks like you already ________ ________________________, and three are overdue.

M: Are you saying I can't check these books out?

W: I'm afraid not. At least until you return the overdue books and ________________________.

M: But I have a paper due tomorrow and I need all of the books.

W: ________________________________. I can't make the computer do anything else.

M: What if I pay my fine now and ____________ ________________________?

14

W: Excuse me, can you tell me why the plane hasn't taken off yet?

M: ________________________________ because of the heavy rains.

W: We have been sitting ______________________ for an hour.

M: Yes, ma'am. I just spoke to the pilot and he said it may be another 30 minutes.

W: That is ridiculous! It isn't even raining anymore.

M: It isn't raining at the airport, but ______________ ______________________, which is the direction we need to fly.

W: Can't we go over or around the storm?

M: We can do that as soon as ____________________ ______________________.

W: I don't think ____________ that we should wait for others to take off before us.

15

M: Michelle is Jody's supervisor at the coffee shop they work at, but she is also his friend. Jody __________ ________________________ every day for two weeks. At first he made excuses to Michelle and ________________________________, but for the last few days, he didn't say anything, not even "I'm sorry." Michelle ________________________ ____________________ Jody when he is late and, therefore, there haven't been any big problems with customers. However, she feels that as his supervisor she must say something. She thinks that Jody is abusing their friendship and __________ ____________________________ of Michelle's position at work. In this situation, what would Michelle most likely say to Jody?

16-17

W: Good morning, everyone. Recently, we've talked a lot about ______________________________. Today, we'll discuss a few everyday ways to burn calories that don't require going to the gym. For example, as many as 250 calories can be burned when shopping for groceries. Simple decisions like taking the stairs instead of an elevator can also ____________________________________ your health. House chores are another opportunity for exercise. For instance, vacuuming for half an hour burns around 100 calories. If you have a large family, even ______________________________. In fact, if you wash fast enough, you will gain the benefits of aerobic exercise. Mopping the floor is even more work for the body, which means it ____ ______________. Ironing doesn't take that long, but ______________________ that you can still burn up to 130 calories in an hour while doing it. Outside of the home, there are many other simple, everyday ways to stay in shape. What can you think of?

실전모의고사

21 PRACTICE TEST

01 다음을 듣고, 남자가 하는 말의 목적으로 가장 적절한 것을 고르시오.

① 농업의 중요성을 강조하려고
② 유기농 식품의 구매를 촉진하려고
③ 새로 개장한 주말농장을 홍보하려고
④ 다양한 주말 여가 활동을 추천하려고
⑤ 올바른 식습관에 대한 정보를 제공하려고

02 대화를 듣고, 두 사람이 하는 말의 주제로 가장 적절한 것을 고르시오.

① 조기 영어교육의 장단점
② 모국어와 영어의 차이점
③ 외국 유학 계획 시 고려할 사항
④ 외국어 학습을 시작하기 적절한 연령
⑤ 회화를 통한 효과적인 외국어 학습법

03 대화를 듣고, 두 사람의 관계를 가장 잘 나타낸 것을 고르시오.

① 건축가 - 조수
② 인테리어 디자이너 - 목수
③ 부동산 중개업자 - 고객
④ 경비원 - 거주자
⑤ 집주인 - 세입자

04 대화를 듣고, 그림에서 대화의 내용과 일치하지 않는 것을 고르시오.

05 대화를 듣고, 여자가 남자에게 부탁한 일로 가장 적절한 것을 고르시오.

① 티켓 구입하기
② 꽃다발을 찾아오기
③ 꽃다발을 예약하기
④ 좋은 좌석을 맡아놓기
⑤ 연주회 초대장을 가져오기

06 대화를 듣고, 남자가 지불할 금액을 고르시오. [3점]

① $60 ② $90 ③ $100
④ $120 ⑤ $140

07 대화를 듣고, 여자가 상점 판매 담당자로 지원하지 않는 이유를 고르시오.

① 판매 경력이 2년 미만이라서
② 상점 위치가 집과 멀어서
③ 근무 시간이 맞지 않아서
④ 스페인어를 하지 못해서
⑤ 급여가 너무 적어서

08 대화를 듣고, Experience Korea 프로그램의 오늘 일정에 관해 언급되지 않은 것을 고르시오.

① 박물관 견학 ② 숙소에서 짐 풀기
③ 환영식 ④ 저녁 식사
⑤ 유적지 방문

09 American mink에 관한 다음 내용을 듣고, 일치하지 않는 것을 고르시오.

① 꼬리가 전체 몸길이의 3분의 1이다.
② 먹이의 목을 물어서 죽인다.
③ 냄새로 영역을 표시한다.
④ 물가 근처의 숲에 서식한다.
⑤ 한곳에 오래 정착한다.

정답 및 해설 p.82

10 다음 표를 보면서 대화를 듣고, 두 사람이 수강할 겨울 학교 프로그램을 고르시오.

2025 Winter School Programs			
Program	Tutor	Fee	Period
① Indoor Sports	Jason	$50	January 2~11
② Ocarina	Melissa	$60	January 14~25
③ Chinese	Tim	$70	January 11~31
④ World Explorer Program - the Philippines	Brent	$400	January 15~17
⑤ World Explorer Program - Japan	Mindy	$600	January 17~19

11 대화를 듣고, 남자의 마지막 말에 대한 여자의 응답으로 가장 적절한 것을 고르시오.

① I'm sorry but we are closed.
② I'll seat you next to the window.
③ I can take your order in a moment.
④ Sorry, we can't find your name on the list.
⑤ No problem. Could you give me your name, please?

12 대화를 듣고, 여자의 마지막 말에 대한 남자의 응답으로 가장 적절한 것을 고르시오.

① I'd like to go there with you.
② It's important for my future career.
③ I had a hard time preparing for this.
④ It's held in the first week of October.
⑤ I'm setting up the stage for the school play.

13 대화를 듣고, 남자의 마지막 말에 대한 여자의 응답으로 가장 적절한 것을 고르시오. [3점]

▶ Woman : ______________________

① Right, sometimes failure teaches success.
② Definitely. Slow and steady wins the race.
③ It was very useful when I searched for jobs.
④ Why not? A problem shared is a problem halved.
⑤ I agree. Let's practice for the written test together.

14 대화를 듣고, 여자의 마지막 말에 대한 남자의 응답으로 가장 적절한 것을 고르시오. [3점]

▶ Man : ______________________

① Kids under 10 cannot use this ride.
② Of course, it will just take a moment.
③ Sorry, but tickets cannot be refunded.
④ Sure. Buying full passes would be better.
⑤ I'm sorry you were unsatisfied with the park.

15 다음 상황 설명을 듣고, Ms. Carver가 Julie의 아버지에게 할 말로 가장 적절한 것을 고르시오.

▶ Ms. Carver : ______________________

① Julie studies hard and always gets good grades.
② It's nice to see that Julie is making many friends.
③ I'll talk with her about that tomorrow after the class.
④ It's just part of growing up, so don't worry too much.
⑤ I hope that after-school activities can raise her confidence.

[16~17] 다음을 듣고, 물음에 답하시오.

16 여자가 하는 말의 주제로 가장 적절한 것은?

① essential steps for whitening your teeth
② dental care tips for better-looking teeth
③ alternative remedies for dental problems
④ methods to avoid bad breath and cavities
⑤ the importance of regular dental check-ups

17 언급된 천연 재료가 아닌 것은?

① strawberry ② peppermint
③ lettuce ④ lemon
⑤ bamboo salt

21 DICTATION

녹음된 내용을 들으면서 빈칸을 알맞게 채워 보세요.

01

M: Are you ______________________ fun, healthy activities to do as a family on the weekends? If so, why not ______________ ______________ with your kids? It is a wonderful experience for kids who have grown up in the city. And Uncle John's farm is ______ ______________________. Uncle John's is a recently established farm that grows organic fruits and vegetables in a lovely, natural setting. And it's just 30 minutes from the city by subway! ______________ ______________ with your kids. It is the perfect way for them to develop healthy eating habits and a love of nature at the same time.

02

W: Hello?

M: Hi, Alice. It's Min-ho. Do you have a minute? I'd like your opinion as an English teacher.

W: Sure. What's up?

M: It's about my daughter. She's turning five, and I'm wondering whether she ______________ ______________.

W: Well, that's a difficult question. Personally, I think five is too young to start studying a foreign language.

M: Really? Many of her friends are already enrolled in language programs. ______________ ______________?

W: I don't think so. Besides, learning two languages at a young age can be confusing.

M: ______________________, but then why are so many parents having their children study English before they even speak Korean?

W: There is a lot of pressure to learn English, but it's ______________________ ______________.

M: I see. Thanks for your advice.

03

M: Good morning. How may I help you?

W: Hello, ______________________ ______________ in today's paper. I'd like some more information about the place on Park Street.

M: Oh, you're talking about the house on the hill, right?

W: Exactly. It looks nice, but I can't see much in the picture.

M: Well, it has a great view, and ______________ ______________.

W: That's good. What else can you tell me?

M: It has a large back yard that would be ideal if you have kids.

W: That sounds perfect. ______________ ______________.

M: Of course. Just tell me when you are free and ______________.

W: How about 2 o'clock tomorrow?

M: Okay. If you come to my office, I'll drive you there.

W: Great. See you then.

04

W: Honey, have you seen the view from our room yet?

M: Oh, it's amazing!

W: I'm glad we chose to stay here ______________ ______________.

M: Yeah. Look at the river in the distance. It looks so peaceful.

W: Oh, there's a cruise ship on the water. __________ ______________.

M: We could do that after dinner. Can you see the island to the right of the ship?

W: Yes, I can. Wow, look down, honey. There is a nice park in front of the hotel.

M: Right. ______________________ is beautiful.

W: The nearby sculptures look pretty, too. The three horses look delicate.

M: I'd like to get a closer look at them.

W: There's a cozy bench to the right of the fountain where we could take a rest. ____________________ ____________________?

M: Okay, let's go.

05

M: Jessica, ____________________ David's recital?

W: My watch says it's 2:30. When is the recital?

M: In two and a half hours, but I want to arrive ____________________.

W: We don't need to hurry too much. The invitations David gave to us ____________________ reserved VIP seats.

M: Oh, that sounds great.

W: Besides, I want to clean the house before we leave.

M: All right. Then ____________________ ____________. Would you like some help?

W: That's okay. Instead, could you pick up the bouquet of flowers ____________________ ________________ on 3rd Avenue?

M: Sure. Do you need anything else?

W: That's all. Thanks, honey.

06

M: Hi, I heard ____________________ ________________. Is that true?

W: Yes. We're ____________________ 70 percent.

M: Okay. Then how much are these pants?

W: They're 30 dollars per pair.

M: Wow, the last time, they were 60 dollars a pair. Can I try a size 32?

W: One moment, sir. Sorry, I've ______________ __________ but those on the hanger are all we have.

M: That's too bad.

W: How about this jacket? I think it's your size.

M: Well, I do like the style. ____________________ ____________?

W: Sure. Its original price was 220 dollars, but it's 50 percent off now.

M: Great. ____________________. I'll take it.

W: How about this tie? It's only 10 dollars for those who spend more than 100 dollars today.

M: Wow, that's a good deal! I'll take it, too.

07

M: Daisy, I saw a help-wanted ad in the newspaper. Avenue Clothing Store is looking for a sales supervisor.

W: Sounds great. ____________________?

M: It's located inside the Westfield Shopping Mall, on Market Street.

W: Good! It's not far from my house.

M: They want someone ____________________ ________________. And it says the pay is $32 per hour.

W: Not bad. I should apply for that.

M: And they want a person with at least 2 years of experience, which you clearly have.

W: Yeah. ____________________?

M: Hmm, most of their customers are Hispanic so they need someone who can speak both English and Spanish.

W: Oh, no. ____________________.

M: Really? Well, there'll be other opportunities!

08

W: Good morning, Mr. Lee. Good to see you again.

M: Hi, Ms. Wang. Thank you for choosing us to lead your "Experience Korea" program. ______________________________________?

W: It was comfortable.

M: Great. Now, the sightseeing bus is waiting outside.

W: Are the students going to their accommodations?

M: Right. After they unpack, as you know, there will be ______________________________________.

W: Sounds great. Actually, I heard on the plane that the Secret Garden in Changdeok Palace is open at night. Is that true?

M: Yes, that is new, ______________________________.

W: Could we go there after dinner? I want my students to visit ______________________________________.

M: Sure. The palace is near the Korean restaurant where you will dine. I'll arrange that right now.

09

W: Good afternoon, class. Today, we'll talk about the American mink. American minks ______________________________ North America. They have slim bodies and long, thick tails. In fact, ______________________________ is its tail! American minks are meat eaters that feed on fish, frogs, and small birds. They kill their prey ______________________________________. Like skunks, minks defend themselves by spraying an unpleasant-smelling liquid. Minks also ______________________________ and will fight with other minks that invade their territory. They live in forested areas that are near rivers, streams, lakes, or ponds. They make their homes near water and ______________________________________.

10

M: Emily, take a look at this.

W: Are those winter school programs?

M: Yes, and some of them look fun. Why don't we take one together?

W: Okay. Let's learn ______________________________________.

M: Well, my friend Charlotte had Tim as a Chinese tutor and said that he gives too much work.

W: Really? Then ______________________________________.

M: Experiencing the Philippines sounds interesting.

W: But it's too expensive. I think ______________________________ 100 dollars for our winter program.

M: Then the other World Explorer Program is not an option either, right?

W: Yeah. What about indoor sports?

M: I'm sorry, but I'll be traveling with my family until January 9th.

W: Then we have only one program left, and I think ______________________________________.

M: You're right. Let's sign up for that program.

11

M: Excuse me, are there any available seats in this restaurant?

W: I'm sorry, but ______________________________. You can probably get a table in 20 minutes.

M: I can wait. Could you ______________________________________?

12

W: You look tired, Jason. Are you ______________________________________?

M: Yes. I'm ______________________________ the school festival these days.

W: Oh, what are you doing for the festival?

13

W: What are you doing with your notebook?

M: I'm practicing with the Excel program ________ ______________________________.

W: Ah. I thought you were playing a game. So, how's it going?

M: I passed the written test, but I still have to take the practical examination.

W: I remember when I had to take that same examination.

M: I'm sure it was easy for you, __________________ ____________________________.

W: Programming and mastering Excel are two different things. I had to begin preparing well in advance, and ________________________________ __________________.

M: Really? It was that difficult? Now I'm even more worried.

W: It's ______________________________________, but you can succeed if you try your best.

M: So, you think I can pass if I study like you did?

14

M: Here are your tickets and your receipt. Enjoy your visit to Green Springs Amusement Park.

W: Excuse me, but I think ____________________ _______________. Why is the total $140?

M: That's one all-access adult pass and two all-access children's passes.

W: No, I said, "admission to the park for one adult." I don't plan to go on any of the rides.

M: Oh, I'm really sorry. I misunderstood and charged you for the full admission price.

W: I see. Then could I ___________________________ ____________________?

M: Yes, of course. I'll need to see your credit card to process the refund.

W: All right. Here you are.

M: I'll fix that right now. And again, _____________ ____.

W: That's okay, but my kids ______________________ _______________________________.

15

M: Ms. Carver is a high school teacher, and Julie is one of her students. Julie always does well on tests and assignments, and she ___________________ ___________________________. Today, Ms. Carver has a meeting with Julie's father. During the meeting, Ms. Carver praises Julie's performance and in-class attitude. To Ms. Carver's surprise, Julie's father expresses _______________________ _________________________. He says he worries about Julie's ability to make friends ____________ _______________________________. However, Ms. Carver knows that students sometimes go through temporary periods where ___________________ __________________, and she wants to explain this to Julie's father. In this situation, what would Ms. Carver most likely say to Julie's father?

16-17

W: Are your teeth well taken care of? If not, you could ____ ____________. So, let me provide you with a few tips on making your teeth presentable. I'll start with evenness. Unfortunately, few of us are born with straight teeth. To get a picture-perfect smile, you ____ and have your teeth straightened. It's worth it. While you're there, it's a good idea to have your teeth professionally whitened. Of course, many of us don't have the time or money for this. Luckily, there are a few basic, natural alternatives. For example, strawberries contain ________________ __________________________________. Common herbs such as peppermint and spearmint have the same power. There are even certain vegetables, especially lettuce, __________________________. And since salt is an ingredient in almost every dish, why not switch to bamboo salt? It also has the power to brighten your smile. Finally, _________ ____ and proper brushing to avoid the biggest mistake of all: bad breath.

실전모의고사
22 PRACTICE TEST

01 다음을 듣고, 남자가 하는 말의 목적으로 가장 적절한 것을 고르시오.

① 카카오의 화학성분을 설명하려고
② 신상품을 일반 대중에게 선전하려고
③ 초콜릿 섭취의 건강상 이점에 대해 알리려고
④ 고객이 자신의 광고를 선택하도록 설득하려고
⑤ 아이들에게 새 제품을 많이 팔 수 있는 전략을 논의하려고

02 대화를 듣고, 여자의 의견으로 가장 적절한 것을 고르시오.

① 각자의 취향에 맞는 책을 찾아야 한다.
② 같은 책을 여러 번 읽는 것이 바람직하다.
③ 어릴 때부터 책 읽는 습관을 들이는 것이 좋다.
④ 학교 차원에서 창의력 교육이 이루어져야 한다.
⑤ 창의력을 키우려면 다양한 장르의 책을 읽어야 한다.

03 대화를 듣고, 두 사람의 관계를 가장 잘 나타낸 것을 고르시오.

① 아들 – 엄마
② 의사 – 환자
③ 학생 – 선생님
④ 고용인 – 고용주
⑤ 자원 봉사자 – 요양원 거주자

04 대화를 듣고, 그림에서 대화의 내용과 일치하지 <u>않는</u> 것을 고르시오.

05 대화를 듣고, 남자가 여자를 위해 할 일로 가장 적절한 것을 고르시오.

① 엘리베이터를 잡고 있기
② Max와 Jim을 데리고 오기
③ 여자의 차를 건물 앞에 주차하기
④ 여자의 물건을 엘리베이터에 싣기
⑤ 아래층에서 여자의 물건을 가져오기

06 대화를 듣고, 여자가 지불할 금액을 고르시오. [3점]

① $15 ② $17 ③ $18
④ $20 ⑤ $22

07 대화를 듣고, 남자가 딸을 Nina's parrot cafe에 데려갈 수 <u>없는</u> 이유를 고르시오.

① 조류 공포증이 있어서
② 입장료가 너무 비싸서
③ 미리 예약을 해야 해서
④ 입장 연령 제한이 있어서
⑤ 음료 외 간식을 팔지 않아서

08 다음을 듣고, cenote에 관해 언급되지 <u>않은</u> 것을 고르시오.

① 위치 ② 형성 과정
③ 전통적 상징 ④ 면적
⑤ 입장 허가 필요 유무

09 공룡에 관한 다음 내용을 듣고, 일치하지 <u>않는</u> 것을 고르시오.

① 여러 종의 공룡들이 깃털을 가졌던 것으로 보인다.
② 새로 발견된 화석은 화산 분출 시 묻힌 공룡의 화석이다.
③ 깃털을 가졌던 공룡 중에는 티라노사우루스 렉스도 있다.
④ 깃털은 체온을 유지하기 위한 용도였을 것이다.
⑤ 대부분의 학자들은 이번 발견을 확증해 주었다.

10 다음 표를 보면서 대화를 듣고, 두 사람이 신청할 요리 강좌를 고르시오.

Howard Community Center: Cooking Classes				
Class	Age	Day	Cost	Spots Available
① Seafood Secrets	all ages	Saturday	$45	4 left
② Cookie Decorating	kids aged 8-12	Monday	$25	2 left
③ Italian Recipe	adults	Sunday	$35	1 left
④ French Cooking	all ages	Wednesday	$55	4 left
⑤ Vegan Bowls	adults	Monday	$60	5 left

11 대화를 듣고, 여자의 마지막 말에 대한 남자의 응답으로 가장 적절한 것을 고르시오.

① He's in Hong Kong.
② We usually shop together.
③ He runs his own business.
④ He passed away three years ago.
⑤ He often stays home on weekends.

12 대화를 듣고, 남자의 마지막 말에 대한 여자의 응답으로 가장 적절한 것을 고르시오.

① It's been at least a year.
② It sure has changed a lot.
③ Let's come here again next week.
④ This restaurant opened 5 years ago.
⑤ Just 15 minutes' walk from my home.

13 대화를 듣고, 여자의 마지막 말에 대한 남자의 응답으로 가장 적절한 것을 고르시오. [3점]

▶ Man : ______________________

① It doesn't really matter what you're wearing.
② Then I would have returned your phone call.
③ Then I wouldn't have worn my school uniform!
④ That's OK. I thought we would go to a museum.
⑤ Then I would have gone to the doctor's yesterday.

14 대화를 듣고, 남자의 마지막 말에 대한 여자의 응답으로 가장 적절한 것을 고르시오.

▶ Woman : ______________________

① Variety is the spice of life.
② Yeah, life couldn't get better.
③ It's a matter of life and death.
④ Sure! You are a good friend of mine.
⑤ No, it's difficult to overcome the problem.

15 다음 상황 설명을 듣고, 지희가 해진에게 할 말로 가장 적절한 것을 고르시오. [3점]

▶ Ji-hee : ______________________

① Leave everything. No one will care.
② Western food is too oily for me, too.
③ Let's ask the server to wrap up the food.
④ Let's go home and cook some Korean food.
⑤ Be polite and try to eat as much as you can.

[16~17] 다음을 듣고, 물음에 답하시오.

16 남자가 하는 말의 주제로 가장 적절한 것은?

① how to make the best coffee
② how to clean up coffee grounds
③ the effects coffee has on the body
④ gardening methods good for plants
⑤ how to use coffee grounds at home

17 청소하기 위해 커피 찌꺼기를 쓰는 방법으로 언급되지 않은 것은?

① 악취 흡수 ② 얼룩 제거
③ 곰팡이 제거 ④ 긁힌 자국 보완
⑤ 벽난로 청소

22 DICTATION

녹음된 내용을 들으면서 빈칸을 알맞게 채워 보세요.

01

M: Good afternoon. I'd like to present our advertising campaign to you. Your company, Candyland, has produced a new product called Choco Balls. Now some ad agencies might ____________________ ____________________. Kids love chocolate, right? But ____________________ ____________________ that your product, Choco Balls, is made from 70% cacao. For a long time now, it has been known that the chemicals in cacao can ____________________. In other words, eating cacao is good for our health. So Ace Advertising is proposing that you choose our advertising campaign, which ____________________ ____________________ of eating chocolate. Now please watch this commercial.

02

M: Hi, Mom. Did you go to the bookstore?

W: I did, and I picked up something that ____________________ ____________________.

M: Oh? What's that?

W: It's about the philosophy of Socrates. I read part of it, and it's very interesting.

M: Thanks, Mom, but you know that I prefer to read mystery novels in my free time.

W: If you continue to read the same kind of thing, ____________________.

M: You have a point. I guess ____________________ ____________________ since I've read anything different.

W: Exactly. ____________________ can help you to become more creative. Why don't you ____________________?

M: All right. I'll check it out.

03

M: Is there anything else I can help you with?

W: No. That's it. You did a great job!

M: ____________________.

W: It's really hard for me to ____________________ ____________________. And the nurses don't like to do those kinds of things.

M: No problem. Just stay healthy, Mrs. Gray.

W: It's hard when you're 85.

M: ____________________. I'm sorry, Mrs. Gray. ____________________.

W: Oh, I was hoping you'd chat for a while.

M: Sorry, I'm really busy. Exams are next week.

W: OK. ____________________. You help out every Wednesday, right?

M: Yes. From 4 to 7 every Wednesday.

W: It's nice of you to spend some of your free time with us.

M: I enjoy it.

04

M: Mi-sun, what's this picture?

W: I took that picture yesterday at my daughter's Doljanchi. It's a traditional Korean first-birthday party.

M: Okay, but ____________________ ____________________ in front of your daughter?

W: We believe that they can predict a baby's future. On the left, there is some thread, which represents long life.

M: Then does the pencil symbolize intelligence?

W: Right, and the computer mouse ____________________ ____________________ represents technological ability. Similarly, a microphone would suggest musical talent, but ____________________ ____________________.

M: That's too bad. Then what does the rice mean?

W: It ____________________. It's related to having a comfortable life.

M: I see. Well, I'm sure that the money represents wealth.

W: Of course, and we were all delighted when she picked it up.

05

W: Matt, are you free? Would you help me for a second, please?

M: Sure, Mrs. Brown. ____________________?

W: I have to get all of these boxes and things downstairs and into my car.

M: Wow. That's a lot of stuff. ____________________ ____________?

W: Up the street a long way, unfortunately. But don't worry. Max and Jim are waiting downstairs to help.

M: ____________________________________?

W: No, I just need someone to hold the elevator for me while ____________________________.

M: Why don't I move these boxes and you hold the elevator?

W: Oh, you're a wonderful boy! Thank you, Matt!

06

M: Good morning. How can I help you?

W: I'd like 3 muffins, please.

M: What kind of muffins would you like? We have plain, blueberry, or cheese. Plain is $3, and ______ ____________________________ $5.

W: Two plain and one blueberry, please.

M: Okay. Would you like something to drink?

W: I'd like one tomato juice and two cranberry juices. ____________________________________?

M: No, they're all $3 each. Is that all?

W: Yes, I have a $3 discount coupon and a membership card that gives me an instant 10% discount. _____ ______________________________?

M: I'm sorry, but I'm afraid you can't. You can ______ ______________________________.

W: Oh, then I'll use a $3 discount coupon, which gives me more of a discount.

M: Okay.

07

W: Ethan, __________________________ Nina's parrot cafe?

M: A parrot cafe? What's that? Is it a place you can bring your parrot?

W: No! You can enjoy roastery coffee ___________ ____________________________________.

M: Sounds interesting. Can I bring my kid there?

W: Why not? I took my niece there. Just __________ ____________________________________.

M: No, she isn't. She loves birds. Do I have to make a reservation in advance?

W: You can book in advance, but you don't have to. You will have to pay an entrance fee, though.

M: Okay. ________________________?

W: They serve baked goods like muffins and cakes. The admission fee is $20, which includes one drink.

M: That's reasonable. I'll take my daughter there this weekend. Since her sixth birthday is this Sunday, ____________________________.

W: I'm sorry! They don't allow kids that are under 8 in the cafe.

M: That's too bad. I have to find another one on the Internet.

08

W: Mexico is the perfect destination for a scuba diving vacation. The Yucatan peninsula is especially great because it ______________________ in a cenote. A cenote is a deep natural well formed by the collapse of surface limestone that exposes ground water underneath. These natural ponds were often the only sources of fresh water in the jungle. ______________________ to the ancient Mayan people. The cenotes were important in Mayan myth and ______________________ to the underworld. You can dive in these amazing underground caves, and you may even see Mayan treasures left behind many years ago. You'll ______________________ for the caves, but to dive in the cenotes, you need no advanced training.

09

M: Did dinosaurs have feathers? You're most likely to say, "No!" Our image of dinosaurs comes from books and movies showing dinosaurs with green or brown skin. But ______________________ that many types of dinosaurs, in fact, had feathers. Because these fossils are of dinosaurs that ______________________, they were perfectly preserved. Among the dinosaurs shown to have had feathers is Tyrannosaurus Rex. It is thought these dinosaurs had feathers not to fly but to keep themselves warm. ______________________ by others, the popular image of dinosaurs in books and movies ______________________.

10

W: I'd like to take a cooking course during my summer vacation. Howard Community Center ______________________.

M: I'm also thinking of taking a cooking course there.

W: Then why don't we take a class together? ______________________ their website. Here's the timetable of their cooking classes.

M: Good. I'm interested in Cookie Decorating.

W: But it's for kids aged 8 to 12. We have to choose ______________________.

M: You're right. What day are you available?

W: I'm ______________________. How about you?

M: I'm free on Monday and the weekend.

W: Okay. We should also consider the cost. I don't think I can spend more than 50 dollars.

M: All right. Then we can choose between these two. Oh, no. ______________________. We can't take it together.

W: No problem. We can take the other class together. Let's register for it!

11

W: I saw you at the store yesterday. ______________________?

M: Just my mom and my sister. My dad is ______________________.

W: What does your father do?

12

M: This was a great idea. The pizza is terrific!

W: The pasta, too. It's ______________________.

M: I can't remember ______________________. How long has it been since we last ate here?

13

W: Good morning, Min-sung. Are you feeling better?

M: Yes, thanks, Ji-hye. ______________________ ______________________ yesterday, so I had to rest at home.

W: I thought you were sick.

M: Anyway, shouldn't you be wearing your school uniform?

W: We can wear casual clothes today. We're going on a field trip. Don't you remember?

M: Umm... I do. But it's raining. Didn't the teacher say ______________________ if it was raining?

W: She did. But yesterday the teacher said we'd be going ______________________.

M: Really?

W: Yes, we're going to a museum, not the nature park.

M: Oh, ______________________ last night.

W: Oh? I'm sorry. ______________________.

14

M: Hi, Pamela. How are you doing?

W: I'm doing well, Peter. Thanks.

M: That's good. A month ago, you were so stressed. Is there any particular reason ______________________ ______________________?

W: I got my college acceptance letter. I'm so happy. I worked hard and didn't give up.

M: ______________________. Work hard and you'll be rewarded.

W: Thanks. How is your winter vacation going?

M: Good so far. And next week, my family and I are going to Jeju Island.

W: ______________________, because I've got a part-time job with a movie production company.

M: Wow! You want to study filmmaking in college, don't you?

W: Yes.

M: ______________________.

15

W: Ji-hee and Hae-jin are first-year university students in America. They are at a party given by Julie, an American classmate. There is a buffet table of ______________________ ______________________. They take some food and go sit down in the living room near Julie and some other American classmates. After a few bites, Hae-jin realizes she doesn't ______________________ ______________________. Since arriving from Korea, she often misses Korean food. Ji-hee knows this and she also knows that Hae-jin can sometimes ______ ______________________. She is worried Hae-jin ______________________ ______________________, which would hurt Julie's feelings. In this situation, what would Ji-hee most likely say to Hae-jin?

16-17

M: Did you know there are lots of ways ______________________ ______________________ instead of just throwing them in the garbage? Let's talk about some of the ways to use coffee grounds. First, ______________________. Sometimes your plants need a little boost in the mornings, too. So simply add a couple of cups of coffee grounds to a bucket of water and let it sit for a day. Then apply it to your plants and watch them grow. Coffee grounds can also be used for cleaning. ______________________ in your closet and refrigerator, use coffee grounds. Rub coffee grounds into old pots and pans to get rid of stains. If you have scratched dark wooden furniture, use coffee grounds to fill in the scratches. They can also help clean your fireplace. Use wet coffee grounds to cover your ashes and ______________________ ______________________.

실전모의고사

23 PRACTICE TEST

01 **다음을 듣고, 여자가 하는 말의 목적으로 가장 적절한 것을 고르시오.**

① 사적지 보존의 중요성을 알리려고
② 인구 과밀화의 대책을 설명하려고
③ 역사 교육 강화의 필요성을 알리려고
④ 지역 개발 사업의 필요성을 알리려고
⑤ 정부의 역사 보존 사업을 홍보하려고

02 **대화를 듣고, 남자의 의견으로 가장 적절한 것을 고르시오.**

① 헌혈 문진 절차를 강화해야 한다.
② 헌혈은 주기적으로 하는 것이 좋다.
③ 헌혈 후에는 충분히 휴식을 취해야 한다.
④ 헌혈의 위험성에 대한 의식 개선이 필요하다.
⑤ 헌혈하기 전에는 자신의 건강상태를 확인해야 한다.

03 **대화를 듣고, 두 사람의 관계를 가장 잘 나타낸 것을 고르시오.**

① 승무원 – 기장
② 승객 – 버스 기사
③ 학생 – 지질학 교수
④ 식당 종업원 – 식당 매니저
⑤ 기상 예보관 – 뉴스 아나운서

04 **대화를 듣고, 그림에서 대화의 내용과 일치하지 <u>않는</u> 것을 고르시오.**

05 **대화를 듣고, 남자가 할 일로 가장 적절한 것을 고르시오.**

① 이삿짐 포장하기
② 안 입는 헌 옷 버리기
③ 업무용 모니터 구매하기
④ 자선센터에 책상 가져가기
⑤ 자선센터의 위치 문의하기

06 **대화를 듣고, 여자가 지불할 금액을 고르시오.**

① $80 ② $95 ③ $110
④ $115 ⑤ $150

07 **대화를 듣고, 남자가 과속한 이유를 고르시오.**

① 아내의 출산이 임박해서
② 장모님이 사고를 당하셔서
③ 환자를 급히 수술해야 해서
④ 자동차 속도계가 고장 나서
⑤ 아기를 응급실에 데려가야 해서

08 **대화를 듣고, 일식(solar eclipse)에 관해 언급되지 <u>않은</u> 것을 고르시오.**

① 발생 예정 시기 ② 발생 원리
③ 최초 발견자 ④ 관측 시 주의사항
⑤ 종류

09 **토론 방송에 관한 다음 내용을 듣고, 일치하지 <u>않는</u> 것을 고르시오.**

① 정규 방송 대신 대통령 후보 토론이 있을 것이다.
② 오늘 토론은 생방송으로 진행된다.
③ 토론의 사회자는 뉴스 앵커이다.
④ 방청객은 토론 중에 즉석 질문을 할 수 있다.
⑤ 다른 정당 후보의 토론도 방영될 예정이다.

10 다음 표를 보면서 대화를 듣고, 두 사람이 주문할 유모차를 고르시오.

Best Baby Strollers: Strolleria.com				
Brand	Stroller Weight (pounds)	Maximum Weight (pounds)	Price	Storage Basket
① A	11	45	$228	×
② B	13	50	$319	○
③ C	16	57	$289	○
④ D	18	67	$256	×
⑤ E	24	33	$110	○

11 대화를 듣고, 여자의 마지막 말에 대한 남자의 응답으로 가장 적절한 것을 고르시오.

① Almost 10 minutes.
② I fell asleep in the library.
③ I hope I didn't fail the exam.
④ He ordered me to stay after class.
⑤ I understand why he was angry with me.

12 대화를 듣고, 남자의 마지막 말에 대한 여자의 응답으로 가장 적절한 것을 고르시오.

① I used to go all the time.
② I think I forgot how to ski.
③ This is going to be so much fun.
④ I haven't been since I was a child.
⑤ I'm going to a resort near Mt. Seorak.

13 대화를 듣고, 여자의 마지막 말에 대한 남자의 응답으로 가장 적절한 것을 고르시오. [3점]

▶ Man : ______________________

① I'm sorry, but I don't know where Rose's house is.
② But you always have to be honest with your friends.
③ Can you please put the roses in the vase with water?
④ OK. Your friend needs you. We can celebrate tomorrow.
⑤ It will be more romantic when your boyfriend comes over.

14 대화를 듣고, 남자의 마지막 말에 대한 여자의 응답으로 가장 적절한 것을 고르시오. [3점]

▶ Woman : ______________________

① I don't know where to go from here.
② Maybe you should look for Main Street first.
③ Main Street is closed. Come back tomorrow.
④ I don't think I have to take a taxi to get there.
⑤ But it's really easy. Let me draw a map for you.

15 다음 상황 설명을 듣고, William이 Jonas에게 할 말로 가장 적절한 것을 고르시오. [3점]

▶ William : ______________________

① I need to study, so I can't play sports.
② Nobody would be able to ignore you anymore.
③ My mother wants you to come over for dinner.
④ Can your mother pick us up from soccer next week?
⑤ Please watch your language. You may offend others.

[16~17] 다음을 듣고, 물음에 답하시오.

16 남자가 하는 말의 주제로 가장 적절한 것은?

① throwing the perfect house party
② the growing popularity of 3D movies
③ how to enjoy a cheap vacation at home
④ ways of cutting down traveling expense
⑤ differences between sunglasses and eyeglasses

17 언급된 3D 안경 재료가 아닌 것은?

① CD 케이스 ② 매직펜 ③ 선글라스
④ 낡은 안경 ⑤ 두꺼운 종이

23 DICTATION

녹음된 내용을 들으면서 빈칸을 알맞게 채워 보세요.

01

W: As more and more people migrate to the cities, more buildings, roads, bridges, and subways must be built. When this happens, historical sites are sometimes discovered and ________________. Cities are often the historical capitals of past kingdoms and peoples. Much can be learned from our ancestors. Therefore, ________________ ________________ before all of their accumulated history is lost. With the current rate of construction, there will be no protected sites left within 10 years. ________________ ________________. It may threaten our future too. The past still ________________ ________________.

02

M: Kate, where are you going?

W: Hi, Peter. I'm ________________. It's something I do once every three months.

M: Wow! I'm so proud of you. By the way, how are you feeling?

W: ________________. Why do you ask?

M: I read that it can be dangerous to donate blood if you aren't feeling well.

W: That's true, but don't worry. I slept well last night and had a big breakfast.

M: Good. And you don't have a cold or any other disease, right?

W: No, I don't. I always ________________ ________________ because it could be dangerous to the receiver.

M: I'm glad to hear that. ________________ ________________ you're following the important rules for donating blood.

W: Thanks for your concern.

03

M: Ma'am, some of the people have been asking ________________ ________________.

W: Just make an announcement that we are passing through a big storm cloud.

M: That might ________________.

W: Then tell them we are going through rough air and it is common over this part of the Pacific Ocean.

M: Maybe it would be better if you told them yourself. Besides, I have to serve drinks soon.

W: Yeah, I guess I can do that. I will keep the "fasten seatbelts" sign on.

M: Great, thanks. I'll ________________ in seat 4-B. She has been crying!

W: Tell her we'll be out of this rough spot soon and that there's nothing at all to worry about.

M: ________________.

04

M: Hello?

W: Hi, Dad.

M: Hi, Kelly. How is everything? Have you finished unpacking?

W: Almost. I just finished ________________ ________________ in my room.

M: Did your brother bring your chest of drawers for you?

W: Yes, and he put them ________________ ________________.

M: Okay. I bet you already hung your graduation picture as well.

W: Actually, I decided to hang a family portrait instead.

M: That sounds nice. Did you ________________ ________________?

W: No trouble. My brother helped me move my bed next to the drawers.

M: What about the floor lamp that I ordered for you?

W: It arrived, and I put it to the right of my bed.

M: ________________. I'll see you when I get home.

정답 및 해설 p.90

05

W: Wow! There is so much stuff. It's very hard packing for the move.

M: Definitely. I can't believe we've kept so many things we don't use anymore.

W: We need to get rid of our old clothes ____.

M: You're right. I have to throw away this desk, too.

W: But you need a desk. You bought it just 3 years ago.

M: I need two monitors for working, but ____. I'm going to buy a larger one.

W: Then ____ the charity center? I'm sure there will be a person who needs a desk.

M: That's a great idea. I'll take it to the center tomorrow.

W: You should probably go there today. It is probably closed tomorrow since it's a Saturday.

M: You're right. I'll go now. Is it on Elm Avenue?

W: Right. ____________________________. We have a lot to do today.

06

M: Welcome to Shoe Town. Are you ______________________________________?

W: I saw the advertisement for your sale in the newspaper.

M: That's right. We're having a "buy one pair, get the second pair for half price" sale.

W: So ____?

M: Right and the lower priced shoes are 50% off.

W: So, these running shoes cost $70. If I bought them, how much will these tennis shoes cost?

M: Well, they are $80, so ____.

W: Oh, I see. Then it's the running shoes that are half price, since ________________________________.

M: Exactly. Would you like both pairs?

W: Yes, please. How much will that be?

07

W: Sir, are you aware of how fast you were going? I'm afraid I have to ________________________________.

M: I'm terribly sorry, officer, but I have an excuse.

W: All right. I'm listening.

M: ________________________________, and I'm on my way to the hospital to be with her.

W: ________________________________ right now?

M: Yes. My mother-in-law called me and said the baby is expected at any moment.

W: Is that the reason you were speeding?

M: Yes, I promised to be with her at the hospital.

W: I ________________________________, but you will still need to pay an $80 fine.

M: I understand, officer.

08

M: Look at this, Jessica. The newspaper says ______________________________________ tomorrow afternoon!

W: Umm, okay, Dad. What's a solar eclipse?

M: Oh, well, a solar eclipse occurs when the moon passes between the Earth and the sun.

W: So we won't be able to see the sun tomorrow afternoon?

M: Well, for a period, the moon will ______________________________________ from the sun.

W: That sounds amazing! Can we watch?

M: Yes, but we need to prepare some special glasses first. Even behind the moon, the sun is still ____.

W: Okay. I guess I thought it would be completely dark.

M: There are ________________________________, a partial eclipse, a total eclipse and an annular eclipse. This will be a partial eclipse, so ____.

W: I understand.

09

M: Tonight's scheduled television program will not be shown. Instead we will present you with the Presidential Candidates' Debate. ______________ ________________________ the three candidates representing the Democratic Party. It will be a live, unscripted question-and-answer session. Network news anchor Christopher Martin will host tonight's debate and will present questions. ____________ ______________________________ by the studio audience as they enter the auditorium. __________ ______________________ our fair and impartial standards, we will be presenting the Republican candidates' debate tomorrow night at this same time. Tomorrow's program is going to feature ____ representing the Republican Party.

10

W: Honey, we need to get another stroller. We need a lightweight stroller that's ____________________ __________ and that we can use for traveling.

M: I agree. Let's choose from this website, Strolleria.com.

W: __________________________________ weight.

M: Definitely. We should buy something that ______ __________________________________.

W: And I have to get a sturdy stroller that can handle more than 50 pounds. Our daughter is getting bigger every day.

M: Good point. How much should we spend?

W: Let's find something for under $300.

M: Then we have these two options. One of the strollers __________________________________. Do you want to get it?

W: That would be convenient but _______________ __________. I prefer the cheaper one.

M: That's nice. Let's order it.

11

W: I heard that Mr. Smith ____________________ ________________. What happened?

M: ____, and I missed the first part of the exam.

W: Why were you late?

12

M: I want to go skiing this weekend. What do you think?

W: Okay, but I might need a lesson. I _____________ ____________________________.

M: When was ________________________________?

13

W: Something smells really good! Are you cooking?

M: Yes. I'm making my famous homemade pizza with eggplant and sweet onions.

W: __________________________________?

M: Did you forget? It's our one-year anniversary!

W: Yes, I did forget. And I made plans with Rose tonight.

M: Can't you see her some other night? I've been ____.

W: I wish I could, but she has been having a hard time since her grandfather died.

M: That's really sad, but ______________________ ______________________________.

W: I know! And it's really romantic. I guess I can call Rose and __________________________, but she has always been there for me when I needed her.

14

M: Can you tell me how to get to Main Street?

W: Sure, just ______________________________; walk three blocks, then cross the street and....

M: Wait, slow down. ______________________________ ______________________ and then what?

W: And then walk three blocks. When you see the library, cross the street and turn left.

M: You mean go left ______________________________ ______________________?

W: What I meant was that you should ____________ ______________________________ you were going.

M: I'm starting to ______________________________. Maybe I should just call for a taxi.

15

W: William and Jonas are good friends. They spend a lot of time playing sports together. Sometimes, during games, Jonas ______________________________ ______________________ and uses a lot of bad language. ______________________________ during a game, as emotions can run a little high. But ______________________________, William's mother has heard Jonas using that language when she ______________________________ ______________________ from the field. She ignored it the first few times. But she eventually told William that if she heard it again, she would not allow William to play sports with Jonas anymore. In this situation, what would William most likely say to Jonas?

16-17

M: Vacation season is coming up, but we need to _____ ______________________. So instead of going somewhere for a vacation, why not stay at home? You can start by inviting your friends to your house for a house party. If you ______________________ ______________________ in your refrigerator and ask your friends to bring something to eat, it won't cost you much. Another cheap and fun idea is to turn your house into a 3D movie theater. Even if you only have a regular PC monitor, don't worry. ______________________________ a 3D video converter. By using this program, you can watch normal videos in 3D. The next step is making 3D glasses. You can ______________ ______________________________ using a spare CD case and some permanent markers. Just color the transparent side of the CD case with red and blue markers to ______________________________ ______________________. Alternatively, you may use an existing pair of sunglasses and ______ ______________________________ of transparent plastic. Or pick an old pair of eyeglasses and color the lenses red and blue.

실전모의고사
24 PRACTICE TEST

01 다음을 듣고, 남자가 하는 말의 목적으로 가장 적절한 것을 고르시오.

① 병원의 새로운 위치를 알려주려고
② 흡연의 해로움에 대해 알려주려고
③ 정부의 금연 정책에 대해 문의하려고
④ 빌딩의 입주자 대표회의를 연기하려고
⑤ 새로운 금연 규정을 시행할 것을 요구하려고

02 대화를 듣고, 두 사람이 하는 말의 주제로 가장 적절한 것을 고르시오.

① 인공조명의 다양한 종류
② 인공조명의 부정적인 영향
③ 자연채광과 인공조명의 차이점
④ 대기오염이 생태계에 미치는 영향
⑤ 에너지 절약과 인공조명의 연관성

03 대화를 듣고, 두 사람의 관계를 가장 잘 나타낸 것을 고르시오.

① 과학자 – 과학자
② 기자 – 과학자
③ 기자 – 지역 주민
④ 기자 – 자원봉사자
⑤ 자원봉사자 – 과학자

04 대화를 듣고, 그림에서 대화의 내용과 일치하지 않는 것을 고르시오.

05 대화를 듣고, 여자가 남자를 위해 할 일로 가장 적절한 것을 고르시오.

① 자원봉사자로 참여하기
② 후원해줄 업체를 알아보기
③ 지역 봉사 활동을 기획하기
④ 쓰레기봉투와 음식물을 준비하기
⑤ 프로젝트를 선전할 전단지 만들기

06 대화를 듣고, 남자가 지불할 금액을 고르시오. [3점]

① $40 ② $45 ③ $50
④ $54 ⑤ $60

07 대화를 듣고, 남자가 여자를 찾아다닌 이유를 고르시오.

① 함께 점심을 먹기 위해서
② Lisa의 연락처를 물어보기 위해서
③ 남동생 일로 도움을 청하기 위해서
④ 음식점 예약 취소를 부탁하기 위해서
⑤ 송별회 장소에 관해 논의하기 위해서

08 다음을 듣고, saiga에 관해 언급되지 않은 것을 고르시오.

① 서식지 ② 생김새
③ 먹이 습성 ④ 털의 특징
⑤ 밀렵 방지 대책

09 다음을 듣고, 내용과 일치하지 않는 것을 고르시오.

① Wapno 성의 주요 난방 공급원은 기름보일러이다.
② 우유로 작동되는 새로운 난방 시스템이 발명되었다.
③ 배출되는 소의 젖은 온도가 약 섭씨 38도이다.
④ 우유를 끓이는 과정에서 증기와 열이 발생한다.
⑤ Wapno 성의 일부는 우유에서 나온 증기와 열로 난방을 한다.

10 다음 표를 보면서 대화를 듣고, 여자가 주문할 커피머신을 고르시오.

Capsule Coffee Machines				
Model	Material	Water Tank Capacity	Auto Power Off	Price
① A	plastic	0.6L	○	$ 69
② B	glass	0.7L	×	$ 140
③ C	glass	1.2L	○	$ 270
④ D	stainless steel	1.8L	○	$ 380
⑤ E	stainless steel	1.5L	×	$ 509

11 대화를 듣고, 남자의 마지막 말에 대한 여자의 응답으로 가장 적절한 것을 고르시오.

① I'd rather have turkey.
② I'm already full, thanks.
③ It'd be better to take it out.
④ Chicken sandwiches, please.
⑤ Thanks for buying me sandwiches.

12 대화를 듣고, 여자의 마지막 말에 대한 남자의 응답으로 가장 적절한 것을 고르시오.

① Well, she'll come home soon.
② Yes, I'll pick up Lily next time.
③ Yes, our new dishwasher is very fast.
④ No, she doesn't finish for another hour.
⑤ No, I have an important meeting at the moment.

13 대화를 듣고, 남자의 마지막 말에 대한 여자의 응답으로 가장 적절한 것을 고르시오.

▶ Woman :

① Count to ten. Then jump!
② It's a really safe thing to do.
③ She will help you to study it.
④ Well, then you can count me in.
⑤ Do you happen to know Carolyn?

14 대화를 듣고, 여자의 마지막 말에 대한 남자의 응답으로 가장 적절한 것을 고르시오. [3점]

▶ Man :

① My first impression wasn't very good.
② I'll be sure to get good grades if I do that.
③ In that case, tell me more about your club.
④ Even if I didn't get the job, I'm glad you did.
⑤ I know what they are going to ask during the interview.

15 다음 상황 설명을 듣고, 영재가 지훈에게 할 말로 가장 적절한 것을 고르시오. [3점]

▶ Young-jae :

① I don't know who you're talking about.
② He's so tired that he can't walk properly.
③ That's not fair. You shouldn't imitate me.
④ You are so funny that you should be on TV.
⑤ You shouldn't make fun of people's handicaps.

[16~17] 다음을 듣고, 물음에 답하시오.

16 여자가 하는 말의 주제로 가장 적절한 것은?

① advantages of learning a foreign language
② important parts of learning a foreign language
③ reasons why it is difficult to learn a new language
④ usefulness of song while learning a foreign language
⑤ necessity of memorizing a song's lyrics for language learning

17 언급된 음악 유형이 아닌 것은?

① hip hop ② jazz ③ opera
④ folk ⑤ musical

24 DICTATION

녹음된 내용을 들으면서 빈칸을 알맞게 채워 보세요.

01

W: This is Ideal Property Managers. ______________ ______________________________. Please leave a message after the beep.

M: Hello. My name is Scott Green. I am one of the doctors running the medical clinic ___________ _________________ of the Delaware Building. Your company manages this building. Last week, the city government passed new non-smoking regulations. ______________________________ _____________ in any public building, including the Delaware Building. So _________________ when I saw office workers still smoking in the staircase. ______________________________ by the security staff in the building. When I informed them that people were smoking in the staircase, they did nothing. Please make sure that this does not happen again.

02

W: Rick, you know what I really miss about our trip to the countryside?

M: If you're like me, you miss the night sky. There were so many stars!

W: Right. I never realized how much I was missing ____.

M: Bright city lighting affects more than just our ability to see stars. It also ___________________ ____________________.

W: I've heard about that. For example, birds alter their migration paths because of artificial lighting.

M: Street lights also ____________________________ insects and small animals hunt.

W: That's too bad. I think we should do something to ____.

M: Some countries are taking steps to reduce its impact. Our country really should join them.

03

M: Were you interviewed last week about your research?

W: Yes, a newspaper reporter came to my laboratory.

M: ____?

W: Not yet. It's going to be ____________________ ____________ on the effects of the oil spill.

M: I know. I was interviewed, too.

W: People are really concerned about ______________ ________________________ caused by negligence.

M: Did you watch the news last night?

W: They showed pictures of residents and volunteers ______________________________.

M: Some birds were covered in oil.

W: It's a tragedy.

M: I agree. But ______________________________ _________________ on the effects of pollution on animals' reproductive systems.

W: ____.

04

W: Ethan, this is the flyer for our farm tour. ______ ____ what you think?

M: Wow, it looks great! You put the title, "AMBURY FARM TOUR," on the left.

W: Yes. I also drew a chicken on top of the letters F-A-R-M. What do you think?

M: Great idea. I love it.

W: Is it okay to have the address and telephone number of our farm below the title?

M: Good. I think it's a good idea to ______________ ____.

W: What do you think about the girl holding a basket full of vegetables next to the title?

M: Looks good to me. I like her big hat.

W: Originally, I was going to draw ________________ ____________________, but I changed my mind.

M: I like this full one better. It shows one of the activities we'll have.

W: I also drew a horse and a cow on the right side.

M: Perfect! They're also ______________________________.

W: Great. I'll print this out.

05

M: I'm planning a community service project for civics class.

W: What will you do?

M: ______________________________ along the river near the park.

W: That's great, but ______________________________?

M: It's a lot of work to organize all by myself.

W: What do you have to do first?

M: Well, first I need to get sponsors to buy trash bags and snacks and drinks for volunteers.

W: Then I guess you need to find volunteers to help with the clean-up.

M: Yes. I'm going to ______________________________ to advertise it. But finding sponsors is urgent.

W: Well, I will ask my Dad if his company will help you.

M: Thanks. I feel like ______________________________.

06

W: Hello there. Can I help you find anything?

M: Yes, sure. I'm shopping for some things for my school festival. I have to make a poster.

W: Okay. ______________________________. I recommend these markers. They're 10 dollars.

M: I'll take those, and I also need some paint. ______________________________?

W: It's 20 dollars, and it comes with two brushes.

M: Great. I'll take that, too. And ______________________________.

W: How about these character stickers? They're 5 dollars each.

M: Hmm, they're nice. I'll take four of them.

W: Okay. ______________________________?

M: With this credit card. I can get 10% off with it, right?

W: I'm sorry, but ______________________________.

M: All right then. Here is my card.

07

M: Amanda, I've been looking everywhere for you.

W: I went to lunch with the boss. What's up?

M: Well, you know ______________________________ Lisa's farewell party, but I have a problem.

W: What kind of problem?

M: The restaurant that I had booked ______________________________.

W: Really? In that case, what about using the cafeteria?

M: That was my first choice, but ______________________________. What am I going to do?

W: You know, my brother works in a restaurant. He ______________________________. I could ask him.

M: Would you do that? And could you find out soon? I'm really ______________________________.

W: I'll check on it and let you know immediately.

08

W: The saiga is an unusual animal that lives in open, dry fields and mild deserts. They are mainly found in Russia and Mongolia. Saigas are ______________________________ because of their large noses. Their noses are flexible and ______________________________ during dusty summers and cold winters. They usually eat moss, herbs, and plants containing salt. They also eat some plants that are ______________________________. Their fur is light brown and thin during the summers, turning very thick and white during the winters. ______________________________, they have been the victim of illegal hunting, and have just recently been put on the critically-endangered species list.

09

M: The owners of one dairy farm in Sweden live in an ancient castle, Wapno Castle. ______________ ______________________________________. But the owners have invented a new heating system that is more environmentally friendly. ______ ______________________________________! The dairy farm has 1,000 cows which are milked every day. As the milk leaves the cows, it is hot, about 38 degrees Celsius. ________________ ______________________________. As it cools, where does all that steam and heat from the milk go? Well, ____________________________ in the castle. The owners hope to ______________ ________________________ in the near future.

10

W: I'm looking for a capsule coffee machine.

M: Good idea. A capsule coffee machine is ________ ________________________ at home.

W: I'm thinking of buying one of these five models.

M: Hmm... I don't recommend this because it's completely made of plastic.

W: Why?

M: It's ____________________________________ glass or stainless steel.

W: Then I won't buy it.

M: And you should look for a coffee machine with a large water tank of at least 1 liter. Otherwise, you'll have to constantly keep refilling.

W: Okay. What is ______________________________ ______________?

M: It reduces the risk of a house fire and saves energy.

W: Then I'll get one of these two that has auto power off mode.

M: Do you want to buy the cheaper one?

W: Yes. I think ______________________________. I don't want to spend over $300.

M: Great! You've made a good decision!

11

M: I'm going to ______________________________. Do you want one?

W: I am really hungry. What kinds do they have?

M: They only have ham and turkey. ______________ ______________________________?

12

W: You know ______________________________ Lily from school, right?

M: Of course. ______________________________. I'm just going to finish ______________ ______________ first.

W: Thanks, but won't you be late if you don't leave soon?

13

M: Hi, Sarah. I'm getting some people together to go bungee jumping this weekend. Would you like to join us?

W: Bungee jumping?

M: ______________________________________?

W: No, but Carolyn and I went parasailing one time. We both had a great time. We always have a great time together.

M: A parasail is like a parachute and ______________ ____________________________ by a boat, right?

W: That's right. It's fun.

M: And bungee jumping will be fun, too. __________ ____________________________.

W: Well, where is it?

M: At Harrison Lake. The company has been in business for 25 years. And ________________ ______________________________.

W: Good. Hmm... Have you asked Carolyn yet?

M: Yes, I have. She's coming, too.

14

M: Hi, Jocelyn. You're looking good these days. ______________________?

W: Actually, I have. I've been working out at a new fitness club.

M: Good for you.

W: Yeah. I'm trying to get ready for all the job interviews ______________________.

M: I also have an interview to go to. The interviewers will ask me about their company and what I studied in school, won't they?

W: Yes, but you've got to make a good first impression. ______________________ ______________.

M: I've been busy studying and I've had no time to work out.

W: Well, you ought to. Just an hour a day is all you'll need to spend working out.

15

M: Ji-hoon is ______________________. At break time and lunchtime it is common to see a lot of students around his desk. He loves to tell jokes, make people laugh and ______________ ______________________. He is usually funny. He often ______________________ of popular stars on TV. But today he is making fun of Chang-hyeon, a student in the same class. Chang-hyeon ______________________ because one leg is shorter than the other. So Chang-hyeon limps. Young-jae doesn't think Ji-hoon's actions are funny. He sees that Chang-hyeon is hurt by Ji-hoon's actions. In this situation, what would Young-jae most likely say to Ji-hoon?

16-17

W: The most important part of learning a foreign language is talking with native speakers. Then what is the second most important part? It's self-study. ______________________ self-study because they make your study sessions fun. Having fun is a really effective way to learn a new language. Did you ever ______________ ______________ in your head? Who hasn't! Music sticks in your brain, which is why songs are so often used in foreign language classes to ______________________. Most people who enjoy music listen to their favorite songs over and over until they know them by heart. This repetition, accompanied by a catchy tune, is the perfect formula for getting new words and phrases stuck in your brain ______________ ______________________. Find songs that you love. You'll want to listen to them on repeat, and you'll want to learn the words so you can sing along. Pop music isn't the whole story. Any style of music, whether it be hip hop, rock, or jazz, can be useful in language learning, ______________ ______________ lyrics. From slow, old folk songs to the latest musicals, singing a song is a really useful tool for language learning. So, go ahead and learn a new language through your favorite songs.

PRACTICE TEST

01 다음을 듣고, 여자가 하는 말의 목적으로 가장 적절한 것을 고르시오.

① 내일 시험이 있음을 알려주려고
② 시험에 대비한 스터디 그룹을 만들려고
③ 축구 연습이 언제 끝나는지 알아보려고
④ 자기 책을 학교에서 가져와 달라고 부탁하려고
⑤ 학교 도서관에 빌린 책을 돌려주도록 당부하려고

02 대화를 듣고, 남자의 의견으로 가장 적절한 것을 고르시오.

① 불법 주차는 바로 견인되어야 한다.
② 구급차의 진로 방해는 처벌해야 한다.
③ 지하 주차장을 더 많이 만들어야 한다.
④ 소방도로에는 잠시라도 주차하면 안 된다.
⑤ 화재 대피 경로 표시를 명확하게 해야 한다.

03 대화를 듣고, 두 사람의 관계를 가장 잘 나타낸 것을 고르시오.

① 의사 – 환자
② 영화배우 – 팬
③ 공무원 – 기자
④ 선거 후보자 – 유권자
⑤ 광고 대행사 직원 – 고객

04 대화를 듣고, 그림에서 대화의 내용과 일치하지 않는 것을 고르시오.

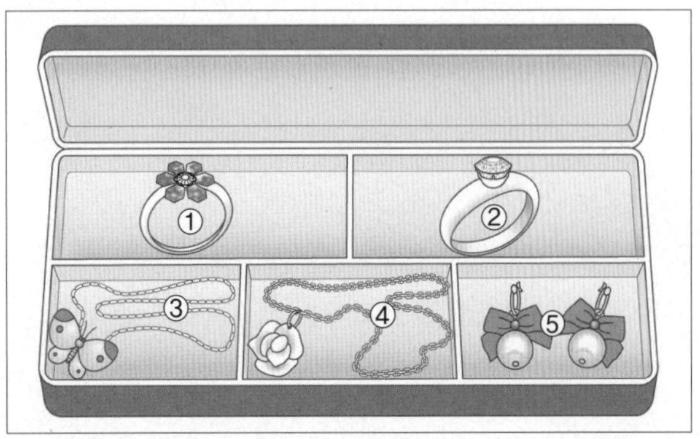

05 대화를 듣고, 여자가 남자에게 부탁한 일로 가장 적절한 것을 고르시오.

① 개 목욕시키기
② 개 산책시키기
③ 개를 위해 문 열기
④ 조부모님 모셔오기
⑤ 요리하는 것 도와주기

06 대화를 듣고, 남자가 지불할 금액을 고르시오.

① $60 ② $65 ③ $120
④ $125 ⑤ $180

07 대화를 듣고, Lee 선수가 계약을 거절한 이유를 고르시오.

① 계약 기간이 너무 길어서
② 이미 다른 회사와 계약해서
③ 계약 금액이 부족하다고 생각해서
④ 한 회사와만 계약하고 싶지 않아서
⑤ 제품 이미지와 어울리지 않는 것 같아서

08 대화를 듣고, 발해에 관해 언급되지 않은 것을 고르시오.

① 시조 ② 신분 제도 ③ 별칭
④ 멸망 원인 ⑤ 유적지의 소재

09 모금 행사에 관한 다음 내용을 듣고, 일치하지 않는 것을 고르시오.

① 홍수 이재민들을 돕기 위한 행사이다.
② 4월 25일 토요일에 개최될 예정이다.
③ 중고 물품들은 이재민들에게 직접 전달된다.
④ 기부할 물품은 학교로 가져와야 한다.
⑤ 모든 수익금은 적십자사로 보내진다.

정답 및 해설 p.98

10 다음 표를 보면서 대화를 듣고, 두 사람이 선택할 장소를 고르시오.

	Buffet	Wheelchair Accessible	Photographer Included
① Century Hall	○	○	×
② Beijing Garden	×	○	○
③ Skyview 41	×	○	×
④ Place Hotel	○	×	○
⑤ Citizen's Hall	○	○	○

11 대화를 듣고, 여자의 마지막 말에 대한 남자의 응답으로 가장 적절한 것을 고르시오.

① Delivery charges can vary.
② Everything will be 20% off.
③ You can resell these for $100.
④ I'm afraid they are not on sale.
⑤ The sales margin is roughly 10%.

12 대화를 듣고, 남자의 마지막 말에 대한 여자의 응답으로 가장 적절한 것을 고르시오.

① You can ask for a refund.
② In that case, don't bother.
③ The sale ended yesterday.
④ The pork was really good.
⑤ You know I'm a vegetarian.

13 대화를 듣고, 여자의 마지막 말에 대한 남자의 응답으로 가장 적절한 것을 고르시오. [3점]

▶ Man : ______________________

① You can use my computer and shop online.
② Let's get indoors before the dust gets worse.
③ I think the movies will be too crowded today.
④ OK. Let me repeat what I said a moment ago.
⑤ I mean the protests downtown are getting too big.

14 대화를 듣고, 남자의 마지막 말에 대한 여자의 응답으로 가장 적절한 것을 고르시오. [3점]

▶ Woman : ______________________

① Wow, that will be a long interview.
② The subway is the fastest way to get back.
③ I have an important commitment that night.
④ I need someone to take notes in my lectures today.
⑤ No problem! I have a car. I'll be there within an hour.

15 다음 상황 설명을 듣고, Maya가 Brooke에게 할 말로 가장 적절한 것을 고르시오. [3점]

▶ Maya : ______________________

① You don't like me, do you?
② I need to read self-help books.
③ I'm sorry I haven't written to you.
④ Why don't you think before complaining?
⑤ I've missed you. What has happened to you?

[16~17] 다음을 듣고, 물음에 답하시오.

16 남자가 하는 말의 주제로 가장 적절한 것은??

① some ways to avoid excess packaging
② how to reduce waste at a birthday party
③ reasons why excess packaging is unavoidable
④ importance of eco-friendly packaging materials
⑤ effects of excess packaging in the supermarket

17 언급된 물품이 아닌 것은?

① paper bags ② styrofoam trays
③ wooden boxes ④ glass jars
⑤ tin cans

25 DICTATION

녹음된 내용을 들으면서 빈칸을 알맞게 채워 보세요.

01

W: John, this is Lisa. You're still at school, right? You've got soccer practice. So ______________________ ______________________. Actually, it's an emergency so I really ______________________ ______________________ after soccer practice. The problem is that I've left my history textbook at school and ______________________. I was going to go to school right now and get it, but then I realized you were still there. I hope you can bring it to your home. I can go to your house to get it. It'd ______________________. And I have to do my math homework first, anyway. Thanks. Give me a call, OK?

02

W: Let's park here near the entrance.

M: Look! There's a sign over there. It's a fire lane.

W: Oh, I didn't know that. But ______________________ ______________________ around here.

M: I don't think we can, Bella. It's a lane for emergency vehicles. ______________________ at any time.

W: You're right. But we're only going to be half an hour. I think it's okay to park here as long as there's no fire.

M: You never know when an emergency will occur. When there's a fire, ______________________ ______________________.

W: I guess we'll have to go to the underground parking garage. I'm not sure if there's any vacancy though.

M: We have to find some other place. Fire lanes are vital for providing quick fire and emergency medical response.

W: I agree. It's important to keep these lanes clear.

M: Right. ______________________ ______________________ at all times.

03

W: Good morning! ______________________ ______________________?

M: Ms. Goh? I recognize your face from posters around town.

W: Well, my volunteer staff worked hard ______________________ ______________________.

M: It's nice to see you out meeting the local people.

W: I've lived here all my life. That's why you should choose me.

M: Ms. Goh, ______________________, what's your plan for health care?

W: The Green Party and I support more comprehensive health care for all families.

M: Really?

W: Yes, especially we'll ______________________ ______________________ for very low-income families.

M: That's interesting.

W: If you'd like more details, check out the campaign site: www.greensfor2015.net.

04

M: Hello?

W: Hi, honey. I need you to ______________________ ______________________.

M: Sure. What's up?

W: I want you to get my flower-shaped stone ring out of my jewelry box and bring it tonight. Can you do that?

M: Of course. ______________________. Yes, I see it beside your diamond ring.

W: Okay, great. Thank you so much.

M: This butterfly pendant necklace is nice. ______________________ ______________________, also?

W: No thanks, but ______________________ ______________________. Can you bring that?

M: Hmm, I don't see it. I see a pearl necklace.

W: What else?

정답 및 해설 p.98
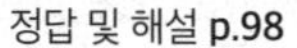

M: ____.

W: Oh, that's right. I lent my rose pendant necklace to my sister. Don't worry about it.

M: Okay. See you tonight.

05

W: Oh, not again! That dog! David, can't you hear that?

M: What, Mom?

W: Max is barking. When we bought you that dog, ____.

M: But I do, Mom. I even gave him a bath this afternoon.

W: I know and you feed him, too. But he's barking like crazy now. I'm sure he wants to go outside and play in the backyard. ____?

M: OK, Mom. I'm sorry.

W: I'm too busy cooking and his barking ____.

M: So sorry. Can I help you with that? My grandparents are coming over tonight, aren't they?

W: That's right. So, I'm preparing special food for them.

M: ____! Can I chop up all the vegetables on the cutting board?

W: No, thanks. Please just do ____.

06

M: Hi, I'd like to register for a Chinese conversation class please.

W: Great. How long would you like?

M: I was thinking just ____.

W: OK, every one-month conversation class is $60.

M: Really? My friend said it was only $40 a month here.

W: Are you sure that your friend goes to this institute? It's definitely $60.

M: Hmm. How much is it if I ____?

W: It is $120. And for six months, it's $180.

M: Oh, then my friend ____ for three months of classes. I'll do that too.

W: Certainly. And before registration, you need to ____. It costs $5.

M: But I'm just a beginner. I'm ____.

W: Then you don't need a placement test.

07

W: We want P.J. Lee to wear and advertise our golf clothing.

M: We ____. We're content with the money and the length of the contract you've suggested.

W: Good. We hope she'll improve our sales to young golfers. When does her present clothing contract finish?

M: In two months. Unfortunately, we do have one problem. She has told me she doesn't ____ with other companies.

W: But that's important to us. We don't want her to be in another company's advertisement.

M: Well, ____, but not an exclusive one.

W: I'm afraid that's not acceptable to us.

M: I'm sorry, then we can't take your offer. She is the youngest LPGA winner ever. At this point, ____ is not good for her.

08

W: Hi, Martin. What are you reading?

M: It's a book about the history of the Korean kingdom of Balhae. It's very interesting.

W: Ah, that's one of the kingdoms that ______________ ______________ of the Goguryeo kingdom.

M: Right. Goguryeo was conquered by Unified Silla, and then Dae Jo-yeong established Balhae.

W: If I remember right, Balhae society was separated into two social classes, one of which ______________ ______________ by the other.

M: Yes, but in other respects, it ______________ ______________. It was nicknamed "the flourishing land of the East."

W: I remember learning that in school. We also learned that Balhae collapsed ______________ ______________.

M: This book says that was the traditional theory, but some scholars believe the eruption of Mt. Baekdu ______________ of Balhae's end.

09

W: Centennial School ______________ ______________ for the flood victims. These people ______________, so the students want to help. On Saturday, April 25th this fundraiser will be held from 10 a.m. to 8 p.m. There will be an arts and handicrafts sale, musical performances, various games, a bake sale plus a sale of second-hand goods. The school requests the entire community ______________ ______________ to be sold at this event. So please ______________ ______________ and bring items to Centennial School before April 23rd. All the proceeds made at the fundraiser will be sent to the Red Cross ______________.

10

M: Where are we having our son's first birthday party? Everyone wants to know.

W: I have ______________ right here. They're all a similar price.

M: Hmm.... Having a party at this place would be great. ______________!

W: Yes, but they don't offer a buffet. It's a three-course western meal.

M: I'd prefer a buffet. ______________, wouldn't they?

W: I think so. Hmm.... Have you invited your oldest uncle yet?

M: I have. So the place must be wheelchair accessible.

W: Well, this one is wheelchair accessible and, as a bonus, an in-house photographer will ______________ ______________.

M: Honey, my brother is a photographer. He'll take the pictures and he'd be angry if he saw someone else taking pictures. No free photography.

W: ______________ then. I'll call now.

11

W: I'd like these three dresses. ______________ ______________?

M: That's $150. But ______________ ______________, in case you'd like to wait.

W: Oh, I didn't know that. How much of a discount will there be?

12

M: I'm going to the store. Do you want me to get anything?

W: Please get some more pork ______________ ______________.

M: Good idea. But ______________ ______________?

13

W: Today is my last day in Seoul. Let's go out.

M: Right, you're going back to Busan tomorrow. Do you want to see a movie?

W: No, I want to buy clothes for summer.

M: ______________________________. Hmm... Going out isn't such a good idea.

W: Why? Is it ______________________________ downtown?

M: No, I just got a text message ____________________ ______________________________ today.

W: Really? That's not good. I have asthma and allergies.

M: Well, we should stay indoors. __________________ __________________________.

W: Aww! I really wanted to go shopping for summer clothes today.

M: You don't have to ____________________________ __________________________.

W: I don't understand.

14

M: Grove Mart, Bruce Carter speaking.

W: Hello, this is Jamie Quan. I'm calling about your ad for casual staff.

M: ____ on Friday and Saturday nights.

W: That's perfect. I'm always free then.

M: May I ask how old you are?

W: Eighteen. I'm in my first year at Swinburne University.

M: OK, do you __________________________________?

W: Yes, four years at my mom's restaurant.

M: Waiting tables or kitchen work?

W: Everything. __________________________________.

M: OK, can you come in for a short interview?

W: Yes, anytime. __________________________________.

M: Then, stop by anytime today.

W: Oh, one more question; what are the hours?

M: 5:30 p.m. to 12:30 a.m. You'll need ____________ ____.

15

W: Maya has been reading self-improvement books. She finds them inspiring and ________________ __________________________ much of the advice she has read, in particular, the advice to think before you complain. She has promised herself to be positive and kind, even in situations where she would usually get angry and _____________ ________________________. Maya has lost touch with her best friend Brooke since they graduated from elementary school. Brooke ____________ __________________________________ to Maya's emails. Maya feels angry and insulted by this. One day, her phone rings. It's Brooke, saying hello. Maya ____. In this situation, what would Maya most likely say to Brooke?

16-17

M: We all enjoy giving and receiving presents on a birthday, and unwrapping them is half the fun. But at the end of the day, ___________________ ____________________________________ more packaging than is necessary? Many products that you buy are over-packaged, and packaging materials account for a third of all household waste. Excess packaging _______________________________ ______________. Is there anything you can do about this? One way is to avoid buying things with lots of packaging. __________________________ _________________ fruit and vegetables packed only in paper bags, rather than in plastic or styrofoam trays. Buy food and drinks in recyclable packaging such as glass jars or tin cans. If you have storage space, buy dried goods in bulk. This means fewer individual packages. Buy basic ingredients and ___________________________, rather than small prepackaged portions. Organic fruit and vegetables in supermarkets are often highly packaged, because they are marketed as high-value luxury produce. Complain about this to your supermarket, or, better still, have unpackaged fruit, vegetables and other produce ________________________________. And, of course, reuse or refuse supermarket carrier bags!

실전모의고사

26 PRACTICE TEST

01 다음을 듣고, 남자가 하는 말의 목적으로 가장 적절한 것을 고르시오.

① 외국인의 한국 방문을 독려하려고
② 비자 면제 프로그램의 시행을 알리려고
③ 한국 관광 산업의 발전 방향을 설명하려고
④ 비자 없이 갈 수 있는 국가들을 소개하려고
⑤ 간단한 비자 신청 수속의 필요성을 알리려고

02 대화를 듣고, 여자의 의견으로 가장 적절한 것을 고르시오.

① 쉬운 운동부터 시도하는 것이 좋다.
② 일상에서 자주 운동하는 것이 중요하다.
③ 건강 검진은 정기적으로 받는 것이 좋다.
④ 유산소 운동보다는 근력 운동이 필요하다.
⑤ 의사의 조언에 따른 체중 조절이 필요하다.

03 대화를 듣고, 두 사람의 관계를 가장 잘 나타낸 것을 고르시오.

① 남편 – 아내
② 지배인 – 바텐더
③ 요리사 – 종업원
④ 가게 주인 – 고객
⑤ 주방장 – 주방 보조

04 대화를 듣고, 그림에서 대화의 내용과 일치하지 않는 것을 고르시오.

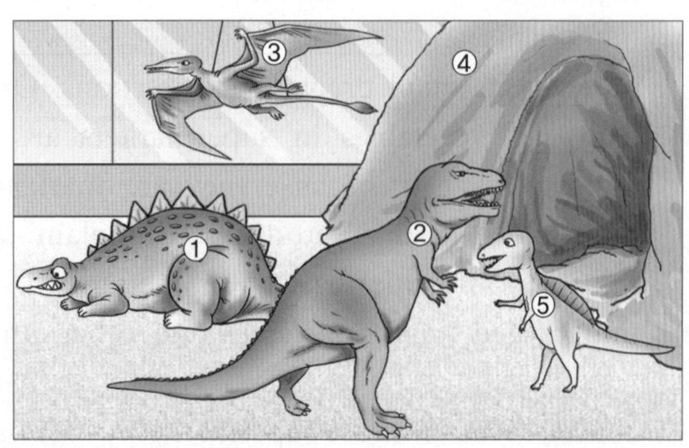

05 대화를 듣고, 남자가 오늘 오후에 할 일로 가장 적절한 것을 고르시오.

① 과학 수업 듣기
② 조교직에 지원하기
③ Miller 교수를 찾아가기
④ Miller 교수에게 전화하기
⑤ 성적 증명서와 이력서 제출하기

06 대화를 듣고, 여자가 지불할 금액을 고르시오. [3점]

① $105 ② $130 ③ $150
④ $155 ⑤ $205

07 대화를 듣고, 남자가 일을 그만두려는 이유를 고르시오.

① 급여가 불만족스러워서
② 한의사 자격시험에 합격해서
③ 더 좋은 일자리를 제의받아서
④ 공부를 다시 시작하고 싶어서
⑤ 자원봉사 단체에서 일하고 싶어서

08 대화를 듣고, 빈센트 반 고흐(Vincent van Gogh)에 관해 언급되지 않은 것을 고르시오.

① 국적 ② 활동 시기
③ 대표작 ④ 작품의 특징
⑤ 미술에 미친 영향력

09 다음 라디오 방송의 발표 내용을 듣고, 일치하지 않는 것을 고르시오.

① 공립학교들은 오늘 등교 시간을 늦추었다.
② 대부분의 사립학교들은 오늘 하루 휴교임을 알렸다.
③ 한 회사는 일부 사원들에게 재택근무를 요청했다.
④ 도로가 폐쇄된 곳도 있다.
⑤ 한 대학교는 오늘 모든 수업이 휴강이다.

정답 및 해설 p.102

10 다음 자료를 보면서 대화를 듣고, 여자가 받게 될 치과 서비스를 고르시오.

Cosmetic Dental Services

	Basic Whitening	Gum Reshaping	Scaling	Price
① Basic			✓	$60
② Deluxe A		✓		$100
③ Deluxe B	✓		✓	$130
④ Super-deluxe A	✓	✓	✓	$190
⑤ Super-deluxe B	✓	✓	✓	$200

11 대화를 듣고, 남자의 마지막 말에 대한 여자의 응답으로 가장 적절한 것을 고르시오.

① No, you'd better watch it later.
② Yes, I'm happy to watch the movie.
③ No, I'll be wearing my headphones.
④ Sure, I usually study in the living room.
⑤ Well, I guess the DVD player is broken.

12 대화를 듣고, 여자의 마지막 말에 대한 남자의 응답으로 가장 적절한 것을 고르시오.

① Sure, I can fix the sink.
② I'll do it right after breakfast.
③ Thanks for taking care of that.
④ I don't think it will cost too much.
⑤ I'd be happy to get a new refrigerator.

13 대화를 듣고, 남자의 마지막 말에 대한 여자의 응답으로 가장 적절한 것을 고르시오.

▶ Woman : ____________________

① My suit fits me just fine, thanks.
② Sorry, I don't have time to get measured.
③ Great. I will be right in to make my choice.
④ I don't want to change the color of the suit.
⑤ Fabric and color are very important in a suit.

14 대화를 듣고, 여자의 마지막 말에 대한 남자의 응답으로 가장 적절한 것을 고르시오. [3점]

▶ Man : ____________________

① They can help you at the bank.
② It isn't easy being single these days.
③ It is important to save for the future.
④ No. I need something with a photo on it.
⑤ That'll be fine, but I also need a second ID.

15 다음 상황 설명을 듣고, Max가 Becky에게 할 말로 가장 적절한 것을 고르시오. [3점]

▶ Max : ____________________

① We would love to have you work with us.
② I didn't know you were running for office.
③ You are far too busy to help with planning.
④ Can you help me select a tie for the banquet?
⑤ I heard you got asked to go to the dance party.

[16~17] 다음을 듣고, 물음에 답하시오.

16 여자가 하는 말의 주제로 가장 적절한 것은?

① healthy recipes for energetic mornings
② necessity of having breakfast every day
③ reasons why people skip their breakfast
④ four effective ways of losing weight without exercise
⑤ how to go on a diet fast and safely to be healthy

17 언급된 식품이 아닌 것은?

① milk ② soup ③ cheese
④ cereal ⑤ cracker

26 DICTATION

녹음된 내용을 들으면서 빈칸을 알맞게 채워 보세요.

01

M: A new agreement between the U.S. and Korean governments will allow more people to visit the United States ______________________________. With this new agreement, called a "Visa Waiver," it is expected that an extra 300,000 Koreans will tour the U.S. To apply for a visa before, people ______________________________. But the process will now be as simple as buying a plane ticket. Although this will benefit many Koreans, the government fears this will ______________________________ for Korea. Koreans who would normally visit places in their own country might choose to go to America instead.

02

W: Hi, Jerome. How was your regular medical check-up?

M: It's not that good. My doctor suggested that I do some exercise, but ______________________________.

W: If you don't do exercise, your health will get worse.

M: I know. But ______________________________ is tough.

W: You don't have to go to the gym. Find other ways to fit activity into your daily life. You can climb up and down the stairs.

M: Yeah. But my doctor said I need some weight training.

W: You can work out in the office with water bottles. ______________________________.

M: Oh, that's a good idea. Then I should use water bottles like dumbbells?

W: Exactly. I'll send you that exercise video. It's ______________________________ anywhere, anytime.

M: Thank you. I'll give it a try.

03

M: How did you say the customer wanted the steak cooked?

W: He said ______________________________. Like, bright red.

M: But, the health department in this state doesn't let us serve any meat cooked less than medium-rare.

W: I tried to tell him that, but he told me that ______________________________.

M: Hmm.... I'm pretty sure ______________________________.

W: Well, what do you want me to tell him?

M: Tell him that the man in charge of the kitchen ______________________________ at anyone getting sick.

W: OK. But he isn't going to be happy. Maybe you should take off your apron and tell him yourself.

04

W: What do you think of the dinosaur exhibit, Peter?

M: It's great, Mom! Look at the one on the left. It has triangle-shaped horns on its back.

W: ______________________________, but it only eats plants.

M: There's a meat-eating dinosaur next to it. It has two short arms and it's standing on two legs.

W: You're right. Oh, Peter, look up at the ceiling!

M: Wow, a dinosaur that can fly. ______________________________!

W: They are! Look! There's a big cave.

M: ______________________________.

W: There are some eggs by the entrance.

M: And they look like they are hatching ______________________________.

W: Let's stay and watch. Maybe something will happen.

05

M: Excuse me, Professor Miller?

W: Yes, that's right. How may I help you?

M: I am looking for a position as a teaching assistant in the spring. I heard you were the best professor in the science department.

W: I usually choose a T.A. from ________________ ________________________ who go on to pursue a Master's.

M: I understand, but I am ____________________ from State University.

W: Do you ________________________________?

M: Yes, they're right here.

W: Well, this looks impressive. Do you have time tomorrow to come to my office?

M: ______________________________________.

W: Then would you call me at this number around 4 this afternoon? So I can schedule an interview.

M: Thank you.

06

W: Hi, I'd like to join this fitness club.

M: Just yourself, or would you like to ____________ _______________________?

W: I don't know if it would be worth signing my husband and daughter up.

M: If you become a member, it's only an extra $50 a month for additional family members.

W: _____________________________________?

M: If you want the deluxe package, which includes tanning and massage, it is $100 per month.

W: And what about a package without tanning and massage?

M: That would be our standard package. It is $80 a month.

W: I think I'll sign up for the deluxe package for me and my husband.

M: OK. Yourself and one extra family member.... ____ ____________________ for the deluxe package.

W: Oh, ________________________________?

M: We usually charge a $5 registration fee, but this month it's free.

07

W: Are you really quitting your job? Isn't it the third job _________________________________?

M: Yes. It is, but this time I have a plan.

W: But this is ______________________________. I know you are satisfied with the pay. You already ____?

M: No, actually, I'm leaving the corporate world, and I'm planning to study again.

W: Really? What are you going to study?

M: Well, I want to be a traditional oriental doctor. That was my dream 10 years ago, and I just realized that ______________________________.

W: Wow. That's great.

M: Yes, I think I will be happier if I am helping people and ____________________________________.

W: Good luck.

08

W: Today, we're going to talk about Vincent van Gogh, ____ of the 19th century.

M: Mrs. Johnson, didn't he paint *Starry Night*?

W: That's right. And he also painted *Sunflowers*, *The Bedroom*, and several self-portraits.

M: ________________________________ of his paintings?

W: His paintings can be recognized by their bold use of color, rough beauty, and emotional honesty.

M: Oh, that sounds similar to the work of Matisse, who we talked about last month.

W: That's right! Vincent van Gogh's influence on art has been tremendous. Characteristics from his work ____ ______________, including Matisse.

M: I'm starting to see why Vincent van Gogh is _____ ______________________________.

09

W: This is WMAL Radio's ____________________. Due to last night's snow storm, all public schools in the county today will open two hours late. If you attend a private school, please contact the school directly to find out ______________________ ______________. Ecstatic Software Corporation is requesting that employees who can work from home do so. Queen Lake road is closed. And finally, Waterloo University ______________ __________________ today. We will keep you updated on ______________________________ every 10 minutes.

10

M: Congratulations! You're getting married in a month!

W: I know! And my father told me to get __________ __________________________.

M: Great!

W: Oh! You have various sets of services. I can get several dental services at once and save money.

M: That's right. Which set do you prefer?

W: I don't know. What do you recommend?

M: Think about ______________________________ ___________________. You want your smile to be perfect at the wedding.

W: OK, but ________________________________ $200.

M: That means you will not choose Super-deluxe B.

W: Yeah, and since my teeth look kind of short, _____ ______________________________.

M: Sure. And you need scaling too?

W: Yes, actually that is the most important thing.

11

M: ____ a movie in the living room?

W: Not at all. I have to study in my room anyway.

M: ______________________________________?

12

W: I think our refrigerator is broken. We need to call a repairman.

M: Yeah, we also need to ______________________ ______________________.

W: Well, if you aren't too busy, ___________________ _________________________?

13

M: Hello, Patrick's Fashion House. How may I help you?

W: Hi. My husband, Walter Kimmel, ____________ ______________________ at your store.

M: Oh, yes. I remember Mr. Kimmel.

W: Well, I was wondering if you could make him another suit from ____________________________ _______________________.

M: Is this going to be a surprise?

W: Yes, his birthday is coming.

M: We can do that. What color do you want?

W: ______________________________ was dark blue. I think charcoal gray would be nice.

M: A classic color. What kind of fabric and style would you prefer?

W: Hmm, I'm not sure.

M: Then, how about if you _____________________ _______________________?

14

W: I'd like to open a bank account.

M: Yes, ma'am. I'll ________________________________ ____________________.

W: OK. Is there a minimum deposit to____________ ______________________?

M: Yes, there is a $50 minimum for savings.

W: I also want to open a checking account. Can I do both today?

M: Of course. But we have a single form for a combined account.

W: One form ________________________________. Do you need anything else?

M: I'll need to see two forms of identification.

W: ____?

15

M: Max ____ ________________ for the Senior Class Spring Banquet at his high school. His twin sister, Becky, wants to be part of the committee, but Max knows his sister ______________________ __________________, like soccer and French lessons. Becky thinks she should _____________ _______________________ in the group because Max is her brother. Max __________________ ______________________ in the committee and must tell his sister that she isn't in the group. In this situation, what would Max most likely say to Becky?

16-17

W: Many people ____________________________ often skip breakfast to reduce their daily caloric intake. While this may work to a certain extent, you might make up for the calories later in the day due to overeating at lunch and dinner. Because you're so hungry by lunch, it's ______________________ _______________________. On top of that, you'll have almost no fuel to run on in the morning, which means you won't be able to perform at full capacity. You might even feel unhappy ________________________________. If you skip breakfast, you will also eat more for dinner. Eating a big dinner means that you won't be hungry for breakfast the next day. Studies suggest that if you eat a high-protein, low-fat breakfast and a small dinner, you will __________________________ ______________________ and maintain a healthy body weight. Skipping breakfast is obviously not good for your overall health. So if you don't have the appetite for a full breakfast, have a small one that's ________________________________. Eat something — milk, fruit, soup, or yogurt. And use your midmorning snack, such as cheese or a wholegrain cracker, to ________________________ ______________________________________ and energy needs. Eating breakfast every day will be an excellent foundation for a long and healthy life.

PRACTICE TEST

01 다음을 듣고, 남자가 하는 말의 목적으로 가장 적절한 것을 고르시오.

① 청중을 고려한 연설문 작성을 권유하려고
② 연설을 위한 사전 준비와 연습을 강조하려고
③ 청중의 공감을 얻는 화법의 중요성을 알리려고
④ 연설할 때 청중과 시선을 맞출 것을 조언하려고
⑤ 연설할 때 덜 긴장할 수 있는 방법을 소개하려고

02 대화를 듣고, 여자의 의견으로 가장 적절한 것을 고르시오.

① 조언은 원하는 사람에게 해줘야 한다.
② 잘못에 대한 사과는 빠르게 해야 한다.
③ 화가 나면 스스로 진정할 시간을 줘야 한다.
④ 농담에 지나친 과잉반응을 보일 필요는 없다.
⑤ 겉모습만 보고 사람을 평가하지 말아야 한다.

03 대화를 듣고, 두 사람의 관계를 가장 잘 나타낸 것을 고르시오.

① 환자 – 의사
② 감독 – 코치
③ 학생 – 선생님
④ 배구 선수 – 감독
⑤ 리포터 – 야구 선수

04 대화를 듣고, 그림에서 대화의 내용과 일치하지 <u>않는</u> 것을 고르시오.

05 대화를 듣고, 남자가 여자를 위해 할 일로 가장 적절한 것을 고르시오.

① 새 블렌더 사기
② 한국어 가르치기
③ 여자의 일정을 세우기
④ 바나나 스무디 만들기
⑤ 예비 부품 제조업자를 찾기

06 대화를 듣고, 여자가 지불할 금액을 고르시오. [3점]

① $56 ② $64 ③ $70 ④ $72 ⑤ $80

07 대화를 듣고, 남자가 대출을 받을 수 <u>없는</u> 이유를 고르시오.

① 서류를 제출하지 않아서
② 시장 조사를 하지 않아서
③ 이미 다른 대출이 있어서
④ 거래 기간이 너무 짧아서
⑤ 주택 구매 대출이 아니라서

08 다음을 듣고, Toco Toucan에 관해 언급되지 <u>않은</u> 것을 고르시오.

① 부리의 특징 ② 깃털의 기능
③ 번식력 ④ 인기 이유
⑤ 전통적 의미

09 우주 김치에 관한 다음 내용을 듣고, 일치하지 <u>않는</u> 것을 고르시오.

① 우주 김치의 주요 개발자는 이원주라는 연구원이다.
② 2003년에 우주 음식으로 정식 인증되었다.
③ 개발 시 가장 큰 난관은 냄새를 줄이는 것이었다.
④ 김치 박테리아를 없애는 처리 과정이 개발되었다.
⑤ 우주 김치는 여느 김치와 같은 맛을 가지고 있다.

정답 및 해설 p.106

10 다음 표를 보면서 대화를 듣고, 두 사람이 예약할 패키지를 고르시오.

Orlando Hotel Packages

Package Type	View	Meals	Price	Included activity
① A	Beach	breakfast and dinner	$1,020	city bus tour
② B	Beach	only breakfast	$880	theme park visit
③ C	Beach	only breakfast	$780	city bus tour
④ D	Beach	only breakfast	$1,150	theme park visit
⑤ E	Garden	breakfast and dinner	$690	walking tour

11 대화를 듣고, 여자의 마지막 말에 대한 남자의 응답으로 가장 적절한 것을 고르시오.

① He's always late.
② I thought you told him.
③ We can't start without him.
④ I'll tell him later if it's possible.
⑤ He said he would come next time.

12 대화를 듣고, 남자의 마지막 말에 대한 여자의 응답으로 가장 적절한 것을 고르시오.

① Time is going by so quickly.
② I guess it wouldn't hurt to ask.
③ That means we only have four hours.
④ We should have submitted it on time.
⑤ At 3 p.m. tomorrow, I'll be in Beijing.

13 대화를 듣고, 여자의 마지막 말에 대한 남자의 응답으로 가장 적절한 것을 고르시오. [3점]

▶ Man : ______

① Do you think I can pay by credit card?
② Great. Then I can leave my wallet here.
③ OK. Let's go and find a good restaurant.
④ That's OK. I'd rather do my work right now.
⑤ I'll do it for an hour and I'll bring 10 dollars back.

14 대화를 듣고, 남자의 마지막 말에 대한 여자의 응답으로 가장 적절한 것을 고르시오.

▶ Woman : ______

① She's a very stylish woman.
② You can try it on if you'd like to check.
③ Your mother takes a medium, doesn't she?
④ I wear a large, so you should get her a small.
⑤ I wear a medium in this brand, so she should too.

15 다음 상황 설명을 듣고, Elizabeth가 Peter에게 할 말로 가장 적절한 것을 고르시오. [3점]

▶ Elizabeth : ______

① Sir, would you like to go ahead of me?
② Are you having steak for dinner tonight?
③ You can get a cart over there in the corner.
④ Please don't cut in the line. Wait your turn.
⑤ Could you help me carry my groceries, please?

[16~17] 다음을 듣고, 물음에 답하시오.

16 여자가 하는 말의 주제로 가장 적절한 것은?

① key factors influencing family health
② facts about National Family History Day
③ effects of physical health on family relationships
④ diseases to predict through a family health history
⑤ health benefits of making a family health history tree

17 언급된 질병이 아닌 것은?

① heart disease
② cancer
③ allergy
④ diabetes
⑤ liver disease

27 DICTATION

녹음된 내용을 들으면서 빈칸을 알맞게 채워 보세요.

01

M: As you know, the audience is an important element in public speaking. A presentation will ______________________________. This is why you need to make your speech worthy of your listeners' time. There is one simple thing you can do to ______________________________. It is purposeful eye contact with one person at a time. When you fail to do it, you ______________________________. When you don't look people in the eye, they are less likely to look at you. That makes them start thinking about something other than what you're saying, and when that happens, they stop listening. So, if you want to ______________________________, look people in the eye, one at a time.

02

W: James, ______________________________?

M: I actually had an argument with Chris a few minutes ago.

W: What happened?

M: Well, everyone wanted a good laugh so I called him a cucumber because of all the pimples on his face. Chris got all upset.

W: Oh, that wasn't very nice of you. ______________________________?

M: Well, no. I thought it was just a joke but he overreacted. Chris said he would never talk to me again.

W: I can understand why he did that. ______________________________. Call him now and tell him you're sorry. You need to apologize and make up right away.

M: I think he needs ______________________________ since he's so angry now.

W: No, you have to make it timely. The sooner you offer an apology, ______________________________.

M: That's right. I'd better call him right away. Thanks for your advice.

03

W: Sue played well against Western High School on Monday.

M: Yes, but she can't play tomorrow because ______________________________.

W: Have you talked to her today? What did she say?

M: She said the doctor ______________________________ for a couple more days.

W: OK.

M: Tomorrow we play Northern High School. They hit the ball hard.

W: We need to ______________________________.

M: I have an idea. I'll show it to you later on the whiteboard.

W: OK. We can teach it to the girls at practice this afternoon. And I want Jill to play a lot tomorrow.

M: Yes, I agree. ______________________________.

04

W: Mary's Interior Design. How may I help you?

M: Hi, this is Greg. I talked to you before about the bakery that I'm opening?

W: Yes, of course. Did you ______________________________ about the exterior?

M: I decided to ______________________________, like you suggested. I also ______________________________ that says "The Bakery."

W: That sounds good. Did you install an entrance door?

M: Yes, I went with ______________________________.

W: Okay. Have you considered placing a three-layer cake in the display window, like we talked about?

M: Yes, ______________________________. It is much more impressive than my two-layer cakes.

W: Good. I also suggest ______________________________ to attract customers.

M: I already have one. It says "Grand Opening."

W: Then everything sounds great.

정답 및 해설 p.106

05

W: Hey, Ji-hoon! You know how I make banana smoothies for breakfast every day?

M: Yum. ______________________________!

W: Sure, but ______________________________. I need a replacement part for a Mixmaster blender.

M: Blender? Oh, we call that a "mixer" in Korea.

W: Right. I looked on the Internet for ____________ ____________________________ in Seoul, but my Korean isn't so good.

M: No problem. ______________________________ ______________. What's the brand name again?

W: Mixmaster.

M: And how about if I teach you some Korean?

W: That sounds great. But not right now. My schedule is too busy nowadays. But thank you anyway.

M: OK, then.

W: You're so good, Ji-hoon.

06

M: We are very lucky. Look, it says membership holders ________________________________ on Fridays.

W: Really?

M: Yes, they give a 20 percent discount for gold membership cards, and a 10 percent discount for silver membership cards.

W: Even 10 percent off can save us a lot of money!

M: But ______________________________!

W: Of course you do! How much is the bill? 70 dollars?

M: No, it's a total of 80 dollars. So if we can get a 20 percent discount, ______________________________.

W: That's a lot.

M: Yeah. I agree. But ______________________________. I'm a silver member.

W: I can get it. I'm a gold member. ________________ ______________.

M: Oh, really? Thanks. I had a really great time.

07

M: Hello, Ms. Lowell. I called you yesterday.

W: Hello, Mr. Miles. Please have a seat. So, __________ ________________________ for your new coffee shop, right?

M: Yes, I'd like to open a coffee shop on Harbor Street.

W: Have you done any market research on that area?

M: Sure I did. That's why I chose that location. I also already sent all the documents you asked for.

W: Yes. Well, unfortunately, it looks like __________ ________________________ at this time.

M: May I ask why? I've had an account with this bank for 12 years now.

W: I realize that, but ____________________________.

M: I took out that loan because I needed money to buy my house.

W: I'm sorry but we can't give you a business loan ______________________________.

M: Oh, I see.

08

M: The Toco Toucan is a type of South American bird characterized by its huge but light beak. Their bright feathers are the colors of flowers and fruits, and ____________________________________ in the broken light of the rain forest. However, these birds are generally noisy, which suggests that they are not trying to remain hidden. They produce two to four eggs each year, and ____________________ ________________________ for about six weeks. These well-known birds are very popular pets, and ____________________________________ in commercials for various products. Native peoples regard the bird ____________________________ ________________; they are traditionally seen as messengers between the worlds of the living and the spirits.

09

W: You're an astronaut doing research in outer space. You're hungry, but not for ________________ ________________. You want some of your mother's kimchi, a taste of home. Now you can have it — thanks to researcher Lee Won-ju, who began working on space kimchi in 2003. To make kimchi a space food, Mr. Lee solved several problems. ________________________________ by 30 to 50%, so ________________________ ________________. Mr. Lee also had to invent a process to kill the bacteria in kimchi without changing the taste. He succeeded. So space kimchi ________________________________ as regular kimchi, but also has the same taste.

10

W: I'm so excited about our trip to Orlando. It's been so long since we've had a vacation.

M: The hotel ________________________________ is offering several special packages. Let's see what we have here.

W: I think we should pay more to get the beach view.

M: I think so, too. Fortunately, ________________ ________________________ have beach views.

W: Good. What about our meals? I want to have breakfast at the hotel.

M: Don't worry. Breakfast is ____________________ ____________________. There are also packages that offer breakfast and dinner.

W: That's not necessary. We'll be sightseeing until evening and there are so many great restaurants there.

M: Okay. And I'd ____________________________ $1,000.

W: I agree. Then there are two we can choose from.

M: How about the cheaper one?

W: I ____________________________________. I think it's worth more than $100.

M: I see. Then let's reserve this package.

11

W: Jacob still isn't here. ________________________ ________________________.

M: Well, I'm not sure that he knows we are meeting today.

W: ____, did you?

12

M: I don't think we can finish this report tonight. Let's meet tomorrow.

W: But ________________________ by 3 p.m. and I don't have time in the morning.

M: Oh, that's right. Do you think ________________ ________________________?

13

M: Clara, do you want to eat dinner at a restaurant in the hotel?

W: Sounds good.

M: I'd like to work out before dinner. Do you know ____________________________________ for hotel guests?

W: You can look in the hotel directory. I've just seen it somewhere. Hmm... Here, I've got it.

M: Can you ________________________________?

W: OK, let's see. ____________________________, an indoor driving range.

M: Really? Is it free?

W: No, it says it's 10 dollars won an hour for hotel guests.

M: Well, I like golfing, but I just want to work out right now. Does it say where the fitness center is?

W: It's on the 11th floor. And ____________________ ________________________.

14

W: Can I help you with anything, sir?

M: I'd like to get ______________________________ for my mother.

W: The size?

M: Medium. Yes, those will do fine. And I need a present for my wife.

W: ______________________________?

M: She asked for a sweater this year.

W: Our sweaters are over here, sir.

M: Getting a present for my wife is hard. I often get ______________________________.

W: This style is very popular this year. I'm sure she'll love it.

M: OK. I'll trust your opinion. ______________________________.

W: And the size?

M: Hmm... it depends on the brand. Actually, she's about your size.

15

M: Elizabeth is doing the weekly grocery shopping. She pushes the cart ______________________________ picking out the groceries. When her cart is full, ______________________________. She is next in line. One person ______________________________ now and there is no one behind her. Then Peter gets in line behind Elizabeth. He has three items: steak, milk and potatoes. He looks anxious and seems to be in a hurry. Elizabeth looks around at the other aisles. There doesn't ______________________________. She wants to help him. In this situation, what would Elizabeth most likely say to Peter?

16-17

W: Do you know what November 24 is? You may think it is Thanksgiving Day, but it is actually National Family History Day. ______________________________ in 2004 to encourage American families to learn about their family health history. It is an important part of routine medical care, and the family gathering on Thanksgiving will be ______________________________ a family health history tree. A family health history helps you see any increased risk of developing serious health problems, like heart disease or cancer. It also ______________________________, such as, say, diabetes, hypertension, and liver disease, that are passed from one generation to the next. Although you can't change your genes, you can ______________________________ with good lifestyle habits and regular medical screenings. So before you join your family for your annual turkey meal, do some research, and make a family health history tree. To get started, talk to your parents and siblings. Then move on to second-degree relatives, like grandparents, aunts, uncles, nieces and nephews. If your grandparents ______________________________, ask your parents or any living aunts, uncles or cousins about them. Making a family tree of health history ______________________________ and to make appropriate health care decisions.

실전모의고사

28 PRACTICE TEST

01 **다음을 듣고, 남자가 하는 말의 목적으로 가장 적절한 것을 고르시오.**

① 도시의 역사에 관해 설명하려고
② 역사적 건축물 보존을 강조하려고
③ 새로운 쓰레기 처리장 건설을 주장하려고
④ 환경과 관련된 새 법률 제정을 요구하려고
⑤ 시의회의 업무 태만에 대해 불만을 표하려고

02 **대화를 듣고, 두 사람이 하는 말의 주제로 가장 적절한 것을 고르시오.**

① 시간이 부족한 이유
② 효율적인 시간 관리 요령
③ 이삿짐을 쌀 때의 주의사항
④ 자투리 시간을 활용하는 방법
⑤ 동시에 여러 가지 일을 처리하는 비결

03 **대화를 듣고, 두 사람의 관계를 가장 잘 나타낸 것을 고르시오.**

① 학생 – 교수
② 독자 – 저자
③ 손님 – 서점 직원
④ 도서관 이용객 – 사서
⑤ 서점 주인 – 출판사 직원

04 **대화를 듣고, 그림에서 대화의 내용과 일치하지 않는 것을 고르시오.**

05 **대화를 듣고, 여자가 할 일로 가장 적절한 것을 고르시오.**

① 추가 면접 준비하기
② 시험 점수 합산하기
③ 신입사원 소개 연설하기
④ 지원자의 법률 지식 검사하기
⑤ 지원자에게 면접 결과 통보하기

06 **대화를 듣고, 남자가 지불할 금액을 고르시오.**

① $46 ② $49 ③ $52
④ $56 ⑤ $59

07 **대화를 듣고, 여자가 약속을 미뤄야 하는 이유를 고르시오.**

① 집을 지켜야 해서
② 교통 체증이 심해서
③ 동생의 학교에 들러야 해서
④ 다른 음식점을 찾아야 해서
⑤ 운동 경기를 보러 가야 해서

08 **대화를 듣고, 남극에 관해 언급되지 않은 것을 고르시오.**

① 위치 ② 면적 ③ 탐험사
④ 생태 ⑤ 기후

09 **Borderland에 관한 다음 내용을 듣고, 일치하지 않는 것을 고르시오.**

① 1900년대 초에 Ames 부부가 산 땅이다.
② 1,782에이커의 부지가 주립공원이 되었다.
③ 승마와 낚시를 즐길 수 있는 곳이 있다.
④ Ames 부부의 저택은 일반인에게 공개되지 않는다.
⑤ 이곳의 연못 근처에서 영화가 촬영되었다.

정답 및 해설 p.110

10 다음 표를 보면서 대화를 듣고, 여자가 구입할 책을 고르시오.

Secondhand Book Search Results:
Go Your Own Way

Seller	Edition	Price	Binding	Shipping Date
① Maggie	1st	$32	Hardcover	same day
② Andrew	3rd	$22	Paperback	two days from the order date
③ Norah	2nd	$18	Paperback	same day
④ Steve	3rd	$28	Hardcover	same day
⑤ Karen	2nd	$24	Hardcover	two days from the order date

11 대화를 듣고, 남자의 마지막 말에 대한 여자의 응답으로 가장 적절한 것을 고르시오.

① The budget is not final.
② You'll conduct the next meeting.
③ There were no changes to that team.
④ I think Jim will make a fine manager.
⑤ He'll cover for you while you're away.

12 대화를 듣고, 여자의 마지막 말에 대한 남자의 응답으로 가장 적절한 것을 고르시오.

① They will charge you $10.
② Hit Tracks is having a huge sale.
③ Sorry, but I don't have my receipt.
④ That shop has various headphones.
⑤ Why don't you go and ask about it?

13 대화를 듣고, 남자의 마지막 말에 대한 여자의 응답으로 가장 적절한 것을 고르시오. [3점]

▶ Woman :

① Sorry, it is unlikely to be achieved.
② I'm not in charge of judging applicants.
③ You'd better prepare for the test immediately.
④ I knew you had the ability to succeed on the test.
⑤ Those who excel receive scholarships for one year.

14 대화를 듣고, 여자의 마지막 말에 대한 남자의 응답으로 가장 적절한 것을 고르시오. [3점]

▶ Man :

① I'm not sure, but you could try.
② It would be better to work without coffee.
③ I regret not starting to drink herbal tea sooner.
④ If I were you, I'd try my best to cut down on coffee.
⑤ Of course. You may not like the taste of herbal teas.

15 다음 상황 설명을 듣고, Robert가 Susie에게 할 말로 가장 적절한 것을 고르시오. [3점]

▶ Robert : Susie,

① can I go with you to help you prepare?
② you should remember that practice makes perfect.
③ I don't want the time I spent preparing to be wasted.
④ your full recovery is more important than the competition.
⑤ you shouldn't swim unless you have the confidence to win.

[16~17] 다음을 듣고, 물음에 답하시오.

16 여자가 하는 말의 주제로 가장 적절한 것은?

① the reasons behind the global energy shortage
② potential crises that nuclear energy might bring
③ the most effective solution to the energy shortage
④ how to enhance the use of new alternative energies
⑤ the relationship between energy and the environment

17 언급된 대체 에너지가 아닌 것은?

① 수력 ② 풍력 ③ 태양열
④ 조력 ⑤ 원자력

28 DICTATION

녹음된 내용을 들으면서 빈칸을 알맞게 채워 보세요.

01

M: Good evening, fellow council members. ________ ________________________, many of the public buildings and facilities in our city were built nearly sixty years ago. Some of these structures, like our beautiful courthouse, will continue to function for many more years, ________________________ ________________________. And our current waste-treatment facility is a perfect example. It is both ________________________________ ________________________ and so inefficient that it is harming our environment. Because our city is growing rapidly, a new facility is necessary _____ ____ overrun with garbage and waste. As city council members, it is our duty ____________________ ____________________________.

02

W: What's wrong, Nate?

M: Oh, Mom. I'm worried about all the reading I have to do for my English essay. _____________ ______________________.

W: Why don't you use the method I used when we moved?

M: What do you mean?

W: When I had to pack, I was busy _______________ ______________________.

M: Yeah, I remember.

W: ____, I chose to pack for an hour every day.

M: That's right. You know, one of my friends usually reads when he's on the subway or waiting for a friend.

W: That's another great way to _________________ ________________. You can also try making a list of tasks before going to bed.

M: Thanks, Mom. I'll give it a try.

03

M: Excuse me, do you possibly have *The History of Russian Translation*?

W: I'll check if we have it for you. _________________ ________________________.

M: All right.

W: I'm afraid the book you want is ______________ ________________________.

M: No way! I really need that book for the essay I'm writing. My grade depends on it.

W: Well, ______________________________, the first edition was released in 1998. We may have a copy somewhere.

M: Okay. I'll wait. Do you have one?

W: I'm afraid not. But I can call the publisher of the book to find out if they have any copies in stock.

M: I really appreciate your help. __________________ ____________________________.

04

M: Hi, Stella. What's that?

W: It's ____.

M: I want to see. Oh, it's your family!

W: Right. We went to the beach in Busan.

M: Who's the man ____________________________?

W: He's my brother. He likes to surf.

M: I see. Oh, there's a row of parasols on the beach.

W: Yeah. It looked great. And the woman __________ ________________________________ in front of the parasols is my mom.

M: Okay. And I guess the girl making a sand castle is your sister, right?

W: Right. I remember she cried because she lost her flag before she could ________________________ ____________________.

M: Did she? Oh, and the man __________________ ____________________________________ must be your father.

W: Yes. It was really hot that day.

정답 및 해설 p.110

05

M: Good morning, Ms. Davis. Here are the results of yesterday's interviews.

W: Great. ________________________________. Thank you.

M: As you can see, Dan Benson did fairly well.

W: What do you think of him?

M: Well, he is a strong speaker and he ____________ ____________________________. But his score on the written test wasn't great.

W: As you know, thorough knowledge of the law is ____. What about Helen Simpson? She scored the highest on the written exam.

M: She is obviously intelligent, but she seems to lack confidence.

W: It's hard to choose between the candidates. Do you have any ideas?

M: The best we can do is ____________________ ______________________ and pick the best.

W: Okay. I'll do that.

06

W: Good afternoon. May I help you?

M: I'd ____. How much is it?

W: It's $8 for an automatic wash and $16 for a hand washing.

M: My car hasn't been washed ________________ ____________________. Which would be better?

W: In that case, I recommend the hand washing. It includes a high-pressure cleansing spray.

M: Then, I'll choose that. Also, ________________ __________________________.

W: Waxing costs $22. It is a reduction from the old price of $25.

M: Sounds good. Lastly, I'd ____________________ ________________________ as well.

W: We charge $10 for vacuuming, but you can get a 20 percent discount since you selected a hand washing.

M: Great. How long until everything is finished?

W: Come back in an hour, and __________________ ________________________.

M: Got it. I'll be back at 3 p.m.

07

M: Hello?

W: Hi, Richard. It's Emily.

M: Hi, Emily. I'm just leaving my house now.

W: Wait. I'm afraid we have to delay our appointment.

M: Why? ____________________________________?

W: No, but I have to take care of something for my brother.

M: Is it urgent? ______________________________ ________________ for dinner.

W: I'm so sorry, but it's important and I'm the only one at home.

M: I know your brother has a big hockey game at his school tonight. ____________________________?

W: Exactly. He forgot to bring his stick to school and he wants to use it for the game.

M: Couldn't he just borrow a stick from someone?

W: No, it has to be that stick. __________________ ________________________.

M: I understand. Just call me back when you are finished.

W: I will.

08

W: I heard you've just come back from the South Pole. What made you decide to study the South Pole?

M: ____. It is located on the continent of Antarctica, and it is nearly 3,000 meters above sea level.

W: It must have been difficult for the first explorers to establish a base.

M: Extremely difficult. It wasn't until 1911 that ______ ________________________________ to the South Pole.

W: And there is no plant life, correct?

M: Right. But, amazingly, there are birds called Snow Petrels that have been spotted there.

W: Incredible. ____________________ ________________ in such a place.

M: Yes, especially considering that the highest temperature ever recorded at the pole was lower than minus twelve degrees Celsius.

W: Will you be going back?

M: I will. ________________________________.

09

W: Borderland is a Massachusetts state park located in the towns of Easton and Sharon. In 1906, a botanist named Oakes Ames and his wife Blanche Ames, an artist and feminist, ________________ ________________________ "Borderland." Sixty-five years later, two years after the death of Blanche Ames, the Massachusetts government acquired the 1,782-acre estate and __________ ____________________________. Here the public can enjoy walking and horseback riding on its woodland trails, as well as fishing, canoeing, ice skating, and sledding. The mansion which the Ameses once lived in ________________ ________________, and its twenty rooms contain many of Blanche Ames' original paintings. Today, ________________ ______________ from the movie *Shutter Island*, directed by Martin Scorsese, which was shot near the park's Leach Pond.

10

M: Sharon, what are you doing on the computer?

W: I'm looking at some used books, but it's ______ ____________________ among these copies.

M: I'll help. How about this? ________________ ____________ since it's a first edition.

W: Hmm.... I don't want to spend more than $30.

M: Okay. Then this one looks good because it's the cheapest.

W: But I'd prefer a hardcover so it will last. What do you think of this one?

M: Well, ______________________________, but it will take more than two days for it to arrive. Is that okay with you?

W: Oh, ______________________________ ________________.

M: Then I think you should buy this one. Moreover, it was published recently.

W: Alright. ______________________________ right now. Thanks for your help.

M: My pleasure.

11

M: I heard Jim ________________________ from tomorrow.

W: Right. Several departments were reorganized during your vacation.

M: Then ______________________________ the finance team?

12

W: Oh, you and I have the same headphones. ______ ____________________________?

M: I bought them at Hit Tracks for $20.

W: Really? I paid $30 at the same shop this morning. ________________________________!

13

W: You must be Kevin. Please, have a seat.

M: Thank you for ______________________________ ______________, Ms. Wilson.

W: Don't mention it. So, how can I help you?

M: Well, my dream is to become an actor. And I heard that the curriculum here is ______________________ ___________________________.

W: Right, our curriculum ______________________ __________________ of young artists and actors.

M: Great. What should I do to apply to your school?

W: To major in acting, you'll have to pass a performance test. This is a performance that __________ ______________________.

M: Are there any ______________________________ ____________________________________?

14

W: I'm glad we decided to study outside. It's a beautiful day.

M: Yeah, but ________________________________. I'm going to buy some juice. Want anything?

W: I'd like an iced coffee.

M: Okay, but I thought ___________________________ ___________________________.

W: Well, I tried, but I was so sleepy all the time and I couldn't concentrate.

M: I see. You know, one of my friends, Ken, was able to quit coffee by ___________________________ ______________________________.

W: That really worked? What was he drinking?

M: He switched to herbal tea, and I haven't seen him drink a cup of coffee since.

W: That's interesting. ___________________________ ___________________________?

15

M: Susie is Robert's friend and classmate. Yesterday, their teacher told him that Susie __________ ______________________. Today, Robert goes to the hospital to visit her and asks about what happened. She explains that ________________ ____________________ while training for an upcoming swimming competition. Robert feels sorry because he _________________________ ___________________________. To his surprise, she is sure that she'll recover in time for the race and she plans to compete, even though ________ ______________________. Robert doesn't think this is a good idea, and he wants to ___________ __________________________. In this situation, what would Robert most likely say to Susie?

16-17

W: As we use more and more gas and coal to power our planet, the possibility of an energy shortage is becoming increasingly likely. ______________ __________________________, many alternatives are being developed. Some of these, like dams that use the power of flowing water to generate electricity, have been around for years. But others are relatively new. For example, solar heat ____________________________________ in many desert regions. Meanwhile, some coastal cities are utilizing the power of tides in marine-energy plants. And then there are _____________ __________________________, such as nuclear power. However, there are drawbacks, including high construction costs and a limited number of possible locations. So, the best way __________ _____________________________ is to practice conserving it. This is as simple as choosing energy efficient lights and appliances, and ___________ _____________________________. And always be looking for energy saving alternatives: Don't drive if you can walk, and let the sunshine in instead of turning on a light. Alternative energies are exciting, but the only guaranteed solution ____________________________________.

실전모의고사

29 PRACTICE TEST

01 다음을 듣고, 남자가 하는 말의 목적으로 가장 적절한 것을 고르시오.

① 서울 낚시 축제를 유치하려고
② 낚시 축제의 일정을 홍보하려고
③ 올해 축제의 개선된 점들을 알리려고
④ 각 지역의 다양한 축제에 대해 알리려고
⑤ 올해 새로 출시된 낚시용품을 홍보하려고

02 대화를 듣고, 여자의 의견으로 가장 적절한 것을 고르시오.

① 폐를 보호하려면 외출을 삼가야 한다.
② 덥고 습한 날씨는 기분을 불쾌하게 만든다.
③ 미세먼지에 대한 위험성을 널리 알려야 한다.
④ 건강에 좋은 습관을 갖기 위해 노력해야 한다.
⑤ 미세먼지에 대비하기 위해 마스크를 써야 한다.

03 대화를 듣고, 두 사람의 관계를 가장 잘 나타낸 것을 고르시오.

① 교수 – 학생
② 영화감독 – 배우
③ 지휘자 – 성악가
④ 각본가 – 내레이터
⑤ TV 감독 – 오디오 감독

04 대화를 듣고, 그림에서 대화의 내용과 일치하지 않는 것을 고르시오.

05 대화를 듣고, 여자가 남자를 위해 할 일로 가장 적절한 것을 고르시오.

① 파티 함께 가기
② 에세이 도와주기
③ 역사책 빌려주기
④ 함께 의상 고르기
⑤ 상점 위치 알려주기

06 대화를 듣고, 남자가 지불할 금액을 고르시오. [3점]

① $200　② $600　③ $800
④ $1,000　⑤ $1,500

07 대화를 듣고, 남자가 교복이 좋다고 생각하는 이유를 고르시오.

① 의복비를 줄일 수 있어서
② 학생들 간의 연대를 강화해서
③ 학습 환경 조성에 도움이 돼서
④ 불필요한 위화감을 조성하지 않아서
⑤ 교육자가 학생의 생활지도를 하기 용이해서

08 대화를 듣고, 수원 화성에 관해 언급되지 않은 것을 고르시오.

① 건축 재료　② 건축 목적　③ 건축 기간
④ 건축 장비　⑤ 건축 비용

09 다음 기상 예보를 듣고, 일치하지 않는 것을 고르시오.

① 목포 지역은 기온이 따뜻해질 것이다.
② 건조한 바람 때문에 화재를 경계해야 한다.
③ 일부 지역에서는 눈을 볼 수 있을 것이다.
④ 서해안 지역은 소나기가 그칠 것이다.
⑤ 서울에서는 구름 낀 하늘을 볼 수 있을 것이다.

10 다음 표를 보면서 대화를 듣고, 두 사람이 선택할 보드게임을 고르시오.

Name of Board Game	The time required	Appropriate age(s)	Number of players
① Property Manager	at least 3 hours	adults and children	2 to 6
② Murder Mystery	at least 90 minutes	adults	2 to 6
③ Word Speller	about 40 minutes	adults	only 2
④ Animal Chess	less than one hour	adults and children	only 2
⑤ Chinese Checkers	40 to 50 minutes	adults and children	2 to 6

11 대화를 듣고, 여자의 마지막 말에 대한 남자의 응답으로 가장 적절한 것을 고르시오.

① She's really nice.
② We met in the hall.
③ Please introduce me later.
④ She said she likes this city.
⑤ We aren't in the same class.

12 대화를 듣고, 남자의 마지막 말에 대한 여자의 응답으로 가장 적절한 것을 고르시오.

① I can't, because I'll be in Japan.
② Sure, I'll give you a call tomorrow.
③ My brother is excited to meet you.
④ Yes, I really enjoyed Japanese food.
⑤ Okay, my lunchtime is before yours.

13 대화를 듣고, 여자의 마지막 말에 대한 남자의 응답으로 가장 적절한 것을 고르시오.

▶ Man : ______________________

① Why do you want to go to Boston?
② Canada is great at this time of year.
③ Your future depends on how hard you study.
④ The schools in Korea are very impressive, too.
⑤ It sounds like you've already made your decision.

14 대화를 듣고, 남자의 마지막 말에 대한 여자의 응답으로 가장 적절한 것을 고르시오. [3점]

▶ Woman : ______________________

① I don't know anything about camping.
② Your brother sounds very adventurous.
③ I have been going camping since I was little.
④ When and where can we go camping together?
⑤ This map is really helpful to find a good campsite.

15 다음 상황 설명을 듣고, Ronald가 Thomas에게 할 말로 가장 적절한 것을 고르시오. [3점]

▶ Ronald : ______________________

① It's the best way to find the solution.
② I think I'm going to get a promotion.
③ You should follow the manager's instructions.
④ I don't really like the manager. What about you?
⑤ I agree that this restaurant needs to be renovated urgently.

[16~17] 다음을 듣고, 물음에 답하시오.

16 여자가 하는 말의 주제로 가장 적절한 것은?

① the importance of a résumé
② the process of applying for a job
③ advice for making a good résumé
④ tips for a successful job interview
⑤ suitable clothes for a job interview

17 증명사진을 잘 찍는 방법으로 언급되지 않은 것은?

① 정장 입기 ② 미소 짓기
③ 턱 들기 ④ 정면으로 사진 찍기
⑤ 카메라 렌즈 응시하기

29 DICTATION

녹음된 내용을 들으면서 빈칸을 알맞게 채워 보세요.

01

M: The Seoul Fishing Festival will take place this year along the banks of the Han River between the Banpo Bridge and the Hannam Bridge. In past years, the festival ______________________ ______________ of Yeouido in Western Seoul. This year, participants ______________ ______________ to fish from several floating platforms in the river. There is another upgrade from ______________________________. Many new vendors of both food and fishing & outdoor products will be set up along the riverbank. We have also added paddle boat rides for the kids and a concert for ____________________________.

02

W: Hi, Walter. Did you hear the news?

M: Hi, Sue. ______________________________?

W: The fine dust will be especially bad this week.

M: Oh, I heard my parents talking about that. It's a big problem, right?

W: It's really bad for our health. ______________ ______________________________.

M: That's scary, but what can we do about it?

W: I bought this mask. I'm going to wear it ________ ______________________________.

M: I hate wearing a mask. It's so hot and uncomfortable.

W: I agree with you. But you should do __________ ______________________________________.

M: You're right. Our health is most important.

W: Then you should get a mask soon. You can buy them at drugstores.

M: Thanks for the advice. I'll buy one tomorrow.

03

W: Cut! Joe, did you practice your lines?

M: Yes, ma'am. ______________________________.

W: Do we need to make cue cards for you?

M: No, you don't. I have lots of experience in this field. I've been in plays on Broadway!

W: But Joe, this is a movie, not a play.

M: I know. But can't we just __________________ ______________________________?

W: The producer would not like to find out we had to shoot this simple scene several times. Please, just concentrate this time and we can ______________ ________________________.

M: I will. Believe me, I am as anxious as you are to ______________________________________.

W: I understand. Then, let's do this scene again, shall we?

04

W: Honey, ______________________________ from our family vacation yet?

M: No, I haven't had time. Oh, that one is good.

W: It's one of my favorites, too. You looked good in your flower-patterned swim shorts.

M: Well, I think you ________________________ in your polka-dotted swimsuit.

W: That's sweet. Look, there's Kevin standing next to me and making a "v" with his fingers for the camera.

M: He looks very excited. It's just a shame that Amy lost her tube just before she took this picture. She loved how it looked like a duck.

W: I know. She ______________________________ with it in the picture.

M: Right, but it's still a good picture. The striped beach parasol in the background especially makes it look great.

W: You're right. We should ____________________ ____________________.

정답 및 해설 p.114

05

M: Hey, sorry I'm late.
W: What took you so long? We really ______________ ______________________________________ today.
M: I slept in by accident. I didn't realize how much I slept. I was catching up on my reading for history class.
W: What about the essay that's due next week? Are you done?
M: Are you kidding? I __________________________ ______________________.
W: Well, if you want to go to the Halloween party, you need to finish it this week.
M: I totally forgot about Halloween. What am I going to wear?
W: Well, I've decided to be Wonder Woman.
M: Good choice. It totally suits you. ______________ ____________________________?
W: I got my costume at the Target Store downtown. They have a huge selection of stuff.
M: Well, after our study session, do you think we could go together and pick something out?
W: Of course! ______________________________ ______________ in the afternoon so I'll be happy to.

06

W: What can I help you with today?
M: I want to ______________________________ for my son that will grow as he grows.
W: ____. Which account do you have in mind?
M: I was looking at the Savings Bond account. How does that work?
W: With that account, ________________________ ________________________ in the account and the money will mature in 10 years or 15 years.
M: What do you mean by "mature?"
W: It means the savings account ________________ ________________ what you invested in 10 years. And it will be tripled in 15 years.
M: So if I want to make $300, how much should I invest today?
W: For that, it would take $150 for 10 years or $100 for 15 years.
M: That sounds great. I want to make $3,000 after 15 years.

07

M: Good morning, sweetheart! You look like you're all ready for school.
W: Don't ______________________________________, Dad. You know I hate wearing my school uniform.
M: Of course, you've told me all about how the uniforms make everyone look the same.
W: ____, except that maybe it reduces my preparation time in the mornings.
M: Well, at least it saves time. Anyway, I think the uniforms help to create ____________________ ____________________________. Isn't that a good thing about them?
W: But I have great outfits in my closet. I want to show my friends!
M: You can wear them on the weekends.
W: I guess, but I still feel like this uniform is ________ ____________________________.
M: I know, but we can't change the school's policy.

08

W: Okay, everyone. From this location, we can ______ ____________________ of Suwon Hwaseong Fortress.

M: It's really impressive. I especially like the large bricks.

W: Yes, this is one of the first Korean structures that was built with bricks like this. ______________ ____________________.

M: I think you mentioned that it was finished in 1796. Is that correct?

W: Yes. King Jeongjo began construction in 1794 to pay respect to his father, who ______________ ____________________________________ of the Joseon Dynasty.

M: So, it only took two years to complete. How was that possible?

W: A special crane called a Geojunggi was invented just to complete this job.

M: That's really interesting. Can we see a Geojunggi?

W: There will be one for you to see ______________ ______________.

09

W: This is your News 22 weather report. Starting in the southwest, Mokpo will be seeing some unseasonably high temperatures. There will also be dry winds blowing from the North. This could lead to fires, so ________________________ if you are in a fire-danger area. ____________ ____________, there will be clear skies across Chungcheongbuk-do and Gyeongsangbuk-do all the way through to southern Gyeonggi-do. In the Gangwon-do area, there will be late season snow in some parts of Sokcho and Gangneung, but ________________________________ about. And in areas near the West Sea, __________ ______________________ of Tuesday's rain showers. And the Seoul area expects cloudy weather and cool temperatures.

10

M: ____________________________________ tonight.

W: Good idea. Let's pick a game to play out of these five games.

M: Well, I love the game in which we buy and sell property. ____________________________ ____________ just like in real life.

W: ____________________________________. That game can even go on for days. Let's play something that takes less than an hour.

M: How about this game?

W: But Sarah cannot play. She's only 10. __________ ____________________.

M: Well, what's that game that the children are always playing?

W: It's a strategy board game with lions, tigers, and elephants in it.

M: Is it fun for adults, too?

W: Yes, but the problem is only two people can play it and there are three of us.

M: Hmm.... There's only one choice then. __________ ________________________.

11

W: I heard that you ________________________ ____________.

M: Yeah, her name is Becky. I talked to her this morning.

W: I haven't seen her yet. ____________________ ____________?

12

M: Hi, Lisa. Did you ____________________ ______________ your brother in Japan?

W: It was great, but ________________________ ______________________.

M: Well, I'm glad you're back. Would you like to have lunch together tomorrow?

13

M: What's all this?

W: ______________________________ the study abroad program. These are brochures for schools.

M: Wow, that's great! I never thought your parents would ______________________________.

W: At first they were against it, but they realized ______________________________.

M: Oh, I see.

W: Now, I'm trying to decide among the U.S., Canada and England.

M: I think you will have an interesting time in England.

W: I think so too, but my uncle lives in Boston, so I might want to go there.

M: ______________________________ in Boston.

W: Yeah, but it's one of the most historical cities in America and it is close to New York.

14

M: Hi, Kelly.

W: Hi. Do you have any plans for this holiday?

M: Yes, I'm going camping, but first I ______________________________.

W: Where will you be camping?

M: I'm going to Rocky Mountain National Park for five days.

W: OK. Since ______________________________, you will need a two-season sleeping bag.

M: All right. What about a tent?

W: If you think you will go camping again at other times of the year, you should get an all-season tent. How many people will be sleeping in your tent?

M: Just my brother and me.

W: Well, ______________________________ and buy a four-man tent then. It won't be heavy for hiking to your campsite.

M: This all sounds great. How did you ______________________________?

15

M: Ronald and Thomas work together in a local restaurant. One of the rules to working in a kitchen is to wash your hands every time you come back into the kitchen. Ronald is very careful to ______________________________ so as not to get anyone sick. But Thomas does not. He sometimes even ______________________________ and doesn't clean his hands after touching dirty mops. Ronald has heard the manager warn Thomas about his bad habit, but finds out he doesn't ______________________________. But if the manager knows this, he will be very upset. As a friend and co-worker, Ronald wants to ______________________________. In this situation, what would Ronald most likely say to Thomas?

16-17

W: Today, I'd like to talk about résumés, the documents describing our work history and experience that we must ______________________________. These days, it's all about packaging. A well-packaged résumé will attract the people you want to impress. The key to a successful résumé is ______________________________. First, make sure to use powerful language to sell your skills. For example, instead of writing "I have experience volunteering," write "I was in charge of organizing activities at a senior center." Also, try to add specific details about how you can ______________________________ you are applying for. My second tip is about your ID picture. Your potential employers want to know who they're hiring. If they can match a face to your name and achievements, it will definitely ______________________________. Wear business clothes when getting your photo taken, and don't forget to smile! Also, bring your chin up to prevent double chin. And make sure the photo ______________________________ from the front. When you get the photo printed, place it at the top left-hand corner of your résumé.

PRACTICE TEST

01 다음을 듣고, 여자가 하는 말의 목적으로 가장 적절한 것을 고르시오.

① 병원 입원 절차를 설명하려고
② 자원봉사 활동에 대해 칭찬하려고
③ 자원봉사 활동 시간을 알려주려고
④ 기금 마련 활동 참여를 권장하려고
⑤ 병원에서 일할 학생들을 모집하려고

02 대화를 듣고, 남자의 의견으로 가장 적절한 것을 고르시오.

① 팀 과제는 팀워크를 기를 수 있는 좋은 기회이다.
② 팀 과제의 수행은 팀워크를 통해 이루어져야 한다.
③ 팀 리더의 역량에 따라 과제 수행 결과가 달라진다.
④ 팀원의 의견이 다를 때는 팀 리더의 역할이 중요하다.
⑤ 팀 과제를 하려면 각자 능력에 맞는 역할을 해야 한다.

03 대화를 듣고, 두 사람의 관계를 가장 잘 나타낸 것을 고르시오.

① 남편 – 아내
② 경찰 – 피해자
③ 기자 – 제보자
④ 사설탐정 – 의뢰인
⑤ 보안담당자 – 아파트 주민

04 대화를 듣고, 그림에서 대화의 내용과 일치하지 않는 것을 고르시오.

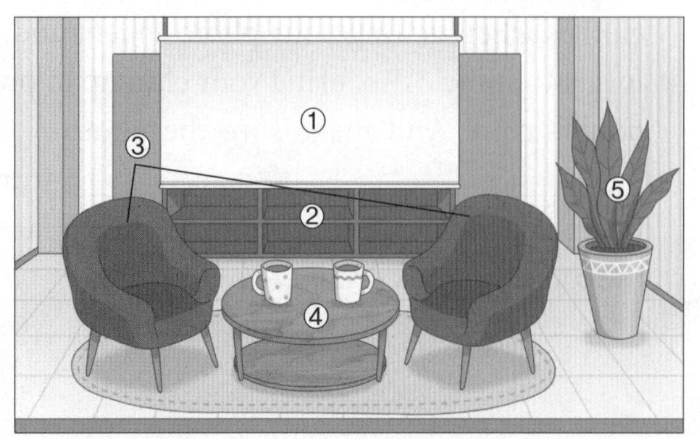

05 대화를 듣고, 남자가 대화 후 여자를 위해 가장 먼저 할 일로 적절한 것을 고르시오.

① 추천서 쓰기
② 함께 점심 먹기
③ 추천서 출력하기
④ 에세이 채점하기
⑤ 질문에 답변하기

06 대화를 듣고, 여자가 지불할 금액을 고르시오. [3점]

① $5　② $10　③ $15
④ $20　⑤ $25

07 대화를 듣고, 남자가 호주에 갈 수 없는 이유를 고르시오.

① 여행 경비가 없어서
② 같이 갈 사람이 없어서
③ 아르바이트를 해야 해서
④ 여름 학기를 들어야 해서
⑤ 할머니를 돌봐 드려야 해서

08 다음을 듣고, 영구 동토층(permafrost)에 관해 언급되지 않은 것을 고르시오.

① 발견 가능 지역　② 거주민의 수
③ 형성 기간　④ 두께
⑤ 주거에 미치는 영향

09 박물관 관람에 관한 다음 내용을 듣고, 일치하지 않는 것을 고르시오.

① 이 투어의 여행객들은 박물관에서 두 시간을 보낼 것이다.
② 이 투어의 모든 여행객들은 일반 입장권을 받게 될 것이다.
③ 특별 전시의 관람을 원하면 요금을 따로 지불해야 한다.
④ 박물관 내에서 가이드 투어를 반드시 할 필요는 없다.
⑤ 관람을 마치고 박물관에서 점심 식사를 하게 된다.

정답 및 해설 p.118

10 다음 표를 보면서 대화를 듣고, 여자가 면접을 위해 연락할 지원자를 고르시오.

Name	Night Shift (from 8 to 12)	Age	Available on weekend	Experience
① Bill Jones	Yes	22	No	Yes
② Mike Smith	No	18	No	No
③ James Hanson	Yes	20	Yes	Yes
④ Peter Parker	Yes	22	Yes	No
⑤ Byran Short	Yes	16	Yes	Yes

11 대화를 듣고, 남자의 마지막 말에 대한 여자의 응답으로 가장 적절한 것을 고르시오.

① See you on Monday, then.
② We also need to pick a topic.
③ Saturday evening would be okay.
④ This meeting room is really great.
⑤ Online discussions have many limitations.

12 대화를 듣고, 여자의 마지막 말에 대한 남자의 응답으로 가장 적절한 것을 고르시오.

① Sorry, it's already sold out.
② Of course. Here's my receipt.
③ I'm hoping that it's still on sale.
④ It had three pockets and a hood.
⑤ I like its design, but not the color.

13 대화를 듣고, 남자의 마지막 말에 대한 여자의 응답으로 가장 적절한 것을 고르시오. [3점]

▶ Woman : ______________________

① That's OK. I'll come along shortly.
② Thanks. Then I'll just walk with you.
③ Great. I'd appreciate it if you understood.
④ OK. I'll take the stairs to the second floor.
⑤ No problem. I'm sure I can find it on my own.

14 대화를 듣고, 여자의 마지막 말에 대한 남자의 응답으로 가장 적절한 것을 고르시오.

▶ Man : ______________________

① OK. I'll have the same as you.
② You're right. Exercising might help.
③ Maybe you're right. I'll give it a try.
④ Don't worry. I can exercise anytime.
⑤ I agree. I'll have some juice this time.

15 다음 상황 설명을 듣고, Jennifer가 어머니에게 할 말로 가장 적절한 것을 고르시오. [3점]

▶ Jennifer : ______________________

① I'm sorry Mom, but the battery died.
② I always turn it off before class starts.
③ Could you please turn down the radio?
④ The homework assignment isn't finished.
⑤ You should go to bed before I come home.

[16~17] 다음을 듣고, 물음에 답하시오.

16 남자가 하는 말의 주제로 가장 적절한 것은?

① the power of positive thinking
② outdoor activities easy to start
③ how to overcome eating disorders
④ importance of healthy eating habits
⑤ the common types of eating disorders

17 body image를 개선하는 방법으로 언급되지 않은 것은?

① 편한 옷 입기
② 마사지 받기
③ 새 향수 사기
④ 자전거 타기
⑤ 패션 잡지 읽기

30 DICTATION

녹음된 내용을 들으면서 빈칸을 알맞게 채워 보세요.

01

W: Good morning, class. Do you remember visiting Happy Oaks Hospital last year? Everyone helped that day. Some students cleaned rooms, ____________ ______________________ and still others washed dishes. Afterwards a few of the students at our school decided to volunteer every Saturday afternoon. Now the principal wants us to ____________________ ______________. The hospital needs money to improve its buildings. You can help raise money ____ for a few hours a week after school. You can sell the tickets on the street, or to family and friends. If you want to participate, please ______________ ______________________________.

02

W: Diego, you look worried. Are you stressed because of your team project?

M: Yes and no. The project itself is a great opportunity, but my team members don't get along well because of the team leader, James.

W: ____?

M: James never listens to our opinions. He is too stubborn.

W: Why don't you ______________________________ ______________________________?

M: No, that won't work. He wants to make decisions based only on his opinion.

W: Maybe he is so self-confident that he closes his ears to other people's opinions.

M: You have a point. ____________________________ __________________ for our project to succeed.

W: That's right. Every team member _______________ _________________________ accomplishing tasks on the job.

M: You're telling me! We have to work together to accomplish the goal. So he should respect our opinions.

03

M: What did they take?

W: They took some jewelry and some money. That's all, I think.

M: I'm really sorry.

W: Mr. Ward, my next-door neighbor, said he heard some loud noises around three.

M: That's helpful. I'll look at _____________________ __________________ around that time.

W: I hope you can see someone clearly.

M: I can't remember ____________________________ ____________________________ in the three years I've been working here.

W: Yes, I usually feel safe.

M: ________________________________ an hour ago. I'll also talk to the person on duty in the afternoon.

W: I'll call the police right now.

M: Yes, do it right away. I'm sorry, Mrs. Foster. ______ ____.

W: I hope this will never happen again.

04

W: Liam, I'm __________________________________ for the talk show. I took a picture of the stage. Look here.

M: You set up a big screen at the back of the stage as I asked.

W: Yes, I also placed a bookcase under the screen. I'm going to ___________________________________.

M: Good idea!

W: I prepared two armchairs for a host and a guest. Do you think I should put out more chairs?

M: No, we don't need more than two chairs. They look comfortable.

W: I also ____ and left two cups on it.

M: Perfect! Wait a minute! You placed a vase with flowers on the right side of the stage.

W: Yes, aren't those roses beautiful? _______________ _________________.

M: Sure, but actually I heard the talk show's guest is __________________________.

W: Really? I'll change it to a green plant right away.

M: That'll be nice.

05

W: Excuse me, Mr. Myers. ____?

M: Hi, Nicole. If you're wondering about your essay, ____.

W: Oh, it's not about that.

M: How can I help you then? Do you have a question about yesterday's lecture?

W: No, actually a few weeks ago I asked you ____ for me.

M: Oh, yes. I've done it.

W: Could you put it in this envelope?

M: Yes, but first I need to ____. Do you want me to do it right away?

W: ____ before your lunch. But the deadline is today.

M: Wait here, then. I'll be back in a minute.

06

W: Is there any discount if I am a member of the museum?

M: Yes, there is. Lifetime members are allowed to enter for free, but ____ must pay $5.

W: And what is the adult ticket price?

M: ____ is $15.

W: Well, I need one regular admission ticket for my friend. And I'm a lifetime member.

M: I'll need to see your lifetime museum membership card, ma'am.

W: Just one moment. Yes, here it is.

M: Thank you. Ma'am, I am afraid you've made a small mistake.

W: What is that?

M: Well, you only have a yearly museum membership.

W: Oh? Really? ____________________________________?

M: No, it hasn't. You are still a yearly museum member.

07

W: Summer vacation starts next week! ________________________________?

M: I don't know. What about you?

W: I had a part-time job during the school year, so I will use the money to travel to Australia. How about joining me?

M: I'd like to go, but _________________________________. I ________________________________ some money.

W: Well, you studied hard instead and got good grades. Maybe we can travel together in the future.

M: I hope so. I guess I'll visit my grandma's home __________________________________. She turned 70 this year.

W: That should be __________________________________.

M: Yes. Maybe I can get a part-time job while I'm there.

08

W: Today, we're going to talk about permafrost, ______________________________. Most permafrost is found in Northern Canada and Russia, but some can be found on tall mountains and on Antarctica. In general, areas with glaciers or thick snow have relatively little or no permafrost because ______________________________ ______________________. Permafrost can form in just a few years, but some is over 500,000 years old and over 600 meters thick. During the summer months, some strong plants can be found living on permafrost. Permafrost can also ________ ______________________________ ____________. The icy ground constantly shifts and sinks, cracking foundations and ruining homes. In places where people live on permafrost, ______________________________.

09

M: Your attention, please. The bus will ____________ ______________________________. We will spend 2 hours here. As you leave the bus, I will give you a ticket. It is a general entrance ticket which ______________________________. You must pay for those exhibits yourself. If you don't want to, you don't have to follow the guided tour. If you walk around on your own and finish quickly, you can ______________________________ and have a coffee. But please do not have a meal. We will be getting back on the bus and driving to a restaurant for lunch. We will meet at 12:30 ______________________________. Thank you very much.

10

M: Here are some recent applicants for part-time work.

W: Thanks. Well, tell me ______________________________ ________________ for an interview.

M: What's the first thing we should consider?

W: Actually, we need someone to work the night shift two nights a week. That's the most important thing.

M: You mean they ______________________________ ________________?

W: Yes, that's right. I think young people can't work that shift.

M: ______________________________ that late?

W: It's not, but for the night shift I insist on someone who is 18 years old or older.

M: Okay. Do they have to work on weekends?

W: Sure. They must work ____________________ ____________________. Oh, and it is better if we can hire someone who has experience.

M: Then, there is only one person __________________ ________________.

W: Let me see his application.

11

M: I think we need to ______________________________ ______________________________.

W: I agree, but I'm really busy for the next few days.

M: In that case, ______________________________ on the weekend?

12

W: Hi, can I help you find something?

M: I'm looking for a jacket that ____________________ ________________ on your website.

W: We have several. ______________________________ ________________?

13

M: ____?

W: Yes, I'm looking for the Bantech phone repair center.

M: It's not in this building.

W: But I was told it was in a building with a Triple B Bank ______________________________.

M: Well, there is a Triple B Bank in this building. But there is also another branch of the Triple B Bank ______________________________.

W: Really?

M: Yes. A block farther up the street is another building with a Triple B Bank branch. My office is in the same building.

W: Oh, really?

M: I'd take you there, but ______________________ ______________________ for a while.

14

W: You drink 8 cups of coffee a day!

M: Yeah. I've tried to stop many times, but I always fail.

W: Try again! Drinking too much coffee is unhealthy.

M: I know. When ______________________________, I still felt terrible until I had coffee. And a few weeks ago, I tried to ______________________________ ______________.

W: That's hard.

M: I know. So I started exercising. I thought if I were healthier, I wouldn't miss coffee.

W: Obviously, ______________________________.

M: No, I had to have my coffee.

W: I've heard acupuncture is good at ______________ ______________________________.

M: Acupuncture?

W: Yeah. ______________________________________ ______________________.

M: Hmm....

W: I don't think you have much choice.

15

W: Jennifer is doing research in the library for a homework assignment. She starts reading a book and ______________________________. She finds the book interesting and before she realizes it, ______________________________. She was told to come home at 9 but it's 10 now. Her mother always ______________________________. And Jennifer realizes she must call her mom to tell her she'll be home soon. So she tries to make a call, but ______________________________. She borrows a friend's cell phone. Her mom answers. She had tried to phone Jennifer. She asks Jennifer why she didn't answer her cell phone. In this situation, what would Jennifer most likely say to her mom?

16-17

M: Did you know that millions of people are ________ ______________________________? Some of them refuse to eat anything, while others eat too much. Today, I'd like to introduce ______________________ ______________________________. First, it's always a good idea to get some counseling about nutrition and healthy eating. The goal of a counselor is to help you ______________________ ______________________________. They can't change your habits overnight, but they can push you in the right direction. Second, you should learn to ______________________________ ____________________. So here are some tips to improve your body image. Wear clothes you feel comfortable in. Dress to express yourself, not to impress others. ______________________________ ____________________. And do nice things for your body once in a while, like getting a massage or a new perfume. Becoming more active can also help. So try to stay active by climbing mountains or riding bikes with friends.

실전모의고사

31 PRACTICE TEST

01 다음을 듣고, 여자가 하는 말의 목적으로 가장 적절한 것을 고르시오.

① 가게의 개점을 알리려고
② 다가올 특별 판매를 알리려고
③ 단골 고객을 연례행사에 초대하려고
④ 유료 음악 스트리밍 서비스를 홍보하려고
⑤ 음악 파일을 온라인으로 할인 판매하려고

02 대화를 듣고, 두 사람이 하는 말의 주제로 가장 적절한 것을 고르시오.

① 연극 관람 시 주의사항
② 연극에 대한 관객의 반응
③ 축제에 올릴 연극 고르기
④ 오디션 참가자들에 대한 평가
⑤ 배우가 되기 위해 필요한 자질

03 대화를 듣고, 두 사람의 관계를 가장 잘 나타낸 것을 고르시오.

① 소설가 – 기자
② 사진작가 – 기자
③ 카메라맨 – 영화감독
④ 미술가 – 미술 비평가
⑤ 조각가 – 미술품 거래상

04 대화를 듣고, 그림에서 대화의 내용과 일치하지 않는 것을 고르시오.

05 대화를 듣고, 여자가 할 일로 가장 적절한 것을 고르시오.

① 수프 만들어주기
② 코치에게 전화하기
③ 약국에서 약 사오기
④ 남자를 응급실에 데리고 가기
⑤ 남자를 축구경기장까지 태워다주기

06 대화를 듣고, 남자가 지불할 금액을 고르시오. [3점]

① \$2,300 ② \$2,500 ③ \$2,700
④ \$3,200 ⑤ \$3,400

07 대화를 듣고, 여자가 오늘 호텔에서 식사를 하지 않는 이유를 고르시오.

① 해산물 알레르기가 있어서
② 친구들을 만나러 나가야 해서
③ 다른 레스토랑을 이미 예약해서
④ 호텔 레스토랑이 마음에 들지 않아서
⑤ 바닷가 산책 후 근처에서 식사하기 위해서

08 대화를 듣고, 기업 채용에 관해 언급되지 않은 것을 고르시오.

① 지원 자격 ② 급여
③ 모집 인원 ④ 지원 방법
⑤ 지원 마감 기한

09 New Town 댄스 대회에 관한 다음 내용을 듣고, 일치하지 않는 것을 고르시오.

① 아마추어와 프로 선수의 경기가 같은 시간에 진행된다.
② 다섯 명의 심사위원이 우승자를 가리게 된다.
③ 아마추어 경기의 우승자는 시의 행사에서 공연하게 된다.
④ 신청서는 온라인으로 제출할 수 있다.
⑤ 참가비는 현장에서 직접 지불할 수도 있다.

정답 및 해설 p.122

10 다음 표를 보면서 대화를 듣고, 여자가 선택할 자전거를 고르시오.

	Off-road cycling	Price	Frame size (inches)
① Mountain MX 34	○	$1,300	19, 21
② City Living	×	$800	19, 21
③ Race Roadster RS 4.5	×	$4,000	15, 21
④ Commute FX	×	$900	15, 17
⑤ Rocky Road 3	○	$600	15, 17, 19

11 대화를 듣고, 남자의 마지막 말에 대한 여자의 응답으로 가장 적절한 것을 고르시오.

① I'm afraid there isn't.
② I recommend the 11:30 train.
③ Let me check your reservation.
④ You'd better come again tomorrow.
⑤ Tickets must be purchased before boarding.

12 대화를 듣고, 여자의 마지막 말에 대한 남자의 응답으로 가장 적절한 것을 고르시오.

① I have no appetite during flights.
② I'd like to change my flight time.
③ Yes, but I don't like eating snacks.
④ No, I finished the last of our food.
⑤ Yes, but sometimes it isn't enough.

13 대화를 듣고, 남자의 마지막 말에 대한 여자의 응답으로 가장 적절한 것을 고르시오. [3점]

▶ Woman : ____________________

① I'll bring Susan out here to check the bill.
② I'll take care of your bill and speak to the chef.
③ It would be best if you mind your own business.
④ I'll ask for strict control over the sales of vegetables.
⑤ We are going to shut down the restaurant for renovation.

14 대화를 듣고, 여자의 마지막 말에 대한 남자의 응답으로 가장 적절한 것을 고르시오. [3점]

▶ Man : ____________________

① You have to bring your marriage certificate.
② There is an extra fee to hyphenate your name.
③ You may not take the form out of the building.
④ Bring the form back when you have more time.
⑤ Your insurance certificate is valid for two years.

15 다음 상황 설명을 듣고, Gary가 Felicia에게 할 말로 가장 적절한 것을 고르시오.

▶ Gary : ____________________

① I'm so excited to see you finally happy!
② You deserve the prize. Congratulations.
③ There is always next year for you to win.
④ I must've made some mistakes on my tests.
⑤ I've never seen you so disappointed. What's wrong?

[16~17] 다음을 듣고, 물음에 답하시오.

16 남자가 하는 말의 주제로 가장 적절한 것은?

① the guidelines to meditate properly
② effective methods to reduce sleeplessness
③ effects of sleep on academic performance
④ why bedroom environment is important in sleep
⑤ various causes and symptoms of sleep disorders

17 좋은 침실 환경을 위한 사항으로 언급되지 않은 것은?

① 조명 끄기
② 귀마개 사용하기
③ 너무 덥지 않게 하기
④ 낡은 침대 교체하기
⑤ 부드러운 이불 사용하기

31 DICTATION

녹음된 내용을 들으면서 빈칸을 알맞게 채워 보세요.

01

W: ______________________________ of CDs, Music Warehouse is having a going-out-of-business sale this weekend. ______________________ every CD in the store for 75% off, but we will also be selling the shelves, light fixtures, sound system and furniture. We knew that ______________________, especially with the growing trends of purchasing music online and the expansion of streaming services. And so, we invite all of our loyal customers to come down to this weekend's sale. We ______________________ and playing all your favorite music until the very last CD is sold.

02

W: OK. ______________________.

M: Sounds good to me. So, who do you think would be best for the hero of the play?

W: I guess my favorite so far is Martin. He ______________________, from plays to movies.

M: Yes. He is already well-known. I liked him but, in my opinion, Chris ______________________. He doesn't have as much experience, but I think he has great natural ability.

W: ______________________. How about Jasper? He's ______________________ between the other two.

M: I'm afraid I couldn't feel any emotion from his performance.

W: In that case, Jasper isn't an option. Honestly, I don't think we've found the right actor.

M: Don't worry. We still have a few more actors to see tomorrow.

03

M: I'd like to show you a few of my more recent pieces.

W: This is very interesting. I like your use of shadow in that painting.

M: Thank you. I feel like my work is heading in a different, more mature direction.

W: ______________________ in my story.

M: I'm very glad to hear that.

W: ______________________. Do you have any sculptures?

M: I did this bronze piece over here.

W: ______________________. Did you do that on purpose?

M: In a way, yes. But it was also my first bronze piece, so ______________________.

W: OK. Well, I can tell you right now you will get a positive review from me.

04

M: Welcome home, Jessica! It's great to have you back.

W: Oh, wow! You didn't have to ______________________ for me!

M: Well, your mother and I were worried about you while you were in the hospital, and we wanted to celebrate your return.

W: I can't believe you even put up a "Welcome Home!" banner. It's great.

M: ______________________. Do you like the teddy bear?

W: Of course I do! The flowers are also lovely.

M: Those were my idea. I also chose a heart-patterned dress, but your mother said it was old-fashioned and she ______________________.

W: I'm happy with the style she picked out.

M: Don't forget about the shoes. ______________________ the dress.

W: They are great, too. I love the ribbons!

정답 및 해설 p.122

05

W: Jason! ______________________. It's past 9:00! You have a soccer game at 11:00! But I want to take you early ______________________ ______________.

M: Mom, I'm hot. I feel really tired and weak.

W: You're sick? I should ______________________ ______________________, but it's Sunday. The hospital emergency room?

M: Mom, it's not that bad. I don't have to go to the emergency room.

W: Well, you can't play soccer today.

M: Yeah. ______________________. I woke up at night and took some medicine, but I don't feel any better.

W: I'll make you some chicken noodle soup.

M: Oh, that would be great. And I guess I'd better phone the coach.

W: Do you want me to do it?

M: No, ______________________.

06

W: FX Office Supplies. How may I help you?

M: Hi. ______________________ one of your copiers for my office.

W: Certainly. Could you tell me which one you are interested in?

M: Well, I'm not sure exactly. I definitely need one that can ______________________.

W: Okay. The PDX is our top-of-the-line copier. It's on sale for $3,200.

M: ______________________. How about the ones in your other line, the PD 1 and the PD 2? What's the difference between them?

W: The PD 1 is last year's model. It's $2,500.

M: So ______________________?

W: Correct. And this year's version, the PD 2, costs an extra $200, making it $2,700.

M: In that case, I think I'll order the PD 1.

W: Great choice.

07

M: May I help you?

W: ______________________. My name's Jessica Conner.

M: Yes, a single room for six nights with an ocean view. You'll be on the seventh floor, in room 712. How would you like to pay?

W: I'll ______________________. By the way, are there any good restaurants nearby?

M: There are ______________________ ______________ on the way to the beach. I'm sure you'll find something you like.

W: What about the hotel's seafood restaurant? I heard it's famous.

M: It's on the second floor and it's also very good. ______________________?

W: No, I'll be meeting some friends in the city.

M: OK. Here is your key card. I will have your bags brought up to you. Enjoy your stay.

08

W: Hi, I hope you are enjoying the job fair. If you have any questions, ______________________.

M: Actually, I'm interested in the position that ________ ______________________. What type of candidate are you looking for?

W: An ideal candidate will possess a four-year degree, have strong TOEIC scores, and have more than 2 years of experience in this field.

M: I saw that your company is ______________ ______________________. But what about the salary?

W: ______________________ you mentioned, we're offering $8,000 per month plus health insurance.

M: Sounds great. Where should I submit my résumé?

W: To apply, submit your résumé and a letter of self-introduction on our website.

M: ______________________ ______________?

W: We'll stop accepting applications on October 16.
M: OK. Thank you for your time.

09

M: The annual New Town dancing contest will be held at the New Town Auditorium. The amateur level dancing contest will be held in the morning, while the professional level contest ______________ ______________ in the afternoon, at the same place. ______________ to score each contestant and determine the winner. The winner of the amateur level dancing contest will ______________. If you are interested, please fill out our online application. The fee can be paid ______________ ______________ before the event. ______________.

10

W: I need a good bicycle.
M: ______________. This is our most popular bike. It's great for off-road cycling.
W: Actually, I don't want a mountain bike for off-road cycling. They're too slow. I'll be using my bike ______________.
M: Great. These days, more and more people are cycling to work.
W: And I want to join them. Wow, this one's expensive. ______________ in the city?
M: No, it's a road racing bike. It's not for you.
W: ______________. I want to spend less than $1,000.
M: Hmm.... The problem is the size. It's near the end of the summer and our selection of bicycles is limited. How tall are you?
W: 165 centimeters.
M: You'll want a 15-inch frame. Hmm.... ______________ ______________.

11

M: Hi, ______________ for the 11:30 train, please.
W: I'm sorry, but the 11:30 train is full. How about the 12:00 train?
M: ______________. Isn't there anything sooner?

12

W: Our flight ______________. Are you ready?
M: Almost, but I want to get some snacks for the plane.
W: ______________ during the flight?

13

W: Your server, Susan, told me you wanted to see me. What can I do to help you?
M: ______________, my coffee is cold.
W: OK. I can take care of that right away.
M: Thank you, but that isn't the only problem.
W: Oh? ______________?
M: There was a hair in my soup and an insect in my salad.
W: Oh, my... I'm terribly sorry about that.
M: ______________. I have been coming here for years.
W: We'll remake the dish right away. And as the manager, I ______________ ______________.
M: If you say so, then I expect you to take serious action.

14

W: I need to change my name. Where do I ____?

M: May I ask why you are changing your name?

W: Well, I ________________________________ and I want to hyphenate my last name and my husband's last name.

M: Oh, I see. Well, we need your passport and your marriage certificate. You will only have to fill out form 10-B.

W: I have my passport and marriage certificate, but where do I get that form?

M: ____. Here you go.

W: What do I do ________________________________?

M: Pay the fee and take a number. Then you must wait for about an hour.

W: I can't stay for that long. Is there ____?

M: I'm afraid not.

W: Then, what am I supposed to do?

15

W: Gary and Felicia are the top two students in their class. Every year, one student becomes the class leader and ________________________________ at an event in the auditorium. The number two student doesn't receive anything. ________________________________, Felicia has been selected as the top student, but ________________________________ she will win this year because of a few low scores on tests. Although Gary ________________________________ at last, he knows how important it is to Felicia and how disappointed she is. Gary wants to say something to Felicia to ________________________________. In this situation, what would Gary most likely say to Felicia?

16-17

M: Do you struggle to get to sleep ________________________________? Or do you often wake up in the middle of the night? Sleeplessness is a common problem. Fortunately, there are a few different ways to ________________________________. First of all, meditation is used to treat sleeplessness because meditation techniques ________________________________. Since natural relaxation is the key to successful meditation, meditation should not be forced. Some experts recommend meditating for about 20 minutes before going to bed, while others recommend meditating in bed. Both techniques can work well and the effects can be the same. ________________________________ is also very important. Make sure that your room is dark enough. ________________________________ and close the curtains. Noise does not help you sleep well. Use earplugs to ________________________________. If your room is too warm, lower the temperature by using a fan or opening a window. Finally, beds should be comfortable. Replace them when they become worn and squeak when you sit or lay on them.

실전모의고사
32 PRACTICE TEST

01 다음을 듣고, 여자가 하는 말의 목적으로 가장 적절한 것을 고르시오.

① 학생들이 특별 조회에 참석하게 하려고
② 증축된 학교 시설의 개관식 일자를 발표하려고
③ 출입금지구역에 들어간 학생들을 주의시키려고
④ 지역 사업체와 학생들에게 감사의 마음을 전하려고
⑤ 학교 일부 시설에 당분간 접근할 수 없음을 알리려고

02 대화를 듣고, 남자의 의견으로 가장 적절한 것을 고르시오.

① 보고서 마감 시한을 지키는 게 중요하다.
② 보고서 제출 전에 맞춤법 검사가 필요하다.
③ 교환학생을 위한 적응 프로그램이 있어야 한다.
④ 인용한 문장에는 반드시 출처 표시를 해야 한다.
⑤ 다른 학생의 보고서를 베끼는 것은 절도 행위이다.

03 대화를 듣고, 두 사람의 관계를 가장 잘 나타낸 것을 고르시오.

① 집주인 – 세입자
② 경찰 – 사고 목격자
③ 아파트 주민 – 경비원
④ 차 주인 – 차량 정비공
⑤ 의뢰인 – 보안업체 직원

04 대화를 듣고, 그림에서 대화의 내용과 일치하지 <u>않는</u> 것을 고르시오.

05 대화를 듣고, 남자가 할 일로 가장 적절한 것을 고르시오.

① 편지에 답장 쓰기
② 이웃에게 항의하기
③ 공사 업체에 전화하기
④ 이웃에게 양해 구하기
⑤ 리모델링 업체 물색하기

06 대화를 듣고, 여자가 지불할 금액을 고르시오.

① $13 ② $18 ③ $20
④ $23 ⑤ $28

07 대화를 듣고, 남자가 회의에 참석하지 <u>못한</u> 이유를 고르시오.

① 늦잠을 자서
② 교통 체증이 심해서
③ 엘리베이터가 고장 나서
④ 보고서를 집에 두고 와서
⑤ 다른 회의에 참석해야 해서

08 대화를 듣고, 남자의 휴대 전화의 화면에 관해 언급되지 <u>않은</u> 것을 고르시오.

① 배경화면 사진의 출처 ② 화면 밝기
③ 배경화면 사진의 풍경 ④ 아이콘 개수
⑤ 글자 크기

09 East Lake Rock Festival에 관한 다음 내용을 듣고, 일치하지 <u>않는</u> 것을 고르시오.

① 자리에 앉아 관람할 수 있다.
② 음식물을 반입할 수 있다.
③ 수익금은 불우이웃에게 전액 기부된다.
④ 이번 주말 동안 열린다.
⑤ 1년에 한 번 개최된다.

10 다음 표를 보면서 대화를 듣고, 여자가 구입할 노트북을 고르시오.

Laptop Computers for Your New Start!

*The Free Gift is a wireless mouse.

Model	RAM (Gigabytes)	Price($)	Free Gift	Screen (Inches)
① VT-30	8	800	●	12
② VT-50	8	850		14
③ BF-200	16	900	●	14
④ BF-400	16	950		15
⑤ BF-700	16	1050	●	17

11 대화를 듣고, 여자의 마지막 말에 대한 남자의 응답으로 가장 적절한 것을 고르시오.

① I'll help you make some more.
② Yes, the party was a lot of fun.
③ Actually, it was put off to seven.
④ We should save some cookies for Kelly.
⑤ Unfortunately, she is allergic to peanuts.

12 대화를 듣고, 남자의 마지막 말에 대한 여자의 응답으로 가장 적절한 것을 고르시오.

① This charity is important to the community.
② I hope you'll be able to donate more next year.
③ That's terrible. I wonder what the difference is.
④ I'm afraid I couldn't donate as much as last year.
⑤ I'm shocked. I thought we did really well last year.

13 대화를 듣고, 여자의 마지막 말에 대한 남자의 응답으로 가장 적절한 것을 고르시오. [3점]

▶ Man : ________________

① I'll go get our car back after dinner.
② Of course. Mr. Steven can repair it faster.
③ You know I'm good at cooking and cleaning.
④ I'll commute by bus so you can use our car.
⑤ Let me recommend some tourist attractions for Amanda.

14 대화를 듣고, 남자의 마지막 말에 대한 여자의 응답으로 가장 적절한 것을 고르시오. [3점]

▶ Woman : ________________

① We do if we divide the work.
② I'm glad that we're working together.
③ I can't help you summarize it on the weekend.
④ I'll be sure to stick to the main points next time.
⑤ Our time limit for this presentation is too strict.

15 다음 상황 설명을 듣고, Jenna가 Tim에게 할 말로 가장 적절한 것을 고르시오. [3점]

▶ Jenna : Tim, ________________

① it was wrong of Paul to make those comments.
② I'm sorry. I shouldn't have lost my temper like that.
③ don't worry, I'll talk to Paul and solve this situation.
④ next time, don't hesitate to explain how you really feel.
⑤ I understand, but you have to learn to let your anger pass.

[16~17] 다음을 듣고, 물음에 답하시오.

16 남자가 하는 말의 주제로 가장 적절한 것은?

① the effects of hobbies on career success
② parents' influence on children's mental health
③ essential tips on enhancing a child's character
④ good hobbies for parents to share with their kids
⑤ reasons parents have to show interest in children

17 아이가 할 수 있는 취미로 언급되지 <u>않은</u> 것은?

① 축구
② 물건 수집
③ 연기
④ 그림 그리기
⑤ 노래 부르기

32 DICTATION

녹음된 내용을 들으면서 빈칸을 알맞게 채워 보세요.

01

W: Good morning, students. Welcome back. I hope you all enjoyed your vacations. Now, I have a special announcement. Thanks to the generosity of local businesses and to ____________________ ____________________, we have commenced the expansion and upgrade of the gymnasium, swimming pool, and auditorium. This means that ____, those areas will be off-limits to all students. Arrangements have been made for students to ____ at our junior campus; your homeroom teacher will ____ after assembly. Under no circumstances will students be permitted onto the construction sites. They are dangerous areas and building workers ____.

02

W: I finally finished my term paper.

M: Good. Do you want me to review your paper before you hand it in to your professor?

W: Yes, please. Because it's my first semester as an exchange student, there must be ______________ ______________________________ in my paper.

M: Okay! Let me see. Hmm, Heidi, you copied some sentences ______________________________ __________________ to the original source.

W: What do you mean?

M: I mean it's wrong to copy someone else's sentence without citation. Your professor will think you steal other people's ideas.

W: Really? I didn't know that would be such a big problem.

M: Well, it's a huge problem. You should write _______ ____.

W: Thanks for telling me. I guess I should rewrite the paper.

03

W: Hello, Mr. Smith. Can I talk to you for a second?

M: Sure. Is there something wrong?

W: Yes. Last night, someone ____________________ ______________ without leaving a note.

M: That's terrible. When did you find out?

W: At about 9 last night. I was ________________ __________________________.

M: I had no idea. ______________________________ __________________.

W: I know. I went to the security office as soon as I found out, but you weren't there.

M: Then, I'll check the parking lot's security camera first. It's in my office.

W: OK. You know ____________________________ ______________, right?

M: Of course. ______________________________ ______________ for almost 5 years.

W: If you find someone, please call my place. I'll stay home today.

M: No problem.

04

W: Wow, Ted! Is this your band's poster?

M: Yeah. It's for our regular fund-raising concert for an orphanage. What do you think?

W: It's great. But ____________________________ "Helping" from the title on top?

M: Our band is about having fun. We don't play ______________________________.

W: I see. That's why you put "Having Fun With" above the original.

M: Right. And below it, there's a picture of us enjoying a performance ______________________________ ______________________________.

W: You look excited. Who's the man ______________ ____________________ in the lower-left corner?

M: That's Ron, our drummer. And you know Jenny, right? That's her in the middle, playing the keyboard and singing.

정답 및 해설 p.126

W: Yes, I like her voice. Oh, is that you playing guitar to the right of her?
M: Right. How do I look?
W: You look professional ______________________ ______________________.
M: Thanks.

05

M: Honey. What's that in your hand?
W: It's a complaint letter from Mr. Smith, one of our neighbors.
M: A complaint letter? Why?
W: He said the noise from our home renovations ________________________________, especially in the mornings.
M: I don't think 8 a.m. is ______________________ ______________________.
W: I agree with you, but we should consider his situation.
M: Hmm.... I guess we don't have a choice. I'll call the builders ______________________________ for the construction.
W: Okay. In the meantime, I'll ________________ ________________________________ and ask them to understand.
M: Sounds good. Oh, and be especially apologetic to Mr. Smith.
W: I will.

06

W: Excuse me. Could I exchange this T-shirt _______ ________________________?
M: Why do you want to exchange it?
W: Actually, my sister bought this one for my son in this shop, but he doesn't like its pattern.
M: Oh, I see. We have many different T-shirts here. I'm sure you can find one you like.
W: Let me see.... Oh, ______________________ ________________________. The white puppy on the chest is so cute. How much is this?
M: It's thirty dollars.
W: ________________________________ ______________, then?
M: The T-shirt you brought back is twenty dollars. So you only ______________________________.
W: Okay. ______________________________.
Oh, these socks are cute. How much is a pair?
M: Their original price was five dollars, but they're 20 percent off now.
W: Okay. I'll buy two pairs then.

07

W: Greg, you missed the morning meeting!
M: I know, and I ______________________________ the sales report in the meeting.
W: Come to think of it, you're never late. What happened?
M: Well, I left home early because I wanted to review some materials for the meeting.
W: I did the same thing, and I was surprised that ________________________________.
M: Right. Everything went smoothly until I arrived at our office building.
W: Then what was it? Did you forget your report?
M: No, the elevator ______________________________ ______________________________.
W: Oh, no! How did you get out of there?
M: I rang the bell and ________________________ ______________. It took almost an hour to get out.
W: That's terrible. I'll ask the maintenance department to check the other elevators.
M: Good idea.

08

M: Stacy, I changed my cell phone's background picture. What do you think?

W: Wow! The scenery is so beautiful! Where did you get this picture?

M: I took it myself. It's from my family trip to Damyang last month.

W: Great. The windmill beside the farm ____________ ____________.

M: I think so, too. I especially ____________ ____________. The weather was so nice.

W: By the way, why are there only four icons at the bottom? Don't you use other applications?

M: Sure, but I deleted their icons for simplicity.

W: I see. Then, I think ____________ ____________ are too small.

M: Hmm. It's fine for me. ____________ ____________, they would block the picture.

W: Oh, I didn't think of that.

09

M: If you're tired of ____________ ____________, you'll love the East Lake Rock Festival. Unlike concerts that force you to stand for long periods of time, the East Lake Rock Festival ____________ ____________. This also means you can bring food or drink and eat a picnic lunch while enjoying the music. Plus, a significant portion of the profits ____________ ____________, so you can feel good about yourself too. ____________ ____________ this Saturday and Sunday at the East Lake Park. It's an annual event, but don't wait until next year to enjoy it!

10

M: What are you looking at, Alice?

W: Some laptop computers. I want to buy one to take to college next month.

M: I see. So why not ____________ ____________?

W: That was my first choice, but I really need more RAM than that.

M: Then what about this model? It has 16 gigabytes of RAM and the largest screen.

W: It's too expensive. I ____________ ____________ $1,000.

M: That narrows it down to two.

W: Right. What do you think of this one, then?

M: Hmm. Look here. The other one is cheaper and ____________.

W: I know, but I really want a larger screen for watching movies.

M: It sounds like ____________.

W: I have. Thanks.

11

W: Wow, ____________! Are they for Kelly's birthday party?

M: Yes. I heard peanut butter cookies are her favorite.

W: She'll love them. ____________ ____________, doesn't it?

12

M: You look serious. Do you have a problem?

W: I think our charity ____________ ____________ compared with last year.

M: You're right. Donations here ____________ ____________.

13

M: Hi, honey. Did anything happen while I was out?

W: My niece, Amanda, just called me. She's going to be here for New Year's Day tomorrow.

M: That's nice. ______________________________, and tell her we'll take her sightseeing in the city.

W: I already did. I love that she's coming, but I don't ____ ______________.

M: Don't worry about it. _________________________ ___________________.

W: Thanks, and I'll make some food. Oh, my! Our car is still at Steven's repair shop. We really need it ____________________________________.

M: When will the repair work be finished?

W: It's already done, but _________________________ ___________________.

M: I understand. You've been so busy recently.

W: Then what should we do?

14

M: Thank you for listening to my presentation. So, how did I do?

W: It wasn't bad, but I think _____________________ ______________________.

M: I see. Were there many errors?

W: No. The contents were great, but you exceeded the time limit.

M: Oh, well, I just wanted to ______________________ ______________________.

W: Our teacher said she will place a lot of importance ____ of the presentation.

M: That's a good point.

W: So, I think the only option is __________________ ______________________.

M: You're right, but I don't see how.

W: Well, we just ___________________________________ ___________________________________.

M: Do we have enough time today to finish that and prepare?

15

W: Jenna is waiting outside of a movie theater for her friend Tim. When Tim arrives, he looks upset and Jenna asks what is wrong. Tim explains that a coworker named Paul ___________________ _________________ about his report. Tim tried to ignore the comments but _________________ ____________________________. Finally, Tim and Paul had an argument about the comments. Jenna understands Tim's situation and sympathizes with him, but she also worries that Tim will hurt himself ____. She wants to comfort Tim and advise him ______ ____________________________________. In this situation, what would Jenna most likely say to Tim?

16-17

M: Children are not born with complete personalities. Instead, a personality is ______________________ __________________________, and as parents, it is our duty to guide this development. Fortunately, this is not ___________________________________. Start by listening to your children when they are trying to tell you something, and make time for them even when your schedule is busy. Children learn by imitation, so __________________________ _______________ of what you'd like your children to become. Also, you must pay attention to the development of certain aspects of your child's personality, such as confidence and self-esteem. In this regard, ________________________________ ______________. For example, soccer is a sound way for kids to make friends and learn about teamwork while exercising. Collecting things, such as stamps or rocks, ___________________________ _______________________ while providing a sense of accomplishment. Acting is especially beneficial because children can see things from other points of view through role playing. Similarly, singing ____ ____________________. And you shouldn't forget that many children have gone on to transform their hobbies into professions later in life.

실전모의고사

33 PRACTICE TEST

01 다음을 듣고, 여자가 하는 말의 목적으로 가장 적절한 것을 고르시오.

① 새로운 시험 일자를 알리려고
② 시험 부정행위에 대해 경고하려고
③ 시험을 치르는 방식을 설명하려고
④ 갑작스러운 시험 취소를 알리려고
⑤ 문제 해결을 위해 도움을 구하려고

02 대화를 듣고, 두 사람이 하는 말의 주제로 가장 적절한 것을 고르시오.

① 면대면 의사소통의 중요성
② 인터넷 예절 교육의 필요성
③ 사이버 범죄를 예방하는 방법
④ 인터넷 익명성의 순기능과 역기능
⑤ 인터넷 실명제를 시행해야 하는 이유

03 대화를 듣고, 두 사람의 관계를 가장 잘 나타낸 것을 고르시오.

① 재단사 – 옷 판매원
② 세탁소 직원 – 고객
③ 쇼핑몰 직원 – 디자이너
④ 옷 가게 주인 – 옷 가게 점원
⑤ 문구점 직원 – 문구 도매업자

04 대화를 듣고, 그림에서 대화의 내용과 일치하지 <u>않는</u> 것을 고르시오.

05 대화를 듣고, 남자가 여자를 위해 할 일로 가장 적절한 것을 고르시오.

① 상담소 약도 그려주기
② 강의실에 데려다 주기
③ 대학원 면접 준비 돕기
④ 취업 설명회에 동행하기
⑤ 현직 디자이너 소개해주기

06 대화를 듣고, 여자가 지불할 금액을 고르시오.

① $550 ② $600 ③ $660
④ $720 ⑤ $840

07 대화를 듣고, 남자가 휴대전화를 수리받을 수 <u>없는</u> 이유를 고르시오.

① 물에 빠뜨려서
② 보험이 만기 돼서
③ 해외에서 구매해서
④ 고장 원인을 발견하지 못해서
⑤ 공식 수리점이 아닌 곳에서 수리받아서

08 다음을 듣고, jatropha에 관해 언급되지 <u>않은</u> 것을 고르시오.

① 별칭 ② 재배 환경 ③ 씨앗 활용
④ 재배 효과 ⑤ 재배 촉진법

09 Thames 강 유람선 여행에 관한 다음 내용을 듣고, 일치하지 <u>않는</u> 것을 고르시오.

① 이 유람선에서 역사적 명소를 볼 수 있다.
② 편도 여행은 1시간 20분가량 소요된다.
③ 선상에서 간식과 음료를 구입할 수 있다.
④ 뜨거운 음식은 식당에서 이용 가능하다.
⑤ 배에서 내릴 때 표가 필요하다.

10 다음 표를 보면서 대화를 듣고, 남자가 선택할 회의실을 고르시오.

Room Name	Capacity (people)	Fee/Hour	Conference Equipment
① Crystal Room	100	$300	audio/video equipment, beam projector
② Jade Room	80	$250	audio equipment, beam projector
③ Ruby Room	70	$200	audio equipment
④ Diamond Room	200	$400	audio/video equipment, beam projector
⑤ Sapphire Room	50	$100	—

11 대화를 듣고, 여자의 마지막 말에 대한 남자의 응답으로 가장 적절한 것을 고르시오.

① Do what you think is right.
② The exam was far too difficult.
③ She'll get upset at your poor grades.
④ I'll overlook your mistake this time.
⑤ I really don't want to get caught cheating.

12 대화를 듣고, 남자의 마지막 말에 대한 여자의 응답으로 가장 적절한 것을 고르시오.

① I left work early today for this.
② Yeah, thanks for letting me rest.
③ Yes, we should have hired some movers.
④ I've already packed everything in the kitchen.
⑤ Actually, I think it will be better to work together.

13 대화를 듣고, 여자의 마지막 말에 대한 남자의 응답으로 가장 적절한 것을 고르시오. [3점]

▶ Man : ______

① I like to correct people's bad English.
② Yeah, I learn a lot about other countries.
③ You have taught me a lot about chatting.
④ Of course! I can improve my English a lot.
⑤ Actually, I often have coffee with messenger friends.

14 대화를 듣고, 남자의 마지막 말에 대한 여자의 응답으로 가장 적절한 것을 고르시오. [3점]

▶ Woman : ______

① Bad news travels fast.
② Misery loves company.
③ Art is long, life is short.
④ A watched pot never boils.
⑤ Too many cooks spoil the broth.

15 다음 상황 설명을 듣고, Steven이 Luke에게 할 말로 가장 적절한 것을 고르시오. [3점]

▶ Steven : Luke, ______

① what is your toughest subject?
② can you introduce them to me?
③ I'm really in trouble with my studies.
④ can I join your friends next weekend?
⑤ I'm here for you. I can help you study anytime.

[16~17] 다음을 듣고, 물음에 답하시오.

16 여자가 하는 말의 주제로 가장 적절한 것은?

① the early stage of social phobia
② phobias caused by teen anxiety
③ tips for teens to overcome fears
④ the warning signs of teen anxiety
⑤ why teens should treat their phobias

17 공포를 느끼게 하는 특정 대상으로 언급되지 않은 것은?

① 거미 ② 폭풍 ③ 밀폐된 공간
④ 주삿바늘 ⑤ 큰 소리

33 DICTATION

녹음된 내용을 들으면서 빈칸을 알맞게 채워 보세요.

01

W: I'd like to have your attention, please. I know you ______________________________ ______________ about what is happening. The problem is this testing center has been doing the same thing. We have been trying to ______________________________. What I can tell you is that the problem is not the computers on-site at this testing center. ______ ______________________________ in America. The computer server is causing problems for testing centers throughout the world. Due to this problem we have been informed that ________ ______________________________. The testing agency will announce new testing dates next week. We are really ______________________________.

02

W: Oh, no! Have you seen the terrible comments that people have written below the video I posted?

M: Yeah, I did. That's unfortunate, but you just _____ ______________________________.

W: They wouldn't have said these things to my face. They only did it because they knew __________ ______________________________.

M: That's the downside of having anonymity on the Internet. Some people behave irresponsibly when ______________________________.

W: I guess that means you think there is an upside?

M: Of course. Anonymity allows people to say unpopular things that need to be said. Freedom of speech and expression is also a very important thing.

W: You have a good point, but I'm still __________ ______________________________.

M: Trust me, your video was great.

03

M: Here are your clothes, Mrs. Smith.

W: Thanks. Let's see... a sweater, a pair of pants and a white shirt.

M: That'll be $8.50.

W: OK. Oh, ______________________________ ______________ out of Jenny's shirt?

M: Not completely. ______________________________ and I cleaned it two times.

W: And it still didn't come out completely?

M: No, it didn't. But remember I didn't promise I could ______________________________?

W: I know. I guess I'll have to buy her another white shirt for school.

M: Probably. Look here, the ink stain is still quite visible.

W: ______________________________.
Anyway, here's $10.

M: Here's your change. Have a good day!

04

W: All right, Dave. Now I'll show you __________ ______________.

M: Okay. I think the bread plate and butter knife usually go at the top left.

W: Yes, of course. We also ______________________ ______________________________.

M: Should I set the forks to the left of the dinner plate?

W: Yes, that's correct. The dinner plate goes in the center and the forks go on the left.

M: Would you like me to ______________________ ______________________________?

W: That was our policy, but now we place the napkin to the left of the forks.

M: No problem. Where should I place the knife and spoon?

W: Those go to the right of the dinner plate, like this. ______________________________?

M: I think I've got it.

05

W: What are you going to do after graduation?

M: I've been accepted to a graduate program for computer science. How about you?

W: Well, ______________ contemporary art, and I really want to be an artist.

M: You're very talented. I bet your parents are proud.

W: Actually, they want me to be a designer because ______________. I don't know what to do.

M: You sound confused. In fact, ______________ ______________, and the school's counseling center was extremely helpful.

W: Really? Maybe I should give it a try. By the way, where is it?

M: It's a little hard to find. I'd take you there now, but I have a class. So, ______________ ______________?

W: That'd be great. Use my notebook.

M: Okay. Just a second.

06

W: I need to order T-shirts and baseball caps for a summer camp for 50 kids.

M: No problem, ma'am. We have ______________ ______________. This one is $5 and that one is $8.

W: ______________?

M: The more expensive one is 100% cotton. The other is a cotton polyester blend.

W: Hmm.... ______________.

M: OK. And for the baseball caps, do you want plain ones or do you need ______________ ______________? Plain ones are $4 each, and printed ones are $6 each.

W: Oh, on the caps, I want the name of the camp, "Outdoor Adventures," and this logo showing a man climbing a cliff.

M: Great. So you need 50 of each?

W: Actually, I need 60 of each. We have 10 support staff. We need shirts and caps for them, too.

07

W: How was your trip to Malaysia?

M: It was good, but my phone broke during the trip and the service center here ______________.

W: You just bought it last month. Didn't you get insurance?

M: I did, and the insurance ______________ ______________.

W: Did your phone fall in the water? What happened?

M: No. It got a little rain on it, but ______________ ______________. Actually, it just stopped working one morning during the trip.

W: Then, why won't the service center fix it?

M: Well, I tried to fix it in Malaysia. The place looked official, but I guess it wasn't ______________ ______________.

W: Oh, insurance won't help you if your phone has been opened.

M: Exactly. Now I have to buy a new phone.

08

M: Jatropha is a small tree, about three to five meters tall. Some people call it "a perfect plant" because it's useful and ______________. It can grow almost anywhere, including harsh desert environments with very little water. The oil from its seeds can be made into biofuel, ______________ ______________ in India and the Philippines. Plus, its strong roots can prevent land from turning into desert and protect crops from high winds. However, its strength is also ______________ ______________. It can quickly take over land and dominate other species, which can ______________. For this reason, many governments don't support planting jatropha trees ______________ ______________.

09

W: Welcome aboard the Thames Riverboat Cruise. It's a very scenic journey which will ____________ ____________________ to take pictures of landmarks in the city, including the Tower Bridge and Big Ben. If you are taking the one-way cruise, it will last 1 hour and 20 minutes. If you are making a round-trip, it will last about 2 hours and 40 minutes. ____________________, there is a snack bar on the boat. It only sells packaged snacks and drinks. It sells coffee and tea, but ____________________. And, finally, please don't lose your ticket. You must show it ____________________.

10

W: Good afternoon. May I help you?

M: I would like to inquire about the rooms for _____ ____________________ for native English teachers.

W: I see. When is the conference and ____________ ____________________, sir?

M: It's on June 10th, which is a Saturday, from 1 p.m. to 4 p.m., and we are expecting about 70 teachers to be there.

W: I see. We have the perfect place for your conference. The Crystal Room, with excellent conference equipment, can fit in 100 people for $300 an hour.

M: ____________________. Don't you have anything cheaper?

W: Well, the Jade Room can seat up to 80 people and it's $250, and the Ruby Room is just $200 per hour, but only 70 people can sit in the room.

M: Both of them seem good. Could I have ________ ____________________?

W: Certainly. We have the Diamond Room, which is the largest at our center, and it can accommodate 200 people and the rate is $400. And our Sapphire Room can fit in 50 people, and we charge $100 for the room.

M: ____________________ for our conference. Oh, I forgot to mention that we need a room ____________________.

W: OK. It seems, then, there is only one room that you can choose.

11

W: The girl beside me ____________________ during the exam.

M: I guess Mrs. Bean didn't see, or she ____________ ____________________.

W: I know... Do you think I should tell her what I saw?

12

M: We need to finish moving out today, but ________ ____________________.

W: Right. Should we start with the kitchen?

M: I think it will be a lot faster if we ____________ ______________.

13

W: I go into Internet messenger chat rooms every night.

M: To practice your English, Mi-hyun?

W: No. ____________________ has too much slang. As an English teacher, do you think chatting on the Internet improves learners' English?

M: Not really. I agree that the English isn't so good.

W: I just like to meet people from different countries. ____________________.

M: That's a good idea. And ____________________ ______________?

W: I promised her ____________________ ____________________ I met in a chat room.

M: Good!

W: Why don't we chat sometime?

M: Sure. I do it ____________________ ____________.

W: Oh, really?

14

W: Your drama club is going to perform a play at the year-end school festival, isn't it?

M: Yes.

W: Which play?

M: We want to ______________________________.

W: So how is the writing going?

M: Not good.

W: ____, isn't it?

M: Yes, but the real problem is that we're having lots of problems ______________________________. There are seven of us.

W: Oh, I've been in that situation. Everyone has different ideas of each character.

M: Not only each character, but the plot of the whole story.

W: ____? You know the saying?

M: What's that?

15

M: Steven has been best friends with Luke since elementary school. Last year, they entered high school together and they ____________________ ____________________. Luke, unfortunately, started to ______________________________ ________________. He found high school a lot harder than middle school, and he started to spend some time with some students who really didn't care about studying hard. It seems that Luke ______________________________. Steven really wants to help Luke. But he can't force Luke to study hard. So he just wants to let Luke know he ______________________________. In this situation, what would Steven most likely say to Luke?

16-17

W: If you are a teen and you have anxiety, you are not alone. Studies indicate that nearly 20% of all teens in the US ______________________________. Teen anxiety is an exaggerated emotional reaction that reflects conscious and unconscious fears. Without treatment, teen anxiety can __________ ________________________. One of the most common is teen social phobia, which typically first appears ______________________________. The primary feature of teen social phobia is extreme fear of social situations and performances, and an exaggerated fear of embarrassment. There are also specific phobias that can be caused by teen anxiety. The first symptoms of these specific phobias usually ________________________ ______________________. Phobic individuals may be irrationally afraid of certain beings like dogs, spiders, or snakes. They may also be afraid of things in the environment like storms, closed spaces, elevators, and loud noises, or even events like vomiting. Having one phobia ____________ ______________________________________.

실전모의고사

34 PRACTICE TEST

01 다음을 듣고, 여자가 하는 말의 목적으로 가장 적절한 것을 고르시오.

① 도서 검색 방법을 설명하려고
② 신간 소설 코너를 홍보하려고
③ 서점 회원 가입을 독려하려고
④ 사은품 증정에 대해 안내하려고
⑤ 작가와의 만남 행사를 알리려고

02 대화를 듣고, 남자의 의견으로 가장 적절한 것을 고르시오.

① 공부가 테니스 수강보다 더 중요하다.
② 다양한 운동은 운동 효과를 높여준다.
③ 많은 경험을 통해 자기계발을 해야 한다.
④ 정해진 일정을 최대한 지키려고 노력해야 한다.
⑤ 새로운 일을 시작하는 것보다 지금 하는 일에 집중해야 한다.

03 대화를 듣고, 두 사람의 관계를 가장 잘 나타낸 것을 고르시오.

① 아내 – 남편
② 기관사 – 검표원
③ 승객 – 버스 기사
④ 승객 – 택시 기사
⑤ 관광객 – 관광 가이드

04 대화를 듣고, 그림에서 대화의 내용과 일치하지 않는 것을 고르시오.

05 대화를 듣고, 남자가 할 일로 가장 적절한 것을 고르시오.

① 시험 치기
② 농구 경기하기
③ 도서관에 가기
④ 가족과 저녁 먹기
⑤ Connor의 집에 가기

06 대화를 듣고, 여자가 일일 경비로 예상하는 총금액을 고르시오.

① $55 ② $65 ③ $70
④ $85 ⑤ $100

07 대화를 듣고, 여자가 Richard에게 전화하려는 이유를 고르시오.

① 점심 약속을 잡기 위해서
② 약속 날짜를 변경하기 위해서
③ 전시회에 가자고 제안하기 위해서
④ 약속 시각에 늦는다고 알리기 위해서
⑤ 정확한 식사 장소를 물어보기 위해서

08 대화를 듣고, 빅토리아 폭포(Victoria Falls)에 관해 언급되지 않은 것을 고르시오.

① 규모 ② 위치
③ 이름의 유래 ④ 처음 발견된 시기
⑤ 관광하기 좋은 시기

09 열차의 지연에 관한 다음 내용을 듣고, 일치하지 않는 것을 고르시오.

① 눈이 많이 와서 기차가 지연될 예정이다.
② 716호 열차의 승객은 열차에서 하차하여야 한다.
③ 716호 열차는 다른 노선에 투입될 것이다.
④ 하루 이상 지연되면 무료 기차표를 제공받게 된다.
⑤ 무료 기차표로 미국 전역에서 Trans America사의 열차를 탈 수 있다.

정답 및 해설 p.134

10 다음 표를 보면서 대화를 듣고, 여자가 임대할 아파트를 고르시오.

	Bed-rooms	Monthly Rent	Security Guard	Area
① Oaktree Lane Apts.	3	$900		200m^2
② Starlight Apts.	2	$900	✓	250m^2
③ Executive Suites.	2	$2,000	✓	400m^2
④ Red Robin Apts.	1	$400		100m^2
⑤ Meadow Acres Apts.	3	$800	✓	200m^2

11 대화를 듣고, 여자의 마지막 말에 대한 남자의 응답으로 가장 적절한 것을 고르시오.

① I've booked one-way tickets.
② Our direct flight will take 14 hours.
③ Unfortunately, they were already full.
④ Yes, I'm looking forward to seeing Tokyo.
⑤ Flight attendants will direct us to our seats.

12 대화를 듣고, 남자의 마지막 말에 대한 여자의 응답으로 가장 적절한 것을 고르시오.

① I haven't seen her for a while.
② A taxi is probably much faster.
③ It was around 9 when I talked to her.
④ She came from the other side of town.
⑤ She didn't say, but let's give her ten minutes.

13 대화를 듣고, 여자의 마지막 말에 대한 남자의 응답으로 가장 적절한 것을 고르시오. [3점]

▶ Man : ____________________

① If you do that, you will be fired.
② Teamwork is essential in this field.
③ The internship is for three months.
④ Please let us know your decision by Friday.
⑤ I will give you your first assignment tomorrow.

14 대화를 듣고, 남자의 마지막 말에 대한 여자의 응답으로 가장 적절한 것을 고르시오. [3점]

▶ Woman : ____________________

① You can do it by yourself if you want.
② OK. I think you can finish it by Friday.
③ I'll help this time, but be prepared next time.
④ Let's just forget about it. We'll try next time.
⑤ We can't just download the software off the Internet.

15 다음 상황 설명을 듣고, Ella가 Jill에게 할 말로 가장 적절한 것을 고르시오. [3점]

▶ Ella : ____________________

① We should come to the gym more often.
② I am worried that you may be overdoing it.
③ Can you tell me your secret to losing weight?
④ The hard work is really paying off. You look great!
⑤ You need to see the doctor for your monthly checkup.

[16~17] 다음을 듣고, 물음에 답하시오.

16 남자가 하는 말의 주제로 가장 적절한 것은?

① why we should drive carefully
② advertisement for a new GPS device
③ the dangers of texting while driving
④ advice for avoiding distracted driving
⑤ the process of getting a driver's license

17 운전 중 방해 요인으로 언급되지 않은 것은?

① 휴대전화 사용
② 음식 섭취
③ 졸음
④ 굽 높은 신발
⑤ 외투 탈의

34 DICTATION

녹음된 내용을 들으면서 빈칸을 알맞게 채워 보세요.

01

W: Good afternoon, shoppers! We hope you're having a pleasant afternoon. Our friendly staff is always here to ____________________. We'd also like to remind you that Bloom Books will be hosting a visit from children's author Anna Walker this Saturday at 3 p.m. Her presentation is for children ages 4 to 8, but ____________________ ____________________. She plans to read a small part of her latest book and show the kids how to draw characters. Signed copies of her picture book will also be ____________________. It's sure to be a good time for everyone, so ________ ____________________. For more information on this and other Bloom Books events, visit www.bloombooks.com. Thank you for choosing Bloom Books, and have a great day!

02

M: What are you looking at, Jane?

W: It's a flyer for lessons at the tennis club. __________ ____________________.

M: It looks like the beginner's course meets every afternoon. Do you have time?

W: I think so. I'll just have to reschedule my guitar lessons.

M: Wow. I think I'd delay taking the tennis course ____________________.

W: Why? Don't you think I'll be a good tennis player?

M: It's not that. You're already so busy with Spanish class, swimming lessons, and everything else.

W: I'm only ____________________. I hate wasting time.

M: I know, but it's important to stay focused. It's like the saying, "If you run after two hares, __________ ____________________."

W: You have a point. I have been feeling distracted lately.

M: Exactly. Doing too much at once can overwhelm your brain.

W: You're right. I'll take your advice.

03

W: Hello?

M: Hello. ____________________?

W: I'm going to Central Station.

M: Sure. No problem.

W: Thank you. Sorry for asking, but do you have any idea ____________________?

M: Oh, it shouldn't be more than 18 dollars.

W: OK. How long does it take to get there?

M: Well, ____________________, but it shouldn't take more than 30 minutes.

W: Oh, and by the way, do you know what time the last train for Chicago leaves?

M: I don't know, but I know there is a train for Chicago at 4:50.

W: Oh, ____________________.

M: Well, I'm afraid you'll have to take the next train. I'm sure the 4:50 is not the last train for Chicago.

04

W: I think ____________________ for the school play.

M: I think so, too. It looks great.

W: I'm glad we found such a nice bookshelf for the left side of the stage.

M: Me too, but I think the heart-shaped light that you made for the background ____________________ ____________________.

W: Thanks, and the square-shaped table is wonderful. ____________________ to pick this one instead of a round table.

M: Right. Plus, we were able to find the perfect old telephone to place on the table. The phone is so important to the story.

W: Yes, and the bed looks really good on the right.
M: ______________________________.
I think the audience is going to love the stage.

05

W: Michael! The basketball! I told you ______________________________.
M: I'm not going to play basketball, Mom.
W: Well, why are you ______________________________?
M: It's Connor's basketball, not mine. I'm going to ______________________________.
W: Are you meeting him tonight?
M: Yes. We're going to study together at the municipal library. We can ______________________________ for our exams.
W: Oh?
M: And he asked me to return the basketball tonight. Can I go now?
W: Yes. ______________________________, so it's not a problem. Will you be home when the library closes?
M: Yes, I'll see you around 10:30.

06

W: Larry, you went backpacking last summer, didn't you?
M: Yes.
W: Well, ______________________________ through Europe this summer. How much money do you think I need to budget?
M: ______________________________. Eastern Europe is much cheaper than Western Europe.
W: I want to go to Western Europe and see all the famous sites.
M: OK. Well, first ______________________________. You need about $20 per day if you stay in youth hostels, but $50 for cheap hotels.
W: I'll stay in youth hostels.
M: And if you cook in the hostel, you need about $15 a day for food. But if you eat meals in restaurants, you'll need $30 or so.
W: I'll definitely ______________________________.
M: And budget about $20 a day for travel and entrance fees.
W: OK. ______________________________ how much I need to save now.

07

M: Sara, shouldn't you be leaving for your lunch meeting with Richard?
W: I'll leave soon, Dad. ______________________________. We're meeting at Tim's Diner.
M: The one by the East Mall? That is at least 45 minutes from here.
W: I think he meant the one downtown. It's not that far.
M: ______________________________ after lunch, right?
W: Yes. Richard is very excited about the exhibition.
M: I'm sure Richard was thinking of the exhibit at the mall. That's the one everyone is talking about. I bet you are eating there, too.
W: Now I'm not so sure. I guess ______________________________.
M: Maybe you should give him a call now, ______________________________.
W: You're right. I'll do that.

08

W: This picture of Victoria Falls looks amazing!

M: ____ by area. The falls are 1.7 kilometers wide and 108 meters high.

W: Wow, I only knew that it's in Africa.

M: The falls lie between Zambia and Zimbabwe in Southern Africa. By the way, do you know ______ ______________________________?

W: I'm not sure, but it makes me think of Queen Victoria.

M: Right. Dr. Livingstone, a Scottish explorer, ______ ______________________________.

W: Interesting. I would love to see the falls in person.

M: If you get to go see them, make sure it's in June or July. That's ______________________________.

W: Why is that a good time?

M: That's when the river has the most water, so the falls are the biggest.

09

M: Attention passengers. Due to heavy snowfall in the mountains, Train 716 to Salt Lake City will be delayed for your safety until ________________ ________________________. If you have placed your luggage aboard the train, please remove all items and exit the train now. This train will now be used for another route. Although ____________ ______________________________, if the delay lasts more than 12 hours, we will ____________ ________________________________ for a free round-trip ticket. You can board TransAmerica Trains to anywhere we travel in the U.S. We will ________________________________ on the status of the departure time. Thank you for your patience.

10

W: I've got the list of apartments for rent.

M: Are you sure you want to live all by yourself?

W: Yes, now ______________________________.

M: OK. What is the most important thing for you?

W: I need at least two rooms: one for sleeping and the other for my office.

M: So that small place ______________________ ________________. What else?

W: I can't afford more than $1,000 a month.

M: Then you won't be living like an 'executive.'

W: At least not yet. But I do want to ____________ ______________________________.

M: Of course. And now you have to choose between these two apartments.

W: Well, I ______________________________. So I'll get the bigger one.

11

W: Our vacation is next month. ________________ ______________________?

M: I did. It's a bit long because it stops in Tokyo, but we'll still arrive in L.A. on the 23rd.

W: That's okay, but weren't there ______________ ________________________?

12

M: Well, it's ten o'clock. I think that ______________ ______________________________.

W: ________________________________ for Jane. She said she might be late.

M: We can wait a few minutes. When did she say she would arrive?

13

M: Tell me why you think you are ____________________ ____________________.

W: Although I am just graduating, I have experience through several intensive internships.

M: I did notice the internships on your résumé, but tell me something specific about you.

W: ____________________ and excellent problem-solving skills.

M: How are you ____________________ ____________________?

W: To be honest, I haven't had much experience with group work.

M: What about at the internships?

W: They pretty much gave me assignments and ____________________ ____________________.

M: I'm impressed. When can you start?

W: Well, I have several more interviews to go to this week.

14

W: Do you ____________________ ____________________ for class tomorrow?

M: Tomorrow? I thought we weren't giving our presentation until Friday!

W: We were, initially, but ____________________ ____________________ because one of their members was in the hospital. Remember?

M: If I remembered, I would be better prepared.

W: Well, you ____________________ ____________________.

M: I have it half done.

W: That's it? You'll never be ready. This is going to ____________________.

M: I was waiting for new software to make the presentation really great.

W: Forget great. ____________________.

M: If you look for some information for me, we can finish in just a few hours.

15

W: Ella and Jill have worked out together three times a week at the gym for more than a year now. Ella ____________________, but Jill says she is trying to lose weight. However, Jill is extremely thin and ____________________ ____________________ to Ella. She has also noticed that Jill ____________________ for sometimes three or four hours at a time and is often there on days when Ella is not there. Ella is concerned that her friend may ____________________. As her workout partner and friend, she wants to ____________________. In this situation, what would Ella most likely say to Jill?

16-17

M: Driving is a grave responsibility that ____________________ ____________________, but distractions can occur at anytime. Today, I'd like to talk about ways to ____________________ while driving. First, there are some things you should do before driving. Review all maps, directions, and any pre-programmed routes on a GPS device before driving. This prevents getting distracted by maps while driving. Also, preset the volume of the radio so that you won't ____________________. There are other ways to ____________________ while driving, as well. Talking on your cell phone, or worse, texting while you drive is a major source of distraction. If you have a good reason to talk on the phone, use a hands-free device. Nowadays, ____________________ for busy people to eat and drink while driving. Remember that it is always safer to eat at home or sitting in a restaurant. If you start to feel sleepy, pull over to the side of the road and take a rest for a while. Finally, ____________________ ____________________ or changing clothes while driving.

PRACTICE TEST

01 다음을 듣고, 여자가 하는 말의 목적으로 가장 적절한 것을 고르시오.

① 연설 대회의 주제를 발표하려고
② 결승전의 세부 사항을 설명하려고
③ 이전 라운드의 결과를 알려주려고
④ 관객들에게 상품 변경 사항을 공지하려고
⑤ 참가자들에게 투표하는 방법을 안내하려고

02 대화를 듣고, 두 사람이 하는 말의 주제로 가장 적절한 것을 고르시오.

① 가족 단위 봉사활동의 장점
② 봉사활동을 할 때 고려할 점
③ 자신의 재능을 활용한 봉사활동
④ 청소년기에 봉사활동을 해야 하는 이유
⑤ 연령대별로 가장 필요한 봉사활동의 종류

03 대화를 듣고, 두 사람의 관계를 가장 잘 나타낸 것을 고르시오.

① 내과의 – 환자
② 사육사 – 조수
③ 보건 교사 – 학생
④ 수의사 – 목장 주인
⑤ 조련사 – 애완동물 주인

04 대화를 듣고, 그림에서 대화의 내용과 일치하지 않는 것을 고르시오.

05 대화를 듣고, 남자가 여자에게 부탁한 일로 가장 적절한 것을 고르시오.

① 가수의 사진 찍어주기
② 가수의 사인 받아주기
③ 온라인으로 티켓 예매하기
④ 음악 잡지를 대신 구독해주기
⑤ 문자 메시지로 번호 보내주기

06 대화를 듣고, 두 사람이 올해 지금까지 기부 받은 총금액을 고르시오.

① $47,000 ② $55,000 ③ $56,000
④ $63,000 ⑤ $64,000

07 대화를 듣고, 여자가 웅변대회에 참가하지 않는 이유를 고르시오.

① 자신감이 부족해서
② 다른 할 일이 많아서
③ 웅변에 흥미를 잃어버려서
④ 대회의 심사를 맡게 되어서
⑤ 다른 대회에 참가하고 싶어서

08 대화를 듣고, 에델바이스(edelweiss)에 관해 언급되지 않은 것을 고르시오.

① 모양 ② 원산지 ③ 재배 방법
④ 개화 시기 ⑤ 이름의 의미

09 George Pearson Memorial 도서관에 관한 다음 내용을 듣고, 일치하지 않는 것을 고르시오.

① 명칭은 최초 설립자의 이름에서 따왔다.
② 처음 세워진 지 100년이 넘었다.
③ 리모델링 공사는 6개월이 걸렸다.
④ 난방시설은 아직 마무리되지 않았다.
⑤ 건물의 입구는 새롭게 디자인했다.

정답 및 해설 p.138

10 다음 표를 보면서 대화를 듣고, 두 사람이 선택할 숙소를 고르시오.

Blue Lake Lodge Information

Name of Lodging	Facilities	Internet	Price
① Leaf House	Barbecue	No	$110
② Starlight House	Hot springs	Yes	$145
③ River House	Swimming pool	Yes	$130
④ Hillside House	Hot springs	Yes	$155
⑤ Wet fog House	Swimming pool	No	$120

11 대화를 듣고, 남자의 마지막 말에 대한 여자의 응답으로 가장 적절한 것을 고르시오.

① Try calling one more time.
② I'll check my voicemail now.
③ Now we can start the meeting.
④ The elevator is out of order again.
⑤ Sorry, I left my phone on my desk.

12 대화를 듣고, 여자의 마지막 말에 대한 남자의 응답으로 가장 적절한 것을 고르시오.

① Your sister majored in history.
② No, the deadline was yesterday.
③ I'll ask the teacher for more time.
④ She is busy preparing for her exam.
⑤ There's too much work in this class.

13 대화를 듣고, 남자의 마지막 말에 대한 여자의 응답으로 가장 적절한 것을 고르시오. [3점]

▶ Woman : ________________

① There aren't enough hours during the day.
② Remember that it's really a matter of effort.
③ I'll recommend an appropriate study guide.
④ The tests have been difficult, so don't worry.
⑤ You should have taken your studies more seriously.

14 대화를 듣고, 여자의 마지막 말에 대한 남자의 응답으로 가장 적절한 것을 고르시오. [3점]

▶ Man : ________________

① Well, you should have asked me first.
② Don't worry, that's what friends are for.
③ You must be sad that the trip was canceled.
④ Your friends told me they were disappointed.
⑤ Breaking a promise is unacceptable in any situation.

15 다음 상황 설명을 듣고, Diane이 Justin에게 할 말로 가장 적절한 것을 고르시오. [3점]

▶ Diane : ________________

① Wow, you've changed a lot!
② We are very close to each other!
③ Where are you going to move to?
④ I used to live near your house when I was young.
⑤ Social networking sites are helpful for finding old friends.

[16~17] 다음을 듣고, 물음에 답하시오.

16 남자가 하는 말의 주제로 가장 적절한 것은?

① the importance of a proper diet
② the results of mishandling stress
③ the correct ways to manage stress
④ the negative effects of stress on diet
⑤ the relationship between stress and food

17 식이장애의 원인으로 언급되지 <u>않은</u> 것은?

① 가족 병력
② 습관적 다이어트
③ 예민한 성격
④ 직업적 특성
⑤ 미디어의 조장

35 DICTATION

녹음된 내용을 들으면서 빈칸을 알맞게 채워 보세요.

01

W: Yesterday, the semi-final stage of the Crown High School Speech Contest took place. More than 20 students competed, and 5 have moved on to the final round. Today, ______________________ ______________. Each of the 5 students will have 5 minutes to give their final speech. In the previous rounds, the students chose the topics, but this time ______________________________________. Contestants will then have 30 minutes to prepare. The speeches will be judged by faculty members, but in this round the audience will also ______________________________________. The winner of this exciting competition will ______________________________________, and the runner-up will receive a tablet PC.

02

M: Linda, what's that?

W: It's a letter from the children's home ___________ ______________________.

M: It's great that you donate your talent to such a worthy cause.

W: I was ______________________________________. In fact, his choir group sings songs for patients.

M: That's cool. I'm not good at singing so I can't imagine doing that.

W: Didn't you take a massage class last year? How about massaging the elderly at nursing homes?

M: I'd love to, but I just ______________________ and my arms are weak.

W: Well, your voice is one of your strengths, so ______ ______________________________________?

M: I could do that. Sometimes, I read to my younger sister and it's fun.

W: I'm sure the children will love it.

03

M: You say that Bart isn't feeling well?

W: Yes, ______________________________.

M: Let's see.... I'll take Bart's temperature.

W: Alright. Oh, I'm so worried about him because he does a great job of ______________________ ______________________________, and he's never been sick before.

M: I see. Yes, he does have a fever. When exactly did he get sick?

W: It was three nights ago, after he was out with the hunting dogs in our field.

M: I think I've discovered the reason. He __________ ____________________. It's probably infected.

W: Will he be alright?

M: Yes. I'll ______________________________, and I'm sure he'll be wagging his tail again soon.

W: ______________________________! Thank you so much.

M: It's no trouble at all.

04

W: John, can we finally discuss ______________________ ______________________________?

M: Sure. I'm ready.

W: Great. I think the picture of a dead planet in the top right corner is appropriate.

M: I agree. It's a good match for a book about protecting the environment.

W: The title right under the picture, "The Last Man on Earth," is also fitting.

M: Right, and the picture below it of a lone man kneeling on the ground ______________________ ______________________________.

W: But I'm surprised that you included plants with flowers instead of dead plants.

M: I felt that ______________________________ ______________. I wanted to show there is still hope.

W: Hmm.... That is ______________________________ ______________.

정답 및 해설 p.138

M: Right. And, of course, I've put our company's name, "Best Book House," in the bottom right corner.
W: It looks great.

05

W: Isn't this a pamphlet for Sunny's concert? ________________________________?
M: Sure. And I heard you went last year. How was it?
W: Fantastic! I even met Sunny ________________________________.
M: That's unbelievable! Did you take a picture?
W: Of course! I also got her autograph. She was really nice. That's why she's my favorite singer.
M: Wow, I'd really love to go to her concert.
W: Would you? I can get a discount ________________________________.
M: Really? That's great.
W: Sure. I just need to give you the coupon number. Can you write it down now?
M: ________________________________. Could you send it to me by text message?
W: No problem. ________________________________ your ticket, because they sell out fast.
M: Got it. Thanks.

06

W: Sam! Come and see ________________________________!
M: Wow! It's amazing!
W: You're right. We collected around 55,000 dollars last year, right?
M: Yes, it was 56,000 dollars. And we've got 8,000 dollars more this year than last year, ________________________________.
W: Oh, wait. I think something is wrong. Did you add the 1,000 dollars we got yesterday?
M: You mean from the old lady who didn't tell us her name? Yes, I input the data here in this line.
W: That's why ________________________________. I also added it right below that line.
M: Then we should subtract 1,000 dollars.
W: Right. Still, ________________________________.
M: I feel really great that people are getting more interested in helping others.
W: So do I.

07

W: Hello, Mr. Nelson.
M: Hi, Emma. ________________________________.
W: Actually, I won't be speaking in the speech contest this year.
M: But you've been the champion ________________________________. Have you lost interest in speaking?
W: No, I still enjoy it, especially sharing my ideas with other people.
M: That's good. You've always had a unique confidence and strong stage presence.
W: Thank you. ________________________________.
M: But I guess you are just too busy this year.
W: No. The truth is that I was asked ________________________________.
M: Oh, that will be a new experience. Good for you.
W: Yes, I'm glad to have been invited, and I'll ________________________________.
M: Alright. In that case, I'll see you at the contest.

08

W: That's a lovely flower, Tom.
M: Thanks. It was a gift from a friend.
W: It's an edelweiss flower, right? I recognize the star shape. ________________________.
M: You're right. My friend said ________________ ________________ of Europe. I'm going to plant it in my garden.
W: ________________________.
Can I come to see it later? I really love edelweiss flowers.
M: Of course. It ________________________ until the end of summer, so you should come then.
W: Great. By the way, ________________________ ________ this flower's name?
M: Does it have a special meaning? What is it?
W: "Edel" means "noble" and "weiss" means "white" in German.
M: So it means noble and white? I didn't know that.
W: It's fascinating, isn't it?

09

M: Good morning, everyone! I'm ________________ ________________ that our city library will reopen today. And I'm proud to say that it will be renamed George Pearson Memorial Library, after the founder of the original library. As you probably know, the old library was over a century old when remodeling began. Now, ________________ ________________, we have a library that everyone can enjoy. Though the heating system won't be finished until winter, the air-conditioning system ________________________ ________. And the new building has kept the beautiful entrance of the old library. A few days ago, local high school graduates ________ ________________________ to the new library. This means ________________ ________ even more books and resources.

10

W: Honey, are these the lodges we can choose for our vacation?
M: Yes, I think we should pick one today.
W: How about this one? ________________________ ________________.
M: The kids would love it, but I'm afraid I need the Internet for my work.
W: I wish ________________________ ________________, but I understand.
M: Also, I think it's a good idea to spend less than $150 per night.
W: I agree. So, what do you think of this place?
M: I like it ________________________ ________________.
W: That would feel nice at night, but I'm sure the kids would prefer to play in a swimming pool.
M: You're probably right, and I want them to really enjoy this trip.
W: Then I think it's settled.
M: Good. ________________________.

11

M: Where have you been? The meeting started already!
W: I'm so sorry. ________________________ for about twenty minutes.
M: Well, ________________________, but your phone went to voicemail.

12

W: Mark, do you think we can ________________ ________________________?
M: I'm not sure. We have only three hours left before the deadline!
W: How about ________________________ ________________?

13

M: Ms. Evans, can I talk to you for a minute?
W: Of course, Henry. What's on your mind?
M: It's about English grammar. My grade isn't improving.

W: ____?
Or is it more of a test-related problem?

M: Both, I guess. Do you have any advice?

W: Well, ____________________________________ ____________________ each day?

M: Around 20 minutes every day.

W: That's not enough, Henry. ____________________ __________________________ foreign grammar.

M: But I'm too busy to put more time into studying English. ______________________________?

W: That couldn't hurt, but it won't solve the problem.

M: Then, what about another dictionary?

14

W: Are you busy, Dad?

M: I have a minute. ___________________________ ________________, Rebecca?

W: Well, my friends are going on a trip for a couple of days, and I want to go with them. Can I?

M: I don't know. Whose family ___________________ ________________?

W: It's just a trip with friends. It would be so much fun!

M: I don't think that's a good idea.

W: Dad, please. I'll call you every few hours, and it's only for a couple of days.

M: No, I'm afraid not. It's too dangerous without adults.

W: But we're grown up ___________________________ ______________________.

M: I'm sorry, Rebecca, but I won't change my mind.

W: But, Dad, I ____________________________________ ______________!

15

W: Diane and Justin ____________________________ ________________________. Then, Diane's family moved to Korea because of Diane's father's work. Unfortunately, Diane lost Justin's phone number during the move, so ___________________________ ____________________. Ten years later, Justin is studying Korean in a university in Korea. And Diane is checking some messages from her friends on a social networking site as usual. She sees that Justin ___________________________________ and left his contact number. She calls Justin immediately and the two ___________________ __________________. During the conversation, Diane learns that Justin now lives in a building near her house. Diane wants to _______________ ____________________. In this situation, what would Diane most likely say to Justin?

16-17

M: We are all exposed to stress in our day-to-day lives, and _________________________________ _________________. When stress is not managed in a healthy manner, there can be unpleasant consequences. For example, many stressed individuals become depressed and avoid social situations or _____________________________ ____________________. They may also experience difficulty finding joy in once enjoyable activities. At the same time, ______________________________ or online games to escape their stress. One particularly unhealthy way of escaping stress is through emotional eating. Emotional eaters eat not because they are hungry but because it comforts them. Unfortunately, this can develop into an eating disorder, especially for those with a family history of eating disorders. ___________________________ ________________ because of the compliments they receive when losing weight. But they aren't alone. Those with stressful jobs that focus on body image, like actors and dancers, _______________ _______________________________. Furthermore, the media's focus on entertainers with slim bodies creates pressure to be thin. So, the next time you're feeling stressed, remember that food isn't the answer.

실전모의고사

36 PRACTICE TEST

01 다음을 듣고, 남자가 하는 말의 목적으로 가장 적절한 것을 고르시오.

① 자원 재활용을 권유하려고
② 복사용지 절약을 요청하려고
③ 복사용지 사용량을 조사하려고
④ 복사실 이용 방법을 안내하려고
⑤ 삼림 보호의 필요성을 강조하려고

02 대화를 듣고, 여자의 의견으로 가장 적절한 것을 고르시오.

① 개인의 행동이 사회 전체에 영향을 미칠 수 있다.
② 수영을 통해 청소년의 정신 훈련이 가능하다.
③ 장거리 수영에는 큰 용기가 필요하다.
④ 바다 수영 전에는 준비운동이 필수적이다.
⑤ 무모한 행동은 청소년에게 부정적 영향을 준다.

03 대화를 듣고, 두 사람의 관계를 가장 잘 나타낸 것을 고르시오.

① 병원 접수원 – 환자
② 구급 대원 – 신고자
③ 약사 – 보건 교사
④ 의사 – 간호사
⑤ 연구소 연구원 – 연구소 사무직원

04 대화를 듣고, 그림에서 대화의 내용과 일치하지 않는 것을 고르시오.

05 대화를 듣고, 남자가 여자에게 부탁한 일로 가장 적절한 것을 고르시오.

① 남자 대신 출장 가기
② 남자의 아내 문병하기
③ 남자의 아내 돌봐주기
④ 남자와 함께 집들이에 가기
⑤ 남자의 출장 일정 변경하기

06 대화를 듣고, 여자가 지불할 금액을 고르시오. [3점]

① $100 ② $108 ③ $109
④ $110 ⑤ $120

07 대화를 듣고, 남자가 지금 청소를 할 수 없는 이유를 고르시오.

① 학교에 가야 해서
② 과제를 마쳐야 해서
③ 약속 시간에 늦어서
④ 게임을 하는 중이라서
⑤ 친구와 영화를 보기로 해서

08 대화를 듣고, 직장에 관해 언급되지 않은 것을 고르시오.

① 근무 장소 ② 근무 시간
③ 유급 휴가 ④ 급여 액수
⑤ 보험 부담금

09 Greenville Costume Contest에 관한 다음 내용을 듣고, 일치하지 않는 것을 고르시오.

① 마을 광장에서 일요일에 개최된다.
② 상은 세 개 부문으로 나누어 시상한다.
③ 참가 등록 서류는 사무실로 직접 제출해야 한다.
④ 작년 수상자의 의상을 웹사이트에서 볼 수 있다.
⑤ 가족 단위로 참가해도 무방하다.

10 다음 표를 보면서 대화를 듣고, 남자가 구입할 가방을 고르시오.

Camelia Outlet – Women's Bags

bag	type	size	material	price
① A	shoulder bag	15 × 12	fabric	$360
② B	tote bag	12 × 10	leather	$579
③ C	tote bag	15 × 12	leather	$320
④ D	tote bag	12 × 10	fabric	$399
⑤ E	tote bag	15 × 12	fabric	$287

*size: length × height

11 대화를 듣고, 여자의 마지막 말에 대한 남자의 응답으로 가장 적절한 것을 고르시오.

① It would be great to say hello to her now.
② It's not every day you celebrate your birthday.
③ I'll be disappointed in you if you don't make it.
④ I'm sorry, but I have to go to Singapore tomorrow.
⑤ I thought I would do some shopping to get her a gift.

12 대화를 듣고, 남자의 마지막 말에 대한 여자의 응답으로 가장 적절한 것을 고르시오.

① Okay. I've just confirmed your reservation.
② No problem. You can call for room service.
③ Don't worry. I'll send someone to your room.
④ I'm sorry. We don't have any available rooms.
⑤ It's too small. I'd like to change rooms for tonight.

13 대화를 듣고, 여자의 마지막 말에 대한 남자의 응답으로 가장 적절한 것을 고르시오. [3점]

▶ Man : ______________

① I hope he will get better soon.
② I'm sure he will benefit from it.
③ He should be on good behavior.
④ He said you're under a lot of stress.
⑤ I appreciate your time and consideration.

14 대화를 듣고, 남자의 마지막 말에 대한 여자의 응답으로 가장 적절한 것을 고르시오.

▶ Woman : ______________

① Don't forget to bring your umbrella.
② I'm afraid we have to put off our plan then.
③ Be sure to close the window before you leave.
④ No problem. I can take care of the sandwiches.
⑤ Don't worry about tomorrow! Tomorrow isn't here yet.

15 다음 상황 설명을 듣고, Luis가 Brian에게 할 말로 가장 적절한 것을 고르시오. [3점]

▶ Luis : ______________

① What are friends for? I'm glad I found it for you.
② You're so irresponsible. I'm so disappointed in you.
③ Everyone makes mistakes. I understand why you did.
④ Tell her that you lost it and apologize. It's the best way.
⑤ You're in big trouble. She can't live without her tablet PC.

[16~17] 다음을 듣고, 물음에 답하시오.

16 여자가 하는 말의 주제로 가장 적절한 것은?

① how to plan a vacation on a budget
② benefits of using public transportation
③ paperless vacations for the environment
④ how to be an environmentally-friendly tourist
⑤ the positive impact of ecotourism on a local community

17 언급된 장소가 아닌 것은?

① 시내　② 산　③ 강
④ 공원　⑤ 해변

36 DICTATION

녹음된 내용을 들으면서 빈칸을 알맞게 채워 보세요.

01

M: This is an announcement for everyone who uses the photocopier. We checked to see __________ __________ in the last two months in the photocopy room. We found that people are __________ and wasting a lot of paper. In many cases, employees carelessly make more copies than needed. As a result, a lot of paper is being thrown away. Needlessly throwing away so much paper is destroying forests. In the future, we ask that you __________. By using our copier efficiently, we are also helping our environment. Thank you for your cooperation.

02

M: __________ what Danny did?

W: Are you talking about Danny Bailey? Yeah, he's the talk of the town right now.

M: I can't believe he swam to Alcatraz and back in that freezing water! He's incredibly brave.

W: Do you really see it as bravery? __________ __________. It's the most foolish thing I've ever heard of.

M: Really? Perhaps it wasn't the smartest thing to do, but I still think it was brave.

W: There's a difference between being brave and reckless. To me, it was reckless.

M: Why do you __________?

W: From what I know, he didn't train for the swim. I know he's a good swimmer, but __________ __________.

M: You have a point. He said he just jumped into the ocean and started swimming.

W: Thank goodness nothing went wrong, but that sort of reckless behavior sets a bad example for kids.

M: Oh, I didn't think about that.

03

M: Hi, Allison.

W: Good afternoon, Dr. Welsh. We have a 16-year-old female, Isabella Paolo.

M: Can I see the chart?

W: Here you are. She came in with a pain in her stomach. She __________.

M: When did she come in?

W: Just five minutes ago from the emergency room. Her mother came with her.

M: __________?

W: Yes, she complains of severe stomachache.

M: Let's see. She has a temperature of 37.1°C.

W: __________.

M: Okay. Please place her on a bed and __________ __________ to a 30°angle. I'm going to see her shortly.

W: I see.

04

M: Mom! I had a great day at school.

W: That's great! Tell me about your day.

M: In art class, I drew a pirate after reading *Treasure Island*. I drew him with a pirate hat and __________.

W: How about a parrot? You love to draw parrots with pirates.

M: Of course I drew a parrot. The parrot is sitting __________.

W: Does he have a weapon?

M: Yes. He is sitting in front of a tree and __________ __________.

W: It sounds great. I'm sure you drew some treasures, too.

M: Sure. I drew a big palm tree behind the pirate and a big box of treasure next to the tree.

W: That's fantastic!

M: My teacher said he especially likes __________ __________.

정답 및 해설 p.142 

05

W: Hi, Bill. You missed Jerry's housewarming party yesterday. Were you sick?

M: No, but my wife came down with a bad case of the flu, so I had to take her to the hospital.

W: How awful! ____________________. How serious is it?

M: I don't know. The doctor said she should stay in the hospital for a couple of days until her fever is gone. He thinks she might have some sort of infection.

W: I hope that's a worst-case scenario. I'm sure ____________________.

M: I hope so. I have to go on a business trip tomorrow, and I don't know what to do.

W: You mean a business trip to Seattle? If that's the case, somebody else can go there.

M: Oh, you're right. Then if you're okay, ____________________?

W: Sure. I'll take your place. After all, we work in the same department, so it shouldn't be a problem.

M: Wow, ____________________. You're an angel.

06

M: Is there anything I can help you with?

W: Yes, please. I ordered three books, and ____________________.

M: Can I have your name, please?

W: Sure. My name is Jessica Reynolds.

M: Oh, here it is. Yes, we just received them today. Here you go. Please ____________________.

W: Yes, they are, thank you. How much are they?

M: One book costs $35, another is $45, and the other is $30.

W: So my total is $110. ____________________?

M: No, shipping is another $10.

W: I see. Here's my credit card.

M: Hold on a minute. These books are currently ____________________.

W: Oh, it's my lucky day. Is the discount just for the books?

M: Yes, that's right.

07

W: Aiden, what did I say about cleaning your room? I told you to clean your room three times today!

M: I'm going to clean it, but I can't do it right now.

W: ____________________?

M: I have to do something important.

W: So what's so important? I don't think computer games or movies are important.

M: Remember ____________________?

W: Yeah, I thought you finished it last week.

M: Well, the teacher ____________________, so I have to work on it tonight.

W: So when are you planning to clean your room?

M: I promise I'll do it after I'm done with my project.

W: ____________________ this time.

08

W: Thank you for your honest answer, Mr. Moore. ________________________.

M: I appreciate the opportunity for this interview.

W: Do you have any questions regarding our company or this position?

M: If I get the job, ________________________ ________________?

W: You'll be spending most of your time in the office. And you'll be working from nine to six.

M: I see. I heard that you get one week of vacation a year. Is it paid vacation?

W: Yes, you get ________________________ ________________. Any questions about the salary?

M: No, I'm happy with the salary. I'd like to know more about the insurance you offer to your employees.

W: The company pays for 80% of your health insurance for you and your family. You'll likely pay about $200 for insurance a month.

M: ________________________. Thank you.

09

W: It's time to hold the annual Greenville Costume Contest. ________________________ in our town square next Sunday, October 12th. Anyone can participate by dressing up in a costume of his or her choice. There will be plenty of prizes for everyone. ________________________ ________________: most creative costume, most elaborate costume, and scariest costume. If you're not sure ________________________, visit our website at www.greenvillecostume.com and sign up. You can browse through last year's winners' costumes. How about making this a family activity and having the whole family dress up in costumes? ________________________ ________________ right now, so sign up today!

10

M: Hello? Sarah?

W: Connor, where are you? I thought you were coming back from your business trip tomorrow. ________ ________________________ already?

M: No. I'm here at the Camelia outlet right now. I wanted to know ________________________ ________________. Do you want a long or short strap?

W: The bag I'm looking for isn't a shoulder bag but a tote bag with very short straps.

M: Okay. What size are you looking for?

W: I'd like something ________________________ ________________ and 10 inches in height.

M: Okay. There are two types of material, fabric and leather. Which do you want?

W: What about the price?

M: The leather bags are more expensive.

W: I'd prefer a leather bag, but I'll take whatever bag you choose ________________________.

M: Got it. I'll see you tomorrow.

W: Thanks, honey.

11

W: Jerry, ________________________ to Emily's birthday party this Friday.

M: Oh, I'm sorry. I meant to tell you, I don't think ________________.

W: What are you talking about? You said you would come.

12

M: I made a reservation last week. My name is John Mitchell.

W: ________________, sir. I'm sorry, we don't have your reservation.

M: Something must be wrong. ________________ ________________? Do you have a room tonight?

13

M: Come on in, Mrs. Johnson. ________________ ________________.

W: It's my pleasure. It's good to see you again.

M: Please have a seat. Would you like something to drink?

W: Some water would be nice. Frankly, ____________ ________________________________.

M: Don't worry, it's nothing serious. He gets along with most of his classmates.

W: That's a relief. So is something wrong?

M: Well, ________________________________ over the last few months.

W: Oh dear. Is there a particular subject that he's having problems with?

M: He's struggling in math. So I ________________ ________________________________ for him to get some tutoring at school.

W: Of course. That's a wonderful idea.

14

W: You didn't forget about our trip to the amusement park with the kids tomorrow, did you?

M: Of course I didn't. Do you think we should take some sandwiches with us?

W: Yes, so ________________________________ ______________. We'll just buy the drinks there.

M: Great idea.

W: I hope we'll get good weather tomorrow. ________ ________________________ tomorrow, are we?

M: I don't think so, but we should check since we'll be outside. Let's check the Internet right now.

W: If it's going to rain, ________________________ ______________.

M: Okay. Oh dear. It says that it'll rain all day tomorrow.

W: All day? The kids are going to be so disappointed if we don't take them.

M: Yeah. ________________________________.

15

M: A few days ago, Brian lost his tablet PC at school. His tablet PC was a birthday gift from his girlfriend. He ________________________________ ________________________________, but he couldn't find it. Then ________________________________, Luis. He told Luis that ________________________ ______________ his girlfriend that he'd lost her gift. This was because his girlfriend saved her money for a month from her part-time job to buy the gift. So ________________________________ her the truth about what had happened. Luis thinks that honesty is the best policy in this type of situation. What would Luis most likely say to Brian?

16-17

W: Today, we travel more than ____________________ ____________________. So extra consideration about the impact of your travels is especially important. One of the best things you can do is to use public transportation. Take a bus or a subway train when you are downtown if possible. Public transportation can ________________________ ________________, but it's greener than renting a car or catching a taxi. Also, conserve water and ________________________________ whenever you can while staying at a hotel. By doing so, you're protecting the environment of ______________ ________________________. Remember not to disrupt the local ecology by killing wildlife or uprooting plants in the mountains. Do not litter. Always be mindful of throwing trash in the river or forest of a park. It's a place for everyone, not just you. You must try to preserve the country's ecology for the sake of future travelers and, more importantly, the people who live there. __________ ________________! Forget collecting a bundle of paper brochures from your travel agent. Instead, save paper ________________________ ____________________, well-traveled friends, and bloggers to plan and book your vacation.

실전모의고사 37 PRACTICE TEST

01 다음을 듣고, 여자가 하는 말의 목적으로 가장 적절한 것을 고르시오.

① 스웨터 세탁 방법을 알려주려고
② 스웨터 전용 세제를 홍보하려고
③ 스웨터 유행 경향을 소개하려고
④ 스웨터 보관 방법을 문의하려고
⑤ 스웨터 전문 세탁소를 광고하려고

02 대화를 듣고, 남자의 의견으로 가장 적절한 것을 고르시오.

① 칭찬을 통한 반려동물 훈련이 중요하다.
② 일관성 없는 개 훈련 방법은 문제가 있다.
③ 놀이를 통해 개의 행동을 교정하는 것이 좋다.
④ 반려동물 훈련은 전문 훈련소에 맡겨야 한다.
⑤ 개의 품종에 따라 훈련 방법이 서로 다르다.

03 대화를 듣고, 두 사람의 관계를 가장 잘 나타낸 것을 고르시오.

① 모델 – 패션 디자이너
② 손님 – 웨딩숍 직원
③ 약혼녀 – 약혼자
④ 손님 – 미용사
⑤ 잡지 편집인 – 사진작가

04 대화를 듣고, 그림에서 대화의 내용과 일치하지 않는 것을 고르시오.

05 대화를 듣고, 남자가 할 일로 가장 적절한 것을 고르시오.

① 양파 썰기
② 손 씻고 오기
③ 반찬거리 만들기
④ 반찬 재료 사 오기
⑤ 아빠에게 전화하기

06 대화를 듣고, 여자가 지불할 금액을 고르시오. [3점]

① $700
② $750
③ $1,000
④ $1,050
⑤ $1,200

07 대화를 듣고, 여자가 과제 제출일 연장을 부탁한 이유를 고르시오.

① 아르바이트를 하느라 바빠서
② 가족을 돌봐야 하는 일이 생겨서
③ 컴퓨터 고장으로 파일을 잃어버려서
④ 생각을 정리하는 게 힘들어서
⑤ 참고 도서를 구하지 못해서

08 대화를 듣고, 벽시계에 관해 언급되지 않은 것을 고르시오.

① 모양
② 테두리의 색
③ 소리
④ 크기
⑤ 숫자 표기 방식

09 Owl Creek 고등학교 사진 전시회에 관한 다음 내용을 듣고, 일치하지 않는 것을 고르시오.

① 지난 5년 동안 개최되어 왔다.
② Owl Creek 고등학교 학생은 누구나 참가할 수 있다.
③ 미술부 선생님들이 전시 작품을 선발한다.
④ 사진의 주제는 자유롭게 선택할 수 있다.
⑤ 총 40점의 작품을 학교 미술관에 전시한다.

10 다음 표를 보면서 대화를 듣고, 두 사람이 가기로 한 야구 경기를 고르시오.

University of Ohio – College Baseball Schedule			
DATE	LOCATION (home/away)	OPPONENT	SEATS AVAILABLE
① April, 4 Saturday	away	Albany	infield outfield
② April, 5 Sunday	home	Albany	outfield only
③ April, 11 Saturday	home	Andrews	infield outfield
④ April, 17 Friday	away	Andrews	infield outfield
⑤ April, 18 Saturday	home	Montgomery	infield outfield

11 대화를 듣고, 여자의 마지막 말에 대한 남자의 응답으로 가장 적절한 것을 고르시오.

① My pleasure. I'm glad that you like it.
② I know you want to show off your watch.
③ He is 48, but he looks young for his age.
④ I'm jealous. I wish I had an uncle like yours.
⑤ Take a guess. I have two uncles and four aunts.

12 대화를 듣고, 남자의 마지막 말에 대한 여자의 응답으로 가장 적절한 것을 고르시오.

① Thanks for keeping in touch.
② This is exactly what I wanted.
③ I'm sure she will love your gift.
④ I understand what you're saying.
⑤ Don't expect too much from her.

13 대화를 듣고, 여자의 마지막 말에 대한 남자의 응답으로 가장 적절한 것을 고르시오. [3점]

▶ Man :

① Thanks for coming. Help yourself.
② No, it's not finished yet. Be patient.
③ Hurry up. We'll be late for the party.
④ No, it's delicious. You're really a great cook!
⑤ Stir the milk so it won't burn. Then add a little salt.

14 대화를 듣고, 남자의 마지막 말에 대한 여자의 응답으로 가장 적절한 것을 고르시오.

▶ Woman :

① That's all right. I understand what you mean.
② She is a world-famous cello player. I envy her.
③ I see who she is. I'll go give it to her right now.
④ I don't mind at all. Go ahead and tell her about it.
⑤ We're all impressed by her amazing performance.

15 다음 상황 설명을 듣고, Emily가 점원에게 할 말로 가장 적절한 것을 고르시오. [3점]

▶ Emily :

① This isn't my purse. I didn't lose my purse.
② You're welcome, ma'am. I'm just doing my job.
③ I'm going to go shop for my dress in a different store.
④ Yes, I think this white dress matches my hair perfectly.
⑤ Thanks for finding my purse! I thought it was gone forever!

[16~17] 다음을 듣고, 물음에 답하시오.

16 남자가 하는 말의 주제로 가장 적절한 것은?

① various types of literature for children
② benefits of reading a work of great literature
③ various ways of enjoying a work of literature
④ a new way of reading literature with computers
⑤ the power of reading to enhance communication

17 언급된 문학 장르가 <u>아닌</u> 것은?

① 시　② 소설　③ 동화
④ 희곡　⑤ 전기

37 DICTATION

녹음된 내용을 들으면서 빈칸을 알맞게 채워 보세요.

01

W: Sweaters are a basic piece of clothing for our cold winters. In order to ______________________ ______________________, you need to take extra care when cleaning them. The number one rule is not to over-clean sweaters. The less you clean them, the longer they will last. Most sweaters can be gently hand washed. Just ____________ ______________________ in a mild detergent and cool water. And rinse in cool water to remove all remaining soap. ______________ ______________________ - roll in a towel and gently push on the towel to remove water. Then lay it flat to dry over something like a clothes rack. Sweaters can last for years ______ ______________________.

02

W: My puppy is super cute but very naughty sometimes.

M: What do you mean?

W: He bites everything he sees and still pees in areas he's not supposed to.

M: It looks like ______________________ ______________________. It's important that you don't punish him every time he does something bad.

W: Unfortunately, I yell at him a lot these days.

M: I can understand, and that's required at times, but you ______________________ when he does something good.

W: Well, he does know how to sit when I command him to do so.

M: Great. Then ______________________ and praise him when he does.

W: That's a great idea. ______________________ ______________________.

M: If he goes to the bathroom in the proper place, praise him several times. Eventually, he will be toilet-trained.

W: I see. Thanks for the advice.

03

W: Excuse me. My name is Victoria Clark. I called you this morning.

M: Oh, please have a seat, Ms. Clark. Would you like some coffee or tea?

W: Just some water, please. I don't have much time, so I'd appreciate it ______________________ right away.

M: Why don't you choose a design that you like in one of these catalogs?

W: Okay. Let me see. What is the latest style trend?

M: These are ______________________. Romantic off-the-shoulder dresses.

W: Hmm, I really like the design of this silk A-line dress.

M: I see that you like a simple design. These are very similar to the dress you've chosen in the catalog. ______________________?

W: Okay. Oh, how long does it take to get the dress prepared? You know my wedding date is June 12th.

M: Don't worry. It should take about two weeks to finish the job.

04

M: I feel a little lonely ______________________ during the late fall weather.

W: I know.

M: Look at the big tree near the park's entrance. The leaves ______________________.

W: Oh, look! There's a nest on the tree branch.

M: Yes, it looks like there's a chick in the nest. The mother bird is feeding the chick.

W: Aww, how sweet! ______________________ ____________ near the tree?

M: Sure. Oh, but there's a trash bin next to the bench.

W: And someone left a scarf on the bench.

M: You're right. Let's leave it there. The owner will probably come back for it.

W: Yeah, ______________________. Should we just leave?

정답 및 해설 p.146

M: Sounds good. Hey, Jessica, what's that thing on top of the arched gate?

W: Oh, it looks like a crown to me. That's fun.

05

W: Jay, could you help me in the kitchen for a few minutes?

M: Sure, Mom. Is this all for the picnic tomorrow afternoon?

W: Yes, I'm almost done. I just need to ____________ ____________.

M: Oh, Dad said he'll pick some up on the way home from work tonight. Didn't he tell you?

W: Yes, he mentioned that. But I already have the ingredients, so ____________ ____________.

M: Yours taste better anyway. But we should probably tell Dad you'll make them.

W: ____________ right after I wash my hands.

M: You don't have to. I'll do it now.

W: Thanks for your help. Now I can finish cutting these onions.

M: Okay. Be careful, ____________.

W: Don't worry. I'll be fine.

06

W: I'm interested in purchasing an annual pass to Wonderland.

M: You have ____________. The basic annual pass costs $250, but this pass will not be valid during the summer.

W: Oh, but I want to go to the park during the summer break. ____________?

M: If that's the case, you'll have to consider the Deluxe and Premium passes. The Deluxe pass is $350, and the Premium is $400.

W: I see. ____________ ____________?

M: Both can be used in the summer, but you can use the Deluxe pass only on weekdays.

W: How about the Premium?

M: It is also valid on the weekends during the summer.

W: Then I'll go with ____________ ____________. I'd like three passes. Here's my credit card.

07

W: Hello, Dr. Martin. I'm Elizabeth Lewis. Well, I was wondering ____________ ____________ next Monday.

M: I already had three students who asked for an extension. Do you have a part-time job?

W: Yes, but that's ____________ ____________.

M: Is it due to a family affair? Or are you having difficulty organizing your ideas?

W: No, it's not that. I'm actually almost done with my paper, but ____________ the other day and I lost all my data.

M: Don't you have a back-up file?

W: No, the computer service center is trying to recover the lost data, but it's going to take a while.

M: Well, I'm sorry about that. Since it's your first time, ____________.

W: Thank you so much for understanding, Dr. Martin.

08

M: I want to buy a wall clock.

W: We have ______________________________.
What kind of shape do you want, round or square?

M: I like round clocks.

W: This round clock with a black frame is very popular.

M: I prefer a brown frame to a black frame. And don't you have ______________________________ ____________________?

W: Oh, you want a clock that doesn't make a "ticking" sound! How about this one with Roman numerals?

M: Well, no. Because I have a little kid, I want a clock ______________________________.

W: Then how about this one? ____________________ ____________________.

M: I think I'll take it. It's unique, and it has black Arabic numerals that are easy to read.

W: All right. Come this way.

09

M: Listen up, everyone! We've had great success ______________________________ for the past five years, and now it's time to hold another one at Owl Creek High School. This exhibition will be an exciting opportunity for many of you. ______________________________ ______________, anyone at Owl Creek High can submit their work to the exhibition. __________ ______________________________ will be selected by teachers from the fine arts department. The theme of this year's exhibition will be "Four Seasons." A total of 40 of the best photos will be presented in the school gallery. ______________ ____________________ is April 10th. If you have a passion for photography, this is your chance to show off your talent!

10

W: ______________________________ in this magazine. Our university's baseball team won the college baseball championship last year.

M: I know. Hey, why don't we go to one of their games? In fact, there are some games ______________ ______________________.

W: That sounds like fun. I'll go with you.

M: What time is good for you?

W: Anytime is okay if it's a Saturday or Sunday.

M: They have a game this Saturday in Georgia. Does that work for you?

W: ______________________. I don't feel like going all the way to Georgia just to see a baseball game. Are there any home games?

M: Of course. I'll pick a home game then. There's a game with Andrews College, but I'm not interested in that one.

W: Why is that?

M: Andrews College has the weakest team, so the game won't be very exciting.

W: Let's watch another game then. ______________ ____________________ for another game?

M: There are some infield seats available for one of the games, so I'll reserve two seats in that section.

11

W: Look at my watch!

M: Wow! It's really fancy! ____________________ ____________________. How did you get it?

W: My uncle gave it to me ____________________ __________.

12

M: I want to get a gift for my mother's birthday. ______ ______________________________?

W: What do you think of this night cream? It's a great anti-wrinkle cream.

M: Okay. I'll take it. I hope ____________________.

13

W: Dan, ____________________?

M: Sure. I don't know what this is, but it smells delicious!

W: It's clam chowder. ____________________ ____________________.

M: When did you have time to prepare all this food?

W: I started yesterday, so there isn't much to do today. It'll be done in a few minutes.

M: It's so impressive. I didn't know ____________________ ____________________.

W: I downloaded some great recipes from the Internet. All I did was follow the recipe.

M: Well, I can't wait to taste all this great food.

W: Have a taste of the soup.

M: Really? Let me get a spoon.

W: So what do you think? ____________________ ____________________?

14

W: Excuse me. I'm afraid ____________________ ____________________ right now.

M: Oh, I'm not?

W: No, they're ____________________ right now.

M: I came here to give this music sheet to my sister. She said she needs to hand it in today.

W: I'll take care of it. Can you tell me who she is?

M: Nicole Williams.

W: Nicole? That name ____________________.

M: She has long black hair.

W: There are a few women with long black hair. Is her hair in a ponytail by any chance?

M: No, she's the person ____________________ ____________________. Oh, there she is. She is the one who is standing up with the cello.

15

W: Emily goes shopping for her prom dress about a month before the dance. ____________________ ____________________ in the store, but she can't find one that satisfies her. She leaves all of the dresses that she tries in a pile in the fitting room. Then she goes to other stores until she finally finds a dress that ____________________. It matches her blonde hair perfectly. When she tries to pay for it, ____________________ ____________________. She thinks she probably dropped it in the previous store, so she goes there immediately. When she arrives at that store, ____________________ ____________________ and gives her the purse. The salesclerk tells her that he found her purse in the fitting room. In this situation, what would Emily most likely say to the salesclerk?

16-17

M: ____________________ in recent times, the habit of reading has been neglected. Many people find little or no time for reading. However, those who have read good literature are aware of ____________________ ____________________ associated with it. Reading great literature broadens the thinking of a person, improves vocabulary, and cultivates sensitivity towards people of different cultures. Reading poetry ____________________. It helps to keep the muscles of the brain in good shape. Reading fiction gives immense satisfaction to a person. Nothing can be more satisfying than to sit with your child and ____________________ ____________________. Also, reading a great novel expands the imagination of a person. You can develop your ability to understand and appreciate the various aspects of life. ____________________ ____________________ issues from different angles, question assumptions, and derive conclusions. Reading a biography or autobiography improves a person's knowledge of various areas of life. This knowledge base helps a person ____________________ ____________________ in different situations. Exercise your mind through great literature.

실전모의고사

38 PRACTICE TEST

03 다음을 듣고, 남자가 하는 말의 목적으로 가장 적절한 것을 고르시오.

① 사진전 우승자를 발표하려고
② 자선 경매 참여를 부탁하려고
③ 환경 단체에 가입하도록 독려하려고
④ 사진전을 관람하는 절차를 알리려고
⑤ 학회 이후 일정에 대해서 설명하려고

02 대화를 듣고, 남자의 의견으로 가장 적절한 것을 고르시오.

① 교육적인 TV 프로그램은 찾기 어렵다.
② 레슬링 경기 시청은 아이에게 무해하다.
③ 스포츠 경기와 폭력성은 상관관계가 있다.
④ TV 광고는 아이들의 정서 발달에 해롭다.
⑤ 아이의 잘못된 행동에는 올바른 훈계가 필요하다.

03 대화를 듣고, 두 사람의 관계를 가장 잘 나타낸 것을 고르시오.

① 도서관 사서 - 자원봉사자
② 출판사 직원 - 작가
③ 신발가게 점원 - 손님
④ 교사 - 학생
⑤ 서점 직원 - 고객

04 대화를 듣고, 그림에서 대화의 내용과 일치하지 않는 것을 고르시오.

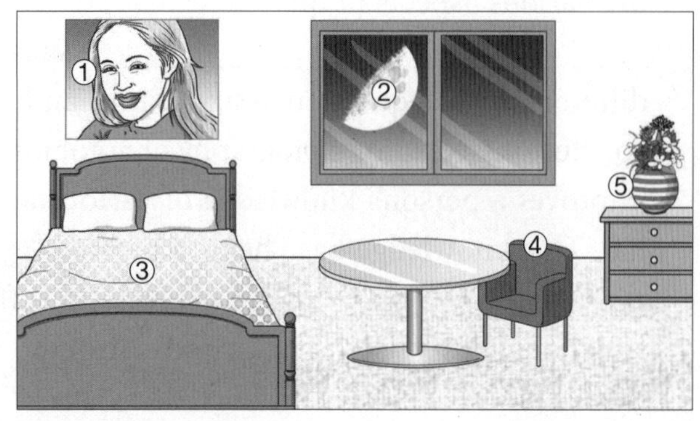

05 대화를 듣고, 여자가 남자를 위해 할 일로 가장 적절한 것을 고르시오.

① 약 사다주기
② 응급실에 데려다주기
③ 휴대전화 가져다주기
④ 아내에게 전화해주기
⑤ 서류 가방 보관해주기

06 대화를 듣고, 여자가 지불할 금액을 고르시오. [3점]

① $80　　② $81　　③ $90
④ $100　　⑤ $110

07 대화를 듣고, 여자가 어제 출근하지 않은 이유를 고르시오.

① 건강 검진을 받아야 해서
② 공항에 친구를 마중 나가야 해서
③ 남동생의 졸업식에 참석해야 해서
④ 어머니를 병원에 모시고 가야 해서
⑤ 대학 교수님을 만나 뵈러 가야 해서

08 대화를 듣고, 국경 없는 의사회(Doctors Without Borders)에 관해 언급되지 않은 것을 고르시오.

① 주요 활동　　② 수상 내역
③ 가입 자격　　④ 활동 국가 수
⑤ 본부 위치

09 Safe Identity에 관한 다음 내용을 듣고, 일치하지 않는 것을 고르시오.

① 한 달에 20달러로 이용할 수 있다.
② 개인 정보가 불법으로 사용되는지 감시한다.
③ 고객명으로 새 계좌가 개설되면 즉시 알려준다.
④ 고객이 피해를 입었을 경우 모든 책임을 진다.
⑤ 1년 계약 시 백신 프로그램을 무료로 제공한다.

10 다음 표를 보면서 대화를 듣고, 두 사람이 선택할 기차 여행을 고르시오.

2025 April Train Tours					
	Train Tour	Time of Departure	Departure Station	Price	Lunch
①	Cave Tour	10:00 a.m.	Suwon	$50	○
②	Sea Fishing Tour	8:30 a.m.	Yongsan	$45	○
③	Rail Bike Tour	9:00 a.m.	Seoul	$65	×
④	Farm Village Tour	9:30 a.m.	Suwon	$40	○
⑤	Gallery Tour	10:30 a.m.	Seoul	$55	×

11 대화를 듣고, 남자의 마지막 말에 대한 여자의 응답으로 가장 적절한 것을 고르시오.

① He's about your size.
② I insist that you should swim later.
③ He is nice enough to do me a favor.
④ Blue and grey will look good on you.
⑤ It's very careless of you to forget them.

12 대화를 듣고, 여자의 마지막 말에 대한 남자의 응답으로 가장 적절한 것을 고르시오.

① Yes, that'll be $40.
② I recommend this model.
③ I'm a little short of money.
④ There's one on the second floor.
⑤ I'm sorry, but we only accept cash.

13 대화를 듣고, 남자의 마지막 말에 대한 여자의 응답으로 가장 적절한 것을 고르시오. [3점]

▶ Woman :

① You can pay the money later if you want.
② What time is your mother leaving for Korea?
③ That's more than enough. Let me get my coat.
④ I don't think I like the way you are talking to me.
⑤ I'll never be able to repay you enough. Thank you.

14 대화를 듣고, 여자의 마지막 말에 대한 남자의 응답으로 가장 적절한 것을 고르시오.

▶ Man :

① It sure is a small world.
② I'd love to meet her one day.
③ Do you happen to know Jenna?
④ Can I meet her in the near future?
⑤ I couldn't imagine meeting you again.

15 다음 상황 설명을 듣고, Gloria가 John에게 할 말로 가장 적절한 것을 고르시오. [3점]

▶ Gloria : Sorry for the misunderstanding.

① We'll give you a complimentary upgrade in your seats.
② We will book a seat for you on the next flight to Hawaii.
③ However, if your wife is sick, she cannot take this flight.
④ My manager has said your economy class tickets are valid.
⑤ But you should check in at least one hour before departure.

[16~17] 다음을 듣고, 물음에 답하시오.

16 여자가 하는 말의 주제로 가장 적절한 것은?

① the academic calendar of the new school year
② how to use the school website
③ changes to school rules
④ difficulties when using the school website
⑤ considerations when choosing classes to take

17 웹사이트에 게시되는 사항이 아닌 것은?

① 교칙
② 학교 축제
③ 견학
④ 수업 일정
⑤ 교사 홈페이지

38 DICTATION

녹음된 내용을 들으면서 빈칸을 알맞게 채워 보세요.

01

M: Our foundation's Rainforest Frogs Photography Competition has ended with over 700 entries. We have selected our winners, and they are now on display here at the Reef Hotel, ______________ ______________________ next Thursday from 5:30 p.m. to raise funds to save our frogs and rainforests. ______________________________ for the charity auction, so please visit the exhibition hall after today's conference. If you can't join us and you have no time to see the exhibition today, you can still take part in the auction by viewing the photographs and ______________________ _________________ on our website. Thank you for your continued support of the Rainforest Foundation.

02

M: The wrestling finals are about to start! Where is the remote control?

W: I don't know, but I wish you wouldn't watch them.

M: Why not? ______________________________ ________________ tonight?

W: No, it's not that. I just don't think it's a very good idea.

M: It's just some harmless fun. _________________ ______________________, you know.

W: Actually, I'm worried Brandon will imitate the wrestlers. I don't want him to become violent. As you know, he is already jumping around the house and pretending to fight.

M: You think watching wrestling _______________ ________________?

W: I'm not sure, but it couldn't have helped.

M: Well, I wouldn't worry so much. I mean, I've watched a lot of violent horror movies and ______ ________________________.

W: Hmmm.... You think I don't have to worry so much?

03

W: Hello. How can I help you?

M: Hi. It's my first day, and ____________________ ________________.

W: Oh, great. You must be one of the new student volunteers.

M: Right. I filled out the volunteer application on the library's website, and I got __________________ ______________________________.

W: Okay, well, you'll be on your feet most of the time. So, you should wear comfortable shoes.

M: I guess I should walk around and ____________ ______________.

W: That's part of it. You also need to help visitors use the self-checkout machines for borrowing books.

M: No problem. By the way, how many other librarians work here?

W: I'm the only one. So, ______________________ ________________________ to help me out.

M: I'm happy to be here.

04

M: Before the play begins, ____________________ ________________?

W: Okay. It looks good! Especially the poster on the wall.

M: I agree. The woman's smiling face will _________ ______________________________________.

W: How about the window? Shouldn't it show a full moon?

M: No, it's supposed to be a half-moon. __________ ______________________________________, but it doesn't start out like that.

W: Now I remember. Well, the bed below the poster is perfect.

M: Yes, it's good to have it on the left side of the stage.

W: And there's a chair beside the table. I remember you prepared two chairs before.

M: Since it's a solo drama that is focusing on loneliness, a single chair will be better.

W: Good idea. Oh, and is that ________________ ________________ on top of the drawers?

M: Yes, it turned out well.

05

W: Are you alright, Robert? You've been sitting here for the past hour.

M: I think I'm ill.

W: ________________________________?

M: I feel like I'm going to pass out, and I'm extremely nauseous. I've been throwing up almost non-stop.

W: It ____________________________, too. I think you need to go to the hospital. Do you want me to give you a ride to the emergency room?

M: No, that's okay. I'll call my wife and __________ ________________________.

W: Okay, where's your cell phone? You stay here, and I'll go get it for you.

M: That would be great. It should be inside my briefcase.

W: And where's your briefcase?

M: Oh sorry, ____________________________.

W: Okay. Hang in there. I'll be right back.

06

M: Welcome to Pine Mountain Resort. How can I help you?

W: ____________________________ today. I need tickets and rental equipment.

M: Well, lift tickets are $30 for an afternoon and $50 for a full day.

W: I definitely want to board for the full day. _______ ____________________________?

M: The rental board is $20 per day, and the boots are $10 per day.

W: I borrowed some boots from my sister, so I only need the board.

M: Great. ____________________________.

W: But I think I also need a lesson, since it's my first time.

M: Lessons are $30 each, and if the total price is at least $100, you can get a 10% discount.

W: Okay, then ____________________________. Here's the money.

M: And here is your ticket and rental pass. Enjoy.

07

M: Hi, Kate. It's good to see you again. I guess you had a relaxing vacation? Did you just get back last night?

W: It was a great trip, but I actually returned on Sunday.

M: Oh? Then ____________________________ __________ yesterday?

W: That's because I wanted to attend my brother's graduation.

M: Did he finish medical school? That's great! _______ ____________________________?

W: He's going to work at a hospital near my mother's house.

M: That's Saint Mary's Hospital, right? __________ ____________________________ there.

W: Right. It's a great position. One of my brother's professors recommended him for the job.

M: I'm really glad to hear that ________________ ____________________________ for him.

W: I'm happy for him, too.

08

M: Sue, do you want to meet tonight?

W: I'm afraid I can't. My father just returned from Africa. We're having dinner together.

M: I see. ________________ for Doctors Without Borders?

W: Yes. There's been an Ebola outbreak in Sierra Leone. He went to help.

M: I really admire his commitment to an organization ________________ in extreme situations, like civil wars, famines, and natural disasters.

W: I do as well. Did you know it received the Nobel Peace Prize in 1999?

M: I'm not surprised. I know it's doing amazing work in almost 70 countries worldwide.

W: I'd love to ________________, but I don't have much interest in medicine.

M: I suppose you could try to get a job at the headquarters in Switzerland.

W: Oh, I had never considered that before.

09

W: About 9 million people ________________ each year. Identity theft is a serious issue that's difficult to resolve. This is where we come in. With $20 per month, Safe Identity will work with banks and credit card companies ________________. We will also actively monitor the Web for personal information ________________. Our company notifies you immediately when new bank or credit card accounts are opened in your name and when suspicious changes to your personal information are detected. If you become a victim ________________, we will take full responsibility to resolve the situation for you. For a limited time, our company is offering free antivirus software for one year when you sign up for our service. Call us today to receive this special offer.

10

W: Honey, look at this flyer of tours.

M: Wow. I'm sure we can find something for our daughter's spring break.

W: Right. Hannah will love it. Why don't we choose ________________?

M: Hmm, Hannah doesn't like to wake up that early, and ________________.

W: Oh, I forgot. Let's see. We shouldn't spend more than 60 dollars per person.

M: Then I guess one of them is not an option.

W: How about the other one that departs from Seoul Station? It would be an educational experience.

M: That's true, but ________________.

W: You have a point. I don't want to worry about finding a restaurant.

M: Then it looks like two choices are left. Which do you prefer?

W: I think ________________ because we only have one day for the tour.

M: I agree. I'm looking forward to it.

11

M: I can't believe ________________ my swim shorts.

W: Don't worry. My brother's got two pairs of shorts. You can borrow one of them.

M: Do you think ________________?

12

W: I'll take this electric fan. And I'll ________________.

M: I'm really sorry, but ________________.

W: That's too bad. Is there a cash machine nearby?

13

M: Are you busy right now?

W: Not really. Do you need help with something?

M: I'm going to pick my mother up at the airport and I wanted to know ______________________________ ______________________.

W: Umm... I guess. Is there any particular reason you want me to come?

M: Actually, yes. It's my mother's first time in Korea, and I want her ______________________________ ______________________.

W: Oh, I see! You want me to be Korea's ambassador to your mother, right?

M: In a way, yes. But I also thought ______________ ______________________________. And since you speak Korean....

W: I should be getting paid as an interpreter! You're lucky we're such good friends.

M: ______________________________. Is that payment enough?

14

M: It's a long flight, so let me introduce myself. I'm Bruce.

W: Hi, I'm Tina.

M: Going to Chicago?

W: I'm transferring in Chicago. Going to New York.

M: So am I. ______________________________ the same connecting flight. AC 345?

W: Yes, I think that's the flight. I'm a high school teacher. What do you do?

M: I'm a dentist. I have a small clinic in Manhattan.

W: Really? One of my best friends is a dentist. ______ __________________________ in Manhattan, too.

M: I'm in the Lakeshore Building.

W: So is she. Her name is Jenna Johnson.

M: Wow. I often say "hi" to her in the elevator! Her clinic is on the floor above mine!

W: ______________________________!

15

M: John and Mary ______________________________. Now they are checking in at the airport for their Hawaiian honeymoon. John booked economy class tickets online, so he hands the ticketing agent, Gloria, the receipt he printed out at home. Gloria spends a minute checking her computer, looking increasingly unhappy as she does. Finally, she tells John ______________________________ and they must wait for a later flight. Mary turns white and looks sick. John is angry and ________ ______________________________. Gloria's manager comes to see what the problem is. When Gloria explains, the manager asks her to check in business class and first class for vacant seats and to give any vacancies to John and Mary. So Gloria checks her computer and ____________________ ______________________. In this situation, what would Gloria most likely say to John?

16-17

W: Good morning, students. This is Principal Catherine. I hope you are all ______________ ______________________________ at Eastpark High School. Now, a few changes have been made since last year. One of them is the addition of our new school website. ___________ __________________________ is easy. Simply find the "new student" tab located on the top left of the page and enter your name and student ID number. You will then be __________________ ________________. The site will be a place for you to find news and important information about our school. Regular notices will be posted about events like school festivals and field trips. Changes to class schedules will also be there. And many of your teachers will have a homepage there as well. Students are also invited to post on the website, and ______________________________ on the "student life" page. However, to post, you will need to speak with the site administrator, Mr. Kim, and receive a special ID. I hope that everyone will ______________________________.

실전모의고사

39 PRACTICE TEST

01 **다음을 듣고, 남자가 하는 말의 목적으로 가장 적절한 것을 고르시오.**

① 미아 방지를 위한 협조를 당부하려고
② 어린이 안전에 관한 강연을 소개하려고
③ 유치원 교통안전 교육 일정을 공지하려고
④ 어린이 이름표 달아주기 캠페인을 안내하려고
⑤ 자녀 건강관리에 관한 학부모회를 홍보하려고

02 **대화를 듣고, 여자의 의견으로 가장 적절한 것을 고르시오.**

① 지속적으로 부모님의 건강을 살펴야 한다.
② 자연 감상은 스트레스 해소에 도움이 된다.
③ 정원 가꾸기에는 심리적인 이점이 존재한다.
④ 부정적인 감정일수록 빨리 표출하는 것이 중요하다.
⑤ 건강을 위해 유기농 작물을 직접 재배하는 것이 좋다.

03 **대화를 듣고, 두 사람의 관계를 가장 잘 나타낸 것을 고르시오.**

① 토크쇼 사회자 – 초대 손님
② 스포츠 캐스터 – 스포츠 해설가
③ 관람객 – 프로게이머
④ 방송 기자 – 야구 감독
⑤ 심사위원 – 오디션 지원자

04 **대화를 듣고, 그림에서 대화의 내용과 일치하지 않는 것을 고르시오.**

05 **대화를 듣고, 여자가 남자에게 부탁한 일로 가장 적절한 것을 고르시오.**

① 함께 병원 가기
② 전단지 나눠주기
③ 동아리 지원자 인터뷰하기
④ 부스 설치하는 것 도와주기
⑤ 여자 대신 오리엔테이션 참석하기

06 **대화를 듣고, 여자가 지불할 금액을 고르시오. [3점]**

① $50 ② $70 ③ $95
④ $115 ⑤ $145

07 **대화를 듣고, 남자가 저녁 식사 메뉴를 바꾼 이유를 고르시오.**

① 여자가 채식주의자라서
② 조리 시간이 오래 걸려서
③ 닭고기를 구입하지 못해서
④ 할머니의 조리법을 잃어버려서
⑤ 여자가 닭고기에 알레르기가 있어서

08 **대화를 듣고, 남자의 아들에 관해 언급되지 않은 것을 고르시오.**

① 소속 고등학교 ② 포지션
③ 포지션 순위 ④ 등번호
⑤ 진학할 대학

09 **수학 경시대회에 관한 다음 내용을 듣고, 일치하지 않는 것을 고르시오.**

① 전국 대회에 참가할 학교 대표 선발 시험이다.
② 5월 17일 오후 4시에 실시한다.
③ 1시간 30분 동안 25문제를 풀어야 한다.
④ 성적순으로 상위 7명을 선발한다.
⑤ Baum 선생님에게 참가 신청을 할 수 있다.

10 다음 표를 보면서 대화를 듣고, 두 사람이 선택할 여행 상품을 고르시오.

Philipsburg Day Activities

Tour	Type of tour	Time span	What to do	Price
① A	sightseeing	full day	guided bus tour & shopping	$140
② B	activity-based	half day	snorkeling (water)	$132
③ C	activity-based	half day	biking (land)	$119
④ D	activity-based	full day	horseback riding (land)	$185
⑤ E	activity-based	half day	fishing (water)	$167

11 대화를 듣고, 여자의 마지막 말에 대한 남자의 응답으로 가장 적절한 것을 고르시오.

① All right. I'll get some aspirin for you.
② It's near the hospital. You can't miss it.
③ No, it's nothing serious. An aspirin will do.
④ Yes, Mom asked me to buy her a cookbook.
⑤ Drink plenty of orange juice and get some rest.

12 대화를 듣고, 남자의 마지막 말에 대한 여자의 응답으로 가장 적절한 것을 고르시오.

① No, that flower shop is too expensive.
② Right, she has a recital twice every year.
③ Okay, I'll wear my black dress for the concert.
④ Yes, buy this rose bouquet and get a vase free.
⑤ I already ordered and they'll be delivered by 4 today.

13 대화를 듣고, 여자의 마지막 말에 대한 남자의 응답으로 가장 적절한 것을 고르시오. [3점]

▶ Man : ____________________

① Got it. I'll be right back.
② The prices are high here.
③ You should have made a shopping list.
④ Take your time. We've got a lot of time.
⑤ You know I don't like shopping very much.

14 대화를 듣고, 남자의 마지막 말에 대한 여자의 응답으로 가장 적절한 것을 고르시오.

▶ Woman : ____________________

① I think you're good at playing the violin.
② Good idea. You have a genuine musical talent.
③ I have a different idea. You should reconsider.
④ Too much confidence in your vision doesn't help.
⑤ Okay! You've given me the courage to pursue my dream.

15 다음 상황 설명을 듣고, Alexis가 Christine에게 할 말로 가장 적절한 것을 고르시오. [3점]

▶ Alexis : ____________________

① Please give my regard to your friends.
② You're so kind. You really helped me out.
③ How sweet of you! But you shouldn't have.
④ It's difficult at first. I'm sure you'll be fine.
⑤ Thanks for inviting me. I'll come to the party.

[16~17] 다음을 듣고, 물음에 답하시오.

16 여자가 하는 말의 주제로 가장 적절한 것은?

① the benefits of eating edible weeds
② the advantages of growing vegetables
③ the growing popularity of wild edibles
④ the importance of buying organic food
⑤ how to get rid of weeds in your garden

17 언급된 식용 잡초가 아닌 것은?

① dandelion
② red clover
③ plantain
④ fireweed
⑤ wild asparagus

39 DICTATION

녹음된 내용을 들으면서 빈칸을 알맞게 채워 보세요.

01

M: There are many parents who often worry they'll lose their children or their children ____________ ____________. As a result, the Wingfield police have continued to campaign for the safety of children and ____________ ____________ over the past five years. Last month, the Wingfield police distributed name cards for all children in the neighborhood. We will also be ____________ ____________ for all parents who have children under the age of six on May 21st at 6:00 p.m. A child psychologist will be on hand to offer valuable advice for any parent. The lecture will be held at 245 Williams Street in the Wingfield Community Center and ____________ ____________. We invite all parents who are interested.

02

W: I think we should help Mom make a garden.

M: That sounds nice. What made you think of that?

W: Well, I know ____________ ____________ recently, and I think a garden will help her greatly.

M: Good idea. It will definitely keep her busy.

W: A garden can be ____________ ____________. I guess it would be a good place to relax and take her mind off things.

M: Watching plants grow can give her ____________ ____________.

W: She will feel like she has a purpose. And it'll also be nice to have fresh organic produce.

M: Right. We can help her make a small pond in the garden. Water has a soothing effect.

W: Great idea. I'll start ____________ I need to build a garden.

M: I'll check out the garden supply store and get some seeds.

03

W: The game is finally over. Let's speak to Jim Gonzalez. Hello, Mr. Gonzalez.

M: Yes, we won!

W: First, ____________ on this fantastic win. Can you say a few words to our audience?

M: It was a great game. We thank all the people who cheered for our team here.

W: The team is still ____________ ____________ right now. Who do you think played the best out there tonight?

M: Everyone did a great job. But I have to say that our pitcher, Eric Morris, did an amazing job.

W: Yes, he was great! I was also very impressed with the player who hit the final home run.

M: Oh, that was Dave Bennett. He is ____________ ____________.

W: Well, congratulations again. We wish you more wins in the future.

M: Thanks for the support.

04

M: Here is a picture of a beautifully decorated party. ____________ for your wedding?

W: I love it. It has a wonderful antique feel. Can we rent this space, too?

M: Of course. This is a chapel in an old castle and can be rented by anyone. The painting in the middle of the wall ____________.

W: The candleholders on both sides of the painting are beautiful.

M: We decorated the ceiling with ____________ ____________.

W: I see that. What a creative idea!

M: Do you see the beautiful lamp on the left wall?

W: Yes. It's another lovely detail of the decor.

M: What do you think about the checkered table cloths we placed over the round tables?

W: I like them.

M: I'll go ahead and contact the chapel and make a reservation for you.

W: I'd appreciate it. ______________________ ______________________.

05

W: Hi, Gabriel. ______________________?

M: Great. What are you doing here?

W: I have something to take care of. I'm glad we met. I need some help and you're the perfect person to help me.

M: What is it?

W: Since we're starting the new school year, it's time for school orientation. ______________________ ______________________ on campus during orientation so that we can recruit some freshmen to our club.

M: That's a fantastic idea. How can I help?

W: I'm putting the booth together, so could you move the poles for me?

M: Sure. I will. ______________________ ______________________? Where are James and Kyle?

W: James hurt his wrist, so he went to see a doctor, and Kyle has a part-time job this afternoon.

M: Oh, I see. And are these the flyers that we will ______________________?

W: Yes.

06

M: Hello, I'm Adrian Sanchez, your stylist. What can I do for you today?

W: Well, I ______________________. Would I look okay with this kind of body wave?

M: I think it would suit you. A body wave would give you more body.

W: How much is the perm?

M: A cut and a perm would cost you $95. How about ______________________?

W: Color? Sounds good. I'm bored with my dark hair.

M: Yes, I think light brown ______________________ ______________________.

W: How much does a coloring cost?

M: It'll cost you $50 to color your hair.

W: Well, coloring my hair and getting a perm ______ ______________________. Give me a cut and coloring for today.

M: Sure. Cuts are $20.

W: Great.

07

M: Jennifer, why don't you come over to my place for dinner tonight? Jonathan and Faith will come, too.

W: I'll definitely be there. I ______________________ ______________________ for a while. By the way, what are we eating?

M: I'm going to make chicken parmesan. It's an old family recipe ______________________ ______________________ the last time she visited!

W: Oh, that really does sound delicious, but unfortunately I can't eat it.

M: What? Why not? Do you have an allergy to something in the dish?

W: No, no allergies. It's just that ______________________ ______________________.

M: Oh, I had no idea! When did this happen?

W: From last year. I can live without meat, and it's better for the animals that way.

M: Well, then chicken parmesan is definitely not a good choice to put on the menu. I'll prepare some pasta.

W: ______________________. Are you sure it's no trouble?

M: No problem. I want you to feel comfortable at the dinner!

08

M: Good morning, Jasmine.

W: Hello, Daniel. ______________________________?

M: Yes, I'm on my way to see a basketball game in Boston.

W: Oh, in Boston? You must really enjoy watching basketball games.

M: I do, but my son will also be playing. He is a player on the Wheeler High School basketball team.

W: Oh, I had no idea your son was such an athlete! What's his name?

M: Sean, Sean Davis. He's ______________________ ____________________________________. That's the position Michael Jordan played. He's number one on the ESPN position rankings.

W: Wow, very impressive. You must be proud of him.

M: He was asked to join the NBA, but ____________ ____________________________. He got accepted to Duke University, and that's where he plans to go.

W: Fantastic! That's one of the top Ivy League schools!

M: Yes, I know. It's not an easy school to get into.

W: ______________________. I hope your son's team wins.

09

W: May I have your attention, please? The national math contest ______________________________ and we are looking for students who would like to compete. We are currently recruiting students to represent our school as a team. _______________ ________________________________ on May 17th, next Wednesday, at 4 p.m. in room 201 for all students who are interested. The test will be composed of three parts, and students will be required to answer 25 questions in 80 minutes. ___________________________________. The seven students with the highest scores will get a spot on the team. Our wonderful math teacher, Mr. Baum, ________________________________, so if you're interested in trying out, drop by his class or email him at baum@kennedyhigh.com. Good luck!

10

M: The cruise ship will have a stopover in Philipsburg for a day and ______________________________ at any time. Is there anything particular you would like to do while we're there?

W: Sounds like fun. What type of activities do they offer?

M: Do you feel like going on a sightseeing tour or an activity-based tour?

W: I don't feel like ______________________________, so let's do something active.

M: Sounds good to me. We can choose an activity for a full or half day. Which do you prefer?

W: Let's do something for half a day so we have some time to ______________________________________.

M: You're right. Then what should we choose? I can't swim, so we can't do any water sports.

W: Oh, you don't need to know how to swim to do this activity. All you need is a life jacket.

M: If that's what you want, it's okay with me. And ____, so we don't want to spend more than $150 per person.

W: Then this is exactly what we want.

11

W: Justin, I'm going to the bookstore. Don't you have anything to buy?

M: Yes. There is a pharmacy ____________________ ____________________________. Could you pick up some aspirin for me?

W: Do you still have a headache? ________________ ____________________________?

12

M: The concert begins at 7 tonight. We should probably ____. I'll be home at five.

W: ____.

M: How could I forget your friend's recital? Did you get some flowers for her?

13

M: Just a minute, Kaitlyn. I think I should wait outside in the parking lot.

W: No, don't do that. I only need to buy a few things.

M: Alright. Only a few things? ______________________.

W: Can you ______________________________?

M: If you're only buying a few things, do you really need a cart? Don't forget that we have to be at the cinema by six.

W: I know. We have plenty of time. ______________________________. First, we need some cans of tuna.

M: Here. What else do we need?

W: Hold on. Let's get the Sunrise tuna cans instead. I have a coupon for them.

M: What's next? ____________________. Then we can save a little time.

W: Okay. We need some paper towels and facial tissues.

14

M: Rachel, I didn't know that you could sing so well.

W: That's very kind of you to say so!

M: You can ______________________________.

W: Do you really think so?

M: Certainly. It was amazing. If I could sing like you, I would be a singer.

W: Do you think I sing well enough to record? Um, actually, I've thought about becoming a singer. It was always my dream.

M: Yeah, why don't you try it?

W: Hmm.... People say I'm a little ______________________________.

M: No, I don't think so. You're ______________________________.

W: Do you think so? I was thinking of trying to audition for a musical.

M: Try it! ____________________________. It is always worth trying.

15

M: Christine moved to Atlanta because of her new job. Christine didn't know anyone in Atlanta. Then ______________________________ Alexis, a co-worker at her company. Last Saturday, Alexis invited Christine to dinner at her house. She introduced her friends to Christine. Christine was very happy and really appreciated it. Today, Christine buys a gift for Alexis ______________________________. She knows that Alexis likes flowers, so she buys her a plant pot. She tells Alexis ______________________________ and hands her the gift. Alexis accepts the gift, but she feels that ______________________________ Christine out and is thus surprised to get such a gift. In this situation, what would Alexis most likely say to Christine?

16-17

W: Have you ever wondered if weeds in the wilderness could be eaten? ______________________________. For example, dandelion is a weed that's most known as a salad green. Red clover ______________________________ for cancer. And several Native American tribes included fireweed in their diet. It's best eaten young, when the leaves are tender. Also, wild asparagus is a great source of vitamin C. ______________________________, you will get an "early harvest" at a time when most gardens are just getting started. As with most other homegrown food, you'll save money. This particular food is especially economical — ______________________________ (you didn't even have to pay for the seeds). In addition, you'll ______________________________. There are approximately 50,000 edible plant species in the world, but the average American eats only 30. Therefore, if you only use three kinds of weeds as part of your diet, you've probably increased your food choices by 10%! Plus, it's easier to avoid using weed killers ______________________________, which helps the environment.

실전모의고사
40 PRACTICE TEST

01 다음을 듣고, 여자가 하는 말의 목적으로 가장 적절한 것을 고르시오.

① 평생 교육의 중요성을 강조하려고
② 온라인 교육의 확대를 촉구하려고
③ 온라인 교육의 한계를 지적하려고
④ 직장인을 위한 온라인 대학을 홍보하려고
⑤ 대학생을 위한 취업 준비 특강을 소개하려고

02 대화를 듣고, 남자의 의견으로 가장 적절한 것을 고르시오.

① 명절에는 가급적 모든 가족이 함께 모여야 한다.
② 관계에 따라 적정한 선물을 주는 것이 중요하다.
③ 연말에는 사람이 많은 쇼핑몰을 피하는 것이 좋다.
④ 상업화된 크리스마스 선물 주고받기는 문제가 있다.
⑤ 선물을 고를 때에는 받는 사람의 취향을 고려해야 한다.

03 대화를 듣고, 두 사람의 관계를 가장 잘 나타낸 것을 고르시오.

① 조카 – 삼촌
② 어머니 – 아들
③ 남편 – 아내
④ 장모 – 사위
⑤ 형수 – 시동생

04 대화를 듣고, 그림에서 대화의 내용과 일치하지 않는 것을 고르시오.

05 대화를 듣고, 여자가 남자에게 부탁한 일로 가장 적절한 것을 고르시오.

① 바이러스 예방 프로그램 설치하기
② 다른 USB 케이블 구매하기
③ 삭제된 사진 앨범 복구하기
④ 카메라의 특징 설명해주기
⑤ 사진을 컴퓨터로 옮기기

06 대화를 듣고, 여자가 지불할 금액을 고르시오. [3점]

① $125 ② $140 ③ $180 ④ $200 ⑤ $235

07 대화를 듣고, 남자가 주문을 취소할 수 없는 이유를 고르시오.

① 제조업체가 폐업해서
② 제품 불량이 아니라서
③ 상품이 배송 중이라서
④ 제품을 이미 사용해서
⑤ 교환하려는 모델이 품절이라서

08 대화를 듣고, 자동차 보험에 관해 언급되지 않은 것을 고르시오.

① 차종
② 자동차 엔진 배기량
③ 보험 보장 범위
④ 차주의 운전 경력
⑤ 차주의 사고 이력

09 Thompson 중고 서점에 관한 다음 내용을 듣고, 일치하지 않는 것을 고르시오.

① 손상이 심한 책은 가격이 할인된다.
② 10권 이상 사면 20% 할인받는다.
③ 서점 회원은 모든 책을 10% 할인받는다.
④ 학생증을 제시하는 대학생은 모든 책을 5% 할인받는다.
⑤ 일요일은 오전 시간에만 문을 연다.

정답 및 해설 p.158

10 다음 표를 보면서 대화를 듣고, 여자가 선택할 일을 고르시오.

Work	Type	Pay per hour	Working Hours
① restroom maintenance	cleaning	$13	Saturday & Sunday 8 a.m. - 1 p.m.
② office assistant	office work	$8	Monday - Friday 11 a.m. - 3 p.m.
③ campus maintenance	cleaning	$10	Monday - Friday 9 a.m. - 11 a.m.
④ library assistant	office work	$6	Monday - Friday 10 a.m. - 4 p.m.
⑤ office maintenance	cleaning	$11	Monday & Thursday 8 a.m. - 1 p.m.

11 대화를 듣고, 여자의 마지막 말에 대한 남자의 응답으로 가장 적절한 것을 고르시오.

① We still have five more hours to go.
② Then try moving your legs up and down.
③ I'll ask the flight attendant for some water.
④ Thank you. I'm so glad you're here with me.
⑤ The sign is on because we're flying through a storm.

12 대화를 듣고, 남자의 마지막 말에 대한 여자의 응답으로 가장 적절한 것을 고르시오.

① Not expensive. It is only $25.75.
② Don't worry. It's due on April 24th.
③ Yes. Thanks for lending me the book.
④ Sure. I'll let you know when I'm done.
⑤ I agree. The story touched us all deeply.

13 대화를 듣고, 여자의 마지막 말에 대한 남자의 응답으로 가장 적절한 것을 고르시오. [3점]

▶ Man : ______________________

① Let's give it our best shot.
② I hope tomorrow goes by quickly.
③ I'll keep my fingers crossed for you.
④ Don't be nervous about your new start!
⑤ Sounds exciting. I'm looking forward to it.

14 대화를 듣고, 남자의 마지막 말에 대한 여자의 응답으로 가장 적절한 것을 고르시오. [3점]

▶ Woman : ______________________

① I'm really sorry. I'm so embarrassed.
② There is no need for you to apologize.
③ Don't be stubborn. Admit you're wrong.
④ That's okay. We know it isn't your fault.
⑤ I understand. These things often happen.

15 다음 상황 설명을 듣고, Jeremy가 남자에게 할 말로 가장 적절한 것을 고르시오.

▶ Jeremy : ______________________

① I'm sorry to say, but you're mistaken.
② Calm down. I don't want to trouble you.
③ Excuse me! I think you've got my phone.
④ Sorry for the delay. I'll be right with you.
⑤ I'm very sorry. I thought it was my phone.

[16~17] 다음을 듣고, 물음에 답하시오.

16 남자가 하는 말의 주제로 가장 적절한 것은?

① benefits of taking a short nap
② harmful effects of medicine abuse
③ positive effects of a natural remedy
④ how to reduce drug users' risk of overdose
⑤ the influence of medicine on body conditions

17 언급된 약이 아닌 것은?

① 감기약 ② 진통제 ③ 수면제
④ 소화제 ⑤ 아스피린

40 DICTATION

녹음된 내용을 들으면서 빈칸을 알맞게 채워 보세요.

01

W: ______________________________?
Looking for something different? There are many people who have a passion but cannot find sufficient education for their new career. For them, getting this education is a must. ______________ ______________ by getting an online degree from Oak Online University. With flexible scheduling, Oak Online ______________ ______________________ who are currently working. Plus, its low student-to-teacher ratio guarantees you will receive __________ ____________________. We offer online courses in a variety of degree programs. Explore how you can earn a college degree online. Visit www.oak.edu for more information.

02

W: ________________________, Matthew?
M: Oh, my family didn't buy presents for each other this year.
W: What? Why not?
M: I think that during Christmas time these days, ________________________ shopping and material gifts.
W: That's true. But giving a gift is a way to show love for family and friends.
M: Right. But today it has become too commercialized. We're pressured to buy something. __________ ____________________.
W: I understand what you mean. But kids love gifts. People just want their kids to be happy.
M: Well, Christmas is not about gifts at all. It is about families coming together and having fun.
W: You're right. ________________________ ______________.
M: I think Christmas has become a celebration of American consumerism.

03

W: Hello?
M: Hello, this is Michael.
W: Oh, hi, Michael. ______________________ ______________. By the way, your parents are here at my house.
M: Yes, I know. ____________________.
W: We're planning to stay at the Green Valley Resort. Can you come? Your brother, Joshua, wants you to spend the weekend with us.
M: I'm not sure yet.
W: I hope you can join us. It's been a long time since your parents came down from Denver to see us. We'd love to see you, too.
M: ________________________. Oh, by the way, how's Jacob?
W: You mean your nephew, Jacob? There are so many Jacobs in our family.
M: You're right. Yes, your son and my nephew, Jacob Junior. I bought him a graduation gift.
W: Oh, ______________________. Hold on. Your mother wants to speak to you.
M: Okay, thanks.

04

W: Can you take a look at our final draft of the poster for the Stern Groove Festival? ______________ ____________________.
M: I see that you placed the title, "Stern Groove Festival," in the middle. I like it.
W: ________________________________.
M: Oh, you drew musical instruments in the tree!
W: Yes, since it's a music festival, I drew musical instruments, like a trumpet, guitar, harp, and violin, as branches for the tree.
M: ________________________!
W: I put the date of the festival under "Admission Free Concert" to the right of the tree.
M: I see there's a couple with a kid enjoying a picnic beside the tree.

W: Yes, I wanted people to know that they can enjoy a family picnic at the festival.

M: Wonderful. ______________________________ ______________________, I'm glad you drew a bird next to the mat. Let's go ahead and print some posters.

W: I'll do it right away.

05

W: David, you're a computer expert, aren't you?

M: I wouldn't call myself an expert, but __________ ____.
Why? Did you get a virus in your computer?

W: No, it's not that. I've already installed anti-virus software on my computer.

M: Good for you.

W: You know that I bought a digital camera last week, right?

M: Yes, I remember. It's really nice.

W: Well, I've taken a ton of photos, and ________ ____, but I don't know how.

M: Not a problem. It's pretty easy once you know how to do it. Just plug one end of the USB cable into your camera and the other into your computer.

W: I'm sorry, but I have no idea _______________ ______________________. Could you do it for me?

M: Of course. I'd be happy to.

06

M: Do you need any help?

W: Yes. I was looking for the Adventurer T2 tent.

M: I'm afraid all the T2 tents ____________________.
All we have at this moment are the T3 models. They're virtually the same.

W: How much is the T3 model?

M: It used to be $140, but now it's on sale for $80.

W: Great! I'll take it then.

M: ____.
You can get $5 off for every $50 you spend.

W: Hmm.... In that case, ________________________ ____________ hiking shoes. How much are these?

M: Those are $60.

W: Okay. I'd like to buy two pairs of the shoes, one for my husband and ___________________________.

M: I think you've made a great choice.

W: Thanks, here's my credit card.

07

W: You've reached EC Mall. How can I help you?

M: I have a question ____________________________ ____________________.

W: Can I have your name and order number?

M: My name is Sebastian Cox, and the order number is 150812.

W: One moment, please. I see that you bought a toaster a week ago.

M: Yes. I just realized that _____________________ _________________________, so I'd like to cancel my order and exchange it for another model.

W: Sorry, sir, but you can't cancel it now, because it was shipped two days ago.

M: ______________________________________?

W: Within 7 days after you've received the item, please return the item and purchase the model you want on our website again.

M: Oh, okay. That's complicated.

W: Sorry, but _________________________________ ______________.

M: Thanks anyway.

08

M: Hello, Mrs. White. I'm Trevor Perez from the Safe Insurance Company. Have a seat.

W: Oh, yes. ______________________________ before I buy any car insurance.

M: Yes, I've heard that you're going to buy a car. ______________________________ a new type of car insurance. Which type of car will you buy?

W: It's a typical mid-size sedan.

M: How about its engine size?

W: It's 2,500 cc. It costs 30,290 dollars.

M: ______________________________?

W: For 13 years, since I got a driver's license at 19.

M: Okay. Have you had any accidents?

W: No, I've never been involved in any car accidents.

M: Okay, that means you ______________________________ for over 10 years. In that case, your insurance costs are cut by 10%.

W: That sounds great.

09

M: Greetings to all customers of Thompson's Used Bookstore! You'll notice that ______________________________ with very competitive prices. For books ______________________________, we offer additional price cuts. If you buy books in bulk, you'll receive a discount. For those who purchase 10 or more books, you'll get 20% off. ______________________________ today, you'll get 10% off all your purchases. College students receive an additional 5% off on all college textbooks with a proper student ID. We are open seven days a week, from 10 a.m. to 9 p.m. from Monday to Saturday and 10 a.m. to noon on Sunday. Please feel free to phone or email us with any questions. Also ______________________________, www.thompsonbooks.com.

10

W: Hi, my name is Olivia Morris. I'd like to do some work on campus during summer break.

M: ______________________________?

W: I'm not sure. Can you tell me what kinds of jobs are being offered?

M: Basically, ______________________________. One is cleaning and the other is office work. What are you interested in?

W: I don't mind either, but I think office work would be better. I'd also like to get something that pays at least $10 per hour.

M: Well, that means you have to do cleaning work. ______________________________.

W: Alright. That's what I'll do then.

M: When are you available to work?

W: I have summer classes on Monday, Wednesday, and Friday mornings, so ______________________________.

M: Okay, then I think this is the job for you. Would you like to take it?

W: Sure, I will. Thank you.

11

W: Air travel is so tiring. ______________________________ because I've been sitting for so long.

M: I know what you mean. Why don't you walk up and down the aisle?

W: But the "______________________________" sign is on. I don't think I should right now.

12

M: Did you buy the book that Dr. Hugh ______________________________?

W: Yes, I'm reading it right now.

M: When you're finished with the book, do you think ______________________________?

13

W: Ian, why aren't you in bed?

M: ______________________________, Mom.

W: But you need a good night's rest for tomorrow.

M: I know, but I just can't fall asleep.

W: ____? It'll help you fall asleep.

M: No, I don't think that's a good idea. I might get an upset stomach.

W: ____. Just think of tomorrow as another ordinary day.

M: I'm trying, but I'm nervous.

W: You've practiced a lot for this audition so I'm sure you'll do fine. ______________________________ ____________________.

14

M: We'll be taking our city tour now, so ____________ ____.

W: Passport? I thought you had everything.

M: No, I gave everyone their documents before we got on the plane.

W: But I hadn't gotten anything.

M: ______________________________. Everyone gave me their passports a minute ago.

W: I'm positive I didn't get my passport. You're supposed to keep these things.

M: If you hadn't have your passport, ____________ ____. Could you double-check your bag, please?

W: I told you that I didn't receive my passport. Look, it's not here! Oh, dear! Here it is!

M: I told you so. ______________________________. Please give me your passport.

15

W: Jeremy is at the airport. He is going on a business trip to Seoul. ______________________________, he goes to a coffee shop in the airport. He orders a cup of coffee and drinks it at a small table. There is a man sitting next to Jeremy, and he's playing a game on his phone. It's the same type of phone as Jeremy's. Jeremy reads the news on his phone while he drinks coffee. When he realizes ______________ ______________, he leaves his phone on the table and returns his coffee and tray. When he returns to his table, ______________________________, but it's not his. Then Jeremy notices that the man who was sitting next to him is leaving the coffee shop with a phone in his hand. Jeremy __________ ____.

In this situation, what would Jeremy most likely shout to the man?

16-17

M: A recent survey has revealed a surprising discovery about prescription medicine. According to the survey, many people are using much more medicine than they should use. Some types of drugs can be dangerous ______________________________. For instance, if you abuse cold medicine, you can do serious damage to your liver, and excessive use of painkillers can harm your heart and brain. Sleeping pills ______________________________ for sleeping, but those effects come at a price - ______________________________. Even aspirin has some side effects. Its main undesirable effects are heartburn and other symptoms of stomachaches. Therefore, you should remember that in some cases taking medicine might not be the best idea. ______________________________ if you get frequent headaches, after a while you need to take more medicine for the pain to go away. This is because taking medicine too often ________ ____, and it doesn't work as well the next time. If the pain or ache is relatively small, sometimes it's a better idea to take a natural remedy, like a cup of hot tea or a nice relaxing nap.

ANSWER

정답

01회
01. ② 02. ⑤ 03. ④ 04. ② 05. ⑤
06. ③ 07. ② 08. ② 09. ⑤ 10. ③
11. ① 12. ① 13. ② 14. ④ 15. ④
16. ⑤ 17. ②

02회
01. ③ 02. ③ 03. ③ 04. ④ 05. ⑤
06. ② 07. ③ 08. ③ 09. ① 10. ②
11. ① 12. ③ 13. ③ 14. ④ 15. ③
16. ④ 17. ⑤

03회
01. ④ 02. ① 03. ① 04. ② 05. ②
06. ① 07. ④ 08. ① 09. ⑤ 10. ④
11. ② 12. ② 13. ⑤ 14. ④ 15. ⑤
16. ④ 17. ④

04회
01. ④ 02. ② 03. ① 04. ③ 05. ③
06. ② 07. ④ 08. ① 09. ⑤ 10. ④
11. ⑤ 12. ③ 13. ④ 14. ③ 15. ③
16. ③ 17. ②

05회
01. ① 02. ⑤ 03. ③ 04. ⑤ 05. ②
06. ③ 07. ⑤ 08. ③ 09. ④ 10. ③
11. ② 12. ④ 13. ④ 14. ④ 15. ④
16. ① 17. ③

06회
01. ① 02. ② 03. ④ 04. ⑤ 05. ②
06. ④ 07. ② 08. ④ 09. ③ 10. ③
11. ③ 12. ① 13. ⑤ 14. ⑤ 15. ③
16. ② 17. ④

07회
01. ① 02. ① 03. ② 04. ④ 05. ③
06. ③ 07. ③ 08. ③ 09. ⑤ 10. ②
11. ② 12. ⑤ 13. ④ 14. ⑤ 15. ④
16. ② 17. ③

08회
01. ④ 02. ③ 03. ③ 04. ⑤ 05. ②
06. ② 07. ① 08. ④ 09. ③ 10. ③
11. ② 12. ① 13. ④ 14. ④ 15. ②
16. ③ 17. ⑤

09회
01. ④ 02. ② 03. ⑤ 04. ③ 05. ④
06. ⑤ 07. ⑤ 08. ① 09. ⑤ 10. ③
11. ③ 12. ⑤ 13. ⑤ 14. ② 15. ⑤
16. ② 17. ④

10회
01. ④ 02. ⑤ 03. ④ 04. ⑤ 05. ⑤
06. ③ 07. ① 08. ③ 09. ④ 10. ④
11. ③ 12. ⑤ 13. ⑤ 14. ① 15. ①
16. ④ 17. ④

11회
01. ④ 02. ⑤ 03. ① 04. ⑤ 05. ④
06. ③ 07. ④ 08. ③ 09. ③ 10. ③
11. ① 12. ⑤ 13. ② 14. ⑤ 15. ③
16. ⑤ 17. ③

12회
01. ⑤ 02. ① 03. ③ 04. ⑤ 05. ⑤
06. ② 07. ④ 08. ③ 09. ④ 10. ⑤
11. ① 12. ① 13. ⑤ 14. ③ 15. ④
16. ⑤ 17. ③

13회
01. ④ 02. ② 03. ③ 04. ⑤ 05. ②
06. ② 07. ⑤ 08. ③ 09. ④ 10. ④
11. ② 12. ④ 13. ② 14. ④ 15. ①
16. ① 17. ③

14회
01. ① 02. ④ 03. ② 04. ③ 05. ⑤
06. ③ 07. ④ 08. ⑤ 09. ② 10. ③
11. ③ 12. ③ 13. ② 14. ① 15. ③
16. ① 17. ④

15회
01. ① 02. ③ 03. ② 04. ② 05. ②
06. ② 07. ④ 08. ① 09. ② 10. ④
11. ④ 12. ③ 13. ② 14. ③ 15. ①
16. ③ 17. ②

16회
01. ③ 02. ④ 03. ④ 04. ③ 05. ⑤
06. ③ 07. ④ 08. ④ 09. ④ 10. ③
11. ④ 12. ④ 13. ⑤ 14. ③ 15. ④
16. ④ 17. ①

17회
01. ⑤ 02. ③ 03. ④ 04. ③ 05. ③
06. ③ 07. ② 08. ② 09. ② 10. ④
11. ① 12. ① 13. ⑤ 14. ⑤ 15. ④
16. ③ 17. ③

18회
01. ① 02. ② 03. ② 04. ④ 05. ④
06. ③ 07. ⑤ 08. ④ 09. ④ 10. ④
11. ③ 12. ① 13. ⑤ 14. ② 15. ③
16. ② 17. ④

19회
01. ④ 02. ④ 03. ⑤ 04. ⑤ 05. ⑤
06. ② 07. ④ 08. ④ 09. ④ 10. ③
11. ① 12. ② 13. ⑤ 14. ⑤ 15. ④
16. ① 17. ④

20회
01. ② 02. ⑤ 03. ⑤ 04. ④ 05. ①
06. ③ 07. ④ 08. ① 09. ⑤ 10. ④
11. ④ 12. ⑤ 13. ⑤ 14. ② 15. ②
16. ③ 17. ③

21회
01. ③ 02. ④ 03. ③ 04. ⑤ 05. ②
06. ④ 07. ④ 08. ① 09. ⑤ 10. ②
11. ⑤ 12. ⑤ 13. ② 14. ② 15. ④
16. ② 17. ④

22회
01. ④ 02. ⑤ 03. ⑤ 04. ③ 05. ④
06. ② 07. ④ 08. ④ 09. ⑤ 10. ①
11. ③ 12. ① 13. ③ 14. ② 15. ⑤
16. ⑤ 17. ③

23회
01. ① 02. ⑤ 03. ① 04. ③ 05. ④
06. ④ 07. ① 08. ③ 09. ④ 10. ④
11. ② 12. ④ 13. ④ 14. ⑤ 15. ⑤
16. ③ 17. ⑤

24회
01. ⑤ 02. ② 03. ① 04. ④ 05. ②
06. ③ 07. ⑤ 08. ⑤ 09. ④ 10. ③
11. ① 12. ④ 13. ④ 14. ③ 15. ⑤
16. ④ 17. ③

25회
01. ④ 02. ④ 03. ④ 04. ④ 05. ③
06. ③ 07. ④ 08. ⑤ 09. ③ 10. ①
11. ② 12. ② 13. ① 14. ⑤ 15. ⑤
16. ① 17. ③

26회
01. ② 02. ② 03. ③ 04. ⑤ 05. ④
06. ③ 07. ④ 08. ① 09. ② 10. ④
11. ③ 12. ② 13. ③ 14. ⑤ 15. ③
16. ② 17. ④

27회
01. ④ 02. ② 03. ② 04. ④ 05. ⑤
06. ② 07. ③ 08. ④ 09. ② 10. ②
11. ② 12. ② 13. ② 14. ⑤ 15. ①
16. ⑤ 17. ③

28회
01. ③ 02. ② 03. ③ 04. ④ 05. ②
06. ① 07. ③ 08. ② 09. ④ 10. ④
11. ③ 12. ⑤ 13. ⑤ 14. ① 15. ④
16. ③ 17. ②

ANSWER

정답

29회

01. ③ 02. ⑤ 03. ② 04. ④ 05. ④
06. ④ 07. ③ 08. ⑤ 09. ④ 10. ⑤
11. ① 12. ② 13. ⑤ 14. ③ 15. ③
16. ③ 17. ⑤

30회

01. ④ 02. ② 03. ⑤ 04. ⑤ 05. ③
06. ④ 07. ① 08. ② 09. ⑤ 10. ③
11. ③ 12. ④ 13. ⑤ 14. ③ 15. ①
16. ③ 17. ⑤

31회

01. ② 02. ④ 03. ④ 04. ④ 05. ①
06. ② 07. ② 08. ③ 09. ① 10. ④
11. ① 12. ⑤ 13. ② 14. ④ 15. ③
16. ② 17. ⑤

32회

01. ⑤ 02. ④ 03. ③ 04. ④ 05. ③
06. ② 07. ③ 08. ② 09. ③ 10. ④
11. ③ 12. ③ 13. ① 14. ① 15. ⑤
16. ③ 17. ④

33회

01. ④ 02. ④ 03. ② 04. ④ 05. ①
06. ③ 07. ⑤ 08. ⑤ 09. ④ 10. ②
11. ① 12. ⑤ 13. ② 14. ⑤ 15. ⑤
16. ② 17. ④

34회

01. ⑤ 02. ⑤ 03. ④ 04. ③ 05. ③
06. ① 07. ⑤ 08. ④ 09. ④ 10. ②
11. ③ 12. ⑤ 13. ④ 14. ③ 15. ②
16. ④ 17. ④

35회

01. ② 02. ③ 03. ④ 04. ④ 05. ⑤
06. ④ 07. ④ 08. ③ 09. ⑤ 10. ③
11. ⑤ 12. ④ 13. ② 14. ① 15. ②
16. ② 17. ③

36회

01. ② 02. ⑤ 03. ④ 04. ③ 05. ①
06. ③ 07. ② 08. ④ 09. ③ 10. ④
11. ④ 12. ④ 13. ② 14. ② 15. ④
16. ④ 17. ⑤

37회

01. ① 02. ① 03. ② 04. ④ 05. ⑤
06. ④ 07. ③ 08. ④ 09. ④ 10. ⑤
11. ④ 12. ③ 13. ④ 14. ③ 15. ⑤
16. ② 17. ④

38회

01. ② 02. ② 03. ① 04. ⑤ 05. ③
06. ③ 07. ③ 08. ③ 09. ⑤ 10. ④
11. ① 12. ④ 13. ③ 14. ① 15. ①
16. ② 17. ①

39회

01. ② 02. ③ 03. ④ 04. ⑤ 05. ④
06. ② 07. ① 08. ④ 09. ③ 10. ②
11. ③ 12. ⑤ 13. ① 14. ⑤ 15. ③
16. ① 17. ③

40회

01. ④ 02. ④ 03. ⑤ 04. ⑤ 05. ⑤
06. ③ 07. ③ 08. ③ 09. ④ 10. ①
11. ② 12. ④ 13. ② 14. ① 15. ③
16. ② 17. ④

1 구문 판매 1위 '천일문' 콘텐츠를 활용하여 정확하고 다양한 구문 학습

끊어읽기 | 해석하기 | 문장 구조 분석 | 해설·해석 제공 | 단어 스크램블링 | 영작하기

2 문법·서술형 쎄듀의 모든 문법 문항을 활용하여 내신까지 해결하는 정교한 문법 유형 제공

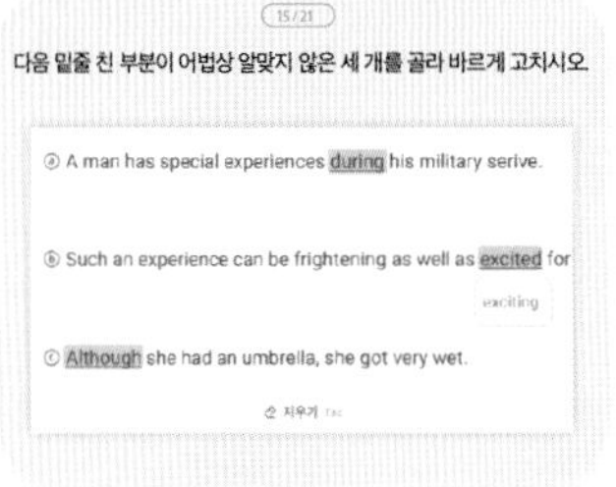
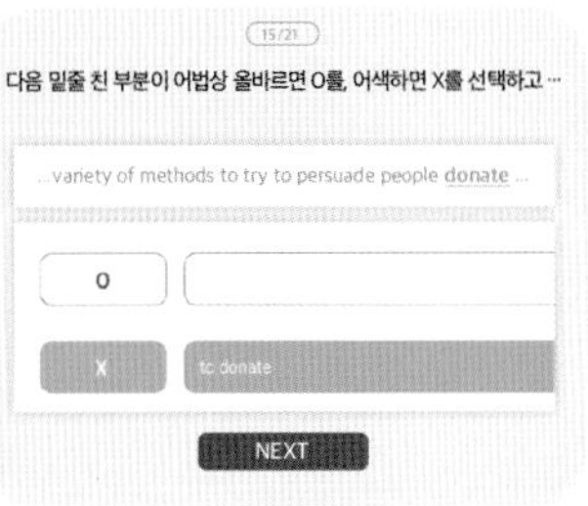
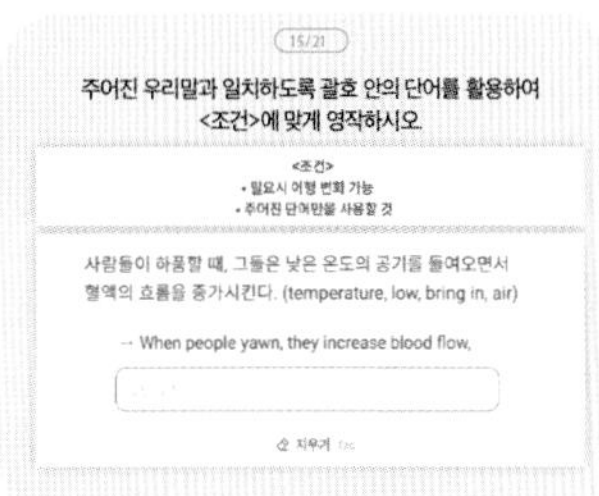

객관식과 주관식의 결합 | 문법 포인트별 학습 | 보기를 활용한 집합 문항 | 내신대비 서술형 | 어법+서술형 문제

3 어휘 초·중·고·공무원까지 방대한 어휘량을 제공하며 오프라인 TEST 인쇄도 가능

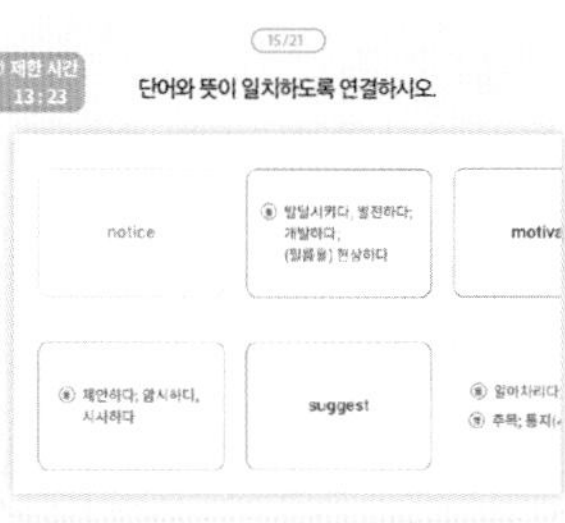

영단어 카드 학습 | 단어 ↔ 뜻 유형 | 예문 활용 유형 | 단어 매칭 게임

4 선생님 보유 문항 이용

Online Test | OMR Test

P

W
E
R

파워업

듣기 모의고사 40회

정답 및 해설

Up

쎄듀

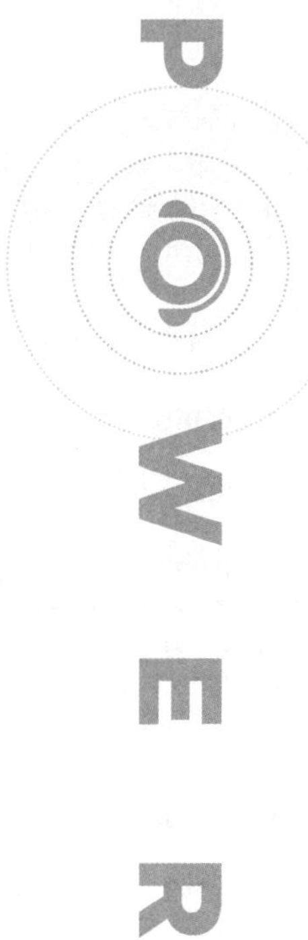

파워업

듣기 모의고사 40회

정답 및 해설

Answers & Explanation

01. ② 02. ⑤ 03. ④ 04. ② 05. ⑤ 06. ③ 07. ② 08. ② 09. ⑤ 10. ③
11. ① 12. ① 13. ② 14. ④ 15. ④ 16. ⑤ 17. ②

01 화자가 하는 말의 목적 | ②

▶ 손님을 받는 시간과, 음식을 제공하는 순서, 연사 연설 시간 등이 나오는 것으로 보아 어떤 행사의 상세일정을 설명하고 있음을 알 수 있다.

M: Doors open for the reception at 6:30, **when food and drink is to be served** and guests have the opportunity to enter the Zero Waste contest. At 6:55 precisely, waiters should remind guests that the Zero Waste video starts in five minutes. An official welcome to the guests and **an introduction to the 30-minute video** is scheduled for 7:00~7:40. After this, guest speaker Olivia James is introduced and gives a 30-minute speech. Then, Zero Waste Discussion Panel members are introduced and **each given five minutes to speak**. Twenty minutes of audience question time follows. Finally, **dessert is served** and guests have their final opportunity to enter the Zero Waste contest.

남: 6시 30분에 환영회를 위해 문이 열립니다. 그때 음식과 음료가 제공될 것이고 손님들은 Zero Waste 대회에 참가할 기회를 갖습니다. 정확히 6시 55분에 웨이터들은 손님들에게 Zero Waste 비디오가 5분 뒤에 시작한다는 것을 상기시켜 주어야 합니다. 손님들에 대한 공식 환영과 30분 길이의 비디오 소개는 7시부터 7시 40분까지로 예정되어 있습니다. 그 후에, 초청 연사 Olivia James 씨가 소개되고 30분간 연설을 합니다. 그런 다음 Zero Waste 토론위원들이 소개되고 각각 5분의 연설시간이 주어집니다. 뒤이어 20여 분간의 청중 질문 시간이 있습니다. 마지막으로 후식이 제공되고 손님들은 Zero Waste 대회에 참가할 마지막 기회를 얻게 됩니다.

어휘 **reception** 환영회; 응접, 접견 / **precisely** 정확히 / **panel** 토론자단, 패널 ((특정한 문제에 대해 조언·견해를 제공하는 전문가 집단, 또는 방송에 나와 토론을 하는 사람들))

02 의견 | ⑤

▶ 스팸 문자 메시지를 많이 받는 남자에게 여자가 스팸 문자 메시지를 차단할 수 있는 방법이 있음을 알려주고 있다.

W: Your phone is buzzing again. I think someone is texting you.
M: No, it's just a spam message. They are probably offering me a loan or some other thing that **I don't care about**.
W: Do you get many messages like that?
M: I get several each day. It's really annoying.
W: You know, there are applications **that will block unwanted messages**. They work just like the spam filter in your email.
M: Something like that might be helpful. Maybe **you could recommend one for me**.
W: I'd be happy to. I can also check if your phone-service provider has an option to block spam. Many do.
M: **That would be great**. Thanks for your help.

여: 네 휴대전화가 또 울리고 있어. 누가 너에게 문자 메시지를 보내는 것 같아.
남: 아니야, 스팸 문자 메시지일 뿐이야. 아마 대출이나 난 관심 없는 다른 걸 제안하는 걸 거야.
여: 그런 문자 메시지를 많이 받아?
남: 하루에 몇 개씩 받아. 정말 귀찮아.
여: 있잖아, 원하지 않는 문자 메시지를 차단해 줄 응용프로그램이 있어. 꼭 이메일의 스팸 차단 프로그램처럼 작동하지.
남: 그런 게 도움이 될 수도 있겠다. 어쩌면 네가 하나 추천해줄 수도 있고.
여: 기꺼이. 네 휴대전화 서비스 사업자가 스팸 차단 옵션을 제공하는지도 확인해줄 수 있어. 그렇게 하는 회사가 많거든.
남: 그거 좋겠다. 도와줘서 고마워.

어휘 **buzz** 윙하는 소리를 내다 / **loan** 대출(금) / **care about** ~에 관심을 가지다 / **application** 응용프로그램

03 관계 | ④

▶ 비행기 탑승 관련 서류 제출을 요구받고 This job ~, We refuel ~ 등의 말을 한 남자는 항공기 조종사이고, 서류를 검사하고 탑승을 허가한 여자는 공항의 보안담당 요원임을 알 수 있다.

W: Excuse me, sir! I have to see your documents!
M: I'm sorry! I usually don't have to show them. Most of the officers here know me. **You must be new**. Here you are.
W: Thank you, sir. **Security has been tightened recently**. I'm sure you understand.
M: Of course, I understand. No trouble at all. It's gratifying **to see you being so thorough**.
W: Flight 381 for Singapore. Is that your final destination?
M: Unfortunately, no. This job is long distance. We refuel in Singapore, **take on some more passengers**, and continue to Auckland.
W: Here are your documents. **Everything is in order**. Fly safely!
M: Thank you.

여: 실례합니다, 선생님! 제가 당신의 서류를 좀 봐야 하는데요!
남: 죄송합니다! 대개는 그것들을 보여줄 필요가 없거든요. 여기서 일하는 담당자들은 대부분 저를 알고 계세요. 새로 오셨나 보네요. 여기 있습니다.
여: 감사합니다, 선생님. 최근에 보안이 강화되어서요. 이해하시리라 믿습니다.
남: 물론 이해합니다. 전혀 문제없어요. 이렇게 철저하게 하시는 것을 보니 만족스럽습니다.
여: 싱가포르행 381편이군요. 그곳이 최종 목적지인가요?
남: 유감스럽게도 그렇지 않아요. 이번 일은 장거리거든요. 싱가포르에서 연료를 채우고 승객들을 더 태운 뒤, 오클랜드로 갑니다.
여: 서류 여기 있습니다. 모든 것이 제대로 되어 있군요. 안전운행하세요!
남: 고맙습니다.

어휘 **tighten** ~을 강화하다 / **gratifying** 만족을 주는 / **thorough** 철저한, 빈틈없는 / **refuel** 연료를 보급하다 / **in order** 제대로 된; 적절한, 타당한

04 그림 불일치 | ②

▶ 여자는 자신이 처음에 고른 3단짜리 책장보다 남자가 사준 5단짜리가 훨씬 더 좋다고 말했다.

[Cell phone rings.]
M: Hello?
W: Hi, Grandpa!
M: Hi, Jessica. How do you like your new study room?
W: It's great! I especially love the world map that **you picked out**. It covers the entire wall.
M: I'm glad it fits. And how about the 5-shelf bookshelf that I bought for you?
W: I think I'll really appreciate the extra space. **It's much better than the 3-shelf one** I originally chose.
M: Good. Also, I heard your father gave you a rectangular desk as a present.
W: Yes, and I have a lamp, too. It's on top of my desk.
M: Great. Are you sure the seat and backrest of your chair are comfortable enough?
W: Of course. It's the same wooden chair **I've been using for years**.
M: Everything sounds great. **I look forward to seeing it**.

[휴대전화 벨이 울린다.]
남: 여보세요?
여: 안녕하세요, 할아버지!
남: 그래, Jessica구나. 새 공부방은 어떠니?
여: 정말 좋아요! 특히 할아버지께서 골라주신 세계 지도가 아주 마음에 들어요. 지도가 벽을 다 덮었어요.
남: 잘 맞는다니 기쁘구나. 그리고 내가 사준 5단짜리 책장은 어떠니?
여: 여분의 공간이 있어서 정말 좋을 것 같아요. 제가 원래 골랐던 3단짜리보다 훨씬 더 좋아요.
남: 잘됐구나. 또, 네 아빠가 선물로 직사각형 책상을 줬다고 들었단다.
여: 네, 그리고 전등도 있는데요, 책상 위에 놓여 있어요.

남: 멋지겠구나. 의자의 앉는 부분과 등받이도 충분히 편안한 거 맞니?
여: 물론이에요. 제가 몇 년 동안 사용해오고 있는 똑같은 나무 의자예요.
남: 모든 게 좋은 것 같구나. 공부방을 보는 게 기대되는걸.

어휘 **backrest** 의자 등받이

05 추후 행동 | ⑤

▶ 대화를 끝내고 여자는 포스터를 만들기 위해 미술 용품을 사러 갈 것이다.

M: Sounds good, honey. You've got a nice voice.
W: Thanks, Dad. I'm practicing for my singing test tomorrow.
M: I'm sure you'll do well. But I'm trying to read some reports for work, so **could you shut the door**?
W: Actually, **I'm finished singing**, Dad.
M: You've got other homework to do?
W: I do. But before I can do it, I have to **go buy some art supplies** to make a poster.
M: Why don't you wait until after dinner?
W: I'm not going to the shopping mall. I'm going to the stationery store on the corner.
M: OK. **Hurry back**. Your mom needs some help getting dinner ready and **setting the table**.
W: OK. I'll just be 10 minutes.

남: 듣기 좋구나, 얘야. 목소리가 정말 좋아.
여: 고마워요, 아빠. 내일 있을 노래 시험을 위해 연습하고 있어요.
남: 네가 잘할 거라고 믿는다. 그런데 회사 일로 보고서를 좀 읽으려고 하니 문을 닫아 줄래?
여: 사실, 노래 연습은 끝났어요, 아빠.
남: 해야 할 다른 숙제가 있니?
여: 네. 하지만 숙제하기 전에, 포스터를 만들기 위해 미술 용품 몇 가지를 사러 가야 해요.
남: 저녁 식사가 끝날 때까지 기다리지 그러니?
여: 쇼핑몰에 가는 게 아니에요. 모퉁이에 있는 문구점에 갈 거예요.
남: 알았다. 빨리 돌아오렴. 엄마가 저녁 식사 준비를 하고 상을 차리는 데 도움이 필요하시단다.
여: 네. 10분이면 돼요.

어휘 **art supplies** 미술 용품 / **stationery store** 문구점

06 금액 | ③

▶ 성인 100달러이고 아동 50달러인 연간 입장권을 성인용 3장과 아동용 1장 샀으므로 350달러인데 Michigan 주민이라서 20% 할인을 받았으므로 남자가 지불할 금액은 280달러이다.

W: Good morning. How can I help you?
M: **I'd like to buy** tickets for the park. How much are they?
W: A single-day ticket is 40 dollars for adults and 20 dollars for children.
M: Is it a one-day ticket?
W: Yes. If you're thinking about visiting our park more than once during the year, consider buying annual passes. You can get a 10% discount on food **as well as free parking**.
M: That sounds great. **How much are they**?
W: 100 dollars for adults and 50 dollars for children.
M: Then I want annual passes for three adults and one child. We're Michigan residents. **Do residents get a discount**?
W: Yes, for Michigan residents, a 20% discount is available on the annual pass. Do you have a valid Michigan ID?
M: Sure. Here are my ID and card.
W: Okay. *[pause]* Here's your receipt. Have a nice day.

여: 안녕하세요. 뭘 도와드릴까요?
남: 공원 티켓을 사고 싶습니다. 얼마인가요?
여: 1일권은 성인이 40달러이고 어린이는 20달러입니다.
남: 1일 티켓인가요?
여: 예. 저희 공원을 일 년에 한 번보다 더 많이 방문할 생각이시면, 연간 입장권을 사는 걸 고려해보세요. 무료주차뿐만 아니라 음식 값의 10퍼센트를 할인받으실 수 있어요.
남: 그거 좋군요. 그건 얼마인가요?
여: 성인은 100달러이고 어린이는 50달러입니다.
남: 그러면 성인 셋과 어린이 한 명의 연간 입장권을 원합니다. 우리는 Michigan 주민인데요. 주민 할인이 되나요?
여: 예, Michigan 주민에게는 연간 입장권의 20% 할인이 가능합니다. 유효한 Michigan 신분증이 있으신가요?
남: 그럼요. 여기 제 신분증과 카드가 있습니다.
여: 좋습니다. *[잠시 후]* 여기 영수증이 있습니다. 좋은 하루 되세요.

어휘 **single-day** 하루 / **consider** 고려하다, 검토하다 / **annual** 연간의, 일 년의 / **resident** 거주자 / **available** 이용 가능한 / **valid** 유효한, 확실한

07 이유 | ②

▶ 남자는 집 안으로 들어오는 모기 때문에 걱정돼서 창문을 닫고 싶다고 했다.

M: Honey, do you mind if I close the window?
W: I'm really enjoying the breeze. So maybe we can keep it open until **it cools down a bit more**?
M: I agree that it's still hot in here, but I'm worried about mosquitoes.
W: Oh, are they **starting to bother you**?
M: Yes, they're coming in through the window.
W: I guess they are getting worse now that it's the rainy season.
M: And **they're really hard to catch** once they are inside the house.
W: In that case, I'll **turn on the air conditioner**. It will be nice to block some of the street noise, too.
M: Good idea.

남: 여보, 창문 닫아도 돼요?
여: 난 산들바람을 정말 만끽하고 있어요. 그러니 좀 더 서늘해질 때까지 혹시 열어 둘 수 있을까요?
남: 여기가 아직 덥다는 데에는 동의하지만, 난 모기 때문에 걱정돼요.
여: 아, 모기가 당신을 귀찮게 하기 시작하고 있나요?
남: 네, 창문을 통해 들어오고 있어요.
여: 장마철이라서 더 심해지고 있는 것 같아요.
남: 그리고 모기가 집 안에 한번 들어오면 잡기가 정말 힘들잖아요.
여: 그렇다면 내가 에어컨을 켤게요. 길거리 소음을 일부 차단하기에도 좋을 거예요.
남: 좋은 생각이에요.

어휘 **breeze** 산들바람, 미풍

08 언급하지 않은 것 | ②

▶ 해석 참조

M: Have you talked to Cindy, the new girl in our class?
W: Not yet, but I heard she is from Morocco. That's a country in North Africa, right?
M: Yes, it's **right on the coast**. Cindy said it's a beautiful country.
W: Can she speak English well?
M: She said that Arabic is her first language, but she **speaks fluent English as well**.
W: That's impressive. I hope she is enjoying her time here.
M: I think she is experiencing a bit of a culture shock. Almost 99% of Moroccans **follow the teachings of Islam**.
W: A lot of things here must be different to her. Morocco also has a different type of government, right?
M: Yeah, it's a constitutional monarchy. They have a king whose power **is restricted by certain rules**.
W: Wow, that's interesting. I look forward to meeting her.

남: 우리 반에 새로 온 여자애인 Cindy와 이야기 나눠봤니?
여: 아직 안 해봤는데, 그 애가 모로코에서 왔다고 들었어. 북아프리카에 있는 나라(① 위치) 맞지?
남: 응, 바로 해안에 있어. 아름다운 나라라고 Cindy가 그랬어.
여: 그 애는 영어를 잘하니?
남: 아랍어가 모국어(③ 언어)라고 했는데, 영어도 유창하게 해.
여: 굉장한데. 그 애가 이곳에서 즐거운 시간을 보내고 있으면 좋겠다.
남: 내 생각엔 문화 충격을 좀 겪고 있는 거 같아. 거의 99%에 달하는 모로코인이 이슬람교의 가르침을 따르거든(④ 종교).
여: 이곳에서의 많은 것이 그 애에게는 분명 다르겠구나. 모로코는 정부 형태도 다르잖아, 맞지?
남: 응, 입헌 군주제(⑤ 정부 형태)야. 특정 법규에 의해 권한이 제한되는 국왕이 있지.
여: 와, 흥미로운데. 그 애를 만나는 게 기대돼.

어휘 **Morocco** 모로코 ((아프리카 북서부의 왕국)) ***cf.* Moroccan** 모로코 사람(의); 모로코의 / **teaching** ((주로 pl.)) (정치적·종교적·사회적) 가르침[사상], 교리 / **constitutional monarchy** 입헌 군주제 / **restrict** ~을 제한[한정]하다

09 내용 불일치 | ⑤

▶ 전통적으로 남성만이 연주한다고 말했다.

W: A jembe is a West African drum played **with bare hands**. The name of the jembe comes from a West African country's saying that means "everyone gather together in peace." The jembe has a body carved of hard wood and the upper part **is usually covered with goat skin**. This drum can be heard clearly when **it is accompanied by other instruments** because its sounds are very loud and various. Another special feature of the jembe is that it is traditionally played only by men. Even today, **it is rare to see women playing** the jembe in West Africa, and many African women are startled when they do see a female jembe player.

여: 젬베는 맨손으로 연주하는 서아프리카식 북이다. 젬베라는 이름은 '모든 사람이 평화 속에 함께 모이다'란 뜻의 서아프리카 속담에서 왔다. 젬베는 단단한 목재를 깎아 만든 몸체를 가지고 있으며 윗부분은 대개 염소 가죽으로 덮여 있다. 이 북은 소리가 매우 크고 다채로워서 다른 악기들과 합주될 때에도 그 소리를 똑똑히 들을 수 있다. 젬베의 또 다른 특별한 특징은 전통적으로 남성만이 연주한다는 점이다. 오늘날에도 서아프리카에서 여성들이 젬베를 연주하고 있는 것을 보기란 드물며, 많은 아프리카 여성들은 여성 젬베 연주자를 실제로 보면 깜짝 놀란다.

어휘 **carve** 조각하다, 깎아서 만들다 / **accompany** ~의 반주를 해 주다; ~을 동반하다, 동행하다 / **rare** 드문, 보기 힘든; 희귀한 / **startle** ~을 깜짝 놀라게 하다

10 도표 이해 | ③

▶ 우선 오후 1시 이후에 시작하면서 공연 시간이 40분 이내의 것을 선택하기로 했다. 입장료가 일인당 30달러가 넘지 않는 것을 고르자고 했고 직접 해보는 활동을 제공하는 것을 택했으므로 답은 ③이다.

W: There are so many great shows that Charlotte would love. Which should we choose?
M: Well, you know **how much she loves birds**. And parrots are her favorite.
W: I know. But look at the time. It's before lunchtime and she'll probably get hungry during the show, so maybe something after lunch **would be better**.
M: You have a point. Then should we choose something after 1 p.m.?
W: Yeah, it'll give us enough time to eat. How about this show?
M: Well, a one-hour show might be too long for Charlotte. She starts to get distracted after about 40 minutes.
W: You're right. Then let's **choose one from these three**. And I don't want to spend too much money on a show.
M: Yes, we should spend our money on other attractions, too.
W: **Let's not spend more than** $30 per person.
M: We have two choices left. Which do you prefer?
W: Oh, this one offers a hands-on activity for Charlotte.
M: That'll be good. Let me go get the tickets.

여: Charlotte이 좋아할 멋진 쇼가 무척 많군요. 어떤 것을 택할까요?
남: 음, 그 애가 얼마나 새를 좋아하는지 알잖아요. 그리고 앵무새는 그 애가 가장 좋아하는 것이고요.
여: 알아요. 하지만 시간을 봐요. 그게 점심시간 전에 있어서 쇼 중간에 아이가 아마 배가 고플 수도 있으니까, 점심 이후에 하는 것이 더 좋을 거예요.
남: 당신 말이 맞아요. 그러면 오후 한 시 이후의 것을 선택해야 할까요?
여: 예, 그게 우리에게 식사할 충분한 시간을 줄 거예요. 이 쇼는 어때요?
남: 음, 한 시간짜리 쇼는 Charlotte에게 너무 길지도 몰라요. 그 애는 약 40분이 지나면 산만해지기 시작해요.
여: 맞아요. 그러면 이 셋 중에서 하나를 선택합시다. 그리고 난 쇼에 너무 많은 돈을 쓰고 싶지 않아요.
남: 그래요, 우리는 다른 인기거리에도 돈을 써야 하니까요.
여: 한 사람 당 30달러 넘게는 쓰지 맙시다.
남: 우리에게 두 가지 선택이 남았군요. 어떤 게 더 좋아요?
여: 아, 이건 Charlotte에게 직접 해보는 활동을 제공하네요.
남: 그게 좋겠군요. 내가 가서 표를 살게요.

어휘 **hands-on** 직접 해보는 / **parrot** 앵무새 / **distract** 산만하게 하다, (주의를) 딴 데로 돌리다 / **attraction** 인기거리, 인기물

11 짧은 대화에 이어질 응답 | ①

▶ 노란색이 어울리지 않는다는 남자에게 어떤 것을 생각하고 있는지 여자가 물었다. 따라서 마음에 드는 것이 없다는 응답이 가장 적절하다.

① 어느 것도 마음에 들지 않아.
② 파란색 스웨터는 몸에 맞지 않아.
③ 세일할 때까지 기다릴 거야.
④ 여기가 내가 가장 좋아하는 상점이야.
⑤ 난 이미 결정했어.

W: I think you should buy the yellow sweater.
M: I don't think so. **Yellow isn't my color**.
W: Oh, really? Then, which one do you have in mind?
M: ______________________________

여: 너 그 노란색 스웨터를 사는 게 좋을 것 같아.
남: 내 생각은 좀 달라. 난 노란색이 안 어울려.
여: 아, 그래? 그럼 넌 어떤 것을 생각하고 있니?
남: ______________________________

12 짧은 대화에 이어질 응답 | ①

▶ 쇼핑하러 갈 계획이라는 여자에게 남자가 쇼핑을 얼마나 자주 하느냐고 물었으므로, 빈도를 알려주는 응답이 가장 적절하다.

① 한 달에 몇 번밖에 안 가.
② 계획을 어제 세웠어.
③ 난 종종 내 차를 타고 가서 거기 주차를 해.
④ 지난번엔 원하던 것을 못 찾았어.
⑤ 난 주말마다 공원에서 산책을 해.

M: I'm going to the park. Do you want to come?
W: Sorry, **I already made plans to go shopping**.
M: You just went shopping yesterday. **How often do you go**?
W: ______________________________

남: 나 공원에 갈 건데. 너도 갈래?
여: 미안하지만, 난 쇼핑하러 가기로 이미 계획을 세웠어.
남: 너 어제도 쇼핑하러 갔잖아. 얼마나 자주 가니?
여: ______________________________

13 긴 대화에 이어질 응답 | ②

▶ 여자가 체육용품을 지하철에 놓고 내렸다고 했으므로 그에 대한 충고나 조언이 적절한 답변이 될 수 있다.

① 내릴 정거장을 놓쳤다니 안됐구나.
② 지하철 회사의 분실물 보관소 번호로 전화를 걸어보렴.
③ 내 생각엔 그것을 더 안전한 장소로 옮겨야 해.
④ 그곳에는 운동화를 보관할 수 있는 사물함이 있어.
⑤ 문제없어. 네 짐은 내가 안전하게 지켜줄게.

M: Good morning, Lisa.
W: Hi, Mr. Park.
M: Lisa? What's the matter? **Is there something wrong**? You look a little upset.
W: Yes! I feel so stupid!
M: Did you forget to bring your P.E. gear to school today?
W: Well, not exactly.
M: **What do you mean**, "not exactly"?
W: I had my sneakers and gym clothes in a shopping bag. **I fell asleep on the subway** and when I woke up I was at my station already. So I jumped up and quickly **got off the train**.
M: Did you forget the shopping bag?
W: Yes. It's probably still **on the overhead luggage rack**.
M: ______________________________

남: 안녕, Lisa.
여: 안녕하세요, 박 선생님.
남: Lisa? 무슨 일이야? 문제라도 있니? 기분이 좀 안 좋아 보이네.
여: 네! 제가 정말 바보같이 느껴져요!
남: 오늘 체육용품을 학교에 가져오는 것을 잊어버렸니?
여: 음, 꼭 그렇지는 않아요.
남: '꼭 그렇지 않다'니, 무슨 뜻이니?
여: 운동화와 운동복을 쇼핑백에 넣어 놨거든요. 지하철에서 잠들어서 일어났을 때는 이미 제가 내릴 역이었어요. 그래서 벌떡 일어나서 열차에서 급하게 내렸어요.

남: 쇼핑백을 잊어버리고?
여: 네. 아마 그게 아직도 좌석 위 수화물 선반에 놓여 있을 거예요.
남: ______________________________

어휘 **lost property** 분실물 (보관소) / **gear** (특정 활동에 필요한) 장비, 복장 / **overhead luggage rack** 좌석 머리 위쪽에 위치한 수화물 선반

14 긴 대화에 이어질 응답 | ④

▶ 여자는 예전에 삼촌과 숙모의 농장에 갔던 일이 즐거웠으므로 올해에도 가기를 고대하고 있다. 그러므로 기대를 나타내는 응답이 적절하다.

① 내일 할게요. 괜찮죠, 아빠? 안녕히 주무세요.
② 글쎄요. 승마를 하지 않을 거라니 안타까워요.
③ 그걸 할 필요가 없으면 좋을 텐데요. 외국으로 여행가고 싶어요.
④ 시험이 다 끝날 때까지 기다릴 수 없을 것 같아요.
⑤ 설마 진심은 아니시죠. 저는 너무 바빠서 어떤 농장 일도 할 수 없어요!

W: Dad, I'm exhausted.
M: It's tough, isn't it, honey? But **final exams are just a week away**.
W: It's so stressful! I have to write two more essays tonight!
M: **Just keep at it**. You'll do great. And think of all the things you can do when you've finished!
W: Yeah, **sleeping as long as I like** will be wonderful.
M: That's right.
W: Actually, you know what I'd really like to do after my exams? To go and work for Uncle Kevin and Aunt Maureen on their farm again.
M: Really, sweetheart?
W: Oh, yeah. It was so much fun that summer, and I **got to ride horses** every day!
M: Well, I'm sure they'd love to have you again. They'll have lots of work for you!
W: ______________________________

여: 아빠, 저 지쳤어요.
남: 힘들지, 얘야? 하지만 기말고사가 일주일밖에 안 남았잖니.
여: 스트레스가 정말 쌓여요! 오늘 밤에 작문 숙제를 두 개나 더 해야 해요!
남: 잘 견뎌내렴. 너는 잘할 거야. 그리고 끝냈을 때 할 수 있는 모든 일을 생각해 봐!
여: 네, 원하는 만큼 오래 자는 것은 멋질 거예요.
남: 맞아.
여: 사실, 시험 끝나고 제가 정말로 하고 싶은 게 뭔지 아세요? Kevin 삼촌과 Maureen 숙모네 농장에 다시 가서 일하는 거예요.
남: 정말이니, 얘야?
여: 그럼요. 저번 여름에 정말 재미있었고, 매일 말도 탔어요!
남: 그럼, 그분들은 네가 다시 오는 것을 분명히 좋아하실 거야. 너에게 일을 많이 주실 거야!
여: ______________________________

어휘 **overseas** 외국으로, 외국에 / **exhausted** 지친 / **keep at it** 견디어 내다, 끝까지 버티다

15 상황에 적절한 말 | ④

▶ 초자연적인 것들을 믿지 않는 Alex는 점술가가 알려줄 운명에 대해 Polly가 너무 진지하게 받아들이지 않기를 원할 것이다.

① 예술은 길고 인생은 짧아요.
② 좋은 생각이에요. 점을 보는 것은 정말 흥미로워요.
③ (실력이) 더 좋고 (비용이) 더 저렴한 점술가를 알아요. 이제 거기로 가죠.
④ 그저 재미로 보는 거라면 좋아요. 하지만 무엇이든 들어맞을 거라고 믿지는 마세요!
⑤ 저는 이미 점을 봤어요. 그렇지만 당신을 위한 돈은 여기 가지고 있어요.

W: Alex studies physics at a university. He believes only science holds the answers to life's mysteries. He firmly rejects fortune tellers, star signs, and **all other supernatural things**. On the other hand, Alex's girlfriend, Polly, **is fascinated by those things**. Alex never tells lies and never says no to Polly. He adores her and hopes to marry her after graduation. One day, **they are out shopping** when Polly says "Look at the sign! It says, 'Your fortune told for $25.' What fun! **Let's get our fortunes told**! Please!" Alex worries Polly will take the fortune too seriously. In this situation, what would Alex most likely say to Polly?

여: Alex는 대학에서 물리학을 공부한다. 그는 오직 과학만이 인생의 신비에 대한 해답을 가지고 있다고 믿는다. 그는 점술가나 별자리 그리고 모든 다른 초자연적인 것들을 단호히 거부한다. 반면 Alex의 여자 친구인 Polly는 그러한 것들에 매혹되어 있다. Alex는 결코 거짓말을 하지 않고 Polly에게 안 된다고 절대 말하지 않는다. 그는 그녀를 아주 좋아하고 졸업 후 그녀와 결혼하길 희망한다. 하루는 그들이 쇼핑을 하러 나갔는데 Polly가 "저 간판 좀 봐요! '당신의 운명을 25달러에 알려드립니다.'라고 적혀 있어요. 정말 재미있겠다! 우리 점 보러 가요! 제발요!"라고 말한다. Alex는 Polly가 그 점을 너무 진지하게 받아들일까 걱정이다. 이러한 상황에서 Alex가 Polly에게 할 말로 가장 적절한 것은 무엇인가?

어휘 **fortune** 운수, 운세; 운, 행운 ***cf.* fortune teller** 점술가 / **physics** 물리학 / **star sign** 별자리 / **supernatural** 초자연적인 / **fascinate** ~을 매혹하다, 황홀하게 하다 / **adore** ~을 아주 좋아하다[흠모하다]

16~17 세트 문항 | 16. ⑤ 17. ②

▶ 16. 아주 오래전부터 허브가 약으로 쓰였음을 밝히면서 바빌론과 고대 그리스에서 사용된 예를 들고 있다.

① 허브의 다양한 용도 ② 페퍼민트의 의학적 효능 ③ 민간요법의 다양한 종류
④ 허브를 알맞게 사용해야 하는 이유 ⑤ 고대의 허브 약용

▶ 17. 해석 참조

M: Herbal medicine, the oldest form of medicine known to humans, is the traditional medical practice of using plants to treat illnesses and disease. Depending on the plant and the illness **that is being treated**; leaves, seeds, flowers, stems, and roots may all be used. People **have been using medicinal plants** on every continent for thousands of years. For example, the records of King Hammurabi of Babylon included instructions for using medicinal plants in 1800 BC. Specifically, Hammurabi prescribed the use of mint for **treating digestive disorders**. Modern research has confirmed that peppermint does indeed relieve nausea and vomiting **by calming and relaxing the stomach**. In ancient Greece, the great physician Hippocrates described valerian, a plant with heads of sweetly scented pink flowers, **as a good remedy for sleeplessness**. However, although valerian root is nontoxic, it sometimes **causes side effects**, such as dizziness and a loss of sense of direction. Also, in rare cases, it causes skin rashes and difficulty breathing. For this reason, small doses have always been recommended.

남: 약초학은, 인류에게 알려진 가장 오래된 형태의 의학으로, 아픔과 질병을 치료하는 데 식물을 이용하는 전통적인 의술이다. 식물과 치료하는 병에 따라, 잎사귀, 씨앗, 꽃, 줄기, 그리고 뿌리가 모두 사용될 수도 있다. 사람들은 수천 년 동안 모든 대륙에서 약초를 사용해오고 있다. 예를 들어, 바빌론의 함무라비 왕에 대한 기록에는 기원전 1800년에 약초를 사용하는 것에 대한 설명이 포함되어 있다. 구체적으로 말하면, 함무라비는 소화불량을 치료하는 데 박하의 사용을 처방했다. 근대의 연구에서는 페퍼민트가 위를 진정시키고 긴장을 풀어줌으로써 메스꺼움과 구토를 실제로 완화해 준다는 것이 확인되었다. 고대 그리스에서는 위대한 의사 히포크라테스가 달콤한 향기가 나는 분홍 꽃송이가 달린 식물인 쥐오줌풀을 불면증에 좋은 치료제로 묘사했다. 그러나 쥐오줌풀 뿌리에 독성이 없긴 하지만 그것은 때때로 ① 현기증 및 ③ 방향감각 상실과 같은 부작용을 유발한다. 또한, 드물게는 ④ 피부 발진과 ⑤ 호흡곤란을 일으킨다. 이러한 이유로 항상 소량 복용이 권장되어왔다.

어휘 **folk medicine** (약초 등을 쓰는) 민간요법 / **in moderation** 알맞게, 적당히 / **herbal** 허브의, 약초의 / **medicinal** 약효가 있는 / **specifically** 구체적으로 말하면; 특히, 특정해서 / **prescribe** ~을 처방하다 / **digestive** 소화의 / **nausea** 메스꺼움 / **vomiting** 구토 / **scented** 향기로운, 강한 향기가 나는 / **remedy** 치료(약); 해결책 / **nontoxic** 무독성의 / **rash** 발진 / **dose** (약의) 복용량

Answers & Explanation

01. ③ 02. ③ 03. ③ 04. ④ 05. ⑤ 06. ② 07. ③ 08. ③ 09. ① 10. ②
11. ① 12. ③ 13. ③ 14. ④ 15. ③ 16. ④ 17. ⑤

01 화자가 하는 말의 목적 | ③

▶ 내일 시험이 선택사항이라는 것과 시험을 치를 시 얻게 될 추가 점수, 출제 범위에 대해 설명하고 있다.

W: Class, I'd like to remind you about tomorrow's speaking test. The test is optional. **You don't have to take it** if you don't want to. But you will **earn extra points** if you do take it. I will give three extra points to **those who do well on it**; two extra points to those who do OK; and one point to those who take it. It also gives you a chance to evaluate how much your speaking skills have improved. The test results will show which part of your speaking skills **needs to be worked on more**. The test will be based on one of the short passages that I've asked you to listen to and recite at home. Are there any questions?

여: 여러분, 내일 있을 말하기 시험에 대해서 일러주고자 합니다. 시험은 선택입니다. 원하지 않으면 치지 않아도 됩니다. 하지만 시험을 치면 추가 점수를 얻게 됩니다. 시험을 잘 친 학생에게는 3점의 추가 점수를, 성적이 보통인 학생에게는 2점의 추가 점수를, 그리고 시험을 치기만 한 학생에게는 1점의 추가 점수를 주겠습니다. 이번 시험은 여러분에게 자신의 말하기 능력이 얼마나 나아졌는지 평가할 수 있는 기회도 줄 것입니다. 시험 결과는 말하기 능력에서 어떤 부분이 더 노력이 필요한지를 보여줄 것입니다. 시험은 집에서 듣고 암송해보라고 했던 짧은 단락들 중 하나를 토대로 할 것입니다. 질문 있습니까?

어휘 **remind A about[of] B** A에게 B를 상기시키다[생각나게 하다] / **optional** 선택 가능한, 마음대로의 / **evaluate** ~을 평가하다 / **recite** (~을) 암송하다, 낭독하다

02 의견 | ③

▶ 여자가 카풀이 돈을 절약할 수 있다고 하자, 남자가 이에 동의하면서 환경에 도움이 되는 여러 이점들도 있다며 이를 설명하고 있으므로 남자의 의견으로는 ③이 가장 적절하다.

W: Lucas! Do you have to work overtime today?
M: No, I'm waiting for Mia and Ethan. **We're in a car pool**.
W: Good. Who drives?
M: We take turns driving each week.
W: That sounds nice. But I think it's a bit inconvenient on days like today when you three have different schedules. Why don't you take the subway?
M: There's no subway station near my home. And carpooling is very convenient **if you decide on some ground rules**.
W: Oh, yes. You can save money on your commute, too.
M: That's right. But most importantly, carpooling **cuts down on the number of cars** on the road.
W: Oh, that's right.
M: That means there is **less carbon and other gasses and pollution** getting into the air. It saves the environment by keeping the air cleaner.
W: I didn't think about that.

여: Lucas! 오늘 야근해야 하나요?
남: 아니오, 나는 Mia와 Ethan을 기다리고 있어요. 우리는 카풀을 하거든요.
여: 좋군요. 누가 운전하나요?
남: 우리는 매주 번갈아 운전해요.
여: 그거 괜찮군요. 하지만 당신들 셋이 일정이 다른 오늘 같은 날에는 좀 불편하겠네요. 지하철을 타지 그래요?
남: 집 근처에 지하철역이 없어요. 그리고 몇몇 기본 원칙들을 결정하면 카풀이 아주 편리해요.
여: 아, 그렇군요. 통근하는 데 돈을 절약할 수도 있고요.
남: 그래요. 하지만 가장 중요한 건 카풀 하는 게 도로에 자동차 숫자를 줄인다는 거예요.
여: 아, 맞아요.
남: 그건 탄소와 다른 가스들 그리고 오염 물질이 대기로 더 적게 들어간다는 걸 의미하죠. 공기를 더 깨끗하게 유지해서 환경을 구하는 거죠.
여: 난 그건 생각하지 못했어요.

어휘 **overtime** 초과근무 / **car pool** 카풀, 승용차 함께 타기(를 하다) / **take turns** 교대하다 / **inconvenient** 불편한 ***cf.*** **convenient** 편리한 / **ground rule** 기본 원칙 / **commute** 통근(하다) / **cut down on** ~을 줄이다 / **carbon** 탄소

03 관계 | ③

▶ 축구 선수의 사인이 있는 기념품을 구입하고자 하는 고객과 기념품 판매상 간의 대화이다.

W: That autograph on the magazine, **whose is it**?
M: That's Pablo Rossini's.
W: My husband would love to have that autograph. He's a big fan of soccer.
M: **It's any soccer fan's dream** to have one of his autographs. But it's very expensive.
W: How much?
M: $5,000.
W: Wow! **Why is it so expensive**?
M: Well, he never gave a lot of autographs. **There are very few on the market** and therefore the price is high. He signed this magazine after the 1992 World Cup.
W: Can you show me anything else for my husband?
M: Sure, over here is a newspaper photograph of the 2002 Korean soccer team. All the players **have signed it**.
W: Oh, **he could hang it on the wall** of his office. How much is it?
M: It's $300.

여: 잡지에 있는 저 사인, 누구의 것이죠?
남: 그건 Pablo Rossini 선수의 것이에요.
여: 저희 남편이 그 사인을 가지고 싶어 할 거예요. 열렬한 축구 팬이거든요.
남: 그의 사인 중 하나를 갖는 것은 모든 축구 팬의 꿈이죠. 하지만 매우 비싸답니다.
여: 얼만데요?
남: 5천 달러요.
여: 와! 왜 그렇게 비싼가요?
남: 음, Rossini 선수가 결코 사인을 많이 해주지 않았기 때문이죠. 시장에 나와 있는 것도 거의 없어서 결과적으로 가격이 높아요. 이 잡지에는 1992년 월드컵 후에 사인했어요.
여: 제 남편을 위해 다른 것도 보여주시겠어요?
남: 물론이죠. 여기 2002년 한국 축구 대표팀의 신문 사진입니다. 모든 선수가 여기에 사인했어요.
여: 아, 남편의 사무실 벽에 걸어둘 수도 있겠어요. 얼마인가요?
남: 300달러요.

어휘 **autograph** 사인, 서명

04 그림 불일치 | ④

▶ 공주 캐릭터는 물방울무늬 드레스를 입고 있다고 했다.

W: Dad, this amusement park looks amazing!
M: It really looks like **there will be plenty to do**. What do you want to do first?
W: I want to start by trying the merry-go-round.
M: All right. I'm sure you also want to visit that castle.
W: I do. Right after trying the merry-go-round.
M: Okay. Then **how about riding** the roller coaster, afterward?
W: Sounds great. I also want to **get my picture taken** with that princess character. She's standing right over there.
M: Oh, you mean the one with a polka-dotted dress?
W: Right. Actually, I expected her to be wearing a star-patterned dress **like she usually does**, but I think her new dress is far more beautiful.
M: I agree. Would you like to have hot dogs at that stand on the right, afterward?
W: Yes, please.

여: 아빠, 이 놀이공원 굉장해 보여요!
남: 정말 할 게 많이 있을 것 같구나. 제일 먼저 뭘 하고 싶니?
여: 회전목마 타는 것부터 시작하고 싶어요.
남: 좋아. 분명 저 성에도 가고 싶어 할 것 같은데.
여: 가고 싶어요. 회전목마를 탄 다음에 바로요.
남: 그래. 그럼 그다음엔 롤러코스터를 타는 게 어떠니?

여: 좋아요. 저 공주 캐릭터와 사진도 찍고 싶어요. 바로 저기 서 있어요.
남: 아, 물방울무늬 드레스를 입고 있는 공주 말이니?
여: 맞아요. 실은 보통 때처럼 별무늬 드레스를 입고 있을 것으로 예상했지만, 새 드레스가 훨씬 더 예쁜 것 같아요.
남: 그런 것 같구나. 그 후에 오른쪽에 있는 저 가판대에서 핫도그 먹을래?
여: 네, 먹을래요.

어휘 **merry-go-round** 회전목마 / **polka-dotted** 물방울무늬의

05 추후 행동 | ⑤

▶ 여자(엄마)는 콘서트 표를 예매해달라는 남자(아들)의 부탁을 들어줄 수 없자 딸에게 대신 전화하여 예매를 부탁해주겠다고 했다.

[Cell phone rings.]
W: Hello?
M: Mom, this is Kevin.
W: What's up? Don't you have class soon?
M: Yes, but I **need to ask a favor of you**.
W: Oh? What do you need?
M: Could you go on your computer and **reserve a ticket** for DJ Dawnstar's concert for me? It's urgent.
W: I'm sorry, but I'm on my way to your grandmother's place. Can't you use the school's computer lab?
M: The computer lab **has been shut down for regular maintenance**, so I can't. And I'm not going to be home until 7, which will be too late.
W: I **won't be home until late** either. Why not ask your sister?
M: Okay, but I have to go to history class right now.
W: Then I'll call her instead. She'll text you if she can help.
M: Thanks, Mom. I'll wait for a text.

[휴대전화 벨이 울린다.]
여: 여보세요?
남: 엄마, 저 Kevin이에요.
여: 무슨 일이니? 곧 수업 있지 않아?
남: 네, 하지만 엄마에게 부탁드릴 게 하나 있어서요.
여: 그래? 뭐가 필요하니?
남: 컴퓨터로 가셔서 저를 위해 DJ Dawnstar의 콘서트 표를 예매해 주실래요? 급해요.
여: 미안하지만 엄마는 할머니 댁에 가는 중이란다. 학교 컴퓨터실을 이용하면 안 되니?
남: 컴퓨터실은 정기 점검 중이라 문이 닫혀 있어 이용할 수 없어요. 그리고 전 7시 이후에나 집에 갈 텐데 그때는 너무 늦을 거예요.
여: 엄마도 집에 늦게 갈 것 같구나. 누나에게 부탁하면 어떻겠니?
남: 좋아요. 그런데 저 지금 역사 수업에 들어가야 해요.
여: 그럼 엄마가 누나에게 대신 전화해 보마. 누나가 도와줄 수 있으면 네게 문자를 보낼 거야.
남: 고마워요, 엄마. 문자 기다릴게요.

어휘 **ask a favor of** ~에게 부탁을 하다 / **maintenance** (정기적으로 점검·보수하는) 유지; (수준·상태 등의) 유지, 지속 / **text** (휴대전화로 주고받는) 문자(메시지); (휴대전화로) ~에게 문자(메시지)를 보내다; (책·잡지 등의) 본문, 글

06 금액 | ②

▶ 두 사람은 남자의 책 한 권(8달러)과 누나의 책 두 권(15달러+10달러)을 구입하기로 했다. 주문 금액이 30달러가 넘으면 배송료는 무료이므로, 지불할 총 금액은 33달러이다.

M: Mom, click on the title of the book.
W: Let's see. It says it is $8.
M: That's 20% cheaper than the bookstore. Is shipping included?
W: I'm not sure.
M: **Click where it says** "Prices and Shipping Policy." On the left.
W: Oh, the two-day shipping cost is $8.
M: Then I'll go to the bookstore.
W: Hold on. **It says if our order is** over $30, shipping is free.
M: But the book is only $8.
W: Well, your big sister needs more study guides to prepare for the SAT.
M: She's not going to be happy if you give her more study books.
W: She has no choice. I'll get this one for $15 and this vocabulary book for $10.
M: Then we're over $30 **if you add my book**.

남: 엄마, 책의 제목을 클릭해 보세요.
여: 어디 보자. 8달러라고 적혀 있어.
남: 서점보다 20% 싼 가격이네요. 배송료가 포함되어 있나요?
여: 잘 모르겠어.
남: '가격과 배송 정책'이라고 적힌 부분을 클릭해 보세요. 왼쪽에 있어요.
여: 아, 이틀 내 배송 비용은 8달러야.
남: 그럼 전 서점에 갈래요.
여: 잠깐만. 주문금액이 30달러가 넘으면 배송료가 무료라고 하는데.
남: 하지만 책 가격이 8달러밖에 안 되는데요.
여: 음, 네 누나는 SAT를 준비하기 위한 학습 입문서가 더 필요해.
남: 엄마가 공부할 책을 더 주면 누나는 좋아하지 않을 거예요.
여: 누나에게는 선택의 여지가 없어. 이 책을 15달러에 사고 이 어휘 책을 10달러에 사야겠다.
남: 그럼 제 책까지 합하면 30달러가 넘는군요.

어휘 **shipping** 운송, 선적

07 이유 | ③

▶ 남자는 누나가 키우는 개가 짖는 소리에 잠이 깼다고 했다.

W: You looked like **you were falling asleep** in class today, Jim. Tired?
M: Yeah, really tired. I woke up at 5 a.m. today.
W: Oh, do you have **a big exam to study for**?
M: No, our dog was barking and woke me up.
W: I didn't know your family had a dog.
M: It's my sister's. She usually wakes up early and goes jogging with it, but she's traveling right now.
W: Oh, poor thing. Why didn't you take it jogging instead?
M: Well, I wanted to get plenty of sleep so I could **stay up and watch the soccer game**.
W: Oh, **I almost forgot about tonight's game**. Why don't you go home and take a nap before it starts?
M: That's a good idea. Talk to you later.

여: 너 오늘 수업 시간에 자고 있는 것 같았어, Jim. 피곤하니?
남: 응, 정말 피곤해. 오늘 아침 5시에 일어났거든.
여: 아, 공부해야 할 중요한 시험이 있니?
남: 아니, 우리 집 개가 짖고 있어서 잠이 깼어.
여: 너희 가족이 개를 키우는지 몰랐어.
남: 누나 개야. 누나는 대개 일찍 일어나서 개와 함께 조깅하러 가는데, 지금은 여행 중이야.
여: 아, 불쌍해라. 왜 네가 대신 조깅에 데려가지 않았니?
남: 음, (밤에) 깨어서 축구경기를 볼 수 있도록 충분히 자고 싶었거든.
여: 아, 오늘 밤 경기를 잊어버릴 뻔했네. 집에 가서 경기 시작 전에 잠깐 자는 게 어때?
남: 좋은 생각이야. 나중에 얘기하자.

08 언급하지 않은 것 | ③

▶ 해석 참조

M: Want to fall in love? Come to Lincoln City during its 33rd annual Rose Festival and you'll **find it hard not to feel the passion**. From April 29th to May 15th, there will be three types of garden roses **on display**: miniatures, shrubs and climbers. Miniature roses are less than 40 centimeters tall, shrubs are **over a meter high** and climbing roses can be 7 meters long. All the types of roses will be on display in both the outdoor and the indoor exhibition areas. The exhibition areas are open from 9 a.m. until 8 p.m. But these areas will close **two hours later on weekends**. Roses symbolize love. Come to Lincoln City this spring and feel the love.

남: 사랑에 빠지고 싶으신가요? 33번째 연례 장미 축제 기간 동안 Lincoln 시로 오시면, 열정을 느끼지 않는 것이 어렵다는 것을 알게 되실 것입니다. 4월 29일부터 5월 15일까지(① 전시 기간) 세 가지 종류의 정원용 장미가 전시될 예정인데, 그것들은 미니 장미, 관목 장미, 덩굴장미(② 전시되는 장미 종류)입니다. 미니 장미는 길이가 40센티미터 미만이고, 관목 장미는 1미터가 넘으며, 덩굴장미는 7미터에 이를 수 있습니다. 모든 종류의 장미는 야외 전시장과 실내 전시장에 모두 전시(④ 전시 장소)될 것입니다. 전시장은 오전 9시부터 오후 8시까지 개방(⑤ 관람 시간)됩니다. 그러나 이 전시장들은 주말에는 2시간 더 늦게 문을 닫을 것입니다. 장미는 사랑을 상징합니다. 올봄에 Lincoln 시에 오셔서 사랑을 느껴보세요.

어휘 **annual** 매년의, 연례의; 1년(간)의 / **miniature** (동·식물의) 미니형, 소형(품)종; 아주 작은, 소형의 / **shrub** 관목(灌木) / **climber** 덩굴 식물 / **symbolize** ~을 상징하다

09 내용 불일치 | ①

▶ 훈련은 테러의 위험 때문이 아니라 다가오는 겨울철을 대비하여 실시된다.

W: To be ready for the upcoming winter season, **we are going to conduct a fire drill** today. When you hear the alarm, please treat it **as though it were a real fire**. Each floor of the building has two fire captains. You will soon **be directed to leave the building**. So please follow their instructions for the evacuation. During the drill you will not be able to use the elevators. But if you have a health problem and **need to use them**, please see your fire captain immediately after this announcement. It is to confirm you don't have to participate in this drill. If you have any question about the drill, **feel free to ask each floor's captains**. Thank you.

여: 다가오는 겨울철을 대비하기 위하여, 오늘 화재 대피 훈련을 실시하고자 합니다. 경보가 들리면 실제 화재가 난 것처럼 행동해 주십시오. 건물의 각 층에는 화재 훈련대장이 두 명 배치됩니다. 여러분은 건물에서 대피하도록 곧 지시를 받을 것입니다. 그러니 대피에 따른 지시사항을 따라 주십시오. 훈련 도중에는 엘리베이터를 이용하실 수 없을 것입니다. 하지만 건강상 문제가 있어서 엘리베이터를 이용하셔야 한다면, 이 방송이 나간 후 즉시 해당 훈련대장을 만나십시오. 이것은 이번 훈련에 참가하지 않아도 된다는 것을 확인하기 위한 것입니다. 훈련에 대해 의문점이 있으시면, 각 층 화재 훈련대장에게 언제든지 문의하십시오. 감사합니다.

어휘 **upcoming** 다가오는 / **conduct** ~을 처리하다, 수행하다 / **drill** 훈련, 반복 연습 / **as though** 마치 ~인 것처럼 / **direct** ~을 지도하다, 지시하다 / **instruction** ((pl.)) 지시, 설명 / **evacuation** 대피 / **announcement** 발표, 공고 / **confirm** ~을 확인[승인]하다

10 도표 이해 | ②

▶ 400달러 이하의 예산에서 가스 그릴이고 버너가 알루미늄으로 만들어진 것 중에서 크기가 적어도 300제곱인치인 것을 택했으므로 답은 ②이다.

W: Honey, we need to buy a new grill for barbecuing in the backyard. We can buy one from this online store.
M: Sure. The success of the barbecue often comes down to the quality of the grill. First, do you **have a certain budget in mind**?
W: I don't want to spend over $400.
M: Then we have great options at that price range. And we need to choose between gas and charcoal.
W: My friend Lily says gas is **more convenient to use and easier to clean up**. So I'd like to buy a gas grill.
M: Okay. Next is the material the burners **are made out of**. I think the best burner is the stainless steel burner.
W: But I've heard aluminum will outlast stainless steel. It's also less expensive than stainless steel.
M: Okay. **Let's go with your opinion**. It looks like we'll have to choose the size. How big do you think the grill should be?
W: I think we need one with at least 300 square inches for our family.
M: Then we should go with this one. Let's order it now.

여: 여보, 우리 뒷마당에서 바비큐를 할 새로운 그릴을 사야 해요. 이 온라인 상점에서 하나를 살 수 있어요.
남: 물론이에요. 바비큐의 성공은 종종 그릴의 품질로 설명되죠. 우선, 특정 예산을 염두에 두고 있나요?
여: 400달러 넘게 쓰고 싶지는 않아요.
남: 그러면 그 가격 범위에서 훌륭한 선택이 될 수 있는 것들이 있군요. 그리고 우리는 가스와 숯 중에서 선택해야 해요.
여: 내 친구 Lily가 가스가 사용하기 더 편리하고 청소하기 더 쉽다고 해요. 그래서 난 가스 그릴을 사고 싶어요.
남: 알겠어요. 다음은 버너를 만든 재료예요. 난 최고의 버너는 스테인리스강 버너라고 생각해요.
여: 그런데 알루미늄이 스테인리스강보다 더 오래 갈 거라 들었어요. 그건 스테인리스강보다 더 저렴하기도 하고요.
남: 알겠어요. 당신 의견대로 합시다. 크기를 골라야 할 것 같네요. 그릴이 얼마나 커야 한다고 생각해요?
여: 난 우리 가족에게는 적어도 300제곱인치인 것이 필요하다고 생각해요.
남: 그러면 우리 이걸로 해야겠어요. 지금 그걸 주문합시다.

어휘 **grill** 그릴; (그릴을 이용하여) 구운 고기[요리] / **charcoal** 숯; 목탄; 짙은 회색 / **material** 재료; 자료 / **square inch** 제곱인치 / **come down to** (한마디로) 설명[요약]되다; ~에 이르다, 결국 ~이 되다 / **certain** 특정한; 확실한 / **budget** 예산 / **range** 범위; 다양성; (범위가) A에서 B 사이이다 / **clean up** 청소하다[치우다] / **outlast** ~보다 더 오래 가다[계속하다] / **go with** ~에 동의하다, 지지하다; 부속되다

11 짧은 대화에 이어질 응답 | ①

▶ 각자 파트너가 없는 상황에서 과제를 함께 하자는 여자의 제안에 가장 적절한 응답을 고른다.

① 정말 좋은 생각이야.
② 나는 일주일 내내 그 과제를 하고 있어.
③ 나는 고궁에서 산책하는 것을 좋아해.
④ 고맙지만 우리는 과제를 혼자서 해야 해.
⑤ 그 과제에는 역사박물관에 가는 것이 포함되어 있어.

W: I don't have a partner for my history project.
M: **Neither do I**. I'm not sure what to do.
W: Why don't we **work on it together**?
M: ______________________

여: 나는 역사 과제를 함께 할 파트너가 없어.
남: 나도 없어. 어떻게 해야 할지 모르겠어.
여: 우리 같이 하는 게 어때?
남: ______________________

12 짧은 대화에 이어질 응답 | ③

▶ 노트북으로 게임을 잘 안 한다는 여자에게 남자가 그럼 노트북을 무엇을 하는 데 사용하는지 묻고 있다. 이에 대한 적절한 응답을 찾는다.

① 더 좋은 노트북이 있으면 좋겠어.
② 난 게임에 관심이 없을 뿐이야.
③ 난 주로 인터넷 서핑하는 데 사용해.
④ 이 노트북은 우리 오빠 거였어.
⑤ 사용 설명서를 오래전에 잃어버렸어.

M: Is your laptop **powerful enough to play games**?
W: No, but I don't play a lot of games anyway.
M: Then **what do you use it for**?
W: ______________________

남: 네 노트북은 게임을 할 만큼 성능이 좋니?
여: 아니, 하지만 난 어차피 게임을 많이 안 해.
남: 그럼 노트북을 뭐 하는 데 사용하니?
여: ______________________

어휘 **instruction manual** 사용 설명서

13 긴 대화에 이어질 응답 | ③

▶ 공원이 쓰레기 더미 위에 만들어졌으며 그 위를 자신이 걷고 있다는 것을 새롭게 알게 된 남자의 응답을 고른다.

① 천천히 가세요. 당신은 너무 빨리 걷고 있어요.
② 조심해요! 밟는 곳을 주의하세요.
③ 놀랍네요. 저는 결코 몰랐을 거예요.
④ 알겠어요. 집안의 온도를 높일게요.
⑤ 쓰레기를 버리지 마세요. 쓰레기는 휴지통에 넣어 주세요.

M: Sang-mi, thanks for bringing me to this beautiful park.
W: You're welcome, Eric.
M: It's relaxing **walking through the forest** and up the mountain.
W: I don't think you know, but this park used to be a garbage dump. For 50 years, **garbage from the city was put here**.
M: Really?
W: Yes. A few years ago they covered all the garbage with layers and layers of plastic. **Then they put down dirt** and planted trees.
M: A garbage mountain! Wow!
W: It is producing energy, too. **As the covered garbage** breaks down, it produces gas.
M: They collect the gas coming out of the mountain?
W: That's right. **It heats nearby homes**.
M: Everything looks so natural and clean.
W: But we're really walking on garbage.
M: ______________________

남: 상미 씨, 이렇게 아름다운 공원에 데리고 와 줘서 고마워요.
여: 천만에요, Eric 씨.
남: 숲을 가로질러 산 위로 걸어 올라가는 것이 마음의 긴장을 풀어 주는군요.
여: Eric 씨는 모를 것 같은데 이 공원은 예전에 쓰레기 더미였어요. 도시의 쓰레기가 50년간 여기에 버려졌죠.

남: 정말이요?
여: 네. 수년 전 모든 쓰레기를 비닐로 겹겹이 덮었어요. 그런 다음 흙을 덮고 나무를 심었죠.
남: 쓰레기 산이라! 와!
여: 산에서 에너지도 나와요. 덮인 쓰레기가 분해되면서 가스를 배출하죠.
남: 산에서 나오는 가스를 모으는 거예요?
여: 맞아요. 그것으로 인근 가정에 난방을 해요.
남: 모든 것이 매우 자연스럽고 깨끗하게 보이는군요.
여: 하지만 우리는 실제로 쓰레기 위를 걷고 있답니다.
남: ______________________________

어휘 **turn up the heat** (실내) 온도를 높이다 ***cf.*** **heat** 온도, 열; ~을 따뜻하게 만들다 / **litter** 쓰레기를 버리다 / **relaxing** 긴장을 풀어주는 / **dirt** 흙 / **plant** ~을 심다 / **break down** 분해되다

14 긴 대화에 이어질 응답 | ④

▶ 세 개의 문 중 하나의 문에만 상품이 있다. 여자가 선택하지 않은 문에서 염소가 나왔으므로, 여전히 상품을 탈 기회가 있는 여자의 응답으로 적절한 것을 고른다.

① 괜찮아요. 아버지께서 농장을 가지고 계세요.
② 와! 잘됐어요! 제가 차를 탔네요!
③ 아, 이런! 염소로 뭘 할 수 있겠어요?
④ 휴! 잘됐어요! 제겐 여전히 기회가 있어요.
⑤ 좋지 않네요. 다른 문을 빨리 열어 봐요.

M: You've defeated the others in the quiz round of our show. Now you're ready to enter **a challenge for the grand prize**, a new car!
W: Oh, this is so exciting! I really want to win the new car.
M: Let me explain how to play. Sharon, there are three doors.
W: Yes, I know.
M: There is a new car behind one door. There are **goats behind the other two doors**.
W: I know. I don't want a goat!
M: Well, choose your door.
W: I'll take door no. 3.
M: Sharon, I'll open door no. 2 first instead of door no. 3. **Is it the car**? *[pause]* No, it's a goat!
W: ______________________________

남: 당신은 우리 방송의 퀴즈 시합에서 나머지 분들을 모두 이기셨습니다. 이제 대상(大賞)인 새 차를 받기 위해 도전하실 준비가 되었군요!
여: 아, 정말 흥분돼요! 새 차를 정말 받고 싶어요.
남: 어떻게 하면 될지 알려드리겠습니다. Sharon 씨, 세 개의 문이 있습니다.
여: 네, 알고 있어요.
남: 하나의 문 뒤에 새 차가 있습니다. 다른 두 개의 문 뒤에는 염소가 있습니다.
여: 알아요. 염소는 필요 없어요!
남: 그럼, 문을 선택하세요.
여: 3번 문으로 하겠습니다.
남: Sharon 씨, 3번 문 대신 2번 문을 먼저 열겠습니다. 이것은 차일까요? *[잠시 후]* 아닙니다. 염소군요!
여: ______________________________

어휘 **defeat** ~을 이기다[패배시키다] / **round** 한 경기, 시합의 한 판

15 상황에 적절한 말 | ③

▶ 주제에서 벗어난 발표를 하고 있는 Sally에게 할 말이 답으로 적절하다.

① 나도 영국을 방문한 적이 한 번 있어.
② 잘했어, Sally. 고마워.
③ 발표 주제에 관해서 계속해 주겠니?
④ 런던을 떠난 후에 어디로 갔니?
⑤ 좀 천천히 말해줄 수 있겠니?

M: Mr. Jones is a teacher at a high school. One of his students, Sally, is giving a presentation. Her presentation is on World War Ⅱ. She is talking about how the people in Britain **survived the bombing** by the Germans. She says that London was bombed particularly hard. Then she says that her family visited London last year. And she talks on and on about **what her family saw**, where they stayed and what they ate. Mr. Jones knows Sally **has gone off the topic**. He wants her to get back to her presentation. **He is getting irritated**. In this situation, what would Mr. Jones most likely say to Sally?

남: Jones 선생님은 고등학교 교사이다. 그의 학생 중 한 명인 Sally가 발표를 하고 있다. 그녀의 발표는 2차 세계대전에 관한 것이다. 그녀는 영국 사람들이 독일의 폭격에서 어떻게 살아남았는지 이야기하고 있다. 그녀는 런던이 특히 맹렬한 폭격을 받았다고 말한다. 그런 다음 자신의 가족이 작년에 런던을 방문했다고 말한다. 그리고 가족이 무엇을 보았는지, 어디서 묵었는지, 무엇을 먹었는지에 대해 계속해서 이야기한다. Jones 선생님은 Sally가 주제에서 벗어났다는 것을 안다. 선생님은 Sally가 그녀의 발표로 다시 돌아오기를 바란다. 선생님은 점점 언짢아진다. 이러한 상황에서 Jones 선생님이 Sally에게 할 말로 가장 적절한 것은 무엇인가?

어휘 **get on with** (특히 중단했다가) ~을 계속하다 / **pace** 속도; 보폭 / **bombing** 폭격 ***cf.*** **bomb** ~을 폭격하다 / **irritated** 짜증이 난, 화가 난

16~17 세트 문항 | 16. ④ 17. ⑤

▶ 16. 변화하는 환경에 가까스로 성공적으로 적응하고 있는 몇몇 동물들을 소개하겠다고 말한 뒤 적응 중인 동물들과 적응 방법을 차례대로 말하고 있다.

① 동물들이 진화하는 속도
② 따뜻해진 지구에서 살아남는 방법들
③ 지구온난화가 동물들에게 미치는 이점들
④ 기후 변화에 적응하고 있는 다양한 종들
⑤ 동물들이 기후 변화에 적응하도록 돕는 방법

▶ 17. 해석 참조

① 북극곰 ② 앵무새 ③ 부엉이 ④ 모기 ⑤ 해파리

W: Good morning, class. As you know, we've been discussing climate change by talking about the animals **most affected by global warming**, such as the polar bear. Today, we'll continue by introducing a few animals that are **managing to adapt successfully** to their changing environments. For example, some parrots living in Australia are growing larger wings to adapt to climate change. Larger wings allow the birds to release more heat from their bodies. This **enables them to survive** in warmer temperatures. A European owl is another adapting species. As less and less snow falls in Europe, more brown owls and fewer white owls are being seen. This is because white is no longer a useful color for hiding when there isn't snow. Unfortunately for us, the mosquitos of North America are also adapting. As the winters get shorter and shorter, their active season is **becoming longer and longer**. This gives them more time to breed and grow. How might other animals adapt to the changing climate?

여: 안녕하세요, 학생 여러분. 여러분도 알다시피, 우리는 ① 북극곰과 같이 지구 온난화에 가장 영향을 받는 동물들에 관해 이야기하며 기후 변화를 논의해 오고 있습니다. 오늘은 변화하는 환경에 가까스로 성공적으로 적응하고 있는 몇몇 동물들을 소개하는 것으로 계속하겠습니다. 예를 들어, 호주에 사는 일부 ② 앵무새들은 기후 변화에 적응하기 위해 날개가 점점 커지고 있습니다. 더 큰 날개는 그 새들이 자신의 몸에서 더 많은 열을 방출하도록 해 줍니다. 이는 그들이 더 따뜻한 기후에서 살아남는 것을 가능하게 합니다. ③ 유럽 부엉이는 (기후에) 적응하고 있는 또 다른 종입니다. 유럽에 눈이 점점 더 적게 내리면서, 갈색 부엉이는 더 많이, 흰색 부엉이는 더 적게 목격되고 있습니다. 이는 눈이 없다면, 흰색이 더는 숨기에 유용한 색이 아니기 때문입니다. 우리에게는 불행히도, 북아메리카 대륙의 ④ 모기들 또한 적응하고 있습니다. 겨울이 점점 더 짧아지면서, 모기의 활동 시기는 점점 더 길어지고 있습니다. 이는 모기가 번식하고 성장하는 데 더 많은 시간을 제공합니다. 그 밖의 동물들은 변화하는 기후에 어떻게 적응할까요?

어휘 **evolve** 진화하다; (점진적으로) 발전하다 / **species** (분류상의) 종(種) / **adapt** 적응[순응]하다; 조정하다; 각색(하다) / **adjust to A** A에 적응하다 / **jellyfish** 해파리 / **affect** 영향을 미치다 / **manage to-v** 가까스로 v하다 / **release** 방출(하다), 내뿜다; 석방(하다); 발매[개봉](하다) / **owl** 부엉이 / **breed** 번식하다; 품종; 사육[재배]하다

Answers & Explanation

01. ④ 02. ① 03. ① 04. ② 05. ② 06. ① 07. ④ 08. ① 09. ⑤ 10. ④
11. ② 12. ② 13. ⑤ 14. ④ 15. ⑤ 16. ④ 17. ④

01 화자가 하는 말의 목적 | ④

▶ 가족 모두가 화재 발생 시 대책을 알고 있어야 하고 각자의 상황에 맞게 대책을 마련해야 한다는 것이 글의 주요 내용이므로, 이를 종합하면 화재 대책 수립 시 유의사항을 설명하기 위한 것이다.

M: In the event of a fire, many people are not prepared. Therefore, they easily panic. When they **get this strong feeling of fear**, it becomes very hard for them to survive even in a small fire. This is why each and every person in the house must know **how to escape fires** at any time and from any place. For taller apartment buildings, each home should be equipped with a fire-proof rope. This is **to lower oneself safely** to the ground. In homes closer to the ground, a rope ladder may be good enough. You should **have a proper fire plan** for your individual situation. If you don't have a fire plan, call your local fire department for a consultation.

남: 화재가 발생했을 때, 많은 사람은 준비가 되어 있지 않습니다. 그러므로 그들은 쉽게 공황상태가 됩니다. 이런 강한 두려움을 느끼면, 작은 화재에서도 살아남기가 매우 어려워집니다. 이것이 바로 가족 구성원 모두가 언제, 어느 곳에서든 화재에서 벗어나는 방법을 알아야 하는 이유입니다. 고층 아파트의 경우, 각 세대는 불연성 밧줄을 갖추고 있어야 합니다. 이는 땅으로 안전하게 내려오기 위함입니다. 지면에 가까운 집들은, 줄사다리가 있으면 충분할지도 모릅니다. 자신의 개별적인 상황에 맞는 적절한 화재 대책이 있어야 합니다. 화재 대책이 없으시다면, 지역의 소방 부서에 전화하셔서 상담하십시오.

어휘 **panic** 공황을 일으키다, 당황하다 / **equip A with B** A에게 B를 갖추게 하다 / **fire-proof** 불연소성의, 불에 타지 않는 / **consultation** 상담, 자문

02 의견 | ①

▶ 여자는 개를 기르는 것은 많은 노력이 필요하고 개를 기르기 전에 진지하게 고려해야 한다고 말하고 있다.

M: Stephanie, this article says that raising companion animals is great for one's mental and physical health.
W: I've heard that, too.
M: I want to raise a dog. Walking a dog would be great for my health.
W: Raising a dog **is not as easy as you think**. Do you know it takes a great amount of effort and care?
M: I know I would be responsible for **feeding and bathing him**.
W: But you aren't home much because you go on so many business trips. Who's going to look after your dog then?
M: Oh, I heard there are places **that will look after your dog when you're away**.
W: I don't think it's a good idea to leave him too often. You really have to treat them like your kids.
M: Oh, you have a point.
W: You have to **give it serious consideration** before you bring a dog into your life.
M: You're right. I didn't really think this through.

남: Stephanie, 반려동물이 사람의 정신과 신체 건강에 아주 좋다고 이 기사에 나왔네요.
여: 나도 그걸 들었어요.
남: 나는 개를 기르고 싶어요. 개를 산보시키는 건 내 건강에 아주 좋을 거예요.
여: 개를 기르는 건 당신 생각처럼 쉬운 게 아니에요. 많은 노력과 돌봄을 필요로 한다는 것을 알고 있나요?
남: 개를 먹이고 목욕시키는 데 책임을 져야 할 거라는 점은 알아요.
여: 하지만 당신은 출장을 많이 가기 때문에 집에 오래 있지 않잖아요. 그때 누가 당신 개를 돌보죠?
남: 아, 부재중일 때 개를 맡아주는 곳이 있다고 들었어요.
여: 개를 너무 자주 두고 가는 건 좋은 생각이 아닌 것 같아요. 정말로 개들을 자식처럼 대우해야 해요.
남: 아, 당신 말이 일리가 있어요.
여: 개를 당신 삶에 끌어들이기 전에 그 점을 진지하게 고려해야 해요.
남: 맞아요. 그 점을 충분히 생각하지 않았어요.

어휘 **companion animal** 반려동물 / **you have a point** 당신 말이 맞아요 / **consideration** 고려 / **think through** 충분히 생각하다

03 관계 | ①

▶ 협진을 하고 수술도 같이 하기로 결정한 것으로 보아 의사 간의 대화이다.

M: Linda, I'd like you to take a look at this X-ray.
W: Oh my, Bob. **That bone is broken in three places**. Where is the patient?
M: He's lying on bed number five. He crashed his motorcycle while delivering food.
W: That's terrible. What have you decided to do?
M: That's the reason I asked you to look at it. What do you think is the best treatment?
W: I think surgery is not necessary, but it will **speed up the healing**.
M: I agree with your opinion. **Will you assist me**?
W: That will be fine. Let me tell my assistant that I will be busy for the next several hours.
M: Great. I'm glad **I can count on you**.
W: You go tell the patient, and I'll meet you downstairs for the operation.

남: Linda, 이 엑스레이를 좀 살펴봐 주었으면 해요.
여: 이런, Bob. 저 뼈는 세 군데가 부러졌어요. 환자는 어디에 있어요?
남: 5번 침대에 누워 있어요. 음식을 배달하다가 자신의 오토바이로 충돌사고를 냈어요.
여: 안됐네요. 당신은 어떻게 하기로 결정했나요?
남: 그것 때문에 당신에게 이걸 봐 달라고 부탁한 거예요. 가장 좋은 치료법이 뭐라고 생각하세요?
여: 수술이 반드시 필요하지는 않지만, 수술을 하면 회복이 빨라질 거라고 생각해요.
남: 당신 의견에 동의해요. 저를 도와주시겠어요?
여: 좋습니다. 제 조수에게 앞으로 몇 시간 동안 제가 바쁠 거라고 말할게요.
남: 잘됐네요. 당신에게 의지할 수 있어서 기뻐요.
여: 당신은 환자에게 가서 알리시고 저는 수술을 위해 아래층에서 뵙지요.

어휘 **assist** (~을) 돕다, 거들어주다 ***cf.* assistant** 조수, 보조 / **count on** ~에 의지하다, 기대다

04 그림 불일치 | ②

▶ 티백은 커피포트 바로 옆 정사각형 접시 위에 놓는다고 했다.

W: Next, I'll show you how to prepare the tables in the guest rooms.
M: Okay. I can see that the black coffeepot **goes on the left**.
W: Yes, please try and remember that, as it is **our hotel's policy to do so**.
M: I think I can handle that. Also, the tea bags go on a square-shaped plate just next to the coffeepot.
W: Right. Then, next to that, we place two mugs that can **be used for drinks**.
M: Okay, so the mugs, and then a magazine next to them?
W: No, please put the notepad and pen in between the mugs and the magazine.
M: All right. **I think I've got it**.
W: Great. I think you are going to do well here.

여: 다음으로, 객실에 있는 탁자를 정리하는 방법을 보여줄게요.
남: 네. 검은색 커피포트는 왼쪽에 놓이는 것을 알 수 있겠네요.
여: 그래요. 그렇게 하는 것이 우리 호텔의 방침이니 해보고 기억하세요.
남: 할 수 있을 것 같아요. 또, 커피포트 바로 옆 정사각형 접시 위에 티백을 놓는군요.
여: 맞아요. 그리고는 그 옆에, 음료를 마실 때 사용할 수 있도록 머그잔 두 개를 놓아요.
남: 그렇군요. 그럼 머그잔, 그러고 나서 그 옆에 잡지인가요?
여: 아니요, 머그잔과 잡지 사이에 메모지와 펜을 두세요.
남: 알겠습니다. 이해한 것 같아요.
여: 좋습니다. 당신 여기에서 잘할 것 같군요.

어휘 **notepad** (한 장씩 떼어 쓰게 된) 메모지

05 추후 행동 | ②

▶ 여자(딸)와 함께 쇼핑을 가기로 했던 엄마가 갈 수 없게 되자, 남자(아빠)가 대신 가주겠다고 했다.

M: Why are you in such a hurry, Nicole?
W: I need to go to the mall **to buy a suit for my job interview**, Dad.
M: I heard your mother was going to take you. Where is she?
W: She just called me and said her meeting **would end much later than expected**.
M: Really? I hope it doesn't finish too late. It's already 7 p.m.
W: I'm so sad that she can't go shopping with me. **She knows what fits me best**.
M: Then, do you want me to accompany you instead? **Not as much as your mother**, but I can be helpful.
W: That would be great. Thanks, Dad.
M: I'll get the car keys. **It will be quicker than taking the bus**.
W: OK. I'll wait for you.

남: 왜 그렇게 서두르니, Nicole?
여: 구직 면접에 입을 정장을 사러 쇼핑몰에 가야 해요, 아빠.
남: 네 엄마가 널 데려갈 거라고 들었는데. 엄마는 어디 계시니?
여: 엄마가 방금 전화하셔서 회의가 예상했던 것보다 훨씬 더 늦게 끝날 거라고 하셨어요.
남: 그래? 너무 늦게 끝나진 않았으면 좋겠구나. 벌써 오후 7시야.
여: 엄마가 저와 쇼핑하러 가실 수 없다는 게 너무 아쉬워요. 엄마는 어떤 게 저한테 제일 잘 어울리는지 아시거든요.
남: 그럼, 내가 대신 너와 함께 가 줄까? 네 엄마만큼은 아니겠지만, 나도 도움이 될 수 있단다.
여: 그러면 좋겠어요. 고마워요, 아빠.
남: 차 열쇠를 가져오마. 버스를 타는 것보다 더 빠를 거야.
여: 알겠어요. 기다릴게요.

어휘 **accompany** (사람과) 동반하다, 동행하다; (일·현상 등이) 동반되다[딸리다]

06 금액 | ①

▶ 초급자의 1개월 수강료는 160달러이고 친구와 함께 등록 시 10달러씩 할인을 받는다. 남자는 친구의 수강료를 함께 지불하고자 하므로 320달러(2인)에서 각각 10달러의 할인(20달러)을 적용하면 지불할 금액은 총 300달러이다.

W: Welcome to Susan's Calligraphy School. How may I help you?
M: Hello, I'd like to sign up for a calligraphy class. **What do you have available**?
W: We have a beginner class and an advanced class.
M: How much are the class fees?
W: It costs $160 a month for beginners and $180 a month for advanced students.
M: I should take a beginner's class since I'm a beginner. What day is the beginner's class?
W: The class **meets once a week**, on Fridays from 7 p.m. to 9 p.m.
M: That's perfect. I want to enroll with my friend. Is there a discount available?
W: Sure. If **you bring a friend to the class**, both of you get a $10 discount each.
M: That sounds great. Then both my friend and I **will sign up for** the beginner's class. I'll pay for the two of us now.
W: All right. If you pay for 3 months in advance, you can receive an additional 10% discount.
M: Thank you, but we'll start with one month.
W: Okay.

여: Susan의 캘리그래피 학교에 온 것을 환영합니다. 무엇을 도와드릴까요?
남: 안녕하세요. 저는 캘리그래피 수업을 등록하고 싶은데요. 어떤 것이 이용 가능하나요?
여: 저희는 초급자 수업과 상급자 수업이 있습니다.
남: 수업료가 얼마인가요?
여: 초급자를 위한 수업은 한 달에 160달러이고 상급 학생을 위한 것은 한 달에 180달러입니다.
남: 저는 초급자니까 초급자 수업을 들어야겠네요. 초급자 수업은 무슨 요일에 있나요?
여: 그 수업은 일주일에 한 번, 금요일마다 오후 7시부터 9시까지 만납니다.
남: 완벽해요. 저는 제 친구와 함께 등록하고 싶어요. 할인을 받을 수 있나요?
여: 물론이죠. 만약 수업에 친구를 데려오면, 여러분 둘 다 각각 10달러의 할인을 받습니다.
남: 좋아요. 그러면 제 친구와 저 둘 다 초급자 수업을 등록할게요. 제가 지금 저희 둘의 수업료를 지불할게요.
여: 좋습니다. 3개월분을 미리 지불하시면, 추가로 10퍼센트 할인을 받으실 수 있습니다.
남: 감사하지만, 저희는 1개월로 시작할게요.
여: 알겠습니다.

어휘 **calligraphy** 캘리그래피; 서예 / **sign up for** ~을 등록[가입]하다 / **advanced** 상급[고급]의; 선진의 / **enroll** 등록하다; 명부에 올리다 / **in advance** 미리; 선금으로 / **additional** 추가의

07 이유 | ④

▶ 여자는 친구인 Hannah가 헬스클럽에서 함께 운동하자고 물어봐서 요가 대신 헬스클럽에 다니기로 했다.

W: I'm going to work out, Dad. I'll be back before dinner.
M: You aren't going to jog in this rain, are you?
W: Of course not! **I signed up for the fitness center** across the street. Didn't I tell you?
M: I don't remember hearing anything about it, but didn't you want to do yoga before?
W: Yes, but Hannah **asked me to exercise with her** at the fitness center, so I decided to go to the fitness center instead.
M: Oh, it's great that you have a friend to exercise with.
W: I agree. It's really **helping my motivation**.
M: Well, have fun. And please let me know if they **are offering any discounts**. I also need to find a new gym.
W: Sure, Dad. I will.

여: 저 운동하러 가요, 아빠. 저녁 식사 전엔 돌아올 거예요.
남: 이 빗속에 조깅하러 가는 건 아니지, 그렇지?
여: 당연히 아니죠! 길 건너편에 있는 헬스클럽에 등록했어요. 제가 말씀 안 드렸나요?
남: 들은 기억이 없구나. 그런데 전에 요가를 하고 싶어 하지 않았니?
여: 네, 하지만 Hannah가 헬스클럽에서 함께 운동하자고 물어봐서, 대신 헬스클럽에 다니기로 결정했어요.
남: 아, 함께 운동할 친구가 있어서 다행이구나.
여: 맞아요. 동기 부여에 정말 도움이 되고 있어요.
남: 음, 잘 다녀오렴. 그리고 거기서 할인을 하고 있는지 내게 알려주렴. 나도 새로운 헬스클럽을 찾아야 하거든.
여: 물론이죠, 아빠. 그럴게요.

어휘 **work out** 운동하다 / **motivation** 동기 부여; 자극

08 언급하지 않은 것 | ①

▶ 해석 참조

M: Hello. I can answer any questions for you about the meerkat exhibit.
W: Great. It's fun to **watch them interact as a group**. Also, that one standing on two feet is really cute.
M: Right now, the others are looking for food. The one that is standing **is watching for danger**.
W: That's a really clever way for them to protect each other. Oh, look, that one just caught a small snake.
M: Yes, they eat many things including insects, reptiles, and even scorpions.
W: And all of these meerkats were brought from South Africa?
M: That's correct. South Africa is **their natural habitat**.
W: I see. How large is a typical adult?
M: Meerkats grow to be 25 to 35 centimeters. And they typically **live for 5 to 15 years**.

남: 안녕하세요. 미어캣 전시에 관해서 어떤 질문에도 답변해 드릴 수 있습니다.
여: 잘됐네요. 무리지어 교류하는 걸 보는 게 재미있어요. 또, 두 발로 서 있는 저건 정말 귀여워요.
남: 지금은 나머지가 먹이를 찾고 있습니다. 서 있는 한 마리는 위험을 경계하고 있는 거죠.
여: 서로를 보호하는 아주 현명한 방법이네요. 아, 보세요, 저게 방금 작은 뱀을 잡았어요.
남: 네, 그것들은 곤충, 파충류, 심지어 전갈까지 포함해 많은 것을 먹어요(② 먹이 습성).
여: 그리고 이 미어캣들은 모두 남아프리카에서 왔나요?
남: 맞습니다. 남아프리카가 자연 서식지(③ 서식지)예요.
여: 그렇군요. 다 자란 것은 보통 얼마나 큰가요?
남: 미어캣은 25에서 35센티미터까지 자랍니다(④ 몸 크기). 그리고 보통 5년에서 15년을 살아요(⑤ 평균 수명).

어휘 **interact** 교류하다; 상호 작용하다 / **scorpion** 전갈 / **habitat** 서식지

09 내용 불일치 | ⑤

▶ 수익의 일부를 기부할 것이라고 말했다.

W: In Cambodia, temples are being damaged by tourists. And throughout the world, **tourists are damaging the environment** they came to see. Ecotours is a different kind of travel company. We pledge to preserve the environment. Our company also **promises to help local people**. Too often, travel companies don't help the local people. So we promise to employ locals to run our trips. And our customers will stay in lodges and hotels owned by locals, too. Finally, we pledge to donate money to conservation activities in the countries **we run tours in**. For example, in Costa Rica, we will donate a percentage of profits **to help endangered birds**.

여: 캄보디아에서는 사원들이 관광객에 의해 파괴되고 있습니다. 그리고 세계 도처에서 관광객은 자신들이 보러 온 환경을 파괴하고 있습니다. Ecotours는 (그와) 다른 종류의 여행사입니다. 우리는 환경을 보호할 것을 서약합니다. 우리 회사는 또한 지역민을 도울 것을 약속합니다. 너무 자주, 여행사들은 지역민을 돕지 않습니다. 그래서 우리는 여행 상품을 운영하는 데 지역민을 고용할 것을 약속합니다. 또한 우리 고객들은 지역민이 소유하고 있는 여관과 호텔에 투숙할 것입니다. 마지막으로 우리가 여행 상품을 운영하는 나라에서의 보호 활동들에 돈을 기부할 것을 서약합니다. 예를 들어, 코스타리카에서 우리는 멸종위기에 처한 새들을 돕기 위해 수익의 일부를 기부할 것입니다.

어휘 **throughout** 도처에 / **pledge** ~을 서약하다 / **local** 지역의; 현지인, 주민 / **lodge** 여관 / **conservation** (자연) 보호, (자원) 보존 / **percentage** 수익의 일부; 백분율, 비율 / **endangered** 멸종 위기에 처한

10 도표 이해 | ④

▶ 100개 넘는 좌석이 있고 대여료가 1000달러가 넘지 않아야 하며 실내 음식 조달이 가능하고 주차가 가능한 두 곳 중에서 더 저렴한 곳을 택했으므로 답은 ④이다.

W: Noah, could you **help me choose a place for** our annual conference next month?
M: Sure. I know a nice website that will help us find a conference venue. *[Typing sound]* Look here.
W: Wow! Thanks. First, we have to think about the size of the venue.
M: **How many people have applied for** the conference?
W: So far 96 people have applied and we're expecting about 120 people.
M: Okay. Then it should have more than 100 seats. Next, what is our budget range for the venue rental?
W: We **can't afford to spend** more than $1,000.
M: All right. And we should think about dining.
W: Of course. I'd like a place where indoor catering is possible in case of rain.
M: We have these two options, then. Both of these places provide parking, so you can choose between them. **Which one would you like**?
W: Of course we should choose the cheaper place.
M: Then this one is perfect for us.

여: Noah, 제가 다음 달 우리의 연례 회의를 위한 장소를 고르는 것을 도와줄 수 있나요?
남: 물론이죠. 우리가 회의 장소를 찾는 것을 도와줄 좋은 웹사이트를 알아요. *[타자치는 소리]* 여기 봐요.
여: 와! 고마워요. 첫째로 우리는 장소의 크기에 대해 생각해야 해요.
남: 회의에 얼마나 많은 사람이 신청했나요?
여: 지금까지 96명의 사람들이 신청했는데 우리는 120명 정도 예상하고 있어요.
남: 알겠어요. 그러면 100개 넘는 좌석이 있어야 하겠네요. 다음으로 장소 대여를 위한 우리 예산 범위가 어떻게 되죠?
여: 우리는 1,000달러 넘게 쓸 여유는 없어요.
남: 좋아요. 그리고 우리는 정찬에 대해 생각해 봐야 해요.
여: 물론이죠. 저는 비가 올 경우에 실내 음식 조달이 가능한 장소면 좋겠어요.
남: 그러면 우리에게 두 가지 선택할 수 있는 것이 있어요. 이 두 장소들은 주차 공간을 제공해서 우리는 그것들 중 선택하면 돼요. 당신은 어느 곳이 좋아요?
여: 물론 우리는 더 저렴한 장소를 선택해야 해요.
남: 그러면 이 장소가 우리에게 완벽하네요.

어휘 **conference** 회의; 회담 / **venue** 장소 / **rental** 대여; 사용(료) / **dining** 정찬, 식사 / **indoor** 실내(용)의 / **catering** (행사에) 음식 조달 / **council chamber** 회의실 / **annual** 연간의; 1년을 주기로 하는 / **apply for** ~에 신청[지원]하다 / **budget** 예산; 비용

11 짧은 대화에 이어질 응답 | ②

▶ 어떤 종류의 음악을 좋아하느냐는 여자의 질문에 가장 적절한 응답을 고른다.

① 나는 라디오 듣는 것을 좋아해.
② 나는 기악곡을 더 좋아해.
③ 그의 공연은 매우 즐거웠어.
④ DJ Antonie의 음악은 힙합이 아니야.
⑤ 나는 그 콘서트가 기대돼.

W: **Do you want to come with me** to see DJ Antonie's performance?
M: Thanks, but I don't really like hip hop.
W: Then **what kind of music** do you enjoy?
M: ____________________

여: 나랑 같이 DJ Antonie의 공연을 보러 갈래?
남: 고맙지만, 난 힙합은 별로 안 좋아해.
여: 그럼 어떤 종류의 음악을 즐기니?
남: ____________________

어휘 **instrumental music** 기악(곡)

12 짧은 대화에 이어질 응답 | ②

▶ 자신이 고른 책보다 더 좋은 책을 추천해달라는 남자의 질문에 가장 적절한 응답을 찾는다.

① 나도 그에게 선물을 사줘야겠어요.
② Kevin Smith의 책이 굉장해요.
③ 죄송합니다만, 그녀의 책은 품절되었어요.
④ 그 책을 온라인으로 구매하는 게 나을 거예요.
⑤ 무엇을 사다주든지 그는 고마워할 거예요.

M: I'm thinking of getting this Mary Clark book for my brother. What do you think?
W: In my opinion, **her books are overrated**.
M: Then could you recommend something better?
W: ____________________

남: 남동생에게 Mary Clark이 쓴 이 책을 사 줄 생각이에요. 어떻게 생각하세요?
여: 제 생각에 그녀의 책은 과대평가되었어요.
남: 그럼 더 좋은 것을 추천해주시겠어요?
여: ____________________

어휘 **overrate** ~을 과대평가하다

13 긴 대화에 이어질 응답 | ⑤

▶ 여자가 휴가를 떠나 있을 동안 신문 배달중지를 요구했으므로 그에 대한 적절한 응답이 필요하다.

① 곧 좋아지시기를 바랍니다.
② 떠나시기 전에 대금을 보내 주십시오.
③ 그 날짜에 배달을 시작하겠습니다.
④ 제가 당신의 새 주소를 그들에게 알려주겠습니다.
⑤ 제가 배달원에게 즉시 알리겠습니다.

[Phone rings.]
M: Hello. This is Daily News. How may I help you?
W: I'm going on vacation for a month, but I don't want to **waste all those newspapers**.
M: Well, we can stop delivery for you, if you would like.
W: **Will it cost anything to do that**?
M: No. We will also **stop charging you for the time** when you are gone.
W: Great. What do I have to do?
M: Just give me your name and address.
W: My name is Lucinda Williams and I live at 722 Fremont Avenue.
M: And **when are you going on vacation**?
W: I am leaving next Friday, the 10th.
M: ____________________

[전화벨이 울린다.]
남: 여보세요. Daily News입니다. 무엇을 도와 드릴까요?
여: 제가 한 달 동안 휴가를 갈 예정입니다만, (그 동안) 신문을 모두 낭비하고 싶지 않아서요.
남: 그럼, 원하신다면 신문 배달을 중지해 드릴 수 있습니다.
여: 그렇게 하는 데 비용이 듭니까?

남: 아닙니다. 또, 안 계시는 기간 동안은 신문 요금을 부과하지 않을 것입니다.
여: 좋아요. 제가 무엇을 해야 됩니까?
남: 제게 성함과 주소를 가르쳐 주세요.
여: 제 이름은 Lucinda Williams이고 Fremont가 722번지에 삽니다.
남: 그리고 언제 휴가를 떠나십니까?
여: 다음 주 금요일, 10일에 떠납니다.
남: ______________________________

어휘 **payment** 대금, 지불금; 지불, 납입

14 긴 대화에 이어질 응답 | ④

▶ 영화를 같이 볼 것을 제안하고 있는 여자가 용돈을 다 써 버려 영화표를 살 수 없는 남자에게 할 수 있는 말을 유추해 본다.

① 누가 이것을 깼는지 아니? ② 너는 왜 그렇게 긴 휴가가 필요하니?
③ 너는 은행에 빚을 갚아야 해. ④ 내가 너에게 돈을 좀 빌려 줄까?
⑤ 너의 어머니께서 너에게 돈을 얼마나 주신 거니?

W: Hi, Sean. What's up?
M: Nothing really. **I've just been hanging out** in the mall all afternoon.
W: By yourself?
M: No, with Cole and Claire. **They've just left**. They're going to a movie at the theater in the mall.
W: That's where I am going. **Why don't you join me**? I want to see *Save Oscar*.
M: I can't.
W: Are you busy? Homework?
M: No, I've done all my homework for this weekend.
W: Well then, come on. Let's go.
M: Mia, I can't. **I spent all my allowance** on my new books yesterday.
W: Oh, that's the problem.
M: Yeah. **I'm broke**.
W: ______________________________

여: 안녕, Sean. 웬일이야?
남: 뭐 특별한 것은 없어. 난 그냥 오후 내내 이 쇼핑몰에서 놀고 있었어.
여: 혼자서?
남: 아니, Cole과 Claire랑 함께. 그 애들은 방금 떠났어. 쇼핑몰에 있는 극장에서 영화를 볼 거래.
여: 나도 거기로 가는 중이야. 같이 가지 않을래? 난 〈Save Oscar〉를 보고 싶거든.
남: 난 못 가.
여: 바쁘니? 숙제라도 있어?
남: 아니, 이번 주말에 하려던 숙제를 모두 해 뒀어.
여: 그럼, 자, 같이 가자.
남: Mia, 난 갈 수가 없어. 어제 새 책을 사느라 용돈을 다 써버렸거든.
여: 아, 그게 문제구나.
남: 응, 나는 파산 상태야.
여: ______________________________

어휘 **repay** ~에게 돈을 갚다, 보답하다 / **debt** 빚, 부채 / **hang out** (사람들과) 시간을 보내다 / **allowance** 용돈 / **be broke** 파산하다, 무일푼이다

15 상황에 적절한 말 | ⑤

▶ Robert는 정직이 최선의 정책이라고 생각하고 있으므로, Sandra에게 정직하게 상황을 설명할 것이다.

① 내가 없어도 이 모임은 괜찮을 거야.
② 나 대신 발표 내용을 좀 써줄 수 있니?
③ 나는 더는 이 공부 모임의 일원일 수 없어.
④ 우리 부모님이 나를 다른 학교로 전학시키실 거야.
⑤ 가족에게 급한 일이 생겨서 공부를 할 수 없었어.

M: Robert has agreed to join Sandra's study group. Each week, a different member of the study group presents a topic that they are currently studying in class and teaches the rest of the group. This week, **he is expected to tell** the rest of the group about photosynthesis in plants. However, during the weekend, his grandmother **got sick** and he had to leave town with his parents to visit her in the hospital. At the time, he was too worried about his grandmother to remember to take along his book, so **he didn't get the work done**. He has always thought that **honesty is the best policy**. In this situation, what would Robert most likely say to Sandra?

남: Robert는 Sandra의 공부 모임에 가입하는 것에 동의했다. 매주, 공부 모임의 회원 한 명이 현재 수업시간에 공부하고 있는 주제에 대해 발표를 하고 모임의 나머지 친구들을 가르친다. 이번 주, 그는 모임의 친구들에게 식물의 광합성에 대해 설명하기로 예정되어 있다. 그러나 주말 동안, 할머니가 편찮으셔서, 그는 부모님과 함께 도시를 떠나 병원에 계시는 할머니의 문병을 가야 했다. 그때 그는 할머니가 너무 걱정되어서 책을 가져가는 것을 잊어버려, 공부를 하지 못했다. 그는 정직이 최선의 방책이라고 항상 생각해왔다. 이러한 상황에서 Robert가 Sandra에게 할 말로 가장 적절한 것은 무엇인가?

어휘 **currently** 현재, 지금 / **photosynthesis** 광합성

16~17 세트 문항 | 16. ④ 17. ④

▶ 16. 2100년까지 소멸할 것으로 예상되는 언어로 아이누어와 만주어를 언급하고 있다.

① 연구되어야 할 고대 언어 목록
② 언어가 보전할 가치가 있는 이유
③ 문화와 사회에 미치는 언어의 본질적인 영향
④ 이번 세기 말까지 사라질지도 모르는 언어들
⑤ 멸종 위기에 처한 언어들을 지키기 위한 다양한 방법들

▶ 17. 해석 참조

W: Experts estimate that only 50% of the languages that are alive today will be spoken by the year 2100. **The disappearance of a language** means the loss of valuable scientific and cultural information. So, I'd like to discuss **a few of the endangered languages** today. The Ainu language is spoken by members of the Ainu ethnic group on the Japanese island of Hokkaido. However, most of the ethnic Ainu in Japan speak only Japanese now. There are **only around 100 speakers left**, out of which only 15 use the language every day. Another endangered language is the Manchu language spoken in Northeast China. Out of nearly 10 million Manchu people, there are **less than 70 native speakers** of the Manchu language. And even those who speak Manchu only use it in specific circumstances, such as ceremonies, proverbs, or songs. Most Manchu **prefer to use** Mandarin Chinese in all situations. **As is the case with** most endangered languages, Manchu is being abandoned for languages spoken by wealthier people.

여: 전문가들은 2100년이 되면 오늘날 존속하는 언어 중 50%만이 구사될 것으로 추정합니다. 언어의 소멸은 귀중한 과학 및 문화 정보의 손실을 의미합니다. 그래서 오늘은 사라질 위기에 처한 몇몇 언어에 관해 논하고자 합니다. 아이누어는 일본 홋카이도 섬에 사는 아이누족 구성원들에 의해 구사됩니다. 하지만 일본에 있는 아이누족 대부분은 현재 일본어만 사용합니다. 언어 사용자가 약 100명 정도만 남아 있지만, 그중에서도 15명만이 그 언어를 매일 사용합니다. 소멸위기에 처한 또 다른 언어는 중국 북동부(① 사용되는 지역)에서 구사되는 만주어입니다. 거의 1천만 명에 이르는 만주 사람 중 만주어 원어민은 70명이 채 되지 않습니다(② 구사하는 사람 수). 그리고 만주어를 구사하는 사람들마저도 의식이나 속담, 노래와 같은 특정 상황(③ 사용되는 상황)에서만 만주어를 사용합니다. 만주인 대부분은 매사에 표준 중국어 사용을 선호합니다. 소멸위기에 처한 언어 대부분이 그렇듯, 만주어는 더 부유한 사람들이 구사하는 언어 때문에 버림받고 있습니다(⑤ 쇠퇴 이유).

어휘 **endangered** 멸종 위기에 처한 / **estimate** ~을 추정[추산]하다 / **ethnic** 민족[종족]의 / **circumstance** 상황, 환경 / **Mandarin Chinese** 표준 중국어

Answers & Explanation

01. ④ 02. ② 03. ① 04. ③ 05. ③ 06. ② 07. ④ 08. ① 09. ⑤ 10. ④
11. ⑤ 12. ③ 13. ④ 14. ③ 15. ③ 16. ③ 17. ②

01 화자가 하는 말의 목적 | ④

▶ 남자의 말의 목적은 If enough people say no to second-hand smoke, smoking itself will become a thing of the past.에서 명확히 나타나 있다.

M: Every year, more than 10 million people die from illnesses related to smoking. Whether it is lung cancer, or **other diseases related to breathing**, they can be avoided simply by not smoking and avoiding being around those who do smoke. Second-hand smoke **causes almost as many deaths as smoking itself**. Until more laws are passed to protect the lungs of non-smokers, children and **even unborn babies**, the best choice is to stay away. If enough people say no to second-hand smoke, smoking itself will become a thing of the past. **Don't become an unknowing victim of smoking**.

남: 매년 천만 명이 넘는 사람이 흡연과 관련된 질병으로 사망합니다. 그것이 폐암이든 호흡과 관련된 다른 질병이든 간에, 단지 흡연을 하지 않는다거나 담배를 피우는 사람의 주위에 있지 않는 것만으로도 그런 병들을 피할 수 있습니다. 간접흡연은 거의 흡연 자체로 인한 것만큼이나 많이 사망의 원인이 됩니다. 비흡연자와 아이들, 심지어 태어나지도 않은 태아의 폐를 보호하기 위해 더 많은 법안이 통과될 때까지, 최선의 선택은 (흡연자에게서) 떨어져 있는 것입니다. 만약 충분한 사람이 간접흡연을 거절한다면, 흡연 자체는 과거의 일이 될 것입니다. 자신도 모르게 흡연의 희생자가 되지 마십시오.

어휘 **second-hand smoke** 간접흡연 / **unborn** 아직 태어나지 않은 / **unknowing** 자신도 모르는, 알아채지 못하는

02 대화 주제 | ②

▶ 배낭여행에 가져갈 짐을 싸면서 어떤 물품들을 챙겨야 할지 이야기하고 있다.

M: Hi, Gina. What are you doing?
W: I'm trying to pack for our backpacking trip.
M: It looks like you have a good start, but I wouldn't bring those cotton shirts **if I were you**.
W: Oh, really? Why is that?
M: Cotton absorbs sweat and quickly **makes you cold**. Man-made fabrics and wool are better.
W: Okay, I'll trust you about that. Also, I'm bringing **an extra pair of shoes**.
M: That's a great idea. Footwear is the most important thing when hiking. Plus, **don't forget to pack** several pairs of socks.
W: Of course, and I've also purchased some money belts that we can use to safely hide our money.
M: Good thinking. **We don't want to get robbed**.
W: Right. We should always be careful while we're traveling.

남: 안녕, Gina. 뭐 하고 있어?
여: 우리 배낭여행에 가져갈 짐을 싸려는 중이야.
남: 순조롭게 시작하는 것 같긴 하지만, 내가 너라면 그 면 셔츠들은 가져가지 않을 거야.
여: 아, 정말? 왜?
남: 면은 땀을 흡수해서 체온을 빠르게 떨어뜨리거든. 합성 직물과 모직이 나아.
여: 알겠어, 네 말을 믿을게. 그리고 신발도 한 켤레 더 가져갈 거야.
남: 아주 좋은 생각이야. 신발은 하이킹할 때 가장 중요한 거니까. 그리고, 양말 여러 켤레 챙기는 거 잊지 마.
여: 물론이지. 그리고 우리 돈을 안전하게 숨기는 데 쓸 수 있는 전대도 샀어.
남: 잘 생각했네. 도둑맞으면 안 되니까.
여: 맞아. 여행하는 동안에는 항상 조심해야 해.

어휘 **man-made** 합성[인공]의, 사람이 만든 / **money belt** 전대, 돈 숨기는 주머니가 달린 벨트 / **rob** (사람·장소에서[를]) 도둑질하다[털다]

03 관계 | ①

▶ 남자가 최우수 감독상을 수상했고, 잡지에 실을 기사를 위해 여자가 남자를 인터뷰하겠다는 대화 내용으로 보아 영화감독과 잡지 기자의 대화임을 알 수 있다.

[Phone rings.]
M: Hello?
W: Hi. This is Tanya Paulson. How have you been?
M: Great, Ms. Paulson. It's been a while.
W: It has. By the way, **let me congratulate you** on winning the Best Director award for your movie, *Trading Lives*. **You deserved it**!
M: Thank you. I wasn't expecting to win, but it felt great.
W: **As you may have heard**, my magazine, *Hollywood Weekly*, is planning a feature on your movie next month.
M: Yes, and I think **it would be great to write about the scenes** I directed in the desert.
W: Sounds good. And I'd also like to interview you about the script and the actors.
M: That's not a problem. How about Wednesday afternoon?
W: That would be perfect. And we'd like to use still shots from the movie for the article, too.
M: I can **have some sent to you**.
W: Thanks.

[전화벨이 울린다.]
남: 여보세요?
여: 안녕하세요. Tanya Paulson입니다. 어떻게 지내셨어요?
남: 잘 지냈어요, Paulson 씨. 오랜만입니다.
여: 그러네요. 그나저나, 영화 〈생명의 거래〉로 최우수 감독상을 받으신 거 축하드려요. 수상하실 만했죠!
남: 고마워요. 상을 탈 거라고 예상 못 했는데, 기분이 좋았습니다.
여: 들으셨겠지만, 저희 잡지 〈할리우드 위클리〉에서 감독님 영화에 대한 특집기사를 다음 달로 기획하고 있어요.
남: 네, 제가 사막에서 연출했던 장면들에 관해 쓰면 좋겠군요.
여: 좋아요. 그리고 대본과 배우들에 관해서도 감독님과 인터뷰하고 싶습니다.
남: 문제없어요. 수요일 오후가 어떠세요?
여: 아주 좋습니다. 그리고 영화 스틸사진도 기사에 쓰고 싶은데요.
남: 몇 장 보내드릴 수 있어요.
여: 감사합니다.

어휘 **feature** (신문·텔레비전 등의) 특집기사; 특성

04 그림 불일치 | ③

▶ 여자는 선거 포스터에 여자와 남자가 손을 잡고 웃고 있는 사진을 사용했다고 했다.

M: Hi, Nicole. Did you finish our election poster?
W: Yes. I just printed it, so **I can explain some changes to you now**.
M: Okay. What did you change?
W: First, I moved our candidate number **to the upper left corner** like we talked about.
M: Good! What else?
W: Well, the title, "Nicole and Adam for Student Council," is now **in an arch across the top**.
M: Much better. Are the photos back from the studio?
W: Yes. I picked one **where we are smiling hand in hand**.
M: Okay. I like that you put our names and positions in round speech bubbles beside the photo.
W: It looks like we're talking, doesn't it?
M: Exactly. And you didn't forget to show our pledges.
W: Of course not. They are at the bottom in three lines.
M: I think **everything is all set**.

남: 안녕, Nicole. 우리 선거 포스터 마무리했니?
여: 응. 방금 인쇄해서, 이제 몇 가지 바뀐 점을 너에게 설명해 줄 수 있어.
남: 좋아. 뭘 바꿨니?
여: 우선, 우리가 얘기했던 것처럼 후보 번호를 왼쪽 상단 구석으로 옮겼어.
남: 잘했어! 그밖에 다른 것은?
여: 음, 'Nicole과 Adam을 학생회로'라는 타이틀은 이제 포스터 상단을 아치 모양으로 가로지르게 놓여 있어.

남: 훨씬 나은데. 사진은 스튜디오에서 찾아온 거야?
여: 응. 우리가 손을 잡고 웃고 있는 사진으로 골랐어.
남: 좋아. 사진 옆의 동그란 말풍선 안에 우리 이름과 직책을 집어넣은 게 마음에 들어.
여: 우리가 말하고 있는 것처럼 보이지 않니?
남: 맞아. 그리고 우리 공약을 보여주는 것도 잊지 않았구나.
여: 물론이지. 포스터 하단에 세 줄로 집어넣었어.
남: 이제 모든 게 다 된 것 같아.

어휘 **student council** 학생회 / **expand** 확대시키다 / **scholarship** 장학금 / **renovate** 개조하다 / **candidate** 후보자 / **arch** 아치형; 아치형 구조물 / **hand in hand** (두 사람이) 서로 손을 잡고 / **speech bubble** (만화의) 말풍선 / **pledge** 공약, 약속, 맹세

05 추후 행동 | ③

▶ 여러 가지 할 일 중 자동차 배기가스 검사, 비행기 표 인쇄와 Lisa를 발레 강습에서 데려오는 것, 그리고 세탁물 가져오기를 남자가 하기로 했다. 여자가 할 일은 여권사무국에 가서 여권 찾아오는 것이다.

W: There are so many things I have to do before our trip this Friday.
M: I thought **you were caught up with all your chores**. Don't worry. There's nothing to be anxious about. I can help you.
W: I appreciate it. I just got the smog check notice in the mail for our car.
M: **I can handle that**. I can take the car to the repair shop tomorrow after work.
W: That'd be great. Our printer broke down so could you print the flight tickets at your office?
M: Not a problem. By the way, where are you going? Are you going to pick up Lisa from her ballet lesson?
W: No, **I'm going to the passport agency to pick up** the passports. Lisa's lesson will finish at 4. Can you pick her up?
M: Sure. Anything else?
W: One last thing. Since I won't have the car tomorrow, **could you stop by** the dry cleaners and pick up the shirts?
M: No worries. I can take care of that.
W: Thanks for helping me.

여: 이번 금요일 우리 여행 전에 해야 할 일이 아주 많아요.
남: 당신이 모든 집안일에 붙잡혀 있는 것 같군요. 걱정하지 마요. 아무것도 걱정할 게 없어요. 내가 당신을 도울 수 있어요.
여: 고마워요. 난 우리 차 배기가스 검사 공지를 우편으로 막 받았어요.
남: 내가 그것을 처리할 수 있어요. 내일 퇴근 후에 정비소로 차를 가져갈 수 있어요.
여: 그러면 좋겠네요. 우리 프린터가 고장 났는데, 당신 사무실에서 비행기 표를 인쇄해주겠어요?
남: 그럼요. 그런데 어디 가려고요? Lisa를 발레 강습에서 데려오려고요?
여: 아니오, 여권을 받아오려고 여권사무국에 가요. Lisa의 강습은 4시에 끝날 거예요. 당신이 그 애를 데려올 수 있나요?
남: 그럼요. 다른 건 없어요?
여: 마지막 하나요. 내가 내일 차가 없기 때문에, 세탁소에 들러서 셔츠를 가져올 수 있어요?
남: 걱정하지 마요. 내가 그것을 처리할 수 있어요.
여: 도와줘서 고마워요.

어휘 **catch up with** 발목을 잡다 / **chore** 집안일 / **anxious** 염려되는 / **smog check** 배기가스 검사 ***cf.* smog** 연무 ((매연·배기가스가 섞인 안개)), 스모그 / **break down** 고장나다 / **passport agency** 여권국 / **stop by** 들르다

06 금액 | ②

▶ 각각 150달러와 180달러의 새 스케이트를 사지 않고 중고제품을 선택했는데, 금액이 새 스케이트의 50%라고 했으므로, 여자가 지불할 금액은 165달러이다.

M: How can I help you?
W: **I'm looking for two pairs of** inline skates for my daughters.
M: Do you know their exact sizes?
W: My younger daughter takes a size 2 and my older daughter takes a size 4.
M: The inline skates for kids are here. The size 2 pair costs $150 and size 4 is $180.
W: Wow, they're so expensive. My daughters are beginners and they're growing quickly. Do you have **anything less expensive**?
M: Yes, we do. We have used skates **if you're interested**. They are good quality.
W: Can I see them?
M: Sure. Please wait a moment. *[pause]* Okay. Here you are.
W: Hmm, they look brand new. **How much do they cost**?
M: The total is exactly 50% cheaper than the new ones.
W: Wow, that's a great deal! Okay, I'll take these used skates for my daughters.
M: You've made the right choice.

남: 어떻게 도와드릴까요?
여: 제 딸애들에게 줄 인라인 스케이트 두 켤레를 찾고 있어요.
남: 정확한 사이즈를 아시나요?
여: 작은 딸은 사이즈 2를 신고 큰 딸은 사이즈 4를 신어요.
남: 어린이 인라인 스케이트는 여기 있습니다. 사이즈 2는 150달러이고 사이즈 4는 180달러입니다.
여: 와, 무척 비싸네요. 제 딸애들은 초보자이고 애들은 빨리 자라잖아요. 좀 더 싼 것이 있나요?
남: 예, 있습니다. 관심이 있으시다면 중고 스케이트가 있습니다. 품질이 좋습니다.
여: 그것들을 볼 수 있나요?
남: 그럼요. 잠깐 기다리십시오. *[잠시 후]* 좋습니다. 여기 있습니다.
여: 음, 완전 새것처럼 보이는군요. 값이 얼마나 하나요?
남: 새 것보다 총액이 정확히 50% 쌉니다.
여: 와, 그거 상당한데요! 좋아요. 딸들을 위해 이 중고 스케이트들을 살게요.
남: 잘 선택하셨습니다.

어휘 **inline skate** 인라인 스케이트 / **used** 중고의 / **brand new** 완전 새것인 / **exactly** 정확히 / **a great deal** 상당량, 다량

07 이유 | ④

▶ 남자는 여름방학 동안 연구실에서 인턴사원 근무를 해야 해서 아버지를 만나러 갈 수 없다고 했다.

M: Hi, Anna. How was camping with your father?
W: Great! We **set up a tent near the river** and went fishing.
M: Sounds like an unforgettable experience.
W: It was. At night, we **talked for hours beside the campfire**. I feel much closer to my father now.
M: I bet you do. I really miss my father. He's been in England for almost a year.
W: No wonder you miss him. Then, **why don't you book a cheap flight** now to visit him during the summer?
M: I'd love to, but **you know I have an internship** at Dyson Lab during the vacation.
W: Oh, I forgot about that. Dyson is famous for its anti-virus software, right?
M: Yes. It's a great opportunity, so I think my father will understand.
W: I'm sure you're right.

남: 안녕, Anna. 아버지와의 캠핑은 어땠니?
여: 아주 좋았어! 강 근처에 텐트를 치고 낚시도 했어.
남: 잊지 못할 경험이었을 것 같구나.
여: 그랬지. 밤에는 캠프파이어 옆에서 몇 시간 동안 이야기를 나눴어. 이제 아버지와 훨씬 더 가까워진 것 같아.
남: 분명 그럴 거야. 나도 아버지가 많이 그리워. 영국에 거의 일 년 동안 가 계시거든.
여: 네가 아버지를 그리워하는 것도 당연하네. 그러면 지금 싼 항공편을 예약해서 여름 동안 아버지를 뵈러 가는 게 어때?
남: 그러고 싶지만, 방학 동안 Dyson Lab에서 인턴사원 근무를 하는 걸 너도 알잖아.
여: 아, 그것을 잊고 있었네. Dyson은 바이러스 퇴치 소프트웨어로 유명하지, 맞지?
남: 그래. 정말 좋은 기회니까, 아버지도 이해하실 거라고 생각해.
여: 네 말이 맞아.

어휘 **internship** 인턴사원 근무 (기간) / **anti-virus** 바이러스 퇴치용인

08 언급하지 않은 것 | ①

▶ 해석 참조

W: Dan, what are you doing?
M: **I'm working on my report** about the problems that cities have.
W: I see. When's the deadline?
M: There are only two days left, so I have to hurry.
W: Isn't it a team project? What about your team members?
M: We have five members in our team, so we each chose one topic to research.
W: **That's a good way to divide the work**. Then what topic are you

researching?
M: I'm researching about **the growth of urban populations**.
W: Then you should present accurate numbers in the report.
M: You're right. I've put lots of graphs and tables about the topic.
W: It seems like you are working hard.
M: Of course. **We are all doing our best** for this 50-page report.
W: Okay. I'm glad to hear that.

여: Dan, 뭐 하고 있니?
남: 도시가 갖는 문제점에 대해 보고서를 작성하고 있어.
여: 그렇구나. 제출 기한이 언제야?
남: 이틀밖에 안 남아서(② 제출 기한) 서둘러야 해.
여: 그 보고서는 팀 프로젝트 아니니? 팀 구성원들은 뭐 하고?
남: 우리 팀은 구성원이 다섯 명(③ 작성 인원)인데, 조사할 주제를 각자 하나씩 골랐어.
여: 과제를 분담하는 좋은 방법이구나. 그럼 네가 조사하고 있는 주제는 뭐야?
남: 난 도시 인구의 증가에 관해 조사하고 있어.
여: 그렇다면 보고서에 정확한 수치를 제시해야 하겠네.
남: 맞아. 주제에 대한 그래프와 표(④ 구성 자료)를 많이 넣었어.
여: 열심히 준비하고 있는 것 같구나.
남: 당연하지. 이 50페이지(⑤ 작성 분량)짜리 보고서를 위해 우리 모두 최선을 다하고 있어.
여: 좋아. 그 얘기를 들으니 기쁘다.

어휘 **urban** 도시의, 도회지의

09 내용 불일치 | ⑤

▶ 12세 미만 어린이는 무료입장 혜택을 받을 수 있다고 했다.

W: Do you like to look at the night sky? If so, the Big Tree Observatory is the perfect place for you. We are open from 2 to 10 p.m., Tuesday through Sunday, during the summer. Our afternoon program **consists of a night-sky exhibition**, a small theater presentation, and hands-on instruction with telescopes. Additionally, our professional instructors **guide you to a deeper understanding of space** and basic astronomy during these programs. Our evening program, starting at 8 p.m., is the highlight of what we offer and **gives you the chance to observe the night sky** with a telescope. All of our programs are open to the public for $5, but children under 12 **receive free admission**. Due to the popularity, reservations are highly recommended. For more information, visit our website www.bigtreeobservatory.com.

여: 밤하늘을 보는 것을 좋아하십니까? 그렇다면 Big Tree 천문대는 여러분을 위한 완벽한 장소입니다. 저희는 여름철에는 화요일에서 일요일, 오후 2시부터 10시까지 개관합니다. 저희의 오후 프로그램은 밤하늘 전시와 소극장 상연, 그리고 망원경을 직접 다뤄보는 교육으로 구성되어 있습니다. 또한, 이러한 프로그램이 진행되는 동안 저희 전문 강사진이 우주와 기초 천문학에 대해 더 깊이 이해할 수 있도록 안내해 드립니다. 오후 8시에 시작하는 저녁 프로그램은 저희가 제공하는 것 가운데 하이라이트로서 망원경으로 밤하늘을 관측하는 기회를 드립니다. 모든 프로그램은 일반인에게 5달러에 개방되지만, 12세 미만 어린이는 무료입장 혜택을 받을 수 있습니다. 인기가 많으므로, 예약하시기를 강력히 권해드립니다. 더 자세한 정보를 보시려면 저희 웹사이트인 www.bigtreeobservatory.com을 방문해 주십시오.

어휘 **observatory** 천문대; 관측소 ***cf.* observe** ~을 관찰하다[보다]; (법을) 준수하다 / **hands-on** 직접 해보는 / **astronomy** 천문학 / **admission** 입장(료); (잘못에 대한) 시인, 인정

10 도표 이해 | ④

▶ 남자는 테니스 강좌는 자신에게 요일과 연령층이 맞지 않고, 요일이 맞는 요가 강좌 역시 너무 어려울 것이라 했다. 따라서 두 사람은 강좌 수준도 적합하고 시간대도 잘 맞는 초급 수영 강좌를 선택할 것이다.

W: Brad, have you seen this? It's a schedule of courses **at our local gym**.
M: A few of them look interesting.
W: What do you think about tennis? You've mentioned before that you want to learn.
M: Unfortunately, **I have my piano practice on Wednesdays**. Besides, it's for young children.
W: Have you considered yoga?
M: I'm worried that **an advanced course would be too difficult** because I'm not very flexible.
W: Well, that only leaves swimming classes.
M: I'm interested in that, especially if it's for beginners. Also, I think **the schedule fits me well**.
W: I should sign up too, **since I swim like a brick**.
M: Good idea. Let's take it together.
W: I'm looking forward to it.

여: Brad, 이거 봤어? 우리 동네 체육관의 강좌 일정표야.
남: 그중 몇 개는 흥미로워 보인다.
여: 테니스 어때? 전에 배우고 싶다고 했잖아.
남: 안타깝지만, 수요일에는 피아노 연습이 있어. 게다가 수요일 테니스 강좌는 유소년 대상이야.
여: 요가는 생각해 봤어?
남: 상급 코스는 내게 너무 어려울 것 같아 걱정돼. 나는 몸이 그다지 유연하지 않거든.
여: 그럼, 수영 강좌만 남는구나.
남: 수영 강좌에는 관심 있어, 특히 초보자를 위한 강좌라면 말이야. 그리고 일정도 내게 잘 맞는 것 같아.
여: 나도 수영을 전혀 못 하니까 등록해야겠어.
남: 좋은 생각이야. 같이 듣자.
여: 기대돼.

어휘 **sign up** (강좌에) 등록하다 / **swim like a brick** 헤엄을 전혀 못 치다, 맥주병이다

11 짧은 대화에 이어질 응답 | ⑤

▶ 마감일이 지났으므로 남자의 과제를 받아줄 수 없다는 여자의 말에 다음번에는 제때 제출하겠다는 응답이 가장 적절하다.

① 마감시한 한 시간 전에 제출했습니다.
② 기회를 한 번 더 주셔서 감사합니다.
③ 독후감에서 더 좋은 점수를 받겠습니다.
④ 과제 마감시한이 연기되었습니다.
⑤ 죄송합니다. 다음번에는 과제를 제때 제출하겠습니다.

W: Fred, you didn't send your book report to me.
M: Oops, **when was the due date**? Can I send it now?
W: It's too late. The due date was yesterday, and it would be unfair **to allow you to submit the assignment today**.
M: ______________________________

여: Fred, 나한테 독후감을 내지 않았더구나.
남: 이런, 마감일이 언제였지요? 지금 보내드려도 될까요?
여: 너무 늦었단다. 어제가 마감일이었어. 그리고 네게 과제를 오늘 제출하도록 허락하는 것은 공평하지 않을 거야.
남: ______________________________

12 짧은 대화에 이어질 응답 | ③

▶ 무작정 셔틀버스를 기다리다가는 회의에 늦을지도 모르는 상황에서 남자는 좀 더 일찍 택시를 탔어야 했다며 어떻게 할지 묻고 있다. 이에 대한 여자의 적절한 응답을 찾는다.

① 서둘러, 그러지 않으면 지하철을 놓칠 거야.
② 넌 저기서 셔틀버스를 탈 수 있어.
③ 지금이라도 타자. 저기 택시 승차장이 있어.
④ 회의가 거의 한 시간이나 늦게 끝났어.
⑤ 버스 탈 돈이 충분하지 않아.

M: **When on earth** will the shuttle bus to the conference come?
W: I don't know, but if we continue to wait, we'll be late for the meeting.
M: You're right. We **should have taken a taxi earlier**. What should we do?
W: ______________________________

남: 회의장으로 가는 셔틀버스는 도대체 언제 오는 거야?
여: 모르겠어. 그런데 우리가 버스를 계속 기다린다면 회의에 늦을 거야.
남: 네 말이 맞아. 좀 더 일찍 택시를 탔어야 했는데. 어떻게 하지?
여: ______________________________

어휘 **의문사+on earth** ((의문사 강조)) 도대체 (어떻게, 왜, 어디서, 누가 등)

13 긴 대화에 이어질 응답 | ④

▶ 여자의 발표 연습에 피드백을 주겠다고 제안한 남자에게 여자는 바쁘진 않은지 묻고 있다. 이러한 상황에서 남자가 할 수 있는 적절한 대답을 유추해 본다.

① 너를 도울 수 있어서 기뻤어.
② 네 리허설은 정말 인상적이었어.
③ 조금 바쁘지만, 발표를 할 수는 있어.
④ 그렇게 바쁘지 않아. 데이터 분석이 끝나면 전화해줘.
⑤ 네가 준비될 때까지 회의를 연기해야 해.

M: Hi, Carolyn. Here's the USB you asked to borrow.
W: Oh. Thanks, Paul.

M: Is it for next Friday's economics presentation?
W: Yes. **I've been working on it nonstop** for the past few days.
M: Really? **No wonder you look so tired**. What do you have left to do?
W: Well, first **I need to analyze some data** that's on my friend's laptop.
M: Ah, that's why you need the USB.
W: Right. And then I have to rehearse the presentation.
M: You know, I'd **be happy to listen to your rehearsal** and give you some feedback.
W: Really? That would be helpful, but I thought you were busy.
M: ______________________

남: 안녕, Carolyn. 네가 빌려달라고 했던 USB 여기 있어.
여: 아, 고마워, Paul.
남: 다음 주 금요일에 있는 경제학 발표 때문이지?
여: 응, 지난 며칠 동안 쉴 새 없이 여기에만 매달려 있었어.
남: 그래? 그래서 이렇게 피곤해 보이는구나. 아직 뭐가 더 남았니?
여: 음, 우선 친구 노트북 컴퓨터에 있는 데이터를 좀 분석해야 해.
남: 아, 그래서 USB가 필요한 거구나.
여: 맞아. 그다음에는 발표 리허설을 해야 해.
남: 있잖아, 네가 리허설 하는 걸 들어보고 피드백을 주고 싶어.
여: 정말? 그래 주면 도움이 될 텐데, 나는 네가 바쁜 줄 알았어.
남: ______________________

어휘 **rehearsal** 리허설 ***cf.* rehearse** 리허설[예행연습]을 하다 / **postpone** ~을 연기하다[미루다] / **nonstop** 휴식 없이, 연속적으로; 직행 운행; 직행의

14 긴 대화에 이어질 응답 | ③

▶ 칼슘이 철분 흡수를 방해하므로 칼슘과 철분 보충제 중 하나를 끊는 게 좋겠냐는 남자의 물음에 대한 적절한 대답을 찾는다.

① 제시간에 보충제를 먹는 걸 잊으면 안 돼.
② 건강보조제는 먹지 않아도 돼.
③ 음, 한 번에 하나씩 먹으면 괜찮아.
④ 이것이 네가 병에 걸리는 걸 막을 수도 있다고 생각해.
⑤ 맞아. 정해진 복용량을 초과하지 않는 게 중요해.

W: Hi, Luke. Is that medicine? Are you sick?
M: No, but I haven't been eating right. So, I bought these dietary supplements last week.
W: That's smart, but it's best **to get vitamins from the foods you eat**.
M: I agree, but people say supplements are helpful **for those who don't get enough calcium**.
W: I see. So, what else are you taking?
M: Well, these are iron supplements.
W: You're taking iron and calcium?
M: Don't sound so concerned. I **stick to the recommended dosages**.
W: That's not what I mean. Iron and calcium **should not be taken together**, because calcium blocks the absorption of iron.
M: Then what should I do? Would it be better to quit taking one of them?
W: ______________________

여: 안녕, Luke. 그거 약이야? 아프니?
남: 아니, 제대로 먹질 못했어. 그래서 지난주에 식이보충제를 좀 샀어.
여: 현명한 방법이긴 하지만 네가 먹는 음식에서 비타민을 섭취하는 게 가장 좋아.
남: 맞아. 그렇지만 칼슘을 충분히 섭취하지 않는 사람에게는 보충제가 도움이 된다고 하더라.
여: 그렇구나. 그래서 그것 말고는 또 뭘 먹니?
남: 음, 이건 철분 보충제야.
여: 철분과 칼슘을 먹고 있다고?
남: 너무 걱정하지 않아도 돼. 권장 복용량을 지키고 있으니까.
여: 그런 뜻이 아니야. 철분과 칼슘은 같이 섭취하면 안 돼. 칼슘이 철분 흡수를 방해하거든.
남: 그럼 어떻게 해야 해? 둘 중 하나를 끊는 게 좋을까?
여: ______________________

어휘 **exceed**~을 넘다, 초과하다 / **dose** (약의) 복용량(=dosage) / **dietary supplements** 식이보충제 / **absorption** 흡수; 몰두

15 상황에 적절한 말 | ③

▶ 무절제하게 게임을 하느라 학업을 게을리하는 Jacob에게 화가 난 Jacob의 엄마가 할 수 있는 말을 골라야 한다.

① 과욕은 금물이란다.
② 돈을 저축하는 습관을 들이는 게 좋아.
③ 숙제를 마칠 때까지 게임 금지야.
④ 네가 그 돈을 스스로 벌었다니 정말 놀랍구나.
⑤ 네가 하기로 선택한 것이 무엇이든지 거기에 완전히 주의를 집중해라.

W: During the winter vacation, Jacob decided to buy a new game console. To pay for it, he **got a part-time job at a local convenience store** and started saving. Two months later, he purchased the console and began playing. These days, **he spends a minimum of six hours per day** playing games. He rarely studies and sometimes doesn't **complete his assignments** because he is so focused on his games. Jacob's mother is concerned. She knows that Jacob even has an important exam next week but still continues to play his games. So, **she can no longer tolerate** Jacob's behavior. In this situation, what would Jacob's mother most likely say to Jacob?

여: 겨울방학 동안, Jacob은 새 게임기를 사겠다는 결정을 내렸다. 게임기 비용을 지불하기 위해 Jacob은 동네 편의점에서 아르바이트를 구해 돈을 모으기 시작했다. 두 달 후, 그는 게임기를 사서 게임을 하기 시작했다. 요즘 그는 하루에 최소 여섯 시간을 게임을 하는 데 보낸다. 그는 게임에 너무 열중해 있어서 공부를 거의 하지 않고, 가끔은 과제를 끝마치지 않는다. Jacob의 엄마는 걱정된다. 엄마는 Jacob이 다음 주에 중요한 시험이 있는데도 게임을 계속한다는 것을 알고 있다. 그래서 엄마는 Jacob의 행동을 더는 용인할 수 없다. 이러한 상황에서 Jacob의 엄마가 Jacob에게 할 말로 가장 적절한 것은 무엇인가?

어휘 **bite off more than you can chew** 너무 욕심을 부리다 ***cf.* bite off** ~을 물어 끊다 / **get in the habit of v-ing** ~하는 습관을 들이다 / **forbid A to-v** A가 v하는 것을 금지하다 / **game console** 게임기 ((비디오 오락기)) / **tolerate** ~을 용인하다[참다]

16~17 세트 문항 | 16. ③ 17. ②

▶ 16. 밝은 색의 옷 입기, 사용하지 않는 전기기구의 플러그 뽑기, 에어컨 올바르게 사용하기 등 여름철 전기 요금을 줄이는 방법에 대해 설명하고 있다.

① 기후 변화의 주된 원인
② 한여름 무더위의 위험성
③ 여름철 전기 요금을 줄이는 방법
④ 더운 날씨에 안전하게 지내는 것을 도와주는 조언들
⑤ 에어컨의 장점과 단점

▶ 17. 해석 참조

M: This summer has been particularly hot, hasn't it? In fact, the entire Earth **is getting hotter and hotter** because of global warming. As a result, many of us are suffering from skyrocketing electricity bills for air conditioning. To save yourself some money, there are a few things you can do. First, **wearing lighter colors can help you remain cool** without spending money because light colors reflect heat and sunlight. Second, unplug electronic devices when you aren't using them. This is because electronics **not only consume electricity but also produce unwanted heat**. Third, use your air conditioner properly. Air conditioning is energy intensive and can quickly run up a huge bill. To use it properly, there are several things you must do. To begin with, **set up the air conditioner in a shady location**. Then, remember to clean its filter at least once every two weeks because blocked filters waste electricity. For the same reason, leave some space in front of the unit. Finally, **don't turn it on and off frequently**, since additional electricity is required to activate the unit. By following these tips, you can hopefully remain cool without breaking the bank.

남: 이번 여름은 특히 더웠습니다, 그렇지 않았나요? 사실 지구 전체가 지구 온난화로 점점 더 더워지고 있습니다. 그 결과, 우리 중 다수가 냉방 장치 때문에 치솟는 전기 요금으로 고생하고 있습니다. 돈을 절약하기 위해서, 당신이 할 수 있는 일이 몇 가지 있습니다. 우선, 밝은 색상은 열과 햇빛을 반사하기 때문에 밝은 색상의 옷을 입으면 돈을 들이지 않고도 시원하게 있는 데 도움이 될 수 있습니다. 둘째, 전기기구를 사용하지 않을 때는 플러그를 뽑아두십시오. 전기기구는 전기를 소모할 뿐 아니라 불필요한 열을 발생시키기 때문입니다. 셋째, 에어컨을 올바른 방법으로 사용하십시오. 에어컨은 에너지를 많이 소모하기 때문에 금세 어마어마한 전기세가 나올 수 있습니다. 에어컨을 올바른 방법으로 사용하기 위해, 당신이 해야 하는 몇 가지가 있습니다. 우선, 에어컨은 ① 그늘진 장소에 설치하십시오. 그리고 필터가 (먼지 등으로) 막히면 전기를 낭비하니, ③ 적어도 2주에 한 번 필터를 청소할 것을 기억해두십시오. 같은 이유로, ④ 에어컨 장치 앞에 약간의 공간을 남겨두십시오. 마지막으로, 에어컨 장치를 가동하는 데 별도의 전기가 필요하니, 에어컨의 ⑤ 전원을 자주 켰다 껐다 하지 마십시오. 이 조언들을 따르면 당신은 큰돈을 들이지 않고도, 바라건대 시원하게 지내실 수 있을 것입니다.

어휘 **contributor** 원인 (제공자); 기부[기여]자 / **skyrocketing** 치솟는 / **energy intensive** 많은 에너지를 소비하는 / **run up a bill** 청구서가 쌓이다; 빚을 지다 / **set up** (기계·장비를) 설치하다; ~을 시작[설립]하다; ~을 세우다 / **shady** 그늘이 드리워진 / **activate** ~을 작동시키다; ~을 활성화시키다 / **break the bank** 파산시키다, 무일푼이 되게 하다

Answers & Explanation

01. ① 02. ⑤ 03. ③ 04. ⑤ 05. ② 06. ③ 07. ⑤ 08. ③ 09. ④ 10. ③
11. ② 12. ④ 13. ④ 14. ④ 15. ④ 16. ① 17. ③

01 화자가 하는 말의 목적 | ①

▶ Veggie-Wash라는 제품의 기능과 효능을 설명한 것으로 보아 제품 홍보가 목적이라는 것을 알 수 있다.

W: It doesn't matter how long you wash an apple under tap water. Water alone can't remove all those harmful pesticides **you're trying to get rid of** because the pesticides are trapped under the wax coating **that is sprayed onto the apple** to make it look 'perfect.' But Veggie-Wash can do the job! It is a type of soap for your fruits and vegetables made from all natural ingredients. **It is guaranteed to remove** 98% of the pesticides on the fruits and vegetables you eat. It comes in an easy-to-use spray bottle **which can be refilled**. Start using it today for the health of your family.

여: 수돗물에서 사과를 얼마나 오랫동안 씻는지는 상관이 없습니다. 물만으로는 제거하려고 하는 그 유해한 살충제들을 다 없애기는 불가능한데, 왜냐하면 사과를 '완벽하게' 보이도록 하기 위해 그 위에 뿌려진 왁스 코팅 아래 살충제가 있기 때문입니다. 하지만 Veggie-Wash가 그 일을 할 수 있습니다! 이것은 과일과 채소를 씻기 위한 비누의 일종으로 모두 천연 성분으로 만들어졌습니다. 여러분이 섭취하는 과일과 야채에 남아 있는 살충제의 98%를 제거할 수 있다고 장담합니다. 이것은 리필이 가능한, 사용하기 쉬운 스프레이 병으로 출시되어 있습니다. 가족의 건강을 위해서 오늘부터 사용해 보세요.

어휘 **tap water** 수돗물 / **pesticide** 살충제 / **trap** 흐름을 막다, 모아두다; 덫으로 잡다 / **ingredient** 성분; (요리의) 재료 / **guarantee** ~을 보증[보장]하다

02 대화 주제 | ⑤

▶ 중국 만리장성에서 열리는 마라톤 대회의 개최 시기, 종류, 특징 등에 관해 이야기하고 있다.

M: I think our report on The Great Wall of China is almost finished.
W: It's good, but I'd like to include something about The Wall's modern role.
M: We could **mention the annual marathon** that is held on The Wall in May.
W: Good idea. I remember reading that they have 5 km, 10 km, half marathon, and full marathon races.
M: And competitors in the full marathon must climb **more than 5,000 steps**.
W: Yes, it's a very challenging race. It takes even well-prepared runners five to six hours to complete the run.
M: **That must be very difficult**, but I heard the race is for everyone. There are no time limits and the course remains open with full support **until the last runners finish**.
W: In that case, I'd like to try it.

남: 중국의 만리장성에 대한 우리 보고서가 거의 완성된 것 같아.
여: 잘됐다. 그런데 난 그 성벽의 현대적 역할에 관한 내용을 포함하고 싶어.
남: 5월에 성벽에서 열리는 연례 마라톤에 대해 언급할 수 있어.
여: 좋은 생각이야. 5km, 10km, 하프 마라톤, 풀 마라톤 경주가 있다는 것을 읽은 기억이 나.
남: 그리고 풀 마라톤 참가자들은 5,000개가 넘는 계단을 올라가야 하지.
여: 맞아, 그건 아주 도전 의식을 북돋는 경주야. 철저히 준비한 주자들조차 완주하는 데 대여섯 시간이 걸려.
남: 그건 분명 몹시 힘들 테지만, 누구나 그 경주에 참가할 수 있다고 들었어. 시간제한이 없고, 마지막 주자가 완주할 때까지 전폭적으로 지원해주면서 코스를 열어 둔대.
여: 그렇다면 나 한번 해보고 싶어.

어휘 **annual** 연례의, 매년의 / **competitor** (시합) 참가자; 경쟁자 / **challenging** 도전 의식을 북돋우는, 도전적인

03 관계 | ③

▶ 두 사람은 엘리베이터에서 만나 최근 근황을 물어보았다. 또한 남자는 여자 집의 보수 공사로 인한 소음 때문에 불만도 호소하고 있다.

M: Thanks for holding the elevator.
W: No problem, Sam. I haven't seen you for a while.
M: Well, I've gotten a promotion and **it's meant I've had to do** a lot of work in the evenings and on weekends.
W: Oh, that's too bad.
M: Yeah. But **I've taken this week off** so I can rest.
W: Good for you.
M: But I can't seem to get much rest in my apartment.
W: Oh! Sam. I'm sorry about the renovations. **It is kind of noisy**, isn't it?
M: It really is! I was trying to read in my living room this morning and all I heard was 'Bang! Bang!'
W: We're putting in a new bathroom. The plumber was installing the pipes today.
M: **Will the work be done soon**?
W: Yes, by tomorrow.

남: 엘리베이터를 잡아주셔서 감사합니다.
여: 천만에요, Sam. 얼마간 뵙지 못했네요.
남: 음, 제가 승진을 해서 저녁과 주말에도 일을 많이 해야 했거든요.
여: 아, 안됐네요.
남: 네. 하지만 이번 주는 휴가를 내서 쉴 수 있습니다.
여: 잘됐네요.
남: 그런데 아파트에서는 많이 쉴 수 있을 것 같지 않습니다.
여: 아! Sam. 보수 공사 건에 대해서는 죄송합니다. 좀 시끄러워요, 그렇죠?
남: 정말 그래요! 오늘 아침 거실에서 책을 읽으려고 했는데 들리는 것이라고는 '꽝! 꽝!' 소리밖에 없더군요.
여: 저희는 욕실을 새로 공사하고 있거든요. 배관공이 오늘 파이프를 설치하고 있었어요.
남: 공사가 곧 끝날까요?
여: 네, 내일쯤 끝납니다.

어휘 **promotion** 승진 / **take ~ off** ~간의 휴가를 얻다 / **renovation** 보수 공사; 혁신 / **bang** 쾅 하는 소리; 쿵쿵 소리를 내다 / **plumber** 배관공

04 그림 불일치 | ⑤

▶ 여자가 서랍장 위에 있던 책들과 다른 물건들을 치웠다고 했지만, 그림에는 세 권의 책과 탁상시계가 있으므로 대화의 내용과 일치하지 않는다.

W: I rearranged the living room this morning, honey. What do you think?
M: I like this round table on the carpet. Is it new?
W: Actually, one of our neighbors **was throwing it out**. I took it home instead.
M: Good job. There's something different about the sofa, too. The teddy bear!
W: Right. I bought it at a small shop and put it on the sofa. I think it's cute.
M: It's nice. Our family picture looks good **hanging above** the sofa, as well.
W: That's what I thought.
M: Now, you placed the floor lamp **to the left of the sofa**.
W: I thought it would be good for reading, but I'm thinking about moving it again.
M: You can if you want. Do you have **anything special in mind**?
W: No, I'll think about it. Oh, I also threw out the books and other things that were on the chest of drawers.
M: That's good. The room looks more neat and tidy.
W: I agree.

여: 오늘 아침에 거실을 다시 배치했어요, 여보. 어떻게 생각해요?
남: 카펫 위의 이 둥근 탁자가 마음에 들어요. 새것이에요?
여: 사실, 이웃 사람들 중 한 분이 그것을 버리고 있었어요. 제가 대신 집으로 가져왔죠.
남: 잘했어요. 소파도 무언가가 달라졌어요. 곰돌이 인형이네요!
여: 맞아요. 어떤 조그만 가게에서 샀는데 소파 위에 놓아두었죠. 귀여운 것 같아요.
남: 좋네요. 우리 가족사진이 소파 위에 걸려있는 것도 보기 좋아요.
여: 그럴 것 같았어요.
남: 자, 소파 왼쪽에 플로어 스탠드를 배치했군요.

여: 독서에 좋을 거라 생각했지만, 다시 옮기는 것을 생각 중이에요.
남: 당신이 원한다면 그렇게 해요. 특별히 생각해 둔 것이 있어요?
여: 아니요, 생각해 볼게요. 아, 서랍장 위에 있던 책들과 다른 물건들도 치웠어요.
남: 좋네요. 방이 더 깔끔하고 잘 정돈되어 보여요.
여: 저도 그렇게 생각해요.

어휘 **rearrange** 다시 배치하다 / **floor lamp** (방바닥에 세우는) 플로어 스탠드 / **chest of drawer** 서랍장 / **neat** 깔끔한; 정돈된, 단정한 / **tidy** 잘 정돈된, 단정한

05 추후 행동 | ②

▶ 여자는 오래된 도서관을 헐겠다는 시의회의 계획에 반대하는 시위운동을 하고 있는데 남자가 이에 관심을 보이며 도울 수 있는 방법을 물었다. 온라인으로 후원할 수 있다는 여자의 말에 남자가 바로 집에 가서 온라인으로 후원하겠다고 응했다.

W: Can I have everyone's attention?
M: Oh, Emma. What are you doing with a picket sign? Are you demonstrating against something?
W: Oh, Lucas. The city council **is planning to approve the plan to tear down** the Bridgeport Library. Look at this flyer.
M: You mean that beautiful old library? It's a historically significant structure in our city.
W: Yes! They say there is a new city library, so they want to tear down the old one and build a 30-story hotel there.
M: That's a terrible idea! **We should preserve the library**.
W: That's why we're protesting here. We sent a letter of protest to the city council.
M: **I'm proud of you for taking part in** this kind of campaign. How can I help you?
W: You can support us by making an online donation.
M: That sounds nice. I'll go home and sponsor you online right away.
W: Thanks a lot! **Your interest means a lot to us**.

여: 여러분 집중해주시겠어요?
남: 아, Emma. 너 피켓 간판을 들고 뭐 하고 있는 거야? 무언가에 대한 시위운동을 하고 있니?
여: 아, Lucas. 시의회에서 Bridgeport 도서관을 헐겠다는 계획을 허가할 예정이래. 이 전단을 봐.
남: 저 아름답고 역사가 긴 도서관 말이야? 그것은 우리 시에서 역사적으로 중요한 건축물이잖아.
여: 그래! 그들이 말하길 새로운 시립 도서관 있어서, 오래된 것을 헐고 거기에 30층짜리 호텔을 짓기를 원한대.
남: 그건 끔찍한 생각이다! 우리는 그 도서관을 보존해야 해.
여: 그래서 우리가 여기서 항의하고 있는 거야. 우리는 시의회에 항의 편지를 보냈어.
남: 이러한 종류의 캠페인에 참여하다니 네가 자랑스러워. 어떻게 내가 너를 도울 수 있을까?
여: 너는 온라인 기부를 해서 우리를 후원할 수 있어.
남: 그거 괜찮네. 내가 바로 집에 가서 온라인으로 너를 후원할게.
여: 정말 고마워! 네 관심은 우리에게 많은 것을 의미해.

어휘 **demonstrate against** ~에 대한 시위운동을 하다 / **council** 의회; 위원회 / **approve** 허가[승인]하다 / **tear down** (건물 등을) 헐다; 파괴[해체]하다 / **flyer** (광고·안내용) 전단 / **preserve** 보존[관리]하다; 지키다 / **protest** 항의(하다); 이의 제기 / **make a donation** 기부[기증]하다 / **sponsor** 후원하다, 지지하다; 후원자

06 금액 | ③

▶ 한 벌에 20달러인 반바지를 두 벌 구매하고, 티셔츠는 4장 구매해 20달러이며, 카디건은 30달러이므로, 여자가 지불할 총 금액은 90달러이다.

W: I need shorts for this summer weather.
M: Summer shorts are over here. Pure cotton, soft and comfortable.
W: **The sign says** they are $20 a pair.
M: That's right.
W: Well, they look nice, so I'll take the brown ones and the blue ones in a 24 waist.
M: Good. **I have plenty in that size**. What about summer T-shirts? These ones here are 2 for $15 or 4 for $20.
W: Hmm... very cheap. **The cotton feels comfortable**, too. I'll take 2 blue ones and 2 pink ones. I need a small size.
M: OK. $20 for the T-shirts.
W: Oh, and I need a long-sleeved white cardigan in a cool summer material.
M: How about **that one hanging over the pants**? I have it in your size. It's $30.
W: Fine. **How much do I owe you**?

여: 올여름 날씨에 입을 반바지가 필요한데요.
남: 여름 반바지는 이쪽에 있습니다. 순면에 부드럽고 편안합니다.
여: 표지판에 한 벌에 20달러라고 쓰여 있네요.
남: 그렇습니다.
여: 음, 좋아 보이니까 허리 24로 갈색과 파란색을 살게요.
남: 알겠습니다. 그 치수로는 많이 있습니다. 여름 티셔츠는 어떠세요? 여기 이것들은 2장에 15달러 또는 4장에 20달러입니다.
여: 음… 아주 싸네요. 면도 편안하게 느껴져요. 파란색 두 장과 분홍색 두 장을 살게요. 스몰 치수가 필요해요.
남: 알겠습니다. 티셔츠들은 20달러입니다.
여: 아, 그리고 시원한 여름 소재의 하얀색 긴 소매 카디건이 필요해요.
남: 저 바지 위에 걸려 있는 저것은 어떠세요? 고객님의 치수가 있습니다. 30달러예요.
여: 좋아요. 얼마를 드려야 하나요?

어휘 **sleeved** ~한 소매가 달린 / **cardigan** 카디건 / **How much do I owe you?** 얼마를 드려야 하나요?

07 이유 | ⑤

▶ 남자는 Lee 교수님이 자기 분야에서 최고이기 때문에 그 밑에서 공부하는 게 아주 좋은 기회라고 했다.

M: Hey, Karen. Have you chosen your classes for next semester?
W: Almost. **I have everything set** except for history.
M: Why don't you take history from Professor Lee? I'm taking it.
W: I heard that **his classes are tough**. I don't have time for a lot of extra assignments and group projects.
M: I'm sure you can handle it. Besides, he is **at the top of his field**. Studying under Lee is a great opportunity.
W: Hmm... I guess it does **fit into my schedule**. And are you sure I can pass his class?
M: Of course. You **got good grades in much harder classes** in the past.
W: Okay, I'll do it. Thanks for your advice.
M: Anytime.

남: 저기, Karen. 다음 학기에 들을 수업 결정했니?
여: 거의 다 했어. 역사 수업을 제외하고는 다 정했어.
남: Lee 교수님의 역사 수업을 듣는 게 어때? 난 그거 들을 거야.
여: 그 교수님 수업은 힘들다고 들었어. 난 많은 추가 과제와 그룹 프로젝트를 할 시간이 없어.
남: 분명 넌 감당할 수 있을 거야. 게다가, 그 교수님은 자기 분야에서 최고이셔. Lee 교수님 밑에서 공부하는 건 아주 좋은 기회야.
여: 음… 내 시간표에 맞는 거 같긴 해. 그리고 정말 내가 그 수업을 통과할 수 있다고 생각해?
남: 물론이야. 넌 예전에 훨씬 더 힘든 수업들에서도 좋은 성적을 받았잖아.
여: 알겠어, 그렇게 할게. 조언해줘서 고마워.
남: 천만에.

어휘 **assignment** 과제, 임무

08 언급하지 않은 것 | ③

▶ 해석 참조

M: These pictures from your trip are great. Where is this?
W: That's the Rainbow Bridge. It's **a popular tourist attraction**.
M: Really? It looks like a typical steel bridge. Why is it famous?
W: It's built across the Niagara river, and the famous Niagara Falls are located nearby.
M: Oh, I understand. Then **this must be at the border** of Canada and the U.S. Right?
W: Exactly. It's only 290 meters in length, so it can be crossed **on foot in under 10 minutes**.
M: Did you cross it on foot, too?
W: Well, I rode a bicycle. Cars can drive on it, too, but commercial trucks are not allowed.
M: I see. By the way, **isn't a passport required** to cross the bridge?
W: That's right. My nephew, Franklin, **didn't have his with him**, so he couldn't cross.
M: That's too bad.

남: 네 여행에서 찍은 이 사진들 멋지구나. 이건 어디니?
여: Rainbow Bridge야. 인기 있는 관광 명소지.
남: 정말? 일반 철교처럼 보이는데. 왜 유명해?
여: 그건 Niagara 강을 가로질러 지어졌고, 유명한 Niagara 폭포가 근처에 있거든.
남: 아, 알겠어. 그럼 이 다리는 분명 캐나다와 미국 국경(① 위치)에 있겠구나, 그렇지?
여: 맞아. 길이가 290미터(② 길이)밖에 안 돼서, 걸어서 10분 이내로 건널 수 있어.
남: 너도 걸어서 건넜니?
여: 음, 난 자전거를 탔어. 자동차도 그 위로 지나갈 수 있는데, 영업용 트럭은 지나갈 수 없어 (④ 통행 수단).
남: 그렇구나. 그런데 다리를 건너려면 여권이 필요(⑤ 통행 허용 요건)하지 않니?
여: 맞아. 내 조카인 Franklin은 여권을 가지고 있지 않아서 건널 수 없었어.
남: 그건 정말 안 좋구나.

어휘 **tourist attraction** 관광 명소

09 내용 불일치 | ④

▶ 볼리비아에는 퀴노아 재배에 적합한 땅이 많지 않다고 했다.

M: Quinoa is a grain-like crop grown in the Andes mountains of Peru and Bolivia. While usually **considered to be a whole grain**, what we call "quinoa grain" is actually the plant's seed. For centuries, quinoa **has been thought of as a food** for the poor, but in recent years, things have changed rapidly. Quinoa has become popular for its high protein and dietary fiber content. In the last few years, Peru has almost **doubled its income** from quinoa exports. Bolivia has also **made a good profit** from quinoa, although it doesn't have much land suitable for growing quinoa. Ironically, the local consumption of quinoa still remains low because **selling it abroad is so profitable**.

남: 퀴노아는 페루와 볼리비아의 안데스 산맥에서 재배되는 곡물과 비슷한 농작물이다. 대개 통알곡으로 여겨지지만, 우리가 '퀴노아 곡물'이라 부르는 것은 사실 그 식물의 씨앗이다. 수 세기 동안, 퀴노아는 가난한 사람들을 위한 음식으로 여겨져 왔지만, 최근에 상황이 급속하게 변했다. 퀴노아는 단백질과 식이섬유 함량이 높다는 이유로 인기를 얻게 되었다. 지난 몇 년간, 페루는 퀴노아 수출로 소득이 거의 두 배가 되었다. 볼리비아 역시, 퀴노아 재배에 적합한 땅이 많지 않음에도, 퀴노아로 상당한 수익을 얻어 왔다. 얄궂게도, 퀴노아를 외국에 판매하면 수익이 많이 남기 때문에 해당 지역의 퀴노아 소비량은 여전히 낮다.

어휘 **protein** 단백질 / **dietary fiber** 식이성 섬유; 섬유질 식품 / **content** 함유량, 함량; ((pl.)) 내용(물) / **make a profit** 이익을 얻다 / **ironically** 얄궂게도; 반어적으로 / **consumption** 소비(량) / **profitable** 수익성이 있는; 유익한

10 도표 이해 | ③

▶ 500달러 이하의 예산에서 4킬로그램이 넘는 것은 제외했다. HEPA 필터가 있는 것들 중 더 긴 작동 시간을 가진 것을 택했으므로 여자가 구매할 무선 진공청소기는 ③이다.

M: How can I help you?
W: I'm looking for a cordless vacuum cleaner.
M: Come this way. These five are the best-selling cordless vacuum cleaners these days. What is **the most you want to spend**?
W: No more than $500. And I want a lightweight vacuum cleaner that **I can easily carry around**.
M: Okay. We need to eliminate this one. It weighs more than 4 kg.
W: All right. And my husband and I have allergies. I heard there's a vacuum cleaner that has a special filter.
M: You're talking about the HEPA filter. These ones have HEPA filters.
W: Great. Now I have these two options.
M: **The price difference** between these two is around $60. Do you want the cheaper one?
W: It doesn't matter. I'd like a vacuum cleaner **with a longer run time**.
M: Then this one is for you. Good choice.
W: Okay. I'll take it.

남: 무엇을 도와드릴까요?
여: 무선 진공청소기를 찾고 있습니다.
남: 이쪽으로 오세요. 이 다섯 개가 요즘 가장 잘 팔리는 무선 진공청소기입니다. 최대 얼마까지 쓰기를 원하시나요?
여: 500달러 넘게 쓰고 싶지는 않습니다. 그리고 제가 쉽게 들고 다닐 수 있는 가벼운 진공청소기를 원해요.
남: 알겠습니다. 이것은 제외해야겠군요. 이건 4킬로그램이 넘네요.
여: 좋습니다. 그리고 제 남편과 제가 알레르기가 있어요. 특별한 필터를 가진 진공청소기가 있다고 들었는데요.
남: HEPA 필터를 말씀하시는 거군요. 이것들이 HEPA 필터가 있습니다.
여: 좋아요. 이제 이 두 개가 있네요.
남: 이 두 개의 가격 차이는 약 60달러입니다. 더 저렴한 것을 원하세요?
여: 상관없어요. 전 작동 시간이 더 긴 진공청소기를 원해요.
남: 그러면 이것이 손님을 위한 것이군요. 좋은 선택입니다.
여: 알겠어요. 이것으로 선택할게요.

어휘 **cordless** 무선의 / **vacuum cleaner** 진공청소기 / **run time** 실행 시간 / **lightweight** 가벼운 / **eliminate** 제외[제거]하다

11 짧은 대화에 이어질 응답 | ②

▶ 가장 좋아하는 과목을 묻는 말에 적절한 대답을 찾는다. 남자가 수학을 좋아하지 않는다는 점에 유의한다.

① 수학이 내가 가장 좋아하는 과목이야.
② 미술이야. 왜냐하면 그림 그리는 것을 아주 좋아하거든.
③ 난 내일 역사 수업이 있어.
④ 내가 네 숙제를 도와줄게.
⑤ 그 과학 동아리는 우리 학교에서 아주 인기 있어.

W: You're really good at math. You must love it.
M: **Not really**. I only study it **because I need to**.
W: Then what is your favorite subject?
M: ______________________________

여: 너 수학 정말 잘하는구나. 수학을 분명 좋아하겠네.
남: 꼭 그렇지는 않아. 해야 하기 때문에 공부할 뿐이야.
여: 그럼 네가 가장 좋아하는 과목은 뭐야?
남: ______________________________

12 짧은 대화에 이어질 응답 | ④

▶ 마지막 교차로에 약국이 있지 않았냐는 남자의 말에 몸이 아픈 여자가 할 수 있는 응답을 찾는다.

① 어떤 약은 중독성이 있을 수 있어.
② 동네 약국에 물어봐.
③ 내 생각엔 좀 쉬는 게 도움이 될 거야.
④ 잘 모르겠어. 신경 쓰지 않고 있었거든.
⑤ 맞아. 하지만 처방전을 가져가야 해.

M: How are you doing? **Are you still feeling sick**?
W: I really don't feel well. Can we stop and get some medicine?
M: Of course. **Wasn't there a pharmacy** at the last intersection that we just passed?
W: ______________________________

남: 어때? 아직도 아프니?
여: 몸이 정말 안 좋아. 잠시 멈춰서 약을 좀 사도 될까?
남: 물론이야. 우리가 지금 막 지나온 마지막 교차로에 약국이 하나 있지 않았니?
여: ______________________________

어휘 **addictive** 중독성의, 중독성이 있는 / **prescription** 처방(전) / **intersection** 교차로

13 긴 대화에 이어질 응답 | ④

▶ 여자는 매진된 〈The Ghosts of Gettysburg〉라는 책이 정말 필요하다고 했으므로 남자가 할 말을 유추할 수 있다.

① 좋습니다. 손님께 그 책을 팔겠습니다.
② 기다리시는 동안 커피 한 잔 드릴까요?
③ 한국 전쟁에 관한 책을 원하십니까?
④ 손님을 위해 한 권 주문해 드릴 수 있습니다만, 일주일은 걸릴 것입니다.
⑤ 제가 게티즈버그에 대해서 손님의 질문에 전부 답해 드릴 수 있습니다.

W: I'm looking for a book about the U.S. Civil War.
M: We have a large selection on that war. **Is there anything specific you want**?
W: There was a famous battle in Pennsylvania. I can't remember what it was called.
M: That was the battle of Gettysburg. Let me see **what we have about it**.
W: If there isn't one about that battle, then maybe just **an overview of**

the war would be OK.

M: *[pause]* Well, I have good news and bad news.

W: Uh-oh! That doesn't sound promising.

M: We carry a book called *The Ghosts of Gettysburg*, but, unfortunately, **we are sold out** now.

W: I really need that book.

M: ______________________________

여: 미국 남북 전쟁에 관한 책을 찾고 있습니다.
남: 저희는 그 전쟁에 관한 많은 책을 보유하고 있습니다. 구체적으로 원하시는 것이 있습니까?
여: 펜실베이니아에서 유명한 전투가 있었습니다. 이름이 무엇이었는지 기억이 나지 않습니다.
남: 그것은 게티즈버그 전투입니다. 그에 관해 어떤 책이 있는지 알아보겠습니다.
여: 그 전투에 관한 책이 없다면, 전투의 개요만이라도 괜찮을 것입니다.
남: *[잠시 후]* 음, 좋은 소식과 나쁜 소식이 있습니다.
여: 저런! 가망 있게 들리지 않네요.
남: 〈The Ghosts of Gettysburg〉라는 책을 판매는 합니다만, 유감스럽게도 현재 매진되었습니다.
여: 저는 그 책이 정말 필요합니다.
남: ______________________________

어휘 **copy** (책·잡지의) 한 부; (~을) 복사하다 / **the Civil War** 미국 남북 전쟁 / **selection** 선택 가능한 것들; 선발, 선정 / **overview** 개요, 개관 / **promising** 가망이 있는 / **carry** (가게에서 품목을) 취급하다; ~을 운반하다

14 긴 대화에 이어질 응답 | ④

▶ 남자는 오랜만에 만난 학교 친구에게 예전에 좋아했다고 고백하고 있다. 아마도 그 사실을 이제야 알게 되었을 여자의 응답으로 가장 적절한 것을 고른다.

① 그만해! 난 너무 바빠서 지금 너와 이야기할 수 없어.
② 나도 그랬어. 우리가 왜 헤어졌는지 기억이 나지 않아.
③ 미안해. 너를 그렇게 많이 놀리려던 게 아니었어.
④ 정말? 하지만 너는 나에게 데이트 신청을 한 적이 한 번도 없잖아.
⑤ 맞아. 그 머리 모양 때문에 너 정말 어려 보인다.

W: It's great **to run into you**, Matt.

M: Yeah. It's been 10 years.

W: **You haven't changed**! Your hairstyle is even the same.

M: Yes, I've still got the same hairstyle. Umm... I think **I used to tease you** about your hairstyle.

W: Yes. My hair was short, so you said I had a boy's hairstyle.

M: Well, I'm sorry. By the way, in high school you wanted to be a teacher, right?

W: Yes. **My dream came true**. And yours?

M: Not yet. **I am acting though**. It's a small part in a new play at the Royal Playhouse.

W: That's great. I remember **you were the lead actor** in several school plays.

M: Yeah. Umm, you know, I used to tease you because I really liked you.

W: ______________________________

여: 우연히 만나니 반가워, Matt.
남: 응, 10년 만이지.
여: 너는 하나도 안 변했구나! 심지어 머리 모양도 같고.
남: 응, 난 아직도 같은 머리 모양을 하고 있어. 음… 네 머리 모양을 내가 놀리곤 한 것 같은데.
여: 응, 머리가 짧아서 내가 남자 머리 모양을 하고 다닌다고 말했어.
남: 음, 미안하다. 그건 그렇고, 고등학교 때 너는 선생님이 되고 싶어 했지, 맞지?
여: 응, 내 꿈은 이루어졌어. 그런데 네 꿈은?
남: 아직 이루지 못했어. 하지만 연기를 하고 있어. Royal Playhouse의 새로운 연극에서 작은 역할을 맡고 있어.
여: 멋지다. 학교의 여러 연극에서 네가 남자 주인공이었던 게 기억나.
남: 응, 음, 있잖아, 내가 너를 놀리곤 했던 건 널 정말 좋아했기 때문이야.
여: ______________________________

어휘 **tease** 놀리다; 괴롭히다 / **ask A out** A에게 데이트 신청을 하다 / **run into** ~을 우연히 만나다 / **lead actor** 남자 주인공

15 상황에 적절한 말 | ④

▶ 미용사는 긴 머리가 어울리겠다고 했지만, 머리를 짧게 자르지 않으면 어머니께서 용돈을 압수하실 거라서 귀 위까지 자르러 간 것이므로 ④번 대답이 가장 적절하다.

① 아뇨, 그냥 조금만 다듬어 주세요.
② 아니요, 전 긴 머리를 하고 싶어요.
③ 먼저 제 머리를 감겨 주세요. 괜찮겠지요?
④ 그러면 좋겠어요. 하지만 어머니께서 허락하지 않으실 거예요.
⑤ 헤어 왁스를 올바르게 쓰는 방법을 알려 주세요.

W: Andrew spends a lot of time on his hair. **It's not too long** but a little below his ears. At home he styles his hair with lots of hair wax. At school, he frequently checks his hair. His mom is angry. Andrew's mom **orders him to get it cut short**. It must be above his ears. If he doesn't, **she'll take away his allowance**. Andrew walks unhappily into a hairdresser's near his house. The hairdresser says he looks good with long hair and suggests that **she just trim his hair**. In this situation, what would Andrew most likely say to the hairdresser?

여: Andrew는 머리 손질에 많은 시간을 보낸다. 머리카락이 그렇게 길지는 않지만 귀밑으로 조금 내려온다. 집에서 그는 헤어 왁스를 많이 사용하여 머리를 손질한다. 학교에서 그는 자주 머리 스타일을 확인한다. 그의 어머니께서는 화가 나셨다. Andrew의 어머니께서는 그에게 머리를 짧게 자르라고 말씀하신다. 머리 길이가 귀 위에 와야 한다. 그렇게 하지 않으면, 어머니께서는 그의 용돈을 압수하실 것이다. Andrew는 불만에 차서 집 근처의 미용실로 걸어 들어간다. 미용사가 그는 긴 머리가 어울린다고 말하며 머리를 조금 다듬기만 할 것을 제안한다. 이러한 상황에서 Andrew가 미용사에게 할 말로 가장 적절한 것은 무엇인가?

어휘 **trim** ~을 다듬다[손질하다] / **take away** 빼앗다

16~17 세트 문항 | 16. ① 17. ③

▶ 16. 알레르기를 소개하면서 땅콩 알레르기와 벌침 알레르기의 예를 들어 특히 위험한 알레르기에 대해 알려주고 있다.

① 매우 위험한 알레르기들의 위협
② 알레르기 반응에 대처하는 가장 좋은 방법
③ 음식과 알레르기 사이의 연관성
④ 당신이 벌침을 피해야 하는 이유
⑤ 음식과 곤충 알레르기를 피하는 방법

▶ 17. 해석 참조

M: There are millions of people who suffer from allergies worldwide, and many of these people can **have severe allergic reactions**. Allergies occur when your immune system **overreacts to a substance** that normally shouldn't cause a reaction. Although allergic reactions can be caused by many things, there are a few that are especially dangerous. Peanut allergies are **one of the most common causes** of life-threatening reactions. More than 3 million people in the United States report being allergic to peanuts, and about 150 of them **die annually from** allergic reactions. That's more than the number of people killed by lightning strikes. Bee stings are also very dangerous to anyone who is allergic. At least 40 Americans die each year from bee stings. To avoid getting stung, **be extremely cautious** whenever bees are nearby. Stay calm, and slowly move away. You can somewhat **discourage bees from coming** near you by not wearing bright clothing and not using perfume. Also, if you're picnicking outdoors, don't open the food **until you're ready to eat**, and cover up high-sugar foods and drinks like sodas that can attract bees.

남: 전 세계에 알레르기로 고생하는 사람들이 수백만 명 있으며, 이들 중 많은 사람들이 극심한 알레르기 반응을 보일 수 있습니다. 알레르기는 보통 때는 반응을 일으키지 않을 물질에 면역 체계가 과잉 반응을 보일 때 발생합니다. 알레르기 반응은 많은 것에 의해 생길 수 있지만, 특히 위험한 것이 몇 가지 있습니다. 땅콩 알레르기는 생명을 위협하는 반응의 가장 흔한 원인 중 하나입니다. 미국에서 3백만 명이 넘는 사람들이 땅콩 알레르기가 있다고 말하며, 매년 그 중 약 150명이 알레르기 반응으로 사망합니다. 이는 벼락을 맞아 사망하는 사람들의 수보다 많습니다. 벌침 또한 알레르기가 있는 사람에게 매우 위험합니다. 해마다 최소 40명의 미국인이 벌에 쏘여서 사망합니다. 벌에 쏘이는 것을 피하기 위해서, 벌이 근처에 있을 때마다 극도로 주의하십시오. 침착함을 유지하다가 ① 천천히 멀어지십시오. ② 밝은 색 옷을 입는 것을 피하고 ④ 향수를 사용하지 않음으로써 벌이 가까이 오는 것을 어느 정도 막을 수 있습니다. 또한, 야외에서 소풍을 즐기고 있다면, 먹을 준비가 될 때까지 음식을 개봉하지 말고, 벌을 유인할 수 있는 ⑤ 당도 높은 음식과 탄산음료 같은 음료를 덮어 두십시오.

어휘 **bee sting** 벌침; 벌에 쏘인 상처 ***cf.* sting** (곤충의) 침; 쏘인 상처; (곤충 등이) 쏘다, 찌르다 / **stay clear of** ~을 피하다 / **immune system** 면역 체계 / **overreact** 과잉 반응을 보이다 / **substance** 물질 / **discourage A from v-ing** A가 v하는 것을 하지 못하게 하다

Answers & Explanation

01. ① 02. ② 03. ④ 04. ⑤ 05. ② 06. ④ 07. ② 08. ④ 09. ③ 10. ③
11. ③ 12. ① 13. ⑤ 14. ⑤ 15. ③ 16. ② 17. ④

01 화자가 하는 말의 목적 | ①

▶ 학교 기념행사를 자선 장터 행사로 대체하겠다는 내용이므로 학교 행사 계획의 변경을 알리는 것이 목적이다.

M: I'm terribly sorry to inform you that our school's anniversary event **cannot be held this year**. Since our neighborhood is still suffering from the terrible damage done by last summer's typhoon, we decided to cancel this event. Instead, **to demonstrate our care and concern**, we are planning a charity bazaar event. Soon your homeroom teacher will **give you a note with details** of next week's event, which every student should attend. Of course, your family members are most welcome too. This is **a time to gather our thoughts and efforts** for those who lost everything overnight. Please bring anything that would **help them to overcome** this difficult time.

남: 우리 학교의 개교 기념행사가 올해에는 열리지 못하게 된 점을 알려드리게 되어 상당히 유감입니다. 우리 이웃이 지난여름 태풍으로 인한 극심한 피해로 여전히 고통 받고 있기 때문에 우리는 이번 행사를 취소하기로 결정했습니다. 대신 우리의 걱정과 관심을 보여주기 위해서 자선 장터 행사를 계획 중입니다. 곧 여러분의 담임 선생님께서 다음 주에 있을 행사에 관한 상세한 사항이 적힌 쪽지를 나누어 주실 것인데, 이번 행사에는 학생 모두가 참가해야 합니다. 물론 여러분의 가족들 또한 매우 환영합니다. 지금이야말로 하룻밤에 모든 것을 잃어버린 분들을 위해 우리의 생각과 노력을 모을 때입니다. 그들이 이 어려운 시기를 극복하는 데 도움이 될 어떤 것이라도 가지고 오십시오.

어휘 **anniversary** 기념일의; 기념일 / **damage** 피해, 손해 / **typhoon** 태풍 / **demonstrate** (행동으로) 보여주다 / **charity** 자선 (행위) / **bazaar** 자선 장터, 자선 특매장 / **overcome** ~을 극복하다

02 의견 | ②

▶ 여자는 공원에 치워지지 않은 배설물을 보고, 사람들이 반려견에 더 주의해야 한다고 말하면서 다른 사람이 대신 그것들을 치우는 것을 용납할 수 없다고 했다.

M: It was a great idea to come to the park. The weather is perfect.
W: Yeah, but **I wish people would be more careful** with their dogs.
M: I guess I haven't even noticed any dogs since we got here.
W: I don't think there are any. But **that's not what I'm talking about**. Look at that.
M: Ugh, is that dog waste?
W: How could the owner of that dog just walk off and leave that there? **Who is going to clean that up**?
M: I suppose some unfortunate park employee will have to.
W: That's simply unacceptable. Sometimes the careless behavior of others really **makes me sick**.
M: You have a point.

남: 공원에 오는 건 정말 좋은 생각이었어. 날씨가 완벽해.
여: 응. 그렇지만 사람들이 자신의 반려견에 더 주의하면 좋겠어.
남: 난 여기 온 이후로 개를 한 마리도 못 본 것 같은데.
여: 한 마리도 없는 것 같아. 하지만 내가 말하고 있는 건 그게 아니야. 저걸 봐.
남: 윽, 저거 개 배설물이야?
여: 저 개의 주인은 어떻게 그냥 휙 가버리고 저걸 저기에 내버려둘 수가 있지? 저걸 누가 치울 거야?
남: 어떤 운 없는 공원 직원이 해야 할 것 같아.
여: 그건 정말 용납할 수 없어. 때때로 다른 사람들의 경솔한 행동은 정말 나를 화나게 해.
남: 네 말이 맞아.

어휘 **simply** ((강조하여)) 정말로, 완전히; 단순히, 그저 / **unacceptable** 용납할 수 없는, 받아들일 수 없는 / **make A sick** A를 아주 화나게 하다

03 관계 | ④

▶ 남자는 박사이기는 하지만 caller, show, listen과 같은 단어를 보아 현재는 라디오 방송 진행자임을 알 수 있다. 여자는 방송 프로그램 청취자이다.

M: ... and our next caller is Andrea from Sydney.
W: Hi, Dr. Karl. I love your show. I listen every week.
M: That's terrific, Andrea. **Have you got a question for me** today?
W: Yes. Dr. Karl, I'm always tired. Mom says **I should go to bed earlier**, but I can never sleep until 2 a.m.
M: How old are you, Andrea?
W: Sixteen.
M: Oh, that's a natural teenage sleep pattern. Teenagers have very special sleep needs.
W: You mean **falling asleep late is natural for my age**?
M: Yes, so you don't have to worry about it too much. **Just sleep as much as you can** on weekends.
W: OK, thank you.
M: Thanks for calling, Andrea.

남: … 그리고 다음 전화 연결은 시드니에 사시는 Andrea 양입니다.
여: 안녕하세요, Karl 박사님. 저는 박사님 방송을 아주 좋아해요. 매주 들어요.
남: 굉장하네요, Andrea 양. 오늘 저에게 질문이 있나요?
여: 네. Karl 박사님, 저는 항상 피곤해요. 엄마가 말씀하시길 제가 더 일찍 자야 한대요. 하지만 저는 새벽 2시가 되어서야 잠이 들어요.
남: Andrea 양, 몇 살이죠?
여: 16살이요.
남: 아, 그건 청소년의 자연스러운 수면 패턴입니다. 청소년은 매우 특별한 수면 욕구가 있지요.
여: 늦게 자는 것이 제 나이에 자연스럽다는 말씀이세요?
남: 네, 그러니 너무 많이 걱정하지 않아도 됩니다. 주말에 될 수 있으면 수면을 많이 취하도록 하세요.
여: 알겠습니다. 감사합니다.
남: 전화 감사합니다, Andrea 양.

어휘 **pattern** (정형화된) 패턴, 양식 / **need** 욕구, 필요한 것; 필요로 하다

04 그림 불일치 | ⑤

▶ 꽃이 케이크와 카드 사이에 있다고 했으므로 그림 속의 선물 상자가 대화 내용과 일치하지 않는다.

[Cell phone rings.]
M: Hello?
W: Hi, Chuck. It's me. Sorry I couldn't be there to **help you set things up**.
M: That's okay. I think we can **manage by ourselves**.
W: Good. I really want Ms. Wilson's farewell party to be a success. Did you get balloons?
M: Yes, and I taped them on the board.
W: Okay, but the board still says "Thank You, Teacher," right?
M: Of course. And I **put the candle in the cake** and set it on the table.
W: Great. Do you need me to bring any flowers?
M: No, I already have some on the table. They're between the cake and the cards from the other students.
W: Then I'll just bring my card and add it to the pile.
M: Right. **That's all you need to do**.

[휴대전화 벨이 울린다.]
남: 여보세요?
여: 안녕, Chuck. 나야. 준비하는 것을 도와주러 가지 못해서 미안해.
남: 괜찮아. 우리끼리 그럭저럭할 수 있을 거 같아.
여: 잘됐다. 난 Wilson 선생님 송별 파티가 정말 잘되면 좋겠어. 풍선은 가져왔니?
남: 응. 그리고 칠판에 테이프로 붙였어.
여: 그래. 하지만 칠판에 '고맙습니다, 선생님'이라고 여전히 쓰여 있지, 맞지?
남: 당연하지. 그리고 케이크에 초를 꽂아서 교탁 위에 올려놨어.
여: 아주 잘했네. 내가 꽃을 가져가야 할까?
남: 아니, 내가 교탁 위에 이미 좀 갖다 놨어. 케이크랑 다른 학생들이 쓴 카드들 사이에 있어.
여: 그럼 난 그냥 내 카드를 가져가서 그 (카드) 더미 위에 합쳐야겠네.
남: 그래. 그것만 하면 돼.

어휘 **set up** ~을 준비[마련]하다; ~을 설립하다 / **tape** (접착) 테이프로 붙이다; (접착용) 테이프 / **pile** 더미, 포개[쌓아] 놓은 것

05 부탁한 일 | ②

▶ 자전거를 타러 가자는 남자의 제안에 여자가 타이어에 바람이 빠졌는데 수리점이 없어 자전거를 못 타고 있다고 말했다. 그때 남자가 수리하는 법을 안다고 하자 여자가 토요일 오전에 고쳐달라고 부탁하고 있다.

M: Are you busy on Saturday afternoon, Julie?
W: I don't have any plans. **What do you have in mind**?
M: I'd love to go bicycling in Lake Park with you. I remember that you once said you love bicycling in the park.
W: That was right after I had bought my new bike. But **I haven't been riding for a while**.
M: Why not?
W: My bicycle is broken. OK, it's not really broken. There's a hole in my tire and **it's flat**. But there aren't any bicycle repair shops near my house.
M: I know how to fix a flat tire. I've patched a hole before.
W: Well, then **can you come over and fix it** on Saturday morning? Afterwards, I'd love to go to the park with you.
M: OK. No problem.

남: Julie, 토요일 오후에 바쁘니?
여: 별다른 계획은 없어. 넌 생각하는 거 있니?
남: 너와 호수 공원에 자전거를 타러 가고 싶어. 네가 공원에서 자전거 타기를 아주 좋아한다고 예전에 말했던 것을 기억하고 있어.
여: 그건 새 자전거를 산 직후였어. 하지만 난 한동안 자전거를 타지 않고 있어.
남: 왜 안 타는데?
여: 내 자전거가 고장 났거든. 좋아, 정말로 고장 난 것은 아니야. 타이어에 구멍이 나서 바람이 빠졌거든. 그렇지만 집 근처에 자전거 수리점이 한 군데도 없어.
남: 내가 바람 빠진 타이어를 어떻게 수리하는지 알아. 전에 구멍을 때워본 적이 있어.
여: 음, 그럼 토요일 오전에 와서 그것을 고쳐줄 수 있니? 그 뒤에 너와 공원에 가고 싶어.
남: 좋아. 문제없어.

어휘 **flat** (타이어가) 바람이 빠진; 평평한 / **patch** (구멍 등을 헝겊으로) 때우다, 덧대다; ~을 수선하다, 고치다

06 금액 | ④

▶ 15달러짜리 A4 용지 10박스(150달러)와 5달러짜리 바인더 10개(50달러)를 주문하고 5% 할인(10달러)을 받으므로 190달러가 된다. 여기에 배송비로 20달러를 추가로 지불해야 하므로 남자가 지불할 금액은 210달러이다.

[Telephone rings.]
W: Glory Office Supplies. How can I help you?
M: Hi, this is Michael Whittier of Lloyd Trading Company. **I'd like to place a rush order** for some office supplies.
W: Okay, Mr. Whittier. **What would you like to order**?
M: First, we'd like to purchase 10 boxes of A4 printer paper. How much is it?
W: It costs $15 a box.
M: I see. And we need 10 plastic binders. I want the one with 40 pockets.
W: It's $5 each, and you need 10 binders. Will there be anything else?
M: No, **that's all for now**. You offer a bulk discount, right?
W: I can give you 5% discount as usual.
M: Okay. We need them today. **Is there a delivery charge** for a rush order?
W: Yes, you'll have to pay $20 for delivery. We can get it to you today after 3 p.m.
M: Okay. We'll pay with our corporate credit card.
W: Thanks.

[전화벨이 울린다.]
여: Glory 사무용품입니다. 무엇을 도와드릴까요?
남: 안녕하세요. 저는 Lloyd 무역회사의 Michael Whittier입니다. 몇몇 사무용품을 급하게 주문하고 싶습니다.
여: 알겠습니다, Whittier 씨. 무엇을 주문하고 싶으신가요?
남: 우선, 저희는 A4 프린터 용지 10박스를 구매하고 싶어요. 얼마인가요?
여: 한 박스에 15달러입니다.
남: 알겠습니다. 그리고 저희는 플라스틱 바인더 10개가 필요해요. 40개 포켓이 달린 것을 원해요.
여: 하나당 5달러이고, 10개의 바인더가 필요하시군요. 다른 것도 필요하실까요?
남: 아뇨, 지금은 그게 다입니다. 대량 구매 가격을 할인해주시죠, 그렇죠?
여: 평소대로 5퍼센트 할인을 해드릴 수 있습니다.
남: 좋습니다. 저희는 그것들이 오늘 필요해요. 급한 주문에는 배송비가 있나요?
여: 네, 배송을 위해 20달러를 지불하셔야 할 겁니다. 오늘 오후 3시 이후에 가져다드릴 수 있습니다.
남: 알겠습니다. 저희 법인카드로 결제할게요.
여: 감사합니다.

어휘 **office supplies** 사무용품 / **trading company** 무역회사, 상사(商社) / **rush order** 급한 주문 / **binder** (종이 등을 함께 묶는) 바인더; 제본 기계 / **bulk discount** 대량 구매 가격 할인 / **corporate** 법인의; 기업(체)의

07 이유 | ②

▶ 여자의 친구가 이사를 하는데 여자가 이미 도와주겠다고 약속해서 내일 열리는 시사회에 갈 수 없다고 했다.

M: Today is truly my lucky day. My brother just called and told me the best news ever.
W: Well, what did he say?
M: **He got tickets to a preview** of the movie *Blue Moon*, but he can't make it. So he's giving them to me. Do you want to see it?
W: Are you kidding me? Of course I do. I heard it's a great movie.
M: We can get some autographs from the actors **after watching the movie**.
W: Really? I'm a big fan of Timothy Dalton! I can't believe it! By the way, why can't he go?
M: He had an unexpected business trip to Seattle so he'll be **out of town**. Anyway, it begins at 6 p.m. tomorrow, so let's meet at 5.
W: Tomorrow? Oh, no! My best friend is moving tomorrow and **I've offered to help** her move. I already promised to go.
M: Oh, I understand.
W: I really want to go and get Timothy's autograph.
M: If you want, I'll get his autograph for you.
W: Great! That's very nice of you! I really appreciate it!

남: 오늘은 정말 내 행운의 날이야. 내 남동생이 방금 전화 와서 최고의 소식을 말해줬어.
여: 음, 그 애가 뭐라 했는데?
남: 그 애가 영화 〈푸른 달〉의 시사회 티켓을 구했는데, 그 애는 갈 수 없대. 그래서 내게 그것들을 주기로 했어. 너 보러 가고 싶니?
여: 장난해? 물론 가고 싶지. 그건 굉장한 영화라고 들었어.
남: 우리는 영화를 본 다음에 배우들에게 사인을 받을 수 있어.
여: 정말? 나는 Timothy Dalton의 열혈 팬이야! 믿을 수 없어! 그건 그렇고, 그 애는 왜 못가는 거야?
남: 시애틀로 예기치 않은 출장이 생겨서 도시에 없을 거야. 그건 그렇고, 시사회가 내일 오후 6시에 시작하니까 5시에 만나자.
여: 내일? 세상에! 내 가장 친한 친구가 내일 이사를 해서 그녀가 이사하는 것을 도와주겠다고 했는데. 가겠다고 이미 약속했어.
남: 아, 이해해.
여: 정말로 가서 Timothy의 사인을 받고 싶다.
남: 네가 원한다면 내가 너에게 그의 사인을 구해다 줄게.
여: 굉장해! 정말 친절하구나! 정말로 고마워!

어휘 **preview** 시사회; 시사평 / **make it** (모임 등이) 가다[참석하다]; 성공하다; 해내다 / **autograph** (유명인의) 사인; 사인을 해주다 / **unexpected** 예기치 않은, 예상 밖의

08 언급하지 않은 것 | ④

▶ 해석 참조

M: American dancer, singer, and actress Josephine Baker spent most of her career in France, captivating audiences with her wonderful performances and outgoing personality. Nicknamed "The Black Venus," she left the U.S. for France **while still a teen**. She made the decision because she wanted to experience the freedom of acting in Paris. After arriving, her style of dance quickly **made her a star**. During the late 1920s, Baker was the highest-paid entertainer in Europe and the most photographed. She **was also active in the French resistance** during World War II, and remained a lifelong fighter against racism. She even **adopted 12 children** from varying ethnic backgrounds and named them her "Rainbow Tribe."

남: 미국의 무용수이자 가수, 여배우인 Josephine Baker는 경력 대부분을 프랑스에서 보냈으며 훌륭한 연기와 외향적인 성격(① 성격)으로 관객들을 사로잡았다. '검은 비너스'란 별명(② 별명)을 가진 그녀는 아직 십 대일 때 미국을 떠나 프랑스로 갔다. 그녀는 파리에서 연기하는 자유를 경험하고 싶어서(③ 고국을 떠난 이유) 그런 결정을 내렸다. (프랑스에) 도착 후 그녀는 무용 스타일 때문에 곧 스타가 되었다. 1920년대 후반에, Baker는 유럽에서 가장 많은 보수를 받은 연예인이었으며 사진도 가장 많이 찍혔다. 그녀는 제2차 세계대전 동안 프랑스의 저항 운동에도 적극적이었으며 인종차별에 저항(⑤ 참여한 사회 운동)하는 투사로 평생을 살았다. 심지어 인종 배경이 다양한 아이들을 12명 입양하고 그들을 자신의 '무지개 부족'이라 명명하였다

어휘 **captivate** ~의 마음을 사로잡다[매혹하다] / **outgoing** 외향적인, 사교적인 / **resistance** (지하) 저항 운동, 레지스탕스; 저항, 반항 / **racism** 인종 차별(주의); (폭력적인) 인종 차별 행위 / **varying** 변화하는, 다양한 / **ethnic** 인종의, 민족의

09 내용 불일치 | ③

▶ Tour de France 경기의 최초 부정행위는 1904년 발각되었다.

W: The Tour de France is the world's most famous bicycle race. It is held in France every July. Cyclists ride for 22 days across a distance of more than 3,000 kilometers. Unfortunately, some cyclists **want to win so badly** that they cheat. The very first cheats on the Tour de France were caught in 1904. They **had secretly ridden on trains** in between towns. More recently, cheats have used performance-enhancing drugs. These drugs **make muscles bigger and stronger**, reduce pain, and give enormous energy. They are forbidden because they are not fair. American Floyd Landis won the 1997 Tour de France, but then a blood test showed he had used performance-enhancing drugs. **His prize was taken away from him**, and he returned to America in disgrace.

여: Tour de France는 세계에서 가장 유명한 자전거 경주이다. 이것은 매년 7월 프랑스에서 개최된다. 사이클 선수들은 22일간 3천 킬로미터가 넘는 거리를 횡단한다. 유감스럽게도 일부 사이클 선수는 너무나 우승하고 싶어서 부정행위를 한다. Tour de France에서 최초의 부정행위자들은 1904년에 발각되었다. 그들은 마을 사이를 잇는 열차를 몰래 탔다. 최근 들어 부정행위자들은 경기력을 향상시켜주는 약물을 사용해왔다. 이러한 약물은 근육을 더 크고 더 강하게 만들고, 고통을 줄여주며, 엄청난 에너지를 준다. 그것들은 정당하지 않으므로 금지되었다. 미국인 Floyd Landis는 1997년 Tour de France에서 우승했지만, 그 후 혈액검사 결과 그가 경기력을 향상시켜주는 약물을 사용했음이 밝혀졌다. 상은 압수되었고, 그는 불명예스럽게 미국으로 돌아갔다.

어휘 **cyclist** 사이클 선수 / **cheat** 부정행위를 하다; 부정행위자, 속임수를 쓰는 사람 / **performance** 성적, 성과; 공연 / **enhance** ~을 높이다, 강화하다 / **enormous** 거대한, 막대한 / **disgrace** 불명예, 망신

10 도표 이해 | ③

▶ 두 사람은 투자 강좌는 우선 제외했고 5주나 6주 과정을 택하기로 했다. 수업료가 300달러가 넘지 않는 두 가지 중 수업료가 더 싼 것보다는 강좌 평가가 더 좋은 것을 택하기로 했으므로 답은 ③이다.

M: Miranda, you said you're interested in getting a real estate license.
W: Yes, I am. **I'm thinking of taking** an online real estate course. I've already downloaded the course list.
M: Good. How about taking a course together?
W: Sure. Why don't we take a look at the course list? Do you have **a particular field of interest**?
M: I'm afraid we can't take the investment course because we are beginners.
W: You're right. And I need to finish this course within 6 weeks because I'll leave on my two-month vacation in December.
M: I also think a 5-6 week course would be perfect. By the way, fees are very expensive. **What's your price range**?
W: I don't want to spend more than $300 for just one course.
M: Me either. Well, it seems we have two choices. The difference is the course fee. Want to choose the cheaper one?
W: But the student ratings of that course are **lower than the other**.
M: You're right. Then I guess we need to take this course.
W: It looks like it.

남: Miranda, 부동산 중개사 자격증을 따는 데 관심 있다고 말했죠.
여: 예, 그래요. 온라인 부동산 강좌를 듣는 것을 생각하고 있어요. 전 벌써 과정 목록을 다운받았어요.
남: 좋군요. 함께 과정을 듣는 건 어때요?
여: 좋아요. 과정 목록을 살펴볼까요? 특별한 관심을 가진 분야가 있나요?
남: 우리는 초보자이기 때문에 투자 강좌는 들을 수 없을 것 같군요.
여: 맞아요. 그리고 저는 12월에 2달 휴가를 떠날 거라서 이 강좌를 6주 안에 끝내야 해요.
남: 나도 5주에서 6주짜리 강좌가 완벽할 거라고 생각해요. 그런데 수업료가 아주 비싸군요. 당신의 가격대는 얼마인가요?
여: 난 단 한 강좌에 300달러 넘게는 쓰고 싶지는 않아요.
남: 나도 그래요. 음, 우리가 두 가지 선택이 있는 것 같군요. 차이는 강좌 수업료인데요. 더 싼 것을 선택하고 싶나요?
여: 하지만 그 강좌의 학생 평가가 다른 것보다 더 낮은데요.
남: 맞아요. 그러면 우리가 이 강좌를 택해야겠네요.
여: 그런 것 같아요.

어휘 **rating** 평가, 등급 / **real estate** 부동산 중개업 / **license** 자격증, 면허증 / **particular** 특별한, 특정한 / **range** 범위, 한도

11 짧은 대화에 이어질 응답 | ③

▶ 여자는 공포영화를 보기에 적절한 나이를 묻고 있다.

① 저 영화 굉장한 것 같아.
② 나는 지난 일요일에 21살이 되었어.
③ 열다섯 살이 넘어야 할 것 같아.
④ 원작은 10년 전에 제작되었어.
⑤ 공포영화는 그 애에게 정말 무서울 거야.

W: Let's go watch that new horror movie with your brother.
M: Sounds great. But I don't think he's old enough.
W: **How old do you have to be**?
M: ______________________________

여: 네 남동생과 함께 새로 나온 저 공포영화를 보러 가자.
남: 좋은 생각이야. 하지만 내 동생은 (그 영화를 볼) 나이가 아직 안 된 것 같아.
여: 몇 살이어야 하는데?
남: ______________________________

12 짧은 대화에 이어질 응답 | ①

▶ 하루에 문자를 몇 통 보내는지 묻는 남자의 말에 가장 적절한 응답을 고른다.

① 확실히는 모르지만, 많이 보내.
② 그게 전화하는 것보다 훨씬 더 저렴해.
③ 문자를 너무 많이 보내는 것을 그만하려고 노력할 거야.
④ 문자에 오류가 많이 있어.
⑤ 최대 크기는 80자야.

M: **It seems like** you are always texting these days.
W: I **prefer texting to talking** on the phone.
M: How many texts do you think you send in a day?
W: ______________________________

남: 넌 요즘 항상 문자를 보내고 있는 것 같아.
여: 전화로 얘기하는 것보다 문자를 보내는 것이 더 좋아.
남: 하루에 문자를 몇 통이나 보내는 것 같니?
여: ______________________________

어휘 **character** 글자; 성격; 등장인물

13 긴 대화에 이어질 응답 | ⑤

▶ 갈 길은 바쁘지만 운전 중 졸음이 오는 운전자에게 할 수 있는 말로 ⑤번이 적절하다.

① 하지만 걸어가기에는 너무 멀어.
② 조금만 더 가면, 그것을 보게 될 거야.
③ 고맙지만, 이번에는 그냥 넘어갈게.
④ 우리 돌아가야 할 것 같아. 점점 어두워지고 있어.
⑤ 내가 운전할게. 너는 뒷자리에서 잠을 자도 돼.

W: Look. **There's a sign up ahead** — "Lake Victoria National Park, 320 kilometers."
M: Three hours to go.
W: I can't wait! I hope we get the same campsite we had last summer.
M: We need to get there before the school holiday crowds. **Just keep up your good driving** and we'll get there in time.
W: We don't have any time to stop, do we?

M: No, we don't. Ha-bin, I just **saw you rubbing your eyes** and yawning!
W: Yeah, I'm feeling really sleepy.
M: Take a rest! You've been driving too long. **What if you fall asleep** at the wheel?
W: But we can't stop. We have to keep going if we want to get our campsite!
M: ___________________________________

여: 봐, 앞에 표지판이 있어. 'Victoria 호수국립공원, 320킬로미터'.
남: 세 시간 더 가야 해.
여: 빨리 가고 싶어! 우리가 지난여름에 이용했던 곳과 같은 야영지를 잡을 수 있으면 좋겠다.
남: 방학한 학생들보다 먼저 그곳에 도착해야 돼. 네가 계속해서 운전을 잘하면 거기에 제시간에 도착할 거야.
여: 차를 세웠다가 갈 시간이 없겠지, 그렇지?
남: 응, 없어. 하빈아, 방금 네가 눈을 비비면서 하품하는 것을 봤어!
여: 응, 정말 졸려.
남: 쉬어! 너무 오랫동안 운전을 했구나. 만일 운전하다 잠들면 어떻게 되겠니?
여: 하지만 멈출 수가 없잖아. 우리가 원하는 야영지를 잡고 싶으면 계속 가야 해!
남: ___________________________________

어휘 **nap** 선잠, 낮잠 / **campsite** 야영지 / **keep up** ~을 지속하다, 유지하다 / **at[behind] the wheel** 운전하고 있는

14 긴 대화에 이어질 응답 | ⑤

▶ 남자는 점심식사로 두 명 예약을 해 두었지만, 같이 식사하기로 한 상대가 오지 못하는 상황이다. 곤란함을 표하는 남자에게 여자의 응답으로는 같이 먹자고 말하는 ⑤번이 가장 적절하다.

① 그 일자리에 그녀를 고용하지 않았어야 했는데.
② 응, 나도 알아. 그녀가 30분 전에 나에게 전화했어.
③ 그녀는 일하러 너무 늦게 와서 곤란해질 거야.
④ Mario's에서 그녀와 점심 먹게 서둘러야겠어!
⑤ 음, 나는 점심 먹을 시간 있는데, 같이 가면 어떨까?

W: Hi, Ben. What are you doing here?
M: Waiting for someone.
W: **It's too hot to be waiting outside**!
M: I know. **I've been waiting for ages**. I wonder where she is.
W: Why don't you call?
M: I can't. Stupidly, **I left my cell phone** at home! And I can't remember her number.
W: Oh! Anyway, are you meeting for something important?
M: Oh, no. She's a friend. We have lunch together every Tuesday at Mario's.
W: Oh, I love Mario's! **The pizza is great there**! So, who's the friend?
M: Do you know Joanna?
W: Joanna! I saw her just before. She's working at Smokey's Burgers.
M: Oh, I completely forgot! She told me last week she got a new job! But **I still have a reservation for two**.
W: ___________________________________

여: 안녕, Ben. 여기서 뭐 하니?
남: 누굴 기다리고 있어.
여: 밖에서 기다리기에는 너무 더운 날씨다!
남: 맞아. 오랫동안 기다리고 있었거든. 난 그 애가 어디에 있는지 모르겠어.
여: 전화하지 그래?
남: 못 해. 바보같이, 전화기를 집에 두고 왔어! 그리고 그 애의 전화번호도 기억이 안 나고.
여: 아! 어쨌든, 중요한 일 때문에 만나는 거니?
남: 아니, 그 애는 친구인데, 우리는 화요일마다 Mario's에서 함께 점심을 먹어.
여: 아, 나도 Mario's를 정말 좋아해! 거기 피자가 정말 맛있어! 그래, 그 친구가 누구니?
남: Joanna라고 아니?
여: Joanna! 방금 전에 그 애를 봤어. Smokey's Burgers에서 일하고 있던데.
남: 아, 완전히 잊어버렸어! 새 일자리를 얻었다고 지난주에 말해줬는데! 하지만 2명 예약이 아직 되어있는데.
여: ___________________________________

어휘 **get[be] in trouble** 곤란에 처하다 / **reservation** 예약

15 상황에 적절한 말 | ③

▶ 학교에서 의기소침해진 학생의 어머니와 선생님이 이야기를 나누는 상황이다. 최근에 생긴 여동생에게 관심이 몰린 것이 원인일 수 있는 상황에서 선생님이 어머니에게 할 말로는 ③이 가장 적절하다.

① 그게 도움이 된다고 생각하신다면 우리가 그걸 해봐요.
② 그는 자기 문제를 나와 의논하기를 원하지 않아요.
③ 우리가 그에게 더 많은 주의를 기울이도록 노력해야 한다고 생각합니다.
④ 그에게 무슨 일이 일어나고 있는지 알아내실 수 있기를 바랍니다.
⑤ 그의 문제가 학업과 관련되어 있다고 생각하지 않습니다.

M: Sylvia is Anthony's mother. Today she comes to Anthony's school to meet his teacher, Mr. Grant, because he wants to talk with her about Anthony. Mr. Grant says Anthony **has been one of the best students** in the class, but recently he rarely participates and he doesn't get along with his classmates. He says Anthony looks stressed. Sylvia is very surprised to hear this at first, but she says it's probably because **Anthony got a younger sister** last month. She thinks he is upset because everyone in the family **is giving his sister all the attention**. Mr. Grant thinks it would **affect his behavior at school**. In this situation, what would Mr. Grant most likely say to Sylvia?

남: Sylvia는 Anthony의 어머니이다. 오늘 그녀는 그의 선생님인 Grant 선생님이 Anthony에 대해서 이야기를 나누기를 원하기 때문에 선생님을 만나러 Anthony의 학교로 간다. Grant 선생님은 Anthony가 반에서 가장 뛰어난 학생 중 하나였지만 최근에 그가 거의 참여하지 않고 친구들과 잘 어울리지 않는다고 말한다. Sylvia는 이것을 듣고 처음에는 무척 놀라지만 아마 Anthony가 지난달에 여동생을 생겼기 때문인 것 같다고 말한다. 그녀는 가족의 모든 사람들이 그의 여동생에게 모든 관심을 쏟기 때문에 그가 속상해한다고 말한다. Grant 선생님은 그것이 학교에서의 그의 행동에 영향을 주었을 것이라고 생각한다. 이 상황에서 Grant 선생님이 Sylvia에게 뭐라고 말하겠는가?

어휘 **pay attention** 관심을 갖다 / **figure out** 알아내다, 이해하다 / **participate** 참가하다 / **get along with** ~와 잘 지내다 / **attention** 관심; 주목

16~17 세트 문항 | 16. ② 17. ④

▶ 16. 스포츠에서 가장 빠르게 움직이는 물체에 대한 몇 가지 사실을 소개하겠다는 말 뒤에 빠른 순서에 따라 물체를 차례대로 소개하고 있다.

① 스포츠 세계 기록
② 스포츠에서 가장 빠른 물체
③ 스포츠에서 공의 역사
④ 사람들이 스포츠를 좋아하는 이유
⑤ 전 세계적으로 인기 있는 스포츠

▶ 17. 해석 참조

① 배드민턴 ② 골프 ③ 테니스 ④ 야구 ⑤ 축구

W: Hello, everyone. At the end of last class, we spent some time talking about popular sports and why people love them. Certainly, one reason for their popularity is the fast-paced action that attracts a viewer's attention. Continuing with this idea, I'd like to introduce some facts about **the fastest moving objects in sports**. Surprisingly, the fastest object recorded in a major sport isn't a ball. It's the shuttlecock from badminton, **which has been recorded** traveling at 493 km/h. In second place is the golf ball. In 2012, one was recorded traveling at 340 km/h. Now, you might have already guessed that tennis balls **would be on this list**. In fact, tennis serves have been recorded traveling at over 260 km/h, making the tennis ball the fifth-fastest object in sports. The objects **mentioned so far** have all been small. So, you might not expect that a soccer ball can travel at over 210 km/h. What other sports **would you guess** belong on this list?

여: 안녕하세요, 여러분. 지난 수업이 끝날 무렵에, 우리는 인기 있는 스포츠와 왜 사람들이 그것을 좋아하는지에 대해 이야기하는 시간을 가졌습니다. 분명히, 그것들이 인기 있는 한 가지 이유는 관객의 주의를 끌어당기는 빠른 속도의 행동입니다. 이 생각에 이어, 저는 스포츠에서 가장 빠르게 움직이는 물체에 대한 몇 가지 사실을 소개해 드리고자 합니다. 놀랍게도, 주요 스포츠에서 기록된 가장 빠른 물체는 공이 아닙니다. 그 물체는 ① 배드민턴의 셔틀콕인데, 시속 493km로 움직이는 것으로 기록된 적이 있습니다. 2위는 ② 골프공입니다. 2012년에 골프공 하나가 시속 340km로 이동하는 것으로 기록되었습니다. 이제, 여러분은 ③ 테니스공이 이 목록에 있을 것이라고 벌써 짐작했는지도 모르겠습니다. 실제로, 테니스 서브는 시속 260km가 넘게 이동하는 것으로 기록되어, 테니스공을 스포츠에서 다섯 번째로 빠른 물체로 만들었습니다. 지금까지 언급된 물체들은 모두 작았습니다. 그래서 여러분은 ⑤ 축구공이 시속 210km가 넘는 속도로 이동할 수 있다는 것을 예상하지 못할지도 모르겠습니다. 여러분은 다른 어떤 스포츠가 이 목록에 속해 있을 거라 추측하시나요?

어휘 **popular** 인기 있는; 대중[통속]적인 ***cf.* popularity** 인기; 대중성 / **pace** 속도를 유지하다; 속도 / **attract** 마음을 끌어당기다 / **object** 물체; 대상; 목표 / **mention** 언급하다, 말하다 / **so far** 지금까지 / **belong** (~에) 속하다, (~의) 소유이다

Answers & Explanation

01. ① 02. ① 03. ② 04. ④ 05. ③ 06. ③ 07. ③ 08. ③ 09. ⑤ 10. ②
11. ② 12. ⑤ 13. ④ 14. ⑤ 15. ④ 16. ② 17. ③

01 화자가 하는 말의 목적 | ①

▶ 음악 교사의 결혼식을 알리며 결혼식에서 노래를 부를 합창단원을 찾는 내용이므로 결혼식에서 축가를 부를 사람을 모집하는 것이 목적임을 알 수 있다.

M: Great job today, class. **As your choir instructor**, I'm very pleased to see that your singing is improving. You're sure to do well at this fall's competition. Now, before you leave for the day, **I have an announcement to make**. Ms. Hathaway, the music teacher, is getting married next month. She has asked if someone from our choir **would be willing to sing** at her wedding. I believe this is a great opportunity to show your appreciation for one of the nicest and most dedicated teachers at our school, **as well as to sing in public**. Those who are interested should speak to me after class. I will be happy to help with selecting a song and practicing for the performance. Let's show Ms. Hathaway **how much we care**!

남: 학생 여러분, 오늘 굉장히 잘했습니다. 여러분의 합창 교습 강사로서, 여러분의 노래가 나아지고 있는 것을 보게 되어 매우 기쁩니다. 이번 가을에 열리는 대회에서 분명히 잘할 거예요. 자, 여러분이 떠나기 전에 알려드릴 사항이 있습니다. 음악 교사인 Hathaway 선생님께서 다음 달에 결혼하십니다. Hathaway 선생님께서 우리 합창단의 누군가가 결혼식에서 노래를 부를 의향이 있는지를 물어보셨습니다. 이는 사람들 앞에서 노래를 부르는 것뿐 아니라, 우리 학교에서 가장 훌륭하고 헌신적인 선생님 중 한 분께 여러분의 감사를 표할 좋은 기회라고 생각합니다. 관심이 있는 학생들은 수업이 끝난 후 제게 말해주세요. 곡 선정과 공연 연습을 기꺼이 도와주겠습니다. Hathaway 선생님께 우리가 얼마나 (선생님을) 위하는지를 보여줍시다!

어휘 **choir** 합창단, 성가대 / **instructor** (특정한 기술이나 운동을 가르치는) 강사[교사] / **announcement** 공지, 공고; 발표 (내용), 소식; 안내 방송 / **dedicated** 헌신적인, 전념하는

02 의견 | ①

▶ 여자는 휴대 전화가 가격이 비쌀뿐더러 아이들의 주변 인식을 어렵게 하고, 두뇌 발달에도 해롭다는 이유를 들어 아이들에게 휴대 전화를 사주는 것이 좋지 않다고 말하고 있다.

W: Hi, Tony. What are you reading?
M: It's an article in today's paper about a new cell phone.
W: Oh, I saw that phone on TV.
M: It has several amazing features and applications, but the price is high.
W: They say it's selling well **despite its high cost**.
M: Right. It's especially popular with younger children. I think parents buy it **to stay in touch with their kids**.
W: I'm not sure if that's right.
M: What do you mean?
W: It's dangerous because young kids can't control themselves. They focus entirely on their phones and **are unaware of what is going on** around them.
M: True. Kids these days become **completely absorbed in their phones**.
W: In addition, there's evidence that suggests cell phone radiation is harmful to developing brains.
M: That is something to worry about.

여: 안녕, Tony. 뭘 읽고 있어?
남: 새 휴대 전화에 관한 오늘 신문 기사야.
여: 아, TV에서 그 휴대 전화를 봤어.
남: 여러 가지 놀라운 기능과 애플리케이션이 있지만, 가격이 높아.
여: 사람들이 값이 비싸도 잘 팔린다고 하더라.
남: 맞아. 이 휴대 전화는 어린아이들에게 특히 인기 있어. 부모님들이 아이들과 연락하기 위해서 사는 것 같아.
여: 그게 옳은 일인지 잘 모르겠어.
남: 무슨 말이야?
여: 어린아이들은 자신을 통제할 수 없어서 위험해. 그 애들은 휴대 전화에 완전히 집중해 있어서 주변에서 무슨 일이 일어나는지 알아차리지 못해.
남: 맞는 말이야. 요즘 아이들은 휴대 전화에 완전히 몰입해.
여: 게다가, 휴대 전화에서 나오는 방사선이 두뇌 발달에 해롭다는 걸 암시하는 증거도 있어.
남: 그거 걱정할 일이구나.

어휘 **application** ((약어: app)) 응용 프로그램; 지원(서); 적용, 응용 / **stay in touch** 연락을 유지하다 / **unaware** 알지[눈치 채지] 못하는 (↔ aware 알고[눈치 채고] 있는) / **absorb** (사람의 마음을) 열중시키다; ~을 흡수하다[빨아들이다] ***cf.* absorption** 흡수; 통합; 몰두 / **radiation** 방사선; (열·에너지 등의) 복사

03 관계 | ②

▶ 남자는 여자가 알아야 할 규칙과 할 일을 알려준 뒤, 자신의 요리를 먹으러 올 단체 손님을 위해 요리를 잘해야 한다고 말하고 있고, 여자는 남자를 위해 일하게 돼서 영광이라고 하며 남자를 돕기 위해 최선을 다하겠다고 말하는 것으로 보아 주방 보조원과 주방장의 대화이다.

W: Hello, I'm Jenny Harper.
M: It's nice to meet you, Jenny.
W: **It's an honor to work for you**. I saw your interview in a cooking magazine last month.
M: I'm glad to hear that. Now, let's go over **what you will be doing today**.
W: Okay. I'm ready.
M: First, **wash your hands thoroughly**. That's the first rule you should never forget while working here.
W: Got it. And then?
M: Peel the onions in this bowl and **cut this lettuce into small pieces**.
W: No problem. By the way, I heard a group is coming to taste your special dish, salmon with salad.
M: Right. I should cook especially well for them.
W: **I'll do my best to help you**, as well. Please tell me if you need anything.
M: Great. Let's get started.

여: 안녕하세요. 저는 Jenny Harper입니다.
남: 만나서 반가워요, Jenny.
여: 선생님을 위해 일하게 돼서 영광입니다. 지난달에 요리 잡지에서 선생님의 인터뷰를 봤어요.
남: 그 말을 들으니 기쁘군요. 이제, 당신이 오늘 무엇을 할지 점검합시다.
여: 네, 준비됐어요.
남: 우선 손을 철저히 씻으세요. 그게 당신이 여기서 일하는 동안 절대 잊지 말아야 할 첫 번째 규칙입니다.
여: 알겠습니다. 그러고는요?
남: 이 그릇에 있는 양파를 까고 이 양상추를 잘게 썰어주세요.
여: 문제없습니다. 그런데 선생님의 특별 요리인 샐러드를 곁들인 연어를 맛보러 단체 손님이 오신다고 들었어요.
남: 맞아요. 전 그분들을 위해 요리를 특별히 잘해야 하죠.
여: 저도 최선을 다해서 선생님을 도와드릴게요. 뭔가 필요하시면 제게 말씀해 주세요.
남: 좋습니다. 이제 시작하죠.

어휘 **thoroughly** 철저히, 철두철미하게; 대단히 / **lettuce** 양상추

04 그림 불일치 | ④

▶ 남자의 여동생인 Carol이 긴소매 셔츠를 입고 있다고 했는데 그림에는 반소매 셔츠를 입고 있으므로 ④가 일치하지 않는다.

W: What **did you do over the weekend**, Harry?
M: I went to the park with my friends. Do you want to see a picture?
W: Of course. *[pause]* Oh, the wooden hut beside the bench looks great.
M: Yes, we ate lunch inside of it.
W: Wonderful. Who are the people **chatting on the bench**?
M: They're Sandra and Nick. They hadn't met for a while, so they had a lot to talk about. And the man **leaning against the tree** is my friend Jake.
W: Since he's holding a racket, he **must have played badminton**.
M: That's right. And the girl with a long-sleeved shirt is my younger sister Carol.
W: She looks excited, and the puppy running in front of her is so cute. Is it her dog?
M: Yeah. It loves to run with her.

여: Harry, 주말 동안 뭐 했어?
남: 친구들이랑 공원에 갔어. 사진 한 장 볼래?
여: 물론이야. *[잠시 후]* 아, 벤치 옆에 있는 통나무 오두막이 좋아 보인다.
남: 응, 우리는 그 안에서 점심을 먹었어.
여: 멋지다. 벤치에서 이야기를 나누고 있는 사람들은 누구니?
남: Sandra랑 Nick이야. 그 애들은 한동안 만나지 않아서 할 얘기가 많았어. 그리고 나무에 기대어 있는 남자는 내 친구 Jake야.
여: 그가 라켓을 들고 있으니까, 분명 배드민턴을 쳤겠네.
남: 맞아. 그리고 긴소매 셔츠를 입은 여자아이는 내 여동생 Carol이고.
여: 신나 보인다. 그리고 그 애의 앞에서 달리고 있는 강아지가 정말 귀여워. Carol의 강아지야?
남: 응. 그 강아지는 Carol이랑 달리는 걸 정말 좋아해.

어휘 **hut** 오두막, 막사

05 부탁한 일 | ③

▶ 남자는 여자에게 거실을 청소해 달라고 부탁했다. 여자는 처음에는 간접적으로 거절 의사를 보였지만, 엄마에게 야단맞을 거라는 남자의 말에 바로 치우겠다고 했다.

M: It's almost 1:00 p.m. What should we have for lunch?
W: We have leftover pizza in the refrigerator. We **could warm it up**.
M: That's not an option.
W: **You're tired of it already**?
M: No, I ate it all last night. How about ordering some food?
W: That's fine with me. I'm **in the mood for chicken**.
M: Sounds good. I have the number saved in my cell phone.
W: Could you order it while I clean the kitchen table? It's **too messy to eat on**.
M: I think the living room is worse. Could you please take care of it first?
W: I'm too hungry to bother with the living room.
M: If Mom sees it, **we'll get a scolding**.
W: Alright. I'll do that right now.

남: 오후 한 시가 다 됐네. 점심으로 뭘 먹어야 할까?
여: 냉장고에 남은 피자가 있어. 그걸 데우면 돼.
남: 그건 선택사항이 아니야.
여: 너 벌써 피자가 싫증 난 거야?
남: 그게 아니라, 내가 어젯밤에 다 먹었어. 음식을 주문하는 게 어떨까?
여: 난 좋아. 난 치킨을 먹고 싶어.
남: 좋아. 내 휴대 전화에 저장된 전화번호가 있어.
여: 내가 부엌 식탁을 치우는 동안 그걸 주문해줄래? 음식을 먹기엔 식탁이 너무 지저분해.
남: (식탁보다) 거실이 더 엉망인 것 같은데. 그곳을 먼저 처리해줄래?
여: 거실을 신경 쓰기엔 너무 배고픈데.
남: 엄마가 거실을 보시면, 우리는 야단맞을 거야.
여: 알았어. 지금 바로 청소할게.

어휘 **be in the mood for** ~할 기분이 나다 / **messy** 지저분한, 엉망인; 지저분하게 만드는 / **get a scolding** 야단맞다, 꾸지람을 듣다

06 금액 | ③

▶ 카메라 가방은 50달러이고 15달러짜리 메모리 카드도 두 개 사기로 했으므로 원래 총 금액은 80달러이다. 그런데 10퍼센트 할인 쿠폰을 사용하기로 했으므로 8달러를 할인받아 여자가 지불할 총 금액은 72달러가 된다.

W: Excuse me. How much are your camera bags?
M: They **range anywhere from** $15 to $150. What are you looking for?
W: I want something decent that's under $70.
M: Then **I recommend this one**. It's priced at $50, but it's very well-made.
W: Great! I'll take it. Can I also get two 16GB memory cards?
M: Of course. They're $15 each. **Would that be all**?
W: Yes. I have two coupons I'd like to use: one is for 10% off and the other is for $5 off the total price.
M: I'm sorry, but you can't combine the two coupons. Our store policy is to accept only one at a time. **It's indicated on** the coupons.
W: Oh, then I guess I'll use the 10% off coupon today. Here's my credit card.
M: OK. Thank you for shopping with us!

여: 실례합니다. 카메라 가방이 얼마인가요?
남: 15달러에서 150달러까지 다양합니다. 어떤 것을 찾으시나요?
여: 70달러 아래로 괜찮은 것을 원해요.
남: 그럼 이것을 추천합니다. 가격은 50달러인데, 아주 잘 만들어졌어요.
여: 좋아요! 그것을 살게요. 16GB 메모리 카드도 두 개 살 수 있을까요?
남: 물론입니다. 한 개에 15달러입니다. 그게 필요하신 전부인가요?
여: 네. 사용하고 싶은 쿠폰이 두 가지 있는데요. 하나는 10퍼센트 할인 쿠폰이고, 다른 하나는 총 금액에서 5달러를 할인해주는 거예요.
남: 죄송합니다만, 두 가지 쿠폰을 함께 쓰실 수 없습니다. 가게 방침이 한 번에 한 가지만 받는 것이라서요. 쿠폰에 나와 있습니다.
여: 아, 그럼 오늘은 10퍼센트 할인 쿠폰을 사용할게요. 신용카드 여기 있어요.
남: 알겠습니다. 저희 가게를 이용해주셔서 감사합니다!

어휘 **range** (범위가) 다양하다, (~의 범위에) 이르다 / **decent** 괜찮은, 제대로 된; 점잖은, 예의 바른 / **be priced at** 가격이 ~이다 / **at a time** 한 번에, 따로따로

07 이유 | ③

▶ 두 사람이 이야기하는 자원봉사 프로그램은 최소 3개월 동안 지원에 전념해야 할 것을 요구하는데 남자는 다음 달에 유럽 여행을 가게 되어 최소 봉사 기간을 채울 수가 없으므로 자원봉사 프로그램에 지원할 수 없는 이유는 ③이다.

W: Jonathan, I've just signed up for a volunteer program.
M: What kind of volunteer program?
W: Have you heard of Evergreen Youth Club? They are looking for people **to participate in** their voluntary work project.
M: This is the first time I've heard of it. Can you tell me more?
W: **They host various volunteer activities**, such as opening sports classes for underprivileged children, doing environmental clean-ups and so on.
M: It sounds quite rewarding. I'd like to sign up, too. **Are there any special requirements** or skills that I need?
W: No, just sign up as a member of the club. I think you can volunteer in the soccer class.
M: That would be great. Thanks for the information.
W: Oh, most importantly, they require that **you commit to helping** for the minimum period of three months from next month.
M: Oh, no. Then I can't. I'm planning a trip to Europe for a month next month.
W: Too bad. Okay, then you can apply next time.

여: Jonathan, 나 방금 자원봉사 프로그램을 신청했어.
남: 어떤 종류의 자원봉사 프로그램이니?
여: Evergreen Youth Club이라고 들어 봤니? 그들이 자원봉사 활동 프로젝트에 참여할 사람들을 찾고 있어.
남: 나는 그걸 처음 들어 봐. 내게 더 말해줄 수 있니?
여: 그들은 혜택을 받지 못하는 아이들을 위한 스포츠 교실을 열고 환경 정화 작업을 하는 등 다양한 자원봉사 활동을 주최해.
남: 꽤 보람 있는 것 같다. 나도 신청하고 싶어. 내가 필요한 어떤 특별한 요건이나 기술이 있니?
여: 아니, 단지 클럽의 회원으로 신청하면 돼. 내 생각에 넌 축구 교실에서 자원봉사할 수 있을 거 같아.
남: 그거 멋지겠다. 알려줘서 고마워.
여: 아, 가장 중요한 건 그들은 다음 달부터 3개월의 최소 기간 동안 네가 지원에 전념하기를 요구해.
남: 아 이런. 그럼 난 못하겠다. 난 다음 달에 한 달 동안 유럽 여행을 갈 계획이야.
여: 어쩔 수 없지 뭐. 알겠어. 그러면 너는 다음번에 지원할 수 있어.

어휘 **host** 주최하다; 진행하다; 주최자 / **underprivileged** (사회·경제적으로) 혜택을 못 받는 / **clean-up** 정화 (작업) / **rewarding** 보람 있는; 돈을 많이 버는 / **requirement** 요건, 필요(조건); 요구 / **commit to** ~에 전념[헌신]하다 / **apply** 지원하다; 신청하다

08 언급하지 않은 것 | ③

▶ 해석 참조

M: Do you have any questions about the equipment?
W: No, I think I'm ready to dive.
M: Good. Then the only thing left before we enter the sea is **to warn you about the jellyfish**.
W: Jellyfish? You mean the fish that looks like an umbrella?
M: That's right. Most aren't deadly, but they **release a poison when touched**. It's extremely painful.
W: How can I avoid them?

M: These jellyfish are about a meter in length and will be easy to see.
W: One meter? That's **bigger than I expected**. How many years do they usually live?
M: It **varies by species**. Most large coastal jellyfish live for 2 to 6 months.
W: I guess jellyfish are something **all divers must worry about**.
M: That's true, but don't worry too much. I'll be with you.
W: Okay. Let's go.

남: 장비에 관해 질문이 있으신가요?
여: 아니요, 다이빙할 준비가 된 것 같아요.
남: 좋습니다. 그러면 우리가 바다에 들어가기 전에 남은 한 가지는 해파리에 관해 주의를 드리는 것이군요.
여: 해파리요? 우산처럼 보이는(① 모양) 물고기를 말씀하시는 건가요?
남: 맞아요. 대부분은 치명적이지 않지만, 건드리면 독을 방출(② 유독성)하거든요. 굉장히 아프죠.
여: 제가 그것들을 어떻게 피할 수 있죠?
남: 이 해파리들은 길이가 약 1미터 정도(④ 크기)라서 발견하기 쉬우실 겁니다.
여: 1미터요? 제가 생각했던 것보다 더 크네요. 해파리들은 보통 몇 년을 살죠?
남: 종마다 달라요. 큰 해안 해파리 대부분은 2개월에서 6개월 동안 살죠(⑤ 수명).
여: 해파리는 분명 모든 잠수부가 걱정하는 것이겠군요.
남: 사실이지만, 너무 많이 걱정하지는 마세요. 제가 함께 있을게요.
여: 알겠어요. 가요.

어휘 **extremely** 극도로, 극히 / **coastal** 해안[연안]의

09 내용 불일치 | ⑤

▶ 금요일과 토요일에만 자정까지 운영한다고 했으므로 ⑤가 일치하지 않는다.

W: Attention shoppers. Thank you for visiting Shiny Department Store, **the largest department store** in the city. This announcement is to invite you to the Shiny Pool, which opens this Friday. **Located on the rooftop**, it offers an incredible view of the city for you to enjoy while you swim. **The pool itself can accommodate** up to 300 people and there are shower facilities available. The entrance fee is $10 per person and children under 14 can swim for free. And **admission is half off** for those with department store membership cards. If you aren't already a Shiny Member, **now is a great time to join**. The pool is open every day from 10 a.m. until 10 p.m., and it's open until midnight on Fridays and Saturdays. So come to the Shiny Pool and enjoy your summer.

여: 고객 여러분께 알려드립니다. 시에서 가장 큰 백화점인 Shiny 백화점을 방문해주셔서 감사합니다. 이 안내방송은 이번 주 금요일에 개장하는 Shiny 수영장에 여러분을 초대하기 위함입니다. 옥상에 자리 잡고 있기 때문에 Shiny 수영장은 여러분이 수영하시는 동안 즐기실 수 있는 대단히 멋진 시내 전망을 제공합니다. 수영장 자체는 300명까지 수용할 수 있으며 이용 가능한 샤워 시설이 있습니다. 입장료는 한 명당 10달러이고 14세 미만 어린이는 무료로 수영할 수 있습니다. 또한, 백화점 회원카드를 소지하신 분들께는 입장료가 반값입니다. 아직 Shiny 백화점의 회원이 아니시라면, 지금이 가입하시기 매우 좋은 때입니다. 수영장은 매일 오전 10시에 개장하여 오후 10시까지 운영하며, 금요일과 토요일에는 자정까지 운영합니다. 그러니 Shiny 수영장에 오셔서 여름을 즐기시기 바랍니다.

어휘 **rooftop** (건물의) 옥상 / **accommodate** (건물 등이 사람·물건을) 수용하다; (의견 등을) 수용하다 / **admission** 입장(료); (잘못에 대한) 시인, 인정

10 도표 이해 | ②

▶ 남자는 80달러를 넘지 않는 모델 중에서 GPS 내비게이션 시스템이 있으며 수용 인원이 다섯 명인 차를 빌릴 것이다.

W: Hello, sir. How may I help you?
M: I need to rent a car for a trip.
W: You've come to the right place. As you can see, we have five options. **Do you have a budget in mind**?
M: I think $80 is the most I'm willing to spend.
W: Okay. And would you like a GPS navigation system?
M: I definitely need one. **I won't be familiar with the roads** where I'm going.
W: Then I recommend this model. It has a navigation system and **enough room for seven people**.
M: That sounds good, but I really don't need that much space. A car **with seating for five** would be fine.
W: Then we have just the thing for you. And it will save you some money.
M: Great. I'll take it.

여: 어서 오세요, 손님. 무엇을 도와드릴까요?
남: 여행 갈 때 쓸 차 한 대를 빌려야 해서요.
여: 제대로 오셨네요. 보시다시피, 저희는 다섯 가지의 선택사항이 있습니다. 생각해 두신 예산이 있습니까?
남: 80달러가 제가 쓸 수 있는 최대인 것 같아요.
여: 알겠습니다. 그리고 GPS 내비게이션 시스템을 원하세요?
남: 꼭 필요합니다. 제가 가는 도로가 익숙하지 않을 거예요.
여: 그러면 이 모델을 추천해 드립니다. 내비게이션 시스템이 있고 일곱 명이 탈 수 있는 충분한 공간이 있죠.
남: 괜찮은 것 같은데, 전 그렇게 큰 공간은 별로 필요하지 않아요. 다섯 명이 앉을 자리가 있는 차면 좋겠어요.
여: 그러면 손님께 딱 맞는 게 있네요. 그리고 돈도 약간 절약하실 겁니다.
남: 잘됐네요. 그걸로 할게요.

11 짧은 대화에 이어질 응답 | ②

▶ 공상 과학 영화를 보자고 제안하는 남자에게 여자는 다른 종류의 영화를 보고 싶다고 했으므로, 이에 가장 적절한 응답을 고른다.

① 나도 다양한 장르의 영화를 좋아해. ② 알았어. 이번에는 네가 고르게 해줄게.
③ 그 로맨틱 코미디 영화 정말 재미있게 봤어. ④ 그러면 다음번에 다시 와도 돼.
⑤ 이 영화는 원래 것보다 액션이 더 적어.

W: It looks like there are three movies we could see.
M: Oh, let's watch *Iron Man 3*! **It's supposed to be great**!
W: Another sci-fi movie? I **want to try something different**.
M: ______________________

여: 우리가 볼 수 있는 영화가 세 편 있는 것 같아.
남: 아, 〈아이언맨 3〉를 보자! 굉장할 거야!
여: 또 공상 과학 영화야? 뭔가 다른 걸 시도해보고 싶어.
남: ______________________

어휘 **sci-fi** 공상 과학 영화[소설] ((science fiction의 줄임말, 약어: SF))

12 짧은 대화에 이어질 응답 | ⑤

▶ 여자에게 뜨개질 수업에 다니는지 묻는 남자의 말에 가장 적절한 응답을 고른다.

① 물론이야, 나는 학생들을 가르치는 게 정말 좋아.
② 아니, 지금 집에 가는 길이야.
③ 점점 추워지고 있어서 그걸 만들었어.
④ 네가 원한다면, 너에게 하나 만들어줄 수 있어.
⑤ 실은, 이모가 날 가르쳐주고 계셔.

M: Jenny, did you make this muffler? It's great!
W: Thank you. **I've been learning to knit** since last month.
M: Oh, **are you going to a knitting class**?
W: ______________________

남: Jenny, 이 목도리 네가 만든 거야? 멋지다!
여: 고마워. 지난달부터 뜨개질을 배우고 있어.
남: 아, 뜨개질 수업에 다니는 거야?
여: ______________________

13 긴 대화에 이어질 응답 | ④

▶ 비가 많이 오고 있고, 일이 끝나기 전에 지하철이 끊길 수도 있으므로, 집까지 데려다 주겠다는 여자의 제안을 수락하는 응답이 가장 적절하다.

① 미안해하지 마. 친구 좋다는 게 뭐야?
② 그러면 내일 우리 집에 들르자.
③ 고맙지만 괜찮아. 한 시간 안에 나가야 하거든.
④ 음, 그러면 달리 방법이 없네. 너에게 신세지는구나.
⑤ 정말 지하철 안 타고 싶어?

W: Do you think we'll finish by tonight, Matthew?
M: We have to. That's the deadline. Besides, we can finish in a few hours.
W: Okay, then I'll start on this next file. *[pause]* Did you hear something?
M: It sounds like rain. Look out the window! **It's raining cats and dogs** outside!

W: It's quite a storm. Will you **be able to make it home** after work?
M: I'm not worried. The rain will probably stop later.
W: I don't think so. I heard the rain will last through the night.
M: Oh, I **should have brought an umbrella**.
W: I could drive you home. It's no trouble.
M: Thanks, but my house is **much farther than yours**. I'll take the subway.
W: **It's not a big deal**. Also, the subway might stop before we finish tonight.
M: ____

여: 오늘 밤까지 우리가 끝낼 것 같니, Matthew?
남: 끝내야 해. 마감 기일이니까. 게다가, 우린 몇 시간 후면 끝낼 수 있어.
여: 그래, 그러면 나는 바로 다음 파일을 시작할게. *[잠시 후]* 무슨 소리 들었니?
남: 비가 오는 것 같아. 창밖을 봐! 밖에 비가 억수같이 내리고 있어!
여: 엄청난 폭풍우네. 일 끝나고 집에 갈 수 있겠어?
남: 난 걱정 안 해. 비는 아마 나중에 그칠 테니까.
여: 난 그렇게 생각하지 않아. 비가 밤새 내릴 거라고 들었거든.
남: 아, 우산을 가져왔어야 했는데.
여: 내가 차로 널 집에 태워다줄 수 있어. 어려울 거 없어.
남: 고맙지만, 우리 집이 너희 집보다 훨씬 더 멀잖아. 지하철을 탈게.
여: 그건 별문제 아니야. 또, 지하철은 우리가 오늘 밤에 일을 끝내기 전에 끊길 수도 있어.
남: ____

어휘 **owe** 신세지다; (돈을) 빚지고 있다 / **rain cats and dogs** 비가 억수같이 내리다

14 긴 대화에 이어질 응답 | ⑤

▶ 남자가 새 자전거를 사서 이전에 쓰던 자전거를 버리려하자 여자는 자신의 중고 물품 세일 때 자전거를 팔 것을 제안한다. 이때, 남자가 판매날까지 집에 그 자전거를 둘 곳이 없다고 했으므로 여자는 자기가 대신 보관해주겠다고 할 것이다.

① 내게 더 큰 마당이 있으면 좋겠어. ② 네가 경주에서 잘하길 바랄게.
③ 그들이 일요일에 올 거라니 행복해. ④ 그 자전거를 얼마에 팔기 원해?
⑤ 그러면 내가 널 위해 주말까지 보관해줄 수 있어.

W: Where are you going, Tony? Oh, nice bicycle!
M: Hi, Mina. Thanks, I just bought it at the mall and **I'm on my way home**.
W: It looks great! By the way, don't you already have one?
M: Yes, but I had to buy this high-performance bicycle for next month's race.
W: I see. So, what are you going to do with your old one?
M: **Throw it away**, I guess.
W: Is there **something wrong with it**?
M: No, but I don't need it anymore.
W: Hey, my family **is having a garage sale** on Sunday. You could sell it there.
M: That's a great idea, but I don't have room in my yard to keep both bicycles until then.
W: Your yard isn't **big enough for two bicycles**?
M: Well, my brother and sister each have bicycles also.
W: ____

여: 어디 가니, Tony? 아, 자전거 멋지다!
남: 안녕, 미나. 고마워. 지금 막 쇼핑몰에서 샀고 집에 가는 길이야.
여: 아주 좋아 보인다! 그런데, 너 이미 하나 가지고 있지 않아?
남: 있긴 한데, 다음 달에 있는 경주를 위해서 이 고성능 자전거를 사야 했어.
여: 그렇구나. 그러면 예전 것은 어떻게 할 거야?
남: 버릴 것 같아.
여: 그 자전거에 무슨 문제 있니?
남: 아니, 하지만 더는 필요 없으니까.
여: 얘, 우리 가족이 일요일에 차고에서 중고 물품 세일을 해. 거기에서 그걸 팔아도 돼.
남: 좋은 생각이긴 한데, 우리 집 마당에 그때까지 자전거 두 대를 다 둘 공간이 없어.
여: 마당이 자전거 두 대를 둘 만큼 크지 않다고?
남: 음, 우리 형이랑 여동생도 자전거가 하나씩 있거든.
여: ____

어휘 **high-performance** 고성능의 / **garage sale** (자기 집 차고에서 하는) 중고 물품 세일

15 상황에 적절한 말 | ④

▶ Kyle의 엄마는 매번 시험을 앞두고 벼락치기를 하는 Kyle에게 매일 조금씩 복습을 하라고 권유할 것이다.

① 서두를 필요 없으니 천천히 공부하렴.
② 네 건강이 늘 최우선이다.
③ 괜찮다. 항상 다음 기회가 있잖니.
④ 지금부터는 방과 후에 복습하는 게 좋겠구나.
⑤ 넌 열심히 공부했으니까 좋은 점수를 받을 수 있어.

M: It's late on a Thursday night, and Kyle is studying history for next week's final exam. Since Kyle did not prepare for the exam in advance, **he has stayed up late all week** to study. In fact, Kyle has gotten less than four hours of sleep each night this week. Kyle's mom has noticed that this behavior is **part of a regular pattern** that is repeated each semester. She thinks it is a poor study habit and bad for Kyle's health, **not to mention his performance** at school. Furthermore, she believes Kyle could **avoid this type of studying** by spending a little time each day **going over his classwork**. Since Kyle doesn't seem to realize this, she decides to tell him her opinion. In this situation, what would Kyle's mom most likely say to Kyle?

남: 목요일 늦은 밤, Kyle은 다음 주 기말고사를 위해 역사를 공부하고 있다. Kyle은 시험을 미리 준비하지 않았기 때문에, 이번 주 내내 공부하려고 밤늦게까지 깨어 있다. 사실, Kyle은 이번 주에 밤마다 네 시간 미만으로 자고 있다. Kyle의 엄마는 이러한 행동이 학기마다 반복되는 주기적 패턴의 일부임을 알게 됐다. 그녀는 이것이 학교에서의 학업 성과는 말할 것도 없거니와 나쁜 공부 습관이며 Kyle의 건강에 좋지 않다고 생각한다. 게다가, 그녀는 Kyle이 매일 조금씩 시간을 들여 학교 공부를 복습함으로써 이런 형태의 공부를 방지할 수 있다고 생각한다. Kyle이 이 사실을 깨닫지 못하는 것처럼 보여서, Kyle의 엄마는 자신의 의견을 Kyle에게 말하기로 결심한다. 이 상황에서 Kyle의 엄마가 Kyle에게 할 말로 가장 적절한 것은 무엇인가?

어휘 **not to mention** ~은 말할 것도 없고[물론이고]

16~17 세트 문항 | 16. ② 17. ③

▶ 16. 휴가 기간 동안 할 수 있는 일들을 설명하고 있다.

① 날씨가 여행에 어떻게 영향을 미치는지 ② 휴가를 즐기기 위한 좋은 방법들
③ 새 도서관의 특징들 ④ 가족들을 위한 휴가 계획
⑤ 여행 중에 돈을 절약하기 위한 조언들

▶ 17. 해석 참조

W: We all **look forward to time off**, but it can sometimes be difficult to find fun and interesting activities to do. But there are a few tips that can help you out. For example, a one-day trip outside the city can be fun. **Start by doing a little research online** about the best local foods and places to explore. Then take **public transportation** for a cheap and relaxing journey to your destination. While exploring, you can listen to music. And don't forget to take pictures. Now, if the weather isn't so nice, you can **go to a nearby library instead**. You will be surprised how many things you can do there. Watching a DVD in a multimedia room will be a great start. Special lectures from authors or professors also make a nice change of pace. **More and more libraries hold events** such as mini concerts or plays. Watching one is a great way to spend an evening. And finally, don't forget the cafeteria. It may not be the best, but there will be **a variety of food at reasonable prices**.

여: 우리는 모두 휴가를 몹시 바라지만, 때때로 재미있고 흥미로운 해볼 만한 활동들을 찾는 것이 어려울 수 있습니다. 하지만, 당신을 도와줄 수 있는 몇 가지 방법들이 있습니다. 예를 들어, 시외로의 당일치기 여행이 재미있을 수 있습니다. 그 지역에서 가장 맛있는 음식과 답사할 장소들에 관해 인터넷에서 조사를 조금 하는 것으로 시작하세요. 그런 다음 당신의 목적지까지 저렴하고 편안한 여행을 위해 대중교통을 이용하세요. 답사를 하면서 당신은 음악을 들을 수 있습니다. 그리고 사진 찍는 것을 잊지 마세요. 자, 만약 날씨가 그리 좋지 않으면, 대신에 근처 도서관으로 가도 좋습니다. 거기에서 당신이 할 수 있는 것이 얼마나 많은지에 놀랄 것입니다. 멀티미디어실에서 ① DVD를 보는 것은 멋진 시작이 될 것입니다. 작가나 교수들의 ② 특별 강연도 좋은 기분전환이 됩니다. 점점 더 많은 도서관들이 ④ 미니 콘서트나 연극과 같은 이벤트를 개최합니다. 한 편 관람하는 것은 저녁을 보내는 훌륭한 방법입니다. 그리고 마지막으로, ⑤ 구내식당을 잊지 마세요. 최고는 아닐지 모르지만, 합리적인 가격에 다양한 음식들이 있을 것입니다.

어휘 **day off** 휴가, 휴식 (= time off) / **strategy** 계획, 전략 / **help out** (특히 곤경에 처한 ~을) 도와주다 / **destination** 목적지

Answers & Explanation

01. ④ 02. ③ 03. ③ 04. ⑤ 05. ② 06. ② 07. ① 08. ④ 09. ③ 10. ③
11. ② 12. ① 13. ④ 14. ④ 15. ② 16. ③ 17. ⑤

01 화자가 하는 말의 목적 | ④

▶ 여러 가지 면모를 살펴 자격 있는 후보를 학급 회장으로 선출해야 한다는 취지의 내용이다.

M: Selecting a class president is a very important choice. Although someone may be popular among the students and teachers, it will not necessarily **make them the right candidate**. Other things to consider are whether the candidate can handle **the pressure of being class president**. Will it interfere with doing school work and other activities? Will they **put in enough effort** to represent your voice in school matters? Will they bring about positive changes, or will they simply use the position to **make their college applications look better**? Ask the candidates these questions and choose the one who will best serve you, not just themselves.

남: 학급 회장을 선출하는 것은 매우 중요한 선택을 하는 것입니다. 어떤 사람이 학생들과 선생님들 사이에서 인기가 있을지도 모르지만, 그렇다고 해서 그 사람이 반드시 적절한 후보인 것은 아닐 것입니다. 고려해야 할 다른 사항들은 후보가 학급 회장이라는 중압감을 다스릴 수 있는가 하는 것입니다. 그것이 학업이나 다른 활동들을 방해할 것인가? 후보들이 학교 문제에 있어 여러분의 목소리를 대변하는 데 충분한 노력을 쏟을 것인가? 긍정적인 변화를 가져올 것인가, 아니면 대학입학지원서를 더 좋아 보이게 하기 위해 단순히 지위를 이용할 것인가? 후보들에게 이러한 질문들을 하고 자기 자신만이 아니라 여러분을 위해 가장 잘 봉사할 사람을 선택하십시오.

어휘 **not necessarily** 반드시 ~은 아닌 / **candidate** 후보 / **interfere with** ~을 방해하다[간섭하다] / **put in** (노력 등을) 쏟다[들이다] / **represent** ~을 대변[대표]하다 / **bring about** ~을 야기하다 / **application** 지원[신청](서); 적용

02 의견 | ③

▶ 여자는 학교에서 겪는 문제들에 관해 이야기를 나눌 사람이 있으면 좋겠다고 하면서 학교 상담 체계가 그런 문제들에 도움이 될 수 있을 거라고 말했다.

W: Hi, Jim. You look really tired. Are you feeling alright?
M: **I'm really stressed out**. I'm failing two of my classes and I'm thinking about changing my major.
W: That's too bad. Actually, I'm also **having trouble focusing** on my school work. **I wish we had someone to talk to** about our problems.
M: I think you're right. I know that many of our classmates are feeling a lot of pressure right now.
W: There are also a lot of students that are **having trouble with other students** who are making them feel uncomfortable. A school counseling system might be able to help with those things.
M: That's a great idea. I would really appreciate having someone to talk to.
W: Don't forget that you can talk to me anytime.

여: 안녕, Jim. 너 정말 피곤해 보여. 괜찮니?
남: 난 스트레스가 정말 쌓였어. 강의 중 두 가지를 낙제할 것 같아서 전공을 바꿀까 생각 중이야.
여: 그거 안됐구나. 사실, 나도 학업에 집중하기가 어려워. 우리 문제에 관해 이야기를 나눌 누군가가 있다면 좋겠어.
남: 네 말이 맞는 것 같아. 내가 알기론 우리 반에 많은 애들이 현재 압박감을 많이 느끼고 있어.
여: 마음을 불편하게 만드는 다른 학생들 때문에 곤란해하고 있는 학생들도 많이 있어. 학교 상담 제도가 그런 일들에 도움이 될 수 있을지도 몰라.
남: 그거 정말 좋은 생각이야. 이야기할 누군가가 있다면 정말 고마울 거야.
여: 너는 언제든지 나에게 말할 수 있다는 거 잊지 마.

어휘 **stressed out** 스트레스가 쌓인 / **counseling** 상담, 카운슬링

03 관계 | ③

▶ your honor, to proceed to a trial, select a jury, guilty, getting a lawyer to represent you 등의 표현에서 두 사람이 판사와 피고인 관계임을 알 수 있다.

M: Do you understand the charges against you?
W: I understand, your honor.
M: It is my job to see that there is justice and **that truth wins**.
W: That's why I want it known that **I did not rob** the convenience store.
M: So you are saying you are not guilty?
W: **That is correct**. I am not guilty.
M: We will then have to **proceed to a trial**. This means we will have to select a jury who will decide whether or not you are guilty.
W: I understand. Then how should I start to prepare for the trial?
M: You should start **by getting a lawyer to represent you**.

남: 당신은 자신의 혐의를 알고 있습니까?
여: 알고 있습니다, 판사님.
남: 정의가 있다는 것과 진실이 승리한다는 것을 보여주는 것이 내 일입니다.
여: 그것이 바로 제가 그 편의점에서 훔치지 않았다는 것을 알리고 싶은 이유입니다.
남: 그래서 자신이 무죄라는 것입니까?
여: 그렇습니다. 저는 무죄입니다.
남: 그렇다면 재판을 해야 합니다. 이는 당신이 유죄인지 아닌지를 결정할 배심원단을 우리가 선택해야 할 것이라는 뜻입니다.
여: 알겠습니다. 그럼 제가 재판 준비를 어떻게 시작해야 합니까?
남: 당신을 대변할 변호사를 선임하는 것으로 (준비를) 시작해야 합니다.

어휘 **charge** 혐의; 고소 / **honor** 각하 ((판사·시장 등에 대한 존칭어)) / **rob** ~에서 훔치다, 약탈하다 / **guilty** 유죄의 / **proceed to** ~로 나아가다, ~에 이르다 / **trial** 재판, 공판 / **jury** 배심원단 / **represent** ~을 대변[변호]하다

04 그림 불일치 | ⑤

▶ 남녀가 보고 있는 사진에는 3개의 초가 꽂혀 있는 케이크가 있다고 했으므로 ⑤가 대화의 내용과 일치하지 않는다. 숫자 2 모양의 초는 여자가 아이의 생일 파티에 놓을 계획이라고 했다.

W: Honey, Sean is having his second birthday next month. I'd like to **decorate a special table** for him like this photo.
M: Let me see. Wow! Its theme is the Baby Shark.
W: He really loves the Baby Shark song and dance. What do you think of the triangular flags **hung from the wall**?
M: I like them. They give it a festive mood. I also like the banner behind the table.
W: It has Papa, Mama, and Baby Shark. They put their son's name on the banner, too.
M: Good idea. They decorated the table with three balloons on the right.
W: That's another decoration detail.
M: They also **spread a fish net over the left side** of the table. What a great idea!
W: That's my favorite part. They put a cake with three candles on the fish net.
M: Are you going to organize Sean's birthday party just like this picture?
W: Almost the same, **except for the candles**. I'm going to put a number 2-shaped candle on the cake.
M: That would be great!

여: 여보, Sean이 다음 달에 두 번째 생일을 맞이해요. 그 애를 위해 이 사진처럼 특별한 테이블을 꾸미고 싶어요.
남: 봅시다. 와! 그것의 주제는 아기상어네요.
여: 그 애가 아기상어의 노래와 춤을 정말 좋아하잖아요. 벽에 걸려 있는 삼각형 모양의 깃발에 대해 어떻게 생각해요?
남: 난 그것들이 좋아요. 그것들이 축제 분위기를 만드네요. 나는 또 테이블 뒤에 있는 현수막이 마음에 들어요.
여: 그것에는 아빠, 엄마, 아기상어가 있어요. 그들은 자기 아들의 이름도 현수막에 놓았어요.
남: 좋은 생각이에요. 그들은 테이블을 오른쪽에 세 개의 풍선으로 장식했네요.
여: 그건 또 다른 장식 세부사항이에요.
남: 그들은 또한 테이블 왼쪽에 그물을 펼쳐 놓았어요. 정말 멋진 생각이에요!
여: 그게 제가 가장 좋아하는 부분이에요. 그들은 그물 위에 세 개의 초가 꽂힌 케이크를 두었어요.
남: Sean의 생일 파티를 이 사진과 꼭 같이 준비할 계획이에요?

여: 초만 제외하고, 거의 똑같이요. 케이크 위에 숫자 2 모양의 초를 놓을 계획이에요.
남: 훌륭하겠어요!

어휘 **theme** 주제, 테마 / **hang** 걸다, 매달다 / **festive** 축제의, 축하하는 / **mood** 분위기; 기분 / **banner** 현수막; (국가·군대·단체의) 기 / **spread** 펼치다, 펴다 / **fish net** 그물 모양 직물; 어망 / **organize** 준비[조직]하다; 정리하다

05 추후 행동 | ②

▶ 남자(아들)가 공원에서 롤러블레이드를 타다가 넘어지자 여자(엄마)가 약국에서 붕대를 사 온다고 했다.

W: Johnny! Watch out! You're going to hit that other rollerblader.
M: Ahhh! *[crash]* Ouch!
W: Oh, no! Oh, no! Are you OK? **Your knee is all bloody**.
M: It hurts, but I think I'm OK. Let me try to get up.
W: No, **stay lying down**. I'll get some help. I'll call an ambulance.
M: Mom, it's not that bad. Ouch! I can sit down on that bench.
W: Hmm.... There's a pharmacy **just outside the entrance** of the park. I'll go and get some bandages.
M: OK. I'll wait here. I guess I should have worn my knee pads.
W: I told you to go back and get your knee pads and helmet, but you said it was alright.
M: Well, I **might have learned my lesson** today.
W: I hope so.

여: Johnny! 조심해! 너 저 롤러블레이드 타는 다른 사람과 부딪칠 거야.
남: 아아아! *[쾅]* 아야!
여: 오, 이런! 세상에! 괜찮니? 무릎이 전부 피투성이야.
남: 아프지만 괜찮은 것 같아요. 일어서 볼게요.
여: 안 돼, 그대로 누워 있으렴. 내가 도움을 좀 청해볼게. 구급차를 부를게.
남: 엄마, 그렇게 심각하지 않아요. 아야! 저 벤치에 앉을 수 있어요.
여: 음…. 공원 입구 바로 밖에 약국이 있어. 가서 붕대를 좀 사올게.
남: 알겠어요. 여기서 기다릴게요. 무릎 보호대를 착용했어야 했는데 말예요.
여: 내가 돌아가서 무릎 보호대와 헬멧을 가져오라고 말했지만, 네가 괜찮다고 했잖아.
남: 음, 오늘 교훈을 얻었을지도 몰라요.
여: 그랬으면 좋겠구나.

어휘 **rollerblader** 롤러블레이드를 타는 사람 / **bloody** 피투성이의 / **bandage** 붕대; 붕대를 감다 / **knee pad** 무릎 보호대 ***cf.*** **pad** (손상을 막는) 덧대는 것, 패드, 보호대

06 금액 | ②

▶ 65세 이상인 어머니(20달러), 12세 이상이지만 생일을 맞은 아이(25달러), 그리고 일반 가격(30달러)에 해당하는 남자 자신의 티켓 가격을 모두 합하면 남자가 지불할 금액은 75달러이다.

M: I would like three tickets, please, for my mother, my son and myself. Do any of us qualify for a special ticket?
W: A regular ticket costs $30. If your child is under 12 years old, **he gets in for half price**. And anyone 65 years old or older gets in for $20.
M: Oh, no! Today is my son's 13th birthday. **He just missed the special price**.
W: Actually, we also have a birthday special. If you **have proof of his birthday**, then you can take $5 off the price of a regular ticket.
M: That would be $25? *[pause]* Here's his passport.
W: And how about the rest of your family?
M: **My mother is a senior citizen**. That means she can get in for $20. And I guess I just get a regular ticket.

남: 티켓 세 장 부탁드립니다. 제 어머니와 아들, 그리고 저입니다. 우리 중 누구라도 특별 티켓에 자격이 됩니까?
여: 일반 티켓은 30달러입니다. 아이가 12세 미만이면, 반값으로 입장이 가능합니다. 그리고 65세 이상일 경우 20달러에 입장하실 수 있습니다.
남: 아, 이런! 오늘이 우리 아들의 13번째 생일인데요. 특별가를 놓쳐 버렸네요.
여: 사실, 생일 특별가도 있습니다. 아이의 생일이란 증명서가 있으면, 일반 티켓 가격에서 5달러를 할인받으실 수 있습니다.
남: 그럼 25달러가 되겠네요? *[잠시 후]* 여기 아들의 여권입니다.
여: 그리고 다른 가족분은 어떻게 되십니까?
남: 어머니는 고령자세요. 20달러로 입장이 가능하다는 것이지요. 그리고 저는 그냥 일반 티켓을 사야겠네요.

어휘 **qualify for** ~할 자격이 있다 / **proof** 증명(서), 증거(물) / **senior citizen** 고령자, 노인

07 이유 | ①

▶ 여자는 어제 산 하이힐의 끈이 끊어져 있어서 환불했다고 했다.

M: Honey, **do you mind if I use the computer** for a while?
W: Can you wait just a little longer? I'm buying some shoes online.
M: Really? I thought you went shopping yesterday and bought a pair of high heels.
W: I did, but **the straps were broken** when I got home.
M: Were you able to get your money back?
W: Sure. I paid in cash and I kept the receipt. I **had no problem getting a refund** this morning.
M: That's good. So what kind are you ordering today?
W: I've decided to get these walking shoes. I think I have too many high heels that are hurting my feet, anyway.
M: Good idea. And please **let me know** when you are finished with the computer.

남: 여보, 컴퓨터 잠시 써도 돼요?
여: 조금만 더 기다려줄래요? 온라인으로 신발을 좀 사고 있어요.
남: 정말요? 당신이 어제 쇼핑가서 하이힐 한 켤레를 산 줄 알았는데요.
여: 샀죠, 그런데 집에 오니 끈이 끊어졌더라고요.
남: 돈을 돌려받을 수 있었나요?
여: 물론이죠. 현금으로 지불하고 영수증을 가지고 있었거든요. 오늘 아침 환불받는 데 아무 문제가 없었어요.
남: 잘됐네요. 그래서 오늘은 어떤 종류를 주문할 거예요?
여: 이 워킹 슈즈를 사기로 결정했어요. 어차피, 발을 아프게 하는 하이힐을 너무 많이 가지고 있는 것 같아서요.
남: 좋은 생각이에요. 그리고 컴퓨터 사용이 끝나면 내게 알려줘요.

08 언급하지 않은 것 | ④

▶ 해석 참조

W: Starting tonight, performances of some musicals, including *The Lion King*, are cancelled **until further notice**. The workers who operate the theater **have gone on strike**. The workers' union and theater owners tried very hard but **could not reach a new agreement**. Tickets for any performance that is cancelled will be refunded. Some musicals performed in other parts of the city **are not affected by the strike**. Those theater workers are represented by a different union. *Phantom of the Opera*, *Cats* and *West Side Story* are going on without a problem. Phone the theater if you have tickets to a show and **are unsure if it has been closed down** because of the strike.

여: 오늘 밤을 시작으로 〈라이온 킹〉을 포함한 일부 뮤지컬 공연이 다음 공지가 있을 때까지(① 취소 기간) 취소됩니다. 극장을 관리하는 근로자들이 파업(② 취소 이유)에 들어갔습니다. 노동조합과 극장 소유주들은 매우 노력했지만 새로운 합의점에 도달하지 못했습니다. 취소되는 모든 공연의 티켓은 환불될 것(③ 환불 여부)입니다. 도시의 다른 지역에서 공연되는 일부 뮤지컬은 파업의 영향을 받지 않습니다. 그 극장의 근로자들은 다른 노동조합 소속입니다. 〈오페라의 유령〉, 〈캣츠〉 그리고 〈웨스트 사이드 스토리〉는 문제없이 공연될 것입니다. 공연 티켓을 소지하고 계신데 파업으로 인해 공연이 취소되었는지 확실치 않으신 분들은 극장으로 전화(⑤ 공연 여부 문의처)해 주시기 바랍니다.

어휘 **go on strike** 파업에 들어가다 / **workers' union** 노동조합 / **reach an agreement** 합의에 도달하다 / **refund** 환불하다

09 내용 불일치 | ③

▶ 검은색 봉지는 담배꽁초와 같은 쓰레기를 위한 것이다.

M: Welcome to the annual Amity Beach Clean-Up Day. **As you can see around you**, the recent bad weather has made our once-beautiful beach quite ugly. To my left, you will see a table with trash bags and gloves. The orange bags **will be used for recyclable materials**, such as glass, plastic and aluminum. The black bags will be used for trash, such as cigarette butts and old shoes. The table to my right has food and drinks, so please, help yourselves. Now, if everyone will get a partner and **line up for supplies**, each team will get one orange bag, one black bag and two pairs of gloves. Let's make this beach **the pride of our community** once again!

남: Amity 해변 연례 청소의 날에 오신 것을 환영합니다. 여러분 주위에서 보시다시피, 최근 궂은 날씨로 인해 한때 아름다웠던 우리의 해변이 흉하게 변했습니다. 제 왼쪽으로 쓰레기봉투와 장갑이 놓인 테이블이 보이실 것입니다. 오렌지색 봉투는 유리, 플라스틱 그리고 알루미늄과 같은 재활용품을 담기 위해 사용될 것입니다. 검은색 봉투는 담배꽁초나 낡은 신발과 같은 쓰레기를 담기 위해 사용될 것입니다. 제 오른쪽에 있는 테이블에는 음식과 음료가 있으니 마음껏 드십시오. 이제, 모든 분이 파트너와 짝지어서 용품을 배급받기 위해 줄을 서시면, 각 팀은 오렌지색 봉투 한 장과 검은색 봉투 한 장, 그리고 두 켤레의 장갑을 받으실 것입니다. 다시 한 번 이 해변을 우리 지역 사회의 자랑거리로 만들어 봅시다!

어휘 **annual** 연례의, 매년 열리는 / **recyclable** 재활용할 수 있는 / **cigarette butt** 담배꽁초 / **line up** 줄을 서다

10 도표 이해 | ③

▶ 미끄럼틀 구매의 조건으로 우선 4세에서 6세 아이를 위한 것이어야 했고, 그 다음에는 금속이 아닌 플라스틱을 선택했다. 또한 미끄럼틀의 개수는 2개를 선택했고 마지막으로 500달러 이하의 가격을 선택했으므로 모든 조건을 충족하는 미끄럼틀은 ③이다.

W: Bill, I think we need to replace the slide climber in the kindergarten playground.
M: I thought about that, too. **Which one should we get**?
W: I have a catalog here. Let's take a look.
M: Oh, very nice! We need to find something for kids between the ages of 4 and 6.
W: You're right. **Don't you think** plastic would be better for the kids? Metal can be dangerous.
M: Of course. They could **hurt themselves**, and it can also rust over time.
W: How many slides should it have?
M: There should at least be two slides so that the kids don't have to wait long.
W: You're right. The kids can start fighting if they wait too long. But three slides **would take up too much space**. It would be too big for our playground.
M: Then let's get one with two slides. How much should we spend?
W: We can't spend more than $500.
M: Well, we'll have to get this one. Let's hurry and order.

여: Bill, 유치원 놀이터에 있는 미끄럼틀을 교체해야 할 것 같아요.
남: 나도 그렇게 생각했어요. 어떤 것을 사야 할까요?
여: 여기 카탈로그가 있어요. 한 번 보죠.
남: 아, 아주 좋네요! 우리는 4살에서 6살 연령 사이의 아이들을 위한 것을 찾아야 해요.
여: 맞아요. 플라스틱이 아이들에게 더 좋을 것 같지 않아요? 금속은 위험할 수 있잖아요.
남: 물론이죠. 아이들이 다칠 수 있고, 그게 시간이 흐르면서 녹이 날 수도 있어요.
여: 미끄럼틀이 몇 개나 있어야 할까요?
남: 적어도 두 개는 있어야 아이들이 오래 기다릴 필요가 없어요.
여: 당신 말이 맞아요. 너무 오래 기다린다면 아이들은 싸우기 시작할 거예요. 하지만 3개의 미끄럼틀은 너무 많은 공간을 차지할 거예요. 우리 놀이터에 너무 클 거예요.
남: 그러면 2개짜리를 삽시다. 우리가 얼마나 지출해야죠?
여: 500달러를 초과해서 지출할 수는 없어요.
남: 음, 그러면 이것을 사야겠군요. 서둘러서 주문합시다.

어휘 **replace** 교체하다, 대체하다 / **slide** 미끄럼틀 / **playground** 운동장, 놀이터 / **catalog** 카탈로그, 목록 / **rust** 녹슬다

11 짧은 대화에 이어질 응답 | ②

▶ 개들을 돌보기가 힘들지 않느냐고 묻고 있으므로 가끔은 힘들 수 있다는 응답이 가장 적절하다.

① 네가 개를 키워야 한다고 생각해. ② 가끔은 힘들 수 있어.
③ 까만 개가 내가 가장 좋아하는 개야. ④ 네게 개 사료를 좀 줄 수 있어.
⑤ 난 동물 병원에서 일하고 있어.

M: **I'm thinking of getting a dog**. You have one, right?
W: Actually, I have three. They are so much fun to play with.
M: **Aren't they hard to care for**?
W: ______________________________

남: 난 개를 한 마리 키우려고 생각하고 있어. 너도 한 마리 키우지, 그렇지?
여: 실은, 세 마리를 키우고 있어. 같이 놀면 정말 재미있어.
남: 개들을 돌보기가 힘들진 않니?
여: ______________________________

12 짧은 대화에 이어질 응답 | ①

▶ 여자가 우선 Jennifer에게 전화해서 괜찮은지 물어봐야 하지 않겠느냐고 했으므로 이에 대한 적절한 응답을 찾는다.

① 내가 지금 바로 할게. ② 나는 Jennifer와 공부하는 게 좋아.
③ 난 괜찮아. 집으로 가자. ④ 도서관이 문을 너무 일찍 닫네.
⑤ 그 애의 집이 어디 있는지 알아.

W: The library is closing soon. We need to find **somewhere else to study**.
M: Let's go to Jennifer's house.
W: Shouldn't we call her first **to ask if she minds**?
M: ______________________________

여: 도서관이 곧 문을 닫아. 우리 공부할 다른 곳을 찾아야 해.
남: Jennifer 집으로 가자.
여: 우선 그 애에게 전화해서 괜찮은지 물어봐야 하지 않을까?
남: ______________________________

13 긴 대화에 이어질 응답 | ④

▶ 남자가 원하는 스카프는 작년에 나왔던 제품이라 현재 구입이 불가능하다. 판매원(여자)은 아마도 이 상황에 적절한 대응을 할 것이다.

① 여기서는 의류를 팔지 않습니다. 옆 가게로 가보시지요.
② 고객 고충 처리부는 4층에 있습니다.
③ 쿠폰을 가지고 계시면, 기꺼이 울 제품을 팔겠습니다.
④ 죄송합니다만, 엄선된 신제품 스카프가 준비되어 있습니다.
⑤ 우리 가족은 함께 사진에 찍히는 것을 좋아하지 않아요.

M: I saw a red scarf in your catalogue. Do you have it here?
W: We might. Do you remember what it was called?
M: I thought it was called a red wool scarf. Sorry, I didn't notice the style name.
W: That's OK. I have the current catalogue right here.
M: That isn't the same catalogue I was looking at. **Mine had a family on the cover** wearing ski clothes.
W: I'm sorry, but I think you were looking at last year's book!
M: How could that happen? **I just got it yesterday**.
W: Well, we **have had a number of people call** and complain that the old one was sent to them.
M: Does that mean you don't **have that exact scarf** in your store?
W: ______________________________

남: 카탈로그에서 붉은색 스카프를 봤는데요. 여기 있나요?
여: 아마도 있을 것입니다. 제품명이 무엇인지 기억하십니까?
남: 붉은색 울 스카프라고 부르는 것 같던데요. 죄송해요. 스타일 명이 있는지 몰랐어요.
여: 괜찮습니다. 현재 유통되고 있는 카탈로그가 여기 있습니다.
남: 이것은 제가 보고 있던 것과 같은 카탈로그가 아니네요. 제 것은 표지에 스키복을 입은 가족이 있었어요.
여: 죄송합니다만, 손님께서 작년 책을 보고 계셨던 것 같습니다!
남: 어떻게 그런 일이 있을 수 있죠? 어제 받았는데요.
여: 글쎄요, 많은 분이 전화하셔서 오래된 카탈로그를 받았다고 항의하셨습니다.
남: 그 말은 그것과 같은 스카프가 이 매장에 없다는 뜻인가요?
여: ______________________________

어휘 **selection** 선택된 것

14 긴 대화에 이어질 응답 | ④

▶ 남자는 공연 대부분을 서 있어야 하는 오케스트라석보다는 위층의 좌석과 무대 측면 좌석 중에서 선택할 것이다. 그 두 가지의 비용을 알아보는 남자의 말로 적절한 것을 고른다.

① 그 록 공연을 정말 보고 싶습니다.
② 그것들은 제가 생각했던 만큼 편안하군요.
③ 혼잡한 시간에 열차에서 서 있는 것을 좋아하지 않습니다.
④ 그건 비싸군요. 위층의 자리는 어떤가요?

⑤ 오케스트라석을 구하기 위해서라면 두 배라도 내겠습니다.

[Phone rings.]

W: Thank you for calling Ticketron. What can I do for you?

M: I'd like to buy two tickets for the rock concert on Saturday at the concert hall.

W: OK. **We have seats available** in the orchestra pit and seats in the upper deck.

M: Which ones **have a better view**?

W: The orchestra seats have a better view, but you will find yourself standing for most of the show.

M: Hmm. I was hoping to enjoy the concert from **the comfort of my own seat**.

W: Oh, there is another option, but they are very expensive.

M: What option is that?

W: We have stage-side seats. There are **only a dozen seats in total** and we have two left.

M: Great. How much are they?

W: They are $250 each.

M: ______________________________

[전화벨이 울린다.]

여: Ticketron에 전화해 주셔서 감사합니다. 무엇을 도와 드릴까요?

남: 콘서트 장에서 토요일에 열리는 록 공연의 표를 두 매 구입하고 싶습니다.

여: 알겠습니다. 현재 오케스트라석과 위층의 좌석을 구입하실 수 있습니다.

남: 어느 쪽 좌석이 더 잘 보이나요?

여: 오케스트라석이 더 잘 보입니다만, 공연 대부분 서 있게 되실 것입니다.

남: 음. 저는 좌석에 편히 앉아서 공연을 즐기기를 바랐는데요.

여: 아, 선택권이 하나 더 있지만, 매우 비쌉니다.

남: 그게 무엇이죠?

여: 무대 측면 좌석이 있습니다. 총 열두 좌석뿐이고 두 좌석이 남아있습니다.

남: 좋습니다. 얼마입니까?

여: 좌석당 250달러입니다.

남: ______________________________

어휘 **rush hour** 혼잡한 시간 / **deck** (배·경기장 등의) 층; 갑판 / **orchestra pit** (극장의) 오케스트라석(席) / **dozen** 12개

15 상황에 적절한 말 | ②

▶ 친구들과 영화를 같이 보고 싶지만 자신이 봤던 영화는 두 번 보고 싶지 않은 Jess의 답변을 유추해 본다.

① 걱정하지 마. 두 번 보는 것도 나는 괜찮아.
② 우린 우리들 중 아무도 보지 않은 영화를 봐야 해.
③ 난 액션 영화를 보면서 옆 영화관에 있을게.
④ 그 영화는 환상적이야. 뜻밖의 결말을 보여 줘.
⑤ 즐거운 시간 보내! 나는 커피숍에서 너희를 기다릴게.

M: Every Saturday, Jess and Lucinda go out with their friends, Carter and Patty. They usually go to dinner and then a movie and then for a late night cup of coffee. Every week, Carter **insists that he choose the movie**. Even if Jess doesn't want to see the movie Carter has chosen, he doesn't want to argue with his good friend, so **he just goes along**. This week, Carter says he wants to see a movie that Jess has already seen. Carter says that it isn't his or the girls' fault that Jess **saw it without them**. Although Jess does want to see a movie with her friends, she doesn't **feel like seeing the same movie twice**. And she thinks Carter should respect his friends' opinion this time. In this situation, what would Jess most likely say to Carter?

남: 매주 토요일, Jess와 Lucinda는 친구인 Carter와 Patty와 함께 외출한다. 그들은 주로 저녁을 먹은 후 영화를 보고 밤늦게 커피를 마신다. 매주, Carter는 자신이 영화를 고르겠다고 고집한다. Jess는 Carter가 고른 영화가 보고 싶지 않지만, 친한 친구와 논쟁을 벌이고 싶지 않아서, 그냥 따른다. 이번 주, Carter는 Jess가 이미 본 영화를 보고 싶다고 말한다. Carter는 Jess가 자신들 없이 그것을 본 것은 자신의 잘못도 여자 친구들의 잘못도 아니라고 한다. 비록 Jess는 친구들과 영화를 보고 싶긴 하지만, 같은 영화를 두 번 보고 싶지는 않다. 그리고 그녀는 이번에는 Carter가 친구들의 의견을 존중해야 한다고 생각한다. 이러한 상황에서 Jess가 Carter에게 할 말로 가장 적절한 것은 무엇인가?

어휘 **argue** 논쟁하다

16~17 세트 문항 | 16. ③ 17. ⑤

▶ 16. 카페인 중독 인정하기, 보이는 곳에 결심 적어두기, 카페인 대용 찾기 등 카페인 중독을 다스리는 방법에 대해 말하고 있다.

① 카페인의 효능
② 카페인의 중독성이 강한 이유
③ 카페인 중독을 다스리는 방법
④ 커피가 신체에 미치는 다양한 영향
⑤ 커피와 허브티 간의 차이점

▶ 17. 해석 참조

카페인이 제거된 커피라도 카페인이 있을 수 있으므로 대신 허브티를 마시라고 했다.

W: You can't work before your morning coffee? Does your IQ jump a couple of points after a cup from your favorite coffee shop? If so, **you may be addicted to coffee**. You might think this is a harmless addiction, but caffeine can hurt you if you have too much. In order to get rid of your caffeine addiction, you will first have to accept the fact that you are addicted to it. Then, write down your resolution to quit caffeine on a piece of paper and paste it in a place where you will see it every day. You can also try to find a caffeine alternative whenever **your cravings for caffeine get out of hand**. Even decaffeinated coffee may contain caffeine, so **stick to herbal teas instead**. A hot cup of tea can provide an uplifting sensation that is similar to coffee. And **make sure to eat breakfast**. Having a healthy breakfast makes it much easier to get through the morning. Finally, try to stay active. **Physical exercise really helps** to prevent fatigue. Even **talking with your friends** will help take your mind off caffeine.

여: 모닝커피를 마시기 전에는 일할 수 없나요? 가장 좋아하는 커피숍에서 커피 한 잔을 마시고 나면 IQ가 2~3점 급상승하나요? 그렇다면, 커피에 중독된 것일지도 모릅니다. 이것이 (인체에) 무해한 중독이라고 생각할 수도 있지만, 카페인을 너무 많이 섭취하면 몸이 상할 수 있습니다. 카페인 중독에서 벗어나기 위해서는, 카페인에 중독되었다는 사실을 먼저 인정해야 할 것입니다. 그러고 나서, 카페인을 끊겠다는 다짐을 종이에 적어 매일 보는 장소에 붙여놓으십시오. 카페인에 대한 갈망을 통제할 수 없게 될 때마다 카페인 대용을 찾아볼 수도 있습니다. 카페인을 제거한 커피에도 카페인이 들어있을 수 있으므로, 대신 ① 허브티만 마시도록 하십시오. 따뜻한 차 한 잔은 커피와 비슷하게 행복감을 줄 수 있습니다. 그리고 반드시 ② 아침 식사를 하십시오. 건강에 좋은 아침 식사를 하면 오전을 견뎌내는 게 훨씬 더 쉬워집니다. 마지막으로, 활동적으로 생활하려고 노력하십시오. ③ 육체 운동은 피로를 예방하는 데 정말 도움이 됩니다. ④ 친구들과 이야기하는 것도 카페인을 잊는 데 도움이 될 것입니다.

어휘 **addictive** 중독성이 있는; 중독성의 ***cf.*** **addiction** 중독 ***cf.*** **addicted** 중독된 / **herbal** 허브의, 약초의 / **resolution** 다짐, 결심; (문제 등의) 해결 / **alternative** 대안, 선택 가능한 것 / **craving** 갈망, 열망 / **get out of hand** 통제할 수 없게 되다, 과도해지다 / **decaffeinated** 카페인을 제거한 / **uplifting** 행복감을 주는, 사기를 높이는 / **sensation** 느낌, 기분 / **fatigue** 피로

실전모의고사 09

Answers & Explanation

01. ④ 02. ② 03. ⑤ 04. ③ 05. ④ 06. ⑤ 07. ⑤ 08. ① 09. ⑤ 10. ③
11. ③ 12. ⑤ 13. ⑤ 14. ② 15. ⑤ 16. ② 17. ④

01 화자가 하는 말의 목적 | ④

▶ 사고로 인해 열차가 운행되지 않으므로 대체 교통수단인 셔틀 버스를 이용하라는 안내이다.

W: Attention please, passengers. There has been a major accident involving an express train and several cars **at the level railway crossing** at Church Street. Emergency services **are working at the scene**. All trains have been stopped until further notice. We sincerely apologize for the inconvenience. **To get you to your destinations**, we have several shuttle buses waiting at exit 4. Each of the buses will **stop at different suburban stations**, so please check the destination before you get on a bus. **For further updates on the situation**, please call our information hotline at 111-333. That's 111-333. Thank you.

여: 승객 여러분께 알려드립니다. Church가의 평면 철도 건널목에서 특급 열차와 여러 차량이 관련된 큰 사고가 있었습니다. 긴급 구조 활동이 사고 현장에서 진행되고 있습니다. 추후 통보가 있을 때까지 모든 열차 운행이 중단됩니다. 불편을 끼쳐드려서 진심으로 죄송합니다. 여러분을 목적지까지 모셔다드리기 위해 4번 출구에 셔틀 버스 몇 대를 준비해 두었습니다. 버스는 각각 다른 시외 정류장에 정차할 것이니 버스에 타시기 전에 목적지를 확인해 주시기 바랍니다. 상황에 대한 최신 정보를 알고 싶으시면 정보 핫라인 111-333으로 연락 주십시오. 111-333입니다. 감사합니다.

어휘 **involve** ~을 관련시키다, 연루시키다 / **crossing** 건널목; 횡단 / **suburban** 교외의, 시외의 / **update** 최신 정보 / **hotline** 핫라인, (특정 문제에 대한) 상담[서비스] 전화; 긴급 직통 전화

02 의견 | ②

▶ 남자는 공연을 혼자 보는 것의 장점들을 말하면서 그것이 사교 활동이 될 필요가 없다고 이야기하고 있다.

M: Hi, Yumi. Did you just come from the ballet performance?
W: Jason! You surprised me. Yes, I just watched it with my friends.
M: Oh? So did I. I was in row C.
W: Wow, **you were right near the stage**. Who did you come with?
M: No one. I was able to get one good seat for myself.
W: That's too bad. **We could have sat together** if I'd known.
M: Yeah, but don't worry about it. I really enjoyed the performance.
W: Do you mind doing things alone? I go with friends whenever I watch something.
M: Friends are great, but I can focus on the performance when I'm alone. It **doesn't have to be a social activity**.
W: I see what you mean. Maybe I should try it someday.
M: Plus, it gives me a chance to meet new people.
W: That's true, too. But **we can still go together sometime**.
M: I'd love to. Talk to you later.

남: 안녕, Yumi. 발레 공연을 보고 방금 나온 거니?
여: Jason! 깜짝 놀랐네. 응, 방금 친구들이랑 봤어.
남: 오? 나도 그랬는데. 난 C열에 있었어.
여: 와, 무대 바로 가까운 곳에 있었구나. 누구와 함께 갔니?
남: 아무와도 함께 가지 않았어. 난 나를 위한 좋은 자리 하나를 얻을 수 있었어.
여: 그거 정말 유감이다. 내가 알았다면 우리가 함께 앉을 수도 있었을 텐데.
남: 그러게, 하지만 걱정하지 마. 난 공연을 정말로 즐겼어.
여: 넌 혼자 무언가를 하는 것이 괜찮니? 나는 어떤 것을 볼 때마다 친구들과 함께 가는데.
남: 친구도 매우 좋지만, 혼자 있으면 공연에 집중할 수 있어. 그것이 사교 활동이 될 필요는 없잖아.
여: 무슨 말인지 알겠어. 아마 나도 언젠가 시도해봐야겠다.
남: 게다가 그건 내게 새로운 사람들을 만나는 기회를 제공해주지.
여: 그것도 맞아. 하지만 그래도 우리 나중에 함께 갈 수 있을 거야.
남: 좋아. 나중에 다시 이야기할게.

어휘 **social activity** 사교 활동

03 관계 | ⑤

▶ 치료에 대한 비용 청구를 하고 진료 예약을 담당하는 사람과 치과 의사 간의 대화이다.

W: Sam, I've finished with Ms. Walsh. Here are her charts. Please **bill her for a full set** of oral X-rays.
M: As well as the regular clean-and-polish treatment?
W: Yes, and I need to see her again next week.
M: OK, **what procedure is she having**?
W: Implants. So please make it a 60-minute appointment.
M: Yes, I'll ask her **what time and day suit her** when she comes through to reception.
W: Good. Now, who's next?
M: Ken Chang. Wisdom tooth removal. He's not here yet. Here are his records.
W: Thanks. **Send him in** as soon as he arrives.

여: Sam, Walsh 씨의 치료를 끝냈습니다. 여기 차트가 있어요. 그분에게 구강 엑스레이 전체에 대한 청구서를 보내주세요.
남: 치아 세척과 광을 내는 치료 비용도 함께요?
여: 네, 그리고 다음 주에 그분을 다시 진료해야 해요.
남: 알겠습니다. 어떤 시술을 받게 되나요?
여: 인공 치아를 심는 치료요. 그러니 60분간의 진료 예약을 잡아 주세요.
남: 네, 그분이 접수처를 지나가실 때 어떤 시간과 날짜가 괜찮은지 여쭤볼게요.
여: 좋아요. 이제, 다음은 누구죠?
남: Ken Chang 씨입니다. 사랑니 발치예요. 아직 도착하지 않으셨는데요. 여기 그분의 진료 기록입니다.
여: 고마워요. 오시는 대로 들여보내 주세요.

어휘 **bill** ~에게 청구서[계산서]를 보내다 / **oral** 구강(口腔)의, 입의 / **procedure** 의료 시술 / **implant** (인공 치아) 이식, 임플란트 / **reception** 접수처; 응접 / **removal** 제거

04 그림 불일치 | ③

▶ 여자를 위한 선물은 꽃 모양 펜던트가 달린 목걸이라고 했다.

W: Welcome home, brother. How was your trip to Europe?
M: It was very exciting! I bought some gifts for the family. Can you guess which one is for you?
W: Is it the mug on the left?
M: No, that's for Mom. **That's why I placed it** next to Dad's gift.
W: Oh, that's great. Dad will love a checkered handkerchief.
M: I hope so, and the necklace with a flower-shaped pendant is for you. Do you like it?
W: I love it. **It's even better than the necklace** with a heart-shaped pendant that you gave me for my birthday.
M: **I'm glad you like it**. Next to it, I placed a teddy bear for our little sister.
W: That's so sweet, but what about the star-shaped box of chocolates?
M: That's for all of us to share.

여: 집에 온 걸 환영해, 오빠. 유럽 여행은 어땠어?
남: 정말 즐거웠어! 가족을 위해 선물을 좀 샀는데. 어떤 게 네 건지 알아맞힐 수 있겠어?
여: 왼쪽에 있는 머그잔이야?
남: 아니, 그건 엄마를 위한 거야. 그래서 아빠 선물 옆에 놓았지.
여: 아, 멋진데. 아빠가 체크무늬 손수건을 정말 좋아하실 거야.
남: 그러시면 좋겠어. 그리고 꽃 모양 펜던트가 달린 목걸이가 너를 위한 거야. 마음에 드니?
여: 정말 마음에 들어. 오빠가 내 생일에 준 하트 모양 펜던트 목걸이보다 훨씬 더 좋아.
남: 네가 좋아하니 기쁘다. 그 옆에는 우리 여동생에게 줄 곰 인형을 놓았어.
여: 정말 다정하다. 그런데 별 모양 초콜릿 상자는 뭐야?
남: 그건 우리 다 같이 나눠 먹을 거야.

어휘 **checkered** 체크무늬의

05 추후 행동 | ④

▶ 여자는 퇴근길에 안경점에 들러서 안경을 찾아가겠다고 말했다.

[Phone rings.]
M: Goodman Optical, Gary speaking.
W: Hi, Gary. This is Stephanie Lee. You called and left a message earlier. You said **my new glasses are ready**?
M: Oh, I'm afraid **there's been a mix-up**.
W: What's wrong?
M: Your glasses won't be ready until 8 p.m. tonight. I can have them delivered to you by 10 a.m. tomorrow.
W: That's OK. **I'll stop by and get them** on my way home from work tonight.
M: Are you sure?
W: Definitely. I can't stand another day wearing contact lenses. **They are so uncomfortable**.
M: I know what you mean.

[전화벨이 울린다.]
남: Goodman Optical의 Gary입니다.
여: 안녕하세요, Gary 씨. 저는 Stephanie Lee입니다. 이전에 전화하셔서 메모를 남기셨더군요. 제 새 안경이 준비되었다고 말씀하셨죠?
남: 아, 착오가 있었던 것 같습니다.
여: 무엇이 잘못됐나요?
남: 손님의 안경은 오늘 밤 8시가 되어야 준비될 것 같습니다. 내일 아침 10시까지 배송해 드릴 수 있습니다.
여: 괜찮습니다. 제가 오늘 밤 퇴근길에 들러서 가지고 가겠습니다.
남: 정말 괜찮으시겠습니까?
여: 물론이죠. 콘택트렌즈를 착용하고서는 하루도 더 견딜 수가 없어요. 너무 불편하거든요.
남: 무슨 말씀이신지 알겠습니다.

어휘 **mix-up** 혼란, 혼동 / **stop by** 들르다, 방문하다 / **stand** ~을 참다, 견디다

06 금액 | ⑤

▶ 두 사람은 300원짜리 붉은색 꼬치 4개, 400원짜리 파란색 꼬치 2개, 500원짜리 흰색 꼬치 2개를 먹었다.

W: I'm full, but this is so tasty. What's it called again?
M: Eomuk Kkochi.
W: Eomuk Kkochi? Yum. **What's it made of**?
M: It's just mashed fish **with some seasonings**.
W: What a great snack! But why are the sticks different colors?
M: They're different prices. Red sticks are 300 won each, blue are 400 won, and white sticks are 500 won.
W: That's cheap.
M: Isn't it? Here, **let me pay**.
W: No! You can pay next time.
M: OK, **I had four red sticks**. That's 1,200 won.
W: And I had two blue sticks at 400 won per stick, and two white sticks at 500, right?
M: Right.

여: 배가 부르지만 이건 아주 맛있네요. 이걸 뭐라고 부르는지 다시 한 번 말씀해 주시겠어요?
남: 어묵 꼬치요.
여: 어묵 꼬치라고요? 맛있어요. 무엇으로 만든 거죠?
남: 그냥 양념을 조금 한 으깬 생선이에요.
여: 정말 좋은 요깃거리예요! 하지만 꼬치들이 왜 다양한 색이죠?
남: 가격이 달라서 그래요. 붉은색 꼬치는 300원씩이고, 파란색은 400원, 그리고 흰색은 500원이에요.
여: 싸군요.
남: 그렇죠? 여기, 제가 낼게요.
여: 아니에요! 다음에 내세요.
남: 좋아요. 저는 붉은색 꼬치 4개를 먹었어요. 1,200원이군요.
여: 그리고 저는 한 개에 400원인 파란색 꼬치 2개와 500원 하는 흰색 꼬치 2개를 먹었어요. 맞죠?
남: 맞아요.

어휘 **mash** ~을 으깨다 / **seasoning** 양념

07 이유 | ⑤

▶ 노래 대회에 참가하기 위해 오디션을 통과해야 하는데 여자가 오디션 날에 알래스카로 가는 여행을 예약해서 참가할 수 없다고 했다.

M: Sophia, did you hear about the English Song Contest that's being held at Merriam College?
W: Yes, I did. I really want to enter but I **don't know if I can**. I'm not a college student.
M: Of course you can. College and high school students are all accepted this time.
W: I'm so excited. I **would definitely like to sign up**. I'd like to know about the cost to participate.
M: It's $20.
W: That's not as expensive as I thought. When is the contest?
M: It's September 20th, but you **have to go through** an audition. The audition is on August 17th and 18th.
W: Really? Then I won't be able to participate.
M: Why? Is it because of your part-time job? You can switch shifts with someone.
W: My family **has booked a trip** to Alaska from August 11th to 19th. I'm afraid I'll have to wait for another chance.
M: I'm sorry to hear that.

남: Sophia, 너 Merriam 대학에서 개최될 영어 노래 대회에 대해 들었어?
여: 응, 들었어. 나는 정말로 참가하고 싶지만 할 수 있을지 모르겠어. 나는 대학생이 아니잖아.
남: 물론 넌 할 수 있어. 이번에 대학생과 고등학생들을 모두 받거든.
여: 정말 신난다. 나는 꼭 등록하고 싶어. 참가하기 위한 비용에 대해 알고 싶어.
남: 20달러야.
여: 내가 생각했던 것만큼 비싸진 않네. 대회가 언제야?
남: 9월 20일이야. 하지만 너는 오디션을 통과해야 해. 오디션은 8월 17일과 18일에 있어.
여: 정말? 그러면 나는 참가할 수 없을 거야.
남: 왜? 네 시간제 근무 때문에? 너는 다른 사람과 근무 시간을 바꿀 수 있잖아.
여: 우리 가족이 8월 11일부터 19일까지 알래스카로 가는 여행을 예약했거든. 안타깝지만 나는 다른 기회를 기다려야 할 것 같아.
남: 그 말을 들으니 안타깝다.

어휘 **hold** 개최하다; 붙들다 / **participate** 참가[참여]하다 / **go through** 통과하다; 경험하다 / **switch** 바꾸다; 전환하다 / **shift** (교대제의) 근무 시간; 옮기다 / **book** 예약하다

08 언급하지 않은 것 | ①

▶ 해석 참조

W: I brought some snacks for you to eat while you work on your presentation.
M: Thanks, Mom. I was getting really hungry.
W: Are you researching about global warming?
M: Right now, I'm reading about carbon dioxide. It's **one of the major causes** of global warming.
W: Okay. You know it's **a natural part of the air**, right?
M: Yes, but it's only around 0.03% of the atmosphere. However, it's **an important ingredient in many everyday products**.
W: Oh, I know that it can be turned into dry ice and that it's used in fire extinguishers.
M: Right. I've also learned that **it's colorless and has no smell**, which is why it can be added to soda pop.
W: You're really learning a lot from this presentation.

여: 발표를 준비하는 동안 먹을 간식을 좀 가져왔단다.
남: 고마워요, 엄마. 정말 배고팠는데.
여: 지구 온난화에 대해 조사 중이니?
남: 지금은 이산화탄소에 관해서 읽고 있어요. 지구 온난화의 주요 원인 중 하나잖아요.
여: 그렇구나. 그게 본래 대기의 일부분이라는 건 알지, 그렇지?
남: 네, 그런데 대기 중 겨우 0.03% 정도(② 대기 중 비율)예요. 하지만 많은 일상생활용품의 중요한 재료죠.
여: 아, 이산화탄소가 드라이아이스로 바뀔 수 있고 소화기에 쓰인다(③ 용도)고도 알고 있단다.
남: 맞아요. 또 무색(④ 색깔)이고 냄새가 없다(⑤ 냄새)는 것도 배웠어요. 그래서 탄산음료에 첨가될 수 있는 거고요.
여: 너 이번 발표로 정말 많은 것을 배우는구나.

어휘 **carbon dioxide** 이산화탄소 / **atmosphere** 대기, 공기; 분위기 / **fire extinguisher** 소화기

09 내용 불일치 | ⑤

▶ 규제가 있기는 했으나 그로 인해 오히려 가부키의 인기가 증가했다고 말했다.

M: As you can see, we are now inside the Japanese kabuki theater. The history of kabuki **began in 1603 in Japan**. As a new form of drama, kabuki satisfied the tastes of the new social classes, **the lower and middle classes of society** who began to increase in the urban centers. With beautiful costumes, exaggerated movements, and **amazing special effects**, it is no wonder that this spectacular event has remained popular for centuries. The stories deal with a wide range of subjects from historical events to daily life. Sometimes the stories **make fun of political figures**. So, during the 1600s, government officials banned some performances that they felt were too controversial. However, these bans seem to have made kabuki **all the more popular**.

남: 보시다시피, 우리는 지금 일본 가부키 극장 안에 있습니다. 가부키의 역사는 1603년 일본에서 시작되었습니다. 가부키는 새로운 연극 형태로서 신 사회 계층, 즉 도시 중심부에서 증가하기 시작한 사회 중산층과 하류층의 취향을 만족시켰습니다. 아름다운 의상, 과장된 동작, 그리고 놀라운 특수 효과 때문에, 이런 장관의 쇼가 수 세기 동안 계속 인기 있는 것은 전혀 놀랄 일이 아닙니다. 줄거리는 역사적 사건에서 일상생활에 이르기까지 광범위한 주제를 다룹니다. 때로는 정치인을 풍자하기도 합니다. 그래서 1600년대에 정부 관리들은 자신들이 느끼기에 지나치게 논란이 많은 일부 공연을 금지했습니다. 하지만 이러한 규제들은 가부키를 더욱더 인기 있게 만들었던 것으로 보입니다.

어휘 **taste** 기호, 취향; 맛 / **urban** 도시의, 도회지의 / **exaggerate** 과장하다, 부풀려 말하다 / **special effects** 특수 효과 / **official** 공무원, 관리; 공식적인 / **controversial** 논란이 많은

10 도표 이해 | ③

▶ 남자는 자전거 중에서 가격이 300달러 이하이고 바퀴 크기는 26인치인 것을 원한다. 종류는 컴포트나 하이브리드가 좋다고 했고, 그중에서 보증기간이 긴 제품을 선택할 것이다.

M: This website has **huge discounts on bikes**.
W: You should buy one.
M: I know. Which one, though?
W: The Apollo folding bike is a bargain.
M: And **it would be easy to carry** on the subway.
W: **The price is still a bit high**, though.
M: Um, I really can't afford more than $300.
W: Hybrid-style bikes are great for city riding.
M: True. OK, I'll get the Giant Hybrid!
W: That was easy!
M: Oh, no. It's only 24 inches. I need a 26-inch.
W: How about the Milo road bike?
M: No, **I want a comfort or a hybrid**.
W: That leaves two. **It would be better** to get the one with the longer warranty.
M: Good thinking. I'll do that.

남: 이 웹사이트에서는 자전거를 많이 할인하는구나.
여: 하나 구매해.
남: 그래. 그런데 어떤 것으로?
여: Apollo 접이식 자전거가 특가품이야.
남: 그리고 지하철에서 들고 다니기도 쉬울 거야.
여: 하지만 가격은 여전히 조금 비싸.
남: 음, 나는 300달러가 넘는 금액은 감당할 여유가 정말 없어.
여: 하이브리드 스타일 자전거는 시내에서 타기에 정말 좋겠다.
남: 맞아. 좋아, 나는 Giant 하이브리드로 할래!
여: 간단하네!
남: 아, 안 돼. 이건 24인치밖에 안 되는구나. 나는 26인치짜리가 필요하거든.
여: 그럼 Milo 로드 자전거는 어떠니?
남: 싫어, 나는 컴포트나 하이브리드가 좋아.
여: 그럼 두 개만 남는구나. 보증기간이 더 긴 것으로 하는 편이 더 좋을 것 같아.
남: 좋은 생각이야. 그렇게 할래.

어휘 **hybrid bike** 산악용 자전거와 경주용 자전거를 혼합해서 만든 자전거 *cf.* **hybrid** 혼성물, 합성물; (동식물의) 잡종 / **folding bike** 접이식 자전거 / **retail** 소매의, 소매상의 / **warranty** 보증, 보증서 / **bargain** 특가품, 싼 물건

11 짧은 대화에 이어질 응답 | ③

▶ 아무것도 잊은 게 없는지 묻는 남자의 말에 적절한 응답을 찾는다.

① 교대로 운전해요.
② 다시 돌아가서 문단속을 할게요.
③ 내가 모든 것을 이미 두 번씩 확인했어요.
④ 여행은 잊지 못할 추억을 줘요.
⑤ 나는 우리가 대신 기차를 탔어야 했다고 생각해요.

M: I put our luggage in the trunk and **locked up the house** properly.
W: Then let's **get in the car and get going**.
M: Are you sure we aren't forgetting anything?
W: ______________________________

남: 우리 짐을 트렁크에 넣었고 문단속도 제대로 했어요.
여: 그럼 차 타고 떠나요.
남: 우리 아무것도 잊어버리지 않은 게 확실하죠?
여: ______________________________

어휘 **take turns** ~을 교대로 하다 / **lock up** (~에) 문단속을 하다 / **properly** 제대로, 적절히

12 짧은 대화에 이어질 응답 | ⑤

▶ 좋은 웹사이트를 추천해 달라는 요청에 가장 적절한 응답을 고른다.

① 다른 인터넷 브라우저를 사용해 봐.
② 우리가 보고서를 끝낼 수 있을 것 같지 않아.
③ 인터넷상의 정보는 그다지 믿을 만하지 않아.
④ 나는 내 보고서를 인터넷에 올릴 거야.
⑤ 물론이지, 나중에 이메일로 보내줄게.

W: I'm **having trouble finding ideas** for my report.
M: I found most of my ideas on the Internet.
W: Really? **Can you recommend any good websites** for me?
M: ______________________________

여: 난 보고서에 쓸 아이디어를 찾는 데 어려움을 겪고 있어.
남: 난 아이디어 대부분을 인터넷에서 찾았어.
여: 정말? 좋은 웹사이트 있으면 나에게 추천해줄래?
남: ______________________________

어휘 **reliable** 믿을 수 있는, 신뢰할 수 있는 / **post** (웹사이트에 정보·사진을) 올리다, 게시하다

13 긴 대화에 이어질 응답 | ⑤

▶ 남자는 약속 장소 지역이 통제되어 친구들을 만날 수 없을 것이므로, 여자는 전화해서 약속 장소를 바꾸는 것이 좋겠다고 말할 것이다.

① 좋아. 즐거운 회의와 좋은 하루가 되기를 바랄게.
② 음, 너는 서두르는 게 나아. 그렇지 않으면 기차를 놓칠 거야.
③ 나도 오페라를 보고 싶어. 같이 가도 되니?
④ 걱정하지 마. 내가 가서 그 애들에게 네가 오는 중이라 말할게.
⑤ 그 애들에게 전화해서 다른 장소에서 만나자고 해.

[Cell phone rings.]
W: Hey Joe, what are you up to?
M: **I'm heading downtown** to meet up with Dan and Tim.
W: Oh, yeah? Where are you meeting them?
M: Museum Station. **We're going to check out** the Opera House.
W: But you can't! The APEC conference is on. Leaders from all over the world are there. The Opera House area **is closed to the public**.
M: That's all right. We'll do something else.
W: Joe, you won't find them. Museum Station is off-limits too, and the police are everywhere to stop people from going there.
M: Dan and Tim will **be wondering where I am**. I have to go find them.
W: ______________________________

[휴대전화 벨이 울린다.]
여: 안녕 Joe, 뭐 하니?
남: Dan과 Tim을 만나러 시내로 가는 중이야.

여: 아, 그래? 그 애들을 어디서 만나니?
남: Museum 역에서. 우리는 Opera House를 보러 갈 거야.
여: 하지만 너희는 못 봐! APEC 회의가 개최 중이거든. 세계 각국의 지도자들이 그곳에 와 있어. Opera House 지역은 일반인에게 공개되지 않아.
남: 괜찮아. 다른 것을 하지 뭐.
여: Joe, 너는 그 애들을 못 찾을 거야. Museum 역도 역시 출입 금지고 일반인들이 그곳에 들어가는 것을 막기 위해 경찰이 도처에 있어.
남: Dan과 Tim은 내가 어디에 있는지 궁금해하고 있을 거야. 가서 그 애들을 찾아야 해.
여: ______________________________

어휘 **conference** 회의 / **the public** 일반 대중 / **off-limits** 출입 금지의

14 긴 대화에 이어질 응답 | ②

▶ 식사 준비는 남자가 언제 식료품점에서 돌아오느냐에 달려있다는 여자의 말에 가장 적절한 응답을 찾는다.

① 하지만 그때까지는 준비가 되지 않을 거예요.
② 15분 넘게 걸리지는 않을 거예요.
③ 그때 내가 점심을 준비하는 것을 당신이 도와줬으면 해요.
④ 하지만 저는 그리스 샐러드를 어떻게 만드는지 몰라요.
⑤ 어서 가서 점심 먹어요. 저를 기다리지 마세요.

W: Matt, can you go to the grocery store for me?
M: Why?
W: I'm making a Greek salad for lunch. I need some Greek-style cheese and olives.
M: I love Greek salad. And I'm starving. I'll go right away.
W: Thanks. Black olives please, not green. Oh, and **I need red onions too**.
M: OK, anything else? **How about bread to go with it**?
W: Oh, yeah. Some wholemeal bread would be nice. We've got some tomatoes and cucumbers. So don't worry about them. Do you want some money?
M: No, that's okay. I'll pay. **When will lunch be ready**?
W: That depends on when you get back with the cheese and other things.
M: ______________________________

여: Matt, 날 위해 식품점에 다녀 올래요?
남: 왜요?
여: 점심식사로 그리스 샐러드를 만들고 있어요. 그리스식 치즈와 올리브가 필요해요.
남: 난 그리스 샐러드가 정말 좋아요. 그리고 배도 너무 고파요. 금방 다녀올게요.
여: 고마워요. 녹색 올리브 말고 검은 올리브로 부탁해요. 아, 그리고 붉은 양파도 필요해요.
남: 알겠어요. 다른 건 없나요? 같이 먹을 빵은 어떤가요?
여: 아, 맞아요. 통밀 빵이 약간 있으면 좋을 것 같아요. 토마토와 오이는 있어요. 그러니 그건 걱정하지 마세요. 돈이 필요해요?
남: 아니요, 괜찮아요. 내가 낼게요. 점심식사가 언제쯤 준비될까요?
여: 그건 당신이 치즈랑 다른 것들을 사가지고 언제 돌아오는지에 달려있어요.
남: ______________________________

어휘 **cucumber** 오이

15 상황에 적절한 말 | ⑤

▶ 아이의 사고를 엄마에게 전하는 데 적합한 표현을 유추해야 한다.

① 따님에 대한 좋은 소식이 있습니다.
② 따님께서 당신을 매우 걱정하고 있습니다.
③ 이 수영장은 너무 붐벼요, 엄마. 집에 가도 될까요?
④ 따님이 오늘 수영 강습에 빠졌습니다.
⑤ 유감입니다만 따님에게 사고가 있었습니다.

W: Miriam is a lifeguard and swimming instructor at the local swimming pool. One day she **notices a girl floating motionless** in the crowded pool. Miriam **immediately dives in** and checks if the girl is OK, but the girl is unconscious and not breathing. Shouting, "Call an ambulance!" she **lifts the girl out of the water** and applies emergency rescue techniques. Miriam saves the girl's life, but the girl still has to go to a hospital. The ambulance arrives. Miriam asks the girl for her mother's phone number **so that she can tell her** what has happened. Miriam calls and the mother answers the phone. In this situation, what would Miriam most likely say to the girl's mother?

여: Miriam은 구조요원이며 지역 수영장의 수영 강사이다. 어느 날 그녀는 붐비는 수영장에서 한 여자아이가 꼼짝하지 않고 물에 떠 있는 것을 발견한다. Miriam은 즉시 뛰어들어서 여자아이가 괜찮은지 확인하지만, 여자아이는 의식이 없고 숨을 쉬지 않는다. "구급차를 불러요!"라고 소리치며 그녀는 여자아이를 물 밖으로 들어 올려 응급 처치를 실시한다. Miriam은 여자아이의 목숨을 살리지만, 여자아이는 여전히 병원에 가야 한다. 구급차가 도착한다. Miriam은 어떤 일이 있었는지를 아이의 어머니에게 말하기 위해 여자아이에게 어머니의 전화번호를 물어본다. Miriam이 전화를 걸고 어머니가 전화를 받는다. 이러한 상황에서 Miriam이 여자아이의 어머니에게 할 말로 가장 적절한 것은 무엇인가?

어휘 **concerned** 걱정스러운, 염려하는 / **lifeguard** 구조요원 / **instructor** 강사, 지도자 / **unconscious** 의식을 잃은

16~17 세트 문항 | 16. ② 17. ④

▶ 16. 지적 재산권 침해와 바이러스가 감염된 파일을 수신할 수도 있다는 점을 이유로 들어 음악을 불법으로 내려받지 말아야 함을 말하고 있다.

① 저작권법이 음악 산업에 어떻게 영향을 미치는가
② 음악을 불법으로 내려받지 말아야 할 이유들
③ 지적 재산권이 어떻게 독창성을 보호하는가
④ 파일 공유 사이트와 저작권법 사이의 갈등
⑤ 파일을 불법으로 내려받는 것을 예방하는 시스템 구축

▶ 17. 해석 참조

바이러스 감염과 관련된 백신 프로그램 오류에 관한 내용은 언급되지 않았다.

M: When a song is produced and marketed, it is protected by copyright law so that it cannot be copied, reproduced or resold without the copyright holder's permission. If you do not pay for a song that is under copyright, then downloading that song is a crime. Today, I'd like to talk about **why we shouldn't download music illegally**. I'll start by explaining intellectual property. Intellectual property is something that someone has created or invented and that no one is legally allowed to make, copy, or sell. It is basically **the ownership of ideas**. Intellectual property rights were created to reward people for their efforts and stimulate investment. In the music industry, intellectual property rights **motivate companies to invest in artists** by providing a guarantee that the company will end up making money. Violating these rights hurts these companies. Another reason not to download music illegally **has to do with receiving viruses**. Illegally downloaded files are typically passed through file sharing sites, some of which contain viruses designed to steal your identity. Other viruses might **erase important data or slow your Internet connection**. And at the very least, you will probably have to **deal with excessive pop-up ads**.

남: 노래가 제작되어 시중에 나올 때, 그것은 저작권 소유자의 허락 없이 복제, 혹은 재생산하거나 되팔 수 없도록 저작권법의 보호를 받습니다. 저작권 하에 있는 노래에 대해 비용을 지불하지 않는다면, 그 노래를 내려받는 것은 범죄입니다. 오늘, 저는 음악을 불법으로 내려받으면 왜 안 되는지에 대해 얘기하고 싶습니다. 지적 재산을 설명하는 것으로 시작하겠습니다. 지적 재산은 어떤 사람이 창조하거나 발명한 것으로, 다른 사람은 법적으로 (그것을) 만들거나 복제하거나 팔도록 허용되지 않는 것입니다. 이것은 기본적으로 아이디어의 소유권입니다. 지적 재산권은 사람들에게 노력에 대해 보상하고 투자를 자극하기 위해 만들어졌습니다. 음악 산업에서 지적 재산권은 회사가 수익을 내게 될 것이라고 보장함으로써 회사로 하여금 예술가들에게 투자하도록 동기를 부여합니다. 이 권리를 위반하는 것은 이런 회사에 피해를 주는 것입니다. 음악을 불법으로 내려받지 말아야 할 또 다른 이유는 바이러스 수신과 관련이 있습니다. 불법으로 내려받은 파일들은 일반적으로 파일 공유 사이트를 거치는데, 그 사이트 중 일부에는 ① 개인 정보를 훔치도록 고안된 바이러스가 포함되어 있습니다. 다른 바이러스들은 ② 중요한 자료를 지우거나 ③ 인터넷 연결 속도를 느리게 할 수도 있습니다. 그리고 최소한이라도, 아마 ⑤ 과도한 팝업 광고를 처리해야 할 것입니다.

어휘 **copyright** 저작권, 판권 / **intellectual property** ((법률)) 지적 재산 / **market** (상품을) 내놓다, 광고하다 / **ownership** 소유(권) / **stimulate** ~을 자극[격려]하다 / **investment** 투자 ***cf.* invest in** ~에 투자하다 / **end up v-ing** 결국 ~하게 되다 / **have to do with** ~와 관련이 있다 / **excessive** 과도한, 지나친

Answers & Explanation

01. ④ 02. ⑤ 03. ④ 04. ⑤ 05. ⑤ 06. ③ 07. ① 08. ③ 09. ④ 10. ④
11. ③ 12. ⑤ 13. ⑤ 14. ① 15. ① 16. ④ 17. ④

01 화자가 하는 말의 목적 | ④

▶ 300회 공연을 마치기까지 함께 해준 팬들에게 감사의 마음을 전하고 있다.

W: This is it! This is my last performance. I can't believe that after four years and 300 performances, it's over. It was really hard at the beginning. I **gave birth to a son** and wanted to quit. But you, **you kept me going**. Some of you saw the show 50, 60, even more than 70 times. At the beginning I had my critics, but you stood by me. I also want to thank the supporting cast of dancers and musicians. Thank you! I'll miss you. I'm going to work on a new album; then **I'll tour**. But I'll never forget all of you!

여: 이제 이걸로 끝이네요! 이것이 저의 마지막 공연입니다. 지난 4년간 300회의 공연을 하고 이제 끝이라니 믿기지 않네요. 처음에는 매우 힘들었습니다. 아들을 출산하고 나서 그만두고 싶기도 했어요. 하지만 여러분, 여러분 덕택에 공연을 계속할 수 있었어요. 여러분 중 일부는 이 공연을 50번, 60번 심지어 70번도 넘게 보셨습니다. 처음에는 비판하시는 분도 있었지만, 여러분께서 제 곁에 계셨어요. 또한 보조 출연을 해주신 무용수분들과 연주자 여러분께도 감사드리고 싶습니다. 감사합니다! 여러분이 그리울 거예요. 저는 새 앨범 작업을 할 계획입니다. 그리고 순회공연도 할 것이고요. 하지만 여러분 모두를 결코 잊지 못할 거예요!

어휘 **critic** 비평가 / **supporting cast** 보조 출연자, 조연 / **work on** 일을 계속하다 / **tour** (극단·배우 등이) 순회하다

02 의견 | ⑤

▶ 남자는 자유여행에 대한 부정적인 의견을 밝히면서 패키지 단체 여행의 장점을 말하고 있다.

M: Honey, have you thought about our trip?
W: Well, it's our first trip to Europe. I want it to be special.
M: Right. **There are so many things to see**.
W: I know! Why don't you reserve the hotels? Then I'll plan the flights.
M: What do you think about a package tour? We don't have much time to plan.
W: I don't want **to be on a tight schedule**, though. I want to feel free.
M: I'm afraid we'll spend too much time on small details. A group tour would allow us to see all the famous sights.
W: What about the price? **Wouldn't it be cheaper to plan** our own holiday?
M: If we book a package tour soon, we can probably get a good deal. Then we can see everything without wasting money.
W: Okay. I agree. **Let's look at some tour packages**.
M: Great. This is going to be so much fun.

남: 여보, 우리 여행에 대해 생각해 봤어요?
여: 음, 유럽으로 가는 우리의 첫 여행이네요. 특별한 여행이 되면 좋겠어요.
남: 그래요. 정말로 볼 것이 많아요.
여: 그러게요! 당신이 호텔을 예약하는 게 어때요? 그럼 내가 항공편을 계획할게요.
남: 패키지여행에 대해 어떻게 생각해요? 우리는 계획할 시간이 많지 않아요.
여: 그런데, 일정이 빡빡하지 않으면 좋겠어요. 자유를 느끼고 싶어요.
남: 우리가 사소한 부분에 너무 많은 시간을 소비할 것 같아요. 단체 여행은 모든 유명한 장소를 볼 수 있게 해줄 거예요.
여: 가격은요? 우리만의 휴가를 계획하는 것이 더 싸지 않을까요?
남: 만약 우리가 패키지여행을 빨리 예약한다면, 아마 좋은 조건에 구매할 수 있을 거예요. 그럼 돈을 낭비하지 않고 모든 것을 볼 수 있어요.
여: 알겠어요. 동의해요. 여행 패키지 상품들을 좀 보도록 합시다.
남: 좋아요. 정말 재미있을 거예요.

어휘 **tight** (여유가 없이) 빡빡한[빠듯한] / **detail** 사소한 부분, 세부사항; 정보 / **sight** 장소, 관광지; 시력; 시야 / **deal** 조건, 거래; (문제 등을) 처리하다, 다루다

03 관계 | ④

▶ 잡지사에서 일하는 남자는 사진을 찍을 수 있도록 허락을 얻고 있으며, 여자는 자신의 새 영화를 홍보하고 있다는 사실에서 두 사람의 관계를 유추할 수 있다.

M: Beth! Beth! Look over here.
W: Yes?
M: Is it all right if I take a few pictures?
W: Sure. **Are you a freelancer**?
M: No. I work for *Stars* magazine.
W: Well, take good pictures for the magazine. **How should I pose**?
M: We're not in the studio. Just walk down the street holding your daughter and I want to **snap a few photographs** of the two of you.
W: OK. *[pause]* Finished?
M: Yes. Thanks for being understanding.
W: Well, **I want good press**. I am promoting my new movie, *The Good Girl*.
M: I hope it'll be a blockbuster.

남: Beth! Beth! 여기 좀 봐주세요.
여: 네?
남: 제가 사진을 몇 장 찍어도 괜찮을까요?
여: 물론이죠. 당신은 프리랜서인가요?
남: 아니요. 저는 〈Stars〉 잡지에서 일합니다.
여: 그럼, 잡지에 잘 나오게 찍어주세요. 제가 어떻게 포즈를 취해야 하나요?
남: 스튜디오에 있는 게 아니니까요. 따님과 손잡고 길을 걸어 주시면, 제가 두 분의 사진을 몇 장 찍고 싶어요.
여: 좋아요. *[잠시 후]* 끝났나요?
남: 네. 이해해주셔서 감사합니다.
여: 음, 보도가 잘 나가면 좋겠어요. 제 새 영화 〈The Good Girl〉을 홍보 중이거든요.
남: 영화가 큰 성공을 거두길 바랍니다.

어휘 **pose** 자세를 취하다 / **snap** 스냅 사진을 찍다 / (a) **good press** 신문[잡지] 등의 호의적인 소개, 호평 / **blockbuster** 대히트작, 초대작

04 그림 불일치 | ⑤

▶ 빵은 집에 남은 게 있어서 사지 않았다고 했으므로 그림 속의 빵이 대화 내용과 일치하지 않는다.

[Cell phone rings.]
M: Hi, Mom.
W: Jimmy, **are you almost finished** at the store?
M: I think so. I got **a packet of spaghetti**.
W: That's good. And you got some broccoli, too?
M: Yes, of course. I **got two heads**, just to be safe.
W: Okay. Hmm... I can't remember what else I sent you to buy.
M: You told me to get bacon and onions. I got **two slices of bacon**, and three onions.
W: Oh, that's right, and don't forget to get **a block of cheese**. Parmesan cheese is the most important ingredient for the cream spaghetti that you love so much.
M: I didn't forget anything. Don't worry. And I didn't buy bread because we have leftovers at home.
W: Okay. I'll see you at home soon.

[휴대전화 벨이 울린다.]
남: 여보세요, 엄마.
여: Jimmy, 장을 거의 다 봤니?
남: 그런 것 같아요. 스파게티를 한 봉지 샀어요.
여: 잘했구나. 그리고 브로콜리도 좀 샀지?
남: 네, 물론이에요. 혹시 몰라서 두 송이 샀어요.
여: 그래. 음… 그밖에 뭘 사오라고 널 보낸 건지 기억이 안 나는구나.
남: 베이컨과 양파를 사오라고 하셨어요. 베이컨 두 조각이랑 양파 세 개를 샀어요.
여: 아, 맞아, 그리고 치즈 한 덩어리 사오는 거 잊지 마라. 파르메산 치즈는 네가 정말 많이 좋아하는 크림 스파게티에 가장 중요한 재료란다.
남: 아무것도 잊지 않았어요. 걱정하지 마세요. 그리고 빵은 집에 남은 게 있어서 안 샀어요.
여: 그래. 곧 집에서 보자.

어휘 **packet** 한 묶음, 다발; 소포, 꾸러미 / **ingredient** 재료, 성분 / **leftover** ((주로 pl.)) 남은 음식; (과거의) 잔재

05 부탁한 일 | ⑤

▶ 중간 정도 부분의 여자의 말에 Please, don't show them to anyone!이라는 말이 있으며, them은 앞에 나온 the video files를 뜻한다.

W: What are you doing?
M: Just downloading these pictures and video files from the camera.
W: Are those the pictures from when you visited my dance academy?
M: Yeah, you danced well.
W: Thanks.
M: I'm going to show the video files to William **when he comes over** in a few minutes.
W: What? Please, don't show them to anyone!
M: Do you **want me to delete them**?
W: No, I just don't want you to show them to anyone.
M: Tell me why.
W: **I was a little bit embarrassed**. That dance clothing was too tight.
M: Don't worry. Your dance was so great that **no one would notice that**.

여: 뭐 하고 있니?
남: 카메라에서 사진과 비디오 파일을 내려 받는 중이야.
여: 그 사진들은 네가 우리 댄스 학원에 왔을 때 찍은 것들이니?
남: 응, 너 춤을 잘 추던데.
여: 고마워.
남: 잠시 후에 William이 오면 그에게 비디오 파일을 보여 줄 거야.
여: 뭐? 제발 아무에게도 보여 주지 말아 줘!
남: 파일을 지웠으면 좋겠어?
여: 아니, 그저 누구에게도 보여 주지 않았으면 해.
남: 이유를 말해봐.
여: 좀 창피했었거든. 그 댄스복이 너무 달라붙어서.
남: 걱정하지 마. 네 춤이 아주 근사해서 아무도 그것을 알아차리지 못했을 거야.

어휘 **embarrassed** 창피한, 난처한

06 금액 | ③

▶ 슈퍼 클린 서비스가 기본 세차(25달러)보다 10달러 더 비싸므로 35달러이고, 왁스로 닦기 위해 추가 비용 20달러를 더해야 하므로 총 55달러이다. 여기에 5달러 할인 쿠폰을 적용하면 여자가 지불해야 할 총금액은 50달러이다.

M: How can I help you, ma'am?
W: I'd like to have my car hand washed.
M: Welcome. You've come to the right place. Is this your car?
W: Yes, how much is it?
M: If you have a Basic Car Wash, it's $25. **This service includes** hand wash, vacuum, windows, and tire shine.
W: Does it include full interior cleaning?
M: No. The Super Clean service, which is 10 dollars more expensive, includes full interior cleaning and wheel shine.
W: Then I'd like a Super Clean service. And **do I have to pay extra for** waxing?
M: Yes, if you pay an extra $20, we'll treat your car's surface with premium wax.
W: Okay. I want that. And I have this discount coupon **downloaded from your website**. Can I use it now?
M: Sure. We'll give you a $5 discount on the total.
W: Thank you. I'll be in the waiting room.

남: 어떻게 도와드릴까요, 손님?
여: 제 차를 손 세차 맡기고 싶어요.
남: 환영합니다. 제대로 오셨습니다. 이게 손님 차인가요?
여: 네, 얼마인가요?
남: 기본 세차를 하시면, 그건 25달러입니다. 이 서비스는 손 세차, 진공 청소, 창문과 타이어 광택을 포함합니다.
여: 전체 내부 청소도 포함되어 있나요?
남: 아뇨, 슈퍼 클린 서비스가 10달러 더 비싼데, 전체 내부 청소와 휠 광택을 포함합니다.
여: 그러면 슈퍼 클린 서비스로 할게요. 그리고 왁스로 닦기 위해 제가 추가 비용을 지불해야 하나요?
남: 네, 20달러를 추가로 내시면, 저희가 고급 왁스로 차 표면을 처리할 겁니다.
여: 알겠어요. 전 그걸 원해요. 그리고 웹사이트에서 내려 받은 이 할인 쿠폰이 있어요. 이것을 지금 사용할 수 있나요?
남: 물론입니다. 전체에서 5달러를 할인해 드립니다.
여: 감사합니다. 저는 대기실에 있을게요.

어휘 **vacuum** 진공청소기를 이용한 청소; 진공청소기로 청소하다 / **interior** 내부(의); 안에 있는 / **wax** 왁스로 닦다; 왁스; 밀랍 / **treat** (화학물질로) 처리하다; 다루다 / **surface** 표면

07 이유 | ①

▶ 발표회가 화요일인데 남자는 월요일 뉴욕으로 출장을 떠나 목요일에 돌아온다고 했다.

W: Honey, do you remember Cindy's violin recital next Tuesday?
M: Next Tuesday? Isn't it next Friday?
W: No, it's Tuesday. Actually, I **have a dental appointment** that afternoon, but I cancelled it.
M: Oh, I may be mixed up on the dates. I'm sorry, but I can't make it.
W: What are you talking about? It's our daughter's first violin recital!
M: I have to go to New York on business on Monday. I'll return on Thursday.
W: **Could you reschedule it**? This is such an important event. Cindy will be disappointed if you don't come.
M: I'll tell Cindy about it. And I'll order a beautiful flower bouquet for her. Where will the recital be held?
W: It's the Riverside Youth Center, near City Hall.
M: I see. By the way, **isn't it too small to hold** a recital?
W: It seats 50 people, and it's okay because it's just for the students and their families.

여: 여보, 다음 주 화요일에 Cindy의 바이올린 발표회 기억하죠?
남: 다음 주 화요일이요? 다음 주 금요일이 아니었어요?
여: 아뇨, 화요일이에요. 사실 난 그날 오후에 치과 예약이 있는데 취소했어요.
남: 아, 내가 날짜를 혼동했나 봐요. 미안하지만 난 참석할 수 없어요.
여: 무슨 말이에요? 우리 딸의 첫 번째 바이올린 발표회잖아요!
남: 나는 월요일에 뉴욕으로 출장을 가야 해요. 목요일에 돌아올 거예요.
여: 일정을 변경할 수 있어요? 정말 중요한 행사잖아요. 당신이 오지 않는다면 Cindy가 실망할 거예요.
남: 내가 그것에 대해 Cindy한테 말할게요. 그리고 그 애를 위해 예쁜 꽃다발을 주문할게요. 발표회가 어디서 열리죠?
여: 시청 근처 Riverside 청소년 센터요.
남: 알았어요. 그런데, 거기 발표회를 열기에 너무 작지 않아요?
여: 50명을 수용하는데, 발표회가 학생들과 그 가족만을 위한 거라서 괜찮아요.

어휘 **recital** 발표회 / **dental** 치과의 / **cancel** 취소하다 / **mix up** 혼동하다 / **make it** 참석하다, 가다 / **reschedule** 일정을 변경하다 / **bouquet** 꽃다발 / **seat** 수용하다

08 언급하지 않은 것 | ③

▶ 해석 참조

W: Are you going camping this summer? Instead of listening to mosquitoes buzzing, **why not listen to pop music**? Come to the Vincent Island Music Camping Festival 2011. Running from July 3rd to the 4th, the festival **lets you enjoy the great outdoors** while listening to James Johnson, Bonnie Blue, the Lawrence Sisters and other pop stars. There are two sizes of tents for rent: a 2-to-3 person tent or a 4-to-6 person tent. Two-day festival passes **can be bought for $150 per person**. The pass doesn't include the tent rental. During the festival, you can take a ferryboat to get to Vincent Island. If you're interested, please **get further details** on the festival website at www.vincentmusic.com.

여: 올여름에 캠핑을 가실 예정입니까? 모기가 윙윙대는 소리를 듣는 대신 팝 음악을 듣는 것이 어떠신가요? 2011 Vincent 섬 음악 캠핑 축제에 오세요. 축제는 7월 3일부터 4일까지(① 축제 기간) 계속되며 James Johnson, Bonnie Blue, the Lawrence Sisters와 다른 팝 스타들(② 출연진)의 음악을 들으면서 대자연을 즐기게 됩니다. 대여가 가능한 텐트는 두 가지 크기로, 2~3인용 텐트 혹은 4~6인용 텐트가 있습니다. 이틀 축제 입장권은 한 사람당 150달러(④ 입장료)에 구매하실 수 있습니다. 입장권에는 텐트 대여료가 포함되어 있지 않습니다. 축제 동안에는 연락선을 타고 Vincent 섬으로 오실 수 있습니다(⑤ 교통편). 관심이 있으시다면 웹사이트 www.vincentmusic.com에서 축제에 관한 더 자세한 내용을 확인하세요.

어휘 **the (great) outdoors** 대자연, 시골 지역 / **pass** 입장[탑승]권, 출입증 / **rental** 대여(료) / **ferryboat** 연락선 (= ferry)

09 내용 불일치 | ④

▶ 청혼 영상은 미리 녹화해야 한다.

M: Where is the perfect place to ask your loved one to marry you? Of course it is the famous Brockton Point of Fraser Stream **in the heart of the city**. In a special ceremony last Monday, Mayor Moore came to this special place and named Brockton Point as "the marriage proposal spot." At Brockton Point, a big screen TV and a speaker system **have been set up**. Citizens can prerecord their marriage proposal, and then **take their loved one to the spot** on a specific day and at a specific time. And **their proposal will be played on a huge screen** for them. Citizens can apply to use the service by logging onto the city government's website.

남: 연인에게 청혼을 하기에 완벽한 장소는 어디일까요? 당연히 도심에 위치한 Fraser 강의 유명한 Brockton Point입니다. 지난 월요일의 특별 행사 때, Moore 시장이 이 특별한 장소에 와서 Brockton Point를 '청혼 장소'로 명명하였습니다. Brockton Point에는 대형 스크린 TV와 스피커 시스템이 설치되었습니다. 시민들은 자신의 청혼을 미리 녹화한 후, 특별한 날 특별한 시간에 이 장소로 연인을 데리고 오면 됩니다. 그러면 그들의 청혼이 그들을 위해 대형 화면에서 상영될 것입니다. 시민들은 시정부의 웹사이트에 접속하여 서비스 이용을 신청할 수 있습니다.

어휘 **spot** 장소, 자리; (작은) 점 / **set up** ~을 설치하다 / **log onto** (인터넷 사이트 등에) 접속하다

10 도표 이해 | ④

▶ 우선 200달러 이하의 가격에 10시간 이상의 배터리 수명이 있고 스테레오 스피커를 원했고 마지막에 방수 기능이 있는 것을 선택했으므로 여자가 주문할 블루투스 스피커는 ④이다.

W: I'm looking for a portable Bluetooth speaker to **take with me on my camping trip** next weekend. Could you help me choose one from this website?
M: Sure. First, what's your budget?
W: I can't spend over $200.
M: Okay. Now you need to think about battery life. I recommend one that **can last for 10 hours or more**.
W: Okay. What is the difference between mono and stereo Bluetooth speakers?
M: Hmm, to put it simply, mono speakers come with a single speaker while stereo ones contain two.
W: Then stereo speakers **must sound relatively louder than** mono speakers. I'd like a stereo speaker.
M: Now you've narrowed the choice down to these two options. The more expensive one is waterproof and the other isn't.
W: I'll choose the one that's waterproof. There's a chance of rain and **I might be close to a lake** when I'm camping, so that feature is important.
M: Good choice.
W: I'll order it now. Thanks for helping me.

여: 다음 주말에 캠핑 여행에 가지고 갈 휴대용 블루투스 스피커를 찾고 있어요. 이 웹사이트에서 하나 고르는 것을 도와주실 수 있나요?
남: 물론이죠. 우선, 예산이 어떻게 되나요?
여: 200달러 넘게 쓸 수는 없어요.
남: 알았어요. 이제 배터리 수명에 대해 생각해 볼 필요가 있어요. 나는 10시간 이상 견딜 수 있는 것을 추천해요.
여: 좋아요. 모노 블루투스 스피커와 스테레오 블루투스 스피커의 차이점은 뭔가요?
남: 음, 간단히 말해서, 모노 스피커는 하나의 스피커가 딸린 반면 스테레오 스피커는 두 개의 스피커를 포함해요.
여: 그렇다면 스테레오 스피커는 모노 스피커보다 상대적으로 소리가 더 큰 게 분명하군요. 난 스테레오 스피커를 원해요.
남: 이제 이 두 가지 선택으로 좁혀졌네요. 더 비싼 것은 방수가 되고 다른 것은 안 돼요.
여: 방수가 되는 것으로 선택할게요. 비가 올 가능성이 있고 캠핑할 때 호수 가까이에서 있을 수도 있으니까, 그 특징이 중요해요.
남: 잘 선택했어요.
여: 지금 주문할게요. 도와줘서 고마워요.

어휘 **water-resistant** 물이 잘 스며들지 않는, 내수성의 / **portable** 휴대용의 / **budget** 예산 / **last** 견디다, 오래 가다 / **to put it simply** 간단히 말하면 / **contain** 포함하다 / **relatively** 비교적 / **narrow down** 좁히다, 줄이다 / **waterproof** 방수의

11 짧은 대화에 이어질 응답 | ③

▶ 실수로 Jemma를 화나게 한 것 같다는 남자의 말에 그것을 어떻게 알아챘는지 묻고 있다. 이에 대한 가장 적절한 응답을 찾는다.

① 그 애를 기쁘게 하기란 매우 힘들어.
② 다음번엔 같이 가자.
③ 그 애가 나에게 말을 거의 하지 않으려고 했거든.
④ 그 애가 늦어서 난 기분이 상했어.
⑤ 우리는 근사한 레스토랑에서 저녁을 먹었어.

W: How was your date with Jemma?
M: Not so good. I think **I accidentally made her angry**.
W: How could you tell that she was upset?
M: ______________________________

여: Jemma와의 데이트는 어땠니?
남: 별로 안 좋았어. 내가 실수로 Jemma를 화나게 한 것 같아.
여: 그 애가 기분이 상한 줄은 어떻게 알 수 있었니?
남: ______________________________

어휘 **barely** 거의 ~아니게; 간신히

12 짧은 대화에 이어질 응답 | ⑤

▶ 수업 중에 음식물 섭취가 허용되는지 물었다. 이에 대한 적절한 대답을 찾는다.

① 그럼, 우리 둘 다 배고픈 것 같아.
② 아니, 선생님들은 구내식당에서 드셔.
③ 응, 너와 나눠 먹어서 기뻐.
④ 아니, 그래서 난 요리 수업을 듣고 싶어.
⑤ 안 되지, 하지만 쉬는 시간에는 먹을 수 있잖아.

M: Are you going to bring that sandwich to class?
W: Yeah, I didn't eat breakfast. I'll give you some **if you want**.
M: **We aren't allowed to eat** in class, are we?
W: ______________________________

남: 너 그 샌드위치 수업시간에 가져갈 거야?
여: 응, 아침을 안 먹었거든. 원한다면 너도 조금 줄게.
남: 수업 중에 먹으면 안 되잖아, 그렇지?
여: ______________________________

13 긴 대화에 이어질 응답 | ⑤

▶ 여자아이는 날씨가 춥지 않아 낄 필요 없다는 장갑을 끼고 있다.

① 문을 잡고 있어 줘서 고맙다.
② 좋은 생각이구나. 네가 감기에 걸릴 수도 있으니.
③ 잠깐만. 그 장갑은 잘 맞는걸.
④ 걱정하지 마. Brad는 혼자서도 괜찮을 거야.
⑤ 내 얘기를 안 들었구나! 너는 그게 필요 없단다.

M: Lisa, you've got to get ready as soon as I ask you to.
W: I was playing with Brad.
M: Lisa, you're not a baby anymore. **No excuses**. If I ask you to do something, you do it right away.
W: Yes, Dad. I'll try. **I'm hurrying as fast as I can**. I've got my jacket, gloves....
M: You don't need gloves. It's not cold today.
W: Huh?
M: Hurry up! You'll be late for your piano lesson.
W: No problem, Dad. It only takes a few minutes to walk there.
M: OK. Let's go then.
W: Hold on. **I'm just putting on my gloves**.
M: ______________________________

남: Lisa, 내가 시키면 곧바로 준비해야지.
여: Brad랑 놀고 있었어요.
남: Lisa, 너는 더는 아기가 아니란다. 변명하지 마. 내가 너에게 뭔가를 시키면 너는 그걸 바로 해야 해.
여: 네, 아빠. 노력할게요. 가능한 빨리 서두르고 있어요. 재킷이랑 장갑도 챙기고….

남: 장갑은 필요 없어. 오늘은 춥지가 않구나.
여: 네?
남: 서둘러라! 피아노 교습에 늦겠구나.
여: 문제없어요, 아빠. 거기까지 걸어가는 데 몇 분밖에 안 걸려요.
남: 좋아. 그럼 가자꾸나.
여: 잠깐만요. 지금 장갑을 끼고 있어요.
남: ______________________________

어휘 **excuse** 변명

14 긴 대화에 이어질 응답 | ①

▶ 남자는 여자의 그림을 돈을 지불하고 사려고 한다. 두 사람이 친구 관계인 것을 미루어 보아 여자의 반응을 유추할 수 있다.

① 말도 안 돼. 너는 내 친구잖아. 하나 가져.
② 그 책들을 얼마 주고 살 거니?
③ 이렇게 좋은 직장을 제안하다니 넌 정말 친절하구나.
④ 고맙지만 괜찮아. 나를 위해서 아무것도 그려 주지 않아도 돼.
⑤ 그것들은 매우 귀중한 그림이야. 굉장히 비싸.

M: You are really good at drawing, Betty.
W: Thanks, Peter. **I've been taking art classes for years**.
M: During a recess **you're always inside drawing and sketching**, aren't you?
W: Yeah. I like to play outside, but I love to draw.
M: Well, **these all look like characters** from cartoon books.
W: They are. These are my favorite characters.
M: They are some of my favorite characters, too.
W: Do you want one of the drawings? I've got so many.
M: Sure, but I don't want you **to give them away**.
W: What do you mean?
M: Let me pay even just a little for your work.
W: ______________________________

남: 넌 정말 그림에 소질이 있구나, Betty.
여: 고마워, Peter. 난 수년간 그림 교습을 받고 있어.
남: 쉬는 시간에도 너는 항상 안에서 그림을 그리거나 스케치를 하고 있지, 그렇지 않니?
여: 응. 나가서 놀고도 싶지만, 그림 그리는 게 정말 좋아.
남: 음, 이것들은 모두 만화책의 캐릭터처럼 보이는데.
여: 맞아. 내가 가장 좋아하는 캐릭터들이야.
남: 몇몇은 나도 가장 좋아하는 캐릭터들이네.
여: 이 그림들 중 갖고 싶은 것이 하나 있니? 나는 아주 많이 가지고 있어.
남: 물론이지. 하지만 네가 그것들을 거저 주지 않았으면 좋겠어.
여: 무슨 뜻이니?
남: 네 그림에 조금이라도 값을 치르게 해 줘.
여: ______________________________

어휘 **cost a fortune** 엄청나게 비싸다 ***cf.* fortune** 큰돈, 거금 / **recess** 쉬는 시간, 휴식 / **give A away** A를 거저 주다[선물로 주다]

15 상황에 적절한 말 | ①

▶ Harry의 어머니는 Harry에게 방과 후와 주말에 외출하면 안 된다고 하셨으므로 Harry는 Paula의 제안을 거절해야 할 것이다.

① 갈 수 없어. 난 외출 금지거든.
② 너는 내게 너무 부당하게 굴고 있어.
③ 좋아. 8시에 만나자.
④ 내게는 전혀 문제가 안 돼.
⑤ 좋아. 난 최근에 내 행동을 변화시켰어.

W: Harry's mother, Mrs. Henderson, is really angry at him. He doesn't clean his room **nor does he turn off the computer** when she tells him to. And he doesn't speak politely to her. **She has tried taking away** his cell phone and not giving him money. But Harry **hasn't changed**. So last night, Mrs. Henderson told him he couldn't go anywhere with his friends. He must stay in his room after school and on weekends. Today, Harry's friend, Paula, **phones the house**, asks to speak to Harry and invites him to a movie tonight. In this situation, what would Harry most likely say to his friend, Paula?

여: Harry의 어머니인 Henderson 부인은 아들에게 정말 화가 나 있다. 그는 어머니께서 말씀하셔도 방을 치우지 않고 컴퓨터도 끄지 않는다. 그리고 어머니께 공손하게 말하지도 않는다. 그녀는 그의 휴대전화를 압수하기도 하고 용돈을 주지 않기도 해봤다. 하지만 Harry는 변하지 않았다. 그래서 어젯밤 Henderson 부인은 그에게 친구들과 아무 데도 갈 수 없다고 말했다. 그는 방과 후와 주말에 방에만 있어야 한다. 오늘은 Harry의 친구인 Paula가 집으로 전화해서 Harry를 바꿔 달라고 한 후 그에게 오늘 밤에 영화를 보러 가자고 한다. 이러한 상황에서 Harry가 친구인 Paula에게 할 말로 가장 적절한 것은 무엇인가?

어휘 **grounded** 외출이 금지된 / **take away** 빼앗다

16~17 세트 문항 | 16. ④ 17. ④

▶ 16. 처음에는 차가 기운을 북돋아주고 마음을 느긋하게 해준다는 내용으로 시작했지만, 대부분의 내용은 차로 인한 여러 부작용을 언급하고 있다.

① 카페인이 신체에 미치는 영향 ② 커피를 마시는 것의 불리함
③ 건강을 위해 차를 선택하는 법 ④ 차를 마시는 것의 잠재적 부작용
⑤ 다양한 허브 차의 특성

▶ 17. 해석 참조

① 홍차 ② 녹차 ③ 로즈마리 차 ④ 재스민 차 ⑤ 캐모마일 차

M: What kind of tea do you drink? Everyone likes a good cup of tea. In the morning, black tea can provide the boost of energy you need to start your day. In the evening, herbal tea can **serve as a relaxing drink** before bed. Depending on how much tea you drink and its specific type, however, tea **has the potential to lead to** some unpleasant side effects. Drinking green tea can cause problems with sleeplessness, as coffee can. **For this reason it is recommended** to drink green tea only in the morning. Trouble with sleeping, however, isn't the only potential downside to drinking tea. Drinking herbal teas, like rosemary tea, can have a negative impact on the medicine you are currently using. So, be sure to speak with your doctor if you are currently taking any medications. It is also known that some herbal teas contain chemicals which **can be blamed for** getting kidney stones. Although rare, allergic reactions to chamomile tea may occur. If you experience symptoms of a serious allergic reaction, including difficulty breathing, you should stop drinking chamomile tea. Despite these side effects, drinking herbal tea **is considered to be extremely good for** health. Side effects are related to people who drink more than 5-6 cups of tea a day, and most people don't.

남: 어떤 종류의 차를 드십니까? 모든 사람이 맛있는 차를 좋아합니다. 아침에는, ① 홍차가 하루를 시작하는 데 필요한 기운을 북돋아줄 수 있습니다. 저녁에는 허브 차가 잠자기 전의 마음을 느긋하게 해주는 음료로서의 역할을 할 수 있습니다. 그러나 여러분이 차를 얼마나 많이 마시는가와 그 특정한 종류에 따라서, 차는 좀 불쾌한 부작용으로 이끌 가능성을 갖고 있습니다. ② 녹차를 마시는 것은 커피가 그럴 수 있듯이 불면증 문제를 일으킬 수 있습니다. 이런 이유로 녹차는 아침에만 마시도록 권장됩니다. 그러나 수면 문제가 차를 마시는 것의 유일한 잠재적인 부정적인 면은 아닙니다. ③ 로즈마리 차와 같은 허브 차를 마시는 것은 여러분이 현재 복용하는 약에 부정적 영향을 줄 수 있습니다. 그러므로 현재 어떤 약물을 복용하고 있다면 의사에게 반드시 이야기하십시오. 일부 허브 차는 신장 결석이 생기는 데 책임이 있을 수 있는 화학물질을 함유하고 있다고 알려져 있습니다. 드물긴 하지만 ⑤ 캐모마일 차에 대한 알레르기 반응이 일어날 수도 있습니다. 여러분이 호흡곤란을 포함해 심각한 알레르기 반응 증세를 겪는다면 캐모마일 차를 마시는 것을 중단해야 합니다. 이러한 부작용에도 불구하고 허브 차를 마시는 것은 건강에 매우 좋다고 여겨집니다. 부작용은 하루에 차를 5잔에서 6잔보다 더 마시는 사람들과 관련된 것이지 대부분의 사람들은 아닙니다.

어휘 **potential** 잠재적인 / **property** 특성, 속성 / **boost** 부양, 증대, 밀어 올리기 / **relaxing** 마음을 느긋하게 해주는 / **unpleasant** 불쾌한 / **side effect** 부작용 / **sleeplessness** 불면(증) / **downside** 부정적인[불리한] 면 / **impact** 영향 / **medication** 약물, 약물 치료 / **blame** ~책임으로 보다, ~을 탓하다 / **kidney** 신장 / **symptom** 증세, 증상

Answers & Explanation

01. ④ 02. ⑤ 03. ① 04. ⑤ 05. ④ 06. ③ 07. ④ 08. ③ 09. ③ 10. ③
11. ① 12. ⑤ 13. ② 14. ⑤ 15. ③ 16. ⑤ 17. ③

01 화자가 하는 말의 목적 | ④

▶ 개인정보 유출의 위험성과 이를 방지하기 위한 주의사항을 설명하고 있으므로 남자의 말은 개인정보 유출의 위험성을 인식시키기 위한 것임을 알 수 있다.

M: Has your personal information ever been shared **without your knowledge**? Unfortunately, many of us **have gone through this unpleasant experience**. If you're lucky, it will only result in an increase in spam mail, but it can be much worse. Your resident registration number could **be used to commit a serious crime**. Often, we are partly to blame when this happens. For example, we might use passwords that include our date of birth or phone number, or use identical passwords for several websites. Moreover, some free websites sell their data to other sites **where it may fall into the wrong hands**. To protect ourselves, we need to change passwords frequently and investigate websites before we join them. Otherwise, **we'll likely lose control of** our personal information, and it may be used for illegal purposes.

남: 당신의 개인정보가 당신도 모르게 공유된 적이 있습니까? 안타깝게도, 우리 중 많은 이들이 이 불쾌한 경험을 한 적이 있습니다. 운이 좋다면, 스팸메일의 증가만 가져오겠지만, 훨씬 더 심각할 수 있습니다. 중대한 범죄를 저지르는 데 당신의 주민등록번호가 사용될 수 있습니다. 이런 일이 일어날 때, 우리는 종종 어느 정도 책임이 있습니다. 예를 들어, 우리는 자신의 생년월일 혹은 전화번호를 포함하는 비밀번호를 사용하거나, 여러 웹사이트에서 동일한 비밀번호를 사용하는지도 모릅니다. 게다가, 일부 무료 웹사이트는 그들의 자료가 잘못된 사람의 손에 넘어갈 수도 있는 다른 사이트에 그것을 팝니다. 우리 자신을 지키기 위해, 우리는 비밀번호를 자주 변경하고 가입하기 전에 웹사이트를 살펴볼 필요가 있습니다. 그러지 않는다면, 우리의 개인정보를 관리할 수 없게 될 것이고, 이것이 불법적인 목적에 사용될지도 모릅니다.

어휘 **resident registration number** 주민등록번호 ***cf.* registration** 등록, (출생·혼인 등의) 신고; (우편물의) 등기 처리; 등록 서류 / **be to blame** (~에 대하여) 책임이 있다 / **investigate** (~을) 살피다, 수사하다; (~을) 조사하다, 연구하다 (= explore)

02 대화 주제 | ⑤

▶ 두 사람은 환경을 위해 테이크아웃을 줄이고 더 큰 용량의 음료를 사는 등 일상생활에서 환경을 보호하기 위해 많은 일들을 실천할 수 있다고 말하고 있다.

M: Thanks for bringing takeout for dinner, but next time, let's eat out instead.
W: Sure, honey, but I thought **you preferred to eat at home**.
M: I do, but recently **I've started to notice** how much waste there is after we eat takeout.
W: I know what you mean. We can recycle these plastic containers, but **they're still bad for the environment**.
M: Right. I've also begun to buy larger containers of juice and cola for the same reason.
W: Good idea. **I'm trying to buy products without excessive packaging**.
M: Good thinking. I'm also doing some other things for the environment. For instance, I bought natural soaps and detergents the other day.
W: That's great. I'm glad we won't be pouring so many harsh chemicals down the drain anymore.

남: 저녁으로 먹을 테이크아웃 음식을 가져와 줘서 고맙지만, 다음에는 대신 밖에서 먹읍시다.
여: 그래요, 여보, 그런데 난 당신이 집에서 먹는 걸 더 좋아하는 줄 알았어요.
남: 그렇긴 한데, 우리가 테이크아웃 음식을 먹은 후에 쓰레기가 얼마나 많은지 최근에 의식하기 시작했거든요.
여: 무슨 뜻인지 알겠어요. 이 플라스틱 용기들을 재활용할 수는 있지만, 환경에는 여전히 나쁘죠.
남: 맞아요. 난 같은 이유로 주스랑 콜라도 더 큰 용기에 든 것으로 사기 시작했어요.
여: 좋은 생각이에요. 난 과대 포장되지 않은 물건을 사려고 노력하고 있어요.
남: 잘 생각했어요. 난 환경을 위해서 다른 것들도 하고 있어요. 이를테면, 얼마 전에 천연 비누와 세제를 샀어요.
여: 훌륭해요. 더는 독한 화학 물질을 그렇게나 많이 배수관에 쏟아붓지 않을 거라니 다행이에요.

어휘 **container** 용기, 그릇; (화물 수송용) 컨테이너 / **excessive** 과도한, 지나친 / **packaging** 포장; 포장재 / **detergent** 세제 / **harsh** (손상을 줄 정도로) 너무 강한; 가혹한 / **drain** 배수관

03 관계 | ①

▶ 여자는 남자에게 쇼와 관련된 질문을 하며 자신의 신문 독자들에게 할 말을 물어보았고, 남자는 자신이 진행하는 쇼에 관해 이야기했으므로 신문 기자와 방송 진행자 간의 대화이다.

W: It's really exciting to be **on the set of my favorite show**!
M: My pleasure. But I only have an hour before the show will be aired live.
W: OK, **I'll get to the point**. Isn't it difficult because it's a live show?
M: It's not an easy job, but it's a lot of fun to host my own show and talk with different celebrities every week.
W: I see. So, **what would you say** is the most challenging? It must be stressful sometimes.
M: Exactly. I can't make any mistakes. It's also thrilling, though. *[pause]* Oh, **it's time for makeup**.
W: OK. Then, quickly, is there anything you'd like to say to our newspaper readers?
M: I truly appreciate all of my fans. **I'll keep trying to be the best**.
W: Alright. Thank you for answering my questions.
M: It was no trouble.

여: 제가 제일 좋아하는 쇼의 세트장에 있으니 정말 신나네요!
남: 저도 기쁩니다. 그런데 쇼가 생방송으로 방영되기 전에 한 시간밖에 안 남았네요.
여: 알겠습니다. 본론으로 들어갈게요. 생방송 쇼라서 힘들지 않으신가요?
남: 쉬운 일은 아니지만, 저만의 쇼를 진행하고 매주 여러 유명 인사들과 이야기를 나누는 게 굉장히 재미있습니다.
여: 그렇군요. 그럼, 무엇이 가장 힘들다고 말씀하시겠어요? 가끔 스트레스가 많으실 텐데요.
남: 맞습니다. 전 어떤 실수도 하면 안 되죠. 그래도 스릴 있기도 해요. *[잠시 후]* 아, 화장을 할 시간이네요.
여: 알겠습니다. 그러면 빨리, 저희 신문의 독자들께 하시고 싶은 말씀이라도 있나요?
남: 제 모든 팬 여러분께 진심으로 감사드립니다. 최고가 되기 위해 계속 노력하겠습니다.
여: 네. 제 질문에 답해주셔서 감사드려요.
남: 어려운 일이 아닌걸요.

어휘 **get to the point** 핵심에 이르다, 요점을 언급하다 / **host** ~을 진행하다; ~을 주최하다; 주인; (행사의) 주최국[측]; (TV·라디오 프로의) 진행자 / **thrilling** 아주 신나는, 황홀한, 흥분되는

04 그림 불일치 | ⑤

▶ 남자는 소파 옆에 공간이 없어서 화분을 책장 옆에 두었다고 했다.

[Phone rings.]
M: Hello?
W: Hi, Martin. Have you finished **arranging your new house**?
M: Almost, Mom. I just finished putting the couch with two cushions on one side of the living room.
W: Wasn't it hard to move it?
M: Not really. **It's not as heavy as it looks**.
W: And I'm sure the table is in front of the couch, too.
M: Yes, **just like you said**. I also put up some curtains. They have a nice striped pattern.
W: Sounds nice. And what about your 4-shelf bookshelf?
M: **I put it in the corner** to the right of the window. It's more space efficient.
W: Also, don't forget to place the flower pot that I bought for you next to the couch.
M: I tried to, but there was very little room, so I put it beside the bookshelf.
W: Hmm.... Okay. **I'm excited to see it for myself**.

[전화벨이 울린다.]
남: 여보세요?

여: 여보세요, Martin. 네 새집 정리하는 건 끝났니?
남: 거의 끝났어요, 엄마. 방금 거실 한쪽에 쿠션 두 개가 있는 소파 놓는 것을 이제 막 마쳤어요.
여: 그것을 옮기는 데 힘들지 않았니?
남: 별로요. 그건 보이는 것만큼 무겁지는 않아요.
여: 그리고 탁자도 분명히 소파 앞에 있겠구나.
남: 네, 엄마가 말씀하신 대로예요. 커튼도 달았어요. 멋진 줄무늬가 있고요.
여: 잘했구나. 그리고 네 4단 책장은 어떠니?
남: 창문 오른쪽 구석에 두었어요. 공간이 더 효율적이에요.
여: 그리고, 내가 사준 화분을 소파 옆에 놓는 것도 잊지 마라.
남: 그러려고 했는데, 공간이 거의 없어서 책장 옆에 두었어요.
여: 음…. 알았다. 직접 볼 게 기대되는구나.

어휘 **flower pot** 화분

05 부탁한 일 | ④

▶ 일을 분담하는 상황에서 여자는 크리스마스카드를 우편으로 보내야 하지만 우체국 근처에 못 갈 것 같다고 하면서 남자에게 이 일을 부탁했고 남자는 승낙했다.

W: I have **so many errands to run** today.
M: Well, maybe I can help you.
W: That would be great. Here's my list.
M: Wow. It looks like you have to drive all over town.
W: Maybe **we can split it up**. Let's see.... If I go to the supermarket to buy bread and milk, I will have to go past the dry cleaners, **where my shirts are**.
M: That's true. And you can also go to the computer repair shop to pick up your laptop.
W: OK, I will do those three things. But I won't be anywhere near the post office to mail my Christmas cards. **Would you handle it**?
M: Sure. But you'll be closer to the library. These books are all late.
W: It looks like I have a lot more to do than you.
M: **Meet you back here for lunch**?
W: Sure! See you then.

여: 오늘 처리할 일이 정말 많아요.
남: 음, 아마 내가 도울 수 있을 거예요.
여: 그러면 좋죠. 여기 목록이 있어요.
남: 와, 마치 시내 전체를 운전하고 다녀야 할 것 같네요.
여: 어쩌면 일을 나눌 수 있을 거예요. 가만 보자…. 내가 슈퍼에 가서 빵과 우유를 사려면, 세탁소를 지나가야 할 건데, 거기에 내 셔츠가 있어요.
남: 맞아요. 그리고 당신은 노트북을 찾으러 컴퓨터 수리점에 갈 수 있고요.
여: 좋아요, 내가 그 세 가지 일을 할게요. 하지만 내 크리스마스카드를 우편으로 보내야 하는데 내가 우체국 근처로는 안 갈 것 같네요. 그걸 처리해 주시겠어요?
남: 물론이죠. 하지만 당신이 도서관에 더 가까이 있겠네요. 이 책들은 모두 연체되었어요.
여: 내가 할 일이 당신보다 훨씬 더 많아 보이네요.
남: 점심 먹으러 여기서 다시 만날까요?
여: 좋아요! 그때 봐요.

어휘 **errand** 볼일, 용무; 심부름 / **split up** ~을 나누다, 쪼개다

06 금액 | ③

▶ 남자는 방수가 되는 노란색 하이킹 재킷(380달러)과 하이킹 양말 두 켤레(10달러×2)를 구입하고, 회원으로 가입하여 10% 할인을 받을 수 있으므로 남자가 지불할 총금액은 360달러이다.

W: Can I help you find anything, sir?
M: Yes, thanks. **I'm interested in** buying a new hiking jacket, and I heard you have a good selection.
W: We certainly do. All of our hiking jackets are on this rack here.
M: Okay. Now **what's the difference between** these two jackets?
W: The blue one is a standard jacket that is $300. The yellow one costs $380 because it's waterproof.
M: I see. Well, I should be prepared for rain. I'll take the waterproof one.
W: Excellent choice. And how about some hiking socks? They **keep your feet dry** and cost only $10 per pair.
M: Why not? I'll take two pairs.
W: Great. Now, **if you're willing to become** a member of our store, you can get 10% off on everything you buy today.
M: Great! Then I'll sign up now.

여: 찾으시는 물건 있으신가요, 손님?
남: 네, 감사합니다. 하이킹 재킷을 새로 사고 싶은데, 여기 좋은 제품들이 있다고 들었습니다.
여: 분명히 그렇습니다. 저희 상점의 하이킹 재킷은 모두 여기 이 선반에 있습니다.
남: 알겠습니다. 그럼 이 두 재킷의 차이점은 무엇인가요?
여: 파란색 재킷은 일반적인 재킷으로 300달러입니다. 노란색 재킷은 방수가 되기 때문에 380달러입니다.
남: 그렇군요. 음, 저는 비에 대비해야겠어요. 방수되는 것으로 할게요.
여: 훌륭한 선택이에요. 그리고 하이킹 양말은 어떠세요? 손님의 발을 건조하게 유지해 주고 한 켤레에 10달러밖에 안 합니다.
남: 그거 좋겠네요. 두 켤레를 살게요.
여: 좋습니다. 이제, 손님께서 저희 가게의 회원이 되신다면, 오늘 구매하시는 모든 물건에 대해 10% 할인을 받으실 수 있습니다.
남: 잘됐군요! 그렇다면 지금 가입할게요.

어휘 **certainly** 분명히, 확실히; 물론이지요, 그럼요 / **rack** 선반; 걸이 / **standard** 일반적인; 기준(의), 표준(의) / **waterproof** 방수가 되는 / **sign up** 가입[등록]하다; 신청하다

07 이유 | ④

▶ 여자는 수학여행 장소인 제주도에 가족들과 얼마 전에 다녀왔기 때문에 다시 가는 게 신나지 않다고 했다.

M: Jenna, why didn't you mention next week's school trip?
W: I didn't tell you **because I'm not going**. Is that okay, Dad?
M: I guess so, but it sounds like it would be fun.
W: Well, it would be fun to fly. I guess I'm just not excited to go back to Jeju Island **since we just went there** as a family.
M: We did see most of the island on your mom's birthday, but it would be **a different experience with your classmates**.
W: You're right, but several of my friends won't be going either. I don't think I'll miss anything interesting.
M: Okay. You don't have to go, but I still think it would be **a chance to make some good memories**.

남: Jenna, 다음 주에 가는 수학여행에 대해 왜 말하지 않았니?
여: 전 가지 않을 거라서 말하지 않았어요. 괜찮죠, 아빠?
남: 괜찮을 것 같지만, 재미있을 것처럼 들리던데.
여: 음, 비행기를 타는 건 재미있을 거예요. 가족들과 바로 얼마 전에 제주도에 갔기 때문에 거기 다시 가는 게 그다지 신나지 않는 것 같아요.
남: 네 엄마 생신 때 그 섬 대부분을 구경하긴 했지만, 반 친구들과 함께라면 (그것과) 다른 경험이 될 거란다.
여: 아빠 말씀이 맞지만, 제 친구들 몇 명도 가지 않을 거예요. 재미있는 것을 놓칠 것 같지 않아요.
남: 그래, 갈 필요는 없지만, 수학여행은 여전히 좋은 추억을 만들 기회인 것 같구나.

08 언급하지 않은 것 | ③

▶ 해석 참조

M: Mom, the weather is so nice today. Let's go on a family picnic.
W: Why not? Do you **have a nice place in mind**?
M: How about Lake Park? I heard the Rose Festival **is being held there** right now.
W: Great idea! I'm sure your dad and Sally will love it.
M: Why don't we invite Grandma? She'd like some fresh air.
W: You're so sweet. Then, that makes five including your grandmother.
M: Right. So, **what should we have for lunch**?
W: Hmm. I think restaurants in the park will be too crowded. I'll make sandwiches and bring some fruit.
M: Great. I love your homemade sandwiches. I'll call Grandmother **while you're preparing lunch**.
W: Alright. Tell her that we're going to leave home at eleven and get there at eleven thirty.
M: Got it.

남: 엄마, 오늘 날씨가 정말 좋아요. 우리 가족 소풍을 가요.
여: 그거 좋겠구나. 생각해둔 괜찮은 장소가 있니?
남: 호수 공원(① 장소) 어때요? 지금 그곳에서 장미 축제가 열리고 있다고 들었어요.
여: 좋은 생각이구나! 네 아빠와 Sally도 그곳을 분명 좋아할 거야.
남: 할머니도 초대하는 게 어때요? 할머니도 상쾌한 공기를 좋아하실 거예요.
여: 정말 다정하구나. 그러면, 할머니를 포함해서 다섯 명(② 인원수)이 되는구나.

남: 맞아요. 그러면, 우리 점심으로 뭘 먹어야 할까요?
여: 음. 공원에 있는 음식점은 너무 붐빌 것 같아. 샌드위치를 만들고 과일(④ 점심 메뉴)을 좀 가져가마.
남: 좋아요. 전 엄마가 집에서 만드시는 샌드위치가 정말 맛있어요. 엄마가 점심을 준비하시는 동안 제가 할머니께 전화 드릴게요.
여: 알겠다. 할머니께 우리가 열한 시에 집에서 떠나(⑤ 출발 시각) 그곳에 열한 시 반에 도착할 거라고 말씀드리렴.
남: 알았어요.

09 내용 불일치 | ③

▶ 매년 두 번의 정기 콘서트와 크리스마스 스페셜 콘서트를 한다고 했으므로 총 세 번이다.

W: Hi, I'm Jennifer Taylor, a junior in the Department of Music. If you are looking for **a fun way to meet new people**, why not join the Monarch Band? Named for the Monarch butterflies commonly found around the band practice room, the Monarch Band is the university's original club band. **Since we were established** 25 years ago, hundreds of students have formed lasting friendships within the Monarch Band. But there is **more than just hanging out**. We play 2 regular concerts and a Christmas special each year. Our annual summer concert, where we choose one country and **perform its traditional music**, is especially popular. Anyone can join, but unlike other clubs that recruit twice a year, we do so annually. So **don't pass up this opportunity** for fun and friendship.

여: 안녕하세요. 저는 음악학과 3학년생인 Jennifer Taylor입니다. 새로운 사람들을 만날 재미있는 방법을 찾고 계신다면, Monarch 밴드에 가입하는 것은 어떨까요? 밴드 연습실 주위에서 흔히 발견되는 왕나비의 이름을 따서 지은, Monarch 밴드는 (저희) 대학의 원조 동아리 밴드입니다. 저희 동아리는 25년 전에 창설되었기 때문에, 수백 명의 학생이 Monarch 밴드 내에서 지속적인 교우 관계를 맺어 왔습니다. 하지만 단지 어울리는 것보다 더 많은 것이 있습니다. 저희는 매년 두 번의 정기 콘서트와 크리스마스 스페셜 콘서트를 합니다. 저희의 연례 여름 콘서트는 한 나라를 골라 그 나라의 전통 음악을 연주하는데, 특히 인기가 있습니다. 누구든지 가입하실 수 있지만, 일 년에 두 번 (회원을) 모집하는 다른 동아리들과는 달리, 저희는 일 년에 한 번 모집합니다. 그러니 재미와 교우 관계를 위한 이 기회를 놓치지 마세요.

어휘 **hang out** 어울려 지내다, 함께 시간을 보내다 / **annually** 일 년에 한 번 / **pass up** (기회를) 놓치다, ~을 거절하다, 퇴짜 놓다

10 도표 이해 | ③

▶ 남자는 먼저 주중에 하는 일은 제외했고, 경험이 필요하지 않은 것 중에서 급여가 높은 것을 선택했다.

M: Hi, Vanessa. **Do you have a minute**?
W: Sure, Derrick. What's up?
M: I'm trying to pick one of these five part-time jobs at a department store, and I'd like your opinion.
W: I see. Well, how about being a greeter? It seems easy.
M: Yeah, but **I'm too busy on weekdays**.
W: Then how about this job? I think you'd be great at it. Plus, it's on weekends and it pays more.
M: Ah, I see. But I don't have any experience.
W: Hmm.... **Why don't you apply for this one**, then? You're an English major, so it'd be easy for you.
M: That's true, but I'd really **prefer to make a better wage**.
W: Then there's only one left.
M: I guess so. I'll apply now.

남: 안녕, Vanessa. 시간 좀 있니?
여: 물론이지, Derrick. 무슨 일이니?
남: 내가 백화점에서 하는 이 다섯 가지 시간제 일 중에서 하나를 고르려고 하는데, 네 의견을 듣고 싶어.
여: 알겠어. 음, 손님맞이 일은 어때? 쉬워 보여.
남: 응, 하지만 난 주중에는 너무 바빠.
여: 그러면 이 일은 어때? 내 생각엔 네가 잘할 것 같아. 게다가, 주말에 하는 거고 급여도 더 많이 주네.
남: 아, 그렇구나. 하지만 난 경험이 없어.
여: 음…. 그러면 여기에 지원하는 건 어때? 넌 영어 전공이니까, 너한테 쉬울 거야.
남: 맞아, 하지만 난 급여가 더 좋은 일을 정말 선호해.
여: 그러면 하나만 남았네.
남: 그런 것 같아. 지금 지원할래.

어휘 **proficiency** 숙달, 능숙

11 짧은 대화에 이어질 응답 | ①

▶ 필름을 현상하기 위해 특별히 생각해둔 크기가 있느냐는 여자의 물음에 남자는 자신이 원하는 크기를 구체적으로 설명할 것이다.

① 이 액자에 맞으면 좋겠어요.
② 죄송합니다만, 중간 치수는 매진되었습니다.
③ 사진이 내일까지 준비되면 좋겠어요.
④ 적어도 각각 세 장씩 필요할 거예요.
⑤ 물론이죠, 30달러면 충분할 거예요.

W: Hello. How can I help you today?
M: I'd like to **have this film developed**, please.
W: Alright. Do you **have a specific size in mind**?
M: ______________________________

여: 안녕하세요. 오늘은 무엇을 도와드릴까요?
남: 이 필름을 현상하고 싶어요.
여: 알겠습니다. 특별히 생각해두신 (사진의) 크기가 있으신가요?
남: ______________________________

어휘 **fit into** ~에 꼭 들어맞다; 적합[적응]하다; 어울리다 / **develop** (필름을) 현상하다; 성장[발달]하다; ~을 개발하다; 발생하다

12 짧은 대화에 이어질 응답 | ⑤

▶ 졸업을 앞두고 있는 남동생이 졸업 후에 친구들을 그리워할 것 같다며 자신이 무엇을 해줄 수 있을지를 묻는 남자의 말에 가장 적절한 응답을 찾는다.

① 그 애는 확실히 빨리 자라는구나.
② 그러면 우리가 준비할 시간이 2주 있구나.
③ 기운 내! 네 친구들을 다시 만나게 될 거야.
④ 너도 같은 학교를 졸업하지 않았니?
⑤ 그 애와 친구들을 위해 파티를 열어주는 건 어때?

M: My little brother's graduation is two weeks from now.
W: Oh, he **is graduating from elementary school**.
M: Yes. I'm afraid that he'll miss his friends. **What can I do for him**?
W: ______________________________

남: 내 남동생의 졸업식이 앞으로 2주 후야.
여: 아, 그 애가 초등학교를 졸업하는구나.
남: 응. 그 애가 친구들을 그리워할 것 같아 유감이야. 내가 무엇을 해줄 수 있을까?
여: ______________________________

13 긴 대화에 이어질 응답 | ②

▶ 여자(학생)가 설명회에 가고 싶지만 수업 시간과 겹쳐서 고민하고 있는 상황에서 남자(교사)가 할 수 있는 적절한 응답을 고른다.

① 너에게 행운을 빌어줄게.
② 괜찮단다. 내가 너희 선생님께 짧은 쪽지를 써줄게.
③ 설명회에서 그 선생님께 여쭤보지 그러니?
④ 유감이지만 수업을 네 마음대로 선택할 수는 없을 것 같구나.
⑤ 그 학교의 수업 시간표는 우리랑 같단다.

M: Great work today, Stacy.
W: Thank you, Mr. Cho. I really love studying Chinese.
M: It shows. **That's why you're being given the chance** to visit Shanghai High School in China.
W: Really? You mean our sister school? I'm so excited! Please, tell me everything about the trip.
M: Actually, one of the teachers from Shanghai High School is coming to visit our school tomorrow.
W: Then, can I **have a chance to talk to the teacher**?
M: Of course. She will lead an information session about the trip in the auditorium at 3 p.m.
W: I really want to go, but **I'm not sure if I can**.
M: Why not?

W: I'm worried because **it overlaps with my last class**.
M: ______________________________

남: 오늘 아주 잘했어, Stacy.
여: 감사합니다, Cho 선생님. 전 중국어 공부하는 게 정말 좋아요.
남: 그래 보이는구나. 그래서 네게 중국에 있는 상하이 고등학교에 방문할 기회가 주어질 거란다.
여: 정말요? 자매학교 말씀이세요? 정말 신나요! 제발 그 여행에 대해서 다 말씀해주세요.
남: 실은, 상하이 고등학교에서 선생님 중 한 분이 내일 우리 학교에 방문하실 거란다.
여: 그러면 제가 그 선생님과 이야기할 기회를 가질 수 있어요?
남: 물론이지. 그 선생님께서 오후 세 시에 강당에서 그 여행에 관한 설명회를 하실 거란다.
여: 정말 가고 싶긴 한데, 그럴 수 있을지 모르겠어요.
남: 왜 그러니?
여: 제 마지막 수업이랑 (시간이) 겹쳐서 고민이에요.
남: ______________________________

어휘 **information session** 설명회 ***cf.* session** (특정 활동을 위한) 시간, 기간; 학년; 연주회 / **overlap** 겹치다; ~을 겹치게 하다, 포개다; 겹침

14 긴 대화에 이어질 응답 | ⑤

▶ 영화를 보는 대신 함께 Janice의 병문안을 하러 가기로 한 남자에게 여자가 할 수 있는 응답을 찾는다.

① 맞아. 자동차를 조심해야 해.
② 네 병문안을 가지 못해 미안해.
③ 좋아. 진료 예약을 할게.
④ 영화 보고 나서 뭐 좀 먹는 게 어때?
⑤ 좋아. 그럼 병원 앞에서 만나자.

[Phone rings.]
M: Hi, Rachel. It's Dan.
W: Oh, hi. What's up?
M: Are you free this afternoon?
W: No, I'm going to the cooking class that I have at 4 every Friday.
M: Oh, now I remember. **You've talked about that before**. How's the class?
W: So far, so good. The instructor said **I have a talent for cooking**.
M: Good for you! Then, what about after class? Actually, I got two free tickets to a newly released movie.
W: Sorry, but **I need to drop by** the West Lake Hospital to visit Janice.
M: What happened to Janice?
W: She had a minor car accident last night. **Why don't you come with me**? She'll be glad.
M: Sure. I want to see if she's okay. We can use the free tickets later.
W: ______________________________

[전화벨이 울린다.]
남: 여보세요, Rachel. 나 Dan이야.
여: 아, 안녕. 어쩐 일이야?
남: 오늘 오후에 시간 있니?
여: 아니, 금요일마다 네 시에 있는 요리 수업을 들으러 가거든.
남: 아, 이제 기억난다. 그 수업에 대해서 전에 말했었지. 수업은 어때?
여: 지금까지는 괜찮아. 강사님께서 내가 요리에 소질이 있다고 하셨어.
남: 잘됐구나! 그럼, 수업 끝나고는 시간 되니? 사실, 새로 개봉한 영화의 공짜 표가 두 장 생겼거든.
여: 미안하지만, Janice 병문안하러 West Lake 병원에 들러야 할 것 같아.
남: Janice에게 무슨 일이 생겼니?
여: 어젯밤에 가벼운 자동차 사고를 당했대. 너도 같이 가는 게 어때? Janice가 좋아할 거야.
남: 그래. Janice가 괜찮은지 보고 싶어. 공짜 표는 나중에 써도 돼.
여: ______________________________

어휘 **instructor** (특정한 기술이나 운동을 가르치는) 강사, 교사 / **release** 개봉[발표]하다; 풀어 주다

15 상황에 적절한 말 | ③

▶ Roger는 Harrison 씨에게 적임자인 친구 Amy를 추천하는 말을 할 것이다.

① Amy가 이 일자리를 얻게 되어 무척 신이 날 것입니다.
② 제게 기회를 주시면, 최선을 다할 것을 약속드리겠습니다.
③ 제가 (이 직책에) 꼭 알맞을 사람을 알고 있는 것 같습니다.
④ 제게 이사회의 결정을 최대한 빨리 알려주십시오.
⑤ 새 마케팅부장으로서의 제 제안을 수락해주시길 바랍니다.

W: Roger is an employee at a large company, and Ms. Harrison is his boss. Two weeks ago, Ms. Harrison recommended Roger **for the position of marketing manager**. Today, the board accepted her recommendation. So, Ms. Harrison gives the good news to Roger, and Roger thanks Ms. Harrison **for her efforts**. Then, Ms. Harrison tells Roger that a replacement is necessary for Roger's current position and **asks if he knows anyone**. At the moment, Roger's friend Amy is looking to **transfer to a different company**. Roger knows that Amy is well-qualified and **a good fit for the position**, so he wants to recommend her. In this situation, what would Roger most likely say to Ms. Harrison?

여: Roger는 대기업의 사원이고 Harrison 씨는 그의 상사이다. 2주 전에, Harrison 씨는 마케팅부장 직에 Roger를 추천했다. 오늘, 이사회는 그녀의 추천을 받아들였다. 그래서 Harrison 씨는 Roger에게 이 좋은 소식을 전하고 그는 Harrison 씨의 노력에 감사해 한다. 그러고 나서, Harrison 씨는 Roger에게 그의 현재 자리에 후임자가 필요하다고 말하며 아는 사람이 있는지 물어본다. 지금, Roger의 친구 Amy는 다른 회사로의 이직을 고려하고 있다. Roger는 Amy가 그 자리에 충분한 자격을 갖추고 있으며 잘 맞는다는 것을 알기에, 그녀를 추천하고 싶어 한다. 이러한 상황에서, Roger가 Harrison 씨에게 할 말로 가장 적절한 것은 무엇인가?

어휘 **thrilled** 아주 신이 난, 황홀해하는 / **board** 이사회, 위원회 / **replacement** 후임자; 대신할 사람; 교체, 대체 / **qualified** 자격(증)이 있는

16~17 세트 문항 | 16. ⑤ 17. ③

▶ 16. 콜레스테롤 수치를 낮출 수 있는 다양한 방법을 소개하고 있다.

① 균형 잡힌 식단의 중요성
② 고(高)콜레스테롤의 가능한 원인
③ 콜레스테롤에 대해 걱정해야 하는 이유
④ 다양한 종류의 건강에 좋은 차를 소개하기
⑤ 콜레스테롤을 줄이는 데 좋은 방법

▶ 17. 해석 참조

M: If you are worried about your cholesterol, there are a few things to keep in mind. First, fatty foods raise cholesterol levels, so **it helps to eat a balanced diet** with lots of fruits and vegetables. Exercise is also important. Studies have shown that even **moderate exercise is enough to lower** cholesterol levels. Now, if you are still worried, there are some specific foods that can actually lower cholesterol, such as oatmeal, fish, and nuts. And along with these, try a cup of maté since it also has the ability to fight cholesterol. It is a type of tea made from the maté tree, which is grown mainly in South America. **After grinding the dried leaves** of the tree, you add them to hot water and drink it. Traditionally, people serve it in a special container and drink it through a metal straw. The flavor is strongly herbal and grassy, similar to green tea. Though it's rich in vitamins and low in caffeine, large quantities of hot maté may **increase the risk of oral cancer**. So, drink less than one liter per day. By following these tips, you'll soon be **on the path to better health**.

남: 만약 당신이 콜레스테롤을 걱정한다면, 마음에 새겨야 할 몇 가지가 있습니다. 먼저, 기름진 음식은 콜레스테롤 수치를 올리므로, 과일과 채소가 많이 있는 균형 잡힌 식사를 하는 것이 도움이 됩니다. 운동 또한 중요합니다. 연구에 따르면 가벼운 운동이라도 콜레스테롤 수치를 낮추기에 충분합니다. 자, 여전히 걱정된다면 오트밀(귀리 가루), 생선, 견과류와 같이 실제로 콜레스테롤을 낮출 수 있는 특정한 음식들이 있습니다. 그리고 이 음식들을 비롯해서, 마테차도 콜레스테롤을 퇴치하는 효능이 있으니 한 잔 마셔보십시오. 그것은 마테 나무로부터 만들어진 차의 일종인데, 마테 나무는 남아메리카(① 원료의 주요 재배지)에서 주로 자랍니다. 나무의 마른 잎을 빻은 후, 뜨거운 물을 부어서 그것을 드십시오(② 음용 방법). 전통적으로, 사람들은 그것을 특별한 용기에 담아내어서 금속 빨대로 마십니다. 향미는 녹차와 비슷하게, 허브와 풀의 향이 강합니다(④ 향미). 비타민이 풍부하고 카페인도 적긴 하지만, 다량의 뜨거운 마테차는 구강암의 위험성을 증가(⑤ 부작용)시킬 수도 있습니다. 그러니 하루에 1리터 미만을 드십시오. 이러한 방법들을 따르는 것으로 당신은 곧 더 좋은 건강으로 가는 길에 있을 것입니다.

어휘 **moderate** 보통의, 중간의; (정치적인 견해가) 온건한; 적당한 / **grind** (곡식 등을) 갈다, 빻다; (날을) 갈다 / **oral** 구두[구전]의; 구강[입]의

실전모의고사 12

Answers & Explanation

01. ⑤ 02. ① 03. ③ 04. ⑤ 05. ⑤ 06. ② 07. ④ 08. ③ 09. ④ 10. ⑤
11. ① 12. ① 13. ⑤ 14. ③ 15. ④ 16. ⑤ 17. ③

01 화자가 하는 말의 목적 | ⑤

▶ 유해한 폐기물이 매립지에 버려져 환경이 오염되지 않도록 폐기물을 안전하게 처리하도록 노력하자는 것이 말의 요지이다.

M: Do you know where your trash goes once you put it in the bag and set it outside? **It is piled up** on trash mountains called 'landfills.' Often, these landfills are filled with common household items such as batteries, motor oil and old computers. **Throwing away such things in landfills** causes a lot of problems. When it rains, toxic chemicals from these items **drip into the ground**. From here, some harmful substances make their way into rivers and **the sources of the local water supply**. We used to think we could throw anything into landfills. But some things have to go to special recycling centers. To ask for a list of harmful household items and **the safest way to remove them**, call your local government office now.

남: 쓰레기를 봉지에 넣어 밖에 내놓으면 그것이 어디로 가는지 아십니까? 그것은 '매립지'라고 불리는 쓰레기 산에 쌓입니다. 종종 이런 매립지들은 건전지, 자동차 기름 그리고 오래된 컴퓨터 같은 흔한 가정용품들로 채워집니다. 이러한 물품들을 매립지에 버리는 것은 많은 문제를 야기합니다. 비가 오면 이 물품들에서 나오는 독성 화학물질이 땅으로 흘러 들어갑니다. 여기서부터 일부 유해 물질들이 강과 지역 상수도의 수원으로 흘러 들어가게 됩니다. 우리는 매립지에 무엇이든 버릴 수 있다고 생각하곤 했습니다. 하지만 어떤 것들은 전문 재활용 센터로 가야 합니다. 유해한 가정용품의 목록과 그것들을 가장 안전하게 처리하는 방법에 대해 문의하시려면, 지방 자치 단체 사무실로 지금 전화 걸어 주십시오.

어휘 **landfill** 매립지 / **household** 가정의; 가구 / **toxic** 유독한; 중독성의 / **chemical** 화학 물질[제품] / **drip** (액체가) 뚝뚝 떨어지다 / **substance** 물질 / **make one's way** 나아가다 / **water supply** 상수도

02 의견 | ①

▶ 여자는 취직 시 인턴십 경험이 중요한데, 그 경험을 졸업 전에 쌓는 게 더 유리할 것이라고 생각한다.

W: Well, the semester is over. Are you going to be around this summer?
M: No, I'll be traveling in South America. What about you?
W: I managed to get an internship. I'll be staying in the city and working.
M: You're going to work all summer? Don't you need a vacation?
W: This is the only chance **to do an internship before graduation**, and I think I'll need internship experience to get a job.
M: Hmm... I assumed I would start getting work experience after I graduated. I **prefer to enjoy myself** now.
W: I'm afraid that those who gain work experience before graduation will **have a significant advantage over** those who don't. Employers like to hire people who have experience.
M: It certainly **won't hurt to have** some internship experience.

여: 자, 이번 학기가 끝났어. 올여름에 (어디 안 가고) 근처에 있을 거니?
남: 아니, 남아메리카를 여행할 거야. 넌 어떻게 할 거야?
여: 난 간신히 인턴십 일자리를 구했어. 이 도시에 머물면서 일할 거야.
남: 여름 내내 일할 거라고? 휴가가 필요하지 않니?
여: 이건 졸업 전에 인턴십을 할 유일한 기회고, 취직하기 위해서는 인턴십 경험이 필요할 거라고 생각해.
남: 음… 난 졸업하고 나서 업무 경험을 쌓기 시작할 거라고 생각했어. 지금은 즐기는 게 더 좋아.
여: 아무래도 졸업 전에 업무 경험을 쌓는 사람들이 그렇게 하지 않는 사람들보다 상당히 유리할 것 같아. 고용주들은 경험이 있는 사람을 채용하기 원하니까.
남: 인턴십 경험을 좀 쌓는 게 결코 나쁘진 않을 거야.

어휘 **internship** (학생 등의) 실무 연수, 인턴직; (의대생의) 인턴 기간 / **assume** ~라고 간주하다, 여기다 / **significant** 상당한, 현저한; 중요한

03 관계 | ③

▶ 비행기의 상승, 가속, 착륙 등에 관한 대화를 통해 비행 강사가 수강생을 가르치고 있는 상황임을 유추할 수 있다.

M: OK. Now just gently pull the stick toward you and you will feel the airplane climb.
W: Wow. This is very exciting.
M: All right. **At your feet are two pedals**. If you push the pedals left and right, one at a time, you will feel **the back end of the plane** swing gently behind us.
W: You mean like this?
M: Just like that. You'll notice it doesn't **take much effort to move the airplane**.
W: Yeah. It's very sensitive.
M: And now if you pull that knob right there out a bit, the plane will go faster.
W: Oh boy! It's getting louder too!
M: Do you think you are ready to **try landing by yourself**?
W: I'm afraid to try that. Maybe next time.

남: 좋습니다. 이제 조종간을 몸 쪽으로 서서히 당기시면, 비행기가 상승하는 것을 느끼실 것입니다.
여: 와. 이거 정말 신나는데요.
남: 네. 발쪽에 두 개의 페달이 있습니다. 왼쪽과 오른쪽의 페달을 한 번에 하나씩 밟으면, 비행기의 후미 부분이 우리 뒤에서 부드럽게 흔들리는 것을 느끼실 것입니다.
여: 이렇게 말인가요?
남: 바로 그렇게요. 비행기를 움직이는 데 많은 노력이 들지 않는다는 것을 알아챌 것입니다.
여: 네. 이건 정말 민감하군요.
남: 그리고 이제 바로 저기 있는 저 손잡이를 밖으로 조금 당기면 비행기가 더 빨라질 것입니다.
여: 세상에! 소음도 심해지는군요!
남: 혼자서 착륙을 시도할 준비가 되신 것 같습니까?
여: 그건 해보기가 겁나네요. 다음에 하죠.

어휘 **gently** 서서히, 부드럽게 / **stick** (비행기) 조종간(桿) / **knob** 손잡이

04 그림 불일치 | ⑤

▶ 여자는 탁자 위에 호박을 두 개 올려놨다고 했다.

[Cell phone rings.]
W: Hello?
M: Amanda. It's me. **Have you finished decorating** the table for Halloween?
W: I'm almost done, Dad.
M: Great! Did you have any trouble putting up the "Trick or Treat!" banner by yourself?
W: Not at all. **It was easy to hang**. I also put the tablecloth on our round table.
M: Good job. Also, **don't forget to put out** the witch's hat.
W: Right. I've already set it on the table, and it looks great.
M: You also have candy and chocolates, right? That's the most important thing.
W: Of course, they're on the rectangular plate.
M: Fantastic. Oh, I almost forgot about the pumpkins.
W: Don't worry, I placed two pumpkins on the table, just like every Halloween.
M: Okay. Then everything **seems to be set up**.

[휴대전화 벨이 울린다.]
여: 여보세요?
남: Amanda. 나란다. 핼러윈 테이블 장식하는 거 끝났니?
여: 거의 다 했어요, 아빠.
남: 굉장한데! '과자를 안 주면 장난칠 거예요!' 플래카드를 혼자서 붙이는 데 힘들진 않았니?
여: 전혀요. 걸기 쉬웠어요. 둥근 탁자에 테이블보도 씌워놨어요.

남: 잘했구나. 또, 마녀 모자를 꺼내놓는 거 잊지 말렴.
여: 네. 이미 탁자 위에 올려놨는데 멋져 보여요.
남: 사탕이랑 초콜릿도 있지, 맞지? 그게 가장 중요한 거란다.
여: 물론이죠. 직사각형 접시 위에 있어요.
남: 멋진데. 아, 호박을 잊을 뻔했구나.
여: 걱정하지 마세요. 매년 핼러윈처럼 탁자 위에 호박 두 개를 올려놨어요.
남: 그래, 그러면 모든 게 준비된 것 같구나.

어휘 **Halloween** 핼러윈 ((10월 31일 밤)) / **banner** 플래카드, 현수막 / **set up** ~을 준비[마련]하다; ~을 설립하다

05 추후 행동 | ⑤

▶ 남자는 수학 성적이 좋지 않아 도움이 필요한데 수학 교수인 아빠가 실망하실까 봐 쉽게 도움을 청할 수 없다. 그러나 다른 방법이 없기 때문에 결국 대화 마지막에 아빠께 부탁하기로 한다.

M: My math grade is so terrible. My father is going to be so disappointed.
W: He'll understand.
M: Ji-won! My father is a mathematics professor. It should be "**Like father, like son**."
W: Oh, that's not true. My mother is good at piano, but I hate it. Just ask him for help.
M: He wants to help me, but I don't want his help. **I'll just disappoint him**.
W: Then join a study group. Your friends can help you.
M: All my classmates have different schedules. **Agreeing on a time is impossible**. I tried a month ago.
W: Lessons at an academy?
M: My mom won't agree since she knows my father said he'd teach me.
W: Then you **have no option but to ask** your dad.
M: Hmm.... I know. I'll do it tonight.

남: 내 수학 성적이 아주 형편없어. 아빠가 매우 실망하실 거야.
여: 이해하시겠지.
남: 지원아! 우리 아빠는 수학 교수님이셔. '그 아버지에 그 아들'이 되어야 해.
여: 오, 그건 사실이 아니야. 우리 엄마는 피아노를 잘 치시지만, 나는 피아노가 질색이야. 그냥 아빠께 도움을 청해 봐.
남: 아빠는 날 도와주고 싶어 하시지만, 나는 아빠의 도움을 바라지 않아. 아빠를 실망시키기만 할 거야.
여: 그럼 스터디 모임에 가입해봐. 친구들이 널 도와줄 수 있어.
남: 반 친구들 모두 다른 일정이 있어. 시간을 맞추는 것은 불가능해. 한 달 전에 시도해봤어.
여: 학원에서 수업은?
남: 엄마가 동의하시지 않을 거야. 아빠가 나를 가르치시겠다고 말씀하셨던 것을 알고 계시거든.
여: 그럼 아빠께 부탁하는 수밖에 없겠네.
남: 음…. 알아. 오늘 밤에 할 거야.

어휘 **have no option but to-v** v하는 수밖에 없다

06 금액 | ②

▶ 소형 차량으로 주중 이틀(2×50달러)과 주말 하루(75달러)를 빌릴 예정이다.

W: I'd like to rent a car.
M: OK. We have different cars and different rates.
W: **What is the price range**?
M: For a compact car, it is $50 a day during the week and $75 a day on the weekends.
W: $50 and $75, hmm... how much is a convertible?
M: A convertible is $100 a day during the week and $150 a day on Saturdays and Sundays.
W: OK. I think I will just **stick to a compact car**. It only costs half as much as a convertible.
M: And **how many days will you need it**?
W: I would like it for Thursday through Saturday.
M: So **that will cost you** two weekdays and one weekend day.
W: Right.

여: 차를 한 대 빌리고 싶습니다.
남: 네. 다양한 차량과 다양한 요금제가 있습니다.
여: 가격대가 어떻게 됩니까?
남: 소형 차량의 경우 주중에는 하루에 50달러이고 주말에는 하루에 75달러입니다.
여: 50달러와 75달러라. 음… 그럼 컨버터블은 얼마입니까?
남: 컨버터블은 주중에는 하루에 100달러, 토요일과 일요일에는 하루에 150달러입니다.
여: 알겠습니다. 그냥 소형 차량을 고수해야겠는데요. 컨버터블의 반값밖에 들지 않는군요.
남: 그리고 며칠 동안 필요하십니까?
여: 목요일에서 토요일까지 빌리고 싶어요.
남: 그럼 주중 이틀과 주말 하루를 더한 가격이 되겠습니다.
여: 알겠습니다.

어휘 **range** 범위, 영역, 폭 / **compact car** 소형차 / **convertible** 컨버터블, 지붕을 접을 수 있게 된 승용차 / **stick to** ~을 고수하다

07 이유 | ④

▶ 남자는 우연히 발견한 책의 삽화를 친구가 그린 것을 알고 그 책을 사려고 한다.

M: Mary, take a look at this book.
W: I really don't think that's a good gift for my sister. She's a bit old for picture books.
M: No, no, take a look inside, **next to the author's autograph**.
W: Oh, wow! It was illustrated by Neil Jurgen, your old roommate.
M: Yeah! You know, **it's been so long** since I've talked to him. I didn't know that he was illustrating books these days.
W: Well, you always said he was talented. And I remember being impressed by the pictures he drew for his art classes.
M: You're right. **He always had talent**. I'm glad he's doing well.
W: So, are you going to get the book?
M: I am, and **I'm going to give him a call** when we get home.

남: Mary, 이 책 좀 봐.
여: 그건 내 여동생에게 줄 선물로 별로 안 좋은 것 같아. 동생은 그림책을 읽기에는 나이가 좀 있어.
남: 아냐, 그게 아니라, 안을 봐, 저자 서명 옆에.
여: 오, 와! 네 옛날 룸메이트인 Neil Jurgen이 삽화를 그렸네.
남: 응! 있잖아, 그 애와 얘기해본 지 꽤 오래돼서 요즘 책에 삽화를 그리고 있는지 몰랐어.
여: 음, 재능이 있다고 네가 항상 말했잖아. 그리고 그 애가 미술 시간에 그린 그림이 인상 깊었던 게 기억나.
남: 네 말이 맞아. 그 앤 항상 재능이 있었어. 잘하고 있어서 기뻐.
여: 그럼, 그 책 살 거야?
남: 응, 그리고 집에 가서 그 애에게 전화할 거야.

어휘 **autograph** 서명, (유명인의) 사인 / **illustrate** (책 등에) 삽화를 넣다

08 언급하지 않은 것 | ③

▶ 해석 참조

W: Honey, let's stop for a minute. I want to get a copy of that magazine.
M: Okay. *[pause]* Who is that on the cover?
W: That's Waris Dirie. She was a model, and is now **a human rights activist**.
M: Oh, right. I didn't recognize her. She's also an author, right?
W: Yeah. She wrote *Desert Flower* in 1998, which was turned into a movie, and *Letter to My Mother* in 2007. **They are both based on** her experiences.
M: I remember watching the movie *Desert Flower*. Anyway, she was born to a poor tribe in Somalia, right?
W: Yes, and she had to **leave her hometown** at the age of 13 to avoid an arranged marriage.
M: She had a difficult life, but she **overcame her hardships** and is now an inspiration to many.

여: 여보, 잠시 멈춰요. 저 잡지를 한 권 사고 싶어요.
남: 그래요. *[잠시 후]* 표지에 있는 저 사람 누구예요?
여: Waris Dirie예요. 모델이었고, 지금은 인권 운동가예요(① 직업).
남: 아, 맞아요. 내가 못 알아봤네요. 작가이기도 하지요(① 직업), 맞죠?
여: 네. 1998년에 〈사막의 꽃〉을 썼는데 영화로 제작됐고요, 2007년에 〈엄마에게 쓰는 편지〉를 썼어요(② 저서). 두 권 다 그녀의 경험을 바탕으로 했어요.
남: 영화 〈데저트 플라워〉를 본 게 기억나요. 그런데, 그녀는 소말리아(④ 출신 국가)의 가난한 부족에서 태어났죠, 맞죠?
여: 네, 그리고 중매결혼을 피해 열세 살의 나이(⑤ 고향을 떠난 나이)에 고향을 떠나야 했어요.
남: 힘든 삶을 살았지만, 어려움을 극복했고 이제 많은 사람에게 영감을 주는군요.

어휘 **copy** (책·신문 등의) 한 부; 복사(본) / **activist** (정치적·사회적) 운동가, 활동가 / **arranged marriage** 중매결혼 / **overcome** ~을 극복하다 / **hardship** 어려움, 곤란 / **inspiration** 영감[자극]을 주는 사람[것]; 영감

09 내용 불일치 | ④

▶ 정치적 이유로 나치당에 의해 폐교되었다고 했다.

W: Bauhaus was a design school in Germany that operated from 1919 to 1933. Bauhaus designers primarily tried to **combine crafts and the fine arts** through a new design philosophy. Its name means "School of Building" in German; however, Bauhaus did not have an architecture department **during the first years of its existence**. However, in pursuit of the establishment of a unified school of the arts, an architecture department was eventually added. Bauhaus **had a profound influence upon** art and design before being forever shut down by Adolf Hitler's Nazi party, which was opposed to it for political reasons. However, through the many modern buildings, offices, and pieces of furniture that **have been built** in the style of Bauhaus, we can see that its influence still remains today.

여: Bauhaus는 1919년에서 1933년까지 운영되었던 독일의 디자인 학교였다. Bauhaus의 디자이너들은 주로, 새로운 디자인 철학을 통해 공예와 미술을 결합하고자 했다. Bauhaus라는 이름은 독일어로 '건축 학교'라는 뜻이지만, 설립 초기 몇 년 동안 Bauhaus에는 건축학과가 없었다. 하지만 통합 예술 학교를 설립하려는 노력으로, 결국 건축학과가 추가되었다. Bauhaus는 Adolf Hitler의 나치당에 의해 영구 폐교되기 전까지 예술과 디자인에 지대한 영향을 미쳤는데, 나치당은 정치적 이유로 Bauhaus를 반대했다. 하지만 Bauhaus 양식으로 지어진 많은 현대 건축물, 사무실, 가구들을 통해 그 영향력이 오늘날 여전히 남아있음을 알 수 있다.

어휘 **primarily** 주로 / **craft** (수)공예; 기술 / **fine art** 미술 / **architecture** 건축학; 건축 양식 / **existence** 존재, 실재 / **in pursuit of** ~을 추구하여 / **establishment** 설립; 기관 / **profound** (영향 등이) 지대한, 엄청난 / **shut down** (가게·학교 등이) 문을 닫다; (기계가) 멈추다 / **party** 정당, 당파; 파티 / **be opposed to** ~에 반대하다

10 도표 이해 | ⑤

▶ 수영장이 있는지 여부는 상관이 없으며 인터넷 접속이 되면서 부엌이 달려있고 하루 100달러보다는 싼 호텔을 선택할 것이다.

W: I can't wait for our trip to Cancun!
M: Yeah, me too. Now all we need to do is choose a hotel.
W: Well, I want to go swimming every day!
M: All of these hotels in this brochure are right on the beach. You can swim in the sea. I don't think **a pool is important at all**.
W: Right, and since you have to check in with work every morning on the big project, we need to have access to the Web.
M: Well, that **eliminates a few more choices**.
W: What will we do about eating? With your special diet, it looks like a kitchen would be helpful.
M: Sure, and **what about the hotel rate**?
W: The rate should be cheaper than $100 per night.
M: I guess that leaves only one choice.

여: Cancun으로의 여행이 정말 기대돼요!
남: 네, 저도요. 이제 우리가 해야 할 일은 호텔을 정하는 것뿐이군요.
여: 음, 전 매일 수영하러 가고 싶어요!
남: 이 책자에 나와 있는 이 호텔들은 모두 바로 해변에 위치해 있어요. 바다에서 수영할 수 있어요. 수영장은 전혀 중요한 것 같지 않아요.
여: 맞아요, 그리고 당신은 큰 프로젝트 때문에 매일 아침 (회사에) 연락해서 일을 확인해야 하니까, 우린 인터넷에 접속할 수 있어야 해요.
남: 그럼, 몇 가지 선택사항이 더 제외되네요.
여: 식사는 어떻게 할 건가요? 당신의 특별 식단 때문에 부엌이 있으면 유용할 것 같은데요.
남: 물론이죠. 그리고 호텔 비용은 어떻게 할까요?
여: 호텔비는 하룻밤에 100달러보다 싸야 해요.
남: 그럼 한 군데만 남는군요.

어휘 **facility** 시설, 설비 / **have access to** ~에 접근하다 / **eliminate** ~을 제거하다

11 짧은 대화에 이어질 응답 | ①

▶ 학교 야구팀에 등록하지 않겠다는 남자에게 여자는 이번 시즌에는 경기하고 싶지 않은지 묻고 있다. 이에 대한 적절한 응답을 찾는다.

① 하고는 싶은데, 그냥 너무 바빠. ② 그 경기를 놓쳐서 아쉬워.
③ 야구를 놓치고 싶지 않아. ④ 응, 하지만 내일 등록할 것 같아.
⑤ 야구는 전통적으로 여름에 해.

W: Today is the last day to **sign up for school baseball**.
M: I know, but I don't think **I will bother**.
W: Don't you want to play this season?
M: ________________

여: 오늘이 학교 야구팀에 등록하는 마지막 날이네.
남: 알고 있지만, 신경 쓰지 않으려고 해.
여: 이번 시즌에는 경기하고 싶지 않니?
남: ________________

어휘 **sign up (for)** (~에) 등록하다

12 짧은 대화에 이어질 응답 | ①

▶ 과제가 조금밖에 남지 않은 상황에서, 내일 마무리하자는 여자에게 남자는 그냥 지금 끝마칠 것을 제안하고 있다. 이에 가장 적절한 응답을 고른다.

① 미안하지만 난 지금 가봐야 해. ② 다음 과제가 곧 시작될 거야.
③ 마감일이 빠르게 다가오고 있어. ④ 이 과제는 우리 능력 밖이야.
⑤ 난 네가 내일 시간이 없을 줄 알았어.

M: I think we can complete this project **in another hour or so**.
W: Great. Let's meet tomorrow and finish it up.
M: Wouldn't you rather stay and **get it over with**?
W: ________________

남: 우리 한 시간 정도면 이 과제를 마칠 수 있을 것 같아.
여: 잘됐다. 내일 만나서 끝내자.
남: 차라리 남아서 끝마치지 않을래?
여: ________________

어휘 **get over with** ((구어)) ~을 끝내다

13 긴 대화에 이어질 응답 | ⑤

▶ 동생을 집까지 데리고 가야 해서 중요한 연습에 참가하지 못하는 친구를 위해 할 수 있는 반응을 찾아본다.

① 네 남동생은 테니스를 정말 잘 치는구나.
② 우리 가족은 주말에 여행을 떠나.
③ 어차피 난 너무 바빠서 너랑 테니스 못 쳐.
④ 네가 우승하지 못하면 어머니께서 정말 기분 상해하실걸.
⑤ 내가 코치님께 너희 집에 급한 일이 생겼다고 말씀드릴게.

M: Where are you going, Valerie?
W: I have to pick up my little brother from school.
M: But we have tennis practice **in a half hour**.
W: I know, but my mother is too busy to get Oscar, so **I have to walk him home**.
M: But the finals are coming up this weekend! Can't your little brother walk home by himself?
W: No. He's only in first grade and he has to **cross some really busy roads**. It might be dangerous for him to go back home by himself. Family comes first.
M: I guess you're right, but the coach is really going to be mad.
W: Hopefully he'll understand. Anyway, **I'm going to run**.
M: ________________

남: 어디 가니, Valerie?
여: 내 남동생을 학교에서 데리고 와야 해.
남: 하지만 우린 30분 뒤에 테니스 연습이 있잖아.
여: 알지만, 어머니께서 너무 바쁘셔서 Oscar를 데려오실 수 없어서, 내가 그 애를 집으로 데려와야 해.
남: 하지만 결승전이 이번 주말로 다가오고 있잖아! 네 남동생은 혼자서 집에 못 걸어오니?
여: 응, 그 애는 겨우 1학년이고 아주 혼잡한 도로를 몇 개 건너야 하거든. 그 애 혼자서 집으로 돌아오는 것은 위험할 수도 있어. 가족이 우선이야.

남: 네 말이 맞는 것 같지만, 코치님께서 정말 화내실 거야.
여: 이해해 주시길 바라야지. 어쨌든 난 뛰어가야겠다.
남: ______________________________

어휘 **go away** (휴가 등을) 떠나다 / **walk** (같이 걸어서) ~을 바래다주다 / **finals** (경기의) 결승전

14 긴 대화에 이어질 응답 | ③

▶ 남자는 주문한 제품이 오지 않고 다른 물건이 배달되어 판매점에 전화를 했다. 이에 판매점의 적절한 대응을 찾는다.

① 저희 모델은 모두 프랑스제입니다.
② 전자레인지는 이번 달에 세일하고 있습니다.
③ 지금 올바른 제품을 전해 드리러 사람을 보내겠습니다.
④ 콤보 식사 세트에는 디럭스 버거가 나옵니다.
⑤ 건조기의 가격을 청구서에 추가하겠습니다.

[Phone rings.]
W: Sammy's Appliances, this is Gladys. How may I help you?
M: Hi. **I ordered a washing machine** to be delivered from your store yesterday.
W: Have you received the machine yet?
M: A machine was delivered today, but **it is the wrong one**.
W: OK. **Let me bring up your order** on my computer. What is your name and address, sir?
M: My name is Bill Bixby. 115 Oak Street.
W: Yes sir. It looks like you ordered the deluxe washer-dryer combo.
M: Well, **that is what they delivered**, but I didn't order that. I asked for the deluxe washer, but no dryer.
W: It looks like we made a mistake at the store. Are you sure you don't want to keep the model we sent?
M: No. That one was more expensive. I just want the one I ordered.
W: ______________________________

[전화벨이 울린다.]
여: Sammy 전자제품 점의 Gladys입니다. 무엇을 도와 드릴까요?
남: 안녕하세요. 제가 어제 귀 판매점의 세탁기를 배달해 달라고 주문했습니다.
여: 물건을 벌써 받으셨습니까?
남: 물건은 오늘 배달되었습니다만, 잘못 왔네요.
여: 알겠습니다. 컴퓨터에서 주문하신 사항을 찾아보겠습니다. 성함과 주소가 어떻게 되시는지요, 손님?
남: 제 이름은 Bill Bixby입니다. Oak가 115번지입니다.
여: 네, 손님. 손님께서 디럭스 세탁 건조기 콤보를 주문하신 것 같군요.
남: 음, 배달된 것이 바로 그것인데, 저는 그것을 주문하지 않았습니다. 디럭스 세탁기를 주문했지만, 건조기는 아닙니다.
여: 판매점에서 실수를 한 것 같습니다. 저희가 보내드린 모델을 원하시지 않는 것이 확실합니까?
남: 그렇습니다. 그게 더 비쌌어요. 전 제가 주문한 것만을 원합니다.
여: ______________________________

어휘 **appliance** (가정용) 기기 / **bring up** (컴퓨터 화면에) 띄우다

15 상황에 적절한 말 | ④

▶ 친한 친구에게 남자 친구가 생겨서 둘 사이가 소원하게 되었을 경우 친구의 기분이 상하지 않게 자신의 마음을 표현할 수 있는 방법을 생각해 본다.

① 나는 네 남자 친구를 좋아하지 않아. 그는 나에게 아주 심술궂게 굴거든.
② 안색이 안 좋아 보인다. 괜찮아?
③ 나도 남자 친구가 생겼으니 우리 더블 데이트할 수 있겠다.
④ 네게 남자 친구가 생긴 것은 기쁘지만 난 너를 잃고 싶지 않아.
⑤ 불평하고 싶은 건 아니지만 나에게 솔직해 줄래?

M: Susan and Jane have been friends all their lives. Now Jane has a boyfriend and she doesn't **have as much time** to spend with Susan as before. In fact, Jane sees her boyfriend almost every evening and doesn't **even call her friend anymore**. This hurts Susan's feelings, but she doesn't want to upset her best friend by complaining. If Jane **keeps acting that way**, Susan is afraid they will not be friends anymore. In this situation, what would Susan most likely say to Jane?

남: Susan과 Jane은 평생 친구로 지내왔다. 지금 Jane은 남자 친구가 생겨서 Susan과 같이 보내는 시간이 예전만큼 많지 않다. 사실, Jane은 거의 매일 저녁 남자 친구를 만나느라 친구에게 더는 전화도 하지 않는다. 이런 상황이 Susan의 감정을 상하게 하지만, 불평을 해서 가장 친한 친구를 속상하게 하고 싶지는 않다. 만약 Jane이 계속 이런 식으로 행동한다면, Susan은 자신들이 더는 친구가 될 수 없을까 봐 두렵다. 이러한 상황에서 Susan이 Jane에게 할 말로 가장 적절한 것은 무엇인가?

어휘 **mean** 심술궂은 / **upset** ~을 속상하게 만들다

16~17 세트 문항 | 16. ⑤ 17. ③

▶ 16. 천연 직물과 염색제의 예를 들면서 의류가 환경에 미치는 영향을 최소화하기 위한 패션 경향에 대해 설명하고 있다.

① 친환경 패션의 오랜 역사
② 헌 옷을 재사용하는 것의 장단점
③ 패션 업계에서 인기 있는 천연 직물
④ 의류 염색에 가장 좋은 천연 염색제를 추천하기
⑤ 환경을 보호하는 것을 목표로 하는 패션 경향

▶ 17. 해석 참조
대나무는 천연 염색제가 아니라 천연 직물의 재료로 언급되었다.

W: Many of the fabrics, materials, and dyes that are used to create today's clothing **have a huge impact on** the Earth's ecosystems. For example, nylon and polyester are both made from petroleum and harmful to the ozone layer. **In an effort to limit the impact** on the environment, there is a new trend toward eco-fashion. Eco-fashion is simply the use of natural fabrics and dyes **in the production of clothing**. Examples of this include using organic raw materials, such as cotton grown without pesticides, or reused materials such as recycled plastic from old soda bottles. Bamboo is especially useful to eco-fashion designers because it grows quickly and can be turned into a soft, breathable fabric that is biodegradable. This means that old clothing made from bamboo **will simply disappear if buried**. Also, eco-fashion avoids the use of harmful chemicals and bleaches to color fabrics, and instead uses natural sources of dyes. For example, apples **can be used to produce** shades of green, while blackberries can make deep purples. Roses can be used for lighter shades of red, and lavender can produce darker shades.

여: 오늘날 의류를 만드는 데 쓰이는 직물, 재료, 염색제의 다수가 지구 생태계에 엄청난 영향을 미칩니다. 예를 들어, 나일론과 폴리에스테르는 둘 다 석유로 만들어져 오존층에 해롭습니다. 환경에 미치는 영향을 제한하려는 노력으로, 에코패션을 추구하는 새로운 경향이 있습니다. 에코패션은 의류 생산에 단순히 천연 직물과 염색제를 사용하는 것입니다. 이러한 사례에는 살충제를 쓰지 않고 재배한 면직물 같은 유기농 원료나 낡은 탄산음료 병에서 재활용한 플라스틱 같은 재사용 재료를 사용하는 것이 포함됩니다. 대나무는 에코패션 디자이너에게 특히 유용한데, 성장이 빠르며, 부드럽고 통기성이 있는 자연 분해성 직물이 될 수 있기 때문입니다. 이는 대나무로 만들어진 낡은 옷이 땅에 묻히면 그냥 없어질 것이라는 의미입니다. 또한, 에코패션은 천을 염색하는 데 유해한 화학 약품과 표백제 사용을 피하고, 대신 천연자원의 염색제를 사용합니다. 예를 들어, ① 사과는 초록색 색조를 생산하는 데 쓰일 수 있는 한편, ② 블랙베리는 짙은 자주색을 만들 수 있습니다. ④ 장미는 보다 연한 색조의 붉은색에 쓰일 수 있으며, ⑤ 라벤더는 더 짙은 색조를 생산할 수 있습니다.

어휘 **eco-friendly** 친환경적인 / **pros and cons** 장단점, 찬반 양론 / **fabric** 직물, 천 / **dye** 염료, 염색제; ~을 염색하다 / **petroleum** 석유 / **ozone layer** 오존층 / **raw material** 원료 / **pesticide** 살충제 / **breathable** (옷감이) 통기성이 있는 / **biodegradable** 자연 분해성의 ((미생물에 의해 무해 물질로 분해되어 환경에 해가 되지 않는)) / **bleach** 표백제 / **shade** 색조; 그늘

Answers & Explanation

01. ④ 02. ② 03. ③ 04. ⑤ 05. ② 06. ② 07. ⑤ 08. ③ 09. ④ 10. ④
11. ② 12. ④ 13. ② 14. ④ 15. ① 16. ① 17. ③

01 화자가 하는 말의 목적 | ④

▶ 웹사이트에 발생한 문제의 원인, 해결 과정, 대책 등을 설명하고 있으므로 이 말의 목적은 ④이다.

W: Important message concerning last night's network happenings. Although all of our servers were fine, Domain Name Service — which was outside our direct control — **became unavailable for** many of our websites. We outsource DNS to a specialist company which has many redundant servers. These also didn't work. We resolved the problem early this morning **by setting up and migrating to** our own DNS service. We intend to make this permanent so that we do not **rely on a third party** in the future. We appreciate your understanding in this matter, especially if you were affected. You can **find a description of what happened**, and what we're doing to **prevent it from happening** again, on our website. Thank you.

여: 어젯밤 네트워크에 발생한 일에 관한 중요한 메시지입니다. 저희 서버는 전부 괜찮았지만, 저희의 직접적인 통제를 벗어나는 도메인 이름 서비스가 저희 웹사이트 많은 곳에서 이용할 수 없게 되었습니다. 저희는 도메인 이름 시스템을 많은 예비용 서버가 있는 전문 기업에 위탁합니다. 이 서버들도 작동하지 않았습니다. 자체 도메인 이름 시스템 서비스를 구축하고 (그것으로) 바꿈으로써 오늘 아침 일찍 문제를 해결했습니다. 앞으로 제삼자에 의존하지 않도록 이것을 영구적인 것으로 만들 생각입니다. 특히 여러분께서 피해를 입으셨다면 이 문제에 대해 이해해주셔서 감사합니다. 무슨 일이 일어났는지, 그리고 그 일이 다시는 발생하지 않도록 하기 위해 무엇을 하고 있는지에 관한 설명은 저희 웹사이트에서 찾으실 수 있습니다. 감사합니다.

어휘 **concerning** ~에 관해 / **domain name** 도메인 이름 ((인터넷 주소)) / **outsource** 외부에 위탁하다 / **DNS** 도메인 이름 시스템 ((Domain Name System의 약어)) / **redundant** (장치 등이) 예비용의; (중복되어) 불필요한 / **resolve** ~을 해결하다; 결심하다 / **migrate** (컴퓨터 시스템을) 바꾸다; 이동[이주]하다 / **permanent** 영구적인 / **third party** 제삼자

02 의견 | ②

▶ 소셜 미디어에 중독된 여자에게 남자는 소셜 미디어 사용을 그만두는 방법으로 먼저 사용 시간을 제한하는 것을 권하며 이를 위한 앱도 소개하고 있다.

M: Evelyn, you keep checking your smartphone every few minutes.
W: I am checking to see **if there are any notifications** on Facebook and Instagram.
M: Have you heard about FOMO? It stands for "Fear of Missing Out."
W: What does it mean?
M: It's the uneasy feeling that **you're missing out on things** that your peers are doing. It's among the biggest causes of social media addiction.
W: You're right. I'm depressed when I have no internet access.
M: I stopped using it. Now I have more free time to do other things. You should try it.
W: But it's very difficult to quit using social media.
M: The first step is **to limit the time you spend on it**. I use a smartphone app that enables you to monitor your screen time and limit it.
W: That's a good idea.
M: Keep one thing in mind when you spend all your time staring at pictures on social media. **It's your life you're missing out on.**

남: Evelyn, 너는 몇 분마다 네 스마트폰을 계속 확인하는구나.
여: 나는 페이스북과 인스타그램에 어떤 알림이 있는지 보기 위해 확인하고 있어.
남: FOMO에 대해 들어본 적 있니? 그것은 '놓치게 되는 것에 대한 두려움'을 의미해.
여: 그게 무슨 의미야?
남: 그건 네 친구들이 하는 것을 네가 놓치고 있다는 불안한 감정이야. 그것은 소셜 미디어 중독의 가장 큰 원인에 속해.
여: 맞아. 나는 인터넷 접속이 안 되면 우울해.
남: 나는 그것을 사용하는 것을 그만뒀어. 이제 나는 다른 것을 하기 위한 자유 시간이 더 많이 생겼어. 너도 시도해 봐야 해.
여: 하지만 소셜 미디어 사용을 그만두는 것은 정말 어려워.
남: 첫 번째 단계는 네가 그것에 쓰는 시간을 제한하는 거야. 나는 네가 네 전자기기 사용 시간을 관찰해서 그것을 제한할 수 있게 해주는 스마트폰 앱을 사용해.
여: 그거 좋은 생각이다.
남: 소셜 미디어에 있는 사진들을 응시하는 데 네 모든 시간을 쓸 때 한 가지를 명심해. 네가 놓치고 있는 것은 네 인생이야.

어휘 **notification** 알림, 통지; 신고 / **stand for** 의미하다, 나타내다; 상징하다 / **miss out (on)** (참석하지 않아 즐거운 것을) 놓치다 / **uneasy** 불안한; 불안정한 / **peer** 또래 / **addiction** 중독 / **depressed** 우울한, 낙담한 / **enable A to-v** A가 v할 수 있게 하다 / **screen time** 전자기기 사용 시간 / **stare at** ~을 응시하다

03 관계 | ③

▶ 대화 중에 periodicals section, microfilm catalogue, make copies, reference section 등의 표현이 등장하는 것으로 보아 도서관 사서와 도서관 이용자 사이의 대화임을 알 수 있다.

M: Hi, where can I find newspapers and magazines?
W: **Downstairs in the periodicals section.** Are you looking for something in particular?
M: Actually, I am researching a local murder that happened in 1925.
W: Oh, in that case, you need to search our microfilm catalogue. All newspapers from 1970 or earlier **are stored on microfilm.**
M: Is it possible to make copies?
W: Of course, you can buy a copier card downstairs.
M: I'm also looking for **war service records**. Do you keep those?
W: No, I suggest you try the National War Archives website. You can use the computers **in the reference section** just over there.
M: Thanks for your help!

남: 안녕하세요. 신문과 잡지는 어디에서 찾을 수 있나요?
여: 아래층의 정기 간행물 구역에 있습니다. 특별히 찾고 계신 것이 있나요?
남: 실은, 1925년에 발생한 지역 살인사건을 조사하고 있습니다.
여: 아, 그런 경우라면 마이크로필름 목록을 찾아 보셔야 되겠네요. 1970년 이전의 신문은 모두 마이크로필름으로 보관되고 있습니다.
남: 복사가 가능한가요?
여: 물론이죠, 아래층에서 복사카드를 구입하시면 됩니다.
남: 전쟁 참전 기록도 찾고 있는데요, 그 기록들도 보관하고 계신가요?
여: 아니요, 국가 전쟁 기록 보관소 웹사이트를 찾아보시길 권합니다. 바로 저쪽 참고 문헌 구역에 있는 컴퓨터를 사용하시면 됩니다.
남: 도와주셔서 고맙습니다!

어휘 **periodical** 정기 간행물; 정기 간행의 / **murder** 살인 사건 / **microfilm** 마이크로필름, 축소 사진 필름 / **catalogue** 도서 목록 / **archive** 기록 보관소 / **reference** 참고 문헌

04 그림 불일치 | ⑤

▶ 대화에서는 남자가 사진 속의 자신은 일광욕용 의자에 앉아 열대과일 주스를 마시고 있다고 했으므로 의자에 누워 잠을 자고 있는 모습의 ⑤가 대화의 내용과 일치하지 않는다.

W: Josh, **what does this picture show**?
M: It's a picture of my family's vacation to Hard Rock Resort. This is the kids' pool.
W: It's quite a big swimming pool. **What is this on the left**? It looks like a mushroom.
M: It's a kind of waterfall. That's my daughter, Stephanie, who is standing under the mushroom and **enjoying the splashing water**.
W: That looks fun. They also have a big water slide in the pool.
M: Yeah. I especially like the waterfall bucket at the top of the slide.
W: That looks great. Where is your son? Is he the boy **who is holding a ball in the pool**?
M: No, he is my nephew. My son is sitting with his feet in the water.
W: He is so cute. Oh, you are sitting on a sun chair near your son. You look very comfortable.
M: Yeah. I was drinking tropical fruit juice **while watching the kids**.

W: I want to go there with my family, too. Let me know some information about this place.
M: Sure. I'll send you a link to the resort's site.

여: Josh, 이 사진은 무엇이에요?
남: Hard Rock 리조트로 간 우리 가족의 휴가 사진이에요. 여긴 유아 풀이죠.
여: 꽤 큰 수영장이군요. 왼쪽에 이것은 무엇인가요? 버섯처럼 생겼네요.
남: 그것은 일종의 폭포예요. 저 애가 제 딸 Stephanie인데 그 애는 버섯 아래에 서서 튀기는 물을 즐기고 있어요.
여: 재미있어 보여요. 풀에 큰 물 미끄럼틀도 있네요.
남: 맞아요. 전 특히 미끄럼틀 위에 있는 폭포 버킷이 좋아요.
여: 저것은 굉장해 보여요. 당신 아들은 어디 있나요? 풀에서 공을 들고 있는 소년인가요?
남: 아뇨, 그 애는 내 남자 조카예요. 내 아들은 발을 물에 담근 채로 앉아 있었어요.
여: 그 애는 아주 귀엽군요. 아, 당신은 아들 근처에 일광욕용 의자에 앉아 있군요. 당신은 아주 편안해 보여요.
남: 맞아요. 나는 아이들을 보면서 열대과일 주스를 마시고 있었어요.
여: 나도 거기에 가족들과 가고 싶어요. 이 장소에 대해 정보 좀 제게 알려줘요.
남: 물론이죠. 내가 리조트 사이트 링크를 보내줄게요.

어휘 **waterfall** 폭포 / **splash** 튀기다; ~에 튀다 / **nephew** 남자 조카 / **tropical** 열대(지방)의; 열대성의 / **link** (인터넷) 링크; 고리; 유대

05 부탁한 일 | ②

▶ 바빠서 컴퓨터를 수리하러 갈 시간이 없는 여자는 기술자를 집으로 보내달라고 했다.

[Phone rings.]
M: Hello, Total Computer Solutions, Kevin speaking.
W: Hi, Kevin. This is Carolyn Jones. It's an emergency!
M: What's wrong?
W: I have a major assignment due tomorrow and **my computer keeps freezing**!
M: Do you have virus protection?
W: Umm... no, I don't think so.
M: You really should **get it installed**. If you bring your computer in, we'll probably have it repaired for you by this afternoon. We can **thoroughly clean it up** for you too.
W: But I can't bring it in! I'm too busy! **Could you please send a technician to my house**?
M: Of course I can do that.
W: How much will that cost?
M: $30 per hour, **not including any replacement parts**.
W: OK. How quickly can someone come?
M: Right away. What's your address?

[전화벨이 울린다.]
남: 여보세요, Total Computer Solutions의 Kevin입니다.
여: 안녕하세요, Kevin 씨. 저는 Carolyn Jones입니다. 급한 일이에요!
남: 무슨 일입니까?
여: 제가 내일까지 해야 할 중요한 숙제가 있는데 제 컴퓨터가 계속 멈춰요!
남: 바이러스 방지 프로그램이 있나요?
여: 음… 아니요, 없는 것 같아요.
남: 그것을 꼭 설치하셔야 합니다. 컴퓨터를 가지고 오시면, 아마 오늘 오후까지 고쳐 드릴 수 있을 것 같습니다. 철저히 청소도 해 드릴 수 있고요.
여: 하지만 가지고 갈 수가 없어요! 제가 너무 바빠서요! 기술자 한 분을 저희 집으로 보내주실 수 있나요?
남: 물론 그렇게 해 드릴 수 있습니다.
여: 그 비용이 얼마나 들까요?
남: 교체 부품을 제외하고, 시간당 30달러입니다.
여: 알겠습니다. 얼마나 빨리 오실 수 있나요?
남: 지금 바로 됩니다. 주소가 어떻게 되십니까?

어휘 **assignment** 숙제, 연구 과제 / **due** ~할 예정인; 만기가 된 / **freeze** (기계 등이) 멈추다 / **thoroughly** 철저히, 완전히 / **technician** 전문가, 기술자 / **replacement** 교체, 교환; 대체물, 교환품 / **part** 부품

06 금액 | ②

▶ 이동할 때마다 드는 요금이 1달러이므로 일주일간 하루에 네 번 이동하면 총 28달러이고 여기에 지하철 카드 구입 가격 3달러를 더해야 한다.

M: See you tonight, Aunt Heather. **I'm going sightseeing**!
W: Make sure you buy a subway card.
M: Oh? Why is that?
W: **You get a discounted fare**. And you don't have to buy a new ticket each time you go somewhere.
M: Cool, how much is it?
W: The blank card costs $3, but **you have to add more money** before you can use it.
M: How much do I need to add?
W: As much as you like. You're in town for seven days. The discounted fare is $1 per trip.
M: So, $1 for each trip. And I'll probably **make around four trips a day**. Then the total amount for one week is....
W: Don't forget to add the $3 fee for the blank card.

남: 저녁에 뵈어요, Heather 이모. 전 관광하러 갑니다!
여: 지하철 카드를 꼭 사렴.
남: 아? 왜요?
여: 할인된 요금으로 이용할 수 있단다. 그리고 어딘가로 이동할 때마다 매번 표를 새로 살 필요가 없거든.
남: 좋네요. 가격이 얼마죠?
여: 빈 카드는 3달러란다. 하지만 그것을 사용하기 전에 돈을 충전해야 한단다.
남: 얼마나 충전해야 하는데요?
여: 네가 원하는 만큼. 너는 이 도시에 7일간 있을 거잖니. 한 번 이동할 때마다 할인된 요금으로 1달러씩 든단다.
남: 그럼, 한 번 이동할 때마다 1달러네요. 그리고 저는 아마 하루에 네 번 정도 이동할 것 같아요. 그러니 일주일간 총 요금은….
여: 빈 카드를 사는 데 드는 3달러를 추가하는 것을 잊지 마라.

어휘 **sightseeing** 관광

07 이유 | ⑤

▶ 여자는 할아버지를 병원에서 모셔 와야 하기 때문에 오늘 만날 수 없다고 했다.

[Cell phone rings.]
M: Hello?
W: Hi, David. It's me, Gina. Listen, I'm sorry, but I don't think I'll be able to meet you today.
M: Oh, really? Did something happen?
W: Yeah, unfortunately. I need to **pick my grandfather up** from the hospital.
M: Okay. It's nothing serious, is it?
W: No, not at all. Normally his nurse takes him and picks him up, but someone **bumped into her car** last night. It's a long story.
M: I heard there were several accidents last night. It was quite a snowstorm.
W: Right. So, anyway, I hope **we can reschedule**. Tomorrow, maybe?
M: Well, **I have some errands I have to do** tomorrow. How about Friday?
W: Sounds good. See you then.

[휴대전화 벨이 울린다.]
남: 여보세요?
여: 안녕, David. 나야, Gina. 들어 봐. 미안한데, 오늘 너를 만날 수 없을 것 같아.
남: 아, 정말? 무슨 일이 생겼니?
여: 응, 유감스럽게도 말이야. 할아버지를 병원에서 모셔 와야 해.
남: 알겠어. 심각한 일은 아니지, 그렇지?
여: 응, 전혀 아니야. 보통은 간호사가 할아버지를 모셔다 드리고 모시고 오는데, 어젯밤 누군가가 그 사람의 차를 들이받았대. 얘기하자면 길어.
남: 어젯밤에 사고가 몇 건 있었다고 들었어. 눈보라가 심했잖아.
여: 맞아. 자, 그건 그렇고, 일정을 변경할 수 있으면 좋겠어. 혹시 내일 어때?
남: 음, 내일은 해야 할 심부름이 몇 가지 있어. 금요일은 어때?
여: 좋아. 그때 보자.

어휘 **bump into** ~와 부딪치다; ~와 (우연히) 마주치다 / **reschedule** 일정을 변경하다

08 언급하지 않은 것 | ③

▶ 해석 참조

W: Green Motors has finally done it! We've made a **reasonably priced** hydrogen-powered car costing as much as a gasoline-powered car. Now you don't have to spend a lot of money **to be environmentally**

conscious. Hydrogen-powered cars are environmentally friendly because they don't discharge harmful chemicals into the air. Hydrogen engines produce only water as they run. Green Motors' hydrogen cars can travel 200 kilometers on a tank of hydrogen. You can drive only **about half as far as** that on one tank of gasoline, but when you drive this car, you can feel good that **you're not hurting the environment**.

여: Green Motors가 드디어 해냈습니다! 우리는 휘발유를 동력으로 하는 차와 비용이 비슷하게 드는 합리적인 가격(① 경제성)의 수소를 동력으로 하는 차를 개발했습니다. 이제 환경을 의식하기 위해 많은 돈을 쓸 필요가 없습니다. 수소를 동력으로 하는 차는 해로운 화학물질을 대기로 배출하지 않기 때문에 환경친화적(② 환경친화성)입니다. 수소 엔진은 구동 시 오직 물만 배출(④ 배출 물질)합니다. Green Motors의 수소 차는 수소 한 통 분량으로 200킬로미터를 이동(⑤ 연비)할 수 있습니다. 휘발유 한 통으로 갈 수 있는 거리의 대략 반 정도만 주행할 수 있지만, 이 차를 운전할 때 환경을 해치지 않는다는 점에서 만족감을 느끼실 수 있습니다

어휘 **reasonably** 합리적으로 / **hydrogen** 수소 / **powered** ~의 동력을 장치한 / **conscious** 의식하고 있는 / **discharge** ~을 배출[방출]하다

09 내용 불일치 | ④

▶ 행사는 일주일이 아니라 5일간 지속된다.

M: Welcome to the Korea International Toilet EXPO and Conference at the Seoul COEX convention center! Experts from more than 40 nations **have gathered to raise awareness** of global sanitation issues and to find solutions to the problems. Over the five days of the conference, we will plan direct action **to improve water and toilet sanitation** around the world. Today's keynote speaker is the distinguished German scientist, Lisa Kirchner. **Don't forget to register** at the reception desk for her keynote address, and for the afternoon tour of the famous toilets in Suwon.

남: 서울 코엑스 컨벤션 센터에서 개최되는 한국 국제 화장실 엑스포와 회의에 오신 것을 환영합니다! 전 세계의 공중위생 문제에 대한 인식을 일깨우고 그 문제에 대한 해결책을 찾고자 40개가 넘는 국가에서 전문가들이 모였습니다. 5일간의 회의 동안, 세계의 수질과 화장실 공중위생을 개선하기 위한 직접적인 활동을 계획할 것입니다. 오늘의 기조 연설자는 저명한 독일 출신 과학자인 Lisa Kirchner 씨입니다. 기조연설을 들으시고 오후에 수원의 유명한 화장실을 돌아보시려면 접수처에서 접수하는 것을 잊지 말아주십시오.

어휘 **awareness** 인식, 의식, 자각 / **sanitation** 공중위생 / **keynote** (연설 등의) 기조(基調), 원리원칙 / **distinguished** 저명한 / **address** 연설, 인사말

10 도표 이해 | ④

▶ 가격이 4천 달러 이하여야 한다고 했고 그 다음에 보증이 필수적이라고 했다. 그리고 경력이 최소 10년인 회사를 원했으며 마지막으로 남은 두 개의 선택지 중 고객 평가가 더 좋은 곳으로 선택하자고 했다.

W: James, I've contacted five different bathroom remodeling companies, since **we have to remodel our bathroom**. I want to discuss it with you.
M: Okay. How should we do this?
W: **I made a list that compares** the five companies. Take a look.
M: Let me see. The price is the most important factor for us.
W: Right. We can spend up to $4,000.
M: We'll have to go with the company that **offers us the cheapest price**.
W: But that company doesn't offer any warranty.
M: Really? Then we must rule it out. A warranty is essential **in case there are problems with the work**.
W: I think experience is also important in ensuring that the remodeling is done correctly.
M: Sure. I think we have to choose a company with at least ten years of experience. Then, there are two options left.
W: We also need to check customer reviews. Let's **choose the one that got better reviews**.
M: Sounds good. I think we've found one.

여: James, 화장실을 리모델링해야 해서, 내가 서로 다른 다섯 곳의 화장실 리모델링 회사와 연락했어요. 당신과 이것을 의논하고 싶어요.
남: 좋아요. 어떻게 해야 하나요?
여: 내가 다섯 회사를 비교하는 목록을 만들었어요. 한 번 보세요.
남: 어디 봅시다. 가격이 우리에게 가장 중요한 요소죠.
여: 맞아요. 우리는 4천 달러까지 쓸 수 있어요.
남: 가장 싼 가격을 제시하는 회사를 선택해야겠어요.
여: 하지만 그 회사는 아무런 보증을 제공하지 않아요.
남: 정말이요? 그러면 거긴 제외해야 해요. 작업에 문제가 있을 경우를 대비해서 보증은 필수예요.
여: 리모델링이 정확하게 되는 것을 보장하는 데 있어서 경험도 중요하다고 생각해요.
남: 물론이죠. 적어도 10년의 경력이 있는 회사를 골라야 한다고 생각해요. 그러면, 두 가지 선택지가 남는군요.
여: 고객 평가도 확인해야 해요. 더 좋은 평가를 받은 곳으로 선택해요.
남: 좋은 생각이에요. 우리가 하나 찾은 것 같군요.

어휘 **remodel** 리모델링하다, 개조하다 / **warranty** 보증 / **go with** 선택하다, 받아들이다 / **rule out** 제외시키다 / **in case** 경우에 대비해서 / **ensure** 보장하다, 확실하게 하다

11 짧은 대화에 이어질 응답 | ②

▶ 사촌의 생일 파티에 함께 가자는 여자의 말에 거기에 아는 사람이 있을지 남자가 묻고 있다.

① 난 선물을 가져갈 거야.
② 아니, 하지만 내가 너를 소개할게.
③ 매우 재미있을 거야.
④ 30명도 넘는 사람들이 거기에 올 거야.
⑤ 파티는 그 애의 집에서 열릴 거야.

M: Beth, what are you doing this weekend?
W: I'm going to my cousin Amy's birthday party. **Everyone is welcome**. You should come.
M: **Will I know anyone there**?
W: ______________________________

남: Beth, 이번 주말에 뭐 할 거야?
여: 내 사촌 Amy의 생일 파티에 갈 거야. 누구든 환영이야. 너도 가자.
남: 거기 내가 아는 사람이 있을까?
여: ______________________________

12 짧은 대화에 이어질 응답 | ④

▶ 어떤 운동 기구를 사야 할지 고민하는 남자에게 여자가 차이점을 설명해 주기 원하는지 묻고 있다. 이에 적절한 남자의 응답을 찾는다.

① 저는 색깔이 마음에 안 들어요.
② 저는 그걸 매일 사용할 계획이에요.
③ 기본 모델은 너무 단순해요.
④ 네, 부탁해요. 결정하는 데 도움이 될 거예요.
⑤ 그것들은 광고에서 달라 보였어요.

W: Here are two exercise machines **that might interest you**.
M: I like both of them. Should I get the basic model or the more expensive one?
W: **That depends**. Would you like me to explain the differences?
M: ______________________________

여: 여기 손님이 관심이 있을 만한 운동 기구가 두 가지 있습니다.
남: 둘 다 좋은데요. 기본 모델을 사야 할까요, 아니면 더 비싼 걸 사야 할까요?
여: 상황에 따라 다릅니다. 차이를 설명해 드릴까요?
남: ______________________________

어휘 **it[that] depends** ((구어)) 그것은 상황[때]에 따라 다르다

13 긴 대화에 이어질 응답 | ②

▶ 남자의 친구가 독일산 진정 크림(soothing cream)에 대해 말해주었다는 말을 듣고 여자는 어떤 상품인지 궁금해할 것이다.

① 그렇게 나쁘지는 않아요. 걱정하지 마세요.
② 잘됐네요. 상표명이 뭐죠?
③ 전 아이스크림 안 먹어요. 다이어트 중이거든요.
④ 물론이죠, 당신의 독일 친구를 만나고 싶어요.
⑤ 괜찮아요. 저는 이미 약을 먹었어요.

M: What's the matter, Yun-hee? You've been scratching yourself all day.
W: I'm itchy! **It's driving me crazy**!
M: Are you allergic to something?
W: I don't know. The itching started yesterday and **just keeps getting worse**.

M: Have you taken anything for it?
W: No, but **I've got an appointment** at an allergy clinic on Saturday.
M: Then you could get some medicine that stops the itching **in the meantime**.
W: Do you know any medicine for this?
M: Yes, sure, but it can make you very sleepy.
W: **If it helps at all**, I'll try it. I can't stand this!
M: You should get some soothing cream, too. **It will help ease the itching**.
W: I should do that.
M: A friend of mine told me about a really good German brand.
W: ______________________________

남: 윤희 씨, 무슨 일이에요? 하루 종일 몸을 긁고 있군요.
여: 가려워서요! 정말 미치겠어요!
남: 무언가에 알레르기가 있나요?
여: 모르겠어요. 어제부터 가렵기 시작해서, 계속 심해지고 있어요.
남: 약을 좀 복용했나요?
여: 아니요. 하지만 토요일에 알레르기 클리닉을 예약해 두었어요.
남: 그렇다면 그 사이에 가려움을 멈추게 하는 약을 좀 먹을 수 있겠네요.
여: 아는 약이 있나요?
남: 네, 물론이죠. 하지만 먹으면 아주 졸릴 수 있어요.
여: 조금이라도 도움이 된다면 시도해 볼게요. 가려움을 견딜 수가 없어요!
남: 진정 크림도 바르셔야 해요. 가려움이 진정되는 데 도움이 될 거예요.
여: 그래야겠어요.
남: 제 친구가 아주 좋은 독일산 제품에 대해서 말해 주더군요.
여: ______________________________

어휘 **brand name** 상표명 / **be on a diet** 다이어트 중이다 / **itchy** 가려운 ***cf.*** **itching** 가려움 / **be allergic to** ~에 알레르기가 있다 / **in the meantime** 그 사이에, 그럭저럭 하는 동안에 / **soothe** (고통 등을) 덜어 주다 / **ease** (통증 등을) 진정시키다

14 긴 대화에 이어질 응답 | ④

▶ 여자는 일자리를 소개해 주면서 주말까지 답을 달라고 했으므로 그에 대한 적합한 응답이 와야 한다.

① 나는 그것에 대해 항상 생각해. ② 할인을 해 줄 수는 없니?
③ 네가 말하는 것만큼 재미있다면, 물론이지. ④ 당연하지. 알려줘서 고마워.
⑤ 고맙지만 괜찮아. 난 해변에 가고 싶지 않아.

M: Sonia, hi. **What have you been up to**?
W: Hi, Won-jun. I've been working. I got myself a part-time job for the summer.
M: Really? Where?
W: Charmaine's ice-cream parlor at Sandy Beach. It's lots of fun. I'm really enjoying it.
M: **Are they still hiring**? I'm looking for a summer job, too.
W: Sorry, no. But my dad needs summer workers at his construction company. **I could introduce you**!
M: I don't know. Construction work is really hard....
W: It can be. But the pay is high. Think about it and let me know by the end of the week.
M: ______________________________

남: Sonia, 안녕. 어떻게 지냈어?
여: 안녕, 원준아. 나 일하고 있어. 여름 동안 할 아르바이트를 구했거든.
남: 정말? 어디서?
여: Sandy 해변의 Charmaine 아이스크림 가게야. 아주 재미있어. 일이 정말 즐거워.
남: 거기 아직도 사람을 뽑고 있니? 나도 여름 아르바이트를 찾고 있거든.
여: 미안하지만 뽑고 있지 않아. 하지만 우리 아버지의 건설 회사에서 여름 동안 일할 사람이 필요해. 내가 너를 소개해 줄 수 있어!
남: 잘 모르겠어. 건설 일은 정말 힘들잖아….
여: 그럴 거야. 하지만 임금이 높아. 생각해 보고 이번 주말까지 알려 줘.
남: ______________________________

어휘 **parlor** 가게; 응접실 / **construction** 건설

15 상황에 적절한 말 | ①

▶ Jeff는 마지막 지하철을 놓쳤고, 마침 Jeff의 집 근처에 사는 Mandy가 집으로 가는 도중 그를 보고 차를 세웠으므로 Mandy에게 차를 태워달라고 할 것이다.

① 우리 집까지 태워 줄래?
② 오랜만이다! 어떻게 지냈니?
③ 지하철역까지 어떻게 가는지 알려 줄래?
④ 왜 이렇게 오래 걸렸니? 오랫동안 기다리고 있었어.
⑤ 왜 나랑 야구 경기를 보러 가지 않았니?

W: Jeff had a great time at a baseball game Friday night. After the game, his friends decided to go to a barbecue restaurant. But since he had to get up early the next day, Jeff said goodnight to his friends and **headed for the subway**. Unfortunately, **he took the wrong street** and got lost. When he found the subway at last, it was too late. **The last train had gone**. Disappointed, he stood on the sidewalk, wondering what to do. **A car drove by slowly** and then suddenly stopped. It was his friend Mandy. She had been at the game with Jeff and their friends. She's on her way home, and her house is near Jeff's. In this situation, what would Jeff most likely say to Mandy?

여: Jeff는 금요일 밤 야구 경기장에서 즐거운 시간을 보냈다. 경기가 끝난 후 그의 친구들은 바비큐 음식점에 가기로 결정했다. 하지만 Jeff는 다음날 일찍 일어나야 해서 친구들에게 작별 인사를 하고 지하철역으로 향했다. 공교롭게도 그는 길을 잘못 들어 길을 잃었다. 그가 마침내 지하철역을 찾았을 때에는 너무 늦었다. 마지막 전철이 떠난 것이다. 그는 실망하여 보도 위에 앉아 어떻게 해야 할지 생각하고 있었다. 차 한 대가 천천히 지나가다가 갑자기 멈추었다. 친구인 Mandy였다. 그녀는 Jeff와 친구들과 함께 경기를 보러 갔었다. 그녀는 집으로 가는 중이고 그녀의 집은 Jeff네 근처에 있다. 이러한 상황에서 Jeff가 Mandy에게 할 말로 가장 적절한 것은 무엇인가?

16~17 세트 문항 | 16. ① 17. ③

▶ 16. 우주에는 눈으로 볼 수 있는 많은 물체들이 있다는 말 뒤에 어떤 물체들이 있는지 차례로 설명하고 있다.

① 밤하늘에서 볼 수 있는 물체들
② 어떻게 망원경이 천문학을 발전시켜 왔는가
③ 밤하늘에서 다양한 행성의 정확한 위치를 찾는 방법
④ 인공위성과 별의 차이점
⑤ 태양계에서 지구라는 행성에 가장 가까운 물체들

▶ 17. 해석 참조

① 금성 ② 수성 ③ 토성 ④ 화성 ⑤ 목성

M: Hello, class. I want to thank all of you for showing so much interest in astronomy. Of course, most professional astronomy research today is done with large telescopes. However, there are **a number of objects in space** that can be seen with the eye. For instance, the planet Venus is often the second-brightest object in the night sky after the moon. It **can easily be found** on any clear night. Mercury, being so close to the sun, is much harder to find, but **it's still possible with practice**. For something a bit easier, try to find Mars. With a telescope, you can even see it in the late afternoon. Asteroids can also be seen at certain times of the year. They are easy to spot when they **light up the night sky**. Though it is quite far from us, Jupiter is also visible on some nights. Incredibly, those with very good vision can sometimes even see three or four of its moons. Finally, there are hundreds of man-made satellites and thousands of stars **that can be seen by anyone** each night.

남: 안녕하세요, 학생 여러분. 천문학에 이렇게 많은 관심을 보여주신 것에 대해 여러분 모두에게 감사드리고 싶습니다. 물론, 오늘날 대부분의 전문적인 천문학 연구는 대형 망원경으로 이뤄집니다. 그러나, 우주에는 눈으로 볼 수 있는 많은 물체들이 있습니다. 예를 들어, ① 금성은 흔히 달 다음으로 밤하늘에서 두 번째로 밝은 물체입니다. 그것은 어떤 맑은 날 밤이면 쉽게 발견될 수 있습니다. ② 수성은, 태양에 매우 가까워서, 찾기에 훨씬 더 힘들지만 그럼에도 연습을 통해 (찾는 것이) 가능합니다. 좀 더 쉬운 것을 찾으려면, ④ 화성을 찾으려 노력하세요. 망원경으로, 늦은 오후에 여러분은 그것을 볼 수도 있습니다. 소행성 또한 일 년 중 특정한 시기에 보일 수 있습니다. 그것들은 밤하늘을 밝힐 때 발견하기 쉽습니다. 우리에게서 꽤 멀리 있긴 하지만, 어떤 밤에는 ⑤ 목성 또한 보입니다. 놀랍게도, 매우 좋은 시력을 가진 사람들은 때때로 목성의 위성들 중 서너 개를 볼 수도 있습니다. 마지막으로, 매일 밤 누구나 볼 수 있는 수백 개의 인공위성과 수천 개의 별이 있습니다.

어휘 **object** 물체; 대상; 목표 / **telescope** 망원경 / **advance** 발전[진보]시키다 / **astronomy** 천문학 / **locate** ~의 정확한 위치를 찾아내다 / **man-made satellite** 인공위성 / **solar system** 태양계 / **asteroid** 소행성 ((화성과 목성 사이에서 태양을 공전하는 수많은 작은 행성)) / **spot** 발견하다, 찾다; 장소; 얼룩; 점 / **visible** (눈에) 보이는; 뚜렷한, 명백한 ***cf.*** **vision** 시력; 시야; 선견지명, 비전

Answers & Explanation

실전모의고사 14

01. ① 02. ④ 03. ② 04. ③ 05. ⑤ 06. ③ 07. ④ 08. ⑤ 09. ② 10. ③
11. ③ 12. ③ 13. ② 14. ① 15. ③ 16. ① 17. ④

01 화자가 하는 말의 목적 | ①

▶ 남자는 노숙자 문제를 묻어두기보다는 쟁점화하는 것으로부터 노숙자 문제에 접근해 보자고 주장하고 있다.

M: The homeless, or people living on the streets, are a serious problem in many cities around the world. These people **are ignored and seen as** an "unpleasant" problem. Thus, homelessness is not an issue that people will talk about because **it brings forth images** of dirty, poor and sometimes mentally-ill people. Sometimes homelessness is **a battle between good and evil**. The good inside of every person is tested **each time one sees a homeless person**. Can we make a difference by ourselves? I believe the answer is "yes," and the first step is to talk about it and **make it an issue** that can no longer be ignored.

남: 노숙자, 즉 길에서 사는 사람들은 전 세계의 많은 도시에서 심각한 문제입니다. 이 사람들은 무시당하며, '불쾌한' 문젯거리로 간주됩니다. 그래서 노숙은 사람들이 이야기하게 되는 쟁점이 안 되는데, 왜냐하면 그것은 더럽고 가난하며 때때로 정신 질환이 있는 사람들의 이미지를 불러일으키기 때문입니다. 가끔 노숙 문제는 선과 악의 싸움이 되기도 합니다. 모든 이의 내면에 있는 선의는 노숙자들을 볼 때마다 시험을 받게 됩니다. 우리 스스로 변화를 가져올 수 있을까요? 저는 그 대답이 '그렇다'라고 믿으며, 그 첫 단계는 그것에 대해서 논의하고 더는 무시할 수 없는 문제로 만드는 것입니다.

어휘 **unpleasant** 불쾌한, 마음에 들지 않는 / **bring forth** ~을 생기게 하다, 낳다 / **mentally-ill** 정신적으로 병든

02 대화 주제 | ④

▶ 열대우림이 파괴되는 것을 여행지에서 보고 온 여자가 그 악영향에 관해 남자와 이야기하고 있다.

M: Hi, Pam. How was your trip to South America?
W: I'm glad I went, but to be honest, **I was shocked by** how much of the rainforest is being destroyed.
M: That's a shame. The rainforests are so important to the environment.
W: On the third day that I was there, it started raining heavily. There were terrible landslides in areas where **all the trees had been cut down**.
M: I saw a bit about that on the news.
W: The worst areas were places where forests are being cut down to **make space for cattle**.
M: Raising cattle is an important business, but I'm worried about the effect on the native people.
W: Me, too. Many of them are losing their villages and their way of life. **I wish there had been more** I could do to help.

남: 안녕, Pam. 남아메리카 여행은 어땠어?
여: 거기에 간 건 기쁘지만, 솔직히 열대우림이 얼마나 많이 파괴되고 있는지를 보고 충격 받았어.
남: 유감이네. 열대우림은 환경에 아주 중요하잖아.
여: 내가 거기 간 세 번째 날에, 비가 내리퍼붓기 시작했어. 나무가 다 잘려나간 지역에서 산사태가 아주 심하게 일어났고.
남: 그거 뉴스에서 조금 봤어.
여: 가장 심한 지역은 소를 키울 공간을 만들려고 숲을 훼손하고 있는 곳들이었어.
남: 소를 키우는 게 중요한 사업이긴 하지만, 난 토착민들에게 미칠 영향이 걱정 돼.
여: 나도. 그들 중 많은 이들이 마을과 생활 방식을 잃고 있어. 돕기 위해 내가 할 수 있는 게 더 많으면 좋겠어.

어휘 **landslide** 산사태

03 관계 | ②

▶ 여자가 남자의 스케줄을 확인하고 수정해주는 것으로 보아 사장과 비서의 대화이다.

M: Good morning, Christine.
W: Mr. Kruger, Suzzane Gorey from Bellcore Manufacturing called just a moment ago.
M: **Did she leave a message**?
W: Yes. She hopes tomorrow's conference call can be moved to Tuesday afternoon.
M: I see. Is my schedule free that afternoon?
W: Actually, **you're supposed to meet** Mr. Anderson, the CEO of DIA Lighting, in your office at that time.
M: **I forgot to mention that** Mr. Anderson would prefer to meet that evening.
W: Then I'll check your schedule for that day.
M: Please do. If I'm free, **let him know that I'll meet him** at the Lexington Hotel at 7 p.m.
W: I'll set that up right away, sir.
M: Thank you, Christine. I'll be in my office. **Please keep me informed.**

남: 안녕하세요, Christine.
여: Kruger 씨, Bellcore 제조사의 Suzzane Gorey 씨가 조금 전에 전화하셨어요.
남: 그분이 메시지를 남겼나요?
여: 네. 내일 예정된 전화 회의를 화요일 오후로 옮기길 원하세요.
남: 알겠어요. 그날 오후에 내 일정이 비어 있나요?
여: 사실, 그 시간에 사무실에서 DIA 조명의 CEO인 Anderson 씨를 만나시기로 되어 있어요.
남: Anderson 씨가 그날 저녁에 만나기를 더 원하신다고 얘기하는 걸 깜빡했군요.
여: 그러면 그날 사장님 일정을 확인해 보겠습니다.
남: 그렇게 해줘요. 시간이 비면 Lexington 호텔에서 저녁 7시에 봤으면 한다고 Anderson 씨에게 전해줘요.
여: 네, 곧장 그렇게 조치하겠습니다.
남: 고마워요, Christine. 사무실에 있을게요. 계속 보고해줘요.

어휘 **manufacturing** 제조업 / **conference call** 전화 회의 / **set up** (어떤 일이 있도록) 마련하다; ~을 설치하다[세우다]

04 그림 불일치 | ③

▶ 남자는 책상 위에 휴대전화가 있으면 공부할 때 방해가 되므로 휴대전화 거치대를 치웠다고 했다.

W: Dan, did you **rearrange your desk**?
M: Yes, Mom. What do you think?
W: You put a bookshelf to the right of the monitor. Where did you get it?
M: I bought it at Kelly's garage sale. The pencil vase in front of it is also from there.
W: I like the polka-dot pattern of the vase. Oh, you put a calendar next to it. That will **help you organize your schedule**.
M: Right. Do you see anything else that is different?
W: **Let me guess**.... You put away the duck-shaped cell phone holder that was on the left side of your desk.
M: You're right. Instead, I placed a lamp there.
W: Why did you put it away? There is still room in front of the lamp.
M: If my cell phone is on my desk, **it disturbs me when I'm studying**.
W: Okay. I understand.

여: Dan, 네 책상 새로 정리했니?
남: 네, 엄마. 어때요?
여: 모니터 오른쪽에 책꽂이를 두었구나. 책꽂이는 어디서 구했니?
남: Kelly네 창고 세일에서 샀어요. 책꽂이 앞에 놓아둔 연필꽂이도 거기서 산 거예요.
여: 연필꽂이의 물방울무늬가 마음에 드는구나. 아, 그 옆에 달력도 놓았네. 일정을 계획하는 데 도움이 될 거야.
남: 맞아요. 그 밖에 달라진 게 보이세요?
여: 어디 보자…. 책상 왼쪽에 있던 오리 모양의 휴대전화 거치대를 치웠구나.
남: 맞아요. 대신 거기에 스탠드를 놓았어요.
여: 그걸 왜 치웠니? 스탠드 앞에 아직 공간이 있는데.
남: 책상 위에 휴대전화가 있으면 공부할 때 방해가 되거든요.
여: 그렇구나. 무슨 말인지 알겠어.

어휘 **rearrange** ~을 재배치하다; (행사 시간·날짜·장소 등을) 재조정하다 / **garage sale** (자기 집 차고에서 하는) 창고 세일, 중고 물품 세일 / **polka-dot** 물방울(모양)의

05 추후 행동 | ⑤

▶ 남자는 여자에게 자신이 작년에 일했던 초등학교 영어 캠프의 구인 메일을 전달해주겠다고 했다.

M: Tina, do you have any plans for summer vacation?
W: Actually, my goal is to find a part-time job.
M: Oh? Are you **saving up for anything in particular**?
W: Mainly, it's to pay next semester's tuition.
M: I see. Well, last year I helped out at an elementary school English camp. The work was meaningful, and I saved enough for school.
W: That sounds perfect. I want a rewarding job like that, but I can't find any.
M: If you are interested, you could **apply for the same camp**. The school recently sent out an email looking for helpers.
W: Really? Wow, I'd love to work there.
M: I'll **forward you the email right away** so you can decide.
W: Oh, what about the hours and pay?
M: I'm not sure **what it will be like this year**, but everything is in the email.
W: OK, that'll be very helpful. Thanks.

남: Tina, 여름방학 때 특별한 계획 있니?
여: 사실 내 목표는 아르바이트를 찾는 거야.
남: 그래? 뭔가 특별한 일로 돈을 모으는 거야?
여: 다음 학기 등록금을 내려는 게 주된 이유야.
남: 그렇구나. 음, 나는 작년에 초등학교 영어 캠프를 도와줬어. 의미 있는 일이었고, 학비도 충분히 모았어.
여: 그거 좋구나. 나도 그렇게 보람 있는 일을 원하는데, 찾을 수가 없네.
남: 관심 있으면, 같은 캠프에 지원해 봐도 돼. 그 학교에서 최근에 도우미를 구한다는 이메일을 발송했더라고.
여: 정말? 와, 거기서 일하고 싶어.
남: 네가 결정할 수 있도록 당장 그 이메일을 네게 전달해줄게.
여: 아, 근무시간과 보수는 어떻게 돼?
남: 올해는 어떨지 모르겠지만, 이메일에 다 있어.
여: 좋아, 큰 도움이 될 거야. 고마워

어휘 **tuition** 등록금, 수업(료) / **send out** (많은 사람에게) ~을 발송하다, 보내다 / **forward** (~에게 정보·물건을) 전달하다, 보내다; 앞으로

06 금액 | ③

▶ 여자는 개당 2달러인 하트 모양 풍선 100개(2x100)와 개당 3달러인 토끼 모양 풍선 100개(3x100)를 사기로 했다. 200개 이상 구입하면 10퍼센트 할인을 받을 수 있다는 점에 유의한다.

M: Good morning. What can I do for you?
W: I need to **buy some balloons for an event**, but I'm not sure how many I need.
M: Where are you going to decorate with them?
W: They are for the Pinebrook Primary School's auditorium.
M: School auditoriums usually need around 150 balloons.
W: Hmm.... I think our auditorium is **larger than other school auditoriums**.
M: Well, then how about 50 more? I can give you a 10 percent discount if you buy 200 or more.
W: Okay, I'll get 200. **What kinds of balloons do you recommend** for elementary school students?
M: I have round and heart-shaped balloons that are two dollars each. I also have rabbit and bear-shaped balloons that are three dollars each.
W: Then **I'll take 100 each** of the hearts and the rabbits.
M: Yes, that would be great.

남: 안녕하세요. 뭘 도와드릴까요?
여: 행사에 사용할 풍선을 좀 사야 하는데, 몇 개나 필요한지 잘 모르겠어요.
남: 풍선으로 어디를 장식하실 건데요?
여: Pinebrook 초등학교 강당이요.
남: 학교 강당이면 보통 풍선 150개 정도면 돼요.
여: 음…. 제 생각에 우리 학교 강당은 다른 학교 강당보다 더 큰 것 같아요.
남: 아, 그렇다면 50개 더 하시는 게 어떨까요? 200개 이상 구입하시면 10퍼센트를 할인해 드릴 수 있어요.
여: 좋아요. 200개로 할게요. 초등학교 학생들에게 추천할 만한 풍선으로 어떤 게 있나요?
남: 개당 2달러씩 하는 원형 풍선과 하트 모양 풍선이 있어요. 개당 3달러씩 하는 토끼 모양, 곰 모양 풍선도 있고요.
여: 그럼 하트 모양 100개와 토끼 모양 100개로 할게요.
남: 네, 그렇게 하시면 되겠네요.

어휘 **auditorium** 강당

07 이유 | ④

▶ 여자는 지방이 많은 음식의 위험성에 관한 다큐멘터리를 보고 기름진 음식을 끊기로 결심했다고 했다.

M: Liz, let's go out for hamburgers. **I'd like to try** Burger Queen's new menu.
W: I don't want a hamburger, Robert.
M: You aren't hungry?
W: I am.
M: Then why? Just the other day, **you mentioned that you wanted a burger**.
W: Yes, but that was a few days ago.
M: I don't understand why you don't want one all of a sudden. Are you on a diet again?
W: Actually, **I watched a shocking documentary** last night called *Grease: The Silent Killer*.
M: I think I've heard of that. It's on the dangers of greasy foods, right?
W: Right! So, I decided to **stop eating fatty foods**.
M: Then why don't we go shopping and cook dinner instead? We can make soup and some salad.
W: Great idea! Sounds delicious.

남: Liz, 햄버거 먹으러 나가자. Burger Queen의 새 메뉴를 먹어보고 싶어.
여: 난 햄버거를 먹고 싶지 않아, Robert.
남: 배고프지 않은 거니?
여: 배고프기는 해.
남: 그럼 왜? 바로 며칠 전만 해도 햄버거 먹고 싶다고 했잖아.
여: 맞아, 하지만 그렇게 얘기한 건 며칠 전이었지.
남: 나는 네가 왜 갑자기 햄버거가 먹고 싶지 않은지 이해가 안 가. 또 다이어트 하는 거야?
여: 실은 어젯밤에 〈지방: 무언의 살인자〉라는 충격적인 다큐멘터리를 봤어.
남: 나도 들어본 것 같아. 기름기 많은 음식의 위험성에 관한 내용이지, 맞지?
여: 맞아! 그래서 난 기름기 많은 음식을 끊기로 했어.
남: 그러면 대신 우리가 장을 봐서 저녁을 만들면 어떨까? 수프와 샐러드를 만들 수 있어.
여: 좋은 생각이야! 맛있겠다.

어휘 **grease** 지방, 기름; 기계의 윤활유 ***cf.*** **greasy** 기름기 많은 / **fatty** 지방이 많은, 지방으로 된

08 언급하지 않은 것 | ⑤

▶ 해석 참조

M: What did you do on the weekend, Sara?
W: I went with some friends to see a movie at the new theater.
M: You mean the one that is on 10th avenue?
W: Right. **Construction was finished a few weeks ago**, but it just opened on Saturday.
M: **I'd like to check it out** while it's still new.
W: Then, you should **take advantage of their Monday discounts**. Tickets are 50% off.
M: That's a good deal. How are the facilities?
W: Great. **It's supposed to be the largest multiplex** in the city.
M: In that case, I'll definitely go there.

남: 주말에 뭐 했니, Sara?
여: 친구 몇 명과 새 영화관에 영화를 보러 갔어.
남: 10번가에 있는(① 위치) 그 극장 말이지?
여: 맞아. 몇 주 전에 완공했는데 지난 토요일에야 개관(② 개관일)했어.
남: 아직 새 건물일 때 가보고 싶은데.
여: 그럼 월요일 할인을 이용해봐. 표가 50퍼센트 할인(③ 할인 혜택)되거든.
남: 괜찮은걸. 시설은 어때?
여: 아주 좋아. 시에서 제일 큰 멀티플렉스(④ 규모)일 거야.
남: 그렇다면 거기에 꼭 가봐야겠다.

어휘 **take advantage of** ~을 이용하다 / **multiplex** 멀티플렉스, 복합 영화관 ((10개 이상의 상영관과 쇼핑몰을 가진 영화관))

09 내용 불일치 | ②

▶ 공원의 철제 울타리는 야생 동물의 침입을 막기 위해서가 아니라 토착 동물을 가두기 위한 것이다.

W: Theodore Roosevelt National Park **consists of three geographically separate areas** of western North Dakota in the United States. The park was founded to pay respect to President Theodore Roosevelt on a location **where he visited to hunt**. To keep the native animals in, the entire park has been surrounded with a 7-foot tall wire fence. More than 185 different bird species live in the park, and most of them are migratory. Despite its current landscape, fossil evidence suggests that the park **used to be much wetter than it is** today. Today, there are no glaciers in the park, but the evidence of their geologically recent presence is everywhere. For those who are looking for adventure, camping is permitted in the park, but **a permit must be obtained beforehand**.

여: Theodore Roosevelt 국립공원은 미국 노스다코타 주(州) 서부의 지리적으로 분리된 세 개의 지역으로 이루어져 있습니다. 이 공원은 Theodore Roosevelt 대통령이 사냥하기 위해 방문했던 곳에 그에 대한 존경을 표하기 위해 설립되었습니다. 토착 동물을 가두어 놓기 위해 공원 전체는 7피트(약 2미터) 높이의 철제 울타리로 둘러싸여 있습니다. 이 공원에는 185종이 넘는 각양각색의 새가 살고 있으며 그중 대부분이 철새입니다. 현재의 경관에도 불구하고, 화석상의 증거는 이 공원이 과거에 오늘날보다 훨씬 더 습했다는 사실을 보여줍니다. 오늘날 이 공원에는 빙하가 없지만 최근까지도 지질학적으로 빙하가 존재했었다는 증거가 어디나 있습니다. 모험을 찾고 계시는 분들을 위해 공원 내 캠핑이 허용되어 있습니다만, 사전에 허가증을 받으셔야 합니다.

어휘 **geographically** 지리(학)적으로 ***cf.* geologically** 지질학상으로 / **pay respect to** ~에 경의를 표하다, ~을 존중하다 / **be surrounded with** ~에 둘러싸이다 / **wire fence** 철제 울타리 / **migratory** 이주하는, 이동하는 ***cf.* migratory bird** 철새 / **permit** (특히 한정된 기간 동안 유효한) 허가증; ~을 허락하다, 허용하다

10 도표 이해 | ③

▶ 두 사람은 먼저 작은 크기의 포토북은 제외했고, 캡션을 넣을 수 있으며 30페이지가 넘는 포토북 중 더 저렴한 것을 선택하기로 했다.

M: Kate, did you choose our honeymoon photo book?
W: Not yet, honey. I'm still **looking over the options**. Can you help me with the choice?
M: Sure, let me see. Let's start with the size.
W: **Any size but small** would be okay.
M: I agree. Would you like to add some captions to the photos?
W: Sure. I'd like the captions to bring back memories **whenever we see them together with the pictures**.
M: That'll be great. And how about the length? We need more than 30 pages, don't you think?
W: I think you're right. The remaining choices have the same number of pages, so **I'll choose the cheaper one**.
M: Okay. So, you've decided?
W: Yes. Thanks for your help, honey.

남: Kate, 우리 신혼여행 포토북 골랐어요?
여: 아직요, 여보. 아직 선택 사항을 살펴보고 있어요. 당신이 고르는 것 좀 도와줄 수 있어요?
남: 그래요, 어디 봐요. 크기부터 정하죠.
여: 작은 것만 아니면 어떤 사이즈든지 괜찮을 것 같아요.
남: 나도 그렇게 생각해요. 사진에 캡션을 넣고 싶어요?
여: 물론이죠. 사진과 함께 캡션을 볼 때마다 기억이 되살아나도록 캡션을 넣고 싶어요.
남: 그거 좋겠네요. 그런데 분량은 어때요? 30페이지가 넘는 게 필요하잖아요, 그렇지 않나요?
여: 당신 말이 맞아요. 남은 선택사항들은 페이지 수가 같으니까 더 싼 걸 고르겠어요.
남: 좋아요. 그럼 결정한 거죠?
여: 네. 도와줘서 고마워요, 여보.

어휘 **caption** 캡션 ((삽화나 사진 따위에 붙는 짧은 설명문))

11 짧은 대화에 이어질 응답 | ③

▶ 여자가 남자에게 Bella의 전화번호를 아는지 묻고 있으므로 이에 가장 적절한 응답을 고른다.

① 그날 그녀에게 전화해야 했어. ② 비밀번호는 내 고양이 이름이야.
③ 내 휴대전화에서 찾아볼게. ④ 그녀는 조금 늦게 오겠다고 했어.
⑤ 난 그녀가 왜 그렇게 행동했는지 이해할 수 없어.

W: Bella **didn't attend the reunion last weekend** and nobody knows the reason.
M: Really? I thought she would definitely come. **Why don't we contact her**?
W: But I don't have her number now. Do you?
M: ______________________________

여: Bella가 지난 주말 동창회에 안 나왔는데 아무도 그 이유를 몰라.
남: 그래? 나는 Bella가 꼭 올 거라고 생각했는데. 우리가 연락해 볼까?
여: 하지만 나에겐 지금 Bella의 전화번호가 없는걸. 너에겐 있니?
남: ______________________________

어휘 **reunion** (오랫동안 못 본 사람들의 친목) 동창회, 모임

12 짧은 대화에 이어질 응답 | ③

▶ 사람들로 붐비는 세일 중인 상점에 들어가 보고 싶으냐는 남자의 물음에 가장 적절한 응답을 고른다.

① 이 제품은 세일하고 있지 않아.
② 그래. 나는 밖에서 기다릴게.
③ 그러고 싶지만, 너무 붐비는걸.
④ 아쉽지만 세일 기간이 이미 끝난 것 같아.
⑤ 오늘 밤까지는 모두 팔 수 있으면 좋겠어.

M: Unbelievable! Look over there! **That store is full of people**!
W: That's because it's having a huge clearance sale.
M: Do you want to **go inside to look for some deals**?
W: ______________________________

남: 굉장하다! 저길 봐! 저 가게는 사람들로 가득해!
여: 대규모 창고 정리 세일 중이라 그래.
남: 살 게 있는지 들어가서 찾아보고 싶니?
여: ______________________________

어휘 **clearance sale** 창고 정리 판매, 재고 정리 판매 / **deal** 거래; 일, 물건; 계약

13 긴 대화에 이어질 응답 | ②

▶ 남자는 노트 필기만 가지고 시험을 준비해야 해서 걱정하고 있는 여자를 도와주려는 말을 할 것이다.

① 걱정하지 마. 네 최종성적은 아주 좋았어.
② 이해 안 되는 게 있으면 내가 설명해 줄 수 있어.
③ 너는 하루 더 누워 있는 게 좋겠어.
④ 장기 결석에는 의사 진단서가 있어야 해.
⑤ 너는 강의시간에 항상 노트 필기를 꼼꼼히 하는구나.

M: Jessica! **Where have you been**? I didn't see you in the lecture last week.
W: I've been sick. I spent last week in the hospital.
M: Why were you in the hospital? **Are you feeling better now**?
W: I had a bad cold, but I'm fine now. Anyway, I'm worried because I've already missed a week of class.
M: Don't worry. You can copy my notes. But we are also having a quiz next week.
W: Oh, I didn't know about that. Is it part of the final grade?
M: Yes, Professor Han said that.
W: Really? I'm not ready for a quiz.
M: It'll be next Friday. So **we have enough time to study**.
W: You're right, but I'm a little worried about **trying to catch up with only the notes**.
M: ______________________________

남: Jessica! 어디 갔었니? 지난주 강의시간에 보이지 않던데.
여: 아팠어. 지난주에는 병원에 있었고.
남: 왜 병원에 있었어? 이제 좀 괜찮아졌니?

여: 감기가 심했는데 이제 괜찮아. 그건 그렇고, 이미 일주일이나 수업을 놓친 게 걱정돼.
남: 걱정하지 마. 내 노트를 복사하면 돼. 그런데 다음 주에 쪽지 시험도 있어.
여: 아, 그건 몰랐어. 그거 최종성적에 들어가는 거니?
남: 응, Han 교수님께서 그렇게 말씀하셨어.
여: 그래? 시험 준비를 못 했는데.
남: 시험은 다음 주 금요일에 있을 거야. 그러니 공부할 시간은 충분해.
여: 네 말이 맞아. 하지만 노트만 가지고 놓친 수업을 따라잡으려 해야 하는 게 조금 걱정돼.
남: ______________________________

어휘 **doctor's note** 의사 진단서[소견서] / **absence** 결석, 결근; 부재 / **quiz** 간단한 시험[테스트] / **catch up with** ~을 따라잡다

14 긴 대화에 이어질 응답 | ①

▶ 여자의 새 휴대전화가 고장 난 이유를 묻는 남자에게 여자는 고장의 이유를 설명할 것이다.

① 휴대전화를 실수로 싱크대에 떨어뜨렸어.
② 휴대전화를 진동 모드로 해놨거든.
③ 내 남동생이 네 책에 우유를 쏟았어.
④ 어젯밤에 휴대전화를 충전했어야 했는데.
⑤ 가방에 여분의 배터리를 갖고 있지 않았거든.

M: Charlotte! **I've been looking for you all day**.
W: Really? Why?
M: I need **the book I lent to you**. I called you several times, but you didn't answer.
W: Oh, I didn't know that you called me.
M: Well, I did, but all I got was a message saying that your mobile phone is turned off.
W: I'm so sorry, but I couldn't turn on my phone. Here's your book.
M: Thanks. You were busy **working on your presentation**, I guess.
W: No. My cell phone is broken.
M: Come on. **You just bought your cell phone**, didn't you?
W: You're right, but now the battery won't charge.
M: **What happened to it**?
W: ______________________________

남: Charlotte! 종일 널 찾고 있었어.
여: 그래? 왜?
남: 네게 빌려준 그 책이 필요해서. 몇 번이나 전화했는데 안 받더라.
여: 아, 네가 전화한 줄 몰랐어.
남: 음, 전화했더니 네 휴대전화가 꺼져 있다는 메시지만 나왔어.
여: 정말 미안해. 휴대전화를 켤 수가 없었어. 네 책 여기 있어.
남: 고마워. 발표 준비하느라 바빴나 보구나.
여: 아냐. 휴대전화가 고장 났어.
남: 에이, 너 휴대전화 산 지 얼마 되지도 않았잖아. 그렇지 않아?
여: 맞아. 그런데 지금은 배터리 충전이 안 돼.
남: 무슨 일이라도 있었어?
여: ______________________________

어휘 **vibration mode** 진동 모드 / **charge** 충전되다, ~을 충전하다; 요금; ~을 청구하다

15 상황에 적절한 말 | ③

▶ Nina는 축제에서 사회를 보다가 실수를 할까 걱정하는 Andy에게 격려의 말을 할 것이다.

① 축제 때 아주 잘했어.
② 너는 리허설에 참석했어야 했는데.
③ 자신감을 갖고 네 능력을 믿어.
④ 방심하지 말고 계속 경계해.
⑤ 네가 내게 행운을 빌어주면 기쁠 거야.

M: Andy is the MC for his high school's annual festival. He has a passion for presenting, and all of his friends think he is very talented. However, **as the festival is about to begin**, Andy becomes nervous. He begins to focus on **some mistakes that he made** during rehearsal. His friend Nina sees that he is worried and asks him about it. Andy explains that **he is scared of forgetting his lines** and worried that other students will make fun of him. Nina listens to this and **wants to do something to encourage Andy**. In this situation, what would Nina most likely say to Andy?

남: Andy는 자신이 다니는 고등학교에서 연례 축제의 사회자를 맡고 있다. 그는 사회 보는 것을 아주 좋아하고 그의 친구들은 모두 그가 매우 재능이 있다고 생각한다. 그러나 축제가 막 시작될 무렵 Andy는 긴장이 된다. 그는 리허설에서 했던 몇 가지 실수에 집중하기 시작한다. 그의 친구인 Nina는 그가 걱정하는 것을 보고는 왜 그러는지 묻는다. Andy는 대사를 잊어버리는 것이 두렵고 다른 학생들이 자신을 놀리지 않을까 걱정된다고 설명한다. Nina는 이 말을 듣고 Andy에게 용기를 북돋아 줄 수 있는 뭔가를 하고 싶다. 이러한 상황에서 Nina가 Andy에게 할 말로 가장 적절한 것은 무엇인가?

어휘 **stay[be] on one's guard** 경계를 늦추지 않다 / **line** (연극·영화의) 대사

16~17 세트 문항 | 16. ① 17. ④

▶ 16. Desert Fox 항공사에서 5월 한 달간 제공하는 이벤트에 대해 안내하고 있다.

① 기내 이벤트와 서비스에 대한 정보
② 보상제도 변경 사항 공지
③ 아이들과 함께 비행기를 탈 때 유용한 여행 조언들
④ 모든 승객이 이용 가능한 특가 상품
⑤ 가족 여행 패키지 추천

▶ 17. 해석 참조

W: Good morning, passengers. **Thank you for flying with** Desert Fox Airlines. Throughout May, Desert Fox Airlines will be offering **several exciting discounts and events** to celebrate Children's Day and Parents' Day. First, passengers will receive an additional 5% of their total bonus mileage when traveling during the month of May. Also, we'll be offering packages of tickets for families who are traveling together. **For kids under the age of seven**, we will provide free, specially-made in-flight meals. We also provide animated films for children as part of our VOD service. If your children prefer to read, our flight attendants have a selection of storybooks. And of course, we provide child safety seats **at no additional cost**. If you have children under seven, **take advantage of these offers** by letting us know when you reserve your tickets. For further details, please check inside your copy of *Desert Fox Airlines Magazine*, **which is located in the seat pocket** in front of you. We hope you have a pleasant flight today with Desert Fox Airlines.

여: 안녕하세요, 승객 여러분. Desert Fox 항공을 이용해 주셔서 감사합니다. 5월 한 달 동안 Desert Fox 항공에서는 어린이날과 어버이날을 기념하여 몇 가지 짜릿한 할인과 이벤트를 제공할 예정입니다. 우선, 5월 한 달 동안 이용해 주시는 승객 여러분께 전체 보너스 마일리지의 5%를 추가로 적립해 드립니다. 또한, 함께 여행하시는 가족분들을 위해 패키지 항공권을 제공하려고 합니다. 7세 미만 아동에게는 ① 특별 기내식을 무료로 제공할 예정입니다. 더불어 저희 VOD 서비스의 일부로 어린이를 위한 ② 만화영화를 틀어드립니다. 만약 자녀가 책 읽는 것을 더 좋아한다면 저희 항공사 승무원들은 ③ 이야기책 선집을 준비해두고 있습니다. 그리고 저희는 당연히 추가 비용 없이 ⑤ 아동용 안전 의자를 제공합니다. 7세 미만의 자녀를 두셨다면, 항공권을 예약하실 때 저희에게 알려주셔서 이러한 기회들을 활용하십시오. 더 자세한 사항은 승객 여러분 앞의 좌석 주머니에 있는 〈Desert Fox 항공 잡지〉를 참고하시기 바랍니다. 오늘 저희 Desert Fox 항공과 함께 즐거운 여행 하시기를 바랍니다.

어휘 **in-flight** 기내의 / **animated** 만화영화의; 활기찬 / **VOD** 주문형 비디오 ((Video On Demand의 약어))

Answers & Explanation

01. ① 02. ③ 03. ② 04. ② 05. ② 06. ② 07. ④ 08. ① 09. ② 10. ④
11. ④ 12. ③ 13. ② 14. ③ 15. ① 16. ③ 17. ②

01 화자가 하는 말의 목적 | ①

▶ 이메일을 통해 은행이나 신용카드 회사라고 사칭하여 개인의 금융 정보나 신용카드 정보를 묻는 금융사기를 조심할 것을 경고하고 있다.

W: The Internet is a sea of information. And some 21st century pirates **are trying to steal your money** by using the Internet. When you open an email, **they deceive you by making you believe** they represent your bank or your credit card company. Then they ask you for your bank account numbers and account passwords, or credit card numbers. These pirates want this information so that they can **break into your accounts** or use your credit card. You need to be careful. Banks or credit card companies don't ask for this kind of information. You should never **give it out while you are online**.

여: 인터넷은 정보의 바다입니다. 그리고 21세기의 해적들은 인터넷을 이용하여 여러분의 돈을 훔치려고 하고 있습니다. 여러분이 이메일을 열 때, 그 해적들은 자신들이 여러분이 이용하는 은행이나 신용카드 회사를 대신한다고 믿게 만들어서 여러분을 속입니다. 그런 다음 여러분의 은행 계좌 번호와 계좌 비밀번호 혹은 신용카드 번호를 요구합니다. 이 해적들은 여러분의 계좌에 침입하거나 신용카드를 사용하고자 이런 정보들을 요구합니다. 여러분은 조심할 필요가 있습니다. 은행과 신용카드 회사는 이런 종류의 정보를 요구하지 않습니다. 온라인상에 있을 때 절대로 이런 정보를 줘버려서는 안 됩니다.

어휘 **pirate** 해적; 저작권을 침해하다, ~을 불법 복제하다 / **deceive** ~을 속이다 / **represent** ~을 대리하다, 대표하다 / **bank account** 은행 예금 계좌 / **break into** ~에 침입하다

02 대화 주제 | ③

▶ 두 사람은 산의 높이가 측정 기술 발전과 산맥의 나이에 따라 변한다고 이야기하고 있다.

W: I think our report about mountain ranges is almost finished. What about you?
M: It's almost finished, but we are still missing a few details.
W: Like what?
M: Well, I **have several different heights** for Mount Whitney. Why is that?
W: Oh, that's the highest peak in the US. As measurement techniques have become more accurate, the official height has changed.
M: Okay. I thought maybe **the mountain was still growing**.
W: It is growing slowly, about a millimeter a year.
M: We should mention that in our report, also. Is every mountain getting taller?
W: **Most of the younger mountain ranges**, like the Alps and the Himalayas, are still growing.
M: And the older ones are slowly shrinking, right?
W: That's right. **Let's include that in our report**, too.

여: 산맥에 대한 우리 보고서가 거의 완성된 것 같아. 넌 어때?
남: 거의 다 됐는데, 우리 아직 몇 가지 세부사항을 놓치고 있어.
여: 예를 들면?
남: 음, Whitney 산의 높이가 몇 가지로 달라. 왜 그렇지?
여: 아, 그 산은 미국에서 가장 높은 봉우리야. 측정 기술이 더 정확해지면서 공식 높이도 변했거든.
남: 그렇구나. 난 어쩌면 산이 아직 높아지고 있다고 생각했어.
여: 일 년에 약 1mm 정도로 천천히 높아지고 있어.
남: 그것도 우리 보고서에서 언급해야겠다. 모든 산이 점점 높아지고 있어?
여: 알프스나 히말라야 같은 더 어린 산맥은 대부분 여전히 높아지고 있어.
남: 그리고 더 오래된 산맥들은 천천히 낮아지고 있지, 맞지?
여: 맞아. 그것도 우리 보고서에 넣자.

어휘 **range** 산맥; 범위 / **peak** (산의) 봉우리, 꼭대기; 정점, 최고조 / **measurement** 측정, 측량

03 관계 | ②

▶ 대화를 통해 두 사람 모두 책을 쓰고 책을 홍보하기 위해 북 투어를 다니는 사람들이라는 것을 알 수 있다.

M: Austin is sending me on a book tour to **promote my new book**.
W: Oh, I like going on book tours.
M: I don't really like going on them.
W: Really? I like meeting the people who read my stories.
M: Not me. I just like writing. **Book tours are so tiring**. I'll be visiting 10 cities in 10 days.
W: And you will visit two or three bookstores in every city, won't you?
M: That's right. It's exhausting. **How's your latest book going**?
W: Good. When it's done, Austin will **send me off on a book tour**, too.
M: What's the new book called?
W: It's called *The Lover's Triangle*.
M: **I'll look forward to reading it.**

남: Austin 씨가 새로 나온 제 책을 홍보하도록 저를 북 투어에 보낼 거예요.
여: 아, 전 북 투어 가는 것을 좋아해요.
남: 저는 거기 가는 것을 그다지 좋아하지 않아요.
여: 정말이요? 저는 제 이야기를 읽은 사람들을 만나는 게 좋아요.
남: 저는 아니에요. 그냥 글 쓰는 것이 좋아요. 북 투어는 너무 힘들어요. 전 10일간 10개 도시를 방문할 거예요.
여: 그리고 각 도시마다 두세 군데의 서점에 들르겠죠, 그렇지 않나요?
남: 맞아요. 정말 피곤하죠. 당신의 신간은 어떻게 되어가고 있나요?
여: 잘되고 있어요. 작업이 끝나면 Austin 씨가 저도 북 투어에 보내겠죠.
남: 새 책의 제목이 무엇인가요?
여: 〈The Lover's Triangle〉이에요.
남: 빨리 읽어 보고 싶네요.

어휘 **exhausting** 심신을 피로하게 하는, 고단한 / **send off** ~을 보내다, 배웅하다

04 그림 불일치 | ②

▶ 드럼 연주자는 줄무늬 셔츠를 입고 있다고 했다.

[Cell phone rings.]
W: Hello?
M: Hi, Vanessa. How's the concert?
W: It's great. A huge banner that says "Beautiful Day" **is hanging above the stage**. I wish you could be here.
M: That's cool. Maybe we can go together next time. Do you **have a good view** of the stage?
W: I can see the drummer clearly. He's wearing his usual striped shirt.
M: Okay. I'm sure the guitarist still has long hair.
W: Right. **He never changes his look**. And the lead singer is wearing sunglasses as always.
M: Can you see the second guitarist?
W: Yes. He's at **the far right of the stage**, wearing checkered pants.
M: It sounds like you have a great seat.
W: Yes, I booked the tickets early.

[휴대전화 벨이 울린다.]
여: 여보세요?
남: 안녕, Vanessa. 콘서트 어때?
여: 굉장해. '아름다운 날'이라고 쓰여 있는 커다란 현수막이 무대 위에 걸려 있어. 네가 여기 올 수 있으면 좋을 텐데.
남: 멋진데. 아마 다음엔 같이 갈 수 있겠지. 무대는 잘 보이니?
여: 드럼 연주자가 뚜렷하게 보여. 평소에 입는 줄무늬 셔츠를 입고 있어.
남: 그래. 분명 기타 연주자는 여전히 긴 머리를 하고 있겠지.
여: 맞아. 그는 외모를 절대 바꾸지 않잖아. 그리고 리드 보컬은 언제나처럼 선글라스를 쓰고 있어.
남: 세컨드 기타 연주자는 보이니?
여: 응. 체크무늬 바지를 입고 무대 오른쪽 맨 끝에 있어.

남: 너 아주 좋은 자리에 앉은 것 같구나.
여: 응, 표를 일찍 예매했거든.

어휘 **banner** 현수막 / **checkered** 체크무늬의

05 추후 행동 | ②

▶ 마지막 부분에서 남자가 회원들과 손님들의 사진을 찍어줄 사람이 필요하다고 했고 여자는 자신이 하겠다고 말했다.

W: Sorry **I couldn't go to** the photography club meeting yesterday.
M: That's OK, Sally.
W: Did you discuss our exhibition for the school festival this Friday?
M: Yes. Everyone has a job.
W: What's mine?
M: Oh, no. We forgot about you. Hmm.... Eddie's setting up the easels **to put the pictures on**.
W: I could help him.
M: Ted will help him. And Johnny and Fred are going to bring the easels down from the art room.
W: I can make promotional signs.
M: Carol's doing that. And **I'm going to set up** a drink's table.
W: I have nothing to do!
M: I know; we need **someone to take photographs of** the club members and important guests.
W: Good idea. I'll do that. That's the best job for me!

여: 어제 사진 동호회 모임에 가지 못해서 미안해.
남: 괜찮아, Sally.
여: 이번 주 금요일에 열리는 학교 축제에서 할 전시회에 대해 의논했어?
남: 응. 모든 사람이 일을 하나씩 맡았어.
여: 내가 할 일은 뭐야?
남: 아, 이런. 널 잊어버렸다. 음…. Eddie는 사진을 올려놓을 이젤을 설치할 거야.
여: 내가 그를 도울 수 있어.
남: Eddie는 Ted가 도와줄 거야. 그리고 Johnny랑 Fred는 미술실에서 이젤을 가져올 거야.
여: 내가 홍보용 표지판을 만들 수 있어.
남: 그건 Carol이 할 거야. 그리고 난 음료수 탁자를 설치할 거고.
여: 난 할 게 없잖아!
남: 알아. 우리는 동아리 회원들과 중요한 손님들의 사진을 찍어줄 사람이 필요해.
여: 좋은 생각이야. 내가 그 일을 할게. 내게 딱 맞는 일인걸!

어휘 **set up** ~을 설치하다; ~을 세우다 / **easel** 이젤, (칠판 등의) 받침대 / **promotional** 홍보의, 판촉의

06 금액 | ②

▶ 메인 요리를 주문하지 않고 점심 가격으로 샐러드 바를 이용할 수 있으므로 두 사람은 총 16달러를 내야 한다.

W: Are you ready to order?
M: Umm... **I'm a little confused**. If we order a main dish, like this steak for $20, then is the salad bar free?
W: No, it isn't. The salad bar is $4 extra with any main dish.
M: And **if we don't order a main dish**?
W: Then the salad bar is $12 per person.
M: Umm... but it says right here that it's $8.
W: The lunch price is $8, but it's only available between 11 a.m. and 2 p.m.
M: **Is it past two**?
W: Yes, it's a few minutes past two.
M: Could you check with the manager? **My friend and I walked in 5 minutes ago**.
W: OK. *[pause]* The manager has agreed to the lunchtime price.
M: We'd just like the salad bar then. **We won't be having a main dish**.
W: OK.

여: 주문하시겠습니까?
남: 음… 조금 헷갈리는데요. 20달러인 이 스테이크 같은 메인 요리를 주문하면 샐러드 바는 무료입니까?
여: 아니요, 그렇지 않습니다. 어떤 메인 요리에든 샐러드 바는 4달러를 추가로 내셔야 합니다.
남: 메인 요리를 주문하지 않으면요?
여: 그러면 샐러드 바는 일인당 12달러입니다.
남: 음… 하지만 바로 여기에는 8달러라고 적혀 있는데요.
여: 점심 가격이 8달러인데 오전 11시에서 오후 2시까지만 이용 가능합니다.
남: 2시가 지났나요?
여: 네, 2시에서 몇 분 더 지났습니다.
남: 매니저분께 확인을 해주시겠어요? 제 친구와 저는 5분 전에 들어왔거든요.
여: 알겠습니다. *[잠시 후]* 매니저께서 점심 가격으로 해드리는 데 동의하셨습니다.
남: 그럼 우리는 샐러드 바로 하겠습니다. 메인 요리는 주문하지 않을 거고요.
여: 알겠습니다.

07 이유 | ④

▶ 남자가 여자에게 식물을 돌볼 수 없는 이유를 묻자 여자는 엄마가 몇몇 꽃들에 알레르기가 있다고 답했다.

W: Hi, Chris. I was hoping to meet you.
M: Why, Susan? Can I help you with something?
W: I hope so. I'd like you to **look after my house plants** for a couple of weeks.
M: Does that mean you're taking a vacation?
W: Unfortunately not. My mom is quite sick.
M: I'm really sorry to hear that. Are you going to visit her?
W: No. I was going to, but I decided to **have her stay with me instead**.
M: I see. Then, why do you want me to care for your plants?
W: Well, she's allergic to some of my flowers. I want you to keep them at your house.
M: I understand. Are there any special instructions for **taking care of them**?
W: No, they just need water and sunlight.
M: Okay. **I don't mind looking after them**.
W: Thanks. You're the best.

여: 안녕, Chris. 널 만나고 싶었어.
남: 왜, Susan? 내가 도와줄 것이 있니?
여: 그러길 바라. 네가 2주 정도 우리 집 식물들을 돌봐주면 좋겠어.
남: 네가 휴가를 간다는 의미니?
여: 안타깝게도 그건 아냐. 우리 엄마가 꽤 아프셔.
남: 정말 유감이구나. 어머니를 방문하러 갈 거니?
여: 아니, 그러려고 했지만, 대신 엄마가 우리 집에서 머무시게 하는 거로 결정했어.
남: 알겠어. 그러면 왜 내가 너의 식물들을 돌보길 원하는 거니?
여: 그게, 엄마에게 내 몇몇 꽃들에 알레르기가 있으시거든. 네가 그것들을 너의 집에 보관해줬으면 좋겠어.
남: 알겠어. 그것들을 돌보는 데 특별히 설명해 줄 것이 있니?
여: 아니, 그냥 물과 햇빛만 있으면 돼.
남: 알겠어. 난 그것들을 돌봐도 괜찮아.
여: 고마워. 넌 최고야.

어휘 **look after** ~을 돌보다[보살피다](= care for, take care of) / **be allergic to A** A에 알레르기가 있다 / **instruction** (무엇을 하는 데 필요한) 설명; 지시; 교육, 지도 / **sunlight** 햇빛, 햇살, 일광

08 언급하지 않은 것 | ①

▶ 해석 참조

W: Hi, Chris. Are you enjoying your time in Korea?
M: **I've had a lot of fun**, but I don't feel like I've seen enough Korean culture.
W: If you want to experience Korean culture, why don't you visit the Jeonju Hanok Village?
M: I've heard about that place. They have **traditional houses that tourists can stay in overnight**.
W: They also have souvenir shops, traditional restaurants, museums, and temples.
M: It sounds like **there will be plenty to see and do**.
W: You won't be disappointed. There are over 500 traditional houses that still have people living in them.
M: That's a lot. How was the village first formed?
W: The village was established by Koreans in the 1930's to **protect their culture** during the period when Korea was controlled by Japan.

여: 안녕, Chris. 한국에서 즐거운 시간 보내고 있니?

남: 아주 재밌었지만, 한국 문화를 충분히 경험한 것 같지는 않아.
여: 한국 문화를 경험하고 싶다면, 전주 한옥마을을 방문하는 게 어때?
남: 그곳에 관해 들어본 적이 있어. 관광객들이 숙박할 수 있는 전통 가옥들(② 숙박 가능 여부)이 있다던데.
여: 기념품점, 전통 음식점, 박물관, 절도 있어(③ 보유 시설).
남: 볼 것도 많고 할 것도 많을 것 같네.
여: 실망하지 않을 거야. 사람들이 여전히 살고 있는 전통 가옥이 500채 넘게 있어(④ 전통 가옥 수).
남: 많구나. 그 마을은 처음에 어떻게 형성됐니?
여: 한국이 일본의 지배를 받던 시절에 한국인들이 자신들의 문화를 지키고자 1930년대에 조성(⑤ 조성 시기)했어.

어휘 **souvenir** 기념품

09 내용 불일치 | ②

▶ 새들이 개복치 몸에서 작은 벌레들을 없앨 수 있도록 개복치들은 해수면 가까이 떠 있기도 한다고 했다.

M: The ocean sunfish is one of the heaviest fish on Earth, with an average weight of about a ton. It lives in temperate and tropical seas and oceans. It is flat and it often **floats near the surface of the water** so birds can remove tiny worms from its body. Besides its unique appearance and habits, the ocean sunfish **has the ability to change colors**. For example, its skin is usually gray or white, but it can become lighter or darker in color **when it's under attack**. They are not aggressive toward humans, so the largest danger they can pose is damage to boats **because of their tremendous weight**. Meanwhile, the meat of ocean sunfish is eaten in many Asian countries. However, the meat **should be inspected for poisons** before consumption.

남: 개복치는 지구상 무게가 가장 많이 나가는 어류 중 하나로, 평균 무게가 대략 1톤이다. 개복치는 온대성 및 열대성 바다와 해양에 서식한다. (모양은) 납작하며 새들이 자기 몸에서 작은 벌레들을 없앨 수 있도록 수면 가까이에 떠 있기도 한다. 이처럼 특이한 외양과 습성 외에도, 개복치는 몸의 색깔을 바꿀 수 있는 능력이 있다. 이를테면, 개복치의 피부는 주로 회색 또는 흰색이지만, 공격을 받으면 색깔이 더 연해지거나 더 짙어질 수 있다. 인간에게 공격적이지 않기 때문에 개복치가 가할 수 있는 가장 큰 위험은 그 어마어마한 무게로 인해 배를 훼손시키는 정도이다. 한편, 많은 아시아 국가에서 개복치 고기를 먹는다. 하지만 먹기 전에 고기에 독이 없는지 점검해야 한다.

어휘 **temperate** 온대성의, (기후·지역이) 온화한 / **pose** (위험·문제 등을) 제기하다 / **tremendous** 엄청난; 굉장한, 대단한 / **inspect** ~을 점검[검사]하다 / **consumption** 소비[소모](량)

10 도표 이해 | ④

▶ 여자는 두부를 좋아하지 않으며 점심에 지방 섭취량을 20그램으로 제한한다고 했으므로 Asian Chicken과 Tuna만 남는데 이 중 칼로리가 낮은 것을 선택했다.

M: I'm having the Italian Meatball sandwich. I love that barbecue sauce.
W: Yikes! It's got 35 grams of fat!
M: But it tastes great! And I didn't have any breakfast. It's what I want.
W: My doctor told me to have only 50 grams of fat a day. Then **I'd lose some weight**.
M: Do you like tofu? **It is low in fat**.
W: No, I don't like it. Hmm... let's see, my doctor recommended I **limit my fat intake** to 20 grams at lunch.
M: Well, you still have two choices.
W: Actually **I don't really like either of them**.
M: Really? Should we go somewhere else?
W: No, I don't have much time. I will take the one which has fewer calories between the two.
M: Good. Let's order then.

남: 난 이탈리안 미트볼 샌드위치를 먹을래. 그 바비큐 소스를 아주 좋아하거든.
여: 헉! 이건 지방이 35그램이나 들어 있어!
남: 하지만 정말 맛있는걸! 그리고 난 아침식사도 안 했어. 이게 먹고 싶어.
여: 의사선생님께서 지방을 하루에 50그램만 섭취하라고 내게 말씀하셨어. 그럼 살이 좀 빠질 거야.
남: 너 두부 좋아하니? 그건 지방이 적은데.
여: 아니, 좋아하지 않아. 음… 어디 보자, 의사선생님께서 점심에는 지방 섭취를 20그램으로 제한하라고 권하셨어.
남: 그럼, 아직 두 가지를 선택할 수 있네.
여: 사실 둘 다 별로 좋아하지 않아.
남: 정말? 다른 데로 가야 하나?
여: 아니, 난 시간이 별로 없어. 둘 중에 칼로리가 더 적은 것으로 먹을래.
남: 좋아. 그럼 주문하자.

어휘 **tofu** 두부 / **tuna** 참치 / **lose weight** 체중이 줄다 / **intake** 섭취(량)

11 짧은 대화에 이어질 응답 | ④

▶ 지하철을 몇 번이나 갈아타야 하느냐는 여자의 질문에 횟수를 말하는 응답이 가장 적절하다.

① 15 정거장밖에 안 돼. ② 난 오늘 4호선을 탔어.
③ 대신 버스를 타봐야겠어. ④ 두 번. 그렇지만 별로 불편하진 않아.
⑤ 적어도 15분은 절약돼.

W: Jeff, you **take the bus to come to school**, right?
M: Actually, I take the subway. **It's faster even though I have to transfer**.
W: Oh, really? How many times do you have to transfer?
M: ______________________________

여: Jeff, 너 학교 올 때 버스 타고 오지, 맞지?
남: 사실, 지하철을 타. 환승을 해야 하긴 하지만 더 빠르거든.
여: 아, 정말? 몇 번이나 갈아타야 해?
남: ______________________________

12 짧은 대화에 이어질 응답 | ③

▶ 남자는 프랑스에 갔다 온 여자에게 사진은 찍었는지 묻고 있다.

① 내가 사진이 잘 받으면 좋을 텐데.
② 여기 네게 줄 기념품이 좀 있어.
③ 물론이지, 기꺼이 네게 보여줄게.
④ 그건 네게 보여준 사진들만큼 아름다웠어.
⑤ Claude Monet의 작품집을 샀어.

M: Hi, Karen! **I haven't seen you** for a few weeks.
W: That's because I went to France with my sister. It was amazing.
M: Sounds like you had a great time. **Did you take any pictures**?
W: ______________________________

남: 안녕, Karen! 몇 주 동안 못 봤네.
여: 왜냐하면 언니와 함께 프랑스에 갔었거든. 굉장했어.
남: 정말 좋은 시간을 보낸 것 같구나. 사진은 찍었어?
여: ______________________________

어휘 **photogenic** 사진이 잘 받는

13 긴 대화에 이어질 응답 | ②

▶ 아들의 친구들을 집으로 초대해 생일 파티를 하자고 주장하는 어머니에게 생일 파티를 원하지 않는 아들이 할 수 있는 응답을 찾는다.

① 멋져요. 저도 그걸 생각했어요.
② 괜찮아요, 엄마. 걱정하지 마세요.
③ 아니요, 이번에는 피자와 치킨이 좋겠어요.
④ 축하하기 위해 제가 그 애들을 이미 초대했어요.
⑤ 고맙습니다. 케이크와 음료로 하겠어요.

W: How are your plans for your birthday party going?
M: My birthday party?
W: Yes. **We used to have a party** in our apartment. You and your friends had pizza and chicken.
M: We did that when I was a child.
W: You're still a child.
M: No, I'm not. I'm in high school.
W: So you don't want a birthday party at home this year?
M: No. **We haven't had one** for two or three years.
W: I know, but I thought maybe this year you would have one. **What are you going to do** on your birthday then?
M: I just want to spend some time with my friends. Maybe they'll buy me some lunch and we'll have some cake.
W: But **wouldn't it be nicer** if we invite them to the apartment?
M: ______________________________

여: 네 생일 파티 계획은 어떻게 되어가고 있니?
남: 제 생일 파티요?
여: 그래. 집에서 파티를 하곤 했잖아. 너랑 네 친구들이 피자와 치킨을 먹었지.
남: 제가 어렸을 때 그랬죠.
여: 너는 아직도 어린애란다.
남: 아니요, 그렇지 않아요. 전 고등학생인걸요.
여: 그래서 올해는 집에서 생일 파티를 하고 싶지 않다고?
남: 네. 2, 3년간 파티를 하지 않았잖아요.
여: 알아. 하지만 아마 올해는 할 것이라고 생각했는데. 그럼 생일에는 무엇을 할 거니?
남: 그냥 친구들이랑 함께 시간을 보내고 싶어요. 아마 그 애들이 저에게 점심을 사줄 테고 우린 케이크를 먹을 거예요.
여: 하지만 그 애들을 집으로 초대하면 더 좋지 않을까?
남: ______________________________

어휘 **have A over** (집으로) A를 초대하다, 부르다

14 긴 대화에 이어질 응답 | ③

▶ 요즘 건망증이 있는 여자는 리필을 하러 가면서 남자의 컵을 가지고 가지 않았다. 이런 상황에서 여자가 할 수 있는 말을 유추해보면 된다.

① 제가 제 컵이 왜 필요하죠?
② 이것들을 리필해 주세요.
③ 오, 바보 같아요. 컵을 가지고 가야 하는데 말예요.
④ 괜찮아요. 나는 패스트푸드를 먹지 않을 거예요.
⑤ 와! 햄버거가 이렇게 맛있는지 잊고 있었어요.

W: I'm becoming **so forgetful that it worries me**.
M: You've just been working hard. You're tired.
W: I'm getting old!
M: **Stop worrying for nothing**! Let's finish our shopping after we eat.
W: OK. How's your hamburger? Mine is great. I haven't had a hamburger in a long time.
M: Well, **you shouldn't be eating them** too frequently.
W: Simon, don't worry. I don't eat too much fast food. I rarely visit food courts like this.
M: Are you finished with your cola?
W: Yeah. All that walking and shopping has **made me thirsty**.
M: Me, too. Can you **go get refills for both of us**?
W: Good idea. Just a minute.
M: Gloria, Gloria, wait! You've forgotten my cup.
W: ______________________________

여: 건망증이 심해져서 걱정돼요.
남: 일을 열심히 해왔잖아요. 당신은 지쳐 있어요.
여: 제가 나이가 드나 봐요!
남: 아무 일도 아닌 일로 그만 걱정하세요! 식사하고 나서 쇼핑을 마치죠.
여: 알겠어요. 햄버거는 어때요? 제 것은 맛있어요. 전 햄버거를 먹은 지 정말 오래되었어요.
남: 음, 너무 자주 먹어서는 안 돼요.
여: Simon, 걱정하지 마세요. 난 패스트푸드를 너무 많이 먹진 않아요. 이런 푸드 코트도 거의 오지 않아요.
남: 콜라는 다 마셨어요?
여: 네. 그렇게 걸어 다니며 쇼핑을 했더니 목이 말랐어요.
남: 저도요. 우리 둘 다 마시게 리필을 해 올래요?
여: 좋은 생각이에요. 잠깐만요.
남: Gloria, Gloria, 기다려요! 제 컵을 잊고 갔어요.
여: ______________________________

어휘 **forgetful** 건망증이 있는, 잊기 잘하는

15 상황에 적절한 말 | ①

▶ 사이트에서 물건을 주문했는데 물건이 오지 않아 우울한 David에게 Sylvia는 온라인으로 물건을 살 때마다 사이트의 신뢰성을 알아봐야 한다는 것을 말하고 싶어 할 것이다.

① 넌 쇼핑을 하기 전에 사이트를 확인해봐야 해.
② 더 빠른 운송을 위해서는 추가 요금을 지불해야 해.
③ 후기를 정말 확인하더라도, 나는 그것들을 신중하게 다뤄.
④ 난 고객 후기를 쓸 때 완전히 솔직하려고 해.
⑤ 내가 너라면, 난 불평하지 않고 그냥 잠시 기다릴 거야.

W: Sylvia happens to meet her friend David at school. **He looks depressed and Sylvia asks him why**. David says he ordered sunglasses online 20 days ago and they still have not shipped them. When Sylvia asks him if he's contacted the seller, David says he sent them an e-mail but **they didn't reply**. He also called them, but **their phone number is no longer in service**. Sylvia asks David to show her what site he bought the item on. She's never heard of that site and **there aren't any customer reviews**. Sylvia thinks it's **necessary to see if the site is reliable** whenever people buy something online. She wants to say that to David. In this situation, what would Sylvia most likely say to David?

여: Sylvia는 친구 David를 학교에서 우연히 만난다. 그가 우울해 보여서 Sylvia는 그에게 이유를 묻는다. David는 자신이 20일 전에 온라인으로 선글라스를 주문했는데 그들이 아직 그것들을 보내지 않았다고 말한다. Sylvia가 그에게 판매자와 연락이 되었는지 묻자 David는 그들에게 이메일을 보냈지만, 답이 없었다고 한다. 그는 그들에게 전화도 했지만, 그들의 전화번호는 더는 사용되지 않는다. Sylvia는 David에게 어느 사이트에서 그가 물건을 샀는지 보여 달라고 요청한다. 그녀는 그 사이트에 대해 들어본 일이 없으며 그곳에는 어떠한 고객 후기도 없다. Sylvia는 사람들이 온라인으로 어떤 것을 살 때마다 그 사이트가 믿을 만한지 알아봐야 할 필요가 있다고 생각한다. 그녀는 David에게 그것을 말하고 싶어 한다. 이러한 상황에서 Sylvia가 David에게 할 말로 가장 적절한 것은 무엇인가?

어휘 **check out** (이상이 없는지) 확인하다, 살펴보다 / **extra charge** 추가 요금 / **shipping** 해상 운송; 선박 ***cf.* ship** (배 등으로) 실어 나르다; 수송[운송]하다 / **with caution** 신중하게 / **item** 물품, 품목 / **reliable** 믿을 만한; 믿을[신뢰할] 수 있는

16~17 세트 문항 | 16. ③ 17. ②

▶ 16. 세계 난민의 날과 난민의 정의 및 그들이 겪는 어려움을 언급한 뒤, 자원봉사 프로그램에 참여하여 난민을 도와줄 것을 장려하고 있다.

① 사람들이 난민이 되는 네 가지 이유
② 세계 난민의 날의 의미와 목적
③ 난민들이 마주하고 있는 어려움과 그들을 돕는 방법
④ 국제연합에 의해 주최되는 난민들을 위한 모금 행사
⑤ 난민들을 위한 자원봉사 단체들의 성과

▶ 17. 해석 참조

M: As you may already know, June 20th is World Refugee Day. Each year the United Nations and other civic groups celebrate this day. But **who exactly are refugees**? Refugees are people who have left their home country and **are afraid to return**. This often happens because a refugee's race, religion, or political opinion isn't respected in his or her home country. Also, when countries go to war, people may choose to leave their home country or **be forced out by invading armies**. In 2020, there were 26.4 million refugees around the world. These people typically have few rights and limited access to food, shelter, and medical care. They need our help. Fortunately, **it's not difficult to help** them. You can start by participating in a volunteer program for refugees. You can help them to understand the culture and language of their new country. **Starting over in a new country** is difficult, but a little effort from you can help refugees to overcome the challenges.

남: 이미 알고 계실지도 모르지만, 6월 20일은 세계 난민의 날입니다. 매년 국제연합과 다른 시민 단체들이 이날을 기념합니다. 하지만 난민이 정확히 누구일까요? 난민은, 조국을 떠났고 (그곳으로) 돌아가길 두려워하는 사람들입니다. 이런 일은 흔히 발생하는데 난민의 ① 인종이나 ③ 종교, 혹은 ④ 정치적 견해가 그들의 조국에서 존중되지 않기 때문입니다. 또한, 나라에서 ⑤ 전쟁이 일어나면 사람들은 조국을 떠나기를 선택하거나 침략군에 의해 강제로 내몰릴 수도 있습니다. 2020년, 세계적으로 2,640만 명의 난민들이 있었습니다. 이 사람들에게는 대개 권리가 거의 없고 식량, 쉼터, 의료 혜택이 제한되어 있습니다. 그들은 우리 도움이 필요합니다. 다행히도 그들을 돕는 것은 어렵지 않습니다. 난민을 위한 자원봉사 프로그램에 참여하는 것부터 시작할 수 있습니다. 그들이 새로운 나라의 문화와 언어를 이해하도록 도와줄 수 있습니다. 새 나라에서 다시 시작하는 것은 힘들지만, 여러분의 작은 노력으로 난민들이 난관을 극복하도록 도울 수 있습니다.

어휘 **refugee** 난민, 망명자 / **fundraiser** 모금 행사 / **accomplishment** 성과, 업적 / **the United Nations** 국제연합 ((전쟁방지와 평화유지를 위해 설립된 국제기구)) (= the UN) / **civic** 시민의; (도)시의 / **force** ~을 강요하다, (어쩔 수 없이) ~하게 만들다 / **shelter** 쉼터, 피난처

실전모의고사 16

Answers & Explanation

01. ③ 02. ④ 03. ④ 04. ③ 05. ⑤ 06. ③ 07. ④ 08. ④ 09. ④ 10. ③
11. ④ 12. ④ 13. ⑤ 14. ③ 15. ④ 16. ④ 17. ①

01 화자가 하는 말의 목적 | ③

▶ 과일과 채소가 건강을 유지하는 데 필요한 영양소를 제공하므로 많이 섭취해야 한다고 주장하고 있다.

M: It is important to eat **a balanced diet** in order to stay healthy. This means eating a wide variety of foods every day. The most important foods are fruits and vegetables. **In their raw form**, they provide the nutrients you need to stay healthy, **along with vitamins, minerals and fiber**. The best way **to ensure a healthy variety of nutrients** is to make sure you eat fruits and vegetables of many colors, because the colors reflect what kinds of vitamins are in the food. **The recommended amount to eat** is five fist-sized servings a day.

남: 건강을 유지하기 위해서는 균형 잡힌 식사를 하는 것이 중요합니다. 이는 매일 다양한 종류의 음식을 섭취하는 것을 뜻합니다. 가장 중요한 음식은 과일과 야채입니다. 그것들은 가공되지 않은 상태에서 비타민, 미네랄 그리고 섬유질과 더불어 건강을 유지하는 데 필요한 영양소들을 제공합니다. 건강에 좋은 다양한 영양소를 확실히 섭취하기 위한 가장 좋은 방법은 다양한 색깔의 과일과 채소를 반드시 먹는 것인데, 색깔이 음식에 어떤 종류의 비타민이 함유되어 있는지를 나타내주기 때문입니다. 섭취 권장량은 하루에 다섯 주먹 정도를 먹는 것입니다.

어휘 **balanced** 균형 잡힌 / **raw** 가공하지 않은, 날것의 / **mineral** 미네랄, 광물질 / **fiber** 섬유질 / **serving** 한 그릇의 음식

02 의견 | ④

▶ 여자는 경기장에서 응원 판으로 다른 관중의 시야를 가리는 사람들에 대해 불만을 표하면서 그에 관한 규정이 있어야 한다고 말했다.

M: It sure is a great day to watch a baseball game.
W: Yeah, but I feel bad for Susan. She can't see very well.
M: You're right. Those people in front of her are **holding up a large sign**.
W: I know they just want to support their team, but it's rude to the people behind them.
M: I agree with you, but I think **they are allowed to do that**.
W: Well, maybe there should be **rules against blocking the view** of another spectator. After all, we all paid the same amount to see the game.
M: I understand your point. In the meantime, I'll ask them to **put their sign down**.
W: That's a good idea.

남: 확실히 야구 경기를 보기에 정말 좋은 날이네요.
여: 그래요. 하지만 Susan이 안타까워요. 그 애는 잘 보이지 않잖아요.
남: 맞아요. 그 애 앞에 앉은 저 사람들이 큰 응원 판을 들고 있어요.
여: 자기 팀을 응원하고 싶을 뿐이라는 건 알지만, 뒤에 앉은 사람들에겐 실례예요.
남: 동의해요. 하지만 저 사람들이 그렇게 하는 게 허용되는 것 같아요.
여: 글쎄요. 어쩌면 다른 관중의 시야를 가리는 것을 금지하는 규정이 있어야 할지도 몰라요. 어쨌든 우리는 경기를 보려고 모두 같은 돈을 지불했으니까요.
남: 당신 말을 이해해요. 그동안은 저 사람들에게 응원 판을 내려달라고 부탁할게요.
여: 좋은 생각이에요.

어휘 **spectator** (특히 스포츠 행사의) 관중 / **in the meantime** (두 가지 시점·사건들) 그동안[그사이]에

03 관계 | ④

▶ 집까지 물건을 배달해주는 사람과 물건을 받는 고객 간의 대화이다.

[Doorbell rings.] [Door opens.]
M: Are you Mary Ellen Park?
W: Yes, I am. What can I do for you?
M: I just need you to **sign your name right here**.
W: Right here, next to the X?
M: Yes, that's right. And this is for you.
W: Wow! It's from Korea. But **I don't recognize the name**.
M: Do you have family there? How about an old high school friend?
W: Hmm... **I do have some family there**, but I only know their Korean names.
M: Well, the family name is 'Kim.'
W: Maybe 'June' is the Western name of my cousin Ji-eun.
M: **You won't know until you open it**. Have a nice day!

[현관 벨이 울린다.] [문이 열린다.]
남: Mary Ellen Park 씨 되십니까?
여: 네, 그렇습니다. 무슨 일이시죠?
남: 여기에다 사인을 해 주시기 바랍니다.
여: 여기, X표시 옆이요?
남: 네, 맞습니다. 그리고 이것은 고객님께 온 것입니다.
여: 와! 한국에서 왔네요. 하지만 이름을 보니 누군지 잘 모르겠어요.
남: 그곳에 가족이 있습니까? 예전 고등학교 때 친구는요?
여: 음… 가족이 그곳에 있기는 하지만 한국 이름밖에 몰라서요.
남: 음, 성은 '김'씨군요.
여: 아마 'June'이 제 사촌 지은의 서양식 이름인가 봐요.
남: 이것을 열어보셔야 알 수 있으시겠네요. 좋은 하루 되십시오!

04 그림 불일치 | ③

▶ 여자는 아치형 출입문을 포기한 것이 유일하게 아쉬운 점이라고 말했다.

M: Wow, your house looks great. I guess the remodeling went well.
W: It did. My daughter and I especially love **the wooden swing in the yard**.
M: That's lovely. By the way, you didn't have a fence before, correct?
W: That's right. **My husband and I had no plan to get one**, but the remodeling company offered us a discount, so we decided to have it built.
M: I think you two made the right choice. It is **much safer to fence the yard**, especially when you have a kid.
W: I hadn't thought of that. Good point! The only disappointment was **giving up on the arch-shaped doorway**.
M: I remember that you were really excited about that. What happened?
W: It was going to cost a lot of money, and my daughter really wanted the swimming pool. Therefore, it was either the door or the swimming pool.
M: And you decided **to go with the swimming pool**. Good choice!
W: Yeah, it's going to be a lot of fun in the summer. And I put a table and chairs next to it.
M: Awesome!

남: 와, 집이 멋져 보여요. 리모델링이 잘된 것 같아요.
여: 잘됐어요. 제 딸과 저는 특히 마당에 있는 나무 그네가 정말 마음에 든답니다.
남: 멋지네요. 그런데 예전에는 울타리가 없었지 않나요. 그렇죠?
여: 맞아요. 제 남편과 저는 울타리를 지을 계획이 없었는데, 리모델링 회사에서 할인을 제안해서 울타리를 짓기로 결정했어요.
남: 두 분이 옳은 결정을 하신 것 같아요. 특히 아이가 있을 때는 마당에 울타리를 치는 것이 훨씬 더 안전해요.
여: 그 점에 대해서는 생각하지 못했어요. 중요한 점이네요! 유일하게 아쉬운 점은 아치형 출입문을 포기한 거였어요.
남: 그 생각에 정말 들떠 있던 것으로 기억하는데. 무슨 일이 있었나요?
여: 비용이 많이 들 거였고 딸아이가 수영장을 정말 원했어요. 그래서 문 아니면 수영장이었어요.
남: 그리고 수영장으로 하기로 했군요. 잘 선택했어요!
여: 네, 여름에 정말 재밌을 거예요. 그리고 그 옆에 테이블과 의자를 두었어요.
남: 근사하네요!

어휘 **remodeling** 리모델링, 주택 개보수 / **fence** 울타리; 울타리를 치다 / **disappointment** 실망, 실망스러운 것 / **arch** 아치형(의 것)

05 추후 행동 | ⑤

▶ 남자가 고통을 호소하자 여자는 진료를 당장 받을 수 있을지 알아보겠다고 답변했다.

W: Welcome to Kim's Dental Clinic. What can we do for you today?
M: **I have a very bad toothache** and would like to see a dentist.
W: Have you ever been here before?
M: No. **I just moved to this area**. My regular dentist is back in Denver.
W: Well, **we have one slot open** to see the dentist at 1 p.m., if you don't mind waiting an hour.
M: That's a long time. Ouch! **There goes that tooth again**.
W: Here are a few forms to fill out for now.
M: OK. But I don't know **how long I can stand this pain**.
W: Well, if it's that bad, I'll see if I can get Dr. Kim to see you right now.
M: That would be great.

여: 김 치과에 잘 오셨습니다. 오늘 무엇을 도와드릴까요?
남: 치통이 매우 심해서 진찰을 받고 싶습니다.
여: 전에 여기에 오신 적이 있나요?
남: 아니요. 이 지역으로 이사 온 지 얼마 되지 않았어요. 제가 원래 다니던 치과는 덴버에 있습니다.
여: 음, 한 시간 정도 기다리는 게 괜찮으시면 오후 1시쯤에 진료를 받으실 수 있는 빈 시간이 있습니다.
남: 너무 오래 기다리네요. 아야! 이가 또 아프네요.
여: 여기 지금 작성해 주셔야 할 몇 가지 양식이 있습니다.
남: 알겠습니다. 하지만 제가 이 통증을 얼마나 오랫동안 참을 수 있을지 모르겠어요.
여: 음, 그렇게 심하다면 김 선생님이 지금 손님을 진찰하실 수 있을지 알아보도록 하겠습니다.
남: 그렇게 해 주시면 좋겠네요.

어휘 **regular** 단골의; 통상의, 정기적인 / **slot** (시간표상의) 시간대

06 금액 | ③

▶ 마지막에 여자가 미키필름 한 묶음(15달러)과 컬러필름 두 묶음(10달러×2)을 사겠다고 말하므로 지불해야 할 총 금액은 35달러이다.

W: I need film for this instant camera.
M: Color or black and white?
W: Color, please.
M: Well, 10 exposures is $10.
W: It's very expensive. $1 a picture. I never knew because I just **got this instant camera as a gift** a few weeks ago.
M: Well, black and white film is $6 for 10 exposures.
W: **Don't you have any larger packages**? Say packs of 20 or 30 exposures. Larger packs would be cheaper per exposure, wouldn't they?
M: Sorry, not right now.
W: Hey, what are these?
M: Films which print cartoon characters on **the border surrounding the picture**. There's Mickey, Winnie the Pooh....
W: Mickey's cute. I love Mickey. **Give me two packs of those**.
M: They're $15 a pack.
W: One pack of Mickey, then, and two packs of color film.
M: OK. Thank you for shopping with us!

여: 이 즉석카메라에 쓸 필름이 필요한데요.
남: 컬러와 흑백 중 무엇으로요?
여: 컬러로 주세요.
남: 자, 10장에 10달러입니다.
여: 아주 비싸네요. 사진 한 장당 1달러군요. 이 즉석카메라를 몇 주 전에 선물로 막 받은 참이라 전혀 몰랐네요.
남: 음, 흑백필름은 10장에 6달러랍니다.
여: 더 많이 포장된 건 없나요? 20장이나 30장 분량의 묶음이라든지요. 더 큰 묶음의 한 장당 가격이 더 쌀 것 같은데, 아닌가요?
남: 죄송해요. 지금은 없습니다.
여: 저기, 이것들은 뭐예요?
남: 사진을 둘러싼 가장자리에 만화 캐릭터를 인화하는 필름들이에요. 저기 미키도 있고, 위니 더 푸우도 있고요….
여: 미키가 귀엽네요. 전 미키가 좋아요. 그거 두 묶음 주세요.
남: 그건 한 묶음당 15달러예요.
여: 그럼 미키필름 한 묶음과 컬러필름 두 묶음을 주세요.
남: 네. 저희 매장에 와주셔서 감사합니다!

어휘 **instant camera** 즉석카메라 / **exposure** (필름에서) 사진을 한 장 찍을 수 있는 분량 / **border** 가장자리

07 이유 | ④

▶ 여자가 감독도 언급하고 영화가 뮤지컬인지, 각본이 마음에 안 드는지, 여배우가 누구인지 물었지만, 남자가 영화에 참여하지 않는 이유로 언급한 것은 내년 7월까지 TVB의 다른 드라마에 출연한다는 것이다. 그러므로 답은 ④이다.

W: Michael. I heard you're going to appear in a movie directed by John Williams.
M: You heard that? I **can't help but wonder** at how fast word travels.
W: Is it a musical? I know you'd like to appear in a musical.
M: No, it's a historical drama. I read the script last week but I **decided not to join the movie**.
W: Oh, I'm sorry to hear that. You don't like the script?
M: Well, I do. Its ending is sad but **the story is unforgettable**.
W: Then what's the problem? The director is John Williams!
M: Yeah, I know that he **has made three consecutive commercial successes**.
W: Definitely. Who is the main actress in that movie?
M: Jennifer Anderson. I really wanted to work with her, but I'm busy making another drama show for TVB until next July.
W: I see. You have to **concentrate on your role in that drama**.
M: Yes, so I didn't really have a choice.

여: Michael, 당신이 John Williams가 감독하는 영화에 출연한다고 들었어요.
남: 그걸 들었어요? 말이 얼마나 빨리 퍼지는지 놀라지 않을 수가 없군요.
여: 그거 뮤지컬인가요? 당신이 뮤지컬에 출연하고 싶어 하는 걸 알아요.
남: 아니오, 사극이에요. 지난주에 각본을 읽었지만 난 영화에 참여하지 않기로 결정했어요.
여: 아, 그거 안 됐군요. 각본이 마음에 안 든 거예요?
남: 음, 마음에 들어요. 그 결말은 슬프지만 이야기는 기억에 남아요.
여: 그러면 뭐가 문제예요? 감독이 John Williams라고요!
남: 그래요, 그가 세 편의 연속적인 상업적 성공을 거두었다는 걸 알아요.
여: 그럼요. 그 영화의 여주인공은 누구예요?
남: Jennifer Anderson이요. 정말 그녀와 같이 작업하고 싶었지만 나는 내년 7월까지 TVB에서 또 다른 드라마를 만드느라 바빠요.
여: 그렇군요. 그 드라마의 역할에 집중해야 하는군요.
남: 네, 그래서 선택의 여지가 없었어요.

어휘 **appear** 출연하다; 나타나다 / **direct** 감독하다 / **script** 각본, 대본 / **unforgettable** 기억에 남는 / **consecutive** 연속적인 / **commercial** 상업적인

08 언급하지 않은 것 | ④

▶ 해석 참조

W: It's not often you come across a real "floating island," but they do exist in Lake Titicaca in Peru. These floating islands **are made from reeds**, a type of grass that grows in the lake, and are large enough for people to live on. The islands **vary in size**, and more are being created as the need arises. The Uros, the people that live on the islands, originally moved onto the floating islands centuries ago to **defend against enemies**. This strategy turned out to be effective, so they have lived like that ever since. Since the islands are slowly sinking, every 6 months or so they have to lift all the houses and other buildings to **add more grass to the islands**. The residents must also wear layers of clothing, to protect themselves from the cold, the wind, and the intense sunshine.

여: 실재하는 '떠다니는 섬'을 발견하는 것은 흔한 일이 아니지만, 페루의 Titicaca 호수에는(① 위치) 정말로 이러한 섬이 존재한다. 이 떠다니는 섬들은 호수에서 자라는 풀의 일종인 갈대로 형성(② 형성 물질)되고, 그 위에서 사람들이 살 수 있을 정도로 크다. 섬들은 크기가 다양하며 필요에 따라 더 많이 지어지고 있다. 섬에 사는 사람들인 Uro 족은 원래 수 세기 전 적의 공격을 막기 위해(③ 최초 거주 이유) 이 떠다니는 섬으로 이주했다. 이 전략은 효과적인 것으로 드러나서 그들은 그 이후로 그렇게 살아 왔다. 섬들이 천천히 가라앉고 있기 때문에 섬에 풀을 더 보충하기 위해 대략 6개월마다 집과 다른 건물들을 전부 들어내야 한다. 또한 주민들은 추위, 바람, 강렬한 햇빛(⑤ 날씨 형태)으로부터 몸을 보호하기 위해 옷을 여러 겹 껴입어야 한다.

어휘 **reed** 갈대 / **resident** 주민 / **layer** (쌓인 것 등의) 겹, 층 / **intense** 강렬한, 극심한

09 내용 불일치 | ④

▶ 참가하지 않는 학생들에게는 오디션이 공개되지 않을 것이라고 했다.

M: The annual spelling championship for Rockville High School **will take place one week from today**. In order to enter, interested students must attend an audition tomorrow. During the audition you will be asked **to spell five words out loud** in front of the judges. If you miss any of the words in the audition, you will not make it to the championship round next Monday. The audition will not be open to non-participating students. **Those of you who do advance** will be given further information about when and where to go, and the format of the contest. **Good luck to all who try out**!

남: Rockville 고등학교의 연례 철자 말하기 선수권 대회가 오늘로부터 일주일 후에 개최됩니다. 참가하기 위해서는, 관심이 있는 학생들은 내일 오디션에 참가해야 합니다. 오디션에서는 다섯 단어의 철자를 심사위원 앞에서 크게 소리 내어 말하도록 요청받을 것입니다. 오디션에서 한 단어라도 못 맞출 경우에는 다음 주 월요일에 있을 선수권 라운드에 진출하지 못하게 될 것입니다. 오디션은 참가하지 않는 학생들에게는 공개되지 않을 것입니다. 진출한 학생들은 시간과 장소 그리고 대회의 형식에 관한 추가 정보를 받을 것입니다. 출전하는 모든 학생에게 행운이 있기를 빕니다!

어휘 **spell** 철자를 말하다 / **championship** 선수권 대회 / **judge** 심사위원; 재판관 / **round** (토너먼트 시합의) 라운드, 한 경기 / **advance** 진출하다, 나아가다, 전진하다 / **format** 형식 / **try out** (선발 등에) 출전하다

10 도표 이해 | ③

▶ 남자는 티셔츠와 모자만 주고 머그잔은 주지 않는 40달러 미만의 회원 자격을 선택할 것이다.

W: What are you doing, Max?
M: I'm going to join the 'Save the Polar Bears Club.'
W: Oh, **that's a great cause**. Good for you.
M: Thanks. Look at this membership form. There are five memberships available.
W: Right.
M: **I definitely can't afford** Lifetime Membership. It costs almost two hundred dollars.
W: I see they give T-shirts, hats and coffee mugs to certain members.
M: Hmm... if I wear the Save the Polar Bears Club T-shirt, that will let people know.
W: Yes, **you will be like a walking billboard**!
M: True. And I would like a hat too.
W: If I **donate some money for your membership**, would you give me the hat?
M: Sure.
W: But I don't think we need the coffee mug.
M: No, we don't. Then, the membership will cost less than $40.

여: 뭐 하고 있니, Max?
남: '북극곰 살리기 동호회'에 가입하려고 해.
여: 아, 좋은 목적이구나. 잘 해봐.
남: 고마워. 이 회원 종류 좀 봐. 가능한 회원 자격이 5개 있어.
여: 그러네.
남: 나는 평생회원에 가입할 여유가 전혀 없어. 거의 2백 달러나 들잖아.
여: 티셔츠와 모자, 그리고 커피 머그잔을 특정 회원들에게 주는구나.
남: 음… 내가 북극곰 살리기 동호회 티셔츠를 입으면 사람들에게 선전이 될 거야.
여: 응, 너는 걸어 다니는 광고판 같을 거야!
남: 맞아. 그리고 나는 모자도 가지고 싶어.
여: 내가 네 회원 자격을 얻는 데 돈을 좀 기부하면 그 모자를 나에게 주겠니?
남: 물론이지.
여: 하지만 커피 머그잔은 필요 없는 것 같아.
남: 맞아, 필요 없어. 그럼 회원권은 40달러 미만이겠네.

어휘 **lifetime** 평생의 / **cause** (자선 등의) 목적, 대의 / **billboard** 광고 게시판

11 짧은 대화에 이어질 응답 | ④

▶ 캠퍼스가 어떠냐고 물었으므로 소감을 밝히는 응답이 가장 적절하다.

① 저는 제가 외로울 거라고 생각했어요. ② 제 고향은 여기서 꽤 멀어요.
③ 구내식당 가는 길 좀 알려주세요. ④ 사진에서 봤던 것처럼 좋아요.
⑤ 제 형은 근처에 있는 학교를 졸업했어요.

W: You're a new student, right?
M: Yes, today is **my first day** at this school.
W: Well, I hope you like it here. **What do you think of the campus** so far?
M: ______________________________

여: 신입생이시죠, 맞죠?
남: 네, 오늘이 이 학교에서의 첫 날이에요.
여: 음, 여기가 마음에 드셨으면 좋겠네요. 지금까지 캠퍼스에 대해 어떻게 생각하세요?
남: ______________________________

12 짧은 대화에 이어질 응답 | ④

▶ 더 비싼 선물을 사자는 여자에게 남자가 선물의 가격이 중요한지 물었다. 따라서 질문에 대한 응답과 이유를 설명하는 말이 가장 적절하다.

① 난 항상 기프트 카드를 선호해.
② 점원에게 도와달라고 해 봐.
③ 난 돈을 그렇게 많이 쓰면 안 돼.
④ 아니, 하지만 뭔가 더 좋은 것을 주고 싶어.
⑤ 가격표를 먼저 확인해야지.

M: What do you think of this book as a present for Carol?
W: It's nice, but I think **we can afford to spend a bit more**.
M: Does the cost of the gift really matter?
W: ______________________________

남: Carol에게 줄 선물로 이 책 어때?
여: 좋지, 하지만 우리가 돈을 좀 더 쓸 여유가 될 것 같아.
남: 선물의 가격이 그렇게 중요하니?
여: ______________________________

어휘 **gift card** 기프트 카드 ((상품권의 기능과 신용카드의 편리함을 합친 선불카드))

13 긴 대화에 이어질 응답 | ⑤

▶ 판매원은 다이아몬드를 권하지만 남자는 가격이 비싸서 사지 않으려고 하고 있다.

① 고맙습니다! 당신은 정말 친절하시군요.
② 하지만 이 다이아몬드도 매우 좋군요.
③ 제 투자는 대부분 손해를 봤습니다.
④ 죄송합니다만, 저는 진짜 다이아몬드를 사야 합니다.
⑤ 네, 그렇지만 더 저렴한 제품을 찾아보고 싶습니다.

W: Welcome to the Jewelry Barn. What can I do for you today?
M: I'm trying to find a gift for my wife's birthday.
W: Oh, how romantic! What do you have in mind?
M: I was thinking about diamond earrings, but **I don't know how much they cost**.
W: Well, we have a small pair for $300.
M: Wow. **That's a lot more than I expected**.
W: We do have small diamond pendants that start at $150. We also have synthetic diamonds that look like the real thing **for even less than that**.
M: No, I couldn't get her a fake diamond. I would **feel guilty trying to trick her**. But $300 is too expensive.
W: **Think of it as an investment** in your future!
M: ______________________________

여: Jewelry Barn에 잘 오셨습니다. 오늘은 무엇을 도와드릴까요?
남: 아내의 생일 선물을 찾고 있습니다.
여: 아, 정말 로맨틱하시군요! 생각하고 계신 것이 있나요?
남: 저는 다이아몬드 귀걸이를 생각하고 있었는데요, 가격이 얼마인지를 몰라서요.
여: 음, 작은 제품으로는 300달러짜리가 있습니다.
남: 와, 제가 예상했던 것보다 훨씬 더 비싸군요.
여: 150달러부터 시작하는 작은 다이아몬드 펜던트도 있긴 합니다. 또한 그보다 훨씬 더 싸지만 진짜처럼 보이는 인조 다이아몬드도 있습니다.
남: 아닙니다, 아내에게 가짜 다이아몬드를 선물할 수는 없어요. 아내를 속이려고 하는 것 같아서 죄책감이 들 거예요. 하지만 300달러는 너무 비싸군요.
여: 미래를 위한 투자라고 생각하십시오!
남: ______________________________

어휘 **investment** 투자 / **genuine** 진짜의 / **look around for** ~을 찾기 위해 둘러보다 / **synthetic** 인조의, 합성의 / **fake** 가짜의; 모조품; ~을 위조하다 / **guilty** 죄책감이 드는; 유죄의

14 긴 대화에 이어질 응답 | ③

▶ 남자는 뮤지컬 오디션에 대해 문의하며 연기 경험과 노래실력이 있다고 했으므로, 여자는 오디션을 통해 남자를 테스트하려고 할 것이다.

① 어느 누구도 그 인물을 연기할 수 없을 거예요.
② 벽에 포스터를 붙이려면 허가를 받아야 합니다.
③ 좋아요, 토요일 오전 11시에 오디션이 있습니다.
④ 그 등장인물에 대해서 설명해 주시겠습니까?
⑤ 네, 사실입니다. 제 어머니는 꽤 유명한 가수였습니다.

[Phone rings.]
W: Roundhouse Theater Company.
M: Hello, may I speak to Jenna Paine, please?
W: Speaking.
M: Oh, **I'm calling about the poster** outside the community center.
W: For the musical?
M: Yes, **I'd like to audition for a part**.
W: OK, do you have any acting experience?
M: Yes, **I've been in quite a few plays**.
W: And singing?
M: Oh yes, I love singing. Actually, I won some prizes for my singing.
W: Lovely. Can I get your name, please?
M: It's Blake Lee.
W: OK. Now, do you know the musical at all?
M: *Jesus Christ Superstar*? Yes, **it's one of my favorites**.
W: ______________________________

[전화벨이 울린다.]
여: Roundhouse 극단입니다.
남: 여보세요, Jenna Paine 씨와 통화할 수 있을까요?
여: 전데요.
남: 아, 저는 시민 문화 회관 외부에 붙어있던 포스터를 보고 연락드렸습니다.
여: 뮤지컬 때문인가요?
남: 네, 배역 오디션을 보고 싶습니다.
여: 좋아요, 연기 경험이 있나요?
남: 네, 상당수의 연극에서 공연한 적이 있습니다.
여: 그리고 노래는요?
남: 아 네, 저는 노래 부르는 것을 좋아합니다. 실은, 노래로 상을 몇 번 탔습니다.
여: 좋아요, 성함이 어떻게 되시죠?
남: Blake Lee입니다.
여: 네, 자, 이 뮤지컬에 대해 조금이라도 아시나요?
남: 〈지저스 크라이스트 슈퍼스타〉요? 네, 가장 좋아하는 작품 중 하나입니다.
여: ______________________________

어휘 **permission** 허가 / **theater** 극단 / **quite a few** 상당수의 / **at all** ((의문문에서)) 조금이라도, 도대체

15 상황에 적절한 말 | ④

▶ 시험지를 보여 달라는 Sarah의 제안을 거절하는 답변을 찾는다.

① 너의 파티에 갈 수 있다면 무엇이든 할게!
② 글쎄, 그것은 위험해. 우린 조심해야 해.
③ 나는 이번에 좋은 성적을 얻도록 최선을 다해야 해.
④ 너를 도와주고 싶지만, 이건 아냐. 네가 부정행위를 하도록 도와주지 않을 거야.
⑤ 나도 이번 주말에 파티를 열 거야. 네가 와 주면 좋겠어.

M: Mary and Sarah sit next to each other in math class. Mary **has always gotten high grades** and Sarah has always gotten average grades. Mary sometimes lets Sarah see her homework **to check if her answers are correct**. On the day of the final exam, Sarah confronts Mary with an offer. She says that she is having a party on the weekend and will invite Mary if she will **let her copy off of her test**. Although Mary would like to go to the party, she knows that cheating is not right and **wants to turn down her offer**. In this situation, what would Mary most likely say to Sarah?

남: Mary와 Sarah는 수학 수업 시간에 서로 옆자리에 앉는다. Mary는 항상 높은 성적을 받고 Sarah는 항상 평균 정도의 성적을 받는다. Mary는 답이 맞는지 확인하도록 Sarah에게 때때로 자신의 숙제를 보여준다. 기말시험 날 Sarah는 Mary에게 제안을 한다. 그녀는 주말에 파티를 열 계획인데 Mary가 시험지를 베껴 쓰게 해 준다면 파티에 초대하겠다고 말한다. Mary는 그 파티에 가고 싶긴 하지만, 부정행위를 하는 것이 옳지 않다는 것을 알고 있기에 그 제안을 거절하고 싶어 한다. 이러한 상황에서 Mary가 Sarah에게 할 말로 가장 적절한 것은 무엇인가?

어휘 **cheat** 부정행위를 하다, 속임수를 쓰다 / **confront** (힘들거나 좋지 않은 것에) 직면하게 만들다; ~에 맞서다 / **turn down** ~을 거절하다

16~17 세트 문항 | 16. ④ 17. ①

▶ 16. 다양한 요가 스타일, 수련장의 환경 등 요가 수련장을 선택할 때 고려해야 할 사항에 대해 조언하고 있다.

① 요가 기술을 향상시키기 위해 필요한 요소들
② 초심자에게 적절한 요가 수련장 종류
③ 최근 수년간 개발된 요가의 다양한 스타일
④ 요가 수련장을 선택하기 전에 고려해야 할 것들
⑤ 요가 철학의 기본 원칙에 대한 개요

▶ 17. 해석 참조

① 온도 ② 수련장 크기 ③ 밝기 ④ 소음 ⑤ 청결함

W: As yoga has become popular over the years, you can now find yoga studios in most major cities. With a number of options available, it may be difficult to decide **which studio is best for you**. There are a few things to consider. First of all, it's a good idea to check out **what style of yoga** the studio offers. There are classes that focus more on the physical aspect of yoga and others that focus more on the spiritual. The latter might include meditation and yoga philosophy. Once you identify what appeals to you, you can choose a studio that has classes of that style. **The environment for yoga practice** is also important. Would you prefer **large classroom sizes or smaller spaces**? Some studios **keep their classroom lights dim** for calm practices and others have bright rooms for an active atmosphere. If you want to focus on the spiritual practice, look for ones **away from possible noises outside**. For some people, **the cleanliness of their facilities** is the most important factor. You can check out all of the information by simply visiting them.

여: 요가가 수년간 인기를 끌게 됨에 따라 이제 대부분의 주요 도시에서 요가 수련장을 찾아볼 수 있습니다. 가능한 선택 사항이 많기 때문에 어떤 수련장이 당신에게 가장 좋은지 결정하기가 어려울 수 있습니다. 고려해야 할 사항이 몇 가지 있습니다. 우선, 수련장이 어떤 스타일의 요가를 제공하는지 살펴보는 것은 좋은 생각입니다. 요가의 육체적 측면에 더 주력하는 수업과 정신적인 것에 더 초점을 맞추는 수업이 있습니다. 후자는 명상과 요가 철학을 포함할 수도 있습니다. 일단 어떤 것이 마음에 드는지 확인하면, 그 스타일의 수업이 있는 수련장을 선택할 수 있습니다. 요가 수련을 하는 환경도 중요합니다. ② 크기가 넓은 수련장이 더 좋은가요, 아니면 더 좁은 공간이 좋은가요? 어떤 수련장은 차분한 수련을 위해 방의 ③ 조명(밝기)을 어둡게 유지하고, 다른 수련장은 활동적인 분위기를 위해 방을 밝게 합니다. 정신 수련에 집중하고 싶다면 ④ 외부에서 들어올 수 있는 소음에서 벗어난 곳을 찾아보십시오. 몇몇 사람들에게는 시설의 ⑤ 청결함이 가장 중요한 요소입니다. 수련장을 방문하는 것만으로 모든 정보를 살펴볼 수 있습니다.

어휘 **studio** 연습실; (방송국의) 스튜디오 / **overview** 개요, 개관 / **fundamental** 기본 원칙; 핵심 / **cleanliness** 청결, 깨끗함/ **spiritual** 정신적인, 정신의; 종교의 / **latter** ((the ~)) (둘 중에서) 후자 / **identify** ~을 확인하다, 알아보다 / **appeal (to)** (~의) 마음에 들다, 관심을 끌다 / **dim** 어둑한, 흐릿한

실전모의고사 17

Answers & Explanation

01. ⑤ 02. ③ 03. ④ 04. ③ 05. ③ 06. ③ 07. ② 08. ② 09. ② 10. ④
11. ① 12. ① 13. ⑤ 14. ⑤ 15. ④ 16. ③ 17. ③

01 화자가 하는 말의 목적 | ⑤

▶ 회사를 떠나는 여자는 작별 인사를 하러 모인 동료들에게 감사의 인사를 하고 있다.

W: Thank you all for coming! In a company as big as ours, we see many people come and go, so **I'm very touched** that you all came to say farewell. You brought such wonderful gifts and food, thank you! Now, I understand that **on these occasions** we are expected to say something about our plans for retirement. But all of you know I'm joining the Red Cross **as a volunteer coordinator**. So, I'll just say this: I'll never forget these last six years. I may be closing one chapter of my life, but the next chapter will **contain plenty of fond memories**. Thanks to all of you.

여: 모두들 와 주셔서 감사합니다! 우리 회사같이 큰 회사에서는 사람들이 입사하고 퇴사하는 것을 많이 보게 되는데 작별 인사를 하기 위해 여러분 모두가 와 주신 것에 저는 매우 감동 받았습니다. 여러분이 주신 이런 멋진 선물과 음식, 감사합니다! 이제, 이런 자리에서는 은퇴 계획에 대해서 말하길 기대하시리라 생각합니다. 하지만 여러분 모두 아시다시피 저는 자원 봉사 책임자로 적십자에서 일하게 되었습니다. 그래서 이것만 말씀 드리겠습니다. 저는 지난 6년을 절대 잊지 않을 것입니다. 제 인생의 한 장은 끝날지도 모르지만, 그 다음 장은 행복한 추억들로 가득할 것입니다. 여러분 모두에게 감사드립니다.

어휘 **occasion** (특정한) 때, 경우; 특별한 행사 / **retirement** 은퇴 / **coordinator** 책임자; 조정자 / **fond memory** (떠올리면) 행복한 추억

02 대화 주제 | ③

▶ 남자가 밤새 운전하면서 깨어 있을 수 있었던 방법에 관해 여자에게 이야기하고 있다.

W: Chris, you're home! I didn't expect to see you until tomorrow.
M: Well, I wasn't tired, so I decided to **drive all night**.
W: But you usually stay at a hotel. **How were you able to stay awake**?
M: If I had gotten tired, I would have stopped for a nap, but I was able to stay awake by eating nuts and chewing gum.
W: I guess **the effort required to chew** might be enough to keep you awake.
M: It worked well, and I also listened to the radio and tried not to turn the heat up very high.
W: Those are good tips, but I hope you aren't **pushing yourself too hard**.
M: Don't worry. I know how dangerous it can be to drive while sleepy.

여: Chris, 너 집에 왔구나! 내일이 되어야 볼 수 있을 거라고 예상했는데.
남: 음, 피곤하지 않아서 밤새 운전하기로 결심했거든요.
여: 하지만 넌 보통 호텔에 묵잖니. 어떻게 깨어있을 수 있었어?
남: 피곤해졌다면 잠깐 자려고 멈췄을 테지만, 견과류를 먹고 껌을 씹으면서 깨어있을 수 있었어요.
여: (음식물을) 씹는 데 필요한 노력이 널 깨어있게 하기에 충분했던 것 같구나.
남: 그게 효과가 좋았고, 라디오도 듣고 온도를 너무 높게 하지 않으려고 노력했어요.
여: 좋은 비법들이긴 한데, 지나치게 애쓰고 있는 건 아니길 바란다.
남: 걱정하지 마세요. 졸릴 때 운전하는 게 얼마나 위험할 수 있는지 알고 있으니까요.

어휘 **push oneself** (무리하게) 애쓰다; 스스로 채찍질하다

03 관계 | ④

▶ 남편과 함께 외출을 하려는 여자는 남자에게 아이들을 어떻게 돌봐주어야 하는지를 설명하고 있다. 이를 통해 남자가 베이비시터임을 알 수 있다.

W: Now, John, you've got my cell phone number?
M: Yes, Ms. Bennett. And your husband's is on the kitchen counter?
W: Yes, **shall I give you the number** for the restaurant too?
M: Sure.
W: Um... **on second thought**, that won't be necessary.
M: Okay. Where are Tom and Nicky?
W: Their father is dressing them in their pajamas. *[ding dong]* Darling, hurry! We'll be late!
M: Are they going to bed already?
W: No! I told them they can watch a DVD, but they must go to bed **as soon as it's finished**.
M: Got it.
W: Help yourself to the cake and sandwiches **I left out for you**, won't you?
M: Thanks, Ms. Bennett. Have a good time!

여: 자, John, 내 휴대전화 번호 가지고 있지?
남: 네, Bennett 아주머니. 그리고 남편분 것은 부엌 조리대 위에 있죠?
여: 그래, 음식점 전화번호도 줄까?
남: 네.
여: 음… 다시 생각해보니, 그럴 필요는 없을 것 같구나.
남: 알겠어요. Tom과 Nicky는 어디에 있나요?
여: 애들 아빠가 잠옷을 입히고 있어. *[초인종 소리]* 여보, 서둘러요! 우리 늦겠어요!
남: 애들이 벌써 자려고 하나요?
여: 아니! 애들에게 DVD를 봐도 좋다고 말했단다. 하지만 그것이 끝나는 대로 애들은 바로 잠자리에 들어야 해.
남: 알겠어요.
여: 널 위해 남겨둔 케이크와 샌드위치를 맘껏 먹으렴, 응?
남: 고맙습니다, Bennett 아주머니. 즐거운 시간 보내세요!

04 그림 불일치 | ③

▶ 남자는 축구 트로피가 없어졌고, 별 모양 트로피는 바닥에 떨어져 있다고 했다.

[Phone rings.]
W: Grimeville Police Department. How may I help you?
M: I think someone **has broken into my house**!
W: Okay, sir. Please describe the scene to me first.
M: The first thing I noticed is that the window was open. I think that's how they came in.
W: Okay. What else?
M: They broke my vase. Oh, why would they do that?
W: **Can you tell if anything is missing**?
M: I had several trophies, and now my soccer trophy is gone and my star trophy is on the floor.
W: Okay. Did they take anything else?
M: I'm not sure. **Everything is a mess**. Oh, they broke my guitar, too.
W: Alright. Any detail can be helpful.
M: I guess they also **knocked over my lamp**. It's on the floor now.
W: Alright, sir. Please tell me your address.

[전화벨이 울린다.]
여: Grimeville 경찰서입니다. 무엇을 도와드릴까요?
남: 누군가 우리 집에 침입했던 것 같아요!
여: 네, 선생님. 먼저 현장을 설명해 주세요.
남: 처음 눈에 띈 것은 창문이 열려 있던 거예요. 그렇게 안으로 들어온 것 같아요.
여: 네, 또 다른 건요?
남: 꽃병을 깨뜨렸어요. 아, 왜 그랬을까요?
여: 무언가 없어진 것이 있는지 말씀해 주시겠어요?
남: 트로피가 몇 개 있었는데요, 지금 축구 트로피는 없어졌고 별 모양 트로피는 바닥에 있어요.
여: 그렇군요. 그 외에 다른 것을 가져갔나요?
남: 잘 모르겠어요. 모든 게 엉망이에요. 아, 제 기타도 망가뜨렸네요.
여: 알겠습니다. 어떤 세부 사항이라도 도움이 될 수 있습니다.
남: 전등도 넘어뜨렸나 봐요. 지금 바닥에 있어요.
여: 알겠습니다, 선생님. 주소를 말씀해 주세요.

어휘 **break into** ~에 침입하다 / **mess** (지저분하고) 엉망(진창)인 상태 / **knock over** ~을 넘어뜨리다, 치다

05 부탁한 일 | ③

▶ 여자는 음식물 쓰레기 버리는 것을 싫어하여 남자에게 대신 버려줄 것을 부탁하고 있다.

W: Honey! What are you doing at the moment?
M: **I'm almost done downloading the movie**. Do you want to watch it with me?
W: I'd love to, but I've got things to do.
M: Anything I can help you with? **Washing the dishes**?
W: Actually, the dishes are done. You know how much I **hate taking the food waste out**?
M: Yeah, that big food waste bucket downstairs really stinks.
W: So, could you do that for me? **I'll run to the shops** and buy some things for our dinner.
M: OK, see you soon. Anyway, where is the food waste?
W: In the yellow plastic bag near the back door.

여: 여보! 지금 뭐 해요?
남: 영화를 다운받는 게 거의 끝나가요. 같이 볼래요?
여: 그러고 싶지만 난 할 일이 있어요.
남: 내가 도울 일이라도 있어요? 설거지요?
여: 사실, 설거지는 끝났어요. 내가 음식물 쓰레기 버리러 가는 것을 정말 싫어한다는 것을 알고 있죠?
남: 네, 아래층에 있는 그 큰 음식물 쓰레기통은 정말 냄새가 지독하더군요.
여: 그러니, 당신이 나 대신 그걸 해 줄래요? 난 가게에 가서 저녁 찬거리를 좀 살게요.
남: 좋아요, 이따 봐요. 그런데 음식물 쓰레기는 어디에 있어요?
여: 뒷문 근처에 있는 노란색 비닐 봉투 안에요.

어휘 **stink** 악취를 풍기다

06 금액 | ③

▶ 왕복승차권 가격이 성인은 40달러, 어린이는 성인 요금의 반값인 20달러이므로 어른 2명, 아이 2명의 표를 따로따로 구매할 때 합계는 120달러이다. 그런데 30% 할인되는 가족 티켓을 구매하기로 했으므로 남자가 지불할 총 금액은 84달러가 된다.

M: Excuse me, **when is the next train** to Wally's Land?
W: The next train leaves in 20 minutes. There's one **every half an hour** until 2 in the afternoon during any national holiday.
M: Great. **How much is the fare for adults**?
W: It's $40 **for a return ticket**.
M: And for children?
W: Children's tickets are 50% off the adult price.
M: Well, I need tickets for two adults and two children.
W: May I suggest buying our Wally's Land Family Ticket? The family ticket is good for a family of four to travel to and from Wally's Land.
M: **Is it any cheaper than buying the tickets separately**?
W: Yes, it's 30% cheaper. It's our holiday gift to families.
M: Oh, that's great. I'll take one family pack, please.

남: 실례합니다. Wally's Land로 가는 다음 기차가 언제 있나요?
여: 다음 기차는 20분 후에 출발합니다. 공휴일 동안에는 오후 2시까지 30분마다 기차가 있습니다.
남: 잘됐네요. 성인 요금은 얼마인가요?
여: 왕복승차권이 40달러입니다.
남: 그리고 어린이는요?
여: 어린이용 승차권은 성인 가격에서 50% 할인됩니다.
남: 음, 어른 두 명과 어린이 두 명의 승차권이 필요합니다.
여: 저희 Wally's Land 가족 티켓을 구매하시는 것은 어떠세요? 가족 티켓은 4인 가족이 Wally's Land를 오가는 데 좋습니다.
남: 표를 따로따로 사는 것보다 더 저렴한가요?
여: 네, 30% 더 저렴합니다. 가족들에게 드리는 휴일 선물입니다.
남: 오, 잘됐네요. 가족 티켓 한 묶음 주세요.

어휘 **return ticket** 왕복표 (= round-trip ticket) / **separately** 따로따로, 개별적으로

07 이유 | ②

▶ 남자는 고양이를 한 마리 입양하기 위해 여자에게 동물 보호소에 함께 가 달라고 했다.

M: Helen, you have a cat, right?
W: Yes, I have had one for years. Why?
M: I've been kind of lonely these days and I want to get a cat, but **I don't know where to start**.
W: There are several ways to get a cat. You could buy one in a shop or get one from someone who wants to **give one away**. You could also adopt one from an animal shelter.
M: I think I'll **adopt one from a shelter**. It will feel good to take in an abandoned animal. Would you go there with me?
W: Of course. My friend works in a shelter and I'm sure he can help you.
M: Great. How about this Saturday?
W: Sounds good. Also, I can **give you some advice about caring for your cat**.
M: Thanks a lot.

남: Helen, 너 고양이 키우지, 맞지?
여: 응, 몇 년간 키우고 있어. 왜?
남: 요즘 좀 외로워서 고양이를 한 마리 키우고 싶은데, 어디서부터 시작해야 할지 모르겠어.
여: 고양이를 구하는 데는 여러 방법이 있어. 가게에서 사거나, 그냥 주길 원하는 누군가에게서 한 마리 분양받을 수도 있어. 또 동물 보호소에서 입양할 수도 있지.
남: 보호소에서 한 마리 입양할까 봐. 유기 동물을 거둬들이는 건 기분 좋을 거야. 거기 함께 가 줄래?
여: 물론이지. 내 친구가 보호소에서 일하는데 분명 널 도와줄 수 있을 거야.
남: 잘됐다. 이번 주 토요일 어때?
여: 좋아. 또, 고양이를 보살피는 데 조언도 해줄 수 있어.
남: 정말 고마워.

어휘 **shelter** 보호소, 쉼터 / **take in** ~을 거둬들이다 / **abandoned** 유기된, 버려진 / **care for** ~을 보살피다, 돌보다

08 언급하지 않은 것 | ②

▶ 해석 참조

W: Hi, Ted. **How was your trip** to Dubai?
M: It was good. I had a great time with my uncle.
W: That's great. Did you see much of the city?
M: Sure. On the second day, we went to see the Burj Khalifa. It's **currently the tallest skyscraper** in the world, at 829 meters.
W: I've heard about that. The project cost 1.5 billion dollars to complete.
M: It's truly an amazing structure. I heard the Dubai government decided to **construct it in order to gain international recognition**.
W: In that case, I would say it's worth the money.
M: I agree. Having such a tall building definitely impresses visitors.
W: Right! And I think **it took them a long time to complete the project**.
M: It sure did. Construction of the Burj Khalifa began in September of 2004, and **wasn't completed until** October of 2009.
W: I hope I get the chance to see it someday.

여: 안녕, Ted. 두바이 여행 어땠니?
남: 좋았어. 삼촌과 즐거운 시간을 보냈지.
여: 잘했네. 도시는 많이 둘러봤니?
남: 물론이야. 둘째 날에 우리는, Burj Khalifa를 보러 갔어. 829미터(① 높이)로, 현재 세계에서 가장 높은 마천루야.
여: 그것에 대해 들어본 적이 있어. 그 프로젝트는 완수하는 데 15억 달러(③ 건축 비용)가 들었지.
남: 정말이지 굉장한 건축물이야. 두바이 정부가 국제적인 명성을 얻기 위해 그 건물을 건설하기로 결정했다(④ 건설한 이유)고 들었어.
여: 그런 이유라면, 그만한 값어치가 있다고 말하고 싶어.
남: 동의해. 그렇게나 높은 빌딩이 있는 것은 분명 방문객들에게 깊은 인상을 줄 거야.
여: 맞아! 그리고 프로젝트를 끝마치는 데 시간이 오래 걸렸을 거 같은데.
남: 정말 그랬어. Burj Khalifa 건설은 2004년 9월에 시작(⑤ 준공 시기)했고, 2009년 10월이 되어서야 완공됐어.
여: 언젠가 그걸 볼 기회가 생기면 좋겠다.

어휘 **currently** 현재, 지금 / **skyscraper** 마천루, 초고층 건물 / **construct** 건설하다 *cf.* **construction** 건설, 공사; 구조

09 내용 불일치 | ②

▶ 전투용이 아니라 전쟁 중 화물을 운송하기 위해 만들어졌다.

M: Welcome to the Springfield Aviation Museum. Did you know that the plane with **the largest wingspan ever built** was nicknamed the Spruce Goose? It measured almost 100 meters from wing tip to wing tip, and weighed 200 tons. It needed **an unprecedented eight engines** to power it. This U.S. plane was designed **to carry a large cargo** during the war. It was made of wood because wood is **a less critical material** in wartime than metal. The plane was so difficult to build that it never really got used. It was flown one time only on November 2, 1947. Today, the Spruce Goose is **on exhibit for the public to see** in Long Beach, California.

남: Springfield 항공 박물관에 오신 것을 환영합니다. 지금까지 제작된 비행기 중 가장 큰 날개를 가진 비행기의 별명이 Spruce Goose라는 것을 알고 계셨습니까? 그 비행기는 날개 끝에서 끝까지 거의 100미터이며 무게는 200톤이었습니다. 비행기에 동력을 공급하기 위해서는 전례 없는 8개의 엔진이 필요했습니다. 이 미국 비행기는 전쟁 중 대량 화물을 운송하기 위해 고안되었습니다. 그 비행기는 목재로 만들어졌는데 목재가 전시에 금속보다 덜 중요한 물자이기 때문입니다. 그 비행기는 만들기가 매우 어려워서 실제로 이용된 적이 한 번도 없습니다. 그것은 1947년 11월 2일에 단 한 번 비행했습니다. 오늘날 Spruce Goose는 일반인들이 볼 수 있도록 캘리포니아의 롱비치에 전시되어 있습니다.

어휘 **aviation** 항공(술), 비행 / **wingspan** 날개 길이 / **spruce** 말쑥한, 단정한 / **unprecedented** 전례가 없는 / **power** 동력을 공급하다 / **cargo** 화물 / **wartime** 전시(戰時)

10 도표 이해 | ④

▶ 오후 8시 30분 이후에 시작하면서 자정 전에 끝나는 영화를 찾는다.

W: Let's go see a movie at the Astor Cinema tomorrow. **Look at this ad** with the screening times. *Citizen Kane* is showing at 4:10.
M: Great! Some critics say it's **the best movie of all time**. Oh, no! I forgot. I'm having dinner at my grandmother's tomorrow. I have to be there by 6. Sorry.
W: Oh, well. How about one of the earlier movies?
M: Umm, I don't like gangster movies. What about a fantasy movie?
W: That's a good one, but **I've already seen it**.
M: Really? Wait! I can leave Grandma's place at 8:30. How about one of the late movies?
W: Sure, but **it needs to be finished** before midnight. I have an early class the following day.
M: OK. Let's see this one. I'll have to hurry from Grandma's place to **make it on time**.

여: 내일 Astor Cinema에 영화 보러 가자. 여기 상영 시간이 적힌 광고를 봐. 〈시민 케인〉이 4시 10분에 상영되네.
남: 좋아! 어떤 평론가들은 그것이 역대 최고의 영화라고 말하던데. 아, 안 돼! 잊고 있었어. 내일 할머니 댁에서 저녁을 먹기로 했는데, 거기 6시까지 가야 해. 미안해.
여: 아, 그래. 더 일찍 상영하는 영화 중 한 편을 보는 것은 어때?
남: 음, 나는 갱스터 영화는 좋아하지 않아. 판타지 영화는 어때?
여: 그건 좋은 영화지만 난 이미 봤어.
남: 정말? 잠깐! 할머니 댁에서 8시 30분에는 나올 수 있어. 저녁 늦게 상영하는 영화 중 하나는 어때?
여: 좋아, 하지만 영화가 자정 전에는 끝나야 해. 다음 날 일찍 수업이 있거든.
남: 알겠어. 이걸 보자. 제시간에 오려면 할머니 댁에서부터 서둘러야 하겠어.

어휘 **gangster** 폭력배, 갱[범죄 조직]의 일원 / **critic** 평론가 / **of all time** 역대, 지금껏

11 짧은 대화에 이어질 응답 | ①

▶ 인턴십 일자리를 어떻게 구했는지 묻는 말에 남자가 할 수 있는 대답을 찾는다.

① 온라인으로 지원했어.
② 너 빨리 지원해야겠다.
③ 한 달 동안만 일했어.
④ 그건 매우 좋은 경험이었어.
⑤ 시간제 번역가로 일했어.

W: Nate, didn't you **have an internship** last summer?
M: I did. I worked in the mayor's office.
W: **How did you get the job**?
M: ______________________________

여: Nate, 너 지난여름에 인턴십 하지 않았니?
남: 했지. 시장실에서 일했어.
여: 그 일을 어떻게 구했니?
남: ______________________________

어휘 **apply (for)** (~에) 지원하다, 신청하다

12 짧은 대화에 이어질 응답 | ①

▶ 원형의 책상 배치가 마음에 들지 않는다는 여자에게 남자가 어떤 배치가 좋은지 물었다. 따라서 일렬로 앉는 게 좋다는 응답이 가장 적절하다.

① 난 차라리 일렬로 앉는 게 좋아.
② 책상들을 전부 청소할 필요가 있어.
③ 난 현대적 디자인의 새 책상을 원해.
④ 선생님께서 요즘 새로운 배치에 대해 생각하고 계셔.
⑤ 둥글게 앉는 것은 토론할 때 좋다고 생각해.

M: I really love going to Ms. Carpenter's class. Don't you?
W: She's a great teacher. But I hate **how our desks are in a circle**.
M: How would you prefer to **have them arranged**?
W: ______________________________

남: 나는 Carpenter 교수님의 수업에 들어가는 게 정말 좋아. 넌 그렇지 않니?
여: 교수님은 정말 좋은 선생님이시지. 하지만 난 책상이 원형으로 되어 있는 게 싫어.
남: 어떻게 배치되어 있는 게 더 좋은데?
여: ______________________________

어휘 **in a row** 일렬로, 한 줄로; 계속해서, 연이어 / **arrangement** 배치, 배열; ((주로 pl.)) 준비, 마련; 합의 ***cf.* arrange** ~을 배치하다, 정리하다; 마련하다 / **circular** 원형의; 순회하는

13 긴 대화에 이어질 응답 | ⑤

▶ 교수들의 동의서를 받아 오면 수강 정정이 가능하게 해준다는 제안을 한 여자에게 할 수 있는 응답을 골라야 한다.

① 제가 의사선생님의 진단서를 지금 당장 받아 오겠습니다.
② 교수님들은 저를 만나서 기쁘실 거예요.
③ 저는 어쨌든 이 강의에서 중도하차하고 싶지 않았어요.
④ 의사선생님의 진단서를 내일 가지고 오면 어떨까요?
⑤ 알겠습니다. 점심시간 이후에 오겠습니다. 정말 감사합니다!

W: What can I do for you today, Chris?
M: I'd like to drop out of my Calculus class and switch into Advanced Psychology.
W: Well, **the last day for dropping and adding classes** was yesterday.
M: I know, but I was very sick yesterday.
W: I'm sorry, but I don't think there is anything I can do for you.
M: **What if I bring in a note** from a doctor?
W: That won't be good enough. Yesterday was **the deadline for a reason**.
M: It's really important that **I switch classes**. I'm changing my major!
W: I'll tell you what, if **you bring me a note from both professors** today, then I'll change it for you.
M: ______________________________

여: 무슨 일인가요, Chris 군?
남: 미적분학 강의에서 중도하자하고 고등 심리학으로 바꾸고 싶습니다.
여: 음, 어제가 수강 정정 기간의 마지막 날이었는데요.
남: 알고 있습니다. 하지만 제가 어제 많이 아팠습니다.
여: 미안하지만 내가 해 줄 수 있는 것이 없는 것 같군요.
남: 의사선생님의 진단서를 받아오면 어떻게 됩니까?
여: 그것으로는 충분하지 않을 거예요. 어제가 마감일이었던 것에는 이유가 있습니다.
남: 강의를 바꾸는 것이 제겐 정말 중요해요. 저는 전공을 바꿀 예정이거든요!
여: 이렇게 하면 어떨까 하는데, 만일 학생이 오늘 양쪽 강의 교수님께 동의서를 받아 오면 내가 바꿔줄게요.
남: ______________________________

어휘 **drop out of** ~에서 중도하차하다 / **calculus** 미적분학 / **deadline** 마감 시간[일자] / **major** 전공

14 긴 대화에 이어질 응답 | ⑤

▶ 남자는 친구 어머니가 자신과 친구들을 태워주기로 한 약속을 지키지 못하게 되어 곤란한 상황이다. 어차피 응원차 경기를 관람하러 갈 예정이던 남자의 어머니의 반응을 유추하면 된다.

① Midlands는 여기서 너무 멀어.
② 셔틀 버스표는 왜 그렇게 비싸지?
③ 네가 제시간에 가지 못했다니 유감이구나.
④ 축구 팬은 너무 공격적인 경향이 있지.
⑤ 내가 기꺼이 너희 모두를 거기에 데려다 주마.

M: Hi, Mom. I'm home.
W: Hi, Luke. How was soccer training this evening?
M: OK. We play Midlands High School on Saturday. It's the finals.
W: I know. **I'm really excited for you**.
M: We're playing an away game though, and Midlands is **an hour away from here**.
W: Don't worry. You'll have lots of supporters there. And I'm coming to watch you!
M: You know **I was going to get a ride** there with Dan and Chris and their mom?
W: Uh-huh.
M: Well, she can't go now. She has to work on Saturday. And **there are no seats left** on the coach's shuttle bus!
W: ______________________________

남: 엄마, 저 왔어요.
여: 그래, Luke. 오늘 저녁 축구 연습은 어땠니?
남: 괜찮았어요. 토요일에 Midlands 고등학교와 시합을 해요. 결승전이에요.
여: 알고 있단다. 정말 기대되는구나.
남: 그런데 우린 원정 경기를 할 거고 Midlands는 여기서 한 시간 정도 걸려요.
여: 걱정하지 마. 많은 팬이 거기에 갈 거야. 그리고 나도 너를 보러 갈 거고!
남: 제가 Dan과 Chris 그리고 걔네 어머니랑 같이 차를 타고 거기 가려던 것을 아시죠?
여: 응.
남: 음, 걔네 어머니께서 못 가신대요. 토요일에 일을 하셔야 해서요. 그리고 코치님의 셔틀 버스에 남는 좌석이 없대요!
여: ______________________________

어휘 **supporter** (특정 스포츠 팀의) 팬, 서포터; 지지자, 옹호자 / **aggressive** 공격적인 / **finals** 결승전; 기말 시험 / **away** 원정 경기로, 상대팀 구장에서

15 상황에 적절한 말 | ④

▶ Angelina는 코트를 살 여유가 없고 그냥 한번 입어 보는 것이므로 이에 적당한 대답을 할 것이다.

① 벌써 45분이나 기다리고 있어요!
② 이 옷을 교환할 수 있을까요? 사이즈가 맞지 않아요.
③ 이 옷을 드라이 클리닝해 주세요.
④ 지금은 그냥 둘러보고 있어요, 고마워요.
⑤ 이 크림색 코트는 당신에게 정말 잘 어울려요.

W: Angelina and her friends are going to see a movie together. She goes to the subway station to meet her friends. She is 45 minutes early, so she **decides to kill some time** in the nearby department store. She only has enough money to pay for the movie and lunch. She goes up to the young fashion department. There's a 50% discount sale on winter coats, so she happily **tries some of them on**. She loves one cream-colored coat in particular, though she **can't afford it**. When she tries it on and **looks at herself in the mirror**, the sales assistant comes and asks, "How may I help you?" In this situation, what would Angelina most likely say to the sales assistant?

여: Angelina와 그녀의 친구들은 함께 영화를 보러 갈 것이다. 그녀는 친구들을 만나러 지하철역으로 간다. 그녀는 45분 일찍 도착했기 때문에 근처 백화점에서 시간을 보내기로 결정한다. 그녀는 영화를 보고 점심을 먹을 정도의 돈만 가지고 있다. 그녀는 영 패션 매장으로 올라간다. 겨울 코트가 50% 세일을 하고 있어서 즐겁게 몇 벌을 입어 본다. 크림색 코트가 특히 마음에 들지만, 그것을 살 여유는 없다. 그 옷을 입고 거울에 자신의 모습을 비춰보고 있을 때, 판매원이 다가와서 '도와드릴까요?'라고 물어본다. 이러한 상황에서 Angelina가 판매원에게 할 말로 가장 적절한 것은 무엇인가?

어휘 **browse** 훑어보다, 이것저것 구경하다 / **sales assistant** 판매원

16~17 세트 문항 | 16. ③ 17. ③

▶ 16. 자원봉사가 심리적, 신체적으로 자원봉사자에게 끼치는 긍정적인 영향을 설명하고 관심 분야에 따른 봉사활동을 제안하며 봉사할 것을 권하고 있다.

① 적절한 자원봉사 활동을 찾는 방법
② 사교 기술을 발전시키는 방법으로서의 자원봉사
③ 자원봉사의 심리적 신체적 건강의 이점
④ 경력 개발을 위한 기회로서의 자원봉사
⑤ 모든 개인의 흥미를 위한 다양한 자원봉사 활동

▶ 17. 해석 참조

① 동물 보호소 ② 병원 ③ 국립공원 ④ 어린이집 ⑤ 유치원

M: Volunteers make a big difference in the lives of others. Oftentimes, they work with the core **intention of helping others**. But did you know that volunteering can do more than that? Research has shown that volunteering **leads to lower rates of depression**. By enjoying time spent in service to others, you will feel a sense of meaning and appreciation, which can have a stress-reducing effect. Volunteer activities also get you moving and thinking at the same time. One study found that adults age 60 and over who volunteered received **benefits to physical and mental health**. According to another research study, in general, volunteers are physically healthier than are non-volunteers. Older volunteers experience greater increases in life satisfaction and greater positive changes in their health. In addition, **volunteering adds fun to your life**. If you enjoy caring for animals, you can walk dogs for an animal shelter. **If you're interested in nursing**, you could volunteer at a hospital or a nursing home. If you like children, you can volunteer to help at a daycare center or kindergarten. Now, how about experiencing some of those yourself? Go volunteer today!

남: 자원봉사자들은 다른 사람의 삶에 큰 변화를 일으킵니다. 종종 그들은 다른 이들을 돕는 데 핵심적인 의도를 갖고 일합니다. 그러나 자원봉사가 그보다 더 많은 것을 할 수 있다는 것을 알고 계셨나요? 연구는 자원봉사가 더 낮은 비율의 우울증을 야기한다고 밝혔습니다. 다른 사람에게 봉사하는 데 들인 시간을 즐김으로써 여러분은 의미와 감사의 감정을 느낄 것이고 이것은 스트레스를 줄이는 효과를 가질 수 있습니다. 자원봉사 활동은 또한 여러분이 동시에 움직이며 생각하게 합니다. 한 연구는 자원봉사를 한 60세 이상의 성인들이 신체와 정신 건강에 이익을 얻는다고 발견했습니다. 또 다른 연구 조사에 따르면, 일반적으로 자원봉사자들은 봉사하지 않은 사람들보다 신체적으로 더 건강합니다. 더 나이가 많은 봉사자들은 삶의 만족도가 더 크게 증가하는 것과 자신의 건강에서 더 큰 긍정적 변화가 생김을 경험합니다. 게다가 자원봉사는 여러분의 삶에 기쁨을 더합니다. 만약 여러분이 동물을 돌보는 것을 즐긴다면 ① 동물 보호소에서 강아지를 산책시킬 수 있습니다. 만약 여러분이 간호에 관심이 있다면 ② 병원이나 양로원에서 봉사할 수 있습니다. 만약 아이들을 좋아한다면 ④ 어린이집이나 ⑤ 유치원에서 돕기 위해 봉사할 수 있습니다. 이제 직접 그것들 중 일부를 경험해 보시는 건 어떨까요? 오늘 봉사하러 가세요!

어휘 **appropriate** 적절한 / **career** 경력; 직업 / **animal shelter** 동물 보호소 / **daycare center** 어린이집, 탁아소 / **kindergarten** 유치원 / **core** 핵심적인 / **depression** 우울증; 우울함 / **service** 봉사; 공헌; 근무 / **appreciation** 감사; 감상; 이해 / **satisfaction** 만족; 만족시키는 것 / **nursing** 간호; 보육 / **nursing home** 양로원

실전모의고사 18

Answers & Explanation

01. ① 02. ② 03. ② 04. ④ 05. ④ 06. ③ 07. ⑤ 08. ④ 09. ④ 10. ④
11. ③ 12. ① 13. ⑤ 14. ② 15. ③ 16. ② 17. ④

01 화자가 하는 말의 목적 | ①

▶ 작가의 순회 강연이 학교에서 열릴 것임을 말하고 있으므로 작가의 강연 소식을 알리는 것이 목적임을 알 수 있다.

M: May I have your attention, please? I'm your principal, Mr. Baker. If you like reading, I'm sure you've heard of Nathan Jenkins. He is **one of the most promising new writers** of the year and has attracted attention with his first book, *The Sound of Your Mind*. Also, he is **currently on a lecture tour** to meet and communicate with his audience. Fortunately, he's chosen to speak at our school. He will lecture about his teenage years and **how he became a writer**, next Friday in our school auditorium. After the lecture, there will be a question-and-answer session, where you may ask anything you like. I hope many students **will attend this unforgettable experience**.

남: 주목해 주시겠습니까? 저는 여러분의 교장인 Baker입니다. 여러분이 책 읽기를 좋아한다면, Nathan Jenkins라는 이름을 분명 들어본 적이 있을 것입니다. 그는 올해 가장 촉망받는 신예 작가 중 한 명이고 첫 번째 책인 〈당신 마음의 소리〉로 주목을 받고 있습니다. 또한, 그는 현재 독자들과 만나서 소통하고자 순회 강연을 하고 있습니다. 운 좋게도, 그가 우리 학교에서 연설하기로 했습니다. 그는 자신의 십 대 시절과 어떻게 작가가 되었는지에 관하여 다음 주 금요일에 학교 강당에서 강연할 것입니다. 강연 후에는 질의응답 시간이 있을 것이고, 거기에서 여러분이 원하는 건 무엇이든지 물어봐도 됩니다. 이 잊지 못할 경험에 많은 학생이 참석하기를 바랍니다.

어휘 **promising** 촉망되는, 유망한; 조짐이 좋은 / **currently** 현재, 지금 / **session** (특정한 활동을 위한) 시간[기간]; (의회 등의) 회기[회의]

02 의견 | ②

▶ 여자는 직장 선택 시 직장의 위치가 중요하다고 했다.

W: Jason, I heard **you've been offered two jobs**. Is that true?
M: It is. One is Yescom, a software company, and the other is ComHealer, an anti-virus software company.
W: **Which are you going to accept**?
M: Yescom. The salaries are similar, but for me, the work is more interesting at Yescom.
W: Isn't Yescom **located in another city**? You'll have to find a house, and rent is high these days.
M: I know. **I'll look for a roommate** who's joining the company at the same time. We can help each other.
W: I guess we're different. I'd choose ComHealer.
M: How come?
W: They are similar companies, so I think location is the most important factor.
M: What if Yescom offered a higher salary?
W: **I still couldn't live apart from my family and friends**.
M: I understand.

여: Jason, 네가 두 곳에서 일자리를 제의받았다고 들었어. 정말이니?
남: 맞아. 한 곳은 소프트웨어 회사인 Yescom이고, 다른 한 곳은 바이러스 퇴치 소프트웨어 회사인 ComHealer야.
여: 어떤 곳을 수락할 거야?
남: Yescom. 급여는 비슷하지만, 내게는 Yescom에서의 일이 더 흥미롭거든.
여: Yescom은 다른 도시에 있지 않니? 넌 집을 구해야 할 거고 요즘은 집세가 비싸잖아.
남: 나도 알아. 같은 시기에 입사하는 룸메이트를 찾을 거야. 우린 서로 도울 수 있어.
여: 우린 다른 것 같아. 나라면 ComHealer를 택하겠어.
남: 어째서?
여: 두 곳은 비슷한 회사니까 난 위치가 가장 중요한 요소라고 생각해.
남: Yescom이 더 높은 급여를 제안하면 어떻게 할 거야?
여: 난 그래도 가족과 친구들에게서 떨어져 살 수 없을 거야.
남: 그렇구나.

어휘 **anti-virus** 바이러스 퇴치용인

03 관계 | ②

▶ 남자는 여자의 티켓을 확인하고 여자는 목적지까지의 소요 시간과 음식 카트에 대해 묻는다. 이에 남자가 예상 소요 시간을 알려주고 다른 차량에 스낵바가 있다고 말하는 것으로 보아 기차 승무원과 승객 간의 대화이다.

M: Excuse me, ma'am. May I see your ticket, please?
W: Of course. I have it in my phone. Electronic tickets are **so much more convenient than** paper ones.
M: Aren't they? *[pause]* Alright. Thank you for your cooperation.
W: Oh, wait. **How much farther is it** to Busan?
M: We'll arrive in about two hours.
W: I see. Will the food cart be coming anytime soon? I'm a bit hungry.
M: No, but **there's a snack bar on board**. It is in the fourth car.
W: Oh, I didn't know that. I think I'll visit it now.
M: Is there **anything else I can do for you**?
W: I think everything's fine. Thank you.
M: Great. Enjoy the rest of your trip and **don't forget your luggage when you arrive**.

남: 실례합니다, 손님. 손님의 티켓을 볼 수 있을까요?
여: 물론이죠. 그건 제 휴대 전화에 있어요. 전자 티켓은 종이 티켓보다 훨씬 더 간편하죠.
남: 그렇죠? *[잠시 후]* 네. 협조해 주셔서 감사드립니다.
여: 아, 잠시만요. 부산까지 얼마나 더 가야 하죠?
남: 약 두 시간 후면 도착할 겁니다.
여: 그렇군요. 음식 카트가 곧 올까요? 배가 좀 고파서요.
남: 아니요, 하지만 기차 내에 스낵바가 있습니다. 네 번째 차량에 있어요.
여: 아, 그건 몰랐네요. 지금 그곳에 가봐야겠어요.
남: 제가 도와드릴 것이 더 있나요?
여: 전부 괜찮은 것 같네요. 감사합니다.
남: 좋습니다. 남은 여행 즐기시고 도착하시면 손님의 짐을 잊지 마시길 바랍니다.

어휘 **snack bar** 스낵바 ((샌드위치와 같은 간단한 식사 거리를 파는 곳)), 간이식당 / **on board** 기차 안에; 선상에; 승차[승선]한

04 그림 불일치 | ④

▶ 남자와 여자가 주문한 꽃은 민지가 학교에 오면서 찾아온다고 했다.

W: How long before class begins?
M: I'll check. *[pause]* Hey, where's the clock?
W: I put it above the left side of the blackboard so **we'd have room to decorate**.
M: Oh, I see. We still have plenty of time.
W: Well, everything looks nice, **including the row of balloons** on the blackboard.
M: Yes, that was a good idea.
W: **What do you think of** the heart-shaped frame with "Happy Teacher's Day!" written inside of it in the middle of the board?
M: You did a great job! And I'm sure the flowers we ordered will **look good on the teacher's desk**.
W: You reminded Min-ji **to pick them up on her way to school**, right?
M: Of course. I also put our teacher's rectangular desk in front of the blackboard for the party.
W: Great. I can't wait for the party.

여: 수업이 시작하려면 얼마나 남았지?
남: 내가 확인할게. *[잠시 후]* 저기, 시계가 어디 있어?
여: 우리가 장식할 공간이 있도록 칠판 왼쪽 위에 놓았어.
남: 아, 알겠어. 시간은 아직 충분해.
여: 음, 칠판 위에 일렬로 된 풍선을 포함해서 모든 게 좋아 보여.
남: 응, 그건 좋은 생각이었어.
여: 칠판 가운데 있는, 안에 '축 스승의 날!'이라고 쓰인 하트 모양의 액자는 어때?
남: 정말 잘했어! 그리고 우리가 주문한 꽃은 교탁 위에 두면 분명히 좋아 보일 거야.
여: 민지에게 학교에 오면서 꽃을 찾아오라고 다시 한번 알려줬지, 맞지?

남: 물론이지. 파티를 위해 직사각형 교탁도 칠판 앞에 놓았어.
여: 좋아. 파티가 정말 기다려진다.

어휘 **rectangular** 직사각형의; 직각의

05 추후 행동 | ④

▶ 남자는 호텔 결정에 관해 남편과 상의하고 싶어 하는 여자를 위해 호텔 웹사이트를 메일로 보내주겠다고 했다.

[Phone rings.]
M: Hello, Golden Travel Agency. How may I help you?
W: I'm planning a trip to Canada next month.
M: I see. **Is there any place in particular** that you wish to visit?
W: Yes. I want to visit Niagara Falls, and I'd like to stay nearby.
M: In that case, the Maple Leaf Hotel is the perfect place for you. It is offering 20 percent discounts **to celebrate its 20th anniversary**.
W: Oh, that sounds good. But I'd like to discuss it with my husband **before making a decision**.
M: Then, I'd be happy to send a free brochure to you by mail or give you the website of the hotel.
W: The website of the hotel would be helpful.
M: Great. Then **I'll send it to you by email**.
W: Thanks for your help.

[전화벨이 울린다.]
남: 여보세요. Golden 여행사입니다. 무엇을 도와드릴까요?
여: 제가 다음 달에 캐나다로 여행을 갈 계획인데요.
남: 그러시군요. 특별히 방문하고 싶은 곳이 있으신가요?
여: 네. 나이아가라 폭포를 보고 싶고, 그 근처에 머물고 싶어요.
남: 그렇다면, Maple Leaf 호텔이 고객님께 꼭 맞는 곳입니다. 이곳은 20주년 기념일을 맞아 20퍼센트 할인을 제공하고 있어요.
여: 아, 그거 좋네요. 하지만 결정을 내리기 전에 제 남편과 상의하고 싶어요.
남: 그러시다면, 고객님께 우편으로 무료 안내 책자를 보내드리거나 호텔의 웹사이트 주소를 알려드릴 수 있습니다.
여: 호텔 웹사이트가 유용하겠네요.
남: 좋습니다. 그럼 웹사이트를 메일로 보내드리겠습니다.
여: 도와주셔서 감사해요.

어휘 **brochure** (안내·광고용) 책자

06 금액 | ③

▶ 여자는 100달러보다 20퍼센트 저렴한 의자를 2개(80달러×2) 사기로 하였고, 여자의 집은 20킬로미터 이내이므로 10달러의 배송료가 더해져, 여자가 지불할 금액은 170달러이다.

M: Honey, look! These are exactly the same chairs we saw at the department store!
W: Oh, they are! You said they would **look good with our new table**.
M: Yes. They were 100 dollars each at the department store, but they're 20 percent cheaper here.
W: **What a deal**! How about buying them here?
M: That would be great. How many should we buy?
W: Well, I think four will be too many. How about two?
M: Two will be enough. Wait, the sign says **they charge a delivery fee**.
W: Really? How much is it?
M: It's 10 dollars within 20 kilometers from here and 20 dollars in other areas.
W: Our house is **pretty close to here**. It will be less than 5 kilometers.
M: Great. Let's buy them here.
W: Okay. I'll **pay for them with my credit card**.

남: 여보, 봐요! 이거 우리가 백화점에서 봤던 그 의자랑 정말 똑같아요!
여: 아, 그러네요! 우리 새 탁자랑 잘 어울릴 거라고 당신이 그랬지요.
남: 그래요. 백화점에서는 하나에 100달러였는데, 여기서는 20퍼센트 더 저렴하네요.
여: 싸네요! 여기서 사는 게 어떨까요?
남: 그게 좋겠어요. 몇 개를 사야 할지요?
여: 음, 네 개는 너무 많을 것 같아요. 두 개가 어때요?
남: 두 개면 충분할 거예요. 잠깐, 배송료를 청구한다는 표시가 있어요.
여: 정말요? 그건 얼마예요?
남: 여기에서 20킬로미터 이내는 10달러이고 그 밖의 지역은 20달러에요.
여: 우리 집은 여기서 꽤 가깝잖아요. 5킬로미터 미만일 거예요.
남: 좋아요. 여기서 사요.
여: 알겠어요. 내 신용카드로 계산할게요.

07 이유 | ⑤

▶ 남자는 과제를 끝마치기 위해 커피와 에너지 음료를 너무 많이 마셔서 잠이 오지 않는다고 했다.

W: Justin, are you still awake?
M: Yes, Mom. Why?
W: I'm worried about you. It's 2 a.m. **Haven't you finished studying** for tomorrow's math test?
M: Yes. Actually, the test was delayed until next week.
W: Then are you still memorizing your lines for the school play?
M: No, I already did that. **I'm just wide awake** and can't go to bed.
W: Hmm.... You aren't normally this energetic late at night.
M: Well, I guess I drank too much coffee and too many energy drinks.
W: Then **it's no wonder you can't sleep**! What were you thinking?
M: Well, I had some important assignments for class. **I had to get them done**.
W: I understand, but too much caffeine can cause **stomachaches as well as sleep disorders**.
M: I promise I'll be more careful in the future.

여: Justin, 아직 깨어있니?
남: 네, 엄마. 왜요?
여: 네가 걱정된단다. 새벽 두 시야. 내일 있을 수학 시험공부가 안 끝난 거니?
남: 네. 실은, 시험이 다음 주로 연기됐어요.
여: 그러면 학교 연극의 네 대사를 아직 외우고 있는 거니?
남: 아니요, 대사는 이미 외웠어요. 그냥 정신이 말짱해서 잘 수가 없어요.
여: 음…. 너 보통 밤늦게는 이렇게 활동적이지 않잖니.
남: 음, 아무래도 커피와 에너지 음료를 너무 많이 마신 것 같아요.
여: 그렇다면 잘 수 없는 것도 당연하지! 무슨 생각으로 그랬니?
남: 음, 수업에 몇 가지 중요한 과제가 있었어요. 그 과제들을 끝내야 했고요.
여: 이해하지만, 너무 많은 카페인은 수면 장애뿐만 아니라 복통도 일으킬 수 있단다.
남: 앞으로는 더 주의하겠다고 약속할게요.

어휘 **line** (연극·영화의) 대사 / **wide awake** 완전히 깨어 있는, 정신이 말똥말똥한 / **sleep disorder** 수면 장애

08 언급하지 않은 것 | ④

▶ 해석 참조

W: Hello. Are you looking for something?
M: Yes. I'd like to buy an electric fan before summer starts.
W: Let's see. First, **you need to decide on a size**. We have 35-, 40-, and 50- centimeter fans.
M: Forty centimeters sounds appropriate.
W: Good. Do you have a specific color in mind?
M: **What colors do you have**?
W: We have black, white, and blue right now.
M: Hmm.... **I'll think about it**. Also, I wonder about the difference between 3- blade and 4-blade fans.
W: More blades offer more cooling power.
M: Oh, I didn't know that. And **I'd like it to be energy efficient**.
W: Okay. The ones with this mark will save on power.
M: Sounds good. Thanks for your help.

여: 안녕하세요. 찾으시는 물건이 있으신가요?
남: 네. 여름이 시작하기 전에 선풍기를 사고 싶어요.
여: 봅시다. 우선, 크기를 결정하셔야 해요. 저희는 35, 40, 그리고 50센티미터 선풍기(① 크기)가 있습니다.
남: 40센티미터가 적당한 것 같네요.
여: 좋습니다. 특별히 생각해두신 색이 있으신가요?
남: 어떤 색이 있나요?
여: 지금은 검은색, 흰색, 그리고 파란색(② 색상)이 있습니다.
남: 음…. 생각해 볼게요. 또, 날이 세 개인 선풍기와 네 개인 선풍기(③ 날개의 날 수)의 차이점이 궁금해요.
여: 날이 많으면 냉각력이 더 좋죠.
남: 아, 그건 몰랐네요. 그리고 에너지 효율이 높으면 좋겠어요.
여: 네. 이 표시가 있는 것들이 전력을 절약(⑤ 절전 기능)할 거예요.

남: 좋네요. 도와주셔서 감사합니다.

어휘 **blade** (칼·도구 등의) 날; (엔진·헬리콥터 등의) 날개깃 / **save on** (식량·연료 등을) 절약하다

09 내용 불일치 | ④

▶ 자원봉사자의 약 25퍼센트가 정규직에 지원한다고 했으므로 ④가 일치하지 않는다.

W: If you are **interested in making a real difference**, consider volunteering for Helping Hands. Helping Hands is an NGO that does its work primarily in Africa. As a volunteer, you will have many jobs, but most of your time will be spent **building houses for the poor**. There is no need to worry about money, because Helping Hands pays for most of its volunteers' expenses. And it's such a rewarding experience that each year around 25 percent of its volunteers **apply to become regular workers**. Unlike some NGOs, Helping Hands welcomes university students. So, if you are thinking of **taking a year off to volunteer abroad**, Helping Hands is the ideal choice for you.

여: 진정한 변화를 만드는 것에 관심이 있으시다면, Helping Hands에서 자원봉사하는 것을 고려해 보십시오. Helping Hands는 주로 아프리카에서 활동하는 NGO입니다. 여러분은 자원봉사자로서 여러 일을 하겠지만, 대부분 시간을 빈민을 위한 집을 짓는 데 보낼 것입니다. 돈에 관해서는 걱정할 필요가 없는데, Helping Hands가 자원봉사자의 경비 대부분을 지불하기 때문입니다. 또한, 이는 대단히 보람 있는 경험이어서 매년 자원봉사자의 약 25퍼센트가 정규직이 되고자 지원합니다. 일부 NGO와는 다르게, Helping Hands는 대학생을 환영합니다. 그러니, 해외에서 자원봉사하기 위해 (대학교를) 일 년 휴학하는 것을 생각하고 계신다면, Helping Hands가 당신에게 가장 알맞은 선택입니다.

어휘 **primarily** 주로; 처음으로; 본래 / **rewarding** 보람 있는; 돈을 많이 버는

10 도표 이해 | ④

▶ 두 사람은 먼저 수요일(9월 4일)을 제외했고, Royal 극장에서 열리는 것 중에서 어린이용 영화가 아니며, 대화에 참여할 수 있는 것을 선택했다.

M: Mary, you remember we planned to visit an independent film festival this week, right?
W: Of course. I saved the schedule on my phone. Take a look.
M: Wow, there's a lot to see. **Which one are we going to**?
W: Actually, I've got an important meeting with a client on Wednesday.
M: No problem. We can choose another day. So, how about this one? I love science fiction.
W: I know you do, but the Big Culture Center is **too far from my house**.
M: That's true. Hmm.
W: Let's go on Thursday. It's at the Royal Theater.
M: I think those films are for kids. How about going on Friday?
W: I do like romantic movies, but I think **I'd rather be able to participate in** a conversation.
M: That would be fun. Okay, **then it's settled**.
W: Great.

남: Mary, 우리 이번 주에 독립 영화제 가기로 계획한 거 기억하지, 그렇지?
여: 물론이지. 내가 휴대전화로 일정표를 저장했어. 봐.
남: 와, 볼 것이 많네. 어느 것을 갈까?
여: 실은, 나 수요일에 고객과 중요한 회의가 있어.
남: 문제없어. 다른 날을 고르면 돼. 그럼 이건 어떨까? 난 공상과학이 정말 좋아.
여: 네가 좋아하는 거 알긴 하지만, Big Culture 센터는 우리 집에서 너무 멀어.
남: 맞아. 음.
여: 목요일에 가자. Royal 극장에서 열려.
남: 그 영화는 어린이용인 것 같아. 금요일에 가는 건 어떨까?
여: 난 로맨틱한 영화를 좋아하긴 하지만, 그보다 대화에 참여할 수 있으면 해.
남: 재미있겠다. 좋아, 그러면 결정됐네.
여: 잘됐다.

어휘 **independent** 독립된, 별개의; 자립적인

11 짧은 대화에 이어질 응답 | ③

▶ 여자는 몽골 음식점을 잘 아는 듯이 말하는 남자에게 그 음식점의 단골손님인 것 같다고 했다. 이에 가장 적절한 응답을 찾는다.

① 여기서 겨우 세 블록 떨어진 곳에 있어.
② 연극이 그곳에서 공연될 거야.
③ 그렇진 않지만 내 여동생이 그곳을 추천해줬어.
④ 아니, 나 몽골 음식은 좋아하지 않아.
⑤ 나는 작년에 두 번 그 극장에 갔어.

W: You know, **I think we have time for dinner** before the play.
M: Let's go to the Mongolian place beside the theater. It's the best in the city.
W: Wow, it sounds like **you are a regular customer**.
M: ______________________________

여: 있잖아, 연극이 시작하기 전에 저녁 식사할 시간이 있는 것 같아.
남: 극장 옆에 있는 몽골 음식점에 가자. 그곳은 시내에서 최고야.
여: 와, 너 단골손님인 것 같다.
남: ______________________________

어휘 **care for** ~을 좋아하다; ~을 보살피다 / **Mongolian** 몽골(인)의; 몽골 사람

12 짧은 대화에 이어질 응답 | ①

▶ 남자가 여자에게 입장료가 얼마인지 아느냐고 묻고 있으므로 확인하고 알려주겠다는 응답이 가장 적절하다.

① 내가 확인한 뒤에 알려줄게.
② 우리는 표를 미리 사야 할 거야.
③ 전시회는 (앞으로) 5주 더 계속될 거야.
④ 스무 점이 넘는 조각품이 전시될 거래.
⑤ 그녀의 조각품은 수천 달러의 가치가 있어.

M: Did you hear that the sculptures of Sarah Milburn are on display?
W: I didn't know **you like her artwork**. Why don't we go see it this weekend?
M: Sounds great! Do you know **how much the admission fee is**?
W: ______________________________

남: Sarah Milburn의 조각품이 전시 중이라는 얘기 들었니?
여: 네가 그녀의 작품을 좋아하는지 몰랐어. 이번 주말에 우리 그걸 보러 가면 어때?
남: 좋아! 입장료가 얼마인지 아니?
여: ______________________________

어휘 **on display** 전시[진열]된

13 긴 대화에 이어질 응답 | ⑤

▶ 녹화방송을 앞두고 긴장한 여자가 방송 도중에 해야 할 일을 잊을까 봐 걱정하고 있다. 이에 방송 관계자인 남자가 할 가장 적절한 응답을 고른다.

① 당신을 도울 수 있어서 정말 기뻐요.
② 전 당신이 다음번에는 더 잘할 수 있을 거라고 믿어요.
③ 음, 이미 지나간 일을 후회해도 소용없어요.
④ 생방송에 익숙해지려면 연습이 필요해요.
⑤ 제가 카메라 옆에 서 있다가 신호를 줄게요.

M: How are you feeling, Ms. Edwards?
W: A little nervous, but I'm **looking forward to hearing from the callers**.
M: I'm sure you'll do well, but I'll just check a few things before we begin, **starting with your microphone**.
W: Oh, alright. Can you hear me clearly?
M: Yes, it's working perfectly. Now, when we begin recording, please remember to face camera number two.
W: It's that one on the left, correct?
M: Right. When this red light comes on, **we are on air**.
W: There's a lot to remember. I'm starting to **get butterflies in my stomach**.
M: There's no need to be nervous. We're going to do a rehearsal first, so you'll have time to get comfortable.
W: **What if I forget what to do** when we're on air?
M: ______________________________

남: 기분이 어떠세요, Edwards 씨?
여: 조금 긴장되는데, 전화 건 분들의 이야기 들을 게 정말 기다려져요.
남: 분명 아주 잘하실 거지만, 시작하기 전에 몇 가지만 확인할게요. 마이크부터요.
여: 아, 알겠어요. 제 말 잘 들리나요?
남: 네, 아주 잘 작동하는군요. 자, 우리가 녹화를 시작하면 2번 카메라를 정면으로 봐야 하는 것을 기억하세요.
여: 왼쪽에 있는 거죠, 맞죠?
남: 맞아요. 이 빨간 불이 들어오면 방송 중인 거예요.

여: 기억할 게 많네요. 가슴이 두근거리기 시작해요.
남: 긴장하실 필요 없어요. 우선 리허설을 할 거니까, 편안해질 시간이 있을 거예요.
여: 방송 중에 제가 뭘 해야 할지 잊어버리면 어쩌죠?
남: ________________________

어휘 **cry over spilled milk** 이미 지나간 일을 후회하다 / **get butterflies in A's stomach** 가슴이 두근거리다, 안절부절못하다

14 긴 대화에 이어질 응답 | ②

▶ 여자는 노트북 컴퓨터에 갑자기 문제가 생겨서 남자에게 전화로 도와줄 수 있는지 물었고, 남자는 해결하는 방법이 복잡해서 직접 봐야 한다고 했으므로 자신이 있는 곳으로 와줄 수 있는지 묻는 게 가장 적절하다.

① 네 도움으로 자료를 복구했어.
② 그러면 우리 집으로 와줄 수 있니?
③ 컴퓨터 실습실로 가지 그러니?
④ 미안하지만 널 도와줄 수 없을 것 같아.
⑤ 어려울 것 같아. 네가 설명하는 것을 이해할 수 없어.

[Cell Phone rings.]
M: Hello?
W: Hi, Chris. It's Lindsey.
M: Oh. Hi, Lindsey. What's up?
W: Well, I know you're good with computers, so I'm hoping you can help me. **It's an emergency**.
M: I'll try. What's the problem?
W: I was working on an assignment on my laptop when, all of a sudden, **the screen went blank**.
M: Sounds serious. Were you able to reboot?
W: Yes, but now it won't connect to the Internet. **What's worse is that my assignment is gone**. It's due tomorrow! Can anything be done?
M: Sure. I know a few tricks for recovering lost data.
W: I was hoping you'd say that! So, what do I do?
M: Oh.... Well, **it's sort of complicated**. I think I'd have to see the laptop.
W: ________________________

[휴대전화벨이 울린다.]
남: 여보세요?
여: 안녕, Chris. 나 Lindsey야.
남: 아. 안녕, Lindsey. 웬일이야?
여: 음, 네가 컴퓨터를 잘한다고 알고 있는데, 나를 좀 도와줄 수 있으면 좋겠어. 급한 일이야.
남: 한번 해볼게. 문제가 뭐야?
여: 내 노트북 컴퓨터로 과제를 하고 있었는데, 그때 갑자기 화면이 꺼졌어.
남: 심각한 것 같네. 재부팅은 할 수 있었어?
여: 응, 그런데 이제 인터넷에 연결이 안 돼. 더 심각한 건 내 과제물이 날아갔다는 거야. 내일까지인데! 할 수 있는 게 있을까?
남: 물론이지. 손실된 자료를 복구하는 요령을 몇 가지 알아.
여: 네가 그렇게 말해주길 바랐어! 그러면 뭘 해야 해?
남: 아···. 음, 그게 좀 복잡해. 내가 그 노트북 컴퓨터를 봐야 할 것 같아.
여: ________________________

어휘 **go blank** (글씨·그림 등이) 갑자기 사라지다, 텅 비다 / **reboot** ((컴퓨터)) 재시동[리부트]하다 / **complicated** 복잡한 (= complex)

15 상황에 적절한 말 | ③

▶ Amanda는 밖에서 달리기하는 것에 관심을 보이는 Billy에게 자신과 함께할 의향이 있는지 물어볼 것이다.

① 네 건강에 관심이 없니?
② 밖에서 달리는 것이 헬스클럽에서 하는 것보다 더 좋아.
③ 나랑 밖에서 달리기를 해보는 게 어때?
④ 네가 하는 달리기 중 하나를 너와 함께 한다면 기쁠 거야.
⑤ 네 제안은 고맙지만, 요즘 초과근무를 하고 있어.

M: Amanda is on her way to a cafe to meet her friend Billy. When she arrives, Billy mentions that Amanda has seemed especially positive and energetic recently. Amanda tells him that **she's been running for an hour** every day after work. Billy looks interested and asks whether **it's different from running on a treadmill**. So, Amanda explains about **the benefits of exercising outdoors** in the fresh air and seeing a variety of scenery. While Amanda talks, she notices Billy becoming **increasingly interested and excited**. Since Amanda has been wanting a workout partner for some time, she decides to find out if Billy **is willing to join her**. In this situation, what would Amanda most likely say to Billy?

남: Amanda는 친구인 Billy를 만나러 카페에 가는 중이다. 그녀가 도착했을 때, Billy는 최근 Amanda가 유난히 긍정적이고 활기차 보인다고 말한다. Amanda는 그에게 퇴근 후 매일 한 시간씩 달리기를 하고 있다고 말한다. Billy는 관심이 있는 것처럼 보이고 그것이 러닝머신에서 뛰는 것과 다른지 묻는다. 그래서 Amanda는 상쾌한 공기가 있는 바깥에서 운동하는 것과 다양한 풍경을 보는 것의 이점에 관해 설명한다. Amanda는 이야기를 하면서 Billy가 점점 더 흥미로워하고 들뜨는 것을 알아차린다. Amanda는 한동안 운동 파트너를 바라왔기 때문에 Billy가 그녀와 함께할 의향이 있는지를 알아보기로 한다. 이러한 상황에서 Amanda가 Billy에게 할 말로 가장 적절한 것은 무엇인가?

어휘 **overtime** 초과근무, 잔업 / **treadmill** 러닝머신, 트레드밀 ((걷기나 달리기용 운동 기구)); 다람쥐 쳇바퀴 같은 일

16~17 세트 문항 | 16. ② 17. ④

▶ 16. 눈 운동, 숫자를 거꾸로 세기, 짧은 산책, 명상 등 집중력을 높이는 방법에 관해 이야기하고 있다.

① 우리가 운동해야 하는 이유
② 우리의 집중력을 증진하는 방법
③ 가벼운 운동이 어떻게 우리의 능률에 영향을 미치는가
④ 명상이 신체에 미치는 다양한 효과
⑤ 명상을 위한 가장 적절한 장소

▶ 17. 해석 참조

① 침실 ② 도서관 ③ 공원 ④ 휴게실 ⑤ 버스

W: How many times have you tried to focus on a task, **only to find that your mind is wandering**? Just like muscles, the mind needs training **in order to perform at its best**. So, I'd like to discuss some useful tips for when we're distracted. The next time you lose focus, **try a minute or two of eye exercises**. These are accomplished by closing your eyes and rolling your eyeballs clockwise and counterclockwise. Then try counting backwards from 100 by multiples of 2. And if that's not helping, take a short walk. Research has shown that walking helps **to increase our ability to pay attention**. Now, if you're truly serious about improving your mind, consider meditation. Start by meditating in your bedroom, or **somewhere equally private**, for a few minutes every day. After that, you can try meditating in other quiet places, such as libraries. Meditating in a park can also be a wonderful experience. When you have truly mastered your technique, you will even be able to meditate in noisy places, like buses. It's an amazing way **to focus your mind on** what is going on in the present.

여: 일에 집중하려 했다가, 결국 당신의 정신이 산만하다는 것을 알게 된 것이 몇 번이나 됩니까? 근육과 마찬가지로, 정신이 가장 잘 작동하려면 훈련이 필요합니다. 따라서 집중이 안 될 때를 위한 몇 가지 유용한 조언에 관해 이야기하고 싶습니다. 다음에 당신이 집중하지 못할 때, 눈 운동을 1분 혹은 2분가량 해보십시오. 이것은 눈을 감고 안구를 시계 방향과 반시계 방향으로 굴림으로써 완수할 수 있습니다. 그리고 나서 2의 배수를 100부터 거꾸로 세어보십시오. 그리고 그것이 도움이 되지 않는다면, 잠깐 산책을 하십시오. 연구에 따르면 산책이 우리의 주목하는 능력을 높이는 데 도움이 됩니다. 이제, 당신이 정신을 수양하는 것에 진정으로 진지하다면, 명상을 고려해보십시오. ① 침실 혹은 그와 같이 혼자 있을 수 있는 곳에서 날마다 몇 분 동안 명상을 하는 것으로 시작하십시오. 그다음에는, ② 도서관과 같은 조용한 다른 장소에서 명상하는 것을 시도할 수 있습니다. ③ 공원에서의 명상 또한 굉장한 경험이 될 수 있습니다. 당신이 기법을 진정으로 통달했을 때, ⑤ 버스 같은 시끄러운 장소에서도 명상할 수 있을 것입니다. 이것은 당신의 정신을 현재 일어나고 있는 것에 집중시키는 놀라운 방법입니다.

어휘 **efficiency** 능률, 효율(성) / **meditation** 명상, 묵상 / **eyeball** 안구, 눈알 / **clockwise** 시계(바늘) 방향으로 (↔ counterclockwise 반시계 방향으로) / **multiple** ((수학)) 배수; 많은, 다수의

Answers & Explanation

01. ④	02. ④	03. ⑤	04. ⑤	05. ⑤	06. ②	07. ④	08. ④	09. ④	10. ③
11. ①	12. ②	13. ⑤	14. ⑤	15. ④	16. ①	17. ④			

01 화자가 하는 말의 목적 | ④

▶ 수업이 끝날 때까지는 학교 축제 연습을 금지한다는 새로운 방침을 발표하고 있다.

W: Your attention, please. **This is the principal speaking**. Between classes and during lunchtime today, I noticed that different groups of students were practicing dances and songs. They were also practicing other material that **they will be performing during the school festival** next week. Everywhere in the school it was too noisy. And the teachers told me that when classes began, the students were not focusing on their lessons. As a result, **I am forbidding students to practice** for the festival until the school day has finished at 3:30. **Students caught breaking this new policy** will automatically be given an after-school detention for three days.

여: 여러분 주목해 주세요. 저는 교장입니다. 오늘 저는 수업 사이 쉬는 시간과 점심시간에 여러 무리의 학생들이 춤과 노래를 연습하는 것을 알게 되었습니다. 그 학생들은 다음 주 학교 축제 때 공연할 다른 것들도 연습하고 있더군요. 학교 여기저기가 너무 시끄럽습니다. 그리고 수업이 시작되어도 학생들이 수업에 집중하지 않는다고 선생님들이 말씀하십니다. 그래서 3시 30분에 수업이 끝날 때까지 학생들이 축제를 위해 연습하는 것을 금지하도록 하겠습니다. 이 새로운 방침을 어기다가 적발되는 학생들은 3일간 방과 후에 학교에 남는 벌칙을 자동적으로 받을 것입니다.

어휘 **material** (공연) 내용; 재료; 자료 / **forbid** ~을 금(지)하다 / **detention** 방과 후 학교에 남기; 구금

02 의견 | ④

▶ 남자는 새집을 지을 때 친환경 건축 재료를 사용할 것을 고려해야 한다고 했다.

M: I think we should use stone for the walls of our new house.
W: That might look really nice. Where did you get the idea?
M: I was watching a show about construction and they said that **stone is good for the environment**.
W: Is that because it's a natural material?
M: Yes, and it's very good at maintaining its temperature. Homes made of stone **stay cool throughout the summer**.
W: Okay, and how about using some bamboo for the floors?
M: I was going to suggest that, too. Bamboo grows more quickly than most trees, which means its use **has less of an impact on the environment**.
W: Great. What other materials could we include in our house?
M: We could consider using straw and earth as **other environmentally friendly ways** to save energy.
W: I'm interested in all of those options.

남: 난 우리 새집 벽에 돌을 사용해야 한다고 생각해요.
여: 정말 멋져 보일 수도 있겠네요. 어디서 그런 아이디어를 얻었어요?
남: 건축에 관한 TV 프로그램을 보고 있었는데, 거기서 돌이 환경에 좋다고 하더라고요.
여: 천연 재료라서요?
남: 네, 그리고 온도 유지에 아주 좋아요. 돌로 만든 집들은 여름 내내 시원하게 유지돼요.
여: 그렇군요. 그리고 바닥에는 대나무를 좀 사용하는 게 어때요?
남: 그것도 제안하려고 했어요. 대나무는 대부분의 나무보다 더 빨리 자라고, 그건 대나무를 사용하면 환경에 영향을 덜 미친다는 걸 의미하니까요.
여: 좋아요. 다른 어떤 재료를 우리 집에 포함할 수 있을까요?
남: 에너지를 절약하기 위한 다른 친환경적인 방법으로 짚과 흙을 사용하는 것을 고려해볼 수 있어요.
여: 그 방법들 전부 다 관심이 가네요.

어휘 **environmentally friendly** 환경친화적인

03 관계 | ⑤

▶ 남자의 건강 상태에 맞는 운동 프로그램을 만들고 식습관에 대해 조언을 해주려는 것으로 보아 여자는 헬스클럽의 트레이너임을 알 수 있다.

M: In university my waist was 30 inches, and **I wore tight-fitting pants**.
W: We all **put on weight as we age**.
M: I really want to be slim again.
W: I'll help you **lose weight and get into shape**.
M: Great. My doctor warned me to lose 10 kilograms or I'd develop health problems.
W: 10 kilograms?
M: Yes.
W: Exercising will help, but I can also give you some advice on your eating habits.
M: Great. Where should we start?
W: **I want to check your fitness level**. Let's go over to the stationary bikes.
M: Do you want to **check my heart rate**?
W: That's right. I want to design a program that's appropriate for your current fitness level.

남: 대학 다닐 때 제 허리는 30인치였고 딱 붙는 바지를 입었어요.
여: 나이가 들면서 모두 살이 찌기 마련이죠.
남: 정말 다시 날씬해지고 싶어요.
여: 제가 살을 빼고 몸매를 가꾸도록 도와 드리겠습니다.
남: 잘됐네요. 제가 10킬로그램을 빼지 않으면 건강에 문제가 생길 거라고 의사가 경고했거든요.
여: 10킬로그램요?
남: 네.
여: 운동이 도움이 되겠지만 식습관에 대해서 조언도 몇 가지 해 드릴 수 있습니다.
남: 좋아요. 어디서부터 시작해야 하나요?
여: 건강 상태를 검사하겠습니다. 고정 자전거 쪽으로 가시죠.
남: 제 심박수를 검사하고 싶으신가요?
여: 그렇습니다. 회원님의 현재 건강 상태에 적합한 프로그램을 만들고 싶습니다.

어휘 **fitting** (옷이) 꼭 맞는 / **put on weight** 체중이 늘다 / **develop** (병·문제가) 생기다 / **fitness** 건강, 체력 / **stationary** 고정된, 움직이지 않는

04 그림 불일치 | ⑤

▶ 남자가 평소와는 달리 왜 바퀴 없는 의자를 내놓았냐고 묻자 여자가 작가의 요청이라고 했으므로 그림에서 바퀴 있는 의자는 내용과 일치하지 않는다.

M: Sandra, have you finished the preparations for the Megan Kelly book signing event?
W: Yes, I'm all finished! **I did everything you asked for** and sent you a photo.
M: Hold on, let me check. Oh, you did a good job. You set a stage in front of a bookcase.
W: Yes, I hung up the banner that says the author's name, "Megan Kelly," above the bookcase.
M: Make sure you have the correct spelling of her name. It's **a good idea to display her books** on the bookshelves.
W: What do you think about the table decoration? I placed a flower vase on the left side of the table.
M: That's a great idea. Flowers **make the table more decorative**. By the way, what is the basket next to the flower vase for?
W: Oh, I put some bookmarks there. They're gifts for the participants.
M: Good. Well, we normally provide a movable chair with wheels for the author. **Why did you put out a chair without wheels** this time?
W: It's because the author asked. She said she wants a chair with no wheels.
M: You really thought of everything! Thanks for all your help.

남: Sandra, Megan Kelly의 책 사인회 행사를 위한 준비를 끝냈나요?
여: 네, 모두 끝냈어요! 요청하신 모든 것을 했고 사진을 보내드렸습니다.
남: 잠깐만요, 확인해볼게요. 아, 정말 잘했군요. 책장 앞에 무대를 세웠군요.
여: 네, 작가 이름인 'Megan Kelly'가 쓰인 현수막을 책장 위쪽에 매달았어요.
남: 반드시 그녀 이름의 철자가 정확하도록 하세요. 그녀의 책을 책 선반에 전시한 건 좋은 생각이에요.

여: 탁자 장식은 어떻게 생각하세요? 제가 탁자 왼쪽에 화병을 두었어요.
남: 좋은 생각이에요. 꽃 때문에 탁자가 더 예쁘게 보이네요. 그런데 화병 옆의 바구니는 무엇을 위한 것인가요?
여: 아, 거기 책갈피를 좀 두었어요. 그것들은 참가자들을 위한 선물이에요.
남: 좋아요. 음, 우리는 보통 작가를 위해서 바퀴가 달린 움직일 수 있는 의자를 제공하잖아요. 이번에는 왜 바퀴 없는 의자를 내놓았나요?
여: 그건 작가가 요청했기 때문이에요. 그녀는 바퀴가 없는 의자를 원한다고 말했어요.
남: 정말 모든 것을 다 생각했군요! 모든 도움에 감사해요.

어휘 **signing event** 사인회 / **bookcase** 책장 / **bookshelf** 책꽂이 / **decoration** 장식 ***cf.*** **decorative** 장식적인 / **bookmark** 책갈피 / **movable** 이동시킬수 있는

05 부탁한 일 | ⑤

▶ 남자는 휴대전화 충전기를 잃어버린 것 같다며, 다른 충전기를 하나 가져다 달라고 말했다.

[Phone rings.]
M: Hello.
W: Hi, honey. How are you doing this afternoon?
M: **It's pretty painful**.
W: Well, the doctor did say it'd be a few days before you could go home.
M: **The good news is I took a few steps** this morning.
W: Won't you need crutches for a few weeks?
M: Yes, I will.
W: I'll look for some this afternoon.
M: You don't need to. Dylan is going to lend me the crutches **he bought when he broke his leg skiing** last year.
W: OK. Do you want me to bring today's newspaper?
M: It's OK. **I've read someone else's copy**. I normally keep my phone charger in my bag, but now I can't find it.
W: You've lost it.
M: Maybe. Could you bring me another one?
W: Sure. I'll be right there.

[전화벨이 울린다.]
남: 여보세요.
여: 안녕, 여보. 오늘 오후는 어때요?
남: 정말 아파요.
여: 음, 의사 선생님께서 당신이 집으로 돌아올 수 있으려면 며칠 걸린다고 하셨죠.
남: 좋은 소식은 오늘 아침에 내가 몇 걸음 걸었다는 거예요.
여: 몇 주 정도는 목발이 필요하지 않을까요?
남: 네, 그럴 거예요.
여: 내가 오늘 오후에 목발을 좀 구해볼게요.
남: 그럴 필요 없어요. Dylan이 작년에 스키 타다가 다리가 부러졌을 때 샀던 목발을 빌려줄 거예요.
여: 알겠어요. 오늘 신문을 가져갈까요?
남: 괜찮아요. 다른 사람 것을 읽었어요. 보통 가방에 휴대전화 충전기를 가지고 다니는데, 지금은 그것을 못 찾겠어요.
여: 잃어버렸군요.
남: 아마도요. 다른 충전기를 가져다줄래요?
여: 물론이죠. 금방 갈게요.

어휘 **crutch** 목발 / **copy** (책·잡지 등의) 한 부(部), 한 권 / **charger** 충전기

06 금액 | ②

▶ 여자는 선글라스의 백화점 가격인 400달러보다 60% 저렴하게 구매하여 결과적으로 240달러를 절약하였으므로 선글라스 구매 가격은 160달러이다.

W: Blake, look at my new Gangster Shades sunglasses.
M: Gangster Shades sunglasses! **They must have cost a fortune**.
W: Well, AM Department Store sells them for $400.
M: $400! Did you pay all that money?
W: I didn't buy them at AM Department Store. I bought them at a second-hand shop that **specializes in selling** brand-name luxury items.
M: Shopping in second-hand shops. Wow! You're really changing.
W: Well, **someone else might have owned them before me**, but they still look brand new.
M: They do look good. And the price?
W: They were 60% less than the price the department store **sells them for**.
M: That means you saved more than $200. Good for you.

여: Blake, 새로 산 제 Gangster Shades 선글라스 좀 봐요.
남: Gangster Shades 선글라스요! 정말 비쌌겠네요.
여: 음, AM 백화점에서 이걸 400달러에 팔아요.
남: 400달러요! 그 돈을 다 주고 샀나요?
여: 전 AM 백화점에서 사지 않았어요. 유명 상표의 고급 제품들을 전문으로 파는 중고 가게에서 샀어요.
남: 중고 가게에서 쇼핑했다니. 와! 당신 정말 변하고 있군요.
여: 음, 전에 다른 사람이 소유했을지도 모르지만 선글라스는 아직 새것 같아요.
남: 정말 좋아 보이는군요. 가격은요?
여: 백화점에서 파는 가격보다 60% 더 저렴하더군요.
남: 그럼 200달러 넘게 절약했다는 뜻이네요. 잘됐어요.

어휘 **cost a fortune** 엄청나게 비싸다 ***cf.*** **fortune** 거금, 큰돈 / **second-hand** 중고의; 전해 들은 / **specialize in** ~을 전문적으로 하다 / **luxury** 고급품; 사치

07 이유 | ④

▶ 남자는 오랫동안 만나지 못한 친구와 함께 지내려고 인도에 가는 거라고 했다.

W: Ted, are you going to take any vacations this summer?
M: **As a matter of fact**, I'm planning to spend two weeks in India in August.
W: You're going to have such a good time. I went two years ago and the scenery and culture were both amazing!
M: Really? I never knew you went to India.
W: I did, and I visited so many great places. If you want, **I could recommend some**.
M: Thanks, but I'll be **staying with a friend** who lives there. I'm sure he'll be able to **show me around**.
W: That will be nice. You haven't seen each other for a long time?
M: Not since he got a job there three years ago. **That's actually why I'm going**.
W: Good for you. India is a wonderful place to visit, and very affordable, too.

여: Ted, 올여름에 휴가 갈 거니?
남: 실은, 8월에 인도에서 2주간 지낼 예정이야.
여: 정말 좋은 시간을 보내겠구나. 난 2년 전에 갔는데 풍경과 문화가 모두 굉장했어!
남: 정말? 네가 인도에 갔다 왔는지 전혀 몰랐어.
여: 갔었어. 그리고 멋진 장소들을 아주 많이 방문했지. 원한다면 몇 군데 추천해줄 수 있어.
남: 고맙지만 난 거기 살고 있는 친구와 함께 지낼 거야. 분명 그 애가 날 안내해줄 수 있을 거야.
여: 그거 좋겠다. 오랫동안 서로 만나지 못했니?
남: 그 애가 3년 전에 거기서 취직한 이후로 못 만났어. 사실 그 때문에 가는 거야.
여: 잘됐네. 인도는 방문하기에 정말 좋은 곳이고 (물가도) 아주 감당할 만해.

어휘 **show A around** A에게 (~을) 둘러보도록 안내하다 / **affordable** 감당할 수 있는, (가격이) 알맞은

08 언급하지 않은 것 | ④

▶ 해석 참조

W: Pamukkale is a natural wonder in southwestern Turkey. **The name literally means** "Cotton Castle," and when you see it, you will understand why. Pamukkale is a collection of seventeen hot springs on top of a small hill. Over time, the calcium from the surrounding rock **has dripped down the side of the hill** and hardened, forming small pools. These pools sit at various levels, each a few meters above or below its neighbor. When approached from below, Pamukkale does indeed **look like a castle**. In the past, Pamukkale was not officially protected, but now the area **is being restored to its natural beauty**. People are allowed to bathe in some of the pools but are not allowed to wear shoes as these may **damage the rocks**.

여: Pamukkale는 터키 남서부에 있는 경이로운 자연경관입니다. 그 이름은 말 그대로 '목화 성'이란 뜻(① 이름의 의미)이며, 그것을 본다면 그 이유를 이해할 것입니다. Pamukkale는 작은 언덕 위에 열일곱 개의 온천(② 온천의 개수)으로 이루어져 있습니다. 시간이 흐르면서, 주변 바위로부터 칼슘이 언덕 비탈로 흘러 내려오고 굳어져 작은 웅덩이들을 형성(③ 형성 과정)하였습니다. 이 웅덩이들은 옆에 있는 것보다 각각 몇 미터 위에 있거나 아래에 있어서, 여러 층으로 되어 있습니다. 아래쪽에서 다가가면, Pamukkale는 진짜 성처럼 보입니다. 과거에 Pamukkale는 공식적으로 보호받지 못했지만, 현재 그 지역은 자연의 아름다운 상태로 복원되는 중입니다. 일부 웅덩이에서 목욕하는 것은 허용되지만 바위를 훼손할 수도 있기 때

문에 신발을 신고 들어가는 것은 허용되지 않습니다(⑤ 구역 내 금지 행위).

어휘 **literally** 말[문자] 그대로 / **hot spring** 온천 / **drip** (액체가) 뚝뚝 흐르다[떨어지다] / **harden** 굳다, 딱딱해지다; ~을 굳히다, 딱딱하게 하다 / **level** (건물·땅의) 층; 수준, 규모 / **restore** ~을 복원[복구]하다

09 내용 불일치 | ④

▶ 최근 발표된 연구 결과는 기존의 연구 결과와 일치한다고 말했다.

M: Do you think arguing is good for your health? Maybe your first reaction is "No!" Well, a recent study revealed that **couples who argue strongly live longer**. The main finding is that partners who try not to argue die 5 to 10 years earlier than those who argue strongly. Not expressing your anger **leads to increased stress**, which can cause health problems. The researchers say **this study of husbands and wives is consistent** with other research which shows that expressing your feelings is good for you. It makes people feel like they are **in control of their lives**. People who don't express themselves can **feel helpless**.

남: 말다툼이 건강에 좋다고 생각하십니까? 아마 첫 반응은 '아니요!'일 것입니다. 글쎄요, 최근 발표된 연구에서는 심하게 말다툼하는 부부가 더 오래 산다고 합니다. 주요 연구 결과에 따르면 다투지 않으려고 노력하는 부부는 심하게 다투는 이들보다 5~10년 더 일찍 사망한다고 합니다. 분노를 표현하지 않으면 스트레스가 증가하고 이는 건강상의 문제를 유발할 수 있습니다. 연구자들은 부부에 대한 이번 연구가 감정을 표현하는 것이 자신에게 이롭다는 것을 보여주는 다른 연구의 결과와 일치한다고 말합니다. 그것은 사람들에게 자신의 삶을 통제하고 있다고 느끼게 해 줍니다. 자신을 표현하지 않는 사람들은 무력하다고 느낄 수 있습니다.

어휘 **reaction** 반응, 반작용 / **finding** 연구 결과, 발견 / **lead to** ~을 야기하다 / **be consistent with** ~와 일치하다 / **be in control of** ~을 통제[관리]하고 있다 / **helpless** 무력한, 어찌할 수 없는

10 도표 이해 | ③

▶ 가운 당 25달러 미만의 가격을 원하고 길이가 36인치 이상이며 섬유는 폴리/면 혼방을 선택했다. 마지막 2개의 선택지 중 가격이 2달러 더 비싸지만 무료 로고 자수가 포함된 실험실 가운을 구매하기로 결정했으므로 답은 ③이다.

M: Sophia, I'm looking at lab coats online. Could you help me choose?
W: Sure. First, what's the laboratory's budget for them?
M: We **need to stay under** $25 per coat.
W: I see. How about the length?
M: Long coats are **helpful in protecting against** accidental spills and drops, so I think the length should be more than 36 inches.
W: Okay. What do you want them to be made of? 100% cotton or polycotton?
M: What do you think about that?
W: I think polycotton coats are **easy to clean and dry**.
M: I agree. Now it looks like we have two choices left. It'd be better to **get the cheaper one out of these two**.
W: It'd saved money, but this one includes free logo embroidery and I think that's **worth more than** $2.
M: You're right. Let's go with this, then.

남: Sophia, 제가 온라인으로 실험실 가운을 보고 있거든요. 고르는 것을 도와줄 수 있어요?
여: 물론이죠. 먼저, 그것에 대한 실험실 예산은 얼마인가요?
남: 가운당 25달러 미만으로 유지해야 해요.
여: 알았어요. 길이는 어때요?
남: 긴 가운은 우발적인 액체 얼룩이나 방울로부터 보호하는 데 도움이 되니까, 길이는 36인치는 넘어야 한다고 생각해요.
여: 좋아요. 그것들이 뭐로 만들어져 있기를 원하나요? 면 100%인가요, 아니면 폴리코튼인가요?
남: 그것에 대해 어떻게 생각해요?
여: 전 폴리코튼 가운이 세탁하고 건조하기가 쉽다고 생각해요.
남: 동의해요. 이제 우리는 두 가지 선택지가 남은 것 같군요. 이 둘 중 가격이 더 싼 것을 사는 게 좋겠어요.
여: 그게 비용을 절감하겠지만, 이건 무료 로고 자수가 포함되어 있고, 전 그것이 2달러가 넘는 가치가 있다고 생각해요.
남: 당신 말이 맞아요. 그럼 이것으로 선택하죠.

어휘 **lab coat** 실험실 가운 / **fabric** 섬유 / **polycotton** 폴리코튼 ((면과 폴리에스테르를 섞어 짠 천)) / **embroidery** 자수 / **laboratory** 실험실 / **accidental** 우발적인, 우연한 / **spill** 얼룩, 엎지름

11 짧은 대화에 이어질 응답 | ①

▶ 지금 살고 있는 곳에 대해 부정적인 견해를 가지고 있는 여자가 할 수 있는 대답을 고른다.

① 응, 가능하다면 이사 가겠어. ② 아니, 여긴 너무 시끄러워.
③ 물론이지. 나도 근처로 이사 올 거야. ④ 응, 이웃 사람들이 착하고 친절해.
⑤ 아니, 난 버스 정류장까지 20분을 걸어야 했어!

M: I think I'm going to move into an apartment near here.
W: Really? **There isn't much transportation**, and the rent is really high.
M: So you don't like **living in this neighborhood**, do you?
W: ______________________________

남: 난 이 근처 아파트로 이사 올 생각이야.
여: 정말? 교통수단도 많지 않고 집세도 정말 비싼데.
남: 그럼 넌 이 근처에서 사는 게 좋지 않니, 그런 거야?
여: ______________________________

12 짧은 대화에 이어질 응답 | ②

▶ 보고서를 혼자 끝낼 테니 집에 들어가라는 남자의 말에 여자가 괜찮은지 물었다. 이에 적절한 응답을 찾는다.

① 신경이 쓰여요. 그러니 묻지 마세요. ② 정말로 전혀 문제없어요.
③ 우리는 내일 이것을 끝낼 수 있어요. ④ 우리는 다음번에 더 잘할 수 있어요.
⑤ 우리 잠시 쉽시다.

W: I'm so tired. It seems like we are never going to finish this report.
M: Actually, **we're almost done**. Just go home and I can finish it myself.
W: Are you sure **you don't mind**?
M: ______________________________

여: 전 정말 피곤해요. 우리 이 보고서를 절대 못 끝낼 것 같아요.
남: 사실, 거의 다 했어요. 그냥 집에 들어가세요. 제가 혼자 끝낼 수 있어요.
여: 정말 괜찮으세요?
남: ______________________________

어휘 **never you mind** ((구어)) (말해주지 않을 테니까) 묻지 마라

13 긴 대화에 이어질 응답 | ⑤

▶ 옷을 치우고 옷장을 닫으라는 여자(엄마)의 말에 남자는 옷장부터 먼저 닫고 있으므로 여자는 다시 한번 주의를 줄 것이다.

① 우리는 그렇게 친하지 않아. ② 게임을 거의 끝내가고 있어.
③ 찬장을 닫아 주어서 고맙구나. ④ 옷이 정말 잘 맞는 것 같구나.
⑤ Harry, 먼저 옷을 그 옷장에 넣도록 해라.

W: Harry, **you're so messy**! I can't understand why your coat is on the floor.
M: I just don't like cleaning up my room. It's not fun.
W: Well, you're old enough **to put away your own clothes**.
M: I'm sorry, Mom. **I'll try harder**.
W: I want you to pick up all your clothes right now and put them in the closet.
M: OK. In a minute, **I've almost finished this game**.
W: Turn the computer off! Right now!
M: OK, OK.
W: And why do you always **leave the closet open**?
M: I don't know.
W: Well, put your clothes away, and then close the closet. You always leave the kitchen cupboards open, too.
M: I guess it's just a bad habit. Look, I'm closing the closet now.
W: ______________________________

여: Harry, 너는 정말 지저분하구나! 왜 네 코트가 바닥에 있는지 모르겠다.
남: 방 청소를 좋아하지 않을 뿐이에요. 그건 재미가 없어요.
여: 글쎄, 네 옷을 직접 정리할 만한 나이잖니.
남: 죄송해요, 엄마. 더 노력할게요.
여: 지금 당장 옷을 모두 주워서 옷장에 넣도록 해라.
남: 알겠어요. 잠깐만요, 이 게임을 거의 끝내가요.
여: 컴퓨터를 꺼라! 당장!
남: 알겠어요, 알겠다고요.
여: 그리고 옷장은 왜 항상 열어 두는 거니?

남: 모르겠어요.
여: 그럼, 옷을 치우고 나서 옷장을 닫도록 해라. 너는 부엌 찬장도 항상 열어두더구나.
남: 그냥 나쁜 버릇인 것 같아요. 보세요. 지금 옷장을 닫고 있잖아요.
여: ______________________________

어휘 **cupboard** 찬장 / **messy** 지저분한, 어질러진 / **put away** ~을 치우다, 간수하다

14 긴 대화에 이어질 응답 | ⑤

▶ 남자가 본인이 추천한 이름 중 하나를 여자가 선택하도록 설득하기 위해 할 수 있는 대답을 찾아보면 된다.

① 그래, 그 이름들이 네게는 너무 현대적이야.
② 그래, 우리는 항상 Jacob의 애칭인 Jake라고 부른단다.
③ 동의해. 변화하는 유행을 따르는 것은 좋지 않은 생각이야.
④ 와, 네가 아기 이름으로 고른 것이 정말 마음에 드는구나.
⑤ 그 이름들은 다시 인기를 얻고 있어서 현대적으로 들린단다.

W: I need a name for my new baby.
M: I think you should call your baby Abraham.
W: But Abraham is **such an old-fashioned first name**.
M: Well, you won't have to use his full first name all the time. You could call him Abe.
W: Hmm... Abe. **That doesn't sound modern to me**.
M: But last year when your mother and I were choosing Jacob **as your nephew's name**, we looked at a list of popular baby names.
W: **Which names were high on the list**?
M: Well, for boys, names like Jacob, Matthew, Joshua and Abraham were high on the list. I like these names.
W: I'm really not sure. Those names seem too traditional.
M: ______________________________

여: 새로 태어난 제 아기에게 이름이 필요해요.
남: Abraham이라고 부르면 될 것 같구나.
여: 하지만 Abraham은 정말 구식 이름인걸요.
남: 글쎄, 항상 이름 전체를 다 부를 필요는 없을 거란다. Abe라고 부를 수도 있으니까.
여: 음… Abe라. 현대적으로 들리지 않는데요.
남: 하지만 작년에 네 엄마와 내가 네 조카의 이름을 Jacob으로 고르고 있었을 때 우린 인기 있는 아기 이름 목록을 봤어.
여: 어떤 이름들이 목록의 상위에 있었어요?
남: 음, 남자 아기에게는 Jacob, Matthew, Joshua 그리고 Abraham 같은 이름들이 목록 상위에 있었어. 나는 이 이름들이 좋더라.
여: 전 잘 모르겠어요. 그 이름들은 너무 전통적인 것 같아요.
남: ______________________________

어휘 **trend** 유행, 경향 / **old-fashioned** 구식의, 유행이 지난

15 상황에 적절한 말 | ④

▶ 가족의 생활비를 초과하는 물건을 사달라는 아들에게 어머니가 해 줄 수 있는 조언을 찾는다.

① 맞아. 모든 악의 근원은 돈이야.
② 항상 돈만 좇으면 안 된단다.
③ 걱정하지 마. 우리 가족은 돈이 엄청나게 많아.
④ 돈은 저절로 생기는 것이 아니라는 것을 알아야 해.
⑤ 신경 쓰지 마. 서투른 목수가 항상 연장 탓하지.

W: Whenever Ben gets his allowance, **he spends it immediately**. His mom wants to teach him to save some money, but she finds it really difficult to do so. Last week, Ben saw **a newly-released e-book reader**. He asked his mom to buy it. Even though it was quite expensive, Ben's mom **bought it**. She thought it might help him. Then a day later, Ben's bike was stolen. **Not only did he ask her to buy** a new bike, but also he asked her to buy one of the most expensive models. She was not happy. What Ben wanted **was exceeding the family budget**. In this situation, what would Ben's mom most likely say to Ben?

여: Ben은 용돈을 받을 때마다, 그 즉시 써버린다. 그의 어머니는 Ben에게 돈을 절약하도록 가르치고 싶어 하지만, 그렇게 하기가 상당히 힘들다는 것을 안다. 지난주 Ben은 새로 출시된 전자책 리더기를 봤다. 그는 어머니께 그것을 사달라고 했다. 그것은 매우 비쌌지만, Ben의 어머니는 그것을 사주었다. 어머니는 그것이 그에게 도움이 될지도 모른다고 생각했다. 그리고 그 다음날, Ben은 자전거를 도둑맞았다. 그는 어머니께 새 자전거를 사달라고 했을 뿐 아니라 가장 비싼 모델 중 하나를 사달라고 했다. 어머니는 언짢았다. Ben이 원하는 것은 가족의 생활비를 초과하는 것이었다. 이러한 상황에서 Ben의 어머니가 Ben에게 할 말로 가장 적절한 것은 무엇인가?

어휘 **root** 근원, 뿌리 / **have money to burn** 돈이 엄청나게 많다 / **allowance** 용돈 / **immediately** 즉시 / **release** ~을 발매하다, (영화 등을) 개봉하다 / **exceed** ~을 초과하다, 넘어서다

16~17 세트 문항 | 16. ① 17. ④

▶ 16. 가족 식사를 많이 하는 학생일 경우 학업 성취도가 더 뛰어나다는 것을 여러 예를 들어 설명하고 있다.

① 가족 저녁 식사의 교육적 이점
② 건강한 식습관의 중요성
③ 가족의 관계 향상법
④ 가족의 결속 시간으로서의 가족 식사
⑤ 가족 식사를 즐겁게 만드는 것의 중요성

▶ 17. 해석 참조

① 사회학 ② 과학 ③ 역사 ④ 수학 ⑤ 문학

M: When's the last time you sat down with your children together for dinner? During the day your children are learning about the world from many sources, often without parental filters or input. Perhaps the only opportunity of the day to talk with each other is at the dinner table. Family meals allow conversations to take place. **Not only do family meals benefit** the body, they benefit the mind too. A national poll of high school seniors showed that students who ate more often with their families **scored higher on** sociology and science than those that did less often. Another study reports that teens who have five to seven family dinners per week compared to **those who have fewer than** three received mostly As and Bs in school. In addition, researchers at the University of Illinois found that children ages 7 to 11 that spent a large amount of time eating meals with their families **did well in** school achievement tests of history and literature. Preschoolers that ate more often with their family did better in language skills than those who didn't as often; it is believed that these meal times give preschoolers more opportunity to hear and have conversations with their parents. Giving your kids **a way to advance in their education** is a great excuse for having more family meals together.

남: 여러분이 자녀와 저녁 식사를 함께 하려고 자리에 앉았던 마지막 때가 언제입니까? 낮에는 자녀들이 종종 부모의 여과기나 조언 없이 많은 공급원으로부터 세상에 관해 배우고 있습니다. 아마도 서로 이야기를 나누기 위한 하루의 유일한 기회는 저녁 식사 테이블에서 일 것입니다. 가족 식사는 대화가 생기게 합니다. 가족 식사는 신체에 이로울 뿐만 아니라 정신에도 이롭습니다. 고등학교 상급생들에 대한 전국 여론 조사는 가족들과 더 자주 먹는 학생들이 덜 자주 먹는 학생들보다 ① 사회학과 ② 과학에서 더 높은 점수를 내고 있음을 보여줍니다. 또 다른 연구는 일주일에 세 번보다 더 적게 가족식사를 하는 학생들과 비교해서 다섯 번에서 일곱 번의 가족 식사를 하는 십 대들이 학교에서 대부분 A와 B를 받는다고 보고합니다. 게다가 Illinois 대학의 연구자들은 가족들과 식사하는 데 많은 양의 시간을 쓰는 7세에서 11세 연령의 아동들이 ③ 역사와 ⑤ 문학의 학교 성취도 시험에서 잘하고 있다는 것을 발견했습니다. 가족들과 더 자주 식사하는 미취학 아동들은 자주 하지 못하는 아동들보다 언어 능력이 더 우수했는데, 미취학 아동들에게 부모들의 말을 듣고 부모들과 대화를 나눌 더 많은 기회를 주는 것이 이러한 식사 시간에서라고 여겨집니다. 여러분 자녀에게 교육적으로 향상할 방법을 주는 것이 함께 더 많은 가족 식사를 하는 것의 큰 이유입니다.

어휘 **benefit** 이점; 이롭다 / **sociology** 사회학 / **source** 공급원, 자료 / **parental** 부모의 / **filter** 여과기, 필터 / **input** 조언, 투입 / **take place** 일어나다, 열리다 / **poll** 여론조사 / **in addition** 게다가 / **achievement** 성취 / **preschooler** 미취학 아동 / **advance** 향상시키다 / **excuse** 이유, 핑계

Answers & Explanation

01. ② 02. ⑤ 03. ⑤ 04. ④ 05. ① 06. ③ 07. ④ 08. ① 09. ⑤ 10. ④
11. ④ 12. ⑤ 13. ⑤ 14. ② 15. ② 16. ③ 17. ③

01 화자가 하는 말의 목적 | ②

▶ 화자는 이민자 아이들이 자신의 문화를 접하지 못하는 현실을 언급하며 화자의 단체가 하는 일을 설명한 후, 어린이 동화를 다양한 언어로 번역하는 자원봉사에 지원하는 신청서를 작성하라고 했다.

M: Many families **leave their countries and settle in other countries**. And many children of immigrant families are growing up without knowledge of their family heritage and first language. They **deserve to have access** to the books of their culture, as well as the majority culture, regardless of where they live. That's why our organization translates children's stories into various languages. We depend upon a network of individuals who **volunteer their time to translate books**. If you want to help children, become a volunteer translator. You don't need to give up a great deal of your time to do it. Please sign up today! Fill out and **submit our online form to us**.

남: 많은 가정이 자신의 나라를 떠나서 다른 나라에 정착합니다. 그리고 이민자 가정의 많은 아이들이 자신의 가문의 유산과 모국어에 대한 지식 없이 자라고 있습니다. 그들은 어디에 사는지에 관계없이 주류 문화뿐만 아니라 그들 자신의 문화에 대한 책에도 접근할 자격이 있습니다. 그것이 바로 우리 단체가 어린이 동화들을 다양한 언어로 번역하는 이유입니다. 우리는 책을 번역하는 데 자신의 시간을 자발적으로 제공할 개인들로 구성된 조직에 의존하고 있습니다. 여러분이 아이들을 돕길 원한다면 자원봉사 번역가가 되십시오. 그것을 하는 데 여러분의 많은 시간을 포기해야 할 필요는 없습니다. 오늘 신청하세요! 저희의 온라인 신청서를 작성하셔서 저희에게 제출하세요.

어휘 **settle** 정착하다; 해결하다 / **immigrant** 이민자(의); 이주하는 / **heritage** 유산; 전통 / **first language** 모국어 / **deserve** ~할 자격[가치]이 있다, ~할 만하다 / **have access to** ~에 접근할 수 있다 / **translate** 번역[통역]하다 ***cf.*** **translator** 번역[통역]가

02 의견 | ⑤

▶ 여자는 각자 능률적으로 일할 수 있는 시간대가 다른 것은 개개인의 생체 리듬과 관련이 있다고 말하며, 일정을 계획할 때 이 생체 리듬을 고려해야 한다고 했다.

M: Jenny! Since we both have interviews soon, **why don't we prepare together**?
W: Great idea! Can we start tomorrow, around 8 a.m.?
M: Eight in the morning is too early. I can't wake up. How about in the evening, after class?
W: Maybe you should find someone else. I'm energetic in the mornings, but I can't concentrate later in the day.
M: **We are complete opposites**. I can't get anything done before noon.
W: **It has to do with our biological rhythms**, like Mr. Watson talked about in science class.
M: I remember. Our biological clocks determine when we are sleepy and alert.
W: Right. He said successful people **follow their biological clocks** and told us to think about this when planning our schedules.
M: You're right, and I see your point.
W: I think you can find someone else like you.
M: Okay, I will.

남: Jenny! 우리 둘 다 곧 면접이 있으니까 함께 준비하는 게 어때?
여: 좋은 생각이야! 내일 오전 여덟 시쯤에 시작할 수 있을까?
남: 아침 여덟 시는 너무 일러. 난 못 일어나. 수업 끝나고 저녁에는 어때?
여: 넌 다른 사람을 찾아야 할 것 같아. 난 아침에는 활동적이지만, 오후 늦게는 집중할 수 없거든.
남: 우리는 완전히 반대구나. 난 낮 열두 시 이전에는 아무것도 못 해.
여: Watson 선생님께서 과학 시간에 말씀하셨던 것처럼 이건 우리의 생체 리듬과 관련이 있어.
남: 기억나. 우리의 생체 시계는 우리가 언제 졸리고 기민한지를 결정하지.
여: 맞아. 선생님께서 말씀하시길 성공한 사람들은 자신의 생체 시계를 따른다고 하셨고 우리가 일정을 계획할 때 이것에 대해 생각해보라고 하셨어.
남: 네 말이 맞아. 그리고 네 요지를 알겠어.
여: 너와 같은 다른 사람을 찾을 수 있을 거라고 생각해.
남: 알았어. 그렇게 할게.

어휘 **biological** 생물학의; 생물체의 / **alert** 기민한, 정신이 초롱초롱한; 경계하는

03 관계 | ⑤

▶ 잉글랜드 팀으로 이적한 운동선수와 그를 취재하는 기자 간에 있을 수 있는 대화이다.

W: Can you tell our audience why you decided to play for the English team?
M: **I really wanted to be challenged** in many different ways.
W: In what ways are you now being challenged?
M: For one thing, the size of the league is much larger, so **it is much more competitive**.
W: What else is challenging?
M: There is also **the cultural aspect**. Living in England like an Englishman — it's not so easy for me as a Korean.
W: I imagine there are some differences. **What do you miss most** about Korea?
M: Umm... I think the thing I miss most is the food. You know I love spicy food.
W: Thank you for your time. That's all the time we have. See you tomorrow!

여: 왜 잉글랜드 팀에서 뛰기로 결정하셨는지 시청자 여러분께 말씀해 주시겠어요?
남: 저는 여러 다른 방식으로 정말 제 기량을 시험해보고 싶었어요.
여: 현재는 어떤 점에서 기량을 시험하고 계신지요?
남: 우선 한 가지는, 리그의 규모가 훨씬 더 커서 경쟁이 훨씬 더 치열하다는 겁니다.
여: 그 외에는 무엇이 도전적인가요?
남: 문화적인 면도 있어요. 잉글랜드에서 잉글랜드 사람처럼 사는 것은 한국인인 제게는 그렇게 쉽지 않아요.
여: 몇몇 문화적 차이가 있을 것으로 짐작되네요. 한국에 대해 가장 그리운 것은 무엇입니까?
남: 음… 가장 그리운 것은 음식이라는 생각이 드네요. 아시다시피 제가 매운 음식을 정말 좋아하거든요.
여: 시간을 내주셔서 감사합니다. 저희는 여기까지입니다. 내일 뵙겠습니다!

어휘 **challenge** ~의 기량[능력]을 시험하다; ~에 도전하다 ***cf.*** **challenging** 도전적인 / **league** (스포츠) 리그, 경기 연맹 / **competitive** 경쟁적인 / **aspect** (사물의) 면, 형세

04 그림 불일치 | ④

▶ 요가는 광고지에 나와 있지 않다고 했다.

[Phone rings.]
M: Kent's Gym. How may I help you?
W: Hi. **I received your flyer** that says "New Kent Gym Center" at the top, and I have a few questions.
M: Certainly. Right now, all new members are getting a 30% discount.
W: Yes, I can see that. What I'd really like to know about are your stationary bikes, **one of which is pictured** in your advertisement.
M: They are all brand new and available to use in our fitness center. A basic membership also includes screen golf as you can see.
W: I'm more interested in yoga classes, but they aren't shown in the flyer. **Do you offer any**?
M: Yoga classes were offered until last month, but they **have now been replaced with** screen golf. However, membership does include swimming classes, which are pictured on your flyer.
W: Okay. Thank you.

[전화벨이 울린다.]
남: Kent 체육관입니다. 무엇을 도와드릴까요?
여: 안녕하세요. 맨 위에 'Kent 체육 센터 새 단장'이라고 쓰여 있는 광고지를 받았는데, 몇 가지 질문이 있어서요.
남: 알겠습니다. 바로 지금 모든 신규 회원은 30% 할인을 받으십니다.
여: 네, 그건 알겠어요. 제가 정말 알고 싶은 것은 고정식 자전거에 대해서인데, 광고에 한 대가 사진으로 나와 있어요.
남: 그것들은 모두 완전히 새것이고, 저희 헬스클럽에서 사용하실 수 있습니다. 보시는 바와 같

이 기본 회원권에는 스크린 골프도 포함됩니다.
여: 저는 요가 수업에 관심이 더 있는데, 광고지에는 안 나와 있네요. 제공되는 것이 있나요?
남: 요가 수업은 지난달까지 제공되었습니다만, 지금은 스크린 골프로 대체되었습니다. 하지만 회원권에 수영 수업이 포함되어 있고, 이는 광고지에 사진으로 나와 있지요.
여: 알겠습니다. 고맙습니다.

어휘 **flyer** 전단, 광고지

05 추후 행동 | ①

▶ 내일 이사를 하는 상황에서 남자가 모든 짐은 이삿짐을 옮기는 사람들이 쌀 것이지만 컴퓨터는 너무 귀중하기 때문에 자신이 직접 챙기겠다고 말했다.

M: I'm glad the real estate agent was able to find a new place that was **cheaper but better than** this place.
W: Yeah. I'm so excited to be moving, too. But **we've got so much to do** tonight.
M: Oh, relax. The movers are coming tomorrow morning, and it's their job to **pack up everything**. Everything, that is, except my computer. I'll do it myself. It's too valuable.
W: Yeah. I'd rather pack my clothes myself, too.
M: Well, I'm going to check my email.
W: You can't! I canceled the cable and Internet service today. We can't use the Internet until we have Internet service available in our new house.
M: OK. Then what are you cooking for dinner? **I'm starving**.
W: Cooking? There is stuff everywhere. I cannot cook. We're having pizza tonight.
M: OK. **You call for delivery**.

남: 부동산 중개인이 이 집보다 더 저렴하면서 더 좋은 새집을 찾을 수 있었다니 기뻐요.
여: 네. 나도 이사하게 되어서 정말 신이 나요. 하지만 우리 오늘 밤에 할 일이 아주 많아요.
남: 오, 진정해요. 이삿짐을 옮기는 사람들은 내일 아침에 올 거고 짐을 다 싸는 것은 그들의 일이에요. 그러니까 내 컴퓨터를 제외한 모든 짐이요. 그건 내가 직접 할 거예요. 컴퓨터는 너무 귀중하니까요.
여: 네. 나도 내 옷을 직접 챙기는 게 좋겠어요.
남: 음, 나는 이메일을 확인할게요.
여: 그럴 수 없어요! 내가 오늘 유선 방송과 인터넷 서비스를 취소했거든요. 새집에서 인터넷 서비스가 이용 가능할 때까지 인터넷을 사용할 수 없어요.
남: 알겠어요. 그럼 저녁으로는 뭘 요리할 거예요? 나는 아주 배고파요.
여: 요리요? 물건들이 여기저기 있잖아요. 요리할 수 없어요. 오늘 밤에는 피자를 먹을 거예요.
남: 좋아요. 당신이 전화해서 배달시켜요.

어휘 **real estate agent** 부동산 중개인 / **starving** 배가 무척 고픈

06 금액 | ③

▶ 어른 입장료가 5달러이므로, 입장권 20장의 금액은 100달러가 된다. 그런데 20장을 묶음으로 구매하면 30% 할인된다고 했으므로, 30달러를 할인받아 남자가 지불할 금액은 70달러이다.

W: Welcome to Mt. Baekdu Sauna. Los Angeles' finest Korean-style sauna.
M: **How much is it for two adults**?
W: It's $5 for adults, and to enter the family sauna area it's $2 extra.
M: We won't be going to the family sauna. Oh, I see you sell books of tickets.
W: Yes, for $40 you get a book of 10 tickets. You can get a 20% discount **compared to buying tickets individually**.
M: We've just moved here. Maybe I should **get a book of tickets**. We'll probably be coming here every weekend.
W: In that case, you can also buy 20 tickets. And the discount is 30%.
M: Sounds good. I'll take the book of 20 tickets. **Here's my credit card**.
W: Thank you. Just a second.

여: 백두산 사우나에 오신 것을 환영합니다. 로스앤젤레스에서 가장 좋은 한국식 사우나입니다.
남: 어른 두 명에 얼마인가요?
여: 어른은 5달러이고 가족 사우나 구역에 들어가시려면 2달러가 추가됩니다.
남: 우리는 가족 사우나에 가지 않을 거예요. 아, 회수권을 판매하시네요.
여: 네, 40달러에 10장 묶음을 구매하실 수 있습니다. 표를 낱개로 구매하시는 것에 비해 20% 할인받으실 수 있습니다.
남: 우린 여기로 막 이사 왔어요. 어쩌면 회수권을 사야 할 것 같네요. 아마 주말마다 여기 올 것 같거든요.
여: 그렇다면 20장을 구매하실 수도 있습니다. 그러면 30% 할인됩니다.
남: 좋은데요. 20장 묶음으로 할게요. 신용카드 여기 있어요.
여: 감사합니다. 잠시만 기다려주세요.

어휘 **a book of tickets** 회수권 ***cf.*** **book** (차표 등의) 묶음 철(綴) / **individually** 개별적으로; 개인으로

07 이유 | ④

▶ 여자는 함께 영화를 보려던 친구가 길이 막혀 영화 시작 부분을 놓치는 바람에 대신 미술관에 갔다고 했다.

W: Good morning, Robert. Did you have a good weekend?
M: Yeah, I took my son to a baseball game. How about you? Did you see that movie you were talking about?
W: No. I planned to go with my friend, but **it didn't work out**.
M: Why? Were the tickets sold out?
W: Well, my friend's house is on the other side of town, so she decided to meet me at the theater. But she **got stuck in traffic**.
M: So you missed the opening?
W: Right. We didn't want to start in the middle, so we **ended up going to an art museum** instead.
M: I guess there is always next weekend.
W: Actually, I'm going by myself tonight. **I don't mind watching it alone**.

여: 안녕하세요, Robert. 주말 잘 보냈어요?
남: 네, 아들을 야구 경기에 데려갔어요. 당신은요? 얘기했던 그 영화 봤나요?
여: 아니요. 친구와 함께 가려고 계획했는데 잘 안됐어요.
남: 왜요? 표가 매진됐나요?
여: 음, 친구 집이 시내 반대편에 있어서 영화관에서 만나기로 했어요. 그런데 친구가 교통 체증으로 꼼짝도 못했어요.
남: 그래서 시작 부분을 놓쳤나요?
여: 네. (영화) 중간에서 시작하고 싶지 않아서 대신 미술관에 가게 됐어요.
남: 다음 주말은 항상 있을 테니까요.
여: 실은, 오늘 밤에 혼자 가려고요. 혼자 봐도 괜찮거든요.

어휘 **work out** (일이) 잘 풀리다, 좋게 진행되다 / **get stuck** 꼼짝 못하게 되다 / **end up v-ing** 결국 v하게 되다

08 언급하지 않은 것 | ①

▶ 해석 참조

[Phone rings.]
W: National Museum. How may I help you?
M: Hi, I'd like to bring my class to visit your museum. **How much is admission**?
W: Admission is free, but there is an extra $5 charge for certain exhibits.
M: All right. I have 23 students. Should I **make a reservation**?
W: Reservations are only required for groups larger than 30.
M: Okay. And you're open from 9 a.m. to 6 p.m. every day, right?
W: Yes, except for Wednesdays and Saturdays, when we close at 9 p.m.
M: Oh, **I almost forgot to ask** about your children's museum.
W: We have a special exhibit on traditional Korean instruments as well as musical performances **until the end of the month**.
M: Great. Thanks so much.

[전화벨이 울린다.]
여: 국립박물관입니다. 무엇을 도와드릴까요?
남: 안녕하세요. 저희 반 학생들을 데리고 박물관을 방문하려고 하는데요. 입장료가 얼마인가요?
여: 입장료는 무료이지만, 일부 전시에 대해서는 5달러의 요금이 별도(② 입장료)로 있습니다.
남: 알겠습니다. 학생이 23명인데요. 예약해야 하나요?
여: 예약은 30명이 넘는 단체에만 필요(③ 예약 필요 여부)합니다.
남: 그렇군요. 그리고 매일 오전 9시부터 오후 6시까지 문을 열죠(④ 관람 가능 시간). 맞죠?
여: 네, 수요일과 토요일은 제외하는데, 그때는 오후 9시에 폐관합니다(④ 관람 가능 시간).
남: 아, 어린이 박물관에 대해 물어보는 것을 잊을 뻔했네요.
여: 이달 말까지 음악 공연뿐만 아니라 한국 전통악기에 관한 특별 전시(⑤ 특별 전시 내용)도 있습니다.
남: 잘됐네요. 정말 감사합니다.

어휘 **be required for** ~을 위해 요구되다

09 내용 불일치 | ⑤

▶ 무료 공부 모임은 조회에서 등록만 하고, 금요일 특별모임은 조회에 참석하지 않는 학생들을 위한 것이다.

W: Attention everyone. Tomorrow at 8:15 a.m., all students **are required to attend an assembly** in the gymnasium. We will be presenting information about the upcoming placement tests in October. These tests will **determine what classes you will be taking** next year. There will also be representatives from several test prep companies and study guide publishers here. They are going to give you information regarding their services and products. We will also **be signing students up for** free study sessions at the school. **Anyone not in attendance tomorrow** will be required to attend a special session on Friday after school.

여: 모두들 주목해 주십시오. 학생들은 내일 오전 8시 15분에 체육관에서 있을 조회에 모두 참석하기 바랍니다. 저희는 10월에 곧 있을 배치 고사에 대한 정보를 제공할 것입니다. 이번 시험으로 여러분이 내년에 어떤 수업을 듣게 될지 결정될 것입니다. 여러 시험 대비 학습지 회사와 학습 지침서 출판사의 관계자분들께서도 여기 참석하실 것입니다. 그분들은 서비스와 제품에 관한 정보를 제공하실 것입니다. 저희는 또한 학교에서 있을 무료 공부 모임에 학생들을 등록시킬 것입니다. 내일 참석하지 않는 학생들은 금요일 방과 후 특별 모임에 참석해야 할 것입니다.

어휘 **assembly** 조회, 모임, 집합 / **gymnasium** 체육관 / **upcoming** 곧 있을, 다가오는 / **placement test** 배치 고사 / **representative** 대리인, 대표자 / **test prep** 시험 준비 / **publisher** 출판업자

10 도표 이해 | ④

▶ 컴퓨터와 프린터를 합한 가격이 천 달러를 넘지 않으며 최신 그래픽카드를 탑재하고 있고 RAM의 용량이 크며 프린터를 공짜로 주는 컴퓨터를 선택할 것이다.

M: I can't wait to start college next year!
W: That's why we're getting you a computer today.
M: **What a sale**! I'm sure we'll find something here. Look at this leaflet.
W: Look, they have one for only $299.
M: But, Mom, the M-550 is a dinosaur! It **has none of the features I want**.
W: Well, you have to decide what is most important. We aren't going to spend more than $1,000 on a computer and printer.
M: **Since I'm studying design**, I will need the top graphics card.
W: I don't know much about computers, but graphics cards use a lot of RAM, right?
M: Yeah, so I don't think the D-425 will have enough. Now **there is only one choice left**.
W: It looks like you're getting a new computer after all.
M: And don't forget the free printer!

남: 내년에 대학교에 가는 게 정말 기대돼요!
여: 그래서 오늘 네게 컴퓨터를 사 주려는 거야.
남: 굉장한 세일이에요! 여기서 좋은 것을 찾을 거라고 확신해요. 이 전단지를 보세요.
여: 봐, 겨우 299달러 하는 물건도 있어.
남: 하지만 엄마, M-550은 무용지물이에요! 제가 원하는 특성이 하나도 없어요.
여: 음, 무엇이 가장 중요한지 결정해야 해. 우린 컴퓨터와 프린터에 천 달러 넘게는 쓰지 않을 거야.
남: 제가 디자인을 공부하고 있으니까 최신 그래픽카드가 필요할 거예요.
여: 난 컴퓨터에 대해서는 잘 모르지만 그래픽카드는 RAM을 많이 사용하지, 맞지?
남: 네, 그래서 D-425는 충분하지 않을 것 같아요. 이제 선택할 남은 것은 한 가지밖에 없네요.
여: 결국 새 컴퓨터를 갖게 되는 것 같구나.
남: 그리고 공짜 프린터도 잊지 마세요!

어휘 **leaflet** 전단, 광고용지 / **dinosaur** 무용지물, 덩치만 크고 쓸모없는 것; 공룡

11 짧은 대화에 이어질 응답 | ④

▶ 어떤 음식이 먹고 싶은지 묻는 말에 가장 적절한 응답을 찾는다.

① 난 하루에 두 끼만 먹어.
② 네가 먹을 음식을 직접 가져와도 돼.
③ 나는 토요일은 안 돼.
④ 파스타와 샐러드를 가장 좋아해.
⑤ 채식주의자가 되는 게 더 좋은 것 같아.

M: **I'm having a barbecue** on Saturday. Want to come?
W: Well, I don't eat meat, so I think I'll pass.
M: I'll have other things too. **What do you like to eat**?
W: ______________________________

남: 토요일에 바비큐를 할 건데, 올래?
여: 음, 나는 고기를 안 먹으니까 안 갈 것 같아.
남: 다른 것들도 있을 거야. 어떤 게 먹고 싶니?
여: ______________________________

어휘 **vegetarian** 채식주의자

12 짧은 대화에 이어질 응답 | ⑤

▶ 여자는 여름 방학 동안 일했다는 남자에게 돈을 좀 모았는지 묻고 있다.

① 아니, 여행하는 데 돈이 너무 많이 들었어.
② 여기에서는 취업 기회가 아주 부족해.
③ 학기 중에는 공부에 집중할 거야.
④ 근무 환경 때문에 그 일을 선택했어.
⑤ 응, 하지만 새 컴퓨터를 사는 데 다 썼어.

W: Kevin, it's good to see you again. Did you go anywhere during the summer?
M: No, **I stayed here** and worked during the vacation.
W: Good for you. Did you **manage to save any money**?
M: ______________________________

여: Kevin, 다시 만나서 반가워. 여름에 어딘가 갔니?
남: 아니, 방학 동안 여기 있으면서 일했어.
여: 잘했네. 돈은 그럭저럭 모았니?
남: ______________________________

어휘 **scarce** 부족한, 드문

13 긴 대화에 이어질 응답 | ⑤

▶ 규정과 다르게 반납 기한이 지난 책들은 다음에 가져오고, 책을 추가로 대출하고자 하는 남자의 말에 대한 적절한 여자의 대답을 유추해 본다.

① 도서관 카드로 대출하실 수 있습니다.
② 그냥 그 책들을 배낭에 넣으세요. 나중에 지불하셔도 됩니다.
③ 책들을 다운받으려면 인터넷을 이용하셔야 합니다.
④ 대여가 안 되는 책들은 복사하시면 안 됩니다.
⑤ 아니요, 가능하지 않습니다. 당신만 예외로 해드릴 수는 없어요.

M: I'd like to check out these four books, please.
W: I'll need your student ID, please.
M: Here you go.
W: Oh, I'm sorry. It looks like you already **have five books checked out**, and three are overdue.
M: Are you saying I can't check these books out?
W: I'm afraid not. At least until you return the overdue books and **pay your fine**.
M: But I have a paper due tomorrow and I need all of the books.
W: **Those are the rules**. I can't make the computer do anything else.
M: What if I pay my fine now and **bring the books back later**?
W: ______________________________

남: 이 책 네 권을 대출하고 싶습니다.
여: 학생증을 주십시오.
남: 여기 있습니다.
여: 아, 죄송합니다. 이미 다섯 권을 대출하신 것 같군요. 그리고 세 권은 반납 기한이 지났습니다.
남: 이 책들을 대출할 수 없다는 말씀입니까?
여: 그렇습니다. 기한이 넘은 책을 반납하시고 벌금을 내실 때까지는 적어도 그렇습니다.
남: 하지만 저는 내일까지 제출할 보고서가 있어서 이 책들이 모두 필요합니다.
여: 이것은 규정입니다. 컴퓨터상으로 다른 어떤 일도 해드릴 수가 없어요.
남: 지금 벌금을 내고 나중에 그 책들을 반납하면 어떨까요?
여: ______________________________

어휘 **photocopy** ~을 복사하다 / **overdue** 기한이 넘은 ***cf.*** **due** ~하기로 되어 있는, 예정된 / **fine** 벌금

14 긴 대화에 이어질 응답 | ②

▶ 자신이 탑승한 비행기가 다른 비행기보다 늦게 이륙한다고 불평하는 승객에 대한 적절한 대답을 찾는다.

① 날씨가 맑으면 비행이 쉽습니다.
② 비행기는 예정된 순서대로 이륙합니다.
③ 손님의 항공편 사정을 바로 확인하겠습니다.
④ 조종사는 방향을 제대로 잡으려고 최선을 다하고 있습니다.
⑤ 손님께서 원하신다면 버스표를 새로 준비해 드리겠습니다.

W: Excuse me, can you tell me why the plane hasn't taken off yet?
M: **There is a delay** because of the heavy rains.
W: We have been sitting **on the runway** for an hour.
M: Yes, ma'am. I just spoke to the pilot and he said it may be another 30 minutes.
W: That is ridiculous! It isn't even raining anymore.
M: It isn't raining at the airport, but **the storm has moved east**, which is the direction we need to fly.
W: Can't we go over or around the storm?
M: We can do that as soon as **it is our turn to take off**.
W: I don't think **it's fair** that we should wait for others to take off before us.
M: ______________________________

여: 실례합니다. 비행기가 왜 아직 이륙하지 않는지 알려주시겠어요?
남: 폭우 때문에 지연되고 있습니다.
여: 우린 활주로에 한 시간 동안 앉아 있잖아요.
남: 네, 손님. 제가 조종사와 방금 얘기를 나눴는데 30분 더 기다려야 할지도 모른다더군요.
여: 말도 안 돼요! 이젠 더 이상 비도 내리지 않는데요.
남: 공항에는 비가 내리지 않지만 폭풍이 비행 방향인 동쪽으로 이동하고 있습니다.
여: 폭풍 위로 가거나 그 주위를 돌아서 갈 수는 없나요?
남: 저희가 이륙할 순서가 되면 곧 그렇게 할 수 있습니다.
여: 다른 비행기들이 우리보다 먼저 이륙하는 것을 기다려야 하는 것은 공평한 것 같지 않아요.
남: ______________________________

어휘 **fair** (날씨가) 맑은; 공평한, 공정한 / **status** 사정, 상태 / **delay** 지연 / **runway** 활주로 / **ridiculous** 말도 안 되는, 터무니없는

15 상황에 적절한 말 | ②

▶ Michelle은 직장 상사로서 Jody에게 주의를 주려고 하고 있다.

① 너의 절친한 친구로서 항상 너를 감싸 줄게.
② 너의 상관으로서 말하는데, 제시간에 오도록 해.
③ 우리가 친구인 게 너에게는 행운이야. 고마워해야 할걸.
④ 네가 이번 주에 일을 하지 않으면 고객 서비스는 어려움을 겪을 거야.
⑤ 다음에 늦으면 네 상관에게 알릴 거야.

M: Michelle is Jody's supervisor at the coffee shop they work at, but she is also his friend. Jody **has been late for work** every day for two weeks. At first he made excuses to Michelle and **it was excused**, but for the last few days, he didn't say anything, not even "I'm sorry." Michelle **has been able to cover for** Jody when he is late and, therefore, there haven't been any big problems with customers. However, she feels that as his supervisor she must say something. She thinks that Jody is abusing their friendship and **is being disrespectful** of Michelle's position at work. In this situation, what would Michelle most likely say to Jody?

남: Michelle은 같이 일하는 커피숍에서 Jody의 상관이지만 또한 친구이기도 하다. Jody는 지난 두 주간 매일 지각했다. 처음에 그는 Michelle에게 변명했고 용서를 받았지만, 지난 며칠간 그는 "미안해."라는 말조차도 하지 않았다. Michelle은 Jody가 늦을 때 그를 대신해 일을 할 수 있었고 이 때문에 손님들과 큰 문제가 없었다. 그러나 상관으로서 (Jody에게) 뭔가 말을 해야 한다고 느낀다. 그녀는 Jody가 친구 관계를 악용하고 있고 직장에서 Michelle의 지위를 존중하지 않고 있다고 생각한다. 이러한 상황에서 Michelle이 Jody에게 할 말로 가장 적절한 것은 무엇인가?

어휘 **cover for** ~을 보호하다, ~을 대신해 일하다 / **supervisor** 감독자 / **make an excuse** 변명하다 ***cf.*** **excuse** ~을 용서하다, 너그러이 봐주다; 변명 / **abuse** ~을 악용하다[남용하다] / **disrespectful** ~을 존중하지 않는, 무례한

16~17 세트 문항 | 16. ③ 17. ③

▶ 16. 체육관에 갈 필요 없이 칼로리를 소모하는 몇 가지 일상적인 방법을 논의하겠다는 말 뒤에 일상생활에서 할 수 있는 여러 가지 운동과 그 효과에 대해 차례대로 소개하고 있다.

① 건강한 생활방식을 결정하는 방법
② 집을 청소하는 가장 효율적인 방법
③ 운동의 역할을 하는 일상적인 활동
④ 운동하기 위해 체육관에 가는 것을 피하는 이유
⑤ 쇼핑을 하며 칼로리를 소모하는 방법

▶ 17. 해석 참조

① 진공 청소 ② 설거지 ③ 요리 ④ 걸레질 ⑤ 다림질

W: Good morning, everyone. Recently, we've talked a lot about **the benefits of regular workouts**. Today, we'll discuss a few everyday ways to burn calories that don't require going to the gym. For example, as many as 250 calories can be burned when shopping for groceries. Simple decisions like taking the stairs instead of an elevator can also **have a big impact on** your health. House chores are another opportunity for exercise. For instance, vacuuming for half an hour burns around 100 calories. If you have a large family, even **doing the dishes can be a workout**. In fact, if you wash fast enough, you will gain the benefits of aerobic exercise. Mopping the floor is even more work for the body, which means it **has the potential to build a small amount of muscle**. Ironing doesn't take that long, but **keep in mind** that you can still burn up to 130 calories in an hour while doing it. Outside of the home, there are many other simple, everyday ways to stay in shape. What can you think of?

여: 안녕하세요, 여러분. 최근 우리는 규칙적인 운동의 이점에 대해 많은 이야기를 나눴습니다. 오늘은, 체육관에 갈 필요 없이 칼로리를 소모하는 몇 가지 일상적인 방법을 논의하겠습니다. 예를 들어, 식료품을 쇼핑할 때에는 무려 250cal가 소모될 수 있습니다. 승강기 대신 계단을 이용하는 것과 같은 간단한 결정 또한 여러분의 건강에 큰 영향을 미칠 수 있습니다. 집안일은 운동을 하는 또 다른 기회입니다. 예를 들어, 30분 동안 ① 진공 청소를 하는 것은 약 100cal를 소모합니다. 만약 식구가 많다면, ② 설거지하는 것도 운동이 될 수 있습니다. 사실, 충분히 빠르게 설거지를 한다면, 유산소운동을 하는 것의 이점을 얻게 될 것입니다. 바닥을 ④ 걸레로 닦는 것은 신체에 훨씬 더 많은 운동이 되는데, 이는 그 일이 약간의 근육을 키울 가능성을 갖고 있음을 의미합니다. ⑤ 다림질은 시간이 그렇게 오래 걸리진 않지만, 그럼에도 다림질을 하며 한 시간 내에 130cal까지 소모할 수 있다는 점을 염두에 두세요. 집 밖에서도, 건강을 유지할 수 있는 다른 간단하고 일상적인 방법이 많이 있습니다. 여러분은 어떤 것을 생각해볼 수 있으신가요?

어휘 **function** 기능하다, 작용하다 / **workout** 운동; 연습 (경기) / **burn calories** 칼로리를 소모하다[태우다] / **vacuum** 진공 청소(를 하다); 진공 / **mop** (대)걸레로 닦다 / **ironing** 다림질 / **benefit** 이점; 이익을 보다; 유익하다 / **grocery** 식료품 / **house chores** 집안일 / **aerobic** 유산소(운동)의 / **potential** 가능성; 잠재력 / **stay in shape** 건강을 유지하다

Answers & Explanation

01. ③ 02. ④ 03. ③ 04. ⑤ 05. ② 06. ④ 07. ④ 08. ① 09. ⑤ 10. ②
11. ⑤ 12. ⑤ 13. ② 14. ② 15. ④ 16. ② 17. ④

01 화자가 하는 말의 목적 | ③

▶ 새로 개장한 주말농장인 Uncle John's 농장을 홍보하고 있다.

M: Are you **struggling to come up with** fun, healthy activities to do as a family on the weekends? If so, why not **try harvesting some organic food** with your kids? It is a wonderful experience for kids who have grown up in the city. And Uncle John's farm is **the perfect place to give it a try**. Uncle John's is a recently established farm that grows organic fruits and vegetables in a lovely, natural setting. And it's just 30 minutes from the city by subway! **Don't hesitate to share this meaningful experience** with your kids. It is the perfect way for them to develop healthy eating habits and a love of nature at the same time.

남: 주말에 가족 단위로 할 수 있는 재미있고 건강한 활동을 찾느라 애쓰고 계십니까? 만약 그렇다면, 아이들과 함께 유기농 식품을 수확해 보지 않으시겠습니까? 이것은 도시에서 자란 아이들에게 멋진 체험입니다. 그리고 Uncle John's 농장은 이를 해 보기에 완벽한 장소입니다. Uncle John's 농장은 멋진 자연환경에서 유기농 과일과 채소를 재배하는, 최근에 지어진 농장입니다. 그리고 시에서 지하철로 30분밖에 걸리지 않습니다! 아이들과 이 의미 있는 체험을 함께하는 것을 주저하지 마십시오. 이것은 아이들이 건강한 식습관과 자연에 대한 사랑을 동시에 기르도록 하는 완벽한 방법입니다.

어휘 **struggle to-v** v하려고 애쓰다[몸부림치다]

02 대화 주제 | ④

▶ 다섯 살이 된 딸이 영어 공부를 시작해야 할지 묻는 남자에게 영어교사인 여자가 초등학교에 들어가서 시작해도 늦지 않는다고 조언해주고 있다.

[Phone rings.]
W: Hello?
M: Hi, Alice. It's Min-ho. Do you have a minute? I'd like your opinion as an English teacher.
W: Sure. What's up?
M: It's about my daughter. She's turning five, and I'm wondering whether she **needs to start learning English**.
W: Well, that's a difficult question. Personally, I think five is too young to start studying a foreign language.
M: Really? Many of her friends are already enrolled in language programs. **Won't she fall behind**?
W: I don't think so. Besides, learning two languages at a young age can be confusing.
M: **That makes sense**, but then why are so many parents having their children study English before they even speak Korean?
W: There is a lot of pressure to learn English, but it's **not too late to start in elementary school**.
M: I see. Thanks for your advice.

[전화벨이 울린다.]
여: 여보세요?
남: 안녕, Alice. 나 민호야. 잠시 시간 있니? 영어교사로서 너의 의견을 듣고 싶어.
여: 그래. 무슨 일인데?
남: 우리 딸에 관한 거야. 우리 딸이 다섯 살이 되는데 영어를 배우기 시작해야 할지 모르겠어.
여: 글쎄, 어려운 질문이네. 나는 개인적으로 다섯 살이면 외국어 공부를 시작하기에 너무 어리다고 생각해.
남: 그래? 딸아이 친구들은 이미 언어 학습과정에 많이 등록되어 있는걸. 우리 애가 뒤처지지 않을까?
여: 그렇지 않을 거야. 게다가 어린 나이에 두 가지 언어를 배우는 건 혼란스러울 수 있어.
남: 그것도 일리가 있는데, 왜 그토록 많은 부모가 아이가 한국어를 구사하기도 전에 영어 공부를 시키는 거지?
여: 영어를 배우는 것에 대한 압박감이 심하기 때문이야. 하지만 초등학교에 들어가서 시작해도 그리 늦지 않아.
남: 알겠어. 조언 고마워.

어휘 **enroll A in B** A를 B에 등록시키다 / **fall behind** (~에) 뒤지다[뒤떨어지다]

03 관계 | ③

▶ 여자는 남자가 광고를 낸 집에 대해 물어보고, 남자는 주인이 집을 개조했다는 말과 함께 정보를 주는 것으로 보아 부동산 중개업자와 고객 간의 대화임을 알 수 있다.

[Phone rings.]
M: Good morning. How may I help you?
W: Hello, **I'm calling about your advertisement** in today's paper. I'd like some more information about the place on Park Street.
M: Oh, you're talking about the house on the hill, right?
W: Exactly. It looks nice, but I can't see much in the picture.
M: Well, it has a great view, and **the landlord recently renovated it**.
W: That's good. What else can you tell me?
M: It has a large back yard that would be ideal if you have kids.
W: That sounds perfect. **I'd love to see it for myself**.
M: Of course. Just tell me when you are free and **I'll set it up**.
W: How about 2 o'clock tomorrow?
M: Okay. If you come to my office, I'll drive you there.
W: Great. See you then.

[전화벨이 울린다.]
남: 안녕하세요. 무엇을 도와드릴까요?
여: 안녕하세요. 오늘 신문에 난 광고를 보고 전화 드립니다. Park 가에 있는 집에 관해 더 많은 정보를 알고 싶어서요.
남: 아, 언덕 위에 있는 집 말씀이시군요, 맞죠?
여: 맞아요. 멋진 집 같은데 사진으로는 많은 걸 볼 수가 없네요.
남: 음, 전망이 아주 좋은 집이고, 주인이 최근에 집을 개조했어요.
여: 그거 좋군요. 그밖에 말씀해주실 건 없으신가요?
남: 뒷마당이 넓어서 아이들이 있다면 더 없이 좋을 거예요.
여: 정말 좋겠네요. 직접 보고 싶은데요.
남: 물론입니다. 한가하신 시간만 말씀하시면 약속을 잡아 두겠습니다.
여: 내일 두 시 어떠세요?
남: 좋습니다. 제 사무실로 오시면 그곳까지 차로 모셔다 드릴게요.
여: 좋아요. 그때 뵐게요.

어휘 **renovate** ~을 개조[보수]하다

04 그림 불일치 | ⑤

▶ 여자는 분수대 오른쪽에 벤치가 놓여있다고 했다.

W: Honey, have you seen the view from our room yet?
M: Oh, it's amazing!
W: I'm glad we chose to stay here **to celebrate our anniversary**.
M: Yeah. Look at the river in the distance. It looks so peaceful.
W: Oh, there's a cruise ship on the water. **I'd like to board it**.
M: We could do that after dinner. Can you see the island to the right of the ship?
W: Yes, I can. Wow, look down, honey. There is a nice park in front of the hotel.
M: Right. **The huge circular fountain** is beautiful.
W: The nearby sculptures look pretty, too. The three horses look delicate.
M: I'd like to get a closer look at them.
W: There's a cozy bench to the right of the fountain where we could take a rest. **Why don't we visit the park right now**?
M: Okay, let's go.

여: 여보, 우리 방에서 내다보이는 경치 벌써 봤어요?
남: 아, 멋지군요!
여: 우리의 기념일을 축하하기 위해 여기 묵기로 해서 기뻐요.
남: 그래요. 저 멀리 있는 강을 봐요. 정말 평화로워 보이는군요.
여: 아, 강물 위에 유람선이 있네요. 타보고 싶어요.
남: 저녁 먹고 타면 돼요. 배 오른쪽에 있는 섬이 보이나요?
여: 네, 보여요. 와, 아래를 봐요, 여보. 호텔 앞에 멋진 공원이 있어요.
남: 그러네요. 둥그렇게 생긴 커다란 분수가 아주 멋져요.

여: 근처에 있는 조각 작품들도 예뻐 보여요. 세 마리 말이 정교해 보이네요.
남: 저 말 조각 작품들을 더 가까이서 보고 싶어요.
여: 분수대 오른쪽에 쉴 수 있는 편안한 벤치가 있어요. 지금 바로 저 공원에 가보는 게 어때요?
남: 좋아요. 가요.

어휘 **circular** 원형의, 둥근 / **delicate** 정교한

05 부탁한 일 | ②

▶ 여자는 남자에게 집 청소를 돕는 대신에 가게에 예약해 놓은 꽃다발을 찾아와 달라고 부탁했다.

M: Jessica, **shouldn't we leave now for** David's recital?
W: My watch says it's 2:30. When is the recital?
M: In two and a half hours, but I want to arrive **early enough to sit in the front row**.
W: We don't need to hurry too much. The invitations David gave to us **allow us to sit in** reserved VIP seats.
M: Oh, that sounds great.
W: Besides, I want to clean the house before we leave.
M: All right. Then **we have some time to spare**. Would you like some help?
W: That's okay. Instead, could you pick up the bouquet of flowers **I reserved at the shop** on 3rd Avenue?
M: Sure. Do you need anything else?
W: That's all. Thanks, honey.

남: Jessica, David의 연주회에 가려면 지금 나서야 하지 않을까요?
여: 내 시계는 두 시 반을 가리키고 있어요. 연주회가 몇 신데요?
남: 두 시간 반 후에 있지만, 앞줄에 앉을 수 있도록 일찍 도착했으면 해요.
여: 너무 서두를 필요 없어요. David가 준 초청장을 가지고 가면 지정된 VIP석에 앉을 수 있거든요.
남: 오, 그거 정말 멋지군요.
여: 그리고 출발하기 전에 집을 청소했으면 해요.
남: 그래요. 그러면 여유 시간이 좀 있군요. 내가 좀 도와줄까요?
여: 괜찮아요. 대신 3번가 가게에 내가 예약해 놓은 꽃다발을 찾아와 줄래요?
남: 그래요. 다른 거 필요한 건 없어요?
여: 그게 다예요. 고마워요, 여보.

어휘 **recital** 연주회, 발표회 / **reserved** 지정된, 예약된; 예비의 ***cf.* reserve** ~을 예약하다; (자리 등을) 따로 잡아 두다

06 금액 | ④

▶ 220달러였던 재킷을 반값에 구매하고, 100달러 넘게 구매하는 고객에게 10달러에 판매하는 넥타이도 사기로 했으므로, 남자가 지불할 금액은 120달러이다.

M: Hi, I heard **you are having a clearance sale today**. Is that true?
W: Yes. We're **offering discounts of up to** 70 percent.
M: Okay. Then how much are these pants?
W: They're 30 dollars per pair.
M: Wow, the last time, they were 60 dollars a pair. Can I try a size 32?
W: One moment, sir. *[pause]* Sorry, I've **checked the stock** but those on the hanger are all we have.
M: That's too bad.
W: How about this jacket? I think it's your size.
M: Well, I do like the style. **Can I try it on**?
W: Sure. Its original price was 220 dollars, but it's 50 percent off now.
M: Great. *[pause]* **It looks good on me**. I'll take it.
W: How about this tie? It's only 10 dollars for those who spend more than 100 dollars today.
M: Wow, that's a good deal! I'll take it, too.

남: 안녕하세요. 오늘 창고 정리 세일을 하신다고 들었어요. 맞나요?
여: 네. 최대 70퍼센트까지 할인해 드리고 있어요.
남: 좋네요. 그럼 이 바지는 얼마죠?
여: 한 벌 당 30달러예요.
남: 우와, 지난번에는 한 벌에 60달러였는데. 32사이즈로 입어 봐도 될까요?
여: 잠시만요, 고객님. *[잠시 후]* 죄송하지만, 재고를 확인해 보니 옷걸이에 걸려 있는 바지가 저희가 가진 전부예요.
남: 유감이네요.
여: 이 재킷은 어떠세요? 손님께 잘 맞을 것 같은데요.
남: 음, 스타일이 정말 맘에 드는군요. 입어 봐도 되나요?
여: 그럼요. 원래 가격은 220달러였는데 지금은 50퍼센트 할인하고 있어요.
남: 좋아요. *[잠시 후]* 저에게 잘 어울리네요. 그걸로 하죠.
여: 이 넥타이는 어떠세요? 오늘 100달러 넘게 구매하시는 고객께는 10달러에 드리고 있어요.
남: 우와, 좋은 조건이네요! 그것도 사겠어요.

어휘 **clearance sale** 창고 정리 판매, 재고 정리 판매

07 이유 | ④

▶ 상점의 위치, 근무 기간이나 판매 경력 모두 문제가 없었지만 스페인어를 말할 수 있는 사람을 필요로 한다고 하자 스페인어를 못한다고 했으므로 답은 ④이다.

M: Daisy, I saw a help-wanted ad in the newspaper. Avenue Clothing Store is looking for a sales supervisor.
W: Sounds great. **Where is it located**?
M: It's located inside the Westfield Shopping Mall, on Market Street.
W: Good! It's not far from my house.
M: They want someone **who can work Tuesday through Saturday**. And it says the pay is $32 per hour.
W: Not bad. I should apply for that.
M: And they want a person with at least 2 years of experience, which you clearly have.
W: Yeah. **Are there any other requirements**?
M: Hmm, most of their customers are Hispanic so they need someone who can speak both English and Spanish.
W: Oh, no. **I can't speak Spanish at all**.
M: Really? Well, there'll be other opportunities!

남: Daisy, 신문에서 구인광고를 봤어. Avenue 의류 매장이 판매 관리자를 찾고 있대.
여: 그거 좋은데. 어디에 위치하고 있니?
남: Market Street에 있는 Westfield 쇼핑몰 안에 위치하고 있어.
여: 좋아! 우리 집에서 멀지 않아.
남: 그들은 화요일에서 토요일까지 일할 수 있는 사람을 원해. 그리고 급여가 시간당 32달러라고 하네.
여: 괜찮은데. 거기 지원해야겠다.
남: 그리고 그들은 적어도 2년 경력을 가진 사람을 원하는데, 넌 분명히 가지고 있잖아.
여: 응. 다른 자격 요건이 있니?
남: 음, 그들 고객 대부분이 히스패닉이라서 영어와 스페인어를 모두 할 수 있는 사람이 필요하대.
여: 아, 이런. 난 스페인어를 전혀 할 줄 몰라.
남: 정말이야? 뭐, 다른 기회가 있을 거야!

어휘 **help-wanted** 구인광고 / **supervisor** 관리자, 주임 / **requirement** 자격, 필요 조건 / **Hispanic** 히스패닉, 라틴 아메리카계 주민

08 언급하지 않은 것 | ①

▶ 해석 참조

W: Good morning, Mr. Lee. Good to see you again.
M: Hi, Ms. Wang. Thank you for choosing us to lead your "Experience Korea" program. **How was your flight from China**?
W: It was comfortable.
M: Great. Now, the sightseeing bus is waiting outside.
W: Are the students going to their accommodations?
M: Right. After they unpack, as you know, there will be **a welcoming party for your students**.
W: Sounds great. Actually, I heard on the plane that the Secret Garden in Changdeok Palace is open at night. Is that true?
M: Yes, that is new, **starting this week**.
W: Could we go there after dinner? I want my students to visit **as many historical sites as possible**.
M: Sure. The palace is near the Korean restaurant where you will dine. I'll arrange that right now.

여: 안녕하세요, 이 선생님. 다시 뵙게 되어 반갑습니다.
남: 안녕하세요, 왕 선생님. '한국 체험' 프로그램을 저희가 진행하게 선택해주셔서 감사합니다. 중국에서 오실 때의 비행은 어떠셨나요?
여: 편안했어요.
남: 잘됐군요. 지금 밖에서 관광버스가 기다리고 있어요.
여: 학생들은 숙소로 가나요?
남: 맞습니다. 아시다시피 짐을 풀고(② 숙소에서 짐 풀기) 나면, 학생들을 위한 환영식(③ 환영

식)이 있을 겁니다.
여: 좋아요. 사실 창덕궁 안에 있는 비원이 야간 개장을 한다고 비행기에서 들었어요. 정말인가요?
남: 네. 이번 주부터 시작되는 새로운 행사입니다.
여: 저녁 식사(④ 저녁 식사) 후에 가볼 수 있을까요? 저는 학생들이 역사 유적지를 되도록 많이 방문(⑤ 유적지 방문)했으면 하거든요.
남: 물론입니다. 창덕궁은 저녁을 드시게 될 한식집 근처에 있어요. 지금 바로 준비할게요.

어휘 **accommodation** 숙소, 숙박시설 / **dine** (잘 차린) 저녁식사를 하다

09 내용 불일치 | ⑤

▶ American mink는 같은 집을 절대로 오랫동안 사용하지 않는다고 했다.

W: Good afternoon, class. Today, we'll talk about the American mink. American minks **are found throughout** North America. They have slim bodies and long, thick tails. In fact, **one third of a mink's length** is its tail! American minks are meat eaters that feed on fish, frogs, and small birds. They kill their prey **by biting it on the neck**. Like skunks, minks defend themselves by spraying an unpleasant-smelling liquid. Minks also **mark their territory with scent** and will fight with other minks that invade their territory. They live in forested areas that are near rivers, streams, lakes, or ponds. They make their homes near water and **never use the same home for long**.

여: 안녕하세요, 여러분. 오늘 우리는 아메리카 밍크(족제빗과 동물)에 관해 이야기하고자 합니다. 아메리카 밍크는 북미 전역에서 발견됩니다. 이들은 날씬한 몸과 길고 두꺼운 꼬리를 가지고 있습니다. 실제로 밍크 몸길이의 3분의 1은 꼬리입니다! 아메리카 밍크는 물고기, 개구리, 작은 새를 먹고 사는 육식 동물입니다. 이들은 목을 물어 먹잇감을 죽입니다. 스컹크처럼 밍크도 불쾌한 냄새가 나는 액체를 뿌려 자신을 방어합니다. 밍크는 또한 냄새로 자기 영역을 표시하고, 자기 영역에 침범하는 다른 밍크들과는 싸움을 벌일 것입니다. 아메리카 밍크는 강, 시내, 호수, 또는 연못 근처의 숲 지대에 서식합니다. 이들은 물가에 집을 짓는데 같은 집을 절대로 오랫동안 사용하지 않습니다.

어휘 **feed on** (동물이) ~을 먹고 살다, 먹다 / **prey** 먹이[사냥감]; 희생, 피해자 / **territory** 영역 / **scent** 냄새(를 맡다); 향기

10 도표 이해 | ②

▶ 중국어는 과제가 너무 많고, 세계탐험 프로그램은 비용이 너무 많이 들며, 실내 스포츠는 남자의 가족 여행 기간과 겹치기 때문에 두 사람은 남은 프로그램인 오카리나 배우기를 선택할 것이다.

M: Emily, take a look at this.
W: Are those winter school programs?
M: Yes, and some of them look fun. Why don't we take one together?
W: Okay. Let's learn **how to speak Chinese over the vacation**.
M: Well, my friend Charlotte had Tim as a Chinese tutor and said that he gives too much work.
W: Really? Then **let's consider the other programs**.
M: Experiencing the Philippines sounds interesting.
W: But it's too expensive. I think **it would be good to spend less than** 100 dollars for our winter program.
M: Then the other World Explorer Program is not an option either, right?
W: Yeah. What about indoor sports?
M: I'm sorry, but I'll be traveling with my family until January 9th.
W: Then we have only one program left, and I think **learning an instrument is always worthwhile**.
M: You're right. Let's sign up for that program.

남: Emily, 이것 좀 봐.
여: 겨울 학교 프로그램이니?
남: 응, 재미있어 보이는 게 몇 개 있는데 같이 하나 듣지 않을래?
여: 좋아. 방학 동안 중국어 회화를 배워보자.
남: 글쎄, 내 친구 Charlotte이 Tim 선생님께 중국어를 개인지도 받았는데, 그분은 숙제를 너무 많이 내주신다고 했어.
여: 그래? 그럼 다른 프로그램을 생각해 보자.
남: 필리핀 체험이 재미있을 것 같아.
여: 하지만 너무 비싸. 우리가 참여할 겨울 프로그램에는 100달러 미만으로 쓰는 것이 좋을 거라고 생각해.
남: 그렇다면 또 다른 세계탐험 프로그램도 선택사항이 아니겠네, 그렇지?
여: 맞아. 실내 스포츠는 어때?
남: 미안하지만, 1월 9일까지 가족들과 여행을 할 거야.
여: 그러면 남은 프로그램은 하나뿐이네. 그리고 악기를 배우는 건 언제나 가치 있는 일이라고 생각해.
남: 네 말이 맞아. 그 프로그램에 등록하자.

어휘 **indoor sports** 실내 스포츠 / **sign up for** (강좌에) 등록하다, ~을 신청[가입]하다

11 짧은 대화에 이어질 응답 | ⑤

▶ 만석인 식당의 대기자 명단에 자신의 이름을 올려달라는 남자의 말에 가장 적절한 응답을 고른다.

① 죄송합니다만 영업시간이 지났습니다.
② 창가 옆자리로 잡아 드릴게요.
③ 곧바로 주문을 받겠습니다.
④ 죄송합니다만, 손님의 이름을 명단에서 찾을 수 없습니다.
⑤ 물론이죠. 성함을 알려주시겠습니까?

M: Excuse me, are there any available seats in this restaurant?
W: I'm sorry, but **we are full at the moment**. You can probably get a table in 20 minutes.
M: I can wait. Could you **put me on the waiting list**?
W: ______________________________

남: 실례합니다. 이 식당에 빈자리가 있나요?
여: 죄송합니다만, 지금은 자리가 모두 찼어요. 아마 20분 후에 자리가 날 겁니다.
남: 기다릴게요. 저를 대기자 명단에 올려주시겠어요?
여: ______________________________

어휘 **waiting list** 대기자 명단

12 짧은 대화에 이어질 응답 | ⑤

▶ 남자가 축제에서 무엇을 하는지 묻는 여자의 말에 가장 적절한 응답을 고른다.

① 거기에 너랑 같이 가고 싶어.
② 그건 내 미래의 직업을 위해 중요해.
③ 이거 준비하느라 힘들었어.
④ 축제는 10월 첫째 주에 열려.
⑤ 학교 연극 무대를 설치해.

W: You look tired, Jason. Are you **on your way home from school**?
M: Yes. I'm **busy preparing for** the school festival these days.
W: Oh, what are you doing for the festival?
M: ______________________________

여: 피곤해 보인다, Jason. 학교에서 집에 가는 중이니?
남: 응. 요즘 학교 축제 준비하느라 바빠.
여: 아, 축제 때 넌 뭘 하는데?
남: ______________________________

13 긴 대화에 이어질 응답 | ②

▶ 여자처럼 엑셀 실기시험을 꾸준히 준비하면 자신도 시험에 합격할 수 있겠느냐는 남자의 물음에 적절한 여자의 응원의 말을 고른다.

① 맞아, 때로는 실패가 성공에 대해 가르쳐 주지.
② 물론이지. 천천히 그리고 꾸준히 하면 해낼 수 있어.
③ 그건 일자리를 찾을 때 아주 유용했어.
④ 당연하지. 백지장도 맞들면 낫잖아.
⑤ 맞아. 필기시험을 같이 준비하자.

W: What are you doing with your notebook?
M: I'm practicing with the Excel program **for my Excel certification test**.
W: Ah. I thought you were playing a game. So, how's it going?
M: I passed the written test, but I still have to take the practical examination.
W: I remember when I had to take that same examination.
M: I'm sure it was easy for you, **since you majored in programming**.
W: Programming and mastering Excel are two different things. I had to begin preparing well in advance, and **I studied a little every day**.
M: Really? It was that difficult? Now I'm even more worried.
W: It's **natural for you to be nervous**, but you can succeed if you try your best.
M: So, you think I can pass if I study like you did?
W: ______________________________

여: 노트북으로 뭐 하고 있니?
남: 엑셀 자격증 시험에 대비해서 엑셀 프로그램을 연습하고 있어.
여: 아. 나는 게임을 하고 있는 줄 알았어. 잘돼 가니?
남: 필기시험은 통과했는데, 아직 실기시험을 봐야 해.
여: 내가 그 똑같은 시험을 봐야 했던 게 생각난다.
남: 너는 프로그래밍을 전공했으니까 분명 쉬웠겠구나.
여: 프로그래밍과 엑셀을 익히는 건 전혀 별개의 일이야. 나도 착실하게 미리 준비를 시작해야 했고, 매일 조금씩 공부를 했지.
남: 정말? 그렇게 어려웠다고? 이제 훨씬 더 걱정되는걸.
여: 네가 걱정하는 건 당연하지만, 최선을 다하면 성공할 수 있어.
남: 그럼, 나도 너처럼 공부하면 합격할 수 있을 거라고 생각하니?
여: ______________________________

어휘 **A problem shared is a problem halved.** 백지장도 맞들면 낫다. / **written test** 필기시험 / **certification** 증명; 자격증 / **practical examination** 실기시험

14 긴 대화에 이어질 응답 | ②

▶ 아이들이 놀이기구를 타고 싶어 한다며 빠른 환불 처리를 원하는 여자의 말에 대한 적절한 대답을 유추해 본다.

① 10세 미만 아동은 이 놀이기구를 탈 수 없습니다.
② 그럼요. 금방이면 됩니다.
③ 죄송합니다만, 티켓 환불은 안 됩니다.
④ 물론이죠. 자유 이용권을 사는 게 더 낫죠.
⑤ 놀이공원에 만족하지 못하셨다니 유감입니다.

M: Here are your tickets and your receipt. Enjoy your visit to Green Springs Amusement Park.
W: *[pause]* Excuse me, but I think **there's been a mistake**. Why is the total $140?
M: That's one all-access adult pass and two all-access children's passes.
W: No, I said, "admission to the park for one adult." I don't plan to go on any of the rides.
M: Oh, I'm really sorry. I misunderstood and charged you for the full admission price.
W: I see. Then could I **have a refund for my ticket**?
M: Yes, of course. I'll need to see your credit card to process the refund.
W: All right. Here you are.
M: I'll fix that right now. And again, **I'm really sorry for the inconvenience**.
W: That's okay, but my kids **can't wait to get on the rides**.
M: ______________________________

남: 여기 티켓과 영수증입니다. Green Springs 놀이공원에서 즐거운 시간 보내세요.
여: *[잠시 후]* 죄송하지만, 실수가 있는 것 같군요. 총액이 왜 140달러죠?
남: 성인 자유 이용권 한 장과 아동 자유 이용권 두 장입니다.
여: 아뇨, 저는 '어른 한 사람은 공원 입장권'을 달라고 했어요. 저는 놀이기구를 안 탈 거거든요.
남: 아, 정말 죄송합니다. 제가 잘못 이해하고 자유 이용권 가격으로 계산했네요.
여: 알겠어요. 그러면 제 티켓은 환불받을 수 있죠?
남: 네, 물론입니다. 환불을 하시려면 손님의 신용카드를 보여주셔야 합니다.
여: 알았어요. 여기 있어요.
남: 지금 바로 조처를 해 드리겠습니다. 불편을 끼쳐드린 것에 대해 다시 한 번 진심으로 사과드립니다.
여: 괜찮아요. 그런데 아이들이 놀이기구를 빨리 타고 싶어 하는군요.
남: ______________________________

어휘 **ride** 놀이기구

15 상황에 적절한 말 | ④

▶ 집에서는 말수가 적은 딸에 대해 걱정하는 아버지에게 일시적 현상임을 설명하기 적합한 표현을 유추해야 한다.

① Julie는 열심히 공부하며 항상 좋은 성적을 받습니다.
② Julie가 친구를 많이 사귀는 것을 보니 흐뭇하군요.
③ 내일 방과 후에 Julie와 그 문제에 대해 얘기해 보겠습니다.
④ 자라는 과정에서 있을 수 있는 일이니 너무 많이 걱정하지 마세요.
⑤ 방과 후 활동을 통해 Julie의 자신감이 향상되면 좋겠어요.

M: Ms. Carver is a high school teacher, and Julie is one of her students. Julie always does well on tests and assignments, and she **gets along well with her classmates**. Today, Ms. Carver has a meeting with Julie's father. During the meeting, Ms. Carver praises Julie's performance and in-class attitude. To Ms. Carver's surprise, Julie's father expresses **concern about Julie's shyness and passive attitude**. He says he worries about Julie's ability to make friends **because she hardly talks at home**. However, Ms. Carver knows that students sometimes go through temporary periods where **they behave differently at home**, and she wants to explain this to Julie's father. In this situation, what would Ms. Carver most likely say to Julie's father?

남: Carver 씨는 고등학교 선생님이고 Julie는 그녀가 가르치는 학생 중 한 명이다. Julie는 언제나 시험도 잘 보고 숙제도 잘해 오고, 반 친구들과도 잘 지낸다. 오늘, Carver 씨는 Julie 아버지와의 면담이 있다. 면담을 하는 동안 Carver 씨는 Julie의 성적과 수업 태도를 칭찬한다. 그런데 Carver 씨에게는 놀랍게도 Julie의 아버지는 Julie의 숫기 없음과 소극적인 태도에 관한 걱정을 드러낸다. 아버지는 Julie가 집에서는 말을 거의 하지 않기 때문에 딸의 사교성에 대해 걱정된다고 한다. 그러나 Carver 씨는 학생들이 때로 집에서 (학교에서와는) 다르게 행동하는 일시적인 시기를 거친다는 것을 알고 있어서, Julie 아버지에게 이를 설명하고자 한다. 이러한 상황에서 Carver 씨가 Julie 아버지에게 할 말로 가장 적절한 것은 무엇인가?

어휘 **passive** 소극적인, 수동적인

16~17 세트 문항 | 16. ② 17. ④

▶ 16. 치아 교정과 미백 등 인상을 개선하기 위한 치아 관리법에 대해 설명하고 있다.

① 치아 미백을 위해 필수적인 단계들
② 더 좋아 보이는 치아를 위한 치아 관리 조언
③ 치아 문제를 위한 대체요법들
④ 나쁜 입냄새와 충치를 피하기 위한 방법들
⑤ 치아 정기검진의 중요성

▶ 17. 해석 참조

① 딸기 ② 페퍼민트 ③ 상추 ④ 레몬 ⑤ 죽염

W: Are your teeth well taken care of? If not, you could **end up giving people the wrong impression**. So, let me provide you with a few tips on making your teeth presentable. I'll start with evenness. Unfortunately, few of us are born with straight teeth. To get a picture-perfect smile, you **have no choice but to visit a dentist** and have your teeth straightened. It's worth it. While you're there, it's a good idea to have your teeth professionally whitened. Of course, many of us don't have the time or money for this. Luckily, there are a few basic, natural alternatives. For example, strawberries contain **enough acid to somewhat whiten teeth**. Common herbs such as peppermint and spearmint have the same power. There are even certain vegetables, especially lettuce, **that can work just as well**. And since salt is an ingredient in almost every dish, why not switch to bamboo salt? It also has the power to brighten your smile. Finally, **keep your teeth clean with regular check-ups** and proper brushing to avoid the biggest mistake of all: bad breath.

여: 당신의 치아는 잘 관리되고 있습니까? 만약 그렇지 않다면 당신은 사람들에게 좋지 않은 인상을 주게 될 수도 있습니다. 그러므로 당신의 치아를 보기 좋게 만드는 몇 가지 팁을 알려드리겠습니다. 우선 (치열이) 가지런해야 합니다. 안타깝게도 우리 가운데 고른 치아를 갖고 태어나는 사람은 별로 없습니다. 흠잡을 데 없이 완벽한 미소를 갖기 위해서는 치과에 가서 치아를 교정하는 수밖에 없습니다. 그건 그럴만한 가치가 있으니까요. 치과에 간 김에, 전문적인 치아 미백 시술을 받는 것도 좋은 생각입니다. 물론 우리 중 많은 사람이 여기에 들일 시간과 비용이 없습니다. 다행히도 몇 가지 기본적인 천연 대체재가 있습니다. 예를 들어 ① 딸기는 치아를 어느 정도 희게 해줄 만큼 충분한 산(酸)을 함유하고 있습니다. ② 페퍼민트와 스피어민트 같은 흔한 허브도 그와 같은 효과가 있습니다. 채소류도 있는데, 특히 ③ 상추가 마찬가지의 효과를 낼 수 있습니다. 그리고 소금은 거의 모든 요리에 사용되는 재료이므로 ⑤ 죽염으로 바꿔보는 건 어떨까요? 죽염도 당신의 미소를 환하게 해주는 힘을 갖고 있습니다. 마지막으로 가장 큰 실수인 입냄새를 피하기 위해서는 정기적인 검진과 올바른 칫솔질로 당신의 치아를 깨끗하게 유지하십시오.

어휘 **alternative** 대안이 되는; 대안, 선택 가능한 것 / **bad breath** 입냄새 / **cavity** 충치; 구멍, 움푹 파진 곳 / **regular check-up** 정기검진 / **presentable** (모습이) 남 앞에 내놓을 만한 / **evenness** 고름; 평편함; 평등 / **picture-perfect** 흠잡을 데 없이 완벽한 / **have no choice but to-v** v할 수밖에 없다 / **straighten** ~을 똑바르게 하다; (자세를) 바로 하다 / **acid** ((화학)) 산; 산성의; (맛이) 신 / **spearmint** 스피어민트 ((유럽 원산의 박하 향신료))

Answers & Explanation

01. ④ 02. ⑤ 03. ⑤ 04. ③ 05. ④ 06. ② 07. ④ 08. ④ 09. ⑤ 10. ①
11. ③ 12. ① 13. ③ 14. ② 15. ⑤ 16. ⑤ 17. ③

01 화자가 하는 말의 목적 | ④

▶ Ace Advertising is proposing that you choose our advertising campaign. ~.에서 남자가 하는 말의 목적을 알 수 있다.

M: Good afternoon. I'd like to present our advertising campaign to you. Your company, Candyland, has produced a new product called Choco Balls. Now some ad agencies might **tell you to market this product to kids**. Kids love chocolate, right? But **that would ignore the fact** that your product, Choco Balls, is made from 70% cacao. For a long time now, it has been known that the chemicals in cacao can **help slow down the aging process**. In other words, eating cacao is good for our health. So Ace Advertising is proposing that you choose our advertising campaign, which **focuses on the health benefits** of eating chocolate. Now please watch this commercial.

남: 안녕하세요. 여러분께 저희 광고를 공개하고자 합니다. 귀사 Candyland는 초코 볼이라는 새로운 제품을 출시했습니다. 지금 몇몇 광고 회사는 이 제품을 아이들에게 판매하라고 권유할 것입니다. 아이들이 초콜릿을 좋아하니까요, 그렇죠? 하지만 이것은 귀사의 제품인 초코 볼이 카카오 70%로 만들어진다는 사실을 간과하는 것입니다. 지금까지 오랫동안, 카카오의 화학성분이 노화 작용을 늦추는 데 도움이 될 수 있다고 알려져 왔습니다. 바꾸어 말하면, 카카오를 섭취하는 것이 건강에 이롭다는 것입니다. 그래서 저희 Ace 광고는 저희 광고를 선택해 주십사 제안하는데, 저희 광고는 초콜릿 섭취가 건강에 이롭다는 것에 초점을 맞추었습니다. 이제 이 광고를 봐주십시오.

어휘 **present** ~을 공개하다, 제공하다 / **advertising campaign** 광고 (캠페인) / **ad** 광고 ((advertisement의 약어)) / **market** (상품을) 내놓다[광고하다] / **aging process** 노화 작용 / **commercial** 광고 방송

02 의견 | ⑤

▶ 여자는 남자에게 같은 종류의 책만 읽으면 창의력이 제한될 수 있다며, 다른 장르의 책을 통해 얻은 새로운 생각이 창의력 향상에 도움이 된다는 내용을 근거로, 다른 장르의 책을 읽도록 권하고 있다.

M: Hi, Mom. Did you go to the bookstore?
W: I did, and I picked up something that **I thought you might enjoy**.
M: Oh? What's that?
W: It's about the philosophy of Socrates. I read part of it, and it's very interesting.
M: Thanks, Mom, but you know that I prefer to read mystery novels in my free time.
W: If you continue to read the same kind of thing, **it could limit your creativity**.
M: You have a point. I guess **it has been a while** since I've read anything different.
W: Exactly. **Exposure to new ideas** can help you to become more creative. Why don't you **give the book a chance**?
M: All right. I'll check it out.

남: 다녀오셨어요, 엄마. 서점 가셨어요?
여: 응, 그리고 내 생각에 네가 재미있어할지도 모르는 책을 사 왔단다.
남: 오? 그게 뭔데요?
여: 소크라테스의 철학에 관한 거란다. 내가 일부 읽어봤는데 아주 흥미롭더구나.
남: 고마워요, 엄마. 하지만 제가 시간이 나면 추리 소설 읽기를 더 좋아하는 거 아시잖아요.
여: 같은 종류의 책만 계속 읽으면 창의력이 제한될 수 있어.
남: 엄마 말씀이 맞아요. 뭔가 다른 것을 읽어본 지가 꽤 된 것 같아요.
여: 바로 그거야. 새로운 생각을 접하면 창의력을 좀 더 키우는 데 도움이 될 수 있단다. 이 책에 기회를 주는 게 어떠니?
남: 알겠어요. 살펴볼게요.

어휘 **exposure** (새로운 생각 등을) 접할 기회; (위험 등에의) 노출

03 관계 | ⑤

▶ 매주 정해진 시간에 요양원의 할머니들을 찾아와서 도움을 주는 학생과 할머니의 대화이다.

M: Is there anything else I can help you with?
W: No. That's it. You did a great job!
M: **It's my pleasure**.
W: It's really hard for me to **put up a picture**. And the nurses don't like to do those kinds of things.
M: No problem. Just stay healthy, Mrs. Gray.
W: It's hard when you're 85.
M: **Keep smiling then**. I'm sorry, Mrs. Gray. **I have to be off now**.
W: Oh, I was hoping you'd chat for a while.
M: Sorry, I'm really busy. Exams are next week.
W: OK. **Run along**. You help out every Wednesday, right?
M: Yes. From 4 to 7 every Wednesday.
W: It's nice of you to spend some of your free time with us.
M: I enjoy it.

남: 도와드릴 일이 더 있나요?
여: 없단다. 그게 다야. 정말 일을 잘하는구나!
남: 천만에요.
여: 그림을 거는 것은 내게는 정말 힘든 일이거든. 그리고 간호사들이 그런 종류의 일을 하는 것을 좋아하지 않아서 말이야.
남: 문제없어요. 건강하기만 하세요, Gray 할머니.
여: 85세가 되면 그게 힘들단다.
남: 그럼 계속 웃으세요. Gray 할머니, 죄송하지만 저는 지금 가야 해요.
여: 아, 너랑 잠시 이야기를 나눴으면 했는데.
남: 죄송해요, 제가 정말 바빠서요. 시험이 다음 주예요.
여: 그래, 빨리 가거라. 매주 수요일에 도와주는 거지, 맞지?
남: 네, 매주 수요일 4시부터 7시까지요.
여: 여가 시간 중 일부를 우리와 함께 보내다니 착하구나.
남: 저는 그게 즐거워요.

어휘 **be off** 떠나다, 출발하다 / **chat** 이야기[담소]를 나누다; 잡담, 담소 / **run along** ((구식)) ((아이에게 명령형으로)) 이제 가야지

04 그림 불일치 | ③

▶ 탁자 중앙에 있는 것은 마이크가 아니라 컴퓨터 마우스이다.

M: Mi-sun, what's this picture?
W: I took that picture yesterday at my daughter's Doljanchi. It's a traditional Korean first-birthday party.
M: Okay, but **why have those items been placed** in front of your daughter?
W: We believe that they can predict a baby's future. On the left, there is some thread, which represents long life.
M: Then does the pencil symbolize intelligence?
W: Right, and the computer mouse **in the middle of the table** represents technological ability. Similarly, a microphone would suggest musical talent, but **we didn't have one**.
M: That's too bad. Then what does the rice mean?
W: It **has to do with not being hungry**. It's related to having a comfortable life.
M: I see. Well, I'm sure that the money represents wealth.
W: Of course, and we were all delighted when she picked it up.

남: 미순 씨, 이 사진은 뭐예요?
여: 어제 제 딸애의 돌잔치에서 그 사진을 찍었어요. 돌잔치는 한국의 전통적인 첫 생일 파티예요.
남: 네, 그런데 왜 아기 앞에 저 물건들을 놓은 건가요?
여: 그것들이 아기의 미래를 예측할 수 있다고 믿거든요. 왼쪽에 실이 있는데, 그건 장수(長壽)를 나타내요.
남: 그럼 연필은 지능을 상징하나요?
여: 맞아요, 그리고 탁자 중앙에 있는 컴퓨터 마우스는 과학 기술 능력을 나타내요. 비슷하게, 마

이크는 음악적 재능을 암시할 테지만 우리에게는 없었어요.
남: 안됐군요. 그럼 쌀은 무엇을 의미하나요?
여: 굶주리지 않는 것에 관한 거예요. 편안한 삶을 사는 것과 관련이 있죠.
남: 그렇군요. 음, 돈은 분명 부(富)를 나타내겠군요.
여: 물론이죠. 그리고 딸애가 그걸 집었을 때 우린 모두 기뻤답니다.

어휘 **symbolize** ~을 상징하다 / **technological** 과학 기술의 / **similarly** 비슷하게; 마찬가지로 / **have to do with** ~와 관계가 있다, 관련되다 / **delighted** 아주 기뻐[즐거워]하는

05 추후 행동 | ④

▶ 여자는 남자가 엘리베이터를 멈추고 있기만을 원했으나 남자는 짐을 엘리베이터에 옮겨 주겠다고 했다.

W: Matt, are you free? Would you help me for a second, please?
M: Sure, Mrs. Brown. **What can I do**?
W: I have to get all of these boxes and things downstairs and into my car.
M: Wow. That's a lot of stuff. **Where is your car parked**?
W: Up the street a long way, unfortunately. But don't worry. Max and Jim are waiting downstairs to help.
M: You want me to go and get them?
W: No, I just need someone to hold the elevator for me while **I load the stuff in**.
M: Why don't I move these boxes and you hold the elevator?
W: Oh, you're a wonderful boy! Thank you, Matt!

여: Matt, 너 한가하니? 잠깐 나 좀 도와주겠니?
남: 네, Brown 부인. 무엇을 할까요?
여: 이 상자와 물건 모두를 아래층으로 가지고 가서 내 차 안에 넣어야 해.
남: 와. 물건이 많네요. 차가 어디에 주차되어 있어요?
여: 안타깝지만 도로를 죽 따라가다 보면 멀리 있어. 하지만 걱정하지 마. Max와 Jim이 도와주려고 아래층에서 기다리고 있거든.
남: 제가 가서 그 애들을 데리고 올까요?
여: 아니, 나는 그저 내가 물건들을 실어 넣을 동안 엘리베이터를 잡아 줄 사람이 필요해.
남: 제가 이 박스들을 옮기고 부인이 엘리베이터를 잡고 계시는 게 어떨까요?
여: 오, 너 정말 멋지구나. 고맙다, Matt!

06 금액 | ②

▶ 여자가 3달러짜리 플레인 머핀 2개, 5달러 하는 블루베리 머핀 1개, 3달러짜리 주스 3잔을 주문했다. 여기에 3달러 할인 쿠폰을 사용했으므로 지불할 금액은 17달러이다. 10% 즉석 할인되는 회원카드는 함께 사용할 수 없다고 했음에 유의한다.

M: Good morning. How can I help you?
W: I'd like 3 muffins, please.
M: What kind of muffins would you like? We have plain, blueberry, or cheese. Plain is $3, and **the other two are** $5.
W: Two plain and one blueberry, please.
M: Okay. Would you like something to drink?
W: I'd like one tomato juice and two cranberry juices. **Is there a difference in cost**?
M: No, they're all $3 each. Is that all?
W: Yes, I have a $3 discount coupon and a membership card that gives me an instant 10% discount. **Can I use them together**?
M: I'm sorry, but I'm afraid you can't. You can **only use one at a time**.
W: Oh, then I'll use a $3 discount coupon, which gives me more of a discount.
M: Okay.

남: 안녕하세요. 뭘 도와드릴까요?
여: 머핀 3개 주세요.
남: 어떤 종류의 머핀을 원하십니까? (아무것도 안 넣은) 플레인, 블루베리, 또는 치즈가 있습니다. 플레인은 3달러이고 다른 둘은 5달러입니다.
여: 플레인 2개하고 블루베리 1개 주세요.
남: 알겠습니다. 마실 것을 원하세요?
여: 토마토 주스 한 잔하고 크랜베리 주스 두 잔을 원해요. 가격에 차이가 있나요?
남: 아뇨, 모두 3달러씩입니다. 그게 다인가요?
여: 예, 제가 3달러 할인 쿠폰을 갖고 있고 즉시 10%를 할인해주는 회원권을 갖고 있어요. 이것들을 함께 사용할 수 있나요?
남: 죄송합니다만, 가능하지 않습니다. 한 번에 한 가지만 사용할 수 있습니다.
여: 아, 그러면 더 많은 할인을 주는 3달러 할인 쿠폰을 사용할게요.
남: 알겠습니다.

어휘 **membership** 회원 / **instant** 즉시의, 즉각적인

07 이유 | ④

▶ 남자의 아이는 조류 공포증도 없고 카페는 미리 예약을 하지 않아도 되고 음료 외 간식도 판매하며 입장료도 비싸지 않다. 그러나 카페에 8살 미만 아이의 입장을 허용하지 않는데 남자의 딸이 다음 일요일에 6살 생일이라고 했으므로 답은 ④이다.

W: Ethan, **have you been to** Nina's parrot cafe?
M: A parrot cafe? What's that? Is it a place you can bring your parrot?
W: No! You can enjoy roastery coffee **while in the company of some beautiful parrots**.
M: Sounds interesting. Can I bring my kid there?
W: Why not? I took my niece there. Just **make sure your kid isn't afraid of birds**.
M: No, she isn't. She loves birds. Do I have to make a reservation in advance?
W: You can book in advance, but you don't have to. You will have to pay an entrance fee, though.
M: Okay. **Do they serve snacks**?
W: They serve baked goods like muffins and cakes. The admission fee is $20, which includes one drink.
M: That's reasonable. I'll take my daughter there this weekend. Since her sixth birthday is this Sunday, **it will be a nice surprise for her**.
W: I'm sorry! They don't allow kids that are under 8 in the cafe.
M: That's too bad. I have to find another one on the Internet.

여: Ethan, Nina의 앵무새 카페에 가봤어요?
남: 앵무새 카페요? 그게 뭐죠? 앵무새를 데려올 수 있는 곳인가요?
여: 아니요! 아름다운 앵무새들 몇 마리와 함께 있으면서 로스터리 커피를 즐길 수 있어요.
남: 흥미롭군요. 거기 아이를 데려가도 되나요?
여: 왜 안 되겠어요? 거기 내 조카를 데려갔거든요. 단지 아이가 새를 무서워하지 않는지 꼭 확인해봐요.
남: 아니오, 안 무서워해요. 아이가 새를 좋아해요. 미리 예약을 해야 하나요?
여: 미리 예약할 수 있지만 그럴 필요는 없어요. 그래도 입장료는 내야 할 거예요.
남: 알았어요. 거기서 간식을 제공하나요?
여: 머핀이나 케이크 같은 구운 음식들을 내놓아요. 입장료는 20달러인데 음료 한 잔이 포함되어 있어요.
남: 비싸지 않군요. 이번 주말에 딸애를 거기 데려가겠어요. 아이의 여섯 번째 생일이 이번 일요일이기 때문에 멋진 깜짝 선물이 될 거예요.
여: 미안해요! 8살 미만의 아이는 카페에 들어오게 하지 않아요.
남: 유감이네요. 인터넷에서 다른 걸 찾아봐야겠어요.

어휘 **roastery** 로스터리((커피 원두를 볶고 가공하는 곳)) / **reasonable** 비싸지 않은, 합리적인 / **surprise** 뜻밖의 일[선물]

08 언급하지 않은 것 | ④

▶ 해석 참조

W: Mexico is the perfect destination for a scuba diving vacation. The Yucatan peninsula is especially great because it **offers the opportunity to dive** in a cenote. A cenote is a deep natural well formed by the collapse of surface limestone that exposes ground water underneath. These natural ponds were often the only sources of fresh water in the jungle. **They were considered to be sacred** to the ancient Mayan people. The cenotes were important in Mayan myth and **were traditionally thought to be entrances** to the underworld. You can dive in these amazing underground caves, and you may even see Mayan treasures left behind many years ago. You'll **need a special permit** for the caves, but to dive in the cenotes, you need no advanced training.

여: 멕시코는 스쿠버 다이빙 휴가를 즐기기에 완벽한 곳입니다. 유카탄 반도(① 위치)는 세노테에서 다이빙할 수 있는 기회를 제공하기 때문에 특히 근사합니다. 세노테는 석회암 표면이 붕괴되어 그 밑에 있던 지하수가 드러나면서 형성(② 형성 과정)된 깊은 천연 우물입니다. 이 천연 연못은 많은 경우에 정글에서 담수를 얻을 수 있는 유일한 원천이었습니다. 이곳은 고대 마야인들에게 신성하게 여겨졌습니다. 세노테는 마야 신화에서 중요했고, 전통적으로 지하 세계의 입구로 여겨졌습니다(③ 전통적 상징). 여러분은 이 놀라운 지하 동굴로 다이빙할

수 있으며, 오래전에 남겨진 마야의 보물들을 보게 될지도 모릅니다. 동굴에 들어가는 데는 특별 허가가 필요할 테지만(⑤ 입장 허가 필요 유무), 세노테에서 다이빙하기 위해서 고도의 훈련이 필요하지는 않습니다.

어휘 **collapse** 붕괴; 붕괴되다, 무너지다 / **limestone** 석회암 / **ground water** 지하수 / **fresh water** 담수, 민물 / **sacred** 신성시되는; 성스러운, 종교적인 / **advanced** (학습 과정이) 고급[상급]의; 선진의

09 내용 불일치 | ⑤

▶ 다른 학자들이 이 발견을 확증해주면, 공룡의 대중적 이미지가 바뀌어야 할지도 모른다고 말했으므로 아직 대부분의 학자들이 이 발견을 확증해 준 것은 아니다.

M: Did dinosaurs have feathers? You're most likely to say, "No!" Our image of dinosaurs comes from books and movies showing dinosaurs with green or brown skin. But **new fossils have provided evidence** that many types of dinosaurs, in fact, had feathers. Because these fossils are of dinosaurs that **were buried in a volcanic eruption**, they were perfectly preserved. Among the dinosaurs shown to have had feathers is Tyrannosaurus Rex. It is thought these dinosaurs had feathers not to fly but to keep themselves warm. **If these findings are confirmed** by others, the popular image of dinosaurs in books and movies **may soon have to be changed**.

남: 공룡들은 깃털이 있었을까요? 여러분은 아마도 "아니요!"라고 대답하실 것입니다. 공룡에 대한 우리의 이미지는 녹색이나 갈색 피부의 공룡을 보여주는 책과 영화에서 비롯된 것입니다. 하지만 새로운 화석들은 사실 다양한 종류의 공룡에게 깃털이 있었다는 증거를 제시하고 있습니다. 이 화석들은 화산 폭발 시 묻힌 공룡의 화석이기 때문에 완전한 상태로 보존되었습니다. 깃털이 있었던 것으로 보이는 공룡 중에는 티라노사우루스 렉스가 있습니다. 이 공룡들은 날기 위해서가 아니라 체온을 유지하기 위해서 깃털이 있었을 것으로 추정됩니다. 이런 결과들이 다른 이들에 의해서 확증되면, 책과 영화에서 보이는 공룡의 대중적인 이미지는 곧 바뀌어야 할지도 모릅니다.

어휘 **feather** 깃털 / **fossil** 화석 / **volcanic** 화산의 / **eruption** 폭발, 분화 / **finding** (조사·연구 등의) 결과, 결론 / **confirm** ~을 확증하다, 확인하다

10 도표 이해 | ①

▶ 우선 8세에서 12세가 대상인 강좌를 제외해야 하고 수강할 수 있는 요일은 월요일과 주말인 토, 일요일이다. 거기에 강좌 비용이 50달러 이하이면서 두 사람이 함께 수강할 수 있는 강좌를 선택했으므로 답은 ①이다.

W: I'd like to take a cooking course during my summer vacation. Howard Community Center **provides reasonable cooking classes**.
M: I'm also thinking of taking a cooking course there.
W: Then why don't we take a class together? **Let's take a look at** their website. *[pause]* Here's the timetable of their cooking classes.
M: Good. I'm interested in Cookie Decorating.
W: But it's for kids aged 8 to 12. We have to choose **a course that adults can participate in**.
M: You're right. What day are you available?
W: I'm **fine with any day except Wednesday**. How about you?
M: I'm free on Monday and the weekend.
W: Okay. We should also consider the cost. I don't think I can spend more than 50 dollars.
M: All right. Then we can choose between these two. Oh, no. **This class has only one spot left**. We can't take it together.
W: No problem. We can take the other class together. Let's register for it!

여: 난 여름방학 동안 요리 강좌를 듣고 싶어. Howard 지역 문화 센터가 적당한 요리 수업을 제공하고 있어.
남: 나도 그곳에서 요리 강좌를 들을까 생각하고 있어.
여: 그럼 우리 같이 수업 듣는 게 어때? 그곳의 웹사이트를 살펴보자. *[잠시 후]* 여기 요리 수업 일정표가 있어.
남: 좋아. 난 쿠키 장식에 관심이 있어.
여: 하지만 그건 8살부터 12살까지의 아이들을 위한 거야. 우리는 어른들이 참여할 수 있는 강좌를 선택해야 해.
남: 네 말이 맞아. 넌 언제 시간이 가능하니?
여: 수요일 빼고는 아무 날이나 괜찮아. 너는 어때?
남: 난 월요일과 주말에 시간이 있어.
여: 좋아. 우리는 비용도 고려해야 해. 난 50달러 넘게는 못 쓸 것 같아.
남: 알았어. 그러면 이 둘 중에 하나를 선택할 수 있구나. 어쩌지. 이 수업은 한 자리만 남았어. 우리가 같이 들을 수 없어.
여: 괜찮아. 우리는 다른 수업을 함께 들을 수 있잖아. 그 수업을 등록하자!

어휘 **spot** 자리 / **available** 이용 가능한; 시간이 있는 / **reasonable** 적당한, (가격이) 비싸지 않은 / **timetable** 일정표, 시간표 / **participate** 참여하다 / **register** 등록하다

11 짧은 대화에 이어질 응답 | ③

▶ 아버지가 무슨 일을 하시는지 묻고 있으므로 개인 사업을 하신다는 응답이 가장 적절하다.

① 아빠는 홍콩에 계셔.
② 우리는 보통 같이 쇼핑해.
③ 아빠는 개인 사업을 하셔.
④ 아빠는 3년 전에 돌아가셨어.
⑤ 아빠는 주말에 보통 집에 계셔.

W: I saw you at the store yesterday. **Who were you with**?
M: Just my mom and my sister. My dad is **away on business**.
W: What does your father do?
M: ______________________________

여: 어제 가게에서 널 봤어. 누구랑 있었니?
남: 엄마랑 누나랑만. 아빠는 출장 중이시거든.
여: 아버지께서는 무슨 일을 하시니?
남: ______________________________

12 짧은 대화에 이어질 응답 | ①

▶ 음식점에서 마지막으로 식사한 지 얼마나 됐는지 묻는 남자의 말에 적절한 응답을 찾는다.

① 적어도 일 년은 됐어.
② 분명히 많이 바뀌었어.
③ 다음 주에 여기 또 오자.
④ 이 음식점은 5년 전에 개업했어.
⑤ 우리 집에서 걸어서 고작 15분 거리야.

M: This was a great idea. The pizza is terrific!
W: The pasta, too. It's **even better than it used to be**.
M: I can't remember **what it used to be like**. How long has it been since we last ate here?
W: ______________________________

남: 이건 정말 좋은 생각이었어. 피자가 훌륭해!
여: 파스타도. 예전보다 훨씬 더 좋아.
남: 예전엔 어땠는지 기억이 안 나. 우리 여기에서 마지막으로 먹은 지 얼마나 됐지?
여: ______________________________

13 긴 대화에 이어질 응답 | ③

▶ 남자는 어제 결석해서 현장 학습을 가는지 모르고 교복을 입고 와서 아쉬워하고 있다.

① 네가 무엇을 입고 있는지는 그다지 중요하지 않아.
② 그랬으면 네게 다시 전화했을 텐데.
③ 그랬으면 교복을 입지 않았을 텐데!
④ 괜찮아. 나는 우리가 박물관에 갈 거라고 생각했어.
⑤ 그랬으면 어제 병원에 갔을 텐데.

W: Good morning, Min-sung. Are you feeling better?
M: Yes, thanks, Ji-hye. **I had a bad stomachache** yesterday, so I had to rest at home.
W: I thought you were sick.
M: Anyway, shouldn't you be wearing your school uniform?
W: We can wear casual clothes today. We're going on a field trip. Don't you remember?
M: Umm... I do. But it's raining. Didn't the teacher say **the field trip would be postponed** if it was raining?
W: She did. But yesterday the teacher said we'd be going **no matter what the weather was like**.
M: Really?
W: Yes, we're going to a museum, not the nature park.
M: Oh, **I wish you'd phoned me** last night.
W: Oh? I'm sorry. **I should have done that**.
M: ______________________________

여: 안녕, 민성아. 괜찮니?
남: 응, 고마워, 지혜야. 어제는 복통이 심해서 집에서 쉬어야 했어.
여: 네가 아픈 거라고 생각했어.
남: 그건 그렇고, 교복 입어야 하는 거 아니니?

여: 오늘은 평상복을 입어도 괜찮아. 현장 학습을 가잖아. 기억 안 나니?
남: 음… 기억나. 하지만 비가 오는 걸. 선생님께서 비가 오면 현장 학습이 연기될 거라고 말씀하시지 않았니?
여: 그랬지. 하지만 어제 선생님께서 날씨가 어떻든 갈 거라고 하셨어.
남: 정말?
여: 응. 자연 공원이 아니라 박물관에 갈 거거든.
남: 아. 네가 어젯밤에 전화를 해주었으면 좋았을 텐데.
여: 아? 미안해. 그랬어야 했는데.
남: ______________________________

어휘 **casual** 평상시의, 격식을 차리지 않는 / **field trip** 현장 학습 / **postpone** ~을 연기하다

14 긴 대화에 이어질 응답 | ②

▶ 여자는 모든 일이 잘 풀리고 있다. 이런 상황에서 여자가 할 수 있는 말로 ②번이 가장 적절하다.

① 다양성은 인생의 묘미야.
② 맞아. 삶이 이보다 더 좋을 수 없지.
③ 그건 생사가 걸린 문제야.
④ 물론이지! 넌 좋은 친구야.
⑤ 아니, 그 문제를 극복하기는 어려워.

M: Hi, Pamela. How are you doing?
W: I'm doing well, Peter. Thanks.
M: That's good. A month ago, you were so stressed. Is there any particular reason **for the change in mood**?
W: I got my college acceptance letter. I'm so happy. I worked hard and didn't give up.
M: **Life's like that**. Work hard and you'll be rewarded.
W: Thanks. How is your winter vacation going?
M: Good so far. And next week, my family and I are going to Jeju Island.
W: **I can't go anywhere**, because I've got a part-time job with a movie production company.
M: Wow! You want to study filmmaking in college, don't you?
W: Yes.
M: **Things are sure looking up for you**.
W: ______________________________

남: 안녕, Pamela. 어떻게 지내니?
여: 잘 지내, Peter. 고마워.
남: 잘됐다. 한 달 전에 너 스트레스를 많이 받았잖아. 기분이 바뀐 특별한 이유라도 있니?
여: 대학 입학 허가서를 받았어. 정말 기뻐. 열심히 공부했고 포기하지 않았거든.
남: 인생이란 그런 거야. 열심히 노력하면 보상을 받지.
여: 고마워. 너는 겨울 방학을 어떻게 지내고 있니?
남: 지금까지는 좋아. 그리고 다음 주에 가족과 함께 제주도에 갈 거야.
여: 난 영화 제작사에서 아르바이트를 하고 있어서 아무 데도 못 가.
남: 와! 넌 대학에서 영화 제작을 공부하고 싶어 하잖아, 그렇지?
여: 응.
남: 너는 일이 정말 잘 풀리고 있구나.
여: ______________________________

어휘 **variety** 다양성, 변화 / **spice** 묘미, 흥취; 양념 / **acceptance** 승인, 동의 / **filmmaking** 영화 제작 / **things are looking up (for)** (~의) 상황이 나아지고 있다

15 상황에 적절한 말 | ⑤

▶ 지희는 해진이 음식을 먹지 않고 남기는 것을 원하지 않으므로 미리 조언을 할 것이다.

① 다 남겨. 아무도 상관하지 않을 거야.
② 서양 음식은 내게도 기름기가 너무 많아.
③ 웨이터에게 음식을 싸달라고 하자.
④ 집에 가서 한국 음식을 좀 만들어 먹자.
⑤ 예의를 차려서 최대한 많이 먹도록 해봐.

W: Ji-hee and Hae-jin are first-year university students in America. They are at a party given by Julie, an American classmate. There is a buffet table of **various American foods that Julie made**. They take some food and go sit down in the living room near Julie and some other American classmates. After a few bites, Hae-jin realizes she doesn't **like the food she took**. Since arriving from Korea, she often misses Korean food. Ji-hee knows this and she also knows that Hae-jin can sometimes **act immaturely or childishly**. She is worried Hae-jin **might leave most of her food uneaten**, which would hurt Julie's feelings. In this situation, what would Ji-hee most likely say to Hae-jin?

여: 지희와 해진은 미국에서 대학교 1학년에 재학 중이다. 그들은 미국인 반 친구인 Julie가 여는 파티에 참석했다. 뷔페 식탁에는 Julie가 만든 다양한 미국 음식이 있다. 그들은 음식을 좀 덜어 거실로 가서 Julie와 다른 미국 친구들 옆에 앉는다. 해진은 몇 입 먹어보고는 가져온 음식들이 마음에 들지 않는다는 것을 깨닫는다. 한국에서 온 이후로 그녀는 한국 음식을 종종 그리워한다. 지희는 이를 알고 있고 해진이 때때로 성숙하지 못한 또는 아이 같은 행동을 한다는 것도 알고 있다. 그녀는 해진이 음식들을 먹지 않고 대부분 남길지도 모르고 그게 Julie의 기분을 상하게 할까 봐 걱정이 된다. 이러한 상황에서 지희가 해진에게 할 말로 가장 적절한 것은 무엇인가?

어휘 **oily** 기름기가 함유된 / **server** 웨이터, 서빙 하는 사람 / **wrap up** ~을 포장하다, 싸다 / **bite** 한 입 / **immaturely** 성숙하지 못하게, 미숙하게 / **childishly** 어린애 같이, 유치하게

16~17 세트 문항 | 16. ⑤ 17. ③

▶ 16. 원예와 집안 청소에 어떻게 커피 찌꺼기를 사용할 수 있는지 설명하고 있다.

① 최고의 커피를 만드는 방법
② 커피 찌꺼기를 청소하는 방법
③ 커피가 신체에 미치는 영향
④ 식물에 좋은 원예 방법
⑤ 집에서 커피 찌꺼기를 사용하는 방법

▶ 17. 해석 참조

M: Did you know there are lots of ways **you can use coffee grounds** instead of just throwing them in the garbage? Let's talk about some of the ways to use coffee grounds. First, **coffee grounds can be useful in your garden**. Sometimes your plants need a little boost in the mornings, too. So simply add a couple of cups of coffee grounds to a bucket of water and let it sit for a day. Then apply it to your plants and watch them grow. Coffee grounds can also be used for cleaning. **To absorb bad smells** in your closet and refrigerator, use coffee grounds. Rub coffee grounds into old pots and pans to get rid of stains. If you have scratched dark wooden furniture, use coffee grounds to fill in the scratches. They can also help clean your fireplace. Use wet coffee grounds to cover your ashes and **prevent them from giving off dust**.

남: 커피 찌꺼기를 그저 쓰레기로 버리는 대신 사용할 수 있는 방법이 많이 있다는 것을 알고 계셨습니까? 커피 찌꺼기를 사용하는 몇 가지 방법에 관해서 이야기해 봅시다. 우선, 커피 찌꺼기는 정원에서 유용할 수 있습니다. 때때로 식물도 아침마다 약간의 활력소가 필요합니다. 그러니 그저 커피 찌꺼기 두 컵을 물 한 양동이에 넣고 하루 동안 그대로 두기만 하십시오. 그러고 나서 그것을 식물에 주고 자라는 것을 지켜보십시오. 커피 찌꺼기는 청소하는 데에도 쓰일 수 있습니다. 옷장과 냉장고의 ① 악취를 흡수하는 데 커피 찌꺼기를 사용하십시오. 커피 찌꺼기를 낡은 냄비와 팬에 문질러 ② 얼룩을 제거하십시오. 긁혀서 흠집이 난 어두운색 원목 가구가 있다면 커피 찌꺼기를 사용해서 ④ 그 긁힌 자국을 메우십시오. 그것은 ⑤ 벽난로 청소에도 도움이 될 수 있습니다. 잿더미를 덮는 데 젖은 커피 찌꺼기를 사용하여 먼지가 날리는 것을 방지하십시오.

어휘 **ground** ((pl.)) 찌꺼기 / **boost** 활력소, 부양(책); 북돋움, 격려 / **stain** 얼룩

Answers & Explanation

01.① 02.⑤ 03.① 04.③ 05.④ 06.④ 07.① 08.③ 09.④ 10.④
11.② 12.④ 13.④ 14.⑤ 15.⑤ 16.③ 17.⑤

01 화자가 하는 말의 목적 | ①

▶ 과거로부터 배울 것이 많이 남아 있으므로 사적지는 보존되어야 한다는 취지의 내용이다.

W: As more and more people migrate to the cities, more buildings, roads, bridges, and subways must be built. When this happens, historical sites are sometimes discovered and **destroyed all at once**. Cities are often the historical capitals of past kingdoms and peoples. Much can be learned from our ancestors. Therefore, **they must be preserved** before all of their accumulated history is lost. With the current rate of construction, there will be no protected sites left within 10 years. **It is time to stop thoughtless development**. It may threaten our future too. The past still **has so much to teach us**.

여: 점점 더 많은 사람이 도시로 이주함에 따라 더 많은 건물과 도로, 다리 그리고 지하철이 건설되어야 합니다. 이런 일이 생기면, 때때로 사적지가 발견되기도 하고 한꺼번에 파괴되기도 합니다. 도시는 종종 과거의 왕국과 선조들의 역사적 수도입니다. 우리 조상들로부터 많은 것을 배울 수 있습니다. 그러므로 축적된 역사를 모두 잃어버리기 전에 그것들을 보존해야 합니다. 현재의 건설 속도라면 10년 내로 보호되는 사적지는 남아있지 않을 것입니다. 무분별한 개발을 멈춰야 할 때입니다. 그것은 우리의 미래도 위협할지 모릅니다. 과거는 우리에게 가르쳐줄 것이 아직 아주 많이 있습니다.

어휘 **migrate** 이주하다 / **historical site** 사적지(史跡地), 역사적인 장소 / **all at once** 한꺼번에, 전부 / **accumulate** ~을 축적하다, 모으다 / **construction** 건설, 건축 / **thoughtless** 무분별한, 경솔한

02 의견 | ⑤

▶ 여자가 헌혈하러 간다고 하자 남자는 여자의 건강상태를 확인하며 헌혈에 관한 중요한 규칙을 따르는지 확인하고 싶었다고 하는 것으로 보아 헌혈하기 전에는 건강상태를 확인해야 한다고 생각한다는 것을 알 수 있다.

M: Kate, where are you going?
W: Hi, Peter. I'm **on my way to donate blood**. It's something I do once every three months.
M: Wow! I'm so proud of you. By the way, how are you feeling?
W: **I've never felt better**. Why do you ask?
M: I read that it can be dangerous to donate blood if you aren't feeling well.
W: That's true, but don't worry. I slept well last night and had a big breakfast.
M: Good. And you don't have a cold or any other disease, right?
W: No, I don't. I always **check my health before giving blood** because it could be dangerous to the receiver.
M: I'm glad to hear that. **I just wanted to make sure** you're following the important rules for donating blood.
W: Thanks for your concern.

남: Kate, 어디 가니?
여: 안녕, Peter. 헌혈하러 가는 길이야. 헌혈은 내가 석 달에 한 번씩 하는 거야.
남: 와! 네가 정말 자랑스러워. 그나저나, 몸은 어때?
여: 최고로 좋아. 왜 물어보니?
남: 몸이 좋지 않으면 헌혈을 하는 게 위험할 수 있다고 읽었거든.
여 그건 사실이지만, 걱정하지 마. 지난밤에 푹 잤고 아침도 많이 먹었어.
남: 잘했어. 그리고 감기에 걸리거나 다른 병이 있는 건 아니지, 그렇지?
여: 그래, 없어. 수혈자에게 위험할 수 있기 때문에 헌혈하기 전에 난 항상 건강을 확인해.
남: 그 말을 들으니 기쁘다. 난 그저 네가 헌혈에 관한 중요한 규칙들을 지키고 있는지 확인하고 싶었어.
여: 염려해줘서 고마워.

어휘 **donate** (~을) 기증[기부]하다

03 관계 | ①

▶ 비행기가 불안정한 기류를 통과할 때 기장과 승무원 사이에 있을 수 있는 대화이다.

M: Ma'am, some of the people have been asking **why it is so bumpy**.
W: Just make an announcement that we are passing through a big storm cloud.
M: That might **make them even more scared**.
W: Then tell them we are going through rough air and it is common over this part of the Pacific Ocean.
M: Maybe it would be better if you told them yourself. Besides, I have to serve drinks soon.
W: Yeah, I guess I can do that. I will keep the "fasten seatbelts" sign on.
M: Great, thanks. I'll **go try to calm down the lady** in seat 4-B. She has been crying!
W: Tell her we'll be out of this rough spot soon and that there's nothing at all to worry about.
M: **That will be a relief for her**.

남: 기장님, 승객 몇몇 분이 왜 이렇게 흔들리는지 궁금해 하십니다.
여: 거대한 폭풍우 구름을 통과하고 있다고 방송을 해 주세요.
남: 승객들이 훨씬 더 불안해하실 수도 있습니다.
여: 그럼 불안정한 기류를 통과하고 있으며 태평양의 이 부근에서는 흔한 일이라고 알려 드리세요.
남: 어쩌면 기장님께서 직접 말씀하시면 더 좋을 것 같습니다. 게다가 전 음료 서비스를 곧 해야 해서요.
여: 네, 제가 할 수 있을 것 같네요. '안전벨트 착용' 표시는 계속 켜놓겠습니다.
남: 좋습니다, 감사합니다. 저는 좌석 4-B에 앉아 계신 여자분을 진정시키러 가야겠습니다. 그 분은 계속 울고 계세요!
여: 이 험한 지점을 곧 벗어날 것이고 걱정할 게 전혀 없다고 말씀드리세요.
남: 그분께 위안이 되겠네요.

어휘 **bumpy** 덜커덩거리는, 울퉁불퉁한; (항공) 돌풍이 있는, 난기류가 있는 / **rough air** 악기류 ((순조롭지 못한 대기의 유동)) / **the Pacific Ocean** 태평양 / **fasten** ~을 단단히 고정시키다 / **spot** (특정한) 장소, 자리 / **relief** 위안, 위로

04 그림 불일치 | ③

▶ 여자는 졸업 사진 대신 가족사진을 걸기로 했다고 말했다.

[Cell phone rings.]
M: Hello?
W: Hi, Dad.
M: Hi, Kelly. How is everything? Have you finished unpacking?
W: Almost. I just finished **putting some flowered curtains up** in my room.
M: Did your brother bring your chest of drawers for you?
W: Yes, and he put them **on one side of the room**.
M: Okay. I bet you already hung your graduation picture as well.
W: Actually, I decided to hang a family portrait instead.
M: That sounds nice. Did you **have any trouble moving things**?
W: No trouble. My brother helped me move my bed next to the drawers.
M: What about the floor lamp that I ordered for you?
W: It arrived, and I put it to the right of my bed.
M: **Everything sounds good**. I'll see you when I get home.

[휴대전화 벨이 울린다.]
남: 여보세요?
여: 여보세요, 아빠.
남: 그래, Kelly. 어때? 짐 푸는 건 끝났니?
여: 거의 다 했어요. 방에 꽃무늬 커튼 다는 것을 이제 막 마쳤어요.
남: 오빠가 네 서랍장을 가져다주었니?
여: 네, 그리고 방 한쪽에 놓아주었어요.
남: 그래. 당연히 네 졸업 사진도 이미 걸었겠지.
여: 실은, 가족사진을 대신 걸기로 결정했어요.
남: 잘했구나. 짐 옮기는 데 문제는 없었니?
여: 없었어요. 오빠가 침대를 서랍장 옆으로 옮기는 걸 도와주었어요.
남: 내가 주문해 준 플로어 스탠드는 어떠니?
여: 도착해서 침대 오른쪽에 두었어요.

남: 모든 게 잘된 것 같구나. 집에 가면 보자꾸나.

어휘 **unpack** (짐을) 풀다 / **chest of drawers** 서랍장

05 추후 행동 | ④

▶ 남자가 책상을 버리겠다고 하자 여자가 책상을 자선센터에 기증할 것을 권유했다. 내일은 자선센터가 문을 닫으므로, 남자는 오늘 책상을 자선단체에 가져다 준다고 했다.

W: Wow! There is so much stuff. It's very hard packing for the move.
M: Definitely. I can't believe we've kept so many things we don't use anymore.
W: We need to get rid of our old clothes **we haven't worn in more than two years**.
M: You're right. I have to throw away this desk, too.
W: But you need a desk. You bought it just 3 years ago.
M: I need two monitors for working, but **it's too small to put two monitors on**. I'm going to buy a larger one.
W: Then **how about donating your desk to** the charity center? I'm sure there will be a person who needs a desk.
M: That's a great idea. I'll take it to the center tomorrow.
W: You should probably go there today. It is probably closed tomorrow since it's a Saturday.
M: You're right. I'll go now. Is it on Elm Avenue?
W: Right. **Make it quick**. We have a lot to do today.

여: 왜! 물건이 무척 많아요. 이사하려고 짐을 싸는 게 너무 어려워요.
남: 정말 그래요. 우리가 더는 사용하지 않는 물건을 그렇게 많이 가지고 있었다는 게 믿을 수가 없어요.
여: 2년 이상 입지 않은 오래된 옷들은 처리할 필요가 있어요.
남: 맞아요. 이 책상도 버려야 해요.
여: 하지만 당신 책상이 필요하잖아요. 그것을 고작 3년 전에 샀잖아요.
남: 난 일하려면 모니터가 2개 필요한데, 그것은 모니터 2개를 놓기엔 너무 작아요. 난 더 큰 것을 살 거예요.
여: 그러면 당신 책상을 자선센터에 기증하는 건 어때요? 분명히 책상이 필요한 사람이 있을 거예요.
남: 그거 좋은 생각이에요. 내가 내일 센터로 그것을 가져갈게요.
여: 거기 오늘 가야 할 거예요. 내일은 토요일이라서 거기는 아마 문을 닫을 거예요.
남: 맞아요. 지금 갈게요. Elm가에 있나요?
여: 맞아요. 서둘러요. 우리는 오늘 할 일이 많아요.

어휘 **get rid of** 처리하다, 없애다 / **charity** 자선

06 금액 | ④

▶ 두 켤레의 신발을 같이 사면 둘 중에 가격이 더 싼 신발을 반값에 판매하는 세일을 하고 있다. 따라서 여자는 운동화를 반값($35)에, 테니스화는 정가($80)를 내고 사게 될 것이다.

M: Welcome to Shoe Town. Are you **looking for anything special**?
W: I saw the advertisement for your sale in the newspaper.
M: That's right. We're having a "buy one pair, get the second pair for half price" sale.
W: So **one pair of shoes is full price**?
M: Right and the lower priced shoes are 50% off.
W: So, these running shoes cost $70. If I bought them, how much will these tennis shoes cost?
M: Well, they are $80, so **you pay full price for those**.
W: Oh, I see. Then it's the running shoes that are half price, since **they cost less**.
M: Exactly. Would you like both pairs?
W: Yes, please. How much will that be?

남: Shoe Town에 오신 것을 환영합니다. 특별히 찾으시는 것이 있습니까?
여: 신문에 난 세일 광고를 봤습니다.
남: 그렇습니다. '한 켤레를 사시면 다른 한 켤레는 반값에 가져가세요' 세일을 하고 있습니다.
여: 그럼 한 켤레는 정가를 내야 하나요?
남: 그렇습니다. 그리고 (둘 중에서) 가격이 더 싼 신발을 50% 할인해 드립니다.
여: 그럼, 이 운동화는 70달러네요. 제가 이걸 사면 이 테니스화는 얼마입니까?
남: 음, 그것은 80달러이니까 정가를 지불하셔야 합니다.
여: 네, 알겠습니다. 그럼 반값인 것은 운동화겠네요. 왜냐하면 그게 더 싸니까요.
남: 그렇습니다. 두 켤레 모두 사시겠습니까?
여: 네, 주세요. 얼마입니까?

어휘 **full price** 정가 / **running shoe** 운동화

07 이유 | ①

▶ 남자는 출산이 임박한 아내 곁에 있어주기 위해 병원에 가는 길이라고 했다.

W: Sir, are you aware of how fast you were going? I'm afraid I have to **give you a ticket**.
M: I'm terribly sorry, officer, but I have an excuse.
W: All right. I'm listening.
M: **My wife is pregnant**, and I'm on my way to the hospital to be with her.
W: **Is she about to give birth** right now?
M: Yes. My mother-in-law called me and said the baby is expected at any moment.
W: Is that the reason you were speeding?
M: Yes, I promised to be with her at the hospital.
W: I **sympathize with your situation**, but you will still need to pay an $80 fine.
M: I understand, officer.

여: 선생님, 얼마나 빨리 달리고 있었는지 알고 계십니까? 딱지를 발부해야 할 것 같습니다.
남: 정말 죄송합니다, 경관님. 하지만 제겐 그럴 만한 이유가 있습니다.
여: 알겠습니다. 듣고 있어요.
남: 제 아내가 임신 중이어서 함께 있어주기 위해 병원에 가는 길이었습니다.
여: 지금 당장 출산하시려는 참인가요?
남: 네. 장모님께서 전화하셔서 아기가 금방이라도 나올 거라고 말씀하셨어요.
여: 그게 과속하고 계셨던 이유입니까?
남: 네, 병원에서 아내와 함께 있어주기로 약속했거든요.
여: 선생님의 상황은 안타깝게 생각하지만, 여전히 벌금 80달러를 내셔야 할 겁니다.
남: 알겠습니다, 경관님.

어휘 **be about to-v** 막 v하려는 참이다 / **sympathize with** ~을 동정하다, 측은히 여기다

08 언급하지 않은 것 | ③

▶ 해석 참조

M: Look at this, Jessica. The newspaper says **there will be a solar eclipse** tomorrow afternoon!
W: Umm, okay, Dad. What's a solar eclipse?
M: Oh, well, a solar eclipse occurs when the moon passes between the Earth and the sun.
W: So we won't be able to see the sun tomorrow afternoon?
M: Well, for a period, the moon will **block most of the light** from the sun.
W: That sounds amazing! Can we watch?
M: Yes, but we need to prepare some special glasses first. Even behind the moon, the sun is still **powerful enough to harm our eyes**.
W: Okay. I guess I thought it would be completely dark.
M: There are **three types of eclipse**, a partial eclipse, a total eclipse and an annular eclipse. This will be a partial eclipse, so **only part of the sun will be blocked**.
W: I understand.

남: 이것 보렴, Jessica. 신문에서 내일 오후에 일식이 있을 거라고 하는구나(① 발생 예정 시기)!
여: 음, 네, 아빠. 일식이 뭐예요?
남: 아, 그래, 일식은 달이 지구와 태양 사이로 지나갈 때 발생(② 발생 원리)한단다.
여: 그럼 내일 오후에는 태양을 볼 수 없을까요?
남: 음, 일정 시간 동안 달이 태양에서 나오는 빛 대부분을 가릴 거야.
여: 놀라운데요! 우리가 볼 수 있어요?
남: 응, 하지만 먼저 특수 안경을 준비(④ 관측 시 주의사항)해야 한단다. 달 뒤에서도 태양은 우리 눈을 상하게 할 만큼 여전히 강력하거든.
여: 알겠어요. 완전히 어두워질 거라고 생각했었나 봐요.
남: 일식에는 부분일식, 개기일식, 금환일식(⑤ 종류) 세 종류가 있어. 이번에는 부분일식이라서 태양의 일부분만 가려질 거야.
여: 그렇군요.

어휘 **solar eclipse** ((천문)) 일식(日蝕) / **partial** 부분적인; 편파적인 / **annular eclipse** ((천문)) 금환일식 ((달이 태양의 한복판을 가리고 둘레를 가리지 못하여 태양이 고리 모양으로 보이는 현상))

09 내용 불일치 | ④

▶ 방청객은 방청석에 들어올 때 질문을 제출하게 된다고 말했다.

M: Tonight's scheduled television program will not be shown. Instead we will present you with the Presidential Candidates' Debate. **The debate will feature** the three candidates representing the Democratic Party. It will be a live, unscripted question-and-answer session. Network news anchor Christopher Martin will host tonight's debate and will present questions. **Questions will be submitted** by the studio audience as they enter the auditorium. **In keeping with** our fair and impartial standards, we will be presenting the Republican candidates' debate tomorrow night at this same time. Tomorrow's program is going to feature **the four candidates for president** representing the Republican Party.

남: 오늘 밤에 예정되어 있던 텔레비전 프로그램은 방송되지 않을 것입니다. 대신 대통령 후보들의 토론을 보내 드리겠습니다. 토론은 민주당을 대표하는 세 명의 후보들을 대상으로 할 것입니다. 토론은 생방송으로 즉석 질문과 대답으로 진행될 것입니다. Network 뉴스 앵커인 Christopher Martin 씨가 오늘 밤 토론의 사회를 맡아 질문을 할 것입니다. 질문은 방청객이 방청석에 들어올 때 제출하게 될 것입니다. 저희의 공정하고 편견 없는 기준에 따라, 내일 밤 똑같은 이 시간에 공화당 후보들의 토론도 방송해 드릴 것입니다. 내일 방송은 공화당을 대표하는 네 명의 대통령 후보를 대상으로 할 예정입니다.

어휘 **debate** 토론 / **feature** ~을 특색으로 삼다, 특집하다 / **candidate** 후보 / **represent** ~을 대표하다 / **Democratic Party** (미국) 민주당 / **unscripted** 즉흥의, 대본이 없는 / **auditorium** 방청석, 청중석 / **in keeping with** ~에 따라, ~와 조화[일치]하여 / **impartial** 공정한, 편견이 없는 / **Republican Party** (미국) 공화당

10 도표 이해 | ④

▶ 두 사람은 우선 유모차의 20파운드보다 가벼우면서 유모차가 견디는 무게는 50파운드가 넘는 것을 원한다. 가격은 300달러보다 저렴한 것을 원해서 ③과 ④의 두 가지 선택지가 있는데 보관 바스켓이 없더라도 가격이 더 싼 것을 사겠다고 했으므로 답은 ④이다.

W: Honey, we need to get another stroller. We need a lightweight stroller that's **easy to fold and carry** and that we can use for traveling.
M: I agree. Let's choose from this website, Strolleria.com.
W: **The first thing we need to check** is weight.
M: Definitely. We should buy something that **weighs less than 20 pounds**.
W: And I have to get a sturdy stroller that can handle more than 50 pounds. Our daughter is getting bigger every day.
M: Good point. How much should we spend?
W: Let's find something for under $300.
M: Then we have these two options. One of the strollers **has a storage basket underneath**. Do you want to get it?
W: That would be convenient but **I can live without it**. I prefer the cheaper one.
M: That's nice. Let's order it.

여: 여보, 우리는 유모차를 하나 더 사야 해요. 접어서 들고 다니기 편하고 여행용으로 사용할 수 있는 가벼운 유모차가 필요해요.
남: 맞아요. 이 웹사이트 Strolleria.com에서 고릅시다.
여: 제일 먼저 확인해야 할 것은 무게예요.
남: 그렇고말고요. 20파운드보다 가벼운 것을 사야 해요.
여: 그리고 50파운드 넘게 처리할 수 있는 튼튼한 유모차를 사야 해요. 우리 딸은 하루가 다르게 크고 있어요.
남: 아주 잘 지적했어요. 우리가 얼마를 써야 할까요?
여: 300달러보다 싼 것을 찾아봐요.
남: 그러면 이 두 선택사항이 있군요. 유모차 중 하나는 아래에 보관 바구니가 있어요. 그걸 사고 싶어요?
여: 편리하겠지만 그건 없어도 살 수 있어요. 난 가격이 더 싼 게 마음에 들어요.
남: 그거 좋네요. 주문합시다.

어휘 **stroller** (접을 수 있는) 유모차 / **storage** 보관 / **lightweight** 가벼운, 경량의 / **sturdy** 튼튼한 / **option** 선택(권)

11 짧은 대화에 이어질 응답 | ②

▶ 왜 늦었는지 묻는 여자의 말에 그 이유를 밝히는 응답이 가장 적절하다.

① 거의 10분.
② 도서관에서 잠들었어.
③ 시험에서 낙제하지 않으면 좋겠어.
④ 교수님께서 나한테 수업 끝나고 남으라고 하셨어.
⑤ 교수님이 왜 내게 화가 나셨는지 이해가 돼.

W: I heard that Mr. Smith **was angry with you**. What happened?
M: **I was really late for class**, and I missed the first part of the exam.
W: Why were you late?
M: ______________________________

여: Smith 교수님께서 너에게 화가 나셨다고 들었어. 무슨 일이 있었니?
남: 내가 수업시간에 너무 늦어서 시험 앞부분을 못 봤거든.
여: 왜 늦었어?
남: ______________________________

12 짧은 대화에 이어질 응답 | ④

▶ 마지막으로 스키를 타러 간 시기가 언제냐는 남자의 질문에 가장 적절한 응답을 고른다.

① 늘 가곤 했어.
② 스키 타는 법을 잊은 것 같아.
③ 이건 매우 재미있을 거야.
④ 아이였을 때 이후로 가본 적이 없어.
⑤ 설악산 근처에 있는 리조트로 갈 거야.

M: I want to go skiing this weekend. What do you think?
W: Okay, but I might need a lesson. I **haven't gone in a long time**.
M: When was **the last time you went**?
W: ______________________________

남: 난 이번 주말에 스키 타러 가고 싶어. 어떻게 생각해?
여: 그래, 하지만 난 강습이 필요할지도 몰라. 오랫동안 안 갔거든.
남: 마지막으로 간 게 언제야?
여: ______________________________

13 긴 대화에 이어질 응답 | ④

▶ 어려울 때 항상 함께해 준 친구를 위하는 여자의 마음을 이해해주는 답변이 적절하다.

① 미안하지만 나는 Rose의 집이 어딘지 몰라요.
② 하지만 친구에게 항상 솔직해야 해요.
③ 이 장미들을 물과 함께 화병에 꽂아 줄래요?
④ 그래요. 친구가 당신을 필요로 하잖아요. 우린 내일 기념하면 돼요.
⑤ 당신의 남자 친구가 오면 더 낭만적일 거예요.

W: Something smells really good! Are you cooking?
M: Yes. I'm making my famous homemade pizza with eggplant and sweet onions.
W: **What's the occasion**?
M: Did you forget? It's our one-year anniversary!
W: Yes, I did forget. And I made plans with Rose tonight.
M: Can't you see her some other night? I've been **working really hard on this meal**.
W: I wish I could, but she has been having a hard time since her grandfather died.
M: That's really sad, but **I have been planning this for days**.
W: I know! And it's really romantic. I guess I can call Rose and **make an excuse**, but she has always been there for me when I needed her.
M: ______________________________

여: 정말 좋은 냄새가 나는군요! 요리하는 중이에요?
남: 네. 가지와 달콤한 양파가 들어간 제가 직접 만드는 그 유명한 피자를 요리 중이에요.
여: 무슨 날인가요?
남: 잊어버렸어요? 우리 1주년 기념일이잖아요!
여: 네, 정말로 잊고 있었어요. 그리고 전 오늘 밤에 Rose랑 약속이 있어요.
남: 다른 날 만나면 안돼요? 이 음식을 정말 공들여 만들고 있어요.
여: 그러고 싶지만 그 애는 할아버지께서 돌아가신 후로 힘든 시간을 보내고 있어요.
남: 정말 슬픈 일이지만, 난 이걸 며칠 동안이나 계획했어요.
여: 알아요! 그리고 정말 낭만적이에요. Rose에게 전화해서 핑계를 댈 수도 있지만, 그 애는 내가 필요할 때 항상 나와 함께 있어준 걸요.
남: ______________________________

어휘 **eggplant** ((식물)) 가지 / **occasion** 특별한 일, 특수한 경우 / **make an excuse** 변명하다

14 긴 대화에 이어질 응답 | ⑤

▶ 길을 안내해 주던 여자가 길 찾기를 어려워하는 남자에게 할 수 있는 적절한 대답을 유추해 본다.

① 여기서 어디로 가야 할지 모르겠어요.
② 아마 Main 가를 먼저 찾아보셔야 할 거예요.
③ Main 가는 폐쇄되었어요. 내일 다시 오세요.
④ 거기에 가려고 제가 택시를 타야 한다고는 생각하지 않아요.
⑤ 하지만 정말 쉬워요. 제가 약도를 그려 드릴게요.

M: Can you tell me how to get to Main Street?
W: Sure, just **take a right at the next corner**; walk three blocks, then cross the street and....
M: Wait, slow down. **Turn right at this corner** and then what?
W: And then walk three blocks. When you see the library, cross the street and turn left.
M: You mean go left **on the other side of the street**?
W: What I meant was that you should **continue going in the same direction** you were going.
M: I'm starting to **get really confused**. Maybe I should just call for a taxi.
W: ______________________________

남: Main 가로 가는 길을 알려주시겠어요?
여: 물론이죠. 다음 모퉁이에서 오른쪽으로 돌아서, 세 블록을 걸어간 다음, 길을 건너시고….
남: 잠시만요, 천천히 말씀해 주세요. 이 모퉁이에서 오른쪽으로 돌아서 어떻게 하라고요?
여: 그러고 나서 세 블록을 걸어가세요. 도서관이 보이면 길을 건너서 왼쪽으로 도세요.
남: 길 건너편에서 왼쪽으로 가란 말씀이세요?
여: 제 말은 가시던 똑같은 방향으로 계속 가시라는 거예요.
남: 정말 혼동되기 시작하네요. 아마 그냥 택시를 불러야 할까 봐요.
여: ______________________________

15 상황에 적절한 말 | ⑤

▶ 나쁜 언어 습관을 가지고 있는 친구에게 할 수 있는 조언을 유추해 본다.

① 난 공부를 해야 해서 운동을 할 수 없어.
② 이제는 누구도 더는 너를 무시할 수 없을 거야.
③ 우리 어머니께서 너보고 저녁 식사하러 오라셔.
④ 네 어머니께서 다음 주에 축구장으로 우리를 데리러 오실 수 있을까?
⑤ 제발 말조심해. 다른 사람의 감정을 상하게 할 수도 있어.

W: William and Jonas are good friends. They spend a lot of time playing sports together. Sometimes, during games, Jonas **gets a little carried away** and uses a lot of bad language. **Everyone usually ignores it** during a game, as emotions can run a little high. But **on more than one occasion**, William's mother has heard Jonas using that language when she **has arrived to pick the boys up** from the field. She ignored it the first few times. But she eventually told William that if she heard it again, she would not allow William to play sports with Jonas anymore. In this situation, what would William most likely say to Jonas?

여: William과 Jonas는 좋은 친구다. 그들은 함께 운동을 하며 많은 시간을 보낸다. 때때로 Jonas는 경기 중에 약간 흥분하여 욕을 많이 한다. 감정이 좀 격해질 수 있어서, 경기 중에는 대개 모두들 그것을 무시해 버린다. 그러나 William의 어머니는 경기장으로 아이들을 데리러 왔을 때 Jonas가 그런 말을 하는 것을 두 번 이상 들으셨다. 어머니는 처음 몇 번은 그것을 무시하셨다. 그러나 결국 어머니는 그런 소리를 다시 듣게 된다면, Jonas와 운동하는 것을 더는 허락하지 않을 것이라고 William에게 말씀하셨다. 이러한 상황에서 William이 Jonas에게 할 말로 가장 적절한 것은 무엇인가?

어휘 **watch[mind] one's language** (남에게 기분 나쁜 말을 하지 않도록) 말을 조심하다 / **offend** ~의 감정을 상하게 하다 / **get[be] carried away** 흥분하다, 넋을 잃다 / **run high** (감정 따위가) 격해지다

16~17 세트 문항 | 16. ③ 17. ⑤

▶ 16. 비용을 적게 들이면서 집에서 휴가를 보내는 방법을 소개하고 있다.

① 완벽한 하우스 파티 열기
② 3D 영화의 증가하는 인기
③ 집에서 저렴한 휴가를 즐기는 방법
④ 여행비용을 줄이는 방법들
⑤ 선글라스와 안경의 차이점

▶ 17. 해석 참조

M: Vacation season is coming up, but we need to **watch our expenses**. So instead of going somewhere for a vacation, why not stay at home? You can start by inviting your friends to your house for a house party. If you **make use of leftovers** in your refrigerator and ask your friends to bring something to eat, it won't cost you much. Another cheap and fun idea is to turn your house into a 3D movie theater. Even if you only have a regular PC monitor, don't worry. **You only need to download** a 3D video converter. By using this program, you can watch normal videos in 3D. The next step is making 3D glasses. You can **build your own 3D glasses** using a spare CD case and some permanent markers. Just color the transparent side of the CD case with red and blue markers to **create lenses to cover your eyes**. Alternatively, you may use an existing pair of sunglasses and **replace the lenses with colored sheets** of transparent plastic. Or pick an old pair of eyeglasses and color the lenses red and blue.

남: 휴가철이 다가오고 있지만, (휴가) 비용에 주의할 필요가 있습니다. 그러니 휴가로 어디엔가 가는 대신 집에서 머무르는 게 어떤가요? 하우스 파티를 위해 친구들을 집으로 초대하는 것부터 시작할 수 있습니다. 냉장고에 남아 있는 음식을 활용하고 친구들에게 먹을거리를 가져오도록 부탁한다면 비용이 많이 들지 않을 것입니다. 돈이 적게 들면서도 재미있는 또 다른 계획은 집을 3D 영화관으로 바꾸는 것입니다. 일반 PC 모니터만 있더라도 걱정하지 마십시오. 3D 비디오 변환기를 내려 받기만 하면 됩니다. 이 프로그램을 사용해서 일반 비디오 영상을 3D로 볼 수 있습니다. 다음 단계는 3D 안경 제작입니다. 남는 ① CD 케이스와 ② 유성 매직펜 몇 개를 사용해서 여러분만의 3D 안경을 만들 수 있습니다. 눈에 댈 렌즈를 만들기 위해 CD 케이스의 투명한 면을 빨간색과 파란색 매직펜으로 색칠하십시오. 그 대신, 기존 ③ 선글라스를 이용해 렌즈를 채색된 투명 플라스틱판으로 대체할 수도 있습니다. 아니면 ④ 낡은 안경 하나를 골라 렌즈를 빨간색과 파란색으로 색칠하십시오.

어휘 **cut down (on)** (~을) 줄이다 / **leftover** 남은 음식 / **converter** 변환기, 전환기 / **spare** 여분의, 예비용의 / **permanent** 영구적인 / **marker** 매직펜; 표시, 표지(물) / **transparent** 투명한; 명백한 / **alternatively** 그 대신에, 그렇지 않으면 / **existing** 기존의, 현재 사용되는 / **sheet** (보통 사각형으로 납작한) 한 장[판]; (종이) 한 장

Answers & Explanation

01. ⑤ 02. ② 03. ① 04. ④ 05. ② 06. ③ 07. ⑤ 08. ⑤ 09. ④ 10. ③
11. ① 12. ④ 13. ④ 14. ③ 15. ⑤ 16. ④ 17. ③

01 화자가 하는 말의 목적 | ⑤

▶ 남자는 자신이 일하는 빌딩에서 새로운 금연 규정이 제대로 시행되고 있지 않는 점을 지적하고 있다.

W: This is Ideal Property Managers. **No one is available at the moment**. Please leave a message after the beep. *[beep]*

M: Hello. My name is Scott Green. I am one of the doctors running the medical clinic **on the fourth floor** of the Delaware Building. Your company manages this building. Last week, the city government passed new non-smoking regulations. **Smoking is no longer allowed** in any public building, including the Delaware Building. So **I was alarmed** when I saw office workers still smoking in the staircase. **I want these regulations enforced** by the security staff in the building. When I informed them that people were smoking in the staircase, they did nothing. Please make sure that this does not happen again.

여: Ideal 자산 매니저 사(社)입니다. 지금은 모두 부재중입니다. 삐 소리 후에 메시지를 남겨 주십시오. *[삐]*

남: 안녕하세요. 저는 Scott Green입니다. Delaware 빌딩 4층에서 병원을 운영하고 있는 의사 중 한 사람입니다. 귀사에서 이 빌딩을 관리하고 계시지요. 지난주 시(市) 정부가 새 금연법을 통과시켰습니다. Delaware 빌딩을 포함한 어떤 공공건물에서도 흡연이 더는 허용되지 않습니다. 그래서 저는 사무실 직원들이 계단에서 여전히 담배를 피우는 것을 보고 놀랐습니다. 저는 건물의 경비 담당자들이 이 규정을 시행해 주시기를 바랍니다. 제가 경비 담당자들에게 사람들이 계단에서 담배를 피우고 있다는 것을 알렸지만 그들은 어떤 조치도 취하지 않았습니다. 이런 일이 다시는 일어나지 않도록 해 주시길 바랍니다.

어휘 **property** 자산, 소유물 / **run** ~을 운영[경영]하다 / **regulation** 규정, 규제 / **alarmed** 깜짝 놀란 / **enforce** ~을 시행하다, 집행하다 / **security** 경비 부서; 안전, 보안

02 대화 주제 | ②

▶ 별을 볼 수 없게 되고, 동물들이 생활 방식에 변화를 겪는 등 인공조명의 부정적인 영향을 이야기하고 있다.

W: Rick, you know what I really miss about our trip to the countryside?

M: If you're like me, you miss the night sky. There were so many stars!

W: Right. I never realized how much I was missing **by living in such a bright city**.

M: Bright city lighting affects more than just our ability to see stars. It also **has an impact on wildlife**.

W: I've heard about that. For example, birds alter their migration paths because of artificial lighting.

M: Street lights also **have an effect on the way** insects and small animals hunt.

W: That's too bad. I think we should do something to **prevent unnecessary light pollution**.

M: Some countries are taking steps to reduce its impact. Our country really should join them.

여: Rick, 우리가 갔던 시골 여행에서 내가 정말 그리워하는 게 뭔지 알아?

남: 나와 같다면 넌 밤하늘을 그리워할 거야. 별이 아주 많았잖아!

여: 맞아. 이렇게 밝은 도시에 살면서 얼마나 많은 것을 놓치고 있는지 미처 깨닫지 못했어.

남: 도시의 밝은 조명은 별을 보는 우리의 능력보다 더 많은 것에 영향을 미쳐. 야생 동물들에게도 영향을 주고.

여: 그것에 대해서 들어본 적 있어. 예를 들면, 인공조명 때문에 새들이 이동 경로를 바꾸는 거 말야.

남: 가로등도 곤충과 작은 동물이 사냥하는 방식에 영향을 미쳐.

여: 그거 정말 유감이다. 불필요한 광공해를 막기 위해 우리가 무언가를 해야 한다고 생각해.

남: 몇몇 국가는 광공해의 영향을 줄이기 위한 조치를 취하고 있어. 우리나라가 그 나라들에 꼭 동참해야 해.

어휘 **lighting** 조명 (장치) / **alter** ~을 바꾸다, 변경하다 / **migration** (사람·동물 등의) 이동, 이주 / **artificial** 인공적인 / **light pollution** 광공해 ((가로등 같은 인공조명이 너무 많아 별빛을 볼 수 없는 것과 같은 상황)) / **take a step** 조치를 취하다

03 관계 | ①

▶ 두 사람 모두 진행하고 있는 연구가 있고 자신의 연구가 기사화되거나 그에 대해 인터뷰를 해주는 위치에 있는 사람들이다.

M: Were you interviewed last week about your research?

W: Yes, a newspaper reporter came to my laboratory.

M: **Have you read the story**?

W: Not yet. It's going to be **a large feature story** on the effects of the oil spill.

M: I know. I was interviewed, too.

W: People are really concerned about **the destruction to the environment** caused by negligence.

M: Did you watch the news last night?

W: They showed pictures of residents and volunteers **cleaning beaches**.

M: Some birds were covered in oil.

W: It's a tragedy.

M: I agree. But **it'll bring attention to my research** on the effects of pollution on animals' reproductive systems.

W: **It's a little ironic that way**.

남: 지난주에 연구에 대한 인터뷰를 하셨어요?

여: 네, 신문 기자 한 분이 제 실험실로 오셨어요.

남: 기사는 읽어 보셨어요?

여: 아직 안 읽었어요. 기름 유출의 영향에 대한 광범위한 특집 기사가 될 거예요.

남: 알고 있어요. 저도 인터뷰를 했거든요.

여: 부주의로 인해 발생한 환경 파괴에 대해 사람들이 아주 우려하고 있어요.

남: 어젯밤에 뉴스 보셨어요?

여: 해변을 청소하고 있는 주민들과 자원봉사자들의 장면을 보여주더군요.

남: 어떤 새들은 기름에 뒤덮여 있었어요.

여: 정말 비극적인 사건이에요.

남: 그래요. 하지만 그로 인해 오염이 동물의 생식 체계에 미치는 영향에 관한 제 연구가 관심을 끌게 될 거예요.

여: 그런 점에선 다소 모순되는군요.

어휘 **laboratory** 실험실, 연구소 / **feature story** 특집 기사 / **spill** 유출, 엎질러짐 / **negligence** 부주의, 태만 / **tragedy** 비극 / **reproductive** 생식의, 번식하는 / **ironic** 모순[역설]적인, 반어적인

04 그림 불일치 | ④

▶ 여자가 빈 바구니를 든 소녀를 그리려고 했지만, 채소가 가득 찬 바구니를 든 소녀를 그리기로 마음을 바꿨다고 했다.

W: Ethan, this is the flyer for our farm tour. **Can you take a look and let me know** what you think?

M: Wow, it looks great! You put the title, "AMBURY FARM TOUR," on the left.

W: Yes. I also drew a chicken on top of the letters F-A-R-M. What do you think?

M: Great idea. I love it.

W: Is it okay to have the address and telephone number of our farm below the title?

M: Good. I think it's a good idea to **keep all the information on the left side**.

W: What do you think about the girl holding a basket full of vegetables next to the title?

M: Looks good to me. I like her big hat.

W: Originally, I was going to draw **a girl holding an empty basket**, but I changed my mind.

M: I like this full one better. It shows one of the activities we'll have.

W: I also drew a horse and a cow on the right side.

M: Perfect! They're also **what our customers expect at our farm**.

W: Great. I'll print this out.

여: Ethan, 이게 우리 농장 투어의 전단이에요. 살펴보고 어떻게 생각하는지 알려줄 수 있어요?
남: 와, 멋져요! 왼쪽에 'AMBURY FARM TOUR'라는 제목을 두었네요.
여: 네. 또 FARM이라는 글자 위에 닭을 한 마리 그렸어요. 어때요?
남: 좋은 생각이에요. 저는 그게 좋아요.
여: 제목 아래에 우리 농장의 주소와 전화번호가 있는 건 괜찮아요?
남: 좋아요. 모든 정보를 왼쪽에 둔 것이 좋은 생각인 것 같아요.
여: 제목 옆에 채소가 가득 찬 바구니를 들고 있는 소녀는 어때요?
남: 좋아 보여요. 그녀의 큰 모자가 좋네요.
여: 원래는 빈 바구니를 들고 있는 소녀를 그리려고 했는데 생각을 바꿨어요.
남: 이 가득 찬 것이 더 좋아요. 우리가 할 활동들 중 하나를 보여주잖아요.
여: 오른쪽에 말 한 마리와 소 한 마리도 그렸어요.
남: 완벽해요! 그것들도 우리 고객들이 우리 농장에 기대하는 것이죠.
여: 좋아요. 이것을 출력할게요.

어휘 **flyer** (광고·안내용) 전단

05 추후 행동 | ②

▶ 현재 시급한 문제는 후원 업체를 찾는 것이라는 남자의 말에 여자가 아버지의 회사가 후원해 줄 수 있을지 알아보겠다고 했다.

M: I'm planning a community service project for civics class.
W: What will you do?
M: **I'll clean up the area** along the river near the park.
W: That's great, but **why don't you seem excited about it**?
M: It's a lot of work to organize all by myself.
W: What do you have to do first?
M: Well, first I need to get sponsors to buy trash bags and snacks and drinks for volunteers.
W: Then I guess you need to find volunteers to help with the clean-up.
M: Yes. I'm going to **put up flyers around town** to advertise it. But finding sponsors is urgent.
W: Well, I will ask my Dad if his company will help you.
M: Thanks. I feel like **I'm halfway there now**.

남: 나는 윤리 수업을 위해 지역 봉사 활동 프로젝트를 계획하고 있어.
여: 무엇을 할 거니?
남: 공원 근처의 강을 따라 그 지역을 청소할 거야.
여: 멋지다. 그런데 왜 즐거워 보이지 않니?
남: 나 혼자 준비하기에는 일이 너무 많아서.
여: 먼저 무엇부터 해야 하는데?
남: 음, 첫 번째로 후원 업체를 구해서 쓰레기봉투와 자원봉사자들을 위한 음식과 음료수를 구입해야 해.
여: 그럼 청소를 도울 자원봉사자들도 찾아야겠구나.
남: 응. 나는 홍보하기 위해 시내 도처에 전단지를 붙일 거야. 하지만 후원 업체를 찾는 것이 급해.
여: 그럼, 내가 아버지 회사가 너를 도와줄지 아버지께 여쭤볼게.
남: 고마워. 이제 절반을 끝낸 것처럼 느껴져.

어휘 **community service** 지역 봉사 활동 / **civics** 윤리학 / **sponsor** 후원자 / **urgent** 긴급한 / **be halfway there** (목표 달성 과정에서) 반은 끝난 셈이다

06 금액 | ③

▶ 남자는 마커펜(10달러)과 그림물감 세트(20달러), 그리고 스티커를 4개(5달러×4) 구입하려고 한다. 카드 할인 이벤트는 종료되어 할인을 받을 수 없으므로 남자가 지불해야 할 금액은 총 50달러이다.

W: Hello there. Can I help you find anything?
M: Yes, sure. I'm shopping for some things for my school festival. I have to make a poster.
W: Okay. **Our art section is right over here**. I recommend these markers. They're 10 dollars.
M: I'll take those, and I also need some paint. **How about this set of paints**?
W: It's 20 dollars, and it comes with two brushes.
M: Great. I'll take that, too. And **I also need some various decorations**.
W: How about these character stickers? They're 5 dollars each.
M: Hmm, they're nice. I'll take four of them.
W: Okay. **How would you like to pay**?
M: With this credit card. I can get 10% off with it, right?
W: I'm sorry, but **that discount event ended two days ago**.
M: All right then. Here is my card.

여: 안녕하세요, 손님. 찾으시는 물건 있으신가요?
남: 네, 물론이에요. 학교 축제를 위한 몇 가지 것들을 사려고 해요. 포스터를 만들어야 하거든요.
여: 그러시군요. 미술 제품은 바로 여기에 있습니다. 이 마커펜들을 추천 드릴게요. 가격은 10달러입니다.
남: 그것들을 사고, 그림물감도 좀 필요해요. 이 그림물감 세트는 어떻게 되나요?
여: 20달러이고, 2개의 붓이 딸려 있습니다.
남: 좋아요. 그것도 살게요. 그리고 다양한 장식품들도 좀 필요한데요.
여: 이 캐릭터 스티커는 어떠세요? 한 개에 5달러씩입니다.
남: 음, 좋습니다. 그것으로 네 개 사겠습니다.
여: 알겠습니다. 어떻게 지불하시겠습니까?
남: 이 신용카드로요. 이것으로 10% 할인을 받을 수 있죠, 맞죠?
여: 죄송하지만, 그 할인 이벤트는 이틀 전에 종료되었습니다.
남: 그럼 어쩔 수 없죠. 여기 제 카드요.

어휘 **paint** 그림물감; 페인트 / **come with** ~이 딸려 있다 / **decorations** 장식(품)

07 이유 | ⑤

▶ 남자는 송별회 장소 예약이 갑자기 취소되어서 어떻게 해결해야 할지 여자와 논의하고 있다.

M: Amanda, I've been looking everywhere for you.
W: I went to lunch with the boss. What's up?
M: Well, you know **I've been put in charge of** Lisa's farewell party, but I have a problem.
W: What kind of problem?
M: The restaurant that I had booked **just cancelled at the last minute**.
W: Really? In that case, what about using the cafeteria?
M: That was my first choice, but **they are busy with another event**. What am I going to do?
W: You know, my brother works in a restaurant. He **might be able to help**. I could ask him.
M: Would you do that? And could you find out soon? I'm really **running out of time**.
W: I'll check on it and let you know immediately.

남: Amanda, 당신을 여기저기 찾아다니고 있었어요.
여: 사장님과 점심 먹으러 갔었어요. 무슨 일이에요?
남: 음, 내가 Lisa의 송별회를 담당하고 있는 거 알죠. 그런데 문제가 있어요.
여: 어떤 문제인데요?
남: 예약한 음식점이 마지막 순간에 (예약을) 그냥 취소해버렸어요.
여: 정말요? 그렇다면 구내식당을 이용하는 게 어때요?
남: 그게 제 첫 번째 선택이었는데 거긴 다른 행사로 바쁘대요. 어떡하죠?
여: 저기, 내 남동생이 음식점에서 일해요. 그 애가 도와줄 수 있을지도 몰라요. 내가 물어볼 수 있어요.
남: 그렇게 해주실래요? 그리고 빨리 알아봐 주시겠어요? 시간이 정말 없어서요.
여: 확인하고 즉시 알려줄게요.

어휘 **put A in charge of** A에게 ~을 담당하게 하다

08 언급하지 않은 것 | ⑤

▶ 해석 참조

W: The saiga is an unusual animal that lives in open, dry fields and mild deserts. They are mainly found in Russia and Mongolia. Saigas are **very distinctive even from far away** because of their large noses. Their noses are flexible and **help them to breathe clean air** during dusty summers and cold winters. They usually eat moss, herbs, and plants containing salt. They also eat some plants that are **poisonous to most other animals**. Their fur is light brown and thin during the summers, turning very thick and white during the winters. **With horns used for medicine**, they have been the victim of illegal hunting, and have just recently been put on the critically-endangered species list.

여: 사이가영양은 탁 트이고 건조한 들판과 심하지 않은 사막지대에 사는(① 서식지) 독특한 동물이다. 그들은 주로 러시아와 몽골에서 발견된다. 사이가영양은 큰 코(② 생김새) 때문에 멀리서도 눈에 아주 잘 띈다. 사이가영양의 코는 유연해서 먼지가 많은 여름철과 추운 겨울철에 깨끗한 공기를 들이마시는 데 도움이 된다. 사이가영양은 주로 이끼, 허브, 그리고 염분이 함유된 식물을 먹는다. 다른 대다수 동물에게는 유독한 일부 식물도 먹는다(③ 먹이 습성). 털은 여름 동안 밝은 갈색이고 가늘지만 겨울에는 아주 굵어지고 흰색으로 바뀐다(④ 털의 특

징). 뿔이 약으로 사용되기 때문에, 불법 포획에 희생되어 왔으며, 최근에는 멸종 위험이 아주 높은 종(種) 목록에 올랐다.

어휘 **distinctive** 눈에 띄는; 독특한 / **dusty** 먼지투성이인 / **moss** 이끼 / **critically** 극도로, 심각하게; 비평[비판]적으로

09 내용 불일치 | ④

▶ 우유를 냉각시킬 때 증기와 열이 배출된다고 말했다.

M: The owners of one dairy farm in Sweden live in an ancient castle, Wapno Castle. **The castle's main heating source is oil-burning boilers**. But the owners have invented a new heating system that is more environmentally friendly. **This new system runs on cow's milk**! The dairy farm has 1,000 cows which are milked every day. As the milk leaves the cows, it is hot, about 38 degrees Celsius. **The milk is quickly cooled down to 3 degrees**. As it cools, where does all that steam and heat from the milk go? Well, **some of it heats up a few rooms** in the castle. The owners hope to **expand their present system** in the near future.

남: 스웨덴의 한 낙농장의 농장주들은 오래된 성인 Wapno 성에 거주합니다. 성의 주요 난방 공급원은 기름보일러입니다. 그러나 농장주들은 더욱 환경 친화적인 새로운 난방 시스템을 발명해 왔습니다. 이 새 시스템은 우유로 작동합니다! 낙농장에는 1,000마리의 젖소가 있는데 매일 젖을 짭니다. 소에서 우유를 짰을 때, 우유는 섭씨 38도 정도로 뜨겁습니다. 우유는 3도로 급속히 냉각됩니다. 우유가 냉각될 때, 우유에서 나온 그 증기와 열은 모두 어디로 가게 될까요? 음, 일부는 성의 방 몇 개를 난방을 하는 데 사용됩니다. 농장주들은 가까운 미래에 현재 시스템을 확장하기를 바라고 있습니다.

어휘 **owner** 소유자 / **dairy farm** 낙농장 / **source** 원천, 근원 / **environmentally friendly** 환경 친화적인 / **milk** 우유; ~의 젖을 짜다 / **Celsius** 섭씨의

10 도표 이해 | ③

▶ 플라스틱 재질은 제외했고 물탱크가 1리터 이상인 것을 선택했다. 또한 자동 전원 꺼짐 기능은 있으면서 가격은 300달러가 넘지 않는 것을 사기로 결정했다.

W: I'm looking for a capsule coffee machine.
M: Good idea. A capsule coffee machine is **a quick and easy way to make coffee** at home.
W: I'm thinking of buying one of these five models.
M: Hmm... I don't recommend this because it's completely made of plastic.
W: Why?
M: It's **not as durable as the ones made of** glass or stainless steel.
W: Then I won't buy it.
M: And you should look for a coffee machine with a large water tank of at least 1 liter. Otherwise, you'll have to constantly keep refilling.
W: Okay. What is **the benefit of the auto power off function**?
M: It reduces the risk of a house fire and saves energy.
W: Then I'll get one of these two that has auto power off mode.
M: Do you want to buy the cheaper one?
W: Yes. I think **that's the one for me**. I don't want to spend over $300.
M: Great! You've made a good decision!

여: 캡슐 커피머신을 찾고 있는데요.
남: 좋은 생각이에요. 캡슐 커피 머신은 집에서 커피를 만드는 빠르고도 쉬운 방법이거든요.
여: 이 다섯 가지 모델 중 하나를 살까 생각 중이에요.
남: 흠… 이건 완전히 플라스틱으로 만들어져 있기 때문에 추천하지 않아요.
여: 왜요?
남: 유리나 스테인리스 스틸로 만들어진 것만큼 내구성이 강하지 않아요.
여: 그렇다면 그것은 안 살래요.
남: 그리고 적어도 1리터의 큰 물탱크가 있는 커피 머신을 찾아야 해요. 그렇지 않으면 계속해서 물을 채워 넣어야 할 거예요.
여: 알겠어요. 자동 전원 꺼짐 기능의 이점은 뭔가요?
남: 집 화재의 위험을 줄이고 에너지를 절약하죠.
여: 그러면 자동 전원 꺼짐 모드가 있는 이 두 개 중 하나를 살게요.
남: 가격이 더 싼 것을 사고 싶어요?
여: 네. 그것이 나한테 딱 맞는 것 같아요. 난 300달러 넘게는 쓰고 싶지 않아요.
남: 아주 좋아요! 잘 선택했어요!

어휘 **durable** 내구력 있는, 오래 견디는 / **constantly** 끊임없이, 빈번히 / **refill** 다시 채우다 / **benefit** 이득, 혜택 / **function** 기능 / **reduce** 줄이다 / **mode** 방식

11 짧은 대화에 이어질 응답 | ①

▶ 햄과 칠면조 중 어떤 샌드위치가 좋은지 묻는 남자의 말에 적절한 대답을 찾는다.

① 칠면조가 좋겠어.
② 고맙지만 난 이미 배불러.
③ 사서 가져가는 게 낫겠어.
④ 치킨 샌드위치로 부탁해.
⑤ 샌드위치를 사줘서 고마워.

M: I'm going to **get a sandwich**. Do you want one?
W: I am really hungry. What kinds do they have?
M: They only have ham and turkey. **Which one sounds good to you**?
W: ______________________

남: 나 샌드위치 사려하는데, 너도 하나 먹을래?
여: 난 정말 배고파. 어떤 종류가 있는데?
남: 햄이랑 칠면조뿐이야. 넌 어떤 게 좋니?
여: ______________________

12 짧은 대화에 이어질 응답 | ④

▶ 아이를 데리러 학교에 가야 하는 남자에게 빨리 나가지 않으면 늦지 않겠느냐고 여자가 묻고 있다. 이에 적절한 응답을 찾는다.

① 음, 그 애는 집에 곧 올 거예요.
② 늦을 거예요. 다음번엔 내가 Lily를 데려올게요.
③ 늦을 거예요. 새로 산 식기세척기가 매우 빠르네요.
④ 늦지 않을 거예요. 그 애는 앞으로 한 시간 동안은 안 끝나거든요.
⑤ 늦지 않을 거예요. 난 지금 중요한 회의가 있어요.

W: You know **it's your turn to pick up** Lily from school, right?
M: Of course. **I haven't forgotten**. I'm just going to finish **doing the dishes** first.
W: Thanks, but won't you be late if you don't leave soon?
M: ______________________

여: Lily를 학교에서 데려오는 게 당신 차례인 거 알고 있죠, 맞죠?
남: 물론이죠. 잊지 않았어요. 단지 설거지를 먼저 끝내려고요.
여: 고마워요. 하지만 빨리 나가지 않으면 늦지 않을까요?
남: ______________________

어휘 **at the moment** 바로 지금

13 긴 대화에 이어질 응답 | ④

▶ 패러세일링을 해 본 경험이 있고 Carolyn과 시간을 보내는 것을 좋아하는 여자는 번지 점프에 참여할 것이다.

① 열을 세. 그리고 뛰어내려!
② 이건 하기에 정말 안전해.
③ 그 애는 네가 그것을 공부하도록 도와줄 거야.
④ 음, 그럼 나도 끼워 줘.
⑤ 혹시 Carolyn을 아니?

M: Hi, Sarah. I'm getting some people together to go bungee jumping this weekend. Would you like to join us?
W: Bungee jumping?
M: **Have you ever tried it**?
W: No, but Carolyn and I went parasailing one time. We both had a great time. We always have a great time together.
M: A parasail is like a parachute and **you're pulled through the air** by a boat, right?
W: That's right. It's fun.
M: And bungee jumping will be fun, too. **It shouldn't be any problem for you**.
W: Well, where is it?
M: At Harrison Lake. The company has been in business for 25 years. And **there haven't been any accidents**.
W: Good. Hmm... Have you asked Carolyn yet?
M: Yes, I have. She's coming, too.
W: ______________________

남: 안녕 Sarah. 이번 주말에 몇몇 사람들과 함께 번지 점프하러 가려고 해. 너도 함께 갈래?
여: 번지 점프?
남: 해 본 적 있니?

여: 아니, 하지만 Carolyn이랑 함께 패러세일링은 한 번 해보러 갔어. 정말 재미있었어. 우리는 늘 함께 즐거운 시간을 보내.
남: 패러세일은 낙하산 같은 것으로, 보트가 공중에 떠 있는 너를 끌고 가는 거지, 맞지?
여: 맞아. 재미있어.
남: 그러면 번지 점프도 재미있을 거야. 네게는 전혀 문제가 되지 않겠다.
여: 음, 장소가 어디야?
남: Harrison 호수야. 이 회사가 25년간 운영을 해왔어. 그리고 사고가 한 번도 없었대.
여: 좋아. 음… Carolyn에게 벌써 물어봤니?
남: 응, 물어봤어. 그 애도 올 거야.
여: ______________________________

어휘 **count** (~을) 세다, 셈에 넣다 / **count A in** A를 끼워주다, 포함시키다 / **parasailing** 패러세일링 ((특수 낙하산을 매고 달리는 보트에 매달려 하늘로 날아오르는 스포츠)) ***cf.* parasail** 패러세일링용 낙하산

14 긴 대화에 이어질 응답 | ③

▶ 여자는 면접에서 좋은 인상을 주기 위해서 운동을 해 보라고 권유를 한다. 운동하는데 시간이 많이 걸리지 않는다는 말에 남자는 운동을 해보려 할 것이다.

① 내 첫인상은 별로 좋지 않았어.
② 그렇게 한다면 난 분명히 좋은 성적을 받을 거야.
③ 그렇다면, 네가 다니는 헬스클럽에 대해서 더 이야기해줘.
④ 비록 난 그 일자리를 얻지 못했지만 네가 (그 일자리를) 얻어서 기뻐.
⑤ 난 그들이 면접에서 무엇을 물어볼지 알아.

M: Hi, Jocelyn. You're looking good these days. **Have you lost some weight**?
W: Actually, I have. I've been working out at a new fitness club.
M: Good for you.
W: Yeah. I'm trying to get ready for all the job interviews **I have lined up**.
M: I also have an interview to go to. The interviewers will ask me about their company and what I studied in school, won't they?
W: Yes, but you've got to make a good first impression. **Looking healthy, strong and fit is sure to help**.
M: I've been busy studying and I've had no time to work out.
W: Well, you ought to. Just an hour a day is all you'll need to spend working out.
M: ______________________________

남: 안녕, Jocelyn. 요즘 좋아 보인다. 살이 좀 빠졌니?
여: 사실, 그래. 새로 생긴 헬스클럽에서 운동하고 있어.
남: 잘됐다.
여: 응. 준비해놓은 모든 면접들에 대비하려고 노력 중이야.
남: 나도 가야 할 면접이 한 군데 있어. 면접관들이 자기 회사에 대한 것이나 학교에서 공부한 것에 관해서 물어보겠지, 그렇지?
여: 응, 하지만 좋은 첫인상을 줘야 해. 건강하고 강하고 탄탄해 보이면 확실히 도움이 될 거야.
남: 공부하느라 바빠서 운동할 시간이 없어.
여: 음, 넌 운동해야 해. 하루에 한 시간이면 운동하는 데 충분해.
남: ______________________________

어휘 **lose weight** 체중이 줄다 / **work out** 운동하다 / **line up** ~을 준비[마련]하다 / **fit** 탄탄한, 좋은 건강 상태인

15 상황에 적절한 말 | ⑤

▶ 영재는 친구를 놀리는 지훈의 잘못된 행동을 지적해 주는 말을 할 것이다.

① 네가 누구에 대해 이야기하고 있는지 모르겠어.
② 그 애는 너무 피곤해서 제대로 걸을 수 없어.
③ 그건 공평하지 않아. 너는 나를 흉내 내면 안 돼.
④ 너는 너무 웃겨서 TV에 나가야 해.
⑤ 사람들의 장애를 놀려서는 안 돼.

M: Ji-hoon is **the class clown**. At break time and lunchtime it is common to see a lot of students around his desk. He loves to tell jokes, make people laugh and **be the center of attention**. He is usually funny. He often **imitates the behavior or voices** of popular stars on TV. But today he is making fun of Chang-hyeon, a student in the same class. Chang-hyeon **has trouble walking** because one leg is shorter than the other. So Chang-hyeon limps. Young-jae doesn't think Ji-hoon's actions are funny. He sees that Chang-hyeon is hurt by Ji-hoon's actions. In this situation, what would Young-jae most likely say to Ji-hoon?

남: 지훈은 학급의 익살꾼이다. 쉬는 시간과 점심시간에 그의 책상 주위로 학생들이 많이 모여 있는 것을 흔히 볼 수 있다. 그는 농담을 하고, 사람들을 웃기고 관심의 중심이 되는 것을 정말 좋아한다. 그는 평소에 재미있다. TV에 나오는 인기 스타들의 행동이나 목소리를 자주 흉내 낸다. 하지만 오늘 그는 같은 반 친구인 창현을 놀리고 있다. 창현은 한쪽 다리가 다른 쪽보다 더 짧아서 걷는 데 어려움이 있다. 그래서 창현은 절뚝거린다. 영재는 지훈의 행동이 웃긴다고 생각하지 않는다. 그는 창현이 지훈의 행동 때문에 상처받는 것을 알고 있다. 이러한 상황에서 영재가 지훈에게 할 말로 가장 적절한 것은 무엇인가?

어휘 **properly** 제대로, 적절히 / **imitate** ~을 모방하다, 흉내 내다 / **make fun of** ~을 놀리다, 조롱하다 / **handicap** 장애; 불리한 조건 / **limp** 절뚝거리다

16~17 세트 문항 | 16. ④ 17. ③

▶ 16. 가사가 있는 좋아하는 외국어 노래를 반복해 들으면서 새로운 단어나 어구를 배우게 된다면서 노래가 외국어 학습에 유용하다고 하고 있다.

① 외국어 학습의 이점
② 외국어 학습의 중요한 부분
③ 새로운 언어를 배우는 것이 어려운 이유
④ 외국어 학습에 노래의 유용함
⑤ 언어 학습을 위해 노래 가사를 외우는 것의 필요성

▶ 17. 해석 참조

① 힙합 ② 재즈 ③ 오페라 ④ 민요 ⑤ 뮤지컬

W: The most important part of learning a foreign language is talking with native speakers. Then what is the second most important part? It's self-study. **Songs are great for** self-study because they make your study sessions fun. Having fun is a really effective way to learn a new language. Did you ever **have a song get stuck** in your head? Who hasn't! Music sticks in your brain, which is why songs are so often used in foreign language classes to **help students memorize new words**. Most people who enjoy music listen to their favorite songs over and over until they know them by heart. This repetition, accompanied by a catchy tune, is the perfect formula for getting new words and phrases stuck in your brain **so you can't get rid of them**. Find songs that you love. You'll want to listen to them on repeat, and you'll want to learn the words so you can sing along. Pop music isn't the whole story. Any style of music, whether it be hip hop, rock, or jazz, can be useful in language learning, **as long as it has** lyrics. From slow, old folk songs to the latest musicals, singing a song is a really useful tool for language learning. So, go ahead and learn a new language through your favorite songs.

여: 외국어 학습에서 가장 중요한 부분은 원어민과 이야기하는 것입니다. 그러면 두 번째로 가장 중요한 부분은 무엇일까요? 그것은 독학입니다. 노래는 여러분의 공부 시간을 재미있게 하기 때문에 독학에 좋습니다. 재미를 갖는 것은 새로운 언어를 배우는 정말로 효과적인 방법입니다. 여러분은 노래가 머릿속에 계속 남아 있던 일이 있습니까? 누구나 그럴 겁니다! 음악은 여러분의 머릿속에 머물러 있는데, 그것이 학생들이 새로운 단어를 암기하도록 돕기 위해 외국어 수업에서 노래가 자주 쓰이는 이유입니다. 음악을 즐기는 대부분의 사람들은 그들이 좋아하는 노래를 외울 때까지 거듭 듣습니다. 외우기 쉬운 곡조가 동반되는 이러한 반복은 새 단어나 어구를 머릿속에 각인시켜 그것을 없앨 수 없게 하는 완벽한 공식입니다. 여러분이 좋아하는 노래를 찾으세요. 여러분은 반복해서 그것들을 듣고 싶을 것이고, 노래를 따라 부를 수 있을 정도로 그 단어들을 배우기를 원할 것입니다. 팝 음악만이 전부는 아닙니다. 그것이 ① 힙합이건, 록이건, ② 재즈이건, 어느 스타일의 음악도 그것이 가사가 있는 한, 언어 학습에 유용할 수 있습니다. 느리고 오래된 ④ 민속 음악에서부터 최신 ⑤ 뮤지컬에 이르기까지 노래를 하는 것은 언어 학습에 정말로 유용한 도구입니다. 그러므로 시작하시고 좋아하는 노래를 통해 새 언어를 배우세요.

어휘 **memorize** 암기하다, 기억하다 / **lyrics** 가사 / **self-study** 독학 / **repetition** 반복 / **accompany** 동반하다 / **catchy** 외기 쉬운 / **tune** 곡조 / **formula** 공식 / **get rid of** 제거하다, 없애다 / **on repeat** 반복해서

Answers & Explanation

01. ④ 02. ④ 03. ④ 04. ④ 05. ③ 06. ③ 07. ④ 08. ⑤ 09. ③ 10. ①
11. ② 12. ② 13. ① 14. ⑤ 15. ⑤ 16. ① 17. ③

01 화자가 하는 말의 목적 | ④

▶ 학교에 두고 온 역사 교과서를 집으로 가져가 달라고 친구에게 부탁을 하고 있다.

[Answering machine beeps.]

W: John, this is Lisa. You're still at school, right? You've got soccer practice. So **after your practice, I need a little favor**. Actually, it's an emergency so I really **hope you check this message** after soccer practice. The problem is that I've left my history textbook at school and **we've got a test tomorrow**. I was going to go to school right now and get it, but then I realized you were still there. I hope you can bring it to your home. I can go to your house to get it. It'd **save me a lot of time**. And I have to do my math homework first, anyway. Thanks. Give me a call, OK?

[자동응답기 신호음이 울린다.]

여: John, 나 Lisa야. 너 아직 학교에 있지, 맞지? 너는 축구 연습이 있잖아. 그러니 연습이 끝나면 부탁 하나 할게. 사실, 급한 일이라 축구 연습 후에 네가 이 메시지를 꼭 확인하면 좋겠어. 문제는 내가 역사 교과서를 학교에 두고 왔는데 내일이 시험이라는 거야. 지금 바로 학교에 가서 가지고 오려고 했는데, 그때 네가 아직 거기 있다는 것을 깨달았지. 네가 그 책을 네 집으로 가져가면 좋겠어. 내가 너희 집으로 가지러 갈게. 그렇게 해주면 내 시간이 많이 절약될 거야. 그리고 어쨌든 나는 수학 숙제부터 해야 하거든. 고마워. 전화해줘, 알았지?

02 의견 | ④

▶ 소방 도로에 주차하려는 여자에게 그렇게 하면 안 되는 이유를 남자가 설명하면서 말리는 상황이다. 그러므로 남자의 의견은 ④가 적절하다.

W: Let's park here near the entrance.
M: Look! There's a sign over there. It's a fire lane.
W: Oh, I didn't know that. But **there isn't anywhere else to park** around here.
M: I don't think we can, Bella. It's a lane for emergency vehicles. **There's no parking allowed** at any time.
W: You're right. But we're only going to be half an hour. I think it's okay to park here as long as there's no fire.
M: You never know when an emergency will occur. When there's a fire, **every second counts**.
W: I guess we'll have to go to the underground parking garage. I'm not sure if there's any vacancy though.
M: We have to find some other place. Fire lanes are vital for providing quick fire and emergency medical response.
W: I agree. It's important to keep these lanes clear.
M: Right. **We must keep these lanes accessible** at all times.

여: 입구 가까이에 주차합시다.
남: 보세요! 저기 표지판이 있어요. 소방 도로네요.
여: 아, 그걸 몰랐어요. 하지만 이 근처에 주차할 다른 곳이 없어요.
남: Bella, 우리는 주차할 수 없어요. 긴급 차량을 위한 통로잖아요. 언제든 주차가 허용되지 않아요.
여: 당신 말이 맞아요. 하지만 우리는 단지 30분 있을 거예요. 화재가 나지 않는 한 여기 주차하는 건 괜찮다고 생각해요.
남: 긴급 상황이 언제 일어날지 절대 알 수 없어요. 화재가 나면 매 순간이 중요해요.
여: 우리가 지하 주차장으로 가야할 것 같군요. 하지만 거기 빈자리가 있을지 모르겠어요.
남: 우리는 다른 장소를 찾아야 해요. 소방 도로는 빠른 화재와 비상 의료 대응을 제공하기 위해 절대 필요해요.
여: 동의해요. 이 통로를 비워두는 게 중요하죠.
남: 맞아요. 항상 이 통로가 접근하기 쉽도록 해야 해요.

어휘 **entrance** 입구, 출입구 / **fire lane** 소방 도로, 긴급 차량 전용 도로 / **emergency** 비상[긴급] 사태 / **vehicle** 차량, 탈것 / **every second counts** 매 순간이 중요하다 / **underground** 지하의 / **parking garage** (실내) 주차장 / **vacancy** 빈 공간 / **vital** 절대 필요한, 필수적인 / **accessible** 접근하기 쉬운

03 관계 | ④

▶ 여자는 선거에서 자신을 뽑아야 하는 이유와 공약에 대해서 설명하고 있고, 지역 주민인 남자는 여자의 의료정책에 대해 문의를 하고 있다.

W: Good morning! **Would you like to read this pamphlet**?
M: Ms. Goh? I recognize your face from posters around town.
W: Well, my volunteer staff worked hard **getting all those posters up**.
M: It's nice to see you out meeting the local people.
W: I've lived here all my life. That's why you should choose me.
M: Ms. Goh, **if you win the race**, what's your plan for health care?
W: The Green Party and I support more comprehensive health care for all families.
M: Really?
W: Yes, especially we'll **fight to introduce free health care** for very low-income families.
M: That's interesting.
W: If you'd like more details, check out the campaign site: www.greensfor2015.net.

여: 안녕하세요! 이 팸플릿을 읽어 보시겠어요?
남: 고 선생님? 마을 주변에 붙어 있는 포스터에서 선생님의 얼굴을 봤습니다.
여: 음, 자원봉사자들이 그 포스터들을 전부 열심히 붙였습니다.
남: 지역 주민을 만나러 나오신 것을 보니 반갑네요.
여: 저는 평생을 이곳에서 살았습니다. 그게 바로 여러분께서 저를 뽑아주셔야 하는 이유입니다.
남: 고 선생님, 선거에서 승리하시면 의료 서비스에 대한 계획은 어떠십니까?
여: 녹색당과 저는 모든 가구를 위해 좀 더 포괄적인 의료 서비스를 지지합니다.
남: 그렇습니까?
여: 네, 특히 소득이 아주 적은 가구를 위한 무료 의료 서비스를 도입하기 위해 투쟁할 것입니다.
남: 그거 흥미롭군요.
여: 자세한 사항을 알고 싶으시면 선거운동 사이트인 www.greensfor2015.net에서 확인해 주십시오.

어휘 **race** 선거전, 경쟁; 경주 / **comprehensive** 포괄적인 / **health care** 의료 서비스, 보건

04 그림 불일치 | ④

▶ 남자가 장미 펜던트 목걸이가 안 보인다고 하자, 여자가 여동생에게 빌려주었다고 했다.

[Cell phone rings.]

M: Hello?
W: Hi, honey. I need you to **help me with something**.
M: Sure. What's up?
W: I want you to get my flower-shaped stone ring out of my jewelry box and bring it tonight. Can you do that?
M: Of course. **Just a second**. *[pause]* Yes, I see it beside your diamond ring.
W: Okay, great. Thank you so much.
M: This butterfly pendant necklace is nice. **Why don't I bring it**, also?
W: No thanks, but **that reminds me of my rose pendant necklace**. Can you bring that?
M: Hmm, I don't see it. I see a pearl necklace.
W: What else?
M: **Just a pair of earrings with a ribbon**.
W: Oh, that's right. I lent my rose pendant necklace to my sister. Don't worry about it.
M: Okay. See you tonight.

[휴대전화 벨이 울린다.]

남: 여보세요?
여: 안녕, 여보. 당신이 뭘 좀 도와줘야겠어요.
남: 그래요. 무슨 일이에요?
여: 내 보석함에서 꽃 모양 보석이 박힌 반지를 꺼내서 오늘 밤에 가져와 주었으면 해요. 해줄 수 있어요?

남: 물론이죠. 잠시만요. [잠시 후] 네, 당신 다이아몬드 반지 옆에 보이네요.
여: 네, 잘됐네요. 정말 고마워요.
남: 이 나비 펜던트 목걸이가 멋지네요. 이것도 가져가면 어때요?
여: 고맙지만 괜찮아요. 하지만 그 덕에 장미 펜던트 목걸이가 생각났어요. 그걸 가져와 줄래요?
남: 음, 안 보이는데요. 진주 목걸이는 보여요.
여: 또 다른 건요?
남: 리본이 달린 귀걸이 한 쌍뿐이에요.
여: 아, 맞아요. 장미 펜던트 목걸이는 여동생에게 빌려줬어요. 걱정하지 마세요.
남: 알겠어요. 오늘 밤에 봐요.

어휘 **remind A of[about] B** A에게 B를 상기시키다, 생각나게 하다

05 부탁한 일 | ③

▶ 개가 짖는 소리 때문에 짜증이 난 여자(엄마)가 남자(아들)에게 개가 뒷마당에서 놀고 싶어 하는 것 같으니 문을 열어달라고 부탁했다.

W: *[woof! woof! woof!]* Oh, not again! That dog! David, can't you hear that?
M: What, Mom?
W: Max is barking. When we bought you that dog, **you agreed to look after it**.
M: But I do, Mom. I even gave him a bath this afternoon.
W: I know and you feed him, too. But he's barking like crazy now. I'm sure he wants to go outside and play in the backyard. **Can you go open the door**?
M: OK, Mom. I'm sorry.
W: I'm too busy cooking and his barking **is driving me crazy**.
M: So sorry. Can I help you with that? My grandparents are coming over tonight, aren't they?
W: That's right. So, I'm preparing special food for them.
M: **I'm looking forward to dinner**! Can I chop up all the vegetables on the cutting board?
W: No, thanks. Please just do **what I asked you to do**.

여: *[컹! 컹! 컹!]* 오, 또야! 저 개! David, 저거 안 들리니?
남: 뭐가요, 엄마?
여: Max가 짖고 있어. 우리가 저 개를 사주었을 때 네가 돌보겠다고 동의했지.
남: 하지만 제가 돌보고 있는 걸요, 엄마. 오늘 오후에 목욕도 시켜주었어요.
여: 알아, 그리고 네가 밥도 주지. 하지만 지금 개가 미친 듯이 짖고 있어. 밖에 나가 뒷마당에서 놀고 싶어 하는 게 확실해. 가서 문을 열어주겠니?
남: 알겠어요, 엄마. 죄송해요.
여: 요리하느라 너무 바쁜데 개가 짖는 소리가 나를 미치게 만들고 있구나.
남: 정말 죄송해요. 제가 그걸 도와드릴까요? 할아버지, 할머니께서 오늘 밤에 오시죠, 맞죠?
여: 맞아. 그래서 그분들을 위해 특별한 음식을 준비하고 있어.
남: 저녁 식사가 정말 기대돼요! 제가 도마 위의 야채를 전부 썰까요?
여: 고맙지만 괜찮아. 그냥 내가 부탁한 일을 해주렴.

어휘 **chop up** ~을 잘게 썰다 / **cutting[chopping] board** 도마

06 금액 | ③

▶ 남자는 수강료를 절약하기 위해 3개월 치 수강료(120달러)를 한꺼번에 내고 강좌에 등록하기로 했다. 그리고 배치고사를 치지 않을 것이므로 배치고사 비용은 낼 필요가 없다.

M: Hi, I'd like to register for a Chinese conversation class please.
W: Great. How long would you like?
M: I was thinking just **one month for a start**.
W: OK, every one-month conversation class is $60.
M: Really? My friend said it was only $40 a month here.
W: Are you sure that your friend goes to this institute? It's definitely $60.
M: Hmm. How much is it if I **pay for three months in advance**?
W: It is $120. And for six months, it's $180.
M: Oh, then my friend **must have prepaid** for three months of classes. I'll do that too.
W: Certainly. And before registration, you need to **take an oral placement test**. It costs $5.
M: But I'm just a beginner. I'm **signing up for the beginner's class**.
W: Then you don't need a placement test.

남: 안녕하세요. 중국어 회화 강좌에 등록하고 싶어요.
여: 네. 얼마 동안 수강하고 싶으세요?
남: 우선 한 달만 수강할까 해요.
여: 알겠습니다. 모든 1개월 회화 강좌는 60달러입니다.
남: 정말이요? 제 친구가 여기 강좌는 한 달에 겨우 40달러라고 했는데요.
여: 친구 분께서 이 학원에 다니시는 것이 확실한가요? 틀림없이 60달러입니다.
남: 음. 3개월 치를 미리 지불하면 얼마인가요?
여: 120달러입니다. 그리고 6개월에는 180달러입니다.
남: 아, 그럼 제 친구가 3개월 치 수강료를 미리 낸 게 틀림없군요. 저도 그렇게 할게요.
여: 그렇게 하시죠. 그리고 등록 전에 구두 배치고사를 치셔야 합니다. 비용은 5달러입니다.
남: 하지만 전 아직 초보자에요. 초급 강좌에 등록할 거예요.
여: 그럼 배치고사를 칠 필요가 없으시네요.

어휘 **for a start** 우선 / **in advance** 미리 / **placement test** 배치고사

07 이유 | ④

▶ 남자의 말에 의하면 Lee 선수는 독점 계약을 원하지 않는다고 했다.

W: We want P.J. Lee to wear and advertise our golf clothing.
M: We **have reviewed your proposal**. We're content with the money and the length of the contract you've suggested.
W: Good. We hope she'll improve our sales to young golfers. When does her present clothing contract finish?
M: In two months. Unfortunately, we do have one problem. She has told me she doesn't **want to be prevented from signing** with other companies.
W: But that's important to us. We don't want her to be in another company's advertisement.
M: Well, **she'll sign a contract**, but not an exclusive one.
W: I'm afraid that's not acceptable to us.
M: I'm sorry, then we can't take your offer. She is the youngest LPGA winner ever. At this point, **being restricted to only one company** is not good for her.

여: P.J. Lee 선수가 저희 골프 의류를 입고 광고해주시길 원합니다.
남: 귀사의 제안서를 검토했습니다. 제안하신 금액과 계약 기간에 만족합니다.
여: 잘됐네요. Lee 선수가 젊은 골퍼들을 대상으로 매출을 올려주시면 좋겠습니다. 현재 의류 계약이 언제 끝나나요?
남: 두 달 후에요. 유감스럽게도, 문제가 한 가지 있습니다. 그녀가 말하길 다른 회사들과 계약하는 게 금지되지 않길 원한다고 했어요.
여: 그렇지만 그건 저희에게 중요합니다. 그녀가 다른 회사 광고에 나오길 원하지 않으니까요.
남: 글쎄요, 계약서에 서명할 테지만 독점 계약은 아니에요.
여: 그건 저희가 받아들일 수 없을 것 같습니다.
남: 죄송합니다만, 그러면 제안을 받아들일 수 없습니다. 그녀는 사상 최연소 LPGA 우승자입니다. 이 시점에서 오로지 한 회사에만 제한되는 건 그녀에게 좋지 않습니다.

어휘 **proposal** 제안, 제의; 프러포즈 / **content** 만족하는 / **contract** 계약(서) / **exclusive** 독점적인, 전용의 / **restricted** 제한된, 제약을 받는

08 언급하지 않은 것 | ⑤

▶ 해석 참조

W: Hi, Martin. What are you reading?
M: It's a book about the history of the Korean kingdom of Balhae. It's very interesting.
W: Ah, that's one of the kingdoms that **were established after the fall** of the Goguryeo kingdom.
M: Right. Goguryeo was conquered by Unified Silla, and then Dae Jo-yeong established Balhae.
W: If I remember right, Balhae society was separated into two social classes, one of which **was forced into slavery** by the other.
M: Yes, but in other respects, it **had a very advanced culture**. It was nicknamed "the flourishing land of the East."
W: I remember learning that in school. We also learned that Balhae collapsed **because of ethnic conflicts**.
M: This book says that was the traditional theory, but some scholars believe the eruption of Mt. Baekdu **may have been the true cause** of Balhae's end.

여: 안녕, Martin. 뭘 읽고 있니?
남: 한국 발해 왕국의 역사에 관한 책이야. 정말 재미있어.
여: 아, 고구려 왕국 멸망 이후에 세워진 왕국 중 하나지.

남: 맞아. 고구려는 통일 신라에 정복당했고, 그런 다음 대조영(① 시조)이 발해를 세웠지.
여: 내 기억이 맞다면, 발해 사회는 두 사회계층으로 나뉘어 있었는데, 한 계층이 다른 계층에 의해 강제로 노예가 되었지(② 신분 제도).
남: 그래, 하지만 다른 면에서는 아주 발달한 문화가 있었어. '해동성국'이라는 별칭(③ 별칭)을 얻었지.
여: 학교에서 그걸 배운 것이 기억나. 또, 발해가 민족 분쟁 때문에 무너졌다고(④ 멸망 원인) 배웠어.
남: 이 책에서 말하길 그게 전통적인 이론이었지만, 일부 학자들은 백두산 폭발이 발해 멸망의 진짜 원인(④ 멸망 원인)이었을 수도 있다고 믿는대.

어휘 **fall** 멸망, 몰락; 하락 / **slavery** 노예 (신분); 노예제도 / **flourishing** 번영하는, 융성한 / **collapse** 무너지다, 붕괴하다 / **ethnic** 민족의 / **eruption** (화산의) 폭발, 분출

09 내용 불일치 | ③

▶ 중고 물품들은 모금 행사에서 판매될 것이라고 말했다.

W: Centennial School **is holding a fundraiser** for the flood victims. These people **need food and basic necessities**, so the students want to help. On Saturday, April 25th this fundraiser will be held from 10 a.m. to 8 p.m. There will be an arts and handicrafts sale, musical performances, various games, a bake sale plus a sale of second-hand goods. The school requests the entire community **to donate second-hand goods** to be sold at this event. So please **look through your house** and bring items to Centennial School before April 23rd. All the proceeds made at the fundraiser will be sent to the Red Cross **to aid their efforts**.

여: Centennial 학교가 홍수 이재민들을 위한 모금 행사를 개최할 예정입니다. 이 사람들은 음식과 기본적인 필수품이 필요해서, 학생들이 돕기를 원합니다. 이 모금 행사는 4월 25일 토요일 오전 10시부터 오후 8시까지 열릴 것입니다. 미술품과 수공예품의 판매, 음악 공연, 다양한 게임, 빵 판매와 더불어 중고품 판매 행사가 있을 예정입니다. 학교는 이 행사에서 판매될 중고품을 기부해 주시기를 전 지역 사회에 부탁드립니다. 그러므로 집안을 살펴보시고 4월 23일 전에 Centennial 학교로 물품을 가져와 주시기 바랍니다. 모금 행사에서 발생한 수익금 전액은 그들의 노력을 돕기 위해 적십자사로 보내질 것입니다.

어휘 **fundraiser** 모금 행사 / **victim** 피해자, 희생자 / **necessity** ((pl.)) 필수품; 필요(성) / **handicraft** 수공예(품) / **second-hand** 중고의; 간접의, 전해들은 / **look through** ~을 훑어보다; ~을 찾다 / **proceeds** 수익금 / **aid** ~을 돕다; 원조, 지원

10 도표 이해 | ①

▶ 두 사람은 뷔페식을 제공하고 휠체어를 타고 이용할 수 있으며 사진작가는 포함되어 있지 않은 장소를 선택할 것이다.

M: Where are we having our son's first birthday party? Everyone wants to know.
W: I have **brochures for the five choices** right here. They're all a similar price.
M: Hmm.... Having a party at this place would be great. **What a view**!
W: Yes, but they don't offer a buffet. It's a three-course western meal.
M: I'd prefer a buffet. **So would most people**, wouldn't they?
W: I think so. Hmm.... Have you invited your oldest uncle yet?
M: I have. So the place must be wheelchair accessible.
W: Well, this one is wheelchair accessible and, as a bonus, an in-house photographer will **take some photos for free**.
M: Honey, my brother is a photographer. He'll take the pictures and he'd be angry if he saw someone else taking pictures. No free photography.
W: **There's only one place left** then. I'll call now.

남: 우리 아들의 돌잔치를 어디서 할 거예요? 모두 알고 싶어 해요.
여: 다섯 가지 선택 사항에 대한 책자가 바로 여기 있어요. 전부 비슷한 가격이에요.
남: 음…. 이 장소에서 파티를 하는 게 좋겠어요. 전망이 멋져요!
여: 네, 그렇지만 뷔페를 제공하지 않네요. 세 코스짜리 양식이에요.
남: 뷔페가 더 좋겠어요. 사람들 대부분도 그렇겠죠, 아닐까요?
여: 그럴 거예요. 음…. 연세가 가장 많으신, 당신의 삼촌을 이미 초대했나요?
남: 초대했어요. 그래서 반드시 장소가 휠체어를 타고 이용하기 쉬워야 해요.
여: 음, 이곳은 휠체어가 접근할 수 있고 보너스로 내부 사진작가가 사진을 무료로 찍어줄 거예요.
남: 여보, 내 남동생이 사진작가잖아요. 그 애가 사진을 찍을 거고 다른 누군가가 사진 찍고 있는 것을 보면 화가 날 거예요. 무료 사진 촬영은 필요 없어요.
여: 그럼 한 장소밖에 남지 않네요. 지금 전화할게요.

어휘 **brochure** (안내·광고용) 책자 / **in-house** (회사·조직) 내부의, 사내의

11 짧은 대화에 이어질 응답 | ②

▶ 내일 드레스가 얼마나 할인되는지 묻는 여자의 말에 적절한 응답을 찾는다.

① 배송비는 달라질 수 있습니다.
② 전부 다 20% 할인됩니다.
③ 이것들을 100달러에 되파실 수 있습니다.
④ 죄송합니다만, 그것들은 할인되지 않습니다.
⑤ 판매 수익은 약 10%입니다.

W: I'd like these three dresses. **How much is the total**?
M: That's $150. But **there will be a sale tomorrow**, in case you'd like to wait.
W: Oh, I didn't know that. How much of a discount will there be?
M: ________________

여: 이 드레스 세 벌로 할게요. 총 얼마지요?
남: 150달러예요. 하지만 기다리셔도 괜찮다면, 내일 세일이 있어요.
여: 아, 그건 몰랐네요. 얼마나 할인되죠?
남: ________________

어휘 **margin** 이윤[이익] 폭 (= profit margin); 여백, 가장자리 / **roughly** 대략, 거의

12 짧은 대화에 이어질 응답 | ②

▶ 돼지고기가 아직 세일 중이면 사다 달라는 말에 남자가 세일이 끝났으면 어떻게 하느냐고 물었다. 이에 적절한 응답을 찾는다.

① 환불해 달라고 할 수 있어.
② 그러면 신경 안 써도 돼.
③ 세일은 어제 끝났어.
④ 그 돼지고기는 정말 좋았어.
⑤ 내가 채식주의자인 거 알잖아.

M: I'm going to the store. Do you want me to get anything?
W: Please get some more pork **if it's still on sale**.
M: Good idea. But **what if the sale has ended**?
W: ________________

남: 나 가게에 갈 건데. 뭐 사다 줄까?
여: 돼지고기가 아직 세일 중이면 좀 더 사다 줘.
남: 좋은 생각이야. 하지만 세일이 끝났으면 어쩌지?
여: ________________

어휘 **vegetarian** 채식주의자

13 긴 대화에 이어질 응답 | ①

▶ 황사 때문에 옷을 사러 나가지 못하게 된 여자에게 남자는 밖에 나가지 않고 옷을 살 수 있는 방법을 알려주려고 하고 있다.

① 내 컴퓨터를 이용해서 온라인 쇼핑을 하면 되잖아.
② 황사가 더 심해지기 전에 안으로 들어가자.
③ 오늘은 영화관이 너무 붐빌 것 같아.
④ 좋아. 방금 한 말을 다시 해줄게.
⑤ 시내에서 시위가 너무 커지고 있다는 뜻이야.

W: Today is my last day in Seoul. Let's go out.
M: Right, you're going back to Busan tomorrow. Do you want to see a movie?
W: No, I want to buy clothes for summer.
M: *[cell phone text message alert sound]* **Wait a minute**. Hmm... Going out isn't such a good idea.
W: Why? Is it **something to do with the protests** downtown?
M: No, I just got a text message **warning about severe yellow dust** today.
W: Really? That's not good. I have asthma and allergies.
M: Well, we should stay indoors. **It's a high risk for you**.
W: Aww! I really wanted to go shopping for summer clothes today.
M: You don't have to **go out to buy clothes**.
W: I don't understand.
M: ________________

여: 오늘이 내가 서울에서 보내는 마지막 날이야. 밖에 나가자.
남: 맞다. 내일 부산으로 돌아가는구나. 영화 보고 싶니?
여: 아니, 여름옷을 사고 싶어.
남: *[휴대전화의 문자메시지 알림음]* 잠깐만. 음…. 외출하는 것은 별로 좋은 생각이 아니야.
여: 왜? 시내의 시위와 관련이 있는 거니?
남: 아니, 오늘 심한 황사가 있을 거라고 경고하는 문자 메시지 안내를 막 받았어.

여: 정말? 그건 좋지 않구나. 난 천식과 알레르기가 있거든.
남: 음, 집에 있어야겠다. 네겐 너무 위험해.
여: 으! 오늘 여름옷을 꼭 사러 가고 싶었는데.
남: 옷을 사러 밖에 나갈 필요는 없어.
여: 무슨 뜻인지 모르겠어.
남: ______________________________

어휘 **protest** 시위[항의]하다 / **be[have] something to do with** ~와 관련이 있다 / **severe** 심한 / **yellow dust** 황사 / **asthma** 천식

14 긴 대화에 이어질 응답 | ⑤

▶ 퇴근 시간이 늦기 때문에 귀가할 때 본인의 차량이 필요할 것이라는 남자의 말에 적절한 대답을 찾는다.

① 와, 긴 면접이 되겠군요.
② 올 때는 지하철이 가장 빠른 방법이에요.
③ 그날 밤엔 중요한 일이 있습니다.
④ 오늘 강의 시간에 노트 필기해 줄 사람이 필요합니다.
⑤ 문제없어요! 자가용이 있거든요. 한 시간 이내로 가겠습니다.

[Phone rings.]
M: Grove Mart, Bruce Carter speaking.
W: Hello, this is Jamie Quan. I'm calling about your ad for casual staff.
M: **That's the evening shifts** on Friday and Saturday nights.
W: That's perfect. I'm always free then.
M: May I ask how old you are?
W: Eighteen. I'm in my first year at Swinburne University.
M: OK, do you **have any work experience**?
W: Yes, four years at my mom's restaurant.
M: Waiting tables or kitchen work?
W: Everything. **I even supervised staff**.
M: OK, can you come in for a short interview?
W: Yes, anytime. **I'm on semester break**.
M: Then, stop by anytime today.
W: Oh, one more question; what are the hours?
M: 5:30 p.m. to 12:30 a.m. You'll need **your own transportation to get home**.
W: ______________________________

[전화벨이 울린다.]
남: Grove 마트의 Bruce Carter입니다.
여: 여보세요, 저는 Jamie Quan이라고 합니다. 임시 직원을 찾는다는 광고를 보고 전화했습니다.
남: 금요일과 토요일 밤에 일하는 저녁 근무조입니다.
여: 잘됐네요. 그 시간은 항상 한가하거든요.
남: 나이를 물어봐도 될까요?
여: 18살이요. Swinburne 대학교 1학년입니다.
남: 알겠습니다. 일을 해본 경험이 있나요?
여: 네, 어머니의 식당에서 4년간 일했습니다.
남: 서빙하는 일이었나요 아니면 주방 일이었나요?
여: 모두 다요. 직원 관리까지도 했습니다.
남: 좋아요. 간단한 면접을 보러 오실 수 있나요?
여: 네, 언제든지요. 지금 방학 중이거든요.
남: 그럼 오늘 아무 때나 오세요.
여: 아, 질문이 하나 더 있는데요. 근무시간이 어떻게 됩니까?
남: 오후 5시 30분부터 밤 12시 30분까지입니다. 퇴근할 때 본인의 차량이 필요할 것입니다.
여: ______________________________

어휘 **commitment** 약속(한 일), 책무 / **casual** 임시의 / **shift** (교대제의) 근무조; 교대 근무 / **wait tables** (식당 등에서) 서빙하다, 손님 시중을 들다 / **supervise** 관리하다, 감독하다

15 상황에 적절한 말 | ⑤

▶ Maya는 자신에게 한 약속에 따라 화가 나더라도 긍정적이고 상냥하게 Brooke의 전화에 응할 것이다.

① 너는 나를 안 좋아하지, 그렇지?
② 나는 자기 수양에 관한 책을 읽어야 해.
③ 편지를 못 써서 미안해.
④ 불평하기 전에 생각을 해 보지 그러니?
⑤ 보고 싶었어. 무슨 일이 있었니?

W: Maya has been reading self-improvement books. She finds them inspiring and **is making an effort to follow** much of the advice she has read, in particular, the advice to think before you complain. She has promised herself to be positive and kind, even in situations where she would usually get angry and **have harsh words with someone**. Maya has lost touch with her best friend Brooke since they graduated from elementary school. Brooke **hasn't responded in over three years** to Maya's emails. Maya feels angry and insulted by this. One day, her phone rings. It's Brooke, saying hello. Maya **reminds herself of her promise to herself**. In this situation, what would Maya most likely say to Brooke?

여: Maya는 자기 계발에 관한 책을 읽고 있다. 그녀는 그런 책들이 영감을 준다는 것을 깨닫고 읽은 조언 중 많은 것들을, 특히 불평을 하기 전에 생각을 하라는 충고를 따르려고 노력하고 있다. 그녀는 대개 화가 나서 다른 사람과 심한 말다툼을 하게 되는 상황에서도 긍정적이고 상냥하게 행동하기로 자신에게 약속했다. Maya는 가장 친한 친구였던 Brooke과 초등학교 졸업 후에 연락이 끊어졌다. Brooke은 Maya의 이메일에 3년이 넘게 답장을 하지 않았다. Maya는 이 때문에 화가 나고 모욕감을 느낀다. 어느 날 전화가 울린다. Brooke이고, 인사를 한다. Maya는 자신에게 한 약속을 떠올린다. 이러한 상황에서 Maya가 Brooke에게 할 말로 가장 적절한 것은 무엇인가?

어휘 **self-improvement** 자기 계발 / **inspiring** 영감을 주는 / **have words (with)** (~와) 말다툼하다 / **harsh** 거친, 불쾌한 / **insult** ~을 모욕하다

16~17 세트 문항 | 16. ① 17. ③

▶ 16. 과대 포장의 문제점을 제시하며 이에 관해 할 수 있는 일을 나열하고 있다.

① 지나친 포장을 피하는 몇 가지 방법들
② 생일 파티에서 쓰레기를 줄이는 방법
③ 과대 포장을 피할 수 없는 이유
④ 환경친화적인 포장재의 중요성
⑤ 슈퍼마켓에서 과대 포장의 효과

▶ 17. 해석 참조

① 종이봉투 ② 스티로폼으로 된 접시 ③ 나무 상자 ④ 유리병 ⑤ 깡통

M: We all enjoy giving and receiving presents on a birthday, and unwrapping them is half the fun. But at the end of the day, **do you ever feel like you have to throw away** more packaging than is necessary? Many products that you buy are over-packaged, and packaging materials account for a third of all household waste. Excess packaging **is costly and damaging to the environment**. Is there anything you can do about this? One way is to avoid buying things with lots of packaging. **You may be able to get** fruit and vegetables packed only in paper bags, rather than in plastic or styrofoam trays. Buy food and drinks in recyclable packaging such as glass jars or tin cans. If you have storage space, buy dried goods in bulk. This means fewer individual packages. Buy basic ingredients and **cook them yourself**, rather than small prepackaged portions. Organic fruit and vegetables in supermarkets are often highly packaged, because they are marketed as high-value luxury produce. Complain about this to your supermarket, or, better still, have unpackaged fruit, vegetables and other produce **delivered straight to your door**. And, of course, reuse or refuse supermarket carrier bags!

남: 우리는 모두 생일날 선물을 주고받는 것을 즐기고, 그것들의 포장지를 푸는 것이 즐거움의 대부분입니다. 그러나 그날의 끝에, 여러분은 필요한 것보다 더 많은 포장재를 버려야 한다고 느낀 적이 있으십니까? 여러분이 구매하는 많은 상품은 과대 포장되어있고 포장 재료가 모든 생활폐기물의 3분의 1을 차지합니다. 지나친 포장은 비용이 많이 들고 환경을 훼손합니다. 이것에 관해 여러분이 할 수 있는 일이 있을까요? 한 가지 방법은 많은 포장이 있는 물건을 사는 것을 피하는 것입니다. 여러분은 플라스틱이나 ② 스티로폼으로 된 접시보다는 ① 종이봉투로만 포장된 과일과 채소를 살 수 있을 겁니다. ④ 유리병과 ⑤ 깡통과 같이 재활용할 수 있는 포장 안에 든 식음료를 사세요. 여러분이 저장 공간이 있다면 마른 식품을 대량으로 구매하세요. 이것은 더 적은 개별 포장을 의미합니다. 판매하기 전에 적은 몫으로 포장된 것보다는 기본 재료를 구매해서 그것들을 직접 요리하세요. 슈퍼마켓의 유기농 과일과 채소는 고가의 고급 농작물로 내놓기 때문에 종종 비싸게 포장됩니다. 이를 여러분의 슈퍼마켓에 항의하거나 더욱더 좋은 것은 포장되지 않은 과일, 채소 그리고 다른 생산품들을 여러분의 문 앞에 곧바로 배송되게 하세요. 그리고 물론 슈퍼마켓 쇼핑백을 재사용하거나 거절하세요!

어휘 **packaging** 포장(재) / **eco-friendly** 환경친화적인 / **unwrap** (포장지를) 풀다 / **half the fun** 즐거움의 대부분 / **over-packaged** 과대 포장된 / **account for** 차지하다; 설명하다 / **household waste** 생활폐기물 / **storage** 저장(고) / **in bulk** 대량으로 / **prepackage** 판매하기 전에 포장하다 / **portion** 몫; 부분, 일부 / **high-value** 고가의 / **produce** 생산품 / **better still** 더욱더 좋은 것은 / **carrier bag** 쇼핑백

Answers & Explanation

01. ② 02. ② 03. ③ 04. ⑤ 05. ④ 06. ③ 07. ④ 08. ① 09. ② 10. ④
11. ③ 12. ② 13. ③ 14. ⑤ 15. ③ 16. ② 17. ④

01 화자가 하는 말의 목적 | ②

▶ 한미 양국 간의 합의에 따라 바뀐 비자 면제 프로그램의 시행을 알리는 내용이다.

M: A new agreement between the U.S. and Korean governments will allow more people to visit the United States **without having to apply for a visa**. With this new agreement, called a "Visa Waiver," it is expected that an extra 300,000 Koreans will tour the U.S. To apply for a visa before, people **had to wait in line for several hours**. But the process will now be as simple as buying a plane ticket. Although this will benefit many Koreans, the government fears this will **result in a loss of revenue** for Korea. Koreans who would normally visit places in their own country might choose to go to America instead.

남: 한미 정부 간에 새로운 합의에 따라 비자 신청을 해야 할 필요 없이 더 많은 사람이 미국을 방문할 수 있게 될 것입니다. '비자면제'로 불리는 이번 합의로 인해, 30만 명의 한국인이 추가로 미국을 여행하게 될 것으로 예상됩니다. 전에는 비자를 신청하기 위해 사람들이 몇 시간 동안 줄을 서서 기다려야 했습니다. 하지만 이제는 그 과정이 비행기 표를 구입하는 것만큼이나 간단해질 것입니다. 비록 이 조치가 많은 한국인에게 혜택을 줄 것이지만, 한국 정부는 이로 인해 국고 수입의 손실이 생길 것을 우려하고 있습니다. 보통 자국의 여행지를 찾아가곤 하던 한국인들이 대신 미국에 가는 것을 선택할 수도 있기 때문입니다.

어휘 **apply for** ~을 신청하다 / **revenue** 국가의 세입; 수입원

02 의견 | ②

▶ 건강 검진 결과가 좋지 않아 의사가 운동을 제안했다는 남자에게 여자는 체육관에 갈 필요 없이 일상에 운동을 끼워 넣으라고 조언하며 가장 중요한 것은 자주 운동하는 거라고 말한다.

W: Hi, Jerome. How was your regular medical check-up?
M: It's not that good. My doctor suggested that I do some exercise, but **I'm too busy to work out**.
W: If you don't do exercise, your health will get worse.
M: I know. But **finding time to stay healthy** is tough.
W: You don't have to go to the gym. Find other ways to fit activity into your daily life. You can climb up and down the stairs.
M: Yeah. But my doctor said I need some weight training.
W: You can work out in the office with water bottles. **The most important thing is to exercise regularly**.
M: Oh, that's a good idea. Then I should use water bottles like dumbbells?
W: Exactly. I'll send you that exercise video. It's **an exercise you can do** anywhere, anytime.
M: Thank you. I'll give it a try.

여: 안녕, Jerome. 당신의 정기 건강 검진은 어땠어요?
남: 그렇게 좋지 않아요. 의사는 내가 운동을 좀 해야 한다고 제안했지만, 너무 바빠서 운동할 수 없어요.
여: 운동을 하지 않으면, 당신의 건강은 더 나빠질 거예요.
남: 나도 알아요. 하지만 건강을 유지할 시간을 찾기가 어렵네요.
여: 체육관에 갈 필요가 없어요. 당신의 일상에 활동을 끼워 넣을 다른 방법을 찾으세요. 계단을 오르내릴 수 있어요.
남: 그래요. 하지만 의사가 내게는 웨이트 트레이닝이 좀 필요하다고 말했어요.
여: 사무실에서 물병을 가지고 운동을 할 수 있어요. 가장 중요한 것은 자주 운동하는 거예요.
남: 아, 그거 좋은 생각이네요. 그러면 내가 아령처럼 물병을 사용해야 하나요?
여: 바로 그거예요. 내가 당신에게 그 운동 비디오를 보내 줄게요. 당신이 어디서나, 언제나 할 수 있는 운동이에요.
남: 고마워요. 한번 해볼게요.

어휘 **check-up** (건강) 검진 / **work out** 운동하다; (일이) 잘 풀리다 / **gym** 체육관 / **dumbbell** 아령; 얼간이 / **give it a try** 한번 해보다, 시도하다

03 관계 | ③

▶ 고기를 익히는 정도에 대해 식당 주방에서 요리사와 종업원이 대화를 나누고 있다.

M: How did you say the customer wanted the steak cooked?
W: He said **he wanted it really rare**. Like, bright red.
M: But, the health department in this state doesn't let us serve any meat cooked less than medium-rare.
W: I tried to tell him that, but he told me that **the rule only applies to hamburgers**.
M: Hmm.... I'm pretty sure **it is for all beef**.
W: Well, what do you want me to tell him?
M: Tell him that the man in charge of the kitchen **would rather not take a chance** at anyone getting sick.
W: OK. But he isn't going to be happy. Maybe you should take off your apron and tell him yourself.

남: 저 손님께서 스테이크를 어떻게 익히길 원한다고 하셨죠?
여: 아주 살짝 익혔으면 좋겠다고 말씀하셨어요. 마치, 선홍색이 나게요.
남: 하지만, 주(州) 보건국에서 미디엄 레어보다 덜 익힌 고기는 제공하지 못하게 하고 있어요.
여: 그것을 손님께 말씀드리려 시도했지만 손님께서 그 규정은 햄버거에만 해당된다고 말씀하셨어요.
남: 음…. 저는 모든 쇠고기에 해당된다고 아주 확신해요.
여: 그럼, 제가 손님께 뭐라고 말씀드리면 좋을까요?
남: 그분께 손님이 탈이 날 수도 있는 일은 주방 책임자가 하고 싶어 하지 않는다고 말씀드려 주세요.
여: 알겠습니다. 하지만 손님께서는 좋아하시지 않을 거예요. 어쩌면 요리사님이 앞치마를 벗고 그분께 직접 말씀해 보시죠.

어휘 **health department** 보건국 / **take a chance** (~을 운에 맡기고) 해보다

04 그림 불일치 | ⑤

▶ 동굴 입구 옆에는 공룡이 아니라 부화하고 있는 것처럼 보이는 알이 몇 개 있다고 했다.

W: What do you think of the dinosaur exhibit, Peter?
M: It's great, Mom! Look at the one on the left. It has triangle-shaped horns on its back.
W: **It looks fierce**, but it only eats plants.
M: There's a meat-eating dinosaur next to it. It has two short arms and it's standing on two legs.
W: You're right. Oh, Peter, look up at the ceiling!
M: Wow, a dinosaur that can fly. **Its wings are huge**!
W: They are! Look! There's a big cave.
M: **Let's take a closer look at it.**
W: There are some eggs by the entrance.
M: And they look like they are hatching **because their tops are broken**.
W: Let's stay and watch. Maybe something will happen.

여: 공룡 전시 어떠니, Peter?
남: 굉장해요, 엄마! 왼쪽에 있는 거 보세요. 등에 세모 모양 뿔들이 있어요.
여: 사나워 보이는데 풀만 먹는구나.
남: 그 옆에 육식 공룡이 있어요. 짧은 팔이 두 개 있고 두 다리로 서 있어요.
여: 맞아. 아, Peter, 천장을 올려다보렴!
남: 와, 날 수 있는 공룡이네요. 날개가 엄청 커요!
여: 그렇구나! 봐! 큰 동굴이 있어.
남: 가까이 가서 봐요.
여: 입구 옆에 알이 몇 개 있네.
남: 그리고 윗부분이 깨져 있어서 부화하고 있는 것처럼 보여요.
여: 그대로 지켜보자. 어쩌면 무슨 일이 일어날지도 몰라.

어휘 **horn** (동물의) 뿔; (차량의) 경적 / **fierce** 사나운, 맹렬한

05 추후 행동 | ④

▶ 남자는 내일 하루 종일 수업이 있어 시간이 없다고 말했고 이에 여자는 오늘 오후 4시에 전화를 주면 면접 일정을 잡겠다고 했다.

M: Excuse me, Professor Miller?
W: Yes, that's right. How may I help you?
M: I am looking for a position as a teaching assistant in the spring. I heard you were the best professor in the science department.
W: I usually choose a T.A. from **among my undergraduate students** who go on to pursue a Master's.
M: I understand, but I am **a transfer student** from State University.
W: Do you **have your transcripts and résumé**?
M: Yes, they're right here.
W: *[pause]* Well, this looks impressive. Do you have time tomorrow to come to my office?
M: I have classes all day long tomorrow.
W: Then would you call me at this number around 4 this afternoon? So I can schedule an interview.
M: Thank you.

남: 실례합니다. Miller 교수님이십니까?
여: 네, 그런데요. 무슨 일이시죠?
남: 저는 봄 학기 조교직을 구하고 있습니다. 자연 과학부에서는 교수님이 최고시라는 말씀을 들었습니다.
여: 난 석사 학위까지 계속 공부하려는 학부 학생 중에서 주로 조교를 선발합니다.
남: 이해합니다만 저는 State 대학교에서 편입한 학생입니다.
여: 성적 증명서와 이력서를 가지고 있나요?
남: 네, 바로 여기 있습니다.
여: *[잠시 후]* 음, 인상적인 것 같네요. 내일 내 연구실로 올 시간이 있나요?
남: 내일은 하루 종일 수업이 있습니다.
여: 그럼 오늘 오후 4시쯤 이 번호로 내게 전화를 주겠어요? 그래서 내가 면접 일정을 잡을 수 있게요.
남: 감사합니다.

어휘 **teaching assistant** 조교(=T.A.) / **pursue** (특정 활동을) 계속해나가다, ~을 추구하다 / **transfer student** 편입생, 전학생 / **transcript** 성적 증명서 / **résumé** 이력서

06 금액 | ③

▶ 디럭스 패키지는 100달러이고, 가족 회원 한 명을 추가한다고 했으므로, 50달러를 더한 150달러를 지불할 것이다.

W: Hi, I'd like to join this fitness club.
M: Just yourself, or would you like to **sign up your whole family**?
W: I don't know if it would be worth signing my husband and daughter up.
M: If you become a member, it's only an extra $50 a month for additional family members.
W: How much will it be for just me?
M: If you want the deluxe package, which includes tanning and massage, it is $100 per month.
W: And what about a package without tanning and massage?
M: That would be our standard package. It is $80 a month.
W: I think I'll sign up for the deluxe package for me and my husband.
M: OK. Yourself and one extra family member.... **Here's an application form** for the deluxe package.
W: Oh, **what about the registration fee**?
M: We usually charge a $5 registration fee, but this month it's free.

여: 안녕하세요. 이 헬스클럽에 가입하고 싶습니다.
남: 손님 혼자십니까, 아니면 가족 전원이 등록을 원하십니까?
여: 제 남편과 딸이 함께 등록할 만할지 모르겠군요.
남: 손님께서 회원이 되시면 다른 가족분들은 매달 50달러만 추가로 내시면 됩니다.
여: 저만 등록하면 얼마인가요?
남: 태닝과 마사지가 포함되어 있는 디럭스 패키지로 하시면 한 달에 100달러입니다.
여: 그러면 태닝과 마사지가 없는 패키지는 어떤가요?
남: 그건 스탠더드 패키지입니다. 한 달에 80달러입니다.
여: 저와 남편이 디럭스 패키지로 등록할까 봐요.
남: 알겠습니다. 손님과 추가 가족 회원 한 분…. 디럭스 패키지 신청서 여기 있습니다.
여: 아, 등록비는 어떻게 되나요?
남: 보통 등록비 5달러를 받습니다만, 이번 달은 무료입니다.

어휘 **sign up** 등록하다 / **tanning** 태닝, 햇볕에 태움 / **application** 신청서

07 이유 | ④

▶ 남자는 예전 꿈이었던 한의사가 되기 위한 공부를 하려고 일을 그만둘 거라고 한다.

W: Are you really quitting your job? Isn't it the third job **you've quit since you graduated**?
M: Yes. It is, but this time I have a plan.
W: But this is **the best job you've ever had**. I know you are satisfied with the pay. You already **have another job lined up**?
M: No, actually, I'm leaving the corporate world, and I'm planning to study again.
W: Really? What are you going to study?
M: Well, I want to be a traditional oriental doctor. That was my dream 10 years ago, and I just realized that **I had lost my way**.
W: Wow. That's great.
M: Yes, I think I will be happier if I am helping people and **living a more relaxed life**.
W: Good luck.

여: 너 정말 일 그만둘 거니? 졸업한 이후로 일을 그만두는 게 세 번째 아니야?
남: 응. 그렇긴 한데 이번엔 계획이 있어.
여: 하지만 지금까지 했던 일 중에 이게 가장 좋잖아. 네가 급여에 만족한다고 알고 있는데. 다른 일자리를 이미 마련해뒀니?
남: 아니, 실은 기업 세계를 떠나서 공부를 다시 할 계획이야.
여: 정말? 뭘 공부할 건데?
남: 음, 난 전통 한의사가 되고 싶어. 그건 10년 전에 내 꿈이었고, 내가 길을 잃었었다는 걸 막 깨달았거든.
여: 와. 잘됐다.
남: 응, 사람들을 도우면서 더 여유로운 삶을 산다면 더 행복할 것 같아.
여: 행운을 빌어.

어휘 **line up** ~을 마련[준비]하다 / **corporate** 기업의, 회사의 / **oriental (medical) doctor** 한의사

08 언급하지 않은 것 | ①

▶ 해석 참조

W: Today, we're going to talk about Vincent van Gogh, **one of the most influential artists** of the 19th century.
M: Mrs. Johnson, didn't he paint *Starry Night*?
W: That's right. And he also painted *Sunflowers*, *The Bedroom*, and several self-portraits.
M: What are the specific features of his paintings?
W: His paintings can be recognized by their bold use of color, rough beauty, and emotional honesty.
M: Oh, that sounds similar to the work of Matisse, who we talked about last month.
W: That's right! Vincent van Gogh's influence on art has been tremendous. Characteristics from his work **have been copied by thousands of artists**, including Matisse.
M: I'm starting to see why Vincent van Gogh is **such a well-respected painter**.

여: 오늘은 19세기(② 활동 시기)의 가장 영향력 있는 예술가 중 한 명인 Vincent van Gogh에 관해 이야기할 거예요.
남: Johnson 선생님, 그가 〈별이 빛나는 밤〉(③ 대표작)을 그리지 않았나요?
여: 맞아요. 그리고 〈해바라기〉, 〈고흐의 방〉(③ 대표작)과 자화상 몇 점도 그렸어요.
남: 그의 그림에는 어떤 특징이 있나요?
여: 그의 그림은 선명한 색채 사용, 야성미, 그리고 솔직한 감정 표현(④ 작품의 특징)으로 인식될 수 있어요.
남: 아, Matisse의 작품과 비슷한 것 같네요. 지난달에 이야기했던 예술가요.
여: 맞아요! Vincent van Gogh가 미술에 끼친 영향력은 대단했어요. 그의 작품 특징은 Matisse를 포함해 예술가 수천 명에 의해 모방돼 왔지요(⑤ 미술에 미친 영향력).
남: Vincent van Gogh가 왜 그렇게 높이 평가되는 화가인지 이해되기 시작하네요.

어휘 **influential** 영향력 있는, 영향력이 큰 *cf.* **influence** 영향(력) / **self-portrait** 자화상 / **bold** 선명한, 굵은; 용감한, 대담한 / **rough** 매끄럽지 않은, 거친 / **tremendous** 대단한, 엄청난

09 내용 불일치 | ②

▶ 사립학교 학생들은 학교에 직접 연락해서 등교 여부와 등교 시간을 확인해야 한다.

W: This is WMAL Radio's **latest news report**. Due to last night's snow storm, all public schools in the county today will open two hours late. If you attend a private school, please contact the school directly to find out **if and when you should arrive**. Ecstatic Software Corporation is requesting that employees who can work from home do so. Queen Lake road is closed. And finally, Waterloo University **has cancelled all classes** today. We will keep you updated on **any additional delays or closures** every 10 minutes.

여: WMAL 라디오 최신 뉴스입니다. 어젯밤의 눈보라로 인해 지역의 모든 공립학교가 오늘 두 시간 늦게 시작할 것입니다. 사립학교에 다니시면 학교로 직접 연락하셔서 등교 여부와 언제 등교를 해야 하는지를 확인하시기 바랍니다. Ecstatic 소프트웨어 회사는 재택근무가 가능한 사원에게는 그렇게 해 주기를 요청하고 있습니다. Queen Lake 도로도 폐쇄되었습니다. 그리고 마지막으로, Waterloo 대학교는 오늘 모든 수업을 취소했습니다. 추가로 발생하는 지연이나 폐쇄 상황에 대한 새로운 소식은 10분마다 계속해서 전해드리겠습니다.

어휘 **county** 미(美) 각 주(州)의 정치행정의 최하위 단위 / **closure** 폐쇄

10 도표 이해 | ④

▶ 여자는 미백, 잇몸 성형, 그리고 스케일링을 함께 받을 수 있으면서 200달러 미만인 서비스를 선택할 것이다.

M: Congratulations! You're getting married in a month!
W: I know! And my father told me to get **anything done I wanted here**.
M: Great!
W: Oh! You have various sets of services. I can get several dental services at once and save money.
M: That's right. Which set do you prefer?
W: I don't know. What do you recommend?
M: Think about **getting your teeth whitened**. You want your smile to be perfect at the wedding.
W: OK, but **the total cost should be less than** $200.
M: That means you will not choose Super-deluxe B.
W: Yeah, and since my teeth look kind of short, **you can reshape my gums**.
M: Sure. And you need scaling too?
W: Yes, actually that is the most important thing.

남: 축하합니다! 한 달 후면 결혼하시는군요!
여: 그러게요! 그리고 아버지께서 여기서 제가 원하는 것은 뭐든 해도 좋다고 하셨어요.
남: 잘됐군요!
여: 아! 다양한 서비스 세트 상품이 있군요. 한 번에 여러 가지 치과 서비스를 받고 돈도 아낄 수 있네요.
남: 맞습니다. 어떤 세트가 더 마음에 드세요?
여: 모르겠어요. 무엇을 추천하시나요?
남: 치아 미백 받는 것을 고려해 보세요. 결혼식에서 손님의 미소가 완벽하기를 원하시잖아요.
여: 좋아요. 하지만 총비용은 200달러 미만이어야 해요.
남: 그렇다면 Super-deluxe B를 선택하지 않으시겠다는 뜻이군요.
여: 네. 그리고 제 치아가 조금 짧으니까 잇몸 성형을 해주셨으면 해요.
남: 물론이죠. 그리고 스케일링도 필요하신가요?
여: 네. 사실 그게 가장 중요한 거예요.

어휘 **gum** 잇몸 / **reshape** 모양을 고치다 / **at once** 동시에; 당장

11 짧은 대화에 이어질 응답 | ③

▶ 영화 소리가 공부에 방해되지 않을지 묻는 말에 가장 적절한 응답을 고른다.

① 방해되지 않아. 넌 그것을 나중에 보는 게 나아. ② 방해되지, 난 영화를 봐서 좋아.
③ 방해되지 않아. 난 헤드폰 쓸 거거든. ④ 물론이지. 난 보통 거실에서 공부해.
⑤ 음. DVD 플레이어가 고장 난 것 같아.

M: **Do you mind if I watch** a movie in the living room?
W: Not at all. I have to study in my room anyway.
M: **Won't the noise bother you**?
W: ______________________________

남: 내가 거실에서 영화를 봐도 될까?
여: 그렇게 해. 난 어차피 방에서 공부해야 해.
남: 소리가 방해되지 않을까?
여: ______________________________

12 짧은 대화에 이어질 응답 | ②

▶ 수리하는 사람을 불러 달라는 여자의 요청에 적절한 응답을 찾는다.

① 물론이에요. 내가 싱크대를 고칠 수 있어요. ② 아침 식사 후에 바로 할게요.
③ 그것을 처리해줘서 고마워요. ④ 비용이 너무 많이 들진 않을 거예요.
⑤ 새 냉장고를 갖게 되어 기뻐요.

W: I think our refrigerator is broken. We need to call a repairman.
M: Yeah, we also need to **call someone to fix the sink**.
W: Well, if you aren't too busy, **would you mind doing it today**?
M: ______________________________

여: 냉장고가 고장 난 거 같아요. 수리기사를 불러야겠어요.
남: 네. 싱크대 고칠 사람도 불러야 해요.
여: 음. 당신이 너무 바쁘지 않으면 오늘 그것을 해줄 수 있어요?
남: ______________________________

어휘 **repairman** 수리기사

13 긴 대화에 이어질 응답 | ③

▶ 전화로는 마음에 드는 양복 천과 스타일을 정할 수 없으므로 직접 보고 선택하려고 할 것이다.

① 양복이 잘 맞네요. 감사합니다. ② 죄송합니다. 치수를 잴 시간이 없어요.
③ 좋아요. 고르러 바로 갈게요. ④ 양복의 색상을 바꾸고 싶지 않아요.
⑤ 양복에서는 천과 색상이 아주 중요해요.

[Phone rings.]
M: Hello, Patrick's Fashion House. How may I help you?
W: Hi. My husband, Walter Kimmel, **had his suit altered** at your store.
M: Oh, yes. I remember Mr. Kimmel.
W: Well, I was wondering if you could make him another suit from **the measurements you took**.
M: Is this going to be a surprise?
W: Yes, his birthday is coming.
M: We can do that. What color do you want?
W: **The suit you fixed for him** was dark blue. I think charcoal gray would be nice.
M: A classic color. What kind of fabric and style would you prefer?
W: Hmm, I'm not sure.
M: Then, how about if you **come in and select them by yourself**?
W: ______________________________

[전화벨이 울린다.]
남: 여보세요. Patrick 패션 하우스입니다. 무엇을 도와드릴까요?
여: 안녕하세요. Walter Kimmel 씨가 제 남편인데 그 가게에서 양복을 수선했어요.
남: 아. 네. Kimmel 씨를 기억합니다.
여: 음. 측정해 놓은 치수로 남편 양복을 한 벌 더 맞출 수 있나 해서요.
남: 깜짝 선물을 하시려고요?
여: 네. 남편의 생일이 다가와서요.
남: 그렇게 해드릴 수 있습니다. 어떤 색상을 원하시는지요?
여: 수선해 주신 양복은 짙은 푸른색이었는데요. 저는 짙은 회색도 좋을 것 같아요.
남: 유행을 안 타는 색상이지요. 어떤 종류의 천과 스타일을 선호하십니까?
여: 음. 잘 모르겠네요.
남: 그럼. 가게에 오셔서 직접 골라 보시는 것이 어떨까요?
여: ______________________________

어휘 **fabric** 천, 직물 / **alter** (의복을) 수선하다; 변하다, 달라지다 / **measurement** ((pl.)) 치수, 양; 측정 / **classic** (스타일이) 유행을 안 타는, 고전적인; 일류의

14 긴 대화에 이어질 응답 | ⑤

▶ 두 종류의 신분증을 보여 달라고 했으므로 여권 이외의 다른 신분증도 보려고 할 것이다.

① 은행에서 당신을 도와줄 수 있을 겁니다.
② 요즘 독신으로 지내는 것은 쉽지 않습니다.
③ 미래를 위해 저축하는 것이 중요합니다.
④ 아니요. 사진이 부착되어 있는 것이 필요합니다.
⑤ 그건 괜찮을 테지만 다른 신분증도 필요합니다.

W: I'd like to open a bank account.
M: Yes, ma'am. I'll **need you to fill out this form**.
W: OK. Is there a minimum deposit to **open a savings account**?
M: Yes, there is a $50 minimum for savings.
W: I also want to open a checking account. Can I do both today?
M: Of course. But we have a single form for a combined account.
W: One form **makes it a lot easier**. Do you need anything else?
M: I'll need to see two forms of identification.
W: **Is a passport good enough**?
M: ______________________________

여: 은행 계좌를 개설하고 싶습니다.
남: 네, 손님. 이 양식을 작성해 주셔야 합니다.
여: 알겠습니다. 보통 예금을 개설하는 데 최소 예치금이 있습니까?
남: 네, 예금의 경우 최소 50달러입니다.
여: 당좌 예금도 개설하고 싶습니다. 오늘 둘 다 가능한가요?
남: 물론입니다. 하지만 통합 계좌를 위한 단일 양식이 있습니다.
여: 양식이 하나라면 훨씬 더 수월하겠네요. 그밖에 필요하신 것이 있습니까?
남: 두 종류의 신분증을 보여 주셔야 합니다.
여: 여권이면 충분한가요?
남: ______________________________

어휘 **ID** 신분증명서, 신분증 ((identity 또는 identification의 약어)) / **minimum** 최저의, 최소한의; 최저, 최소한도 / **deposit** 예치금 / **savings account** 보통 예금 / **checking account** 당좌 예금 ((예금자가 수표를 발행하면 은행이 어느 때나 예금액으로 그 수표에 대한 지급을 하도록 되어 있는 예금)) / **combined** 통합된, 결합된

15 상황에 적절한 말 | ③

▶ Max는 행사 준비를 하기에는 너무 바쁜 Becky에게 준비 위원회에 참여하는 것은 곤란하다는 말을 할 것이다.

① 누나가 우리와 함께 일했으면 좋겠어.
② 누나가 그 직위에 출마한지 몰랐어.
③ 누나는 너무 바빠서 행사 준비를 도울 수 없어.
④ 연회를 위해 넥타이 고르는 것을 도와줄래?
⑤ 누나가 댄스파티에 파트너 신청을 받았다고 들었어.

M: Max **is in charge of the planning committee** for the Senior Class Spring Banquet at his high school. His twin sister, Becky, wants to be part of the committee, but Max knows his sister **is too busy with her other activities**, like soccer and French lessons. Becky thinks she should **automatically get a position** in the group because Max is her brother. Max **has filled all the positions** in the committee and must tell his sister that she isn't in the group. In this situation, what would Max most likely say to Becky?

남: Max는 학교에서 고등학교 3학년 봄 연회 행사의 준비 위원회를 맡고 있다. 그의 쌍둥이 누나인 Becky는 위원회의 일원이 되고 싶어 하지만, Max는 축구와 프랑스어 수업 같은 다른 활동들로 누나가 너무 바쁘다는 것을 안다. Becky는 Max가 자신의 동생이므로 모임의 직위를 자동으로 얻어야 한다고 생각한다. Max는 위원회의 모든 직위를 충원했고 누나에게 그녀가 모임의 일원이 아니라고 말해야 한다. 이러한 상황에서 Max가 Becky에게 할 말로 가장 적절한 것은 무엇인가?

어휘 **run for office** (공직에) 출마하다 / **banquet** 연회 / **be in charge of** ~ 담당이다

16~17 세트 문항 | 16. ② 17. ④

▶ 16. 아침 식사를 건너뛰는 것이 안 좋은 점을 이야기하면서 아침 식사를 해야 장수하고 건강한 생활을 할 수 있다고 말하고 있다.

① 활기찬 아침을 위한 건강 요리법
② 매일 아침 식사를 하는 것의 필요성
③ 사람들이 아침 식사를 거르는 이유
④ 운동 없이 체중을 줄이는 네 가지 효과적인 방법
⑤ 건강을 위한 빠르고 안전한 다이어트 법

▶ 17. 해석 참조

① 우유 ② 수프 ③ 치즈 ④ 시리얼 ⑤ 크래커

W: Many people **trying to lose weight** often skip breakfast to reduce their daily caloric intake. While this may work to a certain extent, you might make up for the calories later in the day due to overeating at lunch and dinner. Because you're so hungry by lunch, it's **highly likely that you will eat more**. On top of that, you'll have almost no fuel to run on in the morning, which means you won't be able to perform at full capacity. You might even feel unhappy **due to the lack of food**. If you skip breakfast, you will also eat more for dinner. Eating a big dinner means that you won't be hungry for breakfast the next day. Studies suggest that if you eat a high-protein, low-fat breakfast and a small dinner, you will **most likely lose weight** and maintain a healthy body weight. Skipping breakfast is obviously not good for your overall health. So if you don't have the appetite for a full breakfast, have a small one that's **packed with nutrients**. Eat something — milk, fruit, soup, or yogurt. And use your midmorning snack, such as cheese or a wholegrain cracker, to **catch up with the rest of your morning nutrition** and energy needs. Eating breakfast every day will be an excellent foundation for a long and healthy life.

여: 체중을 줄이려는 많은 사람들이 일일 칼로리 섭취를 줄이기 위해 아침을 건너뛰는 일이 흔합니다. 이것은 어느 정도 효과가 있을지 모르지만, 점심과 저녁을 과식하기 때문에 그날 후반에 그 칼로리를 보충할지도 모릅니다. 점심때가 되면 배가 몹시 고프기 때문에 더 많이 먹게 될 가능성이 매우 큽니다. 게다가 여러분은 오전에 가동할 연료가 거의 없을 것이고 이는 여러분이 전력을 다해 일을 수행할 수 없음을 의미합니다. 여러분은 음식을 먹지 않아 기분까지 좋지 않을지도 모릅니다. 여러분이 아침을 건너뛴다면 저녁도 더 많이 먹게 될 것입니다. 저녁 식사를 많이 하는 것은 여러분이 다음 날 아침에 배가 고프지 않을 것을 의미합니다. 여러분이 고단백, 저지방의 아침 식사와 저녁 식사를 소식한다면 아마도 체중이 줄고 건강한 체중을 유지할 것이라고 연구들은 시사합니다. 아침을 거르는 것은 분명 여러분의 전반적인 건강에 좋지 않습니다. 그러므로 여러분이 충분한 아침 식사를 할 식욕이 없다면, 영양가로 가득 찬 아침 식사를 적게 드세요. ① 우유, 과일, ② 수프나 요구르트를 드세요. 그리고 나머지 오전 영양과 에너지 필요를 충족하기 위해 ③ 치즈나 통밀 ⑤ 크래커 같은 스낵을 오전 나절에 사용하세요. 매일 아침 식사를 하는 것은 장수하고 건강한 생활을 위한 훌륭한 기반이 될 것입니다.

어휘 **skip** 빠뜨리다 / **caloric** 열량의, 칼로리의 / **intake** 섭취 / **extent** 정도, 범위 / **make up for** 보상하다 / **overeat** 과식하다 / **fuel** 연료, 동력 에너지원 / **capacity** 능력 **high-protein** 고단백의 / **low-fat** 저지방의 / **maintain** 유지하다 / **obviously** 명백하게 / **overall** 전반적인 / **appetite** 식욕 / **nutrient** 영양소 / **midmorning** 아침나절, 오전의 중반 / **catch up with** ~을 따라잡다 / **foundation** 기반, 기초, 토대

Answers & Explanation

01. ④ 02. ② 03. ② 04. ④ 05. ⑤ 06. ② 07. ③ 08. ④ 09. ② 10. ②
11. ② 12. ② 13. ② 14. ⑤ 15. ① 16. ⑤ 17. ③

01 화자가 하는 말의 목적 | ④

▶ 대중 연설을 할 때 영향을 높이기 위해 의도적으로 한 사람씩 시선을 마주치라고 하고 있다. 그러므로 담화의 목적으로는 ④가 적절하다.

M: As you know, the audience is an important element in public speaking. A presentation will **lose its purpose if there are no spectators**. This is why you need to make your speech worthy of your listeners' time. There is one simple thing you can do to **enhance your impact as a speaker**. It is purposeful eye contact with one person at a time. When you fail to do it, you **look less believable and less confident**. When you don't look people in the eye, they are less likely to look at you. That makes them start thinking about something other than what you're saying, and when that happens, they stop listening. So, if you want to **connect with your audience**, look people in the eye, one at a time.

남: 여러분이 아시다시피 청중은 대중 연설의 중요한 요소입니다. 발표는 관중이 없다면 그 목적을 잃어버릴 것입니다. 이것이 여러분이 청중의 시간을 낭비하지 않는 연설을 해야 되는 이유입니다. 연사로서 여러분의 영향력을 높이도록 여러분이 할 수 있는 한 가지 간단한 일이 있습니다. 그것은 한 번에 한 사람씩 의도적으로 시선을 마주치는 것입니다. 여러분이 그것을 하는 것에 실패하면 여러분은 덜 믿음직스럽고 자신감도 덜 해 보입니다. 여러분이 사람들의 눈을 똑바로 쳐다보지 못하면 그들도 여러분을 바라볼 가능성이 적어집니다. 그것은 그들로 하여금 여러분이 말하고 있는 것과는 다른 것에 대해 생각하기 시작하도록 만들고, 그렇게 되면 그들은 듣기를 멈춥니다. 그러므로 여러분이 청중과 연결되고자 한다면, 사람들의 눈을 한 번에 한 명씩 똑바로 바라보십시오.

어휘 **audience** 청중 / **spectator** 관중 / **enhance** 높이다, 향상하다 / **purposeful** 의도적인, 목적이 있는 / **at a time** 한 번에, 따로따로 / **believable** 믿을 수 있는

02 의견 | ②

▶ 친구에게 도가 지나친 농담을 해 친구의 기분을 상하게 한 남자에게 여자는 곧바로 사과하고 화해해야 하며 사과가 빠를수록 치유가 빠르다고 말한다.

W: James, **why do you look so down**?
M: I actually had an argument with Chris a few minutes ago.
W: What happened?
M: Well, everyone wanted a good laugh so I called him a cucumber because of all the pimples on his face. Chris got all upset.
W: Oh, that wasn't very nice of you. **Did you apologize to him**?
M: Well, no. I thought it was just a joke but he overreacted. Chris said he would never talk to me again.
W: I can understand why he did that. **You went too far**. Call him now and tell him you're sorry. You need to apologize and make up right away.
M: I think he needs **some time to cool off** since he's so angry now.
W: No, you have to make it timely. The sooner you offer an apology, **the quicker the healing can begin**.
M: That's right. I'd better call him right away. Thanks for your advice.

여: James, 왜 그렇게 축 처져 있니?
남: 사실 몇 분 전에 Chris와 말다툼을 했어.
여: 무슨 일 있었어?
남: 음, 모두가 큰 웃음을 원해서 내가 그 애의 얼굴에 있는 모든 여드름 때문에 그를 오이라고 불렀어. Chris는 완전히 화가 났지.
여: 아, 그건 너무 좋지 않았어. 그 애에게 사과했니?
남: 음, 아니. 난 단지 농담이었지만 그 애가 과잉 반응을 보였다고 생각했어. Chris는 다시는 나와 이야기를 하지 않을 거래.
여: 난 왜 그 애가 그랬는지 이해할 수 있어. 네가 도를 넘었어. 그 애에게 지금 전화해서 미안하다고 말해. 넌 곧바로 사과하고 화해해야 해.
남: 난 그 애가 지금은 너무 화가 났으니 진정할 시간이 필요하다고 생각해.
여: 아니야, 그건 시기적절해야 해. 네가 더 빨리 사과할수록 치유가 더 빨리 시작될 수 있어.
남: 맞아. 지금 당장 그 애에게 전화하는 게 낫겠다. 조언 고마워.

어휘 **argument** 말다툼; 논쟁 / **pimple** 여드름 / **apologize** 사과하다; 변명하다 *cf.* **apology** 사과 / **overreact** 과잉 반응을 보이다 / **go too far** 도를 넘다, 지나치다 / **make up** 화해하다; 화장을 하다 / **cool off** 진정하다; 시원해지다 / **timely** 시기적절한, 때맞춘 / **healing** 치유[치료](법)

03 관계 | ②

▶ 두 사람은 내일 있을 배구 시합에서 상대팀에 대비하는 방법과 출전할 선수들에 대해 서로 의논하고 있다.

W: Sue played well against Western High School on Monday.
M: Yes, but she can't play tomorrow because **her thumb still hurts**.
W: Have you talked to her today? What did she say?
M: She said the doctor **told her not to play volleyball** for a couple more days.
W: OK.
M: Tomorrow we play Northern High School. They hit the ball hard.
W: We need to **teach the girls a play to block their spikes**.
M: I have an idea. I'll show it to you later on the whiteboard.
W: OK. We can teach it to the girls at practice this afternoon. And I want Jill to play a lot tomorrow.
M: Yes, I agree. **She's good at returning hard shots**.

여: 월요일에 있었던 Western 고등학교와의 시합에서 Sue가 경기를 잘했어요.
남: 네, 하지만 그 애는 엄지손가락이 아직 아파서 내일 시합을 할 수 없어요.
여: 오늘 그 애랑 이야기해 보셨어요? 뭐라고 하던가요?
남: 의사 선생님이 며칠 정도 더 배구를 하지 말라고 하셨대요.
여: 알겠어요.
남: 내일은 Northern 고등학교와 시합하네요. 그들은 공을 세게 쳐요.
여: 아이들에게 그들의 스파이크를 막는 방법을 가르쳐야 해요.
남: 제게 생각이 있어요. 나중에 화이트보드에 그려서 보여 드릴게요.
여: 좋아요. 오늘 오후에 있을 연습에서 아이들에게 가르치면 되겠어요. 그리고 전 Jill이 내일 많이 뛰어 주면 좋겠어요.
남: 네, 동감이에요. 그 애는 강타를 받아내는 데 능숙하니까요.

어휘 **spike** (배구) 스파이크

04 그림 불일치 | ④

▶ 남자는 여자의 조언대로 진열창에 3단 케이크를 놓았다고 했다.

[Phone rings.]
W: Mary's Interior Design. How may I help you?
M: Hi, this is Greg. I talked to you before about the bakery that I'm opening?
W: Yes, of course. Did you **make a decision** about the exterior?
M: I decided to **go with bricks**, like you suggested. I also **put up a sign** that says "The Bakery."
W: That sounds good. Did you install an entrance door?
M: Yes, I went with **a rectangular glass door**.
W: Okay. Have you considered placing a three-layer cake in the display window, like we talked about?
M: Yes, **I followed your advice**. It is much more impressive than my two-layer cakes.
W: Good. I also suggest **standing a signboard in front of the store** to attract customers.
M: I already have one. It says "Grand Opening."
W: Then everything sounds great.

[전화벨이 울린다.]
여: Mary 인테리어 디자인입니다. 무엇을 도와 드릴까요?
남: 안녕하세요. Greg입니다. 제가 개업할 빵집에 관해 전에 말씀드린 적이 있는데요?
여: 네, 물론입니다. (건물) 외부에 관해 결정을 내리셨나요?
남: 제안하셨던 대로 벽돌로 하기로 했습니다. '빵집'이라는 간판도 걸었고요.
여: 잘하셨습니다. 출입문은 설치하셨나요?

남: 네, 직사각형 유리문으로 했습니다.
여: 그렇군요. 우리가 이야기 나눴던 대로 진열창에 3단 케이크를 놓는 건 생각해 보셨나요?
남: 네, 조언하신 대로 했습니다. 제가 말했던 2단 케이크보다 훨씬 더 인상적이에요.
여: 잘됐네요. 또, 손님을 끌도록 가게 앞에 입간판을 세우는 것을 추천합니다.
남: 이미 하나 있어요. '신장개업'이라고 쓰여 있어요.
여: 그럼 다 잘된 것 같네요.

어휘 **exterior** (건물의) 외부; 외부의, 겉의 / **layer** 층, 겹 / **signboard** 간판, 광고판

05 추후 행동 | ⑤

▶ 믹서가 고장 나서 교체 부품을 찾으려고 하지만 한국어가 서툴러서 제조업자를 찾는 것이 어려운 여자를 위해 남자가 도움을 주기로 했다.

W: Hey, Ji-hoon! You know how I make banana smoothies for breakfast every day?
M: Yum. **I wish you'd make me one**!
W: Sure, but **my blender's broken**. I need a replacement part for a Mixmaster blender.
M: Blender? Oh, we call that a "mixer" in Korea.
W: Right. I looked on the Internet for **a spare parts supplier** in Seoul, but my Korean isn't so good.
M: No problem. **I can track one down for you**. What's the brand name again?
W: Mixmaster.
M: And how about if I teach you some Korean?
W: That sounds great. But not right now. My schedule is too busy nowadays. But thank you anyway.
M: OK, then.
W: You're so good, Ji-hoon.

여: 얘, 지훈아! 내가 매일 아침 식사로 바나나 스무디 만드는 거 알지?
남: 맛있겠다. 나에게도 하나 만들어 주면 좋을 텐데!
여: 물론이지. 하지만 내 블렌더가 고장이 났어. Mixmaster사의 블렌더 교체 부품이 필요해.
남: 블렌더? 아, 한국에서는 그걸 '믹서'라고 해.
여: 맞아. 인터넷에서 서울에 예비 부품 제조업자가 있나 찾아봤지만, 내가 한국어를 그렇게 잘 하지 않아서 말이야.
남: 문제없어. 내가 어디에 있는지 찾아볼게. 상표가 뭐라고 했지?
여: Mixmaster야.
남: 그리고 내가 너에게 한국어를 좀 가르쳐 주면 어떨까?
여: 좋은 생각이야. 하지만 지금은 안 돼. 요즘 내 일정이 너무 바쁘거든. 하지만 어쨌든 고마워.
남: 좋아, 그럼.
여: 너는 정말 좋은 아이야, 지훈아.

어휘 **blender** 블렌더, 믹서 / **replacement** 교체, 교환 / **spare** 예비용의; 남는 / **part** (기계 등의) 부품 / **supplier** 부품 제조업자, 공급 회사 / **track down** (흔적 등을) 찾아내다

06 금액 | ②

▶ 계산서에 나온 금액은 80달러이다. 여자가 골드 회원이고 골드 회원은 20% 할인을 받을 수 있다고 했으므로 여자가 지불할 금액은 총 금액 80달러에서 16달러를 뺀 64달러이다.

M: We are very lucky. Look, it says membership holders **can get a special discount** on Fridays.
W: Really?
M: Yes, they give a 20 percent discount for gold membership cards, and a 10 percent discount for silver membership cards.
W: Even 10 percent off can save us a lot of money!
M: But **I want the bigger discount**!
W: Of course you do! How much is the bill? 70 dollars?
M: No, it's a total of 80 dollars. So if we can get a 20 percent discount, **it would be 16 dollars off**.
W: That's a lot.
M: Yeah. I agree. But **I can't get it**. I'm a silver member.
W: I can get it. I'm a gold member. **Let me pay the bill**.
M: Oh, really? Thanks. I had a really great time.

남: 우리 정말 운 좋은데. 봐, 회원들은 금요일마다 특별 할인을 받을 수 있다는데.
여: 진짜?
남: 그래, 골드 카드 회원은 20% 할인을 해주고, 실버 회원 카드는 10% 할인을 해준대.
여: 10% 할인만 되어도 돈을 많이 아끼는 거네.
남: 하지만, 난 할인을 더 많이 받고 싶어!
여: 물론이지. 계산서에 얼마 나왔어? 70달러?
남: 아니, 총 80달러야. 그러니까 우리가 20% 할인을 받으면, 16달러 할인받는 거야.
여: 그거 꽤 되는데.
남: 응, 그렇지. 그런데 나는 그렇게 할인이 안 돼. 실버 회원이라서 말이야.
여: 나는 받을 수 있어. 골드 회원이거든. 내가 계산할게.
남: 정말? 고마워. 정말 즐거운 시간이었어.

어휘 **membership** 회원; 회원자격 / **holder** 소유주, 소지인 / **pay the bill** 계산하다, 돈을 내다

07 이유 | ③

▶ 남자는 시장 조사도 끝냈고 서류도 이미 제출했고 은행과 10년 동안 거래를 했지만 주택 구입 대출을 이미 받았기에 사업 융자를 받을 수가 없다고 했으므로 답은 ③이다.

M: Hello, Ms. Lowell. I called you yesterday.
W: Hello, Mr. Miles. Please have a seat. So, **you want to apply for a loan** for your new coffee shop, right?
M: Yes, I'd like to open a coffee shop on Harbor Street.
W: Have you done any market research on that area?
M: Sure I did. That's why I chose that location. I also already sent all the documents you asked for.
W: Yes. Well, unfortunately, it looks like **we can't approve your loan** at this time.
M: May I ask why? I've had an account with this bank for 12 years now.
W: I realize that, but **you already have another loan**.
M: I took out that loan because I needed money to buy my house.
W: I'm sorry but we can't give you a business loan **unless you pay that off**.
M: Oh, I see.

남: 안녕하세요, Lowell씨. 어제 전화드렸었죠.
여: 안녕하세요, Miles씨. 앉으세요. 그럼, 새로 커피숍을 내려고 대출을 신청하고 싶으신 거죠, 그렇죠?
남: 네, Harbor Street에 커피숍을 열고 싶어서요.
여: 그 지역에 대해 시장 조사를 한 적이 있나요?
남: 그럼요, 했어요. 그래서 제가 그 장소를 선택했고요. 요청하신 서류도 이미 다 보내드렸는데요.
여: 네, 음, 안타깝게도 이번에는 손님의 대출을 승인할 수 없을 것 같아요.
남: 이유를 여쭤봐도 될까요? 전 이 은행에 예금계좌를 12년째 갖고 있는데요.
여: 알고 있습니다만, 이미 다른 대출이 있으시더군요.
남: 집을 살 돈이 필요해서 그 대출을 받았어요.
여: 죄송합니다만 그걸 다 갚지 않으시면 사업 융자를 드릴 수가 없어요.
남: 아, 그렇군요.

어휘 **loan** 대출, 융자 / **document** 서류, 문서 / **approve** 승인하다, 허가하다 / **account** 예금계좌 / **take out** 받다 / **pay ~ off** ~을 다 갚다, 청산하다

08 언급하지 않은 것 | ④

▶ 해석 참조

M: The Toco Toucan is a type of South American bird characterized by its huge but light beak. Their bright feathers are the colors of flowers and fruits, and **help to keep them hidden** in the broken light of the rain forest. However, these birds are generally noisy, which suggests that they are not trying to remain hidden. They produce two to four eggs each year, and **both parents care for the babies** for about six weeks. These well-known birds are very popular pets, and **they are also frequently used** in commercials for various products. Native peoples regard the bird **with a more sacred eye**; they are traditionally seen as messengers between the worlds of the living and the spirits.

남: Toco Toucan은 남아메리카 새의 한 종류로, 거대하지만 가벼운 부리(① 부리의 특징)가 특징이다. 밝은 색 깃털은 꽃과 과일 색깔로, 열대 우림 사이로 부서져 들어오는 햇빛 속에 몸을 숨기도록 도와준다(② 깃털의 기능). 하지만 이 새는 대개 시끄러운데, 이는 새가 숨어 있으려 하지 않음을 암시한다. 매년 두 개에서 네 개의 알을 낳고(③ 번식력), 암수가 함께 약 6주간 새끼를 보살핀다. 이 유명한 새는 매우 인기 있는 반려동물이며, 다양한 상품 광고에도 자주 이용된다. 원주민들은 이 새를 보다 신성한 시각으로 본다. 즉, 그 새는 전통적으로 산 자의 세계와 영혼 세계 사이의 전령(⑤ 전통적 의미)으로 여겨진다.

어휘 **be characterized by** ~가 특징이다 / **beak** (새의) 부리 / **feather** 깃털 / **commercial** (텔레비전 · 라디오의) 광고 (방송) / **sacred** 신성시되는; 성스러운, 종교적인

09 내용 불일치 | ②

▶ 2003년부터 우주 김치의 개발을 시작했다고 했다.

W: You're an astronaut doing research in outer space. You're hungry, but not for **tasteless space food**. You want some of your mother's kimchi, a taste of home. Now you can have it — thanks to researcher Lee Won-ju, who began working on space kimchi in 2003. To make kimchi a space food, Mr. Lee solved several problems. **His biggest challenge was reducing the odor** by 30 to 50%, so **non-kimchi eating astronauts wouldn't complain**. Mr. Lee also had to invent a process to kill the bacteria in kimchi without changing the taste. He succeeded. So space kimchi **not only has the same color and texture** as regular kimchi, but also has the same taste.

여: 여러분은 우주 공간에서 연구를 수행 중인 우주 비행사입니다. 여러분은 배고프지만 맛없는 우주 음식은 먹고 싶지 않습니다. 고향의 맛인, 어머니가 해 주신 김치가 먹고 싶습니다. 이제 2003년부터 우주 김치를 개발하기 시작한 이원주 연구원 덕분에 그것을 먹을 수 있습니다. 김치를 우주 음식으로 만들기 위해, 이원주 씨는 여러 가지 문제점들을 해결했습니다. 그에게 있어 가장 큰 난관은 30~50% 정도로 냄새를 줄여 김치를 먹지 않는 우주 비행사들이 불평하지 않게 하는 일이었습니다. 이원주 씨는 또한 맛을 변하게 하지 않고도 김치에 있는 박테리아를 죽이는 처리 과정을 발명해야 했습니다. 그는 성공했습니다. 그래서 우주 김치는 보통 김치와 색과 씹히는 느낌이 같을 뿐 아니라 맛도 같아지게 되었습니다.

어휘 **tasteless** 맛없는 ***cf.*** **taste** 맛; 기호, 취향 / **challenge** 난제, 과제 / **odor** 냄새, 향기 / **texture** (음식의) 씹히는 느낌, 질감; (직물의) 감촉

10 도표 이해 | ②

▶ 두 사람은 호텔 패키지 중 해변 전망을 선택했고 조식은 원했지만 석식은 필요 없다고 했다. 가격은 1,000달러를 넘지 않는 것을 원했으므로 ②와 ③의 선택지가 남았는데 가격이 100달러 더 비싸지만 포함된 활동이 마음에 든 ②를 선택했다.

W: I'm so excited about our trip to Orlando. It's been so long since we've had a vacation.
M: The hotel **we chose to stay in** is offering several special packages. Let's see what we have here.
W: I think we should pay more to get the beach view.
M: I think so, too. Fortunately, **four of the rooms in the offers** have beach views.
W: Good. What about our meals? I want to have breakfast at the hotel.
M: Don't worry. Breakfast is **included in all of the packages**. There are also packages that offer breakfast and dinner.
W: That's not necessary. We'll be sightseeing until evening and there are so many great restaurants there.
M: Okay. And I'd **prefer not to spend more than** $1,000.
W: I agree. Then there are two we can choose from.
M: How about the cheaper one?
W: I **like the included activity of the other one**. I think it's worth more than $100.
M: I see. Then let's reserve this package.

여: Orlando 여행이 너무 신나요. 우리가 휴가 여행을 간 게 정말 오래됐어요.
남: 우리가 묵기로 선택한 호텔이 몇 가지 특별 패키지를 제공하고 있어요. 여기 뭐가 있는지 봅시다.
여: 해변 전망을 얻으려면 돈을 더 내야 할 것 같아요.
남: 나도 그렇게 생각해요. 다행히도, 제공 객실 중 4개가 해변 전망이에요.
여: 좋아요. 식사는 어쩌죠? 나는 호텔에서 아침 식사를 하고 싶어요.
남: 걱정하지 말아요. 조식은 모든 패키지에 포함되어 있어요. 또 조식과 석식을 제공하는 패키지들도 있어요.
여: 그것은 필요 없어요. 우리는 저녁까지 관광할 건데 거기 훌륭한 식당이 아주 많아요.
남: 알겠어요. 그리고 1,000달러 넘게는 쓰지 않았으면 좋겠어요.
여: 동의해요. 그럼 고를 수 있는 게 두 가지가 있네요.
남: 가격이 더 싼 거 어때요?
여: 난 다른 쪽에 포함된 활동이 좋아요. 그건 100달러가 넘는 가치가 있다고 생각해요.
남: 알았어요. 그럼 이 패키지를 예약합시다.

어휘 **sightsee** 관광하다 / **worth** 가치가 있다 / **reserve** 예약하다

11 짧은 대화에 이어질 응답 | ②

▶ Jacob에게 말해주는 걸 잊은 게 아닌지 묻는 여자의 말에 가장 적절한 답변을 찾는다.

① 그 애는 항상 늦어.
② 난 네가 말한 줄 알았어.
③ 그 애 없이 시작할 순 없어.
④ 가능하면 내가 나중에 그 애에게 말할게.
⑤ 그 애는 다음에 온다고 말했어.

W: Jacob still isn't here. **Maybe we should start without him.**
M: Well, I'm not sure that he knows we are meeting today.
W: **You didn't forget to tell him**, did you?
M: ______________________________

여: Jacob이 아직도 여기에 안 왔어. 아무래도 그 애 없이 시작해야겠어.
남: 음, 우리가 오늘 만난다는 것을 그 애가 아는지 모르겠어.
여: 너 그 애에게 말해주는 것을 잊은 거 아니지?
남: ______________________________

12 짧은 대화에 이어질 응답 | ②

▶ 보고서를 제때에 제출할 수 없는 상황에서 교수님께서 시간을 더 주실 것 같은지 묻는 남자의 말에 가장 적절한 응답을 고른다.

① 시간이 정말 빨리 가고 있어.
② 여쭤봐서 나쁠 건 없을 것 같아.
③ 그건 4시간밖에 안 남았다는 뜻이야.
④ 우리는 그것을 제시간에 제출했어야 했어.
⑤ 내일 오후 3시에 난 베이징에 있을 거야.

M: I don't think we can finish this report tonight. Let's meet tomorrow.
W: But **it's due tomorrow** by 3 p.m. and I don't have time in the morning.
M: Oh, that's right. Do you think **Professor Clark would give us more time**?
W: ______________________________

남: 우리 이 보고서를 오늘 밤에 끝낼 수 없을 것 같아. 내일 만나자.
여: 하지만 이건 내일 오후 3시까지 내야 하고, 난 아침에 시간이 없어.
남: 아, 맞아. 너는 Clark 교수님이 우리에게 시간을 더 주실 거라고 생각하니?
여: ______________________________

어휘 **submit** ~을 제출하다

13 긴 대화에 이어질 응답 | ②

▶ 호텔 내의 헬스클럽은 호텔 투숙객에게는 무료이므로 남자는 돈이 필요하지 않을 것이다.

① 신용카드로 지불할 수 있다고 생각하세요?
② 좋아요. 그럼 지갑을 여기에 두고 갈게요.
③ 좋아요. 좋은 식당을 찾으러 가요.
④ 괜찮아요. 차라리 일을 지금 하는 게 좋겠어요.
⑤ 한 시간 동안 하고 10달러를 다시 가져올게요.

M: Clara, do you want to eat dinner at a restaurant in the hotel?
W: Sounds good.
M: I'd like to work out before dinner. Do you know **if there is a fitness center** for hotel guests?
W: You can look in the hotel directory. I've just seen it somewhere. Hmm... Here, I've got it.
M: Can you **look through it for me**?
W: OK, let's see. **They have a golfing facility**, an indoor driving range.
M: Really? Is it free?
W: No, it says it's 10 dollars an hour for hotel guests.
M: Well, I like golfing, but I just want to work out right now. Does it say where the fitness center is?
W: It's on the 11th floor. And **there is no charge for hotel guests**.
M: ______________________________

남: Clara, 호텔에 있는 음식점에서 저녁 먹을래요?
여: 좋아요.
남: 난 저녁 먹기 전에 운동하고 싶어요. 호텔 투숙객을 위한 헬스클럽이 있는지 아세요?
여: 호텔의 안내 책자를 보면 돼요. 내가 그것을 어딘가에서 막 봤는데. 음…. 여기, 찾았어요.
남: 좀 찾아봐 줄래요?

여: 그래요. 어디 보자. 골프 시설이 있네요. 실내 골프 연습장이요.
남: 정말이요? 무료예요?
여: 아니요. 호텔 투숙객들은 한 시간에 10달러라고 적혀 있어요.
남: 음, 골프를 좋아하지만 지금은 그냥 운동이 하고 싶네요. 헬스클럽이 어디 있는지 적혀 있나요?
여: 11층에 있네요. 그리고 호텔 투숙객은 무료고요.
남: ______________________________

어휘 **directory** 안내 책자; (컴퓨터의) 디렉터리 / **look through** ~을 살펴[훑어]보다 / **facility** 시설, 설비 / **driving range** 골프 연습장

14 긴 대화에 이어질 응답 | ⑤

▶ 아내의 치수가 판매하고 있는 여자의 치수와 비슷하다고 했으므로 여자는 자신의 치수를 알려주려고 할 것이다.

① 아내분은 아주 세련된 분이세요.
② 확인하고 싶으시면 착용해보셔도 됩니다.
③ 어머니께서는 중간 치수를 입으시죠, 맞죠?
④ 제가 큰 치수를 입으니까, 아내분께는 작은 치수를 사 드리셔야 해요.
⑤ 제가 이 상표 제품의 중간 치수를 입으니까 아내분도 그 치수를 입으셔야 해요.

W: Can I help you with anything, sir?
M: I'd like to get **a pair of these winter gloves** for my mother.
W: The size?
M: Medium. *[pause]* Yes, those will do fine. And I need a present for my wife.
W: **What were you thinking of getting her**?
M: She asked for a sweater this year.
W: Our sweaters are over here, sir.
M: Getting a present for my wife is hard. I often get **something unstylish or the wrong size**.
W: This style is very popular this year. I'm sure she'll love it.
M: OK. I'll trust your opinion. **I'll take it in black**.
W: And the size?
M: Hmm... it depends on the brand. Actually, she's about your size.
W: ______________________________

여: 무엇을 도와드릴까요, 손님?
남: 어머니께 드릴 이 겨울 장갑을 사고 싶습니다.
여: 치수는요?
남: 중간 치수요. *[잠시 후]* 네, 그거면 될 거예요. 그리고 아내에게 줄 선물도 필요합니다.
여: 아내분께 어떤 선물을 하시고 싶은가요?
남: 올해는 스웨터를 사 달라고 했어요.
여: 스웨터는 이쪽에 있습니다, 손님.
남: 아내에게 줄 선물을 사는 것은 힘들어요. 세련되지 못하거나 잘못된 치수의 물건을 종종 고르거든요.
여: 이 스타일이 올해 매우 인기 있습니다. 부인께서도 틀림없이 아주 좋아하실 거예요.
남: 알겠습니다. 당신의 의견을 믿을게요. 검은색으로 주세요.
여: 그리고 치수는요?
남: 음… 상표에 따라 다른데요. 실은, 당신 치수 정도 되겠군요.
여: ______________________________

어휘 **stylish** 세련된, 유행을 따르는

15 상황에 적절한 말 | ①

▶ 자신의 카트에 물건이 가득 찬 상태라 계산을 하고 나가는 데 시간이 많이 걸릴 것이므로 Elizabeth는 Peter에게 먼저 계산하도록 배려해 줄 것이다.

① 선생님, 저보다 먼저 계산하시겠어요?
② 오늘 저녁 식사로 스테이크를 드실 건가요?
③ 저쪽 구석에서 카트를 가지고 오시면 됩니다.
④ 줄에 끼어들지 마세요. 차례를 기다리세요.
⑤ 식료품을 나르는 것을 도와주시겠어요?

M: Elizabeth is doing the weekly grocery shopping. She pushes the cart **up and down the aisles** picking out the groceries. When her cart is full, **she pushes it to one of the checkout lanes**. She is next in line. One person **is being checked out by the clerk** now and there is no one behind her. Then Peter gets in line behind Elizabeth. He has three items: steak, milk and potatoes. He looks anxious and seems to be in a hurry. Elizabeth looks around at the other aisles. There doesn't **appear to be an express lane open**. She wants to help him. In this situation, what would Elizabeth most likely say to Peter?

남: Elizabeth는 일주일에 한 번 하는 식료품 쇼핑을 하고 있다. 그녀는 식료품을 고르느라 카트를 밀며 통로를 왔다 갔다 한다. 카트가 다 차자 계산대 통로 중 한 곳으로 카트를 민다. 그녀는 다음 차례이다. 현재 한 사람이 점원에게 계산을 하고 있고 그녀의 뒤에는 아무도 없다. 그때 Peter가 Elizabeth 뒤에 줄을 선다. 그에게는 세 가지 물품, 즉 스테이크, 우유 그리고 감자가 있다. 그는 초조해 보이고 서두르는 것 같다. Elizabeth는 다른 통로를 둘러본다. 신속 처리 계산대가 열려 있지 않은 것 같다. 그녀는 그를 돕고 싶다. 이러한 상황에서 Elizabeth가 Peter에게 할 말로 가장 적절한 것은 무엇인가?

어휘 **go ahead of** ~보다 앞서 가다 / **cut in** 끼어들다 / **express lane** 신속 처리 계산대; 추월 차선

16~17 세트 문항 | 16. ⑤ 17. ③

▶ 16. 가족 건강 역사 족보를 만드는 것이 건강상 위험을 예측해 특정 질병을 예방하도록 돕고 그를 위한 조치를 취하게 한다고 했다. 여러 질병을 언급했지만 예시로 든 것이며 질병에 대해 설명하고 있지는 않다는 것에 유의한다.

① 가족 건강에 영향을 주는 주요한 요인들
② 전국 가족 역사의 날에 대한 사실들
③ 신체 건강이 가족 관계에 미치는 영향
④ 가족 건강 역사를 통해 예측되는 질병들
⑤ 가족 건강 역사 족보를 만드는 것의 건강상 이점

▶ 17. 해석 참조

① 심장 질환 ② 암 ③ 알레르기 ④ 당뇨병 ⑤ 간 질환

W: Do you know what November 24 is? You may think it is Thanksgiving Day, but it is actually National Family History Day. **The day was designed** in 2004 to encourage American families to learn about their family health history. It is an important part of routine medical care, and the family gathering on Thanksgiving will be **a good opportunity to make** a family health history tree. A family health history helps you see any increased risk of developing serious health problems, like heart disease or cancer. It also **helps you prevent specific diseases**, such as, say, diabetes, hypertension, and liver disease, that are passed from one generation to the next. Although you can't change your genes, you can **take steps to lower health threats** with good lifestyle habits and regular medical screenings. So before you join your family for your annual turkey meal, do some research, and make a family health history tree. To get started, talk to your parents and siblings. Then move on to second-degree relatives, like grandparents, aunts, uncles, nieces and nephews. If your grandparents **are no longer alive**, ask your parents or any living aunts, uncles or cousins about them. Making a family tree of health history **gives you the ability to predict disease risks** and to make appropriate health care decisions.

여: 11월 24일이 무슨 날인지 아세요? 여러분은 그것이 추수감사절이라고 생각하겠지만, 사실은 그날은 전국 가족 역사의 날입니다. 그날은 미국의 가족들이 가족 건강 역사에 대해 알기를 장려하기 위해 2004년에 만들어졌습니다. 그것은 중요한 일상적인 의료 관리의 중요한 부분이고, 추수감사절에 가족들이 모이는 것은 가족의 건강 역사 족보를 만드는 좋은 기회가 될 것입니다. 가족의 건강 역사는 ① 심장 질환이나 ② 암 같은 심각한 건강 문제가 생길 위험이 늘어나는 것을 알도록 도와줍니다. 그것은 또한 여러분이 가령 ④ 당뇨병, 고혈압과 ⑤ 간 질환 같이 한 세대에서 다음 세대로 전해지는 특정한 질병을 예방하도록 돕습니다. 비록 여러분이 유전자를 바꿀 수는 없지만, 여러분은 좋은 생활 습관과 정기적인 의료 검사로 건강의 위협을 낮추기 위한 조치를 취할 수 있습니다. 그러므로 여러분이 가족들과 매년 하는 칠면조 식사에 합류하기 전에 연구를 좀 하고 가족 건강 역사 족보를 만드십시오. 시작하려면, 여러분의 부모님과 형제자매와 이야기를 하십시오. 그리고 두 번째 단계의 친척인 조부모, 숙모, 삼촌, 조카딸, 그리고 조카로 이동하십시오. 만약 조부모님이 더는 살아계시지 않는다면 부모님이나 다른 살아계신 고모, 삼촌, 사촌에게 그분들에 대해 물어보십시오. 건강 역사의 가족 족보를 만드는 것은 여러분에게 질병의 위험을 예측하고 적절한 건강 관리 결정을 할 능력을 줍니다.

어휘 **disease** 질병 / **cancer** 암 / **diabetes** 당뇨병 / **liver** 간, 간장 / **routine** 일상의 / **hypertension** 고혈압 / **gene** 유전자 / **threat** 위협, 징조 / **screening** (질병 · 결격 사유 등을 찾기 위한) 검사[심사] / **sibling** 형제, 자매

Answers & Explanation

01. ③ 02. ② 03. ③ 04. ④ 05. ② 06. ① 07. ③ 08. ② 09. ④ 10. ④
11. ③ 12. ⑤ 13. ⑤ 14. ① 15. ④ 16. ③ 17. ②

01 화자가 하는 말의 목적 | ③

▶ 오래전에 지어져 협소하고 비효율적인 쓰레기 처리장의 문제점을 설명하며 새로운 시설의 필요성을 주장하는 내용이다.

M: Good evening, fellow council members. **As you may already know**, many of the public buildings and facilities in our city were built nearly sixty years ago. Some of these structures, like our beautiful courthouse, will continue to function for many more years, **while others are no longer adequate**. And our current waste-treatment facility is a perfect example. It is both **too small to handle our current needs** and so inefficient that it is harming our environment. Because our city is growing rapidly, a new facility is necessary **to prevent our streets from becoming** overrun with garbage and waste. As city council members, it is our duty **to address this issue immediately**.

남: 안녕하세요, 의회 동료 의원 여러분. 여러분도 이미 아시겠지만, 우리 시의 많은 공공건물과 시설은 거의 60년 전에 세워졌습니다. 이러한 건축물 중 일부는 아름다운 법원 청사 건물처럼 앞으로도 수년 동안 계속해서 이용되겠지만, 다른 건물들은 더는 (이용하기에) 적절하지 않습니다. 현재 사용되는 쓰레기 처리 시설이 적합한 예입니다. 이 시설은 현재 우리에게 필요한 만큼을 처리하기에는 너무나 협소하기도 하고 매우 비효율적이어서 환경을 해치고 있습니다. 우리 시는 급속도로 성장하고 있으므로, 길거리가 쓰레기로 넘치게 되는 것을 막기 위해 새로운 시설이 필요합니다. 시 의회 구성원으로서, 이 사안을 즉시 처리하는 것이 저희의 의무입니다.

어휘 **council** (지방 자치 단체의) 의회; (도시나 지방의) 자문 위원회 / **courthouse** 법원 청사 / **adequate** 적절한, 충분한 / **inefficient** 비효율[비능률]적인 / **overrun** 넘침, 초과; ~이 급속히 퍼지다, 들끓다; (예정된 시간·금액을) 초과하다 / **address** (문제·상황 등을) 고심하다[다루다]; 주소; 연설(하다)

02 대화 주제 | ②

▶ 해야 할 일을 나눠서 매일 조금씩 하기, 자투리 시간을 활용하기, 할 일 목록 만들기 등 효율적인 시간 관리 요령에 관해 이야기하고 있다.

W: What's wrong, Nate?
M: Oh, Mom. I'm worried about all the reading I have to do for my English essay. **It's due in one week**.
W: Why don't you use the method I used when we moved?
M: What do you mean?
W: When I had to pack, I was busy **with a new project at work**.
M: Yeah, I remember.
W: **Rather than doing everything at once**, I chose to pack for an hour every day.
M: That's right. You know, one of my friends usually reads when he's on the subway or waiting for a friend.
W: That's another great way to **make use of your time**. You can also try making a list of tasks before going to bed.
M: Thanks, Mom. I'll give it a try.

여: 무슨 일 있니, Nate?
남: 아, 엄마. 제가 영어 에세이를 위해 읽어야 할 모든 것이 걱정이에요. 일주일 뒤가 마감이거든요.
여: 우리가 이사했을 때 내가 썼던 방법을 쓰는 게 어떠니?
남: 무슨 말씀이세요?
여: 내가 이삿짐을 싸야 했을 때, 회사에서 새로운 프로젝트로 바빴단다.
남: 네, 기억해요.
여: 난 모든 것을 한꺼번에 하는 것 대신에, 매일 한 시간씩 짐을 싸기로 택했단다.
남: 맞아요. 있죠, 제 친구 중 한 명은 지하철에서나 친구를 기다릴 때 대개 책을 읽더라고요.
여: 그건 네 시간을 활용하는 또 다른 좋은 방법이구나. 넌 자기 전에 (할) 일의 목록을 만드는 걸 해볼 수도 있단다.
남: 고마워요, 엄마. 한번 해볼게요.

어휘 **make use of** ~을 이용[활용]하다

03 관계 | ③

▶ 남자가 찾고 있는 책의 이름을 말하고, 여자는 그 책이 품절이라고 하며 출판사에 전화해 재고가 있는지 알아보겠다고 하는 것으로 보아 손님과 서점 직원 간의 대화이다.

M: Excuse me, do you possibly have *The History of Russian Translation*?
W: I'll check if we have it for you. **Just wait a second**.
M: All right.
W: *[Keyboard typing sound]* I'm afraid the book you want is **currently out of stock**.
M: No way! I really need that book for the essay I'm writing. My grade depends on it.
W: Well, **as far as I know**, the first edition was released in 1998. We may have a copy somewhere.
M: Okay. I'll wait. *[pause]* Do you have one?
W: I'm afraid not. But I can call the publisher of the book to find out if they have any copies in stock.
M: I really appreciate your help. **I must get this book at any cost**.

남: 실례합니다, 혹시 〈러시아어 번역의 역사〉가 있나요?
여: 저희가 가지고 있는지 확인해 보겠습니다. 잠시만 기다려주세요.
남: 알겠습니다.
여: *[키보드 두드리는 소리]* 유감스럽지만, 손님이 원하시는 책은 현재 품절입니다.
남: 안 돼요! 제가 쓰고 있는 에세이를 위해 그 책이 꼭 필요해요. 제 점수가 그 책에 달려 있어요.
여: 음, 제가 알기로는, 초판이 1998년에 발행되었어요. 저희가 어딘가에 한 권 가지고 있을지도 몰라요.
남: 알았어요. 기다릴게요. *[잠시 후]* 가지고 계신가요?
여: 없는 것 같아요. 하지만 이 책의 출판사에 전화해서 재고로 남은 책이 있는지 알아봐 드릴 수 있어요.
남: 도와주셔서 정말 감사해요. 저는 이 책을 반드시 구해야 해요.

어휘 **currently** 현재, 지금 / **out of stock** 품절[매진]이 되어 (↔ in stock 비축되어, 재고로) / **edition** (출간 횟수를 나타내는) 판; (출간된 책의 형태로 본) 판 ***cf.* first edition** 초판 / **at any cost** 무슨 일이 있어도, 반드시

04 그림 불일치 | ④

▶ 여자의 여동생은 모래성에 깃발을 꽂기 전에 깃발을 잃어버렸다고 했다.

M: Hi, Stella. What's that?
W: It's **a picture from last summer**.
M: I want to see. *[pause]* Oh, it's your family!
W: Right. We went to the beach in Busan.
M: Who's the man **surfing on the water**?
W: He's my brother. He likes to surf.
M: I see. Oh, there's a row of parasols on the beach.
W: Yeah. It looked great. And the woman **putting sunscreen on her arms** in front of the parasols is my mom.
M: Okay. And I guess the girl making a sand castle is your sister, right?
W: Right. I remember she cried because she lost her flag before she could **add it to her sand castle**.
M: Did she? Oh, and the man **wearing a striped swimsuit and having a drink** must be your father.
W: Yes. It was really hot that day.

남: 안녕, Stella. 그게 뭐야?
여: 지난여름에 찍은 사진이야.
남: 보고 싶어. *[잠시 후]* 아, 네 가족이구나!
여: 맞아. 부산에 있는 바닷가에 갔어.
남: 물 위에서 서핑하고 있는 남자는 누구야?
여: 우리 오빠야. 오빠는 서핑하는 것을 좋아해.
남: 그렇구나. 아, 해변에 파라솔이 일렬로 있네.
여: 응. 멋있어 보였어. 그리고 파라솔 앞에서 팔에 자외선 차단제를 바르고 있는 여자분은 우리 엄마셔.
남: 그렇구나. 그리고 모래성을 만들고 있는 여자애는 네 여동생인 것 같아. 맞지?

여: 응. 그 애가 모래성에 깃발을 꽂기 전에 그걸 잃어버려서 울었던 게 기억나.
남: 그랬니? 아, 줄무늬 수영복을 입고 음료를 마시는 분은 네 아빠시겠구나.
여: 응. 그날은 정말 더웠어.

어휘 **sunscreen** 자외선 차단제

05 추후 행동 | ②

▶ 남자가 두 시험 점수를 합산해서 가장 뛰어난 사람을 고르는 방법을 제안하자, 여자는 자신이 그것을 하겠다고 했다.

M: Good morning, Ms. Davis. Here are the results of yesterday's interviews.
W: Great. **I've been waiting for them**. Thank you.
M: As you can see, Dan Benson did fairly well.
W: What do you think of him?
M: Well, he is a strong speaker and he **stood out from the others**. But his score on the written test wasn't great.
W: As you know, thorough knowledge of the law is **the most important quality**. What about Helen Simpson? She scored the highest on the written exam.
M: She is obviously intelligent, but she seems to lack confidence.
W: It's hard to choose between the candidates. Do you have any ideas?
M: The best we can do is **to add up the scores from both tests** and pick the best.
W: Okay. I'll do that.

남: 안녕하세요, Davis 사장님. 어제의 면접 결과입니다.
여: 좋아요. 그것을 기다리고 있었어요. 고마워요.
남: 보시다시피, Dan Benson 씨가 상당히 잘했습니다.
여: 그에 대해 어떻게 생각하나요?
남: 음, 그는 말을 굉장히 잘하고 다른 사람들보다 뛰어났어요. 하지만 필기시험 점수는 좋지 않았어요.
여: 알다시피, 법률에 관한 철저한 지식이 가장 중요한 자질이에요. Helen Simpson 씨는 어떤가요? 필기시험에서 가장 높은 점수를 받았네요.
남: 그녀는 분명히 똑똑하지만, 자신감이 부족해 보여요.
여: 후보자들 중에 선택하는 게 어렵네요. 좋은 생각이 있나요?
남: 저희가 할 수 있는 최선은 두 시험의 점수를 합산하고 가장 뛰어난 사람을 고르는 거예요.
여: 알겠어요. 내가 그것을 하죠.

어휘 **stand out** 튀어나오다; 눈에 띄다, 빼어나다 / **thorough** 빈틈없는, 철두철미한; 철저한 / **candidate** 후보자

06 금액 | ①

▶ 남자는 16달러인 손 세차를 선택했고, 22달러인 왁스칠을 할 것이며, 내부 진공 청소는 10달러에서 20퍼센트 할인을 받아 8달러이다. 따라서 남자가 지불할 금액은 46달러이다.

W: Good afternoon. May I help you?
M: I'd **like to get my car washed**. How much is it?
W: It's $8 for an automatic wash and $16 for a hand washing.
M: My car hasn't been washed **for quite a long time**. Which would be better?
W: In that case, I recommend the hand washing. It includes a high-pressure cleansing spray.
M: Then, I'll choose that. Also, **I need to have my car waxed.**
W: Waxing costs $22. It is a reduction from the old price of $25.
M: Sounds good. Lastly, I'd **like to have the inside vacuumed** as well.
W: We charge $10 for vacuuming, but you can get a 20 percent discount since you selected a hand washing.
M: Great. How long until everything is finished?
W: Come back in an hour, and **your car will be as good as new**.
M: Got it. I'll be back at 3 p.m.

여: 안녕하세요. 무엇을 도와드릴까요?
남: 제 차를 세차하고 싶어요. 얼마인가요?
여: 자동 세차는 8달러이고, 손 세차는 16달러입니다.
남: 제 차를 꽤 오랫동안 세차하지 못했어요. 어떤 것이 나을까요?
여: 그런 경우라면, 손 세차를 추천해드려요. 고압으로 물을 분사하는 세정을 포함하거든요.
남: 그러면, 그것으로 고를게요. 또 제 차에 왁스칠을 해야 해요.
여: 왁스칠은 22달러입니다. 예전 가격인 25달러에서 할인된 가격이에요.
남: 좋네요. 마지막으로, 차 내부도 진공 청소를 하고 싶어요.
여: 진공 청소는 10달러가 드는데, 손 세차를 선택하셔서 20퍼센트 할인을 받으실 수 있어요.
남: 좋습니다. 모든 게 끝날 때까지 얼마나 걸릴까요?
여: 한 시간 뒤에 오세요. 그러면 손님의 차는 새것이나 다름없을 거예요.
남: 알겠습니다. 오후 3시에 돌아올게요.

어휘 **automatic** (기계가) 자동의; 반사적인 / **high-pressure** 고압의, 압력이 강한; 강압적인; 스트레스가 많은 / **wax** 왁스로 광을 내다; 밀랍, 왁스 / **reduction** 할인; 축소, 감소 / **vacuum** 진공청소기로 청소하다; 진공

07 이유 | ③

▶ 여자는 남동생이 하키 경기에서 쓸 스틱을 학교로 가져다주어야 한다고 했다.

[Cell phone rings.]
M: Hello?
W: Hi, Richard. It's Emily.
M: Hi, Emily. I'm just leaving my house now.
W: Wait. I'm afraid we have to delay our appointment.
M: Why? **Are you stuck in traffic**?
W: No, but I have to take care of something for my brother.
M: Is it urgent? **I've already made reservations** for dinner.
W: I'm so sorry, but it's important and I'm the only one at home.
M: I know your brother has a big hockey game at his school tonight. **Is it related to that**?
W: Exactly. He forgot to bring his stick to school and he wants to use it for the game.
M: Couldn't he just borrow a stick from someone?
W: No, it has to be that stick. **He practices with it all the time**.
M: I understand. Just call me back when you are finished.
W: I will.

[휴대전화벨이 울린다.]
남: 여보세요?
여: 안녕, Richard. 나 Emily야.
남: 안녕, Emily. 나 지금 막 집을 나서고 있어.
여: 잠깐만. 미안하지만 우리 약속을 미뤄야 할 것 같아.
남: 왜? 차가 막히니?
여: 아니, 그런데 남동생을 위해 처리할 일이 있어.
남: 급한 일이야? 내가 벌써 저녁 식사 예약했는데.
여: 정말 미안하지만, 중요한 일이고 내가 집에 있는 유일한 사람이야.
남: 네 남동생이 오늘 밤 학교에서 중요한 하키 경기를 한다고 알고 있어. 그것과 관계있는 거니?
여: 바로 그거야. 그 애가 학교에 스틱을 가져가는 것을 잊어버렸는데 경기에 그것을 쓰고 싶어 해.
남: 그 애가 스틱을 다른 사람에게 빌릴 수는 없어?
여: 안 돼. 그 스틱이어야 해. 그 애는 항상 그것으로 연습하거든.
남: 이해해. 다 되면 내게 전화해줘.
여: 그럴게.

08 언급하지 않은 것 | ②

▶ 해석 참조

W: I heard you've just come back from the South Pole. What made you decide to study the South Pole?
M: **I was attracted to its isolation**. It is located on the continent of Antarctica, and it is nearly 3,000 meters above sea level.
W: It must have been difficult for the first explorers to establish a base.
M: Extremely difficult. It wasn't until 1911 that **an exploration team first made it** to the South Pole.
W: And there is no plant life, correct?
M: Right. But, amazingly, there are birds called Snow Petrels that have been spotted there.
W: Incredible. **They must be strong to survive** in such a place.
M: Yes, especially considering that the highest temperature ever recorded at the pole was lower than minus twelve degrees Celsius.
W: Will you be going back?
M: I will. **There is much to study there**.

여: 선생님께서 남극에서 막 돌아오셨다고 들었어요. 왜 남극을 연구하기로 하셨나요?
남: 남극의 고립된 상태에 끌렸어요. 남극은 남극대륙에 있고, 거의 해발 3,000미터에 있죠(① 위치).
여: 최초의 탐험가들이 기지를 세우는 데 힘들었겠네요.

남: 굉장히 어려웠죠. 1911년이 되어서야 탐사대가 처음으로 남극에 기지를 세웠어요(③ 탐험사).
여: 그리고 식물이 없지요, 맞나요?
남: 네. 그렇지만 놀랍게도 흰바다제비라는 이름의 조류(④ 생태)가 거기서 발견되었죠.
여: 굉장하네요. 그런 곳에서 생존하다니 강인한 게 틀림없어요.
남: 맞아요. 특히 지금까지 남극에서 기록된 최고 온도가 섭씨 영하 12도보다 낮았다(⑤ 기후)는 것을 감안하면요.
여: (남극으로) 돌아가실 건가요?
남: 그럴 거예요. 그곳은 연구할 것이 많아요.

어휘 **isolation** 고립, 분리; 외로운[고립된] 상태 ***cf.* isolate** ~을 격리하다, 고립시키다; ~을 분리하다 / **Antarctica** 남극 대륙 / **sea level** 해수면 / **explorer** 답사[탐사]자, 탐험가 ***cf.* exploration** 탐사, 답사, 탐험 / **extremely** 극도로, 극히 / **incredible** 놀라운, (믿기 어려울 만큼) 훌륭한, 대단한 / **Celsius** 섭씨의

09 내용 불일치 | ④

▶ Ames 부부가 살았던 저택은 일반인에게 개방되어 있다고 했으므로 ④가 일치하지 않는다.

W: Borderland is a Massachusetts state park located in the towns of Easton and Sharon. In 1906, a botanist named Oakes Ames and his wife Blanche Ames, an artist and feminist, **purchased the property and named it** "Borderland." Sixty-five years later, two years after the death of Blanche Ames, the Massachusetts government acquired the 1,782-acre estate and **turned it into a state park**. Here the public can enjoy walking and horseback riding on its woodland trails, as well as fishing, canoeing, ice skating, and sledding. The mansion which the Ameses once lived in **is also open to the public**, and its twenty rooms contain many of Blanche Ames' original paintings. Today, **the park is well-known** from the movie *Shutter Island*, directed by Martin Scorsese, which was shot near the park's Leach Pond.

여: Borderland는 이스턴과 샤론 마을에 있는 매사추세츠 주립공원입니다. 1906년에 Oakes Ames라는 이름의 식물학자와 예술가이자 페미니스트인 그의 아내 Blanche Ames가 그 대지를 사들여 'Borderland'라고 이름 붙였습니다. Blanche Ames가 죽은 지 2년 후인 65년 후에, 매사추세츠 정부는 1,782에이커의 대지를 취득했고 그것을 주립공원으로 전환했습니다. 이곳에서, 일반인들은 낚시, 카누 타기, 아이스 스케이팅 그리고 썰매 타기 뿐만 아니라 공원의 삼림 지대에 난 오솔길에서 산책과 승마를 즐길 수 있습니다. Ames 부부가 한때 살았던 저택도 일반인들에게 개방되어 있으며, 이곳에 있는 스무 개의 방에는 Blanche Ames의 그림 원작이 많이 있습니다. 오늘날, 이 공원은 Martin Scorsese가 감독한 영화 〈셔터 아일랜드〉로 잘 알려져 있으며, 이 영화는 공원의 Leach 연못 근처에서 촬영되었습니다.

어휘 **botanist** 식물학자 / **feminist** 페미니스트, 여권(女權) 확장론자 / **woodland** 삼림 지대

10 도표 이해 | ④

▶ 여자는 30달러를 넘지 않으면서 표지가 양장본이고, 이틀 이내에 배송되는 책을 주문할 것이다.

M: Sharon, what are you doing on the computer?
W: I'm looking at some used books, but it's **hard to choose the best** among these copies.
M: I'll help. *[pause]* How about this? **It's the best value** since it's a first edition.
W: Hmm.... I don't want to spend more than $30.
M: Okay. Then this one looks good because it's the cheapest.
W: But I'd prefer a hardcover so it will last. What do you think of this one?
M: Well, **the price seems reasonable**, but it will take more than two days for it to arrive. Is that okay with you?
W: Oh, **I want my book delivered faster than that**.
M: Then I think you should buy this one. Moreover, it was published recently.
W: Alright. **I'll place an order** right now. Thanks for your help.
M: My pleasure.

남: Sharon, 컴퓨터로 뭐 하고 있어?
여: 중고 책을 좀 보고 있는데, 이 책 중에서 제일 좋은 걸 고르기가 어려워.
남: 내가 도와줄게. *[잠시 후]* 이건 어때? 초판이니까 가장 가치 있어.
여: 음…. 30달러 넘게는 쓰고 싶지 않아.
남: 알았어. 그러면 이 책이 가장 저렴하니까 좋을 것 같아.
여: 하지만 난 오래갈 수 있게 양장본이 더 좋아. 이 책은 어때?
남: 음, 가격은 적당한 것 같은데, 이게 도착하려면 이틀 넘게 걸릴 거야. 그래도 괜찮아?
여: 아, 난 내 책이 그거보단 더 빨리 배송됐으면 좋겠어.
남: 그러면 넌 이 책을 사야 할 것 같아. 게다가, 이건 최근에 출판됐어.
여: 알았어. 지금 바로 주문할게. 도와줘서 고마워.
남: 천만에.

어휘 **binding** (제본용) 표지; 법적 구속력이 있는 / **hardcover** 하드커버 ((딱딱한 표지로 제본한 책)), 양장본 ***cf.* paperback** 페이퍼백 ((종이 한 장으로 표지를 장정한 싸고 간편한 책))

11 짧은 대화에 이어질 응답 | ③

▶ 남자는 여자에게서 조직 재편성으로 팀원 이동이 있었다는 소식을 듣고 누가 재무팀을 관리하게 되었는지 묻고 있다. 이에 가장 적절한 응답을 찾는다.

① 그 예산안은 최종이 아니에요.
② 당신이 다음 회의를 진행할 거예요.
③ 그 팀에는 아무 변화가 없었어요.
④ 나는 Jim이 좋은 관리자가 될 거라고 생각해요.
⑤ 당신이 없는 동안 그가 당신의 일을 대신할 거예요.

M: I heard Jim **will be on our team** from tomorrow.
W: Right. Several departments were reorganized during your vacation.
M: Then **who's going to manage** the finance team?
W: ______________________________

남: 내일부터 Jim이 우리 팀이 될 거라고 들었어요.
여: 맞아요. 당신의 휴가 동안 몇몇 부서가 재편성됐거든요.
남: 그러면 재무팀은 누가 관리하죠?
여: ______________________________

어휘 **cover for** ~을 대신하다; ~을 보호하다 / **reorganize** ~을 재편성[재조직]하다 / **finance** 자금; 재정[재무]; 자금을 대다

12 짧은 대화에 이어질 응답 | ⑤

▶ 남자와 같은 헤드폰을 같은 가게에서 더 비싸게 산 여자가 바가지를 쓴 게 틀림없다고 말하고 있다. 이에 가장 적절한 응답을 찾는다.

① 그들은 너에게 10달러를 청구할 거야.
② Hit Tracks에서 큰 세일을 하고 있어.
③ 미안하지만 난 영수증이 없어.
④ 그 가게에는 다양한 헤드폰이 있어.
⑤ 가서 그것에 대해 물어보는 게 어때?

W: Oh, you and I have the same headphones. **Where did you buy yours**?
M: I bought them at Hit Tracks for $20.
W: Really? I paid $30 at the same shop this morning. **I must have been overcharged**!
M: ______________________________

여: 아, 너 나랑 똑같은 헤드폰을 가지고 있구나. 네 것은 어디서 샀어?
남: Hit Tracks에서 20달러에 샀어.
여: 정말? 나는 오늘 아침에 같은 가게에서 30달러를 냈어. 난 바가지를 쓴 게 분명해!
남: ______________________________

어휘 **overcharge** 바가지를 씌우다, (~에게 금액을 너무) 많이 청구하다

13 긴 대화에 이어질 응답 | ⑤

▶ 연기를 전공하려면 연기 시험을 통과해야 함을 알게 된 남자가 시험을 잘 보면 특별 혜택이 있느냐고 물었으므로 여자는 그에 관한 응답을 할 것이다.

① 죄송하지만, 성사될 것 같지 않습니다.
② 저는 지원자 평가를 담당하지 않아요.
③ 시험을 즉시 준비하는 것이 좋겠어요.
④ 전 당신이 시험에서 성공할 능력이 있다는 것을 알았어요.
⑤ 뛰어난 학생들은 한 해 동안 장학금을 받아요.

W: You must be Kevin. Please, have a seat.
M: Thank you for **making the time to see me**, Ms. Wilson.
W: Don't mention it. So, how can I help you?
M: Well, my dream is to become an actor. And I heard that the curriculum here is **aimed at those with artistic talent**.
W: Right, our curriculum **is organized to foster the abilities** of young

artists and actors.

M: Great. What should I do to apply to your school?

W: To major in acting, you'll have to pass a performance test. This is a performance that **you create and star in**.

M: Are there any **special advantages for doing exceptionally well**?

W: ____

여: 당신이 Kevin이겠군요. 앉으세요.
남: 시간 내서 만나주셔서 감사합니다, Wilson 선생님.
여: 별말씀을요. 자, 무엇을 도와드릴까요?
남: 음, 제 꿈은 배우가 되는 거예요. 그리고 이곳의 교육과정이 예술적 재능을 가진 이들을 대상으로 한다고 들었어요.
여: 맞아요. 저희 교육과정은 젊은 예술가와 배우의 능력을 육성하도록 체계화되어 있죠.
남: 좋네요. 이 학교에 지원하려면 무엇을 해야 하죠?
여: 연기를 전공하기 위해서는, 연기 시험을 통과해야 할 거예요. 당신이 창작하고 주연을 맡는 공연이죠.
남: 특별히 잘 보면 특별 혜택이 있나요?
여: ____

어휘 **applicant** 지원자 / **excel** 뛰어나다, 탁월하다; (보통 때보다 훨씬) 뛰어나게 잘하다 / **curriculum** 교육과정 / **be aimed at** ~을 목표로 삼다 / **foster** ~을 조성하다, 발전시키다; (수양부모로서) 아이를 맡아 기르다 / **star in** ~에 주연을 맡다 / **exceptionally** 특별히; 예외적인 경우에만

14 긴 대화에 이어질 응답 | ①

▶ 남자가 자신의 친구가 커피 대신 허브차를 마시면서 커피를 끊었다고 하자 여자는 그 방법이 자기에게도 효과가 있을지 물었다. 이에 가장 적절한 응답을 찾는다.

① 잘 모르겠지만, 시도해볼 수는 있지.
② 커피를 안 마시고 일하는 게 더 좋을 거야.
③ 더 일찍 허브차를 마시기 시작하지 않은 게 후회돼.
④ 내가 너라면 커피를 줄이려고 최선을 다할 거야.
⑤ 물론이지. 네가 허브차의 맛을 좋아하지 않을 수도 있어.

W: I'm glad we decided to study outside. It's a beautiful day.

M: Yeah, but **I'm a little thirsty**. I'm going to buy some juice. Want anything?

W: I'd like an iced coffee.

M: Okay, but I thought **you'd given up coffee for health reasons**.

W: Well, I tried, but I was so sleepy all the time and I couldn't concentrate.

M: I see. You know, one of my friends, Ken, was able to quit coffee by **switching to a different drink**.

W: That really worked? What was he drinking?

M: He switched to herbal tea, and I haven't seen him drink a cup of coffee since.

W: That's interesting. **Would it work for me as well**?

M: ____

여: 밖에서 공부하기로 해서 기뻐. 날씨가 참 좋아.
남: 그래, 그런데 나 목이 좀 말라. 나는 주스를 좀 사러 갈 거야. 원하는 거 있어?
여: 난 아이스커피 마시고 싶어.
남: 그래, 그런데 난 네가 건강상의 이유로 커피를 끊은 줄 알았어.
여: 음, 그러려고 했는데 항상 너무 졸려서 집중할 수가 없더라고.
남: 그렇구나. 있지, 내 친구 중 하나인 Ken은 커피를 다른 음료로 바꾸면서 끊을 수 있었어.
여: 그게 정말 효과가 있었어? 그 애가 마신 건 뭐야?
남: 허브차로 바꿨는데, 그 후로 난 그 애가 커피 마시는 것을 본 일이 없어.
여: 흥미롭다. 그게 나한테도 효과가 있을까?
남: ____

어휘 **herbal** 허브[약초]의; 허브[약초]로 만든 / **cut down on** ~을 줄이다

15 상황에 적절한 말 | ④

▶ Robert는 어깨에 부상을 입었는데도 수영 경기에 참가하려는 Susie에게 휴식을 취해 완전히 회복하는 것이 더 중요하다고 말할 것이다.

① 내가 같이 가서 네가 준비하는 것을 도와줄까?
② 연습하면 완벽해진다는 것을 기억해야 해.
③ 내가 준비하며 보낸 시간을 헛되게 하고 싶지 않아.
④ 경기보다 네가 완전히 회복하는 것이 더 중요해.
⑤ 이길 자신이 있지 않는 한 수영하면 안 돼.

M: Susie is Robert's friend and classmate. Yesterday, their teacher told him that Susie **is in the hospital**. Today, Robert goes to the hospital to visit her and asks about what happened. She explains that **she injured her shoulders** while training for an upcoming swimming competition. Robert feels sorry because he **understands how important swimming is to her**. To his surprise, she is sure that she'll recover in time for the race and she plans to compete, even though **it is only a few days away**. Robert doesn't think this is a good idea, and he wants to **advise her to get some more rest**. In this situation, what would Robert most likely say to Susie?

남: Susie는 Robert의 친구이자 급우이다. 어제 선생님께서 그에게 Susie가 병원에 있다고 말씀하셨다. 오늘 Robert는 그녀를 병문안하러 병원에 가서 무슨 일이 있었는지 물어본다. 그녀는 곧 있을 수영 경기를 위해 훈련을 하던 중에 어깨에 부상을 입었다고 설명한다. Robert는 수영이 그녀에게 얼마나 중요한지 이해하기 때문에 안타까워한다. Robert로서는 놀랍게도, 그녀는 경기에 맞춰 회복할 것이라 확신하고, 경기가 며칠밖에 남지 않았음에도 참가할 계획이다. Robert는 이것이 좋은 생각이라고 생각하지 않으며, 그녀에게 휴식을 좀 더 취하라고 충고하고 싶다. 이러한 상황에서 Robert가 Susie에게 할 말로 가장 적절한 것은 무엇인가?

어휘 **upcoming** 곧 있을, 다가오는

16~17 세트 문항 | 16. ③ 17. ②

▶ 16. 대체 에너지 사용은 문제점이 있으므로, 우리가 보유한 에너지의 절약을 실천하는 것이 최고의 방법이라고 말하고 있다.

① 세계적인 에너지 부족 이면의 이유들
② 원자력 에너지가 가져올지도 모르는 잠재적 위기
③ 에너지 부족에 대한 가장 효과적인 해결책
④ 새로운 대체 에너지의 사용을 증진시키는 방법
⑤ 에너지와 환경 사이의 관계

▶ 17. 해석 참조

W: As we use more and more gas and coal to power our planet, the possibility of an energy shortage is becoming increasingly likely. **To deal with this potential crisis**, many alternatives are being developed. Some of these, like dams that use the power of flowing water to generate electricity, have been around for years. But others are relatively new. For example, solar heat **is now being used to power generators** in many desert regions. Meanwhile, some coastal cities are utilizing the power of tides in marine-energy plants. And then there are **more controversial alternatives to fossil fuels**, such as nuclear power. However, there are drawbacks, including high construction costs and a limited number of possible locations. So, the best way **to guarantee our supply of energy** is to practice conserving it. This is as simple as choosing energy efficient lights and appliances, and **being aware of your energy usage**. And always be looking for energy saving alternatives: Don't drive if you can walk, and let the sunshine in instead of turning on a light. Alternative energies are exciting, but the only guaranteed solution **is to respect what we have**.

여: 우리가 우리 행성에 동력을 공급하기 위해 더 많은 석유와 석탄을 사용하면 할수록, 에너지 부족의 가능성은 점점 더 있을 법해지고 있습니다. 이 잠재적 위기에 대응하기 위해, 여러 대안이 개발되고 있습니다. 전기를 생산하고자 ① 흐르는 물의 동력(수력)을 이용하는 댐처럼, 그것들 중 일부는 수년 동안 (우리의) 주변에 있었습니다. 하지만 다른 것들은 상대적으로 새롭습니다. 예를 들어, ③ 태양열은 현재 많은 사막 지역에서 발전기에 동력을 공급하는 데 사용되고 있습니다. 한편, 일부 해안 도시는 해양 에너지 발전소에서 ④ 조력을 활용하고 있습니다. 그리고 화석 연료에 대해서, ⑤ 원자력 같은 더 논란이 많은 대안이 있습니다. 하지만 고가의 건설비와 한정된 수의 (건설) 가능한 장소를 포함하여 문제점이 있습니다. 따라서 우리의 에너지 공급을 보장하는 가장 좋은 방법은 그것을 아껴 쓰는 것을 실천하는 것입니다. 이것은 에너지 효율이 높은 전등과 가전제품을 선택하는 것과 당신의 에너지 사용을 인식하는 것처럼 간단합니다. 그리고 에너지를 절약하는 대안을 항상 찾으십시오. 예를 들어, 걸을 수 있다면 (걸을 수 있는 거리라면) 차를 이용하지 말고, 전등을 켜는 대신 햇빛이 들어오게 하십시오. 대체 에너지는 흥미롭지만, 유일하게 확실한 해결책은 우리가 가진 것을 소중히 여기는 것입니다.

어휘 **alternative** 대안이 되는; 대안, 선택 가능한 것 / **generate** 발생시키다 ***cf.* generator** 발전기; (~을) 발생시키는 것, 발생기 / **coastal** 연안[해안]의 / **marine** 해양의, 바다의 / **controversial** 논란이 많은 / **fossil fuel** 화석 연료 ((석탄·석유·천연가스 같은 지하매장 자원을 이용하는 연료)) / **drawback** 문제점, 결점 / **conserve** ~을 아껴 쓰다, 아끼다; ~을 보호[보존]하다

Answers & Explanation

01.③ 02.⑤ 03.② 04.④ 05.④ 06.④ 07.③ 08.⑤ 09.④ 10.⑤
11.① 12.② 13.⑤ 14.③ 15.③ 16.③ 17.⑤

01 화자가 하는 말의 목적 | ③

▶ 올해의 낚시 축제에서 변경되고 추가된 사항을 설명하고 있다.

M: The Seoul Fishing Festival will take place this year along the banks of the Han River between the Banpo Bridge and the Hannam Bridge. In past years, the festival **has taken place along the shore** of Yeouido in Western Seoul. This year, participants **will also be given the opportunity** to fish from several floating platforms in the river. There is another upgrade from **previous fishing festivals**. Many new vendors of both food and fishing & outdoor products will be set up along the riverbank. We have also added paddle boat rides for the kids and a concert for **those less interested in fishing**.

남: 올해 서울 낚시 축제는 반포대교와 한남대교 사이의 한강 변을 따라 개최될 예정입니다. 지난 몇 년간 이 축제는 서울의 서쪽 지역에 있는 여의도 강변을 따라 개최되었습니다. 올해, 참가자들은 강에 떠 있는 몇 개의 플랫폼에서 낚시할 기회도 얻게 될 것입니다. 지난 낚시 축제 때보다 개선된 점이 또 하나 있습니다. 음식과 낚시용품 및 야외 용품을 파는 많은 노점상이 강둑을 따라 새로이 개업할 것입니다. 또한 아이들을 위해 발로 페달을 굴려서 가는 보트 타기와, 낚시에 그다지 관심이 없는 분들을 위해 콘서트도 추가했습니다.

어휘 **platform** (역의) 플랫폼, 승강장; (장비 등을 올려놓거나 하기 위한) 대(臺) / **upgrade** 개선, 향상 / **previous** 이전의 / **vendor** 노점상인 / **paddle boat** 발로 페달을 굴려서 가는 보트

02 의견 | ⑤

▶ 여자는 미세먼지에 대비하기 위해 마스크를 착용할 것이며, 남자에게도 구매해야 한다고 말하고 있다.

W: Hi, Walter. Did you hear the news?
M: Hi, Sue. **What news is that**?
W: The fine dust will be especially bad this week.
M: Oh, I heard my parents talking about that. It's a big problem, right?
W: It's really bad for our health. **The dust carries toxic pollution in it**.
M: That's scary, but what can we do about it?
W: I bought this mask. I'm going to wear it **whenever the dust level is high**.
M: I hate wearing a mask. It's so hot and uncomfortable.
W: I agree with you. But you should do **anything you can to protect your lungs**.
M: You're right. Our health is most important.
W: Then you should get a mask soon. You can buy them at drugstores.
M: Thanks for the advice. I'll buy one tomorrow.

여: 안녕, Walter. 너 뉴스 들었니?
남: 안녕, Sue. 무슨 뉴스인데?
여: 이번 주에 미세먼지가 특히 심할 거라네.
남: 아, 부모님께서 그것에 대해 말씀하시는 것을 들었어. 미세먼지가 큰 문제야, 그렇지?
여: 그건 우리 건강에 정말로 좋지 않아. 그 먼지는 독성 오염 물질을 실어 나르거든.
남: 끔찍해, 하지만 우리가 그것에 대해 무엇을 할 수 있지?
여: 나는 이 마스크를 샀어. 먼지 수치가 높을 때마다 이것을 착용할 거야.
남: 난 마스크를 착용하는 걸 싫어해. 너무 덥고 불편하잖아.
여: 나도 동의해. 하지만, 너는 네 폐를 보호하기 위해 할 수 있는 어떤 것이든 해야 해.
남: 네 말이 맞아. 건강이 가장 중요하지.
여: 그럼 곧 마스크를 사야겠구나. 그것들은 약국에서 구매할 수 있어.
남: 조언 고마워. 내일 하나 살게.

어휘 **fine dust** 미세먼지 ***cf.* dust** 먼지; 가루 / **toxic** 독성의, 유독한 / **pollution** 오염(물질), 공해 / **lung** 폐 / **drugstore** 약국

03 관계 | ②

▶ 영화감독과 배우가 촬영을 하면서 주고받을 수 있는 대화이다. cue cards, shoot, scene, filming this movie와 같은 표현에서 힌트를 얻을 수 있다.

W: Cut! Joe, did you practice your lines?
M: Yes, ma'am. **I stayed up all night rehearsing**.
W: Do we need to make cue cards for you?
M: No, you don't. I have lots of experience in this field. I've been in plays on Broadway!
W: But Joe, this is a movie, not a play.
M: I know. But can't we just **shoot it again until you are satisfied**?
W: The producer would not like to find out we had to shoot this simple scene several times. Please, just concentrate this time and we can **move on to the next scene**.
M: I will. Believe me, I am as anxious as you are to **finish filming this movie**.
W: I understand. Then, let's do this scene again, shall we?

여: 컷! Joe, 대사 연습을 했어요?
남: 네, 감독님. 밤새도록 연습했어요.
여: 큐 카드를 만들어 줘야 하나요?
남: 아니요, 그러실 필요 없어요. 전 이 분야에서 경력이 많아요. 브로드웨이에서 연기를 하고 있고요!
여: 하지만 Joe, 이건 연극이 아니라 영화예요.
남: 알아요. 그런데 만족하실 때까지 그냥 다시 찍으면 안 되나요?
여: 이렇게 간단한 장면을 여러 번 찍어야 했다는 사실을 제작자가 알면 좋아하지 않을 거예요. 제발 이번에는 집중 좀 해주세요. 그래야 다음 장면으로 넘어갈 수 있어요.
남: 그렇게 할게요. 정말, 저도 이 영화 촬영을 끝내고 싶은 마음이 감독님만큼 간절하니까요.
여: 알겠어요. 그럼, 이 장면을 다시 해요, 그럴까요?

어휘 **line** ((pl.)) 대사 / **rehearse** (~을) 예행연습하다 / **cue card** 큐 카드 ((촬영 시 보여주는 대사나 지시가 적힌 카드)) / **shoot** ~을 촬영하다 / **anxious to-v** v하기를 간절히 바라는[열망하는]

04 그림 불일치 | ④

▶ 남자는 사진을 찍기 전에 딸인 Amy가 튜브를 잃어버려서 안타깝다고 했다.

W: Honey, **have you seen these photos** from our family vacation yet?
M: No, I haven't had time. *[pause]* Oh, that one is good.
W: It's one of my favorites, too. You looked good in your flower-patterned swim shorts.
M: Well, I think you **looked even better** in your polka-dotted swimsuit.
W: That's sweet. Look, there's Kevin standing next to me and making a "v" with his fingers for the camera.
M: He looks very excited. It's just a shame that Amy lost her tube just before she took this picture. She loved how it looked like a duck.
W: I know. She **would have looked much cuter** with it in the picture.
M: Right, but it's still a good picture. The striped beach parasol in the background especially makes it look great.
W: You're right. We should **hang this on our wall**.

여: 여보, 우리 가족 휴가 중에 찍은 이 사진들 이미 봤나요?
남: 아뇨, 시간이 없었어요. *[잠시 후]* 아, 그거 좋네요.
여: 나도 가장 좋아하는 사진 중 하나예요. 꽃무늬 수영복이 당신에게 잘 어울렸어요.
남: 음, 난 당신이 물방울무늬 수영복을 입은 모습이 훨씬 더 좋아 보였다고 생각해요.
여: 다정하군요. 봐요, Kevin이 내 옆에 서서 카메라를 향해 손가락으로 'V'자를 만들고 있어요.
남: 매우 신이 나 보이네요. 다만 이 사진을 찍기 바로 전에 Amy가 튜브를 잃어버려서 안타까울 뿐이에요. 오리처럼 생긴 모양을 아주 좋아했는데.
여: 그래요. 사진에 그게 있었으면 훨씬 더 귀여워 보였을 거예요.
남: 맞아요. 하지만 그래도 좋은 사진이에요. 배경에 있는 줄무늬 비치 파라솔 때문에 특히 멋져 보이네요.
여: 당신 말이 맞아요. 우리 이 사진을 벽에 걸어야겠어요.

어휘 **polka-dotted** 물방울무늬의

05 추후 행동 | ④

▶ 남자가 스터디를 끝내고 나서 핼러윈 파티에 입을 의상을 고르는 것을 함께 할 수 있냐고 묻

고 여자가 승낙했다.

M: Hey, sorry I'm late.
W: What took you so long? We really **need to get this project done** today.
M: I slept in by accident. I didn't realize how much I slept. I was catching up on my reading for history class.
W: What about the essay that's due next week? Are you done?
M: Are you kidding? I **haven't even started it yet**.
W: Well, if you want to go to the Halloween party, you need to finish it this week.
M: I totally forgot about Halloween. What am I going to wear?
W: Well, I've decided to be Wonder Woman.
M: Good choice. It totally suits you. **What do you think I should wear**?
W: I got my costume at the Target Store downtown. They have a huge selection of stuff.
M: Well, after our study session, do you think we could go together and pick something out?
W: Of course! **I'm not doing anything special** in the afternoon so I'll be happy to.

남: 이런, 늦어서 미안해.
여: 왜 이렇게 늦었니? 우린 정말 이 프로젝트를 오늘 끝내야 하잖아.
남: 어쩌다 늦잠을 잤어. 얼마나 잤는지 깨닫지도 못 했어. 역사 수업에 읽어야 할 책들을 읽고 있었거든.
여: 다음 주까지 내야 하는 에세이는 어떠니? 다 했니?
남: 농담하니? 그건 아직 시작도 못했어.
여: 음, 네가 핼러윈 파티에 가고 싶다면 그걸 이번 주에 끝내야 해.
남: 핼러윈에 대해서는 까맣게 잊고 있었네. 나 뭐 입지?
여: 글쎄, 나는 원더우먼이 되기로 결정했어.
남: 훌륭한 선택이야. 너한테 완전 잘 어울려. 난 뭘 입어야 할 거 같니?
여: 나는 시내에 있는 Target 상점에서 내 의상을 샀어. 거기는 물건 종류가 엄청나.
남: 음, 스터디 시간이 끝나고 나서 우리 같이 가서 뭔가를 고를 수 있을까?
여: 물론이지! 난 오후에 특별히 할 게 없으니까 기꺼이 그렇게 할게.

어휘 **sleep in** 늦잠을 자다 / **by accident** 어쩌다, 우연히 / **catch up on** ~을 따라잡다, 만회하다 / **due** 하기로 된 / **suit** 어울리다 / **costume** 의상 / **session** 시간, 기간 / **pick out** 고르다

06 금액 | ④

▶ 남자는 3,000달러 채권 계좌(15년 만기)를 개설할 것이므로 계좌 가치의 ⅓인 1,000달러를 지불하면 된다.

W: What can I help you with today?
M: I want to **open some kind of account** for my son that will grow as he grows.
W: **That's a very thoughtful gift**. Which account do you have in mind?
M: I was looking at the Savings Bond account. How does that work?
W: With that account, **you invest a set amount of money** in the account and the money will mature in 10 years or 15 years.
M: What do you mean by "mature?"
W: It means the savings account **will be worth double** what you invested in 10 years. And it will be tripled in 15 years.
M: So if I want to make $300, how much should I invest today?
W: For that, it would take $150 for 10 years or $100 for 15 years.
M: That sounds great. I want to make $3,000 after 15 years.

여: 오늘 무엇을 도와드릴까요?
남: 제 아들이 자라는 것에 따라 (수익이) 증가할 종류의 계좌를 아들을 위해 개설하고 싶습니다.
여: 정말 사려 깊은 선물이십니다. 어떤 계좌를 생각하고 계신지요?
남: 저축 채권 계좌를 보고 있었는데요. 그건 어떻게 운영되나요?
여: 그 계좌로, 손님께서 정해진 금액을 계좌에 투자하시면 그 투자금이 10년 또는 15년 후 만기가 되는 것이지요.
남: '만기가 된다'는 것이 무슨 뜻인가요?
여: 저축 계좌가 10년 후에, 손님께서 투자하신 금액의 두 배의 가치가 될 거라는 뜻입니다. 그리고 15년 후에는 세 배가 될 것입니다.
남: 그럼 300달러를 만들고 싶으면 오늘 얼마를 투자해야 하죠?
여: 그 경우에, 10년짜리는 150달러, 15년짜리는 100달러가 될 것입니다.
남: 그거 좋은데요. 저는 15년 후에 3,000달러를 만들고 싶습니다.

어휘 **account** 계좌 / **thoughtful** 사려 깊은 / **bond** 채권 / **mature** (어음 등이) 만기가 되다; 성숙하다

07 이유 | ③

▶ 남자는 교복이 학습에 적합한 환경을 조성하는 데 도움이 되는 것 같다고 했다.

M: Good morning, sweetheart! You look like you're all ready for school.
W: Don't **try to cheer me up**, Dad. You know I hate wearing my school uniform.
M: Of course, you've told me all about how the uniforms make everyone look the same.
W: **There's nothing good about it**, except that maybe it reduces my preparation time in the mornings.
M: Well, at least it saves time. Anyway, I think the uniforms help to create **an environment suitable for learning**. Isn't that a good thing about them?
W: But I have great outfits in my closet. I want to show my friends!
M: You can wear them on the weekends.
W: I guess, but I still feel like this uniform is **a waste of money**.
M: I know, but we can't change the school's policy.

남: 잘 잤니, 얘야! 학교 갈 준비를 다 한 것 같구나.
여: 제 기운을 북돋으려고 하지 마세요, 아빠. 제가 교복을 입기 싫어하는 거 아시잖아요.
남: 물론이지, 교복이 모든 사람을 똑같아 보이게 만든다고 네가 전부 다 말해줬잖니.
여: 아침에 준비 시간을 줄여줄지도 모른다는 것 외에는 좋을 게 하나도 없어요.
남: 음, 적어도 시간은 절약되잖니. 어쨌든, 교복은 학습에 적합한 환경을 조성하는 데 도움이 된다고 생각한단다. 그게 교복의 좋은 점 아닐까?
여: 그렇지만 제 옷장엔 멋진 옷들이 있는걸요. 친구들에게 보여주고 싶어요!
남: 그 옷들은 주말에 입을 수 있잖니.
여: 그렇긴 하지만 이 교복은 여전히 돈 낭비인 것 같아요.
남: 그래, 하지만 우리가 학교 방침을 바꿀 순 없단다.

어휘 **outfit** (한 벌로 된) 옷, 복장

08 언급하지 않은 것 | ⑤

▶ 해석 참조

W: Okay, everyone. From this location, we can **get a great view** of Suwon Hwaseong Fortress.
M: It's really impressive. I especially like the large bricks.
W: Yes, this is one of the first Korean structures that was built with bricks like this. **They are quite heavy**.
M: I think you mentioned that it was finished in 1796. Is that correct?
W: Yes. King Jeongjo began construction in 1794 to pay respect to his father, who **is known to have one of the most tragic life stories** of the Joseon Dynasty.
M: So, it only took two years to complete. How was that possible?
W: A special crane called a Geojunggi was invented just to complete this job.
M: That's really interesting. Can we see a Geojunggi?
W: There will be one for you to see **at the end of the tour**.

여: 자, 여러분. 이 위치에서 수원 화성의 멋진 경관을 보실 수 있습니다.
남: 정말 인상적이군요. 큰 벽돌들이 특히 마음에 들어요.
여: 네, 이것은 한국에서 이처럼 벽돌(① 건축 재료)로 지어진 최초의 건축물 중 하나입니다. 벽돌들은 꽤 무겁습니다.
남: 1796년에 완공되었다고 말씀하신 것 같은데요. 맞나요?
여: 네. 정조는 자신의 아버지께 경의를 표하기 위해(② 건축 목적) 1794년에 공사를 시작했는데, 정조의 아버지는 조선 왕조에서 가장 비극적인 인생 이야기 중 하나를 가진 것으로 알려져 있습니다.
남: 그럼 완공하는 데 2년(③ 건축 기간)밖에 안 걸렸네요. 어떻게 그게 가능했죠?
여: 단지 이 일을 해내기 위해 거중기(④ 건축 장비)라고 불리는 특수 크레인이 발명되었습니다.
남: 정말 흥미롭군요. 거중기를 볼 수 있나요?
여: 관광 마지막에 여러분이 보실 수 있는 게 하나 있을 겁니다.

어휘 **construction** 건축, 공사; 구조

09 내용 불일치 | ④

▶ 서해안 지역은 화요일부터 시작된 소나기가 계속된다고 말했다.

W: This is your News 22 weather report. Starting in the southwest, Mokpo will be seeing some unseasonably high temperatures. There will also be dry winds blowing from the North. This could lead to fires, so **be on the lookout** if you are in a fire-danger area. **Further north**, there will be clear skies across Chungcheongbuk-do and Gyeongsangbuk-do all the way through to southern Gyeonggi-do. In the Gangwon-do area, there will be late season snow in some parts of Sokcho and Gangneung, but **nothing worth worrying** about. And in areas near the West Sea, **there will be a continuation** of Tuesday's rain showers. And the Seoul area expects cloudy weather and cool temperatures.

여: 뉴스 22 기상 예보입니다. 남서부 지역을 시작으로 목포는 때아닌 높은 기온을 보이겠습니다. 또한 북쪽에서 건조한 바람이 불 것으로 예상됩니다. 화재로 이어질 수 있으니 화재 위험 지역에 계신 분들은 조심하시길 바랍니다. 북쪽으로 더 이동하면, 충청북도와 경상북도를 걸쳐서 경기 남부 지역까지 모두 맑은 하늘이 예상됩니다. 강원도 지역은 속초와 강릉 일부 지역에서 때늦은 눈이 예상되지만 우려할 정도는 아닙니다. 그리고 서해안 근처 지역에서는 화요일부터 시작된 소나기가 계속되겠습니다. 그리고 서울 지역은 구름 낀 날씨와 서늘한 기온이 예상됩니다.

어휘 **unseasonably** 때아니게, 계절에 맞지 않게 / **on the lookout** 경계하여 / **continuation** 계속됨

10 도표 이해 | ⑤

▶ 두 사람은 소요 시간이 1시간 미만이고 어린이도 할 수 있으며 세 명이 함께 하는 보드게임을 선택할 것이다.

M: **Let's play a board game** tonight.
W: Good idea. Let's pick a game to play out of these five games.
M: Well, I love the game in which we buy and sell property. **We either get rich or go broke** just like in real life.
W: **It takes too long to play**. That game can even go on for days. Let's play something that takes less than an hour.
M: How about this game?
W: But Sarah cannot play. She's only 10. **It wouldn't be fair**.
M: Well, what's that game that the children are always playing?
W: It's a strategy board game with lions, tigers, and elephants in it.
M: Is it fun for adults, too?
W: Yes, but the problem is only two people can play it and there are three of us.
M: Hmm.... There's only one choice then. **I'll set up the board**.

남: 오늘 밤에 보드게임을 합시다.
여: 좋은 생각이에요. 이 다섯 가지 게임 중에서 할 게임을 하나 골라요.
남: 음, 나는 부동산을 사고파는 게임이 정말 좋아요. 우리는 마치 현실에서처럼 부유해지거나 파산하잖아요.
여: 그건 하는 데 너무 오래 걸려요. 그 게임은 며칠 동안도 계속될 수 있다고요. 1시간이 안 걸리는 것으로 해요.
남: 이 게임은 어때요?
여: 하지만 Sarah가 할 수 없어요. 그 애는 겨우 10살이에요. 공평하지 않을 거예요.
남: 음, 아이들이 항상 하고 있는 저 게임은 뭐예요?
여: 게임에 사자, 호랑이, 코끼리가 나오는 전략 보드게임이에요.
남: 어른들에게도 재미있나요?
여: 네, 그렇지만 문제는 두 사람만이 할 수 있는데 우리는 세 명이라는 거예요.
남: 음…. 그럼 한 가지 선택밖에 없네요. 내가 게임판을 준비할게요.

어휘 **property manager** (부동산) 자산 관리자 / **go broke** ((구어)) 파산하다 / **set up** ~을 준비[마련]하다; ~을 세우다, 설립하다

11 짧은 대화에 이어질 응답 | ①

▶ 신입생이 어떤지 묻는 여자의 말에 가장 적절한 응답을 고른다.

① 그 애는 정말 좋아. ② 우리는 강당에서 만났어.
③ 나중에 나 좀 소개해 줘. ④ 그 애는 이 도시가 좋다고 했어.
⑤ 우리는 같은 반이 아니야.

W: I heard that you **have a new student in your class**.
M: Yeah, her name is Becky. I talked to her this morning.
W: I haven't seen her yet. **What's she like**?
M: ______________________________

여: 너희 반에 신입생이 있다고 들었어.
남: 응, 이름이 Becky야. 오늘 아침에 얘기해 봤어.
여: 난 아직 못 봤는데, 그 애 어때?
남: ______________________________

12 짧은 대화에 이어질 응답 | ②

▶ 내일 점심을 같이 먹자고 제안하는 남자의 말에 가장 적절한 응답을 찾는다.

① 안 돼, 난 일본에 있을 거거든. ② 물론이지, 내가 내일 전화할게.
③ 우리 오빠는 널 만나게 돼서 들떠 있어. ④ 응, 일본 음식을 정말 맛있게 먹었어.
⑤ 그래, 내 점심시간이 너희 점심시간보다 먼저 있어.

M: Hi, Lisa. Did you **have a good time visiting** your brother in Japan?
W: It was great, but **I'm a little tired from the flight**.
M: Well, I'm glad you're back. Would you like to have lunch together tomorrow?
W: ______________________________

남: 안녕, Lisa. 일본에 계신 오빠를 방문해서 좋은 시간 보냈니?
여: 정말 좋았는데, 비행 때문에 좀 피곤해.
남: 그래, 네가 돌아오니까 나는 좋다. 내일 같이 점심 먹을래?
여: ______________________________

13 긴 대화에 이어질 응답 | ⑤

▶ 여자는 삼촌이 살고 계시고 역사적인 장소이기 때문에 유학 갈 장소로 보스턴을 마음에 두고 있다. 이런 상황에서 남자가 할 수 있는 말을 찾아본다.

① 왜 보스턴으로 가기를 원하니?
② 캐나다는 매년 이맘때가 멋져.
③ 너의 미래는 네가 얼마나 열심히 공부하느냐에 달려 있어.
④ 한국의 학교들도 매우 인상적이야.
⑤ 너는 이미 결정을 내린 것 같구나.

M: What's all this?
W: **I'm signing up for** the study abroad program. These are brochures for schools.
M: Wow, that's great! I never thought your parents would **let you leave for a year**.
W: At first they were against it, but they realized **it would be essential for my future**.
M: Oh, I see.
W: Now, I'm trying to decide among the U.S., Canada and England.
M: I think you will have an interesting time in England.
W: I think so too, but my uncle lives in Boston, so I might want to go there.
M: **It gets really cold** in Boston.
W: Yeah, but it's one of the most historical cities in America and it is close to New York.
M: ______________________________

남: 이게 다 뭐니?
여: 해외 유학 프로그램을 신청하려고 해. 이것들은 학교 책자들이야.
남: 와, 잘됐다! 너희 부모님께서 네가 일 년간 떠나있는 것을 허락하시리라고 전혀 생각 못했는데.
여: 처음에는 반대하셨는데, 내 미래를 위해 그것이 필수적이란 것을 깨달으셨어.
남: 아, 그래.
여: 이제, 미국, 캐나다, 영국 중에서 결정하려고 해.
남: 네가 영국에서 재미있는 시간을 보낼 거라 생각해.
여: 나도 그렇게 생각하지만, 삼촌께서 보스턴에 거주하셔서, 그곳에 가고 싶은지도 모르겠어.
남: 보스턴은 날씨가 정말 추워질 거야.
여: 응, 하지만 미국에서 가장 역사적인 도시 중 한 곳이고 뉴욕과도 가깝잖아.
남: ______________________________

어휘 **sign up for** ~을 신청하다 / **brochure** 소책자

14 긴 대화에 이어질 응답 | ③

▶ 여자가 캠핑에 대해 잘 알게 된 이유가 대답으로 와야 한다.

① 나는 캠핑에 대해서 아무것도 몰라.
② 네 형은 모험을 매우 즐기는 것 같구나.
③ 난 어렸을 적부터 캠핑을 다녔어.
④ 우리 언제 그리고 어디로 캠핑을 함께 갈 수 있니?

⑤ 이 지도는 좋은 야영지를 찾는 데 매우 도움이 돼.

M: Hi, Kelly.
W: Hi. Do you have any plans for this holiday?
M: Yes, I'm going camping, but first I **need to buy a few supplies**.
W: Where will you be camping?
M: I'm going to Rocky Mountain National Park for five days.
W: OK. Since **it's almost summertime**, you will need a two-season sleeping bag.
M: All right. What about a tent?
W: If you think you will go camping again at other times of the year, you should get an all-season tent. How many people will be sleeping in your tent?
M: Just my brother and me.
W: Well, **you might as well get more space** and buy a four-man tent then. It won't be heavy for hiking to your campsite.
M: This all sounds great. How did you **get so knowledgeable about camping**?
W: ____________________

남: 안녕, Kelly.
여: 안녕. 이번 휴가 때 어떤 계획이라도 있니?
남: 응, 캠핑을 갈 예정인데, 먼저 용품을 몇 가지 사야 해.
여: 어디서 캠핑을 할 건데?
남: 로키산맥 국립공원에서 닷새 동안 지낼 거야.
여: 좋아. 거의 여름철이니까, 두 계절용 침낭이 필요할 거야.
남: 알겠어. 텐트는 어때?
여: 다른 계절에 캠핑을 다시 갈 생각이라면, 사계절용 텐트를 구매해야 해. 텐트에서 몇 명이 함께 잘 거니?
남: 나랑 형만 잘 거야.
여: 음, 공간이 더 많이 있는 편이 좋을 테니 그럼 4인용 텐트를 사도록 해. 야영지까지 도보로 가지고 가기에 무겁지는 않을 거야.
남: 대단하다. 캠핑에 대해서 어떻게 그렇게 잘 알게 되었니?
여: ____________________

어휘 **adventurous** 모험을 좋아하는 / **supply** 용품 / **sleeping bag** 침낭 / **might as well v** v하면 좋을 텐데, v하는 편이 낫다 / **knowledgeable** 많이 아는, 정통한

15 상황에 적절한 말 | ③

▶ 매니저의 경고를 심각하게 듣지 않는 친구에게 할 수 있는 조언이 적절한 답이다.

① 그것이 해결책을 찾는 최선의 방법이야.
② 나 승진할 것 같아.
③ 넌 매니저의 지시를 따라야 해.
④ 난 매니저를 별로 좋아하지 않아. 넌 어때?
⑤ 이 식당은 긴급히 수리할 필요가 있다는 것에 동의해.

M: Ronald and Thomas work together in a local restaurant. One of the rules to working in a kitchen is to wash your hands every time you come back into the kitchen. Ronald is very careful to **wash his hands thoroughly** so as not to get anyone sick. But Thomas does not. He sometimes even **blows his nose around food** and doesn't clean his hands after touching dirty mops. Ronald has heard the manager warn Thomas about his bad habit, but finds out he doesn't **take it seriously**. But if the manager knows this, he will be very upset. As a friend and co-worker, Ronald wants to **give him some advice**. In this situation, what would Ronald most likely say to Thomas?

남: Ronald와 Thomas는 지역 음식점에서 함께 근무한다. 주방에서 근무할 때의 규칙 중 하나가 주방에 다시 들어올 때마다 손을 씻는 것이다. Ronald는 손님들이 탈이 나지 않게 하기 위해, 손을 철저히 씻는 데 매우 신경을 쓴다. 하지만 Thomas는 그렇지 않다. 때때로 그는 음식 근처에서 코를 풀기도 하고 더러운 대걸레를 만지고 나서 손을 씻지 않기도 한다. Ronald는 매니저가 Thomas에게 그의 나쁜 습관에 대해 경고하는 것을 들었지만, 그가 진지하게 받아들이지 않는다는 것을 알게 된다. 하지만 만약 매니저가 이 사실을 안다면, 크게 화를 낼 것이다. 친구이자 동료로서 Ronald는 그에게 충고를 해 주고 싶다. 이러한 상황에서, Ronald가 Thomas에게 할 말로 가장 적절한 것은 무엇인가?

어휘 **promotion** 승진, 진급 / **renovate** ~을 수리[개조]하다 / **urgently** 긴급히 / **thoroughly** 철저히, 완전히 / **co-worker** 동료

16~17 세트 문항 | 16. ③ 17. ⑤

▶ 16. 좋은 이력서 작성을 위해 구체적인 작성 요령과 증명사진을 잘 찍는 법에 대해 조언하고 있다.

① 이력서의 중요성
② 일자리에 지원하는 과정
③ 좋은 이력서 작성을 위한 조언
④ 성공적인 구직 면접을 위한 조언
⑤ 구직 면접에 적합한 복장

▶ 17. 해석 참조

W: Today, I'd like to talk about résumés, the documents describing our work history and experience that we must **submit to employers**. These days, it's all about packaging. A well-packaged résumé will attract the people you want to impress. The key to a successful résumé is **making yourself stand out**. First, make sure to use powerful language to sell your skills. For example, instead of writing "I have experience volunteering," write "I was in charge of organizing activities at a senior center." Also, try to add specific details about how you can **contribute to the company** you are applying for. My second tip is about your ID picture. Your potential employers want to know who they're hiring. If they can match a face to your name and achievements, it will definitely **boost your chances**. Wear business clothes when getting your photo taken, and don't forget to smile! Also, bring your chin up to prevent double chin. And make sure the photo **shows a clear view of your face** from the front. When you get the photo printed, place it at the top left-hand corner of your résumé.

여: 오늘 저는 고용주에게 제출해야 하는, 경력과 경험을 설명하는 서류인 이력서에 대해 말하고 싶습니다. 요즘에는 포장이 전부입니다. 잘 포장된 이력서는 당신이 깊은 인상을 주고 싶은 사람들의 마음을 끌 것입니다. 성공적인 이력서의 비결은 자신을 돋보이게 만드는 것입니다. 첫 번째, 여러분의 기량을 납득시키도록 반드시 강력한 언어를 사용하십시오. 예를 들어, '저는 자원봉사 경험이 있습니다.'라고 쓰는 대신, '저는 노인 회관에서 행사를 조직하는 일을 담당했습니다.'라고 쓰십시오. 또한, 지원하는 회사에 어떻게 기여할 수 있는지 구체적인 세부 사항을 덧붙이도록 노력하십시오. 두 번째 조언은 증명사진에 관한 것입니다. 여러분의 고용주가 될 수도 있는 사람들은 자신이 고용하는 사람에 대해 알고 싶어 합니다. 그들이 여러분의 얼굴을 이름 및 성적에 연결할 수 있다면, 그것은 여러분의 가능성을 틀림없이 증대시킬 것입니다. 사진을 찍을 때 ① 정장을 입고, ② 미소 짓는 것을 잊지 마십시오! 또한, 이중 턱이 생기지 않도록 ③ 턱을 드십시오. 그리고 반드시 사진에서 ④ 얼굴이 정면으로 선명하게 보이도록 하십시오. 인화된 사진을 받으면 이력서의 왼쪽 맨 위 구석에 붙이십시오.

어휘 **résumé** 이력서 / **apply for** ~에 지원하다 / **suitable** 적합한, 알맞은 / **submit** ~을 제출하다 / **stand out** 두드러지다, 눈에 띄다 / **sell** ~을 (받아들이도록) 납득시키다; 팔다 / **be in charge of** ~을 담당하다, 맡다 / **ID** 신분증명서, 신분증 ((identity 또는 identification의 약어)) / **boost** ~을 증대시키다, 끌어올리다 / **left-hand** (어떤 것의) 왼쪽[좌측]의

Answers & Explanation

01. ④ 02. ② 03. ⑤ 04. ⑤ 05. ③ 06. ④ 07. ① 08. ② 09. ⑤ 10. ③
11. ③ 12. ④ 13. ⑤ 14. ③ 15. ① 16. ③ 17. ⑤

01 화자가 하는 말의 목적 | ④

▶ Happy Oaks 병원의 건물 개선을 위한 기금 마련 활동에 학생들이 참여하도록 요청하고 있다.

W: Good morning, class. Do you remember visiting Happy Oaks Hospital last year? Everyone helped that day. Some students cleaned rooms, **others swept floors** and still others washed dishes. Afterwards a few of the students at our school decided to volunteer every Saturday afternoon. Now the principal wants us to **help the hospital raise money**. The hospital needs money to improve its buildings. You can help raise money **by selling tickets for fundraising concerts** for a few hours a week after school. You can sell the tickets on the street, or to family and friends. If you want to participate, please **sign the sheet on the bulletin board**.

여: 안녕하세요, 여러분. 작년에 Happy Oaks 병원을 방문했던 일을 기억하죠? 모든 학생이 그날 도움을 주었습니다. 어떤 학생들은 방을 청소했고, 다른 학생들은 바닥을 청소했고 또 다른 학생들은 설거지를 했지요. 그 후 우리 학교 학생 몇몇이 매주 토요일 오후에 자원봉사를 하기로 결정했고요. 지금 교장 선생님께서는 병원이 기금을 모으는 데 저희가 도움을 주기를 원하십니다. 병원은 건물을 개선하기 위해 기금이 필요합니다. 여러분이 방과 후 일주일에 몇 시간씩만 기금 마련 콘서트 표를 팔면 기금을 모으는 데 도움을 줄 수 있습니다. 길에서 혹은 가족과 친구에게 표를 팔 수 있겠지요. 참여를 원하면, 게시판의 종이에 서명해 주기 바랍니다.

어휘 **sweep** (~을) 청소하다; ~을 쓸어내리다 / **raise** (돈을) 모으다, 마련하다 / **fundraising** 모금 / **bulletin board** 게시판

02 의견 | ②

▶ 남자는 팀장이 너무 자기 의견대로만 한다고 걱정하면서 팀 프로젝트를 성공시키기 위해서 더 많은 협력이 필요하고 팀장이 다른 팀원의 의견을 존중해야 한다고 말하고 있다.

W: Diego, you look worried. Are you stressed because of your team project?
M: Yes and no. The project itself is a great opportunity, but my team members don't get along well because of the team leader, James.
W: **What do you think is the problem**?
M: James never listens to our opinions. He is too stubborn.
W: Why don't you **discuss it together and meet halfway**?
M: No, that won't work. He wants to make decisions based only on his opinion.
W: Maybe he is so self-confident that he closes his ears to other people's opinions.
M: You have a point. **We need more teamwork** for our project to succeed.
W: That's right. Every team member **has a specific role to play in** accomplishing tasks on the job.
M: You're telling me! We have to work together to accomplish the goal. So he should respect our opinions.

여: Diego, 걱정스러워 보인다. 팀 프로젝트 때문에 스트레스받는 거니?
남: 그렇기도 하고 아니기도 해. 프로젝트 자체는 좋은 기회인데, 팀장인 James 때문에 팀원들이 마음이 잘 안 맞아.
여: 문제가 뭐라고 생각해?
남: James는 우리 의견에 결코 귀 기울이지 않아. 그는 너무 고집이 세.
여: 왜 그것을 함께 의논해서 타협하지 그러니?
남: 아니, 그게 효과가 없을 거야. 그는 오직 자기 의견에 기반해서 결정 내리고 싶어 해.
여: 아마 그는 너무 자신이 넘쳐서 다른 사람의 의견에 귀를 막고 있나 보다.
남: 네 말이 맞아. 우리는 프로젝트를 성공시키기 위해서 더 많은 팀워크가 필요해.
여: 맞아. 모든 팀원들이 그 일에서 과업을 성취하기 위해 해야 할 특정한 역할이 있잖아.
남: 내 말이 그 말이야! 우리는 목표를 이루기 위해 함께 노력해야 하잖아. 그러니 그는 우리 의견을 존중해야 해.

어휘 **get along well** 마음이 맞다, 협조하다 / **stubborn** 고집 센 / **meet halfway** 타협하다, 절충하다 / **self-confident** 자신만만한 / **specific** 특정한 / **You're telling me!** 내 말이 바로 그 말이에요!

03 관계 | ⑤

▶ 도난사고를 당한 주민이 아파트의 보안담당자에게 사건을 설명하고 있는 대화이다. 경찰에게 신고하라고 말하는 대목에서 남자가 경찰이 아님을 알 수 있다.

M: What did they take?
W: They took some jewelry and some money. That's all, I think.
M: I'm really sorry.
W: Mr. Ward, my next-door neighbor, said he heard some loud noises around three.
M: That's helpful. I'll look at **the security camera pictures** around that time.
W: I hope you can see someone clearly.
M: I can't remember **any of our residents being broken into** in the three years I've been working here.
W: Yes, I usually feel safe.
M: **I just came on duty** an hour ago. I'll also talk to the person on duty in the afternoon.
W: I'll call the police right now.
M: Yes, do it right away. I'm sorry, Mrs. Foster. **We should have made you feel safer**.
W: I hope this will never happen again.

남: 그들이 무엇을 가져갔나요?
여: 보석이랑 돈을 좀 가져갔어요. 제 생각엔 그게 다예요.
남: 정말 유감입니다.
여: 옆집에 사는 Ward 씨께서 세 시쯤에 시끄러운 소리를 들었다고 말씀하셨어요.
남: 도움이 되는 정보네요. 그 시간쯤의 보안 카메라의 내용을 조사해 보겠습니다.
여: 어떤 사람인지 명확하게 보이면 좋겠네요.
남: 제가 여기서 근무한 3년간 우리 주민 중 누구의 집에도 도둑이 든 기억이 없는데요.
여: 네, 저도 평소에는 안전하다고 느꼈어요.
남: 저는 한 시간 전에 근무를 막 시작했습니다. 오후 근무자에게도 말해 두겠습니다.
여: 저는 지금 당장 경찰에 신고할게요.
남: 네, 지금 바로 하세요. 유감입니다, Foster 부인. 더 안전하다고 느끼시도록 해드렸어야 했는데.
여: 이런 일이 다시는 일어나지 않기를 바랍니다.

어휘 **break into** ~에 침입하다 / **on duty** 근무 중인, 당번인

04 그림 불일치 | ⑤

▶ 대화 중 남자가 무대 오른편에 꽃병을 둔 것을 지적하자 여자가 그것을 곧바로 녹색 식물로 바꾸겠다고 했다.

W: Liam, I'm **all done setting up the stage** for the talk show. I took a picture of the stage. Look here.
M: You set up a big screen at the back of the stage as I asked.
W: Yes, I also placed a bookcase under the screen. I'm going to **arrange some books on the shelves**.
M: Good idea!
W: I prepared two armchairs for a host and a guest. Do you think I should put out more chairs?
M: No, we don't need more than two chairs. They look comfortable.
W: I also **positioned a round table between the chairs** and left two cups on it.
M: Perfect! Wait a minute! You placed a vase with flowers on the right side of the stage.
W: Yes, aren't those roses beautiful? **They are in full bloom.**
M: Sure, but actually I heard the talk show's guest is **allergic to flowers**.
W: Really? I'll change it to a green plant right away.
M: That'll be nice.

여: Liam, 토크쇼 무대 설치를 다 끝냈어요. 무대 사진을 찍었는데요. 여기를 보세요.
남: 내가 요청한 대로 무대 뒤에 큰 스크린을 설치했군요.
여: 네, 또 스크린 아래 책장을 두었어요. 책꽂이에 책을 몇 권 배열할 거예요.

남: 좋은 생각이에요!
여: 사회자와 초대 손님을 위해서 안락의자 두 개를 준비했어요. 의자를 더 놓아야 한다고 생각하세요?
남: 아니요, 의자는 두 개보다 더 많이는 필요하지 않아요. 의자들이 편안해 보이는군요.
여: 또 의자 사이에 둥근 테이블을 적당한 장소에 놓고 그 위에 컵 두 개를 놓아두었어요.
남: 완벽해요! 잠깐만요! 무대 오른편에 꽃이 든 화병을 두었네요.
여: 네, 장미들이 아름답지 않나요? 완전히 만개했어요.
남: 맞아요, 그런데 사실 토크쇼 초대 손님이 꽃 알레르기가 있다고 들었어요.
여: 정말이요? 곧바로 그것을 녹색 식물로 바꿀게요.
남: 그러면 아주 좋겠군요.

어휘 **set up** 설치하다, 준비하다 / **bookcase** 책장, 책꽂이 / **arrange** 배열하다 / **host** 사회자; 주최하다 / **position** 적당한 장소에 놓다 / **allergic** 알레르기의

05 추후 행동 | ③

▶ 남자는 이미 써놓은 추천서를 아래층에서 출력한 후 봉투에 넣어 여자에게 줄 것이다.

W: Excuse me, Mr. Myers. **Do you have a minute**?
M: Hi, Nicole. If you're wondering about your essay, **I haven't graded it yet**.
W: Oh, it's not about that.
M: How can I help you then? Do you have a question about yesterday's lecture?
W: No, actually a few weeks ago I asked you **to write a letter of recommendation** for me.
M: Oh, yes. I've done it.
W: Could you put it in this envelope?
M: Yes, but first I need to **go downstairs to print it out**. Do you want me to do it right away?
W: **I'm sorry to disturb you** before your lunch. But the deadline is today.
M: Wait here, then. I'll be back in a minute.

여: 실례지만, Myers 선생님, 시간 있으세요?
남: 안녕, Nicole. 에세이에 대해서 궁금해하는 거라면 아직 채점하지 않았단다.
여: 아, 그것 때문이 아니에요.
남: 그럼 무엇을 도와줄까? 어제 강의에 대해 질문이 있니?
여: 아니요, 실은 몇 주 전에 제가 추천서를 써 주십사 하고 부탁드렸는데요.
남: 아, 그렇지. 써놓았단다.
여: 이 봉투에 넣어 주시겠어요?
남: 그래, 하지만 우선 아래층에 내려가서 출력해야 한단다. 지금 당장 해줬으면 좋겠니?
여: 점심시간이 되기도 전에 방해해서 죄송해요. 하지만 마감일이 오늘이어서요.
남: 그럼 여기서 기다리렴. 곧 돌아오마.

어휘 **letter of recommendation** 추천서 / **deadline** 마감일, 최종 기한

06 금액 | ④

▶ 여자는 연회원이기 때문에 입장료가 5달러이고, 친구는 15달러짜리 일반 입장권을 사야 하므로, 모두 20달러를 내야 한다.

W: Is there any discount if I am a member of the museum?
M: Yes, there is. Lifetime members are allowed to enter for free, but **those holding yearly memberships** must pay $5.
W: And what is the adult ticket price?
M: **The regular adult admission fee** is $15.
W: Well, I need one regular admission ticket for my friend. And I'm a lifetime member.
M: I'll need to see your lifetime museum membership card, ma'am.
W: Just one moment. Yes, here it is.
M: Thank you. *[pause]* Ma'am, I am afraid you've made a small mistake.
W: What is that?
M: Well, you only have a yearly museum membership.
W: Oh? Really? **Has it expired**?
M: No, it hasn't. You are still a yearly museum member.

여: 박물관 회원이면 할인이 되나요?
남: 네, 그렇습니다. 평생회원은 무료로 입장이 가능하지만, 연회원은 5달러를 내셔야 합니다.
여: 그리고 성인 입장료는 얼마인가요?
남: 성인 일반 입장료는 15달러입니다.
여: 그럼, 제 친구에게 줄 일반 입장권 한 장이 필요하네요. 그리고 저는 평생회원이에요.
남: 박물관 평생회원카드를 보여 주셔야 합니다, 손님.
여: 잠깐만요. 네, 여기요.
남: 감사합니다. *[잠시 후]* 손님, 작은 실수를 하신 것 같습니다.
여: 어떤 실수요?
남: 음, 손님께선 연회원증만 가지고 계십니다.
여: 아? 정말이요? 기한이 지났나요?
남: 아니요, 그렇지 않습니다. 아직 박물관 연회원이십니다.

어휘 **lifetime** 일생의 / **yearly** 연간의; 1년에 한 번씩 있는 / **expire** (기간이) 끝나다, (계약 등이) 만기가 되다

07 이유 | ①

▶ 남자는 호주에 가고 싶지만, 금전적 여유가 없다고 했다.

W: Summer vacation starts next week! **What will you do**?
M: I don't know. What about you?
W: I had a part-time job during the school year, so I will use the money to travel to Australia. How about joining me?
M: I'd like to go, but **I can't afford it**. I **should have saved** some money.
W: Well, you studied hard instead and got good grades. Maybe we can travel together in the future.
M: I hope so. I guess I'll visit my grandma's home **in the countryside**. She turned 70 this year.
W: That should be **a great way to relax**.
M: Yes. Maybe I can get a part-time job while I'm there.

여: 여름 방학이 다음 주에 시작해! 넌 뭐 할 거야?
남: 모르겠어. 넌?
여: 난 학기 중에 아르바이트를 해서, 그 돈을 호주 여행하는 데 쓸 거야. 나랑 같이 갈래?
남: 그러고 싶지만 금전적 여유가 없어. 돈을 좀 모아놨어야 했는데.
여: 음, 대신 넌 열심히 공부해서 좋은 성적을 받았잖아. 아마 앞으로 함께 여행 갈 수 있을 거야.
남: 그러면 좋겠다. 난 시골에 있는 할머니 댁에 방문할 것 같아. 올해 70세가 되셨거든.
여: 휴식을 취하는 훌륭한 방법이겠는걸.
남: 응. 거기 있는 동안 아마 아르바이트를 구할 수도 있을 거야.

08 언급하지 않은 것 | ②

▶ 해석 참조

W: Today, we're going to talk about permafrost, **ground that is constantly frozen**. Most permafrost is found in Northern Canada and Russia, but some can be found on tall mountains and on Antarctica. In general, areas with glaciers or thick snow have relatively little or no permafrost because **snow and ice protects the ground from cold air**. Permafrost can form in just a few years, but some is over 500,000 years old and over 600 meters thick. During the summer months, some strong plants can be found living on permafrost. Permafrost can also **make it surprisingly difficult to build structures**. The icy ground constantly shifts and sinks, cracking foundations and ruining homes. In places where people live on permafrost, **special building methods must be used**.

여: 오늘은 계속 얼어있는 땅인 영구 동토층(지층의 온도가 연중 0℃ 이하로 항상 얼어 있는 땅)에 대해 이야기하고자 합니다. 영구 동토층 대부분은 캐나다 북부와 러시아에서 발견되지만, 일부는 고산지대와 남극 대륙에서 발견될 수 있습니다(① 발견 가능 지역). 일반적으로 빙하가 있거나 눈이 많은 지역에서는 상대적으로 영구 동토층이 거의 혹은 전혀 없는데, 이는 눈과 얼음이 차가운 공기로부터 지면을 보호해주기 때문입니다. 영구 동토층은 단 몇 년 만에 형성될 수 있지만, 일부는 50만 년도 더 되었으며(③ 형성 기간) 두께도 600미터가 넘습니다(④ 두께). 여름철에는 일부 강인한 식물들이 영구 동토층 위에 살고 있는 것이 발견되기도 합니다. 또, 영구 동토층은 건축물 짓는 것을 놀라울 정도로 어렵게 만들 수 있습니다. 그 빙판의 땅은 계속 이동하고 가라앉아 (건물의) 토대를 갈라지게 하고 집을 망가뜨립니다(⑤ 주거에 미치는 영향). 사람들이 영구 동토층 위에 사는 곳에서는 특수한 건축 기법이 사용되어야 합니다.

어휘 **Antarctica** 남극 대륙 / **glacier** 빙하 / **relatively** 상대적으로 / **structure** 건축물, 구조물; 구조 / **shift** 이동하다, 옮기다 / **foundation** (건물의) 토대, 기초 / **ruin** ~을 망치다, 엉망으로 만들다

09 내용 불일치 | ⑤

▶ 점심 식사는 박물관을 떠나 차를 타고 음식점에 가서 하게 된다.

M: Your attention, please. The bus will **be parking at the museum**

shortly. We will spend 2 hours here. As you leave the bus, I will give you a ticket. It is a general entrance ticket which **does not cover special exhibits**. You must pay for those exhibits yourself. If you don't want to, you don't have to follow the guided tour. If you walk around on your own and finish quickly, you can **shop for souvenirs** and have a coffee. But please do not have a meal. We will be getting back on the bus and driving to a restaurant for lunch. We will meet at 12:30 **at the exit of the museum**. Thank you very much.

남: 주목해 주십시오. 버스가 곧 박물관에 주차할 것입니다. 우리는 이곳에서 두 시간을 보낼 것입니다. 버스에서 내리실 때 표를 배부하겠습니다. 그것은 특별 전시는 적용되지 않는 일반 입장권입니다. 특별 전시는 따로 요금을 지불하셔야 합니다. 원하지 않으시면, 가이드 투어를 따라다니실 필요가 없습니다. 홀로 관람을 하시다가 빨리 끝나시면, 기념품을 사시거나 커피를 드셔도 됩니다. 하지만 식사는 하지 마십시오. 버스에 돌아온 후 점심 식사를 위해 음식점으로 이동할 것입니다. 12시 30분에 박물관 출구에서 모이겠습니다. 대단히 감사합니다.

어휘 **shortly** 곧 / **cover** ~에 적용되다 / **souvenir** 기념품

10 도표 이해 | ③

▶ 여자는 주중에 밤 근무를 할 수 있는 18세 이상의 지원자로 주말 근무가 가능하며 경험이 있는 지원자가 마음에 든다고 했다.

M: Here are some recent applicants for part-time work.
W: Thanks. Well, tell me **who you think I should call in** for an interview.
M: What's the first thing we should consider?
W: Actually, we need someone to work the night shift two nights a week. That's the most important thing.
M: You mean they **must be able to work until midnight**?
W: Yes, that's right. I think young people can't work that shift.
M: Is it illegal for young people to work that late?
W: It's not, but for the night shift I insist on someone who is 18 years old or older.
M: Okay. Do they have to work on weekends?
W: Sure. They must work **at least one day during the weekend**. Oh, and it is better if we can hire someone who has experience.
M: Then, there is only one person **whom you want to call.**
W: Let me see his application.

남: 여기 최근에 아르바이트 일자리에 신청한 지원자들 몇 명입니다.
여: 고마워요. 음, 당신 생각에는 누구에게 면접을 보러 오라고 해야 할지 말씀해 주세요.
남: 우리가 가장 먼저 고려해야 할 점이 무엇인가요?
여: 사실 일주일에 두 번씩 밤 근무를 할 사람이 필요해요. 그게 가장 중요한 부분이에요.
남: 자정까지 일할 수 있어야 한다는 말씀이신가요?
여: 네, 맞아요. 나이가 어린 사람들은 밤 근무를 할 수 없다고 생각해요.
남: 어린 사람들이 그렇게 늦게까지 일하는 것이 불법인가요?
여: 그건 아니지만, 밤 근무를 하려면 18세 이상이 되어야 한다고 생각해요.
남: 알겠습니다. 주말에 일해야 할까요?
여: 물론이죠. 적어도 주말에 하루는 일해야 해요. 오, 그리고 경험이 있는 사람을 고용할 수 있다면 더 좋아요.
남: 그럼, 전화할 지원자는 딱 한 명 있습니다.
여: 그의 지원서를 보여주세요.

어휘 **applicant** 지원자, 신청자 / **call in** ~을 불러들이다 / **shift** (교대제의) 근무 시간, 교대 근무

11 짧은 대화에 이어질 응답 | ③

▶ 주말에 만날 것을 제안하는 남자의 말에 가장 적절한 응답을 찾는다.

① 그럼 월요일에 봐. ② 우리는 주제도 골라야 해.
③ 토요일 저녁이라면 괜찮아. ④ 이 회의실 정말 멋져.
⑤ 온라인 토론에는 제약이 많아.

M: I think we need to **meet soon and discuss our project**.
W: I agree, but I'm really busy for the next few days.
M: In that case, **how about meeting** on the weekend?
W: ______________________________

남: 우리 얼른 만나서 과제에 대해 의논해야 할 것 같아.
여: 나도 그렇게 생각해. 하지만 앞으로 며칠간 난 매우 바빠.
남: 그러면 주말에 만나는 게 어때?
여: ______________________________

12 짧은 대화에 이어질 응답 | ④

▶ 웹사이트에서 광고했던 재킷을 찾는 남자에게 여자는 여러 가지가 있으므로 무엇인지 자세히 말해 달라고 한다. 이에 가장 적절한 대답을 찾는다.

① 죄송해요, 그건 이미 다 팔렸어요.
② 물론이죠. 여기 영수증이에요.
③ 그게 아직 세일 중이면 좋겠어요.
④ 그건 주머니가 세 개고 모자가 달려 있었어요.
⑤ 디자인은 마음에 드는데 색상이 별로예요.

W: Hi, can I help you find something?
M: I'm looking for a jacket that **you had advertised** on your website.
W: We have several. **Could you describe it to me**?
M: ______________________________

여: 안녕하세요, 찾으시는 물건 있으세요?
남: 웹사이트에서 광고했던 재킷을 찾고 있어요.
여: 몇 가지가 있는데요. 그 재킷에 대해 자세히 설명해 주시겠어요?
남: ______________________________

어휘 **hood** (외투 등에 달린) 모자; (기계 등을 보호하기 위한) 덮개

13 긴 대화에 이어질 응답 | ⑤

▶ 남자가 같이 가줄 수 없으므로 여자는 남자가 가르쳐 준 길을 혼자 찾아가겠다고 할 것이다.

① 괜찮습니다. 곧 뒤따라가겠습니다. ② 고맙습니다. 그럼 당신과 함께 걸을게요.
③ 잘됐네요. 이해해 주시면 감사하겠습니다. ④ 알겠습니다. 2층까지 계단으로 갈게요.
⑤ 문제없어요. 혼자서도 분명 찾을 수 있을 거예요.

M: Do you need some help?
W: Yes, I'm looking for the Bantech phone repair center.
M: It's not in this building.
W: But I was told it was in a building with a Triple B Bank **on the ground floor**.
M: Well, there is a Triple B Bank in this building. But there is also another branch of the Triple B Bank **farther up the street**.
W: Really?
M: Yes. A block farther up the street is another building with a Triple B Bank branch. My office is in the same building.
W: Oh, really?
M: I'd take you there, but **I'm not heading back to work** for a while.
W: ______________________________

남: 도움이 필요하신가요?
여: 네, Bantech 전화 수리 센터를 찾고 있는데요.
남: 이 건물에는 없습니다.
여: 하지만 1층에 Triple B 은행이 있는 건물에 있다고 들었어요.
남: 음, 이 건물에 Triple B 은행이 있어요. 하지만 길을 따라 더 가면 Triple B 은행의 다른 지점이 또 있어요.
여: 그래요?
남: 네, 이 길을 따라 한 블록 더 가시면 Triple B 은행 지점이 있는 건물이 또 하나 있어요. 제 사무실이 같은 건물에 있거든요.
여: 아, 그러세요?
남: 제가 그리로 모셔다드리고 싶지만, 얼마 동안은 일하러 돌아가지 않을 예정이라서요.
여: ______________________________

어휘 **come along** 뒤따라가다 / **ground floor** 1층

14 긴 대화에 이어질 응답 | ③

▶ 커피 중독을 끊기 위해 여러 가지 노력을 해 보았지만 모두 실패한 남자에게 여자가 침을 맞으라고 이야기하고 있다.

① 좋아요. 당신이랑 같은 것으로 할게요.
② 당신 말이 맞아요. 운동이 도움이 될 수도 있어요.
③ 아마 당신 말이 맞을 거예요. 한번 시도해 볼게요.
④ 걱정하지 마세요. 전 언제라도 운동할 수 있어요.
⑤ 동의해요. 이번에는 주스를 마실게요.

W: You drink 8 cups of coffee a day!
M: Yeah. I've tried to stop many times, but I always fail.
W: Try again! Drinking too much coffee is unhealthy.

M: I know. When **I switched to juice**, I still felt terrible until I had coffee. And a few weeks ago, I tried to **avoid all places I might find coffee**.
W: That's hard.
M: I know. So I started exercising. I thought if I were healthier, I wouldn't miss coffee.
W: Obviously, **it hasn't worked**.
M: No, I had to have my coffee.
W: I've heard acupuncture is good at **helping people end addictive habits**.
M: Acupuncture?
W: Yeah. **Putting needles in your body's pressure points**.
M: Hmm....
W: I don't think you have much choice.
M: ______________________________

여: 당신은 하루에 커피를 8잔씩 마시는군요!
남: 네. 여러 번 끊으려고 시도했지만 항상 실패해요.
여: 다시 시도해 보세요! 커피를 너무 많이 마시면 건강에 해로워요.
남: 알아요. 주스로 바꿨을 때, 커피를 마실 때까지 기분이 계속 안 좋았어요. 그리고 몇 주 전에는 커피를 찾을 수도 있는 곳이라면 모두 피하려고 노력했어요.
여: 그건 어렵죠.
남: 네. 그래서 운동을 하기 시작했어요. 더 건강해지면 커피가 그립지 않을 거라고 생각했어요.
여: 분명히 그것도 효과가 없었군요.
남: 그래요. 전 커피를 마셔야만 했어요.
여: 침술이 중독적인 습관을 끊는 데 도움이 많이 된다고 들었어요.
남: 침술이요?
여: 네. 신체의 압점에 바늘을 꽂는 거예요.
남: 음….
여: 당신에게는 선택의 여지가 별로 없는 것 같아요.
남: ______________________________

어휘 **give it a try** 시도하다, 한번 해 보다 / **unhealthy** 건강에 해로운 / **switch** 바꾸다, 전환하다 / **obviously** 명백하게, 아무리 보아도 / **acupuncture** 침술 / **addictive** 중독성의 / **pressure point** (피부의) 압점, 지혈점

15 상황에 적절한 말 | ①

▶ Jennifer는 귀가 시간에도 늦었고 전화기도 꺼져 있었기 때문에 먼저 어머니에게 사과하고 전화를 받지 못한 이유(배터리 문제)를 말할 것이다.

① 죄송해요, 엄마, 하지만 배터리가 다 됐어요.
② 전 수업이 시작되기 전에 전화를 항상 꺼둬요.
③ 라디오 소리를 좀 줄여 주실래요?
④ 숙제가 끝나지 않았어요.
⑤ 제가 집에 들어가기 전에 주무세요.

W: Jennifer is doing research in the library for a homework assignment. She starts reading a book and **taking notes for her assignment**. She finds the book interesting and before she realizes it, **three hours have passed**. She was told to come home at 9 but it's 10 now. Her mother always **worries about her**. And Jennifer realizes she must call her mom to tell her she'll be home soon. So she tries to make a call, but **her battery has run out**. She borrows a friend's cell phone. Her mom answers. She had tried to phone Jennifer. She asks Jennifer why she didn't answer her cell phone. In this situation, what would Jennifer most likely say to her mom?

여: Jennifer는 숙제 때문에 도서관에서 조사를 하고 있다. 숙제를 하기 위해 책을 읽고 필기를 하기 시작한다. 그 책이 흥미롭다고 생각해 어느새 세 시간이 지나버렸다. 9시까지 집에 들어오라는 말씀을 들었지만 지금은 10시이다. 어머니는 항상 그녀를 걱정하신다. 그리고 Jennifer는 집에 곧 들어간다고 말씀드리기 위해 어머니께 전화해야 한다는 사실을 깨닫는다. 그래서 전화를 하려고 하지만 배터리가 다 됐다. 그녀는 친구의 휴대전화를 빌린다. 어머니가 전화를 받으신다. 어머니도 Jennifer에게 전화하려고 하셨다. 어머니는 Jennifer에게 왜 휴대전화를 받지 않았는지 물어보신다. 이러한 상황에서 Jennifer가 어머니에게 할 말로 가장 적절한 것은 무엇인가?

어휘 **turn down** (소리·온도 등을) 낮추다 / **assignment** 과제 / **run out** 다 되다, 바닥나다

16~17 세트 문항 | 16. ③ 17. ⑤

▶ 16. 식이 장애 치료법으로 식이 상담을 받는 것과 신체상을 개선하는 방법을 제시하고 있다.

① 긍정적 사고의 힘
② 시작하기 쉬운 야외 활동들
③ 식이 장애를 극복하는 방법
④ 건강한 식습관의 중요성
⑤ 식이 장애의 흔한 종류들

▶ 17. 해석 참조

M: Did you know that millions of people are **suffering from eating disorders**? Some of them refuse to eat anything, while others eat too much. Today, I'd like to introduce **two basic treatments for eating disorders**. First, it's always a good idea to get some counseling about nutrition and healthy eating. The goal of a counselor is to help you **combine healthy eating with your everyday life**. They can't change your habits overnight, but they can push you in the right direction. Second, you should learn to **see yourself in a positive way**. So here are some tips to improve your body image. Wear clothes you feel comfortable in. Dress to express yourself, not to impress others. **Stay away from scales and fashion magazines**. And do nice things for your body once in a while, like getting a massage or a new perfume. Becoming more active can also help. So try to stay active by climbing mountains or riding bikes with friends.

남: 수백만 명의 사람이 식이 장애로 고생하고 있다는 사실을 알고 계셨습니까? 그중 일부는 어떤 것이든 먹기를 거부하는가 하면, 다른 사람들은 너무 많이 먹습니다. 오늘은 식이 장애에 대한 기본적인 치료법 두 가지를 소개하려고 합니다. 첫 번째, 영양과 건강한 식사에 관해 상담을 받는 것은 언제나 좋은 생각입니다. 상담사의 목표는 일상생활에서 건강한 식사를 하도록 돕는 것입니다. 그들이 하룻밤 사이에 여러분의 (식)습관을 바꿀 수는 없지만, 올바른 방향으로 독려할 수는 있습니다. 두 번째, 자기 자신을 긍정적인 방향으로 바라보는 법을 배워야 합니다. 그래서 여기 자신의 몸에 대한 이미지를 개선하는 방법이 몇 가지 있습니다. 여러분이 느끼기에 ① 편안한 옷을 입으십시오. 다른 사람에게 좋은 인상을 주기 위해서가 아니라, 자신을 표현하기 위해 옷을 입으십시오. 체중계와 패션 잡지를 멀리하십시오. 그리고 ② 마사지를 받거나 ③ 새 향수를 사는 것처럼, 때때로 자신의 몸을 위해 기분 좋은 일을 하십시오. 좀 더 활동적이 되는 것도 도움이 될 수 있습니다. 그러니 친구들과 등산을 하거나 ④ 자전거를 타면서 활동적으로 지내려고 시도해 보십시오.

어휘 **eating disorder** 식이 장애 / **counseling** 상담, 카운슬링 ***cf.* counselor** (전문) 상담사, 카운슬러 / **scale** ((pl.)) 저울; 규모, 범위 / **once in a while** 때로는, 가끔

실전모의고사 31

Answers & Explanation

01. ② 02. ④ 03. ④ 04. ④ 05. ① 06. ② 07. ② 08. ③ 09. ① 10. ④
11. ① 12. ⑤ 13. ② 14. ④ 15. ③ 16. ② 17. ⑤

01 화자가 하는 말의 목적 | ②

▶ 주말에 있을 점포 정리 특가 판매를 고객들에게 홍보하고 있다.

W: **With the decline in the use** of CDs, Music Warehouse is having a going-out-of-business sale this weekend. **Not only will we be selling** every CD in the store for 75% off, but we will also be selling the shelves, light fixtures, sound system and furniture. We knew that **this day would eventually come**, especially with the growing trends of purchasing music online and the expansion of streaming services. And so, we invite all of our loyal customers to come down to this weekend's sale. We **will be serving refreshments** and playing all your favorite music until the very last CD is sold.

여: CD 사용이 줄어듦에 따라, Music Warehouse는 이번 주말에 점포 정리 판매를 실시합니다. 가게의 모든 CD를 75% 할인하여 판매할 뿐만 아니라 진열대, 조명 기구, 음향 시스템 그리고 가구도 판매할 것입니다. 특히 온라인에서 음악 파일을 구매하는 경향이 늘어나고 스트리밍 서비스가 확장됨에 따라, 저희는 언젠가 이런 날이 오리라는 것을 알고 있었습니다. 그래서 단골 고객분 모두를 이번 주말에 있을 판매에 초대하는 바입니다. 맨 마지막 CD가 팔릴 때까지 다과를 제공하고 고객들이 좋아하시는 음악을 틀어 드릴 예정입니다.

어휘 **decline** 하락, 감퇴 / **going-out-of-business sale** 점포 정리 판매 / **light fixture** 조명 기구 / **trend** 경향 / **expansion** 확장, 확대 / **refreshment** 다과, 가벼운 음식물

02 대화 주제 | ④

▶ 오디션 참가자들 중 연극 주인공으로 누가 적합할지에 관해 이야기하고 있다.

W: OK. **Let's call it a day**.
M: Sounds good to me. So, who do you think would be best for the hero of the play?
W: I guess my favorite so far is Martin. He **has acted in many different things**, from plays to movies.
M: Yes. He is already well-known. I liked him but, in my opinion, Chris **showed more promise**. He doesn't have as much experience, but I think he has great natural ability.
W: **That's a great point**. How about Jasper? He's **somewhat of a compromise** between the other two.
M: I'm afraid I couldn't feel any emotion from his performance.
W: In that case, Jasper isn't an option. Honestly, I don't think we've found the right actor.
M: Don't worry. We still have a few more actors to see tomorrow.

여: 자, 오늘은 이걸로 끝내죠.
남: 좋아요. 그럼 누가 연극의 주인공으로 가장 적합할 것으로 생각하세요?
여: 제 생각에 지금까지 가장 괜찮은 사람은 Martin이에요. 그는 연극에서 영화까지 여러 다양한 작품에서 연기했거든요.
남: 맞아요. Martin은 이미 잘 알려졌죠. 그가 마음에 들긴 했지만, 제 생각에 Chris가 더 많은 가능성을 보여주었어요. 그는 그만큼의 경험은 없지만 뛰어난 재능을 타고났다고 생각해요.
여: 좋은 지적이에요. Jasper는 어떤가요? 그가 어느 정도 다른 둘 사이의 절충안이 되는 것 같은데요.
남: 아쉽지만 저는 그의 연기에서 어떤 감정도 느끼지 못했어요.
여: 그렇다면, Jasper는 선택할 수 없겠네요. 솔직히 말해서 꼭 맞는 배우를 찾지는 못한 것 같아요.
남: 걱정하지 마세요. 내일 만나볼 배우들이 아직 몇 명 더 있어요.

어휘 **call it a day** (그날 하루 일을) 그만하다, 끝내다 / **compromise** 절충안; 타협, 화해

03 관계 | ④

▶ 미술 작품을 만드는 사람과 그 작품에 대한 평가를 쓰는 사람 사이의 대화이다.

M: I'd like to show you a few of my more recent pieces.
W: This is very interesting. I like your use of shadow in that painting.
M: Thank you. I feel like my work is heading in a different, more mature direction.
W: **I might have to quote you on that** in my story.
M: I'm very glad to hear that.
W: **Show me something else**. Do you have any sculptures?
M: I did this bronze piece over here.
W: **There is a certain imbalance to it**. Did you do that on purpose?
M: In a way, yes. But it was also my first bronze piece, so **some things happened by accident**.
W: OK. Well, I can tell you right now you will get a positive review from me.

남: 저의 좀 더 최근 작품을 몇 점 보여 드리고 싶습니다.
여: 매우 흥미롭군요. 저 그림에서 그림자를 사용한 방식이 마음에 듭니다.
남: 감사합니다. 제 작품이 색다르고 더 원숙한 방향으로 나아가고 있는 것 같습니다.
여: 그 작품에 관한 작가님의 말씀을 제 평론에 인용해야 할지도 모르겠네요.
남: 그렇게 말씀해 주시니 정말 기쁩니다.
여: 다른 작품도 보여 주세요. 조각품도 있습니까?
남: 여기 있는 이 청동 작품을 만들었습니다.
여: 거기에 어떤 불균형이 있네요. 의도적으로 그렇게 하신 건가요?
남: 어떤 면에서는, 그렇습니다. 하지만 제가 청동으로 만든 첫 작품이기도 해서 우연히 그렇게 돼버린 면도 있어요.
여: 알겠습니다. 음, 현재로서는 제가 긍정적인 작품평을 쓸 것이라고 말씀드릴 수 있습니다.

어휘 **mature** 원숙한 / **quote** (남의 말을) 인용하다 / **sculpture** 조각(품) / **bronze** 청동 / **imbalance** 불균형 / **on purpose** 고의로, 일부러

04 그림 불일치 | ④

▶ 남자는 하트 무늬 드레스를 골랐지만 여자의 엄마가 무늬가 없는 드레스로 바꿨다고 했다.

M: Welcome home, Jessica! It's great to have you back.
W: Oh, wow! You didn't have to **throw a party** for me!
M: Well, your mother and I were worried about you while you were in the hospital, and we wanted to celebrate your return.
W: I can't believe you even put up a "Welcome Home!" banner. It's great.
M: **Take a look at your gifts**. Do you like the teddy bear?
W: Of course I do! The flowers are also lovely.
M: Those were my idea. I also chose a heart-patterned dress, but your mother said it was old-fashioned and she **selected a plain dress instead**.
W: I'm happy with the style she picked out.
M: Don't forget about the shoes. **They are supposed to match with** the dress.
W: They are great, too. I love the ribbons!

남: 집에 온 걸 환영한다, Jessica! 네가 돌아와서 정말 기쁘구나.
여: 아, 와! 저를 위해 파티를 열지 않으셨어도 되는데요!
남: 음, 네가 병원에 있는 동안 네 엄마와 난 널 걱정했고, 네가 돌아온 걸 축하해주고 싶었어.
여: '집에 온 걸 환영해!'라는 플래카드까지 붙이셨다니 믿을 수 없어요. 멋져요.
남: 네 선물들 좀 보렴. 곰 인형이 마음에 드니?
여: 당연히 마음에 들죠! 꽃도 예뻐요.
남: 그것들은 내 아이디어였단다. 내가 하트 무늬 드레스도 골랐는데, 네 엄마가 그건 유행에 뒤진다면서 대신에 무늬가 없는 드레스를 선택했어.
여: 엄마가 골라 주신 스타일이 마음에 들어요.
남: 구두도 잊지 말렴. 그 드레스와 어울리도록 한 거야.
여: 그것도 멋져요. 리본이 정말 마음에 들어요!

어휘 **banner** 플래카드, 현수막 / **old-fashioned** 유행에 뒤떨어진, 구식의 / **be supposed to-v** v하기로 되어 있다

05 추후 행동 | ①

▶ 몸이 아파 축구 경기에 참가하지 못하고 쉬어야 하는 남자(아들)에게 여자(엄마)가 닭고기 수프를 만들어주겠다고 말했다.

W: Jason! **Get out of bed**. It's past 9:00! You have a soccer game at 11:00! But I want to take you early **as Grandma is coming over**.
M: Mom, I'm hot. I feel really tired and weak.
W: You're sick? I should **take you to the doctor's**, but it's Sunday. The hospital emergency room?
M: Mom, it's not that bad. I don't have to go to the emergency room.
W: Well, you can't play soccer today.
M: Yeah. **I'd better rest all day**. I woke up at night and took some medicine, but I don't feel any better.
W: I'll make you some chicken noodle soup.
M: Oh, that would be great. And I guess I'd better phone the coach.
W: Do you want me to do it?
M: No, **I should do it myself**.

여: Jason! 일어나. 9시가 지났어! 11시에 축구 경기가 있잖니! 하지만 할머니께서 오실 거라서 너를 일찍 데려다 주고 싶구나.
남: 엄마, 저 열이 나요. 정말 피곤하고 힘이 없어요.
여: 아픈 거니? 병원에 데려가야 하지만, 일요일이야. 병원 응급실에 가야 할까?
남: 엄마, 그렇게 심하지는 않아요. 응급실에 갈 필요는 없어요.
여: 음, 오늘은 축구를 할 수 없겠구나.
남: 네. 하루 종일 쉬는 게 낫겠어요. 밤에 깨서 약을 좀 먹었지만 조금도 나아지지 않아요.
여: 국수를 넣은 닭고기 수프를 만들어줄게.
남: 아, 그래 주시면 좋겠어요. 그리고 코치님께 전화하는 게 좋을 것 같아요.
여: 내가 해줄까?
남: 아뇨, 제가 직접 해야 해요.

06 금액 | ②

▶ 남자는 작년 모델인 PD 1을 사고자 하므로 2,500달러를 지불할 것이다.

[Phone rings.]
W: FX Office Supplies. How may I help you?
M: Hi. **I'm interested in purchasing** one of your copiers for my office.
W: Certainly. Could you tell me which one you are interested in?
M: Well, I'm not sure exactly. I definitely need one that can **handle a large workload**.
W: Okay. The PDX is our top-of-the-line copier. It's on sale for $3,200.
M: **It costs more than I thought**. How about the ones in your other line, the PD 1 and the PD 2? What's the difference between them?
W: The PD 1 is last year's model. It's $2,500.
M: So **the two only differ in design**?
W: Correct. And this year's version, the PD 2, costs an extra $200, making it $2,700.
M: In that case, I think I'll order the PD 1.
W: Great choice.

[전화벨이 울린다.]
여: FX Office Supplies입니다. 무엇을 도와드릴까요?
남: 안녕하세요. 사무용으로 귀사의 복사기 중 한 대를 구입하고 싶은데요.
여: 알겠습니다. 어느 모델을 원하시는지 말씀해 주시겠어요?
남: 음, 정확히는 모르고요. 많은 작업량을 처리할 수 있는 제품이 꼭 필요합니다.
여: 알겠습니다. PDX는 저희 최고급 복사기입니다. 그것은 할인해서 3,200달러입니다.
남: 생각했던 것보다 비용이 더 드네요. 다른 종류의 제품 중 PD 1과 PD 2는 어떤가요? 그 둘의 차이는 뭐죠?
여: PD 1은 작년 모델입니다. 2,500달러고요.
남: 그럼 그 둘은 디자인만 다른 건가요?
여: 맞습니다. 그리고 올해 버전인 PD 2는 200달러가 추가되어서 2,700달러입니다.
남: 그렇다면 PD 1으로 주문해야겠군요.
여: 잘 선택하셨습니다.

어휘 **workload** 작업량, 업무량 / **line** (상품의) 종류

07 이유 | ②

▶ 남자가 호텔에서 저녁 식사를 할 것인지 묻자 여자가 부정하면서 시내에서 친구들을 만날 거라고 했다.

M: May I help you?
W: **I have a reservation**. My name's Jessica Conner.
M: Yes, a single room for six nights with an ocean view. You'll be on the seventh floor, in room 712. How would you like to pay?
W: I'll **charge it to my credit card**. By the way, are there any good restaurants nearby?
M: There are **a wide variety of excellent restaurants** on the way to the beach. I'm sure you'll find something you like.
W: What about the hotel's seafood restaurant? I heard it's famous.
M: It's on the second floor and it's also very good. **Will you be dining here tonight**?
W: No, I'll be meeting some friends in the city.
M: OK. Here is your key card. I will have your bags brought up to you. Enjoy your stay.

남: 도와드릴까요?
여: 예약했습니다. 제 이름은 Jessica Conner입니다.
남: 네, 바다가 보이는 1인용 객실로 6박이시네요. 7층 712호에 묵게 되실 겁니다. 요금은 어떻게 지불하시겠습니까?
여: 신용카드로 할게요. 그런데 근처에 괜찮은 레스토랑이 있나요?
남: 해변으로 가는 길에 아주 다양한 종류의 훌륭한 레스토랑들이 있습니다. 마음에 드는 곳을 분명 발견하실 거예요.
여: 호텔 해산물 레스토랑은 어떤가요? 유명하다고 들었어요.
남: 2층에 있는데 그곳도 아주 좋습니다. 오늘 밤 여기서 식사하실 건가요?
여: 아니요, 시내에서 친구 몇 명을 만날 거예요.
남: 알겠습니다. 키 카드 여기 있습니다. 가방을 옮겨 드릴게요. 머무시는 동안 즐거운 시간 보내시기 바랍니다.

어휘 **dine** (잘 차린) 식사를 하다, 만찬을 들다

08 언급하지 않은 것 | ③

▶ 해석 참조

W: Hi, I hope you are enjoying the job fair. If you have any questions, **please feel free to ask**.
M: Actually, I'm interested in the position that **your company is recruiting for**. What type of candidate are you looking for?
W: An ideal candidate will possess a four-year degree, have strong TOEIC scores, and have more than 2 years of experience in this field.
M: I saw that your company is **offering sick leave and paid holidays**. But what about the salary?
W: **Aside from the benefits** you mentioned, we're offering $8,000 per month plus health insurance.
M: Sounds great. Where should I submit my résumé?
W: To apply, submit your résumé and a letter of self-introduction on our website.
M: **When is the deadline for applications**?
W: We'll stop accepting applications on October 16.
M: OK. Thank you for your time.

여: 안녕하세요. 취업 박람회를 즐겁게 둘러보고 계시길 바랍니다. 질문이 있으시면, 자유롭게 해주십시오.
남: 실은, 귀사에서 채용 중인 일자리에 관심이 있는데요. 어떤 유형의 지원자를 찾고 계신가요?
여: 가장 적합한 지원자는 4년제 학사 학위와 높은 토익 점수, 이 분야에서 2년이 넘는 경력(① 지원 자격)을 갖춘 사람일 것입니다.
남: 귀사에서 병가와 유급 휴가를 제공한다는 것은 보았습니다. 그런데 급여는 어떤가요?
여: 말씀하신 혜택 외에 한 달에 8천 달러(② 급여)이며 의료 보험도 제공합니다.
남: 정말 좋네요. 이력서를 어디로 제출해야 하나요?
여: 지원하시려면 이력서와 자기소개서를 저희 웹사이트로 제출(④ 지원 방법)해 주십시오.
남: 지원 마감일은 언제인가요?
여: 10월 16일에 지원서 접수를 마감할 것입니다(⑤ 지원 마감 기한).
남: 알겠습니다. 시간 내주셔서 감사합니다.

어휘 **recruit** (신입 사원·회원 등을) 모집하다, 뽑다 / **candidate** 지원자, 후보자 / **sick leave** 병가 / **aside from** ~외에 / **benefit** ((주로 pl.)) (직장·보험 등에서 받는) 혜택, 수당; 이득 / **résumé** 이력서 / **deadline** 마감 시간[일자], 기한 / **application** 지원(서); 적용, 응용

09 내용 불일치 | ①

▶ 아마추어와 프로 선수의 경기는 오전, 오후로 나뉘어 따로 진행된다.

M: The annual New Town dancing contest will be held at the New Town Auditorium. The amateur level dancing contest will be held in the morning, while the professional level contest **will be held separately**

in the afternoon, at the same place. **Five judges will be appointed** to score each contestant and determine the winner. The winner of the amateur level dancing contest will **perform in upcoming city events**. If you are interested, please fill out our online application. The fee can be paid **either online or at the box office** before the event. **Good luck to all who participate**.

남: 연례 New Town 댄스 대회가 New Town 강당에서 개최됩니다. 아마추어급 댄스 대회는 오전에 개최될 것이며, 프로급 대회는 같은 장소에서 오후에 별도로 개최될 것입니다. 다섯 명의 심사위원이 선임되어 각 참가자의 점수를 매기고 우승자를 결정할 것입니다. 아마추어급 댄스 대회의 우승자는 다가오는 시(市)의 행사에서 공연하게 됩니다. 관심이 있으시면, 온라인 신청서를 작성해 주시기 바랍니다. 참가비는 온라인상으로 혹은 대회가 열리기 전에 매표소에 지불하실 수 있습니다. 참가하시는 모든 분께 행운이 있기를 빕니다.

어휘 **annual** 연례의 / **amateur** 아마추어 선수, 비전문가 (↔ professional 프로 선수, 전문가) / **judge** 심사위원, 심판 / **appoint** 임명하다, 지명하다 / **score** 채점하다 / **contestant** 경기 참가자

10 도표 이해 | ④

▶ 여자는 비포장도로용이 아니고 가격은 1,000달러 미만이며, 프레임이 15인치인 자전거를 선택할 것이다.

W: I need a good bicycle.
M: **I'll show you what we have**. This is our most popular bike. It's great for off-road cycling.
W: Actually, I don't want a mountain bike for off-road cycling. They're too slow. I'll be using my bike **to travel to work**.
M: Great. These days, more and more people are cycling to work.
W: And I want to join them. Wow, this one's expensive. **Is it for biking** in the city?
M: No, it's a road racing bike. It's not for you.
W: **That's for sure**. I want to spend less than $1,000.
M: Hmm.... The problem is the size. It's near the end of the summer and our selection of bicycles is limited. How tall are you?
W: 165 centimeters.
M: You'll want a 15-inch frame. Hmm.... **I recommend this one here**.

여: 괜찮은 자전거가 한 대 필요해요.
남: 저희가 가진 것을 보여 드릴게요. 이것이 가장 인기 있는 자전거예요. 비포장도로에서 타기에 아주 좋아요.
여: 사실 비포장도로용 산악자전거를 원하지 않아요. 그것은 너무 느려요. 저는 통근하는 데 자전거를 이용할 거예요.
남: 좋습니다. 요즘 점점 더 많은 사람이 자전거로 출근하고 있죠.
여: 저도 동참하고 싶어요. 우와, 이것은 비싸네요. 도시에서 타는 데 쓰이나요?
남: 아뇨, 그것은 도로 경주용 자전거예요. 고객님을 위한 것이 아니에요.
여: 물론이에요. 저는 1,000달러보다 적게 쓰고 싶어요.
남: 음…. 문제는 크기네요. 여름 막바지라서 저희가 구비해놓은 자전거가 한정적이에요. 키가 어떻게 되세요?
여: 165센티미터예요.
남: 15인치 프레임이 필요하시겠네요. 음…. 여기 이것을 추천합니다.

어휘 **off-road** (차량 등이) 일반[포장] 도로 밖에서 사용하게 만든 / **selection** 선택 가능한 것들; 선발, 선택

11 짧은 대화에 이어질 응답 | ①

▶ 11시 30분 기차가 매진되어 12시 기차를 권하는 여자의 말에 남자가 더 빠른 것은 없는지 물었다. 이에 적절한 응답을 찾는다.

① 죄송하지만 없습니다.
② 11시 30분 기차를 권해 드립니다.
③ 손님의 예약을 확인해 드리겠습니다.
④ 내일 다시 오시는 게 좋겠습니다.
⑤ 표는 탑승 전에 구매하셔야 합니다.

M: Hi, **I'd like two tickets** for the 11:30 train, please.
W: I'm sorry, but the 11:30 train is full. How about the 12:00 train?
M: **I'm really in a hurry**. Isn't there anything sooner?
W: ______________________________

남: 안녕하세요. 11시 30분 기차표 두 장 주세요.
여: 죄송하지만, 11시 30분 기차는 다 찼습니다. 12시 기차는 어떠세요?
남: 제가 정말 급해서요. 더 빠른 것은 없나요?
여: ______________________________

어휘 **board** 탑승[승선]하다; (비행기 · 배가) 탑승[승선]에 들어가다

12 짧은 대화에 이어질 응답 | ⑤

▶ 남자가 비행기에서 먹을 간식을 사고 싶다고 하자 여자가 비행 중에 식사가 제공되지 않느냐고 물었다. 이에 대한 적절한 응답을 찾는다.

① 난 비행 중에는 입맛이 없어요.
② 비행시간을 바꾸고 싶은데요.
③ 줄 거예요. 하지만 난 간식 먹는 것을 좋아하지 않아요.
④ 안 줄 거예요. 내가 마지막으로 남은 음식을 다 먹었어요.
⑤ 줄 거예요. 그래도 가끔 그건 충분치 않아요.

W: Our flight **will start boarding soon**. Are you ready?
M: Almost, but I want to get some snacks for the plane.
W: **Won't they be serving meals** during the flight?
M: ______________________________

여: 우리가 탈 비행기의 탑승 수속이 곧 시작될 거예요. 준비됐어요?
남: 거의 다 됐는데, 난 비행기에서 먹을 간식을 좀 사고 싶어요.
여: 비행 중에 식사를 주지 않을까요?
남: ______________________________

어휘 **appetite** 식욕; 욕구

13 긴 대화에 이어질 응답 | ②

▶ 식당에서 입은 피해에 대한 적절한 조치를 원하는 손님에게 할 수 있는 대답을 고른다.

① Susan을 이리로 불러 계산서를 확인하게 하겠습니다.
② 제가 손님의 계산서를 책임지고 주방장에게 말하겠습니다.
③ 남의 일에 간섭하지 않는 것이 가장 좋을 것입니다.
④ 채소 판매에 대한 엄격한 관리를 요청하겠습니다.
⑤ 보수 공사 때문에 음식점의 문을 닫을 예정입니다.

W: Your server, Susan, told me you wanted to see me. What can I do to help you?
M: **For starters**, my coffee is cold.
W: OK. I can take care of that right away.
M: Thank you, but that isn't the only problem.
W: Oh? **What else could be wrong**?
M: There was a hair in my soup and an insect in my salad.
W: Oh, my... I'm terribly sorry about that.
M: **I am shocked by this**. I have been coming here for years.
W: We'll remake the dish right away. And as the manager, I **take full responsibility for this**.
M: If you say so, then I expect you to take serious action.
W: ______________________________

여: 담당 종업원인 Susan 말로는 손님께서 저를 불러달라고 하셨다고요. 무엇을 도와드릴까요?
남: 우선, 커피가 너무 차가워요.
여: 알겠습니다. 바로 처리해 드리겠습니다.
남: 감사합니다만, 문제는 그뿐이 아니에요.
여: 아? 다른 문제가 또 있습니까?
남: 수프에는 머리카락이 있었고 샐러드에는 벌레가 들어 있었어요.
여: 아, 이런… 그 부분은 정말 죄송합니다.
남: 이건 충격적이네요. 저는 수년간 여기 단골이거든요.
여: 당장 음식을 다시 만들어 드리겠습니다. 그리고 매니저로서 이번 문제에 대해 전적으로 책임지겠습니다.
남: 그렇게 말씀하시니, 제대로 된 조치를 취해 주시기를 기대합니다.
여: ______________________________

어휘 **mind one's own business** 남의 일에 간섭하지 않다 / **renovation** 보수 공사, 개조 / **for starters** 우선, 첫째로 / **take responsibility for** ~에 대한 책임을 지다 / **take action** 조치를 취하다

14 긴 대화에 이어질 응답 | ④

▶ 개명 신청을 빨리 처리할 수 있는 다른 방법이 없다는 사실이 정답의 힌트가 된다.

① 결혼 증명서를 가져오셔야 합니다.
② 이름에 하이픈을 넣는 데 추가 비용이 듭니다.
③ 신청 용지를 건물 밖으로 가지고 나갈 수 없습니다.
④ 시간이 더 있을 때 신청 용지를 다시 가져오십시오.

⑤ 손님의 보험증은 2년 동안 유효합니다.

W: I need to change my name. Where do I **get the forms for that**?
M: May I ask why you are changing your name?
W: Well, I **just got married** and I want to hyphenate my last name and my husband's last name.
M: Oh, I see. Well, we need your passport and your marriage certificate. You will only have to fill out form 10-B.
W: I have my passport and marriage certificate, but where do I get that form?
M: **I will get one for you**. *[pause]* Here you go.
W: What do I do **after I fill it out**?
M: Pay the fee and take a number. Then you must wait for about an hour.
W: I can't stay for that long. Is there **any way to get it done quickly**?
M: I'm afraid not.
W: Then, what am I supposed to do?
M: ______________________________

여: 제 이름을 바꾸고 싶습니다. 신청서를 어디에서 받을 수 있나요?
남: 개명하시려는 이유를 여쭤봐도 될까요?
여: 음, 얼마 전에 결혼을 해서 제 성과 남편의 성 사이에 하이픈을 넣고 싶어서요.
남: 아, 그렇군요. 그럼, 여권과 결혼 증명서가 필요합니다. 손님께서는 10-B 용지만 작성하시면 될 것입니다.
여: 여권과 결혼 증명서는 있는데, 그 서식은 어디에서 받는 거죠?
남: 제가 가져다 드리겠습니다. *[잠시 후]* 여기 있습니다.
여: 작성하고 나서 무엇을 하면 되나요?
남: 신청비를 내시고 번호를 받아가세요. 그 다음에 한 시간 정도 기다리셔야 합니다.
여: 그렇게 오래 있지는 못해요. 빨리 처리할 수 있는 방법이 있나요?
남: 없을 것 같습니다.
여: 그럼, 어떻게 해야 하죠?
남: ______________________________

어휘 **certificate** 증명서; 자격증, 면허증 / **hyphenate** ~을 하이픈으로 잇다 / **valid** 유효한

15 상황에 적절한 말 | ③

▶ Gary는 이번에 상을 받지 못하게 된 Felicia에게 위로가 되는 말을 전하려고 한다.

① 네가 마침내 행복해져서 정말 기뻐!
② 넌 상을 받을 자격이 있어. 축하해.
③ 내년에도 네가 상을 받을 기회가 얼마든지 있어.
④ 난 시험에서 실수한 게 틀림없어.
⑤ 네가 이렇게 실망한 건 본 적이 없어. 무슨 일이니?

W: Gary and Felicia are the top two students in their class. Every year, one student becomes the class leader and **receives a special prize** at an event in the auditorium. The number two student doesn't receive anything. **For two years in a row**, Felicia has been selected as the top student, but **it is not likely that** she will win this year because of a few low scores on tests. Although Gary **is excited to win the award** at last, he knows how important it is to Felicia and how disappointed she is. Gary wants to say something to Felicia to **help make her feel better**. In this situation, what would Gary most likely say to Felicia?

여: Gary와 Felicia는 반에서 1, 2등을 다투는 학생들이다. 매년, 한 학생이 반 대표가 되고 강당에서 열리는 행사에서 특별상을 받는다. 2등 학생은 아무것도 받지 못한다. 지난 2년간 Felicia가 연속해서 최고 학생으로 선출되었지만, 올해는 몇 가지 시험에서 낮은 점수를 받아 그녀가 선출될 확률이 적다. Gary는 마침내 상을 타게 되어 기쁘지만, Felicia에게 이 상이 얼마나 중요한지 그리고 그녀가 얼마나 실망한지를 안다. Gary는 Felicia가 기분이 나아지는 데 도움이 될 말을 해주고 싶다. 이러한 상황에서, Gary가 Felicia에게 할 말로 가장 적절한 것은 무엇인가?

어휘 **in a row** 연속적으로, 잇따라

16~17 세트 문항 | 16. ② 17. ⑤

▶ 16. 불면증을 치료하는 방법으로 명상과 좋은 침실 환경 조성을 제시하고 있다.

① 올바르게 명상하기 위한 지침
② 불면증을 줄이는 효과적인 방법
③ 잠이 학업 성적에 미치는 영향
④ 침실 환경이 수면에 중요한 이유
⑤ 수면 장애의 다양한 원인과 증상

▶ 17. 해석 참조

M: Do you struggle to get to sleep **no matter how tired you are**? Or do you often wake up in the middle of the night? Sleeplessness is a common problem. Fortunately, there are a few different ways to **deal with sleeplessness**. First of all, meditation is used to treat sleeplessness because meditation techniques **relax the body and mind**. Since natural relaxation is the key to successful meditation, meditation should not be forced. Some experts recommend meditating for about 20 minutes before going to bed, while others recommend meditating in bed. Both techniques can work well and the effects can be the same. **Having a good bedroom environment** is also very important. Make sure that your room is dark enough. **Turn the lights off** and close the curtains. Noise does not help you sleep well. Use earplugs to **block unwanted noise**. If your room is too warm, lower the temperature by using a fan or opening a window. Finally, beds should be comfortable. Replace them when they become worn and squeak when you sit or lay on them.

남: 아무리 피곤해도 잠들기 힘드십니까? 혹은 한밤중에 종종 잠이 깨곤 하십니까? 불면증은 흔한 문제입니다. 다행히도 불면증에 대처할 다양한 방법이 몇 가지 있습니다. 우선, 불면증을 치료하는 데 명상이 이용되는데, 명상 기법이 몸과 마음의 긴장을 풀어주기 때문입니다. 자연스러운 이완이 성공적인 명상의 비결이므로 명상은 강요되어서는 안 됩니다. 일부 전문가들은 잠자리에 들기 전 약 20분 동안 명상할 것을 권하는 반면, 다른 전문가들은 침대에서 명상할 것을 권합니다. 두 기법 모두 잘 작용할 수 있으며 효과도 똑같을 수 있습니다. 좋은 침실 환경을 조성하는 것 또한 매우 중요합니다. 반드시 방을 충분히 어둡게 만드십시오. ① 조명을 끄고 커튼을 치십시오. 소음은 잠을 잘 자는 데 도움이 되지 않습니다. 원치 않는 소음을 차단하기 위해 ② 귀마개를 사용하십시오. ③ 방이 너무 따뜻하면 선풍기를 사용하거나 창문을 열어서 온도를 낮추십시오. 마지막으로, 침대가 편안해야 합니다. ④ 침대가 낡아 그 위에 앉거나 누울 때 끼익 하는 소리가 나면 침대를 교체하십시오.

어휘 **meditate** 명상하다 / **sleeplessness** 불면증 / **disorder** (신체 기능의) 장애 / **relax** (긴장을) 풀게 하다; 휴식을 취하다 ***cf.* relaxation** 이완, 경감; 휴식 / **earplug** 귀마개 / **squeak** 끽[찍] 하는 소리를 내다

Answers & Explanation

01. ⑤ 02. ④ 03. ③ 04. ④ 05. ③ 06. ② 07. ③ 08. ② 09. ③ 10. ④
11. ③ 12. ③ 13. ① 14. ① 15. ⑤ 16. ③ 17. ④

01 화자가 하는 말의 목적 | ⑤

▶ 학교 시설 일부가 공사에 들어가기 때문에 출입금지구역으로 지정되었음을 알리고 있다.

W: Good morning, students. Welcome back. I hope you all enjoyed your vacations. Now, I have a special announcement. Thanks to the generosity of local businesses and to **your efforts to collect funds**, we have commenced the expansion and upgrade of the gymnasium, swimming pool, and auditorium. This means that **for the coming four months**, those areas will be off-limits to all students. Arrangements have been made for students to **have access to the facilities** at our junior campus; your homeroom teacher will **give you further details** after assembly. Under no circumstances will students be permitted onto the construction sites. They are dangerous areas and building workers **will not tolerate interruptions**.

여: 학생 여러분, 안녕하세요. 돌아온 것을 환영합니다. 모두 방학을 즐겁게 보냈으리라 생각합니다. 이제 특별 발표를 하겠습니다. 지역 기업들의 후원과 기금을 마련하기 위한 여러분의 노력 덕분에, 저희는 체육관과 수영장, 그리고 강당을 증축하고 개조하는 공사에 착수하였습니다. 이는 앞으로 4개월 동안 모든 학생이 그 구역들에 출입할 수 없을 것이라는 뜻입니다. 학생들이 저학년 캠퍼스의 시설을 이용할 수 있도록 조치를 취했습니다. 담임선생님께서 조회 후에 자세한 사항을 더 알려줄 것입니다. 어떤 경우에도 학생들은 공사장에 출입해서는 안 될 것입니다. 그곳은 위험한 지역이고 건설 근로자들도 방해하는 것을 허용하지 않을 것입니다.

어휘 **generosity** 후원, 아량, 관용 / **commence** ~을 개시하다, 시작하다 / **expansion** 확장 / **upgrade** 개선 / **off-limits** 출입금지의 / **arrangement** 준비, 마련; 조정, 협의 / **have access to** ~에 접근할 수 있다 / **assembly** (학교에서의) 조회 / **under no circumstances** 어떠한 일이 있어도 결코 ~이 아니다 / **tolerate** ~을 허용하다, 견디다 / **interruption** 방해

02 의견 | ④

▶ 남자는 원출처에 대한 참고 문헌을 밝히지 않고 문장들을 베낀 것이 큰 문제라고 하면서 인용한 문장의 출처를 밝히라고 말하고 있다.

W: I finally finished my term paper.
M: Good. Do you want me to review your paper before you hand it in to your professor?
W: Yes, please. Because it's my first semester as an exchange student, there must be **a lot of grammatical mistakes** in my paper.
M: Okay! Let me see. Hmm, Heidi, you copied some sentences **without giving any references** to the original source.
W: What do you mean?
M: I mean it's wrong to copy someone else's sentence without citation. Your professor will think you steal other people's ideas.
W: Really? I didn't know that would be such a big problem.
M: Well, it's a huge problem. You should write **where you took these sentences from**.
W: Thanks for telling me. I guess I should rewrite the paper.

여: 내가 마침내 학기말 리포트를 끝냈어.
남: 잘했어. 네가 교수님께 그걸 제출하기 전에 내가 네 보고서를 검토하길 바라니?
여: 응, 부탁이야. 교환학생으로 내 첫 학기이기 때문에 내 보고서에 틀림없이 문법적 실수가 많을 거야.
남: 좋아! 어디 보자. 음, Heidi, 너는 원출처에 대한 참고 문헌을 말하지 않고 일부 문장들을 베꼈구나.
여: 무슨 뜻이니?
남: 내 말은 인용 없이 누군가의 문장을 베끼는 것이 잘못이라는 뜻이야. 네 교수님은 네가 다른 사람의 아이디어를 훔치는 것으로 생각하실 거야.
여: 정말이야? 난 그게 그렇게 큰 문제가 되리라는 것을 몰랐어.
남: 글쎄, 그건 큰 문제야. 넌 이 문장들을 어디서 가져왔는지 적어야 해.
여: 알려줘서 고마워. 보고서를 다시 써야 할 것 같아.

어휘 **term paper** 학기말 리포트 / **semester** 학기 / **exchange student** 교환 학생 / **give reference to** ~에 관해 말하다 / **citation** 인용 / **rewrite** 다시 쓰다, 고쳐 쓰다

03 관계 | ③

▶ 순찰을 하느라 차 사고가 난 것을 몰랐다는 남자의 말과, 경비실에 남자가 (있을 줄 알았는데) 없었다는 여자의 말에서 남자는 경비원임을 알 수 있다. 또한, 남자의 말, You have lived in this apartment for almost 5 years.에서 여자는 아파트 주민임을 알 수 있다.

W: Hello, Mr. Smith. Can I talk to you for a second?
M: Sure. Is there something wrong?
W: Yes. Last night, someone **hit my car and disappeared** without leaving a note.
M: That's terrible. When did you find out?
W: At about 9 last night. I was **returning home from work**.
M: I had no idea. **I was on patrol at that time**.
W: I know. I went to the security office as soon as I found out, but you weren't there.
M: Then, I'll check the parking lot's security camera first. It's in my office.
W: OK. You know **where I usually park my car**, right?
M: Of course. **You have lived in this apartment** for almost 5 years.
W: If you find someone, please call my place. I'll stay home today.
M: No problem.

여: 안녕하세요, Smith 씨. 잠깐 얘기 좀 할 수 있을까요?
남: 그럼요. 무슨 문제라도 있으신가요?
여: 네. 지난밤에 누군가 제 차를 치고는 메모도 남기지 않고 사라져 버렸어요.
남: 끔찍하군요. 언제 알게 되셨나요?
여: 어젯밤 아홉 시쯤에요. 회사에서 집으로 돌아오는 중이었어요.
남: 몰랐네요. 저는 그때 순찰을 하고 있었거든요.
여: 알아요. 제가 알게 되자마자 경비실로 갔지만, 그곳에 안 계시더군요.
남: 그러면, 제가 주차장에 있는 보안 카메라를 먼저 확인해 볼게요. 제 사무실에 있어요.
여: 알았어요. 제가 평소 차를 어디에 주차하는지 아시죠, 맞죠?
남: 물론입니다. 당신은 이 아파트에 거의 5년 동안 살고 계시잖아요.
여: 누군가를 발견하면, 저희 집으로 전화 주세요. 오늘은 집에 있을 거예요.
남: 문제없어요.

어휘 **patrol** 순찰(대); 순찰을 돌다

04 그림 불일치 | ④

▶ Jenny는 키보드를 치며 노래를 하고 있다고 했는데 그림에는 키보드가 없으므로 ④가 일치하지 않는다.

W: Wow, Ted! Is this your band's poster?
M: Yeah. It's for our regular fund-raising concert for an orphanage. What do you think?
W: It's great. But **why did you cross out** "Helping" from the title on top?
M: Our band is about having fun. We don't play **out of pity**.
W: I see. That's why you put "Having Fun With" above the original.
M: Right. And below it, there's a picture of us enjoying a performance **with the kids in the orphanage**.
W: You look excited. Who's the man **holding drum sticks** in the lower-left corner?
M: That's Ron, our drummer. And you know Jenny, right? That's her in the middle, playing the keyboard and singing.
W: Yes, I like her voice. Oh, is that you playing guitar to the right of her?
M: Right. How do I look?
W: You look professional **now that you wear sunglasses**.
M: Thanks.

여: 와, Ted! 이거 네 밴드 포스터니?
남: 응. 보육원을 위한 기금 마련 정기 콘서트용이야. 어때?
여: 멋져. 그런데 위에 있는 제목에서 왜 'Helping'에 줄을 그어서 지웠니?
남: 우리 밴드는 즐기기 위한 거야. 우린 동정심으로 연주하지 않아.
여: 그렇구나. 그래서 원래 글자 위에 'Having Fun With'를 넣은 거구나.
남: 맞아. 그리고 그 아래에는 보육원 아이들과 공연을 즐기는 우리 사진이 있어.
여: 너 신이 나 보이는구나. 왼쪽 아래 구석에 드럼 스틱을 잡고 있는 남자는 누구야?

남: 우리 드럼연주자인 Ron이야. 그리고 너 Jenny 알지, 맞지? 가운데에서 키보드 치며 노래 부르는 사람이 Jenny야.
여: 응, 난 그녀의 목소리가 마음에 들어. 아, Jenny 오른쪽에 기타를 치고 있는 사람이 너야?
남: 맞아. 나 어때?
여: 선글라스를 쓰니까 전문적으로 보여.
남: 고마워.

어휘 **fund-raising** (정당·자선단체의) 모금 활동(의), 자금 조달(의) / **cross out** 줄을 그어 지우다 / **orphanage** 보육원, 고아원

05 추후 행동 | ③

▶ 남자는 공사 시간대를 재조정하기 위해 공사 업체에 전화하겠다고 했다.

M: Honey. What's that in your hand?
W: It's a complaint letter from Mr. Smith, one of our neighbors.
M: A complaint letter? Why?
W: He said the noise from our home renovations **is disturbing him**, especially in the mornings.
M: I don't think 8 a.m. is **an inappropriate time to begin work**.
W: I agree with you, but we should consider his situation.
M: Hmm.... I guess we don't have a choice. I'll call the builders **to rearrange the working hours** for the construction.
W: Okay. In the meantime, I'll **explain the situation to our neighbors** and ask them to understand.
M: Sounds good. Oh, and be especially apologetic to Mr. Smith.
W: I will.

남: 여보, 손에 있는 건 뭐예요?
여: 우리 이웃 중 한 명인 Smith 씨한테서 온 항의 편지예요.
남: 항의 편지요? 왜요?
여: 우리 집을 수리하며 나는 소음이 그를 방해한다고 했어요, 특히 아침에요.
남: 오전 여덟 시가 공사를 시작하기 부적절한 시간인 것 같진 않은데요.
여: 저도 동의하지만, 우리는 그의 입장을 고려해야 해요.
남: 음…. 우리에겐 선택의 여지가 없는 것 같군요. 공사 작업 시간대를 재조정하라고 공사 업체에 전화할게요.
여: 알겠어요. 그동안에, 저는 우리 이웃들에게 상황을 설명하고 양해를 구할게요.
남: 좋은 생각이에요. 아, Smith 씨에게는 특별히 사과해 주세요.
여: 그럴게요.

어휘 **renovation** 수리, 수선; 혁신, 쇄신 / **inappropriate** 부적절한, 부적합한 / **builder** 건축 회사, 건축업자; ~을 만드는[개발하는] 사람[것] / **rearrange** (행사 시간·날짜·장소 등을) 재조정하다; ~을 재배열[배치]하다; (몸의 자세를) 바꾸다 / **in the meantime** 그동안[사이]에 / **apologetic** 미안해하는, 사과하는

06 금액 | ②

▶ 여자는 20달러인 티셔츠를 30달러인 티셔츠로 교환할 것이므로 차액인 10달러와, 켤레당 5달러에서 20퍼센트 할인된 양말을 두 켤레 사겠다고 했으므로 8달러를 지불해야 한다. 따라서 여자가 지불할 총금액은 18달러이다.

W: Excuse me. Could I exchange this T-shirt **for another one**?
M: Why do you want to exchange it?
W: Actually, my sister bought this one for my son in this shop, but he doesn't like its pattern.
M: Oh, I see. We have many different T-shirts here. I'm sure you can find one you like.
W: Let me see.... Oh, **this will look good on my son**. The white puppy on the chest is so cute. How much is this?
M: It's thirty dollars.
W: **How much more do I have to pay**, then?
M: The T-shirt you brought back is twenty dollars. So you only **have to pay the rest**.
W: Okay. **I'll put it on my card**. Oh, these socks are cute. How much is a pair?
M: Their original price was five dollars, but they're 20 percent off now.
W: Okay. I'll buy two pairs then.

여: 실례합니다. 이 티셔츠를 다른 것으로 교환할 수 있을까요?
남: 왜 교환하고 싶으세요?
여: 실은 제 여동생이 우리 아들에게 주려고 이 가게에서 이 옷을 샀는데요, 아이가 옷의 무늬를 좋아하지 않아서요.
남: 아, 그렇군요. 여기 다른 티셔츠가 많이 있어요. 분명히 손님 마음에 드는 것을 찾으실 수 있을 거예요.
여: 어디 보자…. 아, 이게 우리 아들에게 잘 어울릴 거예요. 가슴에 있는 하얀 강아지가 아주 귀엽네요. 이건 얼마예요?
남: 30달러예요.
여: 그러면 제가 얼마를 더 내야 하죠?
남: 손님이 다시 가져오신 티셔츠가 20달러예요. 그러니 나머지만 내시면 돼요.
여: 알겠어요. 제 카드로 계산할게요. 아, 이 양말 귀엽네요. 한 켤레에 얼마예요?
남: 원래 가격은 5달러였는데, 지금은 20퍼센트 할인 중입니다.
여: 알겠어요. 그러면 두 켤레 살게요.

07 이유 | ③

▶ 남자는 엘리베이터가 고장 나서 안에 갇히는 바람에 회의에 참석하지 못했다.

W: Greg, you missed the morning meeting!
M: I know, and I **was supposed to present** the sales report in the meeting.
W: Come to think of it, you're never late. What happened?
M: Well, I left home early because I wanted to review some materials for the meeting.
W: I did the same thing, and I was surprised that **traffic wasn't as bad as usual**.
M: Right. Everything went smoothly until I arrived at our office building.
W: Then what was it? Did you forget your report?
M: No, the elevator **suddenly stopped working and I was stuck**.
W: Oh, no! How did you get out of there?
M: I rang the bell and **waited for help**. It took almost an hour to get out.
W: That's terrible. I'll ask the maintenance department to check the other elevators.
M: Good idea.

여: Greg, 당신 아침 회의를 놓쳤어요!
남: 저도 알아요. 그리고 회의에서 매출 보고서를 발표하기로 되어 있었죠.
여: 그러고 보니, 당신은 절대 늦지 않잖아요. 무슨 일이 있었나요?
남: 음, 회의를 위해 몇 가지 자료를 검토하고 싶어서 일찍 집을 나섰어요.
여: 저도 집에서 일찍 나왔어요, 또 교통이 평소처럼 나쁘지 않아서 놀랐어요.
남: 맞아요. 제가 회사 건물에 도착할 때까지 모든 것이 순조롭게 흘러갔어요.
여: 그러고 무슨 일이 있었나요? 당신 보고서를 잊어버렸나요?
남: 아니요, 엘리베이터가 갑자기 작동을 멈춰서 갇혀 버렸어요.
여: 아, 이런! 거기서 어떻게 나왔어요?
남: 벨을 누르고 도움을 기다렸죠. 나오는 데 거의 한 시간이 걸렸어요.
여: 끔찍하네요. 관리부에 다른 엘리베이터들을 확인해 달라고 요청할게요.
남: 좋은 생각이에요.

어휘 **come to think of it** 그러고 보니 / **stuck** (불쾌한 장소에) 갇힌 / **maintenance** (기계 등을 정기적으로) 관리, 유지, 보수

08 언급하지 않은 것 | ②

▶ 해석 참조

M: Stacy, I changed my cell phone's background picture. What do you think?
W: Wow! The scenery is so beautiful! Where did you get this picture?
M: I took it myself. It's from my family trip to Dam-yang last month.
W: Great. The windmill beside the farm **looks perfect below the mountains**.
M: I think so, too. I especially **like the clouds against the blue sky**. The weather was so nice.
W: By the way, why are there only four icons at the bottom? Don't you use other applications?
M: Sure, but I deleted their icons for simplicity.
W: I see. *[pause]* Then, I think **the letters on the screen** are too small.
M: Hmm. It's fine for me. **If the letters were bigger than now**, they would block the picture.
W: Oh, I didn't think of that.

남: Stacy, 나 휴대 전화의 배경 사진을 바꿨어. 어때?
여: 와! 풍경이 정말 아름다워! 이 사진 어디서 났니?
남: 내가 직접 찍었어. 지난달에 담양으로 간 가족 여행에서 찍은 거야(① 배경화면 사진의 출처).

여: 멋지다. 산 아래 농장 옆에 있는 풍차(③ 배경화면 사진의 풍경)가 아주 멋있어 보여.
남: 나도 그렇게 생각해. 푸른 하늘을 배경으로 한 구름(③ 배경화면 사진의 풍경)이 특히 마음에 들어. 날씨가 정말 좋았어.
여: 그런데, 왜 (화면) 아래에 아이콘이 네 개(④ 아이콘 개수)뿐이야? 다른 응용 프로그램은 사용하지 않니?
남: 사용하지만, 간결함을 위해 그 아이콘들은 삭제했어.
여: 그렇구나. *[잠시 후]* 그리고 화면의 글자가 너무 작은 것 같아(⑤ 글자 크기).
남: 음. 나한텐 괜찮아. 글자가 지금보다 더 크면, 사진을 가릴 거야.
여: 아. 그건 생각하지 못했어.

어휘 **windmill** 풍차; (풍력 발전용) 풍차 터빈 / **application** ((약어: app)) 응용 프로그램; 지원(서); 적용, 응용 / **simplicity** 간단함, 평이함 (↔ complexity 복잡함); 소박함, 순박함

09 내용 불일치 | ③

▶ East Lake 록 페스티벌의 수익금은 전액이 아닌 상당 부분만이 불우이웃을 돕는 데 쓰인다고 했다.

M: If you're tired of **attending the typical concert**, you'll love the East Lake Rock Festival. Unlike concerts that force you to stand for long periods of time, the East Lake Rock Festival **lets you reserve a mat in advance**. This also means you can bring food or drink and eat a picnic lunch while enjoying the music. Plus, a significant portion of the profits **are used to help the needy**, so you can feel good about yourself too. **The concert is being held** this Saturday and Sunday at the East Lake Park. It's an annual event, but don't wait until next year to enjoy it!

남: 틀에 박힌 콘서트에 가는 것이 지겨우시다면, East Lake 록 페스티벌을 아주 좋아하실 것입니다. 오랜 시간 동안 서 있게 만드는 콘서트와는 달리, East Lake 록 페스티벌은 당신이 돗자리를 미리 예약하시도록 해드립니다. 이는 또한 음식이나 마실 것을 가져와서 음악을 즐기면서 소풍 도시락을 먹을 수 있다는 것을 뜻합니다. 게다가, 수익금의 상당 부분이 불우이웃을 돕는 데 쓰이므로, 자신에 대해 뿌듯함도 느낄 수 있습니다. 이 콘서트는 East Lake 공원에서 이번 주 토요일과 일요일에 열릴 것입니다. 연례행사이지만, 즐기는 것을 내년까지 미루지 마세요!

어휘 **portion** 부분; (음식의) 1인분; (부분·몫으로) 나누다 / **the needy** 불우이웃, 빈민

10 도표 이해 | ④

▶ 여자는 남자가 가장 처음에 권한 노트북 컴퓨터보다 램이 큰 것을 원한다고 했으므로, 16기가바이트인 것 중에서 가격이 1,000달러 미만이며 화면이 더 큰 것을 살 것이다.

M: What are you looking at, Alice?
W: Some laptop computers. I want to buy one to take to college next month.
M: I see. So why not **pick the cheapest one**?
W: That was my first choice, but I really need more RAM than that.
M: Then what about this model? It has 16 gigabytes of RAM and the largest screen.
W: It's too expensive. I **can't afford to spend more than** $1,000.
M: That narrows it down to two.
W: Right. What do you think of this one, then?
M: Hmm. Look here. The other one is cheaper and **comes with a free mouse**.
W: I know, but I really want a larger screen for watching movies.
M: It sounds like **you've made up your mind**.
W: I have. Thanks.

남: 뭘 보고 있니, Alice?
여: 노트북 컴퓨터야. 다음 달에 대학에 가져갈 것을 하나 사고 싶어.
남: 그렇구나. 그럼 가장 저렴한 것을 고르는 게 어때?
여: 처음에 그것을 골랐는데, 난 그것보다 더 (용량이) 큰 램이 정말 필요해.
남: 그러면 이 모델은 어때? 램이 16기가바이트이고 화면도 가장 크네.
여: 그건 너무 비싸. 나는 1,000달러 이하로 써야 해.
남: 그러면 두 개로 좁혀지네.
여: 맞아. 그러면 이건 어떨 것 같아?
남: 음, 여기 봐. 나머지 하나가 더 싸고 공짜 마우스가 딸려 와.
여: 알아. 하지만 나는 영화를 보려면 더 큰 화면이 꼭 있었으면 해.
남: 너 결정한 것 같구나.
여: 결정했어. 고마워.

11 짧은 대화에 이어질 응답 | ③

▶ Kelly의 생일 파티가 오후 여섯 시에 시작하는지를 묻는 여자의 물음에 가장 적절한 응답을 고른다.

① 네가 (쿠키를) 좀 더 만들도록 도와줄게.
② 응, 파티는 정말 재미있었어.
③ 실은, 일곱 시로 연기되었어.
④ 우리는 Kelly를 위해 쿠키를 좀 남겨 두어야 해.
⑤ 안타깝지만, 그 애는 땅콩 알레르기가 있어.

W: Wow, **these cookies look so yummy**! Are they for Kelly's birthday party?
M: Yes. I heard peanut butter cookies are her favorite.
W: She'll love them. **The party starts at 6 p.m.**, doesn't it?
M: ______________________________

여: 와, 이 쿠키들 정말 맛있어 보인다! Kelly의 생일 파티에 쓸 거야?
남: 응. Kelly가 땅콩버터 쿠키를 가장 좋아한다고 들었거든.
여: 그 애가 정말 좋아할 거야. 파티는 오후 여섯 시에 시작하지, 그렇지?
남: ______________________________

어휘 **allergic** (~에 대해) 알레르기가 있는; 알레르기성의 / **yummy** 아주 맛있는

12 짧은 대화에 이어질 응답 | ③

▶ 기부금이 작년보다 줄어든 것 같다며 고민하고 있는 여자에게 남자는 거의 20퍼센트나 떨어졌다고 말하고 있다. 이에 여자가 할 가장 적절한 응답을 고른다.

① 이 자선단체는 지역 사회에 중요해.
② 네가 내년에는 더 많이 기부할 수 있길 바라.
③ 그것 참 심하다. (작년과의) 차이점이 무엇인지 궁금해.
④ 내가 작년만큼 기부할 수 없어서 유감이야.
⑤ 깜짝 놀랐어. 우리가 작년에 정말 잘했다고 생각했는데.

M: You look serious. Do you have a problem?
W: I think our charity **is receiving fewer donations this year** compared with last year.
M: You're right. Donations here **have dropped by almost 20 percent**.
W: ______________________________

남: 심각해 보인다. 무슨 문제 있니?
여: 우리 자선단체가 작년에 비해 올해 더 적은 기부금을 받고 있는 것 같아.
남: 네 말이 맞아. 이곳의 기부금이 거의 20퍼센트나 떨어졌어.
여: ______________________________

13 긴 대화에 이어질 응답 | ①

▶ 내일 당장 차가 필요하지만 정비소에서 찾아오지 않은 여자가 남자에게 어떻게 해야 할지 묻고 있으므로 그에 대한 해결책을 제시하는 반응이 답으로 적절하다.

① 저녁 먹고 내가 가서 차를 가져올게요.
② 물론이죠. Steven 씨는 차를 더 빨리 수리할 수 있어요.
③ 내가 요리와 청소를 잘한다는 거 당신도 알잖아요.
④ 당신이 우리 차를 쓸 수 있도록 나는 버스로 출퇴근할게요.
⑤ Amanda를 위한 관광 명소를 몇 곳 추천할게요.

[Doorbell rings.]
M: Hi, honey. Did anything happen while I was out?
W: My niece, Amanda, just called me. She's going to be here for New Year's Day tomorrow.
M: That's nice. **Ask her to stay here**, and tell her we'll take her sightseeing in the city.
W: I already did. I love that she's coming, but I don't **have much time to prepare for her visit**.
M: Don't worry about it. **I'll clean up the guest room**.
W: Thanks, and I'll make some food. *[pause]* Oh, my! Our car is still at Steven's repair shop. We really need it **to show her around the city**.
M: When will the repair work be finished?
W: It's already done, but **I forgot to pick it up**.
M: I understand. You've been so busy recently.
W: Then what should we do?
M: ______________________________

[초인종이 울린다.]
남: 안녕, 여보. 내가 외출한 사이에 무슨 일 있었어요?
여: 제 조카 Amanda가 조금 전에 전화했어요. 새해 첫날을 맞으러 내일 여기에 온대요.
남: 잘됐네요. Amanda에게 우리 집에 묵으라고 하고, 우리가 시내 구경을 시켜줄 거라고 말하고요.
여: 이미 그렇게 말했어요. Amanda가 온다니 좋긴 한데, 그 애의 방문에 준비할 시간이 많지 않네요.
남: 그건 걱정하지 마요. 손님방은 내가 청소할게요.
여: 고마워요. 그러면 나는 음식을 좀 만들게요. *[잠시 후]* 이런! 우리 차가 아직 Steven 씨네 정비소에 있어요. Amanda에게 시내 구경을 시켜주려면 차가 꼭 필요한데 말이에요.
남: 수리는 언제 끝나요?
여: 이미 끝났는데 가져오는 걸 깜빡했어요.
남: 이해해요. 당신 요즘 무척 바빴잖아요.
여: 그럼 어떡하죠?
남: ____________________

어휘 **commute** 통근하다; 통근 / **tourist attraction** 관광 명소

14 긴 대화에 이어질 응답 | ①

▶ 남자는 오늘 안에 발표 내용을 줄이고 준비까지 마칠 수 있을지 물었으므로 이에 가장 적절한 응답을 고른다.

① 일을 분담한다면 충분해.
② 우리가 함께 작업해서 기뻐.
③ 주말에는 네가 그것을 요약하는 것을 도와줄 수 없어.
④ 다음번에는 반드시 요점을 고수할게.
⑤ 이 발표에 대한 우리 제한 시간이 너무 엄격해.

M: Thank you for listening to my presentation. *[pause]* So, how did I do?
W: It wasn't bad, but I think **it could be improved**.
M: I see. Were there many errors?
W: No. The contents were great, but you exceeded the time limit.
M: Oh, well, I just wanted to **explain our topic in detail**.
W: Our teacher said she will place a lot of importance **on sticking to the time limit** of the presentation.
M: That's a good point.
W: So, I think the only option is **to shorten the presentation**.
M: You're right, but I don't see how.
W: Well, we just **need to summarize some of the details**.
M: Do we have enough time today to finish that and prepare?
W: ____________________

남: 제 발표를 들어주셔서 감사합니다. *[잠시 후]* 자, 나 어땠어?
여: 나쁘진 않았는데, 개선할 수 있을 것 같아.
남: 알겠어. 실수를 많이 했니?
여: 아니. 내용은 훌륭했는데, 제한 시간을 초과했어.
남: 아, 음, 우리 주제를 자세하게 설명하고 싶었을 뿐인데.
여: 우리 선생님께서는 발표 제한 시간을 지키는 것을 매우 중요하게 생각할 거라고 하셨잖아.
남: 좋은 지적이야.
여: 그래서 우리가 선택할 수 있는 건 발표를 줄이는 것뿐인 것 같아.
남: 네 말이 맞아. 그런데 어떻게 해야 할지 모르겠어.
여: 음, 세부 내용의 일부를 요약하기만 하면 돼.
남: 오늘 그것을 마치고 준비할 시간이 충분해?
여: ____________________

어휘 **summarize** ~을 요약하다 / **stick to** ~을 고수하다[지키다]; ~을 계속하다 / **exceed** ~을 넘다, 초과하다 / **shorten** ~을 짧게 하다, 단축하다; 짧아지다

15 상황에 적절한 말 | ⑤

▶ Jenna는 화를 참지 못하는 Tim을 위로하는 동시에 화를 넘기는 법을 배워야 한다고 충고할 것이다.

① Paul이 그런 말을 한 것은 잘못이었어.
② 미안해. 그렇게 화를 내지 말았어야 했는데.
③ 걱정하지 마. 내가 Paul에게 이야기해서 이 상황을 해결할게.
④ 다음번에는, 네 기분이 정말 어떤지 설명하는 것을 망설이지 마.
⑤ 이해하지만, (화가 나더라도) 화를 넘기는 것을 배워야 해.

W: Jenna is waiting outside of a movie theater for her friend Tim. When Tim arrives, he looks upset and Jenna asks what is wrong. Tim explains that a coworker named Paul **made some rude comments** about his report. Tim tried to ignore the comments but **was unable to control his anger**. Finally, Tim and Paul had an argument about the comments. Jenna understands Tim's situation and sympathizes with him, but she also worries that Tim will hurt himself **if he continues to respond in this way**. She wants to comfort Tim and advise him **not to express his emotions right away**. In this situation, what would Jenna most likely say to Tim?

여: Jenna는 영화관 밖에서 친구인 Tim을 기다리고 있다. Tim이 도착했을 때, 그의 기분이 안 좋아 보이자 Jenna는 무슨 일인지 묻는다. Tim은 Paul이라는 동료가 자신의 보고서에 관해 무례한 말을 했다고 설명한다. Tim은 그 말을 무시하려고 노력했지만, 자신의 화를 참을 수 없었다. 결국, Tim과 Paul은 그 말에 관해 말다툼을 했다. Jenna는 Tim의 상황을 이해하고 그에게 공감하지만, 그가 계속 이런 식으로 반응하면 스스로를 다치게 할까 봐 걱정되기도 한다. 그녀는 Tim을 위로하고 감정을 곧바로 드러내지 말라고 충고하고 싶다. 이러한 상황에서 Jenna가 Tim에게 할 말로 가장 적절한 것은 무엇인가?

어휘 **lose A's temper** 화를 내다; 흥분하다 / **sympathize** ((**with**)) 공감하다; 동정하다; 지지하다

16~17 세트 문항 | 16. ③ 17. ④

▶ 16. 부모로서 아이의 인성 발달을 돕는 방법에 관해 조언하고 있다.

① 직업적인 성공에 미치는 취미의 영향
② 아이들의 정신적 건강에 미치는 부모의 영향
③ 아이의 인성을 기르는 것에 관한 필수적인 조언
④ 부모가 자녀들과 공유하기에 좋은 취미
⑤ 부모가 아이에게 관심을 보여야 하는 이유

▶ 17. 해석 참조

M: Children are not born with complete personalities. Instead, a personality is **something that develops over time**, and as parents, it is our duty to guide this development. Fortunately, this is not **as difficult as it might sound**. Start by listening to your children when they are trying to tell you something, and make time for them even when your schedule is busy. Children learn by imitation, so **you must be an example** of what you'd like your children to become. Also, you must pay attention to the development of certain aspects of your child's personality, such as confidence and self-esteem. In this regard, **hobbies are especially effective**. For example, soccer is a sound way for kids to make friends and learn about teamwork while exercising. Collecting things, such as stamps or rocks, **teaches kids about sorting and organization** while providing a sense of accomplishment. Acting is especially beneficial because children can see things from other points of view through role playing. Similarly, singing **builds confidence while stimulating emotional intelligence**. And you shouldn't forget that many children have gone on to transform their hobbies into professions later in life.

남: 아이들은 완벽한 인성을 가지고 태어나지 않습니다. 대신에, 인성은 시간이 흐르면서 발달하는 것이고, 이 발달을 지도하는 것이 부모로서 우리의 의무입니다. 다행스럽게도, 이것은 들리는 것처럼 어렵지 않습니다. 아이들이 당신에게 무언가를 말하려 할 때 그들의 말에 귀를 기울여줌으로써 시작하고, 당신의 일정이 빡빡할 때라도 아이들을 위해 시간을 내십시오. 아이들은 모방을 통해서 배우므로, 당신이 아이가 되었으면 하는 모습의 본보기가 되어야 합니다. 또한, 자신감과 자부심 같은 아이 인성의 특정 부분이 발달하는 데 주의를 기울여야 합니다. 이러한 점에서, 취미가 특히 효과적입니다. 예를 들어, ① 축구는 아이가 운동하며 친구를 만들고 협동에 관해 배우는 건전한 방법입니다. 우표나 돌과 같은 ② 물건을 수집하는 것은 아이에게 성취감을 주면서 분류와 체계성에 관해 가르칩니다. ③ 연기는 아이들이 역할극을 통해 다른 사람의 관점에서 사물을 바라볼 수 있기 때문에 특히 유익합니다. 마찬가지로, ⑤ 노래 부르기는 감성 지능을 활발하게 하면서 자신감을 길러줍니다. 그리고 많은 아이가 나이가 들어서 자신의 취미를 직업으로 바꾸었다는 것을 잊으면 안 됩니다.

어휘 **enhance** ~을 높이다[향상하다] / **self-esteem** 자부심; 자존(심) / **sorting** 분류, 구분 / **beneficial** 유익한, 이로운

Answers & Explanation

01. ④ 02. ④ 03. ② 04. ④ 05. ① 06. ③ 07. ⑤ 08. ⑤ 09. ④ 10. ②
11. ① 12. ⑤ 13. ② 14. ⑤ 15. ⑤ 16. ② 17. ④

01 화자가 하는 말의 목적 | ④

▶ 미국에 있는 컴퓨터 서버의 문제로 인해 컴퓨터로 치르는 시험이 갑자기 취소되었다는 내용이다.

W: I'd like to have your attention, please. I know you **have been waiting patiently to be informed** about what is happening. The problem is this testing center has been doing the same thing. We have been trying to **find out what the problem is**. What I can tell you is that the problem is not the computers on-site at this testing center. **The fault lies with a computer server** in America. The computer server is causing problems for testing centers throughout the world. Due to this problem we have been informed that **today's test cannot go on as planned**. The testing agency will announce new testing dates next week. We are really **sorry for the inconvenience**.

여: 여러분 주목해 주세요. 무슨 일이 일어나고 있는지 안내받기 위해 참을성 있게 기다리고 계신 것을 잘 압니다. 문제는 이 시험 센터도 똑같이 기다리고 있었다는 것입니다. 저희는 문제가 무엇인지 알아내기 위해 노력하고 있습니다. 제가 말씀드릴 수 있는 것은 이 시험 센터 현장에 있는 컴퓨터에 의한 문제는 아니라는 것입니다. 잘못은 미국에 있는 컴퓨터 서버에 있습니다. 미국의 컴퓨터 서버가 전 세계의 시험 센터에 문제를 야기하고 있습니다. 이 문제로 인해 저희는 오늘 시험이 계획한 대로 시행될 수 없음을 통보 받았습니다. 시험 대행사는 다음 주에 새 시험 일자를 발표할 것입니다. 불편을 끼쳐 드려 정말 죄송합니다.

어휘 **patiently** 참을성 있게 / **on-site** 현장의, 현지의 / **lie with** (책임이) ~에 있다

02 대화 주제 | ④

▶ 인터넷이 가진 익명성 때문에 사람들이 무책임하게 행동하기도 하지만, 반면에 언론과 표현의 자유를 누릴 수 있다고 이야기하고 있다.

W: Oh, no! Have you seen the terrible comments that people have written below the video I posted?
M: Yeah, I did. That's unfortunate, but you just **have to ignore them**.
W: They wouldn't have said these things to my face. They only did it because they knew **they couldn't be punished**.
M: That's the downside of having anonymity on the Internet. Some people behave irresponsibly when **their identities are hidden**.
W: I guess that means you think there is an upside?
M: Of course. Anonymity allows people to say unpopular things that need to be said. Freedom of speech and expression is also a very important thing.
W: You have a good point, but I'm still **upset by those comments**.
M: Trust me, your video was great.

여: 아, 이런! 내가 올린 동영상에 사람들이 쓴 끔찍한 댓글들 봤어?
남: 응, 봤어. 불쾌하긴 하지만, 그냥 무시해야 해.
여: 내 얼굴에 대고는 이런 말을 하지 않았을 거야. 자기들이 처벌받을 수 없다는 걸 알기 때문에 그랬을 뿐이야.
남: 그건 인터넷 익명성의 부정적인 면이야. 어떤 사람들은 자기 신분이 감춰졌을 때 무책임하게 행동하니까.
여: 긍정적인 면도 있다고 생각한다는 뜻인 것 같네?
남: 물론이지. 익명성이 있기 때문에, 사람들이 할 필요가 있는 평이 좋지 않은 말들을 하게 되지. 언론과 표현의 자유 역시 아주 중요한 거니까.
여: 네 말도 일리가 있지만, 난 그 댓글들 때문에 아직도 속상해.
남: 날 믿어, 네 동영상은 훌륭했어.

어휘 **post** (웹사이트에) ~을 올리다, 게시하다 / **downside** 불리한 면 (↔ upside 괜찮은 면) / **anonymity** 익명성 / **irresponsibly** 무책임하게 / **unpopular** 평이 좋지 않은, 인기가 없는

03 관계 | ②

▶ 옷의 얼룩을 빼는 것에 대해 이야기하는 것으로 보아 세탁소에서 직원과 손님과의 대화로 볼 수 있다.

M: Here are your clothes, Mrs. Smith.
W: Thanks. Let's see... a sweater, a pair of pants and a white shirt.
M: That'll be $8.50.
W: OK. Oh, **were you able to get the big ink stain** out of Jenny's shirt?
M: Not completely. **I put a stain remover on it** and I cleaned it two times.
W: And it still didn't come out completely?
M: No, it didn't. But remember I didn't promise I could **remove it completely**?
W: I know. I guess I'll have to buy her another white shirt for school.
M: Probably. Look here, the ink stain is still quite visible.
W: **I wish she were more careful**. Anyway, here's $10.
M: Here's your change. Have a good day!

남: 옷이 여기 있습니다, Smith 부인.
여: 고마워요. 어디 보자… 스웨터, 바지 그리고 흰색 셔츠.
남: 모두 8달러 50센트입니다.
여: 네. 아, Jenny의 셔츠에 있던 커다란 잉크 얼룩을 뺄 수 있었나요?
남: 완전히 빼진 못했어요. 그 위에 얼룩 지우는 세제를 뿌리고 두 번이나 세탁했지만요.
여: 그런데도 여전히 완전하게 빠지지 않았다고요?
남: 네, 그렇습니다. 하지만 제가 완전히 제거할 수 있다고는 약속하지 않았다는 것을 기억하시죠?
여: 알아요. 학교에 입고 갈 흰색 셔츠를 하나 사 줘야겠네요.
남: 아마도요. 여기 보세요. 잉크 얼룩이 여전히 눈에 잘 띄죠?
여: 애가 좀 더 조심스러우면 좋겠어요. 어쨌든, 10달러 여기 있습니다.
남: 여기 잔돈이요. 좋은 하루 되세요!

어휘 **stain** 얼룩 / **visible** (육안으로) 볼 수 있는

04 그림 불일치 | ④

▶ 남자가 냅킨을 정찬용 접시 위에 두냐고 묻자, 여자가 그건 예전 방침이었고 이제는 포크 왼쪽에 놓는다고 했다.

W: All right, Dave. Now I'll show you **how to set the tables**.
M: Okay. I think the bread plate and butter knife usually go at the top left.
W: Yes, of course. We also **place a water glass at the top right**.
M: Should I set the forks to the left of the dinner plate?
W: Yes, that's correct. The dinner plate goes in the center and the forks go on the left.
M: Would you like me to **leave a napkin on the dinner plate**?
W: That was our policy, but now we place the napkin to the left of the forks.
M: No problem. Where should I place the knife and spoon?
W: Those go to the right of the dinner plate, like this. **Can you remember all of this**?
M: I think I've got it.

여: 자, Dave, 이제 테이블 세팅하는 법을 보여줄게요.
남: 네. 빵 접시와 버터나이프는 보통 왼쪽 위에 놓는 것 같네요.
여: 네, 물론이에요. 또 물 잔은 오른쪽 위에 놓지요.
남: 포크들은 정찬용 접시 왼쪽에 두어야 하나요?
여: 네, 맞아요. 정찬용 접시는 가운데에 놓고 포크들은 그 왼쪽에 놓습니다.
남: 냅킨을 정찬용 접시 위에 두기 원하시나요?
여: 그게 우리 방침이었는데, 이제는 포크 왼쪽에 냅킨을 놓습니다.
남: 알겠습니다. 나이프와 스푼은 어디에 둬야 할까요?
여: 이렇게, 정찬용 접시 오른쪽으로 놓습니다. 이거 다 기억할 수 있나요?
남: 모두 이해한 것 같습니다.

05 추후 행동 | ①

▶ 남자는 진로 문제로 고민하는 여자에게 학교 상담소에 가볼 것을 추천하며, 자신은 수업에 가야 하기 때문에 여자에게 상담소의 약도를 그려주겠다고 했다.

W: What are you going to do after graduation?
M: I've been accepted to a graduate program for computer science. How

about you?

W: Well, **I majored in** contemporary art, and I really want to be an artist.

M: You're very talented. I bet your parents are proud.

W: Actually, they want me to be a designer because **it's more profitable**. I don't know what to do.

M: You sound confused. In fact, **I had a similar decision to make**, and the school's counseling center was extremely helpful.

W: Really? Maybe I should give it a try. By the way, where is it?

M: It's a little hard to find. I'd take you there now, but I have a class. So, **why don't I draw a map for you**?

W: That'd be great. Use my notebook.

M: Okay. Just a second.

여: 졸업하고 뭐할 거니?
남: 나는 컴퓨터공학 대학원 과정에 입학 허가를 받았어. 너는?
여: 음, 나는 현대 미술을 전공했으니까 정말로 화가가 되고 싶어!
남: 너는 정말 재능이 있어. 부모님께서 분명 자랑스러워하시겠다.
여: 사실 부모님은 내가 디자이너가 되길 바라셔, 왜냐하면 돈을 더 많이 벌거든. 어떻게 해야 좋을지 모르겠어.
남: 혼란스러워 보이는구나. 사실 나도 비슷한 결정을 내려야 했었는데, 학교 상담소가 정말 큰 도움이 되었어.
여: 정말? 나도 한번 가봐야겠다. 그런데 상담소는 어디 있어?
남: 찾기가 조금 어려워. 너를 지금 거기에 데려다 주고 싶지만 수업이 있어. 그러니 내가 너를 위해 지도를 그려주면 어떨까?
여: 좋아. 내 노트를 써.
남: 그래. 잠깐만 (기다려).

어휘 **contemporary art** 현대 미술 / **profitable** 수익성이 있는 / **counseling center** 상담소

06 금액 | ③

▶ 여자가 티셔츠는 더 저렴한 5달러짜리를 구매하기로 했고, 모자는 이름과 로고가 인쇄되는 6달러짜리를 구매하기로 했다. 총 60명이 입을 예정이므로 여자가 지불할 총 금액은 660달러이다.

W: I need to order T-shirts and baseball caps for a summer camp for 50 kids.

M: No problem, ma'am. We have **two T-shirts to choose from**. This one is $5 and that one is $8.

W: **What's the difference**?

M: The more expensive one is 100% cotton. The other is a cotton polyester blend.

W: Hmm.... **I'll order the cheaper one**.

M: OK. And for the baseball caps, do you want plain ones or do you need **a design printed on them**? Plain ones are $4 each, and printed ones are $6 each.

W: Oh, on the caps, I want the name of the camp, "Outdoor Adventures," and this logo showing a man climbing a cliff.

M: Great. So you need 50 of each?

W: Actually, I need 60 of each. We have 10 support staff. We need shirts and caps for them, too.

여: 50명의 아이들이 여름 캠프에서 착용할 티셔츠와 야구 모자를 주문해야 해요.
남: 문제없습니다, 고객님. 선택하실 수 있는 티셔츠가 두 가지 있습니다. 이것은 5달러이고 저것은 8달러입니다.
여: 어떤 차이가 있나요?
남: 더 비싼 것은 면 100%입니다. 다른 것은 면과 폴리에스테르의 혼방이고요.
여: 음…. 더 저렴한 것을 주문할게요.
남: 알겠습니다. 그리고 야구 모자는 무늬가 없는 것을 원하십니까, 아니면 모자에 무늬가 인쇄되기를 원하십니까? 민무늬는 각각 4달러이고, 인쇄된 것은 각각 6달러입니다.
여: 아, 모자에 캠프 이름인 '야외모험'과 절벽을 올라가는 한 남자가 있는 이 로고가 필요해요.
남: 좋습니다. 그럼 각각 50개가 필요하신가요?
여: 사실은 각각 60개가 필요해요. 보조해주는 사람들이 10명 있거든요. 그 사람들이 착용할 셔츠와 모자도 필요해요.

어휘 **polyester** 폴리에스테르 섬유 / **blend** 혼합(물); ~을 섞다, 혼합하다 / **logo** (회사·조직의) 로고, 상징 / **staff** 직원

07 이유 | ⑤

▶ 남자의 휴대전화는 말레이시아에 있는 공인 서비스 센터가 아닌 곳에서 수리를 위해 개봉된 적이 있기에 이곳 서비스센터에서 수리를 받을 수 없을 거라고 했다.

W: How was your trip to Malaysia?

M: It was good, but my phone broke during the trip and the service center here **won't fix it**.

W: You just bought it last month. Didn't you get insurance?

M: I did, and the insurance **covers everything except water damage**.

W: Did your phone fall in the water? What happened?

M: No. It got a little rain on it, but **that's not a big deal**. Actually, it just stopped working one morning during the trip.

W: Then, why won't the service center fix it?

M: Well, I tried to fix it in Malaysia. The place looked official, but I guess it wasn't **an authorized center**.

W: Oh, insurance won't help you if your phone has been opened.

M: Exactly. Now I have to buy a new phone.

여: 말레이시아 여행 어땠어?
남: 좋았는데, 여행 중에 휴대전화가 망가졌고 여기 서비스 센터에서는 수리해주지 않을 거야.
여: 너 그거 겨우 지난달에 샀잖아. 보험 안 들었니?
남: 들었어, 그리고 보험은 침수 피해만 제외하고 다 보장해.
여: 휴대전화를 물속에 빠뜨렸니? 무슨 일이 있었던 거야?
남: 안 빠뜨렸어. 비를 좀 맞긴 했지만, 그건 별일 아냐. 사실, 여행 중 어느 날 아침에 작동이 그냥 멈춰버렸어.
여: 그럼, 서비스 센터에서는 왜 수리해주려고 하지 않는 건데?
남: 음, 말레이시아에서 수리하려고 했었어. 공식 수리점처럼 보였는데, 공인 서비스 센터가 아니었나 봐.
여: 아, 휴대전화가 개봉된 적이 있으면 보험이 도움이 안 되는구나.
남: 바로 그거야. 난 이제 휴대전화를 새로 사야 해.

어휘 **authorized** 공인된, 인정받은

08 언급하지 않은 것 | ⑤

▶ 해석 참조

M: Jatropha is a small tree, about three to five meters tall. Some people call it "a perfect plant" because it's useful and **extremely easy to cultivate**. It can grow almost anywhere, including harsh desert environments with very little water. The oil from its seeds can be made into biofuel, **which is already being used** in India and the Philippines. Plus, its strong roots can prevent land from turning into desert and protect crops from high winds. However, its strength is also **one of its drawbacks**. It can quickly take over land and dominate other species, which can **destroy the ecological balance of an area**. For this reason, many governments don't support planting jatropha trees **in spite of the benefits**.

남: 자트로파는 키가 3~5미터 정도 되는 작은 나무이다. 이것은 유용하고 재배하기 매우 쉽기 때문에 몇몇 사람은 '완벽한 식물'(① 별칭)이라고 부른다. 이 나무는 물이 거의 없는 척박한 사막 환경을 포함하여 거의 어디에서든 자랄 수 있다(② 재배 환경). 씨앗에서 나오는 기름은 생물연료로 만들어질 수 있으며(③ 씨앗 활용), 이는 인도와 필리핀에서 이미 사용되고 있다. 게다가, 단단한 뿌리는 토양이 사막화되는 것을 막으며 농작물을 강한 바람으로부터 보호(④ 재배 효과)할 수 있다. 그러나 이러한 강인함은 단점 중 하나이기도 하다. 이 나무는 땅을 재빨리 점령하고 다른 식물 종들도 제압할 수 있는데, 이 때문에 지역 생태계의 균형이 파괴될 수 있다. 이러한 이유로, 이점들에도 불구하고 많은 정부가 자트로파 나무 심기를 지지하지 않는다.

어휘 **extremely** 극도로, 극히 / **cultivate** (식물·작물을) 재배하다; (땅을) 경작하다 / **harsh** (날씨·환경이) 혹독한; 가혹한, 냉혹한 / **biofuel** 생물연료 / **drawback** 단점, 결점 / **dominate** (~을) 지배[군림]하다 / **ecological** 생태학적인, 생태상의

09 내용 불일치 | ④

▶ 커피와 차는 팔지만 뜨거운 음식은 판매하지 않는다고 말했다.

W: Welcome aboard the Thames Riverboat Cruise. It's a very scenic journey which will **give you many great opportunities** to take pictures of landmarks in the city, including the Tower Bridge and Big Ben. If you are taking the one-way cruise, it will last 1 hour and 20

minutes. If you are making a round-trip, it will last about 2 hours and 40 minutes. **For those of you who are hungry**, there is a snack bar on the boat. It only sells packaged snacks and drinks. It sells coffee and tea, but **it doesn't sell any hot food**. And, finally, please don't lose your ticket. You must show it **when getting off the boat**.

여: 템스 강 유람선을 타신 것을 환영합니다. 이 여행은 풍경이 아주 아름다운 여행으로, 타워 브리지와 빅벤을 포함해 도시의 역사적 명소를 사진으로 찍을 수 있는 멋진 기회를 많이 제공할 것입니다. 편도 유람선을 타시면 1시간 20분가량 걸릴 것입니다. 왕복을 하시면 2시간 40분 정도 걸릴 것입니다. 시장하신 분들을 위해 선상에 매점이 있습니다. 포장된 간식과 음료만 판매합니다. 커피와 차는 판매하지만, 뜨거운 음식은 판매하지 않습니다. 그리고 마지막으로, 표를 잃어버리지 마십시오. 배에서 내리실 때 보여주셔야 합니다.

어휘 **cruise** 유람선 여행 / **scenic** 경치가 아름다운 / **landmark** 역사적 건물, 유적 / **one-way** 편도의 / **round-trip** 왕복여행의 / **packaged** 포장된

10 도표 이해 | ②

▶ 남자는 70명 이상 수용 가능하며 시간당 300달러보다는 저렴하고, 빔프로젝터 시설이 갖추어진 방을 선택할 것이다.

W: Good afternoon. May I help you?
M: I would like to inquire about the rooms for **our upcoming conference** for native English teachers.
W: I see. When is the conference and **how many people will be attending it**, sir?
M: It's on June 10th, which is a Saturday, from 1 p.m. to 4 p.m., and we are expecting about 70 teachers to be there.
W: I see. We have the perfect place for your conference. The Crystal Room, with excellent conference equipment, can fit in 100 people for $300 an hour.
M: That's rather expensive. Don't you have anything cheaper?
W: Well, the Jade Room can seat up to 80 people and it's $250, and the Ruby Room is just $200 per hour, but only 70 people can sit in the room.
M: Both of them seem good. Could I have **the rates for the rest of the available rooms**?
W: Certainly. We have the Diamond Room, which is the largest at our center, and it can accommodate 200 people and the rate is $400. And our Sapphire Room can fit in 50 people, and we charge $100 for the room.
M: Neither of them is appropriate for our conference. Oh, I forgot to mention that we need a room **equipped with a beam projector**.
W: OK. It seems, then, there is only one room that you can choose.

여: 안녕하세요. 무엇을 도와드릴까요?
남: 곧 있을 원어민 영어교사 회의를 할 장소를 문의하고 싶습니다.
여: 알겠습니다. 회의가 언제이고 몇 분이나 참석하실 예정이십니까, 손님?
남: 토요일인 6월 10일 오후 1시부터 4시까지고, 선생님 약 70분이 오실 것으로 예상하고 있습니다.
여: 알겠습니다. 회의 장소로 완벽한 곳이 있습니다. 뛰어난 회의 시설을 갖춘 Crystal Room은 100명을 수용할 수 있고 시간당 300달러입니다.
남: 그건 다소 비싸네요. 좀 더 저렴한 회의실은 없습니까?
여: 음, Jade Room은 80명까지 앉을 수 있고 시간당 250달러이며, Ruby Room은 시간당 겨우 200달러이지만 70명만 앉을 수 있습니다.
남: 둘 다 괜찮을 것 같네요. 이용할 수 있는 나머지 회의실들의 요금도 알 수 있을까요?
여: 물론입니다. Diamond Room은 저희 센터에서 가장 큰 회의실로 200명을 수용할 수 있고 요금은 400달러입니다. 그리고 Sapphire Room은 50명에 알맞을 수 있고 100달러입니다.
남: 둘 다 우리 회의에는 적절하지 않군요. 아, 빔프로젝터 시설이 설치된 회의실이 필요하다고 말씀드리는 것을 잊어버렸네요.
여: 알겠습니다. 그럼 선택하실 수 있는 회의실이 하나밖에 없는 것 같네요.

어휘 **upcoming** 곧 있을, 다가오는 / **equipment** 장비, 용품 ***cf.* equip A with B** A에 B를 설치하다, A에게 B를 갖추게 하다 / **accommodate** ~을 수용하다, 공간을 제공하다

11 짧은 대화에 이어질 응답 | ①

▶ 시험 중에 옆 사람이 자신의 시험지를 베끼는 것을 본 여자가 선생님께 말씀드려야 하는지 묻고 있으므로 이에 적절한 응답을 찾는다.

① 네가 옳다고 생각하는 대로 해.
② 시험은 정말 너무 어려웠어.
③ 선생님께서는 네 낮은 점수에 화내실 거야.
④ 이번에는 네 실수를 눈감아 줄게.
⑤ 난 부정행위한 것을 정말 들키고 싶지 않아.

W: The girl beside me **cheated off my test** during the exam.
M: I guess Mrs. Bean didn't see, or she **would have been really upset**.
W: I know... Do you think I should tell her what I saw?
M: ______________________________

여: 시험 중에 옆에 앉은 여자애가 내 시험지를 베꼈어.
남: Bean 선생님께서 못 보신 것 같아. 그렇지 않았으면 정말 화내셨을걸.
여: 나도 알아… 내가 본 걸 선생님께 말씀드려야 한다고 생각하니?
남: ______________________________

어휘 **overlook** (잘못된 것을) 눈감아 주다, 못 본 체하다

12 짧은 대화에 이어질 응답 | ⑤

▶ 일을 분담하면 훨씬 더 빠를 것 같다는 남자의 의견에 대한 적절한 응답을 찾는다.

① 이것 때문에 오늘 일찍 퇴근했어요.
② 네, 쉬게 해줘서 고마워요.
③ 네, 물건 나르는 사람을 몇 명 고용했어야 해요.
④ 부엌에 있는 건 이미 다 쌌어요.
⑤ 사실, 나는 같이 하는 게 더 좋을 거라고 생각해요.

M: We need to finish moving out today, but **we still have a lot to do**.
W: Right. Should we start with the kitchen?
M: I think it will be a lot faster if we **divide up the work**.
W: ______________________________

남: 우리 오늘 이사를 마쳐야 하는데, 아직 할 일이 많네요.
여: 맞아요. 부엌부터 시작해야 할까요?
남: 일을 분담하면 훨씬 더 빠를 것 같아요.
여: ______________________________

13 긴 대화에 이어질 응답 | ②

▶ 여자와 같은 이유로 채팅을 한다고 말했기 때문에 다른 나라에 대해 많은 것을 배운다는 답변이 가장 적절하다.

① 나는 사람들이 잘못 쓰고 있는 영어를 고쳐주는 게 좋단다.
② 응, 다른 나라에 대해서 많은 것을 배우니까.
③ 네가 나에게 채팅에 대해서 많은 것을 가르쳐 줬구나.
④ 물론이지! 내 영어 실력을 많이 향상할 수 있으니까.
⑤ 사실, 메신저로 사귄 친구들과 자주 커피를 마신단다.

W: I go into Internet messenger chat rooms every night.
M: To practice your English, Mi-hyun?
W: No. **The English used in a chat room** has too much slang. As an English teacher, do you think chatting on the Internet improves learners' English?
M: Not really. I agree that the English isn't so good.
W: I just like to meet people from different countries. **I learn a lot**.
M: That's a good idea. And **your mom isn't worried**?
W: I promised her **I would never meet in person anyone** I met in a chat room.
M: Good!
W: Why don't we chat sometime?
M: Sure. I do it **for the same reason you do**.
W: Oh, really?
M: ______________________________

여: 전 매일 밤 인터넷 메신저 채팅 방에 들어가요.
남: 영어를 연습하러 들어가니, 미현아?
여: 아니요. 채팅 방에서 사용되는 영어에는 속어가 너무 많아요. 영어 교사로서, 인터넷 채팅이 학습자들의 영어 실력을 향상한다고 생각하세요?
남: 그렇지는 않아. 거기서 쓰는 영어가 그렇게 좋지 않다는 점에 동의해.
여: 전 다른 나라 사람들과 만나는 것이 좋을 뿐이에요. 많은 것을 배우거든요.
남: 좋은 생각이구나. 그리고 어머니께서는 걱정하지 않으시니?
여: 어머니께 채팅 방에서 만난 사람과 절대로 직접 만나지 않을 거라고 약속드렸거든요.
남: 잘했구나!
여: 저랑 언제 한번 채팅하는 거 어떠세요?
남: 좋지. 나도 너와 같은 이유로 채팅을 한단다.

여: 아, 정말이요?
남: ________________________________

어휘 **in person** 직접

14 긴 대화에 이어질 응답 | ⑤

▶ '여러 사람이 자기 주장만 내세우게 되면 오히려 일을 그르친다.'는 뜻의 속담에 해당하는 것을 찾는다.

① 나쁜 소식은 빨리 퍼져. ② 동병상련이야.
③ 예술은 길고 인생은 짧아. ④ 서두른다고 일이 되는 것은 아니야.
⑤ 사공이 많으면 배가 산으로 가는 법이야.

W: Your drama club is going to perform a play at the year-end school festival, isn't it?
M: Yes.
W: Which play?
M: We want to **perform one we've written**.
W: So how is the writing going?
M: Not good.
W: **It's hard to write a play**, isn't it?
M: Yes, but the real problem is that we're having lots of problems **working together as a group**. There are seven of us.
W: Oh, I've been in that situation. Everyone has different ideas of each character.
M: Not only each character, but the plot of the whole story.
W: **Why don't only two of you write it**? You know the saying?
M: What's that?
W: ________________________________

여: 너희 연극부는 연말 학교 축제에서 연극을 할 예정이지, 맞지?
남: 응.
여: 어떤 연극이니?
남: 우리가 창작한 것을 공연하려고 해.
여: 그럼 희곡 쓰는 것은 어떻게 되어가니?
남: 신통치 않아.
여: 희곡을 쓰는 것은 어렵지, 그렇지 않니?
남: 어려워, 하지만 정말 문제가 되는 것은 우리가 그룹으로 같이 작업하면서 많은 어려움을 겪고 있다는 거야. 우리는 일곱 명이거든.
여: 아, 나도 그런 경우가 있었어. 각 인물에 대해 모두들 다른 생각을 가지고 있지.
남: 인물뿐만 아니라 이야기의 전체 줄거리에 대해서도 그래.
여: 너희 중 두 사람만 희곡을 쓰지 그러니? 이런 속담을 아니?
남: 뭔데?
여: ________________________________

15 상황에 적절한 말 | ⑤

▶ 공부에 흥미를 잃은 친구를 도와주고 싶은 Steven의 마음이 잘 표현된 것을 찾는다.

① 네게 가장 어려운 과목이 뭐니?
② 그 애들을 내게 소개해 주겠니?
③ 나는 공부하는 데 정말 어려움을 겪고 있어.
④ 다음 주말에 내가 네 친구들과 함께해도 되겠니?
⑤ 내가 여기 있잖아. 언제든지 네가 공부하는 것을 도와줄 수 있어.

M: Steven has been best friends with Luke since elementary school. Last year, they entered high school together and they **both met a lot of new classmates**. Luke, unfortunately, started to **have trouble with his studies**. He found high school a lot harder than middle school, and he started to spend some time with some students who really didn't care about studying hard. It seems that Luke **has lost interest in studying**. Steven really wants to help Luke. But he can't force Luke to study hard. So he just wants to let Luke know he **is always willing to help him**. In this situation, what would Steven most likely say to Luke?

남: Steven은 초등학교부터 Luke와 가장 친한 친구 사이다. 지난해 고등학교에 함께 진학했고 둘 다 새로운 친구들을 많이 사귀었다. Luke는, 안타깝게도 공부를 하는 데 어려움을 겪기 시작했다. 그는 고등학교가 중학교 때보다 훨씬 더 어렵다는 것을 알게 되었고, 열심히 공부하는 것에는 정말 관심이 없는 몇몇 학생들과 함께 시간을 보내기 시작했다. Luke는 공부에 흥미를 잃은 것처럼 보인다. Steven은 Luke를 정말 돕고 싶다. 하지만 그는 Luke에게 공부를 열심히 하라고 강요할 수는 없다. 그래서 그는 Luke에게 언제나 자신이 기꺼이 돕겠다는 것을 알리고 싶을 뿐이다. 이러한 상황에서 Steven이 Luke에게 할 말로 가장 적절한 것은 무엇인가?

어휘 **tough** (문제 등이) 어려운, 힘든 / **be willing to-v** 기꺼이 ~하다

16~17 세트 문항 | 16. ② 17. ④

▶ 16. 십 대 불안을 소개한 뒤, 십 대 사회 공포증과 특정 대상에 대한 공포증 등 십 대 불안에 의해 발생하는 공포증을 설명하고 있다.

① 사회 공포증의 초기 단계
② 십 대 불안에 의해 발생하는 공포증들
③ 십 대들이 공포를 극복하기 위한 조언
④ 십 대 불안의 경고 징후
⑤ 십 대들이 공포증을 치료해야 하는 이유

▶ 17. 해석 참조

W: If you are a teen and you have anxiety, you are not alone. Studies indicate that nearly 20% of all teens in the US **suffer from teen anxiety**. Teen anxiety is an exaggerated emotional reaction that reflects conscious and unconscious fears. Without treatment, teen anxiety can **lead to several kinds of phobias**. One of the most common is teen social phobia, which typically first appears **during early to mid teens**. The primary feature of teen social phobia is extreme fear of social situations and performances, and an exaggerated fear of embarrassment. There are also specific phobias that can be caused by teen anxiety. The first symptoms of these specific phobias usually **occur in childhood or adolescence**. Phobic individuals may be irrationally afraid of certain beings like dogs, spiders, or snakes. They may also be afraid of things in the environment like storms, closed spaces, elevators, and loud noises, or even events like vomiting. Having one phobia **increases the likelihood of developing another**.

여: 여러분이 십 대이고 불안해한다면, 여러분 혼자만 그런 것은 아닙니다. 연구 결과 미국의 모든 십 대 중 거의 20%가 십 대 불안으로 고통받는다고 합니다. 십 대 불안은 의식적인 공포와 무의식적인 공포를 반영하는, 과장된 감정 반응입니다. 치료를 하지 않으면, 십 대 불안은 여러 종류의 공포증으로 이어질 수 있습니다. 가장 흔한 것 중 하나는 십 대 사회 공포증인데, 일반적으로 십 대 초반에서 중반에 처음 나타납니다. 십 대 사회 공포증의 주요 특징은 사회적 상황과 수행에 대한 극심한 공포와 당황스러움에 대한 과장된 공포입니다. 십 대 불안에 의해 발생할 수 있는 특정 공포증도 있습니다. 이런 특정 공포증들의 첫 번째 증상은 보통 아동기 혹은 청소년기에 발생합니다. 공포증이 있는 사람은 개나 ① 거미 혹은 뱀 같은 특정한 대상을 비이성적으로 무서워할지도 모릅니다. 그들은 또한 ② 폭풍, ③ 밀폐된 공간, 엘리베이터, 그리고 ⑤ 큰 소리 같은 환경 속에 있는 것들, 또는 구토하는 것과 같은 일도 무서워할 수 있습니다. 한 가지 공포증이 있으면 또 다른 것이 생길 가능성이 높아집니다.

어휘 **phobia** 공포증 ***cf.* phobic** 공포증이 있는 / **anxiety** 불안(감), 염려; 걱정거리 / **exaggerated** 과장된, 지나친 / **embarrassment** 당황스러움, 난처함 / **adolescence** 청소년기 / **irrationally** 비이성적으로, 비합리적으로 / **likelihood** (어떤 일이 있을) 가능성

Answers & Explanation

01. ⑤ 02. ⑤ 03. ④ 04. ③ 05. ③ 06. ① 07. ⑤ 08. ④ 09. ④ 10. ②
11. ③ 12. ⑤ 13. ④ 14. ③ 15. ② 16. ④ 17. ④

01 화자가 하는 말의 목적 | ⑤

▶ 서점을 방문한 고객들에게, 어린이 도서 작가와 만나는 행사의 일시와 상세한 내용을 안내하고 있다.

W: Good afternoon, shoppers! We hope you're having a pleasant afternoon. Our friendly staff is always here to **help you find the perfect book**. We'd also like to remind you that Bloom Books will be hosting a visit from children's author Anna Walker this Saturday at 3 p.m. Her presentation is for children ages 4 to 8, but **adults are welcome to attend**. She plans to read a small part of her latest book and show the kids how to draw characters. Signed copies of her picture book will also be **available for purchase**. It's sure to be a good time for everyone, so **come early and bring your children**. For more information on this and other Bloom Books events, visit www.bloombooks.com. Thank you for choosing Bloom Books, and have a great day!

여: 안녕하세요, 고객 여러분! 즐거운 오후를 보내시고 있길 바랍니다. 여러분이 완벽한 책을 찾을 수 있도록 돕기 위해 저희 친절한 직원들이 항상 여기 있습니다. 저희는 또한 Bloom Books가 이번 주 토요일 오후 3시에 어린이 도서 작가 Anna Walker 씨의 방문 행사를 주최한다는 것을 다시 한번 알려드리고 싶습니다. 그녀의 발표는 4세에서 8세 사이의 어린이들을 위한 것이지만, 어른들도 참석하는 것을 환영합니다. 그녀는 자신의 최신작 일부를 읽어주고 등장인물을 그리는 방법을 아이들에게 보여줄 예정입니다. 그녀가 사인한 그림책들도 구입이 가능합니다. 모두에게 좋은 시간이 될 것이라 확신하오니, 서둘러 아이들을 데리고 방문해주세요. 이 행사와 Bloom Books의 다른 행사에 대한 더 많은 정보를 위해 www.bloombooks.com을 방문해 주십시오. Bloom Books를 이용해 주셔서 감사드리며, 좋은 하루 보내시길 바랍니다!

어휘 **pleasant** 즐거운, 쾌적한, 기분 좋은 / **remind** (기억하도록) 다시 한번 알려[말해]주다 / **host** (행사를) 주최하다; (TV·라디오 프로를) 진행하다 / **presentation** 발표(회); 제출, 제시 / **latest** 최신[최근]의 / **available** 구할[이용할] 수 있는

02 의견 | ⑤

▶ 이미 너무 많은 것을 하고 있는 여자가 또 새로운 것을 시작하려 하자 남자가 이에 대해 충고하는 내용이다. 그러므로 남자의 의견으로는 ⑤가 적절하다.

M: What are you looking at, Jane?
W: It's a flyer for lessons at the tennis club. **I'm thinking of signing up.**
M: It looks like the beginner's course meets every afternoon. Do you have time?
W: I think so. I'll just have to reschedule my guitar lessons.
M: Wow. I think I'd delay taking the tennis course **if I were you**.
W: Why? Don't you think I'll be a good tennis player?
M: It's not that. You're already so busy with Spanish class, swimming lessons, and everything else.
W: I'm only **trying to improve myself**. I hate wasting time.
M: I know, but it's important to stay focused. It's like the saying, "If you run after two hares, **you'll catch neither**."
W: You have a point. I have been feeling distracted lately.
M: Exactly. Doing too much at once can overwhelm your brain.
W: You're right. I'll take your advice.

남: Jane, 무엇을 보고 있니?
여: 테니스 클럽에서 하는 강좌에 대한 전단이야. 나는 등록할까 생각 중이야.
남: 초급자 과정은 매일 오후에 있는 것처럼 보이는데. 너 시간 있니?
여: 그런 것 같아. 다만 난 내 기타 수업 시간을 변경해야 할 거야.
남: 와. 내가 너라면 테니스 수강을 미룰 거 같아.
여: 왜? 너는 내가 훌륭한 테니스 선수가 될 거라고 생각하지 않니?
남: 그런 게 아니야. 넌 이미 스페인어 수업, 수영 강습 그리고 다른 모든 것들로 매우 바쁘잖아.
여: 난 단지 나 자신을 발전시키기 위해 노력하는 중이야. 시간을 낭비하는 게 싫거든.
남: 알아, 하지만 집중하는 것은 중요해. '두 마리 토끼를 쫓으면 두 마리 다 놓칠 것이다.'라는 속담처럼 말이야.
여: 네 말이 일리가 있어. 난 요즘 집중을 못 하고 있어.
남: 바로 그거야. 한 번에 너무 많은 일을 하면 머리가 압도당할 수 있어.
여: 맞아. 네 충고를 받아들일게.

어휘 **flyer** 전단, 광고지 / **sign up** 등록[신청]하다; 참가하다 / **run after** ~을 쫓다[따라가다] / **hare** 산토끼 / **have a point** 일리 있다; 장점이 있다 / **distracted** 집중이 안 되는, 산만한 / **overwhelm** 압도[제압]하다

03 관계 | ④

▶ 목적지와 요금, 그리고 목적지까지의 이동 시간 등에 대한 대화 내용으로 미루어 보아 택시를 탄 승객(여자)과 택시 운전사(남자) 사이의 대화임을 알 수 있다.

W: Hello?
M: Hello. **Where are you off to**?
W: I'm going to Central Station.
M: Sure. No problem.
W: Thank you. Sorry for asking, but do you have any idea **how much the fare will be**?
M: Oh, it shouldn't be more than 18 dollars.
W: OK. How long does it take to get there?
M: Well, **that all depends on the traffic**, but it shouldn't take more than 30 minutes.
W: Oh, and by the way, do you know what time the last train for Chicago leaves?
M: I don't know, but I know there is a train for Chicago at 4:50.
W: Oh, **it's already half past four**.
M: Well, I'm afraid you'll have to take the next train. I'm sure the 4:50 is not the last train for Chicago.

여: 안녕하세요?
남: 안녕하세요. 어디로 가십니까?
여: 중앙역에 가려고요.
남: 알겠습니다. 문제없습니다.
여: 고맙습니다. 여쭤봐서 죄송하지만, 요금이 얼마나 나올지 아세요?
남: 아, 18달러 넘게는 나오지 않을 것입니다.
여: 알겠습니다. 거기 도착하려면 얼마나 걸리나요?
남: 음, 교통 상황에 따라 다르지만 30분 넘게는 걸리지는 않을 것입니다.
여: 아, 그런데 시카고로 가는 마지막 기차가 몇 시에 출발하는지 아세요?
남: 모르겠습니다. 하지만 4시 50분에 시카고로 가는 기차가 있다는 것은 압니다.
여: 아, 벌써 4시 30분이에요.
남: 음, 다음 기차를 타셔야 할 것 같습니다. 4시 50분 기차가 시카고행 마지막 기차가 아닌 것은 확실합니다.

어휘 **fare** (교통수단의) 요금, 운임

04 그림 불일치 | ③

▶ 둥근 탁자 대신 정사각형 탁자를 골랐다고 했다.

W: I think **the stage is almost ready** for the school play.
M: I think so, too. It looks great.
W: I'm glad we found such a nice bookshelf for the left side of the stage.
M: Me too, but I think the heart-shaped light that you made for the background **looks even better**.
W: Thanks, and the square-shaped table is wonderful. **It was a great choice** to pick this one instead of a round table.
M: Right. Plus, we were able to find the perfect old telephone to place on the table. The phone is so important to the story.
W: Yes, and the bed looks really good on the right.
M: **You can say that again**. I think the audience is going to love the stage.

여: 학교 연극을 위한 무대가 거의 준비된 것 같아.
남: 나도 그렇게 생각해. 근사해 보여.
여: 무대 왼쪽에 둘 아주 좋은 책장을 찾아서 기뻐.

남: 나도. 하지만 네가 배경용으로 만든 하트 모양 조명이 훨씬 더 좋아 보이는 것 같아.
여: 고마워. 그리고 정사각형 탁자가 훌륭해. 둥근 탁자 대신 이걸 고른 건 탁월한 선택이었어.
남: 맞아. 게다가, 우리는 탁자 위에 놓을 완벽한 옛날 전화기도 구할 수 있었어. 전화기는 줄거리에서 아주 중요해.
여: 응. 그리고 침대가 오른쪽에 있으니 정말 좋아 보여.
남: 정말 그래. 관객들이 무대를 아주 좋아할 거 같아.

어휘 **bookshelf** 책장, 책꽂이

05 추후 행동 | ③

▶ 남자는 도서관에서 친구를 만나 농구공을 돌려주고 함께 공부할 것이다.

W: Michael! The basketball! I told you **not to play until exams were finished**.
M: I'm not going to play basketball, Mom.
W: Well, why are you **getting it out of the closet**?
M: It's Connor's basketball, not mine. I'm going to **return it to him**.
W: Are you meeting him tonight?
M: Yes. We're going to study together at the municipal library. We can **help each other study** for our exams.
W: Oh?
M: And he asked me to return the basketball tonight. Can I go now?
W: Yes. **You have already eaten**, so it's not a problem. Will you be home when the library closes?
M: Yes, I'll see you around 10:30.

여: Michael! 농구공이라니! 내가 시험이 끝날 때까지는 농구하지 말라고 했잖니.
남: 농구를 하려는 게 아니에요, 엄마.
여: 그럼, 벽장에서 왜 그걸 꺼내고 있는 거니?
남: 이건 제 농구공이 아니라 Connor의 농구공이에요. 그 애에게 돌려주려고요.
여: 오늘 밤에 그 애를 만나기로 했니?
남: 네. 시립 도서관에서 같이 공부할 거예요. 시험공부를 서로 도와줄 수 있잖아요.
여: 그러니?
남: 그리고 그 애가 농구공을 오늘 밤에 돌려달라고 했거든요. 이제 가도 돼요?
여: 그래. 밥은 이미 먹었으니 괜찮겠구나. 도서관이 닫으면 집에 올 거니?
남: 네. 10시 30분쯤 올게요.

어휘 **municipal** 시립의

06 금액 | ①

▶ 여자는 유스호스텔에 묵을 것이므로 숙박비로 20달러, 그곳에서 음식을 만들어 먹을 것이므로 식비로는 15달러가 필요하다. 여행 경비와 입장료로는 20달러가 필요하므로 여자가 일일 경비로 예상하는 총금액은 55달러가 된다.

W: Larry, you went backpacking last summer, didn't you?
M: Yes.
W: Well, **I'm thinking of backpacking** through Europe this summer. How much money do you think I need to budget?
M: **It depends**. Eastern Europe is much cheaper than Western Europe.
W: I want to go to Western Europe and see all the famous sites.
M: OK. Well, first **think about accommodations**. You need about $20 per day if you stay in youth hostels, but $50 for cheap hotels.
W: I'll stay in youth hostels.
M: And if you cook in the hostel, you need about $15 a day for food. But if you eat meals in restaurants, you'll need $30 or so.
W: I'll definitely **stay away from restaurants**.
M: And budget about $20 a day for travel and entrance fees.
W: OK. **I'll figure out** how much I need to save now.

여: Larry, 너 지난여름에 배낭여행 다녀왔지, 그렇지 않니?
남: 응.
여: 저, 내가 올여름에 유럽 배낭여행을 하려고 생각 중이야. 내가 예산을 얼마나 계획해야 할까?
남: 상황에 따라 다르지. 동유럽이 서유럽보다 돈이 훨씬 더 적게 들어.
여: 나는 서유럽에 가서 유명한 유적지를 다 구경하고 싶어.
남: 그래. 음, 먼저 숙박에 대해 생각해봐. 유스호스텔에 묵는다면 하루에 약 20달러가 필요하지만, 저렴한 호텔은 50달러야.
여: 나는 유스호스텔에서 지낼 거야.
남: 그리고 호스텔에서 음식을 만들어 먹는다면, 식비로 하루에 약 15달러가 필요해. 그렇지만 레스토랑에서 식사한다면, 30달러 정도가 필요할 거야.
여: 나는 레스토랑에는 절대로 가지 않을 거야.
남: 그리고 이동 경비와 입장료로 하루에 약 20달러의 예산을 세워.
여: 알겠어. 이제 얼마를 모아야 하는지 계산해볼게.

어휘 **budget** 예산을 세우다; 예산 / **it[that] depends** ((구어)) 그것은 상황[때]에 따라 다르다 / **site** 유적지, (사건 등의) 현장, 장소; 대지, 부지 / **accommodation** 숙박시설 / **youth hostel** 유스호스텔 (= hostel) / **stay away from** ~에서 떨어져 있다, ~을 가까이하지 않다 / **fee** 요금, 수수료

07 이유 | ⑤

▶ 여자는 남자와 대화 중 Richard와 만나기로 한 장소가 헷갈려서 직접 전화해 확인하려고 한다.

M: Sara, shouldn't you be leaving for your lunch meeting with Richard?
W: I'll leave soon, Dad. **I don't have far to go**. We're meeting at Tim's Diner.
M: The one by the East Mall? That is at least 45 minutes from here.
W: I think he meant the one downtown. It's not that far.
M: **You are going to an art exhibition** after lunch, right?
W: Yes. Richard is very excited about the exhibition.
M: I'm sure Richard was thinking of the exhibit at the mall. That's the one everyone is talking about. I bet you are eating there, too.
W: Now I'm not so sure. I guess **I should have asked him**.
M: Maybe you should give him a call now, **just to be safe**.
W: You're right. I'll do that.

남: Sara, Richard와 만나서 점심 식사하려면 출발해야 하지 않니?
여: 곧 출발할 거예요, 아빠. 가려면 멀지 않아요. Tim 식당에서 만날 거라서요.
남: East Mall 옆에 있는 거 말이니? 그 식당은 여기서 최소 45분이 걸리는데.
여: 그 애는 시내에 있는 곳을 말한 것 같아요. 그곳은 그렇게 멀지 않아요.
남: 너희 점심 먹고 미술 전시회에 갈 거지, 맞지?
여: 네. Richard가 전시회 생각에 아주 들떠 있어요.
남: Richard는 분명 쇼핑몰에서 하는 전시회를 생각하고 있었을 거야. 그게 모든 사람이 얘기하고 있는 전시회거든. 점심도 거기서 먹을 게 분명해.
여: 이젠 확실히 모르겠어요. 그 애에게 물어봤어야 했는데요.
남: 혹시 모르니, 지금 전화해봐야 할 것 같구나.
여: 아빠 말씀이 맞아요. 그렇게 할게요.

08 언급하지 않은 것 | ④

▶ 해석 참조

W: This picture of Victoria Falls looks amazing!
M: **It's the world's largest waterfall** by area. The falls are 1.7 kilometers wide and 108 meters high.
W: Wow, I only knew that it's in Africa.
M: The falls lie between Zambia and Zimbabwe in Southern Africa. By the way, do you know **the origin of its name**?
W: I'm not sure, but it makes me think of Queen Victoria.
M: Right. Dr. Livingstone, a Scottish explorer, **named the falls after the Queen**.
W: Interesting. I would love to see the falls in person.
M: If you get to go see them, make sure it's in June or July. That's **the best time to view the falls**.
W: Why is that a good time?
M: That's when the river has the most water, so the falls are the biggest.

여: 이 Victoria 폭포 사진이 굉장해 보여!
남: 그건 면적이 세계에서 가장 큰 폭포야. 그 폭포는 너비가 1.7킬로미터에 높이가 108미터야(① 규모).
여: 와, 난 그게 아프리카에 있다는 것만 알고 있었어.
남: 그 폭포는 아프리카 남부의 잠비아와 짐바브웨 사이에 있어(② 위치). 그런데 너 그 이름의 유래를 아니?
여: 잘은 모르지만 Victoria 여왕이 생각나.
남: 맞아. 스코틀랜드 사람으로 탐험가이자 의사였던 Livingstone이 여왕의 이름을 따서 폭포 이름을 붙였어(③ 이름의 유래).
여: 흥미롭네. 직접 그 폭포를 보고 싶어.
남: 보러 가게 되면, 꼭 6월이나 7월에 가도록 해. 그때가 폭포를 둘러보기에 가장 좋은 시기야(⑤ 관광하기 좋은 시기).
여: 왜 그때가 좋은 시기야?
남: 강에 물이 가장 많은 때여서 폭포가 가장 크거든.

어휘 **area** 면적; 지역

09 내용 불일치 | ④

▶ 하루 이상이 아니라 12시간 넘게 지연되면 무료 왕복 기차표를 제공받게 된다.

M: Attention passengers. Due to heavy snowfall in the mountains, Train 716 to Salt Lake City will be delayed for your safety until **the tracks can be cleared**. If you have placed your luggage aboard the train, please remove all items and exit the train now. This train will now be used for another route. Although **the weather is beyond our control**, if the delay lasts more than 12 hours, we will **provide you with a voucher** for a free round-trip ticket. You can board TransAmerica Trains to anywhere we travel in the U.S. We will **continue to update you** on the status of the departure time. Thank you for your patience.

남: 승객 여러분께 알려 드립니다. 산악 지역에 많은 눈이 내린 관계로, 솔트레이크 시티행 716호 열차는 선로가 치워질 수 있을 때까지 승객 여러분의 안전을 위해 지연될 예정입니다. 짐을 열차에 실어 놓으신 승객 여러분은 물품을 모두 치워 주시고 지금 하차해 주시기 바랍니다. 이 열차는 이제 다른 노선에 투입될 것입니다. 비록 날씨를 통제할 수는 없지만, 12시간 넘게 계속 지연된다면, 여러분께 무료 왕복 열차표의 교환권을 제공할 것입니다. 미국 내에서 저희가 운행하는 곳은 어디든지 TransAmerica사의 열차를 타실 수 있습니다. 출발 시간 현황에 대해 새로운 소식이 들어오는 대로 계속 알려 드리겠습니다. 기다려 주셔서 감사합니다.

어휘 **snowfall** 강설 / **beyond one's control** 제어할 수 없는 / **voucher** 상품권, 할인권 / **status** 현황, 상황 / **patience** 인내심

10 도표 이해 | ②

▶ 여자는 방이 두 개 이상이고, 월세가 1,000달러 이하이며, 경비원도 있는 곳을 원한다. 그리고 그중에서 면적이 더 넓은 곳을 선택하겠다고 말했다.

W: I've got the list of apartments for rent.
M: Are you sure you want to live all by yourself?
W: Yes, now **help me narrow these choices down**.
M: OK. What is the most important thing for you?
W: I need at least two rooms: one for sleeping and the other for my office.
M: So that small place **is out of the question**. What else?
W: I can't afford more than $1,000 a month.
M: Then you won't be living like an 'executive.'
W: At least not yet. But I do want to **have a security guard**.
M: Of course. And now you have to choose between these two apartments.
W: Well, I **do want something spacious**. So I'll get the bigger one.

여: 임대할 아파트의 목록을 뽑았어.
남: 정말 너 혼자 살고 싶니?
여: 응, 이제 선택의 폭을 좁히는 걸 도와줘.
남: 알겠어. 네게 가장 중요한 사항은 뭐니?
여: 방이 최소한 두 개는 필요해. 하나는 침실이고 다른 하나는 사무실로 사용하게.
남: 그럼 장소가 좁은 저곳은 안 되겠구나. 그 밖엔?
여: 한 달에 1,000달러 넘게는 낼 수 없어.
남: 그럼 '사장님'처럼 살지는 않을 거구나.
여: 적어도 아직은 안 돼. 하지만 경비원은 있으면 정말 좋겠어.
남: 물론이지. 그럼 이제 이 두 아파트 중에서 골라야 해.
여: 음, 넓은 곳이면 정말 좋겠어. 그러니 더 큰 곳으로 할래.

어휘 **security guard** 경비원 / **narrow down** ~을 좁히다 / **out of question** 의논해 봐야 소용없는 / **executive** 임원, 중역 / **spacious** 넓은

11 짧은 대화에 이어질 응답 | ③

▶ 남자가 경유 항공편을 예약한 상황에서 직항편이 없었는지 묻는 말에 적절한 응답을 찾는다.

① 편도 승차권을 예약했어요.
② 우리가 이용할 직항편은 14시간이 걸릴 거예요.
③ 안타깝게도 그건 이미 (예약이) 다 찼어요.
④ 있었어요. 도쿄를 구경할 것이 기대돼요.
⑤ 비행기 승무원이 우리를 자리로 안내해 줄 거예요.

W: Our vacation is next month. **Have you booked a flight**?
M: I did. It's a bit long because it stops in Tokyo, but we'll still arrive in L.A. on the 23rd.
W: That's okay, but weren't there **any direct flights available**?
M: ______________________________

여: 우리 휴가가 다음 달이에요. 항공편 예약했어요?
남: 했어요. 도쿄를 경유해서 좀 오래 걸리긴 하지만, 그래도 23일에 L.A.에 도착할 거예요.
여: 괜찮아요. 하지만 이용할 수 있는 직항편이 없었나요?
남: ______________________________

12 짧은 대화에 이어질 응답 | ⑤

▶ 늦는 친구를 기다리는 상황에서 Jane이 언제쯤 도착할 거라고 했는지 묻는 남자의 말에 적절한 응답을 찾는다.

① 한동안 그 애를 못 봤어.
② 아마 택시가 훨씬 더 빠를 거야.
③ 내가 Jane과 얘기했을 때가 9시쯤이었어.
④ 그 애는 시내 반대편에서 왔어.
⑤ 말하지 않았어. 하지만 10분만 기다리자.

M: Well, it's ten o'clock. I think that **we should get going**.
W: **Let's wait a little longer** for Jane. She said she might be late.
M: We can wait a few minutes. When did she say she would arrive?
W: ______________________________

남: 음, 10시야. 우리 가야 할 거 같아.
여: Jane을 조금만 더 기다리자. 늦을 수도 있다고 했어.
남: 몇 분은 기다릴 수 있어. 그 애가 언제 도착할 거라고 했니?
여: ______________________________

13 긴 대화에 이어질 응답 | ④

▶ 여자를 고용하고 싶은 남자가 다른 면접이 아직 남아 있는 여자에게 할 수 있는 대답을 찾는다.

① 그렇게 한다면 당신은 해고될 것입니다.
② 팀워크는 이 분야에서 필수적입니다.
③ 인턴직은 3개월간입니다.
④ 결정하신 바를 금요일까지 알려주세요.
⑤ 내일 첫 업무를 드리겠습니다.

M: Tell me why you think you are **the best candidate for the job**.
W: Although I am just graduating, I have experience through several intensive internships.
M: I did notice the internships on your résumé, but tell me something specific about you.
W: **I have an eye for detail** and excellent problem-solving skills.
M: How are you **when it comes to teamwork**?
W: To be honest, I haven't had much experience with group work.
M: What about at the internships?
W: They pretty much gave me assignments and **left me on my own**.
M: I'm impressed. When can you start?
W: Well, I have several more interviews to go to this week.
M: ______________________________

남: 자신이 이 일에 가장 적합한 지원자라고 생각하는 이유를 말해 보세요.
여: 저는 비록 갓 졸업했지만, 여러 가지 집중 인턴직을 통해 경험을 쌓았습니다.
남: 당신 이력서에서 인턴직 경력을 주목한 건 사실입니다만, 자신에 대해 구체적으로 말해 보세요.
여: 저는 세부사항을 보는 안목이 있고 문제 해결 능력이 뛰어납니다.
남: 팀워크에 있어서는 어떻습니까?
여: 솔직히 말씀드리면, 단체로 일해 본 경험이 많지 않습니다.
남: 인턴 과정에서는 어땠나요?
여: 거의 회사에서 제게 업무를 주고 혼자서 하게 했습니다.
남: 인상적이군요. 언제부터 일을 시작할 수 있습니까?
여: 음, 이번 주에 참석해야 할 면접이 몇 군데 더 있습니다.
남: ______________________________

어휘 **internship** 인턴직 / **assignment** 업무 / **candidate** 후보자 / **intensive** 집중적인, 철저한 / **have an eye for** ~을 보는 눈이 있다 / **when it comes to** ~에 관해 말한다면 / **pretty much** 거의

14 긴 대화에 이어질 응답 | ③

▶ 여자는 남자의 행동이 마음에 들지 않지만 자신의 성적 때문에라도 남자를 돕게 될 것이다.

① 원한다면 너 혼자 해도 돼.
② 좋아. 난 네가 금요일까지 그것을 끝낼 수 있다고 생각해.

③ 이번엔 도와주겠지만, 다음에는 준비가 되어 있어야 해.
④ 그냥 잊어버리자. 다음에 하지 뭐.
⑤ 인터넷에서 그 소프트웨어를 그냥 다운받는 것은 안 돼.

W: Do you **have your part of the presentation ready** for class tomorrow?
M: Tomorrow? I thought we weren't giving our presentation until Friday!
W: We were, initially, but **we switched with another group** because one of their members was in the hospital. Remember?
M: If I remembered, I would be better prepared.
W: Well, you **should have finished most of it**.
M: I have it half done.
W: That's it? You'll never be ready. This is going to **cost me a good grade**.
M: I was waiting for new software to make the presentation really great.
W: Forget great. **Let's just get it done**.
M: If you look for some information for me, we can finish in just a few hours.
W: ______________________________

여: 내일 수업 때 발표할 프레젠테이션에서 네가 맡은 부분에 대해 준비 다 했니?
남: 내일이라고? 난 금요일에야 우리가 발표할 거라고 생각했는데!
여: 처음엔 그랬었는데, 우리가 다른 그룹이랑 순서를 바꿨잖아. 그 애들 중 한 명이 입원해서. 기억나?
남: 내가 기억했으면 더 잘 준비했겠지.
여: 음, 그 대부분을 끝냈어야 했는데.
남: 반은 했어.
여: 그게 다야? 넌 절대 준비가 안 될 거야. 내가 좋은 점수를 받기는 힘들겠어.
남: 정말 멋지게 발표하려고 새 소프트웨어를 기다리고 있었어.
여: 멋지게 만드는 건 잊어버려. 그냥 끝내기나 하자.
남: 네가 나에게 정보를 좀 찾아 준다면, 몇 시간이면 끝낼 수 있어.
여: ______________________________

어휘 **initially** 처음에, 애초에 / **cost A B** A에게 B를 희생하게 하다

15 상황에 적절한 말 | ②

▶ 살을 빼기 위해 필요 이상으로 운동을 하는 친구에게 할 수 있는 조언을 찾는다.

① 우리 체육관에 좀 더 자주 와야 해.
② 네가 운동을 너무 지나치게 하는 것 같아서 걱정돼.
③ 살 빼는 비법을 알려주겠니?
④ 열심히 노력하면 정말 성과를 거두는구나. 멋져 보인다!
⑤ 넌 병원에 가서 매달 검진을 받아야 해.

W: Ella and Jill have worked out together three times a week at the gym for more than a year now. Ella **goes just to stay in shape**, but Jill says she is trying to lose weight. However, Jill is extremely thin and **no longer looks healthy** to Ella. She has also noticed that Jill **stays in the gym** for sometimes three or four hours at a time and is often there on days when Ella is not there. Ella is concerned that her friend may **be hurting herself without realizing it**. As her workout partner and friend, she wants to **show her concern**. In this situation, what would Ella most likely say to Jill?

여: Ella와 Jill은 지금 일 년이 넘게 일주일에 세 번씩 체육관에서 함께 운동을 하고 있다. Ella는 단지 건강을 유지하기 위해 다니지만, Jill은 살을 빼려고 노력 중이라고 말한다. 하지만 Jill은 너무 말라서 Ella에게 더는 건강해 보이지 않는다. 또한 그녀는 때때로 Jill이 한 번에 서너 시간씩 체육관에 머물러 있고, Ella가 가지 않는 날에도 종종 그곳에 간다는 사실을 알게 되었다. Ella는 친구가 부지불식간에 건강을 해칠 수도 있다는 사실이 걱정스럽다. 운동 파트너이자 친구로서 그녀는 자신이 걱정하고 있음을 보여 주고 싶다. 이러한 상황에서 Ella가 Jill에게 할 말로 가장 적절한 것은 무엇인가?

어휘 **pay off** 성과를 거두다 / **checkup** 건강 진단 / **work out** 운동하다 ***cf.*** **workout** 운동 / **stay in shape** 건강을 유지하다

16~17 세트 문항 | 16. ④ 17. ④

▶ 16. 주의가 산만한 운전을 방지하기 위해 운전하기 전과 운전 중에 해야 할 일을 설명하고 있다.

① 운전을 조심해서 해야 하는 이유
② 새 GPS 장치 광고
③ 운전하는 동안 문자 메시지를 보내는 것의 위험성
④ 산만한 운전을 피하기 위한 조언
⑤ 운전면허 취득 과정

▶ 17. 해석 참조

M: Driving is a grave responsibility that **demands your full attention**, but distractions can occur at anytime. Today, I'd like to talk about ways to **avoid getting distracted** while driving. First, there are some things you should do before driving. Review all maps, directions, and any pre-programmed routes on a GPS device before driving. This prevents getting distracted by maps while driving. Also, preset the volume of the radio so that you won't **get distracted by sudden loud noises**. There are other ways to **stay focused** while driving, as well. Talking on your cell phone, or worse, texting while you drive is a major source of distraction. If you have a good reason to talk on the phone, use a hands-free device. Nowadays, **it has become more common** for busy people to eat and drink while driving. Remember that it is always safer to eat at home or sitting in a restaurant. If you start to feel sleepy, pull over to the side of the road and take a rest for a while. Finally, **avoid taking off your coat** or changing clothes while driving.

남: 운전은 모든 집중을 요구하는 중대한 책무이지만, 방해는 언제든지 일어날 수 있습니다. 오늘은 운전 중에 주의가 산만해지는 것을 방지하는 방법에 관해 이야기하려고 합니다. 첫 번째, 운전하기 전에 해야 할 일이 몇 가지 있습니다. 운전하기 전에 모든 지도와 방향, GPS 장치의 미리 정해진 경로를 살펴보십시오. 이것은 운전 중에 지도로 인해 방해받는 것을 방지합니다. 또한, 갑작스러운 큰 소음에 방해받지 않도록 라디오의 볼륨을 미리 맞춰 놓으십시오. 게다가, 운전 중에 집중하기 위한 다른 방법들도 있습니다. 운전하는 중에 ① 휴대전화로 통화하는 것, 더 안 좋게는 문자 메시지를 보내는 것은 주요 방해 근원입니다. 통화할 타당한 이유가 있다면, 핸즈프리 장비를 이용하십시오. 요즘 들어, 바쁜 사람들이 운전 중에 ② (음식을) 먹고 (음료를) 마시는 일이 더욱 흔해졌습니다. 집이나 음식점에 앉아서 먹는 것이 언제나 더 안전하다는 것을 기억하십시오. ③ 졸음이 오기 시작하면, 도로변에 차를 세우고 잠시 휴식을 취하십시오. 마지막으로, 운전 중에 ⑤ 외투를 벗거나 옷을 갈아입지 않도록 하십시오.

어휘 **distracted** (정신이) 산만해진 ***cf.*** **distraction** (주의) 집중을 방해하는 것 / **grave** 중대한, 심각한; 엄숙한 / **pull over** 길 한쪽으로 차를 대다

Answers & Explanation

01.② 02.③ 03.④ 04.④ 05.⑤ 06.④ 07.④ 08.③ 09.⑤ 10.③
11.⑤ 12.④ 13.② 14.① 15.② 16.② 17.③

01 화자가 하는 말의 목적 | ②

▶ 연설 대회 결승전의 진행 방식, 평가 방식, 상품 등이 나오는 것으로 보아 결승전 관련 세부 사항을 설명하고 있음을 알 수 있다.

W: Yesterday, the semi-final stage of the Crown High School Speech Contest took place. More than 20 students competed, and 5 have moved on to the final round. Today, **the final round will take place**. Each of the 5 students will have 5 minutes to give their final speech. In the previous rounds, the students chose the topics, but this time **the topics will be given out at random**. Contestants will then have 30 minutes to prepare. The speeches will be judged by faculty members, but in this round the audience will also **have a chance to vote on their favorite**. The winner of this exciting competition will **receive a brand-new laptop computer**, and the runner-up will receive a tablet PC.

여: 어제 Crown 고등학교 연설 대회의 준결승전이 열렸습니다. 20명이 넘는 학생들이 경쟁을 벌였고, 다섯 명이 결승전에 진출했습니다. 오늘, 결승전이 개최될 것입니다. 다섯 명의 학생 각자에게 5분이 주어져 최종 연설을 할 것입니다. 이전 라운드에서는 학생들이 (연설의) 주제를 선정했지만, 이번에는 주제가 무작위로 주어질 것입니다. 그 후 참가자들은 30분의 준비 시간을 가질 것입니다. 연설은 교수진의 평가를 받겠지만, 이번 라운드에서는 관객들 또한 가장 마음에 드는 연설자에게 투표할 기회가 있을 것입니다. 이 흥미진진한 경쟁의 우승자는 신형 노트북 컴퓨터를, 2등은 태블릿 PC를 받을 것입니다.

어휘 **semi-final** 준결승전 ***cf.*** **quarter-final** 준준결승 / **previous** 이전의, 먼젓번의 / **at random** 무작위로, 임의로 / **contestant** (대회 · 시합 등의) 참가자 / **faculty** 교수진; (대학의) 학부; (타고난) 능력[기능] / **brand-new** 신제품의; 새것인 / **runner-up** 2위 (선수 · 팀); (1위 외의) 입상자 / **tablet PC** 태블릿 PC ((펜으로 문자나 그림을 입력할 수 있으며, 무선 LAN을 통해 어디서나 인터넷 접속이 가능한 모바일 PC))

02 대화 주제 | ③

▶ 자신이 가진 재능과 장점을 활용하는 봉사활동에 관해 이야기하고 있다.

M: Linda, what's that?
W: It's a letter from the children's home **where I do volunteer work as a tutor**.
M: It's great that you donate your talent to such a worthy cause.
W: I was **influenced by my father**. In fact, his choir group sings songs for patients.
M: That's cool. I'm not good at singing so I can't imagine doing that.
W: Didn't you take a massage class last year? How about massaging the elderly at nursing homes?
M: I'd love to, but I just **had a cast removed** and my arms are weak.
W: Well, your voice is one of your strengths, so **why not try reading to younger patients**?
M: I could do that. Sometimes, I read to my younger sister and it's fun.
W: I'm sure the children will love it.

남: Linda, 그게 뭐야?
여: 내가 과외 강사로 자원봉사를 하는 보육원에서 온 편지야.
남: 그런 훌륭한 대의에 네 재능을 기부하다니 멋지다.
여: 우리 아빠의 영향을 받았어. 실은, 아빠가 속한 합창단이 환자들에게 노래를 불러주거든.
남: 멋지다. 나는 노래를 못해서 그런 것을 하는 건 상상할 수 없어.
여: 너 작년에 안마 수업을 듣지 않았니? 양로원에서 어르신들께 안마를 해드리는 건 어때?
남: 그러고 싶지만, 깁스를 막 풀어서 팔에 힘이 없어.
여: 음, 네 목소리는 네 장점 중 하나니까, 어린 환자들에게 책을 읽어주는 건 어떠니?
남: 그건 할 수 있어. 내 여동생에게 가끔 책을 읽어주는데 재밌더라.
여: 아이들이 분명히 좋아할 거야.

어휘 **children's home** 보육원 / **tutor** 개인 지도 교사, 가정교사; ~을 가르치다, 개인 교습을 하다 / **worthy** 훌륭한; ~을 받을 만한, 자격이 있는

03 관계 | ④

▶ 남자는 양치기 개를 진찰한 뒤 적절한 처방을 내려주고 있고, 여자는 이 개가 자기 사육장의 사냥개들과 나간 뒤로 아팠다고 말하는 것으로 보아 수의사와 목장 주인 간의 대화이다.

M: You say that Bart isn't feeling well?
W: Yes, **he has a fever**.
M: Let's see.... I'll take Bart's temperature.
W: Alright. Oh, I'm so worried about him because he does a great job of **rounding up the sheep in my meadow**, and he's never been sick before.
M: I see. *[pause]* Yes, he does have a fever. When exactly did he get sick?
W: It was three nights ago, after he was out with the hunting dogs in our field.
M: I think I've discovered the reason. He **has an injury on his chest**. It's probably infected.
W: Will he be alright?
M: Yes. I'll **give the appropriate shots**, and I'm sure he'll be wagging his tail again soon.
W: **That's such a relief**! Thank you so much.
M: It's no trouble at all.

남: Bart의 몸 상태가 좋지 않다고 말씀하셨지요?
여: 네, 열이 있어요.
남: 한번 봅시다…. Bart의 체온을 잴게요.
여: 알겠어요. 아, 그 녀석은 제 목장에서 양 모는 일을 굉장히 잘하고 전에는 아팠던 적이 없어서 너무 걱정되네요.
남: 그렇군요. *[잠시 후]* 네, 정말 열이 있네요. 정확히 언제부터 아팠죠?
여: 사흘 밤 전부터요. 우리 사육장에 있는 사냥개들과 나간 뒤로요.
남: 이유를 알아낸 것 같네요. Bart의 흉부에 상처가 있어요. 아마 감염되었을 거예요.
여: Bart가 괜찮을까요?
남: 그럼요. 제가 적절한 주사를 놓을 것이고, 녀석은 분명 곧 꼬리를 다시 흔들 거예요.
여: 다행이네요! 정말 감사합니다.
남: 전혀 어려운 일도 아닌데요.

어휘 **round up** ~을 (찾아) 모으다; (경찰 · 군인이) ~을 찾아 체포하다 / **meadow** 목초지 / **shot** 주사 (한 대); (총기) 발사, 발포; 시도; 사진 / **wag** (개가 꼬리를) 흔들다

04 그림 불일치 | ④

▶ 남자는 죽은 식물은 너무 비극적일 것 같아 잎이 있는 식물을 넣었다고 했다.

W: John, can we finally discuss **the book cover we've been working on**?
M: Sure. I'm ready.
W: Great. I think the picture of a dead planet in the top right corner is appropriate.
M: I agree. It's a good match for a book about protecting the environment.
W: The title right under the picture, "The Last Man on Earth," is also fitting.
M: Right, and the picture below it of a lone man kneeling on the ground **emphasizes the message of the book**.
W: But I'm surprised that you included plants with flowers instead of dead plants.
M: I felt that **dead plants would be too tragic**. I wanted to show there is still hope.
W: Hmm.... That is **an important theme of the book**.
M: Right. And, of course, I've put our company's name, "Best Book House," in the bottom right corner.
W: It looks great.

여: John, 우리가 작업해 온 책 표지를 최종적으로 논의할 수 있을까요?
남: 그럼요. 전 준비됐어요.
여: 좋아요. 오른쪽 상단 구석에 있는 죽은 행성의 그림은 적절하다고 생각해요.
남: 동의해요. 환경 보호에 관한 책과 잘 어울려요.

여: 그림 바로 아래에 있는 제목인 '지구 최후의 인간'도 어울려요.
남: 맞아요. 그리고 그 아래 땅 위에 혼자 무릎을 꿇고 있는 남자의 그림은 책의 메시지를 강조하죠.
여: 그런데 당신이 죽은 식물 대신 꽃이 있는 식물을 넣어서 놀랐어요.
남: 죽은 식물은 너무 비극적일 거라고 느꼈어요. 전 아직 희망이 있다는 것을 보여주고 싶었거든요.
여: 음…. 그게 이 책의 중요한 주제죠.
남: 맞아요. 그리고 당연히, 우리 회사 이름인 'Best Book House'도 오른쪽 하단 구석에 넣었어요.
여: 좋아 보이네요.

05 부탁한 일 | ⑤

▶ 남자는 콘서트 티켓의 할인쿠폰 번호를 받아 적을 수 없어서, 여자에게 문자 메시지로 보내 달라고 부탁했다.

W: Isn't this a pamphlet for Sunny's concert? **Are you interested in going**?
M: Sure. And I heard you went last year. How was it?
W: Fantastic! I even met Sunny **on the way to the snack bar**.
M: That's unbelievable! Did you take a picture?
W: Of course! I also got her autograph. She was really nice. That's why she's my favorite singer.
M: Wow, I'd really love to go to her concert.
W: Would you? I can get a discount **through the music magazine I subscribe to**.
M: Really? That's great.
W: Sure. I just need to give you the coupon number. Can you write it down now?
M: **I don't have anything to write with**. Could you send it to me by text message?
W: No problem. **Don't postpone booking** your ticket, because they sell out fast.
M: Got it. Thanks.

여: 이거 Sunny 콘서트의 팸플릿 아니야? (콘서트에) 가는 데 관심 있니?
남: 그럼. 그리고 네가 작년에 (콘서트에) 갔었다고 들었어. 어땠니?
여: 굉장했어! 스낵바에 가는 도중에 Sunny도 만났어.
남: 믿기지가 않아! 사진 찍었니?
여: 물론이지! Sunny의 사인도 받았어. 그녀는 매우 친절했어. 그녀가 내가 제일 좋아하는 가수인 것도 그것 때문이야.
남: 와, 그녀의 콘서트에 정말 가고 싶어.
여: 그래? 내가 구독하는 음악 잡지로 할인을 받을 수 있어.
남: 정말? 대단하다.
여: 응. 너에게 쿠폰 번호만 주면 돼. 지금 받아 적을 수 있니?
남: 쓸 것이 아무것도 없어. 그것을 문자 메시지로 보내줄 수 있어?
여: 문제없어. 티켓이 빨리 팔리니까 예매하는 것을 미루지 마.
남: 알았어. 고마워.

어휘 **subscribe** (신문 등을) 구독하다; (인터넷·유료 TV 채널 등에) 가입하다; 기부하다 / **postpone** ~을 연기하다, 미루다 / **sell out** 다 팔리다[매진되다]

06 금액 | ④

▶ 두 사람은 작년에 기부받은 56,000달러보다 8,000달러를 더 받았다고 했으나 이 중 1,000달러는 중복으로 입력한 것이므로 그 금액을 빼면 된다. (56,000+8,000−1,000=63,000달러)

W: Sam! Come and see **how much has been donated this year**!
M: Wow! It's amazing!
W: You're right. We collected around 55,000 dollars last year, right?
M: Yes, it was 56,000 dollars. And we've got 8,000 dollars more this year than last year, **while we still have 2 months left**.
W: Oh, wait. I think something is wrong. *[Keyboard typing sound]* Did you add the 1,000 dollars we got yesterday?
M: You mean from the old lady who didn't tell us her name? Yes, I input the data here in this line.
W: That's why **this figure is too big**. I also added it right below that line.
M: Then we should subtract 1,000 dollars.
W: Right. Still, **we have more contributions than last year**.
M: I feel really great that people are getting more interested in helping others.
W: So do I.

여: Sam! 이리 와서 올해 얼마나 기부받았는지 봐요!
남: 와! 놀라운걸요!
여: 당신 말이 맞아요. 우리가 작년에는 55,000달러쯤 모았어요, 그렇죠?
남: 네, 56,000달러였어요. 그리고 올해는 아직 두 달이나 남았는데도 작년보다 8,000달러를 더 받았어요.
여: 아, 기다려 봐요. 뭔가 잘못된 것 같아요. *[키보드 두드리는 소리]* 어제 받은 1,000달러를 더 했어요?
남: 이름을 밝히지 않은 노부인이 주신 것 말이지요? 네, 여기 이 줄에 데이터를 입력했어요.
여: 그래서 이 수치가 너무 크군요. 저도 저 줄 바로 아래에 그것을 더했거든요.
남: 그러면 1,000달러를 빼야겠어요.
여: 맞아요. 그래도 작년보다 더 많은 기부금을 받았네요.
남: 사람들이 다른 이들을 돕는 데 점점 더 관심을 두는 걸 보니 정말 기분이 좋아요.
여: 저도요.

어휘 **figure** 수치; 도형; 모습, 형상 / **subtract** (수·양을) 빼다 / **contribution** 기부[금]; 기여[공헌]

07 이유 | ④

▶ 2년 연속 웅변대회의 우승자였던 여자가 올해는 학생 심사위원이 될 것을 요청받아 웅변하지 않는다고 했다.

W: Hello, Mr. Nelson.
M: Hi, Emma. **I'm looking forward to hearing your speech**.
W: Actually, I won't be speaking in the speech contest this year.
M: But you've been the champion **for two consecutive years**. Have you lost interest in speaking?
W: No, I still enjoy it, especially sharing my ideas with other people.
M: That's good. You've always had a unique confidence and strong stage presence.
W: Thank you. **That means a lot to me**.
M: But I guess you are just too busy this year.
W: No. The truth is that I was asked **to participate as a student judge**.
M: Oh, that will be a new experience. Good for you.
W: Yes, I'm glad to have been invited, and I'll **do my best to evaluate the participants**.
M: Alright. In that case, I'll see you at the contest.

여: 안녕하세요, Nelson 선생님.
남: 안녕, Emma. 네 웅변을 듣기를 기대하고 있단다.
여: 사실, 올해는 웅변대회에서 웅변하지 않을 거예요.
남: 하지만 너는 2년 연속 우승을 했었잖니. 웅변에 흥미를 잃었니?
여: 아뇨, 여전히 웅변하는 게 즐거워요, 특히 다른 사람들과 제 생각을 나누는 것이요.
남: 다행이구나. 넌 늘 남다른 자신감과 무대에서의 뛰어난 침착성을 가졌지.
여: 감사합니다. 그 말씀은 제게 큰 힘이 되네요.
남: 그런데 네가 올해는 단지 매우 바쁜가 보구나.
여: 아니에요. 사실은 학생 심사위원으로 참가해 달라는 요청을 받았어요.
남: 아, 새로운 경험이 되겠는걸. 잘됐다.
여: 네, 초청받아서 기뻐요. 그리고 참가자들을 평가하기 위해 최선을 다할 거예요.
남: 알겠다. 그렇다면, 대회에서 널 볼 수 있겠구나.

어휘 **consecutive** 연이은 / **evaluate** (양·가치·품질 등을) 평가하다[감정하다]

08 언급하지 않은 것 | ③

▶ 해석 참조

W: That's a lovely flower, Tom.
M: Thanks. It was a gift from a friend.
W: It's an edelweiss flower, right? I recognize the star shape. **It almost looks like a snowflake**.
M: You're right. My friend said **it's native to the high mountains** of Europe. I'm going to plant it in my garden.
W: **It will look great in your garden**. Can I come to see it later? I really love edelweiss flowers.
M: Of course. It **blooms from late spring** until the end of summer, so you should come then.
W: Great. By the way, **do you know the meaning of** this flower's name?
M: Does it have a special meaning? What is it?
W: "Edel" means "noble" and "weiss" means "white" in German.

M: So it means noble and white? I didn't know that.
W: It's fascinating, isn't it?

여: 꽃 예쁘다, Tom.
남: 고마워. 친구가 준 선물이야.
여: 에델바이스 꽃이네, 맞지? 그 별 모양을 보면 알아. 거의 눈송이처럼 생겼어(① 모양).
남: 네 말이 맞아. 친구가 유럽의 고산이 원산지(② 원산지)라고 말했어. 이걸 내 정원에 심을 거야.
여: 네 정원에서 예뻐 보일 거야. 나중에 꽃을 보러 가도 돼? 난 에델바이스 꽃을 정말 좋아하거든.
남: 물론이지. 늦봄부터 여름 끝 무렵까지 피니까(④ 개화 시기), 그때 와야 해.
여: 좋아. 그런데 이 꽃 이름의 의미를 아니?
남: 그 이름이 특별한 의미가 있어? 뭔데?
여: 독일어로 '에델'은 '고귀한'이라는 뜻이고 '바이스'는 '하얀색'을 뜻해.
남: 그러면 고귀하고 하얗다는 의미네(⑤ 이름의 의미)? 몰랐어.
여: 정말 매력적이지 않니, 그렇지?

어휘 **snowflake** 눈송이 / **bloom** 꽃을 피우다, 꽃이 피다; 꽃; 혈색 / **noble** 고귀한, 숭고한; 귀족(의) / **fascinating** 매력적인, 대단히 흥미로운

09 내용 불일치 | ⑤

▶ 새 건물의 입구는 예전 도서관의 아름다운 입구를 그대로 유지하고 있다고 했다.

M: Good morning, everyone! I'm **very pleased to announce** that our city library will reopen today. And I'm proud to say that it will be renamed George Pearson Memorial Library, after the founder of the original library. As you probably know, the old library was over a century old when remodeling began. Now, **after six months of construction**, we have a library that everyone can enjoy. Though the heating system won't be finished until winter, the air-conditioning system **is fully prepared for the heat of summer**. And the new building has kept the beautiful entrance of the old library. A few days ago, local high school graduates **were kind enough to donate books** to the new library. This means **the enlarged space will contain** even more books and resources.

남: 안녕하세요, 여러분! 저는 오늘 저희 시립도서관의 재개관 소식을 알려드리게 되어 매우 기쁩니다. 그리고 원래의 도서관 설립자 이름을 따서, George Pearson 기념 도서관으로 개명될 것을 말씀드리게 되어 자랑스럽습니다. 여러분도 아마 아시겠지만, 예전 도서관은 리모델링이 시작되었을 때 (지어진 지) 한 세기가 넘었습니다. 이제, 6개월 동안의 공사 끝에, 저희는 모두가 즐길 수 있는 도서관을 갖게 되었습니다. 난방시설은 겨울이 돼서야 완성되겠지만, 냉방시설은 여름 더위에 대비해 완전히 준비되었습니다. 또한, 새 건물은 예전 도서관의 아름다운 입구를 유지하고 있습니다. 며칠 전, 지역 고등학교 졸업생들이 친절하게도 새 도서관에 도서를 기증했습니다. 이는 확장된 공간이 훨씬 더 많은 도서와 자료를 구비할 것을 의미합니다.

어휘 **enlarge** (~을) 확장[확대]하다

10 도표 이해 | ③

▶ 두 사람은 인터넷을 사용할 수 있는 곳 중에서, 150달러 미만이며 수영장이 딸린 숙소를 선택하기로 했다.

W: Honey, are these the lodges we can choose for our vacation?
M: Yes, I think we should pick one today.
W: How about this one? **It would be fun to barbecue**.
M: The kids would love it, but I'm afraid I need the Internet for my work.
W: I wish **you didn't have to bring your work**, but I understand.
M: Also, I think it's a good idea to spend less than $150 per night.
W: I agree. So, what do you think of this place?
M: I like it **because it has access to the hot springs**.
W: That would feel nice at night, but I'm sure the kids would prefer to play in a swimming pool.
M: You're probably right, and I want them to really enjoy this trip.
W: Then I think it's settled.
M: Good. **I'll make the reservations**.

여: 여보, 이 산장들이 우리가 휴가 보낼 곳으로 고를 수 있는 것들이에요?
남: 네, 오늘 하나를 골라야 할 것 같아요.
여: 이건 어때요? 바비큐하면 재미있을 거예요.
남: 아이들이 아주 좋아하겠지만, 내 일 때문에 인터넷이 필요할 것 같아요.
여: 당신이 일을 안 가져가면 좋겠지만, 이해해요.
남: 또, 하룻밤 머무르는 데 150달러 미만을 쓰는 게 좋은 생각인 것 같아요.
여: 나도 동의해요. 그러면 이곳은 어때요?
남: 온천에 출입할 수 있어서 나는 좋아요.
여: 밤에 아주 좋긴 할 텐데, 아이들은 분명히 수영장에서 노는 것을 더 좋아할 거예요.
남: 아마 당신 말이 맞을 거예요. 그리고 나는 아이들이 이 여행을 정말 즐겁게 보내면 좋겠어요.
여: 그러면 정해진 것 같네요.
남: 좋아요. 내가 예약할게요.

어휘 **lodge** 오두막, 산장

11 짧은 대화에 이어질 응답 | ⑤

▶ 여자에게 전화했지만 통화를 할 수 없었다고 말하는 남자에게 여자는 전화를 받지 못한 이유를 설명할 것이다.

① 한 번 더 전화해 주세요.
② 제 음성 메시지를 바로 확인할게요.
③ 이제 우리는 회의를 시작할 수 있어요.
④ 엘리베이터가 또 고장 났어요.
⑤ 죄송해요, 휴대 전화를 제 책상 위에 두고 왔어요.

M: Where have you been? The meeting started already!
W: I'm so sorry. **I was stuck in the elevator** for about twenty minutes.
M: Well, **I tried calling you**, but your phone went to voicemail.
W: ______________________________

남: 어디 있었어요? 회의가 벌써 시작됐어요!
여: 정말 죄송합니다. 약 20분 동안 엘리베이터에 갇혀 있었어요.
남: 음, 당신에게 전화했지만, 음성 메시지로 넘어가더군요.
여: ______________________________

어휘 **out of order** 고장 난; 정리가 안 된 / **voicemail** (전화기의) 음성 메시지 녹음 장치

12 짧은 대화에 이어질 응답 | ④

▶ 남자의 누나에게 보고서 작성을 도와달라고 부탁하는 게 어떠냐고 묻는 여자의 말에 가장 적절한 응답을 찾는다.

① 너희 언니는 역사를 전공했구나.
② 아니, 마감일은 어제였어.
③ 내가 선생님께 시간을 좀 더 달라고 부탁드릴게.
④ 누나는 시험 준비하느라 바빠.
⑤ 이 수업은 과제가 너무 많아.

W: Mark, do you think we can **finish our history report in time**?
M: I'm not sure. We have only three hours left before the deadline!
W: How about **asking your sister to help us**?
M: ______________________________

여: Mark, 우리가 역사 보고서를 제시간에 끝낼 수 있을 거라고 생각해?
남: 잘 모르겠어. 마감 시간 전까지 세 시간밖에 안 남았잖아!
여: 너희 누나한테 우릴 도와달라고 부탁하는 건 어때?
남: ______________________________

어휘 **deadline** 마감 일자[시간], 기한

13 긴 대화에 이어질 응답 | ②

▶ 여자는 영어 성적을 올리려면 공부하는 데 더 많은 시간을 들여야 한다고 말하고 있으므로, 사전을 하나 더 사는 게 어떻겠냐는 남자의 물음에는 노력이 더 중요하다는 응답이 적절하다.

① 낮 동안에는 시간이 충분하지 않아.
② 이건 정말 노력의 문제라는 것을 기억하렴.
③ 적당한 학습 지침서를 추천해줄게.
④ 시험이 어려웠던 거니까 걱정하지 마.
⑤ 너는 네 공부를 더 진지하게 생각했어야 했단다.

M: Ms. Evans, can I talk to you for a minute?
W: Of course, Henry. What's on your mind?
M: It's about English grammar. My grade isn't improving.
W: **Are you having trouble with the concepts**? Or is it more of a test-related problem?
M: Both, I guess. Do you have any advice?
W: Well, **how much time do you spend studying** each day?

M: Around 20 minutes every day.
W: That's not enough, Henry. **It takes a long time to understand** foreign grammar.
M: But I'm too busy to put more time into studying English. **What if I bought a study guide?**
W: That couldn't hurt, but it won't solve the problem.
M: Then, what about another dictionary?
W: ______________________________

남: Evans 선생님, 잠시 말씀 좀 나눌 수 있을까요?
여: 물론이지, Henry. 무슨 일이니?
남: 영어 문법에 관한 거예요. 제 성적이 오르지 않고 있어요.
여: 개념을 이해하는 게 어렵니? 아니면 그것보다는 시험과 관련된 문제니?
남: 둘 다인 것 같아요. 조언 좀 해주시겠어요?
여: 음, 공부하는 데 하루에 시간을 얼마나 쓰니?
남: 매일 20분 정도요.
여: 그건 충분하지 않단다, Henry. 외국어 문법을 이해하려면 시간이 오래 걸려.
남: 하지만 너무 바빠서 영어 공부에 시간을 더 쓸 수가 없는걸요. 학습 지침서를 사면 어떨까요?
여: 나쁠 건 없겠지만, 그게 문제를 해결해주진 않을 거야.
남: 그럼 다른 사전을 하나 사는 건요?
여: ______________________________

14 긴 대화에 이어질 응답 | ①

▶ 여자(딸)의 여행을 완강히 허락하지 않는 남자(아빠)가 친구들에게 같이 갈 거라고 이미 말했다는 여자에게 할 수 있는 말을 유추해 본다.

① 음, 나한테 먼저 물어봤어야지.
② 걱정하지 마, 친구 좋다는 게 뭐니.
③ 여행이 취소돼서 분명 슬프겠구나.
④ 네 친구들이 실망했다고 내게 말했단다.
⑤ 약속을 깨는 것은 어떤 상황에서도 용납할 수 없구나.

W: Are you busy, Dad?
M: I have a minute. **What's on your mind**, Rebecca?
W: Well, my friends are going on a trip for a couple of days, and I want to go with them. Can I?
M: I don't know. Whose family **would you be staying with**?
W: It's just a trip with friends. It would be so much fun!
M: I don't think that's a good idea.
W: Dad, please. I'll call you every few hours, and it's only for a couple of days.
M: No, I'm afraid not. It's too dangerous without adults.
W: But we're grown up **enough to go on a trip by ourselves**.
M: I'm sorry, Rebecca, but I won't change my mind.
W: But, Dad, I **already told my friends I'd join them**!
M: ______________________________

여: 아빠, 바쁘세요?
남: 잠깐 시간이 있단다. 무슨 일이니, Rebecca?
여: 음, 제 친구들이 이틀 동안 여행을 갈 건데, 저도 같이 가고 싶어요. 그래도 돼요?
남: 잘 모르겠구나. 누구의 가족이랑 함께 묵을 거니?
여: 그냥 친구들과의 여행이에요. 정말 재미있을 거예요!
남: 그건 좋은 생각이 아닌 것 같구나.
여: 아빠, 제발요. 몇 시간 간격으로 전화 드릴게요. 그리고 고작 며칠이잖아요.
남: 안타깝지만 안 되겠다. 어른들 없이는 너무 위험하단다.
여: 하지만 저희는 저희끼리 여행 갈 만큼 충분히 자랐어요.
남: Rebecca. 미안하지만 내 마음이 변하진 않을 거야.
여: 하지만 아빠, 친구들에게 같이 갈 거라고 벌써 말했단 말이에요!
남: ______________________________

어휘 **unacceptable** 용납할[받아들일] 수 없는 (↔ acceptable 받아들일 수 있는)

15 상황에 적절한 말 | ②

▶ 단짝 친구였던 Justin과 10년 만에 연락이 닿았고 서로 가까운 곳에 산다는 것을 알게 된 Diane이 할 수 있는 말을 유추해 본다.

① 와, 너 많이 변했구나!
② 우리 서로 매우 가까이 있어!
③ 어디로 이사 갈 거니?
④ 나 어렸을 때 너희 집 근처에서 살았어.
⑤ 소셜 네트워킹 사이트는 옛 친구를 찾는 데 도움이 돼.

W: Diane and Justin **were best friends in middle school**. Then, Diane's family moved to Korea because of Diane's father's work. Unfortunately, Diane lost Justin's phone number during the move, so **they were unable to keep in touch**. Ten years later, Justin is studying Korean in a university in Korea. And Diane is checking some messages from her friends on a social networking site as usual. She sees that Justin **has sent his regards to her** and left his contact number. She calls Justin immediately and the two **discuss their current lives**. During the conversation, Diane learns that Justin now lives in a building near her house. Diane wants to **let him know this fact**. In this situation, what would Diane most likely say to Justin?

여: Diane과 Justin은 중학교 때 단짝 친구였다. 그 뒤, 아버지의 직장 때문에 Diane의 가족은 한국으로 이사를 갔다. 안타깝게도, Diane이 이사 도중 Justin의 전화번호를 잃어버려서 그들은 연락하고 지낼 수 없었다. 10년 후, Justin은 한국에 있는 대학교에서 한국어를 공부하고 있다. 그리고 Diane은 소셜 네트워킹 사이트에서 친구들에게서 온 메시지를 평소처럼 확인하고 있다. 그녀는 Justin이 자신에게 안부를 전하고 연락처를 남긴 것을 본다. 그녀는 Justin에게 즉시 전화를 걸고 둘은 각자의 현재 삶에 관해 이야기를 나눈다. 대화 도중, Diane은 Justin이 현재 자신의 집 근처 건물에 산다는 것을 알게 된다. Diane은 그에게 이 사실을 알려주고 싶다. 이러한 상황에서 Diane이 Justin에게 할 말로 가장 적절한 것은 무엇인가?

어휘 **social networking site** (온라인 인맥 구축을 목적으로 개설된) 커뮤니티형 웹사이트 (= SNS)

16~17 세트 문항 | 16. ② 17. ③

▶ 16. 스트레스에 잘못 대처했을 때 발생할 수 있는 여러 가지 결과에 관해 이야기하고 있다.

① 올바른 식단의 중요성
② 스트레스를 잘못 처리한 결과
③ 스트레스를 관리하는 올바른 방법
④ 식단에 미치는 스트레스의 부정적인 영향
⑤ 스트레스와 음식 간의 관계

▶ 17. 해석 참조

M: We are all exposed to stress in our day-to-day lives, and **it's important to deal with it properly**. When stress is not managed in a healthy manner, there can be unpleasant consequences. For example, many stressed individuals become depressed and avoid social situations or **isolate themselves from friends and family**. They may also experience difficulty finding joy in once enjoyable activities. At the same time, **others may turn to shopping** or online games to escape their stress. One particularly unhealthy way of escaping stress is through emotional eating. Emotional eaters eat not because they are hungry but because it comforts them. Unfortunately, this can develop into an eating disorder, especially for those with a family history of eating disorders. **Habitual dieters are also at risk** because of the compliments they receive when losing weight. But they aren't alone. Those with stressful jobs that focus on body image, like actors and dancers, **may also struggle with eating disorders**. Furthermore, the media's focus on entertainers with slim bodies creates pressure to be thin. So, the next time you're feeling stressed, remember that food isn't the answer.

남: 우리는 모두 일상적인 생활에서 스트레스에 노출되어 있어서, 그것에 올바로 대응하는 것이 중요합니다. 스트레스가 건전한 방식으로 다루어지지 않을 때, 유쾌하지 않은 결과가 있을 수 있습니다. 예를 들어, 스트레스를 받은 많은 사람은 우울해져서 사교적인 상황을 피하거나 자신을 친구와 가족으로부터 고립시킵니다. 그들은 또한 한때 즐거웠던 활동에서 기쁨을 발견하는 데 어려움을 겪을지도 모릅니다. 동시에, 다른 이들은 스트레스를 피하려고 쇼핑이나 온라인 게임에 의지할지도 모릅니다. 특히 건강을 해치면서 스트레스를 피하는 한 가지 방법은 감정적인 식사를 통해서입니다. 감정적인 식사를 하는 사람들은 배고프기 때문이 아니라 그것이 위안을 주기 때문에 먹습니다. 안타깝게도, 이는 식이장애로 발전할 수 있는데, 식이장애에 대한 ① 가족 병력이 있는 이들에게는 특히 그렇습니다. ② 습관적으로 다이어트를 하는 이들 또한 체중을 감량했을 때 그들이 받는 칭찬 때문에 위험에 처해있습니다. 하지만 그들만 그런 것은 아닙니다. 배우나 무용수처럼 신체상(像)에 치중하는 ④ 스트레스가 많은 직업을 가진 이들 역시 식이장애로 고군분투할지 모릅니다. 더욱이, ⑤ 날씬한 몸을 가진 연예인에 대한 미디어의 주목은 날씬해야 한다는 압박감을 불러일으킵니다. 따라서 다음에 당신이 스트레스를 받을 때, 음식이 답이 아니라는 것을 기억하십시오.

어휘 **mishandle** (문제 · 상황을) 잘못 처리[관리]하다; ~을 거칠게 다루다 / **isolate** ~을 고립시키다, 격리하다; ~을 분리[구분]하다 / **turn to** ~에 의지하다 (= rely on) / **disorder** (신체 기능의) 장애; 영망, 무질서 / **habitual** 습관적인 (= customary)

Answers & Explanation

01.② 02.⑤ 03.④ 04.③ 05.① 06.③ 07.② 08.④ 09.③ 10.④
11.④ 12.④ 13.② 14.② 15.④ 16.④ 17.⑤

01 화자가 하는 말의 목적 | ②

▶ we ask that you make the exact number of copies needed에 목적이 드러나 있다. 복사용지가 낭비되고 있으니 필요한 수량을 정확히 복사할 것을 요청하고 있다.

M: This is an announcement for everyone who uses the photocopier. We checked to see **how much paper we threw away** in the last two months in the photocopy room. We found that people are **making unnecessary copies** and wasting a lot of paper. In many cases, employees carelessly make more copies than needed. As a result, a lot of paper is being thrown away. Needlessly throwing away so much paper is destroying forests. In the future, we ask that you **make the exact number of copies needed**. By using our copier efficiently, we are also helping our environment. Thank you for your cooperation.

남: 이것은 복사기를 사용하는 모든 분을 위한 안내입니다. 지난 두 달간 복사실에서 우리가 종이를 얼마나 낭비하는지 확인차 알아보았습니다. 우리는 사람들이 불필요한 복사를 하면서 많은 종이를 낭비하고 있다는 것을 알았습니다. 많은 경우에, 직원들은 무심코 필요한 것보다 더 많이 복사합니다. 결과적으로 많은 종이가 버려지고 있습니다. 너무 많은 종이가 불필요하게 버려짐으로써 삼림이 파괴되고 있습니다. 앞으로는, 필요로 하는 정확한 수량만큼 복사를 해주시기를 부탁합니다. 복사기를 효율적으로 사용함으로써, 우리는 환경을 도울 수도 있습니다. 여러분의 협조에 감사드립니다.

어휘 **announcement** 발표, 공고 / **photocopier** 복사기 / **throw away** ~을 허비하다; (필요 없게 된 것을) 버리다 / **make a copy** 복사하다 / **carelessly** 무심코, 무관심하게; 부주의하게 / **needlessly** 불필요하게 / **efficiently** 효율적으로 / **cooperation** 협조, 협력

02 의견 | ⑤

▶ 여자는 바다에 준비도 없이 뛰어든 건 무모하다고 단정하면서, 그것 때문에 목숨이 위험할 수 있었고 청소년에게 나쁜 본보기가 될 수도 있다고 말하고 있다.

M: **Have you heard about** what Danny did?
W: Are you talking about Danny Bailey? Yeah, he's the talk of the town right now.
M: I can't believe he swam to Alcatraz and back in that freezing water! He's incredibly brave.
W: Do you really see it as bravery? **I completely disagree**. It's the most foolish thing I've ever heard of.
M: Really? Perhaps it wasn't the smartest thing to do, but I still think it was brave.
W: There's a difference between being brave and reckless. To me, it was reckless.
M: Why do you **feel so strongly about this**?
W: From what I know, he didn't train for the swim. I know he's a good swimmer, but **he could've killed himself**.
M: You have a point. He said he just jumped into the ocean and started swimming.
W: Thank goodness nothing went wrong, but that sort of reckless behavior sets a bad example for kids.
M: Oh, I didn't think about that.

남: Danny가 뭘 했는지 들었어?
여: Danny Bailey에 관해 얘기하는 거니? 응, 그 사람 지금 장안의 화제잖아.
남: 그가 그렇게 차가운 물에서 Alcatraz까지 헤엄쳐서 갔다 돌아온 걸 믿을 수가 없어! 그는 엄청나게 용감해.
여: 넌 정말로 그걸 용기라고 생각해? 난 전혀 동의하지 않아. 그건 내가 들어본 것 중에 가장 어리석은 짓이야.
남: 정말? 가장 똑똑하다고 할 만한 일은 아니지만, 난 그래도 그게 용감한 거라고 생각해.
여: 용감한 것과 무모한 것에는 차이가 있어. 나에게는, 그건 무모한 거였어.
남: 왜 넌 이 일에 대해서 그렇게 예민하게 생각하니?
여: 내가 아는 바로는, 그는 수영에 대비해서 훈련하지 않았어. 그가 수영을 잘하는 건 알지만, 그는 죽을 수도 있었어.
남: 네 말이 맞네. 그는 바다에 그냥 뛰어들어서 수영하기 시작했다고 말했지.
여: 아무것도 잘못되지 않아서 다행이지만, 그런 종류의 무모한 행동은 청소년들에게 나쁜 본보기를 보여준다고.
남: 아, 내가 거기에 대해선 생각을 못 했네.

어휘 **the talk of the town** 장안의 화제, 화젯거리 / **freezing** 몹시 추운 / **incredibly** 엄청나게, 믿을 수 없을 정도로 / **brave** 용감한 ***cf.* bravery** 용감함 / **reckless** 무모한, 신중하지 못한 / **feel strongly** 예민하게 느끼다; 통감하다, 절실히 느끼다 / **set a bad [good] example** 나쁜[좋은] 본을 보이다

03 관계 | ④

▶ 간호사가 의사에게 환자의 상태를 설명하고 있는 내용이다.

M: Hi, Allison.
W: Good afternoon, Dr. Welsh. We have a 16-year-old female, Isabella Paolo.
M: Can I see the chart?
W: Here you are. She came in with a pain in her stomach. She **appears to be very anxious**.
M: When did she come in?
W: Just five minutes ago from the emergency room. Her mother came with her.
M: **Is she still complaining of pain**?
W: Yes, she complains of severe stomachache.
M: Let's see. She has a temperature of 37.1℃.
W: **I took it a moment ago**.
M: Okay. Please place her on a bed and **raise the head of the bed** to a 30° angle. I'm going to see her shortly.
W: I see.

남: 안녕하세요, Allison.
여: 안녕하세요, Welsh 박사님. 16살 여성인 Isabella Paolo가 있습니다.
남: 차트 좀 볼 수 있을까요?
여: 여기 있습니다. 그 환자는 위에 통증이 있어서 왔어요. 매우 불안해하는 것 같아요.
남: 언제 왔나요?
여: 바로 5분 전에 응급실에서요. 환자의 어머니가 함께 오셨어요.
남: 여전히 통증을 호소하고 있나요?
여: 네, 극심한 복통을 호소하고 있어요.
남: 어디 봅시다. 체온은 37.1도네요.
여: 제가 조금 전에 체온을 쟀어요.
남: 좋아요. 환자를 침대에 눕히고 침대의 머리를 30도 각도까지 들어 올려주세요. 제가 곧 환자를 볼게요.
여: 알겠습니다.

어휘 **emergency room** 응급실 / **complain of pain** 통증을 호소하다 / **severe** 극심한, 심각한; 엄격한 / **angle** 각도 / **shortly** 곧

04 그림 불일치 | ③

▶ 해적은 칼을 들고 있다고 했다.

M: Mom! I had a great day at school.
W: That's great! Tell me about your day.
M: In art class, I drew a pirate after reading *Treasure Island*. I drew him with a pirate hat and **a striped shirt**.
W: How about a parrot? You love to draw parrots with pirates.
M: Of course I drew a parrot. The parrot is sitting **on top of his right hand**.
W: Does he have a weapon?
M: Yes. He is sitting in front of a tree and **holding his sword in his hand**.
W: It sounds great. I'm sure you drew some treasures, too.
M: Sure. I drew a big palm tree behind the pirate and a big box of treasure next to the tree.
W: That's fantastic!
M: My teacher said he especially likes **the jewels overflowing from the treasure chest**.

남: 엄마! 오늘 학교에서 즐거운 하루를 보냈어요.
여: 멋지구나! 엄마한테 너의 하루를 말해주렴.
남: 미술 수업에서, 〈보물섬〉을 읽은 후에 해적을 그렸어요. 해적 모자를 쓰고 줄무늬 셔츠를 입은 해적을 그렸어요.

여: 앵무새는? 너는 해적과 함께 앵무새를 그리는 걸 아주 좋아하잖아.
남: 물론 앵무새를 그렸죠. 앵무새는 해적의 오른손 위에 앉아 있어요.
여: 해적은 무기를 가지고 있니?
남: 네, 나무 앞에 앉아서 손에 검을 쥐고 있어요.
여: 멋진 것 같구나. 넌 분명히 보물도 좀 그렸을 거야.
남: 당연하죠. 해적 뒤에 커다란 야자나무를 그렸고 나무 옆에는 커다란 보물 상자를 하나 그렸어요.
여: 굉장하구나!
남: 우리 선생님께서는 보물 상자에서 넘쳐흐르는 보석이 특히 마음에 든다고 말씀하셨어요.

어휘 **pirate** 해적 / **striped** 줄무늬가 있는 / **weapon** 무기, 흉기 / **sword** 검, 칼 / **palm tree** 야자나무 / **overflow** 넘쳐흐르다 / **treasure chest** 보물 상자

05 부탁한 일 | ①

▶ 아내가 병원에 입원한 상태에서 시애틀로 출장을 가야 하는 남자가 여자에게 출장을 대신 가 달라고 부탁하고 있다.

W: Hi, Bill. You missed Jerry's housewarming party yesterday. Were you sick?
M: No, but my wife came down with a bad case of the flu, so I had to take her to the hospital.
W: How awful! **I can't believe that**. How serious is it?
M: I don't know. The doctor said she should stay in the hospital for a couple of days until her fever is gone. He thinks she might have some sort of infection.
W: I hope that's a worst-case scenario. I'm sure **she'll recover soon**.
M: I hope so. I have to go on a business trip tomorrow, and I don't know what to do.
W: You mean a business trip to Seattle? If that's the case, somebody else can go there.
M: Oh, you're right. Then if you're okay, **could you go there instead of me**?
W: Sure. I'll take your place. After all, we work in the same department, so it shouldn't be a problem.
M: Wow, **I don't know what to say**. You're an angel.

여: 안녕하세요, Bill. 어제 Jerry의 집들이에 안 오셨더군요. 아프셨어요?
남: 아니에요, 제 아내가 독감이 심하게 걸려서 아내를 데리고 병원에 가야 했어요.
여: 딱하기도 해라! 믿을 수가 없네요. 얼마나 심각한가요?
남: 모르겠어요. 의사 말로는 열이 내릴 때까지 병원에 며칠 입원해야 한대요. 의사는 아내가 일종의 감염이 됐을지도 모른다고 생각해요.
여: 그게 최악의 경우라면 좋겠네요. 분명히 아내께서 곧 회복하실 거예요.
남: 그러길 바랍니다. 제가 내일 출장을 가야 하는데, 어떻게 해야 할지 모르겠어요.
여: 시애틀 출장 말씀이세요? 그렇다면, 다른 누군가가 거기에 갈 수 있어요.
남: 아, 그렇군요. 그러면 만약 괜찮으시면, 저 대신에 당신이 거기 가주실 수 있을까요?
여: 물론이죠. 제가 대신 갈게요. 어쨌든, 우리는 같은 부서에서 일하니까 문제가 안 될 거예요.
남: 와, 이거 뭐라 말씀드려야 할지. 당신은 천사예요.

어휘 **housewarming party** 집들이 / **come down with** (별로 심각하지 않은 병이) 걸리다, 들다 / **infection** 감염; 전염병 / **worst-case scenario** 최악의 시나리오 ((앞으로 닥칠지 모를 최악의 상황을 가정한 시나리오)) / **recover** 회복되다; 되찾다 / **if that's the case** 그렇다면, 그러면 / **take A's place** A를 대신하다

06 금액 | ③

▶ 책 세 권의 가격 110달러에서 10%를 할인하면 99달러이고, 여기에 운송료 10달러를 더하면 모두 109달러이다. 운송료는 10% 할인에서 제외됨에 주의한다.

M: Is there anything I can help you with?
W: Yes, please. I ordered three books, and **I was wondering if my order came in**.
M: Can I have your name, please?
W: Sure. My name is Jessica Reynolds.
M: Oh, here it is. Yes, we just received them today. *[pause]* Here you go. Please **make sure those are the correct books**.
W: Yes, they are, thank you. How much are they?
M: One book costs $35, another is $45, and the other is $30.
W: So my total is $110. **Does this include the shipping cost**?
M: No, shipping is another $10.
W: I see. Here's my credit card.
M: Hold on a minute. These books are currently **10% off the retail price**.
W: Oh, it's my lucky day. Is the discount just for the books?
M: Yes, that's right.

남: 무엇을 도와드릴까요?
여: 네, 부탁합니다. 제가 책 세 권을 주문했는데, 제가 주문한 게 들어왔는지 궁금했어요.
남: 성함을 알려주시겠어요?
여: 네, 제 이름은 Jessica Reynolds예요.
남: 아, 여기 있네요. 네, 저희가 오늘 그 책들을 받았어요. *[잠시 후]* 여기 있습니다. 그게 (주문하신 것과) 맞는 책인지 확인해 주시기 바랍니다.
여: 네, 맞네요, 감사합니다. 얼마인가요?
남: 한 권은 35달러이고, 다른 한 권은 45달러, 그리고 나머지 한 권이 30달러네요.
여: 그러면 합계는 110달러네요. 이건 운송료를 포함하나요?
남: 아뇨, 운송은 따로 10달러랍니다.
여: 알겠어요. 여기 신용카드요.
남: 잠깐만요. 이 책들은 지금 소매가격에서 10퍼센트 할인하고 있습니다.
여: 아, 운이 좋은 날이네요. 이 할인은 책에만 적용되는 거죠?
남: 네, 맞습니다.

어휘 **shipping cost** 운송료 / **currently** 현재, 지금 / **retail price** 소매가격

07 이유 | ②

▶ 오늘 밤에 과학 과제를 수정해야 하며, 그것을 마친 다음에 청소하겠다고 말했다.

W: Aiden, what did I say about cleaning your room? I told you to clean your room three times today!
M: I'm going to clean it, but I can't do it right now.
W: **What do you mean**?
M: I have to do something important.
W: So what's so important? I don't think computer games or movies are important.
M: Remember **the science project I'm working on**?
W: Yeah, I thought you finished it last week.
M: Well, the teacher **asked me to change a few things**, so I have to work on it tonight.
W: So when are you planning to clean your room?
M: I promise I'll do it after I'm done with my project.
W: **I'll let it go** this time.

여: Aiden, 네 방을 청소하는 것에 대해 내가 뭐라고 말했지? 오늘 너한테 방을 청소하라고 세 번 말했어!
남: 방을 청소할 거예요. 하지만 지금 바로 할 수는 없어요.
여: 무슨 말이야?
남: 해야 할 중요한 일이 있어요.
여: 그럼 뭐가 그렇게 중요한데? 컴퓨터 게임이나 영화가 중요한 것 같진 않구나.
남: 제가 작업하고 있는 과학 과제 기억하세요?
여: 그래, 난 네가 그걸 지난주에 끝냈다고 생각했는데.
남: 음, 선생님께서 저에게 몇 가지를 바꾸라고 요청하셔서 오늘 밤에 그걸 해야 해요.
여: 그러면 언제 방을 청소할 계획인 거니?
남: 제 과제를 마친 다음에 하겠다고 약속해요.
여: 이번엔 이쯤 해 두마.

08 언급하지 않은 것 | ④

▶ 해석 참조

W: Thank you for your honest answer, Mr. Moore. **I'm impressed by your positive attitude**.
M: I appreciate the opportunity for this interview.
W: Do you have any questions regarding our company or this position?
M: If I get the job, **will I be working at the factory or at the office**?
W: You'll be spending most of your time in the office. And you'll be working from nine to six.
M: I see. I heard that you get one week of vacation a year. Is it paid vacation?
W: Yes, you get **a week of paid vacation a year**. Any questions about the salary?
M: No, I'm happy with the salary. I'd like to know more about the insurance you offer to your employees.
W: The company pays for 80% of your health insurance for you and your family. You'll likely pay about $200 for insurance a month.
M: **That's everything I wanted to know**. Thank you.

여: 솔직한 답변에 감사드립니다, Moore 씨. 당신의 긍정적인 태도에 깊은 인상을 받았어요.
남: 이 면접을 볼 기회를 주셔서 감사드립니다.
여: 우리 회사나 이 일자리에 관련된 질문이 있으세요?
남: 만약 제가 그 일을 하게 되면, 저는 공장에서 일하게 되나요, 사무실에서 일하게 되나요?

여: 당신은 사무실에서 대부분의 시간을 보낼 겁니다(① 근무 장소). 그리고 9시에서 6시까지 일할 거예요(② 근무 시간).
남: 그렇군요. 일 년에 일주일의 휴가가 있다고 들었습니다. 그건 유급 휴가입니까?
여: 네, 일 년에 일주일의 유급 휴가가 있습니다(③ 유급 휴가). 급여에 관한 질문이 있으세요?
남: 아뇨, 저는 급여에 만족합니다. 저는 회사가 직원들에게 제공하는 보험에 대해서 더 알고 싶습니다.
여: 회사는 당신과 당신 가족에 대한 건강보험의 80%를 냅니다. 보험에 대해서 당신은 한 달에 200달러 정도를 낼 것입니다(⑤ 보험 부담금).
남: 제가 알고 싶었던 건 그게 전부입니다. 감사합니다.

어휘 **regarding** ~에 관하여 / **paid vacation** 유급 휴가 / **salary** 급여, 봉급

09 내용 불일치 | ③

▶ visit our website at www.greenvillecostume.com and sign up에서 온라인으로 참가 등록을 해야 한다는 것을 알 수가 있다.

W: It's time to hold the annual Greenville Costume Contest. **This outdoor event will be held** in our town square next Sunday, October 12th. Anyone can participate by dressing up in a costume of his or her choice. There will be plenty of prizes for everyone. **Prizes will be given for the following categories**: most creative costume, most elaborate costume, and scariest costume. If you're not sure **how to get started**, visit our website at www.greenvillecostume.com and sign up. You can browse through last year's winners' costumes. How about making this a family activity and having the whole family dress up in costumes? **We are accepting application forms** right now, so sign up today!

여: 매년 열리는 Greenville Costume Contest를 개최할 때입니다. 이 야외 행사는 다음 주 일요일, 10월 12일에 우리 마을 광장에서 개최될 것입니다. 누구든지 자신이 고른 의상으로 차려입고 참가하실 수 있습니다. 모두를 위한 많은 상이 마련돼 있을 것입니다. 가장 창의적인 의상, 가장 정교한 의상, 그리고 가장 무시무시한 의상 부문으로 나누어 상이 시상됩니다. 만약 어떻게 시작해야 할지 잘 모르시겠다면, 저희 웹사이트 www.greenvillecostume.com을 방문하셔서 등록하십시오. 작년 우승자들의 의상을 찾아보실 수 있습니다. 이것을 가족 활동으로 만들어서 온 가족이 의상을 차려입게 하는 건 어떨까요? 지금 신청서를 접수하고 있으니, 오늘 등록하십시오!

어휘 **annual** 매년의, 연례의 / **square** 광장; 정사각형(의) / **dress up** 옷을 갖춰 입다 / **category** 범주; 부문, 종류 / **elaborate** 정교한; 공들인 / **get started** 시작하다 / **sign up** 등록하다, 가입하다 / **browse through** ~을 여기저기 읽다, 훑어보다 / **application** 신청(서)

10 도표 이해 | ④

▶ 남자는 여자에게 어떤 가방을 원하는지 묻고 있다. 여자가 원하는 가방은 짧은 끈이 달린 토트백이고 12×10인치의 크기이며, 가죽이든 천이든 500달러를 넘지 않는 것이다.

[Phone rings.]
M: Hello? Sarah?
W: Connor, where are you? I thought you were coming back from your business trip tomorrow. **Have you arrived at the airport** already?
M: No. I'm here at the Camelia outlet right now. I wanted to know **what kind of bag you wanted**. Do you want a long or short strap?
W: The bag I'm looking for isn't a shoulder bag but a tote bag with very short straps.
M: Okay. What size are you looking for?
W: I'd like something **that is about 12 inches in length** and 10 inches in height.
M: Okay. There are two types of material, fabric and leather. Which do you want?
W: What about the price?
M: The leather bags are more expensive.
W: I'd prefer a leather bag, but I'll take whatever bag you choose **as long as it's not over $500**.
M: Got it. I'll see you tomorrow.
W: Thanks, honey.

[전화벨이 울린다.]
남: 여보세요? Sarah?
여: Connor, 당신 어디야? 난 당신이 내일 출장에서 돌아올 거라고 생각했어. 벌써 공항에 도착했어?
남: 아니, 난 지금 Camelia 아울렛에 있어. 당신이 원했던 가방이 어떤 종류인지 알고 싶었어. 긴 끈을 원해, 짧은 끈을 원해?
여: 내가 찾고 있는 가방은 숄더백이 아니라, 아주 짧은 끈이 달린 토트백이야.
남: 알겠어. 어떤 크기의 가방을 찾고 있어?
여: 길이가 12인치 정도이고, 높이가 10인치 정도인 게 좋아.
남: 좋아. 천과 가죽, 두 가지 종류의 소재가 있어. 어느 것을 원해?
여: 가격이 얼만데?
남: 가죽 가방이 더 비싸.
여: 난 가죽 가방이 더 좋지만, 500달러가 넘지만 않는다면 당신이 골라주는 무슨 가방이든지 좋아.
남: 알겠어. 내일 봐.
여: 고마워, 여보.

어휘 **outlet** 아울렛, 할인점 / **shoulder bag** 숄더백 ((끈을 어깨에 메는 가방)) / **tote bag** 토트백 ((상부가 벌어져 있는 핸드백이나 쇼핑백)) / **fabric** 직물, 천 / **strap** 끈, 줄

11 짧은 대화에 이어질 응답 | ④

▶ 같이 가기로 한 생일 파티에 왜 가지 못하게 된 것인지 묻고 있으므로 이유를 말하는 것이 적절하다.

① 그녀에게 지금 인사하는 게 좋을 거야.
② 생일 축하해 주는 것도 매일 있는 일이 아니야.
③ 네가 오지 않으면 난 너에게 실망할 거야.
④ 미안하지만, 나는 내일 싱가포르에 가야 해.
⑤ 그녀에게 줄 선물을 사려고 쇼핑을 좀 할 생각이었어.

W: Jerry, **we're supposed to go** to Emily's birthday party this Friday.
M: Oh, I'm sorry. I meant to tell you, I don't think **I can make it**.
W: What are you talking about? You said you would come.
M: ______________________________

여: Jerry, 우리 이번 주 금요일에 Emily의 생일 파티에 가기로 되어 있어.
남: 아, 미안해. 너한테 말하려고 했는데, 나는 가지 못할 것 같아.
여: 무슨 말을 하는 거야? 너 갈 거라고 했잖아.
남: ______________________________

어휘 **be supposed to-v** v하기로 되어 있다 / **make it** (모임 등에) 참석하다; (간신히) 시간 맞춰 가다

12 짧은 대화에 이어질 응답 | ④

▶ 예약을 했지만 착오가 생겨 예약이 안 된 상황에서 남자가 오늘 밤에 방이 있느냐고 물었으므로 빈방이 있는지 여부를 답하는 것이 적절하다.

① 알겠습니다. 당신의 예약을 지금 확인했습니다.
② 그럼요. 룸서비스를 부르실 수 있습니다.
③ 걱정하지 마세요. 방으로 사람을 보내겠습니다.
④ 죄송합니다. 사용할 수 있는 방이 없습니다.
⑤ 방이 너무 작아요. 오늘 밤에 묵을 방을 바꾸고 싶어요.

M: I made a reservation last week. My name is John Mitchell.
W: **Wait a second**, sir. I'm sorry, we don't have your reservation.
M: Something must be wrong. **What should I do**? Do you have a room tonight?
W: ______________________________

남: 제가 지난주에 예약했습니다. 제 이름은 John Mitchell입니다.
여: 잠깐만요, 손님. 죄송합니다, 손님의 예약이 없습니다.
남: 뭔가 잘못된 게 틀림없어요. 제가 어떻게 하면 되나요? 오늘 밤에 방이 있나요?
여: ______________________________

어휘 **confirm** 확인하다 / **call for** ~을 요구하다

13 긴 대화에 이어질 응답 | ②

▶ 수학 과목에 뒤떨어진 학생에게 학교에서 개인지도 받는 것을 권유하자 학생의 어머니가 동의한 상황이다. 이에 대한 적절한 응답을 고른다.

① 그가 곧 괜찮아지길 바랍니다.
② 분명히 그것이 그에게 유익할 거예요.
③ 그는 예의 바르게 행동해야 해요.
④ 그가 말하길 당신이 스트레스를 많이 받는다고 하더군요.
⑤ 시간을 내어 배려해 주셔서 감사합니다.

M: Come on in, Mrs. Johnson. **Thanks for stopping by**.
W: It's my pleasure. It's good to see you again.
M: Please have a seat. Would you like something to drink?
W: Some water would be nice. Frankly, **I was surprised to get your call**.
M: Don't worry, it's nothing serious. He gets along with most of his classmates.
W: That's a relief. So is something wrong?

M: Well, **his grades have been falling** over the last few months.
W: Oh dear. Is there a particular subject that he's having problems with?
M: He's struggling in math. So I **wanted to ask you if it would be okay** for him to get some tutoring at school.
W: Of course. That's a wonderful idea.
M: ______________________________

남: 어서 들어오세요, Johnson 부인. 들러주셔서 감사합니다.
여: 천만에요. 다시 뵙게 되니 좋네요.
남: 앉으세요. 마실 것 좀 드릴까요?
여: 물을 좀 주시면 좋겠네요. 솔직히 선생님 전화를 받고 놀랐습니다.
남: 걱정하지 마세요. 심각한 건 아닙니다. 아이는 대부분의 학우들과 잘 지낸답니다.
여: 다행이네요. 그러면 뭔가 잘못되었나요?
남: 음, 지난 몇 달 동안 아이의 성적이 떨어지고 있어요.
여: 아 저런. 문제가 있는 특정 과목이 있나요?
남: 수학을 매우 어려워하고 있습니다. 그래서 학교에서 아이에게 개인지도를 좀 해도 괜찮을지 어머님께 여쭤보고 싶었습니다.
여: 물론입니다. 좋은 생각이네요.
남: ______________________________

어휘 **benefit from** ~에서 이익을 얻다 / **consideration** 배려; 숙고; 고려사항 / **stop by** ~에 들르다 / **get along with** ~와 잘 지내다 / **struggle** 고전하다, 투쟁하다 / **tutor** 개인교습을 하다

14 긴 대화에 이어질 응답 | ②

▶ 아이들과 놀이공원을 가려고 계획하던 중, 남자가 일기예보를 보고 큰 폭풍이 온다고 말한다. 이에 여자는 계획을 미뤄야겠다고 응답할 것이다.

① 우산 가져오는 거 잊지 마요.
② 그러면 우리 계획을 미뤄야겠군요.
③ 떠나기 전에 반드시 창문을 닫아요.
④ 그럼요. 내가 샌드위치를 준비할 수 있어요.
⑤ 내일에 관해선 걱정하지 마요! 내일은 아직 오지 않았어요.

W: You didn't forget about our trip to the amusement park with the kids tomorrow, did you?
M: Of course I didn't. Do you think we should take some sandwiches with us?
W: Yes, so **I'm planning to fix some sandwiches**. We'll just buy the drinks there.
M: Great idea.
W: I hope we'll get good weather tomorrow. **We're not expecting rain** tomorrow, are we?
M: I don't think so, but we should check since we'll be outside. Let's check the Internet right now.
W: If it's going to rain, **it's better that we stay home**.
M: Okay. *[pause]* Oh dear. It says that it'll rain all day tomorrow.
W: All day? The kids are going to be so disappointed if we don't take them.
M: Yeah. **A big storm is coming in**.
W: ______________________________

여: 내일 애들이랑 놀이공원으로 소풍 가는 거 잊지 않았죠, 그렇죠?
남: 물론 안 잊었어요. 당신 생각엔 샌드위치를 좀 가져가야 할 것 같아요?
여: 네, 그래서 샌드위치를 좀 준비하려고 계획 중이에요. 마실 것은 거기에서 살 거예요.
남: 좋은 생각이에요.
여: 내일 날씨가 좋길 바라요. 비가 오지는 않을 거예요, 그렇죠?
남: 그럴 것 같지는 않지만, 우리는 내일 야외에 있을 거니까 확인을 해봐야 해요. 지금 인터넷을 확인해 보죠.
여: 만약 비가 온다면, 집에 있는 게 더 나아요.
남: 알겠어요. *[잠시 후]* 아 이런. 내일 하루 종일 비가 올 거라고 하네요.
여: 하루 종일이요? 아이들은 우리가 자기들을 데려가지 않으면 매우 실망할 거예요.
남: 그래요. 큰 폭풍이 오고 있어요.
여: ______________________________

어휘 **be sure to-v** 반드시 v하다 / **fix** (식사를) 준비하다; 고정하다

15 상황에 적절한 말 | ④

▶ 여자친구가 준 선물을 잃어버린 사실을 차마 말하지 못해 고민하는 친구에게 정직이 최선이라는 조언을 하려고 한다.

① 친구 좋다는 게 뭐니? 내가 네게 그것을 찾아주게 되어서 기뻐.
② 넌 매우 무책임하구나. 너에게 매우 실망했어.
③ 누구나 실수를 하잖아. 네가 왜 그랬는지 이해해.
④ 그걸 잃어버렸다고 그녀에게 말하고 사과해. 그게 최선이야.
⑤ 넌 큰일 났어. 그 애는 자기 태블릿 PC 없이는 살 수 없거든.

M: A few days ago, Brian lost his tablet PC at school. His tablet PC was a birthday gift from his girlfriend. He **looked everywhere in the school for it**, but he couldn't find it. Then **he ran into his friend**, Luis. He told Luis that **he couldn't bear to tell** his girlfriend that he'd lost her gift. This was because his girlfriend saved her money for a month from her part-time job to buy the gift. So **he didn't have the heart to tell** her the truth about what had happened. Luis thinks that honesty is the best policy in this type of situation. What would Luis most likely say to Brian?

남: 며칠 전, Brian은 학교에서 태블릿 PC를 잃어버렸다. 그의 태블릿 PC는 여자친구에게 받은 생일 선물이었다. Brian은 그것을 찾으려고 학교의 모든 곳을 뒤졌지만 찾지 못했다. 그러고 나서 그는 자신의 친구인 Luis와 마주쳤다. Brian은 Luis에게 자신의 여자친구가 준 선물을 잃어버린 것을 그녀에게 차마 얘기할 수 없었다고 말했다. 이는 여자친구가 그 선물을 사기 위해 아르바이트를 하며 한 달간 돈을 모았기 때문이었다. 그래서 Brian은 일어난 일에 대해서 여자친구에게 사실을 말할 용기가 없었다. Luis는 이런 유형의 상황에서는 정직이 최선이라고 생각한다. Luis가 Brian에게 할 말로 가장 적절한 것은 무엇인가?

어휘 **irresponsible** 무책임한 / **run into** ~와 우연히 마주치다 / **cannot bear to-v** 차마 v할 수 없다 / **have the heart to-v** v할 용기가 있다, 감히 v하다

16~17 세트 문항 | 16. ④ 17. ⑤

▶ 16. 여행 시 환경의 피해를 줄이기 위해 할 수 있는 일들을 권유하는 내용이다.

① 예산에 맞춰 휴가를 계획하는 법
② 대중교통 이용의 이점
③ 환경을 위해 종이를 쓰지 않는 휴가
④ 환경친화적인 관광객이 되는 방법
⑤ 지역 공동체에 미치는 생태 관광의 긍정적 영향

▶ 17. 해석 참조

W: Today, we travel more than **any previous generation**. So extra consideration about the impact of your travels is especially important. One of the best things you can do is to use public transportation. Take a bus or a subway train when you are downtown if possible. Public transportation can **not only add to your adventure**, but it's greener than renting a car or catching a taxi. Also, conserve water and **unplug electrical appliances** whenever you can while staying at a hotel. By doing so, you're protecting the environment of **the country you're traveling in**. Remember not to disrupt the local ecology by killing wildlife or uprooting plants in the mountains. Do not litter. Always be mindful of throwing trash in the river or forest of a park. It's a place for everyone, not just you. You must try to preserve the country's ecology for the sake of future travelers and, more importantly, the people who live there. **Make it a paperless vacation**! Forget collecting a bundle of paper brochures from your travel agent. Instead, save paper **by using the vast resources of the Internet**, well-traveled friends, and bloggers to plan and book your vacation.

여: 오늘날, 우리는 이전의 어느 세대보다 더 여행을 많이 다닙니다. 따라서 여러분의 여행이 미치는 영향에 관해 각별히 고려해보는 것은 특히 중요합니다. 여러분이 할 수 있는 최선의 것 중 하나는 대중교통을 이용하는 것입니다. 가능하다면 ① 시내에 있을 때 버스나 지하철을 이용하세요. 대중교통은 당신의 모험심을 더해줄 뿐만 아니라, 자동차를 빌리거나 택시를 잡는 것보다 더 환경친화적입니다. 또, 호텔에 머무르는 동안에는 가능할 때마다 물을 아껴 쓰고 전자제품의 플러그를 뽑으세요. 그렇게 함으로써, 여러분이 여행하는 지역의 환경을 보호하게 됩니다. 야생 동물을 죽이거나 ② 산의 식물을 뽑아 지역 생태를 망가뜨리지 않도록 하세요. 쓰레기를 버리지 마세요. ③ 강이나 ④ 공원의 숲에 쓰레기를 던지는 것을 항상 의식하세요. 그곳은 모두를 위한 장소이지, 여러분만을 위한 곳이 아닙니다. 당신은 앞으로 여행 올 사람들을 위해서, 무엇보다 그곳에 사는 사람들을 위해서, 지역의 생태를 보존하도록 노력해야 합니다. 여러분의 휴가를 종이를 쓰지 않는 휴가로 만드세요! 여행사 직원으로부터 받을 한 묶음의 종이 팸플릿을 모으는 것은 잊으세요. 대신에, 여러분의 휴가를 계획하고 예약하는 데에 인터넷의 광대한 자원, 여행 경험이 풍부한 친구들, 그리고 블로거들을 활용해서 종이를 절약하세요.

어휘 **budget** 예산(안); 예산을 세우다 / **paperless** 종이를 쓰지 않는 / **environmentally-friendly** 환경친화적인 / **ecotourism** 생태 관광 ((환경 훼손을 최소화하는 관광)) / **previous** 이전의, 앞의 / **generation** 세대 / **impact** 영향, 충격; 영향[충격]을 주다 / **add to** 늘리다, 증가시키다 / **rent** 빌리다, 임대하다 / **conserve** 아껴 쓰다; 보존하다 (= preserve) / **unplug** (전기) 플러그를 뽑다 / **electrical appliances** 전자제품 / **disrupt** 지장을 주다, 방해하다 / **ecology** 생태 *cf.* **local ecology** 지역 생태 / **uproot** 뿌리째 뽑다 / **litter** (쓰레기 등을) 버리다; (공공장소에 버려진) 쓰레기 / **mindful** 의식하는, 염두에 두는 / **for the sake of** ~을 위해서 / **bundle** 묶음, 꾸러미 / **brochure** 팸플릿, 소책자 / **vast** 막대한 / **well-traveled** 여행 경험이 많은

Answers & Explanation

01. ① 02. ① 03. ② 04. ④ 05. ⑤ 06. ④ 07. ③ 08. ④ 09. ④ 10. ⑤
11. ④ 12. ③ 13. ④ 14. ③ 15. ⑤ 16. ② 17. ④

01 화자가 하는 말의 목적 | ①

▶ 스웨터를 너무 자주 빨지 말고, 차가운 물에 손세탁하여, 짜지 말고 수건으로 물기 제거 후 평평하게 뉘여서 건조하라고 알려주는 내용이다.

W: Sweaters are a basic piece of clothing for our cold winters. In order to **keep sweaters looking their best**, you need to take extra care when cleaning them. The number one rule is not to over-clean sweaters. The less you clean them, the longer they will last. Most sweaters can be gently hand washed. Just **soak them for a few minutes** in a mild detergent and cool water. And rinse in cool water to remove all remaining soap. **Do not squeeze water out of the sweater** — roll in a towel and gently push on the towel to remove water. Then lay it flat to dry over something like a clothes rack. Sweaters can last for years **with the proper care**.

여: 스웨터는 추운 겨울을 위한 가장 기본적인 옷입니다. 스웨터를 최상의 상태로 보관하기 위해서는 세탁할 때 특별한 주의를 기울여야 합니다. 가장 중요한 규칙은 지나친 세탁을 하지 않는 것입니다. 덜 세탁할수록, 스웨터는 더 오래갑니다. 대부분 스웨터는 부드럽게 손빨래할 수 있습니다. 순한 세제를 푼 차가운 물에 몇 분 동안 그저 담가두십시오. 그러고 나서 찬물에 헹구어 남은 세제를 모두 제거하십시오. 스웨터를 비틀어서 물을 짜내지 마시고 수건으로 말아서 부드럽게 눌러 물기를 제거하십시오. 그 후에 옷걸이 같은 것 위에 평평하게 뉘여 말리세요. 스웨터는 적절히 관리해주면 몇 년 동안은 입을 수 있습니다.

어휘 **soak** (액체에) 담그다 / **detergent** 세제 / **clothes rack** (금속봉의) 옷걸이

02 의견 | ①

▶ 남자는 개의 행동을 교정하기 위해 벌을 주지 말고 착한 일을 했을 때 선물을 주거나 칭찬하는 방법으로 훈련하라고 이야기하고 있다.

W: My puppy is super cute but very naughty sometimes.
M: What do you mean?
W: He bites everything he sees and still pees in areas he's not supposed to.
M: It looks like **you need to train your dog properly**. It's important that you don't punish him every time he does something bad.
W: Unfortunately, I yell at him a lot these days.
M: I can understand, and that's required at times, but you **need to reward the puppy** when he does something good.
W: Well, he does know how to sit when I command him to do so.
M: Great. Then **give him a little treat** and praise him when he does.
W: That's a great idea. **I should buy some treats for him**.
M: If he goes to the bathroom in the proper place, praise him several times. Eventually, he will be toilet-trained.
W: I see. Thanks for the advice.

여: 우리 집 강아지가 아주 귀엽긴 한데 때때로 아주 말을 안 들어.
남: 무슨 뜻이야?
여: 보이는 건 전부 이빨로 물고, 아직도 소변 보면 안 되는 곳에 소변을 봐.
남: 네 개를 제대로 훈련해야 할 것 같아. 개가 나쁜 짓을 할 때마다 벌을 주지 않는 게 중요해.
여: 유감스럽게도, 난 요즘 개한테 야단을 많이 쳐.
남: 이해가 되고 그게 때로는 필요하지만, 착한 일을 할 때 강아지에게 보상을 해줘야 해.
여: 음, 그 녀석은 내가 앉으라고 명령하면 어떻게 앉는지 알긴 해.
남: 잘됐네. 그러면 개가 그렇게 했을 때 약간의 선물을 주고 칭찬을 해줘.
여: 좋은 생각이다. 개에게 줄 선물을 좀 사야겠어.
남: 개가 적절한 곳에 변을 보면, 여러 번 칭찬해줘. 결국엔 용변을 가리게 될 거야.
여: 알겠어. 조언 고마워.

어휘 **naughty** 말을 안 듣는 / **pee** 소변을 보다 / **command** 명령(하다); 지휘(하다) / **treat** 선물, 특별한 것 / **go to the bathroom** 대변[소변]을 보다 / **toilet-train** 용변을 가리게 하다

03 관계 | ②

▶ 드레스의 디자인을 정하고 결혼식 날짜에 맞춰 드레스가 완성될 수 있을지 묻고 답하는 것으로 보아 예비 신부인 손님과 웨딩숍 직원의 대화임을 알 수 있다.

W: Excuse me. My name is Victoria Clark. I called you this morning.
M: Oh, please have a seat, Ms. Clark. Would you like some coffee or tea?
W: Just some water, please. I don't have much time, so I'd appreciate it **if we could get started** right away.
M: Why don't you choose a design that you like in one of these catalogs?
W: Okay. Let me see. What is the latest style trend?
M: These are **the hottest styles this season**. Romantic off-the-shoulder dresses.
W: Hmm, I really like the design of this silk A-line dress.
M: I see that you like a simple design. These are very similar to the dress you've chosen in the catalog. **Why don't you try on both of them**?
W: Okay. Oh, how long does it take to get the dress prepared? You know my wedding date is June 12th.
M: Don't worry. It should take about two weeks to finish the job.

여: 실례합니다. 제 이름은 Victoria Clark예요. 오늘 아침에 전화 드렸는데요.
남: 아, 앉으세요, Clark 양. 커피나 차 좀 드릴까요?
여: 물만 좀 주세요. 제가 시간이 많지 않아서, 바로 시작할 수 있으면 감사하겠습니다.
남: 이 카탈로그 중 한 권에서 마음에 드는 디자인을 고르시는 게 어떨까요?
여: 좋아요. 한번 볼게요. 요즘 스타일 트렌드는 뭔가요?
남: 이것들이 이번 시즌에 가장 인기 있는 스타일입니다. 어깨가 드러나는 로맨틱한 드레스죠.
여: 음, 저는 이 실크로 된 A라인 드레스 디자인이 정말 마음에 드는군요.
남: 단순한 디자인을 좋아하시는 것 같군요. 이것들이 손님께서 카탈로그에서 고르신 것과 아주 비슷합니다. 두 벌 다 입어보시겠어요?
여: 좋아요. 아, 드레스가 준비되는 데는 얼마나 걸리나요? 제 결혼식 날짜가 6월 12일인 거 아시죠?
남: 걱정하지 마세요. 마무리되는 데는 2주 정도 걸릴 겁니다.

어휘 **off-the-shoulder** 어깨가 드러나는

04 그림 불일치 | ④

▶ 벤치 위에 놓여 있는 것은 스카프라고 했으므로 그림의 장갑과 일치하지 않는다.

M: I feel a little lonely **sitting in the park** during the late fall weather.
W: I know.
M: Look at the big tree near the park's entrance. The leaves **have all fallen off the tree**.
W: Oh, look! There's a nest on the tree branch.
M: Yes, it looks like there's a chick in the nest. The mother bird is feeding the chick.
W: Aww, how sweet! **Shall we go sit on the bench** near the tree?
M: Sure. Oh, but there's a trash bin next to the bench.
W: And someone left a scarf on the bench.
M: You're right. Let's leave it there. The owner will probably come back for it.
W: Yeah, **it is pretty chilly**. Should we just leave?
M: Sounds good. Hey, Jessica, what's that thing on top of the arched gate?
W: Oh, it looks like a crown to me. That's fun.

남: 늦가을 날씨에 공원에 앉아 있으면 조금 외로워.
여: 맞아.
남: 공원 입구 근처에 있는 큰 나무를 봐. 나무에서 잎이 다 떨어졌어.
여: 아, 봐! 나뭇가지에 둥지가 하나 있어.
남: 응, 둥지 안에 새끼 새가 한 마리 있는 것 같아. 어미 새가 새끼 새에게 먹이를 주고 있어.
여: 와, 정말 사랑스럽다! 나무 근처에 있는 벤치에 가서 앉을까?
남: 그래. 아, 그런데 벤치 옆에 쓰레기통이 있어.
여: 그리고 누가 벤치에 스카프를 놓고 갔어.
남: 그러네. 거기에 놔두자. 주인이 그걸 찾으러 아마 다시 올 거야.

여: 응, 꽤 춥다. 우리 그냥 갈까?
남: 좋아. 얘, Jessica, 아치 모양 문 꼭대기에 있는 저거 뭐야?
여: 아, 내가 보기엔 왕관 같은데. 재밌다.

어휘 **trash bin** 쓰레기통 / **chilly** 쌀쌀한, 추운 / **arched** 아치 모양의

05 추후 행동 | ⑤

▶ 내일 소풍 준비를 하고 있는 엄마와 아들의 대화이다. 엄마가 아빠에게 전화하겠다고 한 말에 아들이 자신이 하겠다고 응답했다.

W: Jay, could you help me in the kitchen for a few minutes?
M: Sure, Mom. Is this all for the picnic tomorrow afternoon?
W: Yes, I'm almost done. I just need to **finish preparing these side dishes**.
M: Oh, Dad said he'll pick some up on the way home from work tonight. Didn't he tell you?
W: Yes, he mentioned that. But I already have the ingredients, so **I'd prefer to make them myself**.
M: Yours taste better anyway. But we should probably tell Dad you'll make them.
W: **I'll give him a call** right after I wash my hands.
M: You don't have to. I'll do it now.
W: Thanks for your help. Now I can finish cutting these onions.
M: Okay. Be careful, **that knife is sharp**.
W: Don't worry. I'll be fine.

여: Jay, 주방에서 잠깐 엄마 좀 도와줄래?
남: 물론이죠, 엄마. 이 모든 게 내일 오후 소풍을 위한 것인가요?
여: 그럼, 거의 다 했단다. 이 반찬들을 준비하는 걸 끝내기만 하면 돼.
남: 아, 아빠께서 오늘 밤 퇴근길에 몇 가지 반찬을 사 오겠다고 말씀하셨어요. 엄마께 말씀 안 하셨나요?
여: 응, 말씀하셨단다. 하지만 이미 재료도 있어서, 내가 직접 만드는 게 더 좋을 것 같구나.
남: 아무래도 엄마가 만드신 게 더 맛있죠. 하지만 엄마가 반찬을 만드신다고 아빠께 말씀드려야겠네요.
여: 내가 손을 씻고 나서 바로 아빠에게 전화할게.
남: 그러실 필요 없어요. 제가 지금 전화할게요.
여: 도와줘서 고맙구나. 이제 이 양파들을 써는 걸 끝낼 수 있겠어.
남: 네. 조심하세요. 그 칼이 날카로워요.
여: 걱정 마라. 괜찮을 거야.

어휘 **side dish** 반찬; 곁들이는 요리 / **on the way** ~하는 중에 / **mention** 말하다, 언급하다 / **ingredient** 재료, 성분; 구성 요소 / **prefer** 더 좋아하다, 선호하다 / **probably** 아마 / **give A a call** A에게 전화하다

06 금액 | ④

▶ 여자는 여름에 사용할 수 있는 두 이용권 중에 더 싼 350달러짜리 주중 이용권 세 장을 사겠다고 했으므로 지불 금액은 1,050달러이다.

W: I'm interested in purchasing an annual pass to Wonderland.
M: You have **several options to choose from**. The basic annual pass costs $250, but this pass will not be valid during the summer.
W: Oh, but I want to go to the park during the summer break. **What else is there**?
M: If that's the case, you'll have to consider the Deluxe and Premium passes. The Deluxe pass is $350, and the Premium is $400.
W: I see. **What's the difference between the two**?
M: Both can be used in the summer, but you can use the Deluxe pass only on weekdays.
W: How about the Premium?
M: It is also valid on the weekends during the summer.
W: Then I'll go with **the less expensive one**. I'd like three passes. Here's my credit card.

여 Wonderland 연간 이용권을 사고 싶은데요.
남: 선택하실 수 있는 몇 가지 사항이 있습니다. 기본 연간 이용권은 250달러인데, 이 이용권은 여름 동안에는 유효하지 않아요.
여: 아, 하지만 전 여름휴가 동안 그 공원에 가고 싶은데요. 그밖에는 뭐가 있나요?
남: 그러시다면, 디럭스와 프리미엄 이용권을 고려해보셔야 할 겁니다. 디럭스 이용권은 350달러이고, 프리미엄 이용권은 400달러예요.
여: 그렇군요. 그 두 가지의 차이점은 뭔가요?
남: 둘 다 여름에 쓸 수 있습니다만, 디럭스 이용권은 주중에만 사용하실 수 있습니다.
여: 프리미엄은요?
남: 그건 여름 동안 주말에도 유효합니다.
여: 그러면 전 덜 비싼 걸로 할게요. 이용권 세 장 주세요. 여기 제 신용카드 있습니다.

어휘 **annual** 연간의, 매년의 / **valid** 유효한; 타당한

07 이유 | ③

▶ 노트북 컴퓨터가 고장 나서 자료를 모두 잃어버리는 바람에 복구에 시간이 걸려서 과제 제출 마감을 연장해달라고 부탁하고 있다.

W: Hello, Dr. Martin. I'm Elizabeth Lewis. Well, I was wondering **if I could hand in my paper** next Monday.
M: I already had three students who asked for an extension. Do you have a part-time job?
W: Yes, but that's **not the reason for the extension request**.
M: Is it due to a family affair? Or are you having difficulty organizing your ideas?
W: No, it's not that. I'm actually almost done with my paper, but **my laptop crashed** the other day and I lost all my data.
M: Don't you have a back-up file?
W: No, the computer service center is trying to recover the lost data, but it's going to take a while.
M: Well, I'm sorry about that. Since it's your first time, **I'll give you an extension**.
W: Thank you so much for understanding, Dr. Martin.

여: 안녕하세요, Martin 박사님. 전 Elizabeth Lewis입니다. 음, 제 과제물을 다음 주 월요일에 제출해도 될지 궁금합니다.
남: 기한 연장을 요청하는 학생이 이미 세 명 있었단다. 아르바이트를 하니?
여: 네, 그런데 그것 때문에 기한 연장을 요청하는 건 아니에요.
남: 가족 행사 때문이니? 아니면 생각을 정리하는 데 문제가 있어?
여: 아니요, 그게 아니에요. 사실 과제물을 거의 다 끝내긴 했는데요, 며칠 전에 제 노트북 컴퓨터가 고장 나서 자료를 전부 잃어버렸어요.
남: 백업 파일은 없니?
여: 없어요. 컴퓨터 수리 센터에서 잃어버린 자료를 복구하려고 노력 중인데, 시간이 좀 걸릴 거예요.
남: 음, 그렇게 돼서 유감이구나. 넌 이번이 처음이니까 너에게 기한을 연장해주마.
여: 이해해주셔서 대단히 감사합니다, Martin 박사님.

어휘 **hand in** 제출하다 / **extension** (기간의) 연장; (세력의) 확대 / **family affair** 가족 행사, 집안일 / **crash** (컴퓨터가) 고장 나다 / **the other day** 며칠 전에, 일전에 / **back-up file** 백업 파일 ((파일 손상 대비용으로 미리 저장해둔 파일))

08 언급하지 않은 것 | ④

▶ 해석 참조

M: I want to buy a wall clock.
W: We have **a great selection of clocks**. What kind of shape do you want, round or square?
M: I like round clocks.
W: This round clock with a black frame is very popular.
M: I prefer a brown frame to a black frame. And don't you have **any silent wall clocks**?
W: Oh, you want a clock that doesn't make a "ticking" sound! How about this one with Roman numerals?
M: Well, no. Because I have a little kid, I want a clock **that has Arabic numerals**.
W: Then how about this one? **It also tells the temperature**.
M: I think I'll take it. It's unique, and it has black Arabic numerals that are easy to read.
W: All right. Come this way.

남: 벽시계를 하나 사고 싶은데요.
여: 아주 다양한 시계가 있습니다. 동그란 것이나 네모난 것 중 어떤 종류의 모양을 원하시나요?
남: 동그란 시계(① 모양)가 좋아요.
여: 검은색 테두리가 있는 이 동그란 시계가 아주 인기가 많습니다.
남: 전 검은색 테두리보다 갈색 테두리가 더 좋아요(② 테두리의 색). 무소음 벽시계는 없나요(③ 소리)?
여: 아, '똑딱' 소리가 나지 않는 시계를 원하시는군요! 이 로마 숫자가 있는 건 어떠세요?

남: 음, 아뇨. 전 어린아이가 있어서, 아라비아 숫자가 있는 시계를 원해요(⑤ 숫자 표기 방식).
여: 그럼 이건 어떠세요? 온도도 알려줘요.
남: 그걸로 할게요. 독특하고, 읽기 쉬운 검은색 아라비아 숫자가 있네요.
여: 좋습니다. 이쪽으로 오세요.

어휘 **a selection of** 다양한 / **ticking** (시계의) 똑딱 소리

09 내용 불일치 | ④

▶ 전시의 주제는 '사계절'이라고 했으므로, 출품 사진의 주제를 자유롭게 선택할 수 있는 것은 아니다.

M: Listen up, everyone! We've had great success **with our annual photo exhibition** for the past five years, and now it's time to hold another one at Owl Creek High School. This exhibition will be an exciting opportunity for many of you. **Aside from the photography club members**, anyone at Owl Creek High can submit their work to the exhibition. **The photos to be displayed at the exhibition** will be selected by teachers from the fine arts department. The theme of this year's exhibition will be "Four Seasons." A total of 40 of the best photos will be presented in the school gallery. **The deadline for photo entries** is April 10th. If you have a passion for photography, this is your chance to show off your talent!

남: 잘 들으세요, 여러분! 우리는 지난 5년 동안 연례 사진 전시회에서 큰 성공을 거두어 왔고, 이제 Owl Creek 고등학교에서 또 한 번의 성공을 거둘 때입니다. 이번 전시는 여러분 중 많은 이들에게 신나는 기회가 될 겁니다. 사진부 회원들 외에도, Owl Creek 고등학교 학생 누구나 자신의 작품을 전시회에 제출할 수 있습니다. 전시회에 전시될 사진은 미술부 선생님들에 의해 선발될 것입니다. 올해의 전시 주제는 '사계절'이 될 것입니다. 최고의 사진 중 총 40점의 사진은 학교 미술관에 전시될 것입니다. 사진 출품 마감 기한은 4월 10일입니다. 사진 촬영에 열정이 있다면, 이번이 여러분의 재능을 뽐낼 수 있는 기회입니다!

어휘 **aside from** ~ 외에도; ~을 제외하고 / **submit** 제출하다 / **deadline** 마감 기한

10 도표 이해 | ⑤

▶ 우선 토요일과 일요일에 열리는 홈경기를 보려고 하고 있고 Andrews 대학과의 경기는 피하려고 한다. 마지막으로 내야석을 구매한다고 했다.

W: **Come take a look at this article** in this magazine. Our university's baseball team won the college baseball championship last year.
M: I know. Hey, why don't we go to one of their games? In fact, there are some games **that are coming up soon**.
W: That sounds like fun. I'll go with you.
M: What time is good for you?
W: Anytime is okay if it's a Saturday or Sunday.
M: They have a game this Saturday in Georgia. Does that work for you?
W: **That's too far for me**. I don't feel like going all the way to Georgia just to see a baseball game. Are there any home games?
M: Of course. I'll pick a home game then. There's a game with Andrews College, but I'm not interested in that one.
W: Why is that?
M: Andrews College has the weakest team, so the game won't be very exciting.
W: Let's watch another game then. **Are there any seats left** for another game?
M: There are some infield seats available for one of the games, so I'll reserve two seats in that section.

여: 와서 이 잡지에 난 이 기사를 봐. 우리 대학교 야구팀이 작년 대학 야구 챔피언십에서 이겼대.
남: 알아. 저기, 우리 그들이 하는 경기 중 하나를 보러 가지 않을래? 사실, 곧 다가오는 경기들이 있거든.
여: 재미있겠다. 너랑 같이 갈게.
남: 넌 몇 시가 좋아?
여: 토요일이나 일요일이라면 아무 때나 괜찮아.
남: 조지아 주에서 이번 토요일에 경기가 있어. 그것 괜찮아?
여: 나한텐 너무 멀어. 그저 야구 경기를 보려고 조지아 주까지 그 먼 길을 가고 싶지는 않아. 홈경기는 없어?
남: 물론 있지. 그럼 홈경기를 고를게. Andrews 대학과 하는 경기가 있는데 난 이건 별로 흥미가 없어.
여: 왜?
남: Andrews 대학 팀은 제일 약해서 경기가 그리 재미있지 않을 거야.
여: 그러면 다른 경기를 보자. 다른 경기에 자리 남은 거 있어?
남: 게임들 중에서 내야석 자리는 살 수 있는 게 몇 자리 있으니까 그 구역으로 두 장 예약할게.

어휘 **opponent** (논쟁, 경기 등의) 상대; 반대자 / **infield** (야구, 크리켓 등에서) 내야 (↔ outfield 외야) / **home game** 홈경기 ((팀의 근거지에서 하는 경기))

11 짧은 대화에 이어질 응답 | ④

▶ 졸업 선물로 삼촌에게 시계를 받았다는 여자의 말에 가장 적절한 응답을 찾는다.

① 천만에. 네가 마음에 들어 하니까 기쁘다.
② 네가 손목시계를 자랑하고 싶어한다는 거 알아.
③ 그분은 48세이시지만 나이에 비해 젊어 보이셔.
④ 부럽다. 나도 너희 삼촌 같은 삼촌이 있으면 좋겠다.
⑤ 추측해봐. 난 삼촌 두 분과 고모 네 분이 있어.

W: Look at my watch!
M: Wow! It's really fancy! **It's got a gold shine to it**. How did you get it?
W: My uncle gave it to me **as a graduation gift**.
M: ______________________________

여: 내 손목시계 좀 봐!
남: 와! 정말 멋지다! 금색 빛이 나. 어디서 났니?
여: 우리 삼촌이 졸업 선물로 주셨어.
남: ______________________________

12 짧은 대화에 이어질 응답 | ③

▶ 남자는 어머니의 선물을 사면서 어머니가 마음에 들어 하시면 좋겠다고 이야기하였다. 이에 적절한 점원의 응답을 고른다.

① 계속 연락하고 지내주셔서 감사합니다.
② 이게 바로 제가 원하던 거예요.
③ 분명히 어머니께서 손님의 선물을 아주 마음에 들어 하실 거예요.
④ 무슨 말씀이신지 이해합니다.
⑤ 어머니에게 너무 많은 걸 기대하지 마세요.

M: I want to get a gift for my mother's birthday. **Could you recommend a good one**?
W: What do you think of this night cream? It's a great anti-wrinkle cream.
M: Okay. I'll take it. I hope **my mother likes it**.
W: ______________________________

남: 저희 어머니 생신 선물을 사고 싶은데요. 괜찮은 것 하나 추천해주시겠어요?
여: 이 나이트 크림은 어떠세요? 아주 좋은 주름 방지용 크림입니다.
남: 괜찮네요. 그걸로 할게요. 어머니께서 마음에 들어 하시면 좋겠네요.
여: ______________________________

어휘 **anti-wrinkle** 주름[구김] 방지용의

13 긴 대화에 이어질 응답 | ④

▶ 여자가 자신이 요리한 것을 맛본 남자에게 소금을 더 넣어야 할지 묻고 있다. 이에 가장 적절한 반응을 찾는다.

① 와주셔서 감사합니다. 마음껏 드세요.
② 아니요, 아직 안 끝났어요. 좀 더 기다리세요.
③ 서둘러요. 우리 파티에 늦겠어요.
④ 아니요, 맛있어요. 당신 정말로 요리를 잘하는군요!
⑤ 타지 않게 우유를 저으세요. 그러고 나서 소금을 약간 넣으세요.

W: Dan, **could you stir the soup for me**?
M: Sure. I don't know what this is, but it smells delicious!
W: It's clam chowder. **It's my father's all-time favorite**.
M: When did you have time to prepare all this food?
W: I started yesterday, so there isn't much to do today. It'll be done in a few minutes.
M: It's so impressive. I didn't know **you were such a good cook**.
W: I downloaded some great recipes from the Internet. All I did was follow the recipe.
M: Well, I can't wait to taste all this great food.
W: Have a taste of the soup.
M: Really? Let me get a spoon.
W: *[pause]* So what do you think? **Do we need more salt**?

M: ____________________

여: Dan, 나 대신 이 수프 좀 저어줄래요?
남: 물론이죠. 이게 뭔지 모르겠는데, 맛있는 냄새가 나네요!
여: 클램차우더예요. 우리 아빠가 가장 좋아하시는 거예요.
남: 언제 시간을 내서 이 음식을 다 준비했어요?
여: 어제 시작해서 오늘은 할 게 많지 않아요. 몇 분 후면 다 될 거예요.
남: 아주 놀라워요. 당신이 이렇게 요리를 잘하는지 몰랐어요.
여: 인터넷에서 아주 좋은 레시피를 몇 개 다운로드 받았어요. 제가 한 거라고는 그 레시피를 따른 것뿐이에요.
남: 음, 이 근사한 음식을 얼른 다 맛보고 싶네요.
여: 수프 맛 한번 보세요.
남: 정말요? 스푼 가져올게요.
여: *[잠시 후]* 어때요? 소금을 더 넣을까요?
남: ____________________

어휘 **stir** 젓다 / **clam chowder** 클램차우더 ((대합을 넣은 야채수프))

14 긴 대화에 이어질 응답 | ③

▶ 남자가 악보를 동생에게 가져다주려고 왔는데 연습 중이라 들어가서 줄 수 없는 상황이다. 남자가 여자에게 자신의 여동생이 누구인지 알려주고 있으므로 이에 적절한 응답은 ③이다.

① 괜찮습니다. 무슨 말씀이신지 이해해요.
② 그녀는 세계적으로 유명한 첼로 연주자예요. 전 그녀가 부러워요.
③ 누군지 보이네요. 지금 바로 그녀에게 가서 악보를 줄게요.
④ 저는 전혀 상관없습니다. 가서 그녀에게 그것에 대해 말씀하세요.
⑤ 그녀의 놀라운 연주에 우리 모두 감동했어요.

W: Excuse me. I'm afraid **you are not allowed inside the classroom** right now.
M: Oh, I'm not?
W: No, they're **in the middle of practice** right now.
M: I came here to give this music sheet to my sister. She said she needs to hand it in today.
W: I'll take care of it. Can you tell me who she is?
M: Nicole Williams.
W: Nicole? That name **doesn't ring a bell**.
M: She has long black hair.
W: There are a few women with long black hair. Is her hair in a ponytail by any chance?
M: No, she's the person **wearing a white blouse**. Oh, there she is. She is the one who is standing up with the cello.
W: ____________________

여: 실례합니다. 죄송하지만 지금은 교실에 들어가실 수 없습니다.
남: 아, 그런가요?
여: 네, 지금 연습을 하는 도중이라서요.
남: 제 여동생에게 이 악보를 주려고 왔는데요. 동생이 이걸 오늘 제출해야 한다고 말했어요.
여: 제가 처리해 드리겠습니다. 여동생이 누구인지 말씀해주시겠어요?
남: Nicole Williams입니다.
여: Nicole이요? 그 이름은 기억이 나질 않는군요.
남: 머리가 길고 검은색이에요.
여: 긴 검은색 머리의 여학생들이 몇 명 있어요. 혹시 머리를 뒤로 묶었나요?
남: 아뇨, 하얀색 블라우스를 입고 있는 사람이에요. 아, 저기에 있네요. 첼로를 가지고 일어서 있는 사람이요.
여: ____________________

어휘 **music sheet** 악보 / **ring a bell** 들어본 적이 있는 것 같다, 낯이 익다 / **ponytail** 포니테일 ((긴 머리를 뒤에서 하나로 묶어 말 꼬리처럼 늘어뜨린 형태))

15 상황에 적절한 말 | ⑤

▶ 잃어버린 지갑을 찾으러 상점에 돌아갔을 때 직원이 지갑을 보관하고 있다가 돌려준 상황이다. 이때 감사를 표하는 것이 가장 자연스럽다.

① 이건 제 지갑이 아니에요. 전 지갑을 잃어버리지 않았어요.
② 천만에요, 손님. 전 그저 제 할 일을 하는 거예요.
③ 다른 상점으로 제 드레스를 사러 갈 거예요.
④ 네, 이 흰색 드레스가 제 머리에 완벽하게 어울리는 것 같아요.
⑤ 제 지갑을 찾아주셔서 감사합니다! 영영 없어진 줄 알았어요!

W: Emily goes shopping for her prom dress about a month before the dance. **She tries on every dress** in the store, but she can't find one that satisfies her. She leaves all of the dresses that she tries in a pile in the fitting room. Then she goes to other stores until she finally finds a dress that **she absolutely loves**. It matches her blonde hair perfectly. When she tries to pay for it, **she finds she doesn't have her purse**. She thinks she probably dropped it in the previous store, so she goes there immediately. When she arrives at that store, **a salesclerk recognizes her** and gives her the purse. The salesclerk tells her that he found her purse in the fitting room. In this situation, what would Emily most likely say to the salesclerk?

여: Emily는 졸업무도회가 있기 한 달 전에 무도회 드레스를 사러 간다. 그녀는 상점에 있는 모든 드레스를 입어보지만, 만족하는 것을 찾지 못한다. 그녀는 입어보는 드레스를 전부 탈의실에 쌓아 놓는다. 그러고 나서 그녀는 다른 상점으로 가서 굉장히 마음에 드는 드레스를 마침내 찾는다. 그것은 그녀의 금발 머리에 완벽하게 잘 어울린다. 계산을 하려고 할 때, 그녀는 자신의 지갑이 없다는 것을 알게 된다. 아마 이전에 갔던 상점에 떨어뜨렸을 거라고 생각해서 그곳에 즉시 간다. 그녀가 그 상점에 도착했을 때, 점원이 그녀를 알아보고는 지갑을 준다. 점원은 지갑을 탈의실에서 발견했다고 말한다. 이러한 상황에서 Emily가 그 점원에게 할 말로 가장 적절한 것은 무엇인가?

어휘 **prom** (대학, 고교 등의 학년말[졸업]) 무도회 / **previous** 이전의, 앞의

16~17 세트 문항 | 16. ② 17. ④

▶ 16. ~ those who have read good literature are aware of the countless advantages에 말의 주제가 나타나 있다. 즉, '훌륭한 문학작품을 읽는 것의 이점'에 대해 이야기하고 있다.

① 다양한 형태의 아동 문학작품
② 훌륭한 문학작품을 읽는 것의 이점
③ 문학작품을 즐기는 다양한 방법
④ 컴퓨터로 문학작품을 읽는 새로운 방법
⑤ 의사소통 능력을 향상하기 위한 독서의 힘

▶ 17. 해석 참조

M: **With the rising popularity of computers** in recent times, the habit of reading has been neglected. Many people find little or no time for reading. However, those who have read good literature are aware of **the countless advantages** associated with it. Reading great literature broadens the thinking of a person, improves vocabulary, and cultivates sensitivity towards people of different cultures. Reading poetry **loosens and enriches the mind**. It helps to keep the muscles of the brain in good shape. Reading fiction gives immense satisfaction to a person. Nothing can be more satisfying than to sit with your child and **read him a fairy tale**. Also, reading a great novel expands the imagination of a person. You can develop your ability to understand and appreciate the various aspects of life. **The mind is forced to think about** issues from different angles, question assumptions, and derive conclusions. Reading a biography or autobiography improves a person's knowledge of various areas of life. This knowledge base helps a person **to make correct decisions** in different situations. Exercise your mind through great literature.

남: 최근 컴퓨터의 치솟는 인기로 인해, 책 읽는 습관은 뒷전으로 밀렸습니다. 많은 사람이 책을 읽을 시간을 거의 혹은 전혀 찾지 못합니다. 하지만 좋은 문학작품을 읽어온 사람들은 그와 관련된 무수한 장점들을 알고 있습니다. 훌륭한 문학작품을 읽는 것은 사람의 사고를 확장해주고, 어휘력을 향상해주고, 다른 문화권의 사람들에 대한 세심함을 길러줍니다. ① 시를 읽는 것은 마음을 느슨하게 해주고 풍요롭게 해줍니다. 그것은 뇌의 근육을 좋은 상태로 유지해줍니다. ② 소설을 읽는 것은 사람에게 굉장한 만족감을 줍니다. 아이와 함께 앉아서 아이에게 ③ 동화를 읽어주는 것보다 더 만족스러운 것은 없습니다. 또한, 훌륭한 장편소설을 읽는 것은 사람의 상상력을 확장해줍니다. 당신은 삶의 여러 측면을 이해하고 그 진가를 알아보는 능력을 키울 수 있습니다. 정신은 문제를 다른 각도에서 생각하고, 가정을 의심하고, 결론을 이끌어내게 됩니다. ⑤ 전기나 자서전을 읽는 것은 삶의 다양한 분야에 대한 개인의 지식을 향상해줍니다. 이 지식 기반은 다양한 상황에서 올바른 결정을 내리도록 도와줍니다. 훌륭한 문학작품을 통해 정신을 단련하십시오.

어휘 **enhance** 높이다, 향상하다 / **neglect** 무시하다; 소홀히 하다 / **countless** 무수한, 셀 수 없이 많은 / **broaden** 넓히다; 넓어지다 / **cultivate** (말 · 행동 방식을) 기르다; 경작하다 / **sensitivity** 세심함; 감성 / **poetry** (문학 형식으로서의) 시 / **loosen** 느슨하게 하다; 완화하다 / **enrich** 풍요롭게 하다, 질을 높이다 / **immense** 거대한, 막대한 / **expand** 확장하다, 확대하다 / **aspect** 측면; 양상 / **assumption** 가정, 추정 / **derive** 이끌어내다, 얻다 / **biography** 전기(문) / **autobiography** 자서전

Answers & Explanation

01.② 02.② 03.① 04.⑤ 05.③ 06.③ 07.③ 08.③ 09.⑤ 10.④
11.① 12.④ 13.③ 14.① 15.① 16.② 17.①

01 화자가 하는 말의 목적 | ②

▶ 기금 조성을 위해 열대 우림 개구리 사진 자선 경매가 있을 예정이니 사진 관람 후 경매 입찰에 참여해 줄 것을 부탁하고 있다.

M: Our foundation's Rainforest Frogs Photography Competition has ended with over 700 entries. We have selected our winners, and they are now on display here at the Reef Hotel, **where they will be auctioned** next Thursday from 5:30 p.m. to raise funds to save our frogs and rainforests. **We want all of you to join us** for the charity auction, so please visit the exhibition hall after today's conference. If you can't join us and you have no time to see the exhibition today, you can still take part in the auction by viewing the photographs and **placing a bid for your choice** on our website. Thank you for your continued support of the Rainforest Foundation.

남: 저희 재단이 주최한 열대 우림 개구리 사진전은 700여 점의 출품작들과 함께 마감되었습니다. 수상작들이 선정되어서 이곳 Reef 호텔에서 현재 전시 중이며, 이 작품들은 개구리와 열대 우림 지역을 살리기 위한 기금을 조성하기 위해서 이 호텔에서 다음 주 목요일 5시 30분부터 경매에 붙여질 것입니다. 저희는 여러분 모두가 자선 경매에 참여해 주시기를 바랍니다. 그러니 오늘 학회가 끝나면 전시 홀을 방문해 주십시오. 저희와 함께 하실 수 없거나 오늘 전시회를 보실 시간이 없으시면, 웹사이트에서 사진을 보시고 선택하신 작품에 대해서 입찰을 하셔서 경매에 참가하실 수 있습니다. 열대 우림 재단에 지속적인 성원을 보내 주셔서 감사합니다.

어휘 **on display** 전시되어, 진열되어 / **auction** 경매에서 팔다; 경매 / **raise fund** 기금을 모으다 / **charity** 자선 (행위); 자선 단체 / **conference** 학회 / **place a bid** 입찰하다

02 의견 | ②

▶ 남자는 자신이 폭력적인 영화를 보고 나쁜 영향을 받지 않은 것처럼 레슬링 경기의 시청이 아이의 행동에 해로운 영향을 주지 않을 것이므로 걱정할 필요가 없다고 이야기하고 있다.

M: The wrestling finals are about to start! Where is the remote control?
W: I don't know, but I wish you wouldn't watch them.
M: Why not? **Did you have something planned for us** tonight?
W: No, it's not that. I just don't think it's a very good idea.
M: It's just some harmless fun. **Not everything can be educational**, you know.
W: Actually, I'm worried Brandon will imitate the wrestlers. I don't want him to become violent. As you know, he is already jumping around the house and pretending to fight.
M: You think watching wrestling **made him want to fight**?
W: I'm not sure, but it couldn't have helped.
M: Well, I wouldn't worry so much. I mean, I've watched a lot of violent horror movies and **it hasn't hurt me**.
W: Hmmm.... You think I don't have to worry so much?

남: 레슬링 결승전이 이제 막 시작하려고 해요! 리모컨이 어디에 있죠?
여: 모르겠어요, 그런데 전 당신이 경기를 보지 않으면 좋겠어요.
남: 왜죠? 오늘 밤에 할 일이라도 계획해 두었나요?
여: 그런 게 아녜요. 전 단지 레슬링 경기를 보는 게 좋은 거라고 생각하지 않아요.
남: 그건 나에게 해롭지 않은 재미를 주는 것뿐이에요. 모든 게 다 교육적일 수만은 없잖아요.
여: 사실, Brandon이 레슬러를 따라 할까 봐 걱정이에요. 그 애가 폭력적으로 변하는 것을 원치 않아요. 당신도 알다시피, 그 애는 이미 온 집안을 뛰어다니며 싸우는 시늉을 하잖아요.
남: 당신은 레슬링 경기를 보는 것 때문에 그 애가 싸우고 싶어 한다고 생각하는 건가요?
여: 확실하진 않지만, 도움이 됐을 리가 없어요.
남: 글쎄요, 나는 그렇게 많이 걱정하지 않을래요. 내 말은, 나도 지금껏 수많은 폭력적인 공포 영화를 봐 왔지만, 그건 나에게 나쁜 영향을 끼치지 않았어요.
여: 음…. 당신은 내가 그리 많이 걱정할 필요가 없다고 생각하는 거죠?

03 관계 | ①

▶ 대화 초반에서 남자는 도서관에서 자원봉사 일을 시작하는 학생임이 드러났다. 여자는 남자가 도서관에서 해야 할 일을 설명하고 있고, 사서가 몇 명이냐는 남자의 질문에 여자가 본인 혼자라고 했으므로 도서관 사서임을 알 수 있다.

W: Hello. How can I help you?
M: Hi. It's my first day, and **I'm not sure where to go**.
W: Oh, great. You must be one of the new student volunteers.
M: Right. I filled out the volunteer application on the library's website, and I got **an email saying I'd been registered**.
W: Okay, well, you'll be on your feet most of the time. So, you should wear comfortable shoes.
M: I guess I should walk around and **help people find books**.
W: That's part of it. You also need to help visitors use the self-checkout machines for borrowing books.
M: No problem. By the way, how many other librarians work here?
W: I'm the only one. So, **I rely on generous students like you** to help me out.
M: I'm happy to be here.

여: 안녕하세요. 무엇을 도와드릴까요?
남: 안녕하세요. 제가 오늘 처음 왔는데, 어디로 가야 할지 모르겠네요.
여: 아, 그렇군요. 당신은 분명히 새로운 학생 자원봉사자들 중의 한 명이겠군요.
남: 그렇습니다. 도서관 홈페이지에서 봉사 신청서를 작성했는데 등록됐다는 이메일을 받았어요.
여: 네, 음, 학생은 대부분의 시간 동안 서 있게 될 거예요. 그러니 편한 신발을 신어야 해요.
남: 돌아다니면서 사람들이 책을 찾는 걸 도와야겠군요.
여: 그건 (학생이 하는 일의) 일부분이죠. 방문자들이 책을 빌리기 위해 도서 자동 대출기를 사용하는 것도 도와야 해요.
남: 문제없습니다. 그런데 얼마나 많은 다른 사서분들이 여기서 일하시나요?
여: 저 하나입니다. 그래서 학생처럼 저를 도와줄 너그러운 사람들이 필요하죠.
남: 여기 오게 되어 기쁘네요.

어휘 **fill out** 작성하다 / **application** 신청서; 적용, 응용; 도포 / **register** 등록하다; 기록하다 / **on one's feet** 일어서서 / **self-checkout machine** 도서 자동 대출기 / **librarian** 사서, 도서관 직원 / **rely on** ~을 필요로 하다; ~에 의지[의존]하다 / **generous** 너그러운, 관대한; 풍부한, 많은

04 그림 불일치 | ⑤

▶ 서랍장 위에 있는 것이 꽃무늬 꽃병이냐는 여자의 물음에 남자는 그렇다고 대답했다.

M: Before the play begins, **why don't you check the stage**?
W: Okay. *[pause]* It looks good! Especially the poster on the wall.
M: I agree. The woman's smiling face will **contrast nicely with her loneliness**.
W: How about the window? Shouldn't it show a full moon?
M: No, it's supposed to be a half-moon. **It turns into a full moon later in the play**, but it doesn't start out like that.
W: Now I remember. Well, the bed below the poster is perfect.
M: Yes, it's good to have it on the left side of the stage.
W: And there's a chair beside the table. I remember you prepared two chairs before.
M: Since it's a solo drama that is focusing on loneliness, a single chair will be better.
W: Good idea. Oh, and is that the **flower-printed vase we ordered** on top of the drawers?
M: Yes, it turned out well.

남: 연극이 시작되기 전에 무대를 확인하는 게 어때?
여: 그래. *[잠시 후]* 근사해 보이는데! 특히 벽에 있는 포스터가 멋져.
남: 나도 그렇게 생각해. 저 여자의 미소 짓는 얼굴이 그녀의 외로움과 잘 대조될 거야.
여: 창문은 어때? 보름달이 보여야 하지 않을까?
남: 아냐, 반달이어야 해. 연극 후반부에서는 보름달로 변하지만, 그렇게 시작하지는 않아.
여: 이제 기억난다. 음, 포스터 아래 있는 침대도 완벽하구나.
남: 그래, 침대를 무대 왼편에 두니까 좋다.
여: 그리고 테이블 옆에 의자도 하나 있어. 전에 네가 의자 두 개를 준비했던 걸로 기억하는데.
남: 외로움에 중점을 둔 일인극이니까, 의자 하나가 더 좋을 거야.

여: 좋은 생각이야. 아, 그리고 서랍장 위에 있는 거 우리가 주문한 꽃무늬 꽃병이야?
남: 응, 좋네.

어휘 **contrast with** ~와 뚜렷한 대조를 보이다 / **turn into** ~이 되다, ~으로 변하다 / **solo** 혼자서 하는, 단독의; 솔로의, 독주[독창]의 / **focus on** ~에 주력하다, 초점을 맞추다 / **turn out** 모습을 드러내다, 나타나다

05 추후 행동 | ③

▶ 남자가 아내에게 전화하겠다고 하자, 여자가 남자의 휴대전화를 가져다주겠다고 했다.

W: Are you alright, Robert? You've been sitting here for the past hour.
M: I think I'm ill.
W: **What symptoms do you have**?
M: I feel like I'm going to pass out, and I'm extremely nauseous. I've been throwing up almost non-stop.
W: It **seems like you have a fever**, too. I think you need to go to the hospital. Do you want me to give you a ride to the emergency room?
M: No, that's okay. I'll call my wife and **ask her to pick me up**.
W: Okay, where's your cell phone? You stay here, and I'll go get it for you.
M: That would be great. It should be inside my briefcase.
W: And where's your briefcase?
M: Oh sorry, **it's underneath my desk**.
W: Okay. Hang in there. I'll be right back.

여: 괜찮아요, Robert? 여기 한 시간 동안 앉아 있잖아요.
남: 몸이 아픈 것 같아요.
여: 어떤 증상이 있는데요?
남: 기절할 것 같고, 속이 아주 메스꺼워요. 거의 계속해서 토했어요.
여: 열도 있는 것 같은데요. 병원에 가야 할 것 같아요. 내가 응급실까지 태워다 줄까요?
남: 아뇨, 괜찮아요. 내가 아내에게 전화해서 태워다 달라고 할게요.
여: 알겠어요. 당신 휴대전화가 어디 있나요? 여기 계세요. 내가 가져다줄게요.
남: 그래 주시면 좋겠어요. 내 서류 가방 안에 있을 거예요.
여: 그럼 서류 가방은 어디 있나요?
남: 아, 미안해요. 내 책상 밑에 있어요.
여: 알겠어요. 조금만 참아요. 금방 돌아올게요.

어휘 **pass out** 기절하다, 의식을 잃다 / **nauseous** (속이) 메스꺼운 / **throw up** 토하다 / **non-stop** 쉬지 않고, 연속으로 / **hang (on) in there** 곤란을 참고 견디다

06 금액 | ③

▶ 여자는 리프트권을 종일권(50달러)으로 구매하고 보드를 대여(20달러)하려고 한다. 여기에 1회 강습료(30달러)를 더하면 총액이 100달러이다. 이 경우 전체 가격의 10%를 할인받을 수 있으므로 여자가 지불할 금액은 90달러이다.

M: Welcome to Pine Mountain Resort. How can I help you?
W: **I'm hoping to go snowboarding** today. I need tickets and rental equipment.
M: Well, lift tickets are $30 for an afternoon and $50 for a full day.
W: I definitely want to board for the full day. **What about rental equipment**?
M: The rental board is $20 per day, and the boots are $10 per day.
W: I borrowed some boots from my sister, so I only need the board.
M: Great. **That will save you some money**.
W: But I think I also need a lesson, since it's my first time.
M: Lessons are $30 each, and if the total price is at least $100, you can get a 10% discount.
W: Okay, then **I'll take one lesson**. Here's the money.
M: And here is your ticket and rental pass. Enjoy.

남: Pine Mountain 리조트에 오신 것을 환영합니다. 무엇을 도와드릴까요?
여: 오늘 스노보드를 타려고 하는데요. 표와 대여 장비가 필요해요.
남: 음, 리프트 오후권은 30달러이고, 종일권은 50달러입니다.
여: 저는 꼭 하루 종일 타고 싶어요. 대여 장비는 어떻게 되나요?
남: 보드 대여는 하루에 20달러이고, 부츠는 하루에 10달러입니다.
여: 제 여동생에게 부츠를 빌려서, 보드만 필요해요.
남: 잘됐네요. 돈을 좀 아끼실 수 있겠네요.
여: 그런데 강습도 필요할 것 같아요. 제가 (보드 타는 것이) 처음이어서요.
남: 강습은 한 번에 30달러이고, 전체 비용이 100달러 이상이면 10% 할인을 받으실 수 있습니다.
여: 좋아요. 그럼 강습을 한 번 받을게요. 여기 돈이요.
남: 그럼 여기 표와 대여권이 있습니다. 즐거운 시간 보내세요.

어휘 **rental** 대여[임대]의; 임대(료) / **equipment** 장비 / **definitely** 꼭; 절대(로)

07 이유 | ③

▶ 여자는 남동생의 졸업식에 참석하고 싶어서 어제 출근하지 않았다고 했다.

M: Hi, Kate. It's good to see you again. I guess you had a relaxing vacation? Did you just get back last night?
W: It was a great trip, but I actually returned on Sunday.
M: Oh? Then **why didn't you come to work** yesterday?
W: That's because I wanted to attend my brother's graduation.
M: Did he finish medical school? That's great! **What is he planning to do next**?
W: He's going to work at a hospital near my mother's house.
M: That's Saint Mary's Hospital, right? **I had my medical checkup** there.
W: Right. It's a great position. One of my brother's professors recommended him for the job.
M: I'm really glad to hear that **things are going so well** for him.
W: I'm happy for him, too.

남: 안녕, Kate. 다시 만나서 반가워. 느긋하게 휴가를 즐긴 것 같은데, 어젯밤에 막 돌아온 거니?
여: 멋진 여행이었지. 그런데 실은 일요일에 돌아왔어.
남: 그래? 그럼 왜 어제는 출근하지 않았니?
여: 남동생의 졸업식에 참석하고 싶어서 그랬어.
남: 그 애가 의과대학 공부를 끝마쳤니? 굉장하다! 이다음엔 뭐할 거래?
여: 엄마 집 근처에 있는 병원에서 근무할 거래.
남: Saint Mary 병원이지? 난 거기서 건강 검진을 받았어.
여: 맞아. 정말 좋은 직장이지. 남동생의 교수님 중 한 분이 그 자리에 추천해주셨어.
남: 그 애가 하는 일이 잘되고 있다는 소릴 들으니 정말 기쁘구나.
여: 나도 기뻐.

어휘 **medical checkup** 건강 검진

08 언급하지 않은 것 | ③

▶ 해석 참조

M: Sue, do you want to meet tonight?
W: I'm afraid I can't. My father just returned from Africa. We're having dinner together.
M: I see. **Was the trip related to his work** for Doctors Without Borders?
W: Yes. There's been an Ebola outbreak in Sierra Leone. He went to help.
M: I really admire his commitment to an organization **dedicated to providing medical care** in extreme situations, like civil wars, famines, and natural disasters.
W: I do as well. Did you know it received the Nobel Peace Prize in 1999?
M: I'm not surprised. I know it's doing amazing work in almost 70 countries worldwide.
W: I'd love to **follow in my father's footsteps**, but I don't have much interest in medicine.
M: I suppose you could try to get a job at the headquarters in Switzerland.
W: Oh, I had never considered that before.

남: Sue, 오늘 저녁에 만날래?
여: 미안하지만 안 될 것 같아. 우리 아빠가 아프리카에서 막 돌아오셨거든. 오늘 저녁에 함께 식사하기로 했어.
남: 그래 알겠어. 국경 없는 의사회와 관련된 일로 다녀오신 거야?
여: 응. 시에라리온에서 에볼라가 발병했거든. 아빠는 그걸 도우러 가셨던 거야.
남: 내전, 기근, 자연 재해와 같은 극한 상황에서 의료 봉사에 힘쓰는(① 주요 활동) 단체에 너희 아버지께서 헌신적으로 참여하시는 게 정말 존경스러워.
여: 나도 그래. 그 단체가 1999년에 노벨 평화상(② 수상 내역)을 수상한 걸 알고 있니?
남: 당연하지. 전 세계 거의 70개국(④ 활동 국가 수)에서 대단한 일을 하고 있잖아.
여: 난 아버지의 뒤를 잇고 싶지만, 의학에는 별로 관심이 없어.
남: 내 생각에 넌 스위스(⑤ 본부 위치)에 있는 본부에서 일하려고 노력해 볼 수는 있을 것 같은데.
여: 아, 그 생각은 전혀 못했네.

어휘 **outbreak** (전쟁 · 사고 · 질병 등의) 발생[발발] / **commitment** 헌신, 전념; 약속 / **dedicate** (시간 · 노력을) 바치다, 전념[헌신]하다 / **famine** 기근; 굶주림 / **disaster** 재해, 재앙 / **follow in one's footsteps** ~의 뒤를 따라가다; ~의 선례를 따르다 / **headquarters** 본부[본사] (직원들)

09 내용 불일치 | ⑤

▶ 마지막 부분에서 한정 기간 동안에 서비스를 신청하면 무료 백신 프로그램을 1년간 제공한다는 내용이 나온다.

W: About 9 million people **have their identities stolen** each year. Identity theft is a serious issue that's difficult to resolve. This is where we come in. With $20 per month, Safe Identity will work with banks and credit card companies **to carefully monitor your account**. We will also actively monitor the Web for personal information **that is being used or sold illegally**. Our company notifies you immediately when new bank or credit card accounts are opened in your name and when suspicious changes to your personal information are detected. If you become a victim **while under our protection**, we will take full responsibility to resolve the situation for you. For a limited time, our company is offering free anti-virus software for one year when you sign up for our service. Call us today to receive this special offer.

여: 매년 약 9백만 명의 사람들이 신분을 도용당합니다. 신분 도용은 해결하기 어려운 심각한 문제입니다. 이것이 저희가 필요한 이유입니다. 월 20달러에 Safe Identity는 은행 및 신용 카드 회사와 함께 일하며 당신의 계좌를 주의 깊게 감시할 것입니다. 또한 불법적으로 사용되거나 판매되는 개인 정보에 관해 웹을 적극적으로 감시할 것입니다. 저희 회사는 고객님의 이름으로 새로운 은행이나 신용 카드의 계좌가 개설될 때, 그리고 개인 정보에 의심스러운 변화가 발견되면 즉시 알려 드립니다. 만약 저희 회사의 보호를 받는 동안에 피해자가 되시면, 저희가 모든 책임을 지고 상황을 해결할 것입니다. 한정 기간 동안 서비스를 신청하시면 저희 회사는 1년간 바이러스 방지 소프트웨어를 무료로 제공합니다. 오늘 전화하셔서 이 특별 제공을 받아보세요.

어휘 **identity** 신분, 신원 / **theft** 홈침, 절도 / **resolve** 해결하다; 결심하다 / **where A comes in** A가 필요한 이유 / **monitor** 감시[관리]하다 / **notify** 알리다, 통지하다 / **suspicious** 의심스러운 / **anti-virus** ((컴퓨터)) 바이러스 퇴치[방지]용의

10 도표 이해 | ④

▶ 바다낚시 여행은 출발 시각이 너무 이른데다 아이가 뱃멀미를 하므로 적합하지 않고, 레일 바이크 여행은 가격이 비싸며, 미술관 여행은 점심이 제공되지 않는다. 두 사람은 남은 두 개 여행 중 더 일찍 출발하는 농장 마을 여행을 선택하였다.

W: Honey, look at this flyer of tours.
M: Wow. I'm sure we can find something for our daughter's spring break.
W: Right. Hannah will love it. Why don't we choose **the one that departs at 8:30**?
M: Hmm, Hannah doesn't like to wake up that early, and **she also gets seasick**.
W: Oh, I forgot. Let's see. We shouldn't spend more than 60 dollars per person.
M: Then I guess one of them is not an option.
W: How about the other one that departs from Seoul Station? It would be an educational experience.
M: That's true, but **lunch isn't provided**.
W: You have a point. I don't want to worry about finding a restaurant.
M: Then it looks like two choices are left. Which do you prefer?
W: I think **an earlier start is better** because we only have one day for the tour.
M: I agree. I'm looking forward to it.

여: 여보, 이 여행 광고전단 좀 보세요.
남: 우와, 우리 딸이 봄방학에 할 수 있는 걸 찾을 수 있겠는데요.
여: 맞아요. Hannah도 아주 좋아할 거예요. 8시 30분에 출발하는 여행을 선택하는 게 어때요?
남: 음, Hannah는 그렇게 일찍 일어나는 걸 좋아하지 않아요. 그리고 그 애는 뱃멀미도 하잖아요.
여: 아, 깜빡했어요. 어디 보자. 우린 1인당 60달러 넘게 쓰지 않는 게 좋겠어요.
남: 그러면 이중 한 가지는 선택할 수 없겠네요.
여: 서울역에서 출발하는 다른 여행은 어때요? 교육적인 체험이 될 거예요.
남: 그건 그렇지만, 점심이 제공되지 않아요.
여: 잘 지적했어요. 식당을 찾는 문제로 걱정하고 싶지 않거든요.
남: 그렇다면 두 가지 선택이 남았네요. 당신은 어느 쪽이 더 좋아요?
여: 내 생각엔 더 일찍 출발하는 쪽이 좋을 것 같아요. 당일치기 여행이니까요.
남: 내 생각도 그래요. 기대되는군요.

어휘 **flyer** (광고 · 안내용) 전단 / **seasick** 뱃멀미

11 짧은 대화에 이어질 응답 | ①

▶ 여자가 오빠의 수영복을 빌려주겠다고 하자 남자가 사이즈가 맞을지 물었다. 이에 대해 가장 적절한 응답을 찾는다.

① 오빠는 너랑 사이즈가 비슷해.
② 난 네가 나중에 수영해야 한다고 생각해.
③ 오빠는 내 부탁을 들어줄 만큼 착해.
④ 파란색과 회색이 너에게 잘 어울릴 거야.
⑤ 그것을 잊다니 넌 정말 조심성이 없구나.

M: I can't believe **I forgot to bring** my swim shorts.
W: Don't worry. My brother's got two pairs of shorts. You can borrow one of them.
M: Do you think **they will fit me**?
W: ______________________

남: 내가 수영복 가져오는 것을 잊어버리다니 믿을 수 없어!
여: 걱정하지 마. 우리 오빠가 수영복을 두 벌 가져왔어. 그중 한 벌을 빌릴 수 있어.
남: 네 생각엔 그게 나한테 맞을 것 같니?
여: ______________________

12 짧은 대화에 이어질 응답 | ④

▶ 여자가 선풍기를 신용카드로 구매하려는데 카드 기계가 고장 난 상황이다. 근처에 현금인출기가 있는지 물었으므로 위치를 알려주는 응답이 가장 적절하다.

① 네, 40달러입니다. ② 이 모델을 추천합니다.
③ 돈이 약간 부족해요. ④ 2층에 하나 있습니다.
⑤ 죄송합니다만, 저희는 현금만 받습니다.

W: I'll take this electric fan. And I'll **pay with my credit card**.
M: I'm really sorry, but **our credit card machine is broken**.
W: That's too bad. Is there a cash machine nearby?
M: ______________________

여: 이 선풍기를 사겠어요. 그리고 신용카드로 계산할게요.
남: 정말 죄송하지만, 카드 기계가 고장 났습니다.
여: 저런, 근처에 현금인출기가 있나요?
남: ______________________

어휘 **short of A** A가 부족한 / **electric fan** 선풍기

13 긴 대화에 이어질 응답 | ③

▶ 저녁을 사주는 것으로 보답이 되겠느냐는 남자의 말에 가장 적절한 응답을 고른다.

① 네가 원하면 그 돈은 나중에 지불해도 돼.
② 너희 어머니께서는 언제 한국으로 떠나시니?
③ 충분하고말고. 내 코트를 가져올게.
④ 네가 나에게 말하는 방식이 마음에 들지 않아.
⑤ 네게 충분히 보답할 수 없을 거야. 고맙다.

M: Are you busy right now?
W: Not really. Do you need help with something?
M: I'm going to pick my mother up at the airport and I wanted to know **if you wanted to come with me**.
W: Umm... I guess. Is there any particular reason you want me to come?
M: Actually, yes. It's my mother's first time in Korea, and I want her **to get a great first impression**.
W: Oh, I see! You want me to be Korea's ambassador to your mother, right?
M: In a way, yes. But I also thought **you would like to join us for dinner**. And since you speak Korean....
W: I should be getting paid as an interpreter! You're lucky we're such good friends.
M: **Dinner is on me**. Is that payment enough?
W: ______________________

남: 지금 바쁘니?
여: 별로. 도움이 필요하니?
남: 공항에 어머니를 모시러 갈 건데 네가 같이 가고 싶은가 해서.
여: 음… 그러지 뭐. 내가 같이 갔으면 하는 특별한 이유라도 있니?

남: 사실, 있어. 어머니께서 한국에 처음으로 오시는 거라, 어머니께 좋은 첫인상을 심어 드리고 싶거든.
여: 아, 알겠다! 내가 너의 어머니께 한국의 대사 역할을 해줬으면 하는구나, 그렇지?
남: 그런 셈이지. 하지만 네가 우리와 식사도 같이 했으면 하고 생각했어. 네가 한국어를 하니까….
여: 통역사로서 비용을 받아야겠는걸! 너는 운이 좋아. 우리가 좋은 친구 사이니 말이야.
남: 저녁은 내가 살게. 그게 충분한 보답이 될까?
여: ______________________________

어휘 **repay** 보답하다, 은혜를 갚다 / **impression** 인상, 감명 / **ambassador** 대사; 사절, 대표 / **interpreter** 통역사 / **payment** 보수, 보상

14 긴 대화에 이어질 응답 | ①

▶ 비행 중에 우연히 만난 두 사람이 같은 사람을 알고 있으므로 '세상 참 좁다'라는 대답을 기대할 수 있다.

① 정말 세상이 좁군요. ② 언젠가는 그분을 만나고 싶군요.
③ 혹시 Jenna 씨를 아세요? ④ 가까운 미래에 그분을 만날 수 있을까요?
⑤ 당신을 다시 만나리라고는 상상도 못했어요.

M: It's a long flight, so let me introduce myself. I'm Bruce.
W: Hi, I'm Tina.
M: Going to Chicago?
W: I'm transferring in Chicago. Going to New York.
M: So am I. **We're probably catching** the same connecting flight. AC 345?
W: Yes, I think that's the flight. I'm a high school teacher. What do you do?
M: I'm a dentist. I have a small clinic in Manhattan.
W: Really? One of my best friends is a dentist. **She has a practice** in Manhattan, too.
M: I'm in the Lakeshore Building.
W: So is she. Her name is Jenna Johnson.
M: Wow. I often say "hi" to her in the elevator! Her clinic is on the floor above mine!
W: **What a coincidence**!
M: ______________________________

남: 정말 긴 비행이네요. 제 소개를 할게요. Bruce라고 합니다.
여: 안녕하세요. Tina예요.
남: 시카고로 가시나요?
여: 시카고에서 갈아탑니다. 뉴욕에 가거든요.
남: 저도 그래요. 아마도 같은 연결 항공편을 타겠군요. AC 345편인가요?
여: 네, 저도 그 비행기인 것 같아요. 전 고등학교 교사예요. 무슨 일을 하세요?
남: 전 치과의사입니다. 맨해튼에서 작은 병원을 하고 있습니다.
여: 그래요? 제 친한 친구 중 한 명도 치과의사예요. 그 친구도 맨해튼에서 개업했어요.
남: 저는 Lakeshore 빌딩에 있어요.
여: 내 친구도 그래요. 그 친구의 이름은 Jenna Johnson이에요.
남: 와, 저는 그분과 엘리베이터에서 종종 인사해요! 그분의 병원은 제 바로 위층에 있어요!
여: 정말 우연이군요!
남: ______________________________

어휘 **transfer** 갈아타다 / **connecting** 연결되는 / **practice** (의사 · 변호사 등의) 업무, 업무 장소 / **coincidence** 우연의 일치

15 상황에 적절한 말 | ①

▶ John은 일반석으로 미리 예약했는데 항공사 측의 잘못된 처리로 자리가 없어 비행기를 타지 못해 화가 나 있다. 매니저는 일등석이라도 빈 좌석이 있다면 John과 Mary에게 주라고 Gloria에게 지시한다. 따라서 일등석에 빈 좌석이 있음을 확인한 Gloria는 John과 Mary의 좌석을 무료로 일등석으로 업그레이드 해주겠다고 할 것이다.

Gloria: 착오가 생겨서 죄송합니다. ______________________________
① 고객님의 좌석을 무료로 업그레이드해 드리겠습니다.
② 하와이행 다음 비행기에 좌석을 예약해 드리겠습니다.
③ 하지만 부인이 아프시면 이 비행기를 타실 수 없습니다.
④ 매니저께서 고객님의 일반석 티켓이 사용 가능하다고 하셨습니다.
⑤ 하지만 최소한 출발 1시간 전에 탑승 수속을 밟으셔야 합니다.

M: John and Mary **have just gotten married**. Now they are checking in at the airport for their Hawaiian honeymoon. John booked economy class tickets online, so he hands the ticketing agent, Gloria, the receipt he printed out at home. Gloria spends a minute checking her computer, looking increasingly unhappy as she does. Finally, she tells John **the flight has been overbooked** and they must wait for a later flight. Mary turns white and looks sick. John is angry and **starts complaining in a loud voice**. Gloria's manager comes to see what the problem is. When Gloria explains, the manager asks her to check in business class and first class for vacant seats and to give any vacancies to John and Mary. So Gloria checks her computer and **finds two seats in first class**. In this situation, what would Gloria most likely say to John?

남: John과 Mary는 이제 막 결혼했다. 지금 그들은 하와이로 신혼여행을 가기 위해 공항에서 탑승 수속을 밟고 있다. John은 온라인으로 일반석 티켓을 예매했기 때문에, 발권 담당 직원인 Gloria에게 집에서 인쇄해 온 영수증을 건네준다. Gloria는 잠깐 동안 컴퓨터로 확인을 하는데 그러는 동안 점점 그녀의 표정이 좋지 않다. 마침내, 그녀는 John에게 비행기 예약이 초과되었고 그들이 다음 비행기를 기다려야만 한다고 말한다. Mary의 얼굴이 하얗게 질리고 아파 보인다. John은 화가 나서 큰소리로 항의하기 시작한다. Gloria의 매니저가 무슨 일이 생겼는지 알아보러 온다. Gloria가 설명하자, 매니저는 그녀에게 비즈니스석과 일등석에 빈 좌석이 있는지 확인하고, (있다면) 어떤 빈 좌석이라도 John과 Mary에게 주라고 요청한다. 그래서 Gloria는 자신의 컴퓨터를 확인하고 일등석에 두 개의 자리를 발견한다. 이러한 상황에서 Gloria가 John에게 할 말로 가장 적절한 것은 무엇인가?

어휘 **complimentary** 무료의; 칭찬하는 / **upgrade** 상위 등급으로 높여주다 / **valid** 유효한 / **departure** 출발 / **check in** 탑승[투숙] 수속을 밟다 / **vacant** 비어 있는, 빈자리의 ***cf.* vacancy** 빈자리, 빈방; 결원

16~17 세트 문항 | 16. ② 17. ①

▶ 16. 새로 만든 학교 웹사이트와 관련하여 로그인하는 법과 축제나 견학 등의 공지사항, 교사 홈페이지, 게시판 글 올리기 기능 등에 대해서 설명하고 있다.

① 새 학기 학사 일정 ② 학교 웹사이트 사용법
③ 교칙 변경 사항 ④ 학교 웹사이트 사용 시 어려움
⑤ 수업 선택 시 고려사항

▶ 17. 해석 참조

W: Good morning, students. This is Principal Catherine. I hope you are all **looking forward to another productive year** at Eastpark High School. Now, a few changes have been made since last year. One of them is the addition of our new school website. **Getting started with the new website** is easy. Simply find the "new student" tab located on the top left of the page and enter your name and student ID number. You will then be **asked to create a password**. The site will be a place for you to find news and important information about our school. Regular notices will be posted about events like school festivals and field trips. Changes to class schedules will also be there. And many of your teachers will have a homepage there as well. Students are also invited to post on the website, and **their posts will be visible** on the "student life" page. However, to post, you will need to speak with the site administrator, Mr. Kim, and receive a special ID. I hope that everyone will **benefit from this new service**.

여: 안녕하세요, 학생 여러분. 저는 교장 Catherine입니다. 여러분 모두 Eastpark 고등학교에서 결실을 맺는 또 한 해를 (보내길) 기대하고 있을 줄 압니다. 자, 지난해부터 몇 가지 변화가 생겼습니다. 그중 하나는 새로운 학교 웹사이트가 생긴 것입니다. 새로운 웹사이트를 시작하는 것은 쉽습니다. 단순히 웹페이지의 왼쪽 위에 있는 'new student' 탭을 찾아서 이름과 학생증 번호를 넣으면 됩니다. 다음에는 비밀번호를 만들라고 할 것입니다. 이 사이트는 여러분이 학교에 대한 소식과 중요한 정보를 찾아보는 곳입니다. ② 학교 축제나 ③ 견학 같은 정기적인 공지사항이 게시될 것입니다. ④ 수업 일정 변경 사항도 게시될 것입니다. 그리고 ⑤ 여러분의 선생님 중 많은 분들이 그곳에 홈페이지도 갖고 계십니다. 학생 여러분도 웹사이트에 글을 올려주세요. 그 글들은 'student life' 페이지에 보이게 됩니다. 웹사이트에 무언가를 게시하고 싶다면 사이트 관리자인 Kim 선생님께 말씀드려서 특별 아이디를 부여 받으세요. 이 새로운 서비스가 모두에게 도움이 되면 좋겠습니다.

어휘 **consideration** 고려 사항; 숙고 / **look forward to** ~을 기대하다 / **productive** 결실을 맺는, 생산적인 / **addition** 추가 / **notice** 공지사항 / **field trip** 견학, 현장 학습 / **post** 게시[공고]하다; 발송[우송]하다 / **visible** (눈에) 보이는 / **administrator** 관리자, 행정인

실전모의고사 39

Answers & Explanation

01. ② 02. ③ 03. ④ 04. ⑤ 05. ④ 06. ② 07. ① 08. ④ 09. ③ 10. ②
11. ③ 12. ⑤ 13. ① 14. ⑤ 15. ③ 16. ① 17. ③

01 화자가 하는 말의 목적 | ②

▶ We will also be holding a lecture on child safety에 담화의 목적이 잘 드러나 있다. 즉, 어린이 안전에 관한 강연을 알리고 있다.

M: There are many parents who often worry they'll lose their children or their children **will get hurt in an accident**. As a result, the Wingfield police have continued to campaign for the safety of children and **more funding for missing-children cases** over the past five years. Last month, the Wingfield police distributed name cards for all children in the neighborhood. We will also be **holding a lecture on child safety** for all parents who have children under the age of six on May 21st at 6:00 p.m. A child psychologist will be on hand to offer valuable advice for any parent. The lecture will be held at 245 Williams Street in the Wingfield Community Center and **will be free of charge**. We invite all parents who are interested.

남: 사고로 자신의 아이들을 잃을까 혹은 아이들이 다칠까 종종 걱정하시는 부모님들이 많이 있습니다. 그래서 Wingfield 경찰은 지난 5년간 어린이 안전 캠페인과 미아 사건에 대한 더 많은 모금 캠페인을 계속해오고 있습니다. 지난달, Wingfield 경찰은 인근의 모든 아이들에게 이름표를 나눠주었습니다. 또한, 5월 21일 저녁 6시에 6세 미만의 아이들을 둔 모든 부모님을 대상으로 어린이 안전에 관한 강연을 개최할 것입니다. 아동 심리학자께서 어느 부모님께든 귀중한 조언으로 도움을 주실 것입니다. 강연은 Williams 245번가에 있는 Wingfield 주민 센터에서 열릴 것이며, 무료입니다. 관심 있으신 모든 부모님을 초대합니다.

어휘 **funding** 모금; 기금 / **distribute** 나누어 주다 / **psychologist** 심리학자 / **on hand** 도움을 얻을 수 있는 / **free of charge** 무료로

02 의견 | ③

▶ 여자는 정원일로 어머니가 편안함과 희망을 찾을 수 있다고 하는 것으로 보아 정원 가꾸기의 심리적인 이점에 관해서 이야기하고 있음을 알 수 있다.

W: I think we should help Mom make a garden.
M: That sounds nice. What made you think of that?
W: Well, I know **Mom has been feeling sad and lonely** recently, and I think a garden will help her greatly.
M: Good idea. It will definitely keep her busy.
W: A garden can be **a place of comfort and peace**. I guess it would be a good place to relax and take her mind off things.
M: Watching plants grow can give her **a sense of hope and renewal**.
W: She will feel like she has a purpose. And it'll also be nice to have fresh organic produce.
M: Right. We can help her make a small pond in the garden. Water has a soothing effect.
W: Great idea. I'll start **making a list of things** I need to build a garden.
M: I'll check out the garden supply store and get some seeds.

여: 우린 엄마가 정원 만드시는 걸 도와드려야 할 것 같아.
남: 좋아. 어떻게 그런 생각을 했니?
여: 음, 내가 알기로는 엄마가 최근에 울적하고 외로워하셨는데, 정원이 엄마에게 많이 도움이 될 것 같아.
남: 좋은 생각이야. 분명 엄마를 바쁘게 지내게 해줄 거야.
여: 정원은 편안하고 평화로운 공간이 될 수 있어. 긴장을 풀고 엄마의 관심을 딴 데로 돌리기에 훌륭한 공간이 될 것 같아.
남: 식물이 자라는 것을 바라보는 게 엄마에게 희망과 소생의 느낌을 줄 수 있어.
여: 엄마는 목적이 생긴 것처럼 느끼실 거야. 그리고 신선한 유기농 작물을 얻는 것도 멋질 거야.
남: 맞아. 우리는 엄마가 정원에 작은 연못을 만드는 것을 도울 수 있어. 물은 마음을 진정시키는 효과가 있어.
여: 좋은 생각이야. 난 정원을 만드는 데 필요한 것들의 목록을 작성하기 시작할게.
남: 나는 정원 용품 가게를 살펴보고 씨앗을 좀 살게.

어휘 **definitely** 분명히, 확실히 / **take one's mind off A** A를 잊다; 관심을 딴 데로 돌리다 / **renewal** 소생, 회복; 새롭게 하기 / **produce** 작물, 농산물 / **soothing** 진정시키는, 달래는

03 관계 | ④

▶ 경기가 끝난 뒤 남자에게 시청자들에게 소감을 말해달라고 하고 경기에서 가장 활약한 선수에 대해 묻는 것으로 보아 여자는 방송 기자이고, 대화 중에 pitcher, the final home run 등의 표현이 등장한 것으로 보아 남자는 야구 감독임을 알 수 있다.

W: The game is finally over. Let's speak to Jim Gonzalez. Hello, Mr. Gonzalez.
M: Yes, we won!
W: First, **I'd like to congratulate you** on this fantastic win. Can you say a few words to our audience?
M: It was a great game. We thank all the people who cheered for our team here.
W: The team is still **celebrating their victory on the field** right now. Who do you think played the best out there tonight?
M: Everyone did a great job. But I have to say that our pitcher, Eric Morris, did an amazing job.
W: Yes, he was great! I was also very impressed with the player who hit the final home run.
M: Oh, that was Dave Bennett. He is **a player I can always trust**.
W: Well, congratulations again. We wish you more wins in the future.
M: Thanks for the support.

여: 경기가 드디어 끝났습니다. Jim Gonzalez 감독님과 이야기 나눠보죠. 안녕하세요, Gonzalez 감독님.
남: 네, 우리가 이겼습니다!
여: 먼저, 이 환상적인 승리에 축하드립니다. 저희 시청자들께 한 말씀 해주시죠.
남: 굉장한 경기였어요. 여기 저희 팀을 응원해주신 모든 분들께 감사합니다.
여: 지금도 팀원들은 경기장에서 승리를 자축하고 있는데요. 오늘 저녁 경기장에서 가장 활약한 선수는 누구라고 생각하십니까?
남: 모두 멋진 활약을 했어요. 하지만 투수인 Eric Morris 선수가 대단한 활약을 했다고 말해야 겠네요.
여: 네, 굉장했지요! 저는 마지막 홈런을 친 선수도 매우 인상 깊었습니다.
남: 오, 그는 Dave Bennett이었죠. 그는 제가 항상 신뢰할 수 있는 선수입니다.
여: 음, 다시 한 번 축하드립니다. 앞으로 더 많은 승리가 있기를 기원합니다.
남: 응원해주셔서 감사합니다.

어휘 **cheer for** 응원하다 / **pitcher** 투수 / **impressed** 인상 깊게 생각하는, 감명을 받은

04 그림 불일치 | ⑤

▶ 대화에서는 식탁보가 체크무늬라고 했는데 그림에는 흰 식탁보가 있으므로 일치하지 않는다.

M: Here is a picture of a beautifully decorated party. **Would you like something similar** for your wedding?
W: I love it. It has a wonderful antique feel. Can we rent this space, too?
M: Of course. This is a chapel in an old castle and can be rented by anyone. The painting in the middle of the wall **is said to be over 200 years old**.
W: The candleholders on both sides of the painting are beautiful.
M: We decorated the ceiling with **balloons in the shape of a heart**.
W: I see that. What a creative idea!
M: Do you see the beautiful lamp on the left wall?
W: Yes. It's another lovely detail of the decor.
M: What do you think about the checkered table cloths we placed over the round tables?
W: I like them.
M: I'll go ahead and contact the chapel and make a reservation for you.
W: I'd appreciate it. **I'm looking forward to everything**.

남: 이건 아름답게 장식된 파티의 사진입니다. 귀하의 결혼식에 비슷한 것을 원하십니까?
여: 마음에 들어요. 멋진 고풍스러운 느낌이 있어요. 이 장소도 빌릴 수 있나요?
남: 물론입니다. 이곳은 오래된 성 안에 있는 예배당이고 누구든 빌릴 수 있습니다. 벽 가운데에 있는 그림은 200년이 넘었다고 합니다.
여: 그림 양옆에 있는 촛대도 아름다워요.
남: 천장에는 하트 모양으로 풍선을 장식했습니다.
여: 그렇네요. 독창적인 아이디어군요!

남: 왼쪽 벽에 있는 아름다운 전등이 보이시나요?
여: 네, 또 다른 사랑스러운 세부 장식이네요.
남: 둥근 테이블을 덮은 체크무늬 식탁보는 어떠신가요?
여: 좋아요.
남: 저는 어서 가서 예배당에 연락하고 예약을 하겠습니다.
여: 감사합니다. 모든 것이 기대되네요.

어휘 **decorated** 장식된, 훌륭하게 꾸민 *cf.* **decor** (실내) 장식 / **antique** 고풍스러운; 골동품인; 골동품 / **chapel** (부속) 예배당 / **candleholder** 촛대 / **checkered** 체크무늬의 / **look forward to A** A를 고대하다

05 부탁한 일 | ④

▶ 여자는 남자에게 동아리 신입생 모집을 위한 부스를 만드는 것을 도와달라고 했다.

W: Hi, Gabriel. **How have you been**?
M: Great. What are you doing here?
W: I have something to take care of. I'm glad we met. I need some help and you're the perfect person to help me.
M: What is it?
W: Since we're starting the new school year, it's time for school orientation. **I'm planning to set up a booth** on campus during orientation so that we can recruit some freshmen to our club.
M: That's a fantastic idea. How can I help?
W: I'm putting the booth together, so could you move the poles for me?
M: Sure. I will. **Why are you doing this job alone**? Where are James and Kyle?
W: James hurt his wrist, so he went to see a doctor, and Kyle has a part-time job this afternoon.
M: Oh, I see. And are these the flyers that we will **hand out to the new students**?
W: Yes.

여: 안녕, Gabriel. 어떻게 지냈니?
남: 잘 지냈지. 여기서 뭐 하고 있니?
여: 처리해야 될 일이 있어. 우리 만나서 다행이다. 도움이 좀 필요한데 네가 나를 도와줄 완벽한 사람이야.
남: 뭔데?
여: 새 학년이 시작됐으니까 학교 오리엔테이션 기간이잖아. 우리 동아리에 신입생을 모집할 수 있게 오리엔테이션 기간에 교정에 부스를 설치하려고 계획하고 있어.
남: 멋진 생각인데. 어떻게 도와줄까?
여: 내가 부스를 설치하고 있는데 기둥을 옮겨줄래?
남: 그래. 그럴게. 이 일을 왜 혼자 하고 있어? James와 Kyle은 어디 있어?
여: James는 손목을 다쳐서 진찰을 받으러 갔고, Kyle은 오늘 오후에 아르바이트가 있어.
남: 아, 그렇구나. 그리고 이것들은 신입생들에게 나눠줄 전단이야?
여: 응.

어휘 **set up** 세우다, 설치하다; 시작하다 / **recruit** 모집하다, 뽑다 / **freshman** 신입생 / **wrist** 손목 / **flyer** (광고, 안내용) 전단 / **hand out** 나눠주다, 배포하다

06 금액 | ②

▶ 여자는 오늘 커트(20달러)와 염색(50달러)만 하겠다고 했으므로 70달러를 지불해야 한다.

M: Hello, I'm Adrian Sanchez, your stylist. What can I do for you today?
W: Well, I **want a new look**. Would I look okay with this kind of body wave?
M: I think it would suit you. A body wave would give you more body.
W: How much is the perm?
M: A cut and a perm would cost you $95. How about **putting some color in your hair**?
W: Color? Sounds good. I'm bored with my dark hair.
M: Yes, I think light brown **would look nice on you**.
W: How much does a coloring cost?
M: It'll cost you $50 to color your hair.
W: Well, coloring my hair and getting a perm **would really damage my hair**. Give me a cut and coloring for today.
M: Sure. Cuts are $20.
W: Great.

남: 안녕하세요, 스타일리스트 Adrian Sanchez입니다. 오늘은 뭘 도와드릴까요?
여: 음, 새로운 머리 스타일을 하고 싶어요. 이런 종류의 보디 웨이브는 괜찮을까요?
남: 손님께 잘 어울릴 것 같네요. 보디 웨이브를 하시면 머리가 더 풍성해질 거예요.
여: 파마는 얼마예요?
남: 커트와 파마는 95달러입니다. 머리에 염색을 좀 하는 건 어떨까요?
여: 염색이요? 괜찮네요. 검은 머리가 지겹거든요.
남: 네, 제 생각엔 밝은 갈색이 손님에게 아주 잘 어울릴 것 같아요.
여: 염색은 얼마인가요?
남: 손님 머리를 염색하는 데는 50달러입니다.
여: 이런, 염색하고 파마하는 건 머리에 정말 손상을 입히겠네요. 오늘은 커트랑 염색만 할게요.
남: 알겠습니다. 커트는 20달러입니다.
여: 좋아요.

어휘 **body wave** 보디 웨이브 ((컬이 거의 없는 파마))

07 이유 | ①

▶ 여자는 작년부터 채식주의자가 되어 고기를 먹지 않는다고 했고 그에 따라 남자는 메뉴를 파스타로 바꿨다.

M: Jennifer, why don't you come over to my place for dinner tonight? Jonathan and Faith will come, too.
W: I'll definitely be there. I **haven't spent time with you guys** for a while. By the way, what are we eating?
M: I'm going to make chicken parmesan. It's an old family recipe **that I learned from my grandmother** the last time she visited!
W: Oh, that really does sound delicious, but unfortunately I can't eat it.
M: What? Why not? Do you have an allergy to something in the dish?
W: No, no allergies. It's just that **I became a vegetarian**.
M: Oh, I had no idea! When did this happen?
W: From last year. I can live without meat, and it's better for the animals that way.
M: Well, then chicken parmesan is definitely not a good choice to put on the menu. I'll prepare some pasta.
W: **I don't want to impose**. Are you sure it's no trouble?
M: No problem. I want you to feel comfortable at the dinner!

남: Jennifer, 오늘 밤에 저녁 먹으러 우리 집에 오는 게 어때? Jonathan이랑 Faith도 올 거야.
여: 꼭 갈게. 너희와 함께 시간을 보내는 것도 정말 오래간만이구나. 그런데 우리 뭐 먹을 거야?
남: 닭고기 파르메산 치즈 요리를 만들 거야. 지난번에 할머니께서 오셨을 때 배운 오래된 우리 가족 조리법이야!
여: 오, 정말 맛있겠지만, 안타깝게도 난 먹을 수 없어.
남: 뭐라고? 왜? 요리에 들어가는 것 중에 알레르기가 있는 게 있니?
여: 아니, 알레르기는 없어. 내가 채식주의자가 됐거든.
남: 오, 난 몰랐어! 언제 그렇게 된 거야?
여: 작년부터야. 나는 고기를 먹지 않아도 살 수 있고, 그게 동물들에게 더 좋아.
남: 음, 그러면 닭고기 파르메산 치즈 요리는 메뉴에 넣기에 결코 좋은 선택이 아니구나. 파스타를 준비할게.
여: 폐를 끼치고 싶지 않은데, 번거롭지 않겠어?
남: 문제없어. 난 네가 저녁 식사 때 편안했으면 좋겠어.

어휘 **parmesan** 파르메산 치즈 / **allergy** 알레르기 / **vegetarian** 채식주의자 / **impose** 폐를 끼치다; (세금 등을) 부과하다; 강요하다

08 언급하지 않은 것 | ④

▶ 해석 참조

M: Good morning, Jasmine.
W: Hello, Daniel. **Are you on your way out**?
M: Yes, I'm on my way to see a basketball game in Boston.
W: Oh, in Boston? You must really enjoy watching basketball games.
M: I do, but my son will also be playing. He is a player on the Wheeler High School basketball team.
W: Oh, I had no idea your son was such an athlete! What's his name?
M: Sean, Sean Davis. He's **one of the top shooting guards on his team**. That's the position Michael Jordan played. He's number one on the ESPN position rankings.
W: Wow, very impressive. You must be proud of him.
M: He was asked to join the NBA, but **he decided against it**. He got accepted to Duke University, and that's where he plans to go.
W: Fantastic! That's one of the top Ivy League schools!
M: Yes, I know. It's not an easy school to get into.
W: **That's for sure**. I hope your son's team wins.

남: 안녕하세요, Jasmine.
여: 안녕하세요, Daniel. 나가는 길이세요?
남: 네, 보스턴에 농구 경기를 보러 가는 길이에요.
여: 오, 보스턴에요? 농구 경기 관람을 정말 좋아하시나 봐요.

남: 그렇기도 하지만, 제 아들이 경기를 하거든요. 그 애는 Wheeler 고등학교(① 소속 고등학교) 농구팀 선수예요.
여: 오, 아드님이 운동선수인지 몰랐네요! 이름이 뭐예요?
남: Sean이에요, Sean Davis요. 그 애는 팀에서 최고 슈팅가드(② 포지션) 중 한 명이에요. Michael Jordan이 뛰었던 포지션이죠. ESPN 포지션 순위에서 1위(③ 포지션 순위)고요.
여: 와, 매우 훌륭하네요. 아드님이 자랑스러우시겠어요.
남: NBA에 진출하라는 권유를 받았지만, 그 애는 그러지 않기로 결정했어요. Duke 대학에서 입학 허가를 받았고(⑤ 진학할 대학), 거기가 그 애가 가려고 하는 곳이지요.
여: 멋지군요! 거기는 최고 Ivy League 학교 중 하나잖아요!
남: 네, 알아요. 들어가기 쉬운 학교는 아니죠.
여: 물론이죠. 아드님의 팀이 이기기를 바랍니다.

어휘 **shooting guard** 슈팅가드 ((농구 포지션에서 중장거리 슛 능력이 좋은 가드)) / **ranking** 순위, 등급

09 내용 불일치 | ③

▶ answer 25 questions in 80 minutes라는 말로 보아 1시간 20분 동안 25문제를 풀어야 한다.

W: May I have your attention, please? The national math contest **is coming up next month** and we are looking for students who would like to compete. We are currently recruiting students to represent our school as a team. **We will be holding a test** on May 17th, next Wednesday, at 4 p.m. in room 201 for all students who are interested. The test will be composed of three parts, and students will be required to answer 25 questions in 80 minutes. **No calculators will be allowed**. The seven students with the highest scores will get a spot on the team. Our wonderful math teacher, Mr. Baum, **will be heading the team**, so if you're interested in trying out, drop by his class or email him at baum@kennedyhigh.com. Good luck!

여: 주목해 주시겠습니까? 전국 수학대회가 다음 달로 다가와, 참가하고자 하는 학생을 찾고 있습니다. 한 팀으로 우리 학교를 대표할 학생들을 현재 모집 중입니다. 다음 주 수요일인 5월 17일 오후 4시 201호실에서 관심 있는 모든 학생들을 대상으로 경시대회를 개최하려고 합니다. 시험은 세 부분으로 구성될 것이며, 학생들은 80분 동안 25문제를 풀어야 합니다. 계산기는 허용되지 않습니다. 가장 높은 점수를 받은 일곱 명의 학생들이 그 팀에 들어가게 됩니다. 우리 학교의 훌륭한 수학 선생님이신 Baum 선생님께서 그 팀을 지도하실 것입니다. 그러니 시험에 참가해보는 데 관심이 있다면, Baum 선생님의 교실에 들르거나 baum@kennedyhigh.com으로 이메일을 보내십시오. 행운을 빕니다!

어휘 **currently** 현재, 지금 / **be composed of** ~로 구성되다 / **calculator** 계산기 / **drop by** ~에 들르다

10 도표 이해 | ②

▶ 관광보다는 활동할 수 있는 것, 반나절짜리 투어, 수상 스포츠를 택했고, 가격은 150달러 이하를 원했다.

M: The cruise ship will have a stopover in Philipsburg for a day and **we're free to leave the ship** at any time. Is there anything particular you would like to do while we're there?
W: Sounds like fun. What type of activities do they offer?
M: Do you feel like going on a sightseeing tour or an activity-based tour?
W: I don't feel like **being stuck on a bus tour**, so let's do something active.
M: Sounds good to me. We can choose an activity for a full or half day. Which do you prefer?
W: Let's do something for half a day so we have some time to **explore the port on our own**.
M: You're right. Then what should we choose? I can't swim, so we can't do any water sports.
W: Oh, you don't need to know how to swim to do this activity. All you need is a life jacket.
M: If that's what you want, it's okay with me. And **we have a tight budget**, so we don't want to spend more than $150 per person.
W: Then this is exactly what we want.

남: 유람선이 필립스버그에 하루 동안 머무를 거고, 우리는 언제든 배에서 나갈 수 있어요. 거기 있는 동안 특별히 하고 싶은 것이 있나요?
여: 재미있겠네요. 어떤 종류의 활동이 있어요?
남: 관광 투어를 하고 싶어요, 아니면 활동 위주 투어를 하고 싶어요?
여: 난 버스 투어에 매여 있고 싶지 않아요. 그러니 활동적인 걸 해요.
남: 나도 좋아요. 온종일 하거나 반나절만 하는 활동 중에 고를 수 있어요. 어떤 게 좋아요?
여: 우리끼리 항구를 돌아다닐 시간을 가질 수 있게 반나절인 것으로 해요.
남: 당신 말이 맞아요. 그러면 뭘 골라야 할까요? 난 수영을 할 수 없으니, 수상 스포츠는 할 수 없어요.
여: 오, 이 활동을 하기 위해서는 수영할 줄 몰라도 돼요. 당신이 필요한 건 오직 구명조끼예요.
남: 그 활동이 당신이 원하는 거라면, 나도 좋아요. 그리고 예산이 빠듯하니까, 1인당 150달러 넘게 써서는 안 돼요.
여: 그러면 이게 딱 우리가 원하는 거네요.

어휘 **time span** 기간 / **snorkeling** 스노클링 ((스노클(숨대롱)을 이용한 잠수)) / **horseback riding** 승마 / **stopover** 여행 중 잠시 머묾, 단기 체류 / **port** 항구 (도시)

11 짧은 대화에 이어질 응답 | ③

▶ 남자가 외출하는 여자에게 아스피린을 사다 달라고 하자 여자가 진찰을 받으라고 권유하고 있다. 이에 가장 적절한 응답을 찾는다.

① 알겠어. 아스피린을 좀 사다 줄게.
② 거긴 병원 근처에 있어. 쉽게 찾을 거야.
③ 아냐, 심각한 거 아니야. 아스피린이면 될 거야.
④ 응, 엄마가 요리책을 사다 달라고 하셨어.
⑤ 오렌지주스를 많이 마시고 좀 쉬어.

W: Justin, I'm going to the bookstore. Don't you have anything to buy?
M: Yes. There is a pharmacy **on your way to the bookstore**. Could you pick up some aspirin for me?
W: Do you still have a headache? **Why don't you see a doctor**?
M: ______________________________

여: Justin, 나 서점에 갈 거야. 뭐 살 거 없니?
남: 있어. 서점 가는 길에 약국이 있어. 아스피린 좀 사다 줄래?
여: 아직도 두통이 있니? 병원에 가서 진찰을 받는 게 어때?
남: ______________________________

어휘 **pharmacy** 약국 / **aspirin** 아스피린 ((해열 진통제))

12 짧은 대화에 이어질 응답 | ⑤

▶ 친구의 연주회에 가기 전에 꽃을 샀는지 묻는 남자에게 여자가 할 말로 가장 적절한 것을 고른다.

① 아뇨, 그 꽃집은 너무 비싸요.
② 맞아요, 그녀는 매년 두 차례씩 연주회를 해요.
③ 알겠어요, 연주회에 내 검은 드레스를 입을게요.
④ 네, 이 장미 꽃다발을 사시면 화병을 무료로 드립니다.
⑤ 이미 주문했고 오늘 4시까지 배달해줄 거예요.

M: The concert begins at 7 tonight. We should probably **leave the house at six**. I'll be home at five.
W: **I'm glad you didn't forget**.
M: How could I forget your friend's recital? Did you get some flowers for her?
W: ______________________________

남: 연주회가 오늘 저녁 7시에 시작해요. 우린 아마 집에서 6시에 나가야 할 거예요. 5시에 집에 올게요.
여: 당신이 잊지 않았다니 기쁘네요.
남: 당신 친구의 연주회를 어떻게 잊을 수 있겠어요? 그녀에게 줄 꽃은 샀어요?
여: ______________________________

어휘 **recital** 연주회, 발표회

13 긴 대화에 이어질 응답 | ①

▶ 쇼핑을 온 여자에게 남자가 서두르자고 하는 상황이다. 시간을 절약하기 위해 남자가 따로 필요한 것을 가져오겠다고 하자 여자가 구매 품목을 말해준다. 이에 대한 남자의 응답으로 가장 적절한 것을 찾는다.

① 알았어요. 곧 돌아올게요.
② 여기는 가격이 비싸네요.
③ 당신은 구입할 물건 목록을 만들었어야 했어요.
④ 천천히 해요. 우린 시간이 많아요.
⑤ 내가 쇼핑을 별로 좋아하지 않는다는 걸 알잖아요.

M: Just a minute, Kaitlyn. I think I should wait outside in the parking lot.
W: No, don't do that. I only need to buy a few things.
M: Alright. Only a few things? **Let's make it quick**.
W: Can you **get me a shopping cart from over there**?
M: If you're only buying a few things, do you really need a cart? Don't

forget that we have to be at the cinema by six.

W: I know. We have plenty of time. **Our refrigerator is completely empty**. First, we need some cans of tuna.

M: Here. What else do we need?

W: Hold on. Let's get the Sunrise tuna cans instead. I have a coupon for them.

M: What's next? **I'll go get it**. Then we can save a little time.

W: Okay. We need some paper towels and facial tissues.

M: ________________________________

남: 잠시만요, Kaitlyn. 난 바깥 주차장에서 기다려야 할 것 같아요.
여: 아니에요, 그러지 마요. 몇 가지만 사면 돼요.
남: 알겠어요. 몇 가지만이죠? 빨리 해요.
여: 저기서 쇼핑 카트를 가져다 줄래요?
남: 몇 가지만 산다면, 카트가 정말 필요해요? 극장에 6시까지 가야 한다는 걸 잊지 마요.
여: 알아요. 시간 많이 있어요. 우리 냉장고가 텅텅 비었어요. 먼저, 참치 통조림 몇 개가 필요해요.
남: 여기요. 또 뭐가 필요해요?
여: 잠시만요. 그것 말고 Sunrise 참치 통조림을 사요. 쿠폰이 있거든요.
남: 다음은 뭐죠? 내가 가서 가져올게요. 그러면 시간을 좀 아낄 수 있어요.
여: 알겠어요. 종이 수건과 화장지가 필요해요.
남: ________________________________

어휘 **take one's time** 천천히 하다; 늑장부리다

14 긴 대화에 이어질 응답 | ⑤

▶ 가수의 꿈을 가진 여자의 노래를 듣고 남자가 오디션에 시도해보라고 격려하고 있다. 이에 대한 적절한 대답을 유추해 본다.

① 넌 바이올린 연주를 잘하는 거 같아.
② 좋은 생각이야. 넌 음악에 진정한 재능이 있어.
③ 난 생각이 달라. 넌 다시 생각해봐야 해.
④ 네 비전에 대한 너무 큰 자신감은 도움이 안 돼.
⑤ 좋아! 넌 내게 꿈을 추구할 수 있도록 용기를 줬어.

M: Rachel, I didn't know that you could sing so well.

W: That's very kind of you to say so!

M: You can **turn professional if you want to**.

W: Do you really think so?

M: Certainly. It was amazing. If I could sing like you, I would be a singer.

W: Do you think I sing well enough to record? Um, actually, I've thought about becoming a singer. It was always my dream.

M: Yeah, why don't you try it?

W: Hmm.... People say I'm a little **too old to become a singer**.

M: No, I don't think so. You're **young enough to start**.

W: Do you think so? I was thinking of trying to audition for a musical.

M: Try it! **Better late than never**. It is always worth trying.

W: ________________________________

남: Rachel, 난 네가 그렇게 노래를 잘 부르는지 몰랐어.
여: 그렇게 말해주다니 정말 고마워!
남: 네가 원하면 전문적으로 할 수 있겠다.
여: 정말 그렇게 생각해?
남: 물론이지. 굉장했어. 내가 너처럼 노래할 수 있다면, 난 가수가 될 거야.
여: 내가 (음반을) 녹음할 수 있을 정도로 노래를 잘한다고 생각해? 저, 실은, 난 가수가 되는 것을 생각해왔어. 그건 항상 내 꿈이었거든.
남: 그래, 해보지 그래?
여: 음…, 사람들이 내가 가수가 되기에는 나이가 좀 많대.
남: 아니야, 난 그렇게 생각 안 해. 너는 시작해도 될 만큼 충분히 어려.
여: 그렇게 생각해? 난 뮤지컬 오디션을 보려고 생각하고 있었어.
남: 해봐! 하지 않는 것보다 늦더라도 하는 게 낫지. 시도하는 건 항상 가치 있어.
여: ________________________________

어휘 **genuine** 진짜의; 진실한 / **reconsider** 다시 생각하다 / **pursue** 추구하다; 뒤쫓다 / **audition** 오디션을 보다

15 상황에 적절한 말 | ③

▶ Alexis는 낯선 곳에 온 Christine과 친구가 되어 식사에 초대하고 자신의 친구들을 소개해 주었다. Alexis가 고마움의 표시로 화분을 선물한 Christine에게 할 말로는 감사를 표하고 선물에 대해 언급을 하는 것이 적절하다.

① 네 친구들에게 안부를 전해줘.
② 넌 아주 친절해. 넌 정말 내게 큰 도움이 됐어.
③ 넌 정말 다정하구나! 하지만 이럴 것까지는 없었는데.
④ 처음에는 어려워. 넌 분명히 잘할 거야.
⑤ 초대해줘서 고마워. 파티에 갈게.

M: Christine moved to Atlanta because of her new job. Christine didn't know anyone in Atlanta. Then **she became friends with** Alexis, a co-worker at her company. Last Saturday, Alexis invited Christine to dinner at her house. She introduced her friends to Christine. Christine was very happy and really appreciated it. Today, Christine buys a gift for Alexis **to express her appreciation**. She knows that Alexis likes flowers, so she buys her a plant pot. She tells Alexis **how thankful she is for dinner** and hands her the gift. Alexis accepts the gift, but she feels that **it's only natural for her to help** Christine out and is thus surprised to get such a gift. In this situation, what would Alexis most likely say to Christine?

남: Christine은 새로운 직장 때문에 애틀랜타로 이사했다. Christine은 애틀랜타에서 아는 사람이 아무도 없었다. 그러다가 회사 동료인 Alexis와 친구가 되었다. 지난 토요일, Alexis는 Christine을 자신의 집으로 저녁 식사에 초대했다. 그녀는 Christine에게 자신의 친구들을 소개해줬다. Christine은 매우 기뻤고 정말 감사했다. 오늘 Christine은 감사를 표하려고 Alexis에게 줄 선물을 산다. 그녀는 Alexis가 꽃을 좋아한다는 것을 알고는 화분을 산다. 그녀는 Alexis에게 저녁 식사에 대해 얼마나 고마움을 느끼는지 말하며 선물을 건넨다. Alexis는 선물을 받지만, 자신이 Christine을 도와준 것을 그저 당연한 일이라고 생각해 그런 선물을 받고는 놀란다. 이러한 상황에서 Alexis가 Christine에게 할 말로 가장 적절한 것은 무엇인가?

어휘 **co-worker** 동료 / **appreciation** 감사; 감상 / **plant pot** 화분 / **hand** 건네주다

16~17 세트 문항 | 16. ① 17. ③

▶ 16. 식용 잡초를 먹음으로써 경제성, 음식 선택의 증가, 환경 보호 등의 이점이 있음을 설명하고 있다.

① 식용 잡초를 먹는 것의 이점
② 채소를 재배하는 것의 장점
③ 야생 식품의 더해가는 인기
④ 유기농 식품 구매의 중요성
⑤ 정원에서 잡초를 없애는 방법

▶ 17. 해석 참조

① 민들레 ② 붉은토끼풀 ③ 질경이 ④ 분홍바늘꽃 ⑤ 야생 아스파라거스

W: Have you ever wondered if weeds in the wilderness could be eaten? **Most of those weeds are edible**. For example, dandelion is a weed that's most known as a salad green. Red clover **has been used for ages as a folk remedy** for cancer. And several Native American tribes included fireweed in their diet. It's best eaten young, when the leaves are tender. Also, wild asparagus is a great source of vitamin C. **By using those weeds as food**, you will get an "early harvest" at a time when most gardens are just getting started. As with most other homegrown food, you'll save money. This particular food is especially economical — **it's totally free** (you didn't even have to pay for the seeds). In addition, you'll **expand your own food knowledge**. There are approximately 50,000 edible plant species in the world, but the average American eats only 30. Therefore, if you only use three kinds of weeds as part of your diet, you've probably increased your food choices by 10%! Plus, it's easier to avoid using weed killers **once you view weeds as food**, which helps the environment.

여: 야생에 있는 잡초를 먹을 수 있는지 궁금하게 여긴 적이 있나요? 그런 잡초 대부분은 먹을 수 있습니다. 예를 들어, ① 민들레는 샐러드용 채소로 가장 잘 알려진 잡초입니다. ② 붉은토끼풀은 암에 대한 민간요법으로 오랫동안 사용되어왔습니다. 그리고 몇몇 아메리카 원주민 부족은 ④ 분홍바늘꽃을 그들의 식단에 포함시켰습니다. 그것은 잎이 부드러운 어린 풀일 때 가장 먹기가 좋습니다. 또한, ⑤ 야생 아스파라거스는 비타민 C의 훌륭한 공급원입니다. 그런 잡초들을 음식으로 사용함으로써, 대부분 정원이 막 (파종되기) 시작하고 있을 때에 여러분은 '이른 수확'을 거둘 수 있게 됩니다. 집에서 기른 다른 음식 대부분과 마찬가지로, 돈을 절약하게 될 것입니다. 이 특별한 음식은 특히 경제적인데, 이것은 완전히 공짜입니다(씨앗을 사려고 지불할 필요도 없었으니까요). 게다가, 음식에 대한 지식이 확장될 것입니다. 세상에는 약 5만 가지의 식용 식물 종이 있지만, 평균적인 미국인은 30가지만 먹습니다. 따라서 식단에 3가지 종류의 잡초만 사용해도, 아마 음식 선택을 10% 늘린 셈이 될 것입니다! 또한, 일단 잡초를 음식으로 보면 제초제 사용을 피하기가 더 쉽고, 이는 환경을 돕습니다.

어휘 **edible** 먹을 수 있는, 식용의; 식품 / **weed** 잡초 / **wilderness** 야생, 황무지; 자연이 보전된 곳 / **salad green** 샐러드용 채소 / **for ages** 오랫동안 / **folk remedy** 민간요법 / **tender** 부드러운 / **homegrown** 자기 집에서 기른; 국내산의 / **economical** 경제적인 / **expand** 확장하다, 팽창하다 / **approximately** 대략, 거의

Answers & Explanation

실전모의고사 40

01. ④ 02. ④ 03. ⑤ 04. ⑤ 05. ⑤ 06. ③ 07. ③ 08. ③ 09. ④ 10. ①
11. ② 12. ④ 13. ② 14. ① 15. ③ 16. ② 17. ④

01 화자가 하는 말의 목적 | ④

▶ 현재 직업을 가진 사람들이 학위를 취득할 수 있는 온라인 대학을 홍보하고 있다.

W: **Are you tired of your current career**? Looking for something different? There are many people who have a passion but cannot find sufficient education for their new career. For them, getting this education is a must. **Take control of your life** by getting an online degree from Oak Online University. With flexible scheduling, Oak Online **can accommodate the special needs of people** who are currently working. Plus, its low student-to-teacher ratio guarantees you will receive **plenty of personal attention**. We offer online courses in a variety of degree programs. Explore how you can earn a college degree online. Visit www.oak.edu for more information.

여: 현재의 직업이 지겨우십니까? 뭔가 다른 것을 찾고 계시나요? 열정은 있으나 자신의 새로운 일을 위한 충분한 교육을 찾지 못하는 분들이 많습니다. 그분들에게는 이 교육을 받는 것이 필수입니다. Oak 온라인 대학교에서 온라인 학위를 받으시고 여러분의 삶을 개척하세요. 탄력적인 일정으로, Oak 온라인 대학은 현재 일을 하고 계신 분들의 특별한 요구를 수용할 수 있습니다. 더불어, 학생 대 교사의 비율이 낮아 여러분이 개인적으로 많은 주목을 받을 것임을 보장합니다. 우리는 다양한 학위 프로그램에서 온라인 과정을 제공합니다. 여러분이 학부 학위를 온라인에서 어떻게 받을 수 있는지 살펴보십시오. 더 많은 정보를 원하시면 www.oak.edu를 방문하세요.

어휘 **be tired of** ~에 싫증나다 / **current** 현재의; 통용되는; 흐름; 전류 ***cf.* currently** 현재, 지금 / **career** (전문적인) 직업; 경력 / **sufficient** 충분한 / **must** 반드시 필요한 것, 필수품 / **take control of** 장악하다, 지배하다 / **flexible** 신축성[유연성] 있는 / **accommodate** 수용하다; 숙박시키다 / **ratio** 비(比), 비율 / **guarantee** 보증[보장]하다; 보증, 약속 / **a variety of** 여러 가지의, 다양한

02 의견 | ④

▶ 남자는 크리스마스 명절에 사람들이 쇼핑과 물질적 선물에만 관심을 갖는다고 하면서 너무 상업화되었다고 말하고 있다.

W: **What did you get for Christmas**, Matthew?
M: Oh, my family didn't buy presents for each other this year.
W: What? Why not?
M: I think that during Christmas time these days, **all people care about is** shopping and material gifts.
W: That's true. But giving a gift is a way to show love for family and friends.
M: Right. But today it has become too commercialized. We're pressured to buy something. **It takes the joy away**.
W: I understand what you mean. But kids love gifts. People just want their kids to be happy.
M: Well, Christmas is not about gifts at all. It is about families coming together and having fun.
W: You're right. **We often forget what's important**.
M: I think Christmas has become a celebration of American consumerism.

여: 넌 크리스마스에 무엇을 받았니, Matthew?
남: 아, 우리 가족은 올해 서로에게 선물을 사주지 않았어.
여: 뭐? 왜 안 샀어?
남: 요즘에 크리스마스 기간 중에 사람들이 신경 쓰는 건 쇼핑과 물질적인 선물이 전부인 것 같아.
여: 사실이야. 하지만 선물을 주는 것은 가족과 친구들에 대한 사랑을 보여주는 하나의 방법이야.
남: 맞아. 그렇지만 오늘날 그건 너무 상업화되었어. 우린 뭔가를 사라고 압박을 받고 그게 즐거움을 앗아가 버려.
여: 네 말이 무슨 뜻인지 이해해. 하지만 아이들은 선물을 아주 좋아해. 사람들은 그저 아이들이 행복하기를 원하는 거야.
남: 음, 크리스마스는 선물 때문에 있는 게 아냐. 가족들이 함께 모여서 즐겁게 지내라고 있는 거지.
여: 네 말이 맞아. 우린 뭐가 중요한지 종종 잊어버려.
남: 난 크리스마스가 미국 소비주의의 기념행사가 된 것 같아.

어휘 **commercialized** 상업화된 / **be pressured to-v** v하라고 압박을 받다 / **celebration** 기념, 축하 / **consumerism** 소비(지상)주의; 소비

03 관계 | ⑤

▶ Jacob은 여자의 아들이자 남자의 조카이고, 여자가 남자의 부모를 your parents라고 하는 것으로 보아 형수와 시동생의 관계임을 알 수 있다.

[Phone rings.]
W: Hello?
M: Hello, this is Michael.
W: Oh, hi, Michael. **It's been a long time since we last spoke**. By the way, your parents are here at my house.
M: Yes, I know. **That's why I called**.
W: We're planning to stay at the Green Valley Resort. Can you come? Your brother, Joshua, wants you to spend the weekend with us.
M: I'm not sure yet.
W: I hope you can join us. It's been a long time since your parents came down from Denver to see us. We'd love to see you, too.
M: **I'll do my best to be there**. Oh, by the way, how's Jacob?
W: You mean your nephew, Jacob? There are so many Jacobs in our family.
M: *[laughing]* You're right. Yes, your son and my nephew, Jacob Junior. I bought him a graduation gift.
W: Oh, **how nice of you**. Hold on. Your mother wants to speak to you.
M: Okay, thanks.

[전화벨이 울린다.]
여: 여보세요?
남: 여보세요, 저 Michael이에요.
여: 아, 안녕하세요, Michael. 지난번에 통화한 이후로 오랜만이네요. 그건 그렇고, 당신의 부모님께서 우리 집에 계세요.
남: 네, 알아요. 그래서 전화 드렸어요.
여: 우리는 Green Valley 리조트에 머무르려고 계획 중이에요. 오실 수 있어요? 형 Joshua가 당신이 우리와 함께 주말을 보내길 원해요.
남: 아직 확실히 모르겠어요.
여: 우리랑 합류하시길 바라요. 당신의 부모님께서 Denver에서 우리를 보러 오신 이후로 시간이 많이 흘렀네요. 우리도 당신을 정말 보고 싶어요.
남: 가도록 최선을 다할게요. 아, 그런데 Jacob은 잘 지내나요?
여: 당신 조카인 Jacob 말이죠? 우리 집안엔 아주 많은 Jacob이 있어서요.
남: *[웃으면서]* 맞아요. 네, 당신 아들이면서 제 조카인 Jacob Junior요. Jacob에게 줄 졸업 선물을 샀거든요.
여: 아, 참 다정하시네요. 잠깐만요. 어머님께서 당신과 통화하고 싶어하세요.
남: 알겠어요, 고마워요.

04 그림 불일치 | ⑤

▶ 돗자리 옆에 새가 앉아있다고 했는데 그림에는 다람쥐가 있으므로 일치하지 않는다.

W: Can you take a look at our final draft of the poster for the Stern Groove Festival? **Let me know what you think**.
M: I see that you placed the title, "Stern Groove Festival," in the middle. I like it.
W: **Look closely at the tree**.
M: Oh, you drew musical instruments in the tree!
W: Yes, since it's a music festival, I drew musical instruments, like a trumpet, guitar, harp, and violin, as branches for the tree.
M: **What a great idea**!
W: I put the date of the festival under "Admission Free Concert" to the right of the tree.
M: I see there's a couple with a kid enjoying a picnic beside the tree.
W: Yes, I wanted people to know that they can enjoy a family picnic at the festival.
M: Wonderful. **Since the festival is being held outside**, I'm glad you drew a bird next to the mat. Let's go ahead and print some posters.
W: I'll do it right away.

여: Stern Groove Festival에 쓸 우리 포스터의 최종안을 봐줄래? 네 생각이 어떤지 알고 싶어.
남: 'Stern Groove Festival'이라는 제목을 가운데 뒀네. 마음에 든다.
여: 나무를 자세히 들여다봐.
남: 아, 나무에 악기를 그렸구나!
여: 응, 음악 축제라서 트럼펫, 기타, 하프, 그리고 바이올린 같은 악기를 나무의 가지처럼 그렸어.
남: 멋진 생각이야!
여: 축제 날짜는 나무의 오른쪽에 있는 '무료 입장 콘서트'라는 글자 아래에다 적었어.
남: 나무 옆에서 아이를 데리고 소풍을 즐기고 있는 부부가 보이네.
여: 응, 축제에서 가족 소풍을 즐길 수 있다는 걸 사람들이 알았으면 했어.
남: 멋져. 축제가 야외에서 열리니까 돗자리 옆에 새 한 마리를 그린 게 아주 마음에 들어. 얼른 가서 포스터를 인쇄하자.
여: 지금 바로 할게.

어휘 **admission** 입장(료); 입학 (허가) / **take a look at** ~을 보다 / **draft** 밑그림, 초안 / **musical instrument** 악기

05 부탁한 일 | ⑤

▶ 남자가 디지털카메라의 사진을 컴퓨터로 옮기는 법을 설명해주었지만 여자는 모르겠다고 하면서 대신 해줄 수 있는지 물었고, 남자가 승낙했다.

W: David, you're a computer expert, aren't you?
M: I wouldn't call myself an expert, but **I know a thing or two about computers**. Why? Did you get a virus in your computer?
W: No, it's not that. I've already installed anti-virus software on my computer.
M: Good for you.
W: You know that I bought a digital camera last week, right?
M: Yes, I remember. It's really nice.
W: Well, I've taken a ton of photos, and **I'd like to transfer them to my computer**, but I don't know how.
M: Not a problem. It's pretty easy once you know how to do it. Just plug one end of the USB cable into your camera and the other into your computer.
W: I'm sorry, but I have no idea **what you're talking about**. Could you do it for me?
M: Of course. I'd be happy to.

여: David, 너 컴퓨터 전문가지, 그렇지?
남: 내 자신을 전문가라고 하진 않지만, 컴퓨터에 관해선 어느 정도 알고 있어. 왜? 네 컴퓨터에 바이러스가 걸렸니?
여: 아니, 그런 건 아냐. 난 벌써 컴퓨터에 바이러스 예방 소프트웨어를 설치했어.
남: 잘했어.
여: 내가 지난주에 디지털카메라 산 것 알고 있지, 그렇지?
남: 응, 기억해. 그건 정말 멋져.
여: 음, 내가 사진을 엄청나게 많이 찍어서 내 컴퓨터로 그걸 옮기고 싶은데, 어떻게 하는지 모르겠어.
남: 어렵지 않아. 어떻게 하는지 알기만 하면 아주 쉬워. 그냥 USB 케이블의 한쪽 끝을 카메라에 꽂고 다른 한쪽은 컴퓨터에 꽂아.
여: 미안하지만 무슨 말을 하는지 모르겠어. 네가 좀 해줄 수 있을까?
남: 물론이야. 해주고말고.

06 금액 | ③

▶ T3 텐트는 80달러이고 한 켤레에 60달러인 하이킹슈즈를 두 켤레 구매하므로 총 200달러이다. 그런데 50달러를 쓸 때마다 5달러가 할인되므로 20달러를 할인받아 여자가 지불할 금액은 180달러가 된다.

M: Do you need any help?
W: Yes. I was looking for the Adventurer T2 tent.
M: I'm afraid all the T2 tents **are sold out**. All we have at this moment are the T3 models. They're virtually the same.
W: How much is the T3 model?
M: It used to be $140, but now it's on sale for $80.
W: Great! I'll take it then.
M: **We're also having a special promotion**. You can get $5 off for every $50 you spend.
W: Hmm.... In that case, **I'd also like to purchase** hiking shoes. How much are these?
M: Those are $60.
W: Okay. I'd like to buy two pairs of the shoes, one for my husband and **the other for myself**.
M: I think you've made a great choice.
W: Thanks, here's my credit card.

남: 도움이 필요하십니까?
여: 네. Adventurer T2 텐트를 찾고 있었어요.
남: 유감스럽게도 T2 텐트는 모두 품절입니다. 현재 있는 것은 T3 모델뿐인데, 그 둘은 거의 같은 것입니다.
여: T3 모델은 얼마인가요?
남: 140달러였는데 지금은 할인해서 80달러입니다.
여: 잘됐네요! 그럼 그걸로 할게요.
남: 저희는 특별 판촉도 진행 중입니다. 50달러를 쓰실 때마다 5달러를 할인받으실 수 있습니다.
여: 흠…. 그렇다면 하이킹슈즈도 구매하고 싶네요. 이것은 얼마인가요?
남: 60달러입니다.
여: 알겠어요. 그 신발 두 켤레 살게요. 한 켤레는 남편, 그리고 다른 한 켤레는 제 것으로요.
남: 탁월한 선택이십니다.
여: 고마워요. 신용카드 여기 있어요.

어휘 **sold out** 품절의, 다 팔린 / **virtually** 거의, 사실상 / **promotion** 판촉; 촉진, 장려; 승진

07 이유 | ③

▶ 제품이 이미 이틀 전에 발송되었기 때문에 지금 취소할 수 없으며, 제품을 받은 후에 반품하라고 하였다.

[Phone rings.]
W: You've reached EC Mall. How can I help you?
M: I have a question **regarding a recent order I made**.
W: Can I have your name and order number?
M: My name is Sebastian Cox, and the order number is 150812.
W: One moment, please. *[pause]* I see that you bought a toaster a week ago.
M: Yes. I just realized that **I got the model numbers confused**, so I'd like to cancel my order and exchange it for another model.
W: Sorry, sir, but you can't cancel it now, because it was shipped two days ago.
M: **Then what should I do**?
W: Within 7 days after you've received the item, please return the item and purchase the model you want on our website again.
M: Oh, okay. That's complicated.
W: Sorry, but **there's nothing we can do now**.
M: Thanks anyway.

[전화벨이 울린다.]
여: EC 쇼핑몰입니다. 무엇을 도와드릴까요?
남: 제가 최근에 주문한 것과 관련해서 질문이 있는데요.
여: 성함과 주문번호를 알려주시겠어요?
남: 제 이름은 Sebastian Cox이고, 주문번호는 150812입니다.
여: 잠깐 기다려주세요. *[잠시 후]* 일주일 전에 토스터를 사셨네요.
남: 네. 제가 모델 번호를 헛갈렸다는 걸 방금 알아서요. 주문을 취소하고 다른 모델로 교환하고 싶어요.
여: 죄송합니다만 손님, 제품이 이틀 전에 발송되어서 지금 취소하실 수가 없습니다.
남: 그럼 어떻게 해야 하죠?
여: 상품을 받으신 후 7일 이내에 그 제품을 반품하시고, 손님께서 원하시는 그 모델을 저희 웹사이트에서 다시 구매하시면 됩니다.
남: 아, 알겠습니다. 복잡하군요.
여: 죄송하지만, 지금 저희가 해드릴 수 있는 게 없네요.
남: 어쨌든 감사합니다.

어휘 **regarding** ~에 관하여 / **toaster** 토스터, 식빵 굽는 기구 / **complicated** 복잡한

08 언급하지 않은 것 | ③

▶ 해석 참조

M: Hello, Mrs. White. I'm Trevor Perez from the Safe Insurance Company. Have a seat.
W: Oh, yes. **I want to compare prices** before I buy any car insurance.
M: Yes, I've heard that you're going to buy a car. **Recently we have released** a new type of car insurance. Which type of car will you buy?
W: It's a typical mid-size sedan.
M: How about its engine size?
W: It's 2,500 cc. It costs 30,290 dollars.
M: **How long have you been driving**?

W: For 13 years, since I got a driver's license at 19.
M: Okay. Have you had any accidents?
W: No, I've never been involved in any car accidents.
M: Okay, that means you **haven't gotten into any accidents** for over 10 years. In that case, your insurance costs are cut by 10%.
W: That sounds great.

남: 안녕하세요, White 부인. 저는 Safe 보험회사의 Trevor Perez입니다. 앉으세요.
여: 아, 네. 자동차 보험을 들기 전에 가격을 비교해 보고 싶어요.
남: 네, 차를 사실 거라고 들었습니다. 최근에 저희가 새로운 유형의 자동차 보험을 출시했답니다. 어떤 종류의 차를 사실 건가요?
여: 일반적인 중간 크기의 세단형 자동차(① 차종)를 살 거예요.
남: 엔진 크기가 어떻게 됩니까?
여: 2,500cc(② 자동차 엔진 배기량)예요. 가격은 30,290달러고요.
남: 운전은 얼마나 하셨습니까?
여: 19살 때 운전면허를 취득한 뒤 13년 동안(④ 차주의 운전 경력)이요.
남: 알겠습니다. 교통사고가 있었나요?
여: 아뇨, 자동차 사고에 연관된 적은 없었어요(⑤ 차주의 사고 이력).
남: 좋습니다. 10년 넘게 사고가 난 적이 없다는 말씀이시네요. 그 경우에는, 손님의 보험료가 10% 삭감됩니다.
여: 잘됐네요.

어휘 **sedan** 세단형 자동차 ((운전석을 칸막이하지 않은 보통의 상자형 승용차)) / **be [become, get] involved in** ~에 관련되다, 휘말리다

09 내용 불일치 | ④

▶ College students receive an additional 5% off on all college textbooks with a proper student ID.에서 대학생은 대학교 교재만 5% 할인받게 됨을 알 수 있다.

M: Greetings to all customers of Thompson's Used Bookstore! You'll notice that **many of our books are in excellent condition** with very competitive prices. For books **that have more wear and tear**, we offer additional price cuts. If you buy books in bulk, you'll receive a discount. For those who purchase 10 or more books, you'll get 20% off. **If you sign up for a membership** today, you'll get 10% off all your purchases. College students receive an additional 5% off on all college textbooks with a proper student ID. We are open seven days a week, from 10 a.m. to 9 p.m. from Monday to Saturday and 10 a.m. to noon on Sunday. Please feel free to phone or email us with any questions. Also **make sure to visit our website**, www.thompsonbooks.com.

남: Thompson 중고 서점을 찾아주신 모든 손님 여러분, 안녕하세요! 저희 책 중에서 상당수가 최상의 상태이며 가격 또한 경쟁력 있다는 것을 아실 것입니다. 닳고 찢어진 부분이 더 많은 책에는, 추가로 가격 인하를 해드립니다. 만약 대량으로 책을 사시면 할인을 받으십니다. 10권 이상을 구매하시는 분들에게는 20%를 할인해 드립니다. 오늘 회원 가입을 하시면, 구매하시는 모든 책에 10%를 할인해 드립니다. 대학생들은 정규 학생증이 있으면 모든 대학교 교재에 5% 추가 할인을 받습니다. 저희는 월요일에서 토요일까지는 오전 10시에서 오후 9시까지, 일요일에는 오전 10시에서 정오까지 일주일 내내 문을 엽니다. 질문이 있으시면 얼마든지 전화를 하시거나 메일을 주십시오. 또한, 저희 웹사이트 www.thompsonbooks.com을 꼭 방문해주십시오.

어휘 **wear and tear** 닳음, 마모 / **additional** 추가의, 부가적인 / **in bulk** 대량으로 / **feel free to-v** 거리낌 없이 v하다/ **make sure to-v** 꼭 v하다

10 도표 이해 | ①

▶ 여자는 처음에 사무직을 원했지만, 그보다는 시급이 10달러 이상인 일을 선택했다. 또한 월, 수, 금요일 오전을 제외한 시간에 일할 수 있으므로 여자가 할 수 있는 일은 ①이다.

W: Hi, my name is Olivia Morris. I'd like to do some work on campus during summer break.
M: **What kind of work are you looking for**?
W: I'm not sure. Can you tell me what kinds of jobs are being offered?
M: Basically, **there are two types of jobs**. One is cleaning and the other is office work. What are you interested in?
W: I don't mind either, but I think office work would be better. I'd also like to get something that pays at least $10 per hour.
M: Well, that means you have to do cleaning work. **Office work pays a lot less**.
W: Alright. That's what I'll do then.
M: When are you available to work?
W: I have summer classes on Monday, Wednesday, and Friday mornings, so **anytime after that is fine with me**.
M: Okay, then I think this is the job for you. Would you like to take it?
W: Sure, I will. Thank you.

여: 안녕하세요, 제 이름은 Olivia Morris입니다. 여름 방학 동안 캠퍼스에서 일을 좀 하고 싶은데요.
남: 어떤 일을 찾고 있나요?
여: 잘 모르겠어요. 어떤 일이 제공되고 있는지 말씀해주실 수 있을까요?
남: 기본적으로 두 가지 종류의 일이 있어요. 하나는 청소를 하는 것이고 다른 하나는 사무직이에요. 무슨 일에 관심이 가요?
여: 어느 것이든 상관없지만, 사무직이 더 나을 것 같아요. 적어도 시간당 10달러는 주는 일을 얻고 싶기도 하고요.
남: 음, 그러면 청소 작업을 해야 한다는 말이네요. 사무직은 훨씬 더 적게 주거든요.
여: 알겠습니다. 그러면 그게 제가 할 일이네요.
남: 언제부터 일할 수 있나요?
여: 월요일, 수요일, 그리고 금요일 아침에는 여름학기 수업이 있어서, 그 시간 이후에는 언제든지 괜찮습니다.
남: 좋아요, 그러면 이 일이 학생에게 맞는 것 같군요. 해보겠어요?
여: 물론이에요, 할게요. 감사합니다.

11 짧은 대화에 이어질 응답 | ②

▶ 비행기에서 오래 앉아 있어서 무릎이 뻐근하다고 하는 여자에게 남자가 통로를 걸어 다니라고 조언하지만 여자는 안전벨트 착용등이 켜진 상황이라 그럴 수 없다고 한다. 이에 적절한 응답은 다른 대안을 제시하는 것이다.

① 아직 5시간 더 가야 해.
② 그러면 다리를 위아래로 움직여봐.
③ 승무원에게 물을 좀 달라고 할게.
④ 고마워. 네가 나랑 여기 같이 있어서 정말 기뻐.
⑤ 지금 폭풍우 속을 날고 있어서 등이 켜졌어.

W: Air travel is so tiring. **My knees feel so stiff** because I've been sitting for so long.
M: I know what you mean. Why don't you walk up and down the aisle?
W: But the "**fasten seat belt**" sign is on. I don't think I should right now.
M: ____________________

여: 비행기 여행은 너무 힘들어. 너무 오랫동안 앉아 있었더니 무릎이 너무 뻐근해.
남: 무슨 말인지 알아. 일어서서 통로를 왔다 갔다 해보는 게 어때?
여: 하지만 '안전벨트 착용' 표시가 켜졌어. 지금은 하면 안 될 것 같아.
남: ____________________

어휘 **flight attendant** 승무원 / **tiring** 힘드는, 피로하게 하는 / **stiff** (근육이) 뻐근한; 뻣뻣한, 딱딱한 / **aisle** 통로 / **fasten** (벨트 등을) 매다; 단단히 고정하다

12 짧은 대화에 이어질 응답 | ④

▶ 지금 읽고 있는 책을 다 읽으면 빌려줄 수 있느냐는 말에 대한 적절한 응답을 고른다.

① 비싸지 않아. 그건 겨우 25달러 75센트야.
② 걱정하지 마. 4월 24일까지야.
③ 응. 그 책을 내게 빌려줘서 고마워.
④ 물론이지. 다 읽으면 너한테 알려줄게.
⑤ 같은 생각이야. 그 이야기는 우리 모두를 깊이 감동시켰어.

M: Did you buy the book that Dr. Hugh **asked us to read**?
W: Yes, I'm reading it right now.
M: When you're finished with the book, do you think **I can borrow it from you**?
W: ____________________

남: Hugh 박사님이 우리에게 읽으라고 하신 그 책 샀니?
여: 응, 지금 읽는 중이야.
남: 그 책 다 읽으면, 너한테 그 책 좀 빌릴 수 있을까?
여: ____________________

어휘 **due** ~하기로 예정된; (지불) 기한이 된

13 긴 대화에 이어질 응답 | ②

▶ 이튿날 오디션을 앞두고 초조해서 잠을 못 이루는 아들에게 어머니가 확신을 가지라며 격려한다. 이에 아들이 할 적절한 응답을 고른다.

① 우리 한번 잘해봐요.
② 내일이 빨리 지나갔으면 좋겠어요.
③ 행운을 빌어줄게요.
④ 새 출발에 대해 걱정하지 마세요!
⑤ 재미있겠는데요. 오디션이 기대돼요.

W: Ian, why aren't you in bed?
M: **I can't fall asleep**, Mom.
W: But you need a good night's rest for tomorrow.
M: I know, but I just can't fall asleep.
W: **Would you like a glass of warm milk**? It'll help you fall asleep.
M: No, I don't think that's a good idea. I might get an upset stomach.
W: **Don't think too much about the audition**. Just think of tomorrow as another ordinary day.
M: I'm trying, but I'm nervous.
W: You've practiced a lot for this audition so I'm sure you'll do fine. **Have confidence in yourself**.
M: ______________________________

여: Ian, 왜 안 자는 거니?
남: 잠이 안 와요, 엄마.
여: 하지만 내일을 위해서 오늘 밤에 푹 자야 하잖아.
남: 알아요, 하지만 그냥 잠이 안 와요.
여: 따뜻한 우유 한 잔 마실래? 잠드는 데 도움이 될 거야.
남: 아뇨, 좋은 생각이 아닌 것 같아요. 배탈이 날지도 몰라요.
여: 오디션에 대해서 너무 생각하지 마라. 내일을 그냥 평범한 하루라고 생각해.
남: 노력하고 있어요. 그런데 긴장돼요.
여: 넌 이 오디션을 위해서 많이 연습했으니까 분명 잘할 거야. 자신감을 가지렴.
남: ______________________________

어휘 **give it one's best shot** 잘해보다, 최선을 다하다 / **keep one's fingers crossed** 행운을 빌다 / **upset stomach** 배탈 / **have confidence in oneself** 자신감을 갖다

14 긴 대화에 이어질 응답 | ①

▶ 여행객이 여행가이드에게 여권을 받지 않았다고 계속 우기다가 자기 가방에서 여권이 나온 상황이다. 따라서 자신의 잘못을 인정하고 사과하는 것이 적절하다.

① 정말 죄송해요. 너무 창피하군요.
② 당신이 사과할 필요는 없어요.
③ 고집부리지 마세요. 당신이 틀렸다는 걸 인정하세요.
④ 괜찮아요. 당신 잘못이 아니라는 걸 알아요.
⑤ 이해해요. 이런 일은 종종 일어나죠.

M: We'll be taking our city tour now, so **let me hold on to your passports**.
W: Passport? I thought you had everything.
M: No, I gave everyone their documents before we got on the plane.
W: But I hadn't gotten anything.
M: **I'm sure I gave it to you**. Everyone gave me their passports a minute ago.
W: I'm positive I didn't get my passport. You're supposed to keep these things.
M: If you hadn't have your passport, **you couldn't have gotten on the plane**. Could you double-check your bag, please?
W: I told you that I didn't receive my passport. Look, it's not here! Oh, dear! Here it is!
M: I told you so. **I was sure I gave it to you**. Please give me your passport.
W: ______________________________

남: 지금 시내 관광을 시작하겠으니, 여권을 저한테 주시기 바랍니다.
여: 여권이요? 당신이 전부 가지고 있는 줄 알았는데요.
남: 아뇨, 비행기를 타기 전에 제가 모든 분께 서류를 드렸어요.
여: 그런데 전 아무것도 안 받았어요.
남: 분명히 드렸는데요. 다들 조금 전에 저에게 여권을 주셨어요.
여: 제 여권을 받지 않은 게 틀림없어요. 당신이 이런 걸 가지고 있기로 되어 있잖아요.
남: 만약 여권이 없으셨다면, 비행기에 타실 수 없었을 겁니다. 가방을 다시 확인해 보시겠어요?
여: 전 여권을 받지 않았다고 말씀드렸잖아요. 보세요, 여기 없어요! 아, 이런! 여기 있네!
남: 그렇다고 했잖아요. 분명히 드렸어요. 저한테 여권을 주세요.
여: ______________________________

어휘 **embarrassed** (실수 등을 하여) 창피한, 당황스러워하는 / **stubborn** 고집스러운, 완고한 / **double-check** 재확인하다

15 상황에 적절한 말 | ③

▶ 착각해서 자신의 전화기를 잘못 가져간 사람에게 할 말을 고른다.

① 이런 말 해서 죄송하지만, 당신이 실수하신 거예요.
② 진정하세요. 당신을 귀찮게 하고 싶진 않아요.
③ 실례합니다! 제 전화기를 가져가신 것 같은데요.
④ 늦어서 죄송합니다. 곧바로 가겠습니다.
⑤ 정말 죄송합니다. 그게 제 전화기인 줄 알았어요.

W: Jeremy is at the airport. He is going on a business trip to Seoul. **While waiting to board**, he goes to a coffee shop in the airport. He orders a cup of coffee and drinks it at a small table. There is a man sitting next to Jeremy, and he's playing a game on his phone. It's the same type of phone as Jeremy's. Jeremy reads the news on his phone while he drinks coffee. When he realizes **it's time to board**, he leaves his phone on the table and returns his coffee and tray. When he returns to his table, **he picks up a phone**, but it's not his. Then Jeremy notices that the man who was sitting next to him is leaving the coffee shop with a phone in his hand. Jeremy **realizes the man probably has his phone**. In this situation, what would Jeremy most likely shout to the man?

여: Jeremy는 공항에 있다. 그는 서울로 출장을 갈 것이다. 탑승을 기다리는 동안, 그는 공항에 있는 커피숍으로 간다. 그는 커피 한 잔을 주문하여 작은 탁자에서 마신다. Jeremy 옆에 한 남자가 앉아 있고, 그 남자는 휴대전화로 게임을 하고 있다. 그것은 Jeremy의 것과 같은 종류의 전화기이다. Jeremy는 커피를 마시는 동안 전화기로 뉴스를 읽는다. 탑승할 시간이 된 것을 깨달았을 때, Jeremy는 탁자 위에 전화기를 두고 커피와 쟁반을 반납한다. 그가 탁자로 돌아왔을 때 전화기를 집어 들었지만, 그것은 자신의 것이 아니다. 그러고 나서 Jeremy는 자신의 옆에 앉아 있던 그 남자가 전화기 하나를 손에 들고 커피숍을 나가고 있는 것을 알아차린다. Jeremy는 그 남자가 아마 자신의 전화기를 가지고 있을 것임을 깨닫는다. 이러한 상황에서 Jeremy가 그 남자에게 외칠 말로 가장 적절한 것은 무엇인가?

어휘 **delay** 지체; 연기; 미루다 / **tray** 쟁반

16~17 세트 문항 | 16. ② 17. ④

▶ 16. 약의 남용이 끼치는 폐해에 관한 내용이다.

① 짧은 낮잠의 이점
② 약물 남용의 해로운 영향
③ 자연 치료법의 긍정적 영향
④ 약물 복용자의 과잉 복용을 줄이는 법
⑤ 신체 상태에 미치는 약의 영향

▶ 17. 해석 참조

M: A recent survey has revealed a surprising discovery about prescription medicine. According to the survey, many people are using much more medicine than they should use. Some types of drugs can be dangerous **if not taken properly**. For instance, if you abuse cold medicine, you can do serious damage to your liver, and excessive use of painkillers can harm your heart and brain. Sleeping pills **tend to be quite effective** for sleeping, but those effects come at a price — **they carry significant risks**. Even aspirin has some side effects. Its main undesirable effects are heartburn and other symptoms of stomachaches. Therefore, you should remember that in some cases taking medicine might not be the best idea. **You might have noticed that** if you get frequent headaches, after a while you need to take more medicine for the pain to go away. This is because taking medicine too often **makes our bodies get used to the medicine**, and it doesn't work as well the next time. If the pain or ache is relatively small, sometimes it's a better idea to take a natural remedy, like a cup of hot tea or a nice relaxing nap.

남: 최근의 조사는 처방약에 관하여 놀라운 발견을 밝혀냈습니다. 조사에 따르면, 많은 사람이 복용해야 하는 것보다 훨씬 더 많은 약을 복용하고 있습니다. 어떤 유형의 약은 잘못 복용하면 위험할 수 있습니다. 예를 들어 만약 ① 감기약을 남용하면 간에 심각한 손상을 입힐 수 있고, ② 진통제의 과도한 복용은 심장과 뇌에 해를 끼칠 수 있습니다. ③ 수면제는 잠을 자는 데 꽤 효과적이지만, 그 효과는 상당한 위험을 동반한다는 대가를 치러야 합니다. 심지어는 ⑤ 아스피린도 부작용이 있습니다. 아스피린의 주요 부작용은 속 쓰림과 복통의 다른 증상입니다. 그러므로 어떤 경우에는 약을 복용하는 것이 최선이 아닐 수도 있다는 것을 기억해야 합니다. 두통이 잦으면 얼마 후에는 통증을 없애기 위해 약을 더 많이 먹어야 한다는 것을 알게 되셨을 겁니다. 약을 너무 자주 복용하면 우리 신체가 그 약에 익숙해지고, 다음번에는 약이 잘 듣지 않기 때문입니다. 통증이 상대적으로 덜하다면, 때로는 따뜻한 차 한 잔이나 긴장을 풀어주는 기분 좋은 낮잠과 같은 자연 치료법이 더 좋은 방법입니다.

어휘 **abuse** 남용(하다), 오용(하다) / **remedy** 치료(약); 해결책 / **overdose** 과다 복용(하다) / **reveal** 드러내다, 폭로하다 / **prescription medicine** 의사의 처방전이 필요한 약 / **liver** 간 / **excessive** 과도한, 지나친 / **painkiller** 진통제 / **effective** 효과적인 / **significant** (양, 정도가) 상당한; 중요한 / **side effect** 부작용 / **undesirable** 탐탁지 않은, 바람직스럽지 못한, 불쾌한 / **heartburn** (소화불량에 의한) 속 쓰림 / **symptom** 증상; (불길한) 징후, 징조 / **frequent** 자주 일어나는, 빈번한 / **relatively** 상대적으로, 비교적(으로) / **relaxing** 마음을 느긋하게 해 주는, 편한

ANSWER

정답

01회

01. ② 02. ⑤ 03. ④ 04. ② 05. ⑤
06. ③ 07. ② 08. ② 09. ⑤ 10. ③
11. ① 12. ① 13. ② 14. ④ 15. ④
16. ⑤ 17. ②

02회

01. ③ 02. ③ 03. ③ 04. ④ 05. ⑤
06. ② 07. ③ 08. ③ 09. ① 10. ②
11. ① 12. ③ 13. ③ 14. ④ 15. ③
16. ④ 17. ⑤

03회

01. ④ 02. ① 03. ① 04. ② 05. ②
06. ① 07. ④ 08. ① 09. ⑤ 10. ④
11. ② 12. ② 13. ⑤ 14. ④ 15. ⑤
16. ④ 17. ④

04회

01. ④ 02. ② 03. ① 04. ③ 05. ③
06. ② 07. ④ 08. ① 09. ⑤ 10. ④
11. ⑤ 12. ③ 13. ④ 14. ③ 15. ③
16. ③ 17. ②

05회

01. ① 02. ⑤ 03. ③ 04. ⑤ 05. ②
06. ③ 07. ⑤ 08. ③ 09. ④ 10. ③
11. ② 12. ④ 13. ④ 14. ④ 15. ④
16. ① 17. ③

06회

01. ① 02. ② 03. ④ 04. ⑤ 05. ②
06. ④ 07. ② 08. ④ 09. ③ 10. ③
11. ③ 12. ① 13. ⑤ 14. ⑤ 15. ③
16. ② 17. ④

07회

01. ① 02. ① 03. ② 04. ④ 05. ③
06. ③ 07. ③ 08. ③ 09. ⑤ 10. ②
11. ② 12. ⑤ 13. ④ 14. ⑤ 15. ④
16. ② 17. ③

08회

01. ④ 02. ③ 03. ③ 04. ⑤ 05. ②
06. ② 07. ① 08. ④ 09. ③ 10. ③
11. ② 12. ① 13. ④ 14. ④ 15. ②
16. ③ 17. ⑤

09회

01. ④ 02. ② 03. ⑤ 04. ③ 05. ④
06. ⑤ 07. ⑤ 08. ① 09. ⑤ 10. ③
11. ③ 12. ⑤ 13. ⑤ 14. ② 15. ⑤
16. ② 17. ④

10회

01. ④ 02. ⑤ 03. ④ 04. ⑤ 05. ⑤
06. ③ 07. ① 08. ③ 09. ④ 10. ④
11. ③ 12. ⑤ 13. ⑤ 14. ① 15. ①
16. ④ 17. ④

11회

01. ④ 02. ⑤ 03. ① 04. ⑤ 05. ④
06. ③ 07. ④ 08. ③ 09. ③ 10. ③
11. ① 12. ⑤ 13. ② 14. ⑤ 15. ③
16. ⑤ 17. ③

12회

01. ⑤ 02. ① 03. ③ 04. ⑤ 05. ⑤
06. ② 07. ④ 08. ③ 09. ④ 10. ⑤
11. ① 12. ① 13. ⑤ 14. ③ 15. ④
16. ⑤ 17. ③

13회

01. ④ 02. ② 03. ③ 04. ⑤ 05. ②
06. ② 07. ⑤ 08. ③ 09. ④ 10. ④
11. ② 12. ④ 13. ② 14. ④ 15. ①
16. ① 17. ③

14회

01. ① 02. ④ 03. ② 04. ③ 05. ⑤
06. ③ 07. ④ 08. ⑤ 09. ② 10. ③
11. ③ 12. ③ 13. ② 14. ① 15. ③
16. ① 17. ④

15회

01. ① 02. ③ 03. ② 04. ② 05. ②
06. ② 07. ④ 08. ① 09. ② 10. ④
11. ④ 12. ③ 13. ② 14. ③ 15. ①
16. ③ 17. ②

16회

01. ③ 02. ④ 03. ④ 04. ③ 05. ⑤
06. ③ 07. ④ 08. ④ 09. ④ 10. ③
11. ④ 12. ④ 13. ⑤ 14. ③ 15. ④
16. ④ 17. ①

17회

01. ⑤ 02. ③ 03. ④ 04. ③ 05. ③
06. ③ 07. ② 08. ② 09. ② 10. ④
11. ① 12. ① 13. ⑤ 14. ⑤ 15. ④
16. ③ 17. ③

18회

01. ① 02. ② 03. ② 04. ④ 05. ④
06. ③ 07. ⑤ 08. ④ 09. ④ 10. ④
11. ③ 12. ① 13. ⑤ 14. ② 15. ③
16. ② 17. ④

19회

01. ④ 02. ④ 03. ⑤ 04. ⑤ 05. ⑤
06. ② 07. ④ 08. ④ 09. ④ 10. ③
11. ① 12. ② 13. ⑤ 14. ⑤ 15. ④
16. ① 17. ④

20회

01. ② 02. ⑤ 03. ⑤ 04. ④ 05. ①
06. ③ 07. ④ 08. ① 09. ⑤ 10. ④
11. ④ 12. ⑤ 13. ⑤ 14. ② 15. ②
16. ③ 17. ③

21회

01. ③ 02. ④ 03. ③ 04. ⑤ 05. ②
06. ④ 07. ④ 08. ① 09. ⑤ 10. ②
11. ⑤ 12. ⑤ 13. ② 14. ② 15. ④
16. ② 17. ④

22회

01. ④ 02. ⑤ 03. ⑤ 04. ③ 05. ④
06. ② 07. ④ 08. ④ 09. ⑤ 10. ①
11. ③ 12. ① 13. ③ 14. ② 15. ⑤
16. ⑤ 17. ③

23회

01. ① 02. ⑤ 03. ① 04. ③ 05. ④
06. ④ 07. ① 08. ③ 09. ④ 10. ④
11. ② 12. ④ 13. ④ 14. ⑤ 15. ⑤
16. ③ 17. ⑤

24회

01. ⑤ 02. ② 03. ① 04. ④ 05. ②
06. ③ 07. ⑤ 08. ⑤ 09. ④ 10. ③
11. ① 12. ④ 13. ④ 14. ③ 15. ⑤
16. ④ 17. ③

25회

01. ④ 02. ④ 03. ④ 04. ④ 05. ③
06. ③ 07. ④ 08. ⑤ 09. ③ 10. ①
11. ② 12. ② 13. ① 14. ⑤ 15. ⑤
16. ① 17. ③

26회

01. ② 02. ② 03. ③ 04. ⑤ 05. ④
06. ③ 07. ④ 08. ① 09. ② 10. ④
11. ③ 12. ② 13. ③ 14. ⑤ 15. ③
16. ② 17. ④

27회

01. ④ 02. ② 03. ② 04. ④ 05. ⑤
06. ② 07. ③ 08. ④ 09. ② 10. ②
11. ② 12. ② 13. ② 14. ⑤ 15. ①
16. ⑤ 17. ③

28회

01. ③ 02. ② 03. ③ 04. ④ 05. ②
06. ① 07. ③ 08. ② 09. ④ 10. ④
11. ③ 12. ⑤ 13. ⑤ 14. ① 15. ④
16. ③ 17. ②

ANSWER

정답

29회

01. ③	02. ⑤	03. ②	04. ④	05. ④
06. ④	07. ③	08. ⑤	09. ④	10. ⑤
11. ①	12. ②	13. ⑤	14. ③	15. ③
16. ③	17. ⑤			

30회

01. ④	02. ②	03. ⑤	04. ⑤	05. ③
06. ④	07. ①	08. ②	09. ⑤	10. ③
11. ③	12. ④	13. ⑤	14. ③	15. ①
16. ③	17. ⑤			

31회

01. ②	02. ④	03. ④	04. ④	05. ①
06. ②	07. ②	08. ③	09. ①	10. ④
11. ①	12. ⑤	13. ②	14. ④	15. ③
16. ②	17. ⑤			

32회

01. ⑤	02. ④	03. ③	04. ④	05. ③
06. ②	07. ③	08. ②	09. ③	10. ④
11. ③	12. ③	13. ①	14. ①	15. ⑤
16. ③	17. ④			

33회

01. ④	02. ④	03. ②	04. ④	05. ①
06. ③	07. ⑤	08. ⑤	09. ④	10. ②
11. ①	12. ⑤	13. ②	14. ⑤	15. ⑤
16. ②	17. ④			

34회

01. ⑤	02. ⑤	03. ④	04. ③	05. ③
06. ①	07. ⑤	08. ④	09. ④	10. ②
11. ③	12. ⑤	13. ④	14. ③	15. ②
16. ④	17. ④			

35회

01. ②	02. ③	03. ④	04. ④	05. ⑤
06. ④	07. ④	08. ③	09. ⑤	10. ③
11. ⑤	12. ④	13. ②	14. ①	15. ②
16. ②	17. ③			

36회

01. ②	02. ⑤	03. ④	04. ③	05. ①
06. ③	07. ②	08. ④	09. ③	10. ④
11. ④	12. ④	13. ②	14. ②	15. ④
16. ④	17. ⑤			

37회

01. ①	02. ①	03. ②	04. ④	05. ⑤
06. ④	07. ③	08. ④	09. ④	10. ⑤
11. ④	12. ③	13. ④	14. ③	15. ⑤
16. ②	17. ④			

38회

01. ②	02. ②	03. ①	04. ⑤	05. ③
06. ③	07. ③	08. ③	09. ⑤	10. ④
11. ①	12. ④	13. ③	14. ①	15. ①
16. ②	17. ①			

39회

01. ②	02. ③	03. ④	04. ⑤	05. ④
06. ②	07. ①	08. ④	09. ③	10. ②
11. ③	12. ⑤	13. ①	14. ⑤	15. ③
16. ①	17. ③			

40회

01. ④	02. ④	03. ⑤	04. ⑤	05. ⑤
06. ③	07. ③	08. ③	09. ④	10. ①
11. ②	12. ④	13. ②	14. ①	15. ③
16. ②	17. ④			

절대평가 대비 수능 영어 실력 충전

POWER Up

쎄듀 초등 커리큘럼

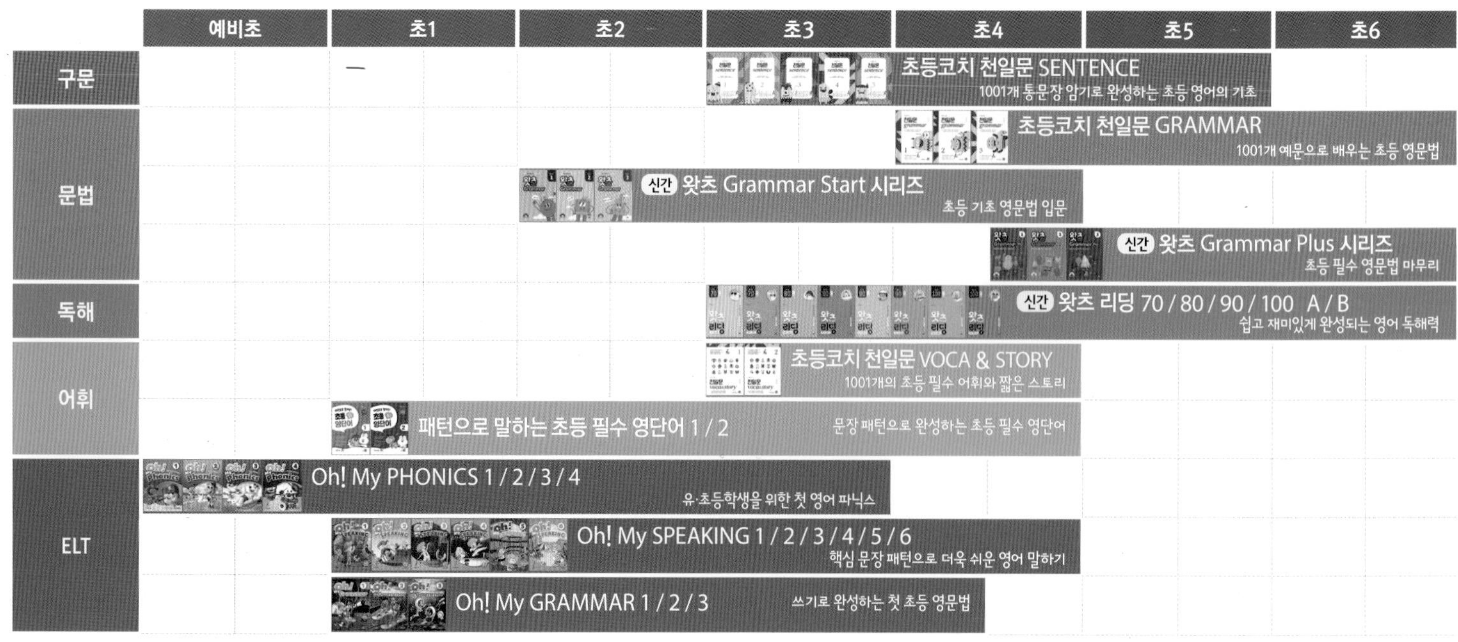

쎄듀 중등 커리큘럼

영역	교재 (예비중 · 중1 · 중2 · 중3)	설명
구문	신간 천일문 STARTER 1 / 2	중등 필수 구문 & 문법 총정리
문법	천일문 GRAMMAR LEVEL 1 / 2 / 3	예문 중심 문법 기본서
	GRAMMAR Q Starter 1, 2 / Intermediate 1, 2 / Advanced 1, 2	학기별 문법 기본서
	잘 풀리는 영문법 1 / 2 / 3	문제 중심 문법 적용서
	GRAMMAR PIC 1 / 2 / 3 / 4	이해가 쉬운 도식화된 문법서
	1센치 영문법	1권으로 핵심 문법 정리
문법+어법	첫단추 BASIC 문법·어법편 1 / 2	문법·어법의 기초
문법+쓰기	EGU 영단어&품사 / 문장 형식 / 동사 써먹기 / 문법 써먹기 / 구문 써먹기	서술형 기초 세우기와 문법 다지기
	올씀 1 기본 문장 PATTERN	내신 서술형 기본 문장 학습
쓰기	거침없이 Writing LEVEL 1 / 2 / 3	중등 교과서 내신 기출 서술형
	개정 중학 영어 쓰작 1 / 2 / 3	중등 교과서 패턴 드릴 서술형
어휘	어휘끝 중학 필수편	중학 필수어휘 1000개
	어휘끝 중학 마스터편	고난도 중학어휘 +고등기초 어휘 1000개
독해	Reading Relay Starter 1, 2 / Challenger 1, 2 / Master 1, 2	타교과 연계 배경 지식 독해
	READING Q Starter 1, 2 / Intermediate 1, 2 / Advanced 1, 2	예측/추론/요약 사고력 독해
독해전략	리딩 플랫폼 1 / 2 / 3	논픽션 지문 독해
독해유형	Reading 16 LEVEL 1 / 2 / 3	수능 유형 맛보기 + 내신 대비
	첫단추 BASIC 독해편 1 / 2	수능 유형 독해 입문
듣기	Listening Q 유형편 / 1 / 2 / 3	유형별 듣기 전략 및 실전 대비
	쎄듀 빠르게 중학영어듣기 모의고사 1 / 2 / 3	교육청 듣기평가 대비